# SAUNDERS BOOKS IN PSYCHOLOGY

LEWIS F. PETRINOVICH     ROBERT D. SINGER

*Consulting Editors*

# MODERN PSYCHOPATHOLOGY

## A BIOSOCIAL APPROACH TO MALADAPTIVE LEARNING AND FUNCTIONING

by

### THEODORE MILLON

University of Illinois

W. B. Saunders Company · Philadelphia · London · Toronto

W. B. Saunders Company:   West Washington Square
Philadelphia, Pa. 19105

12 Dyott Street
London, WC1A   1DB

833 Oxford Street
Toronto, Ontario M8Z 5T9, Canada

Modern Psychopathology

ISBN 0-7216-6385-0

Print No.:      10      9      8      7      6

TO RENÉE

*for being*

# PREFACE

Presumption and vanity, so often the spur to writing books, had little to do with the origins of this text. It began, quite simply, as an exercise in self-education, an attempt on my part to gather and to render the disparate facts and theories of psychopathology into a coherent and orderly framework; such a venture, it was hoped, would enable me to pursue my future research, teaching and clinical responsibilities more effectively. Little did I know that the tasks of authorship would force me to think more presumptuously than I cared—even worse, to feel a measure of pride and vanity in these presumptions. Faced repeatedly with the obscurities, contradictions and confusions that beset the field, I found myself formulating novel "clarifications" and "solutions" to old and perplexing problems. In short, an act of modest self-education became an act of intellectual audacity; only the future will tell whether the venturesome spirit that overtook me will be judged to have been impertinent and foolhardy, or original and persuasive.

If at all successful in its pedagogical aims, this book should provide the student with a logical succession of data and ideas basic to his understanding of pathological behavior. A few words elaborating the purposes and orientation of the author are in order as a précis of the text.

Efforts were made to strike a balance between the twin goals of presenting the scholarship and rigorous thinking of a scientific discipline, on the one hand, and maintaining the curiosity and excitement that first attract the student to the subject, on the other. To create a sense of participation and intellectual challenge, complex and controversial issues were presented in neither predigested nor oversimplified form; at the same time, an ample number of illustrative case histories were included, and professional jargon and pedantic erudition were carefully avoided.

If I have succeeded in striking the proper balance between scholarship and interest, there is no reason why the text could not serve equally well for both majors and nonmajors alike, whetting the appetite and furnishing some solid underpinnings for later work among those who wish to make the study of psychology a career, and exposing a rich vein of information for the intensive study of man among those seeking depth in their liberal arts education.

Toward the end of making the subject meaningful and relevant to the student, and in contrast to most other books on "abnormal psychology," the text devotes two long chapters to what are termed the *mild patterns of personality pathology*. These are not the dramatic and bizarre varieties of mental disorder that are the stock-in-trade of hospital psychiatry; rather, they portray those forms of maladaptive behavior that students are likely to encounter in the course of their everyday lives—in their families and among their friends. In addition to making the text more meaningful and relevant, the inclusion of these milder pathologies enables the student to see the developmental continuity between lesser and more severe disorders, and to trace the insidious manner in which serious pathology unfolds.

As is evident then, it was my intent to write a sequentially unified book, one that was not doctrinaire in its theoretical view, yet one that would demonstrate how the many varieties of psychopathology could logically be derived from a few basic concepts and principles. Most authors in the past split their texts down the middle, so to speak, providing little or no continuity between the varied theoretical notions they presented in the early chapters of their books and the varied pathological syndromes that comprised their later chapters. More recently, several writers have sought to bridge this gap and to develop a degree of sequential consistency in their treatment of the subject. Unfortunately, most have shaped their materials in line with narrow and partisan theoretical models; inevitably, these works compressed the rich diversity of psychopathological data into Procrustean beds, discarding what did not suit their authors' predilections, and imposing a false sense of harmony and order on the remainder. In the hope of gaining the best of both worlds—that is, of being theoretically eclectic, yet logically and sequentially consistent—I have borrowed liberally from several schools of thought, adapting and refashioning what appear to be divergent views to fit a coherent "multidimensional" model. The historical and theoretical background of this model—comprising biophysical, intrapsychic, phenomenological and behavioral data and concepts—is elaborated in chapters 1 through 3; the following 12 chapters illustrate the application of these data and concepts to both the syndromes of psychopathology and their treatment.

As regards the specific sequencing of topics, a conscious effort was made to organize the text in a manner consistent with the teaching of the abnormal psychology course at most colleges and universities. The well-deserved popularity of James C. Coleman's *Abnormal Psychology and Modern Life* derives, in part at least, from its logical progression of chapter subjects, a progression that accepts what the student knows at the beginning of the semester and brings him, in an orderly fashion, to the point at which most instructors want him to be at the end.

To provide a sense of immediacy and to furnish the student with up-to-date and ongoing work in the field, the present text thoroughly integrates, rather than merely notes or describes, the material of the newly revised Diagnostic and Statistical Manual (DSM-II; American Psychiatric Association, 1968), the exciting developments in behavior theory and therapy, the important recent studies on early stimulus impoverishment and enrichment and the new breakthroughs in multivariate classification research.

Many writers have asserted, I believe correctly, that the field of psychopathology has been unnecessarily dependent on nineteenth-century Kraepelinian psychiatry. Given the advances in conceptual and empirical research of the past half-century, the time has come for the development of a new and coherent theoretical framework, one that interweaves both psychological and bio-

logical factors, and from which the principal clinical syndromes could be derived and coordinated. Instead of rephrasing traditional psychiatric categories in the language of modern theories, as several able psychopathologists have done, I have sought to devise a new classification schema, one constructed from its inception by coalescing several basic principles of personality development and functioning. Chapters 4 and 5 provide the theoretical framework of a "biosocial approach" to the learning of pathological behaviors; chapters 6 through 12 illustrate the clinical syndromes that can be derived from this framework. Not only does the schema serve to connect psychopathology to other realms of psychological theory and research, but it demonstrates the developmental continuity of pathological functioning throughout life, and the interconnections that exist among syndromes, still considered discrete clinical entities according to the official Kraepelinian system. To make this developmental continuity explicit, an organizational sequence is arranged in the text in which the secondary and more severe stages of disorder are seen to arise as logical extensions of several basic personality patterns. Although not a fully documented typology, this new classification format has "worked well" in preliminary studies with several hundred institutionalized and clinic patients. Rather surprisingly, the categories derived from this biosocial-learning model correspond closely not only to the traditional clinical syndromes, but also to the "character disorders" formulated by the psychoanalysts and the "typologies" uncovered in recent multivariate research. In recognition of the fact that departures from established terminology and practices can be discomfiting to many, and in order to ensure that students are thoroughly conversant with the official American Psychiatric Association nomenclature (DSM-II), the labels and diagnostic descriptions of the latter are discussed and coordinated fully with their counterparts in the new classification.

No book of this magnitude springs from the mind of one man, nor can its execution be the product of his labors alone; I owe much to many.

My first debt is to five men, all teachers of mine, who set the seeds for many of the ideas contained in the text. The immense erudition and open-mindedness of Gardner Murphy provided not only a sanctuary, but cohesion for the "identity crises" of my adolescence; the generous spirit of Lawrence Frank drew me from sophomoric intellectual exercises and taught me to appreciate the values and rewards of social compassion; the reflective wisdom and personal warmth of Kurt Goldstein assured me that the "organic" approach was neither sterile nor antithetical to humanistic goals; the analytical skills of Ernst Kris guided me as I explored the circuitous labyrinths of my mind and released whatever creative impulses lay therein; the thorough scholarship and deep commitment to the welfare of others of Arthur Noyes served as a model well worth emulating.

To these men must be added a host of other clinicians and scientists who have never formally been my teachers, but from whose writings I have profited greatly; their silent instruction pervades the pages of this book. My debt to those who are still living and active contributors to the field is hereby acknowledged: Norman Cameron, Leon Eisenberg, Erik H. Erikson, Hans J. Eysenck, D. O. Hebb, Maurice Lorr, Paul E. Meehl, Lois B. Murphy, B. F. Skinner, Roger J. Williams, Lewis R. Wolberg and Joseph Zubin.

Many colleagues have generously furnished the stimulus of encouragement and intellectual discourse so necessary to spur an author on through his labors. Heading this list are Addi Geist Agar and Rose Sherman Kutler, two good friends and associates of mine at the Lincoln Consultation Center. I am deeply obliged also to many on the staff of the Allentown State Hospital; for their unstinting support and assistance throughout this and earlier projects, I am particularly grateful to Howard Taft Fiedler, Joshua Epstein, Naomi Hussey Grossman and the late Raymond Shettel. A number of fellow professionals were asked to give me the benefit of their reactions to segments of the manuscript at various stages in its development; those who provided encouragement or constructive criticism include John G. Darley, Howard F. Hunt, Paul E. Meehl, Alan H. Roberts and Joseph Zubin. Among the many who have eased the burdens of preparing the text, a special note of gratitude is due Flo Grabel. I am most appreciative also of the willing and cheerful contributions made by Sally Perlis, Barbara Miller, Shirley Leff and Ann Zarinsky in rendering my inscrutable script legible for publication. Members of the staff of the W. B. Saunders Company deserve no small measure of thanks for their competence and indulgence during these past three and a half years.

The book is affectionately dedicated to my wife, Renée, for bearing the hardships of protecting my time, for being a touchstone of intellectual clarity and for having shared this labor of love with me from start to finish.

THEODORE MILLON

# CONTENTS

## Part 3    CLINICAL SYNDROMES

Chapter 9

# Pathological Personalities of Marked Severity:

Chapter 10

# Symptom Disorders:

# Part 1

## FOUNDATIONS

Sorrow

## Introduction

Psychopathology is probably unique among the sciences in its interest to men in all walks of life. This interest is not new; throughout written history, man has observed, described and pondered strange behaviors and thoughts within himself and his neighbors. The questions that man has posed about these experiences seem so simple and basic. Why do we seek to please our friends, but have incredible difficulty being congenial with our families? Why do we vacillate so often between hopeful fantasy and oppressive despair? Why do we dream and suffer terrifying nightmares? Why do we submit to foolish temptations against our better judgment? Questions such as these have puzzled and intrigued man since ancient times; they persist to challenge us today. Despite their apparent simplicity, they raise some of the most complex issues that face psychological and medical science.

What day has gone by in recent years without encountering news or TV reports of suicide, crime, "nervous breakdowns" and sexual perversion?

Events such as these are intriguing, no doubt, but they are dramatic and extreme; they give us a distorted view of the full scope of psychopathology.

### THE VARIETIES OF PSYCHOPATHOLOGY

It is the undramatic and mundane problems of life, the quiet but persistent anxieties, the repetitive ineffectualities and the immobilizing conflicts that hinder millions of Americans day after day that best represent the true subject matter of psychopathology. These milder disorders usually are "taken for granted" as part of man's "fate" or "nature": the promising college freshman who cannot settle down to his studies, frittering away his time in wasteful daydreaming and TV watching; the "old maid" high school teacher who is extremely permissive with the young boys in her classes, but easily angered and short-tempered with

**1**

the girls; the father who cannot tolerate disagreement from his children and flies into a rage when his authority is questioned; the self-conscious college student who can never gather the courage to call a girl for a date; the housewife who constantly complains of fatigue and headaches, for which no organic disorder can be found; the mother who must be engaged in a whirl of social activity to escape her home responsibilities; the successful businessman who cannot relax on his vacation, checking constantly at the office to see if things are all right without him.

Signs of mental malfunction become more obvious as we shift our focus from these "commonplace" maladjustments to the more moderately severe disorders: the physician who withdraws from a successful practice because he fears that he will do irreparable harm to his patients; the housewife who is unable to sleep in anticipation of someone stealing into her home to murder her family; the college coed who belittles her friends and tests their loyalty so persistently that they ultimately are alienated from her; the ineffectual husband who leans upon his wife for every decision and cannot hold a job for more than a few months; the quiet and scholarly choir boy who steals cars; the shy student who exposes himself in the college library; the alcoholic father who physically attacks members of his family and then threatens suicide to relieve his guilt.

Finally, there are the markedly disturbed individuals whose disordered state is evident to all: the disheveled woman who walks the streets muttering to herself and cursing at passersby; the unemployed man who "knows" that others have conspired to prevent his success and are plotting to take his life; the aged grandfather who wanders at night conversing with long dead relatives; the depressed young mother, immobilized by the responsibilities of caring for her newborn son and dreading her impulse to kill him; the socially isolated college student who seems perennially perplexed, speaks of vague mystical experiences, and shouts at persons unseen by others.

Historically, professionals and public alike considered only the markedly severe disorders to be within the province of psychopathology. They reflected a narrow view that the milder disturbances of personality, which we know today to be the precursors of more serious disorders, were but a measure of moral inferiority, obstinacy, vanity or dissipation. Rather than recognizing that milder disturbances were early stages of potentially more severe disorders, they attacked them with ridicule and condemnation, censuring and exhorting these individuals to mend their ways and to desist from

their foolishness and degeneracy. Fortunately, these archaic and inhumane views have given way in recent years to more sympathetic and psychologically sound attitudes.

## PSYCHOPATHOLOGY AS A CONTEMPORARY PROBLEM

That the incidence of both mild and severe disorders is strikingly high in contemporary society cannot be denied. Perhaps it reflects the strain of life in the twentieth century, or what sociologists have depicted as our *age of anxiety*. Whatever its cause, the inescapable facts are that each year Americans spend more than a hundred million dollars for tranquilizers, tens of billions for liquor and aspirin, and purchase enough books promising successful personal adjustment to fill a good-sized college library.

Famine, epidemics and a majority of the biological ills have been conquered. Americans now have the time to turn to themselves, to their desires for psychological contentment and happiness, for greater social acceptance and for deeper meanings and purposes of existence. Our struggle with the physical environment has been largely won, but a host of new problems has appeared to plague us. Technological innovations have led to industrial automation and to high speed communication and transportation. Not only has the pace of life been heightened, but other societal, economic and religious changes have taken place so rapidly that we can no longer depend upon the traditions and values which gave earlier generations a feeling of stability and regularity. Divorce upsets the pattern of an increasing number of families; the threat of global and atomic war hangs in the balance; racial tension and social resentments have increased. In this rapid whirl of change and ambiguity, an atmosphere of social confusion and psychological instability has arisen to replace the anxieties of starvation, disease and economic insecurity.

No wonder then that the toll of psychological strain, discontent and bewilderment has increased to a point where it accounts for more illness than all other health problems combined. One out of every ten Americans, at the current rate, will spend part of his life in a mental hospital. More than half of all hospital beds in this country are filled with mental patients and, even more startling, is the fact that for every hospitalized patient there are 20 other less severely handicapped Americans who need psychotherapy.

Fortunately, psychopathology is no longer viewed as a remote province of professional study tacked on as a postgraduate specialty for interested physicians. It is a necessary part today not only of the training of psychiatrists, psychologists, teachers and ministers, whose work brings them to serve the needs of the troubled, but is a significant part of the curricula of all colleges. The study of psychopathology can teach us to understand the problems of contemporary man and may lead us to find ways of preventing these problems before they get out of hand.

The growing acquaintance with psychopathology has resulted in changes in the public's attitude. No longer is mental illness viewed as a disgrace, a weird and unnatural phenomenon to be feared and avoided; no longer is it viewed as something apart from other problems of everyday life, to be chalked up as a sign of perversion and to be seen as hopelessly incurable. Mental illness is viewed today as the result of efforts to adjust to real life situations, but with minimal success. These ineffectual and maladaptive efforts can be supplanted or strengthened. Thirty-five thousand competent clinical psychologists, psychiatrists and psychiatric social workers are trained to deal with these problems with compassion and intelligence. In addition, we are spending over a billion dollars a year for research, treatment and care of the mentally ill. We have come to realize, finally, that the problems of psychopathology can be combatted by scientific and humane action.

## *FOCUS OF THE INTRODUCTORY CHAPTERS*

Because psychopathology encompasses a broad field of study and lends itself to many approaches and viewpoints, there are several alternatives available for introducing the subject to the student.

We could begin by tracing the historical development of the field, and thereby give the student a perspective from which he can appraise the growth of current ideas and research. This approach will lead to an appreciation of the difficulties which persistently confront investigators who attempt to unravel the complexities of psychopathology.

A second introduction might begin with a review of contemporary theories. In this way we would initiate our study by focusing on the best that has been distilled from the past—the ideas and concepts that have withstood the test of time. Thus, instead of tracing historical developments, we could present only those theoretical views which have been judged useful to contemporary science and practice.

We could introduce our subject a third and equally fruitful way. Rather than beginning with historical events or abstract theoretical notions, we could present the raw data and procedures of clinical psychopathology. The data of clinical observation and analysis bring the student to the heart of the subject; the procedures by which clinicians observe pathology give the student a taste of what the practitioner does in his everyday work.

To choose one among these three introductory approaches would short-change the student, for each possesses distinct advantages. With this thought in mind, therefore, three introductory chapters have been written to serve as a foundation for the remainder of the text: the first will review *historical trends,* the second will compare *contemporary theories* and the third will examine the various data, concepts and methods of *clinical analysis.*

# Chapter 1

## HISTORICAL TRENDS

Michael Mazur—*Her Place* (1962). (Collection, The Museum of Modern Art, New York. Gift of Mrs. Bertram Smith.)

### INTRODUCTION

Current theories and known facts about human behavior are the product of a long and continuing history of man's curiosity and achievement. Although dependence on the past cannot be denied, progress also occurs because dissatisfaction with the "truths" of yesterday stimulates our search for better answers today. Hopefully, a perspective of historical trends will enable us to decide which achievements are worthy of acceptance and which require further investigation.

As we look back over the long course of scientific history we see patterns of progress and regress, brilliant leaps alternating with foolish pursuits and blind stumblings. Significant discoveries often were made by capitalizing on accidental observation; at other times, progress required the clearing away of deeply entrenched but erroneous beliefs.

Despite these erratic pathways to knowledge, scientists have returned time and time again to certain central themes. What are the causes of abnormal behavior? How can we best conceptualize the structure of psychopathology? Are there but a few basic processes underlying all behavior? What methods are best for alleviating these disorders?

As the study of the science of psychopath-ology progressed, different and occasionally insular traditions and terminology evolved to answer these questions. Separate disciplines with specialized educational and training procedures developed until today we have divergent professional groups involved in the study of psychopathology, e.g., the medically oriented psychiatrist with his tradition in biology and physiology; the psychodynamic psychiatrist with his concern for unconscious intrapsychic processes; the clinical-personology psychologist with his interest in the structure and measurement of personality; and the academic-experimental psychologist with his scientific approach to basic processes of behavior. Each has studied these complex questions with a different emphasis and focus. Yet the central issues remain the same. By tracing the history of each of these diverging trends we will clearly see how different modes of thought today have their roots in chance events, cultural ideologies and accidental discoveries, as well as in brilliant and creative innovation.

### ANCIENT DEMONOLOGY

Primitive man and ancient civilizations alike viewed the unusual and strange within a magical and mythological frame of reference. Behavior which could not be understood was thought to be controlled by animistic spirits. Although both good and evil spirits were conjectured, the bizarre and often frightening behavior of the mentally disordered led to a prevailing belief that demon spirits must inhabit them. The possession of evil spirits was viewed as a punishment for failure to obey the teachings of the gods and priests. Fears that demons might spread to afflict others often led to cruel and barbaric tortures.

Given these explanations of mental disorder, the course of treatment was clear. If placating the gods was insufficient then the demons were to be *exorcised,* or driven from the body. The casting out of evil spirits was attempted initially through prayer, incantation, sharp noises, foul odors and bitter concoctions. If these failed the body of the afflicted was made unwelcome for the spirits by flogging and starving the victim. In several societies operations now called *trephining* were performed by chipping away a circular segment of the skull through which the demons might escape. These primitive "therapies" of shock, starvation and surgery have had their parallels in recent history although the ancients based them on the more grossly naive conception of demonology.

If, by chance, the disordered behavior was viewed to signify mystical powers, as was epilepsy among the early Greeks, the patient was thought to be possessed by sacred spirits with which the gods had honored him. This favorable view of mental affliction, although still based upon a demonic mythology, grew in time into a more uniformly sympathetic approach to the ill. Egyptians and Greeks erected temples in which physician-priests augmented prayers and incantations with kindness, advice, recreation and herbs. In the haven of the Egyptian "hospice" or hospital, priests interpreted dreams and suggested solutions both to earthly and heavenly problems. The Grecian Asclepiad temples of the eighth century B.C., were located in remote regions away from family, trade, war and stress. Here the sick were comforted, fed well, bathed and massaged, given "nepenthic" drugs and surrounded by harmonious music. Despite these promising interludes, the notion of demons persisted and those unable to benefit from humane treatment alone were cast among the evil to be flogged and chained.

## MEDICAL SPECULATIONS IN GREECE AND ROME

Among the few notable advances between 800 B.C. and 400 B.C. were the observations of the sixth century physician-priest, Alcmaeon, who related sensation to brain processes and concluded

that defects in reasoning must result from brain pathology. During the same period Alcmaeon's teacher, the philosopher Pythagoras, proposed the far-sighted view that primary attention be given to modes of prevention rather than to cures.

Not until the fifth century B.C. were truly radical advances made to supplant the superstitions of animistic spirits and temple medicine. It was the genius and courage of Hippocrates (460–367 B.C.) that led to the naturalistic view that the origin of disorders should be sought within the patient and not within spiritual phenomena. The introductory notes to the Hippocratic book on epilepsy state (Grimm, 1838):

It seems to me to be no more divine and no more sacred than other diseases, but like other affections, it springs from natural causes. . . . Those who first connected this illness with demons and described it as sacred seem to me no different from the conjurors, purificators, mountebanks and charlatans of our day. . . . Such persons are merely concealing, under the cloak of godliness, their perplexity and their inability to afford any assistance. . . . It is not a god which injures the body, but disease.

Although the role of developmental experience was not included in his biological view of causation, Hippocrates established the tradition of the personal case history by detailing the course and outcome of disorders he observed. Through these histories we have surprisingly accurate descriptions of such varied disorders as depression, phobias, convulsions and migraine.

Lacking precise observations of bodily structure and prevented by taboo from performing dissections, Hippocratic physicians developed hypothetical but erroneous explanations for disease.

Causation, according to Hippocratic theory, stemmed from an excess or imbalance among four bodily humors—yellow bile, black bile, blood and phlegm. These humors or fluids were the embodiment of earth, water, fire and air which were declared the basic components of the universe by the philosopher Empedocles. Hippocrates' classification of temperaments, choleric, melancholic, sanguine and phlegmatic—terms still in our present day vocabulary—corresponded respectively to excesses in yellow bile, black bile, blood and phlegm. Hysteria, viewed today as a psychogenic reaction, was attributed then to a wandering uterus (*hysterikos*), and believed to be a uniquely female disorder.

Although naive in conception and execution, Hippocrates' approach to therapy followed logically from his view that disorders were of natural origin. To supplant the prevalent practices of exorcism and punishment, he recommended such varied prescriptions as exercise, tranquility, diet, even marriage and, where necessary, venesection or bloodletting.

The Hippocratic proposals of biological causation and naturalistic treatment, together with his theory that temperamental types were exaggerations of normality were profound advances over earlier notions. With but minor revisions, their influence extended over 2000 years.

Plato (429–347 B.C.), a young contemporary of Hippocrates and a distinguished philosopher, argued for humane approaches to the mentally ill and emphasized the role sociocultural factors played in creating them. However, he was unable to transcend the spiritual mythology of his times fully and promulgated the view that many disorders could be attributed to divine intervention.

Aristotle (384–322 B.C.), Plato's most influential student and a physician as well, reactivated the Hippocratic emphasis on bodily functions but minimized the importance Plato gave to psychological factors. He substituted the heart as the major agent of causation. This focus distracted his followers from the earlier and more valid concern with environment and brain function and was particularly regressive by virtue of his authoritative status with succeeding generations.

In early Rome, belief in animistic spirits and divine intervention was gradually replaced by the naturalistic views of Hippocrates. Although the first major figure, Asclepiades (ca. 100 B.C.), rejected the humoral theory of Hippocrates, he vigorously espoused naturalistic diagnosis and humane treatment. Asclepiades stressed the importance of environmental influences and is credited as the first to distinguish among hallucinations, delusions and illusions as well as the subdivision of disorders into acute and chronic. Not only was he ingenious in devising methods of relaxing his patients, but his observations of the effects of bloodletting, mechanical restraints and dungeons led to his open and emphatic opposition to them.

Perceptive observations by Aretaeus (30–90 A.D.) strengthened the notion that mental disorders were exaggerated normal processes. He illustrated direct connections between an individual's normal characteristics of personality and the expression his disorder displayed when afflicted. His insightful differentiation of disorders according to symptom patterns was a striking achievement for his day.

In a manner similar to Aretaeus, his nonmedical contemporary, the encyclopedist, Celsus, reorganized the basic concepts of Hippocrates into distinct groups of disease entities. Among his original contributions to Hippocratic theory was the view that mental disorders pervaded all of an individual's functioning and not one organ alone. This enlightened contribution was overshadowed, however, by his regressive therapeutic suggestions —starvation, intimidation and bloodletting.

The influential practitioner, Soranus (120 A.D), based his teachings on the recommendations of Celsus. Melancholia was viewed as an excess of black bile; hysteria was a disorder of the uterus; phrenitis was a feverish disease related to that part of mind located in the diaphragm (*phren*); hypochondriasis was attributed to the hypochondrium, as hysteria was to the uterus.

This revised and extended Hippocratic system was translated into Latin by the physician Caelius Aurelianus (fifth century A.D.), and remained in circulation, along with similar compilations by Galen (130–200 A.D.) for centuries to come. Although dormant through the oppressive period of medieval demonology, humoral concepts of Hippocrates were revived anew with the Renaissance.

## MEDIEVAL REGRESSION TO PRIMITIVISM AND WITCHCRAFT

The enlightened ideas of Hippocrates were submerged for centuries following the death of Galen and the fall of the Roman empire. During the thousand years of the Dark Ages, superstition, demonology and exorcism returned in full force only to be elaborated with greater intensity into sorcery and witchburning. With but few dissenting voices scattered over the centuries, the naturalism of the Greco-Roman period was all but condemned or distorted by notions of magic. Only in Arabia did the humane and naturalistic aspects of Hippocratic thought remain free of the primitivism and demonology flourishing in Europe.

Signs for detecting those possessed of demons became increasingly indiscriminate. During epidemics of famine and pestilence, thousands wandered aimlessly until their haggard appearance and confusion justified the fear that they were cursed and possessed of demons. The prevalent turmoil, the fear of one's own contamination and the frenetic desire to prove one's spiritual purity, led widespread segments of the populace to use the roaming destitute and ill as convenient scapegoats.

As the terrifying uncertainties of medieval life persisted, fear led to wild mysticism and mass pathology. Entire societies were swept simultaneously. Epidemic manias of raving, jumping, drinking and wild dancing were first noted in the tenth century. Referred to as *tarantism* in Italy, these epidemic manias spread throughout Europe where they were known as *St. Vitus's Dance.*

In the earlier periods of the Middle Ages, before the catastrophes of pestilence and famine, the numbers of destitute and affected were few and treatment was kindly. Monasteries were the chief refuge, providing prayer, incantation, holy water, relic-touching and mild exorcism as prescriptions for cure. As the turmoil of natural calamity continued, mental disorders were equated increasingly with sin and Satanic influence. The interplay between changing theological beliefs and naturalistic catastrophe speeded the acceptance by the secular world of the belief that "madness" and "depravity" were the work of the devil. At first, the mentally ill were thought to have been seized against their will by the devil and were handled accordingly with established exorcistic practice. Soon the afflicted were considered willing followers of Satan; classed now as witches, they were flogged, starved and burned.

Encouraged by the 1484 *Summis Desiderentes Affectibus,* in which Pope Innocent VIII exhorted the clergy to use all means for detecting and eliminating witchcraft, two inquisitional Dominicans, Johann Sprenger and Heinrich Kraemer, issued their notorious manual, *Malleus Maleficarum* (The Witches' Hammer). Published between 1487 and 1489, this "divinely inspired" text set out to prove the existence of witchcraft, to describe methods of identification and to specify the procedures of examination and legal sentence. Given such sanction, witch-hunters persecuted thousands of the mentally ill. With torture recommended as a means of obtaining confession, and feelings of guilt and hopeless damnation characteristic of many of the afflicted, the inevitable consequence for most was the penalty of strangulation, beheading and burning at the stake. This barbaric epidemic swept Protestant and Catholic countries alike, including several American colonies. Although the last execution of a witch occurred in 1782, the notion that the mentally ill were in league with the devil persisted in popular thought well into the nineteenth century.

## THE RENAISSANCE AND HUMANE REFORMS

At the turn of the sixteenth century, amid medieval superstition and inhumane treatment, we see the first outcropping of courageous challenge and scientific questioning.

Not long after the publication of the *Malleus Maleficarum,* Juan Luis Vives (1492–1540), a seclusive Spanish philosopher reared in an orthodox setting, began to question the role of planetary phenomena in mental functioning. His introspectiveness and sensitivity led him to suggest humane compassion for the mentally ill and, perhaps more important, to observe that painful and long-forgotten memories could be recalled through reflective association; in this he anticipated modern psychoanalytic ideas.

Of a different temperament was Vives' Swiss contemporary, Paracelsus (1493–1541), whose inconsistent but strong-willed advocacy of natural causes of mental disorder led to his persecution and the eventual burning of his works. His contribution to the role of psychic factors in disorders was contaminated, unfortunately, with a belief in bodily "magnetism" and a conviction that lunar phenomena determined the course of an illness.

A notable advance in naturalistic explanation was next made by Jean Fernel (1497–1588), the first physician to employ the word physiology. In his anatomically based system he revived and extended the Hippocratic approach of correlating disease to body structure.

### Weyer's Criticism of Demonology

It is to the Dutchman Johann Weyer (1515–1588), often referred to as the father of modern psychiatry, that credit must go for the first effective denunciation of demonology. His major work, *De Praestiguo Daemonum* published in 1563, provided a vigorous attack upon the *Malleus Maleficarum.* Although his views on the general existence of demons is ambiguous, he stated unequivocally that "witches" were ill and insisted that their treatment be medical and humane. Weyer is distinguished, not only as a courageous advocate of naturalism, but as the first physician to specialize in mental disorders. And though he formulated no theories of his own, his talent as a clinician is evident by his sympathetic and skillful description of disorders known well today.

The Renaissance was an age of ambivalence and deep contradiction. Weyer's ideas met with both vehement condemnation and devoted support. His most powerful enemy, the French lawyer, Jean Bodin (1530–1596), attacked his views directly and propounded a vast and detailed argument in favor of the opposing, misguided theological position. In contrast, the Englishman, Reginald Scot (1538–1599), published a daring and forceful exposition of the fallacies of witchcraft and offered a convincing rebuttal to the notion that demons inhabit the mentally ill. As a commentary on the times, it may be noted that Scot's book, *Discovery of Witchcraft,* was ordered burned by King James I, who personally con-

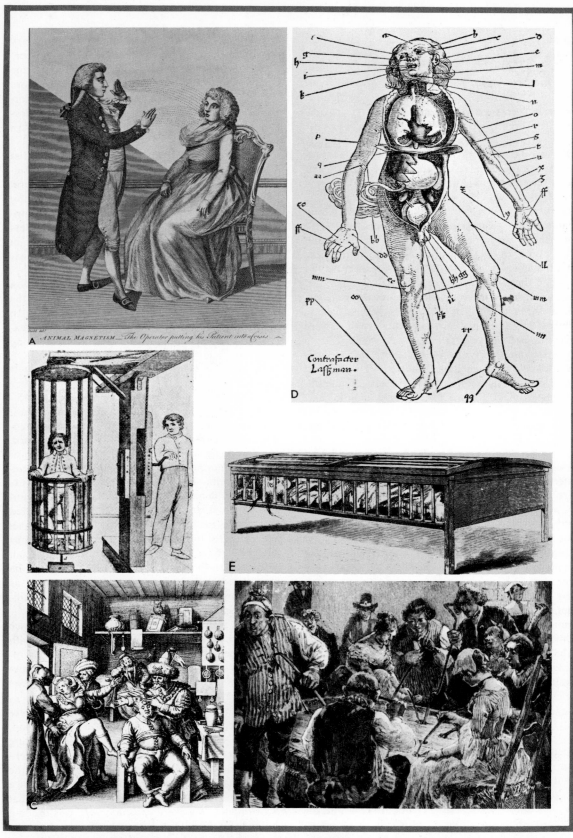

**Figure 1-1   Prescientific therapies.** *A.* Animal magnetism. (National Library of Medicine, Bethesda, Maryland.) *B.* Rotating device. (Bettmann Archive.) *C.* Medieval brain surgery. (Bettmann Archive.) *D.* Bloodletting chart. (Philadelphia Museum of Art.) *E.* The crib. (Bettmann Archive.) *F.* The baquet. (Bettmann Archive.)

demned the work and reasserted the validity of demonology.

In spite of the prevailing dominance of demonology over the next two centuries, some humane attitudes toward the ill and doubts about supernatural causation continued in quiet and undramatic form. In the sixteenth century a beginning search for the natural causes of bodily diseases was made by anatomists and physiologists. Contributions to our knowledge of mental processes were made by philosophers such as Bacon, Descartes, Spinoza, Hobbes, Leibnitz and Locke. The essays and books of Voltaire alerted the mid-eighteenth century French populace to the wretched conditions of the ill and poor, contributing widely to a revived interest in humane and naturalistic treatment.

In the 1760's, great indignation arose in England as a result of the brutal treatment given King George III during his periods of mental confusion. Conflict among physicians engaged to treat the king led to parliamentary investigations, public attention and eventual reforms. By 1796 the York Retreat, devoted to quiet refuge and humane treatment, was established in England by the wealthy Quaker merchant, William Hack Tuke (1732–1822).

### Reforms of Philippe Pinel

It was the distinguished physician and scholar, Philippe Pinel (1745–1826), taking advantage of the French Revolutionary emphasis on individual freedom, who was most effective in proving the success of humane treatment. Placed in charge of the Bicêtre Hospital by the Revolutionary Commune, he quickly instituted the view that the mentally ill were intractable because they were deprived of fresh air and liberty. Fortunately, the removal of chains, the provision of sunny rooms, the institution of free access to hospital grounds and the atmosphere of gentility and kindness resulted in many dramatic recoveries and an overall improvement in patient behavior and manageability. The gratifying success of Pinel's reforms led to his assignment at the larger Salpetrière hospital where he trained personnel to assume more than custodial functions and established the practice of systematic records and case histories.

Pinel's methods were continued by his student and successor at the Salpetrière, Jean Esquirol (1772–1840). In addition to establishing many new hospitals, operated in accordance with Pinel's principles, Esquirol lectured in psychiatry throughout the continent and published the first modern treatise on mental disorders in 1838, *Des Maladies Mentales*.

Although the ideas of Pinel were adopted quickly by Tuke at the York Retreat, and in 1795 by Fricke in Germany, the policy of nonrestraint spread slowly through the Western world. Many segments of the public showed a readiness to accept this view, but forceful opposition arose within the medical community. Thus in England, demonstrations of successful nonrestraint by Gardner Hill and Charlesworth were vigorously condemned by their medical colleagues.

### Dorothea Dix and Public Responsibility

In the United States corrupt and insufficient accommodations for the mentally ill aroused a crusading Massachusetts school teacher, Dorothea Lynde Dix (1802–1887). On her own initiative in 1841 she investigated the deplorable neglect and brutality prevalent in asylums, almshouses and jails. Encouraged by the response of the Massachusetts legislature to her report in 1843, she continued with indefatigable energy for 40 years, influencing the building of over 30 state-supported hospitals, reforming the asylum systems of Scotland and Canada and, above all, establishing firmly the modern principle of public responsibility for the mentally ill. As a measure of the effectiveness of her life's work, we can note the change in the numbers of those cared for in mental hospitals; from 2561, or 14 per cent of the estimated ill in the country in 1840, the figures rose to 74,028 or 69 per cent of those estimated ill in 1890. Thanks to her efforts, the obligation of providing proper shelter, nourishment and medical attention was assumed in responsible fashion through public legislation for the first time.

### Modern Mental Health Movements

Although care for the mentally ill had improved, more was needed than the construction of ominous fortress-like asylums to allay the suspicions and fears of the general public. Prompted by the circumstances of repeated mistreatment as a patient in three such institutions, Clifford W. Beers (1876–1943), wrote an honest and penetrating account of his experiences in the now famous book *A Mind That Found Itself*. When published in 1908, it aroused intense public reaction and the support of such eminent men as William James and Adolf Meyer. With his founding of the Society for Mental Hygiene shortly thereafter, Beers inaugurated a world-wide movement designed not only to encourage improved hospital conditions, but to educate the public on the importance of prevention, and dispel the prevalent belief that mental disorders were a stigma of disgrace and incurable.

Figure 1-2  Leaders in the humanitarian movement.  A.  Johann Weyer. (Bettmann Archive.)  B.  Philippe Pinel. (National Library of Medicine, Bethesda, Maryland.)  C.  Dorothea L. Dix. (National Library of Medicine, Bethesda, Maryland.)  D.  Clifford W. Beers. (Bettmann Archive.)

Although the mental health movement has grown to international proportions through the years, the fact remains that many hospitals today function little better than those to which Beers was confined at the turn of the century. Despite an increasingly better informed public and the recent advent of drugs for easier patient management, there are few state hospitals which cannot justly deplore inadequate appropriations to alleviate persistent overcrowding and understaffing. Idyllic as the present state system might appear to Pinel or Dix, the need for increased funds and staff continues. Without them, advances in scientific knowledge, which could transform futile lives into fruitful ones, remain unused.

The recent conviction that mental health services should be preventively oriented and based in the community has been painfully slow in coming when one notes that Pythagoras made the suggestion 2500 years ago. This "bold new approach" advocated by the Federal Government, known as the "Mental Retardation and Community Mental Health Centers Act of 1963," mobilized both professionals and laymen to participate in the long overdue task of assessing, and judging the capability of, existing resources. Although federal monies for constructing community mental health centers were initially appropriated, strong commitments to bed-centered programs persisted among tradition-bound psychiatrists, thereby slowing the development of this preventive project. To add to the delay, the government's involvement in the prolonged and costly Vietnam war sharply curtailed the necessary funds.

It is not only our public attitude toward the mentally ill which has evolved through a slow and uneven historical progression. In the next section, our attention will turn to the origins of the four major scientific traditions which have shaped our knowledge today. Although each of these traditions—psychiatric medicine, psychodynamic psychiatry, clinical-personology psychology and academic-experimental psychology—reflects differences in training and in scientific emphasis, they evolved from a common naturalistic and philosophical origin in the Greco-Roman period. Despite this commonality and recent efforts at synthesis, they diverged sufficiently over the centuries to result in alternate theories, assumptions and methods of study. Each has made distinctive contributions to our present knowledge of mental disorder; we will focus on the origins of these distinctions next and trace their major contribution to contemporary thinking.

# THE TRADITION OF PSYCHIATRIC MEDICINE

As the custom of recording case histories and detailing observations was established in hospitals, grouping and classification of disorders became a possibility. The trend toward classifying symptom clusters was given additional impetus by the success with which botanical taxonomists had systematized their field in the eighteenth century.

A second major trend within biological medicine, the view that disorders result from organic pathology, can be traced back to the early writing of Hippocrates. With the advent of valid anatomical, physiological and biochemical knowledge in the eighteenth and nineteenth centuries, and the discovery of the role played by bacteria, viruses and lesions, the disease concept of modern medicine took a firm hold. Efforts at developing biophysical methods of treatment, the third phase, followed naturally.

Although these three stages, classification, biological causation and biophysical treatment did not proceed in a smooth or logical fashion, they are the characteristic steps of medical progress and remain the major focus among psychiatrists influenced by the medical tradition.

# EVOLUTION OF CLASSIFICATION SYSTEMS

*Nosology* refers to the science of classifying diseases. Its major value for psychopathology is consistency of communication among scientists seeking the causes of disorder, and clarity among practitioners recommending therapy. These scientific and medical activities, however, presuppose a classification system that is not only communicable but valid. Unfortunately, men classified diseases long before they understood their true nature. Such classifications have persisted because of widespread or authoritative use. They rested most often upon unfounded speculations or, at best, judicious but essentially superficial observations. Criticism of these premature classification schemes and the frequent slavish adherence to them is justified. On the other hand, there is no sound reason to abolish the concept of classifying disorders, because of the important goals they may fulfill. When one recognizes the complexity of human behavior, one can well understand the difficulties involved in formulating acceptable systems.

The classifications proposed in ancient Greece and Rome were founded on the observations of Hippocrates. Mental disorders were divided into five categories: *phrenitis,* an acute disturbance with fever; *mania,* an acute disturbance without fever; *melancholia,* all chronic disorders; *hysteria,* a female disorder noted by agitation, pain and convulsions; and *epilepsy,* the only disorder of the group possessing the same name and meaning today. With but minor variation, this system was adopted by Celsus, Areteus, Soranus, Galen and Caelus Aurelianus. Following the dormant period of the Middle Ages, a reawakened interest in classical writings brought about the return of the Hippocratic system.

## RENAISSANCE SYSTEMS

During the Renaissance, two Swiss physicians, Paracelsus and Felix Plater (1536–1614), attempted classification innovations. Although Paracelsus proposed spiritual and cosmic causes, he was the first to specify a true chemical factor in mental disorder. To the usual Hippocratic classes, he added *vesania,* disorders caused by poisons, *lunacy,* a periodic condition influenced by phases of the moon and *insanity,* diseases caused by heredity.

The scheme developed by Paracelsus was replaced at the turn of the seventeenth century by Plater, who formulated an entirely new logic for classification, one based essentially on observable symptoms. The rationale for his system can be seen in the following categories he proposed: *consternatio mentis,* disturbances of consciousness, *mentis alienato,* disorders of violence, sadness, delirium or confusion, *mentis defatigatio,* mental exhaustion and *imbecillitas mentis,* mental deficiency and dementia.

Seventeenth century physicians adhering to Plater's system were guided by the belief that a close observation of symptoms would reveal an underlying disease entity. Francois Boissier de Sauvages (1706–1767), a French botanist and physician in search of these underlying disease entities, arranged overt symptoms in a manner similar to natural scientists who systematize plants and animals. Grouped into classes, orders and genera, they formed no less than 2400 different "diseases." His contemporaries were extremely impressed by this work and it inspired wide and frequent imitation.

Philippe Pinel was a student of Sauvages and was fully familiar with the nosological entities of his day. Despite his background and the minutely refined system he himself had earlier devised, Pinel bypassed the elegant and detailed nosologies of his time when he assumed the responsibilities of the Bicêtre Hospital. The simple humanitarian and pragmatic concerns faced in the realities of daily patient life led him to a simplified but practical classification. It proved to be not only a reaction against the impractical and ponderous systems of the day, but a departure from the prevalent search for disease entities.

## EARLY GERMAN SYSTEMATISTS

Pinel's departure was short lived. The growth of knowledge in anatomy and physiology strengthened the trend toward disease-oriented classifications. Wilhelm Griesinger (1817–1868), a young

German internist and psychiatrist with little direct patient experience, revived the disease concept in his classic text, *Mental Pathology and Therapeutics,* published in 1845. His statement, "Mental diseases are brain diseases," shaped the course of German systematic psychiatry for more than 40 years. Griesinger's contention that classifications should be formed on the basis of underlying brain lesions was not weakened by the fact that no relationship had been established between brain pathology and mental disorders. In fact, Griesinger's own system of categories—depression, exaltation and weakness—did not parallel his views regarding the importance of brain pathology. Nevertheless, he convinced succeeding generations of German neurologists, led by Thomas Meynart (1833–1892) and Carl Wernicke (1848–1905), that brain diseases would be found to underlie all mental disturbances.

Although the work of Griesinger and his followers dominated continental psychiatry, a different emphasis regarding the basis of classification was developing concurrently. Jean Esquirol, Pinel's distinguished student, had often referred to the importance of age of onset, variable chronicity and deteriorating course in understanding pathology. This idea was included as a formal part of classification in 1856 when Benedict-Augustin Morel (1809–1873) proposed *dementia praecox,* precocious or rapid deterioration, in his manual of disorders. This category was viewed as a separate disorder to be classified entirely on the basis of the course through which an illness had progressed.

It was the German psychiatrist, Karl Ludwig Kahlbaum (1828–1899), who extended Morel's idea by developing a classification system in which disorders were grouped according to their course and outcome. It became the major alternative system to the one proposed by Griesinger and his students. In a series of monographs and books published between 1863 and 1874, Kahlbaum not only established the importance of longitudinal factors, but described the newly observed disorders of *hebephrenia* and *catatonia,* and coined the modern terms *symptom-complex* and *cyclothymia.* His work was not accepted during his lifetime. The brain disease view propounded by Griesinger, and the rather ponderous format proposed by Kahlbaum, operated against the success of his contributions.

## KRAEPELIN'S NOSOLOGY

It was not until the preeminent German synthesist, Emil Kraepelin (1856–1926), that the diverse views and observations of Kahlbaum and Griesinger were bridged. In his outstanding text, revised from a small compendium in 1883 to an imposing two-volume ninth edition in 1927, Kraepelin built a system which integrated the descriptive and longitudinal approach of Kahlbaum with the somatic disease system proposed by Griesinger. By sifting and sorting prodigious numbers of well-documented hospital records and directly observing the varied characteristics of patients, he sought to bring order between symptom pictures and patterns of onset, course and outcome. Kraepelin felt that a classification based on these regularities would lead to specific infections or other bodily conditions which caused these disorders.

Kraepelin constantly revised his nosologic system, elaborating it at times, simplifying it at others. In the sixth edition of 1899, he established the definitive pattern of two modern major disorders: *manic-depressive psychosis* and *dementia praecox.* These were ingenious syntheses of previously independent entities which had been formulated by Morel, Kahlbaum and Ewald Hecker. Within the manic-depressive group he brought together the excited conditions of mania and the hopeless melancholia of depression, indicating the periodic course through which these moods alternate in the same patient. To be consistent with his disease orientation, he proposed that this disorder was caused by an irregular metabolic function transmitted by heredity.

Kraepelin subsumed a wide range of previously known disorders within the category of dementia praecox. He observed two major commonalities which he felt would justify a synthesis among them: each began early in life and then progressed to an incurable dementia. The cause of these disorders, according to Kraepelin, were biologically defective sex glands which led to chemical imbalances in the nervous system. Since puberty was a crucial period in sexual development, defects arose most often at this stage. This fact accounted for the frequency with which dementia praecox occurred in adolescence.

Despite Kraepelin's rigorous application of the disease concept, he recognized, in his seventh edition, that the milder disturbances of neuroses, hysteria and fright were probably of psychogenic origin. All others remained the result of constitution, infection, exhaustion or intoxicants.

While Kraepelin's impressive synthesis of biology and clinical description gave psychiatric medicine a tremendous impetus, his view that inherent bodily defects caused most disorders encouraged a fatalistic attitude toward treatment.

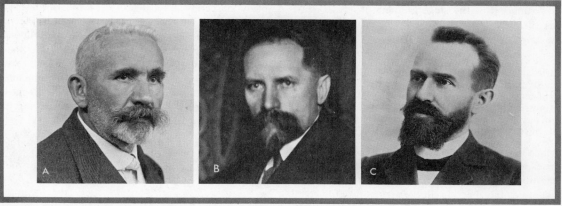

Figure 1-3  Forerunners of modern psychiatry. A. Emil Kraepelin. B. Adolf Meyer. C. Paul Eugen Bleuler. (Photographs courtesy of National Library of Medicine, Bethesda, Maryland.)

Because of this fatalism there was strong motivation to reexamine his hypotheses and ultimately, the nosological classification upon which they were based. Additional criticisms of Kraepelin's system arose from the fact that his observations were limited to hospitalized patients and, of perhaps greater importance, that he failed to offer any insight into the inner thoughts and feelings of these patients.

## MODIFICATIONS BY MEYER AND BLEULER

As early as 1905, Adolf Meyer (1866–1950), a major figure in American psychiatry, espoused the view that a true understanding of the patient could be derived only by a study of the individual's total reaction to his organic, psychological and social experience. Although Meyer was the most prominent psychiatrist to introduce the Kraepelinian system in this country, he believed that these disorders were not disease entities, but "psychobiological reactions" to environmental stress. Through his work, Meyer bridged the physiological orientation of the late nineteenth century and the psychodynamic orientation of the twentieth.

The interrelationship of biological and psychological factors in classifying disorders was stressed also by Meyer's contemporary, the Swiss psychiatrist Eugen Bleuler (1856–1935). Although committed to Kraepelin's view that dementia praecox was primarily an organic disease, Bleuler emphasized the presence of psychological ambivalence and disharmony in this impairment, entitling it *schizophrenia,* to signify the "split" he observed between the intellectual and emotional functions in these patients.

Together, Meyer's notion of reaction-types and Bleuler's focus on cognitive and emotional experience reshaped Kraepelin's original system into our contemporary psychiatric nosology. In this "traditional" classification, Kraepelin's clinical categories are retained as the basic framework, and Meyer's and Bleuler's psychological notions provide guidelines to the patient's inner processes and social reactions.

## MODERN CRITICISMS

In recent years, sharp criticisms have been raised against the current system. Today there are fewer voices heard in defense of the standard nosology than opposed to it. Arthur P. Noyes, an eminent psychiatric teacher and hospital administrator has written (1953):

Except in organic disorders a classificatory diagnosis is less important than a psychodynamic study of personality . . . we should endeavor not so much to fit the symptoms into a classificatory scheme as to understand the sick person in terms of his life experience.

Roe (1949) has noted that too much research time is wasted and too many errors are perpetuated because investigators cling to a classification which has long since been outlived. A sharply different view is expressed by the distinguished psychologist Paul Meehl (1959):

I would explain the viability of the Kraepelin nomenclature by the hypothesis that there is a considerable amount of truth contained in the system; and that, therefore, the practical implications associated with these labels are still sufficiently great, especially when compared with the predictive power of competing concepts.

In contrast, Karl Menninger, the well-known American psychiatrist, has emphasized that all disorders are alike. They differ only quantitatively as a function of the stage of their progress. Szasz has taken a different but equally critical view of the current system (1957):

Categories such as "schizophrenic" may be doubly harmful: first, such categories are unsatisfactory as readily validable concepts for purposes of classification, and secondly, they give rise to the misleading impression that there "exists" a more or less homogeneous group of phenomena which are designated by the word in question.

Views such as those of Menninger and Szasz raise serious questions as to the utility of the traditional psychiatric nosology. Problematic as the topic may be, it reflects a revitalized interest and ferment on an important and age-old issue. We shall turn to it again in later chapters.

## SEARCH FOR BIOLOGICAL CAUSES

There are many psychiatrists and psychologists today who hold the view that a biological defect, or perhaps a subtle combination of defects, will be found ultimately for all mental disorders. Analogies are made with biological medicine where bacteria, viruses, lesions and other traumas foreign to normal functioning have been shown to underlie overt symptoms of disturbance. This notion has a long and stormy history. Theories have been propounded, tested and found wanting when judged by the rigor of time. Significant discoveries have been hailed with much acclaim only to sink into obscurity when reexamined by investigators other than those originally involved. Despite this checkered history, there have been enough valid findings to maintain a continued vigorous search.

### CONCEPT OF MENTAL DISEASE

The view that mental disorders are processes of the nervous system and not abstract spiritual phenomena was first espoused by Alcmaeon in the fifth century B.C. and continued in the work of Hippocrates. In the *Sacred Disease,* Hippocrates wrote (Grimm, 1838):

Men ought to know that from the brain and from the brain only arise our pleasures and joys as well as our sorrows, pains, griefs and tears. . . . It is the same thing which makes us mad or delirious and inspires us with dread and fear.

In the Middle Ages, all progress in anatomy lapsed as the dissection of the human body was forbidden and regressive religious fanaticism took hold. Not until Vesalius (1514–1564) in his *De Humane Corporis Fabrica* was the possibility of cerebral localization of mental disorder reaffirmed. By the seventeenth and eighteenth centuries scientific progress overrode the influence of both Hippocrates' humoral theories and theological supernaturalism. The great English clinician, Thomas Sydenham (1624–1689) enunciated the view that the primary function of diagnosis was to identify the essential disease underlying the overt symptom. He wrote (Latham, 1848):

Nature in the production of disease, is uniform and consistent . . . the self-same phenomena that you would observe in the sickness of a Socrates you would observe in the sickness of a simpleton.

Sydenham's desire to organize accurate symptom patterns was prompted by the belief that specific diseases or bodily dysfunctions could be found to account for them. This view was given a firm foundation in the extraordinary accomplishments of the early nineteenth century by Pierre Louis in pathological anatomy, Louis Pasteur and Joseph Lister in infectious diseases and Rudolf Virchow on cellular pathology. Moreau, in 1845, stated the thesis succinctly:

Insanity is the expression of a lesion of the nervous system, just as dyspnea, palpitations or diarrhea are the symptoms of a disease of the lungs, the heart, or the intestines.

In the mid-nineteenth century Herman Helmholtz, Ernst Brücke and Emil Du Bois-Reymond established a series of physiological research laboratories in Germany which strengthened the physical disease view and dominated the outlook of medical education well into the twentieth century. The role of Griesinger and his students in applying this notion to psychiatry has been noted earlier.

### DISCOVERY OF GENERAL PARESIS

Impressive as these accomplishments were, and convinced as these leaders may have been of the validity of their beliefs, no tangible proof existed that disease did in fact account for any mental disorder. It was not until the painstakingly slow discovery of *general paresis,* that medical science uncovered a biological cause in psychopathology.

The first inkling that a common pattern existed, to be called *dementia paralytica* at first, was noted by John Haslam in 1798. He reported a frequent association between delusions of grandeur and general dementia usually followed by a progressive paralysis. In 1805, Esquirol added his observation that this pattern invariably had a fatal outcome. Credit for a clear delineation of the symptom constellation goes to A. L. J. Bayle in 1822. In postmortem studies of these patients during the mid-nineteenth century, it was discovered that they had marked inflammation and degeneration in brain tissue. By 1869, Argyll-Robertson noted that patients afflicted with syphilis were unable to react with proper pupillary reflexes. This finding implicated the central nervous system in syphilitic disease and strengthened a suggestion that had been made earlier by Esmarch and Jessen in 1857 that a relationship might exist between syphilis and mental disorders. It was not until 1894 that Fournier produced evidence that 65 per cent of all patients classified as dementia paralytica had a history of syphilis. Since the figure of 65 per cent was short of a convincing relationship, doubts arose that syphilis was the cause of dementia paralytica. An ingenious experiment was carried out by Kraft-Ebbing in 1897 to dispel these doubts. He took nine paretic patients who had denied a prior syphilitic infection, and demonstrated their failure to develop syphilis when given an inoculation dose. Their immunity was conclusive proof that in fact they had been previously infected. In 1905 Schaudinn discovered that a spirochete, *Treponema pallidum,* was the cause of syphilis; this was followed in 1913 by Noguchi and Moore in their conclusive verification of this spirochete in the paretic's nerve tissue. With the underlying disease of general paresis so convincingly revealed, and a test for the identification of syphilis already developed by Wassermann, preventive and therapeutic methods progressed rapidly.

## RECENT BIOCHEMICAL RESEARCH

The discovery of general paresis had minor parallels in the specification of thiamine deficiency in Wernicke's syndrome (1881), the role of alcoholism in Korsakoff's psychosis (1887), and the existence of brain tissue degeneration in Alzheimer's presenile syndrome (1906). With the advent of newly refined laboratory procedures and precision instrumentation, these discoveries spurred the twentieth century search for other biological causes of mental disorder. This surge of activity encompassed such diverse fields as neuropathology, psychophysiology, neurochemistry, endocrinology, genetics and psychosomatic medicine. By the 1920's references to physiological "causes" for mental disorders filled the literature. Although a systematic and critical review of these physiogenic findings must be postponed until chapter 4, we may summarize the results briefly by stating that most of the data

has proved to be either incorrect or difficult to identify with any specific nosological disorder. Despite this finding, a final note should be made of the mounting technical armamentarium available to the mid-twentieth century researcher. These new tools, in time, may lead to more conclusive biological discoveries. Of interest in this regard is the statement made by Stern and Mac-Donald in their recent review of physiological correlates of mental disease (1965):

From the electron microscope through time lapse microscopy, from looking at dendritic and nerve cell activity to the vascular bed under finger nails, from studying the web-building activity of spiders, the behavior of fighting fishes, and the rope climbing ability of rats . . . the search for a biological basis of mental disorders continues.

## *DEVELOPMENT OF SOMATOTHERAPIES*

From the early successes of surgery to the recent advent of antibiotic medicines, the conviction has grown that treatment is most effective when directed at the root of a disorder and not its surface symptomatology. An assumption made in psychiatric somatic therapy is that the overt behaviors and feelings of the patient are expressions of an underlying biological affliction best treated at its source. The fact that few if any biological causes have been identified has not deterred the search for such therapies. Somatic treatments that have proved useful have resulted from *serendipity*—the art of accidental discovery. Perhaps the most striking fact about the history of somatotherapy is its progress through error and misconception. Speculative theories regarding new therapies were often far afield and those who discovered effective treatment agents were usually blazing trails to other diseases. By good fortune and happy accident, alert clinical observers noted unanticipated effects which proved empirically useful for mental disorders.

Fortunately, new speculations regarding biological therapy are subject to the scrutiny of a sophisticated professional and scientific public today. The early history of somatotherapy, a curious mixture of humor and horror, did not have these needed controls.

Not all of the biological techniques used in former centuries should be considered forerunners of our present day somatotherapy. Trephining was a religious and magical punishment to allow evil spirits to escape the possessed head of the patient, not to relieve a deficit in his brain. The medications of lizard's blood, crocodile dung and fly specs, prescribed by Egyptian physicians in 1500 B.C. were not disease cures, but magic potions.

Hippocrates, despite his part in specifying the brain as the locus of mental disorder, offered no biological treatment for the disorders he observed. Although the rationale for treating the underlying disease was established in the Renaissance, medical reasoning was naive. For example, the lungs of the fox were given to consumptives because the fox was a long-winded animal, and the fat of a bear, a hairy animal, was prescribed as a cure for baldness. Paracelsus, in the sixteenth century, classified diseases according to the treatments which "cured" them, but the universal remedies of the day included powdered Egyptian mummy, unicorn's horn, bezoar stones and theriac. Several of these contained more than 60 ingredients, all of which were worthless. As a passing note of humor, conferences were held complaining of flagrant tampering with these medications; to the physician of that early day, failures in treatment were best explained by the "pharmaceutical" adulteration of ingredients.

Not all physicians of past centuries were so naive. Many astute observers recognized the crudeness of therapies. Maimonides, in the twelfth century, said rather facetiously, "I call him a perfect physician who judges it better to abstain from treatment rather than prescribe one which might perturb the course of the malady." And Oliver Wendell Holmes, the physician-father of the eminent judge, said as recently as 1860 that nearly all the drugs then in use "should be thrown in the sea where it would be the better for mankind, and all the worse for the fishes." Despite commentaries such as these, patients were subjected to fright, blistering, chloroform, castration, cupping, bleeding, ducking and twirling well into the nineteenth century.

Somatic therapy for a disorder required that a disease first be identified. After syphilis had been established as the cause for general paresis, Julius Wagner-Jauregg, operating more on the basis of a hunch than scientific logic, inoculated paretic patients with malaria in 1917 and successfully cured them of their disease. His effort to extend this treatment technique to other psychotic disorders failed and he concluded correctly that malarial action was specific to the underlying paretic infection and was not a general cure-all for mental disorders.

In 1922, Jacob Klaesi used barbiturates to produce continuous sleep treatment. Although this technique may be considered the precursor to modern "shock" therapy, it was designed to rest fatigued or irritated nerve cells. It was in the mid-1930's that the modern era of somatotherapies started with the almost simultaneous development of insulin-coma therapy, convulsion treatment and cerebral surgery.

## INSULIN COMA THERAPY

Insulin was first administered to mental patients to increase their weight and inhibit their excitement. The step from this symptom-oriented approach to one based on "curing" the disease was made in the early 1930's by Manfred Sakel (1900–1957). He observed that unintentional comas induced by excessive insulin benefited patients. From this observation Sakel was led to the rather extreme hypothesis that psychotic behavior resulted from an overproduction of adrenalin which caused cerebral nerve cells to become hyperactive. This excessive adrenalin made the patient oversensitive to everyday stimulation; insulin was effective because it neutralized adrenalin and restored normal functioning. Sakel's hypothesis was a simple one and easy to test. In brief time it was established that psychotic patients do not overproduce adrenalin. Furthermore, adrenalin is increased rather than decreased during insulin coma. Sakel realized the weakness of his theory and subsequently wrote:

The mistakes in theory should not be counted against the treatment itself, which seems to be accomplishing more than the theory behind it.

An appraisal of these "accomplishments" will be reviewed in chapter 14.

## THE CONVULSION THERAPIES

In 1934 Laszlo Joseph von Meduna (1896–1964) reported the successful treatment of schizophrenia by inducing convulsions with a camphor mixture, known in its synthetic form as *metrazol.* His rationale for its presumed effectiveness was quite different than the one proposed by Sakel. Meduna's thesis was derived from two observations which had been noted frequently in psychiatric literature: that epilepsy and schizophrenia rarely coexist, and that schizophrenic symptoms often disappear following spontaneous convulsions. This same observation had led Nyiro and Jablonsky in 1929 to administer blood transfusions from epileptics to schizophrenics without therapeutic success. Nevertheless, Meduna was convinced that the biochemistry of these two disorders were antagonistic. Subsequent research has entirely disproved Meduna's thesis. First, epilepsy and schizophrenia are neither related nor opposed. Second, clinical experience has shown convulsive treatment to be useful primarily in depressive disorders and only rarely in schizophrenia.

Prior to the advent of pharmacologic agents in the mid-1950's, *electroconvulsive therapy* was the most widely used method of biological treatment in psychiatry. The technique of electrical convulsion, developed as early as 1900 by Leduc and Robinovitch with animals, was well known to Ugo Cerletti (1877–1963) when he first used it with psychotic subjects in 1937. After his initial success Cerletti formulated his own theory regarding its effectiveness; it was quite different from the ones proposed by Meduna and Sakel. He speculated that the convulsion brought the patient close to a state of death. This aroused extraordinary biological defenses which led, in turn, to therapeutic recovery. Whether Cerletti's speculation regarding biological defensive action is correct remains unclear today. Other speculations proposed to account for the beneficial results of convulsive treatment are equally unverified.

## SURGICAL THERAPY

One of the many hypotheses advanced to explain the successful effects of convulsive therapy served to spur the development of psychosurgery. This notion states that psychotic behavior derives from abnormally fixed arrangements in the organization of the brain. It was first proposed by Herman Boerhaave in the early eighteenth century when he devised a special twirling cage in which patients were spun to rearrange connections within the brain. This idea was approached surgically in 1890 when the Swiss psychiatrist, G. Burkhardt, removed portions of the brain cortex to rid patients of their fixed hallucinations.

Egas Moniz (1874–1955), unaware of Burkhardt's earlier work, reactivated this method of treatment in 1935 in what is known as the *prefrontal leucotomy*. This surgical separation of the frontal lobes (thought) from the thalamus (emotion) ostensibly minimized emotional preoccupations. Although the technique was used extensively in this country in the 1940's and 1950's its effectiveness was always in doubt. Its use was sharply curtailed when pharmacologic approaches to somatotherapy emerged in the mid-1950's.

## MODERN PHARMACOLOGICAL THERAPY

The search for biological therapies was given a marked boost in 1952 when two entirely different drugs were discovered accidentally to have beneficial effects in tranquilizing anxious patients. In France, Delay and Deniker reported on the effectiveness of *chlorpromazine,* a drug originally synthesized for hypertensive and surgical patients. Almost simultaneously, another drug, *reserpine,* a product of the Rauwolfia snakeroot which had been used since the 1920's by Indian physicians, was found to calm hyperactive and assaultive patients. Interest in these drugs quickly swept the psychiatric world. Although they possessed undeniable chemical effects, much of their initial success in treating psychotic patients stemmed from *placebo* action—beneficial results arising from increased enthusiasm and high therapeutic expectations. After the early wave of excitement subsided, these agents, along with others since devised, have taken a less impressive, although still useful place in the physician's kit.

The genuine beneficial effects of these agents

Figure 1-4 Founders of somatotherapy. A. Manfred J. Sakel. B. Laszlo J. Meduna. C. Egas Moniz. D. Ugo Cerletti. (From Sackler et al. (eds.): The Great Psychodynamic Therapies in Psychiatry. New York, Hoeber-Harper Publishing Co., 1956.)

encouraged a new wave of biochemical research. The action of many of the new drugs has been deciphered. More important, the search for natural biochemical dysfunctions has been intensi-fied. The growing expectation that a scientific rationale for somatotherapy will be found accounts in large measure for the present strength of the biomedical tradition.

# THE TRADITION OF PSYCHODYNAMIC PSYCHIATRY

The position that mental disorders are primarily caused by internal psychological conflicts is relatively new to psychopathology. The patient's chemistry and nervous system function normally, according to this view, but his inner thoughts and feelings are distorted and his behavior is maladaptive. The major theory espousing this position is known as psychoanalysis, first formulated by Sigmund Freud (1856–1939). Few other schools of medicine have had so pervasive an influence upon the traditions of their society. A review of the origin and development of Sigmund Freud's ideas is not only of value to an understanding of psychopathology, but also offers an illuminating chapter on the impact of one man upon the culture of his time. This flourishing psychodynamic tradition will be traced in the next few sections.

## DISCOVERY OF UNCONSCIOUS PROCESSES

### MESMERISM AND HYPNOSIS

The origin of the concept of the unconscious —inner thought and feelings beyond immediate awareness—began with the dramatic methods of an Austrian physician, Franz Anton Mesmer (1734–1815). Borrowing Paracelsus' notion of planetary magnetism, Mesmer deduced that illness resulted from an imbalance of universal magnetic fluids. This imbalance, he believed, could be restored either by manipulating magnetic devices or drawing upon invisible magnetic forces emanating from one person to another. Mesmer established a successful therapeutic practice of "animal magnetism" in 1778. Patients grasped iron rods protruding from a *baquet*, a tub containing "magnetic" chemicals, while Mesmer coaxed fluids into his patients by the wave of his magnetic wand. Despite the naiveté of his theory, Mesmer's patients responded in extraordinary ways, including the "cure" of several "paralyses." Although Mesmer's success was short lived and his mysterious methods viewed as the work of a charlatan, his introduction of "suggestion" cures indicated that psychological factors could influence mental symptoms.

Mesmer's technique was adopted by several English and French physicians. James Braid (1795–1860), an English surgeon, dispelled the notion of magnetic influence and formulated the modern idea that *hypnosis,* the term he coined for Mesmer's method, was a function only of the suggestive power of the physician's gestures and words. In France, A. A. Liebault (1823–1904), a country doctor from Nancy, included hypnosis among the tools of his otherwise conventional practice. He was instrumental in teaching the technique to both Jean Martin Charcot (1825–1893) and Hippolyte-Marie Bernheim (1840–1914).

### CHARCOT, BERNHEIM AND THEORIES OF HYSTERIA

Charcot's importance in psychodynamic psychiatry stems less from the originality of his ideas than from the role he played in stimulating the thoughts of others. Charcot began a series of detailed studies of the amazingly diverse and puzzling symptoms of hysteria at the Salpetriére hospital. Because of his neurological orientation, he viewed trances, memory loss and bodily anesthesia as diagnostically difficult cases of nervous system disease. Not until his associates demonstrated that the symptoms of hysteria could be induced by hypnosis did Charcot reconsider his views. His inability to differentiate between hypnotized and naturally produced paralyses, the frequently noted migration or disappearance of symptoms and the anatomically impossible location of many of the paralyses he saw, convinced him that hysteria could not be due to an injury or disease of the nervous system. Despite this suggestive evidence, Charcot could not forego the biological tradition of his day. Thus, he proposed that hysteria was a result of congenital neurological deficiency; hypnosis merely served as a stimulant which revealed this inborn defect.

Bernheim, a psychiatrist in the Nancy Med-

Figure 1-5    Charcot demonstrating hypnosis. (Bettmann Archive.)

ical School, vigorously disagreed with Charcot. He maintained that hysteria was a state of heightened self-suggestion and that hypnosis was an equivalent state induced by others. Bernheim advanced the view that hysteria was a psychogenic disorder and coined the term *psychoneurosis* for this and similar symptom patterns. His belief that unconscious self-suggestion might underlie the symptoms of mental disorder played a significant role in the development of the psychodynamic viewpoint. It paralleled the medical tradition of seeking underlying biological causes for disorder with the comparable notion of underlying psychological causes.

## JANET'S CONCEPT OF DISSOCIATION

The study of hysteria was carried on by two distinguished psychiatrists, Pierre Janet (1859–1947) and Sigmund Freud. Janet might very well have been considered the most original thinker of psychodynamic psychiatry had he not been overshadowed by the brilliant Freud. Both Freud and Janet explored the inner thoughts and feelings of hysteric patients. Janet gradually evolved a theory in which these neuroses were seen to result from an inability to integrate conflicting conscious processes; this thesis foreshadowed Bleuler's notion that schizophrenia was a split between thought and emotion. Janet observed that painful experiences and undesirable impulses could not be tolerated by his patients. In his concept of *dissociation,* Janet noted that intolerable thoughts and feelings take on an independent existence within the person and manifest themselves as amnesia, multiple personality, hysterical fits and paralyses. In this formulation, Janet recognized that different systems of thought could become pathologically separated and lost to consciousness. This observation strengthened the idea that unconscious processes reside within the person.

Janet's long association with Charcot limited his perspective. Dissociation was viewed to be the result of either a constitutional defect or a temporary but excessive state of fatigue. Because of this presumed organic deficiency, the patient could not maintain the "psychological tension" he needed to integrate the divergent streams of his consciousness. Janet was unable to bridge the gap between his psychological observations and his neurological training. Despite this, he continued to be a fruitful contributor to the psychodynamic movement. It remained, however, for his erstwhile fellow student, Sigmund Freud, to bring the specific processes of the unconscious into clear focus.

## FREUD AND DEVELOPMENT OF PSYCHOANALYSIS

It would not be misleading to say that Sigmund Freud was the most influential psychologist and physician of the twentieth century. His reinterpretation of the observations first made by Charcot and Bernheim initiated an intellectual revolution of international proportions. Along with Copernicus, who forced man to accept his peripheral place in the universe, and Darwin, who forced him to accept his nonunique and animalistic origins, Freud forced man to recognize that his rational superiority over other animals was but another of his delusions.

A proper understanding of Freud's ideas cannot be achieved without knowing the cultural and intellectual environment within which they developed. The latter half of the nineteenth century was a period of tremendous progress in the world of science: the theory of evolution; the chemistry of metabolism; the cell doctrine; the microbial origin of infection; quantum theory; the rediscovery of Mendelian heredity; and the integration of the nervous system.

Freud was born in Moravia in 1856, moving shortly thereafter to Vienna where he resided for 80 years until Austria was overrun by the Nazis. Antisemitism flourished in Austria throughout his lifetime; Freud may have developed much of his skill for originality by being forced into the role of an outsider from early life. Despite this "outsider's" orientation, three major influences can be seen clearly to have shaped the course of his ideas: the physiological energy theories of Helmholtz, Brücke and Meynart; the concepts of Darwin as elaborated by Jackson; and finally the studies of hypnosis and hysteria initiated by Charcot, Bernheim and Breuer.

### EARLY INFLUENCES UPON FREUD

Freud's ideas are often dated from his contact with Charcot, Bernheim and Breuer. Crucial as these experiences may have been, it is evident that the principles upon which he constructed his theories were first shaped when he was a medical student under Ernst Brücke and elaborated soon thereafter when he was a research associate in the neuroanatomical laboratories of Theodore Meynart. The physicalistic physiology formulated by Helmholtz and taught by Brücke and Meynart influenced both the language and the concepts Freud was to develop in his own psychodynamic theories. Brücke's lectures on physiology in the 1880's note the following (Jones, 1953):

Real causes are symbolized in science by the word "force". . . . Knowledge reduces them to two —attraction and repulsion. Freud, characterizing his own views in 1926, wrote ". . . forces assist or inhibit one another, combine with one another, enter into compromises with one another. . . ."

Freud's concepts were consistently organized as energies interacting in a dynamic play of forces and counterforces. *Libido* was a life force struggling against *thanatos,* a death force; the *id* was an instinctual force regulated by the *ego,* a regulating and controlling force. Freud's entire metapsychology with its mental apparatus, regulating mechanisms and dynamic, topographic and economic modes of description, shows striking parallels with the tenets of his early neurological training. Although he gave up his early efforts to find a physiological basis for mental processes, he was never fully emancipated from the Helmholtzian energy model.

A second and often unrecognized influence upon Freud, came from Darwin's theories of evolution. Hughlings Jackson (1834–1911), the great English neurologist, extended Darwin's basic observations by proposing that the symptoms of brain disorders reflect the emergence of primitive brain functions which had been submerged during evolution. Freud, borrowing this notion, formulated the idea that emotional traumas lead to the loss of mature capacities and are followed by "regression" to more primitive childhood behavior. Jackson further espoused the view that organisms compensate for the loss of a biological function. He viewed these substitutive behaviors as clinically useful signs of an unobservable disease. Freud drew upon this idea, first to formulate his concept of adaptive defense mechanisms, and second, for his view that mechanisms are a sign of an unobservable or unconscious disturbance. Jackson's comments on the diagnostic value of dreams were also adopted by Freud. Although Freud elaborated each of these ideas in an original and insightful manner, it is obvious that as a young neurologist he was fully acquainted with the speculations of Jackson, the most eminent theoretical neurologist of his day.

As early as 1880, Joseph Breuer (1842–1925), a well-known Viennese internist, observed that the recall of early traumatic experiences during hypnosis often resulted in therapeutic relief for hysterical patients. Freud first became acquainted with the relationship between hypnosis and hysteria in 1885 when he received a fellowship to study diseases of the nervous system with Charcot in Paris. Upon Freud's return to Vienna he learned from Breuer, who had been an associate of his in Meynart's laboratory, that emotional catharses among hysterics during hypnosis appeared to benefit these patients. In order to understand this unusual phenomenon better, Freud returned to France in 1889, to study with Bernheim.

After availing himself of Bernheim's psychological interpretations of hysteria, Freud returned to Vienna and adopted the hypnotic-cathartic method of Breuer. After an intensive treatment of several cases of hysteria by this technique, Freud and Breuer reported their studies in an article in 1893, and more fully in their epochal book *Studies of Hysteria* published in 1895. In contrast to the biologically oriented theories of Janet, which failed to explain the personal meaning of hysterical symptoms, the formulations of Freud and Breuer specified the logical relationship of the symptom to the experiences and strivings of the

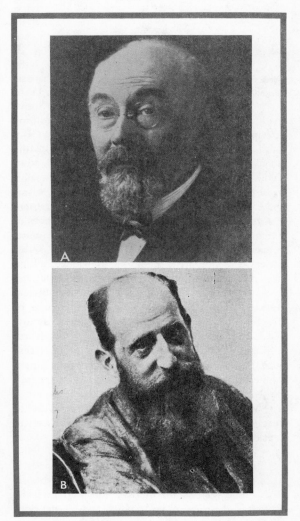

Figure 1-6 A. Pierre M. F. Janet. (Bettmann Archive.) B. Joseph Breuer.

patient. Their thesis was that painful thoughts and feelings were repressed into an unconscious force which exerted powerful pressures within the patient. This pressure expressed itself in symptoms which symbolically represented the repressed thoughts and feelings. Emotional catharsis, known as *abreaction*, relieved the unconscious pressure and, in turn, eliminated the symptom that the pressure had created.

Soon after their joint publication, Breuer gave up their research and left Freud to explore its further development alone. Freud soon found that hypnosis was of limited value. Some patients could not be hypnotized and symptoms often returned after the hypnotic trance. Freud devised an original technique to meet these problems. The technique, called *free association*, consisted merely of requiring that the patient speak aloud every thought and feeling, inhibiting nothing that came to his mind. This method, together with reports of dreams, provided Freud with all the clinical data he needed to build a new system of psychology which he named *psychoanalysis*.

Despite the lonely years following Breuer's withdrawal, Freud remained fascinated by the obscure labyrinths of human thought and emotion. His relentless search into these mysterious and hidden processes proved to be a perilous journey professionally. That he stumbled into blind alleys and held tenaciously to fruitless and obscure concepts does not diminish the courage and inventiveness of his efforts. With rare brilliance he uncovered the inner world of man's psychological make-up. It will suffice for the moment to note only four of his major findings and doctrines.

## ELUCIDATION OF INTRAPSYCHIC PROCESSES

Freud was not the first to uncover the role of unconscious processes. Perceptive men have known it for ages. But Freud was the first to trace the complex manner in which unconscious motives and conflicts weave into intricate and distorted patterns of overt behavior. As he learned to unfold the strategies for self protection and conflict resolution, such seemingly purposeless behavior as dreams, phobias, compulsions and even everyday slips of the tongue took on meaning and clarity. Freud argued that the individual unconsciously adopted extreme defensive maneuvers to deny, falsify or distort the pain of unfulfilled strivings and fears. He recognized clearly that these unconscious processes occurred in normal and abnormal individuals alike. This realization helped close the gap between the study of normal behavior and psychopathology.

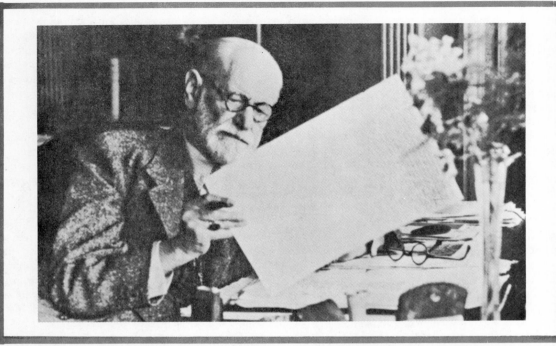

Figure 1-7    Sigmund Freud. (From Jones, E.: The Life and Work of Sigmund Freud. Vol. 3. New York, Basic Books, Inc., 1957.)

## ROLE OF CHILDHOOD EXPERIENCES

In his early writings, Freud believed that disorders resulted primarily from traumatic childhood experience. His later work minimized the importance of trauma and stressed that indulgence or frustration during any of the crucial early stages of development was the major cause of disorders. The remnants of these early experiences were deeply imbedded within the unconscious and were not accessible to the modifying influence of changing circumstance. As the pressure of these memories persisted, the individual anticipated and recreated new experiences similar to those of his childhood. Freud specified different forms of psychopathology depending on the intensity and the stage when these difficulties arose first. From this notion he derived such disorders as the oral and anal characters.

## THEORY OF PERSONALITY STRUCTURE

Personality structure was conceived by Freud to consist of three major components—*id, ego* and *superego*—interacting in dynamic tension and balance. These concepts were merely convenient ways of describing processes involved in personality functioning and were not viewed by Freud as things or entities.

The *id* represented inborn and unmodifiable instinctual strivings within the individual; these strivings seek expression unmindful of reality. The similarities Freud observed between the instinctual behavior of infants and the expression of adult sexuality led him to speak of infantile strivings as sexual in nature; the sequence through which these early instinctual drives unfolded were termed the *psychosexual stages*. The second component of personality, referred to as the *ego,* represented processes geared to reality adaptations. These processes—judgment, memory, knowledge, anticipation and the unconscious mechanisms of defense—controlled the instinctual drives of the id and directed their expression within the boundaries of practical reality. The third personality structure, the *superego,* consisted of internalized social prohibitions that inhibited instinctual impulses; these took the form of guilt feelings and fears of punishment. Practical compromises between the impulses of the id and the inhibitions of the superego are a primary function of the ego; a failure to reconcile these opposing forces led inevitably to tension and emotional disorder.

## TECHNIQUE OF THERAPY

Freud's views on therapy followed logically from his theories of personality and its development; replace the unconscious with the conscious, eliminate conflicts generated during the infantile stages of psychosexual development, and redress imbalances between id and superego by strengthening the resources of the ego. Maladaptive behaviors were eliminated by eliciting memories and developing insights into the past through the techniques of free association and dream analysis; the major goal was the extinction of the patient's disposition to reactivate his childhood difficulties in current life experiences. This was achieved by an analysis of the *transference phenomenon,* that is, the patient's tendency to act toward the therapist with the same attitudes and feelings that he developed in relation to his parents. Through this procedure, the patient became aware of the roots and the persistence of his maladaptive behavior; with these insights, his ego could be reorganized into a more efficient and adaptive pattern.

Freud devoted his long and fruitful life to the development and elaboration of his theories and techniques. Unlike his German contemporary Kraepelin, who sought to classify broad groups of disorders with common symptoms, Freud stressed the personal experience and uniqueness of each patient. And unlike Janet, his French contemporary, who viewed conflicts as precipitants that activate an underlying constitutional deficiency, Freud traced the psychogenic and unconscious processes he perceived as fundamental to each disorder. It was not only the specifics of his findings which proved so epochal; his individualistic philosophy and his orientation toward psychodynamic causation served as the foundation for our twentieth century understanding of man's nature.

## VARIANTS OF FREUD'S PSYCHODYNAMIC THEORIES

Freud's theories underwent continual modification. Although stubbornly adhering to his beliefs despite professional isolation and ridicule, he had sufficient objectivity to modify them when convinced that they were invalid. But he was a jealous guardian of the theories he felt were correct, and tolerated few dissidents in his growing circle of disciples.

The long period of intellectual self-reliance following Breuer's withdrawal, a period spotted only by an obscure and intellectually barren relationship with the internist Wilhelm Fleiss, came to an end in 1902. Weekly discussions with a small group of disciples that year grew into the Vienna Psychoanalytical Society. Many men who would make their own significant contributions to psychodynamic thought were drawn into this group. The Swiss psychiatrist, Eugen Bleuler, became interested in Freud's ideas in 1906 and promulgated the view that his concepts were necessary for an understanding of mental disorder. It was not until 1909, however, when Freud was invited to Clark University in the United States, and later during the First World War, when his theories seemed especially fruitful in explaining the causes of combat neuroses, that his views took on international significance. The acclaim he received was overshadowed, however, by intense criticism and condemnation. As a result Freud became particularly sensitive to criticism from within his own ranks.

### EARLY DEVIATIONS OF JUNG AND ADLER

Carl Gustav Jung (1875–1961) and Alfred Adler (1870–1937) were among the early and most important disciples to diverge from Freud and to develop theories of their own.

Although chosen by Freud as his heir apparent, Jung could not agree with Freud's emphasis on the "sexual" nature of development and motivation, and established his own system of *Analytic Psychology* in 1911. Jung expanded the notion of *libido,* Freud's concept for the basic sexual energies, to include all life-propelling forces. The concept of racial memories, known as the *collective unconscious,* was proposed to suggest that instinctual forces were more than seething animalistic impulses; according to Jung, these forces contained social dispositions as well. These primitive dispositions were often expressed in folklore and mystical beliefs. When no acceptable outlet could be found for them in societal life, they took the form of symptoms such as phobias, delusions and compulsions. Jung's belief in unconscious social dispositions led also to his formulation of two basic personality types, the *extravert* and the *introvert.* Despite these and other original contributions, Jung's views had minimal impact upon the mainstream of psychodynamic theory and practice.

Alfred Adler, founder of the school of *Individual Psychology,* became an outspoken opponent of Freud's views on infantile sexuality at the same time as Jung in 1911. On the basis of his own clinical observations, Adler concluded that superiority and power strivings were more fundamental to pathology than was sexuality. Although many of his patients were not overtly assertive, he observed that their disorder enabled them to dominate others in devious and subtle ways. Phobias and hypochondriasis, for example, not only excused a patient from disagreeable tasks, but al-

Figure 1-8 Early Freudian dissidents. A. Carl G. Jung. (National Library of Medicine, Bethesda, Maryland.) B. Alfred Adler. (Bettmann Archive.)

lowed him to control and manipulate others. Adler hypothesized that these strivings for superiority were a consequence of the inevitable and universally experienced weakness and inferiority in early childhood. In this conception, Adler attempted to formulate a universal drive which would serve as an alternative to Freud's universal sexual strivings. According to Adler, basic feelings of inferiority led to persistent and unconscious compensatory efforts. These were manifested as pathological struggles for power and triumph if the individual experienced unusual deficiencies or weaknesses in childhood. Among healthier personalities, compensation accounted for strivings at self-improvement, and interests in social change and welfare. These compensatory strivings, acquired by all individuals as a reaction to the restrictions imposed by their more powerful parents, led to a general pattern of behavior which Adler called the *style of life*.

## NEO-FREUDIAN SOCIAL THEORISTS

Adler's view that the character of man's development is rooted in social strivings served to guide the ideas of Karen Horney (1885–1952) and Erich Fromm. Although both took issue with Freud's biological orientation, preferring to emphasize sociocultural factors instead, they regarded themselves as renovators rather than deviators from his theories. Along with Harry Stack Sullivan (1892–1949), they have been called neo-Freudian social theorists.

Horney's main contention was that disorders reflected cultural trends learned within the family; biological determinants were minimized and interpersonal relationships stressed. Anxiety and repressed anger were generated in rejected children and led to feelings of helplessness, hostility and isolation. As these children matured, they devel-

oped an intricate defensive pattern of either withdrawal, acquiescence or aggression as a means of handling their basic anxiety. Although Horney felt that adult patterns resulted largely from early experience, she argued, in contrast with Freud, that therapy should focus on its adult form of expression. First, the intervening years between childhood and adulthood caused important changes in adaptive behavior. And second, present day realities had to be accepted and the goals of therapy had to take them into account. Although many of Horney's ideas were presented in an unsystematic and unscientific fashion, the clarity of her expositions and their appropriateness to modern day life influenced the practice and thought of psychodynamic psychiatry in the last two decades in many important ways.

Erich Fromm, a neo-Freudian social philosopher and psychologist, was the first of Freud's disciples to concentrate his writings on the role of society in mental disorder. He advocated the view that the impositions of social conformity force the individual to relinquish his natural spontaneity and freedom. To Fromm, neurotic behavior is a consequence of insufficient encouragement and warmth from one's parents which could have strengthened the individual against the demands of society. Fromm perceived the goal of therapy to be a bolstering of the individual's capacities for self-responsibility, and not the facilitation of a conformist adjustment. Fromm's interest in societal influences led him to modify Freud's neurotic character types into social character types. Along with similar modifications formulated by Horney, these types depicted contemporary patterns of personality disorder with extraordinary clarity.

Harry Stack Sullivan was influenced first by the American psychiatrists Adolf Meyer and William Alanson White, but later adopted many of Freud's concepts regarding intrapsychic processes and early childhood development. His emphasis on the interpersonal aspects of growth and his contributions to the communication process in therapy classify him properly among neo-Freudian social theorists. Because of Sullivan's exposure to the linguist Edward Sapir and the positivist philosopher Percy Bridgman, he became especially critical of the conceptually awkward and frequently obscure formulations of psychoanalysis. As a remedy, he created his own system and terminology. With few exceptions, his terminology has failed to replace that of Freud. However, his highly original studies, especially regarding early development, schizophrenia and the process of therapy, have had a marked impact upon the thinking and practice of contemporary psychodynamic psychiatry.

## NEO-FREUDIAN EGO THEORISTS

Another major contemporary position, to be more fully discussed in chapter 2, has been referred to as neo-Freudian ego theory. Most notable among theorists of this persuasion are Heinz Hartmann, Ernst Kris (1900–1957), David Rapaport (1911–1960) and Erik Erikson. This widespread and growing school of thought minimizes Freud's focus on the sexual instincts, as do the neo-Freudian social theorists. Although recognizing the significance of social and interpersonal factors, ego theorists are especially concerned with the sequence through which consciousness, perception, thought and language unfold in the earliest periods of life. These adaptive and reality-oriented or ego instincts are believed to be crucial to the understanding of pathological behavior. As a result, ego theorists concentrate their research on learning processes leading to the refinement of these ego functions. With this new emphasis, the scope of psychodynamic theory was widened, and a particularly weak link in Freud's original work was strengthened.

Psychodynamic theory took a firm hold in many quarters throughout the globe. In England, Freud's ideas were elaborated by Melanie Klein (1882–1960) in her studies of early development and aggression. W. R. D. Fairbairn (1889–1964), the eminent Scottish psychoanalyst, working along similar lines to Klein, developed a new formulation of ego psychology based on infantile strivings for "object-relations." The Swiss psychoanalysts, Ludwig Binswanger (1878–1967) and Medard Boss, influenced by phenomenological philosophers, laid the groundwork for the contemporary school of *daseinsanalyse,* known best as existential analysis. And not to be overlooked on the current scene is Sigmund Freud's daughter, Anna Freud, who added her own studies of ego development and the mechanisms of defense to those originally formulated by her father.

# THE TRADITION OF PERSONOLOGY AND CLINICAL PSYCHOLOGY

The independent lines along which clinical psychiatric practice and academic psychological research have grown account in part for the scattered and often confused state of psychopathological theory. To be sure, there have been occasions when the ideas and methods of one field have fertilized the other. But many such instances would be difficult to find.

The traditional psychiatric concern with practical problems such as classification and differential diagnosis have resulted in the development of useful but essentially descriptive concepts and terms which have little or no relation to basic psychological processes. While the practical need for this psychiatric language cannot be denied, it rests on a hazardous foundation. Scientific history has shown repeatedly that concepts constructed without reference to fundamental or general laws are extremely fragile and likely to become outmoded.

Unfortunately, concepts formulated in pursuit of general laws of behavior often have little relevance to the practical problems faced by the psychiatrist. Academic researchers derive many of their ideas from studies of normal behavior; these studies concentrate on limited spheres of behavior such as sensation or learning, and frequently are based on animal rather than human subjects. The assumption made by academicians is that a thorough knowledge of these part-functions will lead to a number of basic laws from which the complex behaviors of psychopathology can be logically derived. An attempt to bring basic concepts developed through academic research in line with psychiatric problems has recently begun and we will discuss this rapprochement in another section.

In the present section, however, we will deal with similar efforts in the fields of clinical psychology and personology. These disciplines have sought to bridge the gap between basic psychology and practical psychiatry by the use of personality concepts, that is, concepts which represent *dis-*

*positions to behavior.* Unusual as it may seem, the *conceptualization* of personality structure has evolved quite independently of its *measurement.* As a result, our discussion must trace both of these historical lines of development. There are, however, several assumptions which they share in common.

First, the notion of the *uniqueness* of each individual is implicit in the work of both clinical psychologists and personologists. In contrast to the academic approach, these disciplines are less concerned with general patterns or commonalities among individuals than in the special pattern with which factors combine in a particular individual. From this orientation arises a focus, not upon the elements of functioning, but on their interaction. This approach is often referred to as *idiographic* and *holistic,* signifying a concern with the unique integration of the total personality.

Another assumption shared by clinicians and personologists is that a continuity exists between normal and abnormal behavior. Thus, measurement is designed to establish the relative position of an individual on each of a number of universal dimensions of personality functioning. Viewed in this fashion, abnormality is merely an extension of the study of quantitative individual differences. Diagnosis, in turn, consists of specifying the individual's unique pattern of extreme scores on a set of personality dimensions. Let us now turn to history.

## CONCEPTUALIZATION OF PERSONALITY

Hippocrates formulated the first characterizations of personality. As noted earlier, dominance among any of his four bodily humors resulted in distinct personality temperaments: *sanguine,* or hopeful; *melancholic,* or sad; *choleric,* or irascible; and *phlegmatic,* or apathetic. The longevity of this ancient four-part typology stems not only from its explicit recognition of a relationship between body chemistry and personality, but its success in describing modern personality types as well.

For more than 20 centuries following Hippocrates, personality characterizations took the form of facile and brilliant word portraits drawn in literature and drama. Beginning with the sketches of Theophrastus in the fourth century B.C. and continuing in the work of Chaucer, Ben Jonson, Jean de la Bruyere and George Eliot, the masterful descriptions in drama and fiction, free of the constraints of philosophical discipline, made the clumsy scientific characterizations of their day

seem colorless and restrained. Brilliant and insightful though they were, dramatic portrayals were caricatures, not whole personalities.

### GALL AND PHRENOLOGY

It was not until the late eighteenth century that the first systematic effort was made to analyze the basic elements of which personality might be composed. Despite its discrediting and its disreputable side, *phrenology,* proposed by Franz Joseph Gall (1758–1828), was an honest and serious attempt to construct a science of personology. The rationale that Gall presented for his procedure of measuring contour variation of the skull was not in the least illogical given the limited knowledge of anatomy in his day. Assuming a relationship between mind and body, he proposed that inner characteristics would be reflected in outer structures. Since the brain was the most important biological organ for thought and emotion, it followed, according to Gall, that the expression of these inner characteristics would be represented best by variations in the shape of the cranium. That this gross expression of personality proved invalid is not surprising to us when we think of the exceedingly complex structure of neuroanatomy. Despite his naiveté, Gall's speculation that separate units or *faculties* existed in the brain established a basis for modern factor psychology. His attempt to demonstrate relationships between body structure and personality was also a precursor for the morphological typologies proposed later by Kretschmer and Sheldon.

### EARLY TYPOLOGISTS

Typologies were promulgated by the psychiatrists Janet and Kraepelin during the late nineteenth century. These characterizations were limited, however, to the mentally ill. It was not until Carl Jung's distinction between *extravert* and *introvert* individuals that typological concepts drawn from psychiatry were applied to normal personality. These characterizations were further elaborated by the Swiss psychiatrist Hermann Rorschach, known best for his work on psychodiagnostic tests. The extravert type as described by Jung was a sociable, impulsive and emotionally expressive individual, whereas the introvert was noted as socially awkward, emotionally reserved and self-absorbed.

Credit goes to Ernst Kretschmer (1888–1964) for his synthesis of Gall's notion relating body structure to personality, and Jung's characterization of extravert and introvert types. In his well-documented book, *Physique and Character,* published in 1921, Kretschmer extended an observation he made that schizophrenics possessed elongated physiques and manic-depressives rounded and soft physiques, into a theory connecting body build to normal personality. In a series of studies, he demonstrated that persons with tall and slender physiques were of a schizoid or introversive temperament, whereas those of a heavier and more rotund physique were extraversive. Kretschmer's hypothesis was investigated with more refined measures by William Sheldon, who found that Kretschmer's typology was oversimplified, and that patterns relating body build to personality could take many more than two or three forms; we will analyze Sheldon's research more fully in chapter 4.

## FACTOR AND TRAIT THEORIES

Advances in mathematics in the late nineteenth century led to a reawakened interest in the "basic units" of personality. To replace the hypothetical faculties proposed by Gall, efforts were made to construct *factors*—a set of independent elements of personality derived statistically from commonalities in behavior and test performance. The use of this method in personality research was stimulated by C. Spearman's success in analyzing the basic factors of intelligence. The technique was extended to personality study by Cyril Burt, Lloyd Thurstone, and more recently, in the multivariate research of J. P. Guilford and Raymond Cattell. A notable attempt to correlate body type and extraversion-introversion through factor-analytic methods has been made recently by Hans J. Eysenck. These studies will be treated more fully in chapter 4.

Gordon Allport (1897–1967), the distinguished American personologist, took strong exception to factor-analytic approaches to personality. To him, factors were statistical fictions or mathematical artifacts devoid of intrinsic psychological meaning. His criticism was directed particularly to the notion that factors should be uncorrelated with each other. It seemed highly improbable to Allport that a theory based on independent factors could be consistent with the highly integrated nature of the nervous system. To counter this view, Allport argued for a theory based on trait concepts, that is, relatively enduring personality dispositions which underlie overt behavior. The fact that several traits operate within an individual enabled his theory to deal with the variety of human behavior better than the more restrictive type theories. Since traits, according to All-

port, stabilized during growth, consistency in adult behavior could also be explained. In his major work, *Personality, A Psychological Interpretation,* published in 1937, Allport supported the growing trend toward a belief that personality is best conceived of as a unique and highly integrated or holistic system.

## HOLISTIC THEORIES

The holistic concept states that personality can be understood only in terms of the intrinsic unity between biological functions and environmental stimulation. This view was fostered by the early writings of Hughlings Jackson, Theodor von Uexkuell and the Gestalt psychologists, Max Wertheimer and Kurt Koffka. Its most convincing exposition in personality was made, however, in the brilliant work of Kurt Goldstein (1876–1965) and Kurt Lewin (1890–1947). Although both were influenced by the Gestaltists, they extended the holistic idea along different lines of research. Goldstein, an eminent neurosurgeon, stressed the internal unity of biological functioning whereas Lewin, a psychologist, focused upon the interdependencies of personality and environment.

To Goldstein, personality could not be understood by studying isolated behaviors or functions because the organism operated as a unit that could not be analyzed in terms of its parts. As evidence for his thesis, Goldstein illustrated numerous cases in which neurological damage to the individual led, not to a loss of the affected function, but to a reorganization of his total functioning. This reorganization enabled the individual to keep his drives and goals intact, although more primitively. From this evidence, Goldstein suggested that man possessed a sovereign motive, that of *self-actualization.* Through this concept, he proposed that man's central motive was to realize his inherent potentials by whatever means and capacities available to him.

Kurt Lewin, following a similar philosophy, portrayed personality as a structure composed of interdependent and communicating regions interacting in a dynamic equilibrium with a psychological environment. Of particular note was Lewin's contention that events must be conceived in terms of how each individual consciously perceives them, rather than how they objectively exist; this *phenomenological* viewpoint has grown into one of the major orientations of contemporary psychopathology.

It is Carl Rogers, a contemporary theorist about whom more will be said in later chapters, who has most fully developed both the self-actualization concept of Goldstein and the phenomenological approach of Lewin.

Placed also among the holistic theorists are two other contemporary psychologists, Henry Murray and Gardner Murphy. Their contribution lies more in the scope and depth of their writings than in their originality. Drawing upon a wide knowledge of neurological development, psychodynamic theory, academic psychology and cultural anthropology, both Murray and Murphy formulated independent theories of personality. Their work represents the most sophisticated and integrated conceptions of personality development and structure to date.

# MEASUREMENT OF PERSONALITY

## GALTON, CATTELL AND DIFFERENTIAL PSYCHOLOGY

Although the first attempt to measure psychological differences can be traced to Christian Thomasius' system of "numerical degrees for the principal passions" in the seventeenth century, the true founding of differential psychology began with Francis Galton (1822–1911). Galton followed a suggestion made by Quatelet, a Belgian statistician, to the effect that the principles of probability and mathematics could be applied successfully to the measurement of human attributes. At his anthropometric laboratory in London, established in 1882, Galton constructed tests that were simpler than the psychophysical measures then used, and, more importantly, focused attention on individual differences rather than group characteristics. His use of statistical difference units was an original innovation, and his exploration of psychological traits and temperament went beyond the narrow sensorimotor studies typical of his day.

James McKeen Cattell (1860–1944), despite the objections of his mentor, Wilhelm Wundt, decided to embark on a study of Galton's concepts. Upon returning to the United States from Leipzig, where he received his doctorate, Cattell continued the Galton tradition of studying individual differences. In his laboratories at the University of Pennsylvania established in 1890, he devised statistical procedures to obtain normative and comparative measures among individuals. Here he coined the term "mental tests" to reflect the quantitative or psychometric method he used. He was instrumental also in initiating studies on such varied subjects as reading skills, college aptitudes and the mentally defective. However, the major figure of American psychology at that time, Edward Titchener, had unequivocally condemned tests as unscientific, and as a consequence, the development of test methodology lay dormant for almost two decades.

## ERA OF INTELLIGENCE TESTS AND SELF-REPORT INVENTORIES

It remained for Alfred Binet (1857–1911) a French psychologist, to bring testing out of the laboratory and into systematic use. Binet objected to the measures used by Galton and Cattell on the ground that they were unable to discriminate the more complex higher mental processes. Given the more philosophic temper of French psychology and the support of the French Ministry of Public Instruction, Binet forsook the precise and simple measures constructed by Galton and undertook the study of such complex processes as memory, imagery, comprehension, attention and judgment. By 1905 Binet combined several of the instruments he had devised into the first formal scale of general intelligence.

Revision, translation and the eventual adoption of the Binet scale in this country followed shortly thereafter. Goddard and Kuhlmann published versions in 1911, but the time was not ripe for acceptance until the work of a Stanford psychologist, Lewis M. Terman (1877–1956). In 1916, Terman published *The Measurement of Intelligence* in which his revised scale was described in detail. Revised and improved in 1937, and again in 1960, it remains, along with the scales devised by David Wechsler in the 1930's and 1940's, as one of the standard measures of intelligence in use today.

The early emphasis on intelligence tests was largely a result of the limited instruments available to psychologists during the first decades of this century. These measured a rather limited part of the total range of human functioning. As the need arose to study other aspects of behavior, psychologists were called upon to devise new methods. Unfortunately, when the call came for personality measures, the undeveloped state of personality theory could provide neither suitable concepts nor a suitable format. Instead, the psychometric procedures used with some success in intelligence testing were adopted.

The first of the personality instruments designed in this fashion was constructed by Robert Woodworth (1869–1962) during the First World War. His personal data sheet was devised as an economical replacement for standardized interviews to identify poor prospects for military service. It followed the format of an interview by asking the respondent to answer simple questions about himself. This self-report format became the model for dozens of subsequently devised questionnaire inventories; with a few notable exceptions these instruments failed to survive the scrutiny of scientific analyses or practical use.

## RISE OF PROJECTIVE TECHNIQUES

Personality testing, faced with critical research and indifferent if not hostile academic attitudes, languished during the 1920's and 1930's. Although this period allowed for reappraisal and consolidation of early progress, the use of the psychometric approach seemed restrictive and sterile to most psychologists. An increasing acquaintance with psychodynamic theory led clinically oriented psychologists to search for methods which would portray the complexity of personality and disclose unconscious motivational processes. The search led to the discovery of the little known word-association technique devised in 1905 by Jung, and to the inkblot cards constructed by Hermann Rorschach (1884–1922) in 1921. Rorschach's test was based on an observation Binet had made earlier regarding the use of inkblots for personality diagnosis. The possibilities of this unusual technique were especially intriguing to psychologists accustomed to the simple and straightforward psychometric measures. Obscure though the new method appeared, it promised to reveal the latent and unexpressed aspects of personality. Its logic was novel also, for it was based on the assumption that a person would display the inner

dynamics and full complexity of his make-up when he attempted to interpret or "project" meaning on an ambiguous stimulus. Despite its unusual structure and rationale, the technique was adopted quickly. In 1935, the armamentarium of projective methodology was further extended when Henry Murray devised the Thematic Apperception Test. Combined with similar projective devices these two tests became the major tools available for clinical diagnosis. They are currently in universal use, but they have been justly criticized because procedures for their interpretation are subjective and standards of scientific validation have not been adequately met.

## RETURN TO OBJECTIVE PERSONALITY ASSESSMENT

One gauge of scientific respectability is the degree of objectivity with which an instrument can be administered and interpreted. Thus, to many psychologists, the subjectively obscure procedures followed in the interpretation of projective tests seemed like scientific irreverence. A problem arose, however, since objective psychometric methods were incapable of uncovering complex clinical patterns that projectives ostensibly could uncover. As a means of remedying this impasse, the constructors of the Minnesota Multiphasic Personality Inventory (MMPI) proposed an entirely new rationale for objective test interpretation. They noted that whatever merit a diagnostic technique possesses lies in the validity or accuracy of its conclusions and not in its interpretive procedures. If this gauge was to be applied, the value of any instrument must be determined by the de-

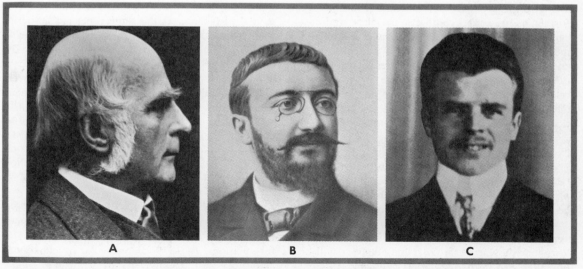

Figure 1-9   Forerunners of modern psychological testing. A. Francis Galton. B. Alfred Binet. (Photographs A and B courtesy of Bettmann Archive.) C. Hermann Rorschach. (Hans Huber Medical Publisher, Berne, Switzerland.)

gree to which it predicted or correlated with *real* and meaningful behavior. Accordingly, the responses which individuals made about themselves on the MMPI were not to be taken at their face value, but were appraised by their correlation with external criteria. Thus, only those test items which showed a significant empirical relationship with

clinical syndromes were included in constructing the final form of the MMPI. The logic underlying the MMPI not only revived standards of objectivity, but showed that simplicity in test interpretation need not be inimical to clinical utility. For the first time, a firm "scientific" basis for psychodiagnostics was established.

# TRADITION OF ACADEMIC AND EXPERIMENTAL PSYCHOLOGY

Academic psychology is distinguished for its commitment to the methods of "science." As usually conceived this entails an acceptance of three guiding principles: the use of objective and technically precise instruments, the application of rigorously controlled procedures in research design and analysis and the search for basic laws that underlie both simple and complex functions. In contrast to those whose concern lies in the intricacies and difficulties of real life, the academician postpones what he knows to be momentary and dubious solutions to pressing problems in order to discover the universally valid and durable principles of human behavior.

The use of objective and technically precise instruments can be seen readily in the laboratory methods preferred by academicians. The perceptionist's use of the tachistoscope, the learning researcher's use of the Skinner box and the psychophysiologist's use of the electroencephalogram all reflect the technical orientation of science.

As a method of achieving objectivity, the academician anchors or "operationally defines" his terms at the level of tangible observables, thereby avoiding the problem of ambiguous concepts. To further assure that hypotheses are clear and susceptible to empirical test, he designs his experiments to eliminate or control extraneous influences which might confuse a proper interpretation of results. To obtain quantitative or functional relationships among his concepts, he compares different magnitudes among variables and statistically analyzes their significance. The rigor and precision demanded in methodology is paralleled by equivalent convictions at the theoretical level. Hypotheses are not accepted because of their facile "explanatory powers," but are tested by their empirical predictive accuracy. Accurate findings must be generalizable and durable since the laws of science, of which psychology is a part, are universal. Since scientific laws are universal, it follows that those governing simple behavior will be operative also in more complex behavior. As such, the most rapid and efficient strategy for investi-

gating complex behavior will be achieved by focusing research on the simpler and less intricate forms. Using this rationale, the academician engages in a systematic study of less complicated functions such as perception and learning, rather than personality as a whole. And, for convenience, he studies them at the simpler animal level.

These methodological and theoretical principles have been breached as often as not. Nevertheless, they have been and remain the major motivating guidelines underlying the development of the academic-experimental approach discussed in this section.

## PSYCHOPHYSICAL AND PERCEPTUAL FOUNDATIONS

The emergence of academic psychology occurred less than a century ago in the study of sensory reactions to physical stimuli. Relationship between the magnitude or frequency of an environmental stimulus, such as a sound wave, and the experience people "sensed" in reaction to it was noted first by a number of German experimental physicists. At the same time, physiologists were uncovering the structure of the internal sense organs which accounted for these sensations. By 1845, the physiologist E. Weber had devised a number of systematic procedures which enabled him to quantify sensory responses to physical stimuli. Gustav Fechner, a physicist, extended and refined Weber's methods and presented them in his highly influential book *Elements of Psychophysics* in 1860.

### WUNDT AND TITCHENER

Wilhelm Wundt (1842–1900), considered by many to be the father of scientific psychology, observed the success of Weber's and Fechner's formulations. In 1879 he opened a psychological laboratory at the University of Leipzig to establish scientific evidence for the view that the "mind" could be measured and that psychology could move from its perennial place as metaphysical speculation into the ranks of science. Wundt's procedure of controlled *introspection* went beyond the study of the simple and pure stimuli investigated by the early German psychophysicists. In his "science of conscious experience" he systematically recorded reactions to complex and impure stimuli, recognizing that consciousness was more than a product of simple sensations. It was in these experiments that he initiated the study of the complex response we call perception.

Wundt's student, Edward Bradford Titchener (1867–1927), continued these studies upon his appointment to Cornell University in 1892. He became a dominant figure in American psychology for more than 20 years during which time he espoused a "core-context theory" of perception. To Titchener, the *core* of perception was composed of immediate sensations fused with residual images of past sensations. Meaning was given to this core by the unique *context* of the individual's past experiences. Combined, the core and context accounted for the meaningfulness of perception. In Titchener's formulation of the context, he conceived it to be an essentially static baseline upon which core stimuli impinged.

## FUNCTIONALISM AND GESTALT PSYCHOLOGY

A differing view of the perceiver's past was developed concurrently by members of the American Functionalist and the German Würzburg schools of psychology. To them the context was viewed as a preestablished attitude or purpose which preceded the perceptual act and actively directed the individual's attention toward selected elements of the stimulus field. In their contention, individuals did not passively receive a stimulus and then give it meaning. Rather, perception was meaningful immediately because of the perceiver's expectation or set. This conception noted that past experiences shape the perception of reality; it established a solid experimental basis for the clinical observation that psychopathology leads to perceptual distortion.

A second and different objection arose to the oversimplified approach of the early psychophysicists and the passively mechanistic conceptions of the core-context theory. Because certain perceptual processes seemed to be universal, the Gestalt school of psychology proposed that they were inherent properties of the nervous system and therefore unlearned. Although this notion received little support, the Gestaltists contended further, through the work of Max Wertheimer, Kurt Koffka and

Wolfgang Kohler, that perception was not a construction of parts merely pieced together. They argued the converse to be true; the whole, or *Gestalt,* was perceived as a unit first, and parts took on meaning only in terms of the Gestalt in which they were imbedded. This holistic notion became a model for comparable conceptions in many fields of psychology and psychopathology. By logical extension, it led to the view that clinical symptoms have meaning only in terms of the personality context of which they are a part. The view that the elements of a complex personality are inextricably interdependent became a central thesis in the study of psychopathology.

## COGNITIVE-HYPOTHESIS THEORIES

Despite their contribution of the holistic viewpoint, Gestaltists bypassed, if not denied, the role that personal experience played in the perceptual process. In the late 1940's and 1950's Gardner Murphy, Jerome Bruner, George Kelly and George Klein revived the Functionalist idea that perception was a learned and adaptive act. To it was added the notion of unconscious motivation stressed by the psychoanalysts. Perception, as elaborated by these men, was an expression of the individual's cognitive attitudes which, in turn, reflected his unconscious drives and adaptive defenses. In attempting to maintain an equilibrium between inner strivings and objective reality, the individual develops cognitive hypotheses or expectancies which enable him to select perceptually those aspects of reality best suited to his needs. In this fashion, perception reconciles needs to reality, and cognition serves as a guide to future adaptive perceptions. An important synthesis was achieved in these theories between the concept of unconscious adaptive striving, first posited by psychodynamic theorists, and the historical interest of academic psychologists in perception and cognition.

## LEARNING THEORIES AND THE BEHAVIORISTIC APPROACH

In contrast with the psychopathologists' concern for complex real-life patterns, learning theorists and behaviorists have traditionally focused on the manipulation of simple laboratory conditions with animal subjects. Despite their attention to simple experimental variables, their work has often produced relevant concepts for understanding clinical phenomena. They virtually eliminate inferred concepts such as the "unconscious," pre-

Figure 1-10    Founders of learning theory and behaviorism. A. Edward L. Thorndike. B. John B. Watson. (Photographs A and B from Murchison, C. [ed.]: A History of Psychology in Autobiography. Vol. III. Worcester, Massachusetts, Clark University Press, 1936. Reprinted by Russell & Russell, Inc., 1961.) C. Ivan P. Pavlov. (National Library of Medicine, Bethesda, Maryland.)

ferring terms which are anchored only to overt behavior. They eschew the notion that "unconscious dynamics" or "underlying diseases" account for symptoms. Rather, clinical symptoms are like all other behaviors, except that they are socially disrupting and maladaptive.

## THORNDIKE AND THE LAW OF EFFECT

The origin of modern learning theory may be traced back to the associative memory studies of Hermann Ebbinghaus and the seminal "law of effect" idea formulated by Edward Lee Thorndike (1874–1949) at the turn of the twentieth century. Thorndike stressed the signal importance of reward and punishment in learning, formulating his concept succinctly in the following statement (1905):

Any act which in a given situation produces satisfaction becomes associated with that situation, so that when the situation recurs the act is more likely than before to recur also. Conversely, any act which in a given situation produces discomfort becomes dissociated from that situation, so that when the situation recurs the act is less likely than before to recur.

## PAVLOVIAN CONDITIONING

Despite the clarity of Thorndike's statement, it remained for the great Russian physiologist, Ivan Petrovitch Pavlov (1849–1936), to demonstrate experimentally that behavior is modified as a function of learning. Although unaware of Thorndike's studies, Pavlov recognized late in his life that the American had preceded him regard-

ing the concept of reinforced learning by two or three years (1928). Pavlov was preceded also by Ivan Sechenov, the father of Russian neurology, who stated as early as 1863 that all animal and human acts were partly cerebral and partly learned or trained.

Pavlov's discoveries resulted from an unanticipated observation made during studies of digestive reflexes. In the year 1902, while measuring saliva secreted by dogs in response to food, he noticed that dogs salivated either at the sight of the food dish or upon hearing the footsteps of the attendant who brought it in. Pavlov realized that the stimulus of the dish or the footsteps had become, through experience, a substitute or signal for the stimulus of food. He soon concluded that this signaling or learning process must play a central part in the adaptive capacity of animals. Because of his physiological orientation, however, he conceived these observations as processes of the brain. Initially, he referred to them as "psychic secretions." When he presented his findings in 1903 before the fourteenth International Congress of Medicine in Madrid, he coined the term *conditioned reflex* (cr) for the learned response and labeled the learned signal as a *conditioned stimulus* (cs). As his work progressed, Pavlov noted that conditioned reflexes persisted over long periods of disuse. They could be inhibited briefly by various distractions and completely extinguished by repeated failure to follow the signal or conditioned stimulus with the usual reinforcement.

Despite his lifelong predilection for conceptualizing these conditioning processes as physiological activities of the "higher nervous system," Pavlov's work proved, to his occasional embarrassment and dismay, to be a major contribution to academic psychology. His early experiments served to replace the focus on subjective introspection traditional among psychologists at the turn of the century. In his substitution of measurable and objective reactions to stimuli, he laid the groundwork, not only for the next half century of Russian research, but for American Behaviorism and modern learning theory as well. But before we discuss the role of Pavlov's ideas upon others, we will note two of his later contributions which are relevant to the history of psychopathology.

Pavlov came to realize that words could replace physical stimuli as signals for conditioned learning. He divided human thought into two signal-systems, stating (1928):

Sensations, perceptions and direct impressions of the surrounding world are primary signals of reality. Words are secondary signals. They represent themselves as abstractions of reality and permit generalizations. The human brain is composed of the animal brain, the first signaling system, and the purely human part related to speech, the second signaling system.

Pavlov noted that under emotional distress behavior shifts from the symbols of the second-signal system to the bodily expression of the first signal-system. Not only did he recognize this "regression" as a part of pathology, but he also used the concept of the second-signal to show how verbal therapy can influence the underlying first-signal system it represents. Thus, words could alter defective or malfunctioning brain processes in the neurotic individual via persuasion and suggestion.

Another of Pavlov's important contributions to psychopathology, his studies of experimentally-produced "neuroses" in animals, was prompted directly by his acquaintance with Freud's writings. In this work, agitation and anger are created in previously cooperative animals by presenting them with conflicting or intense stimuli. These studies generated a marked enthusiasm among a small group of American psychiatrists desirous of finding a more rigorous foundation for psychodynamic theory. The investigations undertaken by W. Horsley Gantt, Howard Liddell and Jules Masserman in the 1930's and 1940's derive largely from an attempt to bridge the ideas of Pavlov and Freud.

## BEHAVIORISM AND NEO-BEHAVIORISTIC THEORIES

Pavlov's work did not have its greatest impact in psychiatry, however. In 1913 an American psychologist, John Broadus Watson (1878-1958) espoused a point of view called *behaviorism* which was intended as an antidote to the preoccupation with consciousness and introspection among his contemporaries. To him, consciousness was a subjectively private experience; as such, it failed to meet a major tenet of science that data should be objective or publicly verifiable. Watson became acquainted with the conditioned reflex studies of Pavlov and his Russian contemporary V. M. Bechterev (1857-1927) in 1915, and saw quickly that this method could be used to circumvent introspective reports and give him the overt and objective data he sought. From that point, and with each succeeding publication, Watson made the conditioned reflex a central concept in behaviorism. He rejected the physiological orientation of Pavlov, however. He had no interest in the inner structure or processes of the organism, stating that concepts defined at the level of behavior were sufficient to account for all learning processes. Watson argued further that learning alone accounts for behavior and personality; this contention gave psychologists a new sense of importance and independence, but it separated psychology even further than before from the mainstream of biological psychiatry.

Although Watson's insistence on objectivity and experimentation contributed greatly to the scientific maturity of psychology, his ideas had little influence upon the study of psychopathology. For the next 30 years, brilliant experiments and theories of learning were devised by such neo-behaviorists as Clark Leonard Hull (1884-1952), Edward Chase Tolman (1886-1961), Edwin Ray Guthrie (1886-1960) and B. F. Skinner. Each of these men took a less adamant behavioristic position than Watson, but retained his emphasis on objectivity and experimentation. In the Second World War, the disciples of neo-behaviorism were called upon to contribute to the solution of problems of mental disorder. As a result, a rapprochement gradually emerged between the orientations of the behaviorist and the psychopathologist. In the absence of any fully convincing theory for psychopathology, and on the assumption that all behavior was based on universal psychological processes, concepts drawn from academic research were applied to the problems of abnormal psychology with justified confidence.

## BEHAVIORAL CONCEPTIONS OF PATHOLOGY AND THERAPY

Theories possessing a common basis in Pavlovian concepts and behavioristic objectivity provided new principles for understanding psychopathology and psychotherapy. The contributions of Hull were elaborated in the late 1940's by O. Hobart Mowrer, Neal Miller, Joseph Wolpe and Hans J. Eysenck, while those of Skinner were developed in the late 1950's by Charles Ferster, Leonard Krasner and Ogden Lindsley. Primary attention was given to the process of reinforcement since reinforcement was the mediating agent through which response habits were acquired and extinguished. The small number of concepts employed in these theories to account for the diverse behaviors involved in psychopathology was an achievement of considerable merit and made them especially attractive to psychologists tired of the obscure and complex explanatory concepts of the psychoanalytic schools. But of even greater importance was the hope that new insights regarding the development and modification of psychopathology could also be provided. For our present purposes it will suffice to note briefly the major ideas of this behavioristic approach to psychopathology; more detailed discussions will follow in later chapters.

Behavior theorists do not postulate the existence of underlying causes or intrapsychic conflicts to account for pathology. Rather, psychopathology is simply a composite of the person's response habits learned as a result of the reinforcements he experienced throughout his life. Distinctions between adaptive and maladaptive behaviors reflect differences only in the reinforcing experiences to which the individual was exposed. There are no "neuroses," "repressions" or "diseases" underlying pathological symptoms since symptoms are merely habits developed and maintained by environmental reinforcements.

The behaviorist's approach to therapy follows logically from his view of pathology; modify the behavior designated as the symptom and "pathology" is eliminated. Therapy, or behavior modification as it is often called, specifies first what behaviors are maladaptive and what behaviors should be reinforced to supplant them. Psychodynamic statements such as "strengthen his ego" are translated into the question, "what differences in his behavior would enable him to function more adequately?" Once the desired changes are specified, a program of reinforcements to shape the new behavior is devised. These reinforcements are given in the form of words, images or direct experience. By creating imaginary or real parallels to situations which previously had evoked maladaptive responses, these responses are extinguished and new, more adaptive ones learned in their stead. Through this "behavior modification," the individual is "cured" of his disorder.

## CONCLUDING COMMENTS AND SUMMARY

We have traveled a long and complex road in this chapter. The vast number of figures, the conflicting theories and the divergent interests which have shaped the historical course of psychopathology can but stagger the beginning student. So broad a sweep as to include ancient demonology and modern behavior conditioning makes for a fascinating story of scientific fact and fancy, prejudice and accident and brilliance and naiveté. Although sketchy in detail, the review has outlined the major trends which have led us to our present attitudes and directions in psychopathology. Hopefully it will serve as a perspective through which future knowledge may be better assessed and properly integrated.

What patterns, trends and directions can we extract from this history? For one, it is likely that the reactions of any group of naive individuals faced with mental disorder in their midst would follow a parallel course to what has in fact taken place. At first, such a group would react with perplexity and fear, followed shortly by efforts to avoid or eliminate the disturbing behavior. Because of their lack of knowledge, their crude efforts would fail, leading to frustration and, in turn, to anger, punitive action and hostility. In due course, the obvious helplessness and innocence of the ill would evoke protests against harshness and cruelty. A new compassion and sympathy would arise and awaken a search for methods of humane treatment. But goodwill alone would not be sufficient to deal with the illness. Proper treatment requires knowledge, and knowledge can be derived best from systematic study and research. And so, in its course of progress, this imaginary group would move step by step from perplexity, fear and cruelty, to scientific analysis and humane treatment. It is at this point that we stand in our study of psychopathology today. Despite periodic regressions and fads, progress toward humanism, naturalism and scientific empiricism has continued.

Our present knowledge in psychopathology has come through many and diverse paths. Competing approaches and theories have stimulated a wide range of speculation and research. Over time, this diverse knowledge and its transmission have taken the form of four professional disciplines: psychiatric medicine, with a focus on disease syndromes, biological causes and somatic therapy; psychodynamic psychiatry, with a focus on unconscious intrapsychic conflict and early interpersonal relations; clinical and personology psychology, with a focus on the structure and measurement of personality; and academic and experimental psychology, with a focus on basic perceptual and behavioral processes. Although these alternate approaches to psychopathology have not produced cumulative knowledge, their studies have given us a broad and fruitful direction for future growth. The major trends and findings of these disciplines are noted briefly in the following summary:

1. Classification of mental disorder, wrought through years of careful clinical observation and given its contemporary form by Emil Kraepelin at the turn of the century, is undergoing vigorous criticism today. Despite its obvious weaknesses, however, no alternative has developed to supplant it.

2. The search for biological causes which underlie psychopathology has a long and substantially fruitless history. Newly devised instruments and procedures, however, hold promise that whatever biological factors do exist will be identified in the near future.

3. Because the search for biological causes has been unproductive, somatotherapy has developed as a result of faulty logic or fortuitous accident. Rational therapies may be devised in the future if biochemical processes associated with psychopathology become better understood.

4. The brilliant insights of Sigmund Freud regarding instinctual strivings, unconscious processes and infantile development established a foundation for contemporary psychodynamic psychiatry. Recent disciples have dissented from Freud's biological orientation and have emphasized early learning processes, interpersonal experiences and sociocultural influences.

5. Early studies in personology focused on the classification of personality types and traits. This has given way to holistic theories which stress the unique integration of personality and the centrality of one motive, that of maintaining one's intrinsic unity and fulfilling one's potentials.

6. The interpretively restrictive psychometric methods used in measuring psychopathology in the 1920's and 1930's were replaced by projective techniques which ostensibly disclosed unconscious attitudes and motives. Because of the subjective and qualitative nature of projective interpretation, new measures were devised to avoid these deficiencies while retaining a degree of diagnostic utility. Most notable among these new instruments is the MMPI.

7. Although academic psychologists have been interested in general laws of behavior, several principles derived from their work have proved useful in describing and modifying psychopathology. Perceptual studies have demonstrated the distorting effects of preestablished attitudes and needs. Conditioning in learning research has become a central concept for understanding how maladaptive behavior is acquired. The procedure of extinction has become a model for eliminating these maladaptive behaviors.

8. Although the late nineteenth century development of state-supported institutions for the mentally ill was an encouraging humanitarian movement, it directed attention toward custodial treatment rather than prevention. In recent decades, a trend has begun toward out-patient clinics designed to prevent disorders and to community-based in-patient centers where disorders may be treated in typical life settings rather than in distantly located and impersonal state institutions.

From this review, the scope of psychopathology may seem overly broad and divided, and its state one of flux or confusion. We should take heart, however, in the fact that controversy and uncertainty are the bases for precise and accurate future knowledge. Skepticism and curiosity characterize the scientific method. Free of the shackles of doctrinaire views, we can be assured that better ways will be devised for the welfare of man.

Now that the past has been outlined, can we predict the course of the future? Such extrapolations require, at least, one additional step—a systematic analysis of present-day ideas and theories. For that we turn to chapter 2.

# Chapter 2

# CONTEMPORARY THEORIES

Michael Mazur—*Cellist* (1945). (Collection, The Museum of Modern Art, New York. Gift of Victor S. Riesenfeld.)

## INTRODUCTION

Nature does not meet our need for a tidy and well-ordered universe. The complexity and intricacy of the natural world make it difficult not only to establish clearcut relationships among phenomena but to find simple ways in which these phenomena can be classified or grouped. In our desire to discover the essential order of nature we are forced to select only a few of the infinite number of elements which could be chosen; in this selection we narrow our choice only to those aspects of nature which we believe best enable us to answer the questions we pose. The elements we have chosen may be labeled, transformed and reassembled in a variety of ways. But we must keep in mind that these labels and transformations are not "realities." The definitions, concepts and theories scientists create are only optional tools to guide their observation and interpretation of the natural world; it is necessary to recognize, therefore, that different concepts and theories may coexist as alternative approaches to the same basic problem. An illustration in the field of bridge design may serve to clarify this point (Hebb, 1958a):

The engineer who designs a bridge must think at different levels of complexity as he works. His overall plan is in terms of spans, piers, abutments; but when

he turns to the design of a particular span, he starts to think in terms of lower-order units such as the I-beam. This latter unit, however, is still quite molar; an engineer is firmly convinced that an I-beam is just a special arrangement of certain molecules, the molecule in turn being a special arrangement of electrons, protons and so forth. Now note: At a microscopic level of analysis, a bridge is nothing but a complex constellation of atomic particles; and a steel I-beam is no more than a convenient fiction, a concession to the limitations of thought and the dullness of human perception.

At another level of analysis, of course, the I-beam is an elementary unit obviously real and no fiction. At this level electrons have a purely theoretical existence, which suggests that "reality" is meaningful as designating, not some ultimate mode of being about which there must be argument, but the mode of being which one takes for granted as the starting point of thought.

With this perspective in mind, let us look at the question: What is psychopathology? Clearly, mental disorders are expressed in a variety of ways; it is a complex phenomenon which can be approached at different levels and can be viewed from many angles. On a behavioral level, for example, disorders could be conceived as a complicated pattern of responses to environmental stress. Phenomenologically, they could be seen as expressions of personal discomfort and anguish. Approached from a physiological viewpoint, they could be interpreted as sequences of complex neural and chemical activity. And intrapsychically, they could be organized into unconscious processes that defend against anxiety and conflict.

Given these diverse possibilities, we can readily understand why psychopathology may be approached and defined in terms of any of several levels we may wish to focus upon, and any of a variety of functions or processes we may wish to explain. Beyond this, each level or angle of approach lends itself to a number of specific theories and concepts, the usefulness of which must be gauged by their ability to solve the particular problems and purposes for which they were created. That the subject matter of psychopathology is inherently diverse and complex is precisely the reason why we must not narrow our choice of approach to one level or one theory. Each has a legitimate and potentially fruitful contribution to make to our study.

In this present chapter, we will discuss first the goals, structure and orientation of scientific systems in general, and with this background in mind, analyze the different theoretical approaches to psychopathology which are currently in use.

## GOALS OF SCIENTIFIC SYSTEMS

Man acquired reliable and useful knowledge about his environment long before the advent of modern scientific thought. Information, skill and instrumentation were achieved without "science" and its methods of symbolic abstraction, research and analysis. If useful knowledge could be acquired by intelligent observation and common sense alone, what special values are derived by applying the complicated and rigorous procedures of the scientific method? Is rigor, clarity, precision and experimentation more than a compulsive and picayunish concern for details, more than the pursuit for the honorific title of "science"? Are the labors of coordinating knowledge and exploring unknown factors in a systematic fashion worth the time and effort involved? There is little question in our "age of science" that the answer would be yes! But why? What are the distinguishing virtues of scientific systems? What sets them apart from the everyday common sense methods of acquiring knowledge? It is these questions to which we must turn next.

Since the number of ways we can observe, describe and organize the natural world is infinite, the terms and concepts we create to represent these activities are often confusing and obscure. For example, different words are used to describe the same behavior, and the same word is used for different behaviors. Some terms are narrow in focus, others are broad and many are difficult to define. Because of the variety of events that can be considered and the lack of precision in language, useful information gets scattered in hodgepodge fashion across the whole landscape of a scientific topic, and communication gets bogged down in terminological obscurities and semantic controversies.

One of the goals of scientific systems is to avoid this morass of confusion. Not all phenomena related to a subject are attended to at once. Certain elements are selected from the vast range of possibilities because they seem relevant to the solution of specific and important problems. To create a degree of consistency among scientists interested in a problem these elements are grouped or classified according to their similarities and differences and given specific labels which describe or define them. This process of classification is indispensable for systematizing observation and knowledge. But it is only a first step.

Classification of knowledge alone does not make a scientific system. The card catalog of a library or an accountant's ledger sheets are well organized classifications but hardly to be viewed as a system of science. The characteristic which distinguishes a scientific classification system from others is its attempt to group elements according to established or hypothesized explanatory propositions. These propositions are formed when certain properties which have been isolated and classified have been shown or have been hypothesized to be related to other classified properties or groupings. The groupings of a scientific system, therefore, are not mere collections of miscellaneous or random information, but a linked or unified pattern of known or presumed relationships. This pattern of relationships is the foundation of a scientific system.

Certain benefits derive from systematizing knowledge in this fashion. Given the countless ways of observing and analyzing a set of complex events, a system of explanatory propositions becomes a useful guide to the observer. Rather than shifting from one aspect of behavior to another, according to momentary impressions of importance, he is led to pursue in a logical and consistent manner only those aspects which are likely to be related.

In addition, a scientific system enables the perceptive scientist to generate hypotheses about relationships that have not been observed before. It enlarges the scope of knowledge by alerting the observer to possible new relationships among phenomena, and then ties these new observations into a coherent body of knowledge. Thus, from a small number of basic explanatory propositions, a scientific system develops broad applicability and subsumes a wide range of phenomena.

This generality or comprehensiveness leads to another important advantage. Because of the scope of the system, different observers are given an opportunity to check or verify the validity of its explanatory propositions. Thus, hasty generalizations, erroneous speculations and personal biases are readily exposed by systematic scrutiny. This exposure assures that propositions are supported by *shared* evidence and that the range of their validity is clearly delimited.

Bringing these points together then, we can see that a scientific system attempts to coordinate and seek relationships among a general but clearly delimited class of phenomena. The means by which a scientific system accomplishes these ends will be our next topic of discussion.

## STRUCTURE AND ORIENTATION OF SCIENTIFIC THEORIES

Scientific endeavor consists of two types of activities. The *first* is the informal and systematic observation of empirical events and objects. The *second* involves the creation of abstract linguistic or mathematical symbols invented by the theorist to represent relationships among observable events, or relationships which he believes exist but have not been observed. This second, or symbolic and theoretical activity of science, will be our focus in this chapter.

As noted earlier, scientific systems consist of explanatory propositions which create order or render intelligible otherwise unrelated phenomena. There are two kinds of propositions in a scientific system, empirical laws and theories. An *empirical law* is a statement representing a universally established relationship observed among a group of empirical phenomena. A *theory,* in contrast, is composed of invented abstractions in the form of models, concepts, rules and hypotheses which function as provisional exploratory tools to aid the scientist in his search for empirical laws. Theories are subject to frequent change; empirical laws are durable.

Before we can discuss intelligently current theories of psychopathology we must examine the structural form into which theories are cast.

### FORMAL STRUCTURE OF THEORIES

Four major components of theory may be distinguished for our purposes: (1) an abstract *model* which serves as an analog or a visualizable pattern representing the overall structure of the theory; (2) a *conceptual terminology* by which various classes of phenomena relevant to the theory are symbolized or labeled; (3) a set of *correspondence rules* which coordinate relationships among the theoretical terms in accordance with the model; and (4) *hypotheses* which specify the manner in which these relationships may be tested in the empirical world.

### Models

A model is an analogy which exploits certain aspects of a familiar or easily visualized system to guide the understanding of a less familiar or difficult subject. For example, theorists have utilized an electronic computer model to describe the processes and structure of psychopathology. Thus, human beings are likened to computers in that both receive complex information from the environment, integrate this information through devious circuits with prior information and emit relatively uncomplicated responses. More commonly, psychopathology has been organized in accordance with a biological disease model. In this format, psychopathology is conceived as if it stemmed from the intrusion of a foreign agent upon normal biological functioning; as in most physical ailments, symptoms are considered to be the organism's reaction to the intrusion.

Few theorists expect the models they adopt to represent accurately all of the features of psychopathology. Rather, the model is used merely as a way to visualize psychopathology "as if it worked like this."

Models pose a number of risks to the theorist. Certain features of a model which may have proved useful in its original setting are often assumed mistakenly to be appropriate elsewhere. Should such a model be adopted, the theorist will waste his time constructing erroneous hypotheses and pursuing unprofitable research. The adoption of the disease model in psychiatry, for example, has been viewed by many psychologists to have led to years of fruitless biochemical research. Similarly, the intrapsychic conflict model underlying psychoanalytic theory has been seen to have delayed the development of more effective psychotherapies. Unfortunately, there are no simple ways to tell beforehand whether a given model will prove to be fruitful or misguided. What should be kept clear in one's thinking is that the model adopted for a theory should not be confused with the theory itself.

### Conceptual Terminology

The elements of a theory are represented by a set of concepts, that is, a language by which members of a scientific group communicate about a subject. Concepts may be seen as serving two functions. *First,* they possess a value in that they facilitate the *manipulation of theoretical ideas.* Concepts are systematically linked to other concepts; it is through the interplay of these concepts that meaningful ideas are formulated and deductive statements are made in the form of propositions and hypotheses. *Second,* most concepts possess an *empirical significance,* that is, they are linked in some explicit way to the observable world; although some concepts may represent processes or events which are not observable, they may be defined or anchored to observables. It is this translatability into the empirical domain that allows the theoretician to test his propositions in the world of "reality."

Ideally, all concepts of a scientific theory should be empirically anchored, that is, correspond to properties in the observable world. This would minimize confusion regarding the objects and events to which a term applies. Moreover, concepts should be more precise than words used in ordinary language; although everyday conversational language has relevance to significant events in the real world, it gives rise to ambiguity and confusion because of the varied uses to which conventional words are often put. Scientific concepts should be defined "precisely" in order to assure that their meaning is clear and specific.

Empirical precision, in the fullest sense of the term, can be achieved only if every concept in a theory is defined by a single observable phenomenon, that is, a different concept or label would be used for every difference that can be observed in the empirical world. This ideal simply is not feasible for reasons which will become apparent shortly. Psychological concepts do differ, however, in the degree to which they satisfy this criterion. A discussion of three types of concepts —operational definitions, intervening variables and hypothetical constructs—will be of value in noting these distinctions and their consequences.

**Operational Definitions.**  Certain concepts are defined literally by observable events and possess no meaning other than these events; they have been termed *operational definitions.* To paraphrase Bridgman (1927), the founder of "operationism," an operational definition is a concept that is defined by the procedure employed to measure the particular empirical event it represents; thus, the meaning of a concept is synonymous with how man measures it, not with what he says about it. For example, the concept "learning" would involve nothing more than the set of operations by which it is measured. There would be a different

concept for learning when it is measured by the number of errors a child makes on a task than when measured by the speed with which he completes the same task. The advantage of operational definitions is obvious; concepts are unambiguous, and propositions utilizing these concepts are translatable directly into the empirical phenomena they represent.

Useful as operational definitions may be, they present several problems. Theoretical concepts should be generalizable, that is, they should enable the theorist to include a variety of observations with his concept. Operational definitions are restrictive; they preclude predictions to new situations that are even slightly different from the original situation. Certainly, one of the primary goals of a theory is to integrate diverse observations with a minimum number of concepts; a strict operational approach would flood us with an infinite number of concepts and clutter thinking with irrelevant distinctions. The major value of operational definitions is cautionary; it alerts the theorist to the importance of conceptual precision and empirical relevance.

**Intervening Variables.**  Certain concepts cannot be measured by currently available techniques (e.g., the earth's core and biochemical processes in memory). Also, internal or organismic processes which connect observable phenomena may not themselves be observable and must be inferred or invented until such time as they can be observed. These unobservables, often referred to as mediating structures or processes, are necessary in all phases of theory construction. Two types of concepts, intervening variables and hypothetical constructs, deal with these mediating factors; their similarities and differences are worthy of note.

An *intervening variable* is a concept which represents a guess regarding an unobserved mediating process which may account for an observed event. Although they signify an unknown mediating process, intervening variables are defined by and entirely reducible to empirical events. For example, the concept "habit," formulated as an intervening variable, may be defined empirically by the number of trials an individual was given to learn a task, or by the demonstrated speed with which he performs it. Although the term "habit" implies a residue of experience within the individual, which cannot be observed, its existence is inferred from a *variety of observables,* e.g., the number of opportunities to learn a task or the skill of performance.

There is a similarity between intervening variables and operational definitions in that both are defined by or anchored to empirical phenomena. But they differ in two important respects. First, a *variety* of empirical phenomena may be used to define an intervening variable; in this respect it is less precise than an operational definition. Second, although both intervening variables and operational definitions are anchored to observables, intervening variables always *imply* the existence of a mediating process whereas operational concepts need not.

**Hypothetical Constructs.** The difference between an intervening variable and a hypothetical construct is largely a matter of degree. *Hypothetical constructs* are admittedly speculative concepts which are formulated without explicit reference to observable phenomena. Their freedom from specific empirical referents distinguishes them from intervening variables. Because they are not defined or anchored to observable events, their use in theory often is questioned. Clarity gets muddled and deductions often are tautological when psychological data are "explained" in terms of a series of hypothetical constructs. For example, statements such as "the mechanisms of the ego are blocked in the anal-character when libidinous energies are dammed up by super-ego introjections," are, at best, puzzling. Postulating connections between one set of hypothetical constructs and another leads to facile but often meaningless "explanations." Such use results in imprecise formulations which are difficult to decipher because we cannot specify observables by which they can be anchored or evaluated.

Vagueness and surplus-meaning are both the weakness and strength of the hypothetical construct. A theory is a human artifact; not every concept of a theory should be linked to empirical events since the purpose of a theory is to extend the range of our knowledge. Moreover, unrealistic standards of empirical anchorage in the early stages of theory construction may discourage the kind of imaginative speculation necessary to decipher elusive and obscure phenomena. Vague and risky as hypothetical constructs may be, they often are necessary tools in the development of a productive theory.

### Correspondence Rules

Even if all the terms of a theory were empirically anchored and precise, something further would have to be added to indicate how these terms are combined and related to one another. Without a set of rules by which its concepts are integrated, a theory lacks internal coherence and its function as a tool for explaining and predicting empirical events is hampered markedly. Many labels have been coined for this linkage or correspondence system; it has often been referred to as the *syntax* of a theory because of its similarity to the rules of grammar.

These rules serve as deductive procedures by which theoretical concepts are arranged or combined to provide new inferences or insights about empirical relations. They give a theory a coherent system of interlocking channels through which diverse facts may be related and derived. For example, the calculational rules of mathematics are frequently used in science as inferential principles which guide the manipulation of concepts and their subsequent derivation into empirical hypotheses. When formulated logically and explicitly, correspondence rules provide tremendous power for systematizing experience and generating research hypotheses.

### Hypotheses

Correspondence rules in psychopathological theories are usually loose and imprecise, if formulated at all. As a consequence, hypotheses, that is, provisional explanations which are stated as predictions about empirical relationships, are rarely derived rigorously from the correspondence rules of a theory. In most undeveloped sciences, hypotheses are formulated as a result of perceptive observations and intuitive hunches.

Whether hypotheses are rigorously derived or intuitively conjectured, it is important that their final form be translatable into empirical terms. We must recall that the ultimate goal of a theory is the development of empirical laws. Such laws develop not only through ingenious speculation or derivation, but also by factual *confirmation*. Unless a hypothesis can be translated into a specific empirical test, its validity cannot be confirmed.

Our discussion has presented a condensation of relatively conventional notions about the structure of theory as formulated by logicians and philosophers of science. Most students may be unacquainted with these terms and may have found them difficult to grasp or see in perspective. Greater clarity may be obtained by reference to Figure 2-1 which summarizes these notions and their interrelationships in pictorial fashion. Although the serious student would do well to obtain a thorough grounding in these fundamental elements of theory, a sophisticated understanding is not essential to follow the major ideas presented later in the chapter. What should be clear, however, is that a theory is not "reality," that it is not an inevitable or predetermined representation of the objective world. Theories are merely optional instruments utilized in the early stages of knowledge. They serve to organize experience in a logical manner, and function as explanatory propositions by which experiences may be analyzed or inferences about them drawn. Their ultimate goal is the establishment of new empirical laws.

Theories arise typically from the perceptive observation and imaginative speculation of a creative scientist. This innovator is usually quite aware of the limits and deficiencies of his "invention" and is disposed in the early stages of his speculation to modify it as he develops new observations and insights. Unfortunately, after its utility has been proven in a modest and limited way, the theory frequently acquires a specious stature. Having clarified certain ambiguities and survived initial criticisms, it begins to accumulate a coterie of disciples. These less creative thinkers tend to accept the theory wholeheartedly and espouse its superior explanatory powers and terminology throughout the scientific market place. They hold to its propositions tenaciously and defend it blindly and unequivocally against opposition. In time it becomes a rigid and sacred dogma

and, as a result, authority replaces the test of utility and empirical validity. Intelligent men become religious disciples; their theory is a doctrine of "truth," not a guide to the unknown.

Should we avoid theories knowing their frequent fate? The answer, of course, is no! Man will interpret his experience either through implicit or formal theories regardless of the dangers and assumptions involved. Rather than dismissing theories as inevitable "religious doctrines," we should formulate criteria by which we can evaluate their genuine utility.

## ORIENTATION OF THEORIES

The previous section dealt with the formal structure of theory, its models, concepts and derivation procedures which serve as its framework or organization. But theories differ not only in these formal attributes. All are designed to guide the discovery of empirical laws, but each has a bias or orientation as to what kinds of laws should be sought, what methods should be used

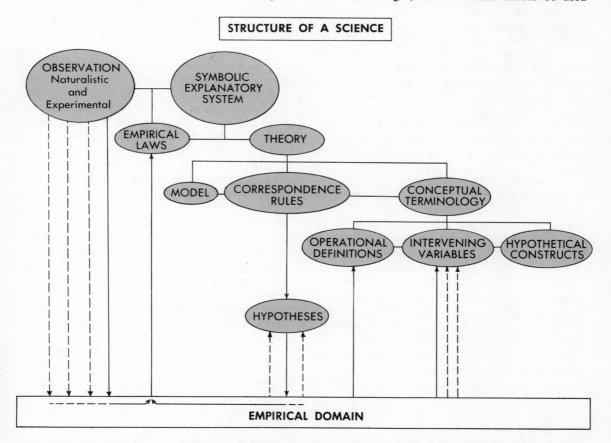

Figure 2-1   Structure of a science. Relationships among the elements of science are signified by connecting lines and arrows. Dotted lines denote a less formal or more imprecise relationship; straight lines indicate greater percision or formality. See text for further elaboration.

to discover these laws and what kinds of empirical phenomena should be observed. Theorists engage in intense debates as to which of several alternative approaches is best; unfortunately, the poor student wastes needless hours in trying to decide which "side" is correct. It is important for the student to recognize at the outset that there is no "correct" choice; no rules exist in nature to tell us which laws are best or most important.

To complicate matters, the orientations of most theories are not explicit. As a result, the student is presented with a fantastic array of overlapping data and concepts which appears disconnected and contradictory and leaves him dazzled and confused. Without differences in orientation clearly in mind, the student is like the young Talmudic scholar who, after immersing himself for weeks in ancient manuscripts, rose suddenly one morning, danced joyously in the streets and shouted, "I have found the most wonderful answer; somebody please tell me the question!"

To make sense and give order to the data of his science, the student must know what kinds of laws each theory seeks to find. Only then can he construct meaning and coherence in his studies. With the goals of each theory clearly before him, he may separate them according to the laws they wish to find and compare them intelligently as to their success in answering the questions they pose in common. It should be obvious that theories seeking biochemical laws cannot be compared to theories seeking behavioral laws. And theories seeking causal sequences between past and present events should not be compared to theories seeking correlation among present events, and so on.

The student might ask at this point why different kinds of theories are needed. Cannot one theory encompass all that need be known in psychopathology? For the time being, at least, the answer must be no. At this stage of our knowledge, theories must serve as instruments to answer particular rather than universal questions. The clinician in the consulting room needs a different kind of theory to facilitate his understanding of verbal therapeutic interaction than does the psychopharmacologist, who seeks to discover the effects of biochemical properties.

A major source of confusion for students stems from their difficulty in recognizing the existence within psychopathology of different levels of scientific observation and conceptualization. No such difficulties seem to exist with regard to drawing distinctions between broad fields such as physics and chemistry or biology and sociology. Students experience problems when they are faced with distinctions *within* each of these wider disciplines; they fail to recognize that scientists refine their focus and concentrate selectively on increasingly narrow bands of data, each of which gives rise to highly delimited concepts and theories. Thus, some physicists concern themselves with elementary particles, whereas others study gravitational fields; similarly, some chemists focus on the bonding of simple molecules, whereas others investigate complex biochemical processes.

Scientists approach "nature" from different vantage points, selecting just those elements of this awesomely complex phenomenon which they believe will best enable them to answer the questions they pose. Not only do chemists focus on different facets of nature than do physicists, but *within* each of these two disciplines, scientists further subdivide the field of study. In effect, then, each of these subdivisions of a science deals with a *different* class of empirical data. Psychopathology is no different than physics or chemistry in this regard. It, too, can be studied from many vantage points. It can be observed and conceptualized in legitimately different ways by behaviorists, phenomenologists, psychodynamicists and biochemists.

It is important to recognize, further, that no single level of observation or conceptualization alone is sufficient to encompass all of the complex and multidimensional features of a field such as psychopathology. The processes and structures which comprise the field may be described in terms of conditioned habits, or reaction formations, or cognitive expectancies, or neurochemical dysfunctions. These different levels of data and conceptualization cannot, and should not, be arranged in a hierarchy, with one level viewed as primary, or reducible to another; nor can they be compared in terms of some "objective truth value." Alternative levels or approaches merely are different; they observe and conceptualize different types of data, and lead, therefore, to different theories and different empirical laws. Despite fruitless debates to the contrary, there is no intrinsic conflict between theories and laws which deal with different data; they are complementary, and *not* contradictory approaches to the subject. No one expects the propositions of a physicist to be the same as those of a chemist; nor should we expect those of a behaviorist to be the same as those of a phenomenologist.

What we wish to stress then, is that theories are best differentiated according to the kinds of data they elect to study and conceptualize. These choices are purely pragmatic, and questions of comparative utility or validity should be asked only of theories which deal with the same kinds of data. Data are the basic ingredients for concepts and for the theories which coordinate these concepts. Irrelevant controversies and confusions are avoided if the conceptual level, or the kinds of data to which they refer, are specified clearly. Where this is done properly, the student and researcher can determine whether two concepts are comparable, whether the same conceptual level refers to different data, whether different theories apply to the same data and so on.

There are many ways in which the subject matter of psychopathology can be differentiated according to "data levels." L'Abate (1964) has proposed levels of integration, interpretation and functioning and development, while Ford and Urban (1963) have organized them in terms of degree of accessibility, order of abstraction and hierarchical structure.

What classification scheme of levels will serve our purpose best? The four major historical traditions presented in chapter 1 suggest a particularly useful basis for us to follow, and one which corresponds closely to the four theoretical orientations in psychopathology today. These contemporary orientations reflect not only relatively distinct historical traditions but, perhaps more importantly, differ also in the kinds of data they elect to conceptualize. For example, followers in the tradition of psychiatric medicine focus upon the *biophysical* substrate of pathology; those within the psychodynamic tradition of psychiatry conceptualize unconscious *intrapsychic* processes; theorists within the clinical-personology tradition tend to be concerned with conscious *phenomenological* experience; and those in the academic-experimental tradition attend primarily to overt *behavioral* data. These four levels—biophysical, intrapsychic, phenomenological and behavioral—reflect, therefore, both different sources of data and the four major theoretical orientations in psychopathology.

In the following sections we will specify these four levels of theoretical analysis in greater detail. This will provide us with a picture of which data a theory has judged significant to its purposes and which it has deemphasized. By arranging contemporary theories according to level of data observation and conceptualization we will be able to understand better the variety of definitions of psychopathology which have been developed. From this basis also, we should have a sound foundation for comparing the varied concepts and explanatory propositions which have been formulated regarding the etiologic development and therapeutic modification of psychopathology.

# CURRENT THEORIES IN PSYCHOPATHOLOGY

The sciences, as we know them, are largely the result of an evolutionary process of haphazard variation and natural selection. The variation is continually being produced by the uncoordinated efforts of innumerable individual investigators, the selection by communication of results and critical appraisal by peers or posterity. An inevitable characteristic of this process is that whenever one surveys the state of any particular field of science one finds it, from the standpoint of organization and elegance, nothing less than a sorry mess. Numerous locally grounded theories, entirely distinct neither from one another nor from the noisy background, vie for attention. Disciplines form along irrational lines and persevere long after interdisciplinary boundaries, originally useful guidelines, have hardened into blockades (Estes, 1965).

It is comforting to know that the discouraging state of affairs described in the above quote is not peculiar to psychopathology. It was inevitable that so broad a subject as psychopathology would produce a scattering of diverse viewpoints. Complex problems lend themselves to many approaches, and divisions of labor in so varied a field become not only a matter of choice but also one of necessity.

The historical evolution of these diverging approaches was described in chapter 1; fortunately, diversification has resulted in a broad spectrum of knowledge about pathological phenomena. But these random evolutions have marked disadvantages as well. Scientists who are preoccupied with only a small segment of the field often have little knowledge of the work of others. Intent on a narrow approach to the subject, they lose sight of perspective, and their respective contributions are scattered and disconnected. What is needed today is a synthesis in which divergent elements of knowledge are brought together to be seen as parts of an integrated whole. Until a psychological Newton or Einstein comes along, however, the student must do the next best thing: develop an attitude by which the various branches and levels of psychopathology are viewed as an interrelated, if not an integrated unit. He must learn the language and orientation of each of the major approaches as if they were all part of an indivisible piece. Until such time as a bridge is created to coordinate each theory and level of approach to the others, no one theory or approach should be viewed as all-embracing, or accepted to the exclusion of the others. A multiplicity of viewpoints must prevail.

An earlier review of the substantive orientations of theories of psychopathology led us to classify them into four levels. These levels were felt to be useful since they corresponded well with historical traditions, contemporary professional orientations and, perhaps most important, with the major types of data which theorists observe and conceptualize. These levels were labeled (1) biophysical, (2) intrapsychic, (3) phenomenological and (4) behavioral. Useful as this division may be, it incorporates many divergent subgroupings: for example, the biophysical category will include theorists whose interests focus more narrowly on either genetics, biochemistry or physiology. Nevertheless, each level is, more or less, distinct from the others by virtue of its attention to a reasonably delimited class of data, a common scientific vocabulary and a central or guiding doctrine.

Any discussion of psychopathological theory should bring us to the question of defining psychopathology. It should be obvious from the foregoing that no single definition is possible. Psychopathology will be defined in terms of the theory one employs. An idiographically oriented theorist who emphasizes the importance of phenomenological experience will include uniqueness and self-discomfort in his definition of psychopathology; a biochemical theorist will formulate his definition in terms of biochemical dysfunctions, and so on. In brief, once a particular level and theory has been adopted, the definition of psychopathology follows logically and inevitably. Clearly, no single definition conveys the wide range of observations and orientations with which psychopathology may be explored.

Unfortunately, the observations and concepts and propositions of the various theoretical approaches to psychopathology have not been collected within one cover. At present, no single journal covers all aspects of psychopathology either, nor is there a permanent professional organization which cuts across disciplinary lines on a regular basis. To fill this void is a monumental task and far beyond the scope of this chapter. At best, we can attempt to provide a brief panoramic view of these approaches and, hopefully, convey certain essential features which they incorporate.

# BIOPHYSICAL THEORIES

Theories at this level assume that biophysical factors such as anatomy and biochemistry are the primary determinants of psychopathology. Ample evidence from medical science exists to justify this assumption. In the present section we will examine the orientation of theorists who hold this view. In addition, we will detail several of the more prominent theories and discuss the basic model they utilize to guide their formulations. Research and data in support of their views will be presented and evaluated in detail in chapter 4.

## GENERAL ORIENTATION

The first question we must ask is: what is the basis of psychopathology according to biophysical theorists? Though by no means mutually exclusive, the theorists have proposed two answers.

One group contends that most pathology can be traced to man's natural biological variability; accordingly, they attempt to relate these variations to measures of personality functioning and psychopathology. Scientists who follow this line of thinking may be considered to be quantitatively oriented since (1) they assume that men differ along the statistical "normal curve," and (2) they seek to discover correlations between biophysical variability and the presence of mental disorder. Roger Williams, the distinguished biochemist, has argued the case for investigating these natural biological variations as follows (1960):

Consider the fact (I do consider it a fact and not a theory) that every individual person is endowed with a distinctive gastrointestinal tract, a distinctive nervous system, and a morphologically distinctive brain; furthermore that the differences involved in this distinctiveness are never trifling and often are enormous. Can it be that this fact is inconsequential in relation to the problem of personality differences?

I am willing to take the position that this fact is of the *utmost* importance. The material in the area of anatomy alone is sufficient to convince anyone who comes upon the problem with an open mind that here is an obvious frontier which should yield many insights. Those who have accepted the Freudian idea that personality disorders arise from infantile conditioning will surely be led to see that, *in addition,* the distinctive bodily equipment of each individual infant is potentially important.

At the risk of being naive, it appears that the whole story we have been unfolding hangs together. Individual infants are endowed with far-reaching anatomical distinctiveness. The same distinctiveness carries over into the sensory and biochemical realms, and into their individual psychologies. It is not surprising therefore that each individual upon reaching adulthood exhibits a distinctive pattern of likes and dislikes not only with respect to trivialities but also with respect to what may be regarded the most important things in life.

That culture has a profound influence on our lives no one should ever deny. The serious question arises, however, as to the relative position that different factors occupy in producing distinctive personalities. To me it seems probable that one's distinctive brain morphology and one's distinctive endocrine system are more important factors than the toilet training one receives as an infant.

The second group of biophysical theorists believe that psychopathology stems from foreign or aberrant factors that intrude and disrupt "normal" functioning. Their focus of interest and observation centers on defects, dysfunctions and diseases that may arise as a result of hereditary errors, toxins, traumas, infections, malignant growths or malnutrition. In contrast to the first group of scientists, who deal with "normal" biological variations, these men concern themselves with biological irregularities.

A second question we may ask in ascertaining the orientation of biophysical theorists is: What specific types of data do they employ to develop their concepts? These may be separated conveniently into three classes: (1) heredity, (2) constitution and (3) neurophysiology. This tripartite division is an oversimplified breakdown of the biophysical realm; we should not be led to conclude that a theorist interested in one class of data fails to see relationships with the others. Classifying theorists in this way merely recognizes their particular sphere of interest or focus.

## HEREDITY THEORIES

The role of heredity in psychopathology is usually inferred from evidence based on correlations in mental disorder among members of the same family. As further support, heredity theorists note that obvious biophysical features such as height, coloration and facial structure are quite similar among close relatives, and that there is every reason to assume that the internal morphology and physiology of their nervous systems must also be alike. Since the nervous system subserves behavior and emotion, it should follow that family members would be disposed to act and feel in similar ways.

Most psychopathologists admit that hereditary factors play a role in personality and behavior, but insist that genetic dispositions can be modified substantially by the operation of environmental factors. This moderate view states that heredity operates not as a fixed constant, but as a disposition which takes different forms depending on the circumstances of an individual's upbringing. Hereditary theorists take a more inflexible position. They refer to a body of impressive data which implicate genetic factors in a variety of pathologies such as "schizophrenia" and "manic-depressive" psychoses. Although they admit that variations in these disorders may be produced by environmental conditions, they are convinced that these are "superficial" influences which cannot prevent the individual from succumbing to his hereditary defect. Research evidence for this more rigid viewpoint will be documented and evaluated in chapter 4. Here we will discuss only general observations and theoretical notions.

Systematic genetic studies were not begun until the early twentieth century. Prior to this period assumptions about inheritance were based on chance observations and superstitious beliefs.

The first authority to initiate a series of systematic investigations of the coincidence of disorders among relatives of mental patients was the German psychiatrist, E. Rüdin. Because of Rüdin's difficulty in separating the role of heredity from that of environment in his human pedigree studies, two German investigators, J. Lange and H. Luxenburger, devised the method of comparing identical and fraternal twins; identical twins had identical genes and, therefore, the specific role of heredity could be isolated partially from environment.

Studies of twins were continued in the mid-1930's by the research psychiatrist, Franz Kallmann. Kallmann presented an amply documented argument to the effect that coincidence in disorder varies directly with degree of genetic similarity; these findings were obtained by comparing the frequency with which relatives were classified similarly according to the Kraepelinian nosological system. Kallmann hypothesized specifically that schizophrenia and manic-depressive disorders arise from the effects of a single gene and are transmitted according to normal hereditary processes. His data are impressive, but several serious questions have been raised about his genetic hypothesis and methodology; these will be elaborated in chapter 4. For the moment let us note that the fact that genetic factors may serve as a predisposition to certain forms of mental disorder does not mean that disordered individuals will not display differences in their symptoms or developmental history. It certainly does not mean that these disorders cannot be helped by psychological therapies, or that similar forms of disorder could not arise without a genetic disposition.

## CONSTITUTIONAL THEORIES

Scientists of this persuasion assume that heredity accounts in large part for temperamental and behavioral dispositions. However, these theorists are not interested in the genetic process itself; rather, they focus on the end product of hereditary action, namely, constitutional variations among individuals and the correlation of these variations with psychopathology.

Constitutional theorists may be divided into two broad groups. The first is concerned chiefly with the covariation of structural body features (e.g., the distribution of body muscle, fat and bone, cardiac output and urinary excretion) and measures of temperament, personality and pathology. The second group of theorists is interested in longitudinal analyses; they concentrate on biophysical characteristics evidenced in early infancy, and seek to trace how these characteristics unfold during development.

The majority of studies undertaken by the first group of theorists deals with constitutional measures of adult physique or body structure. Although the belief that relationships exist between pathology and body build goes back to early Greek and Roman writings, the first of the modern studies was initiated by the German psychiatrist, Kretschmer. He proposed that slender individuals with poor muscular development were prone to introspective and schizophrenic disorders, whereas those with heavy or rotund physiques were vulnerable to mood-alternating and manic-depressive disorders. The American physician, Sheldon, modified both Kretschmer's measurement techniques and hypotheses in his own work, the best known of which relates body type, temperament and delinquency. Details of his research, and that of other body build theorists will be presented in detail in chapter 4.

Work on the relationship between infantile constitutional measures and later pathology is relatively new. The recent studies of Thomas et al. (1963, 1968), Murphy (1962) and Escalona (1964) are among the first longitudinal investigations to have tackled the problem in a comprehensive and detailed nature. Their findings will be discussed in chapter 4.

Constitutional theorists often assume that an underlying hereditary linkage system accounts for the consistencies they observe between body physique, infantile reactivity and pathological behavior. The notion of a genetic linkage of traits is not new (e.g., the well-established findings of characteristics which are sex-linked and hair-pigment correspondences).

Despite the plausibility of the linkage thesis, alternate interpretations for the correspondence between biophysical and behavioral traits also are plausible. For example, the possession of certain biophysical characteristics may lead an individual to certain experiences and these experiences may, in turn, be the real determinant of his behavior. Thus, the correlation found between the biophysical characteristic and the behavior is a function of the individual's experience, not his biophysical make-up. To illustrate, a muscular individual may learn that assertive and aggressive behavior on his part will succeed in getting him what he wants, whereas a thin and weakly individual may find that withdrawal and devious maneuvers are best for him. In these illustrations, any correlation found between the individual's physical make-up and his personality is not the result of an inborn genetic linkage, but a function of learning and experience. More will be said about this "biosocial" interplay in chapters 4 and 5.

## NEUROPHYSIOLOGICAL THEORIES

In contrast to constitutional theorists, who are concerned primarily with relationships between normal biophysical variability and psychopathology, neurophysiological theorists tend to focus on anomalies or aberrant biophysical factors, that is, on irregularities and errors in functioning, or what we shall refer to as diseases, dysfunctions and defects.

The search for these biophysical abnormalities has shifted in recent years from external agents such as bacteria, trauma and toxins to internal anatomical structures and chemical processes, all of which are difficult to locate and analyze. External determinants of mental disorders (exogenous factors) can be readily specified; a discussion of these more obvious sources of impairment will be left for chapter 4. Facts about internal correlates of pathology (endogenous factors) are difficult to establish and, therefore, must be formulated as hypotheses or limited range theories; these will be subdivided for our present brief discussion into two categories: neuroanatomical and physiochemical.

### NEUROANATOMICAL HYPOTHESES

Theories proposing that brain lesions underlie psychopathology have found many adherents since William Greisinger's assertions to that effect in the mid-nineteenth century. Eugen Bleuler, who contributed substantially to the development of a psychological view of mental disorders, wrote the following with regard to the aberrations he entitled "schizophrenia" (1930):

> . . . in all such cases we also find in the autopsy histological alterations of the brain tissue which show some uniformity . . . proof that we are in the presence of a brain lesion.

In the 1930's and the 1940's the eminent neuroanatomists, Spielmeyer, Ferraro and Papez each presented histological evidence of loss, atrophy and demyelinization of brain cells in patients classified as schizophrenic. Others have discovered parasitic microorganisms, inflammations and other histological disease processes in this disorder which could produce pathological emotion, perception and thought.

Several theorists in the last decade proposed specific areas within the brain whose dysfunction may account for various forms of psychopathology. Two sites have been referred to repeatedly: the *reticular formation* and the *limbic system*. These two regions serve as biophysical substrates for activating and integrating motivational and emotional responses; together they alert external receptors and determine whether and how emotion-producing stimuli will be experienced.

The experimental and theoretical work of Magoun, Morruzzi, Lindsley and Hebb has shown that the reticular formation, a previously little understood anatomical no-man's land, plays a key role in the arousal and activation of the central nervous system. The components of this complex system sweep up and down the major organs of the brain to enhance or suppress wakeful activity; it alerts or orients awareness and contributes to the selective focusing of attention. In addition to these experimentally established functions, a number of theorists, (Fessard, 1954; Rimland, 1965) have suggested that it also plays the important function of linking and integrating neural processes. By its unique placement within the brain, impulses from diverse cortical and subcortical sources may readily impinge upon it. As such, it is at least plausible to propose that it serves as a relay station for coordinating interneuronal circuits. If the functions of both arousal and integration are ascribed correctly to the reticular formation, lesions in this system could very well underlie many mental disorders.

Rimland, for example, views the reticular formation as crucial to integrative processes and states that dysfunctions in this system prevent the coordination of present experiences with past memories. In such cases, new perceptions cannot be combined with previous perceptions and thoughts. He suggests that in the childhood disorder known as infantile autism, neural associations are made with extreme difficulty because the reticular system has not developed fully; in childhood schizophrenia, where associations are scattered and disconnected, he proposes that the reticular formation is malfunctioning. Similar theoretical propositions, involving deficient arousal and alerting capacities in the reticular system, have been made by Fish (1961), Rosenzweig (1955), Hebb (1958), Rashkis (1958) and Singer (1960). All of these hypotheses are highly inferential and are based on indirect clinical and experimental data.

Theoretical notions implicating the limbic system in psychopathology likewise are highly speculative. Since the intuitive speculations of Papez in 1937, a substantial body of research has been gathered by Olds (1956, 1962) and Delgado (1954, 1966) to the effect that this system, composed primarily of the hypothalamus, amygdala and septal regions, is deeply involved in the expression and control of both emotional and motivational processes. It is proposed that damage to the limbic system may suppress, magnify or otherwise distort affective reactions and lead, therefore, to pathologic emotions and behavior. Specifically, Gellhorn (1953) and Heath (1954, 1966) have suggested that deficient reactions either at the hypothalamic or septal regions of the limbic system may account for schizophrenic behavior. Consistent also with these views is Bleuler's concept of "anhedonia" and Rado's notion of "integrative pleasure deficiencies" among schizophrenics. Meehl (1962), following the concepts of Bleuler and Rado, hypothesizes that schizophrenia may be traced to endogenous disturbances of synaptic control which lead to functional imbalances among the various limbic regions. Campbell (1953) has proposed that the erratic mood swings of manic-depressives may be attributed also to dysfunctions in the limbic system. There is no direct evidence to date, however, to correlate limbic system defects with any of the traditional categories of psychopathology. Despite this lack of supporting evidence, there is reason to think that defects in either the reticular or limbic systems may be related to a number of different mental disorders.

## PHYSIOCHEMICAL HYPOTHESES

Studies have been undertaken on diverse functions such as general metabolic rate, enzymatic liver reactions, circulatory system patterns and thyroid activity. The belief that physiochemical dysfunctions might underlie psycho-pathology has been supported by findings of greater biophysical variability among the mentally ill than among normals.

Hoskins (1946), reviewing the early litera-ture on endocrine functions, suggested that thyroid dysfunctions were a central factor in schizophre-nia. The failure of schizophrenics to exhibit an adequate response to stress suggested further that their adrenal glands may also be performing deficiently. Hoagland (1952) and Altschule (1953), following this latter proposal of Hoskins, concluded that the deficiency was due to a failure of the adrenals to activate cortical processes. Psy-chopathological symptoms, according to this thesis, result from a breakdown in the connection be-tween neural mechanisms and endocrinologic processes.

Other investigators have attempted to study chemical substances involved in neural transmis-sion. This body of research centers on neuro-hormones, chemical secretions of nerve cells which either facilitate or inhibit synaptic thresh-olds. The fact that certain exogenous chemicals, known as psychotomimetics (LSD, mescaline), can inhibit or stimulate the action of natural neurohumoral substances, and simulate psychotic behavior, led to speculations that natural neuro-hormonal defects also might underlie psycho-pathologic behavior. Of the five major neuro-hormones in the brain—histamine, GABA, norepinephrine, serotonin and acetylcholine—the latter three have been singled out for theoretical speculation.

*Norepinephrine,* from which epinephrine is derived, is present in a small quantity within the brain. Osmond, Smythies and Hoffer (1952, 1954) noted a similarity in chemical structure between epinephrine and mescaline, one of the major psy-chotomimetic agents. In their early work, they hypothesized the existence of an unspecified toxin which caused psychotic symptoms similar to those produced by mescaline. In more recent proposals they have suggested that schizophrenics suffer from a faulty metabolism of norepinephrine lead-ing to the production of two derivatives, adreno-chrome and adrenolutin, which ostensibly create hallucinations. Interesting as this line of specula-tion may be, the theory lacks adequate empirical support.

A second theory involving neurohormones was formulated by Woolley and Shaw (1954, 1962). They observed that the psychotomimetic lysergic acid diethylamide (LSD) was a potent antagonist to the natural neurohormone, *serotonin.* Noting a basic chemical similarity between LSD and serotonin, they proposed that LSD simulated, and then replaced, serotonin in certain essential metabolic processes in the brain, giving rise then to pathologic reactions. Data gathered in support of this thesis have been equivocal. Although not based on ostensive psychotomimetic action, Heath (1958, 1966) has proposed that schizophrenic symptomatology may be due to the operation of a brain antibody, termed taraxein, which presum-ably interferes with neural transmission in the septal region by disrupting the activity of *acetyl-choline.* This speculative thesis remains unverified.

Other theorists have avoided committing themselves to specific hypotheses, preferring to speculate only that a general dysfunction in chemical balance exists in mental disorders. Rubin (1962), for example, has proposed that the in-ability of psychotics to respond effectively to stress may stem from a variety of different hormonal imbalances. Stated simply, he proposes that the adrenergic responses (epinephrine) to stress may be either weakened or suppressed by cholinergic (antiadrenergic) responses. According to Rubin, a matrix of different mental disorders may arise as a function of different patterns of hormonal imbalance, excess or deficiency.

## THE BIOPHYSICAL DISEASE MODEL

The disease model, as adopted from medicine and used by many biophysical theorists as an analogy for psychopathology, possesses two main features. Symptoms, according to this model, are merely surface reflections of either (1) an under-lying biological defect or (2) the compensatory or adaptive reaction to that defect.

The first feature of the model is illustrated in physical medicine by infections, genetic errors, obstructions, inflammations or other insults to normal functioning which display themselves overtly as fevers, fatigue, headaches and so on. Significant progress was made in physical medicine when it shifted its focus from these surface symp-toms to the underlying pathology. Those who accept this model assume that an underlying bio-physical defect ultimately will be found for the "superficial" symptoms of mental disorders, that is, for the maladaptive behavior and poor inter-personal relations of mental patients.

The second feature of the medical disease model, that symptoms represent compensatory adaptations to the basic impairment, derives from the work of the French biologist, Claude Bernard, in the nineteenth century. Of particular interest was his observation that adaptive reactions often are more destructive to the organism than the basic defect itself; adaptive efforts, intended as temporary and reparative, often became continuous and destructive. For example, microorganisms infecting the lung elicit physiological reactions which counter the invasion. Unfortunately, the magnitude of the reaction often is excessive and protracted, leading to lung congestion, pneumonia and death.

Biophysical theorists adopting the disease model are inclined to use only the first feature of the model. To them the only difference between psychological and biological disorders is that the former, affecting the central nervous system, manifested itself in mental symptoms, whereas the latter, affecting other organ systems, manifests itself in physical symptoms. The parallel they see between biological and psychological disorders has led to serious objections, which may be summarized as follows: adherents of the disease model (1) attribute psychopathology to biological defects whose existence is questionable, (2) exclude the role of psychological and interpersonal factors in psychopathology and (3) overlook the second feature of the disease model, that dealing with the individual's compensatory reaction to stress or impairment. Let us elaborate these criticisms briefly.

1. Regarding the first point, Szaaz (1960) questions the wisdom of pursuing the "myth" of neuroanatomical defects and biochemical dysfunctions. To him, the belief that tangible biological phenomena are the cause of mental disorders is a myth, that is, a false verbal analogy founded on an acceptance of the medical disease model. If Szaaz's criticism is taken to mean that not all forms of psychopathology can be attributed to biological causes, it certainly is correct. But this criticism is largely an attack upon a straw man, for no biophysical theorist takes such an extreme position. Biophysical theorists do not deny the role of psychological factors; they merely state that *certain* types of psychopathology can be attributed primarily to biophysical impairments, and that even these are shaped to some extent by the unique environmental experiences of the individual.

2. The second criticism of the disease model, that psychopathology should be viewed as a problem of living (Adams, 1964), also seems irrelevant. Psychopathology can be viewed as a "problem of living" *and* as a physical disease. These are merely different levels of analysis, not incompatible frames of reference. For example, a deaf person may respond in a maladaptive fashion to social life because of his anatomical impairment. Which facet of his overall problem we wish to focus upon depends on the purposes of our investigation—we can stress either his interpersonal difficulties or his biophysical impairment. The failure to recognize that psychopathology likewise can be approached at different levels of analysis will lead only to fruitless controversies.

3. The third criticism leveled at those who have adopted the disease model states that they have overlooked the feature of the model which deals with the organism's adaptive response to his impairment. This criticism perhaps is more justified than the others, but may be unfair given the limited state of biophysical knowledge. Biophysical theorists contend that they must first discover the existence of underlying defects before they can study the manner in which individuals adapt to them. Other theorists, however, feel that little will be gained from a detailed knowledge of biophysical impairments alone. According to their view, it is the adaptive reaction of the individual which is the most significant part of the disease model. The failure of certain biophysical theorists to utilize both aspects of the disease model does not justify condemnation, however. A model, if we will recall, is merely a tool, a heuristic device to stimulate theoretical ideas and empirical research. One may utilize one aspect of a model and overlook others. Certainly, accepting a model in toto does not assure us of its usefulness. Which aspect of the disease model will prove most fruitful will be answered not by debate, but by research. In any event, the adaptation aspect of the disease model has not been intentionally overlooked; it serves as the foundation for the complex and varied intrapsychic theories to which our attention turns next.

# INTRAPSYCHIC THEORIES

Biophysical theories usually are limited in scope and are anchored closely to observable and measurable data. In contrast, theories dealing with intrapsychic processes are organized often into comprehensive systems which lack a firm anchor to the empirical world. They rely heavily on inference and speculation and, as a result, are influenced in large measure by the models that theorists use as their guide. It is for this reason that we must outline the basic model adopted by intrapsychic theorists at the beginning of our discussion. Afterward, we will examine the typical sources they have used to obtain their data and the types of concepts they have devised to represent them. Lastly, we will outline the major theories in use today.

## THE INTRAPSYCHIC ADAPTATION MODEL

The traditional medical disease model, as applied to the study of psychopathology, contains two assumptions about pathological symptoms. The first assumption, which is given primary importance in biophysical theories, states that symptoms reflect the existence of a biological defect. The second assumption, generally overlooked by biophysical theorists, states that symptoms represent compensatory or defensive adaptations to a basic impairment. This second assumption is emphasized by intrapsychic theorists.

Intrapsychic theorists substitute psychological factors for biological diseases in their model, that is, they supplant biological diseases with concepts of psychic trauma or conflict, and supplant the notion of biological defensive reactions with the concept of psychic adaptive compensations. In the same manner as we possess biological stabilizers to correct upsetting defects, we possess adaptive psychological mechanisms by which anxieties and conflicts may be counteracted. And just as defensive biological reactions occasionally prove more destructive than the original assault, so too do psychological mechanisms prove maladaptive.

Anxiety is the primary psychological "defect" resulting in maladaptive reactions. When the individual's basic security is threatened, he invokes intricate defensive maneuvers to deny or distort his awareness of the threat he faces. The intensity of this anxiety will determine, to a great degree, whether the defensive reaction will prove adaptive or maladaptive.

Intrapsychic theorists stress the importance of early childhood anxieties since these experiences may dispose the individual to a lifelong pattern of pathological adaptation. Childhood anxieties establish deeply ingrained defensive systems which may lead the individual to react to new situations as if they were duplicates of what occurred in childhood. These anticipatory defenses persist throughout life and result in progressive or chronic disorders.

Intrapsychic theorists may differ in which experiences they view to be crucial to the production of anxiety, but all agree that psychopathology arises as a result of efforts to relieve anxiety and that these efforts often progress into more serious difficulties.

An illustration of this sequence of maladaptation may be useful at this point. If a youngster avoids his peers as a means of forestalling anticipated rejection, he will prevent himself from engaging in activities that might teach him how to enhance his acceptance by them. Furthermore, withdrawal will deprive him of certain future needs he may have, such as companionship, sexual gratification and love. If, instead of withdrawal, he reacts to his peers with hostility and rage, he will evoke counteraggression and thereby intensify his rejection. As a circular pattern of maladaptation continues, he may become isolated from others entirely and develop highly idiosyncratic patterns of thought which will alienate him only further from society. As a result, he will lose touch with the world of reality and become preoccupied only with his own thoughts and feelings. As his isolation increases, he may be unable to avoid feelings of emptiness and confusion. A sense of futility may emerge and his defensive efforts may collapse, leading him to sink into a state of utter desolation and disorganization.

Intrapsychic theorists hold that childhood experiences of anxiety are the primary cause of pathology; although adult experiences are ceded some importance, their significance is shaped or colored by past influences. Thus, these theorists stress continuity in development, believing that adult personality is related in a determinant way to early experiences.

Three classes of experience have been noted as conducive to pathological development: (1) the extent to which basic needs are frustrated, (2) the conflicts to which the child is exposed and (3) the attitudes and settings in which experiences are learned. A brief discussion of each of these factors will be useful.

1. When we think of how profoundly helpless an infant is in meeting his own survival needs, we can appreciate his dependence upon parental support and nourishment. The security the child feels is tied directly to the manner and extent to which his parents supply his needs. A vital link exists, therefore, between parental attitudes and behaviors, and the security and comfort of the child.

This link is especially crucial during the earliest years of life when the child is completely at the mercy of parental whims and desires. For example, the child's persistent demand for nutrition may evoke parental balking, withdrawal or harshness. Harsh weaning may be experienced as a sign of parental rejection, ridicule and hostility, and may undermine the youngster's self-confidence and security. He may handle the anxieties this experience creates only by distorting or denying what he has experienced.

2.  Difficulties may arise because the child's reasoning processes are undeveloped. He may be unable to grasp and separate conflicting attitudes conveyed by his parents. For example, he may have been admonished, on several occasions, to be kind and considerate to his friends; at other times he may have been urged to be aggressive and competitive. Unclear as to which circumstances call for one or the other of these incompatible responses, he finds himself confused and anxious. As a solution, he may decide that it is best to be indifferent and to disengage himself from others. As another example, a child may have been taught that sexual feelings are degrading and sinful. As a consequence, he may be unable to experience adult sexual satisfaction without feeling conflict and anxiety.

3.  The manner and setting in which attitudes and feelings are taught often are more important than what is taught. If ridicule, intimidation and punishment are employed to inculcate attitudes and behaviors, the child will learn not only to submit to his parents' desires, but to fear and hate his parents. Any method of adverse training adds anxiety and conflict to what is learned. As a result, the child will respond with a variety of maladaptive reactions such as anger, ambivalence, guilt and fear at the same time as he learns "to behave."

## GENERAL ORIENTATION

The emphasis given to early childhood experience by intrapsychic theorists represents their contention that disorders of adulthood are a direct product of the continued and insidious operation of past events. To them, knowledge of the past provides information indispensable to understanding adult difficulties. To the question, "what is the basis of adult disorders?" they would answer: "the anxieties of childhood and the progressive sequence of defensive maneuvers which were devised to protect against a recurrence of these feelings".

Intrapsychic theorists contend that these two determinants of adult behavior, childhood anxieties and defensive maneuvers, are unconscious, that is, cannot be brought to awareness except

under unusual conditions. It is the search for these unconscious processes which is the distinguishing feature of the intrapsychic approach. The obscure and elusive phenomena of the unconscious are the data which they uncover and use for their concepts. These data consist first, of repressed childhood anxieties that persist within the individual and attach themselves insidiously to ongoing experiences, and second, of unconscious adaptive processes which protect the individual against the resurgence of these anxieties. The *intrapsychic* label we have attached to these theorists reflects, therefore, their common focus on these two elements of the unconscious.

How is the unconscious manifested? Essentially, through indirect methods. Since the unconscious cannot be seen by direct means, it must be inferred.

Unconscious processes are revealed most often when we let down our guard, as in "slips of the tongue," or when we put aside the controls of wakeful activity, as in sleep, or when we relinquish our contact with reality, as in serious mental disorders.

Unconscious data may be obtained also in specially designed clinical settings. The technique of *free association,* where the patient is asked to relax his usual controls and to verbalize every passing thought or emotion, often elicits unconscious processes which are not evident in daily life. The seemingly unrelated fragments of free association—memories, hopes and casual commentaries—turn out to be neither random nor irrelevant, but display a pattern of repetitive themes. These themes are interpreted as evidence for the existence of unconscious forces which underlie and direct conscious behavior. *Dream analysis* is another clinical method of uncovering unconscious processes. In sleep, without the controls of reality and responsibility, unconscious processes display themselves freely in symbolic dream imagery. The method of *projective tests* is another clinically created procedure for inferring the unconscious. Here, ambiguous stimuli are presented to the subject and he is forced to draw upon his own inner resources in order to make a response. Idiosyncratic responses result and unconscious processes often are displayed.

Questions have been raised as to whether or not scientific concepts can be founded on unconscious data. Intrapsychic theories have been criticized as unscientific mixtures of metaphorical analogies, speculative notions and hypothetical constructs because their data are anchored so tenuously to the observable world.

Added to this rather harsh judgment is the

equally critical view that the methods of collecting unconscious data are both unreliable and imprecise. How can concepts of the unobservable unconscious be empirically anchored? Can one accept what the patient says without having it corroborated by external evidence? Is the patient an unbiased judge, or is he motivated to agree with his all-knowing therapist? Are free associations really free, or do patients produce what their therapists implicitly suggest?

These and many other questions have been raised about the subjective and methodologically uncontrolled procedures used for the development of intrapsychic theories. Without tools such as tape recorded therapeutic interviews, corroborative data from relatives and experimentally controlled longitudinal studies, the probability of objectifying the concepts and propositions of intrapsychic theories is highly unlikely. To critics, the ingenious speculations of intrapsychic theorists are, at best, a starting point, a preliminary set of propositions which must be articulated into clearly specifiable behaviors which can be confirmed or disproved.

Despite these criticisms, many of which are equally applicable to other theoretical approaches, intrapsychic processes are a necessary part of the study of man's pathological functioning. Although these processes are difficult to formulate according to the tenets of scientific objectivity, their existence cannot be denied or overlooked. Efforts to unravel them will fall prey inevitably to theoretical obscurity and methodological difficulty, yet the search is mandatory. The ideas of those theorists who have ventured upon this troublesome course will be discussed next.

## FREUD'S PSYCHOSEXUAL CONFLICT THEORY

Our presentation of the major intrapsychic theorists will begin with the contributions of Sigmund Freud for two reasons. First, we must recognize his work as the foundation upon which all other intrapsychic theories are based and second, his views serve as a bridge between the biophysical and the intrapsychic orientations. Freud was inclined to anchor many of his concepts to the biological make-up of man; this view was rejected by many of his followers, however.

Freud's theory of psychopathology was developed over a 50-year professional career. Its essential features may be summarized as follows: Man possesses basic biological instincts, the most important of which are the sexual or life-propelling energies known as the *libido*. These energies, together with aggressive death-energies, compose the *id*. A maturational sequence unfolds in which these libidinous energies shift in their primary locus from one organ or zone of the body to another; this sequence is referred to as the stages of *psychosexual development*. Biological instincts must find outlets of expression. In attempting to gain these outlets the child runs into conflict with reality limitations and societal prohibitions. Frustration or conflict associated with these biological drives leads to anxiety. The child learns a variety of techniques to relieve his anxiety and to gratify his instinctual needs; these protective and need-gratifying techniques are referred to as the processes of the *ego*. Ego processes which develop in response to particularly intense infantile anxieties become *fixated* and may persist as lifelong *character disorders*. Experiences in later life which threaten to reactivate these repressed and unconscious anxieties lead to pathological symptoms; these symptoms represent, in symbolic form, both the repressed anxieties and the defensive techniques learned to control them.

Subsequent intrapsychic theorists extended and modified these basic notions. Those features of Freud's theory which characterize his position in distinction to those of his followers will be detailed next.

### The Instincts

Freud believed that the root of all psychopathology could be found in the frustration of certain basic biological instincts. Instincts were viewed as inborn biological energies which excite and direct behavior. They could be satisfied, as can hunger and thirst, by a variety of instinct-gratifying activities. Two major energy sources were proposed by Freud, the life and the death instincts. Because the value of the death instinct as an explanatory concept has been almost universally rejected, we will bypass this concept and deal only with his views regarding the life instinct.

The energies of the life instinct, called the libido, were manifested in what Freud referred to as sexual excitations. To Freud, all of man's interests, tastes and behaviors were but surface expressions or substitutions for more direct gratifications of these excitations. Freud's entire system assumed that "civilized" and social phenomena could be reduced ultimately to the basic biological instincts. Mental disorders, according to Freud, arose as a result of conflicts and frustrations of these instincts.

## Psychosexual Stages

Direct gratification of sexual excitation can be obtained by the manipulation of extremely sensitive surface areas of the body. The primary bodily region of maximal sexual excitation shifts, however, as the individual matures. This progression of *erogenous zones* was termed the psychosexual stages.

In the first year and a half of life, the lips and mouth region are the primary locus of libidinal excitation; during this period sucking and eating behavior produce pleasure and gratification. This *oral* period is followed by a libidinous centering in the *anal* region which lasts about a year; it is replaced, in turn, by an erogenous *phallic* stage in which rubbing and massaging of the genitals serves as the basis of pleasure. These three *pregenital* stages are followed by a *latency* period which lasts until puberty, following which the mature *genital* stage unfolds in preparation for normal adult sexuality.

The three pregenital periods were seen by Freud as prone to conflict and frustration. In early life the young child's needs are entirely dependent upon and subject to the attitudes and whims of his parents. Second, there is a rapid shift in the bodily zones of gratification, leaving little opportunity for resolving or working through whatever frustrations and conflicts arose. To Freud, then, the first few years of life were especially susceptible to unresolved anxiety and defective adaptation.

During the latency period the child learns to accept the restrictions and prohibitions of his parents, establishing thereby what Freud termed the *super-ego*. Henceforth, the child restrains direct gratification of his instinctual impulses by his own volition. Conflicts arise now between the youngster's "ideals" and his instinctual drives. If the prohibitions of the super-ego are too restrictive, however, the individual may be unable to gratify normal adult sexual needs when they emerge during the genital stage. Thus, numerous children have been led by parental teachings and religious admonishments to believe that it is "immoral" to engage in "sex"; the impact of this belief may be so deeply ingrained that they continue to experience feelings of tension and guilt even when sexual activities are fully sanctioned, as in marriage.

## Psychosexual Character Types

Each stage of psychosexual development produces a distinctive set of anxieties and defenses resulting from instinct frustration and conflict. Psychopathological character traits arise from the persistence into adulthood of these distinctive childhood anxieties and defenses. For example, a child may have experienced oral gratification only when he submitted to a rigid feeding schedule imposed by his parents. Anxious lest he lose parental support and fearful of deviating from parental regulations, he may become a cautious and acquiescent person unable to take any step toward adult independence. This pattern of early oral frustration would dispose the individual to retreat or *regress* to this fixated pattern of early adaptation whenever he is faced with anxiety. As a freshman college student, he might develop a psychosomatic ailment if he failed to be accepted into a fraternity and return to the "security" of his parental home; faced with marital or vocational difficulties, he might turn to excessive eating or drinking as a regressive mode of oral gratification.

Freud differentiated the oral period into two phases: the *oral-sucking* phase, in which food is accepted indiscriminately, followed by the *oral-biting* period, in which food is accepted selectively, occasionally rejected and aggressively chewed. Excessive gratifications, conflicts or frustrations associated with each of these phases establish different patterns of adult personality. For example, an overly indulgent sucking stage may lead to imperturbable optimism and naive self-assurance. An ungratified sucking period may lead to excessive dependency and gullibility; for example, the deprived child may learn to "swallow" anything in order to ensure that he will get something. Frustration experienced at the biting stage might lead to the development of aggressive oral tendencies such as sarcasm and verbal hostility in adulthood.

Difficulties associated with the anal period likewise lead to distinctive modes of adult personality. Toilet training occurs in the second year, a time when the child can both control his sphincter muscles and comprehend the desires of his parents. For the first time in his life, he has the power to actively and knowingly thwart his parents' demands; he has the option now of pleasing or foiling their desires. A battle of wits often arises. Depending on the outcome, the child will adopt a pattern of attitudes toward authority which will have a far-reaching effect in shaping his adult traits. If, for example, the child's pleasure in defecation is punished and condemned, his assertive tendencies may be shattered, leading him to become a compliant and conforming person, fearful of expressing independent thoughts. Conceivably, he might accept parental condemnations of his soiling behavior as "right," and thereby attempt to show them how "worthy and clean" he is. He may, in time, become not only compulsively clean and orderly, but may display harsh attitudes toward those who fail to be like him. Thus, he may seek to control others with rules and principles as severe and arbitrary as those his parents imposed upon him. Other reactions to parental severity in toilet training are possible. To avoid toilet training conflict he may learn to hold back his feces; as a result, he may become a retentive, parsimonious and constricted individual, who forever procrastinates and always saves "for a rainy day." As another possibility, harsh training procedures might lead to rage and anger; this may result in a withdrawal of parental demands. Finding himself successful in this maneuver, the child may develop a lifelong pattern of self-assertion, disorderliness and negativism.

Conflicts during the phallic stage were viewed by Freud to be crucial to the development of psychopathology. In the third and fourth year, libidinous energies center upon the genitals, and are manifested in masturbation, sexual curiosity and exhibitionism. At this time there is a shift in the child's attitude toward his parents. Feelings toward the opposite sex become tinged with sexual desire; this is paralleled by jealousy and hostility toward the same-sex parent. A struggle ensues between the child and the same-sex parent for the affection of the opposite-sex parent; this Freud termed the *oedipus complex*. Freud considered his observation of this conflict to be a major discovery and viewed it as the "nucleus" of neurotic disorders. In the young boy this conflict eventuates in an intense fear that his more powerful and jealous father will punish him for his lustful feelings. Anxieties of castration become so intense that he represses his incestuous desire for his mother and denies his hostile feelings toward his father.

If the oedipal conflict is resolved adequately, the boy will not experience a feeling of defeat and humiliation. He will learn to transform his incestuous desire into a more acceptable expression of affection. He will have learned to control his envy and hostility toward his father. He will identify with his father's powerful masculinity and channel his struggle for mastery into acceptable activities such as athletic and social competitions. In brief then, he will transform his sexual and aggressive urges into more realistic modes of expression. In a manner similar to the boy, the young girl will learn to renounce her attraction to the father and her hostile attitudes toward her mother. In healthy resolutions, both boy and girl emerge with a strengthened pattern of ego capacities and an undiminished feeling of self-esteem.

Should the entanglements of the oedipal period be unresolved, the child will forever handle sexual and aggressive impulses in a troubled manner. Sexuality may remain in a conflict between seductive thoughts, on the one hand, and guilt and fear of punishment, on the other. Faulty identification with the same sex parent may lead to a homosexual pattern. Aggressive impulses may persist, turning the individual into a bully and obstructionist.

To Freud, early instinctual frustrations and conflicts remain deeply anchored within the person. Although the anxieties and adaptive reactions they produce are unconscious, they persist as a mold that shapes the entire course of life.

Freud's conception of man's development has not gone unchallenged. In the next section we will turn to a number of intrapsychic theorists who have proposed alternative explanations for the observations which Freud so keenly made. For purposes of simplification these theories have been grouped under three headings:

(1) Adaptive-deficiency theories: These theorists have retained Freud's emphasis on the role of inborn sexual instincts, but in addition, propose the existence of constructive ego instincts which enable the individual to develop in a healthy and mature fashion. Their work focuses on the developmental sequence through which these naturally adaptive ego capacities emerge. In their view, disorders arise not as a function of instinctual conflicts, but because these constructive ego capacities fail to develop.

(2) Object-deprivation theories: These theorists have retained Freud's emphasis on instinctual drives, but have replaced the sexual instincts with instincts which seek nonsexual social relationships or objects for their gratification. It is the deprivation of these innately sought objects and relationships which gives rise to pathology.

(3) Interpersonal-anxiety theories: These theorists deemphasize the role of instincts in pathology and contend that anxiety in interpersonal relations, whatever its original source, is crucial to disorder.

Let us discuss each of these three positions in some detail.

## ADAPTIVE-DEFICIENCY THEORIES

Two major objections to Freud's theories characterize the men to be discussed in this section. First, Freud emphasized a single innate drive within man. These theorists feel that man possesses innate drives other than that of libidinous sexuality. Second, Freud believed that man's drives led inevitably to conflict. These men, referred to in chapter 1 as the *neo-Freudian ego theorists,* conceived man as possessing innate ego drives which are constructive and which facilitate his adaptation to reality. Thus, the focus has shifted from troublesome sexual and aggressive instincts to an interest in constructive instincts.

## HARTMANN AND RAPAPORT

To Freud, the ego was conceived as that part of the personality which served to reconcile the drives of the id to reality and to the restrictions of the superego. Ego processes were not inborn but were learned in order to meet the regulatory and the defensive needs of the individual. The neo-Freudian analyst, Heinz Hartmann (1958), and the psychologist, David Rapaport (1958, 1959), considered this conception of the ego too restrictive.

In a series of papers published in the 1940's and 1950's, they proposed that the ego possessed autonomous inborn capacities (motility, perception, affection and cognition) which matured independently of the instinctual drives of the id. Both ego and id instincts derived from a common matrix of biological potentials, differentiating into separable energy potentials. The *autonomous apparatuses* of the ego, as Hartmann referred to them, were preadapted to handle "average ex-

pectable environments." Thus, as the infant matures, a variety of innate capacities progressively unfold, each appearing in time to enable him to deal competently with the tasks and experiences that typically face youngsters of his age.

Rapaport proposed, further, that the maturation of these ego capacities was dependent on a *stimulus nutriment* diet. What he meant by this concept was that these inborn capacities required periodic stimulation in order to develop properly. To Rapaport, social isolation or environmental deprivation led to a decline in the effectiveness of these capacities. For example, if an infant is overprotected by a mother who "does everything for him," he may be deprived of opportunities to exercise his maturing motor skills, and may fail, as a consequence, to develop his inherent physical competencies.

In summary, Hartmann and Rapaport claimed that man possessed an inherent capacity to adapt to reality, assuming a normal degree of sensory and social stimulation. Pathology, to them, arose when the inborn functions of the ego were deprived of adequate environmental stimulation. Deprivation diminished these capacites to a point where the individual was incapable of responding effectively to everyday situational demands. We will return to these ideas in chapter 5.

## ERIKSON

Erik H. Erikson constructed a sequence for the development of the ego which paralleled the

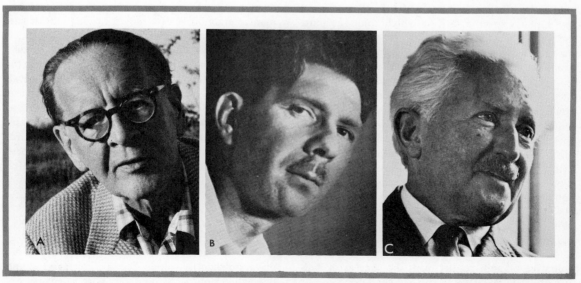

Figure 2-2   Major ego theorists. *A.* Heinz Hartmann. *B.* David Rapaport. (Photograph from the Basic Papers of David Rapaport. New York, Basic Books, Inc., 1967.) *C.* Erik H. Erikson. (Photograph by Olive R. Pierce.)

### Table 2-1    Erikson's Eight Phases of Epigenesis*

| LIFE PHASES | PSYCHOSOCIAL CRISES | SIGNIFICANT RELATIONS | PSYCHOSOCIAL MODALITIES AND TASKS | PSYCHOSEXUAL STAGE (FREUDIAN) |
|---|---|---|---|---|
| I. Infancy | Trust vs. mistrust | Mother | To get; to give in return | Oral-sensory |
| II. Early childhood | Autonomy vs. shame and doubt | Parents | To hold (on); to let (go) | Anal-muscular |
| III. Play age | Initiative vs. guilt | Basic family | To make; to play roles | Genital-locomotor |
| IV. School age | Industry vs. inferiority | Neighborhood school | To make things; to make them together | Latency |
| V. Adolescence | Identity vs. identity diffusion | Peer groups and out-groups; models of leadership | To be oneself (or not to be) | Puberty |
| VI. Young adult | Intimacy and solidarity vs. isolation | Partners in friendship, sex, competition, cooperation | To lose and find one-self in another | Genitality |
| VII. Adulthood | Generativity vs. self-absorption | Divided labor and shared household | To make be; to care for | |
| VIII. Mature age | Integrity vs. despair | "Mankind," "my kind" | To be through having been; to face not being | |

* Adapted from Erikson, 1959.

stages of psychosexual development formulated by Freud (1950, 1959). Erikson called this developmental sequence the *phases of epigenesis.* As with Hartmann and Rapaport, Erikson believed that Freud's focus on psychosexuality was too narrowly conceived. He recognized a broader pattern of sensorimotor, cognitive and social capacities in the infant's biological equipment, and proposed the notion of *developmental modes* which represented the unfolding of these genetically endowed capacities. Each of these modes is characterized by a phase specific task to which solutions must be found. Satisfactory solutions prepared the child to progress to the next phase; unsuccessful solutions led to chronic adaptive difficulties.

Eight stages of ego epigenesis were constructed by Erikson; the expressions, interactions and relationships arising during each of these phases of development are presented in Table 2-1. Each phase is associated with a crisis for the individual, a decisive encounter with others which will shape the course of his future development. For example, the oral-sensory stage, or infancy nursing period, determines whether the child will develop trust or mistrust; the struggle over retention and elimination during the anal-muscular stage influences whether the child will emerge with a sense of autonomy or with shame and doubt; initiative or guilt results from the success or failure of sexual assertiveness in the genital-locomotor period, and so on.

Erikson conceived an innate *mutuality* between the phases of child maturation, on the one hand, and adult phases of development, on the other. He envisioned a mutual regulation, or a *cogwheeling of the life cycles,* such that adult phase specific tasks were innately coordinated to the phase specific needs of the child. For example, infantile helplessness not only elicits a nurturant response from the mother, but fulfills the mother's generative-phase nurturant needs. In all cultures, according to Erikson, the basic timetable of human interaction is determined by this inborn pattern of symbiotic relationships.

Erikson's attempt to coordinate Freud's notion of innate biological dispositions with the formative influences of society and culture parallels the work of the object-deprivation theorists, to whom we shall turn shortly. He proposed, as did the object-deprivation theorists, that man's social behaviors arise largely from genetic or inherent preadaptive dispositions; social experiences merely influence the style or manner in which these inherent dispositions become manifest.

## OBJECT-DEPRIVATION THEORIES

Both adaptive-deficiency and object-deprivation theorists retain Freud's intrapsychic and instinctual approach; however, both reject his exclusive focus on libidinous sexuality, as well as his view that instincts conflict inevitably with reality adjustments. Object-deprivation theorists go beyond the adaptive theorists in claiming that man instinctively seeks specific types of social relationships and objects; more specifically, they contend that psychopathology arises when the person is deprived of these instinctively sought social outlets.

## JUNG

Jung's break with Freud arose largely as a function of two disagreements. First, Jung believed that the libido, or life energies, consisted of several instinctual dispositions, only one of which could be called sexual. Second, he argued that instincts did not necessarily upset the individual's psychic functioning; rather, they could be constructive, that is, facilitate effective and healthy growth. In both these views, he anticipated the ideas of the adaptive-deficiency theorists discussed earlier. However, in addition, Jung believed that man's instincts were oriented or goal-directed to specific objects or activities in the social environment. Thus, he proposed that the instincts possessed not only adaptive potentials, but particular goals which could fulfill these potentials, e.g., the infant not only possessed "ego instincts" that enabled him to recognize and interact with his caretakers, but he actively sought to find and relate to them.

The source of man's goal-directed energies was to be found in what Jung referred to as the *collective unconscious,* a concept representing a hypothetical pattern of inborn predispositions bequeathed by the individual's ancestral past. These "racial" memories were viewed by Jung as a template that shaped the direction in which the individual's general capacities would be best fulfilled; he termed these memories *archetypes.* For example, the infant ostensibly inherited a preformed image of "mother" based on an accumulated racial history of maternal experiences; this primordial image disposed him to relate to his actual mother in a manner similar to his inherited archetype. Archetypal images not only shaped the perception of experience, but drove the individual to find experiences consonant with his heritage. Thus, Jung spoke of the unconscious as possessing a forward or *actualizing* tendency.

Failure to find adequate expression for these archetypal dispositions was viewed by Jung to be the crux of psychopathology. In this formulation, Jung not only rejected Freud's position that unconscious forces inevitably conflict with reality, but offered an entirely opposite hypothesis in which unconscious forces were necessary for healthy functioning. By denying, disavowing or ignoring the unconscious, the individual would invite disorder. If these archetypal tendencies were unexpressed, they would intrude upon the normal processes of perception and behavior, twisting and distorting them into pathological forms such as phobias, delusions and hallucinations.

Unfortunately, many of Jung's contributions have been clouded in a religious and occult "mystique." In addition, Jung's notion of racial inheritance, with its implication of inborn group differences, has been repellent to the humanist orientation of contemporary psychologists. Despite areas of dissent such as these, other ideas formulated first by Jung (e.g., inborn constructive forces which are actualized in social relationships) have been borrowed by subsequent theorists with little recognition of their Jungian origins. Moreover, Freud's olympian role has completely overshadowed the less significant, but nonetheless fertile and impressive contributions made by Jung.

## FAIRBAIRN AND SPITZ

At first glance the ideas of W. R. D. Fairbairn (1952) appear to be entirely unrelated to those of Jung; closer inspection reveals a fundamental similarity. Both reject Freud's focus on the sexual nature of instincts, preferring to emphasize the social relationships and objects through which instincts may be fulfilled. Jung, however, attributed the existence of these instinctive goals to racially derived archetypes which are projected upon the external world throughout the individual's lifetime. Fairbairn, in contrast, proposed infantile *endopsychic objects,* that is, universal pristine images in the unconscious of children which may fail to mature if the child does not obtain satisfying experiences with their real world counterparts. Deprivation of these instinctively sought for relationships results in the loss of social capacities or in the aversion of social contacts, each of which is a forerunner of psychopathology.

The studies of R. A. Spitz on maternally deprived children (1965) has elaborated the importance of developmental social stimulation. To Spitz, neurological maturation depends on experience with specific objects and relationships in the environment. Without these early experiences, pathology is inevitable. Thus, Spitz reports several cases of stuporous infants reared by totally rejecting mothers; weeks of affectionate nurturance and stimulation were necessary to revive these children from their semicomatose state.

## INTERPERSONAL-ANXIETY THEORISTS

Few of Freud's many dissenters have been more influential than the interpersonal-anxiety theorists, known better as the *neo-Freudian social theorists*. Most prominent among them are Harry Stack Sullivan and Karen Horney. To these two we shall add the early Freudian dissident, Alfred Adler, who was the first theorist to stress the role of social and interpersonal experiences. Several beliefs distinguish these theorists from those treated earlier.

First, they contend that the critical determinants of pathology do not arise from the biological properties of the instincts; to them, instincts have significance only in terms of their interpersonal consequences. Freudian stages of psychosexual development are either rejected or reinterpreted to reflect their interpersonal character. Thus, instead of speaking of a biologically based oral stage, they speak of a relationship between parent and child in which the child experiences the interpersonal aspects of dependency; similarly, the anal stage is translated to signify a period when interpersonal obedience or assertiveness is learned.

Second, these theorists reject the Freudian view that adult pathology can be understood simply as a repetition of earlier developmental difficulties. Although they recognize that early experience serves as the basis for later difficulties, they believe that these difficulties often are autonomous of their original source. In this regard, they note that early experiences are modified by intervening experiences, that adaptive reactions often lead to new difficulties and that these, in turn, bring forth new defenses, and so on. By adulthood, there has evolved an extensive and diffusive series of experiences that are far removed from the original childhood difficulties. Because no simple connection was seen between childhood experience and adult pathology, these theorists shifted their focus to adult problems; the past was of value to the extent that it could shed light on the present.

Third, the shift in focus to adult experience led to a decreased interest in the unconscious, which harbored the residues of the past, and an increased interest in the role of the conscious attitudes of adulthood. They recognized that conscious attitudes shaped, in great measure, the individual's way of perceiving and organizing his everyday life; these attitudes transformed the world of objective reality to suit established ways of thinking. This interest in consciousness may be viewed as a bridge between the orientations of the intrapsychic and phenomenological approaches, to be discussed later.

### ADLER

A recurrent theme in Adler's theory is man's universal striving to compensate for basic feelings of inferiority. Adler disagreed with Freud's single-minded view that man is driven by an omnipresent sexual instinct. But Adler fell prey to a similar singular notion, substituting superiority striving for sexuality. Despite this limitation, Adler's thesis extended Freud's theory by adding the social nature of man's motives.

The cardinal concept in Adler's theory is *overcompensation*, an inborn tendency to counteract deficiencies or inadequacies through reparative strivings. According to Adler, all humans suffer an inevitable "inferiority" in childhood and, therefore, all individuals strive to better themselves. Distinctive patterns of striving, referred to by Adler as the individual's *style of life*, derive from unusual shortcomings experienced in childhood. Although all individuals share the common inferiority of childhood, only those experiencing severe inferiorities become disordered.

Adler noted several major sources of inferiority: physical defects, when viewed by others as a sign of weakness; excessive pampering and parental worry, which gave the child a feeling that he could not stand on his own; and rejection and neglect, which led him to believe that he lacked those qualities necessary to be loved.

Compensation for inferiority took the form of *fictive goals*, that is, unrealistic aspirations by which the individual could redress his shortcomings. These aspirations are displayed either in an overt striving for superiority, such as overly aggressive behavior and pomposity, or in a withdrawal from normal social activity, such as seen in homosexuality and schizophrenia. Compensating strategies, which Adler termed *neurotic safeguards*, help the individual keep his fictive goals intact by various protective maneuvers. For example, by assuming the role of a "hippie," a basically insecure, obese youngster asserts his superiority to "all the squares," and displays his physical unattractiveness as a badge of his independence of "bourgeois values."

### SULLIVAN

Sullivan constructed a model of developmental stages in a manner similar to Freud and Erikson. Freud's theory, however, was based on the bodily progression of libidinous instincts, and Erikson's represented the maturation of innate ego capacities. Sullivan, in contrast, devised a system based on the role of interpersonal communication, reflecting his belief that the developmental feature which distinguished man from other animals was not his sexual or adaptive capacities, but his capacity to communicate with others. This is not to say that Sullivan denied the importance of biologically derived functions; he merely deemphasized them in preference to those functions which he felt to be distinctively human.

Anxiety plays a central role in Sullivan's theory. However, in contrast to previously discussed theorists, he did not view anxiety to be a product of instinctual frustration or deprivation, but a direct result of interpersonal experiences; they stemmed, first, from relationships with an anxious and malevolent mother and, later, from social ostracism, ridicule or punishment.

To avoid interpersonal threat, children learn which behaviors are rewarded, that is, lead to feelings of security, and which behaviors are punished, that is, lead to anxiety. In time, a complex pattern of self-protective attitudes and behaviors develop, which Sullivan refers to as the *self-system;* this system consists of a variety of measures that produce the rewards of security and avoid the anxieties of insecurity, a concept not dissimilar from Adler's notion of "neurotic safeguards."

Sullivan's concern with the interpersonal aspect of pathology led him to recognize a pathogenic source that had been overlooked by previous theorists: the detrimental effects of normally well-meaning but inconsistent parents. To Sullivan, contradictory or confusing guides for behavior not only produce anxiety, but have the effect of immobilizing the child. Trapped in what has been referred to as a *double-bind,* the child is unable to act in a single and nonconflictful way to others. As a simple illustration, picture the discomfort and indecision experienced by a youngster whose father appears to be in a friendly and jovial mood, but has on numerous previous occasions quickly changed his "tune" and been harshly critical and deprecating; should he extend himself to his father now, hoping to gain the benefits of his cheerful spirits, or should he keep his distance and not chance a repetition of past humiliations? These inconsistent parental attitudes and behaviors not only produce their own anxiety, but may preclude effective interpersonal relations and effective solutions to other sources of anxiety.

## HORNEY

As with Sullivan, Horney stresses the fact that the central determinant of pathology is anxiety stemming from the child's feelings of insecurity, isolation and helplessness in a potentially hostile world. Without warmth, encouragement and affection, the child's need for basic security will be adversely affected.

According to Horney, the child attempts, at first, to cope with anxiety by adopting a variety of spontaneous strategies; he may be submissive, hostile, ambitious, avoidant, exploitive, independent or perfectionistic, all at different times. Eventually, one of three basic "character patterns"

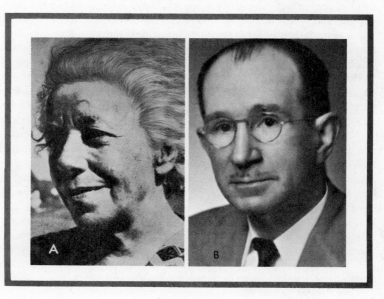

Figure 2-3 Interpersonal anxiety theorists. *A.* Karen Horney. (National Library of Medicine, Bethesda, Maryland.) *B.* Harry S. Sullivan. (Courtesy of William White Psychiatric Foundation, Inc.)

emerges as dominant: *moving toward people,* as manifested in a search for approval and love, and in compliant and submissive behavior; *moving against people,* as evidenced in struggles for power, and in displays of arrogance, rebellion and hostility; or *moving away from people,* as indicated by social withdrawal or detachment.

Disturbances arise when one of these patterns is adopted to the exclusion of the others. A single dominant character style can resolve anxiety and insecurity only partially; more seriously, an inflexible way of relating to others leads often to a vicious circle that creates anew the very problem the individual sought to prevent. For example, by always putting forth a front of haughty arrogance to avoid rejection, an individual may alienate himself further from others, thereby creating, rather than diminishing, his experiences of rejection.

Adherence to a rigid character pattern leads to what Horney calls the *basic conflict,* that is, the individual finds that he cannot relate to others in ways that conflict with his ingrained pattern. Since different behaviors are expected of individuals in the course of life's activities, these conflicts are inevitable. For example, a compliant person will experience severe conflict in situations that call for assertion or competition; likewise, an aggressive person will experience marked discomfort when affection and warmth are expressed to him by others.

The basic conflict is avoided by what Horney terms the *idealized self-image.* What this means is that the individual learns to misrepresent his feelings and thoughts by maintaining a fictional image of himself that caricatures his neurotic character pattern. For example, a compliant person will act completely helpless, and an assertive person will exhibit supreme confidence in himself. Unfortunately, as the person struggles to live up to his false image, he drains his energies and deprives himself of potentially satisfying life experiences. And, in time, he becomes alienated from his real feelings, caught in his own web of pretense.

Horney's use of the concept of self-image brings us to the borderland between the intrapsychic and phenomenological levels of analysis. We will next turn to theorists who cross that tenuous line.

# PHENOMENOLOGICAL THEORIES

## *GENERAL ORIENTATION*

Intrapsychic and phenomenological approaches are similar in many respects. Both gather their data in naturalistic settings, deriving their concepts from clinical observation rather than from experimental laboratory research. Both recognize that their concepts and hypotheses are crude approximations of complex processes, but they contend that less rigorous notions are appropriate in the early stages of a science; thus, methodological quantification and conceptual precision are not devalued, but deemphasized since they are viewed to be premature, given our current state of knowledge.

The major distinction between intrapsychic and phenomenological schools of thought lies in their respective emphasis upon unconscious versus conscious processes. Intrapsychic theorists believe that the most important aspects of functioning are those factors which a person cannot or will not say about himself. In contrast, phenomenologists believe that the person's introspective reports, taken at their face value, are most significant.

Phenomenologists stress that the individual reacts to the world only in terms of his unique perception of it. No matter how transformed or unconsciously distorted it may be, it is the person's way of perceiving events which determines his behavior. Concepts and propositions must be formulated, therefore, not in terms of objective realities or unconscious processes, but in accordance with how events actually are perceived by the individual; concepts must not disassemble these subjective experiences into depersonalized or abstract categories.

The phenomenon of consciousness is one of the most controversial topics in both psychological and philosophical literature, and there are some knotty questions which have been raised about the methods by which conscious data may be obtained. No one doubts that self-awareness exists; but how can phenomenological reality as experienced by another person be categorized, measured or even sensed?

At best, observers must adopt an empathic attitude, a sensing in one's self of what another may be experiencing. But this method is justly suspect, fraught with the distortions and insensitivities of the observer. To obviate this difficulty, phenomenologists assume that the verbal statements of the individual accurately reflect his phenomenal reality. Any datum which represents the individual's portrayal of his experience is grist, therefore, for the phenomenologist's mill.

Serious criticisms have been raised against this introspective method. Are there not deliberate omissions and inaccuracies in verbal reports? How can a scientific theory be founded on subjective reports, reports whose meaning will vary from person to person? Do not patients repress and deny the most crucial elements of their experiences? And, if significant events are hidden or forgotten, of what value are the remaining data? Worse yet, how can deceptive reports be accepted at their face value as the data for a scientific theory?

Several counterarguments have been offered in defense of phenomenological methods. The limitations of self-reports are granted. However, phenomenologists contend that an individual's verbal reports reveal the most important influences upon his behavior. Is it not simple efficiency to ask a person directly what is disturbing him and how this disturbance came to pass? Is his report more prone to error than an observer's speculations gathered from the odds and ends of a case history study? Is it less reliable than deductions which are drawn from dreams and free associations? The fact that some verbal recollections and feelings are misleading is no reason to dismiss them as useless; they summarize events in terms closest to the individual's experience of them, and often embody knowledge that is not otherwise available.

These pro and con arguments miss the point. Phenomenological reports are an important source of data. But they are only one of many sources. There should be no argument between proponents of one method versus another. Each method reflects an arbitrary decision as to which source of data will weigh more in the construction of a theory. Theories using different types of data are complementary frames of reference for investigating the problems of personality and psychopathology. The task for the future is not choosing alternatives between these sources of data, but in establishing a connection between them.

## THE PHENOMENOLOGICAL DISSONANCE MODEL

Most phenomenologists avoid formal theorizing for fear that the unique attributes of individuals will be forced into abstract molds. Nevertheless, their work exhibits certain common conceptions concerning pathological functioning.

Although not formulated as a model of psychopathology, Festinger's notion of cognitive dissonance (1957) captures the essence of most phenomenological theories. Festinger proposed that discomfort is produced when a person holds two attitudes or beliefs that are inconsistent with each other. This discomfort is reduced by a variety of means designed to establish consonance, that is, consistency between these beliefs. Dissonance arises from several sources: a logical inconsistency between two attitudes, contradictory past experiences, conflicting cultural mores and so on. Consonance may be accomplished by changing one of the conflicting attitudes, adding a third set of attitudes which resolve the dissonance and so on.

Festinger notes that an individual will experience particular discomfort when dissonance arises between attitudes that are of special importance to him. According to most phenomenologists, this will occur when the individual's personal feelings and desires run counter to socially approved attitudes. More specifically, disorder arises when the individual's own needs conflict with values imposed upon him by others. Thus, disorder is an estrangement from self, an incongruence between attitudes the person feels are right but which others have told him are wrong. For example, a young man may have been taught to think that masturbation is bad, but his body senses pleasure and gratification in it. The inconsistency between what is phenomenologically felt to be right, and the evaluative judgments of others creates dissonance. Dissonance, in turn, leads to anxiety, and anxiety produces defensive reactions which alienate the person further from his "natural" feelings. By adopting social evaluations that deny or distort his natural feelings, the individual experiences a state of *nothingness*, that is, a sense of inner emptiness and purposelessness.

Of the several phenomenological theories that have been formulated in psychology, only two of those based on the dissonance model are applicable to psychopathology and have gained a wide following: existential theories and Rogers' self-theory; we will turn next to a brief discussion of each.

### EXISTENTIAL THEORIES

There is a growing concern that contemporary man is trapped in the impersonal atmosphere of a mechanistic and mass society; as a result, man finds himself isolated and alienated from his "true" self.

Several European psychiatrists, stimulated by

the work of the philosophers Soren Kierkegaard, Martin Heidegger and Jean-Paul Sartre, have connected this contemporary social problem to the study of psychopathology. In this concern, they are close to the work of the interpersonal-anxiety theorists who have spoken of the child's feelings of loneliness and isolation.

Two important social theorists, Erich Fromm (1947) and David Riesman (1950), also have portrayed the dehumanizing and isolating effects of contemporary society. They see these effects not only in severe disorders but in the behavior and personality of "normal" men. What they portray is a vivid picture of people estranged from themselves, and who wander aimlessly from one meaningless relationship to another.

Although existential theorists share this view of man's fate in contemporary society, they are more concerned with the pathological effects of man's estrangement from himself. Beneath social loneliness and isolation lies a deep and profound alienation from one's own natural feelings. To them, the essential problem lies in man's feeling of futility and despair of ever being what he is and can be. Ludwig Binswanger (1958), Medard Boss (1958), Rollo May (1958) and Abraham Maslow (1962) are the most notable proponents of this view. Although differing on particulars, they agree that pathology results from man's estrangement from self. They agree further that man's capacity for conscious awareness enables him to make choices and to control his existence; man has a unique power to transform events to suit his needs and to create his own distinctive world. The decisions he makes determine whether or not he will progress toward the fulfillment of his inner potentials.

Progress and growth depend on a balance among three modes of experience: the *Unwelt,* signifying the world of biological energies and physical reality; the *Mitwelt,* representing the world of other people; and the *Eigenwelt,* or the inner world of phenomenological experience. Mental health results when the individual can come to terms with all three; disorder results when he fails to do so.

Disorder, according to the existential thesis, reflects more than an inability to fulfill biological urges, as Freud stressed, or to establish significant interpersonal relationships, as Sullivan and Horney stressed. Pleasure, interpersonal security, even survival itself, are viewed as subsidiary to the need to relate to self, that is, to the *Eigenwelt.* Without self, the individual lacks an identity and cannot experience what is termed *being-in-the-world.*

Failing to relate meaningfully to himself, the individual cannot satisfy his instinctual drives and cannot establish satisfying relationships with others. Unable to sense his own inner world, he cannot sense the inner world of others, and without meaningful social interaction, he cannot break the vicious circle to expand experience and develop a sense of identity. As this circle continues, he experiences an *ontological anxiety,* that is, a frightening estrangement from self. This anxiety further isolates him from others and makes him incapable of acting in ways which could alter his existence. Eventually, he succumbs to *nothingness* and disorder.

## ROGERS' SELF-THEORY

There are many commonalities among the ideas of the European existentialists and those of the American psychologist, Carl Rogers (1959). However, Rogers is optimistic about man's capacity to fulfill himself, whereas the existentialists express a tragic and pessimistic attitude. This difference may reflect the confidence and youth of the American ethos, on the one hand, and the atmosphere of totalitarianism and catastrophe which has plagued twentieth century Europe, on the other. To Rogers, man is disposed naturally to be kindly, self-accepting and socially productive. Only if this innate potential is restricted, and feelings of personal worth damaged, will he become ineffective, antagonistic and disturbed.

The principal features of Rogers' theory may be summarized as follows: Every individual is the center of a changing world of experience. Experience is understood only in terms of the individual's perception of his life; thus, Rogers opts explicitly for the phenomenological approach. Rogers recognizes the existence of unconscious processes but contends that only those elements of the unconscious which can be brought into consciousness are relevant to behavior. A portion of the person's phenomenal field becomes differentiated into a conscious perception of self-as-object; this relatively stable pattern of self-perceptions emerges from the individual's interaction with his environment and is shaped, therefore, by the values and judgments of others. Once this self-concept is established it influences the perceptions, memories and thoughts of the individual; experiences that are inconsistent with the self-image are ignored or disowned. If the self-concept is broad and inclusive, the individual will be open to a variety of experiences; conversely, a restricted self-image can tolerate only a small range of experiences,

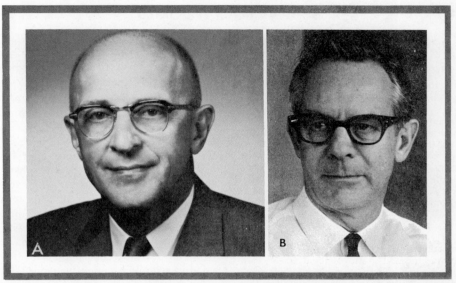

Figure 2-4   Major phenomenological theorists. A. Carl Rogers. (Department of Photography, University of Wisconsin.) B. Rollo May. (Photograph from *Psychology Today*, September, 1967.)

and requires frequent distortions in order to prevent disorder.

From this outline we can see the basis for four of Rogers' major concepts: the *self-actualizing tendency,* the *innate valuing process,* the *need for positive regard* and the *need for self-regard.*

Rogers proposes that man is motivated by a single basic drive, that of extending the range of "pleasurable" experiences. Each individual possesses an innate potential for these experiences and is motivated by a *self-actualizing tendency* to develop and exercise them. This self-actualizing tendency is guided by an *innate valuing process,* that is, an inborn capacity to judge which experiences "feel right" for him and which do not. If the individual develops according to his inherent self-actualizing tendency he will mature as a healthy and well-integrated adult.

This self-actualizing tendency may be interfered with if the individual's personal valuing process does not correspond with the values and judgments of others. Conflicts arise because all persons possess a *need for positive regard,* that is, approval and affection from others. Approval from others may satisfy his need for positive regard, but may require that the person behave in ways that run counter to his innate needs. For example, a child may avoid parental anger and disapproval by refraining from masturbation, but by so doing he must deny the pleasures of his own senses.

When the individual replaces his innate valuing process with the values of others, he has acquired what Rogers refers to as the *need for self-regard.* This second system for appraising experience may supplant or repress his natural valuing process. As a consequence, he will no longer judge his experiences in terms of his own senses, but will use a set of socially learned criteria. Should these conflict with his innate criteria, he will suffer anxiety and threat.

Anxieties often lead to further difficulty, according to Rogers, since they restrict the person's freedom of action and gratification. Thus, he is not only trapped now by the dissonance between his innate judgments and those of others, but because of his anxieties he may be incapable of finding solutions to his dilemma. For example, many young girls who had been cautioned about the "sins" of sex, experience intense anxieties when they wish to express their rather natural affectionate feelings toward boys. The confusion and anguish they experience only complicates their conflict, and therefore decreases the likelihood that they will resolve the problem satisfactorily.

Two major strategies are employed, according to Rogers, to decrease dissonance and anxiety: *denial,* which consists of ignoring the contradictions between self and social judgments, and *distortion,* which refers to the process by which the contradictions are misinterpreted or falsified so as to make them appear consonant. Should these strategies fail, the person's self-structure will *break down* or become *disorganized,* that is, his behavior will become increasingly erratic and unpredictable.

# BEHAVIORAL THEORIES

## GENERAL ORIENTATION

B. F. Skinner, a leading figure in contemporary behaviorism, has phrased the position of the behavioral approach as follows (1956):

Is the scientific study of behavior—whether normal or psychotic—concerned with the behavior of the observable organism . . . or with the functioning of . . . mental processes under the promptings of instincts, needs, emotions, memories, and habits? I do not want to raise the question of the supposed *nature* of these inner entities. A certain kinship between such an explanatory system and primitive animism can scarcely be missed.

The study of behavior, psychotic or otherwise, remains securely in the company of the natural sciences so long as we take as our subject matter the observable activity of the organism, as it moves about, stands still, seizes objects, pushes and pulls, makes sounds, gestures, and so on. . . . Watching a person behave in this way is like watching any physical or biological system. We also remain within the framework of the natural sciences in explaining these observations in terms of external forces and events which act upon the organism.

Taken in its strictest form, the behavioral approach requires that all concepts and propositions be anchored precisely to measurable properties in the empirical world. That behavioral concepts are, in fact, not always formulated as operational concepts is a concession to the limits of practicality. Nevertheless, empirically unanchored speculation is anathema to behaviorists; hypothetical constructs, which abound in intrapsychic and phenomenological theories, rarely are found in behavioral theories.

Behaviorism originated with the view that subjective introspection was "unscientific" and that it should be replaced by the use of objectively observable behaviors. Further, all environmental influences upon behavior were likewise to be defined objectively. If unobservable processes were thought to exist within the individual, they were to be defined strictly in terms of observables which indicate their existence. Bindra states this position strongly in the following (1959):

. . . conscious and unconscious wishes, desires, frustrations, anxieties and other motivational entities as the determiners of normal and abnormal behavior, have failed to contribute significantly to the problems of causation or psychopathology. . . . Research on the problems of causation, diagnosis and treatment of behavior disorders should concentrate, not on "psychodynamics" or other hypothetical processes, but on observed behavior. Descriptions of subjective states, not being subject to publicly observable or objective reliability checks, should not be considered as statements about crucial psychopathological events. The aim of diagnostic and research procedures should be the measurement of significant aspects of behavior . . . rather than *ad hoc* variables which appear temporarily to be of some practical significance.

Recent behavior theories of pathology have used concepts generated originally in experimental learning research. They are not simple translations of psychoanalytic concepts into behavior terminology, as were earlier theories of behavior pathology, but are based on the ostensible "empirical" laws of learning. Theorists using these concepts lay claim to the virtues of science since their heritage lies with the objective studies of systematic learning research and not with the dubious methods of clinical speculation.

That learning concepts are helpful in understanding pathology cannot be denied, but behavior theorists take a stronger position. They state that pathology is learned behavior that develops according to the same laws as those governing the development of normal behavior. Disturbed behavior differs from normal behavior only in magnitude, frequency and social adaptiveness. Were these behaviors more adaptive, or less frequent and extreme, they would possess no other distinguishing features.

## THE BEHAVIOR LEARNING MODEL

The use of learning concepts to explain behavior pathology is based on the assumption that laws demonstrated in simple laboratory settings may be generalized to more complex behavior. Accordingly, psychopathology is considered a complicated pattern of learned maladaptive responses, and nothing else; all patterns of response —normal or abnormal—can be derived from a few basic laws of learning.

Although several concepts have been considered central to the process of learning (e.g., imitation and thinking), most writers in the behaviorist tradition place primary emphasis on the role of *conditioning*. Conditioning has been demonstrated repeatedly in well-controlled laboratory research, but the ingredients involved in establishing a conditioned response are still subject to considerable theoretical controversy.

Two different theories of conditioning are currently in vogue. The simpler theory, known variously as *contiguity* or association, states that any response will become attached to any stimulus as long as the two are associated, usually in temporal sequence. No additional factor need be postulated to account for learning according to theorists of this persuasion. Somewhat more complicated is *reinforcement* theory, which states that the bond between a stimulus and a response is established only if the two are associated in conjunction with the reduction of some need or drive, such as hunger, thirst or anxiety. To both groups of theorists, the strength of the S-R bonds depends on the continued operation of their respective principle of conditioning. Complex learnings, such as those acquired through processes of imitation and thinking, can be understood as more intricate or higher level combinations of basic contiguity or reinforcement principles.

In contiguity theory, if a different stimulus is paired with the response, or in reinforcement theory, if need-reduction fails to occur, the original S-R bond will be weakened and eventually *extinguished*. Both groups of theorists note further that stimuli which are similar to the stimulus in the original S-R bond can evoke the response of the bond. This concept, known as *generalization,* accounts for the observation that individuals transfer old responses to new situations, and do so to the extent of similarity between the old and the new situations.

The following quote illustrates the basic learning model (Eysenck, 1959):

How, then, does modern learning theory look upon neurosis? In the first place, it would claim that neurotic symptoms are learned patterns of behavior which for some reason or other are inadaptive. The paradigm of neurotic symptom formation would be Watson's famous experiment with little Albert, an eleven months old boy who was fond of animals. By a simple process of classical Pavlovian conditioning, Watson created a phobia for white rats in this boy by standing behind him and making a very loud noise by banging on an iron bar with a hammer whenever Albert reached for the animal. The rat was the conditioned stimulus in the experiment, the loud fear-producing noise was the unconditional stimulus. As predicted, the unconditioned response (fear) became conditioned to the C.S. (the rat), and Albert developed a phobia for white rats, and indeed for all furry animals. This latter feature of the conditioning process is of course familiar to all students as the generalization gradient. . . .

The fear of the rat thus conditioned is unadaptive (because white rats are not in fact dangerous) and hence is considered to be a neurotic symptom; a similarly conditioned fear of snakes would be regarded as adaptive; and hence not neurotic. Yet the mechanism of acquisition is identical in both cases. This suggests that chance and environmental hazards are likely to play an important part in the acquisition of neurotic responses. If a rat happens to be present when the child hears a loud noise, a phobia results; when it is a snake that is present, a useful habit is built up!

The point . . . on which the theory here advocated breaks decisively with psychoanalytic thought of any

description is on this. Freudian theory regards neurotic symptoms as adaptive mechanisms which are evidence of repression; they are "the visible upshot of unconscious causes." Learning theory does not postulate any such "unconscious causes," but regards neurotic symptoms as simple learned habits; there is no neurosis underlying the symptom, but merely the symptom itself. *Get rid of the symptom and you have eliminated the neuroses.*

Pathology is defined by most behavior theorists either as socially maladaptive *or* socially deficient behavior. In contrast to most theorists of other schools, where psychopathology is associated exclusively with the presence of undesirable feelings or irrational actions, behaviorists place equal stress on "absent behaviors," that is, indications that the patient has failed to learn social skills and attitudes for effective functioning in his cultural group. Their position differs clearly from biophysical theorists, who define mental illness as physical disease or dysfunction; it differs also from intrapsychic theorists, who consider pathology defined best in terms of unconscious processes; and it differs from the phenomenologists, whose definition is based on subjective feelings of discomfort. Ullmann and Krasner state the behaviorist's position in the following (1965):

. . . the designation of a behavior as pathological or not, is dependent upon the individual's society. Specifically, while there are no single behaviors that would be said to be adaptive in all cultures, there are in all cultures definite expectations or roles for functioning adults in terms of familial and social responsibility. The person whose behavior is maladaptive does not fully live up to the expectations for one in his role, does not respond to all the stimuli actually present, and does not obtain the typical or maximum forms of reinforcement available to one of his status. . . . Behavior that one culture might consider unadaptive, be it that of the shaman or the paranoid, is adaptive in another culture. . . . Maladaptive behavior is behavior that is considered inappropriate by those key people in a person's life.

Several objections have been raised against culturally relativistic and socially adaptive definitions of pathology, such as formulated in the above quote. For example, certain classic types of psychiatric disorder appear in all cultures. How can one account for this uniformity without postulating some universal underlying disease? To this question behaviorists reply that classic textbook cases are figments of a theorist's imagination; moreover, uniformity in diagnostic classification is a psychiatric fiction as evidenced by the fact that classification is highly unreliable, and most nosological systems are constantly revised and rarely hold up under research analysis. Whatever regularities are found to exist can be accounted for, according to behaviorists, by similarities in cultural patterns of conditioning. For example, once an individual is identified as ill, he is exposed to a uniform set of conditions which shape his behavior (e.g., restriction of privileges, threats of "shock" therapy, decreases in social relationships, hospital atmospheres and so on). Regularities observed among these patients are a product, therefore, of common learning experiences, not common "diseases."

Let us turn now to several of the more prominent behavior theorists.

## DOLLARD AND MILLER

The work of John Dollard and Neal Miller (1950), in many respects, is inappropriately classified as behavior theory. It has been pointed out that they merely translated the concepts of traditional Freudian psychoanalysis into the language of Pavlovian conditioning and Hullian learning theory (Bandura, 1961; Mowrer, 1965). These critics note that a proper application of behavioristic principles should have led them to a new conception of psychopathology.

This criticism seems unjust. Dollard and Miller made no pretensions about devising a "new" theory. Further, they were the first of the modern behavior theorists willing to tackle the complex problems of psychopathology, and this they did in a systematic and often brilliant fashion.

Dollard and Miller proposed, as did Freud, that intense emotional conflicts are the basis of behavior pathology. By conflict they meant the existence of two or more mutually incompatible drives; thus, conflicts could occur between innate physiological needs, such as hunger or sex, or socially acquired emotional responses, such as fear, anger or anxiety. The components of these conflicts were categorized as *approach* or *avoidant*. For example, a college student who wished to marry his girl friend (approach) but feared parental disapproval of this desire (avoidant) would experience conflict.

Disorders, according to Dollard and Miller, will not arise unless the individual represses or is otherwise unaware of his conflict; the problem takes on serious proportions because unconscious conflicts are not accessible to realistic thought and intelligent resolution. The consequence of this repression is far reaching. In order to stop thinking about the conflict, the individual tends also to inhibit thinking about other problem areas, as well; as a consequence, the person's overall capacity to reason and plan is impaired.

Symptoms of disorder are seen by Dollard and Miller as efforts to deny painful conflicts.

For example, a phobia of crowded places may cover up conflicting feelings towards others; similarly, antagonisms to women may arise in "moralistic" men as a cloak for disturbing sexual desires.

To Dollard and Miller then, pathology consists of unconscious conflicts which cannot be resolved since they are not available to conscious reasoning. As a result, the individual engages in shortsighted partial resolutions, many of which may invite more serious conflicts and complications.

As is evident from the foregoing, the theory proposed by Dollard and Miller is in no substantial way different from those formulated by intrapsychic theorists. However, their work made the study of psychopathology more palatable to behaviorists; if nothing else then, they built an important bridge between previously incompatible fields of interest.

## WOLPE AND EYSENCK

Although Joseph Wolpe (1958) and Hans J. Eysenck (1965) developed their ideas independently of one another, there is sufficient similarity between them to warrant a single presentation. Both reject Dollard and Miller's acceptance of the basic tenets of Freudian intrapsychic theory. Yet, despite their claim to having formulated a new basis for explaining psychopathology, their systems are strikingly similar to those of Dollard and Miller. The essential difference is that Eysenck and Wolpe present an alternative to the Freudian hypothetical constructs of unconscious conflict and impulse. Their replacement, however, is an equally ill-defined hypothetical construct, that of an innate physiological disposition to anxiety.

Wolpe and Eysenck propose that mental disorders are learned when intense anxiety becomes associated improperly with various environmental conditions. If anxiety is experienced in situations in which no objective threat exists, the individual will acquire a maladaptive fear response. So far this formulation is not unlike that proposed by Freudian theorists. The difference arises with regard to the source of anxiety. Freudians locate anxiety in unconscious conflicts, whereas Eysenck and Wolpe attribute it to an innate physiological disposition to anxiety. Eysenck states his position as follows (1959):

. . . different children have different types of autonomic system, and the same amount of noise produces quite unequal amounts of autonomic upheaval in different children. Consequently, autonomic reactivity must also be considered; the more labile or

Figure 2-5  Major behavior theorists. A. Joseph Wolpe. (Department of Psychiatry, Temple University School of Medicine.) B. B. F. Skinner. (Photograph from *Psychology Today,* September, 1967.) C. Hans J. Eysenck.

reactive the child, the more likely he is to produce strongly conditioned fear reactions, anxieties and phobias . . . the person (is) almost predestined to suffer from anxieties, conditioned fears . . . and so forth.

By introducing the notion of an innate anxiety disposition, Eysenck and Wolpe have intruded a concept into their theory which is as difficult to define behaviorally as is the concept of the unconscious. In so doing, they have muddied the water of their "behavioral" theory as much as if they had invoked the "unconscious."

Innate differences in anxiety proneness may very well exist, but their inclusion as part of a behavior theory is certain to be rejected by pure behaviorists.

## ROTTER AND BANDURA

Another "impure," though highly promising, variant of the behavioral school is that known generally as the "social learning" approach, most clearly formulated in the work of Julian Rotter (1954, 1966) and Albert Bandura (1963, 1968). These two theorists diverge from the behavioristic philosophy to an even greater extent than Eysenck and Wolpe since they apply principles of learning to explain such nonbehavioral data as cognitive expectancies and self-reinforcing thoughts.

Rotter proposes two concepts as basic to his theory: *behavior potential* and *expectancy.* The first refers to the thesis that behaviors that have most frequently led to positive reinforcements (rewarding experiences) in the past have the

greatest potential for occurring again. The second concept is defined as "the probability held by the individual that a particular reinforcement will occur as a function of a specific behavior on his part"; in other words, the likelihood, as the person sees it, that what he does will prove rewarding. For a particular behavior potential to remain high, the individual must continue to expect that it will lead to positive reinforcement. Katkovsky (1968) outlines Rotter's explanation of the learning of maladaptive behavior as follows:

If the behavior is negatively sanctioned by the culture and generally leads to some type of discomfort or punishment, how do we explain the fact that its potential remains high? Should not the individual learn to expect negative consequences rather than rewards for acting in maladjusted ways and therefore become less likely to do so? Apparently this does not happen. The continuation of the behavior indicates that the individual's expectancy for reward for that behavior remains higher than his expectancy for punishment. The problem in understanding maladjusted behavior, then, is to explain why a person subjectively expects to gain some type of satisfaction for a behavior which his culture regards as undesirable and which experience should teach him will lead to negative consequences.

A number of general formulations concerning the bases for maladjustment that are meaningful within a social-learning frame of reference serve as a guide in making such an analysis.

A common, but often overlooked, reason for the existence of maladjusted behavior is that the individual's environment directly encourages it. Sometimes the encouragement is rather blatant, as in the case of a highly dependent and fear-ridden child whose fears are continually reinforced by the fact that his parents respond to them with increased protectiveness, attention, and reluctance to allow him to experience potential dangers. Sometimes the encouragement of maladjustment is very subtle and complex and involves the expectancies, needs, and reactions of important persons in the environment who, without realizing it, are more comfortable if deviant behavior occurs than they would be if it did not occur. Many forms of maladjustment also are positively reinforced by the attention, concern, and special privileges they bring.

In addition to Rotter's expectancy-reinforcement thesis and the other more traditional notions of how learning occurs, Bandura proposes such concepts as *vicarious conditioning* and *self-reinforcement systems*. The first pertains to the fact that people can learn their pathological attitudes simply by observing the experiences and feelings of others; for example, if a youngster happened to be glancing out the window when he saw a neighborhood dog chasing another child, the observing youngster may learn to fear that dog even though he had no frightening experience with it himself. The second concept refers to the fact that persons reinforce their attitudes and emotions simply by thinking about them; moreover, repetitive self-reinforcements often supplant the objective reinforcements of reality. Bandura states this thesis as follows:

Until recently, self-reinforcing behavior has been virtually ignored in psychological theorizing and experimentation, perhaps because of the common preoccupation with animal learning. Unlike human subjects, who continually engage in self-evaluative and self-reinforcing behavior, rats or chimpanzees are disinclined to pat themselves on the back for commendable performances, or to berate themselves for getting lost in cul-de-sacs. By contrast, people typically make self-reinforcement contingent on their performing in ways they have come to value as an index of personal merit. They often set themselves relatively explicit criteria of achievement; failure to meet them is considered undeserving of reward and may elicit self-denial or even self-punishment. Conversely, individuals tend to reward themselves generously when they attain or exceed their self-imposed standards. Self-administered positive and negative stimuli may thus serve both as powerful incentives for learning and as effective reinforcers in maintaining behavior in humans.

. . . behavior can become completely controlled by fictional contingencies and fantasied consequences powerful enough to override the influence of the reinforcements available from the social environment.

For example, a youngster may have gotten the notion that venereal diseases are transmitted by kissing, and every time his natural attraction to girls was stimulated, he would begin to think about the feared consequence. These repetitive thoughts reinforced his belief until it became so deeply ingrained that he began to avoid all contact with girls lest his impulses lead him to engage in "venereal-producing" actions.

Bandura and Rotter's use of such behavior learning principles as conditioning and reinforcement has extended the range of these laboratory-derived concepts to include aspects of maladaptive learning that are overlooked by other behavior theorists. However, it should be noted that these principles have been stretched, so to speak, beyond the data of overt behavior to such internal mediating processes as cognitive expectancies, vicarious learnings and self-reinforcing thoughts.

## SKINNERIAN THEORISTS

The first theory to restrict its concepts entirely to objective behavioral processes, eschewing all reference to internal phenomena such as the unconscious, innate anxiety dispositions or self-reinforcing thoughts, was formulated by B. F. Skinner and his disciples (Skinner, 1956, 1959; Ullmann and Krasner, 1965). According to these strict behaviorists, it is misleading and unnecessary to posit the existence of unobservable emotional states or cognitive expectancies to account for behavior pathology. Thus, in contrast to Eysenck and Wolpe, who believe that disorders stem in part from internal dispositions to anxiety, Skinnerians prefer to view all disorders as a simple product of environmentally based reinforcing experiences. For similar reasons, they disavow Rotter's and Bandura's focus on internal mediating processes such as expectancies and self-reinforcing thoughts. Hypothetical inner states are discarded and explanations are formulated solely in terms of external sources of stimulation and reinforcement. Environmental reinforcements shape the behavioral repertoire of the individual, and differences between adaptive and maladaptive behaviors can be traced entirely to differences in the reinforcement pattern to which individuals are exposed.

Skinner disavows the necessity for theory, and the simplicity of his formulation reflects his conviction that all behavior—normal or pathological—can be reduced to a few objective principles and concepts, most notably that known as *operant conditioning*. This first "pure" behavior theory has had an auspicious beginning in the field of behavior modification therapy (see chapter 15); however, further research will be necessary to appraise Skinner's rather simplified formulation of psychopathology. An effort will be made in subsequent chapters to expand on Skinner's basic concepts, and to demonstrate their special utility in explaining the learning of complex coping (instrumental) strategies.

# CRITICAL EVALUATION

Psychopathology should incorporate a variety of different approaches. But this open-mindedness is not an invitation to ill-conceived notions and random speculations; tolerance of diversity is not license for scientific sloppiness and incompetence.

None of the theories discussed in this chapter approaches the ideal of a complete scientific system for psychopathology, nor do they satisfy all the criteria of a good system. In this section we will note first some of the shortcomings common to all theories of psychopathology, followed by criticisms applicable to each of the four major groups we have presented.

The formal structure of most theories of psychopathology is haphazard and unsystematic; concepts often are vague and procedures by which empirical consequences may be derived are confused. Many theories are written in a hortatory and persuasive fashion. Facts are mixed with speculations, and literary allusions and colorful descriptions are offered as substitutes for testable hypotheses. In short, instead of presenting an orderly arrangement of concepts and propositions by which hypotheses may be clearly derived, these theories present a loosely formulated pastiche of opinions, analogies and speculations. Brilliant as many of these speculations may be, they often leave the reader dazzled rather than illuminated.

Confusion stems further from the interweaving of concepts based on different and occasionally quite distinct sources of data. Thus, concepts generated in experimental learning research are adopted by some theorists and used as if they were synonymous with neurophysiological processes on the one hand and clinical behavior on the other. Terms are interchanged because of some vague similarity in meaning. Further difficulties arise because of the excessive use of hypothetical constructs; even worse, these constructs often are reified into entities. Thus, concepts such as id and Eigenwelt are referred to as if they were real empirical phenomena which possess the power to influence behavior.

Ambiguous concepts in structurally weak theories make it impossible to derive systematic and logical hypotheses; this results in conflicting derivations and circular reasoning. In short, theories of psychopathology have generated brilliant deductions and insights, but few of these ideas can be attributed to either the structure of these theories, the precision of their concepts or their formal procedures for hypothesis derivation.

We will turn to the four major groups of theorists next, beginning with the behaviorists,

since they claim to be the most scientifically sound of the theoretical psychopathologists.

### Behavior Theories

These theorists borrow their concepts from experimental learning research; as such, one would expect their work to be subject to little scientific faulting. The failure to live up to this expectation demonstrates the difficulty of transferring concepts from one field to another. Borrowing concepts from another field may be no more than a specious ennoblement of one's efforts, a cloak of falsely appropriated prestige which duly impresses the naive. One might ask, for example, whether the laboratory-based concepts borrowed from the prestigious field of learning are genuinely useful in psychopathology, or whether they are merely bandied about in an allegorical and superficial manner. Scientific sounding terminology may be no more than a set of flimsy analogies, offering no new explanatory powers or insights; old wine in new bottles is still old wine.

There is reason to suspect, further, that the "basic" laws of learning are not so basic after all; much dissent exists among learning theorists as to which concepts and laws are "basic." Examination of the literature on learning exposes marked disagreements on even the simplest of conditioning processes. Can "laws" of learning be applied to highly complex clinical processes when the existence of these laws in simple situations is a matter of dispute?

Another criticism of behavior theories in psychopathology is their failure to formulate concepts dealing with the development of disorders. What little they say on this matter is usually a rewording of intrapsychic theories. Where they do strike out on their own, as do the Skinnerians, they appear preoccupied with *how* behavior is learned, and not with *when* and *what* is learned. The Skinnerian focus on the process rather than the content of learning has added an important dimension to the study of psychopathology. But without reference to the kinds of experience which lead to pathological learning, the theory creates a sterile and artificial man, an empty creature who behaves according to vacant and abstract principles. By reducing the reality of experience to abstract stimuli and responses, psychopathology becomes a barren pattern of mechanical reactions. Sentimental and "unscientific" as these objections may appear, they bring home the point that an explanation of "real" behavior requires more than a set of abstract principles. Though these principles may be "basic," they remain static until the content and meaning of experience fills them out.

### Phenomenological Theories

The criticism of the behaviorist's conception of man as an empty automaton certainly cannot be leveled at phenomenological theorists. To them, man is a vibrant participant in life, forever shaping the course of his affairs. Rather than a sluggish respondent to the whims of experience, he struggles to "become" his inner potential. He does not succumb to maladaptive "reinforcements," but is depleted by self-frustration and broken by despair. Like a Shakespearean character, man is restrained by inner conflicts until he is an exhausted shadow of himself.

Although the phenomenologist's portrayal of the dilemmas of man are striking, we must distinguish between skillful literary depiction and effective theorizing. No matter how compelling and vivid a theory may be, the crucial test does not lie in elegant persuasion but in explicit hypothesis. Although phenomenologists are among the most acute observers of the human condition, their formulation of these observations into a theory is sporadic and casual. Perhaps these formulations should not be thought of as theory but as a set of loosely connected observations and notions. So discursive a body of work, little concerned with problems of integration, structure and continuity, lacking in tautness of systematic argument, cannot be viewed as a scientific theory at all. At best, it represents a consistent point of view; at worst, it is an ill-constructed social commentary.

Other critics object not to the loose structure of phenomenological theory, but to what these theories propose. Particular exception is taken to their idealistic conception of man's inherent nature. The notion that man would be a constructive, rational and socially conscious being, were he free of the malevolent distortions of society, seems not only sentimental but invalid. There is something grossly naive in exhorting man to live life to the fullest and then expecting socially beneficial consequences to follow. What evidence is there that one's inherent self-interest would not clash with the self-interests of others? There is something as banal as the proverbialism of a fortune cookie in the suggestion, "be thyself." Conceiving man's emotional disorders as a failure to "be thyself" seems equally naive and banal.

### Intrapsychic Theories

Intrapsychic clinicians can hardly be accused of theoretical simplicity or idealistic naiveté.

They have created a highly complicated superstructure of concepts and propositions in support of their notions, and, if anything, their theoretical systems can be justly criticized for their excessive complexity. In further contrast with the phenomenologists, certain intrapsychic theorists, notably Freud, picture man as inherently destructive. Left to his own devices, man generates hostility and sexual conflict. Here there is no sugar-coated view of life, or of man's role in creating its conflicts, tumults and contradictions. Their views contrast sharply also with the automaton simplicity of man as the behaviorist conceives him. Intrapsychic theorists portray man as a fascinating complex of seething unconscious conflicts, an intriguing and complex composite of animal drives and devious social motives.

Most intrapsychic theories would benefit enormously from the excisions of a skillful editor. Although the intricacies and varieties of man's behavior are infinite, there appears to be an excess of principles and concepts to account for them.

A more telling criticism, however, is the rather shoddy empirical foundation upon which these concepts are based. Concepts and propositions were derived from uncontrolled clinical observations and patient reports. Furthermore, the line of reasoning which connected these dubious facts to the theory progressed through tenuous and obscure steps. In short, not only is the source of intrapsychic data suspect, but the sequence of reasoning which ties it to the conceptual system seems excessively involved and imprecise.

### Biophysical Theories

If the chief offense of intrapsychic theorists is the grandiloquence of their system, and the tenuous connection between their concepts and the empirical world, the converse may be said for biophysical theorists. Biophysical scientists propose theories of limited scope and anchor their concepts closely to the observational world. Although these features are commendable, these theorists rarely propose hypotheses that go beyond established facts and, thereby, often fail to generate new knowledge. Biophysical theories can be evaluated best in terms of their factual validity, an appraisal to be undertaken in chapter 4.

### Comment

As a conclusion to this section we might turn to the reflections of two established scientists. Both offer wise counsel to the novice. The first quote was contained in a lecture delivered to an audience of psychoanalysts-in-training (Heilbrunn, 1961):

We cannot continue indefinitely to accept assumptions and theories without testing their validity. . . . At present the scientific journals are replete with articles in which the authors juggle the components of the libido theory until they arrive at the foregone, but nevertheless surprising, results that the patient's difficulties were caused by his unresolved Oedipus complex. So often are simple mechanisms forced into weird double and triple twists to create seemingly new editions of familiar biological situations, full of interpretative sound and psychodynamic fury signifying either nothing or at best the author's compound fantasies. . . . Modern analytic research can flourish only in a multidisciplinary atmosphere which is unafraid . . . of correcting time-honored premises by new facts and substituting radically different vistas for revered, old theories. Specialization grows from the knowledge of many fields and cannot be accomplished through mastery of an isolated vector. It is this very "thinking in multidisciplinary terms" which will induce the analyst to make more stringent therapeutic indications for the benefit of his patients, his professional satisfaction, and the reputation of analysis.

The second quote was delivered by the retiring president of the Division of General Psychology of the American Psychological Association (Dallenbach, 1953):

Theories do not succumb to abstract argumentation. They do not die but—like an occasional old soldier—they just fade away. They pass from the scientific stage not because they have been discredited but because they have been superseded or by-passed—pushed off the stage and replaced by other theories.

Why then become enamored with theory and argue and debate it emotionally as if its issues were of vital concern? The chief and, as I believe, the only justifiable reasons are pride and the obligations of authorship. . . . .

If authors of theories were the only ones to become emotional in defense, the reasons for their fervor would not be far to seek, but others, who espouse and defend theory, are often as ardent and as zealous as the authors themselves. This may be due to youthful loyalties, or to the desire to hold fast to something in this rapidly changing and fluctuating world, even if it be merely theory. In either case, however, it is a mistake because there is such a thing as theory-blindness, i.e., being so blinded by adherence to a specific theory, as to be unable truly to see the facts. When one defends theory, particularly if one is emotional about it, one is very apt to select the data which support it and be blind to all others that do not. . . .

Owing to the training that students of my generation received, my loyalties among the various contending theories were early established. Fortunately for me however, the exalted opinion that I had of theory in general and of my favorite theories in particular did not last for long. At my first conference as a graduate student with Titchener, I had the temerity to ask him in which theory of vision he believed. He replied, "Believe, believe, why, I don't believe in any." Then followed a discourse upon theory and its place in experiment which ended with the admonition "Carry your theories lightly."

Given the knowledge we have, and the knowledge we will continue to seek, Titchener's admonition seems wise counsel.

## Table 2-2  Four Theoretical Approaches to Psychopathology

|  | BIOPHYSICAL | INTRAPSYCHIC | PHENOMENOLOGICAL | BEHAVIORAL |
|---|---|---|---|---|
| Basic model | Disease | Adaptation | Dissonance | Learning |
| Types of concepts | Operational definitions, intervening variables | Hypothetical constructs, intervening variables | Hypothetical constructs, intervening variables | Intervening variables, operational definitions |
| Data | Heredity, anatomy, physiology, biochemistry | Free association, memories, dreams, projective tests | Self-reports of conscious attitudes and feelings | Overt behavior observed and recorded objectively |
| Major theorists | Kraepelin, Bleuler, Sheldon, Meehl, Hoskins, Kallmann | Freud, Hartmann, Erikson, Jung, Fairbairn, Adler, Sullivan, Horney | Rogers, Maslow, May, Boss, Binswanger | Dollard, Miller, Wolpe, Eysenck, Bandura, Rotter, Skinner et al. |
| Major concepts | Genes, temperament, constitution, defects | Instincts, ego, unconscious, defense mechanisms | Self, self-regard, eigenwelt | Conditioning, reinforcement, generalization |
| Cause of pathology | Heredity, constitution, defects | Instinct deprivation, childhood anxieties | Denied self-actualization | Deficient learning, maladaptive learning |
| Definition of pathology | Biological dysfunctions and dispositions | Unresolved conflicts, repressed anxieties | Self-discomfort | Maladaptive behavior |
| Types of pathology | Traditional psychiatric disorders | Symptom disorders, character patterns | Impoverishment, disorganization | Numerable specific behavior symptoms |

# CONCLUDING COMMENTS AND SUMMARY

It has been said that 90 per cent of all the scientists who ever lived are alive today. Given this figure as a gauge we can understand why this chapter on contemporary theories required a more extensive review than the historical survey in chapter 1. A statement written in the summary section of chapter 1 certainly is appropriate again —"the vast number of figures, the conflicting theories and the divergent interests . . . of psychopathology can but stagger the beginning student."

The student may justly ask why the author has not chosen to present a single systematic theory of psychopathology rather than the widely divergent views of different theorists. Although a single doctrinaire presentation might have simplified matters, it would have been not only dishonest scientifically, but pedagogically short-sighted as preparation for further work in the field. Students should be prevented from developing a false sense of theoretical harmony and, even more important, they must recognize that in so complex a field as psychopathology different levels of observation, utilizing different research techniques and directed at different kinds of laws, are not merely possible, but necessary. Although these theorists may be united by a common interest in understanding and treating mental disorders, there is room and need for a variety of approaches.

A summary of some of the major themes of contemporary thought discussed in the chapter follows:

1. The concepts and propositions of scientific theories should not be confused with objective reality. They are optional tools of inquiry chosen by man to guide his observation and analysis of specific aspects of the objective world. The utility of these tools can be evaluated by their success in solving those problems for which they were formulated.

2. There are four fundamental components which comprise the formal structure of theories— a model, a conceptual terminology, correspondence rules and hypotheses. Psychopathological theories usually are based on an implicit model, vary considerably in the empirical precision of their concepts, rarely utilize correspondence rules and generate hypotheses not by systematic derivation but by perceptive observation and intuitive hunch.

3. Theories in psychopathology have biases or orientations as whether to observe biophysical *or* intrapsychic *or* phenomenological *or* behavioral phenomena. These alternatives determine the empirical data upon which a theory will be based; moreover, they correspond to the four professional disciplines involved in psychopathological study (as discussed in chapter 1).

4. Biophysical theorists account for pathology in terms of heredity and constitutional and neurophysiological concepts. Most of these theories are formulated as specific and limited hypotheses, rather than as complicated propositional systems. Despite their narrow formal structure, these theories attempt to account for a wide variety of mental disorders.

5. Modern intrapsychic theories are based on the contributions of Sigmund Freud, and are characterized by their focus upon unconscious processes. Many dissent from Freud's view that pathology arises from conflicts between instinctual drives and social restrictions. Adaptive-deficiency theorists, of whom Hartmann and Erikson are best known, contend that man possesses biologically constructive capacities, and that the primary cause of disorder is the failure of these adaptive capacities to develop adequately. Object-deprivation theorists, of whom we have included Jung, Fairbairn and Spitz, replace Freud's sexual instinct with goal-oriented social instincts. To them, the deprivation of innately sought objects and relationships leads to pathology. Adler, Sullivan and Horney, referred to as interpersonal-anxiety theorists, deny the significance of biological instincts and give primacy to interpersonal and social factors. The key element in disorders for these theorists is the child's experience of insecurity with his parents, and not biological conflict or deprivation.

All intrapsychic theorists have been criticized for the complexity of their theoretical systems and the tenuous connection between their concepts and the empirical world.

6. Phenomenological theorists, of whom Rogers, Binswanger and May are best known, focus on the data of consciousness, and construct their concepts in terms of the individual's perception of the world, rather than as it objectively exists. Disorder, according to these theorists, results from a failure to "actualize" innate potentials and is exhibited in subjective feelings of emptiness and self-alienation. Phenomenological systems are formulated rather loosely and often take the form of social commentaries, rather than theories of psychopathology.

7. It is the intent of behavior theorists to restrict their data to observable phenomena, and to draw their concepts from empirical learning

research. Among the major figures in this movement are Dollard and Miller, Eysenck and Wolpe, Rotter and Bandura and Skinner and his disciples. With the exception of the Skinnerians, most theorists of this persuasion have failed to achieve "pure" behavioristic goals. Moreover, most have been accused of oversimplifying the complexity and variety of psychopathology.

Despite the shortcomings of each approach to psychopathology, taken together they represent a monumental achievement of scientific diversity and discovery. The unfinished business of coordinating theories is an exciting challenge for future generations to tackle with inventiveness and rigor. What better task is there for the intellectually curious and able than to participate in a goal whose purpose is to better understand his fellow man?

# Chapter 3

# CLINICAL ANALYSIS

Vincent van Gogh—*Sorrow* (1882). (Collection, The Museum of Modern Art, New York.)

## INTRODUCTION

Place yourself in the role of the practicing clinician. Your primary daily activity is working directly with troubled and disturbed people. Your day consists largely of gathering information which will enable you to decipher the complex background of each patient's problems and, with this knowledge in hand, to engage in a program of therapy which will relieve their difficulties and give them a fresh approach to life. No matter what therapeutic technique you use, it will be based on an analysis of the patient's present behavior and feelings, the historical sequence and situational context within which these problems arose, and the maladaptive solutions he has adopted to cope with them. Although many of his problems will not be understood fully until therapy is well underway, the clinical study will serve as a useful initial guide in your therapeutic work.

Clinical analysis would be simple if the patient could put into words all we need to know about him. His complaints and self-analyses often are useful, but there are relevant facts which he is unable or unwilling to provide. Deeply ingrained patterns of thought and behavior escape his notice because they are so pervasive and "natural" a part of him. He may lack a means for comparing his thoughts with others and may assume that his feelings and attitudes are typical when in fact they are not. More importantly, he may distort or deny his motives because they are too unbearable to admit to himself or too unacceptable and socially embarrassing. Thus, to preserve his self-esteem and his psychological equilibrium, he may be unable to provide precisely those facts which are most important to our study. Because of these limitations, the clinician must go beyond self-reports; his analysis must rely on a variety of indirect and oblique methods which enable him to fill out, get "beneath" and verify the patient's statements. Direct observation, documentary sources, family interviews, laboratory measures and psychological tests are among the major techniques he may use to obtain a full and hopefully valid clinical picture.

In traditional fields of medical science, the goal of a thorough clinical analysis is accurate diagnosis, that is, establishing the "disease" which underlies the overt clinical symptoms. This diagnostic model is ill-suited to the problems of psychopathology, with but few exceptions, since mental disorders rarely can be ascribed to a single or clearly delineated cause or "disease." Of course, certain events may have played a central role in the development of a disorder, but these initial influences interweave with new influences and reactions which then become an integral part of

74

the disorder. A pervasive network of secondary factors emerge to add fresh momentum to the initial influences and to extend them in ways that are far removed from the original circumstances. Given the complexity of this sequence, any effort to diagnose *the* disease or *the* cause will be futile indeed. To decide what best can be done to remedy the problem then, one must evaluate it in light of the entire configuration of experiences and behaviors which have evolved into the patient's personality make-up.

But this is an awesome task; the clinician cannot survey every aspect of experience and behavior which may be pertinent to a case. The diversity and complexity of a man's life are infinite, and selections must be made only of those aspects which will provide a maximum return for the clinician's efforts. He must use the guidelines of a theory to concentrate on those features of behavior and experience which have proven helpful to other clinicians. The established tools of the clinical profession also will be used as a means of directing his attention to those processes which are most relevant to his goals. With both theory and tool in hand then, the clinician can narrow his focus from the broad sphere of total human functioning and experience to a more limited sphere of maximum pertinence and usefulness. It is the purpose of this chapter to describe the objectives of the clinical analysis, the kinds of data that are gathered and the concepts that are used in making judgments and decisions relevant to these clinical objectives.

## OBJECTIVES OF CLINICAL ANALYSIS

The specific objectives of a clinical study will differ in different settings (psychiatric hospitals, out-patient clinics and private practice), but the central objective of all clinical analysis is to gather information which ultimately will be useful in increasing a patient's well-being. The procedures by which this objective can be attained will be rendered orderly and intelligible if they are divided into four steps.

*First,* the clinician undertakes an examination of the patient's current functioning. This preliminary survey of the problem is based on a variety of symptoms or clinical signs derived from data at each of the four levels of observation and conceptualization discussed in chapter 2. For example, overt behaviors are observed during interviews, testing, and on the ward; phenomenological attitudes and feelings are verbalized to

an interviewer, to nurses and to relatives; intrapsychic conflicts and defensive maneuvers are inferred from a variety of behaviors and test data; biophysical capacities, dispositions and dysfunctions are assessed in physical examinations and laboratory tests.

*Second,* an attempt is made to trace the historical course and situational context within which the patient's problem arose. Family discord, adolescent difficulties and vocational failures all illustrate some of the many experiences which may have contributed to its development. In this phase of his study, the clinician seeks to identify and unravel the complex sequence of events which have shaped the disorder. With this knowledge, he can better understand why the patient has come to express himself as he does.

*Third,* once the elements of past experience and present functioning have been gathered, and the thread of continuity between them established, the clinician next must organize his findings into a coherent pattern or syndrome. He attempts to fashion an internally consistent image or working model of the patient in which the dominant features of his personality make-up are highlighted against the background of his present environment and the major developmental influences of his life. The model or syndrome focuses on the chronic aspects of the patient's maladaptive function, and relates them to his current conflicts and stress.

*Fourth,* the relationship between the patient's personality and his present environmental circumstances is appraised in order to make judgments about prognosis and therapy; the chief purpose of clinical analysis should be intelligent remedial action. Much of the information contained in a thorough clinical study may prove irrelevant or superfluous and may complicate rather than facilitate decisions to be made about the management and treatment of a patient. Unless the analysis lends itself to these practical objectives, it becomes an interesting intellectual exercise, at best, and a consumer of valuable time, at worst.

## PROBLEMS OF CLINICAL ANALYSIS

Significant errors and biases by even the most experienced practitioners arise in most fields of clinical science. These problems are especially prominent, however, in psychopathology. Here, clinicians possess few of the objective and quantitative instruments found in other sciences, and must depend on procedures which are unstandardized, imprecise and highly subjective. Different sources of clinical data (a patient's account of his illness, the observable symptoms he displays and the facts of his past history) frequently lead to contradictory clinical impressions. Conflicting judgments arise also from the tendency of different examiners to ask different questions, emphasize different features of pathology unequally and interpret the information they have gathered in idiosyncratic and biased ways. Thus, not only is there considerable difference in the basic data from which clinical analyses are derived, but this difficulty is compounded by a lack of uniformity in clinical procedures and a low reliability in clinical judgment.

Two factors should be kept in mind by the fledgling clinician. First, there is no evidence to date indicating the unequivocal superiority of one source or one method for obtaining and interpreting clinical information. Second, there are typical errors and biases which frequently intrude and distort the data of clinical analyses.

The precise skills and procedures which produce an excellent clinical study have not been established, but the pitfalls and complications which diminish clinical accuracy are well known. In this section we shall alert the beginning student to some of these problems.

## INTRA-PATIENT VARIABILITY

Man is a capricious creature; his behaviors, thoughts and feelings shift from moment to moment. Consequently, the symptoms or signs of pathology observed in one context or at one point in time may not be displayed in another. In part, this variability signifies differences in the stimulating properties of the environment. To an even greater degree, however, it reflects the complex interaction of myriad internal processes, such as memories, subliminal sensations and moods, which combine in innumerable ways to create changing surface impressions and clinical pictures.

A defective piece of electronic equipment may be a useful analogy to illustrate this point. A malfunctioning hi-fi set may, at one time, sputter and static; for no apparent reason, it may squeal and rumble, the next; the third time the set is on, it may perform well but lose its amplification after a few minutes. The changing symptomatology of the set results from different defective and nondefective components combining in one way the first time, another the second and so on. In the same manner, the inner moods, memories and thoughts which activate overt behavior will combine to produce different clinical

pictures from one time to another. To complicate matters further, research has shown that seriously disturbed persons display greater intra-individual variability than normals (Shakow and Huston, 1936; Silverman, 1964). This marked behavioral inconsistency among patients should warn us against giving excess weight to individual symptoms. Though these rare occurrences may be a valuable clue to the patient's pathology, they tend to divert attention away from his more prosaic but characteristic style of functioning.

## THE SETTING, PROCEDURE AND TIMING OF THE EXAMINATION

Basic to all psychological theory and research is the established fact that behavior is influenced by environmental stimulation. Despite this knowledge, clinicians often assume that the data of their clinical analysis were not influenced by the procedures, settings and timing of their evaluation. The assumption is unjustified; there is ample research to show the many subtle ways in which situational and interpersonal factors do influence clinical data (Sarason, 1954; Masling, 1960). The questions asked of the patient, the examiner's personality (friendly or reserved), his status (intern or senior staff) and physical characteristics (age and sex), the setting (outpatient clinic, hospital ward, private consultation or staff meeting), the clinical procedure (testing or interviews) and the time of evaluation (emergency admission, after drugs or following hospital adjustment) illustrate some of the many factors which may influence and distort the character of clinical data.

To these objective situational influences, the clinician must consider the relationship between the patient's motivations, expectations and the context of the evaluation. The behavior and feelings exhibited by a patient will reflect such matters as his attitudes (e.g., fears of a "state hospital" or "psychiatrists") and the conditions which prompted the clinical study (e.g., involuntary commitment or hospital discharge planning).

The student should keep in mind that the patient's behavior, in large measure, is a product of the situation in which he has been observed. The more the student is aware of these potential influences, the more certain he can be that his data are representative and his interpretations of them are accurate.

## OBSERVATIONAL AND THEORETICAL BIAS OF THE CLINICIAN

Psychopathologists differ in their clinical

judgments because they have different orientations as to what data should be observed and how these observations should be interpreted. Despite protestations that their judgments are dispassionate appraisals of the patient, clinicians committed to a theoretical viewpoint invariably uncover and emphasize data that are consistent with their preferred theory (Pasamanick et al., 1959), whereas characteristics that fit other theoretical biases are overlooked. Furthermore, by probing and asking leading questions, clinicians often evoke responses that support their expectations. Gill and Brenman describe this process as follows (1948):

> If a therapist believes dreams are important in helping a patient, he will show interest in the patient's dreams. Merely asking if the patient has any may result in including many more dreams in the raw data than are gathered by a therapist who is not especially interested in dreams. This is on the grossest level. The subtleties of showing interests in certain kinds of material, often not consciously detected either by therapist or patient, are manifold. They may include a questioning glance, a shifting of visual focus, a well-timed "um-hum," a scarcely perceptible nod, or even a clearing of the throat.

Clearly, what a clinician "sees" often is a product of what he expects to see. Other observers may not record the same findings since their perceptions and behaviors have been conditioned by different theoretical beliefs. It should be obvious then, that the more a clinician looks at and interprets data from alternate viewpoints, the more comprehensive and potentially accurate will be his analysis.

### INTERPRETIVE SKILL OF THE CLINICIAN

Not all of the many inferences which clinicians make are valid or useful. He is limited by the scope of his knowledge of human functioning and that knowledge is restricted by the incomplete state of the science. To compensate for these shortcomings the clinician draws upon an ill-defined "intuitive" sense. Unfortunately, this intuitive process is an elusive and entirely subjective act that can be neither clearly articulated to others nor examined critically.

Given the obscure nature of this intuitive process, and the notable differences in skill even among experienced clinicians, some psychopathologists have suggested that the job of interpretation should be taken out of the hands of the clinician since it can be done more reliably and validly by *actuarial* methods. In the actuarial approach, interpretation is based on statistically demonstrated correlations between such clinical data as test scores, biographical information and behavior signs, on the one hand, and a variety of relevant clinical criteria such as the future course of certain disorders and the response of patients to particular forms of therapy, on the other. For example, instead of sitting down, reflecting and intuitively deciding what certain test scores may mean, the clinician simply looks into a statistical "cookbook" and reads what these scores have been shown to correlate with empirically. With these cookbooks, the task of prediction and decision making is greatly simplified, and the accuracy of interpretations is assured of at least a modicum of validity.

The logic for the statistical or actuarial approach, sketched briefly here, has been convincingly argued by Meehl (1954, 1956 and 1965) and Sarbin (Sarbin, 1943; Sarbin, Taft and Bailey, 1960). Both men recognize that some clinicians are especially skillful, and acknowledge that the actuarial approach may be of fairly limited utility in its present state, but they note that where comparisons of the two methods have been made, the statistical approach is clearly superior.

Despite impressive evidence favoring the statistical method, few actuarial formulas have been devised to handle the varied prognostic and therapeutic decisions which clinicians face daily. Furthermore, it is unlikely that all aspects of clinical judgment can be replaced by a statistical equation. Nevertheless, advances in actuarial prediction and decision making continue to be made, and the student should utilize the results of this work whenever feasible.

## STEPS IN THE CLINICAL ANALYSIS

The basic components of the clinical analysis may be subdivided into four steps: (1) *describing the current clinical picture,* that is, surveying the behaviors, attitudes and other processes displayed by the patient; (2) *tracing developmental influences,* that is, identifying the historical and environmental factors which have contributed to the problem; (3) *constructing the clinical syndrome,* that is, organizing a model which places the dominant features of the clinical picture within the context of the patient's personality make-up and developmental experiences; and (4) *formulating a remedial plan,* that is, outlining and justifying a series of recommendations for the management and treatment of the patient.

In practice, a clinician never progresses through these steps in a smooth sequence. He shuttles back and forth among all four steps, gathering behavioral impressions, making personality inferences, collecting biographical data and so on, in a rather free progression, the shape of which is determined by the chance characteristics displayed at various times by the patient, the available background data he has at his disposal, the tools he uses and the fertility of his clinical hunches. As the examination proceeds he refines his perceptions, retraces old ground and alters earlier hypotheses.

Despite the openness and flexibility of the analytic procedure, the clinician must organize his findings into an orderly pattern for two reasons. First, to clarify in his own thinking the primary observations he has made and the logic for the conclusions he has drawn. And second, he must communicate his findings in a logical and coherent manner to others. The four steps we have outlined enable him to accomplish these goals in a manner insuring both clarity and comprehensiveness.

# DESCRIBING THE CLINICAL PICTURE

### Clinical Data

In chapter 2 we specified four levels of data which theorists observe and conceptualize. These same data levels may be used to study the functions displayed by patients during clinical examination. They include (1) the level of *observable behavior,* that is, the overt actions of the patient as seen by others; (2) the level of *phenomenological experience,* that is, the patient's description of his conscious perceptions, feelings and attitudes as reported to others in conversations, interviews and personality inventories; (3) the level of *intrapsychic functioning,* that is, the unconscious conflicts and defensive processes as inferred from behaviors, fantasies and projective tests; and (4) the *biophysical* level of capacities, temperamental dispositions and biological defects recorded in physical examinations and laboratory tests.

By including all of these levels, the clinician brings his observations into sharp focus and makes sure that he has recorded data relevant to each of the major schools of psychopathological thought. With this as his foundation, he is prepared to utilize a wide range of theoretical ideas for his final clinical work-up.

### Clinical Terminology; Signs and Concepts

Everyday clinical terms do not fit the distinctions made in chapter 2 among operational definitions, intervening variables and hypothetical constructs. Nevertheless, it is possible to group these terms according to the degree to which they are anchored to empirical events.

The first category, referred to as *overt signs,* includes clinical terms which (1) are tied relatively closely to observable phenomena, and (2) deal with a fairly well-circumscribed or delimited area of patient functioning.

To these basic terms may be added a second category of *inferred concepts.* These terms represent generalizations about complex mediating processes, that is, they are inferences about unobservables operating within the patient drawn by the clinician from covariations and interactions he has observed among the overt signs. In this scheme, then, signs represent the basic elements of observation which serve as the raw material for inferences. For example, the behavioral concept "excitement" may be constructed from observable signs such as "distractible," "overtalkative" and "voluble." The phenomenological mood concept "depression" may be derived from patient statements such as "sad," "discouraged" and "guilty."

Since inferred concepts usually imply the existence of an unobservable characteristic of patient functioning, they should be used with considerable care; they are extrapolations drawn from the data of observation and, therefore, depend largely on the clinician's intuitive inferential skills. Despite this hazard, clinicians must use these concepts if they wish to make "sense" and give consistency and order to their observations.

We will turn next to the four levels of data which comprise the clinical picture, dividing them where appropriate into overt signs and inferred concepts. Three points should be kept in mind in reading the following sections. *First,* signs and concepts are abstractions drawn from an ongoing stream of complex activities; thoughts, behaviors and feelings occur simultaneously and are inextricably linked. We separate and label elements of these interrelated phenomena in order to highlight a number of the most significant features of clinical pathology. *Second,* each sign or concept will be found in a variety of disorders, e.g., delusions occur in several pathological conditions, as do fevers in many physical diseases. *Third,* specific clinical signs take on significance only in terms of the larger context within which they occur, e.g., slow and labored speech may signify the beginning of a transitory depressive disorder in one patient, and a longstanding schizophrenic withdrawal in another.

## BEHAVIOR

Physical and verbal behaviors can be readily identified by clinical examiners. These basic observables are recorded by noting what the patient does and how he does it, e.g., walking, chewing, talking, shouting and so on. Through inductive inference, observations of overt behavior may be formed into higher order concepts. These concepts represent either a generalization which brings together, under one label, a variety of superficially different behaviors, or an inference regarding a disposition to behavior which is believed to exist within the patient.

### OVERT SIGNS

For pedagogic purposes, the basic behavioral signs of pathology may be divided into three categories: *deficient, excessive* and *unusual.* Each of these categories may be subdivided further into physical behavior, on the one hand, and verbal behavior on the other. A list of clinical terms appropriate to each of these categories has been noted in Table 3-1. Several of these terms are not in common usage and will be elaborated; reference to the glossary at the end of the text may also prove useful to the student.

*Deficient behaviors* include those physical and verbal acts which are weak, scanty or insufficient for normal adaptive functioning; they fall short of the behaviors expected in our society and **represent** an inadequacy or impairment on the part of the patient. Terms used for these signs range from immobility and physical stupor, signifying the observation that the patient cannot be roused into activity, to the less severe picture of sluggishness and listlessness. Paralleling these physical activities are verbal deficiencies such as muteness, blocked speech and labored, slow and monotonous droning. For example, in the early stages of many depressive disorders, patients often appear lifeless, moving only when prodded, and do so in a plodding and faltering manner; their speech is inaudible, and they emit, in a strained and halting way, only a few monosyllabic words in response to repeated questioning.

### Table 3-1   Overt Behavioral Signs*

| DEFICIENT | EXCESSIVE | UNUSUAL |
|---|---|---|
| *Physical* | *Physical* | *Physical* |
| Immobile | Rage | Compulsions |
| Stuporous | Delirium | Automatisms |
| Sluggish | Tantrums | Mannerisms |
| Listless | Unrestrained | Echopraxia |
| Slow | Fidgety | Posturing |
| Deliberate | Restless | Catalepsy |
| Aimless | Pacing | Waxy flexibility |
| *Verbal* | *Verbal* | *Verbal* |
| Mute | Logorrhea | Circumstantial |
| Blocked | Overtalkative | Tangential |
| Taciturn | Verbigeration | Incoherent |
| Labored | Flight of ideas | Neologisms |
| Monotonous | Accelerated | Word salad |
| Inaudible | Voluble | Echolalia |

* Reference may be made to the glossary for definitions and brief descriptions of several of these terms.

*Excessive behavior* is characterized by unnecessary, unrestrained, extreme and exaggerated activity. Here there is a profusion of unduly intense or frequent behaviors which exceeds the bounds of physical and verbal activity typical of normals. Restlessness and pacing behavior reflect mild overactivity. Tantrums, rage and delirium represent extreme hyperactivity. In the verbal sphere, milder excesses may be noted by the terms, hurried and accelerated speech; pathological repetitions of words and sentences without purpose or meaning are known as *verbigeration;* a rapid and incoherent speech is labeled *logorrhea;* and a skipping from one incomplete idea to another with minimal logic or continuity has been called *flight of ideas.* Several of these signs may be observed among euphorically excited patients, as illustrated in the following brief excerpt from the incoherent and voluble speech of a 36 year old man.

"You better, better; I mean he ain't what he and his thought, what he thought; you better, better; I say he ain't what he and his thought. Gotta get these pants pressed. Yeh! Gotta get these pants pressed; he ain't what his thought."

*Unusual behaviors* include activities that are easy to notice because of their peculiar or bizarre nature; rarely, if ever, are they present in normal persons. *Compulsions* signify uncontrollable and periodic urges to perform a gesture or act which is recognized by the patient to be foolish or irrational; thus, a 27 year old woman would check,

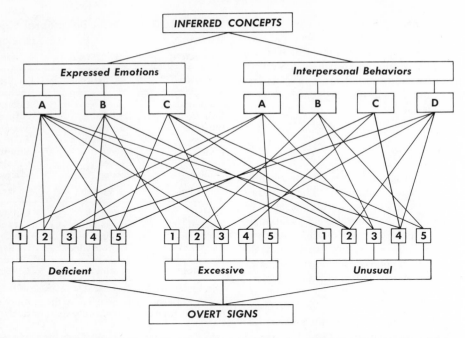

Figure 3-1   Relationship between overt signs and inferred concepts. Inferred concepts are derived from combinations of several of the overt signs. Covariations among the overt signs result in clinical inferences about the emotion that the patient is expressing and the manifest pattern of the patient's interpersonal behavior.

recheck and then check again whether she had closed all of the buttons on her blouse, knowing that what she was doing was foolish and embarrassing, but being unable to refrain from performing the act repeatedly. *Automatisms* differ from compulsions in that they are repetitive stereotyped acts which the patient is unaware of having performed, such as touching one's lips, nose and eyes in sequence.

*Mannerisms* take the form of consciously acknowledged grimaces and gestures which the patient believes are rational and necessary; for example, a 40 year old schizophrenic patient, formerly an army officer, kicked his heels and saluted anyone who asked him a question, claiming that only high-ranking officers ever questioned him. *Echopraxia* signifies the tendency to imitate movements observed in others; thus, an otherwise immobile patient attached herself to a particular attendant, following him around whenever he was on the ward, and quietly duplicating every step and motion he would make.

The terms *posturing, catalepsy and waxy flexibility* represent odd or bizarre positions of immobility assumed by the patient. Posturing is a general term for an unusual position which is maintained over a long period. Catalepsy refers to rigid or fixed postures which the patient is unwilling to modify. In waxy flexibility the patient permits himself to be molded into any posi-

tion desired by others, no matter how discomforting it may be.

Unusual verbal behaviors include *tangential* and *circumstantial* speech; here the patient progresses through tiresome details that are so irrelevant to the topic at hand that he typically loses sight of why he was saying what he was. A more severe form of verbal disturbance is referred to as *incoherence,* a sequence of words and phrases which are so scattered and disconnected as to make meaningful communication impossible. *Neologisms* refer to words which are coined by the patient, usually by the fusion of two or three common words; for example, a schizophrenic patient used the term "crackedop" to mean my cracked open head, and another patient referred to the attendant who cleaned up after patients as the "slimedoc." *Word salad* is a term for unintelligible sequences of meaningful words and phrases intermixed with neologisms and incoherent ramblings; this is illustrated in the following excerpt from a 60 year old schizophrenic: "The Rooskies (meaning Russians) got boomblay (meaning the A-bomb). Can't listen to the liartraps (meaning liars and rapists that will trap you). Don't trust liartraps. Smash boomblay. You got boomblay? No! Can't trust Rooskie liartraps." *Echolalia* notes the tendency of patients to mimic or repeat words and phrases they have just heard; for example, a 19 year old college student who had been institutionalized following a rather terrifying LSD "trip," seemed unable to verbalize on her own, but would repeat verbatim every question that was posed to her.

## INFERRED CONCEPTS

The clinician draws inferences and makes generalizations about pervasive behavior tendencies by combining the raw material of the overt signs; Figure 3-1 portrays the derivation of inferred concepts from observable signs. Several of these higher order concepts which may prove useful in reading later chapters will be presented next. They fall conveniently into two broad subcategories: behaviorally expressed emotions, and manifest interpersonal behaviors.

### Behaviorally Expressed Emotions

Included in this category are inferences made by clinicians from observable physical and verbal acts that convey the patient's feelings and moods. The accuracy of these inferences stands or falls on the examiner's observational and interpretive skills. The "meaning" of extreme emotions is easy to decode, e.g., the hostile and explosive behavior of certain "schizophrenics," or the profound dejection of "depressives." The clinician's task is more difficult, however, and subject more often to interpretive error when he observes subtle and less dramatic behavior.

Before proceeding further, we might note that emotions are conveyed most clearly and directly in verbal self-reports, that is, what the patient says about his feelings; this phenomenological source of emotional data is extremely useful and will be described in a later section. For the moment, however, our attention will focus on feelings and moods as inferred from behavior. Table 3-2 categorizes eight concepts representing inferences about patient emotions. Although patients rarely exhibit only one form of emotional

---

### Table 3-2 Inferred Behavioral Concepts

#### EMOTIONAL EXPRESSION

1. Impassivity:
   Appearance: drab, stuporous, masklike
   Activity: lethargic, listless, retarded
   Speech: monotonous, slow, uncommunicative

2. Confusion:
   Appearance: unkempt, odd, garish
   Activity: disoriented, posturing, mannerisms
   Speech: tangential, rambling, incoherent

3. Dejection:
   Appearance: forlorn, drab, disheveled
   Activity: tearful, sluggish, deliberate
   Speech: spiritless, labored, inaudible

4. Excitement:
   Appearance: slovenly, garish, changing
   Activity: fitful, impetuous, frantic
   Speech: hurried, voluble, boisterous

5. Expansiveness:
   Appearance: garish, bold, ostentatious
   Activity: breezy, histrionic, unrestrained
   Speech: jocular, effusive, bombastic

6. Hostility:
   Appearance: sullen, snappy, surly
   Activity: uncontrolled, assaultive, precipitous
   Speech: caustic, abusive, threatening

7. Restraint:
   Appearance: modest, reserved, proper
   Activity: compulsive, deliberate, repetitive
   Speech: blocked, labored, taciturn

8. Agitation:
   Appearance: untidy, nervous, distraught
   Activity: restless, fretful, distractible
   Speech: nagging, impatient, tremulous

#### INTERPERSONAL BEHAVIOR

1. Asocial:
   passive, reticent, withdrawn; unfeeling, unaware, unresponsive

2. Avoidant:
   shy, ill-at-ease, evasive; guarded, secretive, suspicious

3. Submissive:
   conciliatory, suggestible, placating; helpless, sacrificing, clinging

4. Gregarious:
   frivolous, demonstrative, exhibitionistic; capricious, unpredictable, untrustworthy

5. Narcissistic:
   snobbish, boastful, disdainful; pretentious, grandiose, contemptuous

6. Aggressive:
   arrogant, domineering, dogmatic; derisive, cruel, malicious

7. Conforming:
   conscientious, polite, deferential; autocratic, legalistic, ritualistic

8. Negativistic:
   petty, stubborn, resentful; spiteful, provocative, contentious

expression, they do display a predominance of one or another mood fairly consistently. Each of the eight categories lists subsidiary clinical signs referring to the physical appearance, typical activity level and speech behavior of patients characterized by the conceptual headings, e.g., patients labeled as *dejected* appear "forlorn," evidence a general "sluggishness" and speak in a "labored" manner. A review of the subsidiary descriptive adjectives in each category will convey the clinical picture quite well.

### Interpersonal Behaviors

Concepts selected for these categories attempt to portray the social impact of a patient's actions. Here again the clinician extrapolates from the simple and basic behavior of the patient to construct an image of his general style of relating to others.

Two problems arise in attempting to construct a list of concepts representing manifest interpersonal behaviors. First, interpersonal behaviors vary from situation to situation; for example, a person may be cheerful and friendly with his golf companions, but angry or indifferent with his family. This difficulty is partially resolved by the fact that disturbed patients tend to display a high degree of consistency in their *interpersonal* behavior; preoccupied with their difficulty, they are unable or unwilling to adapt their behavior to suit their environment. Table 3-2 represents a summary of these relatively consistent patterns derived by the author from a variety of clinical and research studies.

A second problem in constructing a list of interpersonal behavior concepts is the inexhaustible number of descriptive adjectives from which labels may be drawn. Two guidelines were followed in selecting the terms noted in Table 3-2. First, the concept selected for each category (asocial, aggressive, etc.) represents a feature common to all of the subsidiary terms listed in the category. Thus, "dogmatic," "arrogant" and "malicious" actions all reflect a basic element of *aggressiveness*. Likewise, acting "shyly," or "secretively" or "evasively" demonstrates a common *avoidance* pattern. The second guide for Table 3-2 attempted to differentiate the subsidiary descriptive adjectives according to their probable severity. Two sets of three adjectives each are listed in each category. The first set of adjectives is well within the bounds of normality, and may, in some cases, be considered "healthy" signs. The second set of adjectives almost invariably signifies interpersonal difficulties.

A brief review of these categories is advisable

as preparation for later discussions of the major varieties of pathological personality patterns.

## PHENOMENOLOGICAL REPORTS

Behavior can be readily and objectively observed by the clinician, but it represents only one of several rich sources of data available to him. Thoughts and feelings "within" the patient often are not expressed in overt behavior; fortunately, patients can recall and comment upon these events and processes. In this respect, the psychopathologist has an advantage over the physicist or the biologist, for they cannot ask the object they study to reflect on their own behaviors and to communicate them in a meaningful and articulate way. Man not only serves as an object of clinical study but can actively participate in it. Moreover, he alone can report on inner attitudes, feelings and memories that cannot be observed by an outside observer.

Subjectively reported experiences will be divided, as in our discussion of behavior, into two categories: overt signs and inferred concepts. The first class of data consists of descriptive comments about himself that the patient consciously communicates to others. He tells us what he is thinking about, how clearly he can think and direct his thoughts and what he sees, feels and recalls; these self-reports, or overt phenomenological signs, are accepted at their face value. Consciously reported statements, however, may not represent the patient's subjective or phenomenological state adequately. He may possess little insight, be scattered and inarticulate, and may deliberately omit obvious thoughts and feelings. Because of these limitations, the clinician must "read between the lines," bring together rambling commentaries and infer, as accurately as possible, what he believes to be the "true" phenomenological state of the patient. In doing this, he extrapolates from overt signs and utilizes higher order concepts that represent inferences and generalizations drawn from the patient's reports.

### OVERT SIGNS

The patient's self-reports may be classified into the six groups outlined in Table 3-3, consciousness, perception, memory, feelings, thought content and pathological preoccupations. Let us comment briefly on each of these.

1. *Disturbances of consciousness* are best described as impairments in discriminative and

reflective awareness. Among normal persons a clear distinction is maintained between fantasied events and those which exist objectively; attention focuses upon pertinent objects in the environment; orientation is clear as to time, place and self; there is an alertness and flexibility in responding to changing events. These functions are impaired among many patients. The term *distractible* is used here when the patient recognizes that he is unable to focus on a single line of thought for any length of time; *clouded* consciousness represents the patient's report that he cannot think clearly or as rapidly as is customary for him; a self-awareness of perplexity and disorganized thinking is signified by the label *confusion.*

2. *Disorders of perception* are gross distortions of objective reality. When the patient reports having seen, heard or felt an object or event which cannot be verified by others, we label his perception an *illusion* or a *hallucination.* Pathological illusions are bizarre misinterpretations of objective stimuli; for example, a suspicious and guilt-ridden patient heard the rustling of leaves as vilifying and castigating voices. Hallucinations are entirely imaginary perceptions, that is, they are not based on an external referent; thus, in an entirely quiet room, an extremely fearful patient heard distant rumblings of bombs falling which became progressively closer, more ominous and loud, and which could be "turned off" only by giving him a sharp slap across the cheek. Hallucinations are total fabrications, but often are experienced phenomenologically as more "real" than objective events.

3. The most common *memory disturbance* found in patients is *amnesia,* an inability to recall experiences and relationships; for example, a well-established physician suddenly was unable to identify who he was, his family and his current colleagues, but did recall the schools he attended and the names of several of his college professors. *Hypermnesia* signifies an unusual capacity to recall the details of distant or insignificant events; thus, an otherwise rather dull patient was able to rattle off, with considerable accuracy, the daily headline news items for a period of a decade more than 20 years ago.

4. Subjective *feelings* reported by patients are listed in Table 3-3 and are, for the most part, self-explanatory. Two terms may require elaboration. *Depersonalization* refers to an estrangement from self in which the patient reports that his identity and feelings have been lost or have no reality. Objects and events seem unreal and the emotions they normally evoke no longer are experienced. In their stead is a frightening sense

of emptiness and strangeness; for example, a rather shy and retiring train conductor would periodically become alarmed over the thought that his "mind" had left his body and that his physical being was not his own but a foreign object that moved and acted like an automaton. The concept of *ambivalence* denotes an awareness of mixed or contradictory attitudes toward the same object, event or person; thus, not uncommonly, patients will vacillate sharply between feelings of rage and guilt toward members of their family.

5. Because thinking is the most highly organized and subtle of man's capacities, disturbances in this sphere of functioning may take innumerable forms. Disorders in the progression and productivity of thought have been presented earlier in our discussion of the overt behavioral signs (e.g., flight of ideas, blocking, circumstantiality or labored speech).

It is in the *content of thought* that the clinician is provided with his single most fruitful source of information. Recollections, attitudes and

## Table 3-3   Overt Phenomenological Signs

| CONSCIOUSNESS | THOUGHT CONTENT |
|---|---|
| Distractible | *About Past* |
| Clouded | Regrets |
| Confused | Shames |
| | Discouragements |
| **PERCEPTION** | Remorse |
| Illusions | *About Others* |
| Hallucinations | Affection |
| | Sex |
| **MEMORY** | Conflict |
| Amnesia | Fear |
| Hypermnesia | Envy |
| | Resentment |
| | Hate |
| **FEELINGS** | Guilt |
| Depersonalized | Jealousy |
| Ambivalent | Suspicion |
| Apprehensive | |
| Despondent | *About Self* |
| Humiliated | Bodily ailments |
| Excited | Unworthiness |
| Angry | Loneliness |
| | Power |
| | Unreality |

### PATHOLOGICAL PREOCCUPATIONS

Obsessions
Phobias
Delusions of:
   Reference
   Influence
   Grandeur
   Persecution

impressions which occupy the patient's mind offer him a rich source of insights that cannot be obtained elsewhere. Table 3-3 lists the most common topics voiced by patients; the meaning of the terms noted in the three listed subsections are apparent.

6. The section on *pathological preoccupations* includes a number of esoteric terms which require elaboration.

*Obsessions* are persistent, intense and unwanted thoughts which the patient cannot dispel; thus, a rather obese, depressed woman with a long and unsuccessful history of dieting could not rid herself of the thought of indulging herself with a table full of cakes and ice cream. An intense and unwarranted fear of an object, situation or person is referred to as a *phobia;* for example, a successful advertising man suddenly developed an unshakable dread of riding an elevator, requiring that he change both his place of employment and his residence. Irrational or bizarre beliefs, maintained despite contrary evidence and logical argument, are known as *delusions.* Delusional beliefs often are classified according to their specific content. Delusions *of reference* pertain to an erroneous belief on the part of the patient that incidental actions and casual remarks of other persons have reference of applicability to him; a patient's belief that others are "magically" controlling him, or that he possesses the power to "telepathically" control others, denotes a delusion *of influence;* delusions *of grandeur* are unrealistic or exaggerated beliefs in one's importance, achievement, significance or identity; the belief that one has been singled out for unjust criticism and hostility signifies a delusion *of persecution.*

## INFERRED CONCEPTS

These concepts reflect the clinician's attempt to bring together the scattered, inarticulated and omitted elements of patient self-reports. In order to describe a patient's phenomenological state accurately, he "reads between the lines" of the patient's verbalizations, drawing inferences that abstract and generalize from the raw data. Numerous concepts have been used by clinicians to represent these inferences, far more than can be covered here, even in their barest details. Only two broad categories will be presented: *self-image* and *interpersonal attitudes.* Table 3-4 out-

### Table 3-4    Inferred Phenomenological Concepts

#### SELF-IMAGE

1. Complacent:
   a. Reflective, untroubled, introversive
   b. Different, strange, unreal

2. Alienated:
   a. Self-conscious, reserved, reticent
   b. Unwanted, rejected, betrayed

3. Inadequate:
   a. Cooperative, considerate, unambitious
   b. Inferior, unworthy, pitiful

4. Sociable:
   a. Charming, affectionate, enthusiastic
   b. Insincere, impetuous, superficial

5. Admirable:
   a. Able, attractive, distinguished
   b. Proud, pretentious, egotistic

6. Assertive:
   a. Energetic, self-reliant, enterprising
   b. Opinionated, unsentimental, overbearing

7. Conscientious:
   a. Practical, prudent, responsible
   b. Tense, perfectionistic, cheerless

8. Discontented:
   a. Sensitive, misunderstood, unappreciated
   b. Disillusioned, petulant, stubborn

#### INTERPERSONAL ATTITUDE

1. Indifferent:
   they are inattentive, disinterested and distant; I am aloof, reserved and uncaring

2. Distrustful:
   they are critical, rejecting and humiliating; I am apprehensive, shy and suspicious

3. Compliant:
   they are friendly, nurturant and thoughtful; I am responsible, obliging and grateful

4. Seductive:
   they are attracted, titillated and lustful; I am affectionate, flirtatious and manipulative

5. Exploitive:
   they are admiring, respectful and envious; I am superior, competitive and contemptuous

6. Vindictive:
   they are fearful, resentful and hostile; I am envious, deprecatory and scornful

7. Respectful:
   they are strict, coercive and punitive; I am brotherly, dutybound and moralistic

8. Vacillation:
   they are impatient, changeable and nonunderstanding; I am confused, cynical and guilt-ridden

lines several of the concepts to be used in later chapters where we discuss the principal varieties of pathological personality patterns. A brief review of the items in the chart will be useful.

### Self-Image

Each person is aware of his "self" as an identifiable being, an "I" or a "me," a distinct self-as-object different from others. As a result of social experiences, and of observations of one's own feelings and behaviors, each person builds up an image of himself, a set of attributes which he feels characterize him. With but few exceptions most individuals have a fairly uniform and consistent conception of themselves, although people differ in the degree to which they are able to articulate this image; some are minimally introspective, lack insight or distort their awareness of self for protective reasons.

Eight categories of self-image concepts are noted in Table 3-4. The term used as the heading of each category best characterizes patients who might be classed as exhibiting a particular self-image. Under each heading are listed also two sets of three adjectives each; these adjectives represent how patients, who differ in degree of self-awareness and insight, would characterize themselves. The first set of three adjectives typifies the comments of nonreflective patients, whereas the second typifies introspective, insightful patients. For example, a minimally insightful patient possessing a self-image of "inadequacy" might describe himself as "considerate," unambitious" and "cooperative." A more introspective and self-examining patient with the same self-image would be inclined to regard himself as "inferior," unworthy" and/or "pitiful."

The characteristic self-image of each of the eight categories can be grasped readily by studying the terms listed in the chart.

### Interpersonal Attitudes

Patients express a variety of attitudes toward others, but there usually is a central theme which runs through their statements, e.g., a feeling of distrust, a need to defend oneself or a desire to exploit or to seduce others. Table 3-4 lists eight such categories. Each of these categories is noted by a concept that conveys the dominant interpersonal attitude characteristic of patients in that category. Two sets of subsidiary terms are listed within each category.

The first set denotes attitudes that the patient believes others feel or express toward him. It is represented by the introductory phrase, "they are. . . ." Whether or not others do in fact convey these attitudes is irrelevant for the moment. What is important is the patient's phenomenological perception of the actions and feelings others convey. The chart notes, for example, that a patient who guides his life in accordance with a *respectful* attitude typically believes that others are "strict," "coercive" and "punitive."

The second set of terms describes the attitudes and feelings that an insightful patient might admit he feels toward others. It is represented by the introductory phrase, "I am. . . ." For example, a patient who conveys "envy," "scorn" and "deprecatory" feelings toward others is conceptualized as displaying a *vindictive* interpersonal attitude.

The concepts and adjectives listed in the interpersonal section are common terms and require no elaboration. A review of the section is advisable, however, since we will use these terms in later chapters.

## INTRAPSYCHIC PROCESSES

The major assumption a clinician makes in utilizing intrapsychic concepts is that manifest behavior and phenomenological reports are largely surface expressions of more complex and essentially unconscious processes. Stated differently, he assumes first, that the patient cannot account consciously for his most troubling difficulties and second, that meaningful connections cannot be made among overt behaviors until they are conceived in terms of unconscious motives, conflicts and mechanisms.

Acceptance of intrapsychic concepts, as pointed out in chapter 2, does not negate the usefulness of either phenomenological or behavioral concepts. Rather, intrapsychic terms are one of a number of different conceptual systems which may assist the clinician in "explaining" pathological phenomena; it is merely a system based on inferences about processes which are neither observable nor amenable to conscious report. All three systems, as well as the biophysical level to be discussed later, should be viewed as complementary conceptual tools to be used in the clinical analysis.

The logic offered in support of the intrapsychic approach may be summarized as follows:

1. The most painful and unresolved problems troubling an individual are unconscious not by accident; these problems are unconscious *because* they are so troubling. The patient intentionally shuts them out of awareness since he would be thrown into a state of anxiety and panic

were he to face them openly. Thus, the unconscious is important because it is composed of fearful memories and conflicts which underlie and create the overt signs of pathology.

2. Behavioral symptoms are merely learned habits which serve to mitigate the intensity of the unconscious problem; overt behavior should not be conceived as the difficulty itself but as a surface maneuver which enables the patient to cover up his problem. The patient's conscious formulation of his problem is equally deceptive. He is conscious only of what he is able to tolerate, that is, of what is least threatening to him. His phenomenological report is a veil, a rational and tolerable cloak to hide his deeper and more troubling problem.

3. Although a conscious conflict or frustration may be painful, it can be identified and dealt with in a direct and intelligent fashion. In contrast, unconscious conflicts cannot be identified and, therefore, cannot be approached in a rational way. The very hidden nature of an unconscious problem renders it effectively more severe, since it is harder to "get to" and resolve.

As noted earlier, one need not agree with all of the doctrinaire arguments of intrapsychic theorists to accept the notion that unconscious processes do exist and that they play a role in psychopathology.

## LOWER LEVEL CONCEPTS

Intrapsychic processes cannot be observed directly; they must be inferred. This contrasts with the other levels of analysis in which the actual responses of the patient (overt behavior, content of verbal reports and biophysical reactions) can readily be separated from inferences about these responses (expressed emotion; self-image). Intrapsychic concepts are based in part on observables, but observables are of minimal interest in themselves; they serve merely as vehicles to enable the clinician to deduce the nature of the unobservables. Overt signs, therefore, are cast immediately into inferred concepts. The "basic data" of the intrapsychic analysis will consist then of lower level concepts, rather than overt signs. These lower level concepts serve, in turn, as the building blocks for higher order concepts which coordinate the simpler concepts into broad and unifying generalizations.

Lower level concepts may be grouped conveniently into three categories: drives, conflicts and adaptive mechanisms. A summary of these concepts and their subdivisions will be found in Table 3-5.

### Drives

Drives are events or stimuli which activate behavior. The child's withdrawal following parental criticism, or the patient's anger in response to a doctor's indifference, illustrate external events which trigger behavior. Drives stem from a variety of internal sources, as well as external ones. Biological needs such as hunger, thirst and rest, and a score of complex psychological desires such as affection, approval and power, all derive from sources within the individual. Many sources which prompt behavior are generated by drives within the person that he may be unaware of but which compel him to act. If these unconscious drives are inordinately intense or are excessively frustrated, they may be expressed in pathological behavior. Intrapsychic theorists believe that the most pernicious drives are those which the patient does not acknowledge, e.g., an unconsciously dominating patient who denies the desire to dominate others would be viewed as more seriously ill than one who accepts this need.

Table 3-5 lists three subcategories of drives which are displayed often in pathology: *protection*, *affection* and *power*. These drives have been separated for purposes of distinction and clarification, but behavior usually is *overdetermined*, that is, prompted by the operation of several simultaneous drives.

Most drives are, in some measure, self-protective, but in some the *protective* objective is primary. The individual may collect a bevy of possessions and property as a backlog for some rainy day; he may hoard and be frugal and miserly with his possessions. Other protective drives relate more to relationships with people than to possessions. Avoiding blame, ostracism or punishment by the inhibition of antisocial behavior signifies a protective effort; avoiding failure and humiliation by refraining from difficult tasks, or justifying one's actions by offering unnecessary excuses and explanations are other signs of self-protection.

The drive for *affection* refers to tender and affiliative needs in one's relationships to others; it varies from an intense desire to be intimate, at one extreme, to the feeling that personal contact is a threat and repulsive, at the other. Concepts which have been coined to represent these drives are legion and we will not attempt a listing of them. It will suffice to note that they range from a dependent seeking of help, sympathy and nurturance through a moderate affiliative drive for social activity and friendships to aversions such as intentionally being different from others,

## Table 3-5 Inferred Intrapsychic Concepts

### LOWER LEVEL CONCEPTS

| Drives | Conflicts |
|---|---|
| Protection | Attachment vs. Mistrust |
| Affection | Autonomy vs. Doubt or Satisfaction |
| Power | Initiative vs. Fear or Guilt |

#### Mechanisms

| Denial | Distortion |
|---|---|
| Repression | Fantasy |
| Isolation | Rationalization |
| Projection | Identification |
| Reaction Formation | Compensation |
| Undoing | Sublimation |
| Fixation | Displacement |
| Regression | |

### HIGHER ORDER CONCEPTS

| Control Level | Interpersonal Coping Strategy | |
|---|---|---|
| Mobilization | Passive-detachment | Passive-independence |
| Defense | Active-detachment | Active-independence |
| Dyscontrol | Passive-dependence | Passive-ambivalence |
| | Active-dependence | Active-ambivalence |

actively resisting their influence and rebuffing others who offer affection or nurturance.

The extremes of the *power* drive are represented in the desire to lead and control others, at one end, and following and submitting, at the other. Power drives may be signified in a striving for personal attainments, a craving for praise, respect and distinction or a desire to dominate, control and influence others or, more blatantly, to belittle and injure them. The avoidance of power may be displayed by a tendency to imitate and agree with others, a need to follow a superior and stronger person or, more dramatically, a desire to be weak, to surrender and be punished.

### Conflicts

There would be few problems in life if needs and drives could be gratified quickly and simply. Unfortunately, there are both real and imagined obstacles to this goal. In this section we will deal with conflicts among drives that often lead to pathology.

Conscious conflicts lend themselves to reflection, reasoning and workable compromises. However, difficulties which reactivate unconscious conflicts are not amenable to easy solution since the individual is unable to grasp the reason for his reaction and distress; unable to fathom the unconscious roots of his difficulty, he cannot "get hold of himself" and cannot work through solutions.

What are the major unconscious conflicts which plague patients? Three may be noted: attachment versus mistrust; autonomy versus doubt or satisfaction; and initiative versus fear or guilt. There are many other conflicts, of course, but these three are particularly pertinent to later discussions.

The conflict between *attachment* and *mistrust* lies at the root of many problems. On the one hand there is a longing, a hunger for affection and acceptance by others, and on the other, a lingering feeling not only that others cannot be depended upon to supply these needs, but that they will actively frustrate, humiliate and abandon one should these needs be displayed. Thus, a 15-year-old patient had been viewed by his peers as being cold and aloof; in actuality, he craved their friendships and affections but had been rebuffed so often in the past that he would not chance further disappointment and, therefore, maintained a front of seeming social indifference. This youngster was trapped, therefore, by an intense search for love and affection which he turned away because of his deep mistrust of others.

*Autonomy* versus *doubt* or *satisfaction* refers to conflicts associated with one's competence in achieving new goals or sources of gratification. Some patients are plagued by doubts regarding their adequacy to attain these goals, and hesitate lest their actions result in failure and humiliation;

they cannot resign themselves to their fate, however, since inaction means minimal gratification and growth. For example, a conscientious and extremely able 40-year-old accountant employed in a large industrial firm suffered intense psychosomatic difficulties that were traced, on the one hand, to his desire to make a "better living" by starting his own company and, on the other, to his fear that he could not "make it" on his own. Other patients are satisfied with things as they are; they defer action not because of a fear of failure, but because any change may require giving up their current gratifications; each act of autonomy elicits anxiety about a potential loss of the security they have gained. Thus, a modestly successful young physician continued to live with his parents despite numerous opportunities to marry well and to take over a lucrative practice in another city; he claimed that all his needs were fulfilled so well staying where he was, and that he "saw no sense in giving them up." Both groups of patients tend, therefore, to "let matters stand" and to display passivity in their interpersonal relationships.

*Initiative* versus *fear* or *guilt* represents a chronic inability to find a middle ground between independence and self-assertion, on the one hand, and submission and conformity, on the other. Some patients are unable to lead others because they fear that self-assertion will result in ridicule, rejection and retribution. Others have been intimidated into conformity by guilt and shame; desires for initiative and self-expression are inhibited by a feeling of responsibility and obligation to others. For example, a 30-year-old dentist had been hospitalized repeatedly for a persistent ulcer; in reviewing his history, it was learned that he practiced with an older brother who had paid for his college and dental school training, and now insisted, against the patient's desires, that the patient "owed it to him to remain his assistant for at least eight years."

### Mechanisms

Drives must be gratified and conflicts must be resolved if the individual is to avoid anxiety and disintegration. Under persistent or extraordinary stress, the individual may be forced to deceive himself and to distort reality in order to mitigate the tensions he experiences. To some degree, all of us avoid conflicts, turn from anxiety and soften blows to our self-image. The mechanisms we adopt to avoid the strains of life often are maladaptive. Self-deception and reality-distortion can interfere with effective functioning and may result in a cycle of events that intensifies the very problems supposed to be circumvented. The more ingrained these mechanisms of self-deception become, the more they will function indiscriminately and the less apt they will be in dealing with reality.

Mechanisms of self-protection and need-gratification may be conscious, of course. Conscious mechanisms can be appraised and adjusted so as to successfully alleviate stress. Mechanisms which operate unconsciously, however, are not subject to reflective appraisal; unaware of their existence, the individual continues to use them even though they may fail to fulfill his needs adequately or appropriately. They are more self-defeating than conscious mechanisms, therefore, not for any intrinsic reason, but because they are less likely to be abandoned if they prove maladaptive.

Two broad classes of unconscious mechanisms may be differentiated. The first group, noted in Table 3-5 as the *denial mechanisms,* represents the banishing from consciousness of intolerable memories, impulses and conflicts. By various maneuvers, the patient disavows these feelings and thoughts, and thereby avoids acknowledging their painful nature. The second class of defenses, noted as *distortion mechanisms,* represents the misinterpretation of painful thoughts and feelings in order to minimize their impact. A discussion of these mechanisms follows.

**Denial Mechanisms.** These concepts represent unconscious processes in which the individual denies the existence of painful or irreconcilable thoughts.

1. *Repression* is the most common of the mechanisms and is a prerequisite to other denial mechanisms. It involves the simple but involuntary process of excluding one's undesirable thoughts and feelings from consciousness; in this way, the individual keeps inaccessible what would otherwise be unbearable.

2. The mechanism known as *isolation* represents a segmented or limited repression; here the painful association between a thought and its emotional counterpart is disconnected. By repressing the feeling associated with a painful event, the individual prevents this feeling from upsetting his equilibrium. For example, a prisoner may isolate his emotional feelings from thoughts about his impending execution; in response to questions about his fate, he may shrug his shoulders and say, "well, that's the way the cookie crumbles." He detaches feeling from the event to protect himself against overwhelming anxiety.

3. *Projection* represents first, a repression of one's own objectionable traits and motives and

second, an attribution of these characteristics to others. The failing college student may claim that "his school has a lousy curriculum and stupid professors"; the tax-dodging businessman may state that he was driven to do it by "mercenary union leaders" and "dishonest government investigators"; the sexually driven patient may accuse the object of his advances as having seduced him.

Projection may allow the individual to vent as well as disclaim his unacceptable impulses. For example, by attributing hostile motives to others, he may claim the right to be hostile to them. Since they have engaged in shameful misdeeds, and he is their victim, he feels justified in seeking retribution.

4. In *reaction-formation* the individual represses his undesirable impulses and assumes a diametrically opposite conscious attitude. A hostile patient may display a façade of exaggerated amiability; a rebellious youngster may become scrupulously polite and gracious; a socially insecure woman puts forth a blasé attitude and gregarious manner.

Reaction-formations not only maintain repression, but strengthen the patient's control over his unconscious tendency, e.g., by being scrupulously polite, the youngster is able to keep his rebellious inclination under constant check. Reaction-formations may also give vent to the repressed desire. Thus, leaders, in condemning public immorality, devote their spare time to "investigating" obscene literature, burlesque houses and neighborhood brothels. They may be gratifying their own unconscious, lascivious desires, while consciously decrying the shameful state of our society.

5. *Undoing* is a self-purification mechanism in which the individual attempts to repent for some misdeed or counteract a repressed "evil" motive. Avaricious financiers donate their fortunes to charity; miserly husbands, unable to tolerate their niggardliness, give exorbitant tips to bellhops and waitresses. In more pathological form, undoing may be displayed in bizarre rituals and "magical" acts. The patient who compulsively washes his hands may symbolically be "cleansing his dirty thoughts"; his intolerable feeling of moral impurity is kept unconscious and counteracted by his ritual. Although his compulsion may cause him considerable discomfort, and consciously may be acknowledged as absurd, he neither has the power to control it nor can he recognize its unconscious significance.

6. *Fixation* denotes the repression of maturing impulses and capacities. The individual refuses to "grow up" and acknowledge feelings and responsibilities appropriate to his age. This attempted cessation of psychological growth stems usually from a fear of adult impulses and responsibilities, or an unwillingness to forego the security of childhood relationships. Thus, in a rather unusual case, an otherwise fully developed and highly intelligent 12 year old boy never learned to drink liquids by any means other than through a nipple; moreover, he refused to wear undershorts, insisting that his parents purchase diapers that fit him.

7. *Regression* is similar to fixation; it differs in that it represents a retreat to an earlier level *after* normal development has progressed. Unable to face the anxieties and conflicts of adult existence, the individual reverts to immature and even infantile behaviors. Thus, disturbed adolescents, fearful of heterosexual impulses and competition, or anxious about their ability to be independent of their parents, often retreat to the safety of an infantile dependency. Their regressive mechanisms may be observed in signs such as incontinence, baby talk, thumbsucking and womb-like postures.

**Distortion Mechanisms.** These concepts represent processes that misinterpret distressing experiences and feelings in order to make them more bearable.

1. *Fantasy* is a semiconscious process of imagination serving to gratify wishes that cannot be fulfilled in reality. Thus, the musings of a shy and withdrawn 15 year old served to "transform" him into an admired and powerful figure, on some occasions, and a noble sufferer whose unjust plight would be redeemed, on others; his fantasies occupied much of his wakeful time and thereby precluded opportunities for realistic gratification.

2. *Rationalization* is the most common mechanism of reality distortion. It represents an unconscious process in which the individual excuses his behavior or relieves his disappointments with reasons that are plausible but not "true." Rational explanations are concocted to cloak unrecognized and unacceptable motives. Thus, the businessman may justify hostility toward his wife by claiming "a hard day at the office"; the failing college student assuages his self-esteem by attributing his failure to "merciless freshman grading"; the spinster aunt alters her feelings of frustration and loneliness by pointing out how much better her life is than that of "those bickering Smiths next door."

3. *Identification* signifies a distortion of self-image in which the individual assigns to himself the power, achievements and stature of those with whom he associates. In this way he experiences

vicariously gratifications which otherwise are not available to him. An alumnus may identify with his college's football team in order to bask in the glory of its athletic victories; an insignificant clerk may read biographies of great men and revel in minor similarities he finds between them and himself. Identification serves important developmental functions in the young, but it may lead to self-repudiation and identity confusion among adults. The belief that one is someone else is a sign of serious pathology; thus, every large mental hospital has one or two patients who claim they are "Napoleon," "Jesus Christ" or some other figure of historical eminence.

4. *Compensation* represents a less pathological attempt to disguise one's deficiencies, frustrations or conflicts. In this mechanism, the individual overcomes his weakness by counteracting it or developing substitute behaviors. Short men may counter their feelings of insignificance by aggressive attention-getting behavior; physically unattractive girls may become preoccupied with their academic studies, and thereby cultivate respect for their "brains"; wives who have been cast aside by their husbands may gratify their need for love symbolically by insatiable appetites for sweets and drink. Well-known examples of successful compensation may be found throughout history. Demosthenes surmounted his early stuttering and became a great orator; Theodore Roosevelt overcame his sickly childhood by turning to feats of physical vigor and courage.

5. *Sublimation* usually is a healthy form of self-distortion. It represents the gratification of unacceptable needs by socially approved substitutes. Through this process the individual keeps his selfish and forbidden impulses out of awareness, yet finds acceptable channels for their expression. An aggressive individual may find gratification in an athletic, military or surgical career; unconscious strivings for power may form the basis of a political or business career; unacceptable desires for recognition may underlie success in science, teaching or acting. In none of these does the person consciously recognize that his occupation is a disguised outlet for unattractive needs or motives.

6. *Displacement* signifies the transfer of negative emotions from one object onto a more neutral or safe object. Through this mechanism, the individual maintains the illusion that his feelings toward the first object do not exist; moreover, he minimizes the risk of counteraction from that object. For example, the professor who displaces upon his students the hostility he experiences at home, protects himself from recognizing his hostile feelings toward his wife and gives vent to his emotions safely; his anger is dissipated in this manner, he maintains the illusion that his marital relations are ideal and he avoids the possibility of retribution from his wife.

## HIGHER ORDER CONCEPTS

The clinician attempts next to bring together the drives, conflicts and mechanisms he has inferred into higher order generalizations. Two classes of higher order concepts will be categorized: (1) the capacity of the patient to control his drives and conflicts, and (2) the interpersonal coping strategies he employs to gratify his needs and to resolve his conflicts.

### Control Levels

How vulnerable is the patient to external and internal stress? Can he withstand minor upsets? At what point will his functioning become disorganized, irrational or self-destructive? These are questions the clinician must answer. In this section we are concerned with the concepts he uses to appraise the overall adaptive capacity of the patient, that is, the efficiency and manner in which he controls and forestalls anxiety and disintegration.

The appraisal the clinician will make depends on answers he has given to the following questions:

1. What resources does the patient possess? Here the clinician evaluates the nature and number of coping behaviors and mechanisms within the patient's repertoire. What he seeks to establish is whether the patient can draw upon alternative modes of reactions for dealing with stress, or whether his capacities are limited and impoverished.

2. Does the patient display flexibility in using his resources? These considerations relate to the patient's capacity to shift and reorient his approach to problems appropriately and effectively. The clinician attempts here to assess whether the patient has become rigid and constrictive, that is, unable to alter his coping pattern; at the opposite extreme, he determines whether the patient lacks persistence and is erratic and scattered and thereby ineffective.

3. Is the patient motivated to change and modify his behavior? Some patients fear change. Facing reality presents the painful prospects of further humiliation and failure; it means giving up the comparative security of invalidism, fantasy

and dependency. Motivated in this fashion, the patient will be unwilling to muster his adaptive resources to effect change.

4. Is the patient in touch with reality and does he possess insight into his difficulty? Imperceptive, distorting and denying patients are unable to interpret the stress they face accurately, nor can they see the logic for change or plan alternative approaches to their difficulties. Distortions preclude realistic appraisals and promote further disharmony and disintegration.

Having answered these questions, the clinician is prepared to assess the patient's capacity to handle stress. Table 3-5 lists three broad levels of control: *mobilization, defense* and *dyscontrol.* They represent a hierarchy of decreasingly adequate levels of adaptive functioning. The term *decompensation* will be employed to represent this progressive breakdown in the effectiveness of controls.

Patients may stabilize at any one of these three levels with a consequent decrease in tension. However, the controls a patient employs may be only partially effective, and may create a series of secondary conflicts and anxieties. For instance, fantasy, which characterizes the level of mobilization, often interferes with reality, and may diminish the patient's chances of succeeding in his aspirations; as a result, he may decompensate to the use of defensive controls, leading to gross distortions of reality, and thereby intensifying his difficulties further.

**Mobilization Controls.** These represent the first line of adjustment to threat and anxiety. Here the individual remains well within the bounds of "normality." He may or may not display insight into the sources of his disturbance, but usually recognizes a growing sense of discomfort. At this stage his motivation is conscious and his resources for relieving discomfort are relatively flexible. He may consciously suppress painful thoughts or impulses, be alert to prevent further stress and remove himself from stress whenever possible. He may "think things through rationally" and engage in a variety of distracting but gratifying activities such as fantasy, hobbies, health fads, alcohol, food and sexual indulgence. In short, his lifelong pattern of handling tensions and conflict has not proven adequate to the stress he feels, and he has begun to devise and mobilize new approaches to maintain his psychic cohesion.

**Defensive Controls.** If his conflicts and anxieties cannot be allayed with the more conscious first-line efforts of mobilization, or if these efforts lead to an increase in anxiety, the individual may invoke second level control methods. At this point, he turns increasingly to the mechanisms of denial and distortion. Repression and rationalization are major adaptive maneuvers. The patient isolates and twists his feelings and thoughts until they give him a measure of solace. Through projection, reaction formation and undoing he denies the threat of his own impulses and conflicts, and transforms reality to suit his needs. His beliefs take on a perverse and delusional quality, and his behaviors become symbolic expressions of his attempt to remove the tensions he experiences. Insight wanes and his adaptive resources become increasingly stereotyped and inflexible. He has been driven to defend his cohesion and to counteract the pressure and strain he feels, even if this requires the denial of feeling and the distortion of reality.

**Dyscontrol.** Defensive or second level controls may fail to keep anxieties and impulses in check, and the patient may give up his attempt to function in an integrated fashion. Efforts to shore up his defenses and counteract his impulses have collapsed, and bizarre thoughts, disjunctive feelings and regressive behaviors begin to emerge. Reality is repudiated, rational feelings and thoughts are abandoned, responsibilities are renounced, emotions are "acted out" excitedly and an overwhelming sense of demoralization and disintegration may result in violent hostility and suicide. As dyscontrol reaches its final stages, the patient disintegrates into a hopeless state of disorganization. He becomes lifeless and disoriented; at this point he is helplessly dependent upon others for his basic survival needs.

The three levels of intrapsychic control described rarely occur in pure form; patients display a mixture of features characteristic of each of the levels. As tension increases or decreases, one level or another may dominate the picture.

*Interpersonal Coping Strategies*

Drives and conflicts are generated and resolved most often in our relations with others. Each of us has learned a variety of interpersonal strategies which enable us to reduce our anxieties and gratify our needs. These interpersonal patterns develop usually as a function of our early experiences with parents and siblings; over time, they become an integral part of our way of relating to all others. Because they are so deeply ingrained, we are generally unaware of their distinctive and automatic character.

The eight coping strategies that follow underlie the overt manifestations of many forms of pathology. Although often developed as a means of coping with conflicts, they frequently prove self-defeating in that they tend to foster rather than resolve conflicts. The following descriptions are brief summarizations of characteristics central to the principal personality patterns to be discussed fully in later chapters.

1. The *passive-detached* strategy is characterized by social impassivity; affectionate needs and emotional feelings are minimal, and the individual functions as a passive observer detached from the rewards and affections, as well as from the dangers of human relationships.

2. The *active-detached* strategy represents an intense mistrust of others. The individual maintains a constant vigil lest his impulses and longing for affection result in a repetition of the pain and anguish he has experienced previously; distance must be kept between himself and others. Only by an active detachment and suspiciousness can he protect himself from others. Despite desires to relate to others, he has learned that it is best to deny these desires and withdraw from interpersonal relationships.

3. The *passive-dependent* strategy is characterized by a search for relationships in which one can lean upon others for affection, security and leadership. This patient displays a lack of both initiative and autonomy. As a function of early experience, he has learned to assume a passive role in interpersonal relations, accepting whatever kindness and support he may find, and willingly submitting to the wishes of others in order to maintain their affection.

4. In the *active-dependent* strategy we observe an insatiable and indiscriminate search for stimulation and affection. The patient's gregarious and capricious behavior gives the appearance of considerable independence of others, but beneath this guise lies a fear of autonomy and an intense need for signs of social approval and affection. Affection must be replenished constantly and must be obtained from every source of interpersonal experience.

5. The *passive-independent* strategy is noted by narcissism and self-involvement. As a function of early experience the individual has learned to overvalue his self-worth; however, his confidence in his superiority may be based on false premises. Nevertheless, he assumes that others will recognize his worth, and he maintains a self-assured distance from those whom he views to be inferior to himself.

6. The *active-independent* strategy reflects a mistrust of others and a desire to assert one's autonomy; the result is an indiscriminate striving for power. Rejection of others is justified because they cannot be trusted; autonomy and initiative are claimed to be the only means of heading off betrayal by others.

7. The *passive-ambivalent* strategy is based on a combination of hostility toward others and a fear of social rejection and disapproval. The patient resolves this conflict by repressing his resentment. He overconforms and overcomplies on the surface; however, lurking behind this front of propriety and restraint are intense contrary feelings which, on rare occasion, seep through his controls.

8. The *active-ambivalent* strategy represents an inability to resolve conflicts similar to those of the passive-ambivalent; however, these conflicts remain close to consciousness and intrude into everyday life. The individual gets himself into endless wrangles and disappointments as he vacillates between deference and conformity, at one time, and aggressive negativism, the next. His behavior displays an erratic pattern of explosive anger or stubbornness intermingled with moments of hopeless dependency, guilt and shame.

## BIOPHYSICAL FACTORS

We are biological as well as psychological creatures. No act, thought or emotion exists without a biological substrate. The chemistry, physiology and anatomy of our body serve as a template to shape our psychological experiences and, in turn, are altered as a product of that experience. As the eminent neurophysiologist, Ralph Gerard, put it with regard to psychopathology, "For every twisted thought, there is a twisted molecule." In short, there is a unity of "mind and body," a unity that is divided only for purposes of conceptualization and analysis.

The assumption made in using biophysical concepts for psychopathological analysis can be stated simply: perceptions, thoughts and behaviors of every animal, including man, are limited and shaped by the characteristics of its biological make-up. For example, the lack of certain brain centers precludes any species lower than man from solving mathematical problems; similarly, the biophysical make-up of deer disposes them to behave in a "gentle" fashion, and the biological characteristics of leopards dispose them to ferocity. All members of a particular species have certain capacities and dispositions in common, but not all possess these attributes to the same degree. Among men there are appreciable differences in obvious features such as muscularity, height and coloration. Other differences reflect "inner" biophysical characteristics which cannot be seen. For example, some children learn to solve complex mathematical problems with ease, whereas others struggle hopelessly with the simplest of arithmetic tasks. Differences in performance such as these cannot be attributed to experience alone; they represent differences in intrinsic biological capacities.

If intellectual attributes stem in large measure from biophysical sources, is it not likely that other biophysical potentials will underlie such temperamental traits as anger, gentility and sadness? If there is reason to believe that biophysical dispositions such as these may be conducive to certain forms of pathological behavior, then one is obligated to investigate and conceptualize them.

## OVERT SIGNS

The variety of defects and dysfunctions which plague man are innumerable. To attempt to catalog these is neither within the scope of this chapter nor necessary for any but the most advanced students. A multitude of inborn errors, toxins, traumas, nutritional abnormalities, infections and growths can disrupt the chemistry, physiology and anatomy of the nervous system and its related structures. These disruptions may result in the maldevelopment or malfunctioning of a variety of perceptual, emotional, intellectual and behavioral processes. Pathological consequences of these disruptions range from the easily identified signs of mental retardation and cerebral convulsion (epilepsy) to a variety of obscure and difficult to diagnose disorders. Definitive signs for these more obscure biophysical dysfunctions must await new biochemical, physiological and histological techniques. Until then, biophysical analyses will be limited to a number of rather gross observational and laboratory methods. A detailed discussion of biophysical defects will be presented in chapters 4 and 13.

## INFERRED CONCEPTS

There is a dearth of basic knowledge about the biophysical substrate of psychopathology, but this has not deterred theoreticians. Most of their biophysical concepts have been formulated on the basis of indirect evidence obtained in studies of infant behavior, familial patterns, animal experiments and overt clinical behavior.

In assessing the presence of a biophysical trait or disposition in a patient, the clinician will seek not only to observe his behaviors, but to establish whether they have characterized him since early childhood. Moreover, he will attempt

### Table 3-6   Inferred Biophysical Concepts

| ACTIVATION | TEMPERAMENT |
|---|---|
| *Threshold:* | Anhedonia |
| Sluggish | Melancholia |
| Irritable | Threctia |
| *Intensity:* | Parmia |
| Languid | Choleria |
| Vigorous | |
| *Rhythmicity:* | |
| Unvariable | |
| Labile | |

to determine whether these traits could have resulted from learning or past experience. Thus, a cranky, irritable and hyperactive child raised by thoughtful and kindly parents would appear *not* to have "learned" these reactions.

Table 3-6 lists two categories of concepts which refer to intrinsic or constitutional dispositions to behavior: *activation* and *temperament;* a brief description of each follows.

### Activation

Duffy (1962) has recently surveyed the literature on activation, a concept which has been referred to in the past by such terms as "arousal," "energy mobilization" and "excitation." The existence of an activation center in the lower brain (Moruzzi and Magoun, 1949) has given support to the notion that individuals may differ in the ease with which they respond to stimuli and expend energy. Duffy's monograph details many neural and chemical studies demonstrating these differences. For purposes of clinical analysis, however, it will be convenient to note only three features of this activation concept: threshold, intensity and rhythmicity.

*Threshold* relates to the ease with which an individual can be roused into activity. All of us know that it is difficult to get a person to respond when he is exhausted; that is, we have a high arousal threshold at that point. But some individuals are chronically *sluggish,* that is, no matter what their state of rest or fatigue may be, they are difficult to rouse and activate. Others seem hyperresponsive, on edge at all times. They always are alert to stimuli and display a chronic *irritability,* that is, an excessive sensitivity, or low threshold, for arousal. During sleep they are fitful and quick to rise at the slightest noise; even in the most calming of circumstances, they are excitable and distractible.

Differences among individuals can be noted

also in their typical level of energy, that is, their *intensity* of activation. Though awake and alert, some individuals are perenially *languid* in their behavior; they move wearily and seem feeble, spiritless and spent; they dawdle, slouch and poke about listlessly; they lack inner vitality and are incapable of expending more than a minimum of energy at any one time. At the other end of the scale are persons who appear to be indefatigable; they are *vigorous,* dynamic, muscular, powerful and spirited. They seem to possess an inexhaustible supply of energy, a persistent and driving vitality that demands constant outlets in physical action and excitement.

The third dimension of activation relates to *rhythmicity,* that is, the existence of cycles of activation. Some persons follow an *unvariable* and fixed level of energy; others are irregular, erratic or *labile.* Rigidity and inflexibility characterize the first group; they display a stable and persistent pattern which will not yield to environmental stimulation. In the second group, there is an inconstant or unstable pattern of activation with unpredictable shifts from languor to frenetic behavior.

### Temperament

Men differ in their susceptibility to emotional reactions; this observation has been recorded since Hippocrates proposed his four bodily humors. The biophysical substrate for various emotions has been explored with increasing precision in the last two decades (Olds, 1956; Delgado, 1966), but as yet no method has been devised to identify the precise biophysical differences among men that correspond to differences observed in their temperamental behavior. In short, we cannot "see" the biophysical correlates of temperamental differences among men. As such, the concepts which represent these temperamental dispositions must be inferred from overt behavior.

Five temperament concepts will be discussed: anhedonia, melancholia, threctia, parmia and choleria. The terms used to label these concepts are uncommon words by intention. First, we wish to differentiate them clearly from terms used to represent behavioral or phenomenological emotions. Second, unfamiliar terms may keep us alert to the fact that temperaments represent an obscure and difficult to specify disposition inherent in the biophysical make-up of the individual.

1. Clinicians have made reference to the concept of *anhedonia* since Bleuler used the term in 1911. According to Rado (1956), this term signifies a constitutionally based "integrative pleasure deficiency," that is, an inherent inability to have fun or experience affection, joy and delight. The anhedonic individual ostensibly lacks the necessary anatomical structures or chemical processes requisite to pleasurable emotions.

2. The term *melancholia* has been in common use since the days of Hippocrates. It signifies a chronic and biophysically based gloomy disposition in which the individual habitually intrudes pessimistic and despairing thoughts into every sphere of his life. This temperament connotes more than a pleasure deficiency, that is, it is not merely a lack of pleasure but an active disposition to pain and displeasure. Thus, the individual's experiences are colored at all times with depressing affects. It is as if the pain threshold within his brain is extremely low, causing him to feel sad and hurt regardless of objective reality. He may experience joy and elation on occasion, but these are rare ventures from his habitual downheartedness.

3. The next two concepts, *threctia* and *parmia,* were coined by Cattell and Scheier (1961) to represent extremes in the constitutional susceptibility to anxiety and threat. The threctic individual is temperamentally disposed to experience anxiety, and is characterized by a general timidity and hesitation when faced with potentially threatening situations. Although the person may be calm and collected in most everyday affairs, he shies from taking chances that may lead to physical injury and emotional stress.

4. *Parmia* signifies a temperamental substrate at the opposite extreme of threctia. Here the individual seems biologically incapable of experiencing intense anxiety; as a consequence, he is inclined to develop a bold venturesomeness, fearlessness and daring character.

5. The term *choleria,* borrowed from Hippocrates, represents a disposition to irascibility, touchiness and ill humor. The choleric individual is prone to anger, is waspish and crabby and is quick to take offense or flare up at the drop of a hat.

These five concepts do not exhaust the list of temperamental dispositions that are likely to be present within man. We have chosen them for this discussion because we believe that they often dispose individuals to pathological behavior; their relevance in this regard will be made more explicit in later chapters.

## COMMENT

Figure 3-2 portrays a hierarchic model of the elements comprising the clinical picture. A

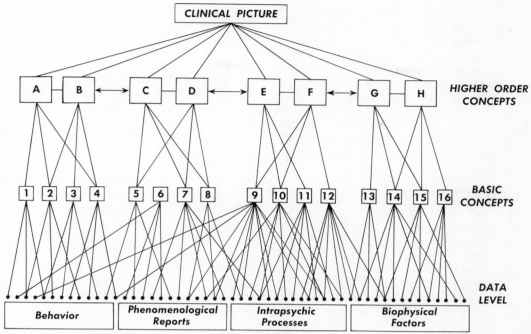

Figure 3-2 Describing the clinical picture. Inferences from the data level (usually overt signs) are formed progressively into basic and higher order concepts. Behavioral, phenomenological, intrapsychic and biophysical concepts are derived in large measure from different data sources, although they often represent the same data viewed from different theoretical orientations. The final clinical picture reflects a synthesis of several higher order concepts drawn from each of the four data sources.

careful study of the figure may be of assistance as an overall schematic of the relationships among the data of clinical observation and the concepts used to represent them.

It should be obvious to the student that considerable similarity exists among the terms and concepts described for each of the four levels of clinical analysis. This should not be surprising since clinicians merely are observing and categor-izing different facets or manifestations of the same basic processes. Different terms should be used for each level, however, in order to maintain clarity as to the source and theoretical outlook associated with each. Difficult though it may be to achieve in everyday practice, every effort should be made to select concepts which convey the observational and theoretical vantage points from which they were drawn.

## TRACING DEVELOPMENTAL INFLUENCES

The patient's clinical picture represents a cross section of his current pathology. Of equal importance are background factors which have contributed to its development. The clinician must attempt to identify and weigh these influences. Difficult though it may be to trace precisely which factors "came first" and which are the "most significant," he should seek to reconstruct the probable sequence of influences which have shaped the problem into its present form. With a clear grasp of the roots of the disorder, the clinician is more apt to make intelligent judgments regarding treatment.

A detailed discussion of these developmental and situational influences will be presented in chapters 4 and 5. For the present, we will merely outline them.

### Heredity

Each individual is endowed at conception with a unique set of chromosomes that shapes the course of his physical maturation and psychological development. The physical and psychological characteristics of children are in large measure similar to their parents because they possess many of the same genetic units. Children are genetically disposed to be similar to their parents not only physically but to be similar to them in stamina, energy, emotional sensitivity and intelligence.

The fact that children of mentally ill parents often become mentally ill suggests that certain forms of pathology may be inherited. Questions remain as to whether any of the major disorders can be attributed entirely to heredity. Despite ambiguity on this point, there is little question that heredity establishes a foundation for biophysical characteristics that may dispose the individual either to health or pathology.

### Prenatal Factors

It is well known that fetal development can be adversely affected by various pregnancy complications or the poor health and nutritional status of the mother. Although many developmental anomalies relevant to psychopathology may originate in utero, the specific nature of these prenatal difficulties or their direct effect upon psychological growth is largely unknown. Nevertheless, an examination of the mother's health and experiences during pregnancy may pinpoint influences which otherwise might be overlooked.

### Constitutional Dispositions

Each infant displays a distinctive pattern of behaviors from the first moments after birth. These characteristics are attributed usually to the infant's "nature," that is, his constitutional make-up, since it is displayed prior to the effects of postnatal influences.

Some infants startle at the slightest of sounds; others seem entirely indifferent to intense noise. Differences in sensitivities such as these dispose children to experience the world differently and, as a consequence, to learn different responses to their environment. For example, tense and easily frightened infants may learn to anticipate distress and may develop a protective aversion to unknown or potentially dangerous situations; in contrast, calm and resilient babies can handle stress and discomfort with equanimity, and may learn to become bold and assertive in their behavior. Thus, different dispositions not only lead to different immediate reactions, but to a complex series of acquired traits.

### Interaction of Maturation and Early Experience

Maturation, that is, the genetically based sequential process through which characteristics of a particular species unfold, is a delicate progression that depends on favorable environmental experiences. Experiences which disrupt or interfere with the normal schedule of development are likely to have serious and long-range consequences. Certain functions may be arrested entirely if there is a deprivation or lack of stimulation. Other functions may be distorted grossly as a result of unusual or traumatic events. Thus, the experiences to which the child is exposed during early maturation can "imprint" a basic pattern of emotional and intellectual capacities which will shape the entire course of his later development.

There are periods during early maturation which appear to be critical to the development of certain psychological functions in that they require special types of stimulation in order to mature. Events experienced during these critical times establish deeply ingrained characteristics within the child that are highly resistant to change. The persistence into adulthood of the effects of these critical period experiences is summarized well in the saying, "as the twig is bent, so the tree is inclined."

### Familial, Social and Cultural Environment

The characteristics of personality which have been shaped by genetic factors and by prenatal and early maturational experience are deeply ingrained, but they are not immutable. They can be molded further by a variety of later experiences, the most important of which are the complex interpersonal influences generated within the family. The young child learns a style and mode of life as a result of the relationships and atmosphere of his home; the tensions, rewards and expectations experienced in relating to his parents and siblings are implicitly accepted as *the* way of life since he has yet to learn of the alternatives which others experience.

In appraising these influences we may ask: What are the models for behavior, thought and feeling to which he was exposed? What characteristics and responsibilities was he expected to assume? Was he capable of meeting these expectations? What rewards and punishments did he receive for success and failure? Did his parents reject him, overprotect him or demand perfection of him? Was discipline meted out fairly, harshly or erratically? Was there open competition and rivalry among siblings for parental approval and love? How did he fare in this competition?

To these questions about childhood family experiences may be added questions about socioeconomic, racial and other demographic factors which may have influenced the attitudes, needs and habits of the child. The entire cultural and social setting within which he was reared may have created strains and may have shaped attitudes and conflicts which were conducive to pathological development.

### Self-Perpetuation of Pathological Trends

Each of us perpetuates the habits, attitudes, needs and conflicts of early life; we are active participants in carrying these early patterns into adulthood. Of interest in this regard are (1) early learned habits of behavior that are generalized or transferred to new situations for which they are ill suited, (2) distorted perceptions of self and others which transform ordinary life experiences into problem situations, (3) unresolved needs or conflicts which have been repressed and therefore persist to color and distort later experiences and (4) behaviors which provoke reactions from others that tend to revive earlier difficulties. Each of these processes, fostered by the individual himself, serves to perpetuate his problems.

### Current Stress

Many of the biological, psychological and and sociological events which bedevil man can produce stress and precipitate a breakdown in his capacity to function adequately. These range from obvious biological disruptions, such as toxins and infections, to more subtle biological weaknesses and ailments which merely lower the individual's resistance to stress.

Realistic psychological problems of everyday life, from nagging wives, occupational failures, family deaths, high pressure jobs, unpaid bills and so on, also may upset the individual's equilibrium in ways he cannot escape or resolve. His environment may not only deprive him of support and comfort but may aggravate inner feelings of distress and turmoil.

Sociological strains, such as family instability, war, racial conflict or the "pace of modern life," may be commonplace today, but they do create tensions, undermine security, intensify pressure, restrict opportunities and frustrate aspirations. The role of these contributors to pathology cannot be overlooked merely because they are shared by many individuals who do not succumb to pathology.

# CONSTRUCTING THE CLINICAL SYNDROME

Clinical analysis attempts to discover the intrinsic and extrinsic factors which have prevented the patient from experiencing personal satisfaction and social adjustment. This is done by carefully reviewing the current clinical picture and reconstructing the developmental forces which have contributed to it. Figure 3-3 depicts the stream and interaction of influences which comprise this development.

## RATIONALE OF CLINICAL SYNDROMES

A clinical study which attempted to unravel all of the elements of a patient's past and present would be an exhausting task indeed. To make the job less onerous, the clinician narrows his attention to certain features of a patient's past history and behavior which may prove illuminating or significant. This reduction process requires that the clinician make a series of discriminations and decisions regarding the data he observes. He must find a core or nucleus of key factors which capture the essential character of the patient, and which will serve as an anchor to guide his analysis.

Several assumptions are made by the diagnostician in narrowing his clinical focus to this limited range of data. He assumes that each patient possesses a core of behaviors and attitudes which are central to his pathology, that these characteristics are found in common among distinctive and identifiable groups of patients and that prior knowledge regarding the features of these distinctive patient groups, known as *clinical syndromes,* will facilitate his clinical responsibilities and functions.

What support is there for these assumptions?

There are both theoretical and empirical justifications for the belief that people display an intrinsic unity and consistency over time in their functioning. Careful study of an individual will reveal a congruency among his behaviors, phenomenological reports, intrapsychic functioning and biophysical disposition. This coherence or unity of psychological functioning is a valid phenomenon; that it is not merely imposed upon clinical data as a function of theoretical bias is evident by the fact that similar patterns of consistency are observed by diagnosticians of differing theoretical persuasions. Moreover, these findings follow logically from the fact that people

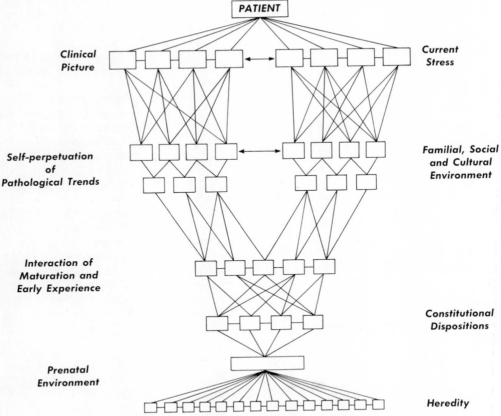

Figure 3-3    Tracing the developmental influences.

possess relatively enduring biophysical dispositions which give a consistent coloration to their experiences, and that the actual range of experiences to which they have been exposed throughout their lives is highly limited and repetitive. It should not be surprising, therefore, that individuals develop a pattern of distinguishing, prepotent and deeply ingrained behaviors, attitudes and needs. Once several of these dominant or key characteristics are identified, the clinician should have a sound basis for inferring the likely presence of other, unobserved, but frequently correlated features of the patient's life history and current functioning.

If we accept the assumption that people display prepotent and internally consistent characteristics, we are led next to the question of whether certain patients evidence a commonality in the central characteristics they display. The notion of clinical syndromes rests on the assumption that there are a limited number of key characteristics which can be used profitably to distinguish certain groups of patients. The hope is that the diagnostic placement of a patient within

one of these groups will clue the diagnostician to the larger pattern of the patient's difficulty, thereby simplifying his clinical task immeasurably. Thus, once he identifies these key characteristics in a particular patient, he will be able to utilize the knowledge he has learned about other patients in that syndrome, and apply that knowledge to his present patient.

The fact that patients can profitably be categorized into syndromes does not negate the fact that patients, so categorized, display considerable differences. The philosopher, Grunbaum, illustrates this thesis in the following (1952):

Every individual is unique by virtue of being a distinctive assemblage of characteristics not precisely duplicated in any other individual. Nevertheless, it is quite conceivable that the following . . . might hold: If a male child having specifiable characteristics is subjected to maternal hostility and has a strong paternal attachment at a certain stage of his development, he will develop paranoia during adult life. If this . . . holds, then children who are subjected to the stipulated conditions in fact become paranoiacs, however much they may have differed in other respects in childhood and whatever their other differences may be once they are already insane.

There should be little concern about the fact that certain "unique" characteristics of each patient will be lost when he is grouped in a category or syndrome; differences among members of the same syndrome will exist, of course. The question that must be raised is *not* whether the syndrome is entirely homogeneous, since no category meets this criterion, but whether placement in the category impedes or facilitates a variety of clinically relevant objectives. Thus, if this grouping of key characteristics simplifies the task of clinical analysis by alerting the diagnostician to features of the patient's past history and present functioning which he has not yet observed, or if it enables clinicians to communicate effectively about their patients, or guides their selection of beneficial therapeutic plans or assists researchers in the design of experiments, then the existence of these categories has served many useful purposes. No single classification schema can serve all of the purposes for which clinical categories can be formed; all we can ask is that it facilitate certain relevant functions.

The next question we must ask is whether such categories or syndromes exist?

If we reflect back to chapter 1, we will recall the checkered history of classification systems in psychiatry and the discontent voiced about the system in current use. Inadequacies have been noted by many writers (Ash, 1949; Rotter, 1954; Phillips and Rabinovich, 1958; Zigler and Phillips, 1961; Phillips, 1968). Some critics believe that the present system should be abandoned as worthless; others have suggested major revisions, whereas a third group claims that it merely needs refinement.

The whole notion of categorization has been indicted by some. This blanket condemnation overlooks the many benefits inherent in an adequate system; it appears as if these critics have overreacted to the shortcomings of the current system without recognizing any of its advantages.

Indeed, there is reason for dismay, especially when one observes that many clinicians are content merely to label a patient as "fitting" a category, and leaving matters stand at that. The slavish adherence on the part of other clinicians to outmoded and ambiguous categories, and their resistance to changes proposed through systematic research, is further reason for dismay. But these legitimate complaints do not justify "throwing out the baby with the bathwater." The notion of categorization should not be abolished if its products have been misused by some, or if they are only partially successful. One need not champion the features of any specific system of categories

in order to recognize the merits of classification itself. Nor should we expect that any one system will encompass all the features which might prove useful to psychopathology.

A classification system of syndromes, at best, is like a theory in that it serves to facilitate the search for relevant variables or characteristics. Thus, if a system enables the clinician to deduce characteristics of the patient's make-up or development which are not otherwise easily obtainable, or if they guide him to a particular course of therapy, or alert him to potentially serious complications, or any other clinical decision-making process, then the system is well worth using.

## EVALUATION OF THE TRADITIONAL NOSOLOGY

Once we accept the idea that syndromes may prove useful, the question arises as to whether the system in current use fulfills as many functions as is possible, given our present theoretical and empirical knowledge. If it does not, then we may ask which features of the present system should be retained, which new features can be added to increase the clarity and utility of its syndromes and how the system may best be reorganized.

Despite its many shortcomings, the present nosological classification system, hereafter termed the DSM-II (American Psychiatric Association, 1968), has a number of *commendable features:*

1.  It distinguishes disorders in terms of their severity. The term psychosis, signifying a markedly severe affliction, and neurosis, denoting a more moderately disabling class of disorders, gives recognition to this dimension.

2.  Although a number of syndrome categories are based exclusively on the presence of a single predominant symptom (e.g., anxiety or phobia), the majority of categories (e.g., schizoid personality) are the result of a combination of several clinical signs which have been found to vary or cluster together. The durability of the present system reflects in part the fact that these clusters have held up well across cultures and over time. Low reliabilities found among clinicians in judging these categories reflect, in part, the large number of signs comprising these clusters, and the fact that many signs are found in a variety of different clusters. Overlapping of signs, however, is inevitable in any system of complex clusters.

3.  The present system distinguishes between biogenic disorders, that is, disorders primarily

due to organic causes (e.g., epilepsy or brain trauma) and those in which the role of biogenic factors is unclear or minimal (e.g., schizophrenia or depression).

4. Efforts have been made to separate disorders precipitated by environmental stress (e.g., transient situational disturbances) from those which reflect longstanding and ingrained life patterns (e.g., personality disorders).

In addition to the merits just noted, the present nosological system possesses a number of *shortcomings:*

**Focus on Dramatic Symptoms.** Categorization in the conventional system is made primarily on the basis of unusual signs such as bizarre behaviors and delusions. There are many other, less dramatic, signs which are available to the sophisticated clinician. Categorization by sign clusters should draw upon all possible sources of data; categories should be constructed only after numerous behavioral, phenomenological, intrapsychic, and biophysical signs and concepts have been analyzed and weighed. By excluding from the pool those variables which deal with the more complex and inferred characteristics of functioning, the system fails to take advantage of many data which might enhance its accuracy and utility as a clinical tool.

Since the present system depends heavily on overt behavioral and phenomenological signs, clinical attention is drawn to surface symptomatology rather than the personality structure of which these surface phenomena are a part. For example, a number of the "symptom disorder" categories are noted in the traditional nosology without reference to the adaptive pattern of the patient's personality. This focus on a single dominant symptom (e.g., anxiety or phobia) gives excess significance to a surface expression of a disorder at the expense of other, potentially more illuminating, features. Classifying patients according to distinctive symptoms may prove useful, *if* it points to other characteristics of a patient's functioning; conceived in this fashion, symptom categories will signify more than the presence of the symptom alone.

**Failure to Incorporate Recent Research.** Not only are the traditional categories based on a limited number of dramatic clinical signs, but these syndrome clusters have remained essentially unchanged since formulated by Kraepelin 70 years ago, despite important advances in research. For example, recent studies using systematic factor analytic techniques with large and varied populations (Lorr et al., 1963, 1965) have suggested numerous modifications that would increase the distinctiveness and homogeneity of clinical syndromes. It is doubtful that these advances will be adopted readily, as evidenced by the fate of previous recommendations (Cameron, 1963; Menninger, 1963), and the failure of the DSM-II revision to take any cognizance of this evergrowing body of empirical research.

**Lack of a Coherent Theory.** The traditional classification schema was not only derived initially in an atheoretical manner, but no coherent theoretical system has since been formulated to provide a consistent overall framework for coordinating the various syndromes. Such a conceptual schema would be helpful even if the established nosology were reliably anchored to empirical research, which it is not. If the principal clinical syndromes could be derived logically from a few basic theoretical variables, this would facilitate our understanding of psychopathology, organize this knowledge in an orderly and coherent fashion and connect the data of abnormal behavior to other realms of psychological theory and research.

**Unspecified Relationships Among Syndromes.** The current DSM-II classification does not spell out the many interrelationships that exist among its clinical categories. The traditional schema is a highly fragmented potpourri of separate diagnostic classes; each syndrome is approached as a discrete cluster of descriptive clinical signs, totally unrelated to other syndromes. For example, the well-known relationship between depressive and hypochondriacal disorders is not noted, nor is there a theoretical framework presented from which this connection might be derived. Obviously, a format that overcomes the fragmented nature of the traditional nosology must be based on principles that would point up the commonalities and interconnections among syndromes.

**Neglect of Milder Personality Pathologies.** Although both the 1952 and 1968 revisions of the traditional nosology include pathological "personality disorders," these diagnostic groups have been relegated to a peripheral place in the psychiatric literature where interest centers on severely disabled hospital cases. In short, little attention is given to patients who manage to adjust to the vicissitudes of everyday life, but whose "personality style" is basically pathological and conducive to decompensation.

Recognition in recent years that psychiatric difficulties are far more prevalent than originally supposed has led to a growth of interest in identifying the early variants of psychopathology, and in preventing them from further decompensation. For these and other reasons, ample justification exists for bringing to the forefront, and elaborating more clearly than does the DSM-II, the clinical features of these "more normal" or milder varieties of personality pathology.

**Disregard for Developmental Continuity.** In line with the aforementioned criticism, the present nosology fails to recognize the continuity in behavior style that exists throughout life and, more specifically, the developmental progression between the patient's premorbid personality pattern and his manifest clinical disorder (Menninger, 1963; Murphy, 1968). Stated differently, the Kraepelinian system neither traces nor systematically connects the more severe or decompensated forms of pathology to their premorbid forms.

Unfortunately, little empirical research of a longitudinal nature is available to demonstrate the developmental continuity between specific premorbid personality patterns and grossly pathological states; however, impressive beginnings in this direction have been undertaken and published (Murphy et al., 1962; Thomas et al., 1963, 1968). Moreover, a substantial psychoanalytic literature exists on "character disorders" (Freud, Horney); this body of clinical data provides us with numerous insights concerning the manner in which mild personality patterns unfold into severe disorders. More recently, empirical studies by Leary (1957), Lorr et al. (1965) and Phillips (1968) have demonstrated correlations between specific premorbid personality styles and specific pathological syndromes. None of the work from this varied and important literature has been incorporated into the DSM-II revision.

**Inattention to Etiological Variables.** It was Kraepelin's hope that an accurate description of the course and clinical picture of a disorder would lead to the discovery of its etiology. He believed that his system would ultimately be founded on an etiological basis. Classification based on etiology is well established in many fields of medicine and would be a commendable attainment. But classification in psychopathology according to etiology alone seems a dim possibility in light of the complex network of influences which shape most disorders.

The fact that those who adhere to the Kraepelinian classification have failed to discover relevant etiological variables, except among the organic conditions, is no reason to abandon the effort. What is called for are revisions in which this deficiency is remedied. The results of etiological research should be included in the reconstruction of syndrome categories to whatever extent possible; there is no reason why they could not play as important a role in a classification scheme as do the descriptive and inferred properties of the clinical picture.

**Omission of Prognostic and Therapeutic Considerations.** Ideally, classification should enable the clinician to make prognostic statements and therapeutic recommendations; the conventional nosology offers little toward these ends. Unfortunately, research in the sphere of therapy has not progressed sufficiently to be used as a basis for revising the present classification scheme. There are promising signs in the recent literature, however; research dealing with the prediction of response to therapy should soon be available for consideration in the classification of patients (Katz et al., 1968; Wittenborn and May, 1966).

## SUGGESTIONS FOR A REVISED NOSOLOGY

In their excellent review of classification problems in psychopathology, Zigler and Phillips made the following comment (1961a):

The authors are impressed by the amount of energy that has been expended in both attacking and defending various systems of classification. We believe that a classification system should include any behavior or phenomenon that appears promising in terms of its significant correlates. At this stage of our investigations, the system employed should be an open and expanding one. . . . Systems of classification must be treated as tools for further discovery, not bases for polemic disputation.

With this philosophy as a basis, what should we retain and what should we seek to revise in the traditional classification system? A list of the decisions which have guided the nosology formulated for the present text will be enumerated:

1.  Syndromes should be differentiated according to severity. Although distinctions of this nature are present in the traditional nosology, their criteria are vague and they are drawn less frequently than they should be. For example, the DSM-II lists ten "personality disorder" syndromes, but makes no distinction among them in terms of degree of pathology; by contrast, chapters 6 and 7 of this text discuss eight *mild* personality patterns, chapter 8 describes three *moderately* severe personality syndromes, and chapter 9 presents three of *marked* severity and one of *profound* severity.

2.  Most categories should be constructed according to the covariation or clustering of clinical signs. This notion was well recognized by Kraepelin in devising his system, but the signs he included consisted largely of dramatic overt behaviors observed among severely disturbed patients. There is need to increase both the number and kind of signs which may prove useful in formulating categories. Thus, clusters should include all sources of clinical data. Moreover, these new signs and correlates should be selected on the basis of systematic empirical research, such as published by Lorr (1963, 1965) and Glueck

(1964). Along this line, chapters 6 and 7 draw upon recent factor-analytic studies in presenting the basic personality patterns, and separate the many subtle as well as obvious elements comprising each clinical picture into the four major data levels.

3. As noted earlier, it would be extremely useful if a consistent theoretical framework were provided to coordinate the various syndromes into a coherent classification system. Toward this end, chapter 5 will describe how the eight coping strategies that are conducive to pathological personality functioning can be derived essentially from a 4 × 2 matrix combining two basic variables: (a) the primary source from which patients gain positive reinforcements and avoid negative ones (no source, termed "detached" patterns; other persons as source, termed "dependent" patterns; self as source, termed "independent" patterns; and conflict between sources, termed "ambivalent" patterns); and (b) the style of instrumental behavior employed by patients to obtain these reinforcements ("passive" versus "active"). These eight coping strategies serve as the basis for understanding the major pathological "personality patterns," and account for the direction in which patients decompensate and the specific "symptom disorders" they display under stress. Chapters 6 to 11 will furnish the clinical details of these theoretically derived and coordinated personality and symptom syndromes.

4. In line with the above, the traditional nosology can be made more useful if the empirically observed relationships among diagnostic categories are specified; thus, rather than standing on their own as discrete pathological syndromes, each diagnostic class should be viewed, where appropriate, as precursors, extensions or modifications of other clinical categories. For example, as noted in point 3 above, all symptom disorders will be considered for purposes of classification to be disruptions of a patient's basic personality, springing forth to dominate his clinical picture under stressful or otherwise unusual circumstances. Viewed this way, symptom disorder categories are not discrete diagnostic entities, but part of a larger complex of clinical features and developmental histories with which they are often correlated.

5. The skimpy treatment in the traditional nosology of the mild personality impairments should be remedied. The shoring up of this important group of syndromes can be aided by reviewing the extensive clinical literature on "neurotic character types" published by intrapsychic theorists, and the recent empirical factor-analytic studies on "interpersonal styles" undertaken by multivariate researchers. As noted, chapters 6 and 7 will be devoted to these milder personality patterns.

6. The failure of the Kraepelinian system to show the psychological continuity and developmental progression between the mild and the more severe disturbances is lamentable. A basic revision is called for in which each patient's premorbid personality is stressed. This will be accomplished by arranging a classification format in which the majority of the secondary or more severe impairments are seen as extensions of a number of the basic or mild personality patterns. Chapter 5 will elaborate several factors that promote this continuity (e.g., resistance of early learning to extinction; reciprocal social reinforcements). Chapters 8 and 9 will demonstrate how these processes lead to decompensation.

7. The separation in the traditional system between disturbances arising primarily from situational stress and those due to other causes should be maintained. Inclusion in a situational stress category should be limited, however, to patients who do not evidence a basic pathological personality.

8. The practice of categorizing in a separate class those disturbances that are attributable to biogenic influences also seems justified and useful. Placement in this category should connote the clear primacy of biophysical causation.

The guidelines enumerated above suggest the following classification scheme:

1. Pathology will be divided according to *severity*. Severity is a continuous function, of course; that is, it is possible to make an infinite number of fine discriminations of degree of severity. However, highly refined discriminations are neither feasible nor necessary. For convenience and utility then, psychopathologies will be differentiated roughly into three groupings: *mild, moderate* and *marked* severity.

2. Four groups will be formed according to etiology and development. These divisions will be noted as: *pathological personality patterns, symptom disorders, pathological behavior reactions* and *biophysical defects*.

3. Syndromes, that is, the major categories of the classification system, are derived by various combinations of the two divisional groupings noted above. Not all of the possible combinations are equally useful, however. Narrowing the list to those categories which appear especially applicable to pathology results in the following syndromes.

a. Pathological personality patterns: *mild* (basic), *moderate* (borderline) and *marked* (decompensated) severity. These patterns will be presented in detail in chapters 6 to 9; a brief discussion of a *profound* (terminal) state of personality deterioration will also be provided.

b. Symptom disorders: moderate or marked severity (a mild symptom disorder would not be significant enough to warrant consideration as a deviation from the patient's basic personality pattern). A wide variety of symptom disorders will be discussed in chapters 10 and 11.

c. Pathological behavior reactions: moderate or marked severity (mild behavior reactions should not be considered as pathological). Typical behavior reactions to transient and circumscribed stimuli will be presented in chapter 12.

d. Biophysical defects: moderate and marked severity (biophysical defects of mild severity usually do not produce psychopathology in and of themselves; they may stimulate the development of pathological personality patterns, however, and would be understood best, under such circumstances, if classified in that group). Biophysical defects will be presented in chapter 13.

A brief discussion of the criteria for assessing severity, and a brief introduction to the subvarieties of the personality patterns and symptom disorders, will give the student a preliminary picture of the classification system of syndromes to be elaborated more fully in later chapters.

## CRITERIA OF SEVERITY

Severity is a continuous variable. Degrees of severity shade imperceptively into one another, and subtle gradations lie between what we have termed mild, moderately and markedly severe.

What gauge can we use to assess degree of severity? Two closely related criteria seem especially appropriate: *level of control* and *reality awareness*. Both of these criteria relate to a number of concepts elaborated in sections pertaining to the clinical picture. Specifically, we may recall the discussion of the intrapsychic concepts listed in the section on "control levels."

What is ascertained first is the level of control to which the patient has retreated in order to maintain a measure of homeostatic balance and psychological cohesion. If environmental stresses have exceeded the patient's habitual adaptive capacities, can he mobilize additional resources to overcome them? Has he been forced to resort to the defensive mechanisms of denial and distortion, or is he so constricted and impoverished that he can muster no defenses and has succumbed to disorientation and dyscontrol?

In addition to control functions, we must appraise whether the patient's capacity to evaluate himself and his environment realistically has been preserved. Does he possess insight into his difficulties? Has his ability to discriminate between subjective experience and objective reality been distorted? Does he falsify reality? Can he respond appropriately and with responsibility to normal social demands? Is his functioning disorganized, bizarre, autistic or delusional?

A combination of judgments about control adequacy and reality awareness, evident in myriad signs, serves as our gauge of severity.

There is no inevitable progression among patients from mildly to markedly severe stages, nor is the progression, if it occurs, irreversible. Many patients remain at a mild level of pathology throughout their lives without decompensating into more severe forms of disorder. Each level of severity should be viewed, therefore, as a transitional phase subject to influences which may move the patient toward greater health or greater illness.

## VARIETIES OF SYNDROMES

Four major divisions of psychopathology were noted earlier: personality patterns, symptom disorders, behavior reactions and biophysical defects. The distinguishing features of the latter three groups are relatively uncomplicated. We will note them here only briefly, leaving details of their subvarieties to be elaborated in later chapters.

1. *Biophysical defects* represent psychopathological states traceable primarily to inborn or acquired biological diseases or dysfunctions.

2. *Behavior reactions* are syndromes either precipitated by objectively stressful, but transient, conditions or learned as maladaptive responses to narrowly circumscribed stimulus events; these categories are reserved for patients who do *not* display a generalized personality pathology. In children, however, these reactions may become internalized as habitual patterns and evolve into ingrained and persistent personality trends.

3. *Symptom disorders* are accentuations or distortions of a patient's basic personality pattern. They are isolated and distinct signs which caricature or stand out in sharp relief against the background of the basic pattern. Symptom disorders are logical extensions of that pattern displayed under exaggerated or special conditions; regardless of how distinctive they may appear, they take on meaning and significance only in light of the patient's preclinical personality and should be described only with reference to that pattern. We will further discuss these disordered states following a presentation of the personality patterns.

4. *Personality patterns* are deeply etched

and pervasive characteristics of an individual's functioning. They develop, in large measure, from interactions between the individual's constitutional make-up and his early life experiences. These patterns tend to perpetuate themselves and aggravate everyday difficulties, but they are so embedded and automatic a way of life, that the patient often is unaware of their character and their self-destructive consequences.

Most individuals possessing these patterns find a niche for themselves in normal social life; on the surface they may appear to function adequately and even successfully. A careful assessment of their relationships and activities, however, will reveal the rather tenuous nature of their existence; there are intense needs which must be met, they experience extreme discomfort with certain types of people or situations and they are markedly distressed if conflicts and frustrations cannot be resolved quickly. Should their balance be upset, they will slip into more pernicious and severe levels of functioning. They will attempt, at first, to mobilize their defenses in order to retain their habitual pattern of adaptive functioning; these coping or self-maintenance efforts often display themselves in what we have termed the symptom disorders. Should their restitutive efforts fail, however, they may regress to more primitive levels of control and retreat to a less adequate relationship with reality.

Under conditions of decompensation, the individual's lifelong pattern of functioning will begin to acquire the features we have termed moderately and markedly severe. Throughout this decompensation, however, the patient retains the basic structure of his personality pattern; we see a continuance throughout this period of the same basic perceptions, attitudes and behaviors as were evident prior to his decompensation. The advanced stages of pathology are merely accentuations of his lifelong pattern of functioning.

Throughout the text we refer repeatedly to the basic pathological pattern of the patient. Whatever syndrome we may discuss will be traced back to underlying patterns of habits and attitudes which have guided the patient throughout his life. *The clinical picture we observe is merely a culmination, a logical extension of his basic personality. Thus, the basic pathological personality pattern serves as the foundation for understanding all of the major clinical syndromes.*

All of us possess characteristic patterns of relating to life. Some of these patterns are self-destructive, conflict producing and socially maladaptive. What features can be used to identify these pathological patterns? How do they develop, and what coherent theoretical framework can we devise to account for the continuity and interrelationships among the various syndromes?

The details of an attempted answer and synthesis will be presented fully in chapters 4 to 9. For the present, we will limit ourselves to a brief textual introduction to the revised nosological system. Figure 3-4 is provided as a visual summary and guide to the following discussion.

### Mild Pathological Patterns

The anchor group of syndromes in Figure 3-4 consists of eight basic (mild) personality patterns. They were derived from the author's clinical and multivariate research, the work of several investigators utilizing a variety of factor-analytic and statistical techniques (Lorr et al., 1963, 1964, 1965, 1966; Overall, 1963, 1967; Zigler and Phillips, 1961b; Katz and Cole, 1963; Phillips and Rabinovitch, 1958; Phillips, 1968; Glueck et al., 1964; Leary, 1957; Wittenborn et al., 1953), and the clinical observations of a number of intrapsychic theorists, most notably Freud, Abraham, Horney, Fromm and Sullivan. Although it reflects a wide number of empirical and clinical studies, it is an interpretive synthesis rather than an established and fully documented typology.

The mild pathological syndromes have been labeled in accordance with the dominant interpersonal behaviors and strategies found among patients. Lorr notes a number of reasons why the interpersonal descriptive label is appropriate (1965):

. . . diagnosis of the milder disorders should be based primarily on characteristic interpersonal behavior patterns. Associated neurotic symptoms and complaints should be regarded as secondary to maladaptive patterns of interpersonal adjustment . . . interpersonal variables are more crucial and relevant therapeutically. Therapists find such variables are more predictive of expected patient behavior in group and individual treatment.

Characteristic interpersonal "styles" or ways of relating to peers, authority figures and subordinates are relatively enduring characteristics. Interpersonal style in turn influences, and is influenced by, preferred defense mechanisms for resolving inner conflicts.

Although labeling is the least important task of the clinical analysis, it serves the purpose of focusing attention upon the characteristic which the clinician considers most important. The interpersonal label seems especially useful, not only in being "therapeutically relevant" or in "influencing and being influenced by the patient's defense mechanisms," but because it reflects the way in which the patient relates to others, the social

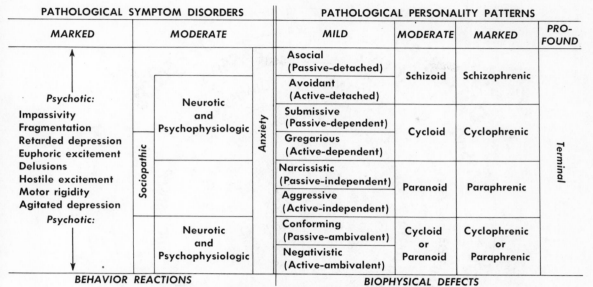

| PATHOLOGICAL SYMPTOM DISORDERS | | | PATHOLOGICAL PERSONALITY PATTERNS | | | |
|---|---|---|---|---|---|---|
| MARKED | MODERATE | | MILD | MODERATE | MARKED | PROFOUND |
| *Psychotic:*<br>Impassivity<br>Fragmentation<br>Retarded depression<br>Euphoric excitement<br>Delusions<br>Hostile excitement<br>Motor rigidity<br>Agitated depression<br>*Psychotic:* | Neurotic and Psychophysiologic | Sociopathic / Anxiety | Asocial (Passive-detached) | Schizoid | Schizophrenic | Terminal |
| | | | Avoidant (Active-detached) | | | |
| | | | Submissive (Passive-dependent) | Cycloid | Cyclophrenic | |
| | | | Gregarious (Active-dependent) | | | |
| | | | Narcissistic (Passive-independent) | Paranoid | Paraphrenic | |
| | | | Aggressive (Active-independent) | | | |
| | Neurotic and Psychophysiologic | | Conforming (Passive-ambivalent) | Cycloid or Paranoid | Cyclophrenic or Paraphrenic | |
| | | | Negativistic (Active-ambivalent) | | | |

*BEHAVIOR REACTIONS*        *BIOPHYSICAL DEFECTS*

Figure 3-4    Major clinical syndromes and their relationships.

machinery by which he works out his conflicts and anxieties, the effects he has had upon others, and the probable reactions he has evoked from them; in short, a whole complex of present relationships, past experiences and future effects may be inferred from the patient's interpersonal style.

The patient can function in everyday social environment at this mild stage of pathology; his interpersonal style of functioning takes on additional significance, therefore, because his relationships with others at this stage will determine the future course of his difficulties. His present interpersonal behavior, in large part, will influence how others react to him, and, in turn, will lead either to a stabilization or a deterioration in his overall functioning.

Figure 3-5 portrays in diagrammatic form several of the major characteristics of the eight mild pathological patterns. For simplification we have termed them: (1) *Asocial:* passive-detached; (2) *Avoidant:* active-detached; (3) *Submissive:* passive-dependent; (4) *Gregarious:* active-dependent; (5) *Narcissistic:* passive-independent; (6) *Aggressive:* active-independent; (7) *Conforming:* passive-ambivalent; and (8) *Negativistic:* active-ambivalent.

The circular grid extending outward from the core numbers in Figure 3-5 lists several concepts characteristic of each syndrome. Progressing from the center of the diagram to the perimeter are (a) self-image, (b) interpersonal attitude, (c) interpersonal behavior, (d) and (e) which, together, represent the interpersonal coping strategy. For example, in (6) the patient's self-image is

that he is an "assertive" person. This image often is correlated with a "vindictive" interpersonal attitude, that is, that betrayal and retribution characterize the nature of man's relationship to man. Patients in this syndrome usually display "aggressive" interpersonal behaviors; we often find that these patients are "actively" striving to assert their "independence" from others. Details about the full clinical picture of each of these patterns, including their developmental roots, will constitute the main body of chapters 6 and 7.

*Moderate and Marked Pathological Patterns*

We have listed terms in Figure 3-4 for moderately and markedly severe pathological patterns. If we view the chart horizontally we will note that each of the moderately and markedly severe patterns runs parallel with certain mild patterns; they have intentionally been placed in this fashion to demonstrate the developmental continuity we believe exists between certain mild and certain more severe patterns. The advanced patterns merely represent an insidious or slow decompensation of a basic or milder pathological personality. They usually evolve gradually, and invariably pervade the whole fabric of the patient's personality. They contrast with the symptom disorders, therefore, in that they do not emerge following a rapid and stormy course, nor are they distinguished by a single dominant symptom. Rather, they usually follow a slow process of deterioration and are deeply etched and pervasive characteristics of functioning.

The horizontal connection in Figure 3-4

Figure 3-5   Eight basic pathological patterns. Diagrammatic representation of typical characteristics of the eight basic pathological patterns. Among those noted on the figure are A. Self-image; B. Interpersonal attitude; C. Manifest interpersonal behavior; D and E. Interpersonal coping strategy.

portrays, for example, the thesis that disintegrating "submissive" and "gregarious" individuals tend to deteriorate into what we have termed the moderately severe *cycloid* pattern. If this decompensation progresses further, these patients will display characteristics we have noted as the markedly severe *cyclophrenic* pattern. In a similar fashion, the "narcissistic" and "aggressive" mild patterns tend to deteriorate first, into the *paranoid,* and later, into the *paraphrenic* pattern. All pathological patterns begin to take on similar features as decompensation progresses; a final stage of severity, signifying a chronic and profound state of disintegration has been labeled the *terminal personality pattern.*

The three terms used to label the moderately severe patterns—*schizoid, cycloid* and *paranoid*—are substantially in line with the nomenclature of the traditional classification. The suffix "oid" has been applied uniformly to signify the common level of moderate personality pathology among these patients. These categories have *not* been labeled in accordance with interpersonal charac-

teristics, as was done in the milder patterns, since the patient's disturbance at this stage of deterioration is better understood in terms of his inner processes than his social relationships. As pathology progresses, behavior is guided less by external reality than by inner thoughts, habits, needs and conflicts. Thus, the change in the descriptive label is designed to direct the clinician's focus to processes within the patient which dominate his behavior. Attention now is turned to problems of control and reality awareness. For example, the paranoid's growing preoccupation with his need for power, independence and recognition leads to distortions in reality, such as the suspicion that people are plotting to prevent his success. The patient no longer is guided by the objective behavior of others; now he sees what he wants to see in order to gratify his drives and assuage his inner feeling of disharmony. Every so often his controls give way, resulting in periodic episodes of severe "disorder."

The markedly severe personality patterns represent a more permanent disintegration of controls and a further loss of reality contact. All of these patients begin to display cognitive disorganization, estrangement from self and a social invalidism. We have adopted the suffix "phrenia" to represent the common level of marked personality deterioration among these patients; this usage maintains a measure of consistency with the conventional nosology in which many of the markedly decompensated patterns are diagnosed as "schizophrenic."

These markedly decompensated patients should not be lumped together; it is our belief that they should be separated in terms of their premorbid personality characteristics. Thus, the label *schizophrenic* will apply only to those patients who have shown a social detachment all their lives. The term *cyclophrenic* is given to patients whose decompensation overlays a lifelong striving for affection and dependency. And the *paraphrenic* category includes those who have displayed a chronic search for independence, power and recognition.

### Symptom Disorders

The left side of Figure 3-4 lists a wide variety of both moderate and markedly severe symptom disorders. As noted earlier, these disorders appear most frequently in conjunction with certain pathological personality patterns; the con-

nection between disorder and pattern can be noted by viewing the chart horizontally.

Although each symptom disorder crops up with greater frequency among certain patterns than others, they do arise in a number of different patterns. For example, neurotic and psychophysiologic disorders occur most commonly among patients exhibiting a basic avoidant, submissive, gregarious, conforming or negativistic personality pattern; sociopathic disorders are found primarily in gregarious, narcissistic and aggressive patterns. This observation points up the importance of specifying the basic personality pattern from which a disorder arises. The dominant symptom a patient displays cannot, in itself, clue us well enough to the basic habits, attitudes and needs of the patient. Thus, we shall make it a practice always to discuss symptom disorders with reference to the specific pathological personality pattern from which it issues.

The label "disorder" has been chosen for these categories because symptoms indicate that the patient's habitual mode of functioning has been upset or disordered. Patients often experience discomfort with their symptoms, frequently are aware that the symptom signifies something discrepant within them and, as a result, are motivated consciously, at least, to rid themselves of it. We shall return to a full discussion of these syndromes in chapters 10 and 11.

# FORMULATING A REMEDIAL PLAN

Clinical analysis is not undertaken for the sake of evaluation and understanding alone. Its purpose is to lead to intelligent remedial action, to answer specific referral questions and to facilitate decisions about the handling or disposition of the patient.

Clinicians are asked different questions for each patient they evaluate. Essentially, these questions deal with two basic points: (1) What is the prognosis? (2) What recommendations can you make regarding management and treatment?

## PROGNOSIS

Traditionally, prognosis refers to predictions about the outcome of a patient's illness. Based on information gathered at the time of his analysis, the clinician ventures a judgment that the future course of an illness is likely to progress in one or another fashion.

Although prediction of the duration, course and outcome of a disorder remains of theoretical and research interest, *clinical* prediction has a more immediate goal. It should be cast in terms of treatment selection; that is, prognostic statements should be designed not as a simple judgment about the patient's likely future, but as an aid in making decisions about management and therapy that will head off or reverse an unfavorable future. In brief, it should guide the therapist to choose the most advantageous methods available to remove the patient's disturbance and replace it with a healthier and more satisfying pattern of behavior.

The notion that prognosis should be stated in terms of suitability for a specific form of therapy is new to psychopathology. Until recently, all seriously disturbed patients were handled as if they were alike—most commonly they received electroconvulsive treatment and custodial care. Mildly disturbed patients also were treated alike

—they were directed into supportive counseling or psychoanalysis. Thus, the specification of the more subtle features of their pathology and prognosis was relatively unimportant since it had little bearing on what form of therapy they would receive.

The last 15 years, however, has seen a burgeoning of systematic research on new and more refined approaches to treatment. These rapid developments may result in the specification of prognostic signs that are predictive of favorable responses to one or another of these newer therapies. To date, however, little has been published which provides a clear prognostic guide to therapeutic alternatives. An impressive number of recent studies have been undertaken with that goal in mind (Wittenborn and May, 1966; Gottschalk and Auerbach, 1966; Katz et al., 1968).

Until this work produces unequivocal prognostic data, we must depend on the rather coarse prognostic guidelines available in the literature. The list that follows consists of signs that are associated with *general* therapeutic success, that is, they cannot be separated according to their special prognostic value for particular types of therapy.

**Constitutional Limits and Capacities.** The resources of the patient's biophysical make-up must be considered in evaluating his potential responsiveness to therapy. Aged patients have less capacity to learn and change; patients with below average intellectual capacities find difficulty in verbal forms of therapy; anhedonic patients are difficult to motivate and choleric patients are often disposed to reject therapeutic efforts. Although the precise contribution of heredity is unclear, a history of frequent mental illness in the family is often a grave prognostic sign. Marked physical abnormalities often aggravate an existent psychopathology and indicate a poor prognosis.

**Chronicity and Pervasiveness.** The longer the duration of the illness, the poorer the prognosis. Maladjustments present from early childhood are extremely resistant to therapy. A slow and insidious development usually indicates that a problem has spread into a wide range of experiences and has penetrated a wide variety of psychological processes (pathological personality patterns); as a consequence, the extinction of the problem will require extensive and long-term efforts. Conversely, difficulties that have a rapid onset or are precipitated by realistic environmental stress (behavior reactions) have a favorable prognosis since they have had little opportunity to pervade the patient's personality structure or life experiences.

**Insight and Motivation.** Insight into the sources of one's discomfort is not a prerequisite to therapy, but it often serves to motivate the patient. A patient who cannot conceive that his symptoms reflect characteristics of his personality make-up will be poorly motivated to join the therapist in self-exploration, and poorly motivated to continue therapy when such explorations are begun.

Many patients receive what are termed *secondary gains* in their disorder, that is, a degree of spurious self-protection or reward by remaining ill. These gains may result in a resistance to therapy. For example, a patient may enjoy the sympathy and attention he receives in being ill, he may avoid exposing his weaknesses by refraining from therapy, escape the onerous responsibilities of health and so on. Any feature which may diminish motivation to get well must be viewed as an unfavorable sign.

**Environmental Support.** The circumstances of the patient's daily life may be so entangled and destructive that an adequate resolution of his inner conflicts and maladaptive behaviors would not be sufficient to overcome them. Family discord, financial circumstances and vocational conflict are just a few of the negative prognostic signs in the patient's environment. Unless the pressures of his situation can be relieved, they will burden him daily and dilute the progress of therapy. Conversely, opportunities for self-realization and growth, or genuinely constructive attitudes within the family will increase the chances of successful treatment.

**Type of Pathology.** The student will assume, no doubt, that the more dramatic and chaotic the symptoms of a disorder may be, the worse will be its prognosis. Actually, there is little relationship between the two. In fact, the absence of severe symptoms often decreases the patient's interest in continuing therapy; intense discomfort serves as a motive to get well.

Although the appearance of severe symptoms, in itself, bears little relationship to prognosis, the patient's less dramatic and characteristic way of relating to others is prognostically significant. For example, detached patients have poor prognoses because they are disinclined to trust and communicate to the therapist. Similarly, dependent patients will lean excessively upon the therapist's guidance and resist making decisions or assuming independent responsibilities.

## MANAGEMENT AND THERAPY

What are the methods that clinicians use to help patients resolve their difficulties? These techniques will be discussed fully in chapters 14 and

15. For the present, we will briefly note seven major approaches, devoting one paragraph each to their essential features.

**Environmental Management.** The object of this approach is to relieve the patient of some of the sources of his difficulties by removing disturbing and aggravating elements in his environment. Management often is undertaken by members of the psychiatric social work profession and consists of such varied procedures as family counseling, foster home placement and rehabilitation guidance. The social and vocational activities of hospitalized patients also fall within the province of environmental management; these are usually combined under the label of "milieu therapy."

**Supportive Therapy.** The primary goal of this method is to reestablish the patient's normal mode of functioning following stress or anxiety. It attempts to shore up and strengthen his habitual way of dealing with his environment and does not seek to alter or modify his basic habits, attitudes and needs. The purpose is to aid the patient in getting "over the hump" of an unusual or brief upset and to bring him back to his previous level of equilibrium.

**Biophysical Treatment.** A variety of pharmaceutical, electrical and surgical methods can be utilized with patients as a means of altering the biological substrate of activity, emotion and thought. The precise neurophysiological effects of these techniques are largely unknown, but a body of empirical evidence has been gathered indicating which types of patients are most responsive to these methods. In the hands of a trained and knowledgeable psychiatrist, these techniques occasionally are sufficient themselves as therapeutic measures. More often, however, they are used as a prelude or adjunct to other therapeutic approaches.

**Behavior Modification.** This approach seeks to extinguish socially maladaptive behaviors and to replace them with new and more adaptive behaviors. Most of these techniques are based on learning theories, and rest on the assumption that disordered behavior is the product of faulty conditioning which can be supplanted by procedures of extinction and relearning. Impressive evidence has been gathered to support the view that these techniques are the most effective methods for handling behavior reactions and symptom disorders.

**Phenomenological Reorientation.** These procedures focus on the patient's self-defeating and distorting attitudes; through direct and indirect means the patient is led to reexamine and reorient his "dissonant" outlook on life. Some therapists confront the patient directly with these unfounded or inconsistent beliefs in an attempt to motivate change and to prevent him from perpetuating his own emotional difficulties. Therapists of a more nondirective persuasion allow the patient to explore his attitudes without therapeutic intervention; in these techniques, the therapist's "accepting attitude" ostensibly enables the patient to examine and clarify his difficulties with equanimity and to find adequate resolutions to them.

**Intrapsychic Reconstruction.** These techniques, based largely on the psychoanalytic theories of Freud, attempt to make the patient aware of his unconscious drives and conflicts. This is done by focusing on the patient's early developmental experiences and by demonstrating the relationship between these experiences and their derivatives in present-day life. The therapist strives to bring unconscious processes into awareness, to expunge or recast them and then assist the patient in rebuilding new and less disabling behaviors.

**Group Methods.** A variety of group procedures have been utilized to provide a setting in which the patient can relate to others without rejection or ridicule. Since all patients suffer some measure of disturbed interpersonal relationships, the therapeutic group allows him to gain greater objectivity and to explore new ways of feeling and relating to others without fear of retribution and humiliation.

# CONCLUDING COMMENTS AND SUMMARY

This third, and last, of our introductory chapters offered no respite for the student; it encompassed in scope and detail as broad a subject as each of the first two.

The number of signs and concepts used by clinicians requires both a broad perspective and a keen perception. Difficult as his task may seem, the clinician has no choice but to enlarge and refine his vision. He cannot do justice to the responsibilities he has assumed, nor experience the rewards that are inherent in them, unless he develops these skills. Research on actuarial clinical prediction may lift some of the burdens of clinical analysis in the near future. Until such time, however, the clinician has no recourse but to extend his theoretical knowledge and validate his technical skills.

The present chapter has exposed the student

to the conceptual tools of clinical analyses; at best, he now has a rough outline of a complex terrain, a schematic drawing rather than a clear picture of the natural topography and buildings themselves. Only through direct experience with patients can these schematic outlines be fleshed out into the vitality and richness of real life. The clinical case histories to be presented in later chapters will provide the student with a more natural picture of human pathology; but not until he observes, interacts and thinks about real patients can the "feel" of the clinical process be fully sensed.

The following may be noted in summary of the chapter:

1. Clinical analysis in pathology is subject to bias and error because of the paucity of objective and quantitative techniques. Inconsistencies arise among clinical judges because they ask different questions, emphasize different clinical features unequally and interpret what they record in terms of different and limited theoretical systems. These errors are compounded by both a failure to observe intra-individual variability, and a failure to account for the effects of the setting, timing and procedures of the examination.

2. Clinical analysis is comprised of four steps: (a) a survey of the patient's current clinical picture, (b) tracing the developmental influences which shaped the problem, (c) constructing a model or syndrome representing the central features of the patient's pathology and (d) formulating a remedial plan for management and therapy.

a. The data of the clinical picture were divided into overt signs, on the one hand, and inferred concepts derived from these signs, on the other. The four major sources of clinical data were described in detail. They are: behavior, phenomenological reports, intrapsychic processes and biophysical factors. Each source provided different signs and concepts which were arranged in a variety of clinically relevant categories of patient functioning.

b. Several influences which shape the course and development of pathology were outlined. Noted briefly were: heredity; prenatal factors; constitutional dispositions; the interaction of maturation and early experience; familial, social and cultural environments; the self-perpetuation of pathological habits, attitudes, needs and conflicts; and the effects of current stress.

c. The clinician attempts next to construct the patient's syndrome, that is, to fashion an internally consistent model of the patient's functioning in which the dominant features of the patient's pathology are brought together and high-

lighted against the background of his development and life experience.

Syndromes found in common among patients serve as the basis of a classification system or nosology. The traditional Kraepelinian classification system was evaluated. A number of commendable features were noted, as were a number of shortcomings. Notable among the shortcomings were failures (1) to construct adequate syndromes for the milder pathological patterns, (2) to discuss interrelationships among various diagnostic categories, (3) to demonstrate the developmental continuity between premorbid pathological trends and the more advanced and severe patterns and disorders, (4) to utilize as wide a variety of clinical signs and correlates as possible, (5) to incorporate the results of a growing body of multivariate clustering research and (6) to provide a coherent theoretical framework from which the major forms of psychopathology could be derived and coordinated.

A revised nosology was proposed to remedy a number of the deficiencies in the present system. Four major classes of pathology were suggested: pathological personality patterns, symptom disorders, pathological behavior reactions and biophysical defects; where appropriate, these were subdivided further in terms of severity. Eight basic pathological patterns were outlined, and their relationship to the more severe patterns and disorders was noted.

d. The last step of clinical analysis consists of prognostic statements and therapeutic recommendations. It was suggested that prognosis be phrased in terms of a remedial plan of management and therapy suitable to the patient's pathology. Alternative approaches to therapy were noted briefly.

With the close of chapter 3, we have concluded our presentation of the historical, theoretical and clinical foundations of psychopathology. We are better prepared now to proceed to a more intensive study of our subject. Attention will turn first to the various biological, psychological and sociological factors which contribute to the etiology and development of psychopathology; two chapters will be devoted to these influences. Following this grounding in the determinants of pathology, we will be ready to study eight chapters devoted to the clinical picture, developmental background, and coping strategies underlying each of the major syndromes. Finally, we will present two chapters dealing with the therapeutic techniques that clinicians use to counter the unfortunate effects of natural defect and environmental learning.

# Part 2

# ETIOLOGY AND DEVELOPMENT

## Introduction

CHAPTER 4
### BIOGENIC FACTORS

CHAPTER 5
### PSYCHOGENIC FACTORS

---

## Introduction

Tracing the causes of psychopathology is one of the most difficult but rewarding phases in the study of medical and psychological science. This study of causation has been termed *etiology*. It attempts to establish the relative importance of a number of determinants of pathology, and seeks to demonstrate how overtly unrelated determinants interconnect to produce a clinical picture. Methods such as laboratory tests, case histories, clinical observation and experimental research are combined in an effort to unravel this intricate developmental sequence.

This introduction will consider briefly the logic, terminology and problems associated with the study of etiology, and will argue that alternative approaches to etiology are reconcilable, necessary and fruitful.

### LOGIC AND TERMINOLOGY OF CAUSAL ANALYSIS

Certain events typically precede others in time and it is often assumed that the second set of events must be an inevitable consequence of the first. Associations of this kind are spoken of as *causal*, that is, earlier events are viewed as the "cause" of later events. It should be noted, however, that causality, as it might be used in the sentence "A is the cause of B," implies nothing more than a description of an empirically observed association between A and B in which A has always preceded B in time.

Philosophers point out that there is no *logical* reason to assume that time sequence relationships which have been demonstrated in the past will, perforce, continue in the future. Naturally, the longer and more consistent an association has been in the past, the stronger will be our confidence in predicting its continuance in the future. But this belief rests on verified empirical observations rather than logical processes of deduction. If we keep this restricted meaning of causality clearly in mind, we can proceed to use the term.

Most people have been conditioned to think of causality in a simple format in which a single event, known as the cause, results in a single

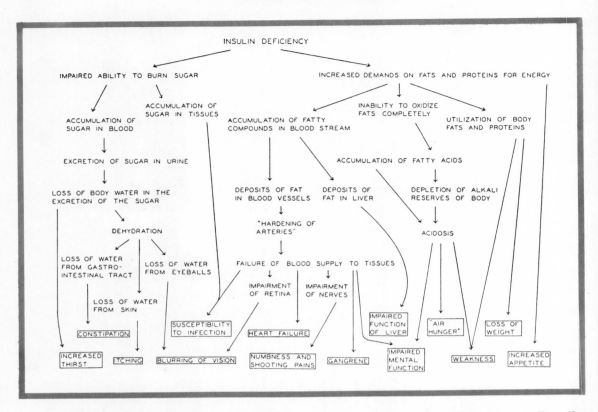

An illustration of causal "chaining." Physiological consequences of the deficiency of insulin in diabetes mellitus. (Reprinted from Human Heredity by J. V. Neel and W. J. Schull by permission of The University of Chicago Press. Copyright 1954 by The University of Chicago.)

effect. Scientists have learned, however, that particular end results usually arise from the interaction of a large number of causes. Furthermore, it is not uncommon for a single cause to play a part in a variety of end results. Each of these individual end results may set off an independent chain of events which will progress through different intricate sequences. The accompanying figure illustrates this pattern of chaining.

The study of etiology is complicated further by the fact that a particular end result, such as a physical disease, may be produced by any one of a number of different and, on occasion, even mutually exclusive causal sequences, e.g., one can get a cold from a chill or a virus. It should be obvious from the foregoing that causation in psychopathology is not a simple matter of a single cause leading to a single effect. Disentangling the varied and intricate pathways to pathology is a difficult task indeed.

In philosophy, causes are frequently divided into three classes: necessary, sufficient and contributory.

A *necessary* cause is an event which *must* precede another event for it to occur. For example,

certain theorists believe that individuals who do not possess a particular genetic defect will not become schizophrenic; they believe further that this inherent defect must be supplemented, however, by certain types of detrimental experiences before the schizophrenic pattern will emerge. In this theory, the genetic defect is viewed as a necessary but not a sufficient cause of the pathology.

A *sufficient* condition is one that is adequate *in itself* to cause pathology; no other factor need be associated with it. However, a sufficient condition is neither a necessary nor an exclusive cause of a particular disorder. For example, a neurosyphilitic infection may be sufficient in itself to produce certain forms of psychopathology, but many other causes can result in these disorders as well.

*Contributory* causes are factors which increase the probability that a disorder will occur, but are neither necessary nor sufficient to do so. These conditions, such as economic deprivation or racial conflict, add to a welter of other factors which, when taken together, shape the course of pathology. Contributory causes usually influence the form in which the pathology is expressed, and play relatively limited roles as primary determinants.

In psychopathology, causes are divided traditionally into predisposing and precipitating factors.

*Predisposing* factors are contributory conditions which usually are neither necessary nor sufficient to bring about the disorder but which serve as a foundation for its development. They exert an influence over a relatively long time span and set the stage for the emergence of the pathology. Factors such as heredity, socioeconomic status, family atmosphere and habits learned in response to early traumatic experiences are illustrations of these predispositions.

No hard and fast line can be drawn between predisposing and precipitating causes, but a useful distinction may be made between them. *Precipitating* factors refer to clearly demarcated events which occur shortly before the onset of the manifest pathology. These factors either bring to the surface or hasten the emergence of a pathological disposition; that is, they evoke or trigger the expression of established, but hidden, dispositional factors. The death of a loved one, a severe physical ailment, the breakup of an engagement and so on, illustrate these precipitants.

## FOCUS AND LEVEL OF CAUSAL ANALYSIS

The things scientists look for as causes of pathology depend largely on their habits of thinking and their theoretical frames of reference. Two aspects of causal analysis may be differentiated for our purposes: *the unit of time* a scientist prefers to focus on, and the *conceptual level* he habitually uses.

### Time Unit

Some scientists focus on *contemporaneous* events, that is, factors in the present environment which influence the individual's behavior. Others are *developmentally* oriented, that is, they attempt to trace the historical sequence of past experiences which have resulted in present behavior.

1. *Contemporaneous analysis* takes as its subject only that which is significant for the moment in the life of the individual; this approach may be pictured as a cross-sectional analysis of current events and processes. Etiologists of this persuasion are *not* concerned with the chain of historical events which has led to the present, but with the state of the individual and his environment as it *currently exists.*

Adherents of this view (Lewin, 1943; Krech and Crutchfield, 1948) claim that a full depiction of an individual's current state can supply all the data necessary for a causal analysis of his behavior. To them, an historical analysis is both unwieldy and unnecessary. For example, let us assume that a patient presently displays a marked hostility to his wife and children. Is it necessary, they ask, to trace the sequence of past events which gave rise to his hostility? Would this not lead to a tortuous and irrelevant search for "first causes?" This search might trace his hostility to an earlier need to compensate for feelings of inadequacy, and that this need stemmed from parental rejection which, in turn, resulted from their preference for a younger sibling. Should his hostility toward his present family be ascribed to his childhood relationship with his brother? The historical analysis may be correct, but is it relevant to the patient's current behavior? The job of disentangling this sequence of causes to its earliest roots not only presents its own difficulties but may lead us to matters far afield from our original interests. Would it not be more expedient to account for his hostility by examining the stresses in his current environment and their impact upon his present personality make-up?

2. Etiologists who prefer a *developmental analysis* of causality contend that a cross-sectional study cannot produce sufficient data to account for present behavior. Furthermore, they believe that contemporary events must be reinterpreted in light of the individual's past history. To them, present experiences can be understood only in terms of their similarity to experiences in the past; likewise, present behaviors take on significance only as extensions of past behaviors.

Developmental theorists assume not only that past conditions exercise an influence on the present, but that the residues of the past, in large measure, continue to operate in the present. Thus, the patient's present responses are being made to past rather than present events. For example, in the previous illustration, they would contend that the patient is reacting to his present family as if its members were duplicates of his childhood family; the feelings and behaviors he expresses now are *not* a function of what his wife and children are doing, but what his brother and parents did. Without knowing what these past experiences were, it would be impossible to understand the causes of his present behavior.

These theorists note further that behaviors

which are indistinguishable in a contemporaneous analysis may be clearly differentiated in a developmental analysis. For example, pacifism in one individual may represent imitative behaviors learned through contact with thoughtful and gentle parents; in another individual, pacifism may have its roots in a fear of hostility based on painful experiences with harsh and brutal parents. According to the developmental viewpoint (Hartmann and Kris, 1945) similar current behaviors often take on very different meanings when analyzed longitudinally.

Contemporary and developmental approaches are neither mutually exclusive nor irreconcilable; they are complementary points of focus. One examines the interplay of current factors on behavior, and the other traces the historical antecedents which preceded that behavior. The philosophical and practical justifications of one approach versus the other may be argued endlessly, but they are merely two sides of the same coin. Both are necessary.

## Conceptual Level

As indicated in earlier chapters, a multiplicity of diverse viewpoints prevails in psychopathology; this extends equally to etiology. Depending on the frames of reference or the kinds of concepts a scientist has become accustomed to deal with, he will explore and organize the causal events of pathology from one of a number of different levels. Biophysical theorists direct their attention to neurological structures and physiochemical processes, expecting to find the key to causality among these phenomena. In a like manner, behavior theorists search for maladaptive reinforcement and conditioning experiences, and ascribe causation in those terms. Conceptual levels are complementary; none, in itself, is sufficient to answer the different kinds of questions which psychopathologists ask, since these questions are posed at the start in different conceptual languages.

Some useful conceptual distinctions can be made in the study of etiology.

*First,* clear-cut biological or psychological sources often can be pinpointed as the primary precipitant of a disorder. For example, a paralysis of an arm due to a gunshot wound of the brachial nerve can meaningfully be differentiated from an emotionally based paralysis of the arm, even though we know that every psychic process is at the same time a process of the nervous system, and vice versa. *Second,* biological and psychological scientists delimit their research to those variables they are best equipped to pursue. As a result, the present literature on etiology is divided rather than coordinated. The division we find corresponds roughly to two classes: *biogenic factors* and *psychogenic factors.* We shall divide our presentation accordingly.

Chapter 4 reviews the work on biogenic determinants, a field that includes genetics, prenatal events, morphology, neurology and physiochemistry. Chapter 5 deals with psychogenic factors and includes the role of experience and social learning.

The age-old issue of whether biogenic or psychogenic factors are more important or basic cannot be decided on *a priori* grounds. As noted in earlier chapters, such questions often rest on a misconception of the nature of theory; that is, the answer depends largely on the conceptual language employed in the questions posed (e.g., to propose a causal interpretation of the "Oedipus complex" in biochemical terms would be irrelevant and specious). Of equal if not greater importance is the fact that answers to these questions are provided *not* by theoretical argument, but through the results of well-designed research. It is the data of such empirical studies to which our attention must turn; these will comprise the main body of the next two chapters.

# Chapter 4

# BIOGENIC FACTORS

José Luis Cuevas—*Madman* (1954). (Collection, The Museum of Modern Art, New York. From the Inter-American Fund.)

## INTRODUCTION

Psychopathologists trained exclusively in the behavioral sciences neglect the role that biological factors play in the etiology of mental disorders. This de-emphasis is lamentable; it is inconceivable that characteristics of anatomical morphology and brain chemistry would not be instrumental in shaping development and behavior. For this reason also, it is necessary in the study of psychopathology to explore fully the structural and functional characteristics of man's biophysical make-up.

Behavioral scientists tend to depict the brain as a passive target receiving and storing a barrage of incoming stimuli. In contrast, biological scientists know that the central nervous system cannot be viewed merely as a faithful follower of what is fed into it from the environment; not only does it maintain a rhythm and activity of its own regardless of external stimulation but it plays an active role in regulating the sensitivity, and in controlling the amplitude of what is picked up by the peripheral sense organs. Unlike a machine which passively responds to all sources of external stimulation, the brain has an orienting and directing function which determines substantially what, when and how events will be experienced. Thus, experiences cannot be thought of in terms of their objective stimulus properties.

Rather, each individual's nervous system selects, transforms and registers the objective events of its life in accordance with its distinctive biological sensitivities. Unusual sensitivities or gross abnormalities in this delicate orienting and selecting system can lead to marked distortions in perception and behavior. A disturbance which produces a breakdown in the smooth integration of functions, or a failure to efficiently retrieve previously stored information, creates chaos and pathology. Howard Fabing offers the following simple analogy to demonstrate this thesis (1956):

The speed, the precision and the grace of a double play in baseball is a thing of beauty which approaches a perfect example of coordinated activity among humans. It has been helpful to me to compare this swift chain-reaction play with neural transmission at the higher levels. The ball, as it moves from pitcher to batter to one infielder after the other, may be likened to the changing, shifting nerve impulse. The split-second handling of the ball by each player along the chain may be regarded as synaptic transmission, and the cheers (or boos) of the spectators may be compared to the emotional side effect of such a neural circuit-in-action.

But if a double play ball were hit, and if the infield were to play it with impedance of the expected time and magnitude of response, it would become meaningless, illogical and ludicrous. If the ball were fielded slowly and apathetically lobbed from base to base instead of being thrown with maximum precision

**115**

and speed, all runners would be safe, and the fans would scream with outrage. Furthermore, all downstream neural responses would be altered, i.e., the whole course of the game would change. If this same sort of disturbance in the time and magnitude of response kept occurring through subsequent innings of the game, both on the part of offensive and defensive players, the result would not be baseball but a buffoonery of the game, a colossal illogical shambles of behavior. Eighteen men exhibiting a partial impedance of their responses in time and volume would be playing hebephrenic baseball, and if they slowed up quite a bit more, they would be playing catatonic baseball.

Those of us who are in good health have a constant play of corrective signals, or counter-excitations, which dampen down and vitiate these patterns of morbid neural activity. When states of impedance exist at the synapses, these balancing counter-mechanisms fail, and excitatory fields continue to fire off in a more or less random and independent way.

As is evident from the foregoing, biogenic theorists hold the view that normal psychological functioning depends on the integrity of certain key areas of the central nervous system, and that any impairment of this biological substrate will result in disturbed thought, emotion and behavior. These theorists concede, however, that the *specific* form in which these disturbed symptoms are expressed are a function of the patient's learning experiences. Biogenic dysfunctions or defects produce the basic break from normality, but psychological and social determinants shape the form of its expression. Eugen Bleuler was the first to speak of this distinction when he referred to the biological defect as the primary symptom, and the psychological content through which it was manifested as the secondary symptom. It should be understood, therefore, that biogenic theorists do not negate the role of social experiences and learning; these experiences throw light on why a patient might display the *particular* content of his delusions or hallucinations. According to them, however, learned experiences cannot explain why the hallucinations or delusions appeared in the first place. For that explanation, it is necessary to track down an anatomical, physiological, chemical or genetic cause.

Although the exact mechanisms by which biological functions influence psychopathology will probably remain obscure for some time, the belief that biogenic factors are intimately involved in mental disorders is not new. Hippocrates, more than 2000 years ago, attributed most forms of pathology to blood disturbances and to imbalances in the bodily humors. In the mid-nineteenth century, Greisinger claimed that brain lesions would be found to underlie all mental diseases, and Thudichum, the father of modern neurochemistry, in the late nineteenth century, stated that "insanity" was unquestionably the external manifestation of the effects of bodily poisons upon the brain.

The confidence and stature of these men stimulated researchers to explore every nook and cranny of man's anatomy and physiology. The questions raised in this chapter are whether their vague beliefs have been refined into precise theoretical hypotheses and whether the recent plethora of biological research has produced findings to substantiate their faith.

In what ways has the existence and role of these biological causes been investigated?

Pertinent data have been gathered by applying a wide variety of research methods across a broad spectrum of biophysical and behavioral functions. The number of techniques used and the number of variables studied is legion. In the present chapter, we will organize this large and growing body of research into six categories: heredity, prenatal experience, infantile reaction patterns, morphological structure, neuroanatomical defects and physiochemical dysfunctions.

We must note at the outset that these categories are not mutually exclusive; often they are merely different avenues for exploring the same basic hypothesis. For example, researchers focusing specifically on biochemical dysfunctions often assume that these dysfunctions are a result of a genetic error. However, the research methods they use and the type of data they produce are quite different from those obtained by investigators who approach the role of heredity directly through family studies and twin research.

# HEREDITY

In 1962, Paul Meehl included the following query in his Presidential address to the American Psychological Association:

Let me begin by putting a question which I find is almost never answered correctly by our clinical stu-

dents on PhD orals, and the answer to which they seem to dislike when it is offered. Suppose that you were required to write down a procedure for selecting an individual from the population who would be diagnosed as schizophrenic by a psychiatric staff; you have to wager $1,000 on being right; you may not include in your selection procedure any behavioral fact, such as a symptom or trait, manifested by the individual. What would you write down? So far as I have been able to ascertain, there is only one thing you could write down that would give you a better than even chance of winning such a bet—namely, 'Find an individual X who has a schizophrenic identical twin.'

The notion that mental disorders are inherited has been among the most controversial of topics in psychopathology. Many theorists are convinced that heredity is the crucial determinant of pathology; others assert with equal conviction that social and interpersonal experiences are primary.

Behavioral scientists have been conditioned to stress environmental learning. Most notable in this regard was J. B. Watson's aggressive denial of the role of heredity back in the 1920's; his disciples and their students retained this viewpoint. At the other extreme are biologically trained theorists who have been conditioned to think that genetic causality is so obvious a factor in behavior as not to require systematic proof through controlled investigation.

In the past decade there has been a rapid growth of theorizing and research in the field of behavioral genetics. We will not attempt to persuade the student to accept one or another of the polar views noted previously. Several of the more prominent hypotheses will be outlined and the results of recent research will be critically evaluated. Before we begin this phase of our presentation, however, it will be useful to provide a review of some of the basic terms, principles and methods of genetics.

## BASIC CONCEPTS AND PRINCIPLES OF GENETICS

The assertion that a trait is subject to genetic influence is a grossly simplified expression of a highly complex physiochemical process, the details of which, for the most part, are beyond our purposes; a few are relevant, however.

The basic units of hereditary transmission are termed *genes*. The existence of the gene as a distinct physical entity is a matter of dispute among geneticists, but it remains a convenient concept for an intricate mosaic of chemical strands arranged in an orderly sequence along a small thread-like body called a *chromosome*. Estimates are that man possesses between 2000 and 80,000 genes; chromosomes are grouped into 23 pairs. During reproduction each parent supplies, on an entirely random basis, one member of each of their respective pairs of chromosomes; these are combined such that the offspring will possess a new complement of 23 pairs of chromosomes consisting exactly of half from each parent. Because of the random nature of these pairings, the number of combinations possible from any set of parents can be calculated as greater than 8 million. The 46 parental chromosomes are transmitted from one generation to the next unchanged, unless altered by some aberration.

Genetic endowment serves as a foundation which predisposes the individual to particular traits; these dispositions are referred to as *genotypes*. Genotypes which do develop into manifest traits are termed *phenotypes*. Many genotypes remain latent or suppressed, however, and are never expressed in the form of overt physical or psychological characteristics. Whether or not a genotype becomes manifest depends on the nature of the gene itself, the modifying influences of other genes and the individual's environmental experiences. Two types of genes currently are distinguished by genetic theorists: *major genes* and *polygenes*.

**Major Genes.** Only one type of hereditary effect was known in early genetic research, namely transmission by single major genes. Current researchers can now identify many of these genes by their precise locus on a chromosome and their frequent correspondence with conspicuous phenotypic traits, e.g., eye color or pigmentation.

Gregor Mendel, the founder of genetics, observed that certain inherited traits were not manifested except under special conditions. He made a simple distinction among genes to represent this difference in visibility, a distinction conventionally known today as dominant and recessive genes. *Dominant genes* reveal themselves even if they occur only in single doses, that is, when they have been inherited from only one parent. *Recessive genes* are discernible only when paired in a double dosage, that is, they must be inherited from both parents to show their effects. If a recessive gene is matched with a dominant gene, the trait with which the recessive gene is normally associated is suppressed by the dominant gene.

The Mendelian concept of dominant and recessive genes accounts only in part, however, for why the effect of a major gene may not be visible. Recent theorists have added a new concept termed *penetrance*. It represents the belief that other genes can further inhibit or otherwise modify the probability of manifestation of a gene. A second new concept, that of *expressivity*, refers to the *degree* to which the effects of a given gene are displayed, *if* they are manifested. To clarify, the concept of penetrance refers to the frequency with which a genotype becomes manifest, whereas expressivity refers to its conspicuousness. Thus, a particular gene may be highly penetrant, being manifest in 90 per cent of the persons possessing the gene, but rather weakly expressed. For example, a major gene for baldness may show up in many men (high penetrance) but result in only partial baldness for the greater majority of those who possess it (low expressivity).

The notions which underlie the concepts of recessivity, penetrance and expressivity are valid. They take recognition of the fact that both the environment and other genes can suppress the action of a single major gene. Unfortunately, these concepts can too readily be drawn upon by theorists as a plausible excuse for their failure to find empirical support for their genetic predictions. They can always claim that unknown "other" genes weakened or distorted the effect of the gene they have postulated. In short, these concepts may too easily rationalize ill-conceived and unverified speculations about genetic causes.

**Polygenes.** It is increasingly evident that Mendelian major genes cannot account for the full range of genetic variability that has been observed. According to Mendelian notions, major genes are displayed in an all-or-none fashion according to patterns of dominance and recessivity. But we know that most physical and psychological traits (e.g., height, weight, intelligence and blood pressure) fall into continuous or normally shaped distributions. Continuous distributions cannot be explained in terms of the all-or-none operation of major genes without invoking the overly pliant concepts of penetrance and expressivity.

As an alternative means of explaining the normal distribution of traits, theorists have proposed the operation of multiple minor genes, or what are generally termed polygenes. Polygenes have individually minute, quantitatively similar and cumulative effects. When a large number of such polygenes have equal probabilities of exerting a small and additive effect upon a particular trait, the resulting distribution within the population will be a normal bell-shaped frequency.

Most genetic theorists are convinced that the great variability among men can be attributed to the presence of polygenes, each of which contributes a minute but cumulatively appreciable effect on a number of different traits. To them, the search for a single gene which might underlie complicated and continuous distributed traits such as those found in personality and psychopathology,

is a fruitless task indeed. Of course, single gene effects do operate in a small number of clearly delineated diseases (e.g., Huntington's chorea). For most traits, however, there seems little doubt that a large number of polygenes are involved.

The fact that the precise effect of each polygene is too slight to be identified accounts, in part, for why most theorists have avoided them for genetic predictions. Perhaps as the science progresses, their effects will be better known and their role as a research variable will become operational.

**Genetic Aberrations.** Brief mention should be made of two rare, and usually lethal, anomalies of heredity: *chromosomal abnormalities* and *genetic mutations*. In both, normal hereditary material has been damaged in the process of transmission.

A small number of physical and mental disorders arise as a result of an abnormal number of chromosomes. For example, Down's syndrome, a form of mental retardation commonly referred to as "mongolism," appears to be associated frequently with the presence of a third small chromosome in *addition* to the normal complement of two units in chromosomal position 21; similarly, recent studies indicate that men who have two rather than the normal one male chromosome give evidence of pathologically aggressive and impulsive behaviors.

Mutations, that is, irregularities and distortions in the molecular composition of the gene itself, have been identified as the source of a number of rare biochemical disorders which result in severe mental deficiency.

Although these two anomalies of hereditary transmission are worthy of note, they appear at this time not to be involved in the major patterns of psychopathology.

## METHODS OF GENETIC RESEARCH

Considerable precision is possible when animals are selectively bred to test the genetic origins of a particular trait. Unfortunately for science this is not possible with humans. Studies of human heredity are dependent on an essentially random pattern of social mating, and such naturalistic studies are far from ideal as a means of testing specific genetic hypotheses. Nevertheless, the investigation of correlations among parents, siblings and other relatives of patients has enabled researchers to obtain fairly reliable estimates of the role of genetic influences.

The role of heredity in psychopathology has

been researched in two ways among humans. The first approach was devised by Rüdin in Germany, and is still widely used by a number of Scandinavian investigators. It compares the degree of correspondence in a disorder among relatives of patients as contrasted to that found in the general population. The second approach, introduced by Luxenburger, a student of Rüdin, and utilized on a wide scale in this country by Kallmann, compares the concordance rates of identical and fraternal twin pairs. Both approaches depend on naturalistic data and are subject, thereby, to the usual interpretive limitations of these materials. Although these data leave much to be desired on methodological grounds, when they are viewed as a whole they amount to an impressive argument favoring genetic hypotheses.

**Correspondence Among Relatives.** The rationale of this method as a technique for exploring genetic hypotheses is rather straightforward. The coincidence of a disorder among family members, whose degree of genetic similarity is fairly well established, can pinpoint the operation of a particular type of genetic agent. For example, if all children of a family with one severely disordered parent were similarly and equally disordered, we would have to conclude that their illness stemmed from the operation of a dominant gene. On the other hand, if all the children were disordered, but varied in intensity from mild to moderate severity, we would be inclined to suggest a polygenic hypothesis. If none of the children were ill, a recessive explanation would be in order. It should be evident then, that the results of a carefully planned family study could supply information about the nature of the genetic agent involved in a disorder.

When the family method was first adopted, researchers fell prey to serious methodological biases and errors. Striking cases of family pathology which caught the eye of curious observers were reported. No attempt was made to check on the possible contribution of common detrimental experiences. No evidence was adduced as to whether the progeny of these families displayed their illness in other environmental settings. Briefly then, cases were selected in a biased fashion; families which "proved" the point of heredity were reported, others were not; no effort was made to control for experiential determinants when they clearly played a role.

In the past quarter of a century, a number of well-controlled studies using large and representative samples have been carried out. The results of these systematic investigations will be discussed later in this section.

**Concordance Among Twins.** Certain interpretive complications which arise in genetic family studies can be avoided by comparing the *concordance* rates among identical and fraternal twins, that is, the degree to which they share a disorder in common. Identical (monozygotic) twins have identical genotypes; as such, differences between them result from environmental sources. Fraternal (dizygotic) twins have similar but not identical genotypes; in these pairs, differences can be attributed either to heredity or environment. A genetic hypothesis is supported when a disorder is shared more often between identical than between fraternal twins. However, we must assume that both types of twins have comparable environmental experiences. This assumption has been questioned. It is pointed out that identical twins often cling together and are treated alike by their parents, whereas fraternal twins experience different reactions from others and tend to develop greater independence.

As a partial antidote to this objection, researchers have investigated twins who were separated in early life and who were reared in different homes. Under these unusual conditions, where environmental similarities are diminished, a higher concordance rate between identical than fraternal pairs would add more convincing support to a genetic hypothesis. From the viewpoint of research design, however, it is unfortunate that twins raised apart from early life are few and far between.

## THEORIES OF GENETIC MODE OF TRANSMISSION

Before we present the findings of genetic research, it will be useful to outline some of the hypotheses that have been proposed about the nature of the genetic defect in psychopathology; the research evidence can be examined then in terms of these hypotheses.

Two points should be noted before we begin. First, researchers have focused on schizophrenia; little work has been done in other categories of pathology. Unless otherwise noted, the discussion that follows refers to this traditional diagnostic classification. Second, most genetic theorists have assumed that schizophrenia is a clearly definable and unitary disease entity; to them, there is no gradation of severity in this disease, that is, either one is, or one is not, schizophrenic. This assumption has disposed theorists to formulate their ideas in accordance with the all-or-none characteristics of single major genes. Continuous gradations in pathological severity that would arise from a polygenic hypothesis are inconsistent with this disease model.

## DOMINANT GENE HYPOTHESIS

A major gene effect would be the simplest biogenic explanation of the etiology of psychopathology, and would be most compatible with the traditional concept of disease. Basically, three modes of transmission of major genes can be postulated: (1) a dominant gene, (2) a recessive gene or (3) a combination of several major genes.

The dominant gene hypothesis has been proposed as logically consistent with empirical data by Schulz (1940) and Böök (1953, 1960). Specifically, they note that parents, siblings and children are affected with equal frequency—a finding they interpret as supporting the dominant gene hypothesis. Both theorists believe that penetrance (phenotypical manifestation) is higher among homozygotes (when there are two paired defective genes) than among heterozygotes (when only one member of a gene pair is defective). Böök calculates the penetrance to be 100 per cent among homozygotes and about 20 per cent among heterozygotes; the respective proportions of these pairings in the population result in an average penetrance of 30 per cent. The assumption that penetrance is lower than 100 per cent when only one member of a dominant gene pair is defective is consistent with other genetic findings.

Schulz and Böök postulate that modifying genes diminish the penetrance in heterozygotic pairs. We must recognize, however, that the operation of genetic modifiers is entirely a matter of speculation. They are calculated by the theorist *after* he finds that his empirical data are inconsistent with the mode of genetic transmission he has hypothesized. The notion that genetic modifiers reduce penetrance gives theorists free rein to fit their hypotheses to any set of empirical data.

## RECESSIVE GENE HYPOTHESES

Schizophrenia has been attributed most frequently to the operation of a recessive gene. Rüdin, the father of modern genetic psychiatry, hypothesized recessivity since schizophrenia did not show up with great frequency among the relatives of patients. Kallmann is the best known proponent of this hypothesis in this country (1938). Two predictions may be derived from a recessive hypothesis: (1) every offspring of two disordered patients should be disordered, and (2) one fourth of the siblings of disordered individuals should be disordered. Since the empirical frequencies are appreciably less than these expected frequencies, Kallmann has invoked the concept of lowered penetrance. Once again, the unpredictable and variable power of modifying genes as suppressors of the effect of a major gene has been used to redeem an otherwise questionable genetic hypothesis.

## MULTIPLE MAJOR GENE HYPOTHESES

Some genetic theorists (Schulz, 1940; Penrose, 1953) have proposed a multifactorial mechanism in which several major genes act in concert to produce pathology. This thesis, which is similar in several respects to the polygenic hypothesis to be discussed shortly, assumes that most persons are heterozygous carriers of a number of pathological genes; however, they do not possess the necessary combination of these genes which would result in the manifestation of disorder.

A second multiple-gene hypothesis suggests that there are several pathological genes which act either in concert or individually to produce different syndromes of psychopathology. Diagnostic classifications such as schizophrenia are not unitary diseases according to this view (Rosanoff et al., 1934; Weinberg and Lobstein, 1943; Essen-Möller, 1952; Rosenthal, 1959). Rather, these classifications comprise different syndromes that are erroneously grouped together; each of these syndromes should be differentiated in terms of the particular combination of defective major genes which give rise to them. This multiple-gene and multiple-syndrome conception contrasts with the views of Kallmann, for example. He believes that schizophrenia is a single syndrome which may be expressed differently depending on the modifying effects of other genes. The difference between these views is not based on empirical evidence; it merely reflects the speculative proclivities of theorists. Until the exact genetic substrate of inherited vulnerability is identified, the choice between them will remain inconclusive.

## POLYGENIC HYPOTHESIS

Most genetic research has been limited to specific categories of hospitalized patients since theorists have assumed that the major forms of psychopathology are well-defined disease entities of marked severity. The sampling of only severely disturbed patients has precluded the possibility of discovering the role of genetic factors in the milder forms of pathology. Despite the paucity of research with these patients, a number of theorists (Schulz, 1940; Luxenburger, 1939; Meehl, 1962) have suggested that milder psychopathologies represent an undeveloped or minimally expressed defective gene, e.g., the schizoid personality possesses the schizophrenic genotype, but the defective gene is weakened by other genes or by fortuitous environmental circumstances. These theorists believe that milder disorders are not fundamentally different from the more severe forms. They retain the notion of schizophrenia as a unitary disease, for example, and account for milder variants by suggesting the operation of beneficial modifying genes or favorable environmental experiences.

An alternate explanation for the milder psychopathologies can be formulated in terms of polygenic action. As mentioned in an earlier section, a continuum or series of graduated pathological patterns can be accounted for by the cumulative effects of a large number of minor genes acting upon the same trait. This hypothesis does not require the assumption of modifying genes or beneficial environments.

No prominent genetic theorist in psychiatry has proposed a polygenic mode of inheritance in mental disorders, despite its appropriateness as an explanatory model for the milder disorders. The resistance reflects the preoccupation of re-searchers with severely ill, hospitalized patients and this preoccupation reflects, in turn, the dominant theoretical belief that psychopathology should be conceived in a dichotomous model of health versus disease, with no intermediary steps.

## RESULTS OF RESEARCH

Both adherents and dissenters of genetic hypotheses have undertaken the study of heredity in psychopathology. Table 4-1 offers a capsule summary of the results of a number of major investigations with patients diagnosed as having schizophrenic and manic-depressive disorders.

One feature worthy of note is the rather wide range of percentages recorded by different researchers. This can be attributed largely to three factors: (1) investigators designed their studies to test specific hypotheses and selected their methods and population samples to maximize the probability of supporting that hypothesis, e.g., Tienari (1963) set out to discover identical twins who were not concordant for schizophrenia by chance and circumstance, investigators selected patient populations that differed in age, socioeconomic status and culture, and thereby confounded their findings with a number of extrane-

Table 4-1   Correspondence in Psychopathology Among Relatives*

| RELATIONSHIP | RANGE OF CORRESPONDENCE REPORTED IN THE LITERATURE* (PER CENT) | THEORETICAL EXPECTANCY (PER CENT) | |
|---|---|---|---|
| | | Completely Dominant Gene | Completely Recessive Gene |
| **Schizophrenic Groups** | | | |
| Nonrelated general population | approx. 1.0 | | |
| First cousins | 2.6 | 13 | 3 |
| Nephews and nieces | 3.9 | 25 | 5 |
| Half siblings | 7.1 | 25 | 15 |
| Parents | 1.0–9.2 | 50 | 9 |
| Full siblings | 5.2–14.2 | 50 | 30 |
| Dizygotic twins | 3.7–17.6 | 50 | 30 |
| Children: one schizophrenic parent | 4.0–16.4 | 50 | 2 |
| Children: two schizophrenic parents | 39.2–68.1 | 75 | 100 |
| Monozygotic twins | 0–91.5 | 100 | 100 |
| **Manic-Depressive Groups** | | | |
| Nonrelated general population | approx. 0.5 | | |
| Parents | 2.0–24.4 | 50 | 9 |
| Full siblings | 1.5–29.1 | 50 | 30 |
| Dizygotic twins | 16.4–23.6 | 50 | 30 |
| Children with one or two disturbed parents | 12.8–38.7 | 50–75 | 2–100 |
| Monozygotic twins | 66.7–92.6 | 100 | 100 |

* From Kallmann (1938, 1953); Shields and Slater (1961); Slater and Shields (1953); Essen-Möller (1952); Fuller and Thompson (1960); Tienari (1963); Kringlen (1964, 1966); Gregory (1960, 1968); Rosenthal (1968); Vandenberg (1966); Gottesman and Shields (1966)

ous factors; and (3) different investigators used different criteria in selecting their patients. It is well known that the criteria for classifying the syndromes of psychopathology differ in different institutions, e.g., a case which one investigator might classify as schizophrenic might be diagnosed as manic-depressive by another.

In short, the findings reported in Table 4-1 represent data gathered with noncomparable patient populations. Whether the findings of these studies would have been more consistent had there been greater uniformity in patient selection cannot be assessed. Despite these methodological complications, Table 4-1 offers strong support for the view that pathology among relatives is substantially higher than in the general population, and that it decreases roughly in proportion to decreasing genetic similarity.

Two questions must be raised, however: can environmental influences be discounted, and can psychogenic hypotheses "explain" the data in Table 4-1 as well as genetic hypotheses?

Psychogenic theorists note that there is a close correlation between genetic similarity and similarity in environmental experience. For example, siblings share parents in common and are exposed to similar patterns of child rearing; in contrast, cousins and nephews experience appreciably less commonality in these early interpersonal relationships. Likewise, identical twins share not only a common set of genotypes but a common uterine environment and a common pattern of reactions from parents and others.

The plausibility of the psychogenic hypothesis is weakened by a number of facts. Most investigators have found the concordance rate among monozygotic twins, whether reared apart or together, to be four to five times greater than among dizygotic twins. The suggestion made by psychogenic theorists that this difference reflects the greater similarity in environmental experience among identical as opposed to fraternal twins cannot be argued persuasively. If environmental factors are primary, the concordance rate among fraternal twins, who share highly similar experiences, should be close to identical twins and appreciably greater than ordinary siblings. This expectancy is controverted by the data. Rates for dizygotic twins and siblings are very similar, whereas the difference between monozygotic and dizygotic twins is substantial.

The greater bulk of twin and family studies is consistent with the conclusion that genetic factors are etiologically significant in psychopathology, but a number of recent investigations have uncovered data which run either contrary

to or require qualifications in the genetic hypothesis.

The most convincing data favoring the genetic hypothesis have been the marked discordance among dizygotic twins and the high concordance among monozygotic twins. These data have been challenged by two recent studies. Tienari (1963) discovered 16 monozygotic twins in which one twin was schizophrenic and the second was not; the concordance rate in this study, in striking contrast to previous work, was zero. Support for this finding was obtained by Kringlen (1964) who discovered only two concordant pairs among eight monozygotic twins. The discrepancy between these two studies and those reported earlier raises a number of questions about not only the methodological merits of previous research (uniformity in criteria, population sampling and design biases), but the whole issue of whether genetic factors do play a role in pathology. More and better designed research clearly is needed.

Two recent studies (Rosenthal, 1959; Gottesman and Shields, 1966) demonstrate that genetic research in psychopathology is growing in methodological and interpretive sophistication. Additionally, the data of these studies suggest an important refinement in the assessment of the role of heredity.

Rosenthal reanalyzed Slater's monozygotic twin data on schizophrenia (1953) and found a substantial history of schizophrenia in the families of concordant pairs (13 out of 22) and a minimal history in discordant pairs (1 out of 13). These results were interpreted as meaning that the classification of schizophrenia consists of biologically heterogeneous individuals. More specifically, these data pointed to a different etiologic basis for the concordant twins than the discordant pairs. The fact that a high rate of pathology was found among relatives of concordant twins indicated that their disorder was based on a hereditary defect; conversely, pathology in the disordered member of discordant pairs resulted from their environmental experiences.

Gottesman and Shields followed up Rosenthal's work in an impressive and well-designed study. They carefully selected 57 monozygotic twins and divided them into four categories graded in terms of degree of concordance with respect to schizophrenia. What they uncovered was a striking relationship between concordance and severity of illness. High concordance corresponded with severe schizophrenic symptomology and vice versa.

If we combine the findings of Gottesman and

Shields and Rosenthal, we may deduce the following: severe cases of schizophrenia are attributable largely to a genetic defect; milder forms of the disorder may be attributed only in part, if at all, to genetic factors. There are many more refinements in our understanding of the role of heredity in schizophrenia to be derived from future studies as well designed as these.

If we accept the evidence that genetic factors do operate in some forms of schizophrenia, we may then ask the question: what kind of genetic transmission (dominant or recessive) fits the data best?

We must proceed with caution in answering this question. The data we have are based on research that is considerably less well designed than that done by Rosenthal and by Gottesman and Shields. Perhaps we should say nothing on this score until a substantial body of carefully derived data has been accumulated. Despite this hesitation, it might be instructive to offer a few comments on the existent theories of genetic transmission, if for no other reason than to indicate their prematurity.

In order to assess the accuracy of a hypothesized mode of transmission it is necessary to calculate the theoretical expected rates of occurrence in various classes of relatives, and compare them to empirically obtained rates. The last two columns of Table 4-1 comprise the theoretical expectancies for dominant and recessive hypotheses (the figures listed assume complete penetrance and expressivity). As can be seen, the empirical figures for schizophrenia and manic-depressive disorders are appreciably less than the theoretical frequencies. The obtained rates appear closer to the recessivity hypothesis, but there is still a substantial margin of error.

Gregory (1960), reviewing the empirical evidence in terms of several alternative theoretical models, concluded that no single or major gene hypothesis is compatible with the data, even when supplemented by auxiliary concepts such as penetrance and expressivity. He suggests two alternate genetic hypotheses: (1) that these syndromes are heterogeneous, that is, they include several sub-varieties, each of which is produced by a different genetic mechanism, or (2) that at least part of the genetic component is polygenic in nature. Penrose, in an earlier paper (1950), remarked that the findings of empirical research do not fit a simple Mendelian pattern of inheritance, unless one accepts a number of questionable assumptions. He concludes that all theories of genetic mode of transmission in psychopathology will remain speculative until more and better research is done.

## EVALUATIVE COMMENTS

Despite ambiguities about the specific mode of transmission involved in psychopathology, there can be little question from the substantial body of data accumulated thus far that genetic factors do play a determinant role in certain disorders. However, these factors are not necessary conditions for all forms of psychopathology nor are they usually sufficient in themselves to elicit pathological behavior. They serve as a predispositional base which makes the individual susceptible to breakdown under environmental stress.

How should future research be planned in order to provide us with more definitive conclusions about the role of genetics? Two major problems must be overcome: the poor methodological design of earlier studies, and the inadequate criteria used in psychiatric diagnosis. These problems are not unique to genetic research. Here we will touch on them only briefly, leaving a more extensive discussion for later chapters.

1. Most genetic studies can be faulted on methodological grounds. Research designs rarely control for potentially confounding variables such as age, sex, socioeconomic level and ethnic group; statistical "adjustments" for these uncontrolled variations are only partially successful, and some authorities feel that these adjustments tend to inflate empirical figures. Whether the consequences of poor design have completely distorted the picture of the role of genetic factors is difficult to tell, but unless methodological problems such as these are carefully resolved our confidence in previous research must be restrained.

2. The usefulness of the current classification system as a basis for etiologic research may be questioned. The assumption that classification categories are homogenous groupings cannot be accepted. If these categories are heterogeneous collections of fundamentally different disorders, then the chances of discovering a common etiologic basis among them are well nigh impossible. An analogy may illustrate this point well. Let us assume that we are to discover the basic principles of a "game." The information we are given, however, consists of the actions of a football quarterback and guard, a baseball pitcher and first baseman, and the pivot man in basketball. Could we make sense, no less discover the basic principles unifying this hodgepodge of behavior?

The resulting confusion is comparable to what would occur if schizophrenia, for example, turns out to be three or more different disorders.

Most investigators accept the traditional diagnostic categories as homogeneous biological unities. The idea that Kraepelinian classification comprises a well-circumscribed disease entity is an attractive assumption for those who wish to find a Mendelian or single gene mode of inheritance. Scientists who seek a single gene difference corresponding to each Kraepelinian category have proposed theoretically archaic simplifications. Recent thinking forces us to question the validity of the Kraepelinian nosology and the adequacy of Mendelian ideas of genetic action. In brief, these early formulations are either erroneous or insufficient for the understanding of genetic factors in pathology. Genetic theorists must take cognizance of the newer concepts of genetic action, and researchers must recognize that traditional categories of pathology are not biologically discrete entities. Until this broader point of view takes hold, the chances of uncovering the precise etiologic significance of heredity will remain bogged down. We must acknowledge that defects in the infinitely complex central nervous system can arise from innumerable genetic anomalies. The different varieties of behavior we classify under the label "schizophrenia," for example, can arise from defects in a multitude of different genes and genetic combinations. Some of these behaviors may be transmitted by a single rare gene, others from the cumulative effects of multiple polygenes and still others may not reflect genetic factors at all.

We must remind ourselves, before closing our discussion of heredity, that genetics is only part of the etiologic story in psychopathology. Even convinced geneticists make reference to the notion of *phenocopies,* a concept signifying the observation that characteristics that usually are produced by genetic action can be simulated by environmental factors. In this concept, geneticists recognize that very similar forms of pathology may arise from genetic and from environmental sources. As such, the manifest picture of a disorder may give us no clue as to its origins. Similar appearances do not signify similar etiologies; biogenic and psychogenic sources can produce equivalent clinical pictures.

It is considered a basic principle among geneticists (David and Snyder, 1962) that the manifest behavior of an individual is a function both of his genetic make-up and the environment in which he develops. They note, further, that different genes vary in their responsiveness to environmental influences; some produce uniform effects under all environmental conditions, whereas the effects of other genes can be suppressed entirely in certain environments. Moreover, it appears highly probable that most genes have specialized effects at particular times during maturational development and that their interaction with environmental conditions is minimal before and after these "critical" periods. More will be said about these time sequence interactions in the next chapter.

It can be seen from the foregoing that pathology cannot be understood in terms of genetic formulations alone. Genetic factors interact with a complex pattern of environmental influences and play a part in promoting an intricate and continuous chain of events, each of which leads to its own sequence of secondary and tertiary consequences. Anastasi describes this network of effects as follows (1958):

> Unlike the blood groups, which are close to the level of primary gene products, psychological traits are related to genes by highly indirect and devious routes.
>
> [For example] heredity may influence behavior through the mechanism of social stereotypes. A wide variety of inherited physical characteristics have served as the visible cues for identifying such stereotypes. These cues thus lead to behavioral restrictions or opportunities and—at a more subtle level—to social attitudes and expectancies. The individual's own self concept tends gradually to reflect such expectancies. All of these influences eventually leave their mark upon his abilities and inabilities, his emotional reactions, goals, ambitions, and outlook on life.
>
> Moreover, hereditary influences cannot be dichotomized into the more direct and the less direct. Rather do they represent a whole "continuum of indirectness," along which are found all degrees of remoteness of causal links.
>
> It should be noted that as we proceed along the continuum of indirectness, the range of variation of possible outcomes of hereditary factors expands rapidly. At each step in the causal chain, there is fresh opportunity for interaction with other hereditary factors as well as with environmental factors. And since each interaction in turn determines the direction of subsequent interactions, there is an ever-widening network of possible outcomes. If we visualize a simple sequential grid with only two alternatives at each point, it is obvious that there are two possible outcomes in the one-stage situation, four outcomes at the second stage, eight at the third, and so on in geometric progression. The actual situation is undoubtedly much more complex, since there will usually be more than two alternatives at any one point.

In short, there is little prospect that psychopathologic science will advance unless investigators are willing to face the fact that genetic influences are infinitely more subtle and complex than they have assumed them to be.

# PRENATAL EXPERIENCE

The period of life between conception and birth, during which diseases and trauma in the uterine environment may upset the normal developmental sequence, has largely been neglected as a field of etiological investigation. Recently, however, researchers have turned to this vital period, but the results of their investigations have proved limited and equivocal to date. Nevertheless, a brief discussion of the rationale and some of the preliminary data gathered relative to intrauterine stress and later psychopathology may be instructive.

## RATIONALE

The organism does not begin its interaction with the environment at birth; birth is merely a transitional point in which the environment is radically changed. Most people assume erroneously that the prenatal environment is both uniform and ideal for all fetuses. This notion is incorrect; it is based on naive conceptions that fail to recognize the complexity and variability of uterine environments. Not only can certain diseases be transmitted directly to the fetus but subtle neurohormonal changes in the mother's chemistry may also disrupt the embryo's delicate nervous system.

Investigators interested in this problem have presented the following rationale for their work (Pasamanick and Knoblach, 1961). Pregnancy complications leading to injury of the nervous system usually result in fetal death but there remains a fraction that does not die. Depending on the degree and location of the damage, these survivors may develop any number of disorders. These range from well-defined symptoms of cerebral palsy and epilepsy to a variety of ill-defined disabilities that retard psychological development and increase the individual's susceptibility to stress.

There are a number of methodological problems in prenatal research. Ethical limits and technical difficulties in human fetal experimentation restrict studies to after-the-fact epidemiological methods. Such studies tend to produce biased data and cannot be used to draw definitive conclusions about the role of prenatal factors. Furthermore, there are an infinite number of complications that can arise during pregnancy and each of these may lead to a variety of complex and different defects. The varied disorders produced by these complications cannot be grouped into clear-cut disease entities; gross diagnostic categories such as "mental deficiency" and "behavior disorder" only pinpoint our ignorance. Until these defects are defined with greater precision, it will be exceedingly difficult to trace their specific etiologies.

## PATHOGENIC FACTORS

Events or agents which give origin to a disorder may be spoken of as pathogenic. In this section we will list and discuss a number of pathogenic factors which produce marked developmental deviations. These factors may upset different developmental processes, depending on their timing, severity and locus of action.

**Diseases.** Smallpox, rubella, scarlet fever, influenza, tuberculosis, toxoplasma and syphilis have been recorded among the pathogenic infectious agents, and high blood pressure and diabetes among the noninfectious diseases. The effect of these ailments upon physical development is usually quite severe; the most common outcome insofar as psychopathology is concerned are various forms of mental retardation.

**Nutritional Deficiencies.** Maternal dietary deficiencies can result in profound physical maldevelopments in the fetus. As regards psychopathology, however, the evidence is largely equivocal with the single exception of an insufficiency in iodine; this deficiency results in congenital *cretinism,* a hormonal disorder associated with severe mental retardation. There is reason to believe, however, that other nutritional deficiencies can produce subtle disruptions in neural development which might escape gross clinical observation.

**Drugs.** The massive intake of potent drugs and medicines which have flooded the pharmaceutical market in the last two decades has given rise to a justified concern about their effects on the unborn fetus. Data regarding specific psychopathological consequences are scanty, however. Nevertheless, it is not unreasonable to assume that disturbances in neural growth can result from these agents, producing a variety of ill-defined brain dysfunctions and susceptibilities to stress.

**Maternal Emotions.** Normal variations in maternal emotionality do not appear to affect the fetus. There is evidence, however, that marked and enduring maternal disturbances do influence fetal behavior and leave dispositional traits that persist beyond birth.

Sontag (1960), summarizing his clinical observations, concluded that disturbing experiences in pregnant mothers result in the birth of disturbed children; he hypothesized that emotional upsets produce neurohormonal imbalances which are transmitted directly to their fetuses. Thompson (1957) has gathered behavioral support for this view. He exposed a group of pregnant rats to frightening experiences and found that their offspring displayed more signs of fear in early postnatal life than did the offspring of a control group. Montague (1962) reported a similar study by Deevey and Keeley; these investigators compared the progeny of pregnant mice kept under crowded and uncrowded conditions and found that the offspring of the crowded mice were more anxious than the control offspring.

**Prematurity.** With the exception of a number of well-substantiated findings of a high incidence of cerebral palsy among premature infants, the evidence of its relation to psychopathology is minimal (MacMahon and Sowa, 1961). However, in a well-designed epidemiological study, Pasamanick and Knoblach (1961) found the frequency of serious neurological abnormalities to be significantly higher in prematures than in controls; they also found a high negative correlation between intellectual potential and degree of prematurity. Prematures displayed what these authors termed "minimal damage," a syndrome associated with a variety of childhood behavior and learning disorders.

**Perinatal Complications.** Difficulties of labor and birth, especially those associated with fetal anoxia (oxygen deprivation) and physical trauma, have been proposed as the source of psychopathology by a number of investigators. The data for this view are equivocal, however, with the exception of cerebral palsy (MacMahon and Sowa, 1961).

It has been noted that difficulties in delivery can arise as a result of a defect already present in the infant's prebirth make-up. For example, previous prenatal neurological damage may be responsible for the infant's difficulty in assuming independent respiration; thus, perinatal anoxia may be merely an insult *added* to an existent injury. There are many gaps in our knowledge of the role of these perinatal complications and additional research is needed to fill them.

## EVALUATIVE COMMENTS

Despite the paucity of definitive research, it would seem warranted to conclude that a continuum of defects, extending from severe to minimal neurological damage, can arise as a result of prenatal and perinatal complications. The pertinence of these defects to psychopathology will depend, of course, on their severity, type and location.

Perhaps of greater importance than the few profound consequences of marked prenatal damage are the pervasive effects of minor disturbances upon the infant's disposition and physical constitution. Maternal disease may diminish the infant's robustness and capacity to handle environmental stress; this may lead to a cycle of events which, in time, may produce behavior pathology. Essentially normal but sluggish or cranky infants will respond to their environment differently than robust infants; this initial weakness may set the stage for diseases, fatigue and even parental discomfort and rejection, each of which may lead to an intensification of the early disability. The circular effect of an infant's early characteristics and behaviors in producing potentially deleterious reactions from others will be discussed more fully in the following section.

# INFANTILE REACTION PATTERNS

Each infant enters the world with a distinctive pattern of behavior dispositions and reaction sensitivities. Every nurse knows that babies differ from the moment they are born, and every perceptive mother notices distinct differences in the behavior of her successive offspring. Some infants suck vigorously from the start; others seem indifferent, hold the nipple feebly and learn to suck slowly. Some infants have a definite cycle of hunger, elimination and sleep, whereas others vary unpredictably from one day to the next. Some twist and turn fitfully in their sleep, while others lie awake peacefully in the most hectic surroundings. Some are robust and energetic; others seem fearful and cranky.

## RATIONALE

Proving that babies are different may seem to be laboring the obvious, but the implications of the obvious may be overlooked. Scientists, for example, have been preoccupied with demonstrating common developmental patterns among infants (Gesell et al., 1940), whereas practitioners have focused on the unique attributes of their individual patients. In recent years, however, an effort has been made to bridge the gap between these two approaches. This new work reflects an interest not only in different patterns of infantile development but in the implications of these differences for later development. The questions posed by these recent investigations may be divided as follows:

1. Are there stable individual differences before postnatal experiences exert their influence, and do these differences persist into childhood?

2. Do these initial patterns have any bearing on the course of later personality characteristics or the development of psychopathology?

Both questions are pertinent to our study. We wish to know not only whether infants differ but whether a whole sequence of subsequent life experiences is associated with these initial differences. Infantile differences would be of little significance if they did not persist and establish a lifelong pattern of functioning.

Among other questions we must ask are (1) whether the experiences a child has are determined by his inborn capacities, temperament and energy; (2) whether his unique characteristics evoke distinctive reactions from his parents and sibs; and (3) whether these reactions have a beneficial or a detrimental effect upon his development. In short, rather than ask what effects the environment has upon the child, we might ask what effect he has on his environment and what the consequences of these are upon his personality development.

## RECENT RESEARCH

Stable patterns of behavior observed in the first few months of life are likely to be of biogenic rather than psychogenic origin. Thomas et al. (1963, 1968) speak of these infantile patterns as *primary* because they appear before postnatal experience can account for them. They have been labeled as *reaction patterns* rather than behavior patterns because they are characterized by the way the child reacts to stimuli, not by the content of behavior; the content of behavior changes with learning, but the basic style or pattern of reactions tends to remain constant.

### STABILITY OF BIOLOGICAL FUNCTIONS

Jost and Sontag (1944) found that infants show an inherited pattern of autonomic system re-

activity. Taking measures such as pulse, respiration, salivation and blood pressure, they were able to show that ordinary siblings are less alike than identical twins but more alike than unrelated children. Other investigators have reported stable infantile differences on such biological measures as sensory threshold (Bergman and Escalona, 1949), quality and intensity of emotional tone (Meili, 1959) and electroencephalographic waves (Walter, 1953).

Despite the value of these findings as evidence of stability in infantile functioning, it remains unclear as to which biological measures are likely to be pertinent to later personality. Our present knowledge of the relationship between physiological processes and behavior is sorely lacking. Thus, the biological variables of infancy that are relevant to future behavior will remain enigmatic until our basic knowledge of psychophysiology has advanced beyond its present stage.

### PERSISTENCE OF REACTION PATTERNS

Because psychophysiological knowledge is limited, investigators have turned their attention to the relationship between the overt behavior of infants and later personality development. The studies of two groups of collaborators, one associated with New York Medical School (Thomas et al., 1963, 1968) and the other with the Menninger Foundation in Kansas (Escalona and Leitch, 1953; Escalona and Heider, 1959; Murphy et al., 1962; Escalona, 1968), have been especially comprehensive and fruitful. They have contributed knowledge not only to an understanding of personality development in general but also to the development of psychopathology in particular. The ensuing discussion will focus on the findings and implications of their work.

Over a hundred infants were observed from birth through the early years of schooling. Reports were made on sleeping, eating, eliminating and a host of other ordinary situations common to infants. As they developed, these children were observed in their reactions to toilet training, learning to drink from a cup, starting to walk, reactions to strangers, trips to a store, being sick, playing with others, getting a pet and so on. With few exceptions, it was found that each infant had a recognizable and distinctive way of behaving in his first weeks of life which persisted through early childhood.

Some babies seemed to have been born with built-in alarm clocks; they did everything on a predictably regular schedule. Others followed a chaotic sequence in which their pattern of sleeping, waking, eliminating and eating changed from day to day. Some reached out for everything presented to them; others avoided anything new, be it food, people or toys. Some jumped at the turn of a door handle, whereas others were indifferent to overloud voices, hot milk and rough handling. Differences were noted in persistence and distractibility; some babies could be turned from their hunger pangs by cooing and soothing, while others remained adamant in their demands through all diversionary tactics.

In summary, there are several behavioral dimensions which differentiated the reaction patterns of infants. They differ in the regularity or irregularity of their basic biological functions; they differ in their autonomic system reactivity, as may be gauged by their initial response to new situations; they differ in their sensory alertness to external stimuli and in their adaptability to change; they display characteristic moods that are either negative or positive; they show differing overall "drive" levels and intensities of response and are different in their distractibility and persistence.

Although infants could be differentiated on each of these dimensions of behavior, one descriptive term seemed to summarize or tie together a number of the characteristics which were felt to be especially relevant, if not crucial, to later development: the infant's *activity* pattern (Murphy et al., 1962). Marked differences in vigor, tempo, smoothness and rhythm colored the infant's style and frequency of relating to his environment, and influenced the character of responses he evoked from others. Of course, all children displayed both active and passive tendencies but in most, one pattern predominated.

Active infants displayed decisiveness, selectivity and vigor; they maintained a continuous relatedness to their environment and were insistent that these relationships should be experienced in accordance with their desires. In contrast, passive infants displayed a more placid and receptive orientation; they appeared to be content to wait and see what was going to be done to meet their needs, and accepted matters until their desires were fulfilled. Of particular interest was the observation that the pattern of activity or passivity shaped the way in which the child learned to manipulate his environment. Active youngsters, for example, came into contact with more aspects of their environment, had more opportunities to develop relationships and interests and developed more ways of coping with frustration, but also encountered more obstacles and risked more failures.

Although early patterns were modified only slightly from infancy to childhood, it was made clear by both groups of researchers that this continuity could not be attributed entirely to the persistence of the infant's innate endowment. Subsequent experiences tend to reinforce characteristics which the infant displayed in early life. The impact of the infant's initial behavior transforms his environment in ways that intensify and accentuate these behaviors. An elaboration of this important notion will comprise our next topic.

## IMPLICATIONS FOR PERSONALITY DEVELOPMENT

There has been little systematic attention to the child's own contribution to the course of his development. Environmental theorists of psychopathology have viewed disorders to be the result of detrimental experiences that the individual has had no part in producing himself. This is a gross simplification. Each infant possesses a biologically based pattern of reaction sensitivities and behavioral dispositions which shape the nature of his experiences and may contribute directly to the creation of environmental difficulties.

It is a stubborn but inescapable fact that the interweaving of biological dispositions with environmental experience is not a simple and readily disentangled web; it is a complicated and intricate feedback system of criss-crossing influences in which the role of each specific etiological agent must be viewed in light of its relationship to the others. Two facets of this interactive system will be elaborated because of their special pertinence to the development of pathology: the relationships between infantile reaction patterns and (1) adaptive learning and (2) social reinforcement.

### ADAPTIVE LEARNING

*The biological dispositions of the maturing child are important because they strengthen the probability that certain kinds of behavior will be learned.*

Highly active and responsive children relate to and learn about their environment quickly. Their liveliness, zest and power may lead them to a high measure of personal gratification. Conversely, their energy and exploratory behavior may result in excess frustration if they overaspire or run into insuperable barriers; unable to gratify their activity needs effectively, they may grope and strike out in erratic and maladaptive ways.

Adaptive learning in constitutionally passive

children also is shaped by their biological equipment. Ill-disposed to deal with their environment assertively and little inclined to discharge their tensions physically, they may learn to avoid conflicts and step aside when difficulties arise. They are less likely to develop guilt feelings about misbehavior than active youngsters who more frequently get into trouble, receive more punishment and are therefore inclined to develop aggressive feelings toward others. But in their passivity, these youngsters may deprive themselves of rewarding experiences and relationships; they may feel "left out of things" and become dependent on others to fight their battles and to protect them from experiences they are ill-equipped to handle on their own.

The thesis that biological patterns are instrumental in the development of adaptive learning is shared by theorists of considerably different persuasions. Behaviorists (Eysenck, 1947, 1957; Franks, 1956) and ego-analysts (Rapaport, 1951; Hartmann, 1958) alike have made this theme a cornerstone of their theories of psychopathology. The studies reported by Thomas et al., Escalona and Murphy add important empirical evidence in support of their views. In later chapters we will expand and illustrate this notion more fully.

### SOCIAL REINFORCEMENT

It appears clear from studies of early patterns of reactivity that *infantile behaviors evoke counterreactions from others which accentuate these initial dispositions.* The child's biological endowment shapes not only his behavior but that of his parents as well.

If the infant's primary disposition is cheerful and adaptable and has made his care easy, the mother will tend quickly to display a positive reciprocal attitude; conversely, if the child is tense and wound up, or if his care is difficult and time consuming, the mother will react with dismay, fatigue or hostility. Through his own behavioral disposition then, the child elicits a series of parental behaviors which reinforce his initial pattern. The manner in which minor features of initial behavior can be strengthened and magnified is illustrated in this quotation (Chess et al., 1960):

It is not infrequently apparent that the disturbed functioning represents an accentuation and distortion of characteristics of primary reactivity to the point of caricature. For example, there are many cases in which the parents respond with growing annoyance and pressure to the manifestations of initial negative mood and withdrawal. The child's response of negativism and increased negative mood to these parental attitudes can produce a vicious cycle which can finally lead to defensive hostility with constant projections of derogation and aggression. Thus we may obtain as an end product an individual with motivated aggressive and hostile behavior who shows a highly suspicious reaction to anything new, be it a person, place or activity. He makes contact by attacking and assumes that every personal contact must involve an overt or hidden antagonism on the other person's part.

Unfortunately, the reciprocal interplay of primary patterns and parental reactions has not been sufficiently explored. It may prove to be one of the most fruitful spheres of research concerning the etiology of psychopathology and merits the serious attention of investigators. The *biosocial approach* that characterizes much of this book stems largely from the thesis that the child's primary reaction pattern shapes and interacts with his social reinforcement experiences.

### EVALUATIVE COMMENTS

Before leaving the present topic, it must be emphasized that innate dispositions can be reversed by strong environmental pressures. A cheerful and optimistic outlook can be crushed by parental contempt and ridicule. Conversely, shy and reticent children may become more self-confident and outgoing in a thoroughly encouraging and accepting family atmosphere.

A further obstacle to the assumption that primary patterns will persist throughout life is our recognition that maturation rates differ from child to child. Not all features of an individual's capacity are activated at the moment of birth. One's potentials may unfold only gradually as maturation progresses. Thus, a number of biologically rooted reactivity patterns may not emerge until the youngster is well past infancy. It is not inconceivable that late-blooming patterns may supplant those displayed earlier. This sequence in the maturation of reaction patterns is a virgin field of study and one which must be explored thoroughly if we are to grasp the full nature of biogenic determinants.

The recognition of the intimate interplay of infantile reactivity patterns and parental counterreactions, though important, is in itself insufficient for an etiological analysis. It is necessary to go one step further and identify those particular types of interactions which are conducive to pathological development. It would be wrong to assume that all children possessing a given reactivity pattern become disordered, since there is ample evidence to the effect that children of closely similar temperaments to those suffering pathology often function normally. Thomas and

Murphy describe several patterns which are frequent precursors of pathology, but they note that the outcome of some youngsters with these unpromising beginnings has been good. A crucial determinant, according to their observations, is parental acceptance of the child's individuality. They believe that parents who learn to accept their child's temperament, and then modify their attitudes and practices accordingly, can deter what otherwise would be pathological. Conversely, if parents are confronted daily with feelings of failure, frustration, anger and guilt, they will contribute to a progressive worsening of the child's adjustment.

These comments bring us back once more to the recognition that biogenic and psychogenic factors interact in complex and varied ways. In the following sections, which deal primarily with biogenic factors in adults, we will see the operation of this interplay again.

# MORPHOLOGICAL STRUCTURE

Heredity and prenatal experience produce not only an initial infantile reaction pattern but a whole constellation of dispositions which endure throughout life. This deeply ingrained pattern of characteristics, referred to as the individual's *constitution,* represents those features of bodily structure and physiology which exert a constant or uniform influence upon behavior and personality development. They are relatively fixed characteristics of an individual's make-up and can be contrasted to other attributes of functioning which are more flexible and more susceptible to modification through experience and learning (e.g., habits, attitudes and values).

There are many characteristics in man which show both marked variability between individuals and relative constancy within single individuals (e.g., height, weight, skin color, hair color and eye color). Only a few of these, however, are relevant to personality growth or psychopathology.

Two broad classes of constitutional factors have been considered relevant by theorists and researchers. The first deals with the *structural composition* of the body; these range from minute anatomical features, such as the histological attributes of brain cells, to characteristics of gross morphology, like body size, body configuration and the relative distribution of muscle, fat and bone. The second sphere of investigation relates to *physiological functioning;* this involves the study of the neurological organization of the autonomic and central nervous systems, as well as the endocrinological and biochemical processes with which they are associated.

One comment should be made as a *précis* to our discussion. Many psychologists display resistance and hostility to the notion that constitutional factors can be related significantly to behavior and development. They are preoccupied with environmental sources of stimulation that change or modify behavior and they evidence a disinclination to consider proposals which imply that certain aspects of behavior may be immutable. Consequently, neither the conceptions nor the data gathered in accord with constitutional theory have marshalled much support in the field. This is most unfortunate. It would befit an experimental science to welcome and judge the results of "alien" fields of research with the same standards it uses for its more cherished notions. Narrow-mindedness among psychologists in this sphere is unfortunate also since the study of behavior change must be founded on a recognition of the limits and dispositions to behavior.

More has been speculated about the association between gross body morphology and behavior than any of the other, more hidden and intricate facets of constitutional make-up. The visibility of our body physique lends it to ready observation and measurement, and accounts for its having served as a convenient starting point for constitutional hypotheses. We will begin our review of the role of biogenic factors in adulthood with theories and findings about this relationship.

## RATIONALE

Shakespeare, a notably perceptive observer of human character, wrote these words in *Julius Caesar:*

> Let me have men about me that are fat;
> Sleek-headed men and such as sleep o'nights:
> Yon Cassius has a lean and hungry look;
> He thinks too much; such men are dangerous.

Observant men since times of antiquity have noted that bodily form and structure were related to particular dispositions and patterns of behavior. What rationale can be offered to account for this relationship?

Biogenic theorists are inclined to believe that correlations between physique and behavior result from the joint operation of linked genes. Body morphology and temperamental disposition may be coupled on the same chromosome or may be produced by the combined action of a single set of genes. Sex-linked characteristics (e.g., height, body form and hirsuteness) arising from associated genetic sources are a well-known phenomenon. In the same manner, associated genes may produce correlated bodily and behavioral attributes. For example, the thesis of a joint genetic basis for morphology and behavior may be illustrated in the disorder known as Down's syndrome (mongolism). Here, distinct physical attributes (slanted eyes and short and squat build) are associated with a particular form of mental retardation; both the morphological and behavioral aspects of this syndrome are consequences of a single anomaly in chromosomal structure.

The constitutional biogenic thesis can be summarized simply: specific biological determinants simultaneously influence both physique and behavior; these determinants account for correlations observed between them.

## MORPHOLOGICAL MEASURES

A question arises as to which features of body structure and form best characterize an individual's constitutional make-up. Despite differences in detail, there is a consensus among constitutional theorists as to the significance of three major dimensions: fat, muscularity and linearity. Before this century, these three features of morphology were put into a three-fold typology in which individuals were classified in accordance with the dominant feature they display. Table 4-2 presents an historical summary of the terms

### Table 4-2 Comparison of Classification of Physical Types*

| INVESTIGATOR | TYPE 1: Fat Dominance | TYPE 2: Muscle Dominance | TYPE 3: Linearity Dominance |
|---|---|---|---|
| Hippocrates (460–400 B.C.) | H. apoplecticus | — | H. pthisicus |
| Rostan (1828) | Digestive | Muscular | Respiratory-cerebral |
| Beneke (1876) | Rachitic | Carcinomatous | Scrofulous-phthisical |
| di Giovanni (1880) | 3rd Comb. | 2nd Comb. | 1st Comb. |
| Manouvrier (1902) | Brachyskeletal | Mesoskeletal | Macroskeletal |
| Virenius (1904) | Connective | Muscular | Epithelial |
| Stiller (1907) | — | Hypertonic | Atonic |
| Sigaud (1908) | Digestive | Muscular | Respiratory-cerebral |
| Bean (1912) | Hypo-entomorph | Meso-entomorph | Hyper-entomorph |
| Bryant (1915) | Herbivorous | Normal | Carnivorous |
| Mills (1917) | Hypersthenic | Sthenic | Asthenic |
| Viola (1919) | Macrosplanchnic | Normosplanchnic | Microsplanchnic |
| Kretschmer (1921) | Pyknic | Athletic | Leptosomatic |
| Bauer (1924) | Hypersthenic | Sthenic | Asthenic |
| Aschner (1924) | Broad | Normal | Slender |
| Bounak (1924) | Euryplastic | — | Stenoplastic |
| McAuliffe (1925) | Round | — | Flat |
| Stockard (1925) | Lateral | Intermediate | Linear |
| Draper (1925) | Gall bladder | — | Ulcer |
| Weidenreich (1926) | Eurysome | — | Leptosome |
| Pearl (1926) | Pyknic | Intermediate | Asthenic |
| Pende (1927) | Macrosplanchnic | Normosplanchnic | Microsplanchnic |
| Von Rohden (1928) | Endodermic | Mesodermic | Ectodermic |
| Boldrini | Brachytype | — | Longitype |
| Wiersma (1933) | Eurysomic | — | Leptosomic |
| Sheldon (1940) | Endomorph | Mesomorph | Ectomorph |
| Conrad (1941) | Pyknomorphy | Metromorphy | Leptomorphy |
| Burt (1947) | Pachysome | — | Leptosome |
| Martigny (1948) | Entoblastique | Mesoblastique | Ectoblastique |
| Hammond (1953) | Pachymorph | — | Leptomorph |
| Hammond (1957) | Eurysome | Mesosome | Leptosome |
| Rees and Eysenck (1945) and Rees (1950) | Eurymorph | Mesomorph | Leptomorph |
| Lindegard (1953) | Fat factor high | Muscle and sturdiness factors high | Length factor high |
| Parnell (1957) | Fat factor (F) dominant | Muscle factor (M) dominant | Linear factor (L) dominant |

* From Eysenck (1961)

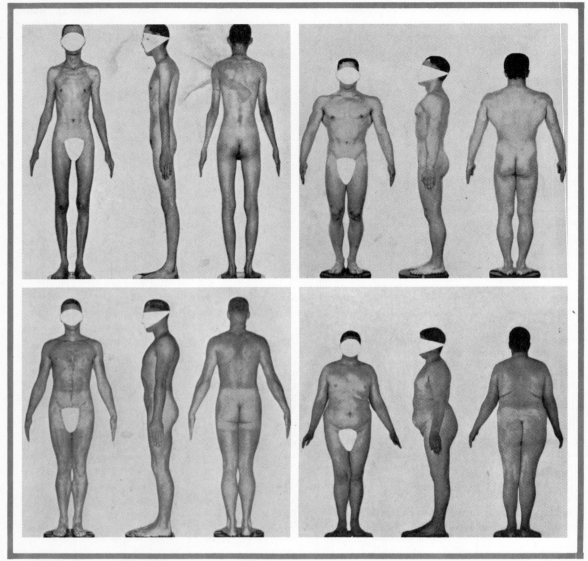

Figure 4-1    Photographs of somatotype extremes. (From Sheldon, W. H.: Atlas of Men. New York, Hafner Publishing Co., 1970.)

that have been coined to represent these typologies.

In recent years, theorists have recognized the naiveté of dividing people into distinct body types. There are a few individuals, of course, who display a marked dominance of one of these morphological features, but the greatest part of the population displays a mixture of all three in varying combinations. It appeared wise, therefore, to devise methods by which the proportionate relationship among these components could be gauged.

Best known among these methods are Sheldon's photographic techniques (1940, 1942, 1949, 1954) in which the magnitude of each of the three body dimensions is rated (anthroscopy) or measured (anthropometry). Sheldon refers to these dimensions as *endomorphy,* in which a predominance of roundness and softness in body structure is evident; *mesomorphy,* which is characterized by muscular and connective tissue dominance; and *ectomorphy,* in which a linearity and fragility of structure is manifest without fat or muscular strength. Each component is measured on a seven point scale, resulting in a *somatotype,* or quantified index of body physique. Extreme endomorphs, for example, are listed as 7-1-1, signifying their marked obesity, minimal endowment of muscularity and a lack of linearity or delicacy of structure. A well-balanced physique would be rated as 4-4-4 somatotype. As is evident, a variety of physical types can be incorporated in this tripolar scheme (Figure 4-1).

Both the technique and the variables proposed by Sheldon have been criticized. For example, his dependence on photographs seemed too restrictive to Lindegard (1953, 1956) for an adequate constitutional analysis. As an alternative, Lindegard developed a system composed of four major factors: length, sturdiness, fat and muscle. In addition to these anthropometric ratings, he obtained direct measures of performance on a number of tasks. Thus, muscularity was measured not only by structural characteristics but also by dynamometers, hand grip, shoulder pull and shoulder thrust. Other researchers (Rees and Eysenck, 1945; Rees, 1961) have included as many as 30 body indices which they combine and weigh by means of factor-analytic techniques.

New components and refined statistical techniques are promising advances in constitutional research, but they have not solved the problem of specifying which physical dimensions are most pertinent to behavior and pathology. As more variables drawn from measures of internal body composition and biomechanics are incorporated, and as new statistical techniques are applied in analysis, the precision and power inherent in the constitutional approach may fully be realized. Until then, the durable tripolar schema formulated in ancient times, as refined by Sheldon, will remain the primary tool.

## THEORIES RELATING MORPHOLOGY AND PSYCHOPATHOLOGY

The long history of body classification and its relation to behavior has been summarized in detail by Sheldon, Stevens and Tucker (1940). As they show, the earliest attempts were entirely subjective.

Hippocrates, the forerunner of many contemporary ideas in medicine, separated men into two categories: the short, heavy and strong; and the tall, slight and weak. These physical types, he felt, differed in their susceptibility to diseases. Hippocrates suggested also that men could be divided into four basic temperaments according to their dominant bodily humors, but he failed to connect his body typology to these temperamental categories. Several centuries later, Galen formulated a scheme in which Hippocrates' four humors were related to variations in body form. This suggestive thesis was not completed and the notion remained dormant until recently. Proposals

were made in the intervening years in which Hippocrates' two-fold body typology was extended and refined (Rostan, 1828; Viola, 1932). The work of Lombroso on criminal types (1889, 1911) was the first systematic attempt, however, to revive Galen's hypothesized relation between behavior and physical constitution.

### KRETSCHMER

The modern trend in constitutional psychology began with the seminal ideas and research of Ernst Kretschmer (1925). In his practice as a psychiatrist, Kretschmer observed a frequent association between certain physical types and particular forms of mental disorder. Prompted by this cursory impression, he set out systematically to categorize individuals according to their dominant physical build and to relate these categories to the two major Kraepelinian disorders of schizophrenia and manic-depressive psychosis. As a third objective, Kretschmer sought to relate physique to normal behavior dispositions.

His physical classification scheme resulted in four types: the *pyknic,* which he described as a compact individual with a large, round head, large thorax and abdomen, soft and poorly muscled limbs and a marked tendency to obesity; the *athletic,* noted for his extensive muscular development and broad skeletal endowment; the *asthenic,* viewed as a fragile individual possessing thin muscularity and a frail bone structure; and the *dysplastic,* which reflected Kretschmer's recognition that the first three types may be mixed in an awkwardly constructed physique.

Using his constitutional system as a basis, Kretschmer rated the physiques of 175 schizophrenics and 85 manic-depressives. His results, presented in Table 4-3, led him to conclude that

Table 4-3  Kretschmer's Physique Types and Psychopathology*

| TYPE | NUMBER OF CASES | |
|---|---|---|
| | Manic-Depressive | Schizophrenic |
| Asthenic | 4 | 81 |
| Athletic | 3 | 31 |
| Asthenic-athletic mixed | 2 | 11 |
| Pyknic | 58 | 2 |
| Pyknic mixture | 14 | 3 |
| Dysplastic | — | 34 |
| Deformed and uncategorized | 4 | 13 |
| | 85 | 175 |

\* From Kretschmer (1925)

there was a clear biological affinity between manic-depressives and the pyknic body build, and a comparable relationship between schizophrenia and the asthenic, athletic and dysplastic types.

To Kretschmer, psychotic disorders were accentuations of normal personality types. He suggested a gradation of temperamental dispositions progressing from pathological schizophrenia to moderately afflicted schizoids to adequately adjusted schizothymic personalities. In a like fashion, cycloids were viewed as moderately ill variants of manic-depressive psychosis, and cyclothymic personalities as essentially normal individuals displaying mild features similar to the more severe types.

Kretschmer's evidence of an association between physique and psychosis, combined with his assumption of continuity between normality and pathology, led him to speculate on the existence of a general relationship between body structure and temperament. Specifically, he contended that normal asthenic individuals would be introversive, timid and lacking in personal warmth, that is, a milder variant of the withdrawn and unresponsive schizophrenics to which they were akin. Normal pyknics were conceived as gregarious, friendly and dependent in their interpersonal relations, that is, a less extreme form of the moody and socially excitable manic-depressive.

Kretschmer's proposal of a graded relationship between body build and behavioral disposition was an imaginative extension of previous constitutional ideas. Unfortunately, he offered no systematic or quantifiable evidence in support of this assertion, nor did he offer a biogenic explanation of why one individual of a particular physique remained normal while a similarly built individual succumbed to a psychosis.

Other criticisms have been leveled at Kretschmer's hypotheses and methodology. For example, he failed to control for the typical age difference between patients classified as schizophrenics and those diagnosed as manic-depressives; the older manic-depressive may be heavier since age usually is associated with an increment in weight. Thus, schizophrenics may have been found to be thinner (asthenic) because they are younger; and manic-depressives fatter (pyknic) because they are older.

Despite the methodological complications which limit the value of Kretschmer's work, he provided more imaginative insights into the association between constitution and behavior than his predecessors. His painstaking research, albeit deficient, served to stimulate more refined quantitative work by others.

## SHELDON

The most notable figure in contemporary constitutional psychology is the research psychiatrist, William H. Sheldon. A brief review of his morphological schema was presented in an earlier section. Here we will outline his hypotheses concerning the relationship between body physique, temperament and psychopathology.

Sheldon contends that the diversity and complexity of man's manifest behavior should be viewed as surface features of a small number of underlying factors. In his search for these basic dimensions he constructed a typology of *temperaments,* that is, persistent dispositions and reaction patterns to the environment that are rooted in the individual's make-up. The temperament scale devised by Sheldon was constructed and rated in a fashion similar to his somatotype system. He narrowed an original list of over 650 traits by correlational analysis to a group of 60 items divided into three clusters of 20 each. Table 4-4 outlines the final items included in the scale.

Sheldon termed the three temperament clusters, viscerotonia, somatotonia and cerebrotonia; they were viewed as parallel to his three basic somatotypes.

The *viscerotonic* component, which parallels endomorphy in Sheldon's theory, is characterized by gregariousness, easy expression of feeling and emotion, love of comfort and relaxation, avoidance of pain and dependence on social approval. *Somatotonia,* the counterpart to mesomorphy, is noted by assertiveness, physical energy, low anxiety, indifference to pain, courage, social callousness and a need for action and power when troubled. *Cerebrotonia,* corresponding to ectomorphy, is defined by a tendency toward restraint, self-consciousness, introversion, social awkwardness, and a desire for solitude when troubled.

How does Sheldon relate these measures of somatotype and temperament to psychopathology?

Sheldon attempted at first to correlate measures of morphology with the traditional system of psychiatric diagnosis and found that the traditional system of diagnosis was inadequate for his purposes (1949). In particular, he rejected the conventional notion in psychiatry of discrete diagnostic categories (e.g., patients were classified as suffering either from manic-depressive psychosis, *or* paranoid schizophrenia *or* catatonic schizophrenia). He proposed, in their stead, that a series of continuous or gradated dimensions should be substituted for the notion of discrete disease entities. Toward this end, he developed three primary components of psychopathology which coexist, in varying proportions, in each disturbed individual; these components parallel not only his somatotype and temperament measures but also psychotic categories found in the traditional classification system (Figure 4-2).

The first psychiatric component is termed *affective*; it is found in its extreme form among manic-depressive patients. Sheldon postulates a high relationship between this component, the endomorphic physique, and the viscerotonic temperament. According to his formulation, the affective component is characterized by a low threshold of behavioral reaction and emotional expression resulting from a weakened or feeble inhibitory capacity. Sheldon speaks of this defect as a pathologically uncontrolled expression of the viscerotonic temperament. With minimal prompt-

ing these individuals display either marked elation or intense dejection, depending on the nature of their immediate environment. The depressed patient is slowed down, overrelaxed, overdependent and overly expressive of his melancholy feelings. During a manic stage, the patient is keyed up, uninhibited, maladaptively hyperactive, euphoric, and overly suggestible.

The *paranoid* component corresponds both in title and in its most intense form of expression with the traditional diagnostic category of the same name. Sheldon proposes that this component corresponds both with mesomorphy and somatotonia. It reflects a "fighting against something," a driving antagonism and resentment which is projected against the environment. Thus, the power delusions and ideas of persecution which

## Table 4-4  Sheldon's Temperament Scale*

| VISCEROTONIA | | SOMATOTONIA | | CEREBROTONIA | |
|---|---|---|---|---|---|
| ( )† | 1. Relaxation in posture and movement | ( ) | 1. Assertiveness of posture and movement | ( ) | 1. Restraint in posture and movement, tightness |
| ( ) | 2. Love of physical comfort | ( ) | 2. Love of physical adventure | | 2. Physiological over-response |
| ( ) | 3. Slow reaction | ( ) | 3. The energetic characteristic | ( ) | 3. Overly fast reactions |
| | 4. Love of eating | ( ) | 4. Need and enjoyment of exercise | ( ) | 4. Love of privacy |
| | 5. Socialization of eating | | 5. Love of dominating. Lust for power | ( ) | 5. Mental overintensity. Hyper-attentionality. Apprehensiveness |
| | 6. Pleasure in digestion | ( ) | 6. Love of risk and chance | ( ) | 6. Secretiveness of feeling, emotional restraint |
| ( ) | 7. Love of polite ceremony | ( ) | 7. Bold directness of manner | ( ) | 7. Self-conscious mobility of the eyes and face |
| ( ) | 8. Sociophilia | ( ) | 8. Physical courage for combat | ( ) | 8. Sociophobia |
| | 9. Indiscriminate amiability | ( ) | 9. Competitive aggressiveness | ( ) | 9. Inhibited social address |
| | 10. Greed for affection and approval | | 10. Psychological callousness | | 10. Resistance to habit and poor routinizing |
| | 11. Orientation to people | | 11. Claustrophobia | | 11. Agoraphobia |
| ( ) | 12. Evenness of emotional flow | | 12. Ruthlessness, freedom from squeamishness | | 12. Unpredictability of attitude |
| ( ) | 13. Tolerance | ( ) | 13. The unrestrained voice | ( ) | 13. Vocal restraint and general restraint of noise |
| ( ) | 14. Complacency | | 14. Spartan indifference to pain | | 14. Hypersensitivity to pain |
| | 15. Deep sleep | | 15. General noisiness | | 15. Poor sleep habits, chronic fatigue |
| ( ) | 16. The untempered characteristic | ( ) | 16. Overmaturity of appearance | ( ) | 16. Youthful intentness of manner and appearance |
| ( ) | 17. Smooth, easy communication of feeling, extraversion of viscerotonia | | 17. Horizontal mental cleavage, extraversion of somatotonia | | 17. Vertical mental cleavage, introversion |
| | 18. Relaxation and sociophilia under alcohol | | 18. Assertiveness and aggression under alcohol | | 18. Resistance to alcohol and to other depressant drugs |
| | 19. Need of people when troubled | | 19. Need of action when troubled | | 19. Need of solitude when troubled |
| | 20. Orientation toward childhood and family relationships | | 20. Orientation toward goals and activities of youth | | 20. Orientation toward the later periods of life |

\* From Sheldon (1942)
† The 30 traits with parentheses constitute collectively the short form of the scale.

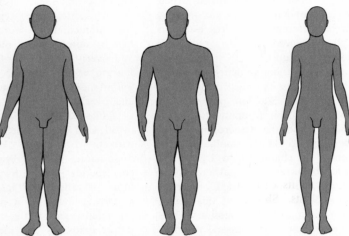

| SOMATOTYPE | ENDOMORPHY | MESOMORPHY | ECTOMORPHY |
|---|---|---|---|
| | Soft and round | Muscular and solid | Lean and fragile |
| TEMPERAMENT | VISCEROTONIA | SOMATOTONIA | CEREBROTONIA |
| | Comfort-loving, pleasure and people oriented | Assertive and competitive, socially callous, action oriented | Emotionally restrained, apprehensive, solitude oriented |
| PSYCHIATRIC COMPONENT | AFFECTIVE | PARANOID | HEBOID |
| | Fluctuates between elation and Depression | Has hostility and delusions of persecution | Is socially withdrawn and indulges in autistic fantasy |

Figure 4-2    Relationships between Sheldon's three somatotypes, temperaments and psychiatric components.

characterize paranoid psychotics can be seen as extremes of this dimension. The patient views his associates as persecutors and as legitimate objects for his scorn and defiance. If he is physically capable, he will be overtly aggressive and arrogant; if he is weak or otherwise deterred from manifesting his hostility, he will use circuitous methods of attack, or become preoccupied ideationally with feelings of persecution. Common to all who possess this component, according to Sheldon, is a "singular lack of compassion," an inability to find joy in social amenities, minimal fulfillment in social situations, intolerance of others, and an inability to achieve reciprocally satisfying personal relationships.

The third component, referred to by Sheldon as *heboid,* is typified by marked withdrawal and regression, features characteristic of the traditional psychiatric diagnosis of hebephrenic schizophrenia. It is found in ectomorphic individuals, according to Sheldon, since these individuals lack both energy and viscerotonic affect. The drive to act, to accomplish and to compete is deficient. In extreme form, the patient learns to relinquish what little affect and energy he may possess as a

means of avoiding the disastrous consequences of his feeble efforts to utilize these attributes. Rather than chance continued failure with his ill-equipped constitution, he withdraws from active social participation and regresses into an infantile state of dependency.

Sheldon's contention that the traditional notion of discrete categories of mental diseases has deterred the effective study of etiology is supported by theorists of considerably different persuasions. His taxonomical system of a continuum of gradated psychiatric components which combine in varying proportions within a single individual is an important contribution not only to constitutional theory but also to our general thinking about mental disorders. Sheldon admits, however, that more research must be done before his specific proposals can be viewed as fully objective and quantitative. Until then we can accept his notions as plausible, although not confirmed.

## RECENT RESEARCH

Few of the empirical studies relating physique to pathology have been well designed. Some of the methodological defects in Kretschmer's work were noted earlier; similar design problems have plagued researchers since. Despite these faults, the results of morphological research have been so impressive that dismissing their findings on methodological grounds alone would appear unwise.

In one of the few well-designed studies relevant to psychopathology, Sheldon set out to explore the correspondence between somatotype and his three psychiatric components (Wittman, Sheldon and Katz, 1948). He devised a checklist for rating each of these components after carefully screening the descriptive records of hospitalized patients; the items finally selected were then organized in terms of his three-fold cluster schema. Two clinicians reviewed and rated the records of 155 psychiatric patients while Sheldon *independently* somatotyped each of these patients; neither the clinicians nor Sheldon saw the patients nor did they have access to each other's judgments. A remarkable consistency was shown in the independent ratings of the clinicians (correlations of +.78 to +.91). Of greater significance, however, were the impressive correlations found between the rated psychiatric components and the independently measured somatotypes; the results are presented in Table 4-5.

Although three of Sheldon's minor expectations were not supported, the major hypotheses of significant relations between endomorphy-affective, mesomorphy-paranoid and ectomorphy-heboid were confirmed. As Sheldon anticipated, there was a complicated pattern of the correlations among these variables, signifying that pathology and morphology are related neither in a simple nor a clear-cut fashion.

Rees (1957, 1961), reviewing the research literature on morphology and psychopathology, concluded that a well-established relationship exists between schizophrenia and ectomorphy and between manic-depressive disorders and endomorphy. He noted further that ectomorphs appear to succumb to their illness at an earlier age, display more marked regressive and withdrawal behavior and follow a more progressive course of deterioration than either endomorphs or mesomorphs.

In the sphere of antisocial behavior, Sheldon (1949) and Glueck and Glueck (1962) conducted longitudinal studies of delinquent youngsters, and found impressive correlations with morphology. Sheldon reported the majority of delinquents to be either mesomorphs or endomorphic-mesomorphs. Glueck and Glueck, comparing delinquents with matched normals, discovered 60 per cent of the delinquents to be mesomorphic, a

**Table 4-5  Correlations Between Sheldon's Somatotypes and Psychiatric Components***

| SOMATOTYPE | PSYCHIATRIC COMPONENT | | |
| --- | --- | --- | --- |
| | Affective | Paranoid | Heboid |
| Endomorphy | +.54 | −.04 | −.25 |
| Mesomorphy | +.41 | +.57 | −.68 |
| Ectomorphy | −.59 | −.34 | +.64 |

* From Wittman, Sheldon and Katz (1948)

figure twice that of the normal group. Less than 15 per cent of the delinquents were ectomorphic, whereas more than 40 per cent of the normals were so grouped. Each of these studies supports the general thesis that body build and deviant forms of behavior are related.

## EVALUATIVE COMMENTS

Two issues must be raised in appraising the research and the hypotheses of morphological theory. The first concerns the methodological shortcomings of most constitutional studies; the second concerns the possibility that psychogenic interpretations can account for relationships found between physique and behavior.

**Methodological Criticisms.**  The data supporting constitutional theory are compelling, but they rest in large measure on methodologically weak research. For example, Kretschmer's ratings were highly subjective, and Sheldon's photographic procedure provided only a surface impression of the complex structure and functional attributes of body morphology. More important, few investigators used adequate controls to guard against the effects of confounding variables. Thus, relationships between endomorphy and manic-depressive psychosis can be attributed, at least in part, to the fact that patients so classified tend to be older than schizophrenics and that people tend to get heavier with age. Similarly, socioeconomic factors are associated both with diagnostic decisions and nutrition, e.g., lower class patients tend to be classified as schizophrenics and have poorer nutritional histories, which may result in ectomorphic physiques. Another telling methodological criticism is the fact that ratings of behavior and physical somatotype were not done independently in many studies, thereby producing spuriously high correlations. For example, an ectomorph may have been rated as withdrawn, self-conscious, restrained and apprehensive because the rater, having an opportunity to observe the patient's physique, was inclined unconsciously to interpret the patient's behavior in this fashion.

Although it is difficult to design a study well, careful controls and proper procedures are necessary if we are to accept the findings of research with confidence. Poorly designed investigations, contaminated with procedural errors and confounding variables, clutter the literature and mislead generations of future researchers.

**Psychogenic Interpretations.** The association between morphology and behavior can reasonably be explained by a number of psychogenic hypotheses; the genetic linkage hypothesis, presented earlier, must be viewed as only one of a number of alternate interpretive possibilities. A review of some of these alternate hypotheses will be instructive, not in that they disprove the validity of the genetic theory, but in that they suggest that the association between morphology and behavior may be the result of the joint action of both biogenic and psychogenic mechanisms.

1. Environmental influences may have a simultaneous effect upon both behavior and physique. For example, overprotective mothers tend to train their children to be emotionally responsive and dependent. Overprotectiveness often leads also to excessive feeding and consequent obesity. Thus, this type of maternal behavior can produce both an endomorphic physique and a viscerotonic (emotionally expressive and socially dependent) temperament. As another example, economic deprivation may give rise to self-consciousness and social withdrawal (cerebrotonic characteristics), as well as to nutritional deficiencies which lead to an ectomorphic physique. This formulation bypasses the contribution of biogenic determinants entirely by proposing that specific environmental conditions can account fully for both physique and behavior.

2. Another psychogenic explanation stresses the influence of social stereotypes and role expectations. Individuals whose physical characteristics fit certain commonly held notions and superstitions such as the "fat, jolly man" or the "mean-tempered redhead" will be expected to play the behavioral role expected of them. Many individuals, reinforced by social expectations, and given implicit sanction to display the expected behaviors, learn to conform to the stereotype. For example, the rotund and cherubic endomorph is not only expected to be jolly and gregarious but he finds that this behavior is rewarded handsomely. Thus, the congruence we observe between physique and behavior may be the result of reinforcing social stereotypes rather than common biological influences.

3. A third psychogenic interpretation recognizes the fact that physical structure facilitates or limits the kinds of behaviors an individual will learn. In other words, to be endowed with a certain body build increases the probability that certain types of behaviors will be successful, while others will fail. Just as it is unlikely for an intellectually deficient youngster to find advanced mathematics rewarding, so too is it improbable that a frail ectomorph will find his efforts at bluff and aggression successful. No matter how persistent a "97 pound weakling" may be, he cannot expect to be able "to push around the boys on the beach." Conversely, it would be quite feasible for an energetic and robust mesomorph to adopt this assertive and domineering behavior. Clearly then, physique does facilitate or limit the range and types of reactions that an individual can—and therefore will—learn. According to this thesis, associations between morphology and behavior do not arise from some biogenic linkage but from adaptive learning.

It seems reasonable to conclude that the psychogenic interpretations just enumerated account in some part for the high correlations found between physique, behavior and psychopathology. The relative contributions of psychogenic and biogenic factors will not be disentangled easily; at this stage in our knowledge it will suffice to say that both types of etiological mechanisms intertwine in a complicated developmental sequence.

# NEUROANATOMICAL DEFECTS

Greisinger's assertion in the mid-nineteenth century that neurological lesions underlie the surface manifestations of psychopathology was given substantive support at the turn of the century by Alzeheimer, who found clear-cut histological defects in the cortex of mental patients. This belief was uncritically accepted by most psychopathologists at the turn of the twentieth century and is clearly evident in the theoretical formulations of Kraepelin and Bleuler. The emergence of psychoanalysis, with its focus on environmental influences, led to a sharp reversal of opinion about the role of pathological lesions. In 1924, for example, Dunlap asserted unequivocally that no neurological evidence could be adduced in support of an organic cause in the major forms of mental disorder; this authoritative position was shared by a growing number of prominent psychopathologists. Not until the mid-1930's were hypotheses of neurological lesions presented again in a favorable light; Speilmeyer, Ferraro and Papez each offered evidence of histopathological processes in the brains of mental patients. With these and subsequent findings, a new period of enthusiasm favoring neurological hypotheses and research was ushered in. Our present review will focus on the rationale, methods, theories and evidence that has appeared during this recent period.

## RATIONALE

The role that neurological lesions may play in producing pathology can be grasped with only a minimal understanding of the structural organization and functional character of the brain. However, certain naive beliefs to the effect that psychological functions can be localized in precise regions of the brain must be avoided. Psychological processes derive from complex interdependent and circular feedback properties of brain activity. Unless we recognize that awesomely intricate connections within the brain subserve psychological functions, we will be inclined to assume that pathological symptoms arise as a direct consequence of the specific neurological lesion itself; the effects of these pathological processes are extremely diverse and complex.

Psychological concepts such as perception, emotion, behavior and thought represent complex and different processes that are grouped together and labeled by theorists as a means of simplifying their observations; these conceptual labels should not be confused with tangible properties of the brain. It is believed erroneously by many students that these theoretical concepts correspond on a one-to-one basis with physical entities, that is, that these terms refer to a specifiable locus in the brain. This unfortunate belief can be traced to the crude notions formulated by nineteenth century anatomists and faculty psychologists; it remains popular today because of our tendency to simplify intrinsically complex processes. Although certain regions of the brain are more directly involved in certain psychological functions than others, it is clear from current research that all of man's higher psychological functions are a product of the interaction of several brain areas.

Figure 4-3 portrays some of the diverse and circular features of interneuronal activity. The figure sketches only crudely the inordinate neurological complexity underlying even simple acts. Thus, writing or talking each requires the proper coordination and timing of innumerable impulses drawn from several neurological structures. The frontal lobes of the cortex, for example, orchestrate a dynamic pattern of impulses by selectively enhancing or diminishing the sensitivity of the receptors, by collating and comparing impulses arising in other spheres of the brain and by guiding them along myriad arrangements and sequences; in this regnant function it facilitates or inhibits a wide range of less dominant brain processes. This modulating capacity operates, therefore, not only to control external sources of stimulation but to regulate stimuli arising from within the brain itself.

In summary, the point we wish to emphasize is that psychological processes cannot be conceived as localized or fixed to one or another sphere of the brain. Rather, they arise from a complex network of interactions and feedbacks. All stimuli, whether generated externally or internally, follow long chains and reverberating circuits which modulate a wide range of other brain activities. Psychological functions must be conceived, therefore, as the product of a widespread and self-regulating pattern of interneuronal stimulation.

The discussion presented thus far has prepared us to better answer the question of how psychological functions are disrupted by neurological impairments. With this précis we will have a sounder basis for understanding some of the diverse consequences of even the simplest neurological lesions, those referred to as focal lesions.

*Focal lesions,* that is, lesions restricted to well-circumscribed neurological zones, should *not* result in the total loss of a psychological function with which it is normally associated (i.e., as noted previously, complex functions are not localized in specific areas of the brain). Focal defects will produce a reduction in the capacity of its associated function; additionally, there will be secondary disruptions in other psychological functions which normally depend on the intactness of the damaged region. Unless the focal lesion involves an area crucial to the overall activation or integration of brain processes, it will have little effect upon functions that usually are not associated with it. For example, a minor lesion in an auditory area rarely will result in impairments of visual functions. However, defects in a cortical area or in the reticular system are likely to have pervasive consequences since both of these regions play important roles in the overall integration and activation of the brain. Similarly, structural defects or

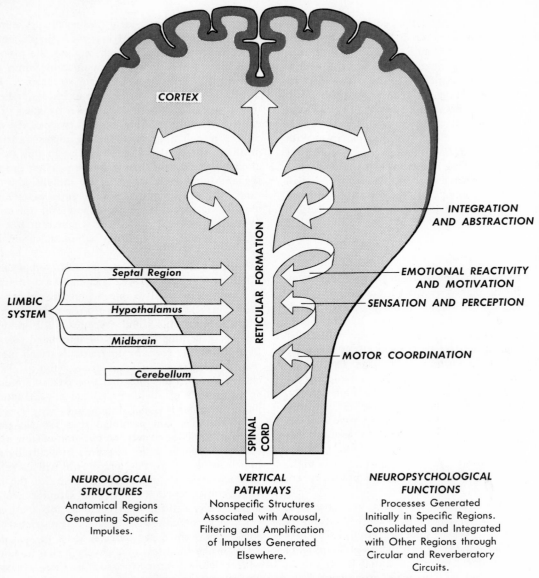

CORTEX

RETICULAR FORMATION

SPINAL CORD

LIMBIC SYSTEM

Septal Region

Hypothalamus

Midbrain

Cerebellum

INTEGRATION AND ABSTRACTION

EMOTIONAL REACTIVITY AND MOTIVATION

SENSATION AND PERCEPTION

MOTOR COORDINATION

NEUROLOGICAL STRUCTURES
Anatomical Regions Generating Specific Impulses.

VERTICAL PATHWAYS
Nonspecific Structures Associated with Arousal, Filtering and Amplification of Impulses Generated Elsewhere.

NEUROPSYCHOLOGICAL FUNCTIONS
Processes Generated Initially in Specific Regions. Consolidated and Integrated with Other Regions through Circular and Reverberatory Circuits.

Figure 4-3    Structural and functional interconnections in the brain

chemical dysfunctions at synapses or in the insulating myelin sheaths of nerve pathways can cause a pervasive impairment of brain activity; in each of these latter cases, several different psychological functions may be simultaneously affected.

Ideally, a careful investigation of the range and the pattern of disturbed psychological functions should enable the clinician to deduce the character of an underlying neurological defect. Unfortunately, the psychodiagnostic and neurological methods that are currently available for correlating neurological and psychological functions are extremely crude. As a consequence, definitive conclusions about the precise nature of these lesions cannot be drawn in any but a few

relatively simple cases. If we keep in mind the intricate neural interdependencies underlying complex psychological processes, we should not fall prey to the errors of interpretive simplifications.

## NEUROPSYCHOLOGICAL METHODS

A detailed review of the techniques available for correlating brain processes with psychological functions is beyond the scope of this book. A brief summary will suffice.

Neuropsychological methods may be divided into *incursive* techniques, that is, those which intrude directly into the brain, and *nonincursive* techniques, that is, those which record neural activity without disrupting the intact brain.

**Incursive Techniques.** Disease, injury and degeneration of brain tissue may be observed directly through surgical methods.

A specific surgical technique, known as extirpation, consists of removing parts of the brain and tracing the consequences of this operation on various psychological functions. Also employed are methods for obtaining direct electrical recordings from the brain; most notable of these are implanted microelectrodes which enable researchers to observe a variety of behavioral, ideational and emotional consequences of focused brain stimulation. Chemicals also have been applied using implanted micropipettes.

Incursive techniques do not produce unequivocal data. Extirpation often results in the destruction of tissue other than that under investigation; consequent behavior changes may be attributable to this more widespread damage. The accuracy of the placement of implanted electrodes is only moderately reliable; given the wide individual differences in anatomical structure, no certainty exists that regions adjacent to the investigated area have not been erroneously stimulated. The locus of action of injected drug solutions is even more difficult to identify since liquid chemicals tend to spread and have secondary physiological effects.

**Nonincursive Techniques.** Two of the major nonincursive methods are the electroencephalogram (EEG) and psychodiagnostic tests. The EEG records rhythmic electrical currents generated by neural activity. By attaching electrodes to the scalp it is possible to pick up sequences of electrical discharge emanating from several regions of the brain; known atypical waves may often be traced to clearly circumscribed lesions. Despite its common use as a diagnostic instrument, the EEG records only gross patterns of neural activity and cannot specify precise neural components involved in most pathological symptoms.

Psychodiagnostic tests often record behaviors that reflect brain dysfunctions, and the level and quality of the subject's performance may clue the examiner to the character of the underlying defect. Most often, however, these tests provide only a gross summary of brain functioning. Thus, it is usually difficult to specify lesions with any precision, since the same pattern of test performance may reflect any number of different neural impairments. For example, disturbances in perceptual-motor coordination may stem from lesions in sensory, motor, frontal or reticular regions.

## KNOWN PATHOGENIC FACTORS

Syndromes attributed clearly to biogenic agents will be discussed fully in chapter 13. Here we will provide a brief synopsis of a number of the well-established neurological defects that can give rise to these syndromes.

**Infections.** The invasion of foreign microorganisms within the brain may cause inflammatory reactions, atrophy and tissue destruction. Most damaging among these infections are syphilis and the virus known as epidemic encephalitis. The consequences of these infections depend on their primary locus and the age of the patient. A fully matured organism usually possesses enough surplus tissue to enable him to relearn those functions that have been impaired.

The effects of disease can be much more severe in younger children since the entire course of their subsequent development may be thrown askew by an infection. Diseases of this kind among infants and toddlers can deter, and even prevent, the maturation of a wide number of capacities.

**Physical Trauma.** Contusions and lacerations of the brain may precipitate pathological reactions, depending on the location and severity of the injury. Traumas in the head region have more serious repercussions among the young for the reason noted above.

**Neoplasm.** The chaotic growth of new tissue in the form of tumors can distort the brain and disrupt a variety of functions. However, slowly expanding lesions frequently fail to produce overt symptoms since adjacent tissues can take over disturbed functions, if given the time to do so. Rapidly expanding neoplasms do not offer sufficient time for the compensation of disturbed functions and often result in profound behavioral changes.

**Degeneration.** The deterioration of brain cells and their supporting circulatory structures usually is pervasive and progressive, producing a gradual overall decline of psychological capacities. Some forms of degeneration are extremely rapid and cause profound destruction, e.g., sudden arterial hemorrhage. Nutritional deficiencies and age-associated cerebral arteriosclerosis (hardening of the arteries) are primary causes of degeneration.

**Aplasia.** The sparse development of neural tissue in certain spheres of the brain may account for many of the intellectual and emotional deficiencies we observe. The rudimentary cortical development of the "microcephalic" retardate illustrates this congenital maldevelopment. The etiological source of these tissue deficits may be either genetic or environmental. The role of environmental stimulation in the underdevelopment of certain neural capacities will be discussed in chapter 5.

Relationships between behavior and the density and spread of neural matter throughout the brain are virgin fields of investigation; the role of "neuroanatomical individuality" may prove to be the crucial variable in relationships between the fields of neurology and psychopathology. Several theorists have begun to speculate along this line; a number of their ideas will be discussed in the next section.

## RECENT THEORIES
## AND RESEARCH

The task of identifying the neuroanatomical substrate of relatively well-defined symptom disorders such as epilepsy and cerebral arteriosclerosis is difficult enough. When we venture into the no-man's land of such variegated and motley syndromes as schizophrenia and manic-depressive psychosis, the task becomes nearly impossible. As has been stated earlier, these latter syndromes comprise, in all probability, heterogeneous groups of ailments which arise from diverse etiological sources. Attempts to specify *the* neurological lesion which corresponds to these syndrome labels will be futile.

Before we can search intelligently for specific neurological defects underlying pathological behavior, we must first differentiate syndromes into those in which neurological (or biochemical) factors are likely to play a significant role from those in which they do not. In the ensuing discussion we will attempt to determine first whether such a distinction is possible. Once we have established that a distinction of this kind is reasonable, we will examine what evidence there is regarding the specific nature of the defects among those classified as neurologically impaired. Of necessity, our attention will focus on the diagnostic classification of schizophrenia since most research has dealt with this group of pathological syndromes.

What evidence is there that some of the patients diagnosed as schizophrenic are neurologically impaired while others are not? Two sources of data will be examined. The first derives from the genetic studies by Rosenthal (1959) discussed in an earlier section, the second from research associated with the distinction known as process-reactive (Kantor, Wallner and Winder,

1953; Becker, 1959; Leonhard, 1961; Higgins, 1964; Garmezy, 1968).

1. Rosenthal's reappraisal of genetic twin data uncovered the fact that the incidence of schizophrenia among families of twins who were concordant for schizophrenia was strikingly higher than that found in families of twins discordant for schizophrenia. Concordant twins had a poorer premorbid history, an earlier onset of the disease, little affect, minimal activity, greater severity and a grave prognosis. In contrast, schizophrenic members in discordant pairs were described as well preserved with minimal loss of affect and a better prognosis. These findings led Rosenthal to conclude that schizophrenia is biologically heterogeneous, that is, one group—those characterized by inactivity and emotional flatness —possesses a primary neurological defect that is genetic in origin, whereas the other, displaying greater affect and activity, is ill as a consequence of environmental experience.

2. The behavior of many schizophrenics on psychodiagnostic tests cannot be distinguished from patients with clear-cut neurological damage. This observation has suggested the possibility that some of the patients classified as schizophrenic possess some form of neurological impairment. Attempts to identify this subgroup have led to the the notion of *process* versus *reactive* schizophrenia. The criteria for this distinction are based on ostensible etiological grounds, developmental histories, test scores and prognoses.

The *process* group presumably suffers from some organic defect which is not present in reactive cases. Although the disorder has an insidious or slow progression over a period of years, pathological signs are present early in life; evidence of childhood social withdrawal and excessive fantasy is the primary indicator of future disorder. These signs become increasingly pronounced in adolescence until a picture of psychosis is clearly manifest. Once manifest, the disorder deteriorates progressively, despite all therapeutic efforts, until the patient succumbs into a chronic and "burned-out" pattern.

The *reactive* group ostensibly possesses no basic neurological impairment. Their early histories are normal in most regards, evidencing no signs of unusual social inadequacy or personal peculiarity. Characteristically, there is a period of marked environmental stress which appears to set off a chain of maladaptive reactions. Once these reactions result in overt pathology the patient manifests, both in severity and type of behavior, the features that have been evident all along in the process group. A careful clinical analysis, however, will uncover their greater capacity for emotional responsiveness and clarity of thought.

The major distinction between the two groups then, in addition to the presumed neurological difference, lies in the favorable prognosis of reactive cases and in their later and rather rapid onset of pathology. Table 4-6 presents a number of the developmental and descriptive features which allegedly differentiate these groups.

Numerous investigators have undertaken to test the validity of the process-reactive distinction. Among the more carefully planned and executed studies is one done by Belmont et al. (1964). They divided schizophrenics according to the age at which their pathology first was evidenced and then made comparisons between them and a third nonschizophrenic group. Early disturbed schizophrenics, in contrast to the late developers, showed markedly inadequate perceptual-analytic functioning, diminished perceptual responsiveness,

bizarre thought and lower I.Q. scores. Their performances resembled those of patients with clear-cut organic deficits. This finding suggested that patients who evidence behavioral abnormalities early in life have a primary neurological impairment which serves as the basis for perceptual, cognitive and interpersonal difficulties throughout their lives. A second finding of their study showed that late developing schizophrenics display minor neurological signs, whereas nonschizophrenic patients are entirely free of such signs.

The gradation in neurological signs that Belmont et al. found suggests that the process-reactive distinction, with its implication of an all-or-none neurological basis, is an oversimplification. An alternative to the notion of a dichotomy of process-reactive schizophrenia is a continuum representing relative degrees of neurological impairment (Garmezy, 1968). The notion of a gradation of neurological involvement would be a more reasonable hypothesis in light of our

**Table 4-6  Case History Distinctions Between Process and Reactive Schizophrenia***

| PROCESS SCHIZOPHRENIA | REACTIVE SCHIZOPHRENIA |
|---|---|
| *Birth to the fifth year* | |
| a. Early psychological trauma | a. Good psychological history |
| b. Physical illness—severe or long | b. Good physical health |
| c. Odd member of family | c. Normal member of family |
| *Fifth year to adolescence* | |
| a. Difficulties at school | a. Well adjusted at school |
| b. Family troubles paralleled by sudden changes in patient's behavior | b. Domestic troubles unaccompanied by behavior disruptions; patient "had what it took" |
| c. Introverted behavior trends and interests | c. Extroverted behavior trends and interests |
| d. History of breakdown of social, physical, mental functioning | d. History of adequate social, physical, mental functioning |
| e. Pathological siblings | e. Normal siblings |
| f. Overprotective or rejecting mother, "momism" | f. Normally protective, accepting mother |
| g. Rejecting father | g. Accepting father |
| *Adolescence to adulthood* | |
| a. Lack of heterosexuality | a. Heterosexual behavior |
| b. Insidious, gradual onset of psychosis without pertinent stress | b. Sudden onset of psychosis; stress present and pertinent; later onset |
| c. Physical aggression | c. Verbal aggression |
| d. Poor response to treatment | d. Good response to treatment |
| e. Lengthy stay in hospital | e. Short course in hospital |
| *Adulthood* | |
| a. Massive paranoia | a. Minor paranoid trends |
| b. Little capacity for alcohol | b. Much capacity for alcohol |
| c. No manic-depressive component | c. Presence of manic-depressive component |
| d. Failure under adversity | d. Success despite adversity |
| e. Discrepancy between ability and achievement | e. Harmony between ability and achievement |
| f. Awareness of change in self | f. No sensation of change |
| g. Somatic delusions | g. Absence of somatic delusions |
| h. Clash between culture and environment | h. Harmony between culture and environment |
| i. Loss of decency (nudity, public masturbation, etc.) | i. Retention of decency |

* From Kantor, Wallner and Winder (1953)

knowledge of the infinite number of neurological components which can go awry, singly or in combination, in so complex an organ as the brain. The cumulative operation of several different minor and major defects of neurological structure is more consonant with the normally distributed and continuous distribution of pathological traits. Whatever role neurological factors play in schizophrenia, their influence is not likely to be a single all-or-none one.

Assuming the reasonableness of the assumption that some schizophrenics are neurologically impaired, we may then ask: What is the specific nature and location of these impairments? To answer this question we must first specify some of the cardinal behavioral features of those classed as schizophrenic.

A number of prominent signs were suggested by Bleuler who gave this disorder its current name. Primary among these is the patient's "loosening of associations," that is, an inability to coordinate and focus his thoughts. Second are features associated with the patient's marked inability to experience pleasure, referred to in chapter 3 as anhedonia.

Given these two cardinal schizophrenic signs as a guide, what neural defects can be hypothesized as their basis? Although our knowledge of the neurological substrate of behavior, thought and emotion has only recently begun (Delafresnaye, 1961; Sheer, 1961), enough information exists to justify certain tentative speculations.

Recent research has shown that the *reticular system* plays a significant role, along with the cortex, in regulating and integrating brain activity (Scheibel and Scheibel, 1958). Others have shown reticular pathways serving as a filter for subcortical impulses en route to the cortex. In addition to these roles, the reticular system is known to be crucially involved in altering states of arousal, attention and activation throughout the brain. Given the nature of these functions, it should be clear that defects in this region can result in either or both of the schizophrenic signs of cognitive loosening and anhedonia. Defects in integration may produce a dyscontrol in thought impulses, and a lowered activation level would diminish the impact of pleasurable reinforcements. A number of hypotheses relating psychopathology to lesions in this region were discussed in chapter 2, e.g., Rimland's notions about infantile autism.

There is little question that the anatomical structures referred to as the *limbic system* are centrally involved in the expression and control of both emotional and motivational processes. Electrodes in this region of the brain can suppress,

magnify or distort a wide range of pleasurable and painful emotions. For example, Delgado (1960) artificially stimulated the limbic system and was able to inhibit motor behavior and aggressiveness in one locale and evoke pleasurable responses or fear in others. It is not inconceivable that defects or natural differences in the density or spread of tissue in these regions would be related to differences among individuals in their proclivities to various emotional behaviors. Likewise, the built-in linkage between the limbic system and other regions of the brain would have a direct bearing on the probability that emotions would become directly involved in other neuropsychological functions. Thus, either peculiarities in neuronal wiring or quantitatively sparse limbic regions may account for the anhedonic characteristic of schizophrenics. Defects such as these may serve as the neurological substrate for Rado's observation that schizophrenic's display an "integrative pleasure deficiency," or Campbell's conception of erratic mood swings among manic-depressives.

Meehl (1962), along similar lines, suggests that the varied emotional and perceptual-cognitive dysfunctions displayed by schizophrenics are difficult to explain in terms of single region defects; the widespread nature of these dysfunctions suggests the operation of a more diffuse integrative deficiency. Although a combination of different neurological defects can account for this deficiency, Meehl opts for an explanation in terms of a deficit in synaptic control. More specifically, he believes that the major problem in schizophrenia lies in a malfunctioning of the two way mutual control system between perceptual-cognitive regions and the limbic motivation center. As another alternative, he refers to Brady's thesis that there may be a synaptic inhibitory defect between the positive and negative reinforcement centers of the limbic system.

Other neurological defects can account for the diffuse nature of schizophrenic symptomatology; most notable among these are cortical lesions. Defects in this regnant control center can upset all subsidiary functions. Thus, either gross aplasia or warped circuitry in this region can result in a wide range of pathological behaviors, thoughts and emotions.

## EVALUATIVE COMMENTS

With the exception of a few well-circumscribed lesions that appear directly associated with specific types of brain syndromes, the data relating neurological damage to psychopathology are scanty and equivocal. We are just beginning to cross the threshold of our knowledge about normal brain processes. When we have a firm grasp of these normal functions, we will have a sounder basis for specifying how disruptions can impair psychological processes. At present, theoretical speculations take the form of deductions extrapolated from surgical and electrical stimulation studies. As such, they must be viewed with a healthy degree of skepticism. Fascinating and ingenious as they may be, these speculations are highly imaginary suppositions based on minimal and indirect empirical data.

Throughout our discussion we have touched on a number of points which must be kept in mind to avoid the many pitfalls involved in ascribing behavioral disorders to neurological defects. Let us recapitulate them briefly.

1. Brain lesions disrupt the functions associated not only with the diseased area but with other areas as well. This occurs because the directly affected region is connected to other brain areas and is thereby involved in a number of different psychological functions. If we acknowledge the complexity and intricacy of neuronal circuitry, we are led to conclude that similar lesions in contiguous areas are likely to produce highly dissimilar effects.

2. The problems of identifying the locus of a neurological defect are complicated immensely by individual differences in the structural organization of the brain; there is at least as much variability in internal morphology as there is in external morphology. As such, the location and interconnections among brain regions differ markedly from person to person. These inter-individual differences are of particular importance in another regard. Natural differences among individuals in the density, range and branching of comparable brain regions will have a direct bearing on their psychological functioning. Possessing more or less of the neurological substrate for a particular function such as pleasure or intelligence will influence the character of a person's experience and the course of his psychological development. It should be evident then, that the role of neurology in psychopathology is not restricted to situations in which tissue has been damaged. Rather, natural differences in anatomical structure can result in a whole continuum of psychologically relevant effects.

3. If we recognize the network of functions that are upset by a specific lesion, and add to it the tremendous natural variability in brain structures, we may begin to see the difficulties involved in establishing the etiological role of neurological factors. If the technical and methodological requirements for assessing the precise psychological consequences of a diffuse brain lesion are difficult, one can only begin to imagine the staggering task of establishing the psychological correlates of natural structural differences. It will be some time before our knowledge of neuropsychology and our technological skills will be up to these tasks. Until then, we must accept on faith the assumption that a substantial part of behavioral pathology is traceable to neurological factors. Unfortunately, this state of affairs applies as well to our next topic.

# PHYSIOCHEMICAL DYSFUNCTIONS

The search for physiochemical dysfunctions in psychopathology has become the most actively pursued field of biogenic investigation of the past decade. The role of physiochemical substances as determinants of psychopathology was suspected and argued persuasively as early as the mid-nineteenth century. Strong support for these early speculations was gathered when the primary determinant of the disease, labeled dementia paralytica (paresis), was discovered to be syphilis. Buoyed by this finding, investigators at the turn of the century began a concentrated search for *exogenous* sources of psychopathology, that is, sources foreign to the body's normal functioning such as toxins or infectious agents which invade the system and destroy its tissues. A number of such agents were uncovered but they failed to account for the great majority of mental disorders.

Attention turned gradually to the possibility that *endogenous,* that is, internal dysfunctions lay at the root of these ailments. Speculations to this effect were offered by the eminent nosologist, Kraepelin; he proposed that most patients possessed an imbalance in metabolic functioning that produced pathogenic toxins which, in turn, led to overt pathological symptomatology. Other theorists rejected Kraepelin's notion of a self-produced toxic substance; to them, disorders reflected the simple and direct consequence of imbalance among natural body chemicals. Arguments for or against one endogenous theory or another proliferated the psychiatric literature, but there were little data to support any of the proposals that were advanced. Technological methods simply were too gross to unravel the intricate and subtle processes of natural physiochemical functioning.

It was not until the 1950's that technical and scientific knowledge enabled biochemists to track down the basic processes of internal physiochemistry. Simultaneous with these advances were the exciting discoveries of the psychotomimetics and tranquilizers, agents which demonstrated that chemicals can both disrupt normal behavior and assuage psychotic behavior. With their advent came a new era of enthusiasm and activity among psychochemists.

The optimism engendered by these discoveries has not been shared by all. Some critics, noting that past enthusiasms waned as the data of newer and better designed research were published, anticipated that the present surge of optimism was doomed to a like fate. The checkered history of ill-conceived hypotheses, poorly designed research and the premature reporting of what turns out to be unsubstantiated findings, gives ample justification for caution, if not pessimism. More significant, however, is the fact that there is no incontrovertible evidence to date specifying physiochemical aberrations in any of the major forms of psychopathology. Despite the inadequacy of data, there is every reason to believe that our increasing technical skills will, in the near future, lead to the discovery of whatever role these dysfunctions may play.

Two points must be kept in mind lest we fall prey to past errors. *First,* every bodily dysfunction results in diverse and far-reaching consequences since biochemical processes are involved intimately in a multitude of functions. When chemical dysfunctions of the body are discovered, the task remains of specifying exactly how they produce psychological pathology. *Second,* the search for biochemical dysfunctions is handicapped by the high degree of natural physiochemical individuality among men. Roger Williams, the eminent biochemist, has alerted us to the fact that each individual possesses a distinctive physiochemical pattern that is wholly unlike others and bears no relationship to a hypothetical norm. These patterns of individuality make us aware of a new and crucial factor that must be evaluated before we can properly appraise the role of chemical dysfunctions in psychopathology. Moreover, natural individual differences in biochemical functioning may prove to be of greater importance in etiology than are defects from a nonexistent biochemical norm.

It will be instructive before we proceed further to survey some of the bodily structures and processes involved in physiochemical functioning. With this as a foundation, we will have a better basis for discussing current theories and research.

## ELEMENTS OF PHYSIOCHEMICAL FUNCTIONING

Physiochemical processes are involved in a wide range of functions ranging from the transduction of environmental stimuli into sensory nerve impulses to the stimulation of muscular and glandular activity. Some of these processes occur throughout the body, while other, more specialized processes, tend to be located within particular organs. All of these processes unfold in a highly complicated chain of reactions and transformations which maintains carefully balanced relationships with a number of other bodily processes.

In searching to uncover which of these myriad processes are central to behavior pathology, scientists have focused their attention on three sources: (1) the autonomic nervous system, (2) the neurohormones and (3) the endocrine glands. These three systems are intricately related in the activation of response to stress; defects in any one may produce deficits in adaptive behavior.

**Autonomic Nervous System.** The major organs of the body are activated by *efferent* nerves. These nerves, collectively termed the autonomic nervous system, form synaptic junctions in ganglia that lie, for the most part, outside and parallel to the spinal cord. At each ganglia, impulses cross one or several synapses and then progress onward to activate certain organs. This chain of transmission can be separated into *preganglionic* fibers, which lead from the cord to ganglia, and *postganglionic* fibers, which proceed from ganglia to organ.

The autonomic nerves have been divided into two groups: (1) the craniosacral group, referred to as the *parasympathetic* division, are composed of nerves which stem from the upper and lower regions of the spinal cord and (2) the thoracolumbar group, called the *sympathetic* division, comprising neurons emerging from the midportion of the spinal column. Figure 4-4 provides a pictorial representation of the distribution and organ connections of these two divisions.

The sympathetic division, connected to the heart, blood vessels and adrenal medulla, tends to serve a mobilizing function, that is, it equips the individual to respond in an accelerated way to emergency or stress conditions. The parasympathetic group is essentially a system of maintenance which facilitates the normal functions of its connected organs. The sympathetic system is often referred to as *adrenergic*, because of its power to activate the mobilizing reactions of the adrenal glands: the counterbalancing characteristics of the parasympathetic division often are referred to as *cholinergic*.

Although many body organs receive impulses from both sympathetic and parasympathetic nerves, certain organs are activated primarily by one division. Normally, a balance exists between these essentially antagonistic nerve groups. Any dysfunction in impulse transmission from one division will give rise to deficit reactions in its

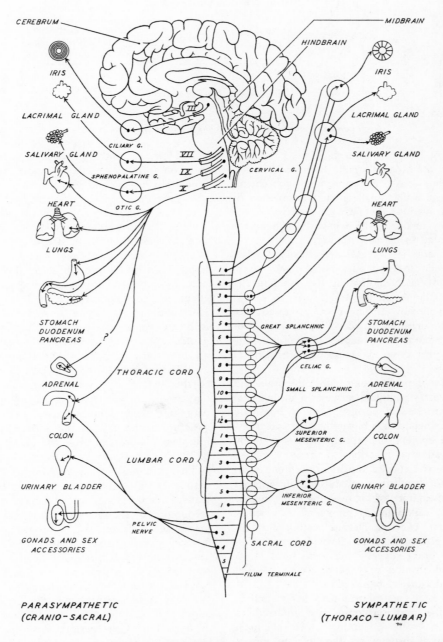

Figure 4-4   The autonomic nervous system. The parasympathetic division is shown on the left, the sympathetic division on the right. Roman numerals refer to cranial nerves. (From Turner, C. D.: General Endocrinology. 3rd edition. Philadelphia, W. B. Saunders Co., 1960.)

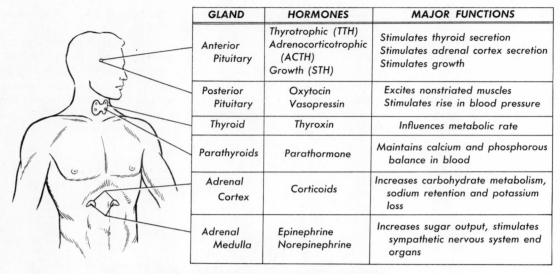

| GLAND | HORMONES | MAJOR FUNCTIONS |
|-------|----------|-----------------|
| Anterior Pituitary | Thyrotrophic (TTH) Adrenocorticotrophic (ACTH) Growth (STH) | Stimulates thyroid secretion Stimulates adrenal cortex secretion Stimulates growth |
| Posterior Pituitary | Oxytocin Vasopressin | Excites nonstriated muscles Stimulates rise in blood pressure |
| Thyroid | Thyroxin | Influences metabolic rate |
| Parathyroids | Parathormone | Maintains calcium and phosphorous balance in blood |
| Adrenal Cortex | Corticoids | Increases carbohydrate metabolism, sodium retention and potassium loss |
| Adrenal Medulla | Epinephrine Norepinephrine | Increases sugar output, stimulates sympathetic nervous system end organs |

Figure 4-5   Hormones and functions of major endocrine glands.

associated organs and overreactions in organs activated by the other, normal, division.

**Neurohormones.** Neurohormones are chemical substances which mediate the transmission of impulses throughout the nervous system; we refer here only to those which have been hypothesized as related to psychopathology.

Most neurons release *acetylcholine* when impulses reach the synaptic junction. An overabundance of acetylcholine at the junction decreases synaptic resistance and results in excess neural transmission. It has been proposed that high or low amounts of acetylcholine may produce dysfunctions in synaptic control, leading either to hyperactive or hypoactive behavioral consequences.

*Norepinephrine* is found within the brain and the peripheral sympathetic nerves. In the adrenal medulla, composed of postganglionic sympathetic nerves, norepinephrine is biosynthesized and transformed into epinephrine; epinephrine is crucially involved in adaptive reactions to stress.

The specific role of the neurohormone *serotonin* has not been fully established. It appears to be a mediator of parasympathetic neural transmission, especially as an agent in vascular and muscular control. Despite ambiguities regarding its precise function, its widespread presence in the brain suggests that deviations in its normal concentration may serve as a potential source of pathological behaviors.

These three neurohormones, acetylcholine, norepinephrine and serotonin, are referred to chemically as brain monamines; their chemical bond usually is broken by the enzyme mono-amine oxidase, and results in a variety of degradation products, that is, nonfunctional and potentially toxic residues.

**Endocrines.** The endocrine system is composed of a number of ductless glands which secrete chemical substances known as *hormones* directly into the blood stream. Hormones are released either by the direct stimulation of neural impulses or by the prompting of other hormones; minute amounts can have powerful regulatory effects on a wide number of bodily functions. Hormones may combine to act either synergistically or antagonistically. The major endocrine glands and their location, principal hormones and functions are presented in Figure 4-5.

The activities and interconnections of one of the endocrine glands, the *pituitary,* are particularly significant from the viewpoint of psychopathology. This gland is located in a small bony structure at the base of the brain, and is divided into two major segments: the anterior and posterior divisions. Secretions from the anterior position are almost as far-reaching as those of the entire nervous system, justifying the title "master gland." Its hormones carry the suffix *trophic* in recognition of the fact that they "seek out" other glands and activate their hormones.

Of special interest in this regard is the adrenocorticotrophic hormone (ACTH) of the pituitary gland which stimulates the adrenal cortex, a gland centrally involved in reactions to stress. We may note, further, that the division of the adrenal gland known as the adrenal medulla is an extension of the peripheral sympathetic nervous system; secretions from this gland also are crucially involved in stress reactions. Thus, both the pituitary-adrenal cortex axis and the sympathetic-adrenal medulla axis demonstrate the close functional interdependence of the nervous and endocrine systems in the production of adaptive reactions to stress.

## EXOGENOUS FACTORS

Before we proceed to discuss some of the theories and research on endogenous physiochemical dysfunctions in psychopathology, let us digress briefly to note a number of the exogenous factors which are known to disrupt normal development and functioning. These external sources of pathology may be divided into two categories: toxic agents and biological deprivations.

1.  Toxic agents fall into three types: poisons, alcohol and drugs.

Poisons include any number of chemicals, gases or metals which cause either acute or chronic disruptions in normal physiochemical functioning and produce a variety of pathological symptoms.

Excessive alcoholic intoxication usually produces a temporary and reversible disorganization of functioning. However, longstanding concentrations of alcohol in the brain may result in permanent impairment, usually signified by disorientation and memory loss.

Marked allergic reactions to various medications may be accompanied by profound alterations in psychological functions; these usually are reversible. Addiction to certain sedatives and opiates can lead to perceptual distortions and prolonged states of delirium. Of particular recent interest are the unusual reactions promoted by drugs known as hallucinogens. Temporary states induced by mescaline, LSD and psilocybin have been particularly useful in experimental and theoretical studies of mental disorder.

2.  Psychopathology can rise from deprivation of biological needs normally provided by external sources; these deprivations can be separated into two sources: nutritional deficiencies and anoxia.

Both the structure and chemical activity of the body depend on nourishment and energy supplied from the environment. Dietary and vitamin deficiencies not only produce marked aberrations such as pellagra but may underlie a multitude of more subtle defects in psychological functioning.

Anoxia is rare among adults, but it is known to be a primary cause of profound brain damage in early infancy. A host of physiochemical oxidation processes are curtailed during brief periods of oxygen deprivation, resulting in destructive accumulations of waste products and the starvation of essential nutrients.

Interest has turned recently to the detrimental effects of sleep deprivation. Although this problem is of rare incidence, research has shown that sleep is a period during which the degradation products of wakeful activity are eliminated, and depleted chemical substances are restored.

## RECENT THEORIES AND RESEARCH ON ENDOGENOUS FACTORS

We have just touched on a number of disorders which arise either from external toxins or from failures to obtain environmental supplies requisite to proper bodily functioning. Next, we will turn to malfunctions caused by defects in the body's own chemical machinery.

**Rationale.** Theorists have proposed two types of endogenous dysfunctions:

1.  Those in which the critical factor derives from a homeostatic imbalance in normal body physiochemistry. This imbalance can arise either from persistent and excessive stress or from a

Figure 4-6   Major biogenic researchers. A. Franz Kallmann. B. Ernst Kretschmer. (Photograph from *American Journal of Psychiatry,* August, 1964.) C. William H. Sheldon. D. Hans Selyé.

constitutionally built-in dominance of one physio-chemical system over the others. In this category are the *prolonged stress* and *autonomic* or *endocrinological imbalance* theories to be discussed shortly.

2. Those in which the critical factor is a failure of the body to convert or metabolize its own chemical products. This failure may result in the production of toxic substances which accumulate and then interfere with normal processes. Some of these consequences may be traced to inborn deficiencies in the functioning of body enzymes which serve to oxidize or bind the accumulation of natural chemicals. For example, the inborn defect known as phenylketonuria is a disease manifested in infancy which results from mass accumulations of phenylalanine; it produces profound mental retardation. Consequences such as these can arise in later life if the requisite enzymes "wear out" gradually and begin to falter in their metabolic functions. This rationale underlies the recent *adrenolutin, taraxein* and *serotonin* hypotheses to be presented shortly.

**Methods.** By what means do investigators trace behavioral observations to these subtle physiochemical dysfunctions? Here we can only outline the major techniques in use.

Naturalistic and experimental designs have been used in research. In *naturalistic* studies, an effort is made to correlate existing individual differences in behavior pathology (e.g., depressions and hallucinations) with existing differences in biological processes (e.g., heart rate and epinephrine). No attempt is made in this work to manipulate conditions experimentally or to produce changes either in psychological or physiochemical functions; measurements are taken as these variables exist in their natural state. The results of these naturalistic-correlational studies are limited by the fact that investigators have no means of determining whether the chemical differences they uncover were the cause or the effect of the behavior pathology. In fact, a third factor may account both for the behavior disturbance and the chemical abnormality, e.g., severe dietary deficiencies can result both in chemical changes and psychopathology.

*Experimental* procedures are restricted to methods to which humans can reasonably be exposed; many procedures can be applied, however, to animals, the results of which may then be generalized to humans. Two experimental designs are in common use. The first consists of manipulating a biochemical agent (e.g., enzymes or psychotomimetics) and observing the action of this agent on a variety of behaviors (e.g., speed of conditioning, motor coordination or hallucinations). Unfortunately, the precise effects of biochemical agents are difficult to specify since they usually disrupt several physiochemical processes and result in a complicated series of secondary effects. The second procedure reverses the sequence by attempting to measure the effect of various behaviors or experiences upon body chemistry. For example, special training experiences in early life may be arranged to see what effect they have upon the structure of various organs or the activity of certain hormones.

Measurement of both behavioral and physiochemical variables has been made by a wide variety of techniques. Behavior measures run the gamut from gross categories such as diagnostic classifications and general moods to precise and quantitative scores such as speed of motor tapping and visual flicker-fusion level. Physiochemical measures fall generally into two classes: direct and indirect. Direct measures are those which attempt to gauge the magnitude of the actual chemicals themselves. Among them are physical tests (e.g., reactions to salt and absorption of ultraviolet), chemical tests (e.g., colorimetric and chromatographic procedures) as well as biological analyses of urine, tissues and so on. The difficulty of assessing the chemical properties of physiological activity in intact humans has led to the development of a number of indirect techniques which enable investigators to measure and infer their locus and character. Primary among these are polygraphic recordings of body activity. They include the electrocardiogram (heart rate), the plethysmogram (blood volume), the sphygmomanometer (blood pressure), the electromyogram (muscular activity), the psychogalvanometer (electrical skin resistance) and, of course, the electroencephalogram (electrical brain rhythms).

With this brief overview of the theoretical rationale and methods of physiochemical research in psychopathology, we can proceed to examine some of the specific proposals and recent findings of work in the field.

## PROLONGED STRESS HYPOTHESIS

Homeostasis, a concept coined by Walter Cannon earlier in this century, represents the observation that internal physiochemical processes attempt to maintain the body's equilibrium under conditions of external and internal stress. More recently, Hans Selyé (1956) has analyzed the sequence through which these homeostatic mechanisms break down. Although Selyé's work focuses primarily on the consequences of physical stress, the theoretical model he has formulated, known as the *general adaptation syndrome,* has fruitfully been applied to the study of psychophysiological disorders. It also has proved instructive as a model for the stages through which the autonomic and endocrine systems react to psychological stress.

Selyé observed that diverse sources of stress produced a common sequence and pattern of physiochemical reaction. This sequence was traced through three stages:

1. Following a brief period of disorganized shock, the organism surges to regain its homeostatic balance in what Selyé terms the *alarm reaction.* Physiochemically, this consists first of the neural activation of the anterior pituitary gland. This gland secretes its adrenocorticotrophic hormone (ACTH) which, in turn, stimulates the adrenal cortex to release its own corticoid hormones. This second discharge precipitates increased muscle tonus, a rapid build up of blood sugar, a quickened heart rate and a deepening of breathing—in general, a sharp increment in adaptive alertness and vigor.

2. The second stage of the adaptation syndrome is termed *resistance.* During this period, physiochemical processes tend to center on the particular sphere of the body that is under primary stress; this more specific focus is associated however, with a concomitant decrement in the body's overall adaptive capacity and flexibility.

3. If the biological processes involved in stress resistance fail to overcome the stressor agent, or if the resistance period is excessively prolonged, the organism may succumb to *exhaus-tion,* the third stage of Selyé's triphasic sequence. At this point, either death or marked physiochemical disorganization occurs.

Throughout these stages, complex chains of autonomic and endocrinological interaction occur. Electrical impulses and neurohormones from the brain activate the endocrines in complicated sequences of reciprocal stimulation. At any point in this concatenation of events, defects or deficiencies may throw delicate response mechanisms awry. For example, the pituitary gland may fail to secrete ACTH, the structural composition of ACTH may prove defective and underactivate the adrenals, the adrenal cortex may produce deficits in corticoid secretions or corticoid secretions may fail to energize their associated organs.

Selyé's notion of adaptive decompensation under prolonged stress is more than a useful description of the physiochemical sequence preceding pathology; his separation of this sequence into specific stages can alert us to the varied physiochemical functions which may go wrong in the adaptive effort. However, Selyé did not specify the precise relation between prolonged stress, physiochemical processes and psychopathology. Other theorists, however, have sought to unravel this connection. We shall turn to their speculations next.

## AUTONOMIC AND ENDOCRINOLOGICAL IMBALANCE HYPOTHESES

Several theorists have proposed that the central factor upsetting the chain of adaptive reactions to stress is an imbalance between the

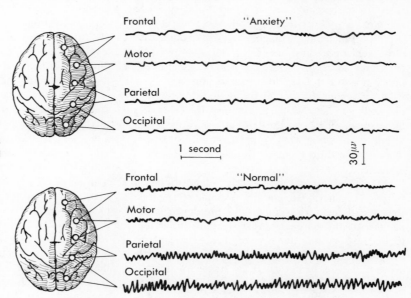

**Figure 4-7** Electroencephalogram records under anxiety and normal conditions.

sympathetic and parasympathetic divisions of the autonomic nervous system. These sets of nerves are crucially involved in initiating and maintaining the sequence of chemical-hormone reactions such as those described in Selyé's three stages. Should the impulses of one of these divisions persist beyond the point of their immediate effectiveness, hormonal secretions may become excessive and overshoot their mark, leading either to pathological overreactions or to pathological underreactions to stress (Gellhorn, 1943).

Hoskins (1946), one of the earliest workers to investigate the relation between autonomic dysfunctioning and psychopathology, found that schizophrenic patients, in general, display considerably greater variability on autonomic measures than do normal control groups. This finding has been corroborated fairly consistently over the years, and the question arises as to why this is the case. Three hypotheses have been proposed: (1) schizophrenics simply are more variable in their sympathetic arousal to stress than normals; (2) acutely disturbed schizophrenics have an excess in sympathetic *reactivity,* whereas chronically disturbed schizophrenics have low sympathetic reactivity; (3) chronic schizophrenics have a persistently high state of sympathetic *arousal,* whereas acute schizophrenics are characterized by a low arousal state.

The first hypothesis claims that each schizophrenic is irregular in his reactivity; the latter two hypotheses assert that each patient is consistent with himself, the variability in the data being attributed to the fact that acute patients have been grouped together erroneously with those who are chronically ill. Let us examine evidence relevant to each of these hypotheses.

1.   Pincus and Hoagland (1950) found that most schizophrenics are more variable in their corticoid secretion (adrenal cortex hormones) under nonstressful conditions than normals. They went one step further than Hoskins, who had obtained similar results, and found that the corticoid reaction in two thirds of the schizophrenics usually *fell* when they were exposed to stress, whereas one third typically displayed the expected increase.

2.   The second hypothesis adheres closely to Selyé's general adaptation schema. It suggests that the defect arises from the prolonged overactivity of the adrenal cortex, leading ultimately to exhaustion and underreactivity. According to this thesis, there is a high state of sympathetic arousal in the *acute* or early stages of schizophrenia. When the stress situation is prolonged and the physiochemical system is extended be-

yond its normal capacities, it eventually is drained and depleted. As a result, the adrenal system in the *chronic* schizophrenic can no longer be activated.

This interpretation does not negate the findings of Pincus and Hoagland. Rather it suggests that the population they studied was predominantly composed of chronic patients. Had they divided their subjects initially into two groups, acute and chronic, they would have observed that their acute patients displayed high reactivity and that their chronic patients displayed low reactivity.

This hypothesis is supported by the findings of Malmo and Shagass (1949, 1951) who observed that an excessive responsiveness to stress and an epinephrine overreactivity characterized the early stages of schizophrenia. Pfister's data (1938) can also be viewed as consonant with this hypothesis; he demonstrated a cardiovascular overresponsiveness among acute patients which progressed to an underresponsiveness in the chronic stage. The data of Pavlov and his disciples (Lynn, 1963), although formulated in terms of cortical inhibitory processes, also are consistent with this thesis; acute and agitated schizophrenics were characterized best by their high sympathetic tone and reactivity, in contrast to chronics who displayed diminished reactivity. All of these findings lend credence to Selyé's notion that emergency overreactions of the adrenal cortex may be depleted under prolonged stress, leading eventually to exhaustion and underreactivity.

3.   The data noted in support of the adrenal depletion hypothesis have been interpreted in a completely opposite fashion by Venables (1964). He suggests that acute patients suffer from a low level of cortical or sympathetic arousal. This diminished activation prevents them from effectively discriminating external stimuli. As a result of this indiscriminate attention, they are flooded and overwhelmed by their environment. Under this pressure their anxiety mounts and leads to a marked increment in adrenal activation. They are now driven into the chronic phase of their illness, a phase characterized by a pervasive and high level of sympathetic arousal. Once at this high activation level, they no longer can react to new stimuli since they have reached the ceiling of their arousal capacity (Wilder, 1950; Lacey, 1956). Thus, they fail, in this chronic phase, to demonstrate sympathetic reactions to stress since they already are operating at their peak level. In the acute phase, they were operating at an abnormally low level of arousal, and thus, "had

room" to be activated by new stress conditions. Venables' thesis reverses Selyé's depletion notion entirely. To Venables, the acute phase is characterized by low corticosympathetic activation, and the chronic phase by high activation.

This brief review of the research literature leads us to a few simple conclusions, the most relevant of which is that the data do not support convincingly any single viewpoint. There is an intriguing simplicity about each of these proposals and each theorist can piece together evidence favoring his preferred hypothesis; unfortunately, matching evidence can be gathered to support an alternative. Our better judgment tells us that the physiochemical processes involved in mental disorders must be not only exceedingly complex but must differ for patients who are uniformly classified as schizophrenic. Each of the hypotheses proposed rests on the assumption that schizophrenia is a unitary disorder; this assumption is a questionable one. Rather than arguing acuteness versus chronicity, or high versus low arousal, it might be best if researchers examined their data to see if some more basic differentiation could be made among "schizophrenics." Inconsistencies in the data of different investigators may reflect substantive differences among their patients, not mere methodological errors or interpretive differences. Perhaps their data can provide us with a better basis for making more fundamental distinctions within the obviously heterogeneous schizophrenic group.

## ADRENOLUTIN HYPOTHESIS

The previous set of hypotheses dealt with the possibility that an overall imbalance in autonomic functioning was basic to psychopathology. The present hypothesis, in contrast, narrows the cause specifically to the faulty metabolism of epinephrine, one of the major hormones produced in the adrenal medulla.

Osmond, Smythies and Hoffer (1954, 1959) noted a similarity in the chemical structure between the psychotomimetic mescaline and the natural hormone epinephrine. They hypothesized that there might be a naturally produced substance within the body, similar both to mescaline and epinephrine, that generated the symptoms of schizophrenia. At first, they believed that adrenochrome, a derivative of epinephrine, was the source of faulty enzymatic oxidation. However, since adrenochrome proved to be a highly unstable substance, they speculated that it was converted within the brain into adrenolutin, an ostensibly more durable neurochemical. This

hypothesized chemical presumably interfered with neural transmission, and gave rise to both perceptual and cognitive dysfunctions.

According to this thesis, a vicious cycle is set into motion when the patient is exposed to stress. Massive outpourings of epinephrine, normally helpful in meeting stress, result in an increase in adrenolutin, leading then to a decrement rather than an increment in adaptive capacity. This decreased adaptive capacity produces further stress, and the cycle is repeated.

Evidence gathered in support of this rather imaginative hypothesis is equivocal. More significantly, there is a question as to the factual existence of either adrenochrome or adrenolutin in normals and schizophrenics.

## TARAXEIN HYPOTHESIS

In chapter 2, note was made of another hypothesis favoring the presence of a toxic substance in schizophrenics. Heath and his co-workers (1957, 1960, 1966) claimed to have discovered a protein substance in the blood of schizophrenics which they named taraxein. They hypothesized that this toxic agent was genetically based, led to the defective functioning of the septal region within the limbic system and resulted in a deficit capacity to experience pleasure or pain. Those who possessed this genetic defect were referred to as schizotypes. According to Heath, the schizotypal syndrome is a prerequisite to the development of the clinical form of schizophrenia. Schizotypes liberate taraxein under stress, and the toxic effects of taraxein, in turn, produce the overt clinical symptoms of schizophrenia.

Evidence for the taraxein hypothesis has come largely from Heath's laboratory. For the most part, other investigators have been unable to verify the existence of this protein either in normals or schizophrenics. Where it has been identified, its power as a pathogenic agent has not been demonstrated convincingly.

## SEROTONIN HYPOTHESIS

In contrast to the adrenolutin and taraxein hypotheses, which contend that self-produced *toxic* substances induce pathological symptoms, the present hypothesis states that either an excess or a deficiency of the *natural* neurohormone, serotonin, can disrupt normal brain functioning and result directly in psychotic symptoms.

The pathogenic role of serotonin was inferred by Woolley and Shaw (1954, 1962) according to the same deductive logic that led

Osmond and Hoffer to formulate their proposals concerning adrenolutin.

Woolley and Shaw observed that LSD was similar in chemical structure to serotonin and hypothesized the following series of steps for the hallucinogenic effect of LSD. *First,* LSD competes with serotonin in attracting an enzyme that normally metabolizes serotonin; *second,* while this enzyme is distracted with LSD, serotonin builds up; *third,* the increased volume of serotonin overcomes the normal secretion of acetylcholine at the synapses of the parasympathetic system; *fourth,* since acetylcholine is necessary for sympathetic transmission, excess serotonin prevents the parasympathetic system from executing its function as a cholinergic counterbalance to the adrenergic action of the sympathetic system; and *fifth,* freed of the counterbalancing effect of parasympathetic controls, the sympathetic system overreacts, leading to excessive emotions and hallucinations.

On the basis of this LSD hypothesis, Woolley and Shaw deduced that proper metabolism of serotonin was a prerequisite for normal psychological functioning. Accordingly, either an excess or a deficiency in serotonin produces imbalances between the parasympathetic and sympathetic divisions. Excesses lead to behavioral signs such as excitement and hallucinations, whereas deficiencies result in lethargy, depression and stupor.

Research support for the LSD-serotonin theory has been equivocal, at best, and critics have raised serious questions about its deductive logic. Most telling are studies that show that the average level of serotonin in the brains of schizophrenics does not differ from that of normals. Acute schizophrenics appear to have less serotonin than chronics, but this variability has been found also in organics differentiated according to chronicity (Feldstein, Hoagland and Freeman, 1959; Toderick, Tait and Marshall, 1960; Halevy, Moos and Solomon, 1965). Without supporting data, the entire thesis rests on the validity of Woolley and Shaw's original deductions regarding the steps through which LSD progresses to create its psychotomimetic effects. This deduction assumes that symptoms induced by LSD are fundamentally akin to those of a true psychosis. This assumption has been questioned by many observers who claim that psychotic hallucinations are not similar to those generated by LSD.

## EVALUATIVE COMMENTS

Physiochemical dysfunction hypotheses have prompted a tremendous increase in research in the past decade. Much of this work is woefully inadequate, especially with regard to methodological controls. It is not possible either to confirm definitively or to reject unequivocally any of the proposals that have been raised on the basis of data currently available. Although some striking differences in physiochemical functioning have been found between psychotics and normals, the data are neither consistent from study to study nor sufficiently orderly to enable a rigorous deduction of the nature of the dysfunctions involved. Furthermore, several of the hypotheses are based on tenuous deductions derived from the effects of psychotomimetic agents. No direct evidence exists that naturally occurring biochemical abnormalities parallel the mechanism of action of foreign chemical agents. Hypotheses based on the ostensible connections between mescaline and adrenolutin and between LSD and serotonin must be viewed only as heuristic models to guide research. They are useful only in that they provide investigators with a frame of reference for exploring potential sources of psychopathology.

Each of the hypotheses presented in this section is an oversimplification of complex chains of physiochemical events. The simultaneous consequences of any single defect in this chain will have to be traced ultimately in order to derive the precise connection between pathological chemistry and pathological behavior. We must recognize that increases or decreases in serotonin, for example, not only can result from several different biochemical mechanisms, but can also produce a sequence of widely disparate effects. Which of these effects is related directly to the symptoms of psychopathology will have to be derived through meticulous research.

We must note, as we have before, that a primary focus on dysfunctions in physiochemistry reflects an acceptance of the disease model of psychopathology. Perhaps our understanding of the etiology of these disorders will be furthered if we were less preoccupied with dysfunctions, and made a concerted attack on the role of "biochemical individuality." Research on normal biochemical variations among men may not only provide us with new insights into the etiological basis of psychopathology but may also lead us to a better understanding of the milder personality pathologies.

A word about some of the methodological flaws in physiochemical research also is in order (Kety, 1959, 1968). Investigators usually fail to control for the fact that hospitalized psychiatric patients typically suffer from poor diets, inadequate physical exercise and a host of other usual experiences and minor ailments, all of which may contribute to their physiochemical dysfunctions. There is little recognition also of the fact that chemical and psychological measures often are unreliable, fluctuating from time to time in the ratings and scores they produce. Along this line is the often overlooked fact that recently admitted patients to a hospital are different in many respects (e.g., family support or effects of heavy tranquilization) from long-term patients.

Perhaps the most important methodological problem, however, has been the tendency to group patients in terms of traditional nosological categories. The detrimental effect of classifying research subjects on this basis has been raised often in this book and cannot be stressed too much. Schizophrenia, for example, is not a homogeneous clinical group; research has shown repeatedly that there is greater variability in physiochemical functioning among this classification of patients than is found in the normal population. The likelihood of obtaining clear-cut results from this heterogeneous population, therefore, is close to zero. Some of the hypotheses that have been presented in this section may ultimately be valid for some of these patients, but not for all. Not only must we recognize the global nature of these diagnostic categories but we must be prepared to divide and rearrange them in accordance with new biological or psychological findings. Unless psychopathologists are sufficiently open minded to reorganize their traditional habits of thinking, the search for clearcut biogenic factors will remain in a hopeless morass for years to come.

Despite the muddle of alternate hypotheses and conflicting research data, there is ample reason to suspect that physiochemical dysfunctions and differences in biochemical individuality will prove to be of etiological significance in psychopathology. It is clear, however, that whatever their role, they interact in complex ways with psychogenic factors. Research must not seek to answer the question of whether physiochemical variables are the cause or the consequence of behavior pathology, but rather *how* they interact with experience. To say that biogenic and psychogenic factors are inextricably intertwined is a truism, however; the intricate strands and sequences of this interaction must be traced as carefully as our methodology will permit.

## CONCLUDING COMMENTS AND SUMMARY

Man's biological equipment does not passively receive and store incoming stimuli from the environment; rather, it plays an active role in regulating what, when and how external events will be experienced. Unusual biological sensitivities or impairments in the internal mechanisms of activation and control can lead to marked distortions in perception and behavior.

Recognizing the validity of these observations, we have attempted in this chapter to review some of the biogenic theories that have been proposed to account for psychopathology and have examined some of the data gathered in support of them. Striking differences between normals and psychotics have been reported frequently, but these data rarely are consistent from one study to another and, in general, do not follow sufficiently ordered patterns to enable the confirmation or rejection of theoretical hypotheses.

The equivocal nature of biogenic data can be attributed in large measure to flaws in research methodology. Much of the work has been based on small samples, questionable procedures and inadequate statistical analyses. Potential confounding variables have been left uncontrolled, making it impossible to evaluate the precise role of the hypothesized factor. Obvious sources of error such as diet, length of hospitalization, prior medication and concurrent physical disease were ignored or bypassed. Thus, the difficult task of unraveling subtle biogenic factors was made all the more difficult by failing to control these unwanted variables.

Perhaps the most serious methodological error vitiating research has been the erroneous assumption that diagnostic groups such as schizophrenia comprise biologically homogeneous disease entities. This grouping of essentially different syndromes into one category may explain the persistent difficulty in finding a common etiological factor; in searching for biophysical causes, it would seem more rational to group patients in terms of their biophysical commonalities, rather than their overt clinical similarity.

Another problem is less a methodological one than a logical one. Psychological disturbances are known to lead to a variety of changes in biological functioning, e.g., anxiety releases excessive amounts of epinephrine in the early stages of most illness. Recognizing that emotional stress can result in biological change leads us to the proverbial "hen-egg" question. Are abnormalities in biological functioning the cause or the consequence of psychological stress? Do patients possess a biological dysfunction because of their emotional illness, or are they emotionally ill because they possess a biological dysfunction?

A summary of some of the major topics and issues raised in this chapter follows.

1.   Despite controversies about the mode of genetic transmission, and inconsistencies in the findings of research, there remains a substantial body of data to indicate that *heredity* does play a determinant role in a limited number of pathological patterns. Recent interpretations of research data suggest that the cumulative effects of multiple minor genes (polygenes) may be of greater significance than single major genes. It should be made clear, however, that whatever mode of transmission proves to be most accurate, genetic factors do *not* operate in all forms of psychopathology nor are they usually sufficient in themselves to elicit behavior disorders where they do occur.

2.   Although *prenatal experiences* are neither uniform nor ideal for all fetuses, only a few types of psychopathology have been ascribed to this period. The primary consequence of deleterious pre- and perinatal experiences is mental retardation. As research progresses, this essentially unexplored field may provide important new leads to the etiology of other clinical conditions.

3.   Every child enters the world with a distinctive and stable pattern of behavior dispositions and reaction sensitivities which evoke special kinds of counterreactions and attitudes from his parents and siblings. These biologically based *infantile reaction patterns* persist into later childhood for two reasons: (1) there is evidence that internal biological functions do not change appreciably with maturation and (2) the child evokes reactions from others which tend to reinforce and intensify these initial dispositions.

4.   There is ample evidence that particular bodily forms and structures, referred to as *morphology,* are related to certain behavioral dispositions. Biogenic interpretations of this correlation tend to focus on the notion of a genetic linkage between morphology and temperament. Psychogenic theorists contend that these relationships can be accounted for equally well by the operation of a variety of environmental influences. One such interpretation, that physical structure may facilitate or limit the kinds of behaviors an individual will experience as rewarding, seems especially promising as a model for handling reciprocal interactions between biogenic factors and learning.

5.   Because of the complicated pattern of interneuronal circuitry, *neuroanatomical defects* within the central nervous system usually upset several psychological functions simultaneously. Theorists have proposed a number of sites of neurological impairment which might underlie the symptomatology of the major forms of psychopathology. Most notable among these are the reticular formation, the limbic system and synaptic junctions within the cortex. These theories must be viewed as speculative, however, given our current limited empirical knowledge of neuropsychological processes.

6.   Many hypotheses have been proposed implicating different *physiochemical dysfunctions* as primary determinants of pathological behavior. Autonomic system imbalances, impairments in adrenal secretion and a host of body toxins are among those most prominently conjectured. Despite the phenomenal increase in recent research activity, the available data are not sufficient to permit either the confirmation or rejection of any of these hypotheses.

7.   The present state of theoretical controversy and the essentially equivocal data gathered in search of biogenic factors have drawn pessimistic and even cynical commentary from some quarters. Psychopathologists of a psychogenic persuasion hasten to point out the methodological flaws of biogenic research. Certainly the checkered history of ill-conceived theories and the tendency on the part of biogenic researchers to report evidence favoring their hypotheses prematurely have given ample justification for caution, if not cynicism. Despite reason for caution, new insights and bold ideas should not be discarded. Cynicism at this point will deter us from seeking suggestive trends that may lead to important discoveries.

8.   The search for biogenic determinants of psychopathology will be handicapped unless researchers recognize the high degree of biophysical individuality among men. Each person's biological make-up is, in many respects, unlike others, and bears no simple relationship to a hypothetical norm. These patterns of individuality should be viewed, however, not as a methodological complication, but as an opportunity to explore a new dimension of etiology. The notion of a continuum composed of natural constitutional variations in neurological structure and physiochemical functioning may, in the long run, prove to be more productive to the study of biogenic factors than

the current search for diseases, defects and dysfunctions.

It would be wise to recognize before we go on to chapter 5 that the line traditionally drawn between biogenic and psychogenic factors does not exist in nature. We separate them largely as a convenience to enable theorists and researchers to focus on different sources and levels of data. Logically speaking, every psychological event experienced by man registers on some biological substrate, and every biological event has some, albeit indirect, bearing on man's psychological functions. The intrinsic isomorphism of biologic and psychologic phenomena is more relevant to philosophical discussion, however, than it is to the scientific study of psychopathology. Distinctions between these two conceptual levels are necessary since without them scientists cannot specify and elaborate the different facets of events which they wish to investigate and communicate to their colleagues. Scientists must apply different conceptual labels to the same set of events in order to highlight those features and dimensions of psychopathology which are most relevant to their research. In chapter 5 we will discuss events and processes which have been formulated most clearly in terms of psychological theories and concepts.

# Chapter 5

# PSYCHOGENIC FACTORS

Sidney Goodman—*Man Waiting* (1961). (Collection, The Museum of Modern Art, New York. Gift of Mr. and Mrs. Walter Bareiss.)

## INTRODUCTION

In the previous chapter we stressed the view that biological functions play an active role in regulating what, when and how events will be experienced; the nervous and endocrine systems do not accept passively what is fed into it. This active process means that unusual biological sensitivities or defects may result in perceptual distortions, thought disorders and pathological behaviors.

Although behavior pathology may be triggered by biogenic abnormalities, the mere specification of a biogenic cause is not sufficient for an adequate etiological analysis. Even in cases where clear-cut biogenic factors can be identified, it is necessary to trace the developmental sequence of experiences which transform these defects into a manifest form of psychopathology; the need for this more extensive developmental analysis is evident by the fact that some individuals with biological defects function effectively, whereas other, similarly afflicted individuals, succumb to maladaptation and psychopathology. Clearly, the biological defect, in itself, cannot account for such divergences in development. Pathological behaviors that are precipitated initially by biological abnormalities are not simple or direct products of these defects; rather, they

emerge through a complex sequence of interactions which include environmental experience and learning.

A major theme of this chapter is that psychopathology develops as a result of an intimate interplay of intraorganismic and environmental forces; such interactions start at the time of conception and continue throughout life. Individuals with similar biological potentials emerge with different personality patterns depending on the environmental conditions to which they were exposed. These patterns unfold and change as new biological maturations interweave within the context of new environmental encounters. In time, these patterns stabilize into a distinctive hierarchy of behaviors which remain relatively consistent through the everchanging stream of experience.

To state that biological factors and environmental experiences interact is a truism; we must be more specific and ask how, exactly, these interactions take place.

Before we begin, let us discount questions about the proportionate contribution of biological factors as contrasted to environmental learning. The search to answer such questions is not only impossible from a methodological point of view, but is logically misleading. We could not, given our present state of technical skill, begin to tease out the relative contribution of these two sources

158

of variance. Furthermore, a search such as this would be based on a misconception of the nature of interaction. The character and degree of contribution of either biogenic or psychogenic factors are inextricably linked to the character and degree of the contribution of the other. For example, biological influences are not uniform from one situation to the next but vary as a function of the environmental conditions within which they arise. The position we take then is that both factors contribute to all behavior patterns and that their respective contributions are determined by reciprocal and changing combinations of interdependence.

Let us return now to the question of how, exactly, biogenic and psychogenic factors interact in the development of personality and psychopathology.

In the previous chapter we examined a number of ways in which biological factors can shape, facilitate or limit the nature of the individual's experiences and learning. For example, the same objective environment will be perceived as different by individuals who possess different biological sensibilities; people register different stimuli at varying intensities in accord with their unique pattern of alertness and sensory acuity. From this fact we should see that experience itself is shaped at the outset by the biological equipment of the person. Furthermore, the constitutional structure of an individual will strengthen the probability that he will learn certain forms of behavior. Not only will his body build, strength, energy, neurological make-up and autonomic system reactivity influence the stimuli he will seek or be exposed to, but they will determine, in large measure, which types of behaviors he will find are successful for him in dealing with these encounters.

We must recognize further, that the interaction between biological and psychological factors is not unidirectional such that biological determinants always precede and influence the course of learning and experience; the order of effects can be reversed, especially in the early stages of development. From recent research we learn that biological maturation is largely dependent on favorable environmental experience; the development of the biological substrate itself, therefore, can be disrupted, even completely arrested, by depriving the maturing organism of stimulation at sensitive periods of rapid neurological growth. The profound effect of these experiences upon biological capacities will be a central theme in this chapter; we will contend that the sheer quantity as well as the quality of these early experiences is a crucial aspect in the

development of several pathological patterns of personality.

Beyond the crucial role of these early experiences, we will argue further that there is a circularity of interaction in which initial biological dispositions in young children evoke counterreactions from others which accentuate their disposition. The notion that the child plays an active role in creating environmental conditions which, in turn, serve as a basis for reinforcing his biological tendencies is illustrated well in this quote from Cameron and Magaret (1951):

. . . the apathy that characterizes an unreactive infant may deprive him of many of the reactions from others which are essential to his biosocial maturation. His unresponsiveness may discourage his parents and other adults from fondling him, talking to him or providing him with new and challenging toys, so that the poverty of his social environment sustains his passivity and social isolation. If such a child develops behavior pathology, he is likely to show an exaggeration or distortion of his own characteristic reactions in the form of retardation, chronic fatigue or desocialization.

This thesis suggests, then, that the normally distributed continuum of biological dispositions which exists among young children is widened gradually because initial dispositions give rise to experiences that feed back and accentuate these dispositions. Thus, biological tendencies are not only perpetuated but intensified as a consequence of their interaction with experience.

The argument that biogenic and psychogenic factors are intimately connected does not mean that psychogenic events cannot produce psychopathology of their own accord. Geneticists, as noted in the previous chapter, refer to the concept of phenocopies, that is, characteristics arising entirely from the action of environmental events which simulate those produced by genes. In a like fashion, psychogenic experiences may lead to pathological behaviors that are indistinguishable from those generated by the interplay of biological and psychological forces. Severe personal trauma, social upheaval or other more insidious pressures can reverse an individual's normal pattern and prompt a pathological reaction. Thus, not only are there exceptions to the general rule that biological dispositions and experiences interact to shape the course of adjustment, but a promising beginning may be upset by unusual or unfortunate circumstances.

Despite the fact that there are cases in which later experience can reverse early behavior patterns, we cannot understand these cases fully without reference to the historical background of events which precede them. We assert that there is an intrinsic continuity throughout life of personality functioning; thus, the present chapter has been organized to follow the sequence of natural development. Furthermore, not only do we contend that childhood events are more significant to personality formation than later events but we also believe that later behaviors are related in a determinant way to early experience.

Despite an occasional and dramatic disjunctiveness in development, there is an orderly and sequential continuity, engendered by mechanisms of self-perpetuation and social reinforcement, which links the past to the present. The format for this chapter demonstrates this theme of developmental continuity.

# EFFECT OF VOLUME AND TIMING OF EARLY STIMULATION UPON MATURATION

Certain forms of pathological behavior appear immutable, resistant to change under all forms of therapy. Psychoanalytic techniques may uncover deeply hidden infantile strivings, environmental management may remove aggravating precipitants and programs of extinction and conditioning may zero in on specific symptoms, but all to no avail. The behavior is so deeply and pervasively ingrained that it is judged to be not only unalterable but an intrinsic part of the individual's biological make-up.

Such deeply rooted traits need not signify the presence of an innate disposition, nor need they stem from the effects of a biological trauma or disease. Embedded patterns of behavior may arise entirely as a product of psychological experience, experience which shapes the development of biological structures so profoundly as to transform it into something substantially different from what it might otherwise have been.

Under what circumstances can psychological experience exert so profound an effect?

An answer that enjoys a great degree of acceptance among psychopathologists is experience during infancy and early childhood. The major impetus for this view can be traced to the seminal writings of Freud at the turn of this century. The observations of a number of eminent European ethologists on the effects of early stimulation upon adult behavior in animals have added substantial naturalistic evidence to support this position in the past twenty years. Experimental work during this period has shown more precisely that environmental stimulation is crucial to the maturation of several psychological functions.

The thesis that early experience has a paramount effect upon personality formation is taken for granted by many theorists and researchers; this consensus is not reason enough, however, to accept it without further elaboration. We must ask why early experience is crucial, and, more

specifically, how this experience shapes the biological substrate of personality.

Several answers advanced in response to these questions will be elucidated throughout the chapter. For the moment we will concentrate on one: the dependence of maturation on early environmental stimulation. The thesis may be stated simply: certain biological capacities will fail to develop fully as a result of impoverished stimulation; conversely, these same capacities may be overdeveloped as a consequence of enriched stimulation.

## PLASTICITY OF THE MATURING BIOLOGICAL SUBSTRATE

Maturation refers to the intricate sequence of ontogenetic development in which initially diffuse and inchoate structures of the body progressively unfold into specific functional units. Early stages of structural differentiation precede and overlap with more advanced stages in which lower level units interweave and connect into a complex and integrated network of functions displayed only in the adult organism.

It was once believed that the course of maturation—from diffusion to differentiation to integration—arose exclusively from inexorable forces laid down in the genes. Maturation was thought to evolve according to a preset timetable that operated autonomously of environmental conditions. This view no longer is tenable. Maturation follows an orderly progression, but the developmental sequence and level of the organism's ultimate biological equipment are substantially dependent on a variety of stimuli and nutritional supplies from the environment. Thus, maturation progresses not in a fixed course leading to a predetermined level, but is subject to numerous variations which reflect the character of the organism's environment.

The answer to why early experiences are more crucial to development than later experiences derives in part from the fact that the peak period of maturation occurs from the prenatal stage through the first years of postnatal life. Granting that experience can influence the course of maturation, it is reasonable to conclude that the organism is subject to more alteration in the early, or more plastic years, than when it has fully matured. An example in the sphere of body structure may illustrate this point well. Inadequate nutrition in childhood may result in stunted bone development, leading to a permanently shortened stature; no amount of nutrition in adult life can compensate to increase the individual's height. However, had adequate nutrition been given during the formative or maturing years, the child might have grown to his full potential. Similarly, in the nervous system, prenatal deficiencies in nutrition will retard or arrest the differentiation of gross tissue into separable neural cells; early postnatal deficiencies will deter or preclude the proliferation of neural collaterals and their integration. However, deficiencies arising later in life will have little or no effect on the development of these neural structures.

## CONCEPT OF STIMULUS NUTRIMENT

The concept of nutrition must be viewed more broadly than we commonly view it if we are to understand its role in the development of biological maturation. Nutrition should be conceived as including not only obvious supplies such as those found in food, but in what Rapaport had termed "stimulus nutriment" (1958). This notion of nutrition suggests that the simple impingement of environmental stimuli upon the maturing organism has a direct bearing on the chemical composition, ultimate size and patterns of neural branching within the brain. Stated simply, the sheer *amount* of stimulation to which the child is exposed has a determinant effect on the maturation of his neural capacities. (We are bypassing, for the moment, any reference to the effects of the timing or quality of the stimulative source, factors which also have a bearing on development.)

The notion that degree of stimulation can produce changes in neural development is not new. Spurzheim, in 1815, proposed that the organs of the brain increase by exercise. Ramon y Cajal suggested in 1895 that since neural cells cannot multiply after birth, cerebral exercise will result in the expansion of neural collaterals and

in the growth of more extended intercortical connections. For more than fifty years, experimental biologists have reported that the development and maintenance of neural connections are dependent on periodic stimulus activation. As early as 1915, Bok showed that nerve fibers grow out along the path of repeated stimuli; he termed this phenomenon *stimulogenous fibrillation*. Similar observations in the 1930's led Kappers to formulate the concept of *neurobiotaxis*. Valid criticisms have been leveled at certain features of these concepts, but there appears to be considerable support from recent research that neurochemical processes, essential to the growth and branching of neural structures, are activated by stimulation; extremes of stimulus impoverishment or enrichment appear to prompt an under or overdevelopment of neural connections and patterns (Conel, 1939, 1955; Pasamanick et al., 1956; Scheibel and Scheibel, 1964; Eisenberg, 1967).

The belief that the maturing organism must receive periodic stimulus nutriments for proper development has led some theorists to suggest that the organism actively seeks an optimum level of stimulation. Thus, just as the infant cries out in search of food when deprived, or wails in response to pain, so too may it display behaviors which provide it with sensory stimulation requisite to maturation. Murphy (1947) and Butler and Rice (1963), for example, have proposed that the maturing organism possesses a series of "adient drives" or "stimulus hungers." They note that although infants are restricted largely to stimulation supplied by environmental agents, they often engage in what appears to be random exercises, exercises which, in effect, furnish them with the stimulation they require. Thus, in the first months of life, infants can be seen to track auditory and visual stimuli; as they mature further, they grasp incidental objects, and then mouth, rotate and fondle them. Furthermore, we observe that the young of all species engage in more exploratory and frolicsome behavior than adults. These seemingly "functionless" play activities may not be functionless at all; they may be essential to growth, an instrumental means of self-stimulation that is indispensable to the maturation and maintenance of biological capacities.

Implicit in the above is the view that the organism's partly matured capacities enable it to provide for itself sources of stimulation necessary for further maturation; according to this thesis, each stage of maturational development establishes a foundation of capacities which are prerequisites for, and conducive to, the development of more advanced stages of maturation. For example, a child with deficient sensory capacities such as vision may be unable to maneuver within its environment, and consequently may be delayed in the development of motor capacities such as walking and running. Similarly, a child with a marked hearing loss may develop inarticulate speech since he is unable to discriminate sounds.

## CONSEQUENCES OF EARLY STIMULUS IMPOVERISHMENT

It should be evident from the foregoing, that unless certain chemicals and cells are activated by environmental stimulation, the biological substrate for a variety of psychological functions may be impaired irrevocably. Furthermore, deficiencies in functions which normally mature in early life may set the stage for a progressive retardation of functions which mature later.

What evidence is there that serious consequences may arise from an inadequate supply of early stimulation?

Beach and Jaynes (1954), Thompson (1961), Melzack (1965), Scott (1968) and Newton and Levine (1968) provide extensive reviews of relevant experimental findings; we shall refer here only briefly to some of the principal conclusions derived from this growing body of work.

Numerous investigators have shown that an impoverished environment in early life results in permanent adaptational difficulties. For example, experimental animals reared in isolation tend to be markedly deficient in such traits as emotionality, activity level, social behavior, curiosity and learning ability. As adult organisms they possess a reduced capacity to manipulate their environments, to discriminate or abstract essentials, to devise strategies and to cope with stress.

Comparable results have been found among humans. Children reared under unusually severe conditions of restriction, such as in orphanages, evidence deficits in social awareness and reactivity, are impulsive, deficient in solving intellectual problems, susceptible to sensorimotor dysfunctions and display a generally low resistance to stress and disease. These consequences have double-barreled effects. Not only is the child hampered by the specific deficiency he suffers, but each of these deficiencies yields progressive and long-range consequences in that they preclude or retard the development of more complex capacities. Thus, early deficits may precipitate a whole series of stunted or distorted adaptive capacities.

## CONSEQUENCES OF EARLY STIMULUS ENRICHMENT

Intense levels of early stimulation also have effects. Several investigators have demonstrated among animals that an enriched environment in early life results in measurable changes in brain chemistry and brain weight. Others have found that early stimulation accelerates the maturation of the pituitary-adrenal system, whereas equivalent stimulation at later stages was ineffective. On the behavioral level, enriched environments appear to enhance problem-solving abilities and increase the capacity of the organism to withstand stress. Comparable data among humans is either lacking or equivocal. Nevertheless, several theorists have proposed that enriching experiences can foster the development of higher intellectual abilities and adaptive coping behaviors.

There has been little systematic exploration of the potentially detrimental effects of environmental enrichment since researchers and clinicians alike are inclined to assume that the opposite side of the coin, that of impoverishment, is more conducive to pathological consequences. This assumption probably is correct, but it should not lead us to overlook the possibility that excessive stimulation can lead to an overdevelopment of certain biological capacities which may prove disruptive to effective psychological functioning. Thus, just as excessive food nutrition leads to obesity and physical ill health, so too may stimulus enrichment produce unhealthy psychological growth. For example, the enhancement or strengthening of certain neural patterns, such as those associated with emotional reactivity, may dispose the organism to overreact to social situations. The predominance of any biological response tendency may throw off key what would otherwise have been a normal or more balanced pattern of psychological functioning. Clearly then, the enrichment of biological capacities does not produce beneficial consequences only; whether enhanced functions prove advantageous or disadvantageous to the individual depends on which of the many and diverse capacities have been enriched, and whether the resultant pattern is balanced or unbalanced.

## NEUROPSYCHOLOGICAL STAGES OF DEVELOPMENT

The previous section focused only on the determinant effects of *volume* of early stimulation. Our attention now will turn from the issue of "how much" to that of "when"; here we will explore the view that the specific time of stimulation has a direct relationship to its effect. The question can be raised: are the effects of extremes in stimulation greater at certain periods of early maturation than others? Interest will be directed and limited to the *interaction* of volume and timing, not to the content or quality of the stimulative source. Questions about the effects of different kinds of stimuli will be discussed in the next section; for the present, we shall deal only with the interplay between "how much" and "when," not with "what." In reality, of course, these three elements are not separable. We distinguish among them, however, not only for pedagogic purposes; we believe that each of these variables can produce different and specifiable effects upon the development of personality; they should be distinguished, therefore, for theoretical clarification and research execution as well.

Two kinds of relationships may be observed between the effect of a stimulus and the time of its occurrence; we may term these *recurrent periods* and *sensitive developmental periods*.

The first relates to recurrent tissue needs, best illustrated in periodic deficit conditions known as hunger and thirst. At various times each day, the depletion of certain nutritional substances leads to increased levels of neurological activation and the selective focusing of sensory receptors. As a consequence, stimuli to which attention is not ordinarily given become dominant and have a marked impact upon the organism. For example, while driving along a road, we tend to notice signs pertaining to food if we are hungry; after a good meal, however, these signs pass by in a blur. The role of these recurrent periods will be elaborated when we discuss, in a later section, the operation of what is known as "motivation" in learning.

The second, and less obvious, relationship between timing and stimulus impact will be our principal focus in this section. It refers to the observation that certain types of stimuli have an especially pronounced effect upon the organism at particular and well-circumscribed periods of maturation. At these periods or stages, the organism is unusually responsive to and substantially influenced by the action of these stimuli.

## CONCEPT OF SENSITIVE DEVELOPMENTAL PERIODS

The contention that stimuli produce different effects at different ages can scarcely be questioned, e.g., the shapely legs of an attractive girl catch the eye of most young and middle-aged men but rarely draw the attention of preadoles-

cent boys and senile men. The concept of sensitive or critical periods of development states more than this, however. It argues, first, that there are limited time periods during which particular stimuli are necessary for the full maturation of an organism and, second, that if these stimuli are experienced either before or after the sensitive period, they will have minimal or no effects. Thus, if critical periods pass without proper stimulus nourishment, the organism will suffer certain forms of maldevelopment which are irremediable, that is, cannot be compensated for by the presentation of the "right" stimuli at a later date.

The rationale for the sensitive period concept was presented initially in the field of experimental embryology. One of the early researchers, Child (1941), found that rapidly growing tissues of an embryo are especially sensitive to environmental stimulation; the morphological structure of proliferating cells was determined, in large part, by the character of the stimulus environment within which it was embedded. At later stages, where growth had slowed down, these same cells were resistant to environmental influences. These embryological findings suggested that the effects of environmental stimuli upon morphological structure are most pronounced *when tissue growth is rapid*.

It is unclear as to what mechanisms operate to account for the special interaction between stimulation and periods of rapid neural growth. *First,* there is evidence that stimulation itself promotes a proliferation of neural collaterals, and that this effect is most pronounced when growth potential is greatest. *Second,* early stimulation may result in a selective growth process in which certain collaterals establish particular interneuronal connections to the exclusion of others. *Third,* we may hypothesize that once these connections are embedded biologically, the first set of stimuli which traverse them preempt the circuit and thereby decrease the chance that subsequent stimuli will have comparable effects. Whatever the sequence and mechanisms may be, it appears clear that the effects of stimulation are maximal at periods of rapid tissue growth; at this point in our knowledge we only can speculate on the apparatus involved.

The notion that brief early experiences may produce a permanent modification of functions has been theorized by scientists in fields other than embryology. Lorenz (1935), the eminent European ethologist, has discovered critical periods during which primary social bonds are permanently established in birds. In human research, McGraw (1943) demonstrated the existence of peak periods for learning specific motor skills, and illustrated the resistance of these skills to subsequent extinction. Murphy (1947) reports a number of studies to support the concept of canalization, a notion signifying an irreversible initial learning process.

Developmental theorists have proposed, either by intention or inadvertently, schemas based on a concept of sensitive periods. Few, however, have formulated this notion in terms of neurological growth stages.

Heinz Werner (1940), for example, has proposed a comparative-developmental approach in which he coordinates the total behavior of organisms in accord with a basic set of developmental principles. His central thesis is that development proceeds from an initially undifferentiated and diffuse state to one that is progressively refined and differentiated. As the organism matures further, these differentiated functions intermesh and become integrated into smoothly coordinated higher capacities. The developmental sequence proposed by Werner is correct as a general descriptive system, but it is too all-encompassing and undifferentiated to serve as a useful model for personality and psychopathology; nevertheless, two efforts to bring Werner's notions in line with pathological behavior have recently been proposed (Goldman, 1962; Bibace et al., 1969).

The theories and studies of Piaget (1952, 1955) provide us with an insightful picture of the invariable and hierarchic order in the developmental progression; he demonstrates how each progressively more complex stage is based on foundations established in preceding stages, and prepares the groundwork for succeeding ones. Pertinent to our own formulations is Piaget's sequence of intellectual development which he divides into several major periods; the first of these is known as "reflexive," the second as "sensorimotor" and the third through fifth are abbreviated as "representational-conceptual"; these periods correspond closely to the three major neuropsychological stages to be presented later in this chapter. Useful as Piaget's schema may be as a model for general psychological development, it is of limited value to us since he did not focus his observations on matters relevant to psychopathology.

Phillips (1968) has formulated a well-researched and promising theory of psychopathology based, in large measure, on a synthesis of Werner's and Piaget's developmental notions. Although his proposals are not founded on the concept of sensitive neurological periods, having as their central thesis the development of "social competence," his derivations concerning the principal types of psychopathological syndromes are highly similar to those presented in this text.

The brilliant speculations of Hebb (1949), phrased according to developmental concepts such as cell-assemblies and phase-sequences, may be viewed as parallel to the neurological orientation proposed here; unfortunately, they have limited applicability to psychopathologic development. More recently, Milner (1967) has furnished a carefully detailed review and theory of maturation with explicit reference to the interrelationships of neural and behavioral development; although the theory is presented in sketchy form, she coordinates the impact of experience on neurological growth with psychopathology, providing a model similar to that formulated in this chapter.

Freud's theory of discrete stages of psychosexual development, in which particular early experiences at specified times in development have deeply etched and lasting effects, may be viewed as the first major psychopathological theory based on a concept of sensitive periods. Despite Freud's early training as a neurologist, his schema was founded *not* in terms of internal neurological maturation, but in terms of a peripheral sphere of maturation, that of sexual development. His concern lay with variations in external sensory erogenous zones (e.g., oral, anal and genital), not with the more central neurological structures which underlie and are basic to them.

It would appear from recent neurological and behavioral research that a more profitable basis for organizing a system of developmental periods would be in terms of internal neurological growth potentials. Relationships certainly will exist between these inner variables and other less centrally involved variables, such as Freud's concept of erogenous zones. But to focus on peripheral spheres of maturation as did Freud, is, from our view, to put the proverbial "cart before the horse."

Other theorists have organized the stages of personality development in accord with interpersonal experience. First among these is Harry Stack Sullivan, whose views were discussed previously in chapter 2. Sullivan's developmental notions stress the progressive capacity of the child to understand and communicate with others. The first stage of infancy represents a period of preverbal and primitive imagery in which generalized feelings of trust and security are the primary features of interpersonal communication. The second stage is characterized by the emergence of verbal communication; communication at this point is highly idiosyncratic, however, and often is illogical and confused. In the final stage, the child's capacities have matured sufficiently to enable him to grasp the consensually validated, that is, the shared meanings of language and communication. Psychopathology arises, according to Sullivan, when the child fails to receive proper experiences requisite to the progressive development of consensually validated communication. Anxiety-producing or deficient and confusing communications lead to distortions in the development of communication capacities, and result in an inability to maintain adequate interpersonal relationships.

As with Freud, Sullivan's schema tends to be somewhat narrow in scope. To Freud, the sexual variable was central to each of the successive periods of development. Sullivan opts for a single and primary variable also, that of interpersonal communication. No doubt, both Freud and Sullivan are correct in specifying two of the crucial elements operative in the developmental sequence; the question that arises, however, is whether the foundation of a comprehensive theory of stages should be constructed from either of the two "peripheral" variables they espouse or from a more central neurological process.

Erikson has formulated an important synthesis of both Freud's and Sullivan's proposals, one enriched further by adding to them the contribution of the "ego" theorists. The major outlines of Erikson's developmental theory, termed the "phases of epigenesis" were presented in chapter 2. To refresh our memory, Erikson extends Freud's focus on childhood psychosexuality, that is, the development of id energies, by adding to them the role of constructive sensorimotor and cognitive capacities, that is, the development of ego energies. These two sources of energy are interconnected within the maturing infant and provide him with a "succession of potentialities for significant interaction with those who tend him." Thus, Erikson attempts to bring together within a single conception of developmental stages the previously separate spheres of sexuality, ego capacity and interpersonal relatedness. Furthermore, he relates this developmental progression to a series of personal and interpersonal crises. At each step in maturation, the child faces a new and decisive encounter with the environment in which his maturing capacities are tested and refined before he progresses toward the realization of his full potentials.

Erikson's theory is the most comprehensive formulation for organizing the varied dimensions of personality growth. Furthermore, his recognition of the crises encountered during each epigenetic period makes his schema relevant to an understanding of psychopathologic development. In presenting the neuropsychological stages of development that have been formulated for this chapter, we will draw freely upon Erikson's seminal ideas; his views owe, in turn, a special indebtedness to Freud, Sullivan and his fellow ego theorists.

Despite the scope and relevance of Erikson's theory to pathological development, it is not coordinated directly to the notion of neurological growth and maturation. As stressed earlier, the central logic for a conception of sensitive periods is founded on evidence that environmental stimuli have their most pronounced effects at times of potentially rapid neural growth. It would seem reasonable, therefore, to revise Erikson's synthesis in line with this neurological viewpoint. Recast in this fashion, it will have a firmer basis as a theory of sensitive periods, and will be formulated in terms consonant with our growing knowledge of the neurological substrate of development.

It is appropriate, before we progress further, to ask a simple but important question: how precise is our knowledge of the character and sequence of neurological maturation? The simplest and most direct answer, given our present state of empirical research, is that we have little knowledge that is clear and relevant; we grasp only the barest outline of the diverse and intricate features which unfold in the developing nervous system. At best, we can make only a few rough distinctions for separating the developmental sequence into identifiable periods of rapid neurological growth. These neurologically sensitive periods must be inferred from sketchy odds and ends gathered from fields as diverse as embryology, neurophysiology, ethology, behavior development and childhood psychopathology. The framework we shall employ to divide these neurological stages will be revised, no doubt, as research progresses.

How shall we divide the maturational sequence, given the sketchy knowledge we possess today?

Keeping in mind the tentative nature of the proposed divisions, and the substantial overlapping which exists between successive stages (all aspects of growth occur simultaneously, though in varying degrees), current theory and research suggests three broad periods of development in which an optimal point of interaction occurs between neurological maturation and environmental stimulation:

1. The first stage, extending in its peak period from birth to 18 months of age, evidences

a rapid maturation of sensory receptors, and is characterized by a substantial dependency of the infant upon others. This stage will be termed the period of *sensory-attachment*.

2. The second period, beginning roughly at 12 months and extending in its peak development through the sixth year, is characterized by a rapid differentiation of motor capacities which combine and coordinate with developed sensory functions; this integration enables the young child to locomote, manipulate and verbalize in an increasingly skillful way. This stage will be referred to as the period of *sensorimotor-autonomy*.

3. The third and final period of maturation begins at about four to five years of age and continues through adolescence; it is characterized at first by the rapid development of higher cortical connections and in its later phases by the turbulent effects of rapidly maturing sexual hormones. These advances enable the child to reflect, plan and act independent of parental supervision. We shall call this stage the period of *intra-cortical-initiative*.

Obviously, this simple tripartite schema does not differentiate the manifold and detailed substages of neurological development; that task awaits future research. We have referred to these periods as the "neuropsychological stages of development" because they group together and summarize what we believe are the psychologically relevant features of neurological growth, that is, they focus on those neurological capacities that are both sensitive to environmental influence and crucial to the individual's capacity to cope with his social environment. Let us keep in mind that although these stages reach their peak periods at different ages, they extend through the entire course of development. As maturation progresses from one stage to the next, the sensitivities of preceding stages do not cease, but merely become less prominent.

### Comment

Let us note a number of qualifications upon the generalizations we shall be making before we elaborate the features and consequences associated with each of these stages.

1. During the sensitive developmental stages, minimal external stimulation produces maximal neuronal patterning; subsequent neural growth, such as in adulthood, requires considerably greater external stimulation. One of the distinguishing features of man's immense brain is that it contains a tremendous number of surplus neural fibers which can be stimulated to develop collaterals throughout adulthood. Thus,

inadequate neuronal connections, especially in the higher cortical areas, may be strengthened after maturity.

2. It is erroneous to assume that children of the same chronological age are comparable with respect to the level and character of their biological capacities. Not only does each infant start life with a distinctive pattern of neurological, physiochemical and sensory equipment, but he progresses at his own maturational rate toward some ultimate but unknown level of potential. Thus, above and beyond initial differences and their not insignificant consequences, are differences in the rate with which the typical sequence of maturation unfolds. Just as some youngsters grow in rapid spurts, reaching their full height by 13, while others progress slowly and steadily until 19 or 20, so too may children follow different courses in the maturational speed and pattern of their neurological substrates. Furthermore, different regions in the complex nervous system within a single child may mature at different rates. To top it all, the potential or ultimate level of development of each of these neurological capacities will vary widely, not only among children but within each child. Thus, a youngster may have a constitutional disposition to mature a sparse neurological substrate for sensory functions, and a dense and well-branched substrate for intracortical or integrative functions.

A brief summary of the rationale of the neuropsychological stages and their relation to psychopathology may be useful before we furnish a detailed description of their separate developmental features and consequences.

The initial capacities of each organism are established by genetic factors. The sequences in which these capacities mature follow a general species-specific order. However, the rate and level to which these capacities develop are determined in large measure by the amount of stimulation the organism experiences at certain peak periods of neural growth. During growth, the organism utilizes its established capacities as a means of providing itself with the stimulus nutriment required for further development. Despite these efforts, the developing organism usually is dependent upon others to supply its nurturant needs. Failure in stimulus nourishment leads to an undermaturation or a retarded progression in development; overstimulation leads to overdevelopment or unbalanced development. When the peak or sensitive period of neural growth has passed, further development is slow and arduous; for all essential purposes, the organism's neuropsychological capacity has reached its likely upper limits.

Continued stimulus nutriment is required, however, to sustain this level of development. Following the peak period, therefore, the organism will continue to engage in activities which provide a level of stimulation consonant with its capacities; undeveloped, that is, previously impoverished individuals, *once past the peak period of neural growth,* will require a lower level of stimulus maintenance than overdeveloped or previously enriched individuals. Each individual will seek to maintain an optimum level of stimulus activation, that is, a level that corresponds to his developed neuropsychological capacities.

The concept of self-actualization, discussed by such theorists as Goldstein (1939) and Rogers (1959) is implicit in the above formulation. Self-actualization has been used in the literature to represent a hypothetical, all-pervasive, and inherent drive *throughout life* for growth and self-expression. We are suggesting something akin to this concept; however, we think it necessary to divide the actualizing process into two phases. The first deals with an intrinsic *seeking of stimuli to promote maturation during peak periods of neural growth potential;* the second deals with a post-developmental *search for stimulus sustenance.* An analogy with food nutrition may be useful; the young child depends on various proteins, vitamins and so on for the growth of his bodily structure, whereas the adult needs them to sustain and replace what already has grown.

The separation between these two phases of self-actualization has been made to distinguish between the present use of the concept and that formulated by other theorists. For most theorists, self-actualization implies an inherent search for growth *throughout life;* we believe there is minimal justification for such a view, given our knowledge of neurological maturation. Self-actualization, as a growth concept, seems valid during periods of peak maturation, but not postdevelopmentally. "Actualizing tendencies" *after the early developmental periods* can be attributed more appropriately to the operation of learned or acquired drives.

Not all individuals are driven to enlarge their stimulus worlds, that is, to "grow" and expand themselves, as self-actualizing theorists propose. Rather, it seems more consistent with the evidence to suggest that after a particular level of neuropsychological capacity has been reached, most individuals seek to find a stimulus level that is consonant with what they are equipped and accustomed to experience. "Enriching and expanding" stimulus experiences will be as disruptive to the underdeveloped individual as constricting or narrow experiences would be to the overdeveloped individual.

The point being made is that the organism does not "seek to grow" postdevelopmentally, but to find better or more satisfying means to sustain his established level of growth. Early stimulus impoverishment or enrichment establishes a deeply ingrained level or *pattern* for subsequent stimulus sustenance. Stimulus intensities which deviate markedly above or below these ingrained patterns may lead to disruptions or *disorders* in the individual's equilibrium.

Let us now turn to the stimulus characteristics and consequences of the three principal stages of neuropsychological development.

## STAGE 1: SENSORY-ATTACHMENT

The first year or two of life is dominated by *sensory* processes; these functions are basic to subsequent development in that they enable the infant to construct some order out of the initial diffusion and chaos he experiences in his stimulus world. This period has also been termed that of *attachment* because the infant cannot survive on his own, and must affix himself to others who will provide the protection, nutrition and stimulation he needs.

### Development of Sensory Capacities

The early neonatal period has been characterized as one of undifferentiation. This descriptive term suggests that the organism behaves in a diffuse and unintegrated way; perceptions are unfocused and behavioral responses are gross. Recent research indicates that certain sensory functions are well matured at birth and that they progress rapidly in their development shortly thereafter.

One of Freud's signal achievements was his recognition that the mouth region was a richly endowed receptor system through which the neonate establishes his first significant relationship to the stimulus world. It is evident, however, that this oral unit is merely the focal point of a more diverse system of sensory capacities in the infant. Freudians have focused on this well-circumscribed region to the exclusion of other less clearly defined spheres of sensitivity; we now know that it is not only through oral contacts that the infant establishes a sense or "feel" of his environment.

Despite the paucity of knowledge about early receptor sensitivities, experimental studies support the view that the near receptors, involving touch, taste, smell and temperature, are dominant in the neonate. This evidence is not inconsistent with Freud's belief in the importance of the oral region, since the mouth, lips and tongue are especially rich in several of these receptor capacities. However, tactual and kinesthetic sensitivities pervade the entire body, and there is every reason to believe that the infant can discriminate and respond to subtle variations in temperature, texture and general physical comfort.

According to the theory espoused earlier, we would expect that the amount and quality of tactile stimulation to which the neonate is exposed will contribute significantly to his neuropsychological development. Not only may extremely low levels of stimulation result in developmental retardations, but the quality and pattern of this stimulation may lead him to experience generalized feelings of isolation, tension or pleasure. (Parenthetically we might note that care must be taken not to attribute subtle or cognitively complex attitudes to the infant; for example, it is unlikely that a two month old can discern the difference between a rough rejecting mother and one that is clumsy and inexperienced.)

The primacy in the first months of life of touch, taste, temperature and smell recedes as the distance receptors of vision and audition come to the foreground. Whereas the near receptors are limited to bodily contact stimuli in the immediate environment, the distance receptors expand the scope of the infant's experiences by enabling him to survey and explore a far-ranging and infinitely more elaborate sphere of stimuli. Here again, variations in the quantity and quality of his stimulus world can have profound effects on his neuropsychological development.

### Development of Attachment

The neonate does not differentiate between objects and persons; both are experienced simply as stimuli. How does this initial indiscriminateness become transformed into specific attachments to particular stimuli, especially the stimulus of the mother? Phrased less abstractly, we may ask why the two month old infant is intrigued and soothed by most forms of stimulation, the five month old by the behavior of certain toys and the antics of most humans, and the 12 month old only by a special blanket and the presence of mother.

A few words should be said first about what appears to be an innate tendency on the part of infants to turn toward and be soothed by stimulation. Soviet psychologists refer to this attraction to stimuli as the "orienting reflex"; Goldstein (1939) has described it simply as a "turning toward the stimulus." For example, normal infants will automatically close their fists when their palm is stroked, and turn their heads toward shimmering leaves, rather than stare at a blank wall. We know also that stimulation-producing activities and devices (e.g., rocking, wheeling, mobiles and radios) are commonly employed by mothers as a means of capturing the attention and calming the discomforts of their infants. Any one of a number of currently popular terms can be applied to describe this behavior—orienting reflex, stimulus hunger, arousal seeking, exploratory curiosity. Whatever the label, it simply signifies that the newborn organism seems intrinsically attracted and responsive to stimulation.

Let us now return to the main question: how does the neonate's diffuse orientation to stimuli become progressively refined into specific attachments? This process can best be described in terms of concepts and mechanisms utilized in the field of learning; in the next major section of this chapter, we will elaborate the process in a detailed manner; the sequence will briefly be described here.

The newborn, for all essential purposes, is helpless and dependent on others to supply its needs. Separated from the womb at birth, the neonate has lost its "attachment" to the mother's body, and the nurturance it provided. It now must turn toward other sources of attachment if it is to survive, be comforted and obtain the requisite stimulation for its further development. The infant's stimulus seeking and attachment behavior may be viewed, albeit figuratively, as an attempt to reestablish the intimate and gratifying unity lost at birth. Since it will be some years before it can provide these needs on its own, the infant progressively discriminates, through its developing sensory capacities, those objects which have a high nurturant and stimulus value. Attachments may occasionally be made to inanimate objects, such as the odor of a doll's hair or the texture of a favorite blanket, but the infant, under normal conditions, will center his attachments to the complexly stimulating and rewarding object of his mother. Gradually distinguishing her as a stimulus source providing warmth, softness, food and comfort, he begins to seek her touch, her odors and her soothing voice. Thus, his attachment to her.

What systematic evidence is there to support the view that sensory processes play a central role in the development of specific attachments? In large measure, this support is obtained from research on subhuman avian and mammalian species; these data are extrapolated or analogized then to similar behaviors displayed among humans.

One body of animal research deals with what has been referred to as "imprinting" behavior; young birds and sheep, for example, are first attracted to the sight of moving objects, then track or follow them as they locomote (Lorenz, 1935; Hess, 1959; Moltz, 1968). The second body of research, referred to as "the establishment of primary affectional and social bonds," has concentrated on the early behaviors of dogs and monkeys (Scott, 1960, 1968; Harlow, 1960, 1963, 1965; Cairns, 1966); for example, these animals demonstrate attachments to surrogate mother objects who provide soft tactual stimulation.

Research on early social bonds points up the primacy of sensory stimulation over conventional rewards. Harlow, for example, found that "ungiving" surrogate mothers covered with a soft terry cloth were preferred to food-nourishing mothers constructed of wire. Furthermore, he showed that young monkeys cling to terry cloth rather than wire mothers when faced with novel and upsetting objects; thus reassured, they venture forth to explore the initially frightening object. If no mother, or if only the wire mother is present under these conditions, the infant displays continued fear and anxiety. In other studies, noxious air blasts were vented from the terry-cloth mother after the primary bond of attachment was established; following the infliction of this pain, the infant monkey, rather strikingly, clung even more tightly to his "unworthy" terry-cloth mother. According to traditional notions of reward and punishment, we would expect the monkey to have avoided the painful terry-cloth mother. However, if we interpret this finding as

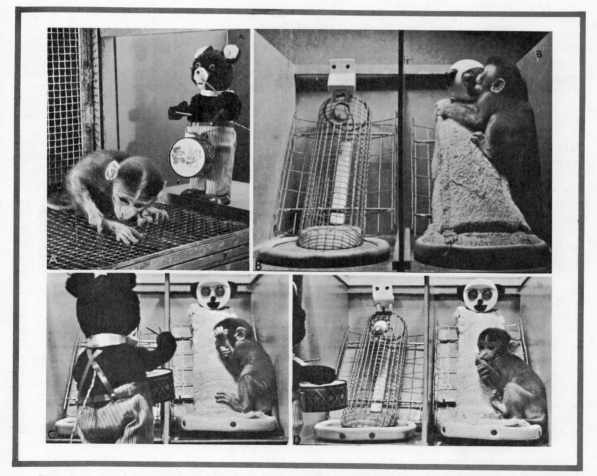

Figure 5-1   A and B. Frightening objects such as a mechanical teddy bear caused almost all infant monkeys to flee to the cloth mother. C and D. After reassurance by pressing and rubbing against the cloth mother they dared to look at the strange object. (Courtesy of Professor Harry F. Harlow.)

evidence of an attachment to the cloth mother, or as a sign of the primacy of sensory stimulation over all other rewards or punishments at this stage, then this seemingly paradoxical result becomes more understandable. In short, these studies support the view that early sensory stimulation gives rise to the development of strong attachment behaviors.

Attachment behavior studies with humans lean heavily on naturalistic evidence. Ribble (1943), Spitz (1965), Bowlby (1952), Gewirtz (1963) and Rheingold (1963), though differing in their interpretation of the mechanisms involved, all conclude that the tactile and kinesthetic stimulation provided by the mother serve as the basis of the infant's attachment. Aspects of their work will be elaborated more fully in later sections.

### Maladaptive Consequences of Impoverishment

What we have stressed thus far is that the simple volume of sensory stimulation is a significant part of the child's environmental experience; let us be mindful, however, that the character or quality of that stimulation is of equal importance; that topic will be dealt with fully in another section in this chapter.

A wealth of clinical evidence is available to show that humans, deprived of adequate maternal care in infancy, display a variety of pathological behaviors. Of course, we cannot design studies to tease out precisely which of the complex of variables that comprise maternal care account for these irreparable consequences; the lives of babies cannot be manipulated to satisfy our scientific curiosity. The value of animal research is clear here since it is possible in these studies to arrange conditions necessary for a more precise analysis of the problem.

Melzack (1965), Riesen (1961) and Beach and Jaynes (1954) have provided extensive reviews of the consequences in animals of early stimulus impoverishment. Briefly, sensory neural fibers atrophy and cannot be regenerated by subsequent stimulation. Almost any means of stimulation (e.g., stroking, tossing, shaking or shocking) will provide the necessary activation for neural development. Inadequate early stimulation in any of the major receptor functions results in marked decrements in the capacity to utilize these and other sensory processes in later life.

Assuming the infant animal has an adequate base of *physical* stimulation, what consequences will follow if it is deprived of *social* stimulation? The profound effects of social isolation have

been studied most thoroughly by Harlow and his associates (1960, 1963, 1965). In a series of studies in which monkeys were totally or partially deprived of social contact, they found that the longer and more complete the social isolation, the more devastating were the behavioral consequences. Deprived monkeys were incapable at maturity of relating to their peers, of participating effectively in sexual activity and of assuming adequate roles as mothers.

Many theorists have sought to relate stimulus impoverishment in human infants to aberrations in later behavior. Most notable in this regard are the views of Bowlby (1952), Goldfarb (1955) and Spitz (1965). According to their observations, an inadequate supply of stimuli from a caretaking environment results in atypical response patterns to nonsocial stimuli and marked deficits in social attachment behaviors; quite often, these are gross developmental retardations, limited capacities for human relationships and a pervasive apathy and depression. These children display inadequate use of their visual and auditory functions; for example, experimenters often are unable to achieve visual contact with these youngsters, and they appear to "look through" observers when approached frontally. Yarrow (1961, 1965) and O'Connor (1968) have furnished amply documented surveys of these findings.

The disorder known as *infantile autism* provides an interesting case in point. These children display excessive preoccupations with inanimate objects, engage in repetitive "self-exercising" activities and seem oblivious to the presence and communications of other humans. Kanner (1949) has suggested that these youngsters received "impersonal" care during infancy, that the warmth and direct human contact requisite to the development of specific human attachment behaviors were denied them either through parental rigidity, remoteness or incompetence. Without cuddling, warmth and a soothing voice, so necessary in the early stages of new receptor development, these infants failed to identify the mother as a stimulus object able to supply their diverse needs. As a result, these youngsters developed a series of diffusive or undifferentiated attachments to random and essentially inanimate objects which, as they mature, they continue to fondle and manipulate to provide themselves with the warmth and stimulation they need. To illustrate, a nine year old "autistic" boy seemed totally oblivious of the presence of other humans, exhibiting no seeming awareness of and response to them, even when efforts were made to intrigue him with comic antics, a soothing voice or the display of bright noise producing toys; rather, his interest was focused on a few colorless blocks and a misshapen doll to which he had become attached in infancy, and which he fondled and smelled nearly all of his waking time. We might note parenthetically that autistic behaviors have been attributed by other theorists to constitutionally defective sensory or arousal systems; thus the child is viewed to be biologically incapable of responding to most stimulative sources and, thereby, cannot become attached to specific stimulus objects. This formulation runs into difficulty, however, since many autistic children do form attachments to inanimate objects; if their defect arose from a generalized sensory or arousal deficiency, any form of attachment would appear unlikely. A more narrowly circumscribed biological deficiency, such as a "social-affect" deficit, seems rather far fetched, but would obviate this inconsistency.

Observers with diverse theoretical views concur on the consequences of inadequate early care; not all agree, however, that it is simply the deficit volume, apart from the nature, of stimulation which is crucial to these aberrations. According to the thesis presented here, variations in the amount of stimulation are more significant during the early neonatal period than is the nature of that stimulation, although both are important. As the infant matures into his second and third year, the nature or quality of the stimulative source becomes the more significant dimension of environmental experience.

Little has been said in the literature about the potential effects of less severe degrees of early sensory impoverishment. We should not overlook the fact that degree of sensory impoverishment is a gradient or continuum, not an all-or-none effect. There is every reason to believe that children who receive less than an optimum degree of sensory stimulation (an amount that will vary, no doubt, in accord with individual differences) will grow up to be less "sensory oriented" and less "socially attached" than those who have experienced more.

### Maladaptive Consequences of Enrichment

What are the consequences of too much early sensory stimulation? Unfortunately, data and theories on this score are few and far between; researchers have been preoccupied with the effects of deficit sensory stimulation rather than excess sensory stimulation. There is a substantial body of theory, but little research, describing the process of overattachment.

It is not unreasonable to hypothesize that excess stimulation in the sensory-attachment stage would result in an overdevelopment of associated neural structures. The work of Rosenzweig et al. (1962), for example, has shown that enriched early environments produce increments in certain neurochemicals. It would not be implausible to hypothesize, further, than an abundance of these chemicals would prove detrimental to subsequent development. Thus, just as too little stimulation may lead to deficit sensory capacities, so too may superfluous stimulations lead to receptor oversensitivities and, in turn, to a maladaptive dominance of sensory functions.

In this vein, Freud hypothesized that excessive indulgence at the oral stage was conducive to fixations at that period; he referred to adult individuals who underwent this childhood experience as "oral characters." According to psychoanalytic theory, these individuals display a lifelong pattern of socially gregarious and dependent behaviors. We will reformulate this conception, eschewing both oral and fixation notions, in terms of the effects of an overdevelopment of early sensory functions. Specifically, we propose that excessive sensory development in childhood would require a high level of stimulus maintenance in adulthood; these maintenance needs would be displayed in persistent sensory activation behavior. Thus, these individuals might be characterized by their seeking of sensory stimulation, their boredom of routine and their capricious searching for excitement and adventure. They would have, in Murphy's terms, an overenriched adient drive or, as Riesen might put it, a need to sustain their established level of neural sensory development. For example, a 14 year old hyperactive girl seemed incapable of "being satisfied" and made inordinate demands upon her parents to "take me here" and "take me there" and "buy me this" then "buy me that"; no sooner would she go somewhere or get something than she would be bored and want to do or get something new. A review of her early history showed that she was a "happy and good baby," but indulged excessively with warm affection and playful stimulation by doting parents and grandparents.

Exactly what neural or chemical mechanisms account for this stimulus-seeking pattern is a matter for speculation: perhaps sensory tissue abundance leads to a rapid adaptation to stimuli; since the effects of stimuli would "wear off" rapidly under these circumstances, the need for new stimulation would build up quickly again. Whatever the mechanisms may be, it appears plausible neurologically, and consistent with clinical observation, to conclude that overenriched early stimulation can result in pathological stimulus-seeking behavior.

Turning briefly to attachment behaviors, it would seem reasonable to assume that excess stimulation, anchored exclusively to the mother, would result in an overattachment to her. This consequence is demonstrated most clearly in the pathological disorder known as the *symbiotic child,* where we find an abnormal clinging by the infant to the mother, an unwillingness to leave or allow her out of sight and a persistent resistance to stimulation from other sources (Mahler, 1952). Feelings of catastrophe, isolation and panic often overtake these children if they are sent to nursery school, or "replaced" by a newborn sibling.

The need to sever the ties of early attachments, so deeply troubling for the symbiotic child, is experienced in some measure by all children. The progression from the first to the second neuropsychological stage is a gradual and overlapping one; a progressive unfolding of newly matured capacities facilitate the shift, however. We next will turn to the characteristics and consequences of this second stage.

## STAGE 2: SENSORIMOTOR-AUTONOMY

All infants possess the rudiments of certain motor capacities at birth; however, it is not until the end of the first year that they are sufficiently matured to engage in actions independent of parental support. A holding of the drinking cup, purposeful crawling, the first few steps or a word or two, all signify a growing capacity to act autonomously of others.

As the child develops the functions which characterize this second stage, he has begun to comprehend with some clarity the attitudes and feelings communicated and intended by stimulative sources. No longer is rough parental handling experienced merely as excess stimulation, undistinguished from the playful tossing of an affectionate father; the child now can discern the difference between parental harshness and good-natured roughhouse. As the meaning or quality of stimulating experiences begins to take on primacy, the importance of pure volume of stimulation itself becomes less significant than it was in the first stage of development. For this reason, discussions regarding the role of psychogenic influences in the second and third stages must focus primarily on the intricate processes and consequences of learning, rather than on the more diffusive processes of neurological growth.

Nevertheless, a brief presentation of the overall role of under or overstimulation during these two periods will be instructive.

### Development of Sensorimotor Capacities

The unorganized gross movements of the neonate progressively give way to differentiated and focused muscular activity. As the neural substrate for muscular control unfolds, the aimless and groping motor behavior of the infant is supplanted by focused, voluntary movements. These newly emergent functions coordinate with previously matured sensory capacities to enable the child to explore, manipulate, play, sit, crawl, babble, throw, walk, catch and talk.

The innately maturing fusion between the neurological substrates of sensory and motor functions is strengthened by the child's exploratory behavior. His absorption in manipulative play, or the formation of babbling sounds, are methods of self-stimulation which facilitate the growth of interneuronal connections; he is building a neural foundation for progressively more complicated and refined skills such as running, handling utensils, controlling sphincter muscles and articulating precise speech. His intrinsic tendency to "entertain" himself is not merely "something cute to behold," but a necessary step in establishing capacities that are more substantial than maturation alone would have furnished. Stimulative experiences, either self-provided or through the actions of others, are requisites then for the development of normal sensorimotor skills. Unless retarded by environmental restrictions, by biological handicaps or by deficits in early sensory development, the toddler's growing sensorimotor capacities prepare him to cope with his environment with increasing competence and autonomy.

### Development of Autonomy

Seminal papers by Erikson (1959) and White (1960) have led the way to a better understanding of the young child's sense of autonomy and competence. In a number of finely executed studies on the achievement-motive concept, McClelland and his associates (1953) have added a fruitful research dimension to the theoretical ideas provided by Erikson and White.

Perhaps the most significant aspect of sensorimotor development is that it enables the child to begin to do things for himself, to exert an influence upon his environment, to free himself from parental domination and to outgrow the attachment and dependencies of his first years

—in other words, to develop a range of competencies by which he can master his world and establish a feeling of autonomy.

This developmental progression can be seen in many spheres of behavior. With his growing skill in locomotion, he can explore new environments. With the advent of speech, he can engage in new social relationships, challenge the thoughts and desires of others, pronounce his own directives, resist, entertain, cajole and manipulate his parents. He becomes aware of his increasing competence and seeks to test his mettle in new ventures. Needless to say, conflicts and restrictions inevitably arise as he asserts himself. These may be seen most clearly during the period of toilet training when youngsters often resist submitting to the demands and strictures of their parents. A delicate exchange of power and cunning ensues. Opportunities arise for the child to manipulate his parents and to extract promises or deny wishes; in response, parents may mete out punishments, submit meekly, register dismay or shift inconsistently among all three. Important precedents for attitudes toward authority and feelings of power and autonomy are generated during this and other periods of parent-child conflict.

## Maladaptive Consequences of Impoverishment

Most of the consequences of this period reflect the quality or kind of stimulation to which the child is exposed, rather than the simple amount of stimulation he experiences. Certain consequences, however, may be attributed primarily to impoverishment.

The failure to encourage and stimulate sensorimotor capacities can lead to serious retardations in functions necessary to the development of autonomy and initiative. This may be seen most clearly in children of overprotective parents. Spoon-fed, helped in dressing, excused from "chores," restrained from exploration, curtailed in friendships and protected from "danger," all illustrate controls which restrict the growing child's opportunities to exercise his sensorimotor skills and develop the means for autonomous behavior. A self-perpetuating cycle may unfold. The child may not be able to abandon his overlearned dependency upon his parents since he is ill-equipped to meet other children on their terms. He is likely to be timid and submissive when forced to venture out into the world, likely to avoid the give and take of competition with his peers, likely to prefer the play of younger children and likely to find an older child who will protect him and upon whom he can lean. Each of these

adaptive maneuvers intensifies his established sensorimotor retardations since it prevents him from engaging in activities that will promote catching up with his peers. He may become progressively more unfit for autonomous behaviors and social competition, and eventually, may display the features of a submissive and dependent adult.

## Maladaptive Consequences of Enrichment

The consequences of excessive enrichment of the second neuropsychological stage are found most often in children of lax, permissive or overindulgent parents. Given free rein to test new skills with minimal restraint, stimulated to explore at will and to manipulate things and others to his suiting without guidance or control, the child will soon become irresponsibly narcissistic and undisciplined in his behaviors. When carried into the wider environment, however, these behaviors normally will run up against the desires of other children and the restrictions of less permissive adults. Unless the youngster is extremely adept, or the larger community unusually lax, he will find that his self-centered and free-wheeling tactics fail miserably. For the few who succeed, however, a cycle of egocentrism, unbridled self-expression and social arrogance may become dominant. To illustrate, a seven year old boy was completely unmanageable both in kindergarten and first grade, talking aloud while the teacher spoke, telling her that he knew "the answers" better than she, intruding and disrupting the play of other children, who referred to him as a "pest" and "bully"; from the family history it was learned that this youngster's parents not only believed in "total permissiveness" but encouraged their son to "speak up and disagree with them" and to "do whatever he wished, short of physically hurting others." The majority of these youngsters will fail to gain acceptance by their peers and will never acquire the give-and-take skills of normal social relationships. In the long run, many of them learn to remain aloof from social activities; the fact that their "talents" have not been esteemed by the wider community is too painful an experience. In general, they come to be characterized by their haughty independence, and maintain their childhood illusions of self-importance through the fanciful workings of their imagination.

## STAGE 3: INTRACORTICAL-INITIATIVE

By the time the major features of this stage begin to unfold, the role played by the amount of stimulus experience, apart from its content, has receded in significance. Volume of stimulation, per se, no longer is as crucial as it was in the first stage when the meaning of incoming stimuli was dimly perceived. Its relevance, at this third stage, serves to remind us that the peak periods of neurological maturation for certain psychological functions occur between the years of four and 18, and that the total amount of environmental stimulation at these times of rapid growth will have a strong bearing on the *degree* to which these functions mature. Thus, the volume of stimulus experience will influence not the character or content of these functions but their magnitude; weak or infrequent stimulation will result in capacity deficits, whereas intense or frequent stimulation will lead to exaggerated capacities.

What capacities unfold during this intracortical and initiative stage, and what consequences can be attributed to differences in the magnitude of relevant stimulus experience?

### Development of Intracortical Capacities

Progressively complex arrangements of neural cells become possible as the infant advances in maturation. Although these higher order connections begin as early as four to six months of age, they do not form into structures capable of rational foresight and planning until the youngster has fully developed his more basic sensorimotor skills. With these capacities as a base, he is able to differentiate, arrange and control the objects of his physical world. As his verbal skills unfold, he learns to symbolize these concrete objects; soon he can manipulate and coordinate these symbols as well as, if not better than, the tangible events themselves. Free now of the need to make direct reference to the concrete world, he can recall past events and anticipate future ones. As more cortical connections are established, higher conceptual abstractions are formulated, enabling him to transfer, associate and coordinate these symbols into ideas of increasingly finer differentiation, greater complexity and broader integration. It is his own internal representations of reality, his own patterns of symbolic thought and his own constructions of events —past, present and future—which take over as the primary units of his stimulus world.

This process of neural growth toward higher forms of cortical integration depends on, and is stimulated by, both his own growing capacity to fantasize, and the evergrowing diversity of his environmental experiences. Without an increase in the complexity in his stimulus environment, and without his own inner symbolic manipula-

tions, the major steps in the growth of potentially more elaborate intracortical connections will fail to materialize.

Somewhere between the eleventh and fifteenth years a rather precipitous series of hormonal changes unsettle the level of intracortical integration so carefully constructed in preceding years. These changes mark the onset of puberty —the emergence of strong sexual impulses and adult-like features of anatomy, voice and bearing. Erratic moods, changing self-images, new urges and hopeful expectancies and a growing physical and social awkwardness, all upset and challenge the relative equanimity of an earlier age. Disruptive as it may be, this turbulent stage of neural and physical growth activates and ties together the remaining undeveloped elements of the youngster's biological potential; it is a preparatory phase for the soon forthcoming independence from parental domination and direction. With it are called forth secretive self-stimulating activities and fantasies; for example, the typical adolescent promotes through masturbation the development of his adult sexual potentials. Once this last of his undeveloped capacities blossoms forth and is coordinated with other more developed functions, he is fully prepared, biologically, to assume the responsibilities of initiating an independent adult course.

### Development of Initiative

When the inner world of symbols is mastered, giving the diverse elements of objective reality an order and integration, the growing youngster is able to create some consistency and continuity in his life. No longer is he buffeted from one mood or action to another by the swirl of rapidly changing events; he now has an internal anchor, a nucleus of stable cognitions which serves as a base, and which imposes a sameness upon an otherwise fluid environment. Increasingly, as he grows in his capacity to organize and integrate his symbolic world, one configuration predominates. Accrued from his experiences with others and from his effects upon them and their reactions to him, an image of the self-as-object takes shape. This highest order of abstraction, the sense of individual identity, becomes the core of personality functioning, the dominant source of stimuli which guides and influences the individual's style of behavior. External sources of stimulation no longer have the power they once exerted; the youngster now has an everpresent and stable sphere of internal stimuli which governs his course of action—he has an established inner base from which *he* initiates events.

It is through fantasy and reflection that the youngster plans goals and devises means of attaining them. Through prior experience he has developed a "conscience" by which he judges the appropriateness of his relations with others; past remembrances provide him with a reservoir from which he can gauge the dangers and values of one course of behavior versus another. He now has the wherewithal to establish the boundaries of self-restriction and constructive action; he now

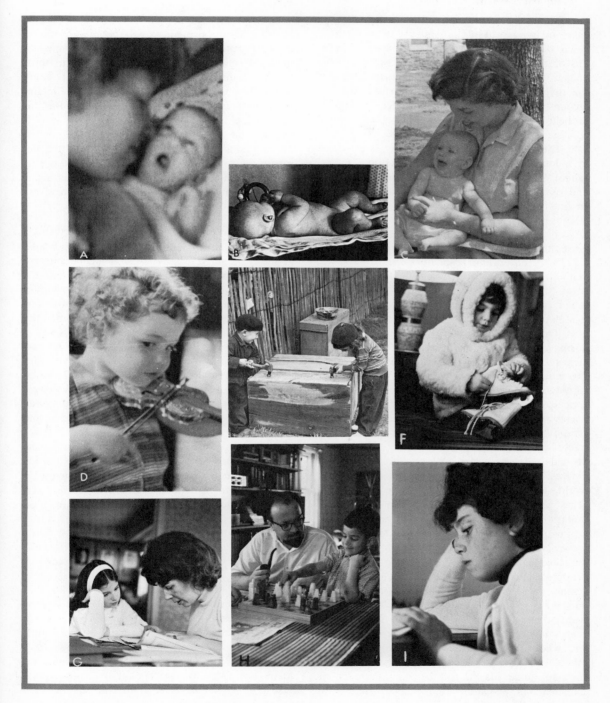

Figure 5-2 Stages of neuropsychological development. A to C. Sensory-attachment. D to F. Sensorimotor-autonomy. G to I. Intracortical-initiative. (Part E, courtesy of L. Stone, parts F to I, courtesy of L. Ross.)

has the anchor of a personal self from which he initiates new directions for growth and adult independence.

### Maladaptive Consequences of Impoverishment

The task of attaining integration is not an easy one in a world of changing events and values. What is best? What is right? How shall I handle this or think about that? Questions such as these plague the growing child at every turn. How can the diverse and everchanging guidelines for behavior be fashioned into a well-integrated system of beliefs and actions? From what source can a consistent image of self be consolidated?

The fabric of organized society is designed to indoctrinate and inculcate the young. Family, school, church and industry set implicit values and explicit rules by which the child is guided to find a means of behaving and thinking that is consonant with those of others. The youngster not only is subject to cultural pressures but requires them to give structure and direction to his rapidly proliferating capacities and impulses. Without them, his maturing potentials may become overly diffuse and scattered; conversely, too much guidance may narrow the scope of his potentials and restrict their flexibility and adaptiveness. Once his basic pattern of thought is shaped during this crucial growth period, it is difficult to alter or reorient it toward new pathways.

Let us elaborate the consequences of understimulation. Erikson (1959) has formulated the concept of *identity diffusion,* a notion we will borrow to represent the effects of inadequate or erratic stimulation during the peak years of intracortical integration. Without direct tuition from his elders, a youngster will be left to his own devices to master the complexities of a varied world, to control intense aggressive and sexual urges which well up within him, to channel his fantasies and to pursue the goals to which he aspires. He may become a victim of his own growth, unable to discipline his impulses or fashion acceptable means for expressing his desires. Scattered and unguided, he cannot get hold of a sense of personal identity, a consistent direction and purpose to his existence. He becomes an "other-directed" person, one who vacillates at every turn, overly responsive to fleeting stimuli and who shifts from one erratic course to another. Ultimately, without an inner core or anchor to guide his future, he may flounder or stagnate. The so-called "hippie" characterizes in mild form this state of diffusion; his aimlessness and disaffiliation from the mainstream of tradi-

tional American life may be traced, in part, to the failure of contemporary society to provide a coherent set of values around which he can focus his life and orient himself toward a meaningful future.

From the foregoing, it is evident that the impoverishment of integrative stimuli, regardless of their kind or quality, will have a profound effect. Fortunately, there is a superabundance of untapped cortical cells in the adult brain; thus, the "immaturity and irresponsibility" of many adolescents who have suffered prolonged identity diffusion may be salvaged in later years. But for others, the inability to settle down into a well-defined and consolidated path becomes a problem of increasingly severe proportions. Given the demands of an overly organized society, the perennially unintegrated adult will find himself ostracized, stereotyped and relegated to progressively inferior positions of responsibility.

### Maladaptive Consequences of Enrichment

The negative consequences of overenrichment at the third stage usually occur when parents are controlling and perfectionistic. The overly trained, overly disciplined and overly integrated youngster is given little opportunity to shape his own destiny. Whether by coercion or enticement, the child who, too early, is led to control his emergent feelings, to focus his thoughts along narrowly defined paths and to follow the prescriptions of parental demands, has been subverted into adopting the identities of others. Whatever individuality he may have acquired is drowned in a model of adult orderliness, propriety and virtue. Such oversocialized and rigid youngsters lack the spontaneity, flexibility and creativeness we expect of the young; they have been trained to be old men before their time, too narrow in perspective to respond to excitement, variety and the challenge of new events. Overenrichment at this stage has fixed them on a restrictive course, and has deprived them of the rewards of being themselves.

## EVALUATIVE COMMENTS

The developmental theory outlined in the preceding pages provides a plausible model for the successive stages of neuropsychological growth. But the model, and several of its particulars, is unproven. Many of the assertions made are based on extrapolations from animal research; what data exist at the human level are founded on naturalistic studies, most of which produce equivocal results, or on findings of undetermined reliability. Moreover, knowledge is sorely lacking of the precise maturational sequence of most of the neurological mechanisms which underlie psychological functions. In short, the empirical verification of relevant biophysical and behavioral variables through careful research remains a task for the future.

It would be a gross error if we left our discussion of neuropsychological development with the impression that personality growth was merely a function of volume and timing of stimulation. Impoverishment and enrichment have their profound effects, especially in the first two years of life, but the quality or kind of stimulation the youngster experiences is often of equal, if not greater, importance. The impact of parental harshness or inconsistency, of sibling rivalry or social failure, is more than a matter of stimulus intensity, volume or timing. Different dimensions of experience take precedence as the meaning conveyed by the stimulating source becomes clear to the growing child. We will turn to this complex facet of psychogenesis in the next section; here the concepts forged in the search for principles and processes of learning will prove most relevant and useful.

## EFFECT OF QUALITY OF EARLY EXPERIENCE UPON LEARNING

Normal psychological functions operate on a substrate of orderly neuronal connections and patterns. The development of this intricate neural substrate unfolds within the organism in accord with genetically determined processes, but there remain substantial numbers of fibers which are unconnected and whose direction of growth is modifiable. As a consequence, many patterns of synaptic association may be influenced by the action of environmental stimuli. To summarize the previous section, then, we might say that the basic architecture of the nervous system is laid down in a relatively fixed and orderly manner, but certain refinements in this linkage system do not develop without the aid of stimulative experience.

We noted further that there are sensitive periods in the maturation of the nervous system when the effects of stimulation are especially pronounced; these occur at points of rapid neural growth. Stimulus impoverishment at these critical stages leads to an underdevelopment among neural connections; deficit neural development will have long-range deleterious effects since early growth serves as a prerequisite to the development of subsequent capacities; comparable complications may arise as a function of stimulus enrichment.

Environmental experiences not only activate the growth of neural collaterals but alter these structures in such ways as to preempt them for similar subsequent experiences. Early stimulus experiences, then, not only construct new neural pathways, but, in addition, selectively prepare these pathways to be receptive to later stimuli which are qualitatively similar. This second consequence of stimulus experience, representing a selective lowering of the threshold for the neural transmission of similar subsequent stimuli, has been described in the conceptual language of psychology as the process of learning; it reflects the observation that perceptions and behaviors which have been subjected to prior experience and training are reactivated with relative ease.

With this second consequence of stimulation in mind, we can begin to speak of the nervous system as more than a network of abstract pathways; it now may be viewed as possessing the residues of *specific* classes of environmental stimuli. These environmentally anchored neural connections interweave to form complex patterns of perception and behavior which relate to discriminable events in the external world. No longer will we be dealing, therefore, with the simple quantitative volume of stimulation; by including qualitatively discriminable features of the stimulus world within our purview, we must begin to shift our attention to observational units that transcend the neural mechanisms of bodily function. It now will be necessary to represent these more complex stimulus events in a conceptual language that is broader in scope than that found in neurology. The eminent neuropsychologist, D. O. Hebb, describes the need for a new level of conceptualization in the following quote (1966):

The essential point is that the simplest behavior of the whole animal involves a fantastic number of firings in individual neurons and muscle cells, as the animal moves, for example, out of the starting box in a maze, or as the student reads a line of this text. There is no possible way of keeping track of more than a few of these cells, and little prospect that it will become possible to do so in the future. To describe mental activity in such terms would be like describing a storm by listing every raindrop and every tiny movement of air.

We must have units on a larger scale for the description. To deal with the storm, the meteorologist speaks of showers or inches of rainfall (instead of counting raindrops), a moving weather system (extending over hundreds of miles) and so forth. For our problem, we can use neurological constructs such as a volley of impulses, the level of firing in the arousal system, or the occurrence of widespread summation in the cortex. But the intricacies of brain function are such that this still does not take us far enough, and we reach a point at which the use of psychological conceptions, on a still larger scale of complexity, becomes inevitable.

We cannot escape the need for large scale units of analysis, nor the need for the special methods of behavioral study on which such analysis is based. Some of the most important aspects of brain function, that is, can only be known and studied by psychological methods.

What conceptual level and units of observation will best enable us to describe and analyze the effects of the *quality* or content of experience?

As noted earlier, the qualitative aspect of stimulation alters the threshold of neural transmission for similar subsequent stimuli. This change in the probability of neural transmission is descriptively similar to the psychological process known as learning; learning often is defined as an increment in the probability that previously experienced stimulus situations will be perceived rapidly, and that responses previously associated with them will be elicited.

Both neurological and learning concepts can be utilized to describe changes in response probabilities arising from prior stimulus exposure. But, since learning concepts are formulated in terms of behavior-environment interactions, it would appear reasonable, when discussing the specific properties of qualitatively discriminable stimulus events, to utilize the conceptual language of learning. In this way, we shall be able to describe the "weather system," as Hebb might put it, rather than the "raindrops." Moreover, the principles derived from learning theory and research describe subtle features of psychological behavior which cannot begin to be handled intelligently in neurological terms. With the principles and conceptual language of learning we can formulate precisely our ideas about the effects of qualitatively discriminable stimulus events, that is, differences not only in the magnitude but in the variety and content of the stimulus world as we experience it.

Let us keep in mind that learning concepts and neurological concepts do not represent intrinsically different processes; we are using the former because they have been more finely differentiated and, therefore, are more fruitful tools for formulating notions about qualitatively different stimulus-behavior interactions.

The following sections will outline some of the basic concepts, principles and processes of learning; second, we will describe a number of the qualitative dimensions of stimulus experience that play an etiological role in psychopathology; and, third, we will discuss some of the strategies which individuals learn as a means of coping with these pathogenic experiences.

## CONCEPTS AND PRINCIPLES OF LEARNING

There are few fields of psychological inquiry that are beset with more theoretical controversy than that of learning. What will be presented in this section represents the author's particular distillations and biases, biases which reflect his belief that certain concepts and principles are especially useful in explaining the acquisition of pathological behavior patterns. Different terms and propositions have been espoused by other psychologists, and it behooves the serious student to examine their comparative utility as tools for psychopathological analysis.

**Principle of Contiguity Learning.** The simplest formulation proposed to account for the acquisition of new behaviors and perceptions has been referred to as contiguity. In essence this principle states that any set of environmental elements which occurs either simultaneously or in close temporal order will become associated with each other. If one of these elements recurs in the future, the other elements with which it had previously been associated will be elicited. Some years ago, for example, the author had the unpleasant experience of running out of gas as his car was crossing a heavily trafficked bridge; for several months thereafter, he sensed an uncomfortable feeling whenever he drove over this particular bridge, and found himself anxiously checking the gas gauge. The essential and sufficient condition for contiguity learning, therefore, is spatial simultaneity or temporal continuity.

The principle of contiguity may be applied to the progressive development of both *response learning* and *expectancy learning*. Response learning refers to associative bonds established between stimulus events and responses. Using the contiguity concept as a model, we can formulate this type of learning as follows: any stimulus pattern accompanying or immediately preceding a response will tend, if it recurs, to elicit that response. Expectancy learning refers to associative bonds established among stimulus events; it does not relate to the learning of responses to stimuli but to the learning of relationships among stimuli. Described in contiguity terms, it states: any environmental stimulus which previously has occurred in temporal or spatial contiguity with other stimuli will, if it recurs, elicit the expectation, i.e., perception, cognition or prediction, that the other stimuli will follow.

We will not go into the particulars of how contiguity notions serve to explain the progressive acquisition of stronger and more complex associative bonds. For our purposes it will suffice to note that it enables us to explain the acquisition of behavioral responses (response learning) and the acquisition of perceptions and cognitions (expectancy learning).

**Role of Motivation and Reinforcement.** Several subsidiary factors, i.e., neither necessary nor sufficient but associated with conditions of contiguity learning, tend to increase the rapidity and strength with which behaviors and expectancies are acquired. We will briefly describe two of these contributing factors: *motivation* and *reinforcement*. The first condition concerns properties of the environment or the organism which facilitate learning by initiating and intensifying behavioral activity; the second term refers to conditions which protect what has been learned by terminating new behaviors that might interfere with or disrupt these learnings.

*Motivation* signifies a state in which the organism is aroused or stimulated into behavior. Motivation may be prompted by internal bodily conditions such as hunger and thirst, or by external sources such as threats to one's security; whatever the impetus, the motivated organism is driven to engage in need-fulfilling behaviors, e.g., obtaining food or withdrawing from a threat.

It would appear reasonable to assume that a large number of neural fibers are activated when the organism is motivated. If this assumption is correct, we would expect that a greater number of contiguity learning bonds will be established when the organism is highly motivated than when it is less motivated. (We might note, parenthetically, that unusually intense motivation produces poor learning since there is a flooding and scattering of neural activity; few clearly defined bonds can be established under these conditions.)

Motivation has other effects upon learning. Specific needs tend to produce a selective focusing upon the stimulus environment. Those fea-

tures of the stimulus world which are relevant to these needs, that is, that enter the sphere of the organism's selective perceptions, will be strongly bonded to each other or to behavioral responses. Thus, specific motivations narrow the effective stimulus field to particular prepotent elements; these elements are most firmly incorporated into learned patterns. For example, a tourist is not likely to register the fact that there were no restaurants along a particular highway if he was not hungry while traveling it; however, if he was searching for a place to eat, the probabilities are high that he would note and remember this fact for future reference.

In a similar manner, attracting environmental stimuli (e.g., intense, incongruous and unusual events; rewards or need satisfiers) tend to catch the attention and activate the organism; these more striking stimuli have a greater probability than less attractive stimuli of entering the effective perceptual sphere of the organism, and hence are subject to stronger learning.

*Reinforcement* is one of the most frequently used, yet one of the most troublesome concepts to define in learning. Historically, the concept of reinforcement has referred to the power of certain events to satisfy the motivational needs of the organism and, thereby, strengthen the associative bond between stimuli and responses. More specifically, the term *positive reinforcement* has been used to signify conditions which, when added to a situation, increase the probability that responses associated with it will be evoked in the future (e.g., food is a positive reinforcer for a hungry animal); the term *negative reinforcement* denotes conditions which, when added to a situation, decrease the probability that responses associated with it will be evoked in the future (e.g., a painful electric shock is a negative reinforcer for all animals).

How do reinforcers (e.g., biological need satisfiers or learned rewards) influence the learning process according to the contiguity point of view?

Briefly, reinforcers serve initially as activators of organismic behavior; second, once the reinforcement is achieved, the organism usually terminates his behavior. For example, the attainment of a *positive reinforcer* (food) will stop a hungry laboratory animal from continuing his food-searching behaviors (exploring alleys of the maze other than the one in which he found food); in this manner the reinforcer protects the specific alley-food association he learned by preventing new bonds from developing. In other words, the receipt of the reinforcer serves to discontinue exploratory behavior, and the early bond is preserved intact since there are no new associative bonds to interfere with it. *Negative reinforcers* (e.g., pain or punishment), in contrast, stir the organism to continue behaving until such time as he learns an appropriate escape response. Thus, positive reinforcers lead to the termination of behavior, whereas negative reinforcers prompt the continuation of activity. As the organism engages in his escape efforts under conditions of negative reinforcement, he acquires new behaviors that interfere with and break each of the associative bonds he has learned along the way. Eventually, he learns one that enables him to successfully escape the negative reinforcement; this last associative bond remains intact since no subsequent ones are learned to replace it.

**Principle of Instrumental Learning.** In time, the organism learns to discriminate between those stimuli which portend pain and those which promise pleasure. This stage of learning takes the form of an expectancy in which he avoids stimuli that lead to discomfort and exposes himself to those that provide rewards. With these cognitions in mind he is able to circumvent future negative reinforcements and invite future positive reinforcements. Moreover, he begins to engage intentionally in a series of acts designed to obtain the reinforcements he seeks. He anticipates and actively manipulates the events of his environment to suit his needs since he has learned that reinforcements are contingent on his performing certain prior acts.

The process of acquiring these anticipations and manipulative behaviors is known as *instrumental learning* or, as Skinner has termed it, operant conditioning. Either through direct tuition or chance events, the organism learns which of his acts ultimately "produces" the desired result of obtaining a positive reinforcement or escaping a negative one. A simple example may prove instructive. A fussy and cranky child is offered candy or ice cream as a means of pacifying him. Although the child has been subdued for the time being, the parent, in effect, has given the child a positive reinforcement consequent to his misbehavior. On subsequent occasions, when the child is desirous of candy or other similar reinforcements, he will engage in cranky and fussy behavior once more since it "succeeded" previously in producing a reward for him.

If these "successful" manipulative acts prove effective in a variety of similar subsequent situations, they may take the form of an ingrained and widely generalized behavior pattern. These learned sequences of instrumental responses serve as the basis for the development of coping strategies, that is, a complex series of manipulative acts, employed in relation to events or people, in which the individual avoids negative reinforcements and obtains positive ones. Instrumental strategies will be elaborated in a later section.

**Vicarious Learning Through Observation and Imitation.** Human patterns of behavior are extraordinarily complex. For each child to learn the intricacies of civilized behavior by fortuitous trial-and-error or reinforcement methods alone would be no less possible than it would be for an isolated primitive culture to advance, in one generation, to a full-fledged industrial and scientific society. Rather than struggling to acquire and integrate each of the many components of human behavior piece by piece, the child learns by adopting whole sequences of behaviors and expectancies provided for him through the incidental actions and the formal precepts espoused by older members of his social group. These highly complex patterns of learning are acquired in toto, therefore, merely by observing, vicariously learning and then imitating what others do and think; it is an efficient and necessary means by which the child becomes a "civilized human" in an amazingly short period of time.

This form of vicarious learning may be acquired quite incidentally by simple contiguity (e.g., being exposed to established associations among stimuli such as are found in social belief systems or observing exemplary forms of behavior) or by complex instrumental strategies (e.g., identifying with and adopting patterns of behavior manifested by parents as a means of obtaining their approval). Thus, intricate sequences of model-matching behaviors and attitudes are learned by incidental exposure to social models, by deliberate parental tuition and reinforcement or by the child's own instrumental maneuvers.

**Implicit Learning Through Thinking.** Much of what is learned, especially after the early years of childhood, occurs implicitly, that is, without being manifest in overt responses or being a direct consequence of external environmental effects. Clearly, the "thinking" organism is capable of arranging the residual memories of his learned experiences into new patterns of association. Furthermore, ideational processes enable him to engage in the self-reinforcements of imaginative fantasy.

As the child develops an extensive symbolic repertoire of words and images, he no longer is dependent on the fortuitous or laboriously attained reinforcements of "real" environmental experience to form and strengthen new learnings. By manipulating his storehouse of symbols and

Figure 5-3   Imitative learning. Children from three to six observed either live or filmed presentations of aggressive behavior. (Parts A to C.) After seeing these models, the children underwent mild frustration and then were photographed in a playroom in which various objects and instruments conducive both to aggressive and nonaggressive behavior were available. The influence of the models was clearly demonstrated by several children who imitated the models' behavior almost exactly. (Parts D to I.) (Courtesy of A. Bandura, Department of Psychology, Stanford University, Stanford, California.)

images, he can mediate new associations among objectively unconnected events; he can reinforce himself by fantasy attainments; he can plan his future by anticipating novel expectancy sequences, and can concoct new instrumental strategies for dealing with his environment. By modeling his internal symbolic world, then, he supplements the objective world with novel thoughts that provide him with new learnings and self-administered reinforcements.

## SOURCES OF PATHOGENIC LEARNING

Attitudes and behaviors may be learned as a consequence of instruction or indoctrination on the part of parents, but most of what is learned accrues from a haphazard series of casual and incidental events to which the child is exposed. Not only is the administration of rewards and punishments meted out most often in a spontaneous and erratic fashion, but the everyday and ordinary activities of parents provide the child with "unintended" models to imitate. The following quote from Bandura and Huston describes well this incidental feature of learning (1961):

During the parents' social training of a child, the range of cues employed by a child is likely to include both those that the parents consider immediately relevant and other cues of parental behavior which the child has had ample opportunity to observe and to learn even though he has not been instructed to do so. Thus, for example, when a parent punishes a child physically for having aggressed toward peers, the intended outcome of the training is that the child should refrain from hitting others. Concurrent with the intentional learning, however, a certain amount of incidental learning may be expected to occur through imitation, since the child is provided, in the form of the parent's behavior, with an example of how to aggress toward others, and this incidental learning may guide the child's behavior in later social interactions.

Without their awareness or intention, parents suggest, through incidental aspects of their behavior, how "people" think, talk, fear, love, solve problems and relate to others. Aversions, irritabilities, attitudes, anxieties and styles of interpersonal communication are adopted and duplicated by children as they observe the everyday reactions of their parents and older siblings. Children mirror these complex behaviors without understanding their significance and without parental intentions of transmitting them. The old saying, "practice what you preach," conveys the essence of this thesis. Thus, as noted in the quote, a parent who castigates the child harshly for failing to be kind to others may create an intrinsically ambivalent learning experience; the contrast between parental manner and their verbalized injunction teaches the child simultaneously to think "kindly" but to "behave" harshly.

The particulars and the coloration of many pathological patterns have their beginnings in the offhand behaviors and attitudes to which the child is incidentally exposed. It is important, therefore, in reading this section, that the student keep in mind that children acquire less from intentional parental training methods than from casual and adventitious experience. People simply do not learn in neatly arranged alley mazes with all confounding effects nicely controlled; the sequence is complicated not only by manifold "extraneous variables" to which learning becomes attached but is subject to highly irregular "schedules of reinforcement."

We might pause briefly, before going further, and note what is meant by the term "pathogenic." Three types of events may be described to illustrate the concept.

1. First, there are events which provoke undue anxiety within the individual because they make demands beyond his capacity, or because they otherwise undermine his feelings of security and comfort. Persistence of these emotionally disruptive events elicit adaptive reactions that, ultimately, lead to the learning of instrumental coping strategies. These strategies may be successful in diminishing feelings of discomfort but they may prove detrimental in the long run to healthy functioning.

2. The second class of pathogenic events are emotionally neutral conditions which lead to the learning of maladaptive behaviors. These conditions *do not* activate protective or defensive behaviors as do emotionally disruptive events; they merely reinforce styles of behavior which prove deleterious when generalized to settings other than those in which they were acquired. The roots of these difficulties, therefore, do not lie in stress, anxiety or unconscious mechanisms of defense but rather in the simple conditioning or imitation of maladaptive behavior patterns.

3. The third source of psychopathology arises from an insufficiency of experiences requisite to the learning of adaptive behavior. Thus, general stimulus impoverishment, or minimal social experience, may produce deficits in learned coping behaviors. The sheer lack of skills and competence for mastering the environment is a form of pathological *underlearning* which may be as severe as those disorders generated either by stressful experiences or by defective models of imitation.

The research and theoretical literature on pathogenic sources do not lend themselves to the three-fold schema outlined above; another format must be used to present this body of work. Nevertheless, it will be helpful to the student if he keeps these distinctions in mind while reading the ensuing pages.

A few preliminary comments are advisable before detailing the pathogenic sources of learning.

The belief that early interpersonal experiences within the family play a decisive role in the development of psychopathology is well-accepted among professionals, but reliable and unequivocal data supporting this conviction are difficult to find. The deficits in these data are not due to a shortage of research efforts; rather, they reflect the operation of numerous methodological and theoretical difficulties which stymies progress. For example, most of the data depend on retrospective accounts of early experience; these data are notoriously unreliable. Patients interviewed during their illness are prone to give a warped and selective accounting of their relationships with others; information obtained from relatives often is distorted by feelings of guilt or by a desire to uncover some simple event to which the disorder can be attributed. In general, then, attempts to reconstruct the complex sequence of events of yesteryear which may have contributed to pathological learning are fraught with almost insurmountable methodological difficulties.

To these procedural complications may be added problems of conceptual semantics and data organization; these complications make comparisons among studies difficult, and deter the systematic accumulation of a consistent body of research data. For example, what one investigator calls a "cold and distant" parent, another may refer to as "hostile or indifferent"; an "indulgent" mother in one study may be referred to as a "worrier" in another or "overprotective" in a third. Furthermore, descriptive terms such as "cold," "overprotective," and so on represent gross categories of experience; variations, timing sequences and other subtleties of interpersonal interaction are lost or blurred when experiences are grouped together into these global categories. The precise element of these experiences which effectively accounts for maladaptive learning remains unclear because of the gross or nonspecific categories into which these experiences are grouped. We must know exactly what aspect of parental "coldness" or "overprotectiveness" is pathogenic. Hopefully, such specifications will be detailed more precisely in future research. Until such time, however, we must be content with the global nature of these categories of psychogenesis.

In the following sections we will differentiate the sources of pathological learning into two broad categories. The first comprises experiences which exert an influence throughout the child's entire developmental sequence; these shall be referred to as *enduring and pervasive experiences*. The second category will include adverse conditions of relatively brief duration which occur at any point in the life span, but which exert a profound influence upon development; they shall be noted as *traumatic experiences*.

## ENDURING AND PERVASIVE EXPERIENCES

An atmosphere, a way of handling the daily and routine activities of life or a style and tone of interpersonal relatedness, all come to characterize the family setting within which the child develops. Events, feelings and ways of communicating are repeated day in and day out. In contrast to the occasional and scattered events of the outside environment, the circumstances of daily family life have an enduring and cumulative effect upon the entire fabric of the child's learning. Within this setting the child establishes a basic feeling of security, imitates the ways in which people relate interpersonally, acquires an impression of how others perceive and feel about him, develops a sense of self-worth and learns how to cope with feelings and the stresses of life. The influence of the family environment is pre-eminent during all of the crucial growth periods in that it alone among all sources exerts a persistent effect upon the child.

In what ways can these enduring experiences be differentiated?

Since the ebb and flow of everyday life consists of many inextricably interwoven elements, any subdivision which can be made must reflect some measure of arbitrariness. The student will not fall prey to the errors of etiological simplification if he keeps in mind that the features separated into each of the five categories listed below represents only single facets of an ongoing and complex constellation of events.

### Parental Feelings and Attitudes

The most overriding, yet the most difficult to appraise, aspect of learned experience is the extent to which the child develops a feeling of acceptance or rejection by his parents. With the exception of cases of blatant abuse or overt deprecation, investigators have extreme difficulty in specifying, no less measuring, the signs of parental disaffiliation and disaffection. Despite the methodological difficulties which researchers encounter, the child who is the recipient of rejecting cues has no doubt but that he is unappreciated, scorned or deceived.

To be exposed throughout one's early years to parents who view one as unwanted and troublesome can only establish a deep and pervasive feeling of isolation in a hostile world. Deprived of the supports and security of home, the child may be ill-disposed to venture forth with confidence to face struggles in the outer world. Rejected by his parents, he may anticipate equal devaluation by others. As a defense against further pain, he may learn the strategy of avoiding others; he may utilize apathy and indifference as a protective cloak to minimize the impact of the negative reinforcements he now expects from others. Different strategies may evolve, of course, depending on other features associated with rejection; children may imitate parental scorn and ridicule, and learn to handle their disturbed feelings by acting in a hostile and vindictive fashion.

Rejection is not the only parental attitude which may result in insidious damage to the child's personality; attitudes represented by terms such as seduction, exploitation and deception contribute their share of damage as well. But it is usually the sense of being unwanted and unloved which proves to have the most pervasive and shattering of effects. A child can tolerate substantial punishment and buffeting from his environment if he senses a basic feeling of love and support from his parents; without them, his resistance, even to minor stress, is tenuous.

### Methods of Behavior Control

What training procedures are used to regulate the child's behavior and to control what he learns? As noted earlier, incidental methods used by parents may have a more profound effect than what the parent intended, that is, the child acquires a model of interpersonal behavior by example and imitation as well as by verbal precept.

What are some of the pathogenic methods of control? Five will be noted (Sears et al., 1957; Glidewell, 1961; Becker, 1964).

**Punitive Methods.** Parents disposed to intimidate and ridicule their offspring, using punitive and repressive measures to control their behavior and thought, may set the stage for a variety of maladaptive patterns.

If the child submits to pressure and succeeds in fulfilling parental expectations (i.e., learns instrumentally to avoid the negative reinforcement of punishment), he is apt to become an overly obedient and circumspect person. Quite typically, these individuals learn not only to keep in check their impulses and contrary thoughts but, by vicarious observation and imitation, to adopt the parental behavior model, and begin to be punitive of deviant behavior on the part of others. Thus, an otherwise timid and hypertense 16 year old boy, whose every spark of youthful zest had been squelched by harshly punitive parents, was observed to be "extremely mean" and punitive when given the responsibility of teaching a Sunday school class for seven year olds.

Should these youngsters fail to satisfy excessive parental demands, and be subject to continued harassment and punishment, they may develop a pervasive anticipatory anxiety about personal relationships, leading to feelings of hopelessness and discouragement, and resulting in such instrumental strategies as social avoidance and withdrawal. Others, faced with similar experiences, may learn to imitate parental harshness and develop hostile and aggressively rebellious behaviors. Which of these reactions or strategies evolves will depend on the larger configuration of factors involved.

**Contingent Reward Methods.** Some parents rarely are punitive, but expect certain behaviors to be performed *prior* to giving encouragement or doling out rewards. In other words, positive reinforcements are contingent upon approved performance. Youngsters reared under these conditions tend to be socially pleasant, and, by imitative learning, tend to be rewarding to others. But, quite often, we observe that they seem to have acquired an insatiable and indiscriminate need for social approval. For example, a 15 year old girl experienced brief periods of marked depression if people failed to comment favorably on her dress or appearance. In early childhood she had learned that parental approval and affection were elicited only when she was "dressed up and looked pretty"; to her, failure on the part of others to note her attractiveness signified rejection and disapproval. It would appear then that contingent reward methods condition children to develop an excessive need for approval; they manifest not only a healthy social affability but also a dependency on social reinforcement.

**Inconsistent Methods.** Parental methods of control often are irregular, contradictory and capricious. Some degree of variability is inevitable in the course of every child's life, but there are parents who display an extreme inconsistency in their standards and expectations, and an extreme unpredictability in their application of rewards and punishments. Youngsters exposed to such a chaotic and capricious environment cannot learn consistently, and cannot devise nonconflictive strategies for adaptive behavior; whatever behavior they display may be countermanded by an unpredictable parental reaction.

To avoid the suspense and anxiety of unpredictable reactions, the child may protectively become immobile and noncommittal. Others, imitatively adopting what they have been exposed to, may come to be characterized by their own ambivalence and their own tendency to vacillate from one action or feeling to another. We know that irregular reinforcements build difficult to extinguish behavior patterns; thus, the immobility or ambivalence of these youngsters may persist long after their environment has become uniform and predictable.

**Protective Methods.** Some parents so narrowly restrict the experiences to which their children are exposed that these youngsters fail to learn even the basic rudiments of autonomous behaviors. Overprotective mothers, worried that their children are too frail or are unable to care for themselves or make sensible judgments on their own, not only succeed in forestalling the growth of normal competencies but, indirectly, give the child a feeling that he is inferior and frail. The child, observing his actual inadequacies, has verification of the fact that he is weak, inept and dependent on others. Thus, not only is this youngster trained to be deficient in adaptive and self-reliant behaviors but he also learns to view himself as inferior, and becomes progressively fearful of leaving the protective "womb."

**Indulgent Methods.** Overly permissive, lax or undisciplined parents allow children full rein to explore and assert their every whim. These parents fail to control their children and, by their own lack of discipline, provide a model to be imitated which further strengthens the child's irresponsibility. Unconstrained by parental control, and not guided by selective rewards, these youngsters grow up displaying the inconsiderate and often tyrannical characteristics of undisciplined children. Having had their way for so long, they tend to be exploitive, demanding, uncooperative and antisocially aggressive. Unless rebuffed by external disciplinary forces, these youngsters may persist in their habits and become irresponsible members of society.

### Family Styles of Communication

The capacity of humans to symbolize experience enables them to communicate with one another in ways more intricate and complex than are found in lower species. Free of the simple mechanisms of instinctive behavior, and capable of transcending the tangibles of his objective world, man can draw from events of the distant past and project to those of the distant future. The symbolic units and syntax of his language provide him with a powerful instrumentality for thought and communication.

Each family constructs its own style of communication, its own pattern of listening and attending and its own way of fashioning thoughts and conveying them to others. The styles of interpersonal communication to which the child is exposed serve as a model for attending, organizing and reacting to the expressions, thoughts and feelings of others. Unless this framework for learning interpersonal communication is rational and reciprocal, he will be ill-equipped to function in an effective way with others. Thus, the very symbolic capacities which enable man to transcend his environment so successfully may lend themselves to serious misdirections and confusions; this powerful instrument for facilitating communication with others may serve instead to undermine social relationships. Although illogical ideas, irrational reactions and irrelevant and bizarre verbalizations often arise as a consequence of extreme stress, its roots can be traced as frequently to the simple exposure to defective styles of family communication.

The effect of amorphous, fragmented or confusing patterns of family communication have been explored by numerous investigators (Singer and Wynne, 1965; Lidz et al., 1958; Bateson et al., 1956; Lu, 1962). Not only are messages attended to in certain families in a vague, erratic or incidental fashion, with a consequent disjunctiveness and loss of focus, but when they are attended to, they frequently convey equivocal or contradictory meanings. The transmission of ambivalent or opposing meanings and feelings produces what Bateson refers to as a *double-bind*. For example, a seriously disturbed ten year old boy was repeatedly implored in a distinctly hostile tone by his equally ill mother as follows: "Come here to your mother; mommy loves you and wants to hug and squeeze you, hug and squeeze you." The intrinsically contradictory nature of these double-bind messages precludes satisfactory reactions; the recipient cannot respond without running into conflict with one aspect of the message, i.e., he is "damned if he does, and damned if he doesn't." Exposed to such contradictions in communication, the youngster's foundation in reality becomes increasingly precarious. To avoid confusion, he learns to distort and deny these conflicting signals; but in this defensive maneuver he succumbs even further to irrational thought. Unable to interpret the intentions and feelings of others and encumbered with a progressively maladaptive pattern of self-distortions, he falls prey to a vicious circle of increasing interpersonal estrangement.

### Content of Teachings

Parents transmit a wide range of values and attitudes to their children either through direct tuition or unintentional commentary. The family serves as the primary socialization system for inculcating beliefs and behaviors. Through these teachings the child learns to think about, be concerned with and react to certain events and people in prescribed ways.

What kinds of teachings lend themselves to the learning of pathological attitudes and behaviors? Just a few will be mentioned.

1. The most insidious and destructive of these teachings is training in anxiety. Parents who fret over their own health, who investigate every potential ailment in their child's functioning and who are preoccupied with failures or the dismal turn of events teach and furnish models for anxiety proneness in their children. Few incidents escape the pernicious effects of a chronically anxious and apprehensive household. Fantasies of body disease, vocational failure, loss of prized objects and rejection by loved ones, illustrate the range of items to which a generalized disposition

to anxiety can become attached. Once learned, this tendency intrudes and colors otherwise neutral events.

2. Feelings of guilt and shame are generated in the teachings of many homes. A failure to live up to parental expectations, a feeling that one has caused undue sacrifices to be made by one's parents and that one has transgressed rules and embarrassed the family by virtue of some shortcoming or misbehavior, illustrate events which question the individual's self-worth and produce marked feelings of shame and guilt. Furthermore, the sacrificing and guilt-laden atmosphere of these parental homes provides a model for behavioral imitation. Youngsters who are admonished and reproached repeatedly for minor digressions often develop a deep and pervasive self-image of failure. If the child admits his misdeeds, and adopts his parents injunctions as his own, he will come to view himself as an unworthy, shameful and guilty person. To protect against feelings of marked self-condemnation, such children may learn to restrict their activities, to deny themselves the normal joys and indulgences of life and to control their impulses far beyond that required to eschew shame and guilt; in time, even the simplest of pleasures may come to be avoided.

3. Other destructive attitudes can be taught directly through narrow or biased parental outlooks; feelings of inferiority and social inadequacy are among the most frequent. Particularly damaging are teachings associated with sexual urges. Unrealistic standards which condemn common behaviors such as masturbation and petting create unnecessary fears and strong guilt feelings; sexual miseducation may have long-range deleterious effects, especially during periods of courtship and marriage.

### Family Structure

The formal composition of the family often sets the stage for learning pathogenic attitudes and relationships. A number of these structural features will be noted (Gregory, 1958; Clausen, 1966).

**Deficient Models.** The lack of significant adult figures within the family may deprive children of the opportunity to acquire, through imitation, many of the complex patterns of behavior required in adult life. Parents who provide undesirable models for imitation, at the very least, are supplying some guidelines for the intricate give-and-take of human relationships.

The most serious deficit usually is the unavailability of a parental model of the same sex.

The frequent absence of fathers in underprivileged homes, or the vocational preoccupations of fathers in well-to-do homes, often produce sons who lack a mature sense of masculine identity; they seem ill-equipped with goals and behaviors by which they can orient their adult lives.

**Family Discord.** Children subject to persistent parental bickering and nagging not only are exposed to destructive models for imitative learning but are faced with upsetting influences that may eventuate in pathological behaviors. The stability of life, so necessary for the acquisition of a consistent pattern of behaving and thinking, is shattered when strife and marked controversy prevail. There is an ever present apprehension that one parent may be lost through divorce; dissension often leads to the undermining of one parent by the other; an air of mistrust frequently pervades the home, creating suspicions and anxieties; a nasty and cruel competition for the loyalty and affections of children may ensue. Children often become scapegoats in these settings, subject to displaced parental hostilities. Constantly dragged into the arena of parental strife, the child not only loses a sense of security and stability but may be subjected to capricious hostility and to a set of conflicting and destructive behavior models.

**Sibling Rivalry.** The presence of two or more children within a family requires that parents divide their attention and approval. When disproportionate affection is allotted to one child, or when a newborn child supplants an older child as the "apple of daddy's eye," seeds of discontent and rivalry flourish. Intense hostility often is generated; since hostility fails to eliminate the intruder and gains, not the sought-for attention, but parental disapproval, the aggrieved child often reverts to regressive or infantile maneuvers, e.g., baby talk or bed-wetting. If these methods succeed in winning back parental love, the youngster will have been reinforced through instrumental learning to continue these childish techniques. More often than not, however, efforts to alter parental preferences fail miserably, and the child may continue to experience deep resentments and a sense of marked insecurity. Such persons often display, in the future, a distrust of affections, fearing that those who express them will prove to be as fickle as their parents. Not unlikely also is the possibility that the intense hostility they felt toward their siblings will linger and generalize into envious and aggressive feelings toward other "competitors."

**Ordinal Position.** It seems plausible that the order of a child's birth within the family would be related to the kinds of problems he faces, and the kinds of strategies he is likely to adopt. For example, the *oldest child,* once the center of parental attention, experiences a series of displacements as new sibs are born; this may engender a pervasive expectation that "good things don't last." However, to counteract this damaging experience, he may be encouraged to acquire the skills of autonomy and leadership, may be more prone to identify with adult models and may learn, thereby, to cope with the complications of life more effectively than his less mature siblings. The *youngest child,* although petted, indulged and allotted the special affections and privileges due the family "baby," may fail to acquire the competencies required for autonomous behaviors. He may be prone to dependency and prefer to withdraw from competition; the higher incidence of mental disorder among the last-born in families lends support to these interpretations (Gregory, 1958; Dohrenwald and Dohrenwald, 1966). *Only children* appear to be especially resilient to severe emotional difficulty. This may reflect their special status as sole recipient of parental attention, approval and affection. In his singular and unhampered state, the child may learn to view himself as especially gifted; with this confidence in self-worth as a base, he may venture into the larger society secure in the conviction that he will be as well-received there as in the parental home. Despite this sound beginning, he is ill-equipped to cope with the give-and-take of peer relationships since he has not experienced the sharing and competition of sibling relationships.

Numerous other features of the family environment, some relating to structural elements (e.g., sex of sibs and presence of "problem" sibs) and some to roles assumed by family members (e.g., domineering or seductive mothers or inadequate or effeminate fathers), can be specified, and their likely consequences upon learning speculated about. A listing of such events and relationships, however, would be too exhaustive for our purposes. A number of these elements will be raised in later chapters when we present case histories.

## TRAUMATIC EXPERIENCES

It is a common belief, attributable in large measure to popularizations of psychology in our literature, that most forms of psychopathology can be traced to a single, very severe experience, the hidden residues of which account for the manifest disorder. Freud's early writings gave impetus and support to this notion, but he reversed himself in his later work when he was made aware of the fact that patient reports of early trauma often were imaginative fabrications of their past. Current thinking in the field suggests that most pathological behaviors accrue gradually through repetitive learning experiences.

Despite the primacy that enduring and pervasive experiences play in shaping most pathological patterns, there are occasions when a particularly painful event can shatter the individual's equanimity and leave a deeply embedded attitude that is not readily extinguished. An untimely frightening experience, or an especially embarrassing and humiliating social event, illustrate conditions which can result in a persistent attitude.

The impact of these events may be particularly severe with young children since they usually are ill-prepared for them and lack the perspective of prior experience which might serve as a context for moderating their effects. If a traumatic event is the first exposure for a youngster to a particular class of experiences, the attitude he learns in reaction to that event may intrude and color all subsequent events of that kind. Thus, an adolescent whose first sexual venture resulted in devastating feelings of guilt, inadequacy or humiliation may carry such feelings within him long after the event has passed.

Traumatic events persevere in their learned effects for essentially two reasons. *First,* a high level of neural activation ensues in response to most situations of marked distress or anxiety. This means that many diverse neural associations become connected to the event; the greater the level of neural involvement, the more deeply and pervasively will be the learned reaction, and the greater the difficulty will be in extinguishing what was learned. *Second,* during heightened stress, there often is a decrement in the ability to make accurate discriminations within the environment; as a consequence, the traumatized individual generalizes his emotional reaction to a variety of objects and persons who are only incidentally associated with the traumatic source. For example, a youngster injured in an auto accident may develop a fear reaction not only to cars but to all red couch covers (the color of the seat of the car in which he was riding), to men in white jackets (the color of the medical intern's uniform who attended to him after the accident) and so on. Because of the seemingly illogical nature of these fears (the difficulty of tracing their connection to the accident), they are not readily amenable to rational analysis and extinction.

Despite the severity and persistence of the effects of certain traumatic events, they tend to be stimulus-specific, that is, limited to stimulus conditions that are highly similar to those in which they were first learned. In certain cases, however, these experiences may give rise to a chain of reactions and events which establish pervasive pathological trends. Thus, in the next section we will see that the conditions of early experience, whatever their nature, may activate coping reactions which persist long after the event which prompted them has passed.

## EVALUATIVE COMMENTS

We have taken the liberty in this section of bringing together many of the diverse notions and findings which theorists have used to identify the principal psychogenic sources of psychopathology; only briefly have we commented on the adequacy of these data, or the methods employed in obtaining them. Our presentation would be amiss if we failed to appraise, albeit briefly, the soundness of the evidence.

The view that the particular setting and events of early experience play a decisive part in determining personality is assumed by psychologists of all theoretical persuasions. But where, in fact, are the "hard data," the unequivocal evidence derived from well-designed and well-executed research? Such data, unfortunately, are sorely lacking. Most of the research in the field can be faulted on methodological grounds, biased populations, poor assessment techniques, unreliable diagnostic categories and, most significantly, failures to include appropriate control groups by which comparative evaluations can be made. Without controls, for example, it is impossible to determine whether the specific parental attitude, training procedure or traumatic event under investigation can be assigned the significance attributed to it.

For the student who is interested in a critical review of the literature on the topic just discussed, we may suggest a reading of any one of several evaluative papers such as those on infant care and personality by Orlansky (1949) and Caldwell (1964), or the role of the family in psychopathology by Frank (1965). To point up the importance of control groups in this field, we offer this illuminating quote from Renaud and Estess (1961):

Students of behavior generally agree that critical tests of hypotheses about the development of mental illness can only be made through the study of control groups of normal or superior subjects. The question with which this paper concerns itself is whether significant numbers of mentally healthy persons have 'pathogenic' childhoods—whether histories of adequately functioning symptom-free normals contain less evidence of 'traumatic' events (parental rejection, parental discord, conflict with siblings, rigid training patterns, repressive sexual attitudes, and oedipal anxieties) than do histories of 'patients' (persons who seek our professional help for neurotic or psychotic symptoms). A belief which grew out of our work with . . . *effectively functioning men* is that their biographies *do not* differ appreciably, if at all, from those of psychiatric patients with respect to the amount of childhood experiences traditionally considered to prognose ineffective functioning and maladjustment.

Such a conclusion is not incompatible with basic assumptions underlying twentieth century behavioral science (e.g., that in substantial degree human behavior is a product of life experience); neither is it in conflict with the basic proposition that the early years of human life are crucial for later development. This view does question, however, elementalistic conceptions of simple, direct causal relations insistently presumed to exist between certain kinds of events and later development of mental illness.

This disconcerting finding shows us that there may be no substantial difference in deleterious childhood experiences between normal men and psychiatric patients. It is known, furthermore, that many adults who have been reared in seemingly devastating childhood environments not only survive but thrive, whereas adults raised under idealistic conditions often deteriorate into severe pathological patterns. Clearly, the combination of factors, and the sequence of events involved in producing pathology, is awesomely complex and difficult to unravel. Unless future lines of research are based on sound premises and executed with the utmost of methodological care, investigators will continue to go around in circles, confirming only what their naive prejudices incline them to find.

The importance of well-reasoned and well-designed studies is nowhere more evident than in the investigation of psychogenic sources of psychopathology; few studies of the past have met the basic criteria of good research. We have minimized reference to specific studies in this section lest we lead the student to believe that there are data from well-designed research to support the notions presented. The student should view these notions as propositions which will be confirmed or disconfirmed as a result of *future* research.

## SIGNIFICANT EARLY LEARNINGS

Because of our primary focus at the moment, we may forget that the child's developmental pattern is a biosocial process in which biophysical dispositions such as reactivity, temperament and physical constitution contribute a part. Learning is vitally important, of course, but we must not overlook the fact that the child's bio-physical make-up influences the character of these learnings. The interaction between biological fac-tors and the nature of what is learned will be touched upon only briefly in this section, but the intimate interplay between them should be kept in mind at all points in our discussion.

## LEARNING INTERPERSONAL AND SELF-ATTITUDES

In the previous section we stressed that the pattern of rearing and the attitudes of parents, to which the child is exposed repeatedly, have a marked and pervasive effect upon his personality; the importance of these enduring influences can-not be underestimated. It will be useful to remind ourselves, however, that experience may have a more profound effect at certain stages in the developmental sequence than at others. In dividing the effects of experience in terms of the time of their occurrence we are reiterating a conviction stated earlier that pronounced environmental in-fluences occur at periods of rapid neurological growth. Thus, a hypothetical event *A* may have a more deleterious consequence if it occurs at stage 2 than at stage 3, because it affects neurological structures which are proliferating rapidly at stage 2, but which are relatively dormant at stage 3.

A further reason for noting the stage-specific significance of experience is the observation that most children are exposed to a succession of dis-tinct social expectancies and tasks which they must fulfill at different points in the developmental sequence. These stage-specific encounters are timed, in general, to coincide with periods of rapid neurological growth (e.g., the training of bladder control is begun in most families when the child has just begun to possess the requisite neural equipment for such control; similarly, children are taught to read when intracortical development has advanced sufficiently to enable a modicum of success). In short, a reciprocity appears to exist in most societies between periods of rapid neuro-logical growth and exposure to related experi-ences and tasks. Each stage may be viewed as a crisis, to use Erikson's terms, in that the child's newly emerging neurological potentials are chal-lenged by a series of decisive encounters with the environment. The child is especially vulnerable to the effects of experience at these critical points since these experiences both shape his neurologi-cal patterns and result in his learning a series of primary attitudes about himself and others.

What experiences arise typically at each of the three neuropsychological stages of develop-ment and, more importantly, what are the central attitudes learned during these periods?

In seeking an answer to these questions, we return once more to the fertile ideas of Freud, and to the brilliant modifications of these ideas by Erikson. The three stages presented earlier in the chapter, and the elaborations concerning the content of learning to be described below, borrow heavily from the work of these men.

Briefly, during the sensory-attachment stage, the central attitude learned deals with one's *trust of others;* the sensorimotor-autonomy stage is noted by the learning of attitudes about *self-competence;* and the intracortical-initiative stage is characterized by learning attitudes regarding one's *personal-identity*. A brief elaboration of the character of these learnings is in order.

### Stage 1: Learning Trust of Others

Trust may be described as a feeling of con-fidence that one can rely on the affections and support of others. Although subsequent events may condition and alter these feelings throughout life, there are few periods in which an individual is so wholly dependent on the good faith and care of others than during the helpless state of infancy. Nothing is more crucial to the infant's survival and well-being than the nurture and protection afforded him by his caretakers. It is through the quality and consistency of this support that deeply ingrained feelings of trust are etched within the child's make-up.

Although the young infant does not possess even the crudest form of symbolism by which he can grasp a concept such as trust of others, he does possess the sensory capacities to register a vague feeling of the "goodness and comfort" of his surroundings. He can learn a rather diffuse expectation that needs are fulfilled, that pain is relieved and that security, warmth and soothing sensations are, or are not, in the offing.

Needless to say, the neonate and young infant can make only the grossest of discrimina-tions at this period. It is as a result of this per-ceptual indiscriminateness, however, that what he does learn is so very significant. Feelings and expectancies arising from his more specific rela-tionship with his caretaker are highly generalized, and come to characterize his entire image of his environment. It is precisely because of his inability to make fine discriminations that these early learnings become pervasive and widespread. Were he able to differentiate among experiences more sharply, their effects would not be as generalized as they are.

Generalized early learnings establish a

foundation of feelings of trust or mistrust with regard to the environment, feelings which will tinge and color every facet of the child's outlook and relationship with others. Nurtured well and given comfort, affection and warmth, he will acquire a far-reaching sense of trust of others; he will learn to anticipate that discomfort will be moderated and that others will assist him and provide for his needs. Should he be deprived of affection, warmth and security or should he be handled severely and painfully, he will learn to mistrust his environment, to anticipate further distress and to view others as harsh and undependable. Rather than developing an optimistic and confident attitude toward the future, he will be inclined to withdraw into himself and to avoid events and people for fear that they will evoke the discomfort and anguish he had experienced in the past.

### Stage 2: Learning Self-Competence

During the sensorimotor-autonomy stage the child becomes progressively less dependent on his caretakers. By the second and third years, he is ambulatory and possesses the power of speech and of physical control over many elements in his environment. Increasingly, he acquires the manipulative skills by which he can venture forth within his world and test his competence to handle events on his own.

In a previous section, we described a number of the consequences of the impoverishment or enrichment of these competencies. Quantity of stimulus opportunity, however, is only part of the story. Subtle as well as obvious, attitudes conveyed by parents will shape the child's confidence in his competencies. These attitudes will markedly influence the child's behavior, since it is not only what he can do which will determine his actions but how he feels about what he can do. The system of rewards and punishments to which he is exposed, and the degree of encouragement and affection surrounding his first performances, will contribute to the child's confidence in himself. He may set out to test his own mettle, of course, but others, through their reactions and attitudes, will have a marked impact in telling him how adequate or inferior are his behaviors.

Severe discipline for minor assertions and transgressions, humiliating comments in response to the first stumbling efforts at self-achievement, embarrassments associated with social awkwardness, deprecations consequent to poor school performance, and shame among one's peers as a result of athletic inadequacies, all weigh heavily as factors diminishing the youngster's sense of self-competence and self-esteem. Faced with re-

buffs and ridicule, the child learns to doubt his adequacy—his capacity to face the frightening array of situations which put his competencies to the test. Whether he actually possesses the requisite skills to handle events no longer is at issue; he simply lacks the confidence to try, to venture or to compete. He may quietly sit by the sidelines, lamenting or rationalizing his self-perceived mediocrity; he may seek the comforts of identifying with a "club" or a "team" or learn to lean on a "stronger" or "virtuous" figure. In summary, then, it is not only the quantity but the qualitative conditions surrounding the development of his competencies which establish attitudes of high or low self-esteem.

### Stage 3: Learning Personal-Identity

With the emergence of the intracortical-initiative stage, and its associated capacities of thinking, evaluating and planning, the child begins to formulate a distinct image of himself as a certain "kind of person," of being an identity discernible from others, one capable of having independent judgments and of fashioning his own course of action.

Several elements of experience which influence the image of self-as-object were discussed in an earlier description of *Stage 3* and need not be reiterated here. It will suffice to recall that the healthy child must acquire a coherent system of internalized beliefs and values which will guide him through the welter of a changing and variegated environment. Free of his earlier dependence on others, he must find his own anchor, his own compass by which he can keep to a steady and independent course through life. Properly equipped by successful efforts toward autonomy, he will have confidence that he possesses a direction and purpose in life which is valued by others, and which can safely withstand the buffeting of changing events. Deprived of rewarding experiences in self-action and unable to get a picture of a valued inner identity, he will lack the means of meeting tasks and challenges, be thrown off-balance by his own aggressive and sexual impulses and be incapable of handling the discouraging and divisive forces which may arise within his personal life.

Should there be a lack of an integrated and coherent sense of self, a consistent set of convictions or beliefs of "who I am" and "where am I going," the growing adolescent or adult will flounder from one tentative course to another, and be beset with an amorphous and vague feeling of discontent and purposelessness. Should circumstances shape a picture of a worthless, unattractive or troublesome person, the youngster will be set on a course of self-deprecation, social with-drawal or aggressive rebellion. Moreover, these reactive behaviors often are self-defeating; self-deprecation, social withdrawal or aggressive be-havior set up vicious circles of reactions from others which tend to perpetuate the image the youngster wishes to change. As his own remedial efforts deepen his plight, he may feel an increasing sense of futility, and may accept his unfortunate self-image as unalterable and permanent.

## LEARNING COPING STRATEGIES

As noted above, children learn complicated sequences of attitudes, reactions and expectancies in response to the experiences to which they were exposed. Initially, these responses are specific to the particular events which prompted them; they are piecemeal, scattered and changeable. Over the course of time, however, through learning what responses are successful in obtaining rewards and avoiding punishments, the child begins to crystal-lize a stable pattern of instrumental behaviors for handling the events of everyday life. These coping and adaptive strategies come to characterize his way of relating to others, and comprise one of the most important facets of what we may term his personality pattern.

The concepts of coping and adaptation have been referred to in the literature since the turn of the century; the brilliant theoretical work of Heinz Hartmann and other "ego" analysts since the mid-1930's has enriched our understanding of the organism's inherent adaptive capacities. In the past ten years, research has explored systematically how these processes unfold, and the types of inte-grated patterns into which they form. The projects undertaken by Lois B. Murphy and her colleagues at the Menninger Clinic (1962) may be pointed to as one of the most comprehensive and illum-inating of these recent studies; our presentation will be drawn largely from the productive ideas generated in this important body of on-going work.

After the first years of groping through trial and error learning, the normal child acquires a set of strategies for coping with events, a pattern of flexible behaviors and mechanisms by which he deals effectively with the challenges of his en-vironment. These resources are not mechanical reactions invariably used in response to all types of situations; rather, the healthy child will display a flexibility in his strategies, deploying only those behaviors which are suited to the particulars of each challenge. When feasible, a direct or task-oriented solution of the problem will be attempted. Once a conscious and objective appraisal of the

conditions of reality has been made, the person will initiate a sequence of behaviors which he previously has learned is successful in com-parable situations. He may alter destructive ele-ments in his own behavior, remove or circumvent obstacles in his way or compromise his goals and accept substitutes for them. Should all of these previously learned strategies fail, he may devise novel approaches until these prove either ade-quate or deficient to the task.

Along with these more rational and con-scious task-oriented behaviors, the individual may employ a number of intrapsychic processes. These essentially unconscious mechanisms amelio-rate the discomforts he experiences when he is unable to resolve his problems in a more direct fashion. Any of the several adaptive mechanisms described in chapter 3 will serve to relieve his anguish; they are useful also in that they enable him to maintain his equilibrium until he can muster a better solution. We should take note, then, that healthy coping may be characterized both by retreat and self-deception *if* the objective conditions of the environment prevent a direct solution to a painful problem; it is not unrealistic and maladaptive to back off and soothe one's wounds if one cannot succeed. Only when the individual persistently distorts and denies the events of the objective world do these uncon-scious mechanisms interfere with effective func-tioning.

What are the principal determinants of the coping strategies that individuals learn to utilize?

Three determinants may be noted: biophysi-cal constitution; past experiences; and current alternatives. These factors have been described previously, but it will be instructive to bring them together at this point to show their rela-tionship to the choice of coping strategies.

*Biophysical Constitution.* The style with which the child copes with his world is rooted initially in basic constitutional factors. His energy, tempo, drive, activity level, temperament, intelligence, sensory sensitivity, physical strength and vulnerabilities, all of the elements of his "reactivity pattern" described in chapter 4, com-prise a given set of capacities and dispositions which colors how he perceives events, and influ-ences the character of his responses to them. Whether elements of his environment will be experienced as overwhelming, and whether he possesses resources for handling strain and dis-harmony, is determined largely by his constitu-tional make-up.

*Past Experiences.* Constitutional factors may be viewed as a set of dispositions which inclines the child to deal in a distinctive way with the events and challenges of his environment. However, the role these factors will play in shaping the child's coping strategies depends largely on the character of the experiences to which he is exposed. Under "normal" environmental circumstances, a child will find some means of coping with events that is suitable to his constitutional disposition. But if pressures and demands are too severe, they may force him to devise strategies that are contrary to his natural inclinations.

To mature the capacities and skills requisite for coping adequately with his environment, the young child must be supplied with an optimum intensity and diversity of stimulus experiences. Early stimulus impoverishment and enrichment during peak periods of maturation result in permanent deficiencies and imbalances which may weaken or distort the coping resources available to him; as a consequence, "normal" events may be experienced as more stressful and discomforting than they might otherwise be.

Through the everyday attitudes and behaviors to which he is exposed the child learns *what is good, where to obtain it and how to act to elicit it.* Parental feelings, attitudes, training methods and interactions with siblings and peers —the whole gamut of odd-and-end personal experiences of life—provide the child with the knowledge of what has been reinforcing for him, where best to gain these reinforcements and which instrumental strategies he must employ to achieve them.

*Current Alternatives.* The full range of coping behaviors available at any particular moment will be narrowed by objective reality. Although a child's resources may be broad and varied, the specific situation with which he is confronted may preclude the use of preferred and effective strategies. For example, a child who typically uses bluff and aggression may back down, or adopt another strategy to win his point, if he is faced with a stronger and more adamant opponent.

In summary, then, there are three primary determinants of a coping strategy: the individual's inborn capacities and dispositions, his history of stimulus nourishments and reinforcements and the realistic alternatives currently available to him.

What we have stressed thus far is that coping strategies enable the individual to handle the tasks of reality, to change the state of events to suit his needs and to maneuver flexibly from one course of action to another. We have noted also that not all aspects of these strategies are conscious or planned according to a rational design; they often entail the use of intrapsychic or unconscious processes which "take the sting" out of difficult situations, and moderate tensions which otherwise would interfere with effective functioning.

But what if these conscious and unconscious strategies fail, what if the cumulation of persistent anxieties erodes the individual's confidence to cope with the problem he faces?

Under such conditions, the person must resort to more circuitous devices, to more distorting and denying mechanisms. If these secondary coping maneuvers restore balance, and enable the individual to obtain some measure of comfort and gratification, he will have a respite, an opportunity to gather his forces and reequip himself with behaviors that are more adequate than those he employed in the past. But if the threat he faces is too severe, or too persistent and unremitting, he dares not divert his attentions, and cannot let down his guard to relax. He must continue his maneuvers, and is forced to keep up his defensive guard lest he be overwhelmed or shattered.

When a person has been exposed to repeated threats, punishments and frustrations, he soon will learn to expect that problems never subside and that he must always be prepared to avoid or react to these events before they recur. Even when no objective strain and discomfort exists, he must be "on his toes," ready to forestall what he expects. As he begins to "cope" with these nonexistent but anticipated events, his behavior becomes inflexible and unadaptive; he traps himself into a vicious circle in which he dares not change and dares not lower his guard. Soon he begins to alienate himself from realistic sources of gratification and begins to elicit reactions from others that only intensify his difficulties. His ingrained coping strategy no longer is adaptive; it has become an indiscriminate and autonomously acting behavior pattern. Designed initially to protect against recurrences of the painful past, it now denies him rewards in the present and thereby perpetuates his anguish. The important notion of self-perpetuation as an element in psychogenesis will be elaborated more fully later in this chapter.

We have asserted in the previous paragraphs that defective strategies can be characterized by their tendency to respond to current events as if they were duplicates of the past. In other words, the individual continues to seek and avoid past reinforcements, and persists in engaging in instrumental behaviors which achieved these aims. Unable to relinquish the bonds of past learnings, he fails to acquire new sources of reinforcement, and new strategies for obtaining them.

It would appear reasonable, from the foregoing, to classify these persistent defective strategies in terms of the *types of reinforcements* an individual has learned to seek, the *sources* he has learned to provide these reinforcements and the *instrumental behaviors* he has learned to employ to achieve them. Describing pathological coping strategies in reinforcement terms casts them merely into a somewhat different language than the one in which they traditionally are formulated, that of "ego psychology." It is hoped, however, that this translation may point up more sharply their basic motivational and behavioral features. By framing our thinking in terms of *what* reinforcements the individual is seeking, *where* he is looking to find them and *how* he performs in order to obtain them, we may see more simply and more clearly the essential strategies which guide his coping behaviors.

Any classification system oversimplifies its subject; the classification herein proposed is no different. However, we cannot criticize a system of categorization for failing to provide for the unique characteristics of individual cases; innumerable differences and variations of behavior will be found among patients who are classified together, no matter what system is used. This loss of individuality is inevitable. What we can ask, however, is whether the central theme of a classification system highlights *important* and *relevant* features of its subject, and whether individuals sharing the same category possess these features in common. Hopefully, and with some confidence, the proposed schema for coping strategies to be described fulfills these criteria.

It is interesting that when one reviews the styles or patterns of personality described by clinical theorists (e.g., Freud, Horney and Fromm) and clinical researchers (e.g., Leary and Lorr), one finds considerable agreement as to the salient types of coping strategies displayed by patients.

What are these coping strategies, and how can they be formulated in terms of the types and sources of reinforcements patients have learned to seek, and the instrumental behaviors they have learned will elicit them?

The formulation we shall propose will be presented here briefly; a more detailed discussion, with case presentations, will be provided in the next few chapters. As noted above, it will be instructive to approach these strategies in terms of three questions: (1) what reinforcements does the individual seek; (2) where does he look to find them and (3) how does he perform to elicit them?

**Reinforcements Sought.** Efforts to categorize patients in terms of the *specific* kinds of rein-

forcements they pursue will not prove fruitful. The particular events or objects which people find rewarding (e.g., sex, sports, art or money) are legion, and for every patient who experiences a certain event as rewarding, one can find another, possessing a similar pathological pattern, who experiences that same event as distasteful or painful, e.g., some patients who are driven to seek attention are sexually promiscuous, whereas others are repelled by sexuality in any form. In short, categorizations based on the specific properties of reinforcing objects will prove not only cumbersome but also futile.

On what basis, then, can relevant and fruitful distinctions among reinforcements be made? Two possibilities present themselves. First, whether or not the patient does find certain events to be reinforcing. And second, what the nature of these reinforcements are, that is, whether he seeks primarily to achieve positive reinforcements, or to avoid negative reinforcements.

1. Certain patients may be characterized by their failure either to seek or to experience *both* positive and negative reinforcements; they have neither a drive for pleasure nor a desire to avoid punishment; they possess either a deficit capacity to experience reinforcement or an inability to discriminate between nonreinforcing and reinforcing events.

These deficiencies may arise from several etiological sources. Some patients may lack the constitutional make-up requisite for seeking, sensing or discriminating reinforcing events. Others may have been deprived of the stimulus nourishment necessary for the maturation of motivational or emotional capacities. A third group may have been exposed to irrational and confusing family communications or to contradictory patterns of reinforcement, both of which may result in cognitive perplexities or motivational apathies. Whatever the complex of causes may have been, these patients acquire little or no body of either positive or negative reinforcing objects to motivate behavior. Thus, a pathetic eight year old "autistic" boy, who may have begun life deficient in the capacity to experience reinforcements, and who was reared by a withdrawn, psychotic mother, exhibited no interest in people or objects, seemed content to sit and stare at a wall, was unmoved by events that surrounded him and appeared indifferent both to threats of pain and to its experience at moderate intensities.

2. Another group of patients may be distinguished by deficits in positive reinforcers, although they possess substantial numbers of negative reinforcers; they get little gratification but

considerable pain from both themselves and others. Although they experience few pleasures in life, they can "feel," and do sense and react to discomfort and punishment.

Etiologically, we may speculate that one of the causes of this pattern is that the neurological or physiochemical make-up of the individual is so constructed as to dispose him maximally to pain and minimally to pleasure, e.g., various centers of the limbic system may be unequally dense, or may be disadvantageously wired to other brain regions. Equally probable in these cases is a history of harsh, rejecting and punitive experiences which may oversensitize these individuals to threat and anxiety. Exposed repeatedly to such events, these persons may have learned not only to anticipate threat but to devise a protective strategy of avoidance so as to minimize its recurrence. To illustrate, a 14 year old schizophrenic girl had been extremely tense and fearful "almost from the moment she was born." This temperamental disposition was aggravated by repeated parental intimidation and humiliation; by the time she was seven, she hid in closets to avoid people, covered her face when asked questions by her teachers and cried whenever she thought someone was making fun of her.

Such individuals usually are deprived of experiences which might strengthen feelings of competence and self-worth; moreover, having a low opinion of themselves, they cannot turn to themselves as a source of positive reinforcement. Ultimately, they seek rewards neither from themselves nor from others, seem perpetually on guard and are oriented solely to the avoidance of negative reinforcers.

Patients either characterized by deficits in the capacity to experience reinforcement or oriented primarily to negative reinforcers, display a *detached* pattern. Incapable of experiencing rewards from themselves or others, they act in a socially detached and self-alienated manner.

**Source of Reinforcements.** Most people experience a wide range of both positive and negative reinforcers. However, some individuals acquire these reinforcements from a narrow band of events and objects; as a consequence, their behaviors and strategies are oriented toward these few prepotent highly rewarding and highly punishing sources.

How can patients be characterized in terms of the *sources* from which they experience their positive and negative reinforcements?

A listing of the varied and sundry places where reinforcements can be acquired will prove fruitless. But one distinction seems relevant and useful. It represents the observation that some

patients turn to others as their source of reinforcement, whereas some turn primarily to themselves. The distinction between *others* and *self* as the primary reinforcement source underlies our categories of *dependent* and *independent* personalities.

1. *Dependent* individuals have learned that feelings of satisfaction, that is, those produced by gaining positive reinforcements and avoiding negative reinforcements, are best provided by others. Behaviorally, most of these persons display an indiscriminate and insatiable need for affection and approval.

Any number of early experiences may set the stage for dependency behavior. For example, some individuals exposed to an overprotective training regime may fail to acquire the competencies for autonomy and initiative; exposure to competitive failures leads them to forego further attempts at self-assertion and self-gratification. In short, they learn early that gratifying experiences are not achieved from themselves but are secured better by leaning on others. Should they be deprived of interpersonal attention, affection and support, they will experience intense discomfort and anxiety.

2. The *independent* personality pattern is characterized by self-reliance. This individual has learned that he obtains a maximum of positive reinforcements and a minimum of negative reinforcements when he depends on himself rather than others.

The tendency to draw upon oneself as the primary source of reinforcement can arise from several different lines of development. For some, this may reflect the acquisition of an image of superior self-worth, learned in response to admiring and doting parents. Rewards produced by oneself are highly valued if one possesses an inflated sense of self-esteem; such persons often display manifest narcissism and egocentricity.

Other patterns of independence may develop as a result of self-protection; these patients turn to themselves to avoid negative reinforcements from others and to supply positive reinforcement which they cannot obtain elsewhere. Where past experience has been characterized by rejection and punishment, the individual learns not only that he cannot depend on others for gratification but that pain and discomfort will be forthcoming if he puts his life in their hands. These patients mistrust others, desire retribution for past punishments and seek independence, strength and prestige to exploit and dominate their environment; only by usurping the power which others possess can they feel secure from threat, and assure the rewards of life.

3. In both dependent and independent patterns, the person demonstrates a distinct preference as to whether to obtain his reinforcements from others or from himself. Such clear-cut commitments are not made by all patients. Some people, those whom we shall speak of as *ambivalent,* remain unsure as to which way to turn, that is, they are in conflict as whether to depend on themselves for reinforcement, or on others. A number of these patients vacillate between submissive conformity, at one time, and aggressive autonomy, the next. Unable to resolve their ambivalence, they weave an erratic course from self-deprecation and guilt to stubborn negativism and resistance.

Other ambivalent patients display a picture of consistent compliance and dependence; their histories indicate that they have been intimidated and subjected to severe discipline for transgressing parental strictures and expectations. Beneath their conforming veneer, however, are intense desires to rebel and to assert their own feelings, impulses and values. But they are trapped in conflict; to avoid punishment and humiliation they must deny the validity of their own feelings as a source of reinforcement, and must adopt the values and guidelines set forth by others. The disparity they sense between their own inner tendencies and the behaviors they must display, leads often to feelings of dissonance, to persistent bodily tensions and to the development of rigid protective controls.

**Instrumental Behaviors.** We noted in a preceding section that any attempt to group together specific types of reinforcements would prove futile or irrelevant; this is equally true of categorizations of types of instrumental activity. Man engages in innumerable forms and sequences of behavior as a means of eliciting the reinforcements he seeks.

On what basis then can a useful distinction be made among instrumental behaviors? A review of the literature in diverse fields such as constitutional psychology, psychoanalytic characterology and multivariate classification research suggests that the behavioral dimension of activity-passivity may prove useful. The causes of differences in the active-passive dimension may include biological dispositions (Murphy, 1962) and competence learnings (White, 1960) as well as specific conditions of training and prior reinforcement (Lefcourt, 1966); whatever the base, people do display consistent and impressive differences in the degree, zealousness and vigor with which they utilize instrumental activities to pursue the reinforcements they seek.

1. *Active* patients may be characterized by their alertness, vigilance, persistence, decisiveness and ambitiousness in goal-directed behavior. They are firmly committed to secure what they want; they plan strategies, scan alternatives, manipulate events and circumvent obstacles, all to the end of eliciting pleasures and rewards, or evading the distress of punishment and anxiety. Although their goals may differ from time to time, they initiate activity and are enterprising, energetic and busily intent on controlling the circumstances of their environment.

2. *Passive* patients initiate few instrumental strategies; they display an inertness, an acquiescence and a seemingly resigned attitude in which they wait for the circumstances of their environment to take their course. They may be temperamentally ill-equipped to assert themselves; perhaps past experience has deprived them of opportunities to acquire a sense of competence, a confidence in their ability to master the events of their environment; equally possible is a naive confidence that things will come their way with little or no effort on their part. From a variety of diverse sources, then, these individuals display minimal overt instrumental activity to control or produce the effects they desire. Passivity is their strategy. They seem suspended, immobile, restrained or listless; they initiate little to shape the course of events, waiting for things to happen and reacting to them only after they occur.

### Classification of Coping Patterns

A classification scheme based on (1) the nature and source of reinforcements and (2) styles of instrumental behavior provides a theoretical framework for what we believe to be the eight principal pathological personality patterns. A 4 × 2 arrangement that combines the detached, dependent, independent and ambivalent reinforcement strategy, with the activity-passivity behavior dimension, results in an eight-fold system that corresponds closely to the basic variants of abnormal functioning uncovered by both clinical theorists and researchers.

In this section, we will briefly outline the features of these eight pathological coping patterns (an earlier summary was provided in chapter 3; a more extensive discussion, with case histories, will be presented in chapters 6 and 7).

1. *Passive-detached (asocial personality)*: These patients lack the drive or capacity to experience either positive or negative reinforcements. They tend to be apathetic, listless, unresponsive, distant, withdrawn and asocial;

2. *Active-detached (avoidant personality)*: These individuals are apprehensive, suspicious and mistrustful. They experience few positive rein-

forcements from life, are vigilant, perennially on guard, ever-ready to avoid actively their anxious anticipation of negatively reinforcing experiences;

3. *Passive-dependent* (*submissive personality*): Here the individual has learned not only to depend on others for reinforcements but to await their leadership in providing them. They appear unambitious, helpless and clinging, display little autonomy or initiative and seem content to sit by compliantly and put their fate in the hands of others;

4. *Active-dependent* (*gregarious personality*): Although these individuals use others as their primary source of reinforcement, they engage busily in a series of socially manipulative maneuvers to secure the attention and approval they seek. They are characterized as gregarious, charming, demonstrative, affectionate and clever, ever-ready to change their tune to attract praise or avoid hostility;

5. *Passive-independent* (*narcissistic personality*): These patients experience their primary rewards simply by being themselves. They display an egocentric self-assurance, an air of snobbish and pretentious superiority which requires little confirmation either through genuine accomplishment or the approval of others. Their sublime confidence that things will work out well provides them with little incentive to engage in the reciprocal give-and-take of social life;

6. *Active-independent* (*aggressive personality*): These individuals counter the expectation of negative reinforcements and the deprivation of positive reinforcements by vigorous, assertive and aggressive actions. As a consequence of their resentment and envy of others, they become self-reliant, domineering, and cunning, strategies designed to exploit and control others for their personal gain;

7. *Passive-ambivalent* (*conforming personality*): These persons have been intimidated and coerced into accepting the reinforcements of others. By a disciplined self-restraint, they inhibit their desires and deny their feelings; they learn to remain passive and conform to the conditions of their environment in a prudent, controlled and perfectionistic way;

8. *Active-ambivalent* (*negativistic personality*): Here the individual struggles between following the reinforcements offered by others as opposed to those desired by himself. He gets into endless wrangles with others for his moodiness and for his erratic and obstructive behaviors; he is restless and discontent and feels misunderstood and unappreciated.

As we have noted earlier in the text, we must be careful not to be carried away by the oversimplifications of classification schemes. What we have proposed in the system of categories outlined above is merely a tool, a way of thinking about the awesomely complicated and diverse patterns of coping behavior manifested by patients. Hopefully, the tool proposed here will sharpen our perception and understanding of relevant characteristics of abnormal behavior. Let us be sure not to "put the cart before the horse." The labels we append to patients are abstractions designed to facilitate our thinking and understanding of them. We first must perceive and understand the distinctive history and attributes of the patient himself; the label we apply is merely a convenient way to coordinate our perceptions and communications; they should not lead us to see more than the patient presents nor to oversimplify what we do see. Furthermore, diagnostic labels should not give us the illusion that we have uncovered the patient's "essence" or "disease." Labels such as "passive-dependent" cannot be viewed as psychological equivalents of physical diseases such as "mumps" or "measles." These terms are conceptual tools of limited utility, and do not represent tangible or rigidly circumscribed illnesses. With these thoughts in mind, we can proceed to our next topic.

## CONTINUITY OF EARLY PATTERNS

We have contended in the two preceding sections that childhood experiences are crucially involved in shaping lifelong patterns of behavior. To support this view we elaborated several conditions of early upbringing and their consequences, noting first the impact of the sheer quantity of stimulation upon maturation and second, the effect of particular kinds of experiences upon the learning of complex behaviors and attitudes. Although few theorists of psychopathology would deny the paramount role we have attributed to early experience, they may differ among themselves as to not only "why" these experiences are important but "how" exactly they come to play their significant role in later behavior.

Is the impact of early experience, as we have asserted in the previous sections, a consequence of the young child's susceptibilities during "sensitive" maturational stages? That is, are early experiences more significant than later experiences because the developing child is more plastic and impressionable than the fully matured adult? Can other explanations be offered to account for the special status in shaping behavior assigned to early experience?

A review of the literature will uncover several alternate explanations, that is, explanations which contend that children are *not* intrinsically different than adults in their responsiveness to experience (Stevenson, 1957). Despite these occasional differences in opinion, most theorists hold the view that early experiences do contribute a disproportionately larger share to learned behavior than later experiences.

Among the alternate interpretations offered for this phenomenon are the following. Influences common both to children and adults arise more often in childhood, that is, there is nothing distinctive about childhood other than the *frequency* with which certain experiences occur; were these events equally frequent in adulthood, there would be no reason to assume that they would effect adults less than they do children. Others state that the difference may be due to the fact that children experience the impact of events more intensely than adults since they have fewer skills to handle challenges and threats. A somewhat similar hypothesis suggests that the importance of childhood experience lies in its *primacy,* that is, the fact that the first event of a set of similar events will have a more marked impact than later ones; according to this view, an event experienced initially in adulthood will have the same effect upon a adult as it does upon a child; these theorists note, however, that it is more likely that the first of a series of similar experiences will occur in childhood.

There is little question that the special status of early experience can be ascribed in part to the simple facts of frequency and primacy; events which come first or more often will have a bearing on what comes later and thereby justify our assigning them special impact value. The question remains, however, as to whether frequency and primacy, in themselves, are sufficient to account for the unusual significance attributed to childhood experiences.

Acceptance of the role which these two factors play does not preclude additional hypotheses which assign unusual vulnerabilities or sensitivities to young children. There is no fundamental conflict between these views; each factor, primacy, frequency and biological sensitivity may operate conjointly and with undiminished singular

effects. A later discussion will attempt to show how these varied influences weave together to give early experience their special role.

We will concentrate in this section on the notion of continuity in behavior, since we believe that the significance of early experience lies not so much in the intensity of its impact but in its durability and persistence. Experiences in early life are not only ingrained more pervasively and forcefully, but their effects tend to persist, and are more difficult to modify, than later experiences. For example, early events occur at a presymbolic level and cannot easily be recalled and unlearned; they are reinforced frequently as a function of the child's restricted opportunities to learn alternatives; they tend to be repeated and perpetuated by the child's own behavior. For many reasons, then, a continuity in behavior—a consistent style of feeling, thinking and relating to the world—once embedded in early life, perseveres into adulthood.

Part of the continuity we observe between childhood and adulthood may be ascribed to the stability of biological constitutional factors, factors described extensively in chapter 4. But there are numerous psychological processes which contribute to this longitudinal consistency. Because these processes enable us to see more clearly how pathology develops, we cannot afford to take them for granted or merely enumerate them without elaboration.

Broadly speaking, the processes which coalesce to bring about continuity may be grouped into three categories: resistance to extinction, social reinforcement and self-perpetuation.

## RESISTANCE TO EXTINCTION

Acquired behaviors and attitudes usually are not fixed or permanent. What has been learned can be modified or eliminated under appropriate conditions, a process referred to as *extinction.* Extinction usually entails exposure to experiences that are similar to the conditions of original learning but which provide opportunities for new learning to occur. Essentially, old habits of behavior change when new learning interferes with, and replaces, what previously had been learned; this progressive weakening of old learnings may be speeded up by special environmental conditions, the details of which are not relevant to our discussion.

What happens if the conditions of original learning cannot be duplicated easily? According to contiguity learning theory, failure to provide opportunities for interfering with old habits means that they will remain unmodified and persist over time; in other words, learnings associated with events that are difficult to reproduce are resistant to extinction.

The question we next must ask is: are the events of early life experienced in such a manner as to make them difficult to reproduce and, therefore, resistant to extinction? An examination of the conditions of childhood suggests that the answer is yes! The reasons for asserting so have been formulated with extraordinary clarity by David McClelland (1951); we will draw upon several of his ideas in the following sections.

## PRESYMBOLIC LEARNING

Biologically speaking, the young child is a primitive organism. His nervous system is incomplete, he perceives the world from momentary and changing vantage points and he is unable to discriminate and identify many of the elements of his experience. What he sees and learns about his environment through his infantile perceptual and cognitive systems will never again be experienced in the same manner in later life.

The infant's presymbolic world of fleeting and inarticulate impressions recedes gradually as he acquires the ability to identify, discriminate and symbolize experience. By the time he is four or five, he views the world in preformed categories and he groups and symbolizes objects and events in a stable way, a way quite different from that of infancy.

Once the growing child's perceptions have taken on discriminative symbolic forms, he can no longer duplicate the perceptually amorphous, presymbolic and diffusely inchoate experiences of his earlier years. Unable to reproduce these early experiences in subsequent life, he will not be able to extinguish what he learned in response to them; no longer perceiving events as initially sensed, he cannot supplant his early reactions with new ones. These early learnings will persist, therefore, as feelings, attitudes and expectancies which crop up pervasively in a vague and diffuse way.

## RANDOM LEARNING

The young child lacks not only the ability to form a precise image of his environment but the equipment to discern logical relationships among its elements. His world of objects, people and events is connected in an unclear and random fashion; he learns to associate objects and events which have no intrinsic relationship; clusters of concurrent but only incidentally connected stimuli

are fused erroneously. Thus, when he experiences fear in response to his father's harsh voice, he may learn to fear not only that voice but the setting, the atmosphere, the pictures, the furniture and the odors, a whole bevy of incidental objects which by chance was present at that time. Unable to discriminate the precise source in his environment which "caused" his fear, he connects his discomfort randomly to all associated stimuli; now each of them become precipitants for these feelings.

Random associations of early life cannot be duplicated as the child develops the capacity for logical thinking and perception. By the time he is four or five he can discriminate cause-and-effect relationships with considerably accuracy. Early random associations do not "make sense" to him; when he reacts to one of the precipitants derived from early learning, he is unable to identify what it is in the environment to which he is reacting. He cannot locate the source of his difficulty, since he now thinks more logically than before. To advise him that he is reacting to a picture or piece of furniture simply will be rejected; he cannot fathom the true features that evoke his feelings since these sources are so foreign to his new, more rational mode of thought. His difficulty in extinguishing the past is compounded since it is difficult not only for him to reexperience the world as it once may have been but he will be misled in his search for these experiences if he applies his more developed reasoning powers.

## GENERALIZED LEARNING

The young child's discriminations of his environment are crude and gross. As he begins to differentiate the elements of his world, he groups and labels them into broad and unrefined categories. All men become "daddy"; all four-legged animals are called "doggie"; all foods are "yum-yum." When the child learns to fear a particular dog, for example, he will learn to fear not only that dog but all strange, mobile four-legged creatures. To his primitive perception, all of these animals are one-of-a-kind.

Generalization is inevitable in early learning. It reflects more than the failure of young children to have had sufficient experiences to acquire greater precision; the child's indiscriminateness represents an intrinsic inability to discriminate events because of his undeveloped cortical capacities.

As the undifferentiated mass of early experiences becomes more finely discriminated, learning gets to be more focused, specific and precise; a ten year old will learn to fear bulldogs as a result of an unfortunate run-in with one, but will not necessarily generalize this fear to collies or poodles, since he knows and can discern differences among these animals.

Generalized learning is difficult to extinguish. The young child's learned reactions are attached to a broader class of objects than called for by his specific experiences. To extinguish these broadly generalized reactions in later life, when his discriminative capacities are much more precise, will require that he be exposed to many and diverse experiences. This may be a difficult point to grasp, and an illustration may be useful to clarify it.

Let us assume that a two year old was frightened by a cocker spaniel. Given his gross discriminative capacity at this age, this single experience may have conditioned him to fear dogs, cats and other small animals. Let us assume further, that in later life he is exposed repeatedly to a friendly cocker spaniel. As a consequence of this experience, we find that he has extinguished his fear, but only of cocker spaniels, not of dogs in general, or cats or other small animals. His later experience, seen through the discriminative eye of an older child, was that *spaniels* are friendly but not dogs in general. The extinction experience applied then to only one part of the original widely generalized complex of fears he acquired. His original learning experience incorporated a much broader range of stimuli than his later experience, even though the objective stimulus conditions were essentially the same. Because of his more precise discriminative capacity, he now must have his fear extinguished in a variety of situations in order to compensate for the single but widely generalized early experience.

These three interlocking conditions—presymbolic, random and generalized learning—account in large measure for the unusual difficulty of re-experiencing the events of early life, and the consequent difficulty of unlearning the feelings, behaviors and attitudes generated by these events.

## SOCIAL REINFORCEMENT

Of the many factors which contribute to the persistence of early behavior patterns, none plays a more significant role than social and interpersonal relationships. These relationships can be viewed fruitfully from the perspective usually taken by sociologists and social psychologists. To these scientists, the varied cultural and institutional forces of a society promote continuity by maintaining a stable and organized class of experiences to which most individuals of a particular group are repeatedly exposed. Reference to these broader social determinants of continuity will be made in a later section. For the present, our focus will be on the more direct and private side of interpersonal experience.

As pointed out in an earlier section, ingrained personality patterns develop as a consequence of enduring experiences generated in intimate and subtle relationships with members of one's immediate family. We described a number of events which lead to the acquisition of particular types of behaviors and attitudes. Here our attention will be not on the content of what is learned but on those aspects of relationships which strengthen what has been learned, and which lead to their perpetuation. Three such influences will be described: repetitive experiences, reciprocal reinforcement and social stereotyping.

### REPETITIVE EXPERIENCES

The typical daily activities in which the young child participates is restricted and repetitive; there is not much variety in the routine experience to which the child is exposed. Day in and day out he eats the same kind of food, plays with the same toys, remains essentially in the same physical environment and relates to the same people. This constricted environment, this repeated exposure to a narrow range of family attitudes and training methods, not only builds in deeply etched habits and expectations but prevents the child from new experiences that are so essential to change. The helplessness of infants, and the dependency of children, keep them restricted to a crabbed and tight little world with few alternatives for learning new attitudes and responses. Early behaviors fail to change, therefore, not because they may have jelled permanently but because the same slender band of experiences which helped form them initially, continue and persist as influences for many years.

### RECIPROCAL REINFORCEMENT

The notion that a child's early behaviors may be accentuated by his parents' response to him was raised in chapter 4; we noted that a circular interplay often arises which intensifies the child's initial biological reactivity pattern. Thus, unusually passive, sensitive or cranky infants frequently elicit feelings on the part of their mothers which perpetuate their original tendencies.

This model of circular or reciprocal influences may be applied not only to the perpetuation of biological dispositions but to behavior tendencies that are acquired by learning. Whatever the initial roots may have been—constitutional or learned—

certain forms of behavior provoke, or "pull" from others, reactions which result in the repetition of these behaviors. For example, a suspicious, chip-on-the-shoulder and defiant child eventually will force others, no matter how tolerant they may have been initially, to counter with perplexity, exasperation and anger; the child undermines every inclination on the part of others to be nurturant, friendly and cooperative. An ever-widening gulf of suspicion and defiance may develop as parents of such children withdraw, become punitive or "throw up their hands in disgust"; controls or affections which might have narrowed the gulf of suspicion and hostility break down. Each participant, in feedback fashion, contributes his share; the original level of hostile behavior is aggravated and intensified. Whether the "cause" was the child or the parent, the process has gotten out of hand, and will continue its vicious and inexorable course until some benign influence interferes, or until it deteriorates into pathological form.

## SOCIAL STEREOTYPES

The dominant features of a child's early behavior form a distinct impression upon others. Once this early impression is established, people expect that the child will continue to behave in his distinctive manner; in time, they develop a fixed and simplified image of "what kind of person the child is." The term "stereotype," borrowed from social psychology, represents this tendency to simplify and categorize the attributes of others.

People no longer view a child passively and objectively once they have formed a stereotype of him; they now are sensitized to those distinctive features they have learned to expect. The stereotype begins to take on a life of its own; it operates as a screen through which the child's behaviors are selectively perceived so as to fit the characteristics attributed to him. Once cast in this mold, the child will experience a consistency in the way in which others react to him, one that fails to take cognizance of the varieties and complexities of his behaviors. No matter what he does, he finds that his behavior is interpreted in the same fixed and rigid manner. Exposed time and time again to the same reactions and attitudes of others, he may give up efforts to convince them that he can change. For example, if a "defiant" child displays the slightest degree of resentment to unfair treatment, he will be jumped on as hopelessly recalcitrant; should he do nothing objectionable, questions will be raised as to the sincerity of his motives. Faced with repeated negative appraisals and unable to break the stereotype into which he

has been cast, the youngster will relapse after every effort to change, and continue to behave as he did originally, and as others expect.

## SELF-PERPETUATION

Significant experiences of early life may never recur again, but their effects remain and leave their mark. Physiologically, we may say they have etched a neurochemical change; psychologically, they are registered as memories, a permanent trace and an embedded internal stimulus. In contrast to the fleeting stimuli of the external world, these memory traces become part and parcel of every stimulus complex which activates behavior. Once registered, the effects of the past are indelible, incessant and inescapable. They now are intrinsic elements of the individual's make-up; they latch on and intrude into the current events of life, coloring, transforming and distorting the passing scene. Although the residuals of subsequent experiences may override them, becoming more dominant internal stimuli, the presence of earlier memory traces remains in one form or another. In every thought and action, the individual cannot help but carry these remnants into the present. Every current behavior is a perpetuation, then, of the past, a continuation and intrusion of these inner stimulus traces.

The residuals of the past do more than passively contribute their share to the present. By temporal precedence, if nothing else, they guide, shape or distort the character of current events. Not only are they ever present, then, but they operate insidiously to transform new stimulus experiences in line with past. We will elaborate four of these processes of perpetuation in this section: protective constriction, perceptual and cognitive distortion, behavior generalization and repetition compulsion.

### PROTECTIVE CONSTRICTION

Painful memories of the past are kept out of consciousness, a process referred to as repression. Similarly, current experiences which may reactivate these repressed memories are judiciously avoided. The individual develops a network of conscious and unconscious protective maneuvers to decrease the likelihood that either of these distressing experiences will occur.

As a consequence of these protective efforts, however, the person narrows or constricts his world. Repression reduces anxiety by enabling the individual to keep the inner sources of his discomfort from awareness, but it also thwarts him from "unlearning" these feelings, or learning new and potentially more constructive ways of coping with them. Likewise, by defensively reducing one's activities to situations which will not reactivate intolerable memories, the individual automatically precludes the possibility of learning to be less anxious than in the past, and diminishes his chances for learning new reactions to formerly stressful situations. For example, a highly intelligent and physically attractive 15 year old boy had progressively withdrawn from school and social activities; for several years there had been marked disharmony at home, culminating in a well-publicized scandal involving his parents. Despite the fact that his teachers and peers viewed him personally in a favorable light and made efforts to show their continued acceptance, his embarrassment and fear of social ridicule led him into increasing isolation and fantasies that he would be humiliated wherever he went.

As a result of his own protective actions, then, the person preserves unaltered his memories of the past; in addition, they persist and force him along paths that prevent their resolution. Moreover, the more vigilant his protective maneuvers and the more constrictive his boundaries, the more limited will be his competencies for effective functioning and the more he will be deprived of the positive rewards of life.

## PERCEPTUAL AND COGNITIVE DISTORTION

Certain processes not only preserve the past but transform the present in line with the past. Cameron (1947) describes this process, which he refers to as *reaction-sensitivity,* with insight and clarity. To him, once a person acquires a system of threat expectancies, he responds with increasing alertness to similar threatening elements in his life situation. For example, persons who develop bodily anxieties often become hypochondriacal, that is, hyperalert to physiological processes which most people experience but ignore.

Kelly's notion of *personal constructs* (1955) may be seen as an extension of the concept of reaction-sensitivity. To him, people acquire anticipatory cognitive attitudes as a consequence not only of threatening but of all forms of past experience; these constructs guide, screen, code and evaluate the stream of new experiences to which the individual is exposed. Thus, a person who has learned to believe that "everyone hates him" will tend to interpret the incidental and entirely innocuous comments of others in line with this premise.

The role of habits of language as factors shaping one's perceptions are of particular interest.

As Whorf (1956) and others have shown, the words we use transform our experiences in line with the meaning of these words. For example, a child who has been exposed to parents who respond to every minor mishap as "a shattering experience" will tend to use these terms himself in the future; as a consequence, he will begin to feel that every setback he experiences is shattering because he has labeled it as such.

The importance of expectancies, reaction-sensitivities and language habits lies in the fact that they lead to the distortion of objective realities. Disturbed individuals may transform what most people would have perceived as a beneficent event into one that is humiliating, threatening and punishing. Instead of interpreting events as they objectively exist, then, the individual selectively distorts them to "fit" his expectancies and habits of thought. These expectancies may channel his attention, and may magnify his awareness of irrelevant and insignificant features of his environment; they intrude constantly to obscure and to warp an accurate perception of reality. The following quote from Beck illustrates this process well (1963):

A depressed patient reported the following sequence of events which occurred within a period of half an hour before he left the house: His wife was upset because the children were slow in getting dressed. He thought, "I'm a poor father because the children are not better disciplined." He then noticed a faucet was leaky and thought this showed he was also a poor husband. While driving to work, he thought, "I must be a poor driver or other cars would not be passing me." As he arrived at work he noticed some other personnel had already arrived. He thought, "I can't be very dedicated or I would have come earlier." When he noticed folders and papers piled up on his desk, he concluded, "I'm a poor organizer because I have so much work to do."

Often *inexact labeling* seems to contribute to this kind of distortion. The affective reaction is proportional to the descriptive labeling of the event rather than to the actual intensity of a traumatic situation.

A man reported during his therapy hour that he was very upset because he had been "clobbered" by his superior. On further reflection, he realized that he had magnified the incident and that a more adequate description was that his superior "corrected an error" he had made. After re-evaluating the event, he felt better. He also realized that whenever he was corrected or criticized by a person in authority he was prone to describe this as being "clobbered."

*Selective abstraction* refers to the process of focusing on a detail taken out of context, ignoring other more salient features of the situation and conceptualizing the whole experience on the basis of this element.

A patient, in reviewing her secretarial work with her employer, was praised about a number of aspects of her work. The employer at one point asked her to discontinue making extra carbon copies of his letters. Her immediate thought was, "He is dissatisfied with my work." This idea became paramount despite all the positive statements he had made.

This distortion process has an insidiously cumulative and spiraling effect. By misconstruing reality in such ways as to make it corroborate his expectancies, the individual, in effect, intensifies his misery. Thus, ordinary, even rewarding events, may be perceived as threatening. As a result of this distortion, the patient subjectively experiences neutral events "as if" they were, in fact, threatening. In this process, he creates and accumulates painful experiences for himself where none exists in reality.

One sometimes sees in patients a progressive worsening of their behavior, despite the fact that the objective conditions of their life have improved. Once the pathological process of distortion has begun, the patient misinterprets experiences in terms of his outlook; he now is caught in a downward spiral in which everything, no matter how objectively "good" it might be, is perceived as distressing, disheartening or threatening. His initial distortions have led to a succession of subjectively experienced stresses; this progressive cumulation of stress drives the patient further and further away from an objective appraisal of reality; all efforts to counter and reverse the pathological trend are utterly useless at this point. The process of perceptual and cognitive distortion has built up its own momentum, resulting not only in its perpetuation but in its intensification.

## BEHAVIOR GENERALIZATION

We have just described a number of factors which lead individuals to perceive new experiences in a subjective and frequently warped fashion; perceptual and cognitive distortions may be viewed as the defective side of a normal process in which new stimulus conditions are seen as similar to those experienced in the past. This process, though usually described in simpler types of conditions, commonly is referred to as *stimulus generalization*. In the present section, we will turn our attention to another closely related form of generalization, the tendency to react to new stimuli in a manner similar to the way in which one reacted in the past; we may speak of this process as *behavior generalization*.

Stimulus generalization and behavior generalization often are two sides of the same coin; thus, if an individual distorts an objective event so as to perceive it as identical to a past event, it would be reasonable to expect that his response to it would be similar to that made previously. For example, let us assume that a child learned to cower and withdraw from a harshly punitive mother. Should the child come into contact with a somewhat firm teacher, possessing physical features similar to those of the mother, the child may distort his perception of the teacher, making her a duplicate of the mother, and then react to her as he had learned to react to his mother.

This tendency to perceive and to react to present events as if they were duplicates of the past has been labeled by intrapsychic theorists as the process of *transference*. This concept signifies the observation that patients in treatment often magnify minor objective similarities between their parents and the therapist, and then transfer to the therapist responses learned within the family setting.

The transference of past behaviors to novel situations is necessary to efficient functioning; we cannot approach each and every new circumstance of life without some prior notion of how to perceive and react to it. From the viewpoint of efficiency, then, generalization enables us to apply what we have learned, that is, to react in the same way to situations that are comparable. A problem arises, however, when we transfer responses incorrectly because we have failed to discriminate between dissimilar situations, e.g., reacting to novel circumstances in the present as if they were duplicates of the past.

The tendency to generalize inappropriate behaviors has especially far-reaching consequences since it often elicits reactions from others which not only perpetuate these behaviors but aggravate the conditions which gave rise to them. Thus, Bateson and Ruesch (1951) have noted that communications between people convey more than a statement; they carry with them some anticipation of what the response will be. Leary (1957), along similar lines, suggests that interpersonal behaviors often are designed unconsciously to "pull" a reaction from others. For example, a phrase such as, "I think I'm doing poorly," is not merely a message denoting one's personal feelings but a social statement which one normally expects will elicit a reciprocal reaction such as, "Of course not! You did beautifully."

How does the generalization of interpersonal behavior perpetuate conditions which give rise to these behaviors?

An example may be useful. A person whose past experiences led him to anticipate punitive reactions from his parents may be hyperalert to signs of rejection from others. As a consequence of his suspiciousness he may distort innocuous comments, seeing them as indications of hostility. In preparing himself to ward off and counter the hostility he expects, he freezes his posture, stares coldly and rigidly and passes a few aggressive comments himself. These actions communicate a message that quickly is sensed by others as unfriendly and antagonistic. Before long, others express open feelings of disaffection, begin to withdraw and display real, rather than imagined, hostility. The person's generalized suspicious behavior has evoked the punitive responses he expected. He now has experienced an objective form of rejection similar to what he received in childhood; this leads him to be more suspicious and arrogant, beginning the vicious circle all over again.

By intruding old behaviors into new situations, individuals will provoke, with unfailing regularity, reactions from others which reinforce their old responses. Almost all forms of generalized behavior set up reciprocal reactions which intensify these behaviors; docile, ingratiating or fearful interpersonal actions, for example, draw domineering and manipulative responses; confident and self-assured attitudes elicit admiration and submissiveness. In short, not only is generalization a form of perpetuation itself but it creates conditions which promote perpetuation.

### REPETITION COMPULSION

Maladaptive behaviors persist not only as a consequence of generalized learned habits. There are intrapsychic sources which "drive" the individual to recreate situations of the past that were frustrating or unresolved. Freud spoke of this process as repetition compulsions; by this he meant the unconscious tendency to reconstruct situations in the present which parallel failures or disappointments of the past, and to persist in the attempt to fulfill these disappointments even though these attempts repeatedly have proven unrewarding.

A contradiction may appear, upon first reading, between "protective constriction," noted earlier, and repetition compulsion. The inconsistency can be resolved if we think of protective constriction as a process of avoiding conditions which have no hope of resolution. Repetition compulsions, in contrast, may be viewed as a process of reinstating conditions which provided partial gratification in the past, and which give promise of ultimate fulfillment. In this process, the individual arranges situations so as to utilize maneuvers which were *periodically* successful. He employs these partially reinforced behaviors again and again in the hope of finally achieving a full measure of the ends he sought.

The derivatives of these partially fulfilled drives constitute a reservoir of strivings which persist and seek gratification. Thus, the individual repeats past patterns not only through generalization but through active efforts to recreate and overcome what was not achieved fully. For example, a highly charged sibling rivalry between two brothers generated intense hostile and destructive feelings on the part of the older brother, a 21 year old college student seen at his university's counseling service. These feelings were vented in a variety of malicious maneuvers, some of which were successful some of the time, but never fully gratified; that is, the drive to undo, humiliate and even destroy the younger brother remained only a partially fulfilled striving. In new interpersonal situations, the older brother recreated the sibling relationship; time and time again he made friends, only to repeat the malicious maneuvers of deprecation and humiliation he had employed with his brother in the past. These relationships only partially fulfilled his needs, however, since the "real" object of his hatred was his brother, and the goal he really sought, that of total destruction of his competitor, never was achieved. He repeated compulsively, in one relationship after another, the same destructive behavior patterns he learned in the past; although he never gratified his unconscious objectives fully, he obtained sufficient symbolic rewards in these peer relationships to perpetuate his behavior.

In contrast to protective constriction, then, a process limited to conditions in which failure and pain were inevitable, repetition compulsions apply to those conditions where rewards are periodically achieved and where the motivation to obtain greater fulfillment persists. As a consequence, intolerable duplicates of the past are recreated.

# SOCIOCULTURAL INFLUENCES

We would be remiss in our presentation if we failed to recognize that psychopathology may be shaped by the institutions, traditions and values which comprise the cultural context of societal living; these cultural forces serve as a common framework of formative influences which set limits and establish guidelines for members of a social group. However, we must be careful to view "society" and "culture" not as entities but as convenient abstractions which characterize the pattern of relationships and responsibilities shared among group members.

The continuity and stability of cultural groups depend largely on the success with which their young are imbued with common beliefs and customs. To retain what has been wrought through history, each group must devise ways of molding its children to "fit in," that is, to accept and perpetuate the system of prohibitions and sanctions which earlier group members have developed to meet the persistent tasks of life. Each infant undergoes a process of "socialization" by which he learns to progressively surrender his impulsive and naive behaviors, and to regulate or supplant them with the rules and practices of his group. Despite the coerciveness of this process and the loss of personal freedom which it entails, children learn, albeit gradually, that there are many rewards for cooperative and sharing behaviors. Societal rules enable him to survive, to predict the behaviors of others, to obtain warmth and security and to learn acceptable strategies for achieving the rich and diverse rewards of life. It is important to recognize, then, that the traditions of a culture provide its members with a shared way of living by which basic needs are fulfilled for the greater majority with minimal conflict and maximal return.

In previous sections we noted that for many children the process of cultural training and inculcation is far from ideal; methods by which societal rules and regulations are transmitted by parents often are highly charged and erratic, entailing affection, persuasion, seduction, coercion, deception and threat. Feelings of stress, anxiety and resentment may be generated within the young, leaving pathological residues that linger, are perpetuated and serve to distort their future relationships; several of these pathogenic experiences have been dealt with earlier.

Attention in this "sociocultural" section will focus, not on the more private experiences of particular children in particular families, but on those more public experiences which are shared in common among members of a societal group. In a sense, we shall be speaking of forces which characterize "society as the patient."

## PATHOGENIC SOURCES IN CONTEMPORARY LIFE

Lawrence K. Frank suggested the following proposal more than thirty years ago (1936):

Instead of thinking in terms of a multiplicity of so-called social problems, each demanding special attention and a different remedy, we can view all of them as different symptoms of the same disease. That would be a real gain even if we cannot entirely agree upon the exact nature of the disease. If, for example, we could regard crime, mental disorders, family disorganization, juvenile delinquency, prostitution and sex offenses, and much that now passes as the result of pathological processes (e.g., gastric ulcer) as evidence, not of individual wickedness, incompetence, perversity or pathology, but as human reactions to cultural disintegration, a forward step would be taken.

The notion that many of the pathological patterns observed today can best be ascribed to the perverse, chaotic or frayed conditions of our cultural life has been voiced by many commentators of the social scene (Fromm, 1955; Reisman, 1950; Goodman, 1960); these conditions have been characterized in phrases such as "the age of anxiety," "growing up absurd" and "the lonely crowd." It is not within the scope of this book to elaborate the themes implied in these slogans; a brief description of three conditions of contemporary life will suffice to provide the student with some idea of what these writers are saying. First, we will note the operation of forces which compel individuals to surpass the standards to which they were exposed in early life; second, we will point up the effects of changing, ambiguous and contradictory social values; and third, we will describe the consequences of the disintegration of social beliefs and goals.

## ACHIEVEMENT STRIVING AND COMPETITION

Few characterizations of American life are more apt than those which portray our society as upwardly mobile. Stated differently, ours has been a culture which has maximized the opportunity of its members to progress, to succeed and to achieve material rewards once considered the province only of the aristocracy and well-to-do. With certain notable and distressing exceptions, the young of our society have been free to rise, by dint of their wits and their talents, above the socioeconomic status of their parents. Implicit in this well-publicized option to succeed, however, is the expectancy that each person will pursue opportunities, and will be measured by the extent to which he fulfills them. Thus, our society not only promotes ambition but expects each of its members to meet the challenge successfully. Each aspiring individual is confronted, then, with a precarious choice; along with the promising rewards of success are the devastating consequences of failure.

Upwardly mobile opportunities are shared by most members of our society; this can only bring forth intense competition. The struggle for achievement is geared, therefore, not only to transcend one's past but to surpass the attainments of others. No better illustration can be seen of the consequences of competitive failure and inadequacy than in the constant testing and grading which children experience throughout their school years; this early form of teaching competitiveness persists and pervades every fabric of societal life. It is evident in athletics, in the desire to be accepted by prestigious colleges, in the search for "pretty" dates, for getting a job with a "title," having the highest income, buying "up" to a status car, belonging to the "right" country club and so on.

The competitive success struggle is insatiable and fruitless since few can reach the "top," and there are no spheres of life in which invidious comparisons cannot be made. Thus, a depressed man of 47, who had risen from a poor immigrant family background to a respected and financially rewarding career as a lawyer, became despondent and considered himself a failure following his unsuccessful bid for the elective office of county judge.

Guilt for having let others down, self-devaluation for one's limitations and self-recrimination for failures, all of these pathogenic feelings well up within many members of our society. We have been well trained to compete and to seek public achievements without examining their aims, their inevitable frustrations and their limited rewards.

## UNSTABLE AND CONTRADICTORY SOCIAL STANDARDS

Achievement strivings refer to the need to surpass one's past attainments; competition describes the struggle among individuals to surpass each other in these achievements. What happens, however, if the standards by which people gauge their achievements keep changing or are ambiguous? What happens if people cannot find dependable and unequivocal standards to guide their aspirations?

It has been the historical function of cultural traditions to give meaning and order to social life, to define the tasks and responsibilities of existence and to guide group members with a system of shared beliefs, values and goals. These traditions, transmitted from parents to child, provide the young with a blueprint for organizing his thoughts, behaviors and aspirations.

One of the problems we face today is the pace of social change, and the increasingly contradictory standards to which members of our society are expected to subscribe (Sherif and Sherif, 1965). Under the cumulative impact of rapid industrialization, immigration, urbanization, mobility, technology and mass communication, there has been a steady erosion of traditional values and standards. Instead of a simple and coherent body of customs and beliefs, we find ourselves confronted with constantly shifting and increasingly questioned standards whose durability is uncertain and precarious. No longer can we find the certainties and absolutes which guided earlier generations. The complexity and diversity of everyday experience play havoc with simple "archaic" beliefs, and render them useless as instruments to deal with contemporary realities. Lacking a coherent view of life, we find ourselves groping and bewildered, swinging from one set of standards to another, unable to find stability and order in the flux of changing events. There have been few times in the history of man when so many have faced the tasks of life without the aid of accepted and durable traditions.

This profusion of divergent standards is compounded by intrinsic contradictions among the beliefs to which people are exposed; we are sermonized to "turn the other cheek," but exhorted to "compete and win," as well. The strain of making choices among conflicting values and loyalties besets us at every turn. Competing claims on our time and divergent demands to behave one way here and another there keep us in constant turmoil, and prevent us from finding a stable anchor or from settling on a fixed course. For example, an anxious and dejected 36 year old mother of three could not resolve the problem of whether to follow her former career as a lawyer, which she had interrupted at the time of her first child's birth, or whether to remain a housewife; when first seen, she was torn between the desire to accept a position as legal counsel for a public agency engaged in humanitarian social programs, and feelings of guilt that by so doing she would fail to fulfill her responsibilities to her husband and children. With no system of consistent values, we drift erratically from one action to another; countervailing pressures only lead us into uncertainty, confusion, conflict and hypocrisy.

## DISINTEGRATION OF REGULATORY BELIEFS AND GOALS

There are large segments of our society that find themselves out of the mainstream of American life; isolated by the unfortunate circumstance of social prejudice or economic deprivation, they struggle less with the problem of achieving in a changing society than with managing the bare necessities of survival. To them, the question is not which of the changing social values they should pursue but whether there are any social values that are worthy of pursuit.

Youngsters exposed to poverty and destitution, provided with inadequate schools, living in poor housing set within decaying communities, raised in chaotic and broken homes, deprived of parental models of "success and attainment" and immersed in a pervasive atmosphere of hopelessness, futility and apathy, cannot help but question the validity of the "good society" (Short, 1966). Reared in these settings one quickly learns that there are few worthy standards to which one can aspire successfully. Whatever efforts are made to raise oneself from these bleak surroundings run hard against the painful restrictions of poverty, the sense of a meaningless and empty existence and an indifferent, if not hostile, world. Thus, the young black people of today reject outright the idea of finding a niche in American society; they question whether a country that has preached equality, but has degraded their parents and deprived them of their rights and opportunities, is worth saving at all. Why make a pretense of accepting patently "false" values or seeking the unattainable goals of the larger society, when reality undermines every hope, and social existence is so evidently and pervasively painful and harsh?

Deteriorating and alienated communities feed upon themselves; not only do they perpetuate their decay by destroying the initiative and promise of their young but they attract the outcast and unstable who drift into their midst. Caught in this web of disintegration, the young and the downwardly mobile join those who already have retreated from the values of the larger society. Delinquency, prostitution, broken homes, crime and addiction increasingly characterize these communities, and the vicious circle of decay and disintegration not only persists but is intensified.

We must keep in mind, however, that harsh cultural and social conditions rarely "cause" psychopathology; rather, they serve as a context within which the more direct and immediate experiences of interpersonal life take place. They color and degrade personal relationships, and establish maladaptive and pathogenic models for imitation.

We have described, in a rather facile way, some of the pathogenic features of contemporary society. In the following discussion we will note several variables of social life which have been subjected to systematic research, and have been shown to be correlates of psychopathology.

## SOME SOCIOCULTURAL CORRELATES OF PSYCHOPATHOLOGY

Many investigators have attempted to specify particular conditions of social life which contribute to mental illness; usually, these studies establish precise correlations between single variables such as socioeconomic class, national and racial origin and marital status and the presence of psychopathology. In this section, we will describe briefly some empirical findings and conclusions of recent research; students interested in detailed reviews would do well to read the articles by Scott (1958) and Dunham (1966).

It is advisable to keep two points in mind while reading this section. First, correlations found between sociocultural variables and psychopathology do not necessarily indicate that these social variables have "caused" the psychological disturbance; the effect may go the other way. Thus, it is just as likely that already disturbed individuals will gravitate toward socially pathological settings, as it is that these settings will produce disturbances in previously healthy individuals. For example, a withdrawn and ineffectual male, raised in a high socioeconomic class, may, as a consequence of his already established illness, drift into a lower class neighborhood; it would be incorrect to assume, in this case, that his illness was a product of his present disadvantaged environment. Psychopathology led to his social disintegration; it did not produce it.

Second, we must recognize that the effects of a social condition can be evaluated only in terms relevant to the personal life of the individual; we cannot assume that our usual conceptions of unfortunate events are effectively experienced as such by an individual. Divorce, for example, may be felt as a crushing personal loss to one individual, but a relief from unbearable anguish to another; in the first case, divorce may be pathogenic; in the second, it may be productive of mental health. Similarly, we normally assume that a high socioeconomic status provides a person with a sense of security and comfort; it may be productive, however, of indolence and irresponsibility, conditions conducive to the development of psychopathology. In short, the significance of any social variable must always be appraised in light of the individual's personal life. Judgments about social conditions will tend to be gross over-simplifications if they fail to be viewed from this context.

## CROSS-CULTURAL STUDIES

It is commonly held that substantial differences in the prevalence (total frequency) of psychopathology exist between cultures. Weinberg (1952), for example, asserts that serious disorders arise less frequently among homogeneous and well-integrated primitive cultures than in those characterized by technological complexities, cultural heterogeneity and intergroup conflict. Ralph Linton (1956) came to a more discriminating conclusion. He noted that overt symptomatology is colored by the beliefs and customs of different social groups, but that the basic patterns of psychopathology can be found with equal frequency throughout the world. To him, the reported prevalence of mental disorder in primitive societies was spuriously low since these groups have little in the way of facilities for identifying and caring for those who are ill.

Carothers, in Africa (1953), and Stainbrook, in Brazil (1952), and Phillips, in Argentina and Japan (1968), found that the proportions of various forms of psychopathology differed substantially from that found in most Western societies. Along similar lines, Rosen and Rizzo (1961) found appreciable differences in the distribution of disorders between subcultures of a single Western society.

An excellent study by Goldhamer and Marshall (1953) investigated hospital admissions in Massachusetts from 1840 to 1940, enabling them to evaluate differences in the incidence (rate of occurrence) and type of disorders as function of time. The per capita incidence of psychopathology doubled during this period, but was accounted for entirely by the increase in patients over 50, a result attributable almost wholly to the increased life span during this period. There was no evidence that serious psychopathology had increased among those in early and middle life; they did note, however, rather striking shifts in the kind of psychopathology reported at different periods in this 100 year span. Similar changes over time in the dominant forms of psychiatric disorder are reported by Malzberg (1959).

In summary, then, there is evidence that cultural factors effect the form of expression, but not the frequency of psychopathology.

## RACIAL AND ETHNIC ORIGIN

Problems in both the definition of race and the ascription of ethnic origins make research on these variables difficult to execute and interpret. If we accept the traditional criteria used by investigators in this field, we are led to conclusions such as the following: Negroes show a higher prevalence of severe pathology than whites; Jews have a lower frequency of severe, but a higher frequency of mild, pathology than non-Jews; Chinese have a particularly low rate of alcoholic and sociopathic disorders; Irish Catholics display different patterns of pathology than Italian Catholics; recent immigrants and foreign-born have higher incidence rates than native-born.

In summarizing his review of research on these correlates, Scott states (1958):

Explanations for the differential rates of mental illness among the different racial and ethnic groups tend to be more speculative than empirically demonstrated. In addition to the problem of controlling socioeconomic status when making interethnic and interracial comparisons, there is the likelihood that differential willingness to care for psychotics within the family, rather than within institutions, might be responsible for some of the apparent differences in incidence.

The findings of the extensive Midtown Manhattan Study corroborate Scott's assertion; they found that racial and ethnic differences in psychopathology disappear when these groups are matched on socioeconomic variables (Srole et al., 1962).

## RESIDENTIAL LOCALE

The admission rate for all forms of mental illness is substantially higher in urban than rural areas (Malzberg, 1940). Furthermore, the larger the city and the more central, congested and overpopulated the region within it, the higher the incidence (Faris and Dunham, 1939).

Differences between urban and rural rates have been attributed primarily to the more benign environment of country life, and to the ability of rural dwellers to care for their mentally ill at home. Other interpretations are possible; however, there are not sufficient data to enable us to choose among them.

The higher rates found within the central and congested tracts of a city, as compared to the more peripheral regions, appear to apply only to larger urban centers (Clausen and Kohn, 1959). It seems reasonable to ascribe the higher rates of psychopathology in central city areas to the fact that these communities usually are poverty stricken, physically decayed and socially disorganized. Not only do these regions breed conditions conducive to pathology but they tend to attract and serve as a haven of anonymity for the unstable and ineffectual who drift into their midst from other regions of society.

## MARITAL STATUS

Married persons have a lower incidence of mental disorder than single people, especially single males, who, in turn, have lower rates than those who are divorced (Rose and Stub, 1955; Odegaard, 1953). There are several ways in which these findings have been interpreted; the two most common assert: that marriage protects the individual from distresses associated with loneliness and disaffection, and that those inclined to psychopathology either are ill-disposed or incapable of establishing a marital relationship, or precipitate difficulties which eventuate in the termination of an existent relationship. Both explanations seem reasonable and, together, are likely to account for the obtained findings. Let us elaborate them briefly.

Single individuals who possess serious emotional difficulties are not likely to desire the involvements of close personal relationships. Because they are ill-equipped or disinclined, single *males* will avoid the pursuit of a wife, or be ineffectual in their courtship attempts. Single males have a higher rate than single females. The lower rate for single females may arise from the fact that women in our society usually assume a passive role in courtship; in contrast to the disturbed male, who must assume initiative, the disturbed woman may be pursued and involved even though she may have initially been disinclined toward marriage.

The high rate of psychopathology among divorced persons may be explained by several factors. Emotionally impaired individuals are likely to provoke conflict with their mates, thereby increasing the likelihood of divorce. Once cut off from support and cast into isolation and disaffiliation, their pathological dispositions may be precipitated into a manifest disorder.

In summary, then, different incidence rates associated with marital status probably reflect both initial dispositions to pathology and the effects of lost affection and affiliation.

## SOCIOECONOMIC CLASS

Numerous studies have sought to demonstrate relationships between socioeconomic condi-

**Table 5-1   Socioeconomic Class Differences in Incidence and Prevalence of Psychopathology***

| CLASS | SIX-MONTH INCIDENCE | PREVALENCE |
|---|---|---|
| *Neuroses* | | |
| I–II | 69 | 349 |
| III | 78 | 250 |
| IV | 52 | 114 |
| V | 66 | 97 |
| *Psychoses* | | |
| I–II | 28 | 188 |
| III | 36 | 291 |
| IV | 37 | 518 |
| V | 73 | 1505 |

* From Hollingshead and Redlich (1958)

tions and prevalence and type of mental disorder. Despite a sprinkling of negative data, two findings appear to hold up fairly consistently. First, members of the lowest socioeconomic class more often are diagnosed as severely impaired than those of the upper classes. Second, the manifest patterns of psychopathology differ among these classes.

Two well-controlled studies, the first based in New Haven, Connecticut (Hollingshead and Redlich, 1958), the other in midtown New York City (Srole et al., 1962), offer evidence that both the prevalence (frequency) and incidence (rate) of serious disorders is greatest among the lowest socioeconomic class, whereas the prevalence of the milder (neurotic) disorders is greatest among the higher social classes; no difference exists between classes in the incidence of milder disorders (Table 5). That these data are not merely a result of the proportion of the overall population that fall within these class categories can be seen from Table 5-2; e.g., the lowest socioeconomic class accounts for 18.4 per cent of the general population, but 38.2 per cent of the psychiatric population.

Analysis of type of pathology found most frequently among the various social strata indicates that apathy and social detachment (traditionally diagnosed as schizophrenia), as well as the more aggressive and antisocial tendencies (traditionally diagnosed as sociopathic disturbances), characterize the mentally ill of the lower classes, whereas feelings of interpersonal anxiety, inadequacy and guilt (traditionally diagnosed as neuroses and depressive disorders) are seen most often in the middle and upper classes (Frumkin, 1955; Hollingshead and Redlich, 1958; Hardt and

Feinhandler, 1959; Srole et al., 1962; Langner and Michael, 1963).

To what can we attribute these class differences?

Essentially, three interpretations have been proposed to account for the greater prevalence of severe pathology in lower socioeconomic classes. *First,* Clark (1949) and Myers and Roberts (1959) suggest that the childhood environment of lower class children contains relatively little love, protection and stability; this establishes a lifelong feeling of rejection that is confirmed by the neglectful and hostile attitude of the larger society. To this is added the persistent stress during adulthood of economic hardship, occupational insecurity and marital instability, conditions which arise from personal histories of poor educational and vocational training, as well as the malignant customs and values often found among lower class groups. *Second,* lower class patients are less likely to be identified early, and less likely to gain the benefits of treatment than those who are well off financially. Differences in income, a major criterion defining socioeconomic class, relate to the probability that a disorder will be spotted and reversed before attaining serious proportions. Since less effective steps are taken in the lower socioeconomic groups, a greater number of these individuals will succumb to severe disorders. The *third* reason offered for the disproportionate number of severely impaired lower class patients relates to the notion of drift, that is, the proclivity of disturbed members of higher social classes to deteriorate to lower socioeconomic states. There is some evidence to indicate that this factor may account only minimally for class differences in severe pathology (Hollingshead and Redlich, 1958; Clausen and Kohn, 1959), but other studies suggest that its role cannot be dismissed (Lystad, 1957; Goldberg and Morrison, 1963). Goldberg and Morrison, for example, examined the socioeconomic status of

fathers of sons who had been diagnosed as schizophrenic; they found an unquestionable drift on the part of these sons toward a lower class status, a trend that became more marked as their illness progressed.

Let us next turn to explanations offered for relationships between class and type of pathology. The tendency for the upper class to develop disorders characterized by interpersonal anxiety, guilt and depression, as contrasted to the characteristic withdrawal, aggressive or antisocial patterns found in the lower classes, is generally viewed to be a function of training differences in these subcultural groups. Myers and Roberts (1959) and Langner and Michael (1963) suggest that middle and upper class youngsters are "oversocialized," that is, learn to inhibit and feel guilt for wasteful, aggressive and sexual behaviors; they experience severe conflict between their impulses and desires and the achievement standards demanded by their parents. Acceptance of these imposed values results in an inner tension; failure to fulfill parental demands results in guilt and depression. In contrast, the lower class child, faced with deprivation and neglect, learns either to withdraw and become indifferent to his surroundings or to assert himself and exploit others who possess what he wants. Since he is exposed to models of aggressive and irresponsible behavior in his environment, and often is admired by his peers for success in using these behaviors, he quickly acquires habits that are judged by society as antisocial or delinquent. Since the alternatives for members of the lower class remain unchanged as they mature into adulthood, these withdrawal or antisocial behaviors persist and become ingrained.

## EVALUATIVE COMMENTS

The obstacles confronting investigators engaged either in the design, the execution or the interpretation of sociocultural studies of psychopathology are formidable. Numerous questions have been raised regarding both the methodological adequacy of earlier research and the likelihood that these studies will prove more fruitful in the future. Let us briefly note some of these problems.

Since it is impossible to design an experiment in which relevant sociocultural variables can systematically be controlled or manipulated, it will be impossible to establish unequivocal cause-effect relationships among these variables and psychopathology. Investigators cannot arrange, no less subvert and abuse, a social group for purposes of

## Table 5-2 Socioeconomic Class Proportions in Normal and Psychiatric Populations*

| CLASS | PER CENT OF NORMAL POPULATION | PER CENT OF PSYCHIATRIC POPULATION |
|---|---|---|
| I | 3.0 | 1.0 |
| II | 8.4 | 7.0 |
| III | 20.4 | 13.7 |
| IV | 49.8 | 40.1 |
| V | 18.4 | 38.2 |

* From Hollingshead and Redlich (1958)

scientific study; research in this field must, therefore, continue to be of a naturalistic and correlational nature. The problem that arises with naturalistic studies is the difficulty of inferring causality; correlations do not give us a secure base for determining which factors were cause and which were effect. We noted in a previous example that correlations between socioeconomic class and psychopathology may signify both that deteriorated social conditions produce mental disorders, *and* that mental disorders result in deteriorated social conditions.

The perennial problem of unreliable and nonuniform diagnostic criteria plagues investigators in this research area even more than in other fields of psychopathology. We know that the basis for assigning one or another diagnostic label varies tremendously from community to community and from state to state. Such unreliability is extremely serious in this field since the purpose of research is to compare prevalence rates among different sociocultural communities; if the criteria among regions are different, comparable figures cannot be achieved.

Despite these and other methodological complications, such as the high frequency of geographic and socioeconomic mobility in our society, there is a sufficient body of well-executed research indicating that sociocultural factors contribute to the course and shape of psychopathology; definitive conclusions indicating the specific factors that influence particular features of pathology will be achieved only by more sophisticated and ingenious research than heretofore.

# CONCLUDING COMMENTS AND SUMMARY

Theorists and researchers are inclined to focus on certain features of psychopathology at the expense of others; they sensitize readers only to those facets related to their work. Narrowness of focus is inevitable since scientists endeavor to probe deeply into the basic elements of their subject; unfortunately, these efforts exact a price, that of losing perspective. Necessary as depth may be to scientific advance, it is fatal, we believe, to the beginning student. Certainly, both depth *and* breadth are requisites to progress; but we contend that perspective must come first to serve as a context within which the details can be fit. Metaphorically speaking, we must survey the terrain of a field before we can judge where our exploratory shafts should be sunk. Chapters 4 and 5 were outlined to meet the goal of providing the student with this perspective; only secondarily did we plumb some depths.

Interaction and continuity were among the major themes presented in the chapters. We stressed the fact that there are manifold biogenic and psychogenic determinants of psychopathology, the relative weights of each varying widely as a function of time and circumstance; these determinants operate conjointly to shape the pattern of an illness. Furthermore, interaction effects operate across time, that is, the course of later events are related in a determinant way to earlier events. *The etiology of psychopathology has been viewed, then, as a developmental process in which intra-organismic and environmental forces display not only a reciprocity and circularity of influence but an orderly and sequential continuity throughout the life of the individual.* A summary of the topics and points described in the present chapter to elucidate these themes follows:

1. The maturation of the biological substrate for psychological capacities is anchored initially to genetic processes, but its development is substantially dependent on environmental stimulation. The concept of *stimulus nutriment* was introduced to represent the belief that the quantity of environmental experience activates chemical processes requisite to the maturation of neural collaterals. Stimulus impoverishment may lead to irrevocable deficiencies in neural development and their associated psychological functions; stimulus enrichment may prove equally deleterious by producing pathological overdevelopments or imbalances among these functions.

2. The notion of sensitive developmental periods was proposed to convey the belief that stimuli produce different effects at different ages, that is, there are limited time periods during maturation when particular stimuli have pronounced effects which they do not have either before or after these periods. It was suggested, further, that these peak periods occur at points in maturation when the potential is greatest for growth and expansion of neural collaterals.

3. Three neuropsychological stages of development, representing peak periods in neurological maturation, were proposed. Each developmental stage reflects transactions between constitutional and experiental influences which

combine to set a foundation for subsequent stages; if the interactions at one stage are deficient or distorted, all subsequent stages will be affected since they rest on a defective base.

a. The first stage, termed *sensory-attachment,* predominates from birth to approximately 18 months of age. This period is characterized by a rapid maturation of neurological substrates for sensory processes, and by the infant's attachment and dependency on others.

b. The second stage, referred to as *sensorimotor-autonomy,* begins roughly at 12 months and extends in its peak development through the sixth year. It is characterized by a rapid differentiation of motor capacities which coordinate with established sensory functions; this coalescence enables the young child to locomote, manipulate and verbalize in increasingly skillful ways.

c. The third stage, called the period of *intracortical-initiative,* is primary from about the fourth year through adolescence. There is a rapid growth potential among the higher cortical centers during this stage, enabling the child to reflect, plan and act independent of parental supervision. Integrations developed during earlier phases of this period undergo substantial reorganization as a product of the biological and social effects of puberty.

4. Maladaptive consequences can arise as a result of either stimulus impoverishment or stimulus enrichment at each of the three stages.

a. From experimental animal research and naturalistic studies with human infants, it appears that marked stimulus impoverishment during the sensory-attachment period will produce deficiencies in sensory capacities and a marked diminution of interpersonal sensitivity and behavior. There is little evidence available with regard to the effects of stimulus enrichment during this stage; it was proposed, however, that excessive stimulation may result in hypersensitivities, stimulus seeking behaviors and abnormal interpersonal dependencies.

b. Deprived of adequate stimulation during the sensorimotor stage, the child will be deficient in skills for behavioral autonomy, will display a lack of exploratory and competitive activity and be characterized by timidity and submissiveness. In contrast, excessive enrichment and indulgence of sensorimotor capacities may result in uncontrolled self-expression, narcissism and social irresponsibility.

c. Among the consequences of understimulation during the intracortical-initiative stage is an identity diffusion, an inability to fashion an integrated and consistent purpose for one's existence and an inefficiency in channeling and directing one's energies, capacities and impulses. Excessive stimulation, in the form of overtraining and overguidance, results in the loss of several functions, notably spontaneity, flexibility and creativity.

5. Several psychological concepts differentiating the various processes of response and expectancy learning were described; these included contiguity learning, instrumental learning, vicarious learning through observation and imitation, and implicit learning through thinking. The roles of motivation and reinforcement were noted to signify the facilitative effects of these conditions. The predominance of learning through incidental circumstances was stressed.

6. Two major sources of pathogenic learning were described in detail: enduring and pervasive experiences, and traumatic experiences. The former was viewed as substantially more important to the development of pathological patterns of personality.

a. Among the more enduring and pervasive experiences were parental feelings and attitudes; methods of behavioral control, notably those which were punitive, used contingent rewards, were inconsistent or were excessively protective or indulgent; family patterns of communication; content of teachings; and, family structure, notably those which provided deficient models or were characterized by marked family discord or sibling rivalry. It was stressed that these influences are complexly and intimately interrelated; in reality, no single element can be isolated from the wider context or constellation of forces which interweave to produce the final result of pathology.

b. Traumatic experiences may shatter the individual's established pattern of integration and may leave a deeply embedded scar which cannot readily be extinguished. The consequences of these severe experiences are especially serious to the young child since he may generalize the attitudes and feelings they evoke, thus coloring his perception of future experience.

7. Significant early learnings were divided into two broad categories; attitudes learned typically during specific developmental stages, and coping strategies acquired to achieve goals. A point stressed was that these learnings not only derive from experience but are rooted in the biological dispositions of the individual.

a. Trust of others is the central attitude learned during the sensory-attachment stage; feelings of self-competence are acquired first during the stage of sensorimotor-autonomy; attitudes concerning one's personal identity are formed primarily during the intracortical-initiative period.

b. Coping strategies were viewed as complex forms of instrumental learning, that is, ways of achieving positive reinforcements and avoiding negative reinforcements. These strategies reflect what reinforcements the individual has learned to seek or avoid, where he looks to obtain these reinforcements and how he performs in order to elicit or escape them. A 4 × 2 classificatory scheme, to be elaborated in greater detail in the next two chapters, was proposed. This scheme is based on three factors: the relative role played by positive and negative reinforcements as determinants of behavior; the tendency to obtain reinforcements either from other persons or from oneself; and the proclivity either to seek these reinforcements actively or to wait passively for their occurrence.

8. The fact that early experiences are likely to contribute a disproportionate share to learned behavior is attributable in part to the fact that their effects are difficult to extinguish. This resistance to extinction stems largely from the fact that learning in early life is presymbolic, random and highly generalized.

Additional factors which contribute to the persistence and continuity of early learnings are social factors such as the repetitive nature of experience, the tendency for interpersonal relations to be reciprocally reinforcing and the perseverance of early character stereotypes.

Beyond these are a number of self-perpetuating processes which derive from the individual's own actions. Among them are protective efforts which constrict the person's awareness and experience, the tendency to perceptually and cognitively distort events in line with expectancies, the inappropriate generalization to new events of old behavior patterns and the repetitive compulsion to create conditions which parallel the past.

9. The traditions, values and customs of a society serve as a template from which the more particular experiences of interpersonal life are shaped and elaborated. Three sources of psychopathology can be traced in part to conditions of contemporary social life: the encouragement of achievement strivings and competition; the unstable and often contradictory nature of standards and values; and the disintegration among certain segments of our society of regulating customs and goals.

A number of research studies have attempted to identify specific social correlates of psychopathology; among those reviewed were variables such as cultural patterns, racial and ethnic origin, residential locale, marital status and socioeconomic class.

Throughout the chapter are comments indicating the appalling lack of definitive research to support assertions regarding the role of psychogenic factors in psychopathology. That psychogenic factors are significantly involved seems axiomatic to most theorists, but science progresses not by supposition and belief but by hard facts gained through well-designed and well-executed research. This paucity of evidence does not signify neglect on the part of researchers; rather, it indicates the awesome difficulties involved in unraveling the intricate interplay of psychogenic factors productive of psychopathology. Despite these apologetics, there is reason for caution in accepting the contentions of psychogenic theorists.

We have no choice but to continue to pursue the suggestive leads provided us both by plausible speculation and exploratory research; difficulties notwithstanding, we must caution against inclinations to revert to past simplifications, or to abandon efforts out of dismay or cynicism. Our increasing knowledge of the multideterminant and circular character of etiology, as well as the inextricable developmental sequences through which it proceeds, should prevent us from falling prey to simplifications which led early theorists to attribute psychopathology to single factors. Innumerable etiologies are possible; the causal elements are so intermeshed that we must plan our research strategies to disentangle, not isolated determinants, but their convergencies, their interactions and their continuities.

This chapter concludes our focus on etiology and development. The groundwork has now been laid for a more thorough examination of the myriad patterns and disorders of psychopathology. Many of the principles provided in this and preceding chapters will be drawn upon to elucidate the complex forms into which psychopathology takes shape; we will have benefit, in the following chapters, of case histories which demonstrate how these abstract principles clarify our understanding of pathological development.

*Part 3*

# CLINICAL SYNDROMES

*Introduction*

# *Introduction*

Recent mental hospital surveys report a resident population of roughly one half million patients (prevalence); equally impaired non-institutionalized individuals may be double the hospitalized figure. Hospital admissions each year average about 100,000 (annual incidence). These figures, of course, merely scratch the surface of a much deeper and wider problem. Epidemiological research suggests that only 15 to 20 per cent of the general population are entirely free of psychopathological symptoms; more than 20 to 25 per cent possess psychological impairments sufficient to interfere seriously with ordinary life adjustments. The billions of dollars spent in this country on liquor and tranquilizers attest to the wide prevalence and severity of emotional difficulties. And predictions are that one out of every ten persons in the United States will spend some part of his life in a mental institution.

Prevalence and incidence figures are difficult to establish with any precision; although the arithmetic procedure for gathering data is theoretically simple, there is little uniformity in the definition and assignment of the various diagnostic categories. Moreover, the sources from which these data are obtained tend to be unrepresentative of the population in general; for example, the lower socioeconomic classes of the general population, cared for primarily in state institutional systems, are overrepresented in most hospital-based studies. The criteria used to define the presence and character of specific psychopathological patterns are highly unreliable; they differ from one population survey to another, and are subject to changing fashions in psychiatric nomenclature. Institutional statistics vary considerably; not only are they markedly influenced by differences in the availability of outpatient and preventive facilities but they reflect differing hospital policies governing admission and diagnostic classification. All of these are minor complications when compared to the problem of identifying and classifying noninstitutionalized patients. Not only is diagnostic terminology especially confusing in the less severe pathological syndromes but research methods are notoriously unreliable and susceptible to the pitfalls of biased population sampling.

Discouraging as these introductory comments may be, we must recognize that current frequency and diagnostic statistics are highly ambiguous at best and misleading at worst. Until steps are taken to obtain greater representativeness in population samples, and greater uniformity in criteria, terminology and methodology, we must view current prevalence and incidence data as both inadequate in scope and unreliable in details.

The next three sections will review a number of points discussed in greater detail in chapter 3. First, we will restate the rationale for the notion of clinical syndromes; second, we will evaluate the attributes of the traditional nosology for psychiatric diagnosis; and third, we will outline the modified system of syndromes to be used in the present text.

## *RATIONALE OF CLINICAL SYNDROMES*

It would be not only exhausting but inefficient and uneconomical for a diagnostician to approach each new case he confronts as if he had no preconceptions as to how psychopathology develops, takes its distinctive form or can be modified. On the basis of his past experience and theoretical knowledge, he focuses his attention upon certain core experiences and features of behavior which, on the basis of foreknowledge, promise to illuminate and simplify his task. In narrowing his attention to this limited class of data, he makes a number of assumptions: that the patient possesses particular characteristics that are central to his disturbance; that these characteristics are found in common among distinctive and identifiable groups of patients; and that prior knowledge regarding these patient groups, known as clinical syndromes, will facilitate his responsibility in diagnosing and treating his patient.

As pointed out in chapter 3, there is considerable support for the assumption that people can be differentiated in terms of certain prepotent and deeply ingrained behaviors, attitudes and needs, and that they evidence consistency and continuity over time in these characteristics. Furthermore, it appears safe to conclude that there are key characteristics which distinguish groups of patients, and that the specification of a patient as a member of one of these groups, or syndromes, will prove clinically expeditious and fruitful.

Differences in characteristics will be found among patients categorized in the same syndrome since all classification systems focus on certain features to the exclusion of others. The question that must be raised with regard to a classification schema is *not* whether its syndromes are entirely homogeneous, since no schema fulfills this criterion, but whether the system facilitates a number of clinically useful objectives. Thus, if a classification system alerts the diagnostician to features of a patient's history or functioning which he had not previously discovered, or if it enables groups of clinicians to communicate effectively about their patients, or guides them to select beneficial therapeutic plans or assists researchers in the design of experiments, then it has served many useful purposes.

The fact that the traditional nosological system of psychiatric classification fails to facilitate many clinical functions does not invalidate the notion of classification itself; no scheme of categories could possibly provide a means for achieving all of the goals of clinical responsibility. All we can ask of such systems is that they expedite as many of these functions as possible, given the limits of our knowledge, and that their shortcomings not impede the fulfillment of these functions. Classification is not, therefore, an end in itself; it is merely a potentially fruitful step in the sequence of clinical analysis, one that should provide a more insightful grasp of the patient's difficulties and a more efficient plan for remedial therapy.

## EVALUATION OF THE TRADITIONAL NOSOLOGY

Once we accept the idea that syndromes may prove useful, the question arises as to whether the system in current use fulfills as many functions as possible, given our present theoretical and empirical knowledge. If it does not, then we must ask which features should be retained, which features should be added to increase its clarity and utility and how the system can best be reorganized. For purposes of reference and comparison in later chapters, the student might profitably scan at this time Table II-1, which outlines the clinical categories and nomenclature of the recently revised "traditional" diagnostic and statistical manual of the American Psychiatric Association, referred to in the text as the DSM-II.

Let us summarize several of the virtues and shortcomings of the DSM-II that were more fully elaborated in chapter 3.

Among the virtues were the following:

1. Syndromes are differentiated in terms of severity.

2. The majority of syndromes are based on combinations of clinical signs which cluster together.

3. Biogenic disorders are distinguished from impairments in which the role of biogenic factors is unclear or minimal.

4. Pathological reactions precipitated by undue environmental stress are separated from those which reflect longstanding and ingrained personality factors.

Notable among the shortcomings are *failures* to:

1. Incorporate a wide variety of clinical signs and correlates so as to minimize the significance of dramatic symptoms. In chapter 3, attention was directed to a variety of traits from each of the four major sources of data (e.g., interpersonal behaviors and strategies, self-image and temperament) that should be considered in appraising the diagnostic picture but are not included as clinical signs in the DSM-II.

2. Revise categories in line with the results of modern research, especially data derived from recent multivariate clustering studies. In this regard, the chapters that follow will draw upon the findings of factor-analytic studies as a basis for selecting the clinical characteristics of the syndromes presented.

3. Provide a coherent theoretical framework from which the principal clinical syndromes can be logically derived and coordinated. The notion of coping strategies, based on a $4 \times 2$ matrix of reinforcement sources and instrumental behaviors, was proposed in chapter 5 to serve as such a framework; the eight major "personality patterns" to be presented in chapters 6 and 7 will furnish the clinical correlates of these strategies; later chapters will detail how the theoretical schema can account for the direction in which patients decompensate and the specific "symptom disorders" they display.

4. Specify the interrelationships and commonalities among its clinical categories. A concerted effort to overcome the discrete and isolated character of the traditional syndromes will be made by spelling out their similarities, interconnections and covariations.

5. Construct adequately detailed syndromes for the milder pathological personality patterns. These widely prevalent and clinically significant diagnostic categories have been briefly summarized in chapters 3 and 5; chapters 6 and 7 will provide extensive descriptions of their clinical features and developmental backgrounds.

6. Demonstrate the developmental continuity between premorbid personality patterns and the more advanced or severe patterns and disorders. Several factors that foster this continuity have been presented in chapter 5 (e.g., resistance to extinction and repetitive and reciprocal reinforcement); chapters 8 and 9 will

**Table III-1    Clinical Categories and Nomenclature of the Recently Revised Diagnostic and**

**I    MENTAL RETARDATION**
- ☐ 310.    Borderline
- ☐ 311.    Mild
- ☐ 312.    Moderate
- ☐ 313.    Severe
- ☐ 314.    Profound
- ☐ 315.    Unspecified

With each: Following or associated with
- ☐ .0    Infection or intoxication
- ☐ .1    Trauma or physical agent
- ☐ .2    Disorders of metabolism, growth or nutrition
- ☐ .3    Gross brain disease (postnatal)
- ☐ .4    Unknown prenatal influence
- ☐ .5    Chromosomal abnormality
- ☐ .6    Prematurity
- ☐ .7    Major psychiatric disorder
- ☐ .8    Psycho - social (environmental) deprivation
- ☐ .9    Other condition

**II    ORGANIC BRAIN SYNDROMES (OBS)**
**A    PSYCHOSES**
*Senile and pre - senile dementia*
- ☐ 290.0    Senile dementia
- ☐ 290.1    Pre - senile dementia

*Alcoholic psychosis*
- ☐ 291.0    Delirium tremens
- ☐ 291.1    Korsakov's psychosis
- ☐ 291.2    Other alcoholic hallucinosis
- ☐ 291.3    Alcohol paranoid state
- ☐ 291.4*    Acute alcohol intoxication*
- ☐ 291.5*    Alcoholic deterioration*
- ☐ 291.6*    Pathological intoxication*
- ☐ 291.9    Other alcoholic psychosis

*Psychosis associated with intracranial infection*
- ☐ 292.0    General paralysis
- ☐ 292.1    Syphilis of central nervous system
- ☐ 292.2    Epidemic encephalitis
- ☐ 292.3    Other and unspecified encephalitis
- ☐ 292.9    Other intracranial infection

*Psychosis associated with other cerebral condition*
- ☐ 293.0    Cerebral arteriosclerosis
- ☐ 293.1    Other cerebrovascular disturbance
- ☐ 293.2    Epilepsy
- ☐ 293.3    Intracranial neoplasm
- ☐ 293.4    Degenerative disease of the CNS
- ☐ 293.5    Brain trauma
- ☐ 293.9    Other cerebral condition

*Psychosis associated with other physical condition*
- ☐ 294.0    Endocrine disorder
- ☐ 294.1    Metabolic and nutritional disorder
- ☐ 294.2    Systemic infection
- ☐ 294.3    Drug or poison intoxication (other than alcohol)
- ☐ 294.4    Childbirth
- ☐ 294.8    Other and unspecified physical condition

**B    NON – PSYCHOTIC OBS**
- ☐ 309.0    Intracranial infection
- ☐ 309.13*    Alcohol* (simple drunkenness)
- ☐ 309.14*    Other drug, poison or systemic intoxication*
- ☐ 309.2    Brain trauma
- ☐ 309.3    Circulatory disturbance
- ☐ 309.4    Epilepsy
- ☐ 309.5    Disturbance of metabolism, growth, or nutrition
- ☐ 309.6    Senile or pre - senile brain disease
- ☐ 309.7    Intracranial neoplasm
- ☐ 309.8    Degenerative disease of the CNS
- ☐ 309.9    Other physical condition

**III    PSYCHOSES NOT ATTRIBUTED TO PHYSICAL CONDITIONS LISTED PREVIOUSLY**
*Schizophrenia*
- ☐ 295.0    Simple
- ☐ 295.1    Hebephrenic
- ☐ 295.2    Catatonic
- ☐ 295.23*    Catatonic type, excited*
- ☐ 295.24*    Catatonic type, withdrawn*
- ☐ 295.3    Paranoid
- ☐ 295.4    Acute schizophrenic episode
- ☐ 295.5    Latent
- ☐ 295.6    Residual
- ☐ 295.7    Schizo - affective
- ☐ 295.73*    Schizo-affective, excited*
- ☐ 295.74*    Schizo-affective, depressed*
- ☐ 295.8*    Childhood*
- ☐ 295.90*    Chronic undifferentiated*
- ☐ 295.99*    Other schizophrenia*

*Major affective disorders*
- ☐ 296.0    Involutional melancholia
- ☐ 296.1    Manic - depressive illness, manic
- ☐ 296.2    Manic - depressive illness, depressed
- ☐ 296.3    Manic - depressive illness, circular
- ☐ 296.33*    Manic-depressive, circular, manic*
- ☐ 296.34*    Manic-depressive, circular, depressed*
- ☐ 296.8    Other major affective disorder

*Paranoid states*
- ☐ 297.0    Paranoia
- ☐ 297.1    Involutional paranoid state
- ☐ 297.9    Other paranoid state

*Other psychoses*
- ☐ 298.0    Psychotic depressive reaction

**IV    NEUROSES**
- ☐ 300.0    Anxiety
- ☐ 300.1    Hysterical
- ☐ 300.13*    Hysterical, conversion type*
- ☐ 300.14*    Hysterical, dissociative type*
- ☐ 300.2    Phobic
- ☐ 300.3    Obsessive compulsive
- ☐ 300.4    Depressive
- ☐ 300.5    Neurasthenic

\* Categories added to ICD-8 for use in U.S. only.

describe some of the more severe syndromes shaped by these factors.

7. Draw sufficiently clear distinctions among the major syndrome classes in terms of etiology and development. The nosology proposed in this text specifies explicit criteria for differen-

tiating these syndromes, as will be discussed shortly.

8. Assign prognostic and therapeutic variables equal weight to that currently given overt clinical symptoms. Though the research literature is sparse, especially with regard to therapeutic

**Statistical Manual (DSM-II)***          *From American Psychiatric Association* (1968)

☐ 300.6   Depersonalization
☐ 300.7   Hypochondriacal
☐ 300.8   Other neurosis

**V      PERSONALITY DISORDERS AND
        CERTAIN OTHER NON—PSYCHOTIC
        MENTAL DISORDERS**

**Personality disorders**
☐ 301.0   Paranoid
☐ 301.1   Cyclothymic
☐ 301.2   Schizoid
☐ 301.3   Explosive
☐ 301.4   Obsessive compulsive
☐ 301.5   Hysterical
☐ 301.6   Asthenic
☐ 301.7   Antisocial
☐ 301.81* Passive - aggressive*
☐ 301.82* Inadequate*
☐ 301.89* Other specified types*

**Sexual deviation**
☐ 302.0   Homosexuality
☐ 302.1   Fetishism
☐ 302.2   Pedophilia
☐ 302.3   Transvestitism
☐ 302.4   Exhibitionism
☐ 302.5*  Voyeurism*
☐ 302.6*  Sadism*
☐ 302.7*  Masochism*
☐ 302.8   Other sexual deviation

**Alcoholism**
☐ 303.0   Episodic excessive drinking
☐ 303.1   Habitual excessive drinking
☐ 303.2   Alcohol addiction
☐ 303.9   Other alcoholism

**Drug dependence**
☐ 304.0   Opium, opium alkaloids and
          their derivatives
☐ 304.1   Synthetic analgesics with morphine -
          like effects
☐ 304.2   Barbiturates
☐ 304.3   Other hypnotics and sedatives or
          "tranquilizers"
☐ 304.4   Cocaine
☐ 304.5   Cannabis sativa (hashish, marihuana)
☐ 304.6   Other psycho - stimulants
☐ 304.7   Hallucinogens
☐ 304.8   Other drug dependence

**VI     PSYCHOPHYSIOLOGIC DISORDERS**
☐ 305.0   Skin
☐ 305.1   Musculoskeletal
☐ 305.2   Respiratory
☐ 305.3   Cardiovascular
☐ 305.4   Hemic and lymphatic
☐ 305.5   Gastro - intestinal
☐ 305.6   Genito - urinary
☐ 305.7   Endocrine
☐ 305.8   Organ of special sense
☐ 305.9   Other type

**VII    SPECIAL SYMPTOMS**
☐ 306.0   Speech disturbance
☐ 306.1   Specific learning disturbance
☐ 306.2   Tic
☐ 306.3   Other psychomotor disorder
☐ 306.4   Disorders of sleep
☐ 306.5   Feeding disturbance
☐ 306.6   Enuresis
☐ 306.7   Encopresis
☐ 306.8   Cephalalgia
☐ 306.9   Other special symptom

**VIII   TRANSIENT SITUATIONAL
        DISTURBANCES**
☐ 307.0*  Adjustment reaction of infancy*
☐ 307.1*  Adjustment reaction of childhood*
☐ 307.2*  Adjustment reaction of adolescence*
☐ 307.3*  Adjustment reaction of adult life*
☐ 307.4*  Adjustment reaction of late life*

**IX     BEHAVIOR DISORDERS OF CHILD—
        HOOD AND ADOLESCENCE**
☐ 308.0*  Hyperkinetic reaction*
☐ 308.1*  Withdrawing reaction*
☐ 308.2*  Overanxious reaction*
☐ 308.3*  Runaway reaction*
☐ 308.4*  Unsocialized aggressive reaction*
☐ 308.5*  Group delinquent reaction*
☐ 308.9*  Other reaction*

**X      CONDITIONS WITHOUT MANIFEST
        PSYCHIATRIC DISORDER AND
        NON—SPECIFIC CONDITIONS**
**Social maladjustment without manifest
psychiatric disorder**
☐ 316.0*  Marital maladjustment*
☐ 316.1*  Social-maladjustment*
☐ 316.2*  Occupational maladjustment*
☐ 316.3*  Dyssocial behavior*
☐ 316.9*  Other social maladjustment*

**Non—specific conditions**
☐ 317*    Non - specific conditions*

**No Mental Disorder**
☐ 318*    No mental disorder*

**XI     NON—DIAGNOSTIC TERMS FOR
        ADMINISTRATIVE USE**
☐ 319.0*  Diagnosis deferred*
☐ 319.1*  Boarder*
☐ 319.2*  Experiment only*
☐ 319.3*  Other*

considerations, the distinctions we shall draw
between the ingrained personality patterns (chapters 6 to 9) and the more transitory and circumscribed behavior reactions (chapter 12) take
cognizance of the prognostic significance of recent
"process-reactive research."

## SURVEY OF THE
## REVISED NOSOLOGY

The nosological system of syndromes to be
used in the present text reflects the primacy of two
factors: *severity* and *etiology and development*.

SEVERITY

Magnitude of illness in psychopathology is a continuous function in which an infinite number of fine discriminations can be made among degrees of impairment. For our purposes, however, a simple, tripartite differentiation will suffice: *mild, moderate* and *marked* severity.

Severity is defined by two closely related criteria: *level of control* and *reality awareness*. The first refers mainly to the adequacy of the coping strategies a patient utilizes to maintain psychological balance and cohesion. The second is gauged by the patient's capacity to evaluate himself and the events of his environment in an objective manner.

Many patients decompensate from mild to markedly severe impairments, but the progression is not inevitable; if it occurs, it often is reversible. Each level of severity may be viewed as a fluid stage subject to influences capable of producing either greater health or greater illness.

ETIOLOGY AND DEVELOPMENT

The second feature used to differentiate patients reflects the type and complexity of influences which have contributed to the development of their impairments. A study of these influences has led to the formulation of four categories: pathological personality patterns, symptom disorders, pathological behavior reactions and biophysical defects.

1. *Pathological personality patterns* are deeply etched characteristics which pervade all facets of an individual's functioning; the term "pattern" has been chosen to represent the embedded and pervasive character of these traits. These patterns derive from the complex and sequential interaction of constitutional and experiential factors. Once established early in life, pathological patterns tend to spread into new spheres and to perpetuate themselves through vicious circles; they are so ingrained and automatic a way of life, that the patient often is unaware of their presence and their self-destructive consequences.

Patterns of mild severity enable the individual to find a niche for himself in normal social life; he may appear to function adequately, even successfully. Should his balance be upset, however, he may slip into a more pernicious level of functioning; initial restitutive efforts often are displayed in the form of "symptom disorders." Should these efforts fail to reestablish equilibrium,

the mildly impaired individual may decompensate to a more primitive level of control, and exhibit increasingly distorted perceptions of reality.

As deterioration continues, the patient displays features which justify the moderate or markedly severe label. Despite these changes, however, the patient's basic or lifelong personality pattern is retained. Thus, although there has been a progressive disintegration of control and reality awareness, the patient exhibits continuity in the perceptions, attitudes and behaviors that characterized him prior to his decompensation; no matter how extreme or dramatic his newly emergent symptoms may be, they are understood best as accentuations or distortions of lifelong habits and coping strategies. Pathological personality patterns will comprise the subject matter of chapters 6 through 9.

2. *Symptom disorders* are isolated and dramatic signs of disturbance which stand out in sharp relief against the background of a patient's pathological personality pattern. These signs spring forth to dominate the clinical picture when the person's coping strategies are disrupted under stressful or otherwise unusual circumstances; regardless of how different and strange these symptoms may appear, they are fully consonant with the patient's basic personality style, and should be viewed as an extension of his lifelong pattern.

The label "disorder" has been chosen for these impairments to signify that the patient's habitual mode of functioning has been upset or disrupted. Many patients are disturbed by these "alien" symptoms, and are motivated, consciously at least, to rid themselves of them. Symptom disorder syndromes will be discussed in detail in chapters 10 and 11.

3. *Pathological behavior reactions* are syndromes either precipitated by objectively stressful conditions in life or learned as maladaptive responses to narrowly circumscribed stimulus events; these categories are reserved for patients who do not display a generalized pathological personality pattern.

The term "reaction" has been chosen to signify the fact that these disturbances are behavioral responses that are tied closely to specific stimulus precipitants. Typical behavior reactions will be described in chapter 12.

4. *Biophysical defects* are impairments attributable primarily to inborn or acquired conditions that have produced deficiencies or dysfunctions in the biophysical substrate. These defects will be described in chapter 13.

# COMMENT

Before we turn to the details of the clinical syndromes, let us be mindful that the classification schema to be outlined is merely an interpretive synthesis, a set of "armchair" prototypes drawn from diverse sources such as hospital psychiatry, multivariate cluster studies, learning research and psychoanalytic theory. It is not a typology documented by systematic empirical research; rather, it is like a theory, a provisional tool which hopefully will aid us in organizing our subject more clearly and with greater understanding, a convenient but essentially fictional format designed to focus and systematize our thinking about psychopathology. Lines of distinction have been drawn between syndromes as if they existed in fact; but many cases will be found which possess features of two or more "distinct" categories, and others will seem alien to all of the categories provided. No classification schema can avoid these problems; every system is of limited utility and must be revised as we gather new data and gain new understanding.

The format for the schema we shall follow has been founded on certain fundamental dimensions—distinctions in pathological *severity* and differentiations among personality *patterns*, symptom *disorders*, behavior *reactions* and biophysical *defects*. Hopefully, this organizational model will serve as a durable framework, lending itself to refinements in internal details as time proceeds rather than to revisions of structure. The chapters that follow will describe syndromes consonant with our present level of knowledge; future theory and research either will verify the system's utility or suggest directions for modification.

To ensure that students are adequately conversant and able to communicate with others familiar with the traditional nomenclature and classification, the labels and diagnostic descriptions of the DSM-II will be presented at appropriate points in conjunction with their parallels in this text. By interweaving and comparing both systems, the reader will have the benefits of a new and coherent classification schema, without foregoing an acquaintance with the terminology and format of the more conventional psychiatric nosology.

# Chapter 6

## PATHOLOGICAL PERSONALITIES OF MILD SEVERITY

### I: Basic Detached and Dependent Patterns

Marc Chagall—*I and the Village* (1911). (Courtesy, The Museum of Modern Art, New York.)

## INTRODUCTION

In the introductory essay to part 1 it was noted that both professionals and the public consider only those who are markedly ill to be within the province of the field of psychopathology. This narrow viewpoint reflects the traditional preoccupation among psychiatrists with hospitalized patients. More significantly, it represents a failure to recognize that milder disturbances signify the presence of pathological processes similar to those seen in advanced cases, and that these less severe patterns are the precursors of more serious disorders.

The historical predominance of hospital psychiatry, with its attendant involvement in dramatic and deteriorated cases, gave the study of psychopathology a restricted and biased focus. The medical and hospital orientation which characterized the field in the past turned the attention of theorists and researchers away from common and mundane psychological problems that comprise the greater body of pathological disorder. In

the last quarter century, however, there has been a growth of interest in preventive psychiatry and "mental health," bringing attention to bear increasingly on premorbid tendencies seen in the less severe variants of mental illness; we now know that the quiet but persistent anxieties, and the minor conflicts and ineffectualities which beset so many of our relatives and friends, serve as forerunners of more serious hospitalized cases. In addition, outpatient clinics, community-based mental health centers and school and family agencies, that is, service groups geared to the needs of the less severely troubled, have shown us that we must refine and extend our conception of clinical psychopathology beyond those syndromes formulated in the service of hospital psychiatry.

Texts in the field no longer can bypass or give lip service to milder personality disturbances; not only are these impairments an integral part of psychopathological study in their own right but they are the foundation for understanding the basic processes which underlie and foster the development of more serious disorders. For these reasons, then, we will, in contrast to most texts in "abnormal psychology," concern ourselves in depth with the mild or less severe clinical syndromes. With these syndromes as a base, we then can grasp better the processes underlying the more severe syndromes, and the sequences through which they unfold.

## CONCEPT OF PERSONALITY PATTERNS

In the first years of life, children engage in a wide variety of spontaneous behaviors. Although they display certain characteristics consonant with their innate or constitutional dispositions, their way of reacting to others and coping with their environment tends, at first, to be capricious and unpredictable; flexibility and changeability characterize their moods, attitudes and behaviors. This seemingly random behavior serves an exploratory function; each child is "trying out" and testing during this period alternative modes for coping with his environment. As time progresses, the child learns which techniques "work," that is, which of these varied behaviors enable him to achieve his desires and avoid discomforts. Endowed with a distinctive pattern of capacities, energies and temperaments, which serve as base, he learns specific preferences among activities and goals and, perhaps of greater importance, learns that certain types of behaviors and strategies are especially successful for him in obtaining these goals. In his interaction with parents, siblings and peers, he learns to discriminate which goals are permissible, which are rewarded and which are not.

Throughout these years, then, a shaping process has taken place in which the range of initially diverse behaviors becomes narrowed, selective and, finally, crystallized into particular preferred modes of seeking and achieving. In time, these behaviors persist and become accentuated; not only are they highly resistant to extinction but they are reinforced by the restrictions and repetitions of a limited social environment, and are perpetuated and intensified by the child's own perceptions, needs and actions. Thus, given a continuity in basic biological equipment, and a narrow band of experiences for learning behavioral alternatives, the child develops a distinctive pattern of characteristics that are deeply etched, cannot be eradicated easily and pervade every facet of his functioning. In short, these characteristics *are* the essence and sum of his personality, his automatic way of perceiving, feeling, thinking and behaving.

When we speak of a personality pattern, then, we are referring to those intrinsic and pervasive modes of functioning which emerge from the entire matrix of the individual's developmental history, and which now characterize his perceptions and ways of dealing with his environment. We have chosen the term pattern for two reasons: first, to focus on the fact that these behaviors and attitudes derive from the constant and pervasive interaction of both biological dispositions and learned experience; and second, to denote the fact that these personality characteristics are not just a potpourri of unrelated behavior tendencies, but a tightly knit organization of needs, attitudes and behaviors. People may start out in life with random and diverse reactions, but the repetitive sequence of reinforcing experiences to which they are exposed gradually narrows their repertoire to certain habitual strategies, perceptions and behaviors which become prepotent, and come to characterize their distinctive and consistent way of relating to the world.

We stress the centrality of personality patterns in our formulations in order to break the long entrenched habit of thinking that all forms of psychopathology are diseases, that is, identifiable foreign entities or intruders which attach themselves insidiously to the person, and destroy his "normal" functions. The archaic notion that all forms of illness are a product of external intruders can be traced back to such prescientific ideas as demons, spirits and witches, which ostensibly "possessed" the person and cast spells upon him. The recognition in modern medicine of the role of infectious agents has reawakened this archaic view; no longer do we see "demons," but we still think, using current medical jargon, that alien, malevolent and insidious forces undermine the patient's otherwise healthy status. This view is a comforting and appealing simplification to the layman; he can attribute his discomforts, pains and irrationalities to the intrusive influence of some external agent, something he ate or caught or some foreign object he can blame that has assaulted his normal and "true" self. This simplification of "alien disease bodies" has its appeal to the physician as well; it enables him to believe that he can find a malevolent intruder, some tangible factor he can hunt down and destroy.

The disease model carries little weight among informed and sophisticated psychiatrists and psychologists today. Increasingly, both in medicine and psychiatry, disorders and disturbances are conceptualized in terms of the patient's *total capacity to cope* with the stress he faces. In medicine, it is the patient's overall constitution—his vitality and stamina—which determine his proclivity to, or resistance against, ill health. Likewise, in psychiatry, it is the patient's personality pattern, his coping skills, outlook and objectivity, which determines whether or not he will be characterized as mentally ill. Physical ill health, then, is less a matter of some alien disease than it is an imbalance or dysfunction in the overall capacity to deal effectively with one's physical environment. In the same manner, psychological ill health is less the product of an intrusive psychic strain or problem than it is an imbalance or dysfunction in the overall capacity to deal effectively with one's psychological environment. Viewed this way, the individual's personality pattern becomes the foundation for his capacity to function in a mentally healthy or ill way.

## DISTINCTIONS BETWEEN NORMAL AND PATHOLOGICAL PERSONALITY PATTERNS

Normality and pathology are relative concepts; they represent arbitrary points on a continuum or gradient. Psychopathology is shaped according to the same processes and principles as those involved in normal development and learning; however, because of differences in the character, timing, intensity or persistence of certain influences, some individuals acquire maladaptive habits and attitudes whereas others do not.

When an individual displays an ability to cope with his environment in a flexible and adaptive manner and when his characteristic perceptions and behaviors foster increments in personal gratification, then he may be said to possess a normal and healthy personality pattern. Conversely, when average responsibilities and everyday relationships are responded to inflexibly or defectively, or when the individual's characteristic perceptions and behaviors foster increments in personal discomfort or curtail his opportunities to learn and grow, then a pathological personality pattern may be said to exist. Of course, no sharp line divides normality and pathology; not only are personality patterns so complex that certain spheres of functioning may operate "normally" while others do not, but environmental circumstances may change such that certain behaviors and strategies prove "healthy" one time but not another.

Despite the tenuous and fluctuating nature of the normality-pathology distinction, it may be useful to elaborate some criteria by which it may be made. We will not concern ourselves with gross aberrations whose pathological character is easily identified. Rather, it is in that nebulous category of *apparently normal* personality that we wish to alert ourselves to subtly concealed signs of an insidious and pervasive pathological process.

Three pathognomonic signs may be noted:

1.  First, the individual displays an *adaptive inflexibility*. This means that the alternative strategies he employs for relating to others, for achieving his goals and for coping with conflict and stress not only are few but are practiced rigidly, imposed upon conditions for which they are ill suited. Not only is he unable to adapt to events but he seeks to change the conditions of his environment so that they do not call for behaviors beyond his meager repertoire; thus, he carefully arranges and restricts his life to minimize failure and discomfort.

2.  Of course, all individuals manipulate their environment to suit their needs. What distinguishes pathological from normal personality patterns is not only their rigidity and inflexibility but their *tendency to foster vicious circles*. As noted in chapter 5, pathogenic experiences lead to perceptions, needs and behaviors that perpetuate and intensify the individual's difficulties. Protective constriction, perceptual and cognitive distortion, behavior generalization and repetition compulsion refer to processes by which individuals restrict their opportunity to acquire new experiences, create stresses where none objectively exist and provoke reactions from others which reactivate earlier problems. Thus, pathological personality patterns are, themselves, pathogenic; the individual himself perpetuates his difficulties, provokes new ones and sets in motion self-defeating vicious circles which cause his discomforts to persist and become intensified.

3.  The third distinguishing feature of these patterns is their *tenuous stability,* that is, their fragility or lack of resilience under conditions of stress. (This notion has often been referred to in the literature as weak "ego strength.") Given the ease with which past sensitivities can be reactivated, and the inflexibility and relative paucity of the coping strategies they have at their command, these individuals are extremely susceptible to disruptions or breakdowns in their established patterns. Faced with the reality of current failure, anxious lest old unresolved conflicts and inadequacies reemerge and unable to recruit new adaptive maneuvers, they are prone to revert to the more pathological mechanisms of denial and distortion, to less adequate controls and to a less objective perception of reality.

Restating matters then, pathological personality patterns are distinguished from normal personality patterns by their adaptive inflexibility, their tendency to foster vicious circles and their tenuous stability under conditions of stress.

## FOCUS ON INTERPERSONAL DIMENSIONS

It was noted in the introduction to part 3 that the various systems of psychiatric classification represent different ways of grouping the same basic clinical phenomena. These diagnostic categories constitute convenient ways for refining and focusing attention on certain features, to the exclusion of others, of that multidimensional complex we call psychopathology. Ostensibly, these categories represent features significant to the accomplishment of a number of useful clinical functions and goals. It is logical, furthermore, that the label designating the title of these categories should reflect some feature or attribute that has proved to be central to these functions.

What label shall we affix, then, to the mild pathological personality patterns?

Numerous writers have suggested that the interpersonal behavior dimension provides particularly useful information for diagnostic and prognostic decisions (Leary and Coffey, 1955). Along the same line, there are others who suggest that interpersonal behaviors should take primacy over other symptoms since interpersonal variables play a crucial role in therapy (Lorr, 1965). It has been proposed, further, that interpersonal classifications would clarify the study of etiology in psychopathology (Haley, 1959); for example, if one specifies the particular deviant manner in

which a patient interacts with others, then one would have a useful basis for tracing the kinds of learning experiences in which he acquired these behaviors. It appears from the above, then, that the interpersonal dimension may provide a focus for pathological syndromes that lends itself to a number of significant clinical goals—diagnosis, prognosis, therapy and etiology.

The logic for this interpersonal thesis applies especially to the less severe or mild personality patterns. These individuals remain in their normal social environment, operating daily in a variety of interpersonal relationships. The style of interpersonal behavior exhibited in these relationships in large measure will determine the future course of their impairments. The strategies an individual uses to achieve his goals and resolve his conflicts with others will evoke counterreactions that will influence whether his problems stabilize, improve or lead to stress and further decompensation.

It is with the preceding considerations in mind that we have designated the mild pathological personality syndromes, to be discussed in the next two chapters, in terms of interpersonal behaviors that perpetuate the very problems they were designed to resolve. This chapter will focus on the basic detached patterns, namely the *asocial* and *avoidant* personalities, and the basic dependent patterns, referred to as *submissive* and *gregarious* personalities. In chapter 7 we will deal with the independent patterns, termed *narcissistic* and *aggressive* personalities, and the ambivalent patterns, entitled the *conforming* and *negativistic* personalities.

# BASIC DETACHED PATTERNS

It is important to recognize that the patterns to be described characterize people who maintain moderately adequate adjustments to life. The "pathological" traits they possess often escape observation and, if noted, are difficult to differentiate from those considered to be "normal"; these individuals rarely seek therapy since their behaviors usually are not viewed to be especially peculiar by others, or discomforting to themselves.

The detached individual typically is introverted, aloof and seclusive; he has difficulty in establishing close friendships, prefers not to become involved with others and seems uninterested in, and tends to avoid, social activities; in general, he gains little gratification in personal relationships.

It will be useful to differentiate the detached pattern into two broad subclasses—the *passive* and the *active*. These groups should be distinguished because they possess basically different developmental histories, behavioral orientations, self-concepts and interpersonal strategies. Neither of these subcategories is entirely homogeneous, of course, but the individuals grouped in each exhibit common etiological trends and clinical features. One group, the passive-detached, is composed of persons who exhibit emotional and cognitive deficits that hinder the development of close interpersonal relationships. The other, active-detached group brings together individuals whose experience of interpersonal anxiety has led them to avoid close relationships.

## THE ASOCIAL PERSONALITY: PASSIVE-DETACHED PATTERN
(DSM-II: *Asthenic Personality*)*

There are people in every walk of life who appear untroubled and function adequately in their chosen professions, but are rather colorless and shy, prefer to remain by themselves and seem devoid of the need to communicate or relate affectionately to others. They remain in the background of social life, work quietly and unobtrusively at their jobs and rarely are noticed or thought about by those who have minimal contact with them. They would fade into the passing scene, to live their lives in undisturbed inconspicuousness, were it not for the fact that there are persons who expect them to be more vibrant, alive and involved. The following case portrays an individual with this personality pattern who might not have come to the attention of a clinician were it not for his wife's discontent.

### CASE 6-1
### Roy L., Age 36, Married, Two Children

Roy was a successful sanitation engineer involved in the planning and maintenance of water resources for a large city; his job called for considerable foresight and independent judgment, but little supervisory responsibility. In general, he was appraised as an undistinguished employee but competent and reliable. There were few demands of an interpersonal nature made of him and he was viewed by most of his colleagues as reticent and shy, and by others as cold and aloof.

Difficulties centered about his relationship with his wife. At her urging they sought marital counseling for, as she put it, "he is unwilling to join in family activities, he fails to take an interest in the children, he lacks affection and is disinterested in sex."

The pattern of social indifference, flatness of affect and personal isolation which characterized much of Roy's behavior was of little consequence to those with whom a deeper or more intimate relationship was not called for; with his immediate family, however, these traits took their toll.

In the early years of marriage, his wife maneuvered Roy into situations which might interest him, getting him involved in bridge clubs, church activities, sports and so on. These not only proved of no avail in activating Roy but they seemed to make him grumpy and antagonistic.

Eventually, it was she who became discontent and irritable, and, in time, she began to cajole,

---

* The DSM-II refers to the official American Psychiatric Association nosology (1968); for reference purposes, we will note in this and following sections the diagnostic label in the official nomenclature that most closely corresponds to the syndrome under discussion, e.g., the DSM designation "asthenic personality" is akin to the diagnostic syndrome *asocial personality* used in this text.

hound and intimidate Roy. Finally, sensing the grave changes that were beginning to take place within herself, she beseeched him to seek help, not so much "because of his behavior, but because I felt I was turning into a frustrated and irritable shrew." It soon became apparent that her difficulties stemmed from Roy's impassivity and self-absorption.

### CLINICAL PICTURE

The brief case presentation of Roy touches upon just a few of the cardinal features of the asocial personality.

In general, these individuals lack the equipment for experiencing the finer shades and subtleties of emotional life; they appear especially insensitive, in this regard, to the feelings and thoughts of others. Their interpersonal passivity may often be interpreted by others as signs of hostility and rejection; in fact, it merely represents a fundamental incapacity to sense the moods and needs which others experience, and which they normally expect will evoke thoughtful or empathic responses. These individuals are unfeeling, then, not by intention, or for self-protective reasons, but because they possess an intrinsic emotional blandness and interpersonal insensitivity. They display a general lack of spontaneity, resonance and color, are clumsy, unresponsive and boring in interpersonal relationships and appear to lead dull, if not bleak and stolid lives.

For purposes of reference and comparison, the "asocial pattern" corresponds, in several respects, to a new diagnostic category, that is, one included for the first time in the recent revision of the traditional nosology; this new classification has been labeled the *asthenic personality,* and is described in the DSM-II as follows:

This behavior pattern is characterized by easy fatigability, low energy level, lack of enthusiasm, marked incapacity for enjoyment and oversensitivity to physical and emotional stress.

Because they experience few rewards in social interaction, asocial personalities often turn their talents and interests toward things, objects or abstractions. In childhood, for example, these individuals typically evidence a disinclination toward the competitive games and frolicsome activities of the young, preferring to concentrate their energies on hobbies such as stamp or rock collecting, mechanical gadgets, electronic equipment or academic pursuits such as mathematics or engineering. They may find considerable gratification with these nonhuman activities and may develop rather intricate fantasy lives with them. Moreover, the drab and withdrawn characteristics of these youngsters often make them easy targets for teasing and condemnation by their peers, leading frequently to an intensification of their withdrawal and self-absorption activities.

With the foregoing sketchy outline as a background picture, let us detail the central clinical characteristics of these individuals in a more systematic fashion.

### Behavior

The inability of these individuals to engage in the give-and-take of reciprocal social relationships can easily be observed. They maintain a rather vague and peripheral interest in group discussions, appearing to be involved in their own preoccupations. It is difficult for them to mix with others in normally pleasant activities, let alone those demanding social leadership. When relationships are mandatory, as in school or work, their social communications are expressed in a perfunctory manner and are impersonal in content.

Their habits of speech typically are slow and monotonous, characterized by obscurities which signify their inattentiveness or their failure to grasp the subtle emotional dimensions of interpersonal communication. Movements are lethargic, and they convey few rhythmic or expressive gestures as they talk. With but little reflection, the student reading this text should be able to identify, among his acquaintances, persons who never appear to "perk up" or who rarely are alert to the feelings of others, but are not intentionally unkind, who seem preoccupied with irrelevant and picayune matters and drift along from class to class, quietly and unobtrusively, as if in a world of their own.

The asocial personality evidences a steady, even state of underresponsiveness to all sources of external stimulation; events which might provoke anger, elicit joy or evoke sadness in others, appear to fall on deaf ears. There is a pervasive imperviousness to most emotions, not only those of joy and pleasure; few feelings of anger, depression or anxiety ever are expressed. This apathy and lack of emotional responsivity is a cardinal sign of the asocial pattern.

Their emotional underreactivity may derive, in part, from a more generalized inability to be activated and aroused. The asocial personality displays a wide-ranging lack of initiative, a failure to respond to most reinforcements that prompt men to action. Thus, they not only are unmoved by emotional stimuli but seem to be generally deficient in energy and vitality. When they do become involved in something, it tends to be in mental activities, such as reading or TV watching, or in physical activities which require minimal expenditures of energy, such as drawing, watch repairing, needlepoint, and so on.

### Phenomenological Reports

Asocial personalities are minimally introspective since the rewards of self-evaluation are relatively few for those incapable of experiencing deep inner emotions. This diminished introspectiveness, with its attendant lowering of insight, derives from another feature of the asocial pattern, that of "cognitive slippage"; that is, these individuals display a vagueness and impoverishment of thought and a tendency to skim the surface of events and to convey inarticulate and confused notions especially regarding interpersonal phenomena. Several of these features are demonstrated in the following case.

CASE 6-2
*Chester A., Age 39, Married, No Children*

Chester, an engineering professor of my acquaintance, would stop by my office repeatedly to chat about "our mutual interests in psychology and philosophy," oblivious of the fact that I thought his ideas obscure and archaic, at best, and that I found him personally tiresome and boring. Despite his obvious competence in engineering and mathematical matters, he seemed completely incapable of formulating his thoughts in a logical manner, let alone of conveying them to others. His superficial grasp and naiveté regarding worldly and social affairs were quite striking, and he appeared totally devoid of any recognition that people might "feel" one way or another about him as a person. He was an extremely inept teacher, a fact he could not understand but nevertheless accepted.

This style of amorphous communication appears related to another trait, which we will refer to as "defective perceptual scanning," characterized by a tendency to miss and blur differences, to overlook, diffuse and homogenize the varied elements of experience. Instead of differentiating events, sensing their discriminable and distinctive attributes, the individual "mixes them up," intrudes extraneous or irrelevant features and perceives them in a cluttered or disorganized fashion. This inability to attend, select and regulate one's perceptions of the environment seems especially pronounced with regard to social phenomena.

Asocial personalities characterize themselves as bland persons who are reflective and introversive. They seem satisfied and complacent about their lives, and are content to remain aloof from the social aspirations and competitiveness which they see in others. As noted earlier, their self-descriptions tend to be vague and superficial; this trait does not indicate elusiveness or protective denial, but rather their deficient powers to reflect on social and emotional phenomena.

Interpersonal attitudes are equally vague and inarticulate. Where their attitudes are adequately formulated, these individuals perceive themselves as being somewhat reserved and distant, experiencing little concern or care for others; similarly, they perceive other persons as being rather inattentive, indifferent, and disinterested in them.

### Intrapsychic Processes

There are few complicated unconscious processes in these personalities. Untroubled by intense emotional experiences, insensitive to interpersonal relationships and difficult to arouse and activate, these individuals hardly feel the impact of events and they have little reason to devise complicated intrapsychic defenses and strategies. Of course, they do possess the residuals of past memories and emotions but, in general, the inner world of the passive-detached personality is devoid of the manifold intricacies typically found in other pathological patterns.

### Biophysical Factors

Despite the many different biophysical techniques that have been utilized in research, few are sufficiently discriminating to be of use in clinical analysis. When taken in concert, several such measures may provide a general picture of the character of a person's biophysical functioning; nevertheless, even these must be supplemented with overt behavioral observation. In the following paragraph we will speculate on some of the biophysical characteristics which we believe may be found in these individuals.

Asocial personalities are likely to display an autonomic-endocrine imbalance favoring the cholinergic or parasympathetic system. Similarly, measures of arousal and activation should indicate high thresholds and sluggish responsivity. An ectomorphic body build, signifying inadequate nutritional reserves and lowered physical and energy capacities, may be found with disproportionately high incidence in this pattern. From behavioral observations we would infer, further, that these individuals have not only an anhedonic temperament but a temperament characterized by a generalized emotional unresponsiveness; thus, the biological substrate for a number of drive states, such as sex and hunger, may be especially weak. Speculations concerning the particular brain regions involved in these deficits will be noted in later sections which deal with the biogenic etiology of this pattern.

## ETIOLOGY AND DEVELOPMENT

Four interrelated features stand out in the clinical picture of the asocial personality; for the sake of simplicity we shall term them: *affectivity deficit* (emotional blandness; inability to experience intense feelings), *cognitive slippage* (obscurity and irrelevance in thought and communication that is inappropriate to the intellectual level), *complacent self-image* (lack of self-insight; unclear but untroubled concept of self) and *interpersonal indifference* (minimal interest in social relationships). The following case may be helpful in illustrating these characteristics:

### CASE 6-3
#### Margaret L., Age 20, College Junior, Unmarried

Margaret was an extremely pretty, petite brunette, who personified the young college coed in appearance. She sought counseling on the urging of her dormitory room-mate because both felt she might have latent homosexual tendencies; this concern proved unjustified, but there were other characteristics of a pathological nature that clearly were evident.

Margaret rarely enjoyed herself on dates; not that she found herself "disgusted" or "repelled" with necking and petting, but she simply "didn't experience any pleasure" in these activities (affectivity deficit). She went out of her way to avoid invitations to parties, preferring to stay in her room, either watching TV or working at her studies. She was an excellent student, majoring in geology and hoping for a field career in forestry, petroleum research or archeology.

Margaret was viewed as rather distant and aloof by her classmates. She rarely engaged in social activities, turned down an opportunity to join a sorority and had no close friends, in fact, few friends at all, except for her room-mate and one girl back home. Despite her good looks, she was asked to date infrequently; when she did date, it usually was a one or two date affair in which either the boy failed to ask again or she refused to accept the invitation. The little reputation she had on campus was that she was a "cold fish" and "a brain," someone who would rather talk about her courses and career plans than dance, drink and be merry.

One relationship with a boy lasted several months. He seemed to be a quiet and introversive young man who joined her in taking hikes, in demeaning the "childish" behaviors of their classmates and in discussing their mutual interest in nature, trees and rock formations. Their relationship faltered after ten to 12 outdoor hiking dates; they seemed to have nothing more to say to each other. Margaret would have liked to continue this friendship, but she experienced no dismay over its termination (interpersonal indifference).

Further explorations showed that Margaret rarely experienced either joy, dismay or anger. She seemed content to "let matters ride along," sitting on the sidelines while others became perturbed, ecstatic or hostile about "silly little things between them." This viewpoint, however, reflected less a well-reasoned philosophy of life than an inability to grasp "what it is that got people so excited."

In describing her few relationships, past and present, she seemed to be vague, superficial and naive, unable to organize her thoughts and tending to wander into irrelevancies such as the shoes certain people preferred or the physical characteristics of their parents (cognitive slippage).

What background factors can account for the emotional and social deficits portrayed in cases such as Margaret's?

Numerous influences may operate singly or in combination to produce the picture we see. Most of these can only be surmised; through careful research and clinical analysis, a few may be specified more definitively. Several contributing factors will be highlighted in this section, but let us keep in mind that these influences do not act independently of one another in the natural course of development. Biogenic and psychogenic determinants, though separated for pedagogic purposes, interact in a complex, reciprocal and circular fashion.

### Biogenic Factors

The role of biophysical structures and processes in psychopathology is largely speculative. It would be presumptuous, given our current state of knowledge, to assert with any degree of confidence that we have conclusive evidence implicating any of the biogenic influences to be hypothesized. The available research data often is contradictory, nonapplicable or based on poorly designed studies. With this caveat in mind, let us advance a few of the more plausible biogenic hypotheses.

**Heredity.** Since children inherit many overt physical features from their parents, it would seem safe to assume that features of internal morphology and physiochemistry may similarly be inherited. Extrapolating further, it would seem plausible that parents who are biologically limited in their capacity to experience intense emotions, or to be vigorous and active, possess certain associated structural and physiological deficiencies which they may transmit genetically to their children. What we are proposing, then, is that the asocial pattern may arise because an individual is at the low end of a genetically based continuum of individual differences in neurological structures and physiochemical processes which subserve affectivity, interpersonal sensitivity, activation and so on. Support for this speculation may be extracted from a variety of genetic studies, espe-

cially in the field of "schizophrenia." However, to select data to fit these conjectures would be borrowing specious evidence for what should be viewed as a frankly speculative hypothesis.

**Passive Infantile Reaction Pattern.** We believe that a substantial number of adult asocial personalities displayed in infancy and early childhood a low sensory responsivity, motor passivity and a generally placid mood. They may have been easy to handle and care for, but it is likely that they provided their parents with few of the joys associated with more vibrant and expressive youngsters. As a consequence of their undemanding and unresponsive nature, they are likely to have evoked minimal stimulation and overt expressions of affectivity from their caretakers; this deficit in sheer physical handling may have compounded their initial tendencies toward inactivity, emotional flatness and general insipidity. The following case illustrates this early pattern and some of its potential consequences.

### CASE 6-4
### Gerald R., Age 9

Gerald's difficulties came to the attention of a therapist after his parents previously brought his eleven year old brother to a mental health clinic; Gerald's brother was excessively aggressive, and Gerald was among his prime targets.

Intense sibling rivalry feelings were engendered at Gerald's birth. Gerald was a "good" baby, gave his parents little trouble, hardly had to be attended to and was undemanding and quiet. Gerald's placid temperament was a welcome relief to a harried mother with five other young children. As she put it, "It was a pleasure never to have to be concerned with him."

Gerald's "ideal" behavior was used repeatedly as an example for his brother to emulate; needless to say, this accomplished little other than to further provoke the brother's general hostile behavior. Gerald's mother was pleased that Gerald "never seemed to mind" his brother's animosity, needling and occasional physical assaults. Only slowly did she realize that Gerald seemed indifferent to all normally provoking emotional situations; she was so pleased with the little he demanded of her, however, that she let this observation pass.

Subsequent clinical study of Gerald indicated that his flatness was not a defense against deeper emotional distress, or an attempt to live up to the "idealistic" model he was made to be, but simply a pervasive apathy and insensitivity to feelings, either his own or others.

**Ectomorphic Body Structure.** Numerous theorists have proposed that individuals with thin and fragile body builds typically are shy and introversive. It is debatable, however, as to whether this correlation can be attributed primarily to an intrinsic genetic linkage between these physical and psychological traits. A more plausible interpretation suggests that persons who possess the frail ectomorphic build tend to conserve their energies, and lack the physical competencies, resilience and mechanical wherewithal to engage in vigorous and assertive behaviors. Given these physical limitations, they may learn quickly to become indifferent to, and to avoid, emotionally charged situations and physically demanding activities.

**Neurological Deficits in the Limbic or Reticular Systems.** Defects in either the limbic or reticular regions of the brain may result in the development of an asocial pattern. However, given the mild form of this personality impairment, it is probable that the correlated biophysical impairment is not that of tissue damage but of a numerical sparseness of neural cells, or a thinly dispersed branching system emanating from these regions.

Congenital aplasia of any of the centers of the limbic system may give rise to an affectivity deficit. Since the subregions of this complex anatomical system may be differentially impaired, no two persons will possess identical affectivity characteristics; for example, some asocial personalities may exhibit the consequences of deficiencies in the "pleasure" center, whereas others may display behaviors associated with an underdeveloped "aversive" center, and so on.

The phlegmatic character of the asocial pattern may derive from deficits in the reticular system as well. Though our understanding of the diverse functions carried out by this widely branched system is far from complete, we do know that it subserves arousal and activation. Thus, a feebly branched reticular formation may account for the mild lethargy and lack of alertness that characterizes the asocial personality.

The view that the reticular system is a major relay station for intrabrain circuitry is unverified but plausible. If this hypothesis is correct, dysfunctions in the reticular system may give rise to chaotic interneuronal transmissions, and these neurological defects may lead, in turn, to deficient emotional learnings; for example, in so disorganized a system, the emotional dimension of an experience may be circuited peculiarly and simply fail to be anchored to the intellectual awareness of that experience. As a consequence of these "discoordinations" the person may possess only an intellectual grasp of human relationships, and may obscure them with irrelevant associations. This "cognitive slippage," or breakdown in reticular coordination, may account, then,

for deficient and irrational connections between normally associated emotions and cognitions.

**Parasympathetic System Dominance.** The activation and affectivity deficits of the asocial personality may stem from an adrenergic-cholinergic imbalance in which the parasympathetic division of the autonomic nervous system is functionally dominant. The inhibitory effects upon alertness and arousal of this dominance could well account for underresponsiveness, apathy and emotional flatness.

**Neurohormonal Synaptic Dyscontrol.** Hypotheses implicating neurohormonal disturbances also are plausible; specific attention may be drawn to the role of these chemicals in maintaining synaptic control. Excesses or deficiencies in acetylcholine and norepinephrine may result in the proliferation and scattering of neural impulses, or in the inhibition of efficient neural sequences. Any form of chemically induced synaptic dyscontrol may give rise to either or both the cognitive slippage or affectivity deficits which characterize the asocial pattern.

In summary then, there are several biogenic factors which may contribute to a developmental course leading to asocial personality patterns. Acceptance of the role of these hypothesized biogenic factors in no way precludes the fact that equivalent effects can be produced purely by psychogenic forces. In fact, no personality pattern can be attributed to biogenic factors alone. Clinical personality syndromes evolve through a lengthy chain of interacting biogenic and psychogenic determinants; the specific weight assigned to the various contributory agents will differ from case to case.

*Psychogenic Factors*

The number and variety of influences which shape personality are legion. Dismayed by the infinite diversity of these determinants, some theorists have avoided assigning more weight to some influences than to others; this "evasion" is unfortunate. Assuming that we have some grasp of the principles by which behavior is learned, we should be able to infer, with some measure of accuracy, the kinds of antecedent conditions which are likely to give rise to these behaviors.

Unfortunately, there is a paucity of well-designed empirical research in this field. Despite this lack of confirmatory data, there is sufficient reason to believe that the psychogenic hypotheses that follow have merit as plausible conjectures.

**Stimulus Impoverishment During the Sensory Attachment Stage.** A lack of functional stimuii normally provided by the infant's caretakers may set the stage for various maturational and learning deficits. Insufficient intake of stimulus nourishment during the first year of life is likely to result in the underdevelopment of the neural substrate for affectivity and in a deficient learning of interpersonal attachments.

Constitutionally unresponsive infants who have a built-in stimulus barrier, or who evoke few reactions from their environment, may experience a compounding of their initial activation and sensory deficits. Such children receive little attention, cuddling and affection from their parents and, as a consequence, are deprived of the social and emotional cues requisite to learning human attachment behaviors. Although they may provide stimulation for themselves, this is likely to take the form of inanimate objects (dolls, blankets or blocks), thereby resulting in the acquisition of attachments to things rather than to people. Given these inborn sensory or energy deficits, then, these infants are likely to be deprived of stimuli necessary for the maturation of the "emotional" brain centers, and the learning of human attachment behaviors.

These same consequences may develop in infants with entirely normal constitutional capacities and dispositions. Thus, an "average" infant reared with minimal human interaction, either in an impersonal atmosphere or with cold and unaffectionate parents, will be deprived of early sensory stimulation necessary for normal development; these youngsters are likely to acquire the interpersonally detached and affectless symptomatology of the asocial pattern.

**Formal or Impassive Family Atmospheres.** Children learn to imitate the pattern of interpersonal relationships to which they repeatedly are exposed. Learning to be stolid, reticent and undemonstrative can be an incidental product of observing the everyday relationships within the family setting. Families characterized by interpersonal reserve, superficiality and formality, or possessing a bleak and cold atmosphere in which members relate to each other in an aloof, remote or disaffiliated way, are likely breeding grounds for asocial children, who evidence deeply ingrained habits of social ineptness or insensitivity.

The following brief sketch portrays this background feature.

*CASE 6-5*
*Lester M., Age 19, College Student*

Lester "wandered in" the door of his college's counseling service, and stood about for over an hour before arranging an appointment. In his first counseling session, he spoke of his inability "to feel" and his awareness that he could not carry on a conversation with his peers of more than a few words at a time. In later sessions, he recounted the impersonal atmosphere of his childhood home; rarely was he allowed to speak unless spoken to, and he could not recall any occasion when he experienced or witnessed affection or anger among the members of his family.

**Fragmented or Amorphous Family Communications.** To relate effectively to others requires the capacity to focus on what others are experiencing and communicating, and to convey appropriate and relevant reactions in response. Some individuals fail to learn how to attend and interpret the signals that others communicate, or fail to learn how to respond in meaningful and rational ways. Learning the skills of interpersonal communication is a requisite to shared social behaviors; without them, the individual cannot function effectively with others, and will appear detached, unresponsive, cold and insensitive—traits which we have assigned to the asocial pattern.

Family styles of communicating in which ideas are aborted, or are transmitted in circumstantial, disjunctive or amorphous ways, are likely to shape the growing child's own manner of communication; in short, the child's pattern of relating to others will assume the vague and circumstantial style of his home. Moreover, exposed to disrupted, unfocused and murky patterns of thought, he will, both by imitation and by the need to follow the illogic which surrounds him, learn to attend to peripheral or tangential aspects of human communication, that is, to signs and cues that most people would view as irrelevant and distracting. This way of attending to, of thinking about and reacting to events, if extended beyond the family setting, will give rise to perplexity and confusion on the part of others. As a consequence, a vicious circle of disjointed and meaningless transactions may come to characterize his interpersonal relations (witness the author's engineering professor friend), leading him into further isolation and social distance. Together, these events will foster increased cognitive obscurities and emotional insensitivities, traits that characterize the passive-detached or asocial pattern.

## COPING STRATEGIES

The notion of strategies implies an instrumental course of action designed either to fulfill certain drives or to resolve certain conflicts; in other words, to seek positive reinforcements and avoid negative reinforcements.

Asocial personalities are essentially devoid of these instrumental behaviors since their drives are meager, and they lack the interpersonal involvements conducive to severe emotional conflicts. This is not to say that they possess no drives or conflicts, but that the few they do experience are of mild intensity and of little consequence. Thus, one of their distinctions as a personality type is the paucity, rather than the character or direction, of their coping strategies.

If any factor in their generally feeble hierarchy of motives can be noted, it is their preference for remaining socially uninvolved. This, however, is not a "driving" need, as it is with the active-detached personality, but merely a comfortable and preferred state. When social circumstances press them beyond comfortable limits, they simply retreat and withdraw to themselves. If the strain of social demands is intense and persists, these individuals may adopt more severe pathological coping patterns such as are found in the "schizoid" or "schizophrenic" syndromes; these advanced states of the detached pattern will be presented in later chapters.

In summary, then, the asocial personality seeks few reinforcements. Given his deeply ingrained deficits and insensitivities, he experiences little discomfort or pleasure either from himself or from others. As a consequence, he has little occasion to develop and employ intrapsychic coping mechanisms.

## SELF-PERPETUATION OF PATTERN

The impassivity and lack of color of the asocial personality enables him to maintain a comfortable distance from others. But this preferred state of detachment is itself pathogenic, not only because it fails to elicit reactions which could promote a more vibrant and rewarding style of life but because it fosters conditions conducive to more serious forms of psychopathology. Among the more prominent factors operating toward this end are the following.

**Impassive and Cognitively Insensitive Behaviors.** The inarticulateness and affective unresponsiveness which characterize these individuals do little to make them attractive to others. Most people are minimally inclined to respond to asocial persons, tend to overlook their presence in social settings and when interacting directly with them, relate in a perfunctory and unemotional way.

Of course, the fact that others view him as a boring and colorless individual suits the passive-detached person's desire to remain apart and alone. However, these social attitudes and experiences only perpetuate and intensify his tendencies toward detachment.

**Diminished Perceptual Awareness.** The asocial person not only is socially imperceptive but tends, in general, to "flatten" all emotional events, i.e., to blur and homogenize that which is intrinsically distinct and varied. In short, he projects his murky and undifferentiated cognitions upon discriminable and complex social experiences. As a consequence of his own perceptual diffusiveness, he precludes learning from experiences which could lead him to a more variegated, alert and socially discriminating life. Thus, no matter how much I sought to point out and clarify concepts and distinctions relevant to human behavior, my engineering colleague, Chester A., would simply acknowledge them, but fail to grasp either their intellectual or personal significance.

**Infrequent Social Activities.** The detached person perpetuates his own pattern by restricting to a minimum his social contacts and emotional involvements; only those activities necessary for performing his job or fulfilling his family obligations are pursued with any diligence. By shrinking his interpersonal milieu, he prevents new and different experiences from coming to bear upon him. This, of course, is his preference, but it fosters the continuation of his isolated and withdrawn existence since it excludes events which might alter his asocial pattern.

## REMEDIAL APPROACHES*

The prognosis for this personality is not promising. Many are limited by a constitutional incapacity for affective expression and physical vigor; whether these liabilities are inborn, or acquired as a consequence of early experience, cannot often be assessed. Regardless of their origin, the activation, cognition, affectivity and interpersonal deficits found in these individuals are chronic and pervasive features of their personality make-up. Coupling these deeply ingrained traits with their characteristic lack of insight and poor motivation for change, we must conclude that the probability is small that they will either seek or succeed in a course of remedial therapy. If their deficits are of mild intensity, however, and if the circumstances of their life are favor-

* The terminology and logic for this and later "remedial approaches" sections will be only partly grasped by the beginning student until he reads chapters 14 and 15 on therapy.

able, these individuals stand a good chance of maintaining an adequate vocational and social adjustment.

Should they come to the attention of a therapist, his efforts would best be directed toward countering their withdrawal tendencies; the primary therapeutic task is to prevent the possibility that these patients will isolate themselves entirely from the support of a benign environment. Furthermore, the therapist should seek to ensure that they continue some measure of social activity so as to prevent them from becoming lost in fantasy preoccupations and separation from reality contacts. Efforts to encourage excessive social activity should be avoided, however, since their capacities in this area are limited.

Biophysical treatment methods may be indicated. Trial periods with a number of the pharmacological "stimulants" may be explored to see if they "perk up" energy and affectivity. These should be used with caution, however, lest they activate feelings that the patient is ill-equipped to handle.

Attempts to reorient the patient's phenomenological attitudes may be made for the purpose of developing self-insight, and for motivating greater interpersonal sensitivity and activity. Techniques of behavioral modification would appear of little value in these patterns. Similarly, little can be expected of intrapsychic approaches since these patients possess a rather uncomplicated unconscious world.

Group methods may prove useful in enabling them to acquire healthier social attitudes. In these benign social settings, they may begin to alter their social image, and develop both motivation and skills for normal interpersonal relations.

## THE AVOIDANT PERSONALITY: ACTIVE-DETACHED PATTERN
(DSM-II: *Schizoid Personality*)

Let us be reminded that "detachment from others" can arise from numerous etiological sources and unfold through a variety of divergent developmental lines.

One group of detached persons, discussed in the previous section, is noted by its passivity. Members of this syndrome lack the affective capacity and cognitive skills requisite to effective social relationships. Because of the deficits they possess, they are unable to respond to the usual incentives and punishments which motivate people to engage in interpersonal behavior, and are unable to communicate to others in a socially relevant and mutually rewarding fashion.

In terms of surface behavior, the second group, referred to as active-detached, appears very much alike the first. Closer inspection, however, reveals that these persons are quite dissimilar from the passive type. They are highly alert to social stimuli and are oversensitive to the moods and feelings of others, especially those which portend rejection and humiliation. Their extreme anxiety in this matter intrudes and distracts their thoughts, interferes with effective behavior and disposes them to avoid, that is, to detach themselves from others as a protection against the stress they anticipate.

The *schizoid personality,* as described in the DSM-II, represents a more severe variant of the "avoidant pattern" to be discussed in this section. Unfortunately, the traditional nosology fails to provide a diagnostic classification for patients who evidence schizoid traits in milder form. In a later chapter, we will detail the clinical features of the "borderline schizoid personality pattern." The following excerpt from the DSM-II, selected from the "schizoid" description, may be useful for comparative purposes:

This behavior pattern manifests shyness, oversensitivity, seclusiveness, avoidance of close or competitive relationships and often eccentricity. . . . These patients react to disturbing experiences and conflicts with apparent detachment.

The following case portrays an avoidant personality, referred for counseling through the personnel office of a large industrial concern.

### CASE 6-6
### James M., Age 27, Unmarried

James was a bookkeeper for nine years, having obtained this position upon graduation from high school. He spoke of himself as a shy, fearful and quiet boy ever since early childhood. He currently was living with his mother, a socially insecure and anxious woman who kept her distance from others. His father, described as an alcoholic, was "mean to his mother" and deprecating to his children; he died when James was 14. A sister, four years older than James, lives in another city, had recently been divorced and was referred to by James as "being just like my father."

James was characterized by his supervisor as a loner, a peculiar young man who did his work quietly and efficiently. They noted that he ate alone in the company cafeteria and never joined in coffee breaks or in the "horsing around" at the office. Some years back he signed up for a company-sponsored bowling league, but withdrew after the first session.

As far as his social life was concerned, James had neither dated nor gone to a party in five years. He dated a girl "seriously" while in high school, but she "ditched" him for another fellow. After a lapse of about three years, he dated a number of different girls rather sporadically, but then stopped "because I didn't know what to say to them, and I thought they must have liked someone else." He now spent most of his free time reading, watching TV, daydreaming and fixing things around the house.

James experienced great distress when new employees were assigned to his office section. Some 40 people worked regularly in this office and job turnover resulted in replacement of four or five people a year. He feared constantly that he was going to be "fired," despite the fact that his work was competent and that the firm almost never dismissed its employees.

In recent months, a clique formed in his office. Although James very much wanted to be a member of this "in-group," he feared attempting to join them because "he had nothing to offer them" and thought he would be rejected. In a short period of time, he, along with two or three others, became the object of jokes and taunting by the leaders of the clique. After a few weeks of "being kidded," he began to miss work, failed to complete his accounts on time, found himself unsure of what he was doing and made a disproportionate number of errors. When his supervisor discussed with him his increasingly poor performance, James displayed extreme anxiety and complained of being "nervous, confused, tired and unhappy much of the time." Although he did not connect his present discomfort to the events in his office, he asked if he could be reassigned to another job where he might work alone.

The counselor to which he was directed found him to be of average intelligence and extremely conscientious, but lacking in confidence and fearful of competition. It became clear in further discussions that many of his traits could be traced to the humiliation and deprecation he suffered at the hands of his father, the rejection he experienced with his peers and in dating and his life-long identification with, and exposure to, his mother's fearful attitudes which he imitated unconsciously.

## CLINICAL PICTURE

The case of James touches briefly on a number of points distinguishing the avoidant from the asocial personality. Active-detached individuals are acutely sensitive to social deprecation and humiliation. They feel their loneliness and isolated existence deeply, experience being out of things and have a strong, though often repressed, desire to be accepted.

Despite this longing to relate and to be an active participant in social life, they fear placing their feelings and welfare in the hands of others, or trusting and confiding in them. Thus, their social detachment does not stem from deficit drives and sensibilities, as in the asocial personality, but from an active and self-protective restraint. Although they experience a pervasive estrangement and loneliness, they dare not expose themselves to the defeat and humiliation they anticipate, as can be seen in the repeated withdrawal behavior that characterizes the social life of James M.

Since their affective feelings cannot be expressed overtly, they cumulate and are vented in an inner world of rich fantasy and imagination. Their need for affect, contact and relatedness may pour forth in poetry, be sublimated in intellectual pursuits or a delicate taste for foods and clothing or be expressed in finely detailed and expressive artistic activities.

Their isolation, that is, their protective withdrawal from others, results, however, in a variety of secondary consequences which compound their difficulties. Their apparently tense and fearful demeanor often "pulls" ridicule and deprecation from others, that is, they leave themselves open to persons who gain satisfaction in taunting and belittling those who dare not retaliate. Thus, the self-protective efforts of the avoidant personality often are self-defeating; the additional humiliation they experience at the hands of others serves not only to confirm their mistrust but reactivates the deep wounds of the past.

With this general introduction in mind, let us separate and detail the four levels of clinical data which characterize the avoidant picture.

### Behavior

A shy and apprehensive quality characterizes these individuals. They not only appear awkward and uncomfortable in social situations but seem to shrink actively from the reciprocal give-and-take of interpersonal relations.

In face-to-face contact they often impose a strain upon others; their discomfort and mistrust take the form of subtle testing operations, that is, a set of carefully guarded maneuvers by which they check whether others are sincere in their friendly overtures, or are deceptive and potential threats to their security. Thus, if a new office employee would be friendly to him on a one-to-one basis, James M. would make it a practice to talk to him when others were around, checking to see if the new employee would continue the conversation with him, or quickly turn his attention to others.

To most observers who have peripheral contact with them, avoidant personalities appear simply to be timid, withdrawn or perhaps cold and strange—not unlike the image conveyed by the asocial personality. Those who relate to them more closely, however, recognize their sensitivity, touchiness, evasiveness and mistrustful qualities.

Speech is generally slow and constrained; there are frequent hesitations, aborted or fragmentary sequences of thought and occasional confused and irrelevant digressions. Physical behavior is controlled and underactive, although it may be marked with periodic bursts of fidgety and rapid staccato movements. The overt expression of emotion typically is flat, but this under-responsiveness overlays tension and disharmony; these people appear to be exerting great restraint to control anxiety, feelings of confusion and anger.

### Phenomenological Reports

The avoidant personality is alert to the most subtle feelings and intentions of others. He is a "sensitizer," an acutely perceptive observer of the passing scene, one who scans and appraises every movement and expression of those with whom he comes into contact. Although this hypervigilance serves to protect him against potential danger, it floods him with excessive stimuli, and distracts him from attending to the ordinary and usually relevant features of his environment. Thus, even in the course of an ordinary day, James M. was so attuned to matters that might have a bearing on how others felt toward him that he could attend to little other than the routine aspects of his job.

Cognitive processes of the avoidant personality are not only interfered with by this flooding of irrelevant environmental details but are complicated further by an inner emotional disharmony which intrudes and diverts his thoughts. Combined with extraneous perceptions, these feelings upset his cognitive processes and diminish his capacity to cope effectively with many of the ordinary tasks of life. "Cognitive interference," one of the cardinal features of the avoidant personality, is especially pronounced in social settings where his perceptual vigilance and his emotional turmoil are most acute; it may be only minimally evident in socially neutral settings.

The active-detached person describes himself typically as tense and fatigued. Feelings of loneliness and of being unwanted and isolated are expressed quite often, as are fear and distrust of others. People are viewed as critical, betraying and humiliating. Given this outlook, we can well understand why his social behavior is characterized by an "interpersonal aversiveness."

Expressions conveying disharmonious emotions and feelings of emptiness and depersonalization are especially noteworthy. Avoidant personalities tend to be extremely introspective and self-conscious, often perceive themselves as different from others and are unsure of their identity and self-worth. The alienation they feel from others is paralleled, then, by a feeling of alienation from self. They voice a sense of futility with regard to their life, have a deflated self-image and frequently refer to themselves with contempt and deprecation.

### Intrapsychic Processes

Protection from real and imagined stress is a paramount goal in these personalities. Avoidance of situations which may result either in personal humiliation or rejection is the guiding force behind their social behavior. Of equal threat is the person's own aggressive and affectional impulses; these are particularly distressful since the person fears that he may himself prompt others to be rejecting, frustrating and condemning. Much of his intrapsychic energy is devoted then to mechanisms which deny and bind these inner urges.

Despite efforts at inner control, painful and threatening thoughts and feelings periodically erupt, disrupting cognitive processes and upsetting emotional equanimity. Fantasies serve as an outlet for venting frustrated impulses, but they too prove distressing in the long run since they reactivate past anxieties, and point up the contrast between desire and objective reality. Repression of all feelings is often the only recourse.

Avoidant personalities are beset by several basic conflicts. The struggle between attachment and mistrust is central; they desire to be close, to show affection with others and to belong to a group, but they cannot shake themselves free of the belief that they will experience pain and disillusion. Strong doubts exist concerning their self-competence; thus, they have grave concerns about venturing into the challenges of a competitive society. Their low opinion of themselves is reflected in their deflated self-esteem; this curtails initiative since they fear that their efforts at autonomy and independence will fail and result in humiliation. Every avenue for gratification seems trapped in conflict. They cannot act on their own because of marked self-doubt; on the other hand, they cannot depend on others because of social mistrust. Positive reinforcements can be obtained, then, neither from themselves nor from others; both sources provide only pain and discomfort. As a consequence, coping strategies are designed to avoid both the distress that surrounds them and the emptiness and wounds that inhere within them.

### Biophysical Factors

The hypervigilance which characterizes the avoidant personality signifies his habitual high level of somatic arousal. The exterior of behavioral sluggishness and inactivity is deceptive, therefore; it overlays an extremely low threshold for alertness and reactive readiness, which the patient goes to great pains to restrain and control. Chronic tension and irritability may be discerned in occasional spasmodic and uncoordinated motor behaviors, and in a high degree of sensory distractibility. Thus, James M. appeared to the undiscerning eye to be a quiet, if shy, man, unperturbed by external events. The converse was true, of course; he was preoccupied with and hyperalert to his surroundings, so much so that he often could not concentrate on the task with which he seemed to be working.

Behavioral signs of hyperarousal may reflect a biophysical sensory irritability, or a more centrally involved somatic imbalance or dysfunction. Using a different conceptual language to refer to this biophysical speculation, we might hypothesize that these individuals possess a constitutionally based threctic temperament, that is, a hypersensitivity to potential threat and anxiety. Stated differently, the perceptual vigilance and motor tension we observe in these patients may derive, in part, from a biological vulnerability to fear.

## ETIOLOGY AND DEVELOPMENT

As we have stated previously, the concept of personality represents an individual's basic and pervasive style of functioning; it arises as a consequence of the intricate and sequential interplay of both biological and psychological influences.

The dominant features of the pathological personality we have termed the avoidant pattern may be summarized in these four traits: *affective disharmony* (confused and conflicting emotions), *cognitive interference* (persistent intrusion of distracting and disruptive thoughts), *alienated self-image* (feelings of social isolation; self-rejection), and *interpersonal distrust* (anticipation and fear of humiliation and betrayal).

As with the asocial personality, and as will be customary with the other pathological patterns to be presented, we will outline several of the more plausible biogenic and psychogenic factors which may underlie the development of pathological personality traits. Let us again stress that the influences hypothesized in these sections are neither necessary, sufficient nor mutually exclusive, nor even contributory causes in all cases.

We merely posit the view that they are plausible as determinants, and that any combination of them may interact to shape the course of pathological personality development.

### Biogenic Factors

As noted earlier, propositions implicating biophysical determinants are highly speculative, given our present state of knowledge. Let us note, further, that the hypotheses suggested below represent, in several circumstances, different conceptual approaches to the same thesis, e.g., a threctic reaction pattern may simply be a "behavioral" term to represent a "biophysical" limbic system imbalance.

**Heredity.**    Genetic predispositions to avoidant behavior cannot be overlooked, despite the lack of empirical data. Many structural elements and physiological processes comprise the biophysical substrate for those complex psychological functions we refer to as affective disharmony, interpersonal aversiveness and so on. It would be naive to assume that these biophysical substrates do not vary from person to person, or that they are not influenced in part by heredity. Studies which demonstrate a higher than chance correspondence within family groups in social apprehensiveness and withdrawal behavior can be attributed in large measure to learning, but there is reason to believe, at least in some cases, that this correspondence may partially be assigned to a common pool of genotypic dispositions within families. The particular regions which may be involved in these ostensive genetic dispositions will be noted in several of the following sections.

**Threctic Infantile Reaction Pattern.**    Infants who display hyperirritability, crankiness, tension and withdrawal behaviors from the first days of postnatal life may not only possess a constitutional disposition toward an avoidant pattern but may prompt rejecting and hostile attitudes from their parents. Frightened and hypertense babies, babies who are easily awakened, cry and are colicky, rarely afford their parents much comfort and joy. Rather, such infants typically induce parental weariness, exasperation and anger, attitudes and feelings which may shape a stereotype of a troublesome, whining and difficult-to-manage child. In these cases, an initial biophysical tendency toward anxiety and withdrawal may be aggravated further by parental rejection and deprecation.

**Slow or Irregular Maturation.**    Delayed or uneven maturation in any of the major spheres of sensory, sensorimotor or cognitive functioning may be conducive to psychopathology. Developmental immaturities and integration deficits may signify an impaired biophysical substrate that can limit the child's capacity to cope adequately with the normal tasks he faces at each developmental stage. These intrinsic deficiencies often are compounded by the child's self-conscious awareness of his inadequacies. Of equal if not greater import in compounding these deficits are parental reactions to the child's atypical development. Parents who expect their children to progress well and rapidly through the usual developmental sequence may experience considerable anxiety and dismay over deviations and failures they observe. Inadequate achievements often result in parental condemnation and ridicule, experiences which will evoke feelings of social alienation and low self-regard on the part of the child. The following case illustrates some of these points.

*CASE 6-7*
*John F., Age 19, Prep School Senior*

John's father was an aggressive and financially successful physician, noted within his specialty as the originator of an important surgical procedure; his mother was a rather shy and retiring woman who had been a high school teacher before her marriage. John had two brothers, one older and one younger than himself.

From the very first, John seemed an unusual baby. He cried incessantly, was difficult to feed and impossible to fit into any schedule of management and care. Colic persisted well into the latter half of his first year. He continued to be easily upset; at eight months, he cried at the sight of anyone other than his mother, and this persisted well into his second year.

His father was easily exasperated with John, especially when the boy failed to stand and walk at the age of ten months; John did not walk at all until 20 months of age, and evidenced a wide variety of other developmental lags in speech and motor performance.

Although his mother sought to compensate for the obvious rejection John experienced at the hands of his father, her efforts and tolerance diminished sharply with the birth of her third child. Throughout his early years, John constantly was compared with his older brother, a robust youngster who was assertive and cheerful in manner, and who matured rapidly in all spheres of motor and cognitive functioning. The advent of the third son in the family, a child who showed signs of progressing in a manner similar to the first, further categorized John as the "slow and difficult one."

John's performance in school was well above average, but far below his father's expectations and his brother's achievements. Although his father's taunting took on a joking tone, he managed, quite effectively, to humiliate and deprecate him. John remained an isolate within his home, and a fearful, quiet and socially withdrawn adolescent among his peers at prep school.

**Limbic Region Imbalances.** Quite possibly, avoidant personalities experience aversive stimuli more intensely and more frequently than others because they possess an especially dense or overabundantly branched neural substrate in the "aversive" center of the limbic system.

Individual differences in brain anatomy have been well demonstrated, but we must recognize that speculations attributing complex forms of clinical behavior to biophysical variations is not only conjectural but also rather simplistic. Even if differences in biological aversiveness ultimately were found, the psychological form and content of these tendencies would take on their specific character only as a function of the individual's particular life experiences and learnings.

**Sympathetic System Dominance.** Another plausible speculation for the threctic or aversive feature of the active-detached pattern centers on a presumed functional dominance of the sympathetic nervous system. Excess adrenalin resulting from any one of a number of possible dysfunctions, either in the autonomic system or in the pituitary-adrenal axis, may give rise to the hypervigilance and irritability characteristic of the avoidant personality. Imbalances of this kind also may account for the affective disharmony and cognitive interference found among these patients.

Although hypotheses implicating adrenal involvement lend themselves more readily to experimental test than those pertaining to the limbic system, no adequately designed studies have been executed, and these hypotheses remain essentially speculative.

**Neurohormonal Synaptic Acceleration.** Deficiencies or excesses in any of the various neurohormones may facilitate rapid synaptic transmission, resulting in the flooding and scattering of neural impulses. Such individuals not only will appear overalert and overactive but may experience cognitive interference, anxiety and a generalized emotional disharmony. Let us briefly note the rationale for these effects.

First, uninhibited neural transmission may generate many pathological consequences; it can make normally discriminable stimuli functionally equivalent, allow irrelevant impulses to intrude upon logical associations, diminish the control and direction of thought and permit the emergence of inappropriate memory traces—in short, it can result in a marked interference with normal cognitive processes.

Second, a lowering of normal resistance at the synapse, with its attendant flooding of impulses, may give rise to anxiety under conditions of normal stimulation. For example, individuals subjected to this impairment may be overwhelmed, overexcited and overaroused by experiences which most people take in their stride. What we observe as anxiety readiness and interpersonal aversiveness in the active-detached pattern may be a protective maneuver to counteract a biologically based inability to control stimulus input and to coordinate impulse transmission.

Along similar lines, the affective disharmony of the active-detached may be a product of his inability to inhibit the intrusion of discordant memories and emotions.

### Psychogenic Factors

Attempts to list and detail the infinite number of life experiences which may shape the development of an avoidant pattern would be not only futile but misleading. It is not so much the particulars of the timing, setting or source of these experiences which make them important but rather the significance of the message they convey to the individual. These diverse experiences possess one central theme in common: they serve to depreciate the individual's self-esteem through either explicit or implicit signs of rejection, humiliation or denigration. Repeated exposure to such events will not only foster an image of deflated self-worth but will tend, ultimately, to produce the affective disharmony, cognitive interference and interpersonal distrust characteristic of the active-detached personality. We will elaborate two of the primary sources of these derogating experiences in the following sections.

**Parental Rejection and Deprecation.** Normal, attractive and healthy infants may encounter parental devaluation, malignment and rejection. Reared in a family setting in which they are belittled, abandoned and censured, these youngsters will have their natural robustness and optimism crushed, and acquire in its stead attitudes of self-deprecation and feelings of social alienation. We can well imagine the impact of these experiences upon John F. who was not especially robust and competent to start with.

The consequences of parental rejection and humiliation are many and diverse. In the following discussion we will outline them as they might arise during each of the three neuropsychological stages of development.

1. Parents who handle their infants in a cold and indelicate manner during the sensory attachment stage will promote feelings of tension and insecurity on the part of their offspring. These infants will acquire a diffuse sense that the world is harsh, unwelcoming and discomforting. They will learn, in their primitive and highly generalized way, to avoid attaching themselves to others; they will acquire a sense of mistrust of their human surroundings and, as a result, feel isolated, helpless and abandoned.

In self-protection, these youngsters may learn to "turn-off" their growing sensory capacities so as to diminish the discomfort they experience. By so doing, however, they may set the stage for a longstanding and generalized habit of stimulus withdrawal.

2. Parents who scorn, ridicule and belittle their offspring's first stumbling efforts during the sensorimotor-autonomy stage will diminish markedly feelings of self-competence and the growth of confidence, e.g., the experience of John F. at the hands of his father. Although normal language skills and motor control may develop, the youngster will often utilize these aptitudes in a hesitant and self-doubting manner. He may accept as "valid" his parents' criticisms and derogations; in time, he may come to disparage and revile himself just as his parents had done.

Harsh self-critical attitudes have far-reaching and devastating consequences. By belittling his own worth, he cannot turn to himself to salve his wounds or gain the rewards he cannot obtain elsewhere. Thus, as a consequence of self-derogation, he not only fails to obtain positive reinforcements from others but cannot obtain them from himself. He is caught in a web of social *and* self-reproval; he, himself, has become an agent of negative reinforcement. Thus, in referring to himself, John F. would characteristically comment first on his stupidity and ineptness, and then note how his father and brothers were so much more able intellectually and socially. A cardinal feature of the active-detached pattern, that of self-alienation, has taken root.

3. The roots of self-deprecation begun in the sensorimotor-autonomy stage take firmer hold as the youngster progresses into the period of intracortical-initiative. The image of being a weak, unlovable and unworthy person takes on a strong cognitive base. He becomes increasingly aware of himself as unattractive, a pitiful person, one who deserves to be scoffed at and ridiculed. Little effort may be expended to alter this image since nothing the youngster attempts can succeed, given the deficits and inadequacies he sees within himself.

Many of these youngsters not only accept their plight but compound it by identifying with a weak and ineffectual parent. Still seeking love and affection, they imitate an unwholesome parental model, and thereby seal their fate. By abdicating their individual identities for the dubious comforts and rewards of parental identification, they subvert their own growth, and undermine whatever possibilities they may have had for finding a more satisfying style of life. They now copy the insecurities and inadequacies of their sorrowful parental prototype, learning to display the same social deficits and ineffectualities they observe. To illustrate, John F. learned to identify with his "quiet and ineffectual" mother, the least threatening figure in his home, but one whose behaviors only reinforced his self-image of ineptitude and social inadequacy.

**Peer Group Alienation.** Signs of avoidant behavior usually are evident well before the child begins to participate in the give-and-take of peer relationships, school and athletic competitions, heterosexual dating, with its attendant anxieties, and so on. These early signs may reflect the operation of constitutional dispositions, or attitudes and habits conditioned by the circumstances of family life. Whatever its origins, many school age children already possess the social hesitations and aversive tendencies which will come to characterize them more clearly in later life.

But for many other youngsters, the rudiments of social withdrawal and self-alienation have developed only minimally when they first encounter the challenges of peer-group activities. For them, the chances of enhancing their competencies and for developing the requisite skills for effective social adaptation remain good, unless they experience rejection, isolation or the devastating ridicule which often can be meted out by their age-mates. As the child ventures to meet his peers at school, on the playground, on the athletic field, at school dances and so on, he is exposed to a variety of challenges which may wear down his sense of self-competence and self-esteem. Many such youngsters will be shattered by daily reminders of their scholastic ineptitude, some will be ridiculed for deficits in athletic prowess, others will be humiliated and experience cruel derogation at the hands of their peers because of physical unattractiveness and their lack of allure, vitality and so on. Unable to prove themselves in any of the myriad intellectual, physical or social spheres of peer competition, they may not only be derided and isolated by others but become sharply critical toward themselves for their lack of worthiness and esteem. Their feelings of loneliness and rejection now are compounded further by severe self-judgments of personal inferiority and unattractiveness. They are unable to turn either to others for solace and gratification or to themselves.

## COPING STRATEGIES

Anxiety-ridden, denied encouragement and belittled and disparaged in childhood, the avoidant personality has a deep mistrust of others and a markedly deflated image of his own self-worth. He has learned through bitter experience that the world is unfriendly, cold and humiliating, and that he himself has few of the personal skills and talents by which he can hope to experience the pleasures and comforts of life. He expects to be slighted or demeaned wherever he turns; he has learned to be watchful, to be on guard against the ridicule and contempt he anticipates from others. He must be ever-alert, exquisitely sensitive to signs of censure and derision. And looking inward offers him no solace since he finds none of the attributes he admires in others.

His goal in life, then, is a negative one. His strategies are designed to avoid pain, to need nothing, to depend on no one and to deny desire. He also must turn from himself, from an awareness of his unlovability and unattractiveness and from his inner conflicts and disharmony. Experience, to him, is a matter of negative reinforcement, both from without and from within.

Let us next detail the characteristic strategies that these patients utilize to cope with this oppressing outlook.

**Aversive Interpersonal Behaviors.** The active-detached person is guided by a need to put distance between himself and others, that is, to minimize involvements that can reactivate or duplicate past humiliations. Privacy is sought; he attempts to eschew as many responsibilities and obligations as possible without incurring further condemnation. Any desire or interest which entails personal commitments to others constitutes a potential threat to his fragile security. He may even deny himself material possessions as a means of protecting against painful loss or disillusionment.

Periodic efforts to comply with the wishes of others, or to assert himself and impose his needs upon others, may have proved fruitless and painful. Appeasement may have brought a loss of what little personal integrity he still may have possessed, and may have led only to greater humiliation and disparagement; aggressive self-assertion may have incurred unbearable counter-hostility and anxiety. The only course he has learned that succeeds is to back away, draw within himself and keep a watchful eye against incursions into his solitude.

To avoid the anguish of social relationships requires remaining vigilant and alert to potential threat; this contrasts markedly with the strategy of the passive-detached asocial personality who is perceptually insensitive to his surroundings. The avoidant person is overly attentive and aware of variations and subtleties in his stimulus world; he has learned through past encounters with threats that the most effective means of avoiding them is to be hyperalert to cues which forewarn their occurrence. He is suspicious and perennially on guard; hypervigilance is the only means at his disposal to minimize the hazards he fears surround him.

**Excessive Dependence on Intrapsychic Mechanisms.** Turning away from one's external environment brings little peace and comfort, however. The avoidant personality finds no solace and freedom within himself. Having acquired a pernicious attitude of self-derogation and deprecation, he not only experiences little reward in his accomplishments and thoughts but finds in their stead, shame, devaluation and anguish.

There may be more pain being alone with one's despised self than with the escapable torment of others. Immersing onself in one's thoughts and feelings presents a more difficult challenge since the person cannot physically avoid himself, cannot walk away, escape or hide from his own being. Deprived of feelings of self-worth, he suffers constantly from painful thoughts about his pitiful state, his misery and the futility of being himself. Efforts as vigilant as those applied to the external world must be expended to ward off the distressing ideas and feelings that well up within him. Unfortunately, these aversive signals pervade every facet of his make-up since it is his entire being that has become devalued; nothing about him escapes the severe judgment of self-derision.

His sole recourse is to break up, destroy or repress these painful thoughts and the emotions they unleash. He must prevent self-preoccupations, intrude irrelevancies, digress, block and make his normal thoughts and communications take on different and less significant meanings. In short, through various intrapsychic ploys, he interferes actively with his own cognitions.

In a similar manner, the mixture of anxieties, desires and impulses which surge forth must be restrained, denied, turned about, transformed and distorted. In short, he muddles his own emotions, and makes his affective life discordant and disharmonious. Better to experience diffuse disharmony than the sharp pain and anguish of being oneself.

## SELF-PERPETUATION OF PATTERN

The strategies employed by the avoidant personality are not a matter of choice; they are the only means he has found effective in warding off the painful humiliation experienced at the hands of others. Discomforting as social alienation

may be, it is less distressing than the anguish involved in extending oneself to others, only to be rebuffed and ridiculed. Distance assures safety; trust invites disillusion.

These coping maneuvers prove self-defeating. There is a compulsive quality to the aversive behavior of avoidant personalities; they are adaptively inflexible and cannot pursue different alternatives without trepidation and anxiety. In contrast to the strategies employed by other personality patterns, the avoidant person's approach is essentially negative. Rather than venturing outward, or drawing upon his realistic aptitude to cope with life, he retreats defensively and becomes more and more remote from others and from sources of potential growth and gratification. As a consequence of his protective withdrawal, the avoidant person is left to himself and to his own inner turmoil, conflicts and feelings of self-alienation. His efforts may have succeeded in minimizing external danger, but he has trapped himself in a situation equally devastating.

Several aspects of coping which foster and intensify the active-detached personality's difficulties will be outlined below.

**Restricted Social Experiences.** Avoidant personalities assume that the atypical experiences to which they were exposed in early life will continue to be their lot forever. In defense, they narrow the range of activities in which they allow themselves to participate. By circumscribing their life in this manner, they preclude the possibility of corrective experiences, experiences which may show them that "all is not lost," that there are kindly and friendly persons who will not disparage and humiliate them.

Moreover, by detaching themselves from others they are left to be preoccupied with their own thoughts and impulses. Limited to these inner stimuli, they can only reflect and ruminate about past events, with all the discomforts they bring forth. Since experience is restricted largely to thoughts of their past, life becomes a series of duplications. They relive the painful events of earlier times rather than experience new and different events which might alter their attitudes and feelings.

Self-preoccupations widen the breach between others and self. A vicious circle is set up. The more they turn inward, the more they lose contact with the typical interests and patterns of thought of those around them. Progressively they become estranged from their environment, increasingly out of touch with reality and the checks against irrational thought provided by interpersonal contact and communication. Away from the controls of human interaction, they may lose their sense of balance and order and begin to feel confused, peculiar, unreal and "crazy."

**Fearful and Suspicious Behaviors.** Withdrawn and mistrustful behaviors not only establish distance from others but evoke reciprocal reactions of disaffiliation and rejection. A demeanor which communicates weakness, self-effacement and fear invariably attracts those who enjoy deprecating and ridiculing others. Thus, the hesitant posture, suspicious manner and self-deprecating attitudes of the avoidant personality will tend to create interpersonal responses which lead further to experiences of humiliation, contempt and derogation—in short, a repetition of the past. Thus, in the cases of both James M. and John F., their obvious sensitivity to rebuff, and their fearful nonassertive manner, evoked ridicule from their peers; this, of course, only reinforced and intensified their aversive inclinations.

**Perceptual Hypersensitivity.** Avoidant personalities are painfully alert to signs of deception and deprecation. They detect the most minute traces of indifference and annoyance expressed by others, make the molehills of a minor and passing slight into a mountain of personal ridicule and condemnation. Their perceptual mechanisms are incredibly sensitive instruments for picking up and magnifying incidental actions, and interpreting them as indications of derision and rejection.

Although their hypersensitivity functions in the service of self-protection, it tends to foster a deepening of the person's plight. As a result of their overalertness and extensive scanning of the environment, the avoidant personality actually increases the likelihood that he will encounter precisely those stimuli he wishes most to avoid. His exquisite defensive antennae pick up and transform what most people overlook. In effect, then, his hypersensitivity backfires; it becomes an instrument that brings to his awareness, time and time again, the very pain he struggles to escape. His protective vigilance thus intensifies rather than diminishes his anguish.

**Intentional Cognitive Interference.** The avoidant personality must counter the flood of threatening stimuli which he registers as a consequence of his perceptual hypersensitivity. To assure a modicum of peace and tranquillity, he engages constantly in a series of cognitive reinterpretations and digressions. He actively blocks, destroys and fragments his thoughts; he seeks to disconnect relationships between what he sees, what meanings he attributes to his perceptions and what feelings he experiences in response to them. Protectively then, he intentionally destroys his own cognitive clarity by intruding irrelevant distractions, tangential ideas and discordant emotions.

This defensive maneuver exacts its price. By upsetting the normally smooth and logical pattern of the cognitive process, he diminishes his ability to deal with events efficiently and rationally. He can no longer attend to the most salient features of his environment; neither can he coordinate his thoughts or respond wisely to events. More importantly, he cannot learn new ways to handle and resolve his difficulties; his thoughts are cluttered and scattered. Social communications take on a tangential and irrelevant quality. Like a car operating on three cylinders and partially locked brakes, he talks and acts in an erratic and halting manner. In his defensive attempt to decrease the flood of threatening stimuli, he falls prey to a coping mechanism that aggravates his original deficits, and intensifies his alienation from himself and others.

## REMEDIAL APPROACHES

The prognosis for the avoidant personality pattern is poor. Not only are his habits and attitudes pervasive and deeply ingrained but he usually is trapped in an environment that provides him with few of the supports and encouragements he needs to reverse his pattern.

Because of the active-detached person's basic mistrust of others, he is unlikely to be motivated either to seek or to sustain a therapeutic relationship. Should he submit to treatment, it is probable that he will engage in maneuvers to test the sincerity and genuineness of the therapist's feelings and motives. In most cases he will terminate treatment long before remedial improvement has occurred.

His tendency to withdraw from therapy stems not only from his doubts and suspicions regarding the therapist's integrity and forthrightness but also from his unwillingness to face the humiliation and anguish involved in confronting his painful memories and feelings. He seems to sense intuitively that his defenses are weak and tenuous, that to face directly his feelings of unworthiness and his repressed frustrations and impulses will overwhelm him, driving him into unbearable anxieties and even to, as he fears it, "insanity."

Furthermore, the potential positive rewards of therapy not only may fail to motivate the avoidant personality but may actually serve as a deterrent. It reawakens what he views will be false hopes; it may lead him back to the dangers and humiliations he experienced with others when he tendered his affections, but received rejection in return. Now that he has carved out a modest degree of comfort by detaching himself from others, he would rather leave matters stand, stick to his accustomed level of adjustment and not "rock the boat" he so tenuously learned to sail.

Should he enter a therapeutic relationship, however, the therapist must take great pains not to push matters too hard or too fast since the avoidant personality has but a fragile hold on reality. He should seek, gently and carefully, to build a feeling of trust. Gradually, he may turn his attention to the patient's positive attributes, seeking to build confidence and enhance his self-image. This may be a slow and laborious process. It may require the reworking of deep, hidden anxieties and past resentments, bringing to consciousness the roots of his mistrustful attitudes and, in time, enabling him to reappraise them more objectively.

If we consider therapy from the viewpoint of formal differences in technique, we might note that a first approach would be to assist the patient in managing a more wholesome and rewarding environment. Here we might seek to facilitate the discovery of opportunities which might enhance self-worth. Supportive therapy may be all the patient can tolerate until he is capable of dealing comfortably with his more painful feelings and thoughts. Biophysical treatment may be used to diminish or control anxieties. Behavior modification techniques may prove useful as a means of learning less fearful reactions to formerly threatening situations. As the patient progresses in trust and security with the therapist, he may be amenable to methods of phenomenological reorientation designed to alter erroneous self-attitudes and distorted social expectancies. No doubt, the deeper and more searching procedures of intrapsychic reconstruction can be useful in reworking unconscious anxieties and mechanisms which pervade every aspect of his behavior. Lastly, group therapy may be employed, where feasible, to assist the patient in learning new attitudes and skills in a more benign and accepting social atmosphere than normally encountered.

## COMMENT

Research relevant to the detached pathological patterns, found largely in literature associated with the more severe impairment entitled "schizophrenia," is rife with methodological defects and contradictory results. Rather interestingly, however, the data generated in this diverse body of work uncover repeatedly a contrasting set of characteristics among these patients. One group of researchers, drawing upon their data, suggests that detached patients (schizophrenic) are distinguished by a number of deficits, their *under*arousal, *under*motivation and *in*sensitivities. The other group asserts, with equal conviction and support, that these patients are best characterized by excessive reactivity, that is, *over*arousal, *over*motivation and *hyper*sensitivity.

It is our contention that both sets of these seemingly contradictory findings are correct, *if* viewed in terms of our two-fold distinction of active and passive detachment. Both detached patterns, as will be elaborated in chapters 8 and 9, are disposed toward the more severe schizoid and schizophrenic patterns. Although the overt symptomatological features of the active and passive patterns are alike, their constitutional dispositions, developmental history and basic coping strategies are quite distinct. Extensive clinical study and experimental research will uncover, we believe, the fundamental distinctions that we contend exist. One group (passive) will display chronic underreactivity, affectivity deficit, cognitive slippage and interpersonal indifference, whereas the other group (active) will show up as chronically overreactive and hyperalert, with affective disharmony, cognitive interference and interpersonal distrust as their essential features. The reason that researchers consistently have turned up paradoxical and contradictory results in schizophrenia, we contend, is because of their failure to recognize the distinction between active and passive-detached personalities.

Despite our convictions in this matter, we have hesitated drawing upon or referring to research which could be viewed as supporting the distinctions we have made between active and passive-detachment. The distinction, as formulated here, is essentially new and highly theoretical. *It would be presumptuous, we believe, to purloin data not designed specifically to test the hypotheses proposed. Any theorist can uncover incidental facts to support his pet convictions if he looks hard enough. This is an unfortunate habit. We would rather let the propositions presented here stand merely as a suggested framework for future research rather than create the illusion that it reflects a well-documented typology.*

A further reason for our hesitation is that available data have been based largely on populations of severely disturbed hospitalized patients; our reference points in this chapter are the moderately well-compensated individuals who only rarely would be seen in an inpatient setting.

Last, but not the least of the reasons for

by-passing reference to the literature, is the fact that previous research on detached patients (schizophrenia) has not been based on the fundamental distinction we have drawn between the active and passive subtypes. These groups, as we conceive them, have been lumped together in a single category; data derived in this manner have proven to be muddled and confused, and they are impossible to separate for our purposes.

For reasons similar to those noted above, we shall be reluctant to make reference to the research literature associated with several of the personality patterns to be described in this and later chapters. As regards research relevant to the detached patterns, we recommend several exceptionally fine reviews such as those by Buss and Lang (Buss and Lang, 1965; Lang and Buss, 1965), Silverman (1964a, 1964b) and Garmezy (1968). More extensive clinical descriptions of "character trends" similar to those presented in this section may be found in the writings of Horney (1945, 1950) and Leary (1957).

# BASIC DEPENDENT PATTERNS

The feature distinguishing dependent personalities from other pathological patterns is their marked need for social approval and affection, and their willingness to adjust their lives in accordance with the values and desires of others.

The dependent person's "center of gravity," as Horney has put it, lies in others, not in himself. He adapts his thoughts and behaviors to appease those upon whom he depends. His never-ending search for love and esteem leads him to deny impulses and ideas which may arouse displeasure; he dreads asserting himself lest his actions be interpreted as aggressive, and thereby arouse resentment and hostility. He often is paralyzed when alone and needs constant bolstering and repeated assurance that he will not be abandoned. He is exceedingly sensitive and vulnerable to signs of disapproval; criticism can be devastating.

Dependent personalities devalue themselves and their accomplishments. What self-esteem they possess is determined entirely by the good will, support and encouragement of others; thus, they are unable to draw upon themselves as a source of comfort and gratification, and must arrange their lives to ensure a constant supply of nourishment and reinforcements from the external world. However, by placing all their "eggs" in someone else's "basket," they make themselves doubly vulnerable and leave themselves open and at the mercy of the whims and moods of others; to lose the affection and protection of those upon whom they depend is to be cast into the frightening void of independence and self-determination. Protectively, then, they must submit and comply with the wishes of others, or make themselves so pleasing and attractive that no one would want to abandon them. The preceding sentence points up the essential distinction between the two basic dependency strategies.

Some persons, to be termed the *passive-dependent* type, willingly submit to others, and comply at all costs to the desires or demands made of them. These personalities tend to be self-effacing, obsequious, ever-agreeable, docile and ingratiating.

The second group, termed *active-dependent* personalities, behaves in a strikingly different manner from the passive type. Their strategy for obtaining reinforcement and protection from others is to captivate or entice their interest; by devious manipulations, they engage, fascinate and seduce those from whom they seek support. Rather than passively submitting to the wishes, whims and tastes of others, they use their talents, charms and cleverness to maneuver the approval and affection they need. Despite their gregarious, flippant and seemingly indifferent exterior, their need for others is no less than that of the passive-dependent type.

## THE SUBMISSIVE PERSONALITY: PASSIVE-DEPENDENT PATTERN
(DSM II: *Inadequate Personality*)

Docility, a clinging helplessness and a poignant search for support, nurture and reassurance characterize these individuals; they are self-depreciating, feel a sense of marked inferiority and avoid displaying initiative and self-determination. Except for their need for signs of belonging and acceptance, they refrain from making any demands of others. They submerge their individuality, subordinate their tastes and desires, deny whatever vestiges they may possess as identities apart from others and often submit to abuse and intimidation, all in the hope of avoiding social isolation and the dread of loneliness and abandonment. They feel paralyzed and empty if left to their own devices; they search for guidance in fulfilling simple tasks or making routine decisions.

Passive-dependent individuals often seek a single, all-powerful "magic helper," a partner in whom they can place their trust, depend on to supply the few comforts they want and to protect them from having to assume responsibilities or face the competitive struggles of life alone. Supplied with a nurturant and dependable partner, they may function with ease, be sociable and display warmth, affection and generosity to others. Deprived of these supports, they may withdraw and become tense, dejected, despondent and forlorn.

Despite the wide prevalence of this pathological pattern, there is no provision in either the old (DSM-1952) or new (DSM-II) official nosology to record these cases. The closest approximation, though far from sufficient in scope and clarity, is the *inadequate personality,* for which the following descriptive phrases may be quoted for comparative purposes:

This behavior pattern is characterized by ineffectual responses to emotional, social, intellectual and physical demands. While the patient seems neither physically nor mentally deficient, he does manifest inadaptability, ineptness, poor judgment, social instability and lack of physical and emotional stamina.

The following case traces the developmental history of a lifelong passive-dependent male who has maintained a tenuous but reasonably adequate level of adjustment.

### CASE 6-8
### Harry G., Age 57, Married, Four Children

Mr. G. was a rather short, thin and nicely featured but somewhat haggard man who displayed a hesitant and tense manner when first seen by his physician. His place of employment for the past 15 years had recently closed and he had been without work for several weeks. He appeared less dejected about the loss of his job than about his wife's increasing displeasure with his decision to "stay at home until something came up." She thought he "must be sick" and insisted that he see a doctor; the following picture emerged in the course of several interviews.

Mr. G. was born in Europe, the oldest child and only son of a family of six children. As was customary of his ethnic group, the eldest son was pampered and overprotected. His mother kept a careful watch over him, prevented him from engaging in undue exertions and limited his responsibilities; in effect, she precluded his developing many of the ordinary physical skills and competencies that most youngsters learn in the course of growth. He was treated as if he were a treasured family heirloom, a fragile statue to be placed on the mantelpiece and never to be touched for fear he might break. Being small and unassertive by nature, he accepted the comforts of his role in a quiet and unassuming manner.

His life was uneventful and inconspicuous until he was called to serve in the army. Despite all kinds of maneuvers on the part of his mother, he was physically removed from his home and trundled off to a training camp. No more than a week elapsed, during which time he experienced considerable anguish, than his eldest sister bribed her way into the camp and spirited him to the home of a distant relative. The records of the government whose army he was to serve were so ill kept that he was able to return to his home several months thereafter with no awareness on the part of local officials that he had failed to fulfill his service obligations.

A marriage was arranged by his parents. His wife was a sturdy woman who worked as a seamstress, took care of his home and bore him four children. Mr. G. performed a variety of odds-and-ends jobs in his father's tailoring shop. His mother saw to it, however, that he did no "hard or dirty work," just helping about and "overlooking" the other employees. As a consequence, Mr. G. learned none of the skills of the tailoring trade.

Shortly before the outbreak of World War II, Mr. G. came to visit two of his sisters who previously had emigrated to the United States; when hostilities erupted in Europe he was unable to return home. All members of his family, with the exception of a young son, perished in the war.

During the ensuing years, he obtained employment at a garment factory owned by his brothers-in-law. Again he served as a helper, not as a skilled workman. Although he bore the brunt of essentially good-humored teasing by his co-workers throughout these years, he maintained a friendly and helpful attitude, pleasing them by getting sandwiches, coffee and cigarettes at their beck and call.

He married again to a hard-working, motherly type woman who provided the greater portion of the family income. Shortly thereafter, the son of his first wife emigrated to this country. Although the son was only 19 at the time, he soon found himself guiding his father's affairs, rather than the other way around.

Mr. G. was never troubled by his "failure" to mature and seemed content to have others take care of him, even though this meant occasional ridicule and humiliation. His present difficulty arose when the factory closed. Lacking the wherewithal of a skilled trade and the initiative to obtain a new position, he "decided" to stay at home, quite content to remain dependent on others.

## CLINICAL PICTURE

Let us next examine the general picture of the submissive personality using the fourfold schema applied previously.

As should be evident from the two patterns described in earlier sections, these four levels of analysis result in a coherent clinical picture. This overall congruity among levels should be expected since one of the criteria of personality traits or patterns is their pervasiveness, that is, their tendency to operate in all major spheres of psychological functioning. It should not be surprising, therefore, that each of the four levels will provide similar clinical impressions.

Despite this congruency, however, each level focuses on a different source of data; as a result, each should highlight or sensitize us to different facets of the overall clinical picture and, perhaps, provide us with information distinctive to that source. For example, it is only through phenomenological reports that we may gather the specific content of an individual's self-perceptions and thoughts.

### Behavior

The absence of self-confidence is apparent in the posture, voice and mannerisms of these persons. They tend to be overly cooperative and acquiescent and prefer to yield and placate rather than assert themselves. Large groups and noisy affairs are abhorrent to them; they go to great pains to avoid public attention by underplaying their attractiveness and achievements.

Friends often view them as generous and thoughtful but may note that they seem unduly apologetic and obsequious. Neighbors and colleagues are impressed by their humility, cordiality and graciousness and by the "softness" and gentility of their behavior.

Beneath the surface of this warmth and affability lies a plaintive and solemn quality, a searching for assurances of acceptance, approval and kindness. These latter features are more clearly manifest under conditions of stress; at these times, they exhibit overt signs of helplessness and clinging behaviors; they may actually plead and solicit encouragement. A depressive tone often colors their mood as they become solemn and mournful. Maudlin and sentimental expressions may be voiced; and they become manifestly conciliatory and self-sacrificing in their relationships.

### Phenomenological Reports

The passive-dependent individual limits his awareness of self and others to a narrow sphere, well within comfortable boundaries. He tends to constrict his world, becoming minimally introspective and Pollyanna-like with regard to the problems and difficulties which may surround him. From a phenomenological viewpoint, then, the submissive personality is naive, unperceptive and uncritical. He attempts to see only the "good" in things, the pleasant and favorable side of troubling events.

Despite this Pollyanna-like veneer, these people feel little of the joy of living; once their "hair is let down" they report feelings of pessimism, discouragement, dejection and gloom. Their "suffering," they claim, is done in silence, away from those with whom they feel they must appear content and pleased.

Their self-image, on the surface, is that of a considerate, thoughtful and cooperative person, prone to be unambitious and modest in achievement. Deeper probing, however, will evoke marked feelings of personal inadequacy and insecurity; they tend to downgrade themselves, claiming a basic lack of abilities, virtues and attractiveness. They magnify their failures and defects; in any area of comparison, they minimize their attainments, underplay their attributes, note their inferiorities and assume personal blame for problems they feel they have brought to others; much of this self-belittling has little basis in reality. Clinically, this habit of self-deprecation may be viewed as a strategy by which they elicit assurances that they are not unworthy and unloved; thus, it serves as an instrument for evoking praise and commendation. The following brief sketch illustrates these maneuvers and their consequences.

### CASE 6-9
#### Ruth S., Age 42, Married, One Child

Ruth was admitted to the psychiatric section of a general hospital in a rather depressed state. The case history showed her to be a passive-dependent personality. For years she had employed self-deprecatory comments which invariably brought forth support, affection and compliments from her husband, despite the meager quality of her household activities. In recent months, however, he began to criticize her, and commented that perhaps she really was inept and inefficient, remarks which prompted her to become depressed and suicidal.

Submissive personalities voice appreciation and gratefulness for the many kindnesses others have provided them. As a consequence, they feel they must sacrifice themselves, and are responsible and obliged to reciprocate. Despite this rationale, they will be sure to note how much a strain these obligations are and how difficult it has been for them to fulfill the expectations others have of them. Thus, on the one hand, they see themselves as incapable, incompetent and helpless; on the other, they feel a deep obligation to assume formidable responsibilities. How pitiful their plight must be, and how unworthy they are of the many kindnesses others have extended.

### Intrapsychic Processes

By claiming weakness and inferiority, the passive-dependent absolves himself of the tasks and responsibilities he knows he should assume, but would rather not. Likewise, self-deprecation evokes sympathy, attention and care from others, for which they are bound to feel guilt.

These maneuvers and conflicts cannot be tolerated consciously. To experience harmony with one's self, the dependent must deny the feelings he experiences and the "deceptive" strategies he employs. He must cover up his fundamental need to be dependent by rationalizing his inadequacies, that is, by attributing them to physical illnesses, unfortunate circumstance and the like. To prevent condemnation, he must restrain assertive impulses and deny feelings which might provoke criticism and rejection.

His social affability and good-naturedness not only forestall social deprecation but reflect a gentility toward himself, a sweet and maudlin sentimentality which protects him from being harsh with his own shortcomings. To maintain a measure of self-equilibrium, then, he must take care of himself, and not overplay expressions of guilt, shame and self-condemnation. He maintains this tenuous balance between moderate and severe self-deprecation by his Pollyanna-like tolerance and naiveté; thus, he "sweetens" his own failures with the same saccharine attitude that he uses to dilute the shortcomings of others.

### Biophysical Factors

Submissive personalities often suffer a chronic state of fatigue. Any form of exertion brings on the need to rest and recuperate; many wake up exhausted, ready to turn over for another night's sleep. Concerted effort, or work out of the ordinary routine, exhausts them. They hesitate engaging in new activities or in any task which may prove demanding or taxing. They frequently lack sexual interest, and often experience impotence. The mere thought of extending themselves beyond their usual narrow boundaries may invite anticipatory feelings of weakness, anxiety and a sense of being "weighted down."

Not infrequently these individuals lack the mesomorphic or muscular body build; they are either thin and weakly or heavy and cumbersome. Deficits in muscularity and energy potential may account in part for the ease with which they are fatigued. We might posit, along the same lines,

that their reticular formation is deficient, incapable of arousing adequate responsivity to the normal tasks of life. Similarly, there may be a dysfunction within the autonomic system such that they experience the physiological reaction of anxiety, but are not energized adequately to effect vigorous coping responses.

The basically anxious and somber quality of their mood suggests an intrinsic melancholic temperament; also plausible is what we have termed a basic threctic temperament. Thus, the submissive person may be constitutionally disposed to feel both sadness and fear more readily than normals.

## ETIOLOGY AND DEVELOPMENT

We shall label the central traits of the passive-dependent personality as follows: *gentle affectivity* (having kind, soft and humanitarian impulses), *cognitive denial* (showing a Pollyanna-like refusal to admit discomforting thoughts), *inadequacy self-image* (viewing self as inferior, fragile and unworthy) and *interpersonal compliance* (willing to submit and oblige others). Let us next turn to hypotheses that refer to the development background of these traits.

### Biogenic Factors

Before listing biophysical influences which ostensibly shape the passive-dependent pattern, let us be reminded of three points. First, most of these hypotheses are conjectural. Second, a contributory role on the part of constitutional determinants in no way denies the thesis that comparable effects can be produced by learning experiences. Thirdly, in all cases, biogenic and psychogenic factors interact; we separate them here only for pedagogic purposes.

**Heredity.** The thesis that dispositions to behavior may in part be rooted in genetic factors is no less plausible in the passive-dependent pattern than in any other; convincing empirical evidence is lacking, however. Similarities among members of a family group suggest the operation of hereditary determinants, but these findings may reflect environmental influences as well.

Despite the paucity of concrete data, and the unquestioned influence of learning, "common sense" tells us that an individual's inherited biological machinery may incline him to perceive and react to experiences in such ways as to result in his learning a passive and dependent style of behavior. Passive-dependency *per se* is never inherited, of course, but certain types of genetic endowments have high probabilities of evolving, under "normal" life experiences, into submissive personality patterns.

**Melancholic or Threctic Infantile Reaction Patterns.** If the assumption is correct that one's constitutional make-up is moderately consistent throughout life, it would seem reasonable to conclude that many adult submissives would have displayed a tendency to moroseness and fearfulness in infancy and early childhood. A soft, gentle and somewhat sad or solemn quality may have characterized their early moods. Similarly, they may have shown a reticence, a hesitance to assert themselves, a restraint in new situations and a fear of venturing forth to test their growing capacities.

Early biophysical dispositions elicit distinctive reactions from parents. A gentle but sad and fearful infant is likely to evoke warmth and overprotectiveness from a concerned mother. Such children invite excessive care and compassion from others, which in turn may result in their learning to be overly dependent and comfortable with their caretakers. Rather than overcoming their initial dispositions, the reactions they draw from others may lead them to be even less assertive and venturesome than they otherwise would have been.

**Ectomorphic or Endomorphic Body Build.** Competencies for independent behavior and initiative depend in large measure upon physical stamina, strength and agility. Deficits in muscularity and vigor may result in a delayed achievement of these competencies, and a consequent tendency to depend on others to assume normal tasks and responsibilities. Heavy and cumbersome youngsters (endomorphic), or youngsters who are frail and easily fatigued (ectomorphic), are less capable and, therefore, less disposed to assert themselves or to experience success in independent actions than physically more well-endowed youngsters.

**Neurological Imbalances Between Reticular and Limbic Systems.** A somewhat intricate pattern of neural organization may be hypothesized to account for the disposition to develop a submissive personality. Conceivably, reticular arousal mechanisms may be sluggish and inactive in these individuals, giving rise to deficit coping reactions under conditions of stress. At the same time, they may be overly endowed in those regions of the limbic system associated with the experience of fear, pain and sadness.

Given these two neural characteristics, such persons may experience considerable stress even with minor discomforts, and learn to turn to others for assistance. Their "limbic" attributes cause them to feel difficulties intensely; their "reticular" attributes prevent them from mustering the reactive powers to cope with these difficulties. If such a person is fortunate in having thoughtful and protective caretakers, he quickly will learn to depend on them to execute the defensive actions he cannot manage on his own. The reinforcement he receives by turning to others to cope with stress "binds" him to them and to the protection they provide. He may drift increasingly, as a consequence, toward greater and greater dependency attachments.

**Adrenal Dysfunctions.** The speculative thesis proposed regarding the effects of neurological imbalances may be applied equally well to physiochemical impairments or variations. It may be conjectured, for example, that adrenal reactivity to stress is more than sufficient for short periods, but is rapidly depleted before adequate restitutive mechanisms can be mustered. Thus, the individual will experience intense emotional turmoil, but lack sustained adrenal reactions necessary for effective coping responses. Experiencing threat, but unable to "follow through" effectively, the individual learns to lean on others either to protect him from distress or to resolve it for him when it occurs.

*Psychogenic Factors*

It would not be difficult to enumerate a score of influences which might contribute to the development of the passive-dependent pattern. We have chosen the determinants to be described below because they arise often in the history of these individuals, and appear to have carried weight in initiating, as well as in shaping, their personality style. Each of these factors contributed, first, to the development of excessive attachment learning and, second, to the avoidance of independent behaviors.

**Parental Attachment and Overprotection.** Every infant is helpless and entirely dependent upon his caretakers for protection and nurturance. During the first few months of life, the child acquires a vague notion of which objects surrounding him are associated with increments in comfort and gratification; he becomes "attached" to these objects since they provide him with positive reinforcements. All of this is natural. Difficulties arise, however, if the attachments the child learns are too narrowly restricted, or so deeply rooted as to deter the growth of competencies by which he can obtain reinforcements on his own. Let us follow the course of these pathological attachments through the three stages of neuropsychological development.

1. The first stage of neuropsychological development, referred to as sensory-attachment, serves as a foundation for future growth. Supplied with adequate amounts of beneficent stimulation, the child is likely to develop both interpersonal sensitivity and trust.

What may go wrong that leads to a pathological passive-dependent pattern?

It seems plausible that infants who receive an adequate amount of reinforcing stimulation, but obtain that stimulation almost exclusively from one source, usually the mother, will be disposed to develop passive-dependent traits. They experience neither stimulus impoverishment nor enrichment, but are provided with stimuli from an unusually narrow sphere of objects. As a consequence of this lack of variety, the infant will form a singular attachment, a fixation if you will, upon one object source to the exclusion of others.

Any number of factors may give rise to this exclusive attachment. Unusual illnesses or prolonged physical complications in the child's health may prompt a normal mother to tend to her infant more frequently than is common at this age. On the other hand, an excessively worrisome and anxious mother may be over-alert to real and fantasied needs she sees in her normal child, resulting in undue attention, cuddling and so on. Occasionally, special circumstances surrounding family life may throw the infant and mother together into a "symbiotic" dependency. The following case, not uncommon during wartime, illustrates the consequences of events such as these.

CASE 6-10
Paul R., Age 7

Paul was born while his father served overseas in the armed forces. Until the age of three he lived in an apartment alone with his mother. With the exception of his mother's parents, both of whom worked, he had little opportunity to relate to anyone other than his mother. Supported by a government allotment, and her parent's gifts, Paul's mother had little to do but devote her attention to, and heap her affections upon him. Two evenings a week, and on Sundays, Paul went with his mother to visit his grandparents. Except for brief and infrequent excursions to a zoo or a park, his contact with people was limited to mother and grandparents.

When Paul's father returned from service he was met by a frightened and withdrawn son. No matter what his father attempted, Paul would turn away, cry and run to his mother. It took several months of good will and considerable patience to get Paul to stay alone with his father;

however, the moment mother came upon the scene, Paul fled to her.

Entrance to kindergarten was traumatic. Paul simulated a variety of ailments each morning. He would develop headaches, vomit or simply cry so intensely that his mother often decided to let him remain at home. After several weeks of this behavior, which often continued in school on those days when he did attend, his mother insisted that he be allowed to remain home for the semester.

The advent of a second child, when Paul was six and ready to enter first grade, further aggravated his attachment and dependency behavior. He could hardly be contained when his mother went to the hospital; only the comforting of his grandparents could assuage his anxiety. Upon his mother's return, Paul began to wet his bed; he had been fully toilet trained two years earlier. His school phobia began again. This time his father insisted that Paul attend despite the morning battles and the teacher's distress over his sulking and weepy behavior in class. The persistence of his resistance to school led to a recommendation for psychological study and treatment.

2. An infant who retains his exclusive attachment to the mother during the second neuropsychological stage, that known as sensorimotor autonomy, will have his earlier training in dependency behaviors strengthened and perpetuated. However, there are many youngsters who were not especially attached to their mothers in the first stage who also develop the passive-dependent pattern; experiences conducive to the acquisition of dependency behaviors can arise independently of an initial phase of exclusive maternal attachment.

The sensorimotor-autonomy stage is distinguished by opportunities to learn skills essential to the emergence of competence and independent behaviors. Circumstances which deter the development of these competencies can foster passive dependency. What conditions, distinctive to this period, result in the learning of these behaviors?

Not uncommon among these is the child's own deficit talents and temperamental disposition, such as his physical inadequacies, his fearfulness of new challenges, his anguish when left to himself and so on. Some children, by virtue of constitutional temperament or earlier learning, elicit protective behaviors from others; their parents may have unwillingly acceded to overprotective habits because the child "forced" them to do so. Similarly, children who have suffered prolonged periods of illness may be prevented from exercising their maturing capacities either because of realistic physical limitations or as a result of the actions of justifiably concerned parents.

Barring the operation of constitutional dispositions and physical deficits, the average youngster in this stage will assert his growing capacities, and strive to do more and more things for himself. This normal progression toward self-competence and environmental mastery may be interfered with by excessive parental anxieties or other harmful behaviors; for example, some parents may discourage their child's independence for fear of losing "their baby"; they place innumerable barriers and diverting attractions to keep him from gaining greater autonomy. These parents limit the child's ventures outside the home, express anxiety lest he strain or hurt himself, make no demands for self-responsibility and provide him with every comfort and reward so long as he listens to mother. Rather than let him stumble and fumble with his new skills, his parents do things for him, make things easier, carry him well beyond the walking stage, spoon feed him until he is three, tie his shoelaces until he is ten and so on. Time and time again he will be discouraged from his impulse to "go it alone."

Ultimately, because of the ease with which he can obtain gratifications simply by leaning on his parents, he will forego his feeble efforts at independence; he never learns the wherewithal to act on his own to secure the rewards of life; he need not acquire any self-activated instrumental behaviors to obtain reinforcements; all he need do is sit back passively, and "leave it to mother."

3. Parental pampering and overprotection, continued into the third neuropsychological stage, often have a devastating effect upon the child's growing self-image.

First, he may fail to develop a distinct picture of himself apart from his caretaker. His excessive dependence upon others for the execution of everyday tasks of life has denied him the opportunity to do things for himself, to form an impression of what *he* is good at and who *he* is. Failing to break his symbiotic dependency upon his mother deprives him of experiences by which he can discover attributes that distinguish him as a person.

Second, it is implicit in parental overprotection that the child cannot take care of himself. The pampered child is apt to view himself as his parents do, as a person who needs special care and supervision because he is incompetent, prone to illness, oversensitive and so on; his self-image mirrors this parental image of weakness and inferiority.

Third, when he is forced to venture into the outside world, he finds that his sense of inferiority is confirmed, that he objectively is less competent and mature than others of his age. Unsure of his identity and viewing himself to be weak and inadequate, he has little recourse but to perpetuate his early pattern by turning to others again to arrange his life and to provide for him. The case of Harry G. illustrates these points well.

**Competitive Deficits among Siblings and Peers.** Let us briefly elaborate some nonparental factors alluded to in the last paragraph which may dispose the child to the passive-dependent pattern. The major theme to be noted here concerns events or relationships that lead the individual either to believe that he cannot compete with others or to learn that a submissive rather than an assertive role will assure less discomfort and greater reward for him.

A family situation in which the youngster is exposed to a more aggressive, competent or troublesome sibling may set the stage for learning a submissive personality style. For example, the presence of a more assertive and competent sibling may result in unfavorable self-comparisons; similarly, a hostile and difficult to manage sibling may invite a child to adopt the "good boy" image, one who, in contrast to his sibling, listens to mother, and acquiesces to her every mood and wish so as to gain comparative favor; in a third family, a child who repeatedly experiences the lashing out of an angry and jealous sibling may run so often for parental cover that he learns to cling to them rather than confront the world on his own. Should the sibling display all of these troubling features—greater competence, unmanageability and a hostile acting out of jealousy—the likelihood is rather high that the child will develop both the sweet submissive strategy and the dependent inadequacy role.

Similar difficulties conducive to passive dependency may be generated in experiences with one's peer group. Feelings of unattractiveness and competitive inadequacy, especially during adolescence, may result in social humiliation and self-doubt. These youngsters, however, are more fortunate than the active-detached adolescent since they usually can retreat to their home where they will find both love and acceptance; in contrast, the active-detached youngster receives little solace or support from his family. Although the immediate rewards of affection and refuge at home are not to be demeaned, they may, in the long run, prove a disservice to the child since ultimately he must learn to stand on his own.

**Adoption of Social Roles.** Brief note should be made of the fact that more women than men develop the passive-dependent pattern. Some theorists attribute this fact to an inherent submissive disposition on the part of the female sex. Equally plausible is the thesis that the cultural roles that are sanctioned in most societies reinforce the learning of passive-dependent behaviors among women.

## COPING STRATEGIES

It may appear strange and paradoxical that the genuine affection and acceptance experienced in childhood by the passive-dependent should dispose him to pathology. Childhood, for most of these individuals, was a time of warmth and security, a period marked by few anxieties and discomforts that were not quickly relieved by parental attention and care. Certainly, the early life of the passive-dependent was idyllic when contrasted to the indifference and humiliation to which the active-detached child was exposed.

But too much of a "good" thing can turn bad. Excessive parental shielding and attachment may establish habits and expectancies which prove detrimental in the long run since they ill prepare the child to cope on his own with the strains and discouragements of later life.

Accustomed to support from others and ill-equipped to obtain rewards without them, the passive-dependent stands implanted, rooted to the deep attachments of his childhood. Unable to free himself from his dependence, he is faced with the constant danger of loss, a dread of desertion and the abyss into which he will be cast if left to himself. Beneath his pleasant and affable exterior, then, lies an extreme vulnerability to rejection, a sense of helplessness and a fear of abandonment. His pathetic lack of resources and his marked self-doubts compel him to seek a safe partner, a trustworthy figure "like his mother" who can be depended on to assure him that he is loved and accepted and will not be deserted.

What instrumental behaviors does the passive-dependent use to maneuver his environment, and how does he arrange and control his feelings and thoughts so as to assure comfort and the achievement of his aims?

**Compliant Interpersonal Behavior.** The passive-dependent individual not only finds little reinforcement within himself but feels that he is inept and stumbling, and thus lacking in the skills necessary to secure reinforcements elsewhere. Only other persons possess the requisite intelligence, talents and experience to attain the rewards of life. Given these learned attitudes, he feels that it is best to abdicate self-responsibility, to leave matters to others and to place his fate in their hands; they are so much better equipped to shoulder responsibilities, to navigate the intricacies of a complex world and to discover and achieve the few pleasures to be found in the tough competitions of life.

To accomplish this goal of dependency, he learns to attach himself to others, to submerge his individuality, to deny points of difference, to avoid expressions of power and independence and to ask for little other than acceptance and support —in other words, to assume an attitude of helplessness, submission and compliance. By acting weak, expressing fear and self-doubt, communicating a need for assurance and direction and displaying a willingness to trust, comply and submit, he may elicit the nurture and protection he seeks.

To secure his "hold" on another, the passive-dependent must be more than meek and docile; he must be admiring and loving, willing to give his "all" for another. Only then can he be assured of consistent care and affection. Fortunately, passive-dependents have been exposed in childhood to parental models of gentility and thoughtfulness; thus, through imitation, they have learned well how to behave affectionately and admiringly. They possess a genuine capacity to reciprocate respect, tenderness and consideration, essential elements in holding their protector. They also have learned well the "inferior" role; thus, they are able to provide their "superior" partner with the rewards of feeling useful, sympathetic, stronger and more competent, precisely those behaviors which the passive-dependent is seeking in his mate. From many viewpoints, then, the submissive personality has learned instrumental interpersonal strategies which succeed in achieving the reinforcements he needs.

**Intrapsychic Mechanisms of Identification and Denial.** The incompetence and inadequacy which the passive-dependent sees within himself provoke feelings of emptiness and anxiety, and to this strain is added the dread of desertion, the fear of being set adrift alone. These terrifying thoughts are countered often by the intrapsychic mechanism of identification, an unconscious process by which he attaches himself to another and imagines himself to be close to, or an integral part of, a more powerful figure. By submerging or allying himself with the competencies and virtues of his partner, he avoids anxieties evoked by thoughts of his own impotence. Not only is he bolstered by the illusion of shared competence but through identification he finds solace in the belief that the bond he has constructed is firm and inseparable: he cannot be deserted.

The pervasive use of denial mechanisms also characterizes the passive-dependent. This is manifested most clearly in the Polyanna-like quality of his perceptions and thoughts. He is ever-alert to "soften" the edges of strain and discomfort. A syrupy sweetness typifies his speech; he persistently sees the "good" side of things and covers up or smooths over troublesome thoughts and events. Especially threatening to him are his own hostile or assertive impulses; any inner feeling or thought that might endanger security is quickly staved off. A verbal torrent of contrition and self-debasement may be vented to expiate transgressions.

## SELF-PERPETUATION OF PATTERN

Despite his claim to ineptness, the submissive personality employs a strategy that recruits the nurture and support he needs, and forestalls his sinking into a deeper level of psychopathology.

In the process of soliciting attention and affection from others the passive-dependent keeps close touch with the "real" world, in contrast to the detached personality who, in his isolation, becomes increasingly lost in internal fantasies; thus, by virtue of seeking to fulfill his dependency needs the submissive person is exposed constantly to social reactions that block him from straying too far into the abyss of subjective distortions.

This protection against the decompensating effects of self-preoccupation and distortion does not prevent some degree of deterioration. There remains the problem that strategies persist long beyond their initial usefulness, and lead the person into self-defeating vicious circles.

Let us next turn to some of the features of the passive-dependent coping style which result in the perpetuation and aggravation of the individual's original misfortunes.

**Self-Deprecation.** Not only does the submissive person observe real deficits in his competence but he deprecates what virtues and talents he may possess so as to prevent others from expecting him to assume responsibilities he would rather avoid. Successful as this maneuver may be as a shield against discomfort and in the service of fulfilling his dependency needs, it is achieved at the cost of a constant demeaning of self-respect and esteem.

Rationalizations of frailty and weakness, offered for the benefit of others, have an impact on the person himself. Each time the passive-dependent announces his defects, he convinces himself as well and deepens his self-image of personal incompetence. Trapped by his own persuasiveness, he feels increasingly the futility of

standing on his own, and tries less and less to overcome his sense of inadequacy. As a consequence of his strategy, then, he fosters a vicious circle of increased helplessness and dependency.

**Avoidance of Competence Activities.** The passive-dependent's sense of inadequacy, fear of failure and hesitations about threatening or antagonizing others, cause him to refrain from many activities which may potentially be constructive. For example, despite ample opportunities to learn a skill and to assume a more "manly" role in his adult family life, Harry G. shied away from these "threats," fearing that he could never succeed, and preferring to remain an inept, though good-natured, "little fellow." These self-imposed restrictions serve, of course, to diminish the probability of anxiety, but they also diminish the probability that the person will learn skills which would enable him to function more effectively. By making himself inaccessible to opportunities for acquiring self-competencies, the submissive personality precludes his own personal growth and becomes increasingly dependent on others.

**Plaintive Social Behavior.** Although the passive-dependent goes out of his way to appease others and to be apologetic for his dependency, his need for nurture, for signs of affection and for assurance that he will not be abandoned, may be so persistent as to exasperate and eventually alienate those upon whom he leans most heavily; these reactions only increase his need for attachment and assurance. As this vicious circle persists, he may become more desperate, more self-ingratiating and more urgently pleading and clinging, until he becomes the proverbial "millstone around his partner's neck." Wearying of demands to prove his fealty of love, the stronger partner may openly express annoyance, disapproval and, finally, rejection.

Once rebuffed seriously by his dependency source, the individual's cycle of decompensation may take on an increased pace. Self-blame, self-criticism and self-condemnation come to the fore. Fearful of expressing hostility toward his partner, lest this result in further loss and rejection, he turns inward, first to reproach himself for his shortcomings and second, to promise to be "different," and to redeem himself for his past mistakes. The "new leaf" he plans to "turn over" takes the form of promises of greater competence and independence—aspirations which run diametrically opposite to his basic personality pattern. Needless to say, these goals rarely are achieved, and it is at this point that we often see the emergence of a serious symptom disorder, or the decompensation into a "cycloid" pattern of functioning.

## REMEDIAL APPROACHES

The prognosis of the passive-dependent pattern is good, for several reasons. *First,* he has had a warm and supporting relationship with at least one of his parents; this has provided him with a reservoir of security and of feelings of being loved and wanted, which may sustain him through many difficult periods. *Second,* his affectionate parent served as a model for imitative learning, equipping him with habits and attitudes for relating with affection and generosity to others. *Third,* his dependency needs assure sufficient interpersonal contact, thereby forestalling the decompensating effects of self-preoccupation and subjective distortion.

Passive-dependents not only are receptive to therapy but are disposed to seek assistance wherever they can find it. The strength and authority of the therapist comforts them, gives them the assurance that an all-powerful and all-knowing person will come to their rescue and harbor them with the kindness and helpfulness they crave; the task of unburdening their woes to a therapist calls for little effort on their part. They may lack true insight into the roots of their difficulties, but they willingly produce evidence to guide the therapist in uncovering them. Furthermore, passive-dependents are disposed to be trustful of the therapist, investing him often with great powers and the highest of virtues.

Unfortunately, the patient's receptiveness and the auspicious beginning of therapy create a misleading impression that future progress will be rapid. The patient desires a dependency relationship with his therapist; despite "promises" to the contrary, the dependent person will resist efforts to assume independence and autonomy. Guiding him to forego his dependency habits proves a slow and arduous process. Building an image of self-competence and self-esteem proceeds one step at a time through a program of strengthening his objective attributes and freeing him from the habit of leaning on others.

Environmental management procedures may be employed to maximize growth and to minimize situations which foster continued dependency. Biophysical treatment, notably certain stimulants, may prove useful toward the end of promoting increased alertness and vigor, since passive-dependents often are plagued by undue fatigue and lethargy, a state that inclines them to postpone efforts at independence. The relationship between therapist and patient must not reestablish the dominance-submission pattern that has characterized the history of these patients. Phenomenological nondirective approaches are more likely to foster the growth of autonomy and self-confidence than more directive reorientation methods. It may be necessary, however, to utilize the intrapsychic approach in order to rework certain deep attachments and to construct a base for competency strivings. Group therapeutic techniques can often be pursued fruitfully as a means of learning autonomous social skills and to assist in the growth of social confidence.

## THE GREGARIOUS PERSONALITY: ACTIVE-DEPENDENT PATTERN
(DSM-II: *Hysterical Personality*)

Dependent personalities experience few positive reinforcements from themselves, and look to others to protect them and provide the rewards of life. Beneath their good-natured affability lies an intense need for attention and affection; they require constant affirmation of approval and acceptance, are exceedingly vulnerable to withdrawal from those upon whom they depend and experience a sense of helplessness, even paralysis, when left alone.

Every dependent personality is different from every other, but two basic groups may usefully be distinguished—the passive and the active. In the previous section we described the passive or submissive type, he who not only experiences his rewards through others but who depends on them to take the initiative in bestowing these rewards. This passivity in securing attention and affection contrasts markedly with the gregarious or active-dependent pattern. Gregarious personalities are no less dependent upon others for reinforcements, but they do not surrender the initiative for achieving these reinforcements. Rather than placing the fate of their needs in the hands of others, and thereby having their security in constant jeopardy, they actively manipulate others through a series of interpersonal maneuvers so as to assure receipt of the stimulation and esteem they need. In this quest they develop an exquisite sensitivity to the moods and thoughts that others experience; this hyperalertness enables them to appraise what reactions and ploys will succeed in attaining the ends they desire. Their extreme "other-directedness," devised in the service of achieving approval, results, however, in a life style characterized by fluidity, an unpredictable and shifting pattern of behaviors and emotions. Unlike the passive-dependent, who anchors himself often to one object of attachment, the active-dependent tends to be capricious and lacks fidelity and loyalty, that is, turns repeatedly from one source of affection and approval to another. The dissatisfaction he experiences with single attachments, combined with his constant need for stimulation and attention, often results in the development of a seductive pattern of personal relationships, and a flair for the dramatic and histrionic.

Fortunately, this well-known syndrome, entirely missing in the official 1952 nosology, has been wisely reinstated in the DSM-II, though under the rather archaic label of *hysterical personality.* (A more modern and appropriate appellation, that of "histrionic personality disorder," is recommended as an alternative designation for this syndrome.) The following excerpt is quoted from the 1968 manual:

These behavior patterns are characterized by excitability, emotional instability, over-reactivity, and self-dramatization. This self-dramatization is always attention-seeking and often seductive, whether or not the patient is aware of its purpose. These personalities are also immature, self-centered, often vain and usually dependent on others.

In the case presented below we can trace some of the features of this pathological pattern in an otherwise successful career woman.

### CASE 6-11
### Suzanne D., Age 34, Twice Divorced, Married, One Child

Suzanne, an attractive and vivacious woman, sought therapy in the hope that she might prevent the disintegration of her third marriage. The problem she faced was a recurrent one, her tendency to become "bored" with her husband and increasingly interested in going out with other men. She was on the brink of "another affair" and decided that before "giving way to her impulses again" she had "better stop and take a good look" at herself. The following history unfolded over a series of therapeutic interviews.

Suzanne was four years older than her sister, her only sibling. Her father was a successful and wealthy business executive for whom children were "display pieces," nice chattels to show off to his friends and to round out his "family life," but "not to be troubled with." Her mother was an emotional but charming woman who took great pains to make her children "beautiful and talented." The girls vied for their parents' approval. Although Suzanne was the more successful, she constantly had to "live up" to her parents' expectations in order to secure their commendation and esteem.

Suzanne was quite popular during her adolescent years, had lots of dates and boyfriends and was never short of attention and affection from the opposite sex. She sang with the high school

band and was an artist on the school newspaper, a cheerleader and so on.

Rather than going to college, Suzanne attended art school where she met and married a fellow student—a "handsome, wealthy ne'er-do-well." Both she and her husband began "sleeping around" by the end of the first year, and she "wasn't certain" that her husband was the father of her daughter. A divorce took place several months after the birth of this child.

Soon thereafter she met and married a man in his forties who gave both Suzanne and her daughter a "comfortable home, and scads of attention and love." It was a "good life" for the four years that the marriage lasted. Her husband was wealthy and had interesting friends. Suzanne attended a dramatic school, took ballet lessons, began to do free-lance artwork and, in general, basked in the pleasure of being the "center of attention" wherever she went. In the third year of this marriage she became attracted to a young man, a fellow dancing student. The affair was brief, but was followed by a quick succession of several others. Her husband learned of her exploits, but accepted her regrets and assurances that they would not continue. They did continue, and the marriage was terminated after a stormy court settlement.

Suzanne "knocked about" on her own for the next two years until she met her present husband, a talented writer who "knew the scoop" about her past. He "holds no strings" around her; she is free to do as she wishes. Surprisingly, at least to Suzanne, she had no inclination to venture afield for the next three years. She enjoyed the titillation of "playing games" with other men, but she remained loyal to her husband, even though he was away on reportorial assignments for periods of one or two months. The last trip, however, brought forth the "old urge" to start an affair; it was at this point that she sought therapy.

Suzanne felt that she had attained what she wanted in life and did not want to spoil it. Her husband was a strong, mature man who "knew how to keep her in check." She herself had an interesting position as an art director in an advertising agency, and her daughter seemed finally to have "settled down" after a difficult early period. Suzanne feared that she would not be able to control her tendency to "get involved" and turned to therapy for assistance.

## CLINICAL PICTURE

The case of Suzanne demonstrates, in mild pathological form, what our society tends to foster and admire in its members—to be well liked, successful, popular, extraverted, attractive and sociable. Unless one examines her life more closely, Suzanne would appear to epitomize the ideal of the American woman; she is intelligent, outgoing, charming and sophisticated, liberated from the traditions of the past, married to an interesting and able husband and pursuing a career commensurate with her talents. But beneath this surface veneer we see a driving quality, a consuming need for approval and a desperate striving to be conspicuous, to evoke affection and attract attention at all costs. Despite the frequent rewards these behaviors produce, the needs they stem from are pathologically inflexible, repetitious and persistent.

Moving from this general description, let us next detail the active-dependent picture in line with the four levels of clinical observation and analysis.

### Behavior

Gregarious personalities impress one, at first, by the ease with which they express their thoughts and feelings, by their flair for the dramatic and by their seemingly natural capacity to draw attention to themselves. This exhibitionistic and histrionic feature is manifested, however, in a series of rapidly changing, short-lived and superficial affects. These persons are highly labile and capricious, easily excited and intolerant of frustration, delay and disappointment; the words and feelings they express appear shallow, fraudulent and simulated, rather than deep or real.

The active-dependent is more than merely friendly and helpful in his interpersonal relationships; he is actively solicitous of praise, "markets" his appeal to others and is entertaining and often sexually provocative. Since affection and attention are his primary goals, he engages in a wide variety of maneuvers to elicit favorable responses. Women typically are charming or coquettish; men are generous in praise and, on occasion, overtly seductive and lascivious.

Both men and women display an interesting mixture of being carefree and sophisticated, on the one hand, and inhibited and naive, on the other. In the sphere of sexuality, for example, they are quite at ease while "playing the game," but become rather immature and apprehensive once matters get serious.

Characteristically, they are unable to follow through or sustain the initial impression of good will and sophistication they convey. Their social life is one in which they have "many acquaintances but few friends." Thus, in most areas of social activity they put up a good show at the start, but falter and withdraw when depth and durability in a relationship is required.

### Phenomenological Reports

Looking inward, gregarious personalities view themselves as sociable, friendly and agreeable people. They lack self-insight, however, failing often to recognize, or admit recognizing, any signs of inner turmoil, weakness, depression or hostility.

Their preoccupation with external rewards and approvals has left them bereft of an identity apart from others. They describe themselves not in terms of their own intrinsic traits, but in terms of their social relationships and their effects upon others. They behave like "empty-organisms" which react more to external stimuli than to promptings from within.

Active-dependents evidence an extraordinarily acute sensitivity to the thoughts and moods of those from whom they desire approval and affection. This well-developed "radar" system serves them in good stead for it not only alerts them to signs of impending rejection but enables them to manipulate the object of their designs with consummate skill.

This exteroceptive orientation, however, leads to a fleeting, impressionistic and scattered attention to details, and accounts in part, for their characteristic distractible, flighty and erratic behaviors. Their susceptibility to transient events parallels their superficial cognitive style, their lack of genuine curiosity and their inability to think in a concentrated and logical fashion. Habits of superficiality and dilettentism also represent their intellectual evasiveness and their desire to eschew knowledge about troublesome thoughts or emotionally charged feelings. Thus, until her recent marriage, Suzanne D. rarely digested anything she had learned, and simply "picked up and left" whenever she was "bothered or bored." Part of the flightiness of the gregarious personality derives, therefore, from an avoidance of potentially disruptive ideas and urges, especially those which might bring to awareness their deeply hidden dependency needs. For these and other reasons they keep running, and "steer clear" of too much self-knowledge and too much depth in personal relationships. In effect, they dissociate themselves from inner thoughts and from people and activities that might upset their strategy of facile superficiality.

### Intrapsychic Processes

As noted above, the active-dependent seeks to avoid introspection and responsible thinking. Not only is he habitually attuned to external rather than internal events but his lifelong exteroceptive orientation has prevented him from learning to deal with inner thoughts and feelings. As a consequence, he is deficient in intrapsychic skills and must resort to gross mechanisms to handle his unconscious emotions; he simply seals off, represses and dissociates entire segments of memory and feeling which may prompt discomfort. In effect, his past is a blank, devoid of many resources he should have acquired through experience.

Deprived of past learnings, he is less able to function on his own, and thereby tends to perpetuate his dependency on others. Furthermore, to compensate for the void of the past, and the guidance these learnings could provide, he remains bound forever to the present. In this he again perpetuates his superficiality and emotional shallowness, his habitual preoccupation with external immediacies rather than with the more durable events of inner life.

### Biophysical Factors

The biophysical attributes of the active-dependent personality are difficult to infer. Conceived in biological terms, their behavior suggests both a high level of energy and activation and a low threshold for autonomic reactivity. They tend, in general, to be quick and responsive, especially with regard to the expression of emotions. Feelings of both a positive and negative variety gush forth with extreme ease, suggesting either an unusually high degree of sensory irritability, excessive sympathetic activity or a lack of cortical inhibition. No single temperament label appears sufficient to capture the intense, erratic and wide range of emotions to which they are disposed.

## ETIOLOGY AND DEVELOPMENT

Using the format of characteristics which has served to summarize the principal features of previous personality patterns, the following distinguishing attributes may be noted in the active-dependent pattern: *labile affectivity* (uncontrolled and dramatic expression of emotions), *cognitive dissociation* (failure to integrate learnings; massive repression of memories), *sociable self-image* (perception of self as attractive, charming and affectionate) and *interpersonal seductiveness* (a need to flirt and seek attention). Next we turn to the question of how these attributes came to pass.

### Biogenic Factors

The role of constitutional dispositions in this, as in most other patterns, is highly speculative. The following hypotheses have the merit of plausibility.

**Heredity.** The role of heredity cannot be overlooked in searching for the biological origins

of the active-dependent pattern. The neural and chemical substrate for tendencies such as sensory alertness and autonomic or emotional reactivity may logically be traced to genetic influences. Evidence demonstrating a high degree of family correspondence in these traits are suggestive of physiological commonalities, of course, but can be explained also as a function of experience and learning. The need for research is obvious, not only in establishing factually the presence of family correspondence but in tracing the manner in which such alleged genetic factors unfold and take shape as psychological traits.

**Hyperresponsive Infantile Reaction Patterns.** It would seem reasonable to expect that gregarious adults would have displayed a high degree of alertness and emotional responsiveness in infancy and early childhood. This inference derives from the assumption not only that constitutional traits are essentially stable throughout life but that an active and responsive child will tend to foster and intensify his initial responsiveness by evoking varied and stimulating reactions from others.

**Neurological Characteristics.** Among the possible sites which may be posited for the high emotional responsivity of the active-dependent are the limbic and reticular systems. A neurally dense or abundantly branched limbic region may account for the intensity and ease with which emotions are expressed. A low threshold for reticular activation, stemming from any number of idiosyncratic features of that region, may underlie part of the excitability and diffusive reactivity typical of the gregarious personality.

**Physiochemical Characteristics.** Ease of sympathetic arousal and adrenal reactivity may be rooted in the individual's constitutional make-up; this can result in the heightened and labile emotions seen among active-dependents. Similarly, neurochemical imbalances may facilitate a rapid transmission of impulses across synaptic junctions, resulting in the tendency of these patients to be distractible and excitable.

The biogenic hypotheses noted above must be viewed as highly conjectural. Even if evidence can be adduced in support of these notions, the question will remain as to why some persons who possess these constitutional characteristics become active-dependents whereas others develop different pathological patterns, and most remain essentially normal.

### Psychogenic Factors

Biogenic influences appear less relevant in the development of the active-dependent pattern than in the personality types previously described. It is logical, then, to focus our attention on psychological experience and learning as the primary etiological variables.

**Stimulus Enrichment and Diversity in the Sensory-Attachment Stage.** Constitutionally alert and responsive infants will experience greater and more diverse stimulation in the first months of life than dull and phlegmatic infants. As a consequence of these early stimulus gratifications, their tendency is reinforced to look "outward" to the external world for rewards rather than "inward" into themselves. In a similar manner, normally alert infants may develop this exteroceptive attitude if their caretakers, by virtue of sensory indulgence and playfulness, expose them to excessive stimulation during the sensory-attachment stage.

Both passive and active-dependents exhibit a focus upon external rather than internal sources of reinforcement. But there is a basic difference between them, one that may be traced in part to differences in the diversity, intensity and consistency in early sensory attachment learning.

Passive-dependents appear to have received their enriched stimulation from a single, perhaps exclusive, source which provided a consistent level of gratification. In contrast, active-dependents appear to have been exposed to a number of different sources that provided brief, highly charged and irregular stimulus reinforcements. For example, the active-dependent may have had many different caretakers in infancy (parents, siblings, grandparents and foster parents) who supplied him with intense, short-lived stimulus gratifications that came at irregular or haphazard intervals. Such experiences may not only have built a high level of sensory capacity, which requires constant "feeding" to be sustained, but may also have conditioned him to expect stimulus reinforcements in short concentrated spurts from a mélange of different sources. (We may note parenthetically that irregular schedules of reinforcement establish deeply ingrained habits that are highly resistant to extinction.) Thus, the persistent yet erratic dependency behaviors of the gregarious personality may reflect a pathological form of intense stimulus seeking traceable to highly charged, varied and irregular stimulus reinforcements associated with early attachment learning.

The shifting from one source of gratification to another so characteristic of the active-dependent, his search for new stimulus adventures, his penchant for creating excitement and his inability to tolerate boredom and routine, all may represent the consequences of these unusual early experiences.

**Parental Control by Contingent and Irregular Reward.** In addition to differences in the variety, regularity and intensity of stimulus enrichments in the sensory-attachment stage, the experiences of the active-dependent child may be distinguished from those of the passive-dependent both during and after the sensorimotor-autonomy stage.

Passive-dependent children continue to receive attention and affection from their caretakers *regardless* of their behavior; it is *not* necessary for them "to perform" in order to elicit parental nurturance and protection. As a consequence of sitting idly by and passively waiting for their parents to tend to their needs, they fail to develop adequate competencies and autonomy.

The active-dependent child, in contrast, appears to learn that he must engage in certain sanctioned behaviors, and must satisfy certain parental desires and expectations in order to receive attention and affection. Thus, Suzanne D. knew that parental approval was contingent on her "looking pretty," or "showing them my latest artistic masterpiece" or the "fancy ballet steps" she had just learned in dancing school. In her quest for attention, she gradually acquired the set of strategies we have described as active-dependent.

What are the conditions of learning which shape these strategies into the active-dependent form?

They seem to be characterized by the following three features: minimal negative reinforcement, e.g., Suzanne's parents rarely criticized or punished her; positive reinforcement contingent upon performance of parentally approved behaviors, e.g., favorable comments were conveyed to Suzanne only if she "was pretty" or "performed"; and irregularity in positive reinforcement, e.g., Suzanne's parents often failed to take cognizance of her "productions" even when she attempted to attract their attention. Stated in conventional language, the parents of the future active-dependent rarely punish their children and distribute rewards only for what they approve and admire, but often fail to bestow these rewards even when the child behaves acceptably.

This pattern of experiences has three personality consequences: strategies designed to evoke rewards, a feeling of competence and acceptance *only* when others acknowledge one's performances and a habit of seeking approval for its own sake. All three of these traits are characteristic of the active-dependent personality. Let us detail their development.

1. The child who receives few punishments and many rewards will develop a strong and unambivalent inclination to relate to others. If he learns that the achievement of rewards is dependent on fulfilling the expectations and desires of others, he will develop a set of instrumental behaviors designed to please others and thereby elicit these rewards. However, if these strategies succeed sometimes but not always, that is, if they are irregularly reinforced, he will persist in using them, or variations of them, well beyond all reason, until they do succeed, which eventually they will. In other words, these instrumental behaviors will not easily be extinguished, even if they fail much of the time.

2. As a consequence of this pattern of experiences, the child will become actively rather than passively oriented toward others. Furthermore, he will learn to look to others rather than to himself for rewards since his behavior is only a preliminary, and *not* a sufficient condition for achieving reinforcements; the same behavior on his part will elicit a reward one time but fail, another. Despite the fact that he acts at all times to please and perform for others, it is always *they* who determine whether and when he will be rewarded. He awaits their judgment as to whether his efforts will bring recognition and approval; as a consequence, it is they who define the adequacy of his behavior, that is, his competence is judged by the reaction of others, not by his own efforts or behaviors.

3. Since favorable recognition of his competence occurs only irregularly, that is, not every time he performs "proper" acts, he is never sure of his adequacy and, therefore, continues to look to others, even after repeated failures to evoke favorable responses. Because of the irregularity of reinforcement, then, his search takes on a "life of its own," a habit of soliciting signs of approval that becomes so firmly established that it eventually is pursued for its own sake.

**Histrionic Parental Models.** Two features of family life often contribute to the development of the active-dependent pattern—histrionic parental models, and sibling rivalry. Let us look into the first.

There is little question that children learn, quite unconsciously, to mimic what they are exposed to. The prevailing attitudes and feelings, and the incidental daily behaviors displayed by family members serve as models which the growing child imitates and takes as his own long before he is able to recognize what he is doing or why. This process of vicarious learning is made especially easy if parental behaviors and feelings are unusually pronounced or dramatic. Under these circumstances, when parents call attention to themselves and create emotional reactions in their child, the child cannot help but learn clearly how people behave and feel. Thus, Suzanne D. reported that she was "just like" her mother, an emotionally labile woman who was "bored to tears with the routines of home life," flirtatious with men and "clever and facile in her dealings with people." The presence of a gregarious and histrionic parent, who exhibits feelings and attitudes rather dramatically, provides a sharply defined model for vicarious and imitative learning.

**Sibling Rivalry.** Children who struggled long and hard to capture the attention and affection of their parents under conditions of sibling rivalry often continue to utilize the devices that led to their periodic successes long after the rivalry ceased in reality. Not only are these behaviors reactivated when they seek attention in the future, but they often misperceive innocuous situations (perceptive distortion) and recreate competitive situations (repetition compulsion) in such ways as to bring forth the strategies they learned in the past. If the child learned to employ cuteness, charm, histrionics, attractiveness and seduction as a strategy to secure parental attention, as did Suzanne D., these interpersonal behaviors may persist, and take the form of a lifelong active-dependent pattern.

**Ease of Interpersonal Attraction.** Esthetically appealing girls and likable or athletic boys need expend little effort to draw attention and approval to themselves. Their mere "being" is sufficient to attract others.

Rewarding as these experiences may be in building up a high sense of self-esteem, they do have their negative consequences. These persons become excessively dependent on others since they are accustomed to approval and have learned to expect attention at all times. They experience considerable discomfort, then, when attention fails to materialize. In order to assure the continuation of these rewards, and thereby avoid discomfort, they learn to "play up" their attractiveness. For example, the formerly pretty young girl, in order to elicit the attention and approval which came so readily in youth, goes to great pains as she matures to remain a pretty woman; similarly the formerly successful young athlete struggles to keep his muscular and trim figure as he progresses into middle life. Both of these attractive individuals may have failed to acquire more substantial talents in their youth since they needed none in order to elicit social rewards. What we observe in their later life, then, is a childish exhibitionism and an adolescent, flirtatious and seductive style of relating, both of which characterize the active-dependent personality.

**Shifting Standards and Values.** An individual can be the master of his fate only if he possesses a personal identity, a sense of self-competence and self-sufficiency based on a framework of internal standards and values. He cannot initiate actions independently of others, nor navigate his own course unless he has a coherent set of goals and aspirations to guide him through changing tides and the buffeting of distracting events.

What happens if the person knows few fixed points of reference, has been exposed to shifting standards and has no stable anchor or reliable rudder by which to orient himself?

In our massively complex and everchanging society more youngsters than ever before grow up devoid of a set of firm and stable standards by which they can guide their lives. Not only are there more things to master and more variety and change to contend with, but children today are provided with less direction than they were years ago.

Of course, not every child raised in our society is plagued with such ambiguity. Most are imbued with unalterable beliefs, rules of conduct and sanctioned goals. Although the straight and narrow path rarely is adhered to anymore, most parents do establish clear boundaries and standards to assure against major digressions.

But there are many parents who fail to provide their children with a consistent or stabilizing set of values. Some fail because they are intellectually committed to a "laissez-faire" policy; others are confused and vacillating themselves; a third group is so preoccupied with their own lives that they have little time or inclination to guide their child's development. Whatever the reason, some children are left to fend for themselves, to discover their own direction in the complex and changing world which surrounds them. These children find no clarity or consistency elsewhere. They are exposed to one set of values here and another, entirely contradictory set, there; what seems right one day, doesn't the next. In short, they find no firm footing anywhere.

Such children learn that the best course of action is to size up each situation as they face it, and guide themselves in accord with the particular demands of that situation, and no other. Rather than acquire a set of uniform and rigid standards, one must acquire flexibility, an adaptiveness to changing circumstances. To be committed for long or to believe in anything wholeheartedly, is foolish since events change and one must be ready to adjust to them.

Such a youngster never establishes a firm image of his personal identity, an internal and stable set of beliefs to which he is committed as his own. His identity is diffuse; life progresses, not with an internal gyroscope but with a radar system oriented and sensitive to the changing values and expectations of others. Unsure of his beliefs, or even who he is, he must be hyperalert and hyperadaptive to his environment. He shifts aimlessly from one brief and fleeting course of action to another and seems dilettante, restless and capricious, all of which are traits that characterize the active-dependent pattern.

## COPING STRATEGIES

All of us seek stimulation, attention and approval, but it is only the gregarious personality who possesses an insatiable striving for these experiences, who feels devoid of an inner self and seeks constant nourishment to fill that void. Lacking a core of self-identity, he *must* draw sustenance from those around him; it is others who supply him the sustenance of life without which he feels emptiness, a fear of collapse and a falling apart in disarray.

What strategies does the active-dependent person employ to assure the stimulation and approval he requires? As before, we will divide these strategies in terms of interpersonal behavior and intrapsychic mechanisms.

**Seductive Interpersonal Behavior.** It may be useful to recall that the interpersonal behavior of mild pathological personalities is not strikingly different from that seen among "normal" individuals. Its distinction lies not in its uniqueness or bizarreness, but in its inflexibility and persistence.

The gregarious personality is often successful in accomplishing the aims of his instrumental behaviors, that of eliciting the stimulation and excitement he craves, or captivating others and winning their attention and approval. His strategies are pathological, however, because he does not limit their use to situations in which they are appropriate or promise success. Rather, they are applied indiscriminately and relentlessly; for example, he seeks to please the most insignificant of people with whom he comes into contact and pursues his strategies with the most unlikely prospects and under the most unsuitable circumstances. Moreover, his need for attention and approval is insatiable; as soon as he receives rewards from one source, he turns his unquenchable thirst for more from others; he appears to possess a bottomless pit into which recognition and esteem may be poured. Furthermore, if he fails to evoke the love and stimulation he seeks, he becomes dejected and anxious; thus, signs of indifference or neutrality on the part of others are interpreted as rejection and failure, and result in feelings of emptiness, unworthiness and anxiety.

To achieve his goals and avoid his fears, the gregarious personality has learned with considerable skill to manipulate others to his suiting. More than being merely agreeable and friendly, he learns to "sell" himself, that is, to employ his talents and charm to elicit approval and esteem; this he does by presenting an attractive front, by seductive pretensions, by a dilettante sophistication and knowledgeability and by little acts to impress and amuse others. Exhibitionistic displays and histrionics, dramatic gestures, attractive coiffures, frivolous comments, clever stories and shocking clothes, all are designed *not* to "express himself," but to draw interest, stimulation and attention to himself. In short, he uses himself as a commodity and as a "personality" with a bag of tricks, a conspicuous talent that corners all of the attention of those with whom he comes into contact.

The active-dependent not only acquires a skill for sensing what is saleable or will "get across" to others but he learns to be alert to signs of potential hostility and rejection. This hypervigilance enables him quickly to adapt his behavior to minimize the dangers of indifference and disapproval. His interpersonal facilities extend, then, not only to the evocation of praise but to the avoidance of rejection. By paying close attention to the varied signals that people transmit, he reshapes and fashions his reactions to conform with their desires and intentions. In this way he need not fear desertion since he maneuvers himself to do things that correspond to the wishes and expectations of others.

Despite his charm and his talent for "pleasing" others, the active-dependent does not provide others with real and sustained affection; in fact, the converse is true. All that the gregarious personality offers in return for the approval he seeks are fleeting and superficial displays of affection. Having failed throughout life to develop any depth and richness of inner feelings and lacking in resources from which he can draw, he is unable to sustain a meaningful and stable relationship with others. Moreover, he senses the disparity between the favorable but superficial impression he gives to others, and his real lack of inner substance; as a consequence, he shies from prolonged contact with others for fear that his fraudulence will be uncovered. In summary, the facile displays of emotion conveyed by these persons are shallow, fleeting and illusory; not only do they lack the capacity to sustain a relationship but they quickly abandon them before the "truth" is out.

**Intrapsychic Mechanism of Repression.** The intrapsychic world of the gregarious personality is skimpy and insubstantial. His exteroceptive orientation has led to an impoverishment of inner richness and depth. In addition, it both reflects and is a consequence of his tendency not to value himself as a source of nourishment and reinforcement. In short, his superficial social facilities and transient emotions are not rooted in a foundation of deep feelings and well-developed cognitions.

To the extent that the gregarious personality possesses an inner world of thought, memory and emotion he tries to repress it and to keep it from intruding into his everyday conscious life. This is done for several reasons. *First,* the worth of his own attributes depends on the judgment of others; there is no reason to plumb his inner self for he alone cannot appraise his personal value or provide self-reinforcements. *Second,* by turning his attention inward he will distract his attention from the outer world. This divided attention will prove troublesome since his strategy requires that he be extraordinarily attuned to the desires and moods of others. To preserve his exteroceptive alertness and vigilance, then, he must cut off "inner" distractions, especially those which may be potentially disturbing. *Third,* the active-dependent must actively blot out an awareness of the objective barrenness of his intrapsychic world. His inner emptiness is most intolerable since it points up the fraudulence that exists between the overt impression he conveys to others and his true cognitive sterility and emotional poverty. The contrast between his pretensions and objective reality leads him to repress not only one or two troublesome aspects of himself, as is the case with most pathological personalities, but all of his inner self since it is the triviality of his entire being, its pervasive emptiness and paucity of substance, which must be kept from awareness. Repression is applied across the board; it is massive and complete.

His dependence on repression also arises from the fact that he has never acquired the skill of more intricate intrapsychic processes. His preoccupation with an "outer life" has prevented him from learning intrapsychic facilities; thus, he applies the mechanism of massive repression because he has no other more discriminating alternative.

## SELF-PERPETUATION OF PATTERN

Each of us, without knowing it, engages in automatic and persistent behaviors that are "senseless" if viewed in terms of their objective utility. The difference between persistent behaviors we call normal, as opposed to pathological, lies in the fact that "normal" senseless and repetitive acts do not create or intensify problems. In contrast, pathological behaviors, no matter what their utility, ultimately foster new difficulties and perpetuate old ones. What features of the active-dependent's instrumental strategy results in these unfortunate consequences?

**Exteroceptive Preoccupations.** We have noted that the active-dependent orients his attention to the external world and that his perceptions and cognitions tend to be fleeting, impressionistic and undeveloped. This scattered preoccupation with incidental and passing details prevents events from being digested and embedded within his inner world; as a result, there is no integration, no well-examined reflective process, that intervenes between perception and action; responses are emitted before they have been connected, organized and refined by the operation of memory and thought.

The disadvantages of hyperalertness and hypersensitivity may outweigh their advantages. Unless experience is digested and integrated, the individual gains little from them. Events and transactions with others pass through the person as if he were a sieve. There is no development of inner skills, no construction of memory traces against which future experience may be evaluated. Rapid and indiscriminate responsiveness leaves the person barren and impoverished and devoid of an inner reservoir of well-developed and articulated memories, a storehouse of examined ideas and thoughts. In short, his excessive preoccupation with external events perpetuates an empty shell and continues his dependence on outer events to guide him and supply him with the nourishment and stimulation he seeks.

**Massive Repression.** The tendency of the active-dependent to seal off, to repress and make inaccessible substantial portions of his meager inner life, further aggravates his dependence on others. By insulating his own emotions and cognitions from the stream of everyday life, he effectively denies himself the opportunity to learn new alternatives for behavior, to modify his self-image or to become a more genuinely skillful and knowledgeable person. As long as he blocks the fusion which should occur between new experiences and self, he remains stagnant, unaltered and impoverished. Deprived of opportunities to learn and to grow, he perpetuates the vicious circle of his dependency on others. He progresses little beyond his childhood, retains the values and modes of behavior of an adolescent and is unable to initiate actions or to venture on his own in a world of more matured adults.

**Fleeting Social Attachments.** Because the active-dependent is devoid of an inner identity, he must lean on others for nourishment; in this respect he is not dissimilar from the passive-dependent. The major distinction between them lies in the durability of their attachments. The submissive personality seeks to ally himself and remain loyal to one strong figure, whereas the gregarious personality requires a retinue of changing events and people to replenish his need for stimulation and approval; as life progresses, he moves capriciously from one source to another. Some of the factors which may underlie this unstable attachment behavior were described in preceding sections.

One of the consequences of these fleeting and erratic relationships is that he can never be sure of securing the affection and support he craves. By moving constantly from one adventure to another and by devouring the affections of one person and then another, he places himself in jeopardy of having nothing to tide him over the times between. He often is left high and dry, in the lurch, alone and abandoned with no one "to love," nothing to do and no excitement with which to be preoccupied. Unlike the passive-dependent who opts for the security of a single and stable relationship, the active-dependent ravenously consumes his source of nourishment.

Cut off from external supplies, the active-dependent either engages in a frantic search for stimulation and approval or becomes dejected and forlorn. He may proceed through cyclical swings, alternating periods of simulated euphoria and illusory excitements, intermingled with moments of hopelessness, futility and self-condemnation. Should these periods of deprivation be frequent or prolonged, the probability is high that these personalities will decompensate into a more entrenched "cycloid" pattern.

## REMEDIAL APPROACHES

The prognostic picture for the active-dependent is favorable. Despite their lack of well-developed inner resources they possess motivation and skills for maintaining satisfactory interpersonal relationships. Given this desire to relate to others, and their facility for eliciting reinforcements, the probability is slight that they will succumb to prolonged and severe pathology.

These personalities rarely seek therapy. When they do, it usually follows a period of prolonged deprivation of stimulation and approval. Their complaints take the form of rather vague feelings of boredom, restlessness, discontent and loneliness. The person often reports a growing disaffection with his mate, a feeling that the interest and vitality, which characterized their earlier years together, have now palled. Sexual interest may have faded, and the frequency of relations may have dropped markedly due to a growing impotence or frigidity. As this disaffection continues, conflicts and tension may arise, prompting the patient to feel not only a sense of loss but rejection and hostility from his mate. Life begins to take on a purposeless and meaningless quality; he begins to dramatize his plight, feeling that matters are hopeless and futile.

A first step in therapy is to curtail the patient's tendency to indulge, overemotionalize and thereby aggravate his distraught feelings; once calmed and more objectively oriented, it is best not to further weaken the patient's previously successful, but currently flagging, gregarious strategy.

In the early stages of treatment, the therapist must be prepared to be viewed by his patient as an object possessing magical powers. This illusion is transient; nevertheless, it may be used to re-establish the patient's equilibrium. It is best at this point to terminate treatment, unless more extensive therapy is indicated.

Few active-dependents retain motivation for therapy; either they again feel capable of securing affection and approval on their own, or they begin to experience intense anxieties upon therapeutic probing and serious self-exploration. Should they be disposed to further treatment, the therapist's efforts are best directed toward the goal of building increased self-reliance, and the capacity to develop sustained and deep emotional attachments.

In general, the techniques of environmental management, biophysical treatment and behavior modification are of minimal value with these personalities. Supportive therapy may be indicated to tide them over the "rough periods." If the patient is sufficiently inclined, the procedures of phenomenological reorientation may prove of assistance in developing deeper insight and a richer inner life. Intrapsychic techniques may be employed if it appears necessary to reconstruct the basic personality style. Of frequent value, also, are group methods designed to aid the person in developing more genuine and sustaining ways of relating to others.

The conclusions and summary for this chapter may be found at the end of chapter 7.

# Chapter 7

## PATHOLOGICAL PERSONALITIES OF MILD SEVERITY

### II: Basic Independent and Ambivalent Patterns

Pablo Picasso—*Girl Before a Mirror* (1932). (Collection, The Museum of Modern Art, New York.)

Let us proceed directly from where we left off in chapter 6 and discuss the remaining four mild personality syndromes.

## BASIC INDEPENDENT PATTERNS

In contrast to dependent personalities, who look to others to provide the reinforcements of life, independent patterns turn inward for gratification, relying on themselves both for safety and comfort. Weakness, inferiority and dependency are threatening; they are overly concerned with matters of adequacy, power and prestige; differences in status and superiority must always be in their favor. They fear the loss of self-determination, are proud of their achievements, strive to enhance themselves and to be ascendant, stronger, more beautiful, wealthier or more intelligent than others. In short, it is what they themselves possess, not what others say or can provide for them, which serves as the touchstone for their security and contentment.

The independent style of life may usefully be divided into two subtypes. The *passive-independent,* who is confident of his self-worth and who needs to be merely himself to feel content and secure, and the *active-independent,* who struggles to "prove" himself, who insists on his rights and will be cunning and ruthless if necessary to gain power over others. For the passive type, self-esteem is based on a blind and naive assumption of personal worth and superiority. For the active-independent, it stems from distrust, a terrifying fear that others will be humiliating and

260

exploitive; to them, self-determination is a protective maneuver, a means of countering, with their own power and prestige, the hostility, deception and victimization they anticipate from their surroundings.

Although both passive and active-independents devalue the standards and opinions of others, finding gratification only within themselves, their life histories, and the strategies they employ for achieving reinforcement, are substantially different.

## THE NARCISSISTIC PERSONALITY: PASSIVE-INDEPENDENT PATTERN

The label "narcissistic" connotes more than mere egocentricity, a characteristic of all individuals driven primarily by their needs and anxieties. Narcissism signifies, more particularly, that the individual overvalues his personal worth, directs his affections toward himself, rather than others, and expects that they will recognize and cater to the high esteem in which he holds himself. This rather fascinating pattern, though well known in contemporary life, and depicted so well in literary writings, has been given but scant theoretical and clinical attention. For example, the recent DSM-II has no diagnostic category that approximates the clinical features of this personality type. This oversight in the professional literature reflects, in part, the relative success with which these individuals function in our society and, perhaps more significantly, their unwillingness to subject themselves to the scrutiny of therapeutic probing.

Self-confidence and a haughty air of self-assurance are conducive to success and the evocation of admiration in our "other-directed" society. It will falter as a style of life, however, if the person's illusion of omnipotence is poorly founded in fact, or if the supercilious air is so exaggerated as to grate and alienate others.

The self-centeredness of the narcissistic personality is *not* tinged with feelings of deep hostility and animosity toward others. Narcissistic individuals display a benign form of arrogance, a disdainful indifference to the standards of shared social behaviors; they feel themselves to be "above" the conventions and ethics of their cultural group, and exempt from the responsibilities that govern and give order and reciprocity to societal living. Others are expected to submerge their desires in favor of the narcissist's comfort and welfare; he operates on the rather fantastic assumption that *his* mere desire is justification

enough for possessing whatever he seeks. Thus, his lofty disdainfulness is matched by his exploitiveness, his assumption that he is entitled to be served and to have his wishes take precedence over others, without expending a shred of genuine effort to merit such favor. In short, he possesses illusions of an inherent superior self-worth, and moves through life with the belief that it is his inalienable right to receive special considerations. Some of the features of this pattern are illustrated in the following case.

### CASE 7-1
#### Steven F., Age 30, Artist, Married, One Child

Steve came to the attention of a therapist when his wife insisted that they seek marital counseling. According to her, Steve was "selfish, ungiving and preoccupied with his work." Everything at home had to "revolve about him, his comfort, moods and desires, no one else's." She claimed that he contributed nothing to the marriage, except a rather meager income. He shirked all "normal" responsibilities and kept "throwing chores in her lap," and she was "getting fed up with being the chief cook and bottle-washer . . . tired of being his mother and sleep-in maid."

On the positive side, Steve's wife felt that he was basically a "gentle and good-natured guy with talent and intelligence." But this wasn't enough. She wanted a husband, someone with whom she could share things. In contrast, he wanted, according to her, "a mother, not a wife"; he didn't want "to grow up . . . he didn't know how to give affection, only to take it when he felt like it, nothing more, nothing less."

Steve presented a picture of an affable, self-satisfied and somewhat disdainful young man. He was employed as a commercial artist, but looked forward to his evenings and weekends when he could turn his attention to serious painting. He claimed that he had to devote all of his spare time and energies to "fulfill himself," to achieve expression in his creative work. His wife knew of his preoccupation well before they were married; in fact, it was his self-dedication and promise as a painter that initially attracted her to him. As Steve put it "what is she complaining about . . . isn't this what she wanted, what she married me for?"

Exploration of Steve's early history provided the following. Steve was an only child, born after his mother had suffered many miscarriages; his parents had given up hope of ever having a child until he came along, "much to their surprise and pleasure." His parents doted over him; he never assumed any household or personal responsibilities. He was given music and art lessons, discovered to have considerable talent in both and given free rein to indulge these talents to the exclusion of everything else. He was an excellent student, won several scholarships and received much praise for his academic and artistic aptitudes. To his family he was "a genius at work"; life at home centered entirely around him.

Socially, Steve recalled being "pretty much of

an isolate," staying home "drawing and reading, rather than going outside with the other kids." He felt he was well liked by his peers, but they may have thought him to be a "bit pompous and superior." He liked being thought of this way, and felt that he was "more talented and brighter" than most. He remained a "loner" until he met his wife.

His relationships with his present co-workers and social acquaintances were pleasant and satisfying, but he did admit that most people viewed him as a "bit self-centered, cold and snobbish." He recognized that he did not know how to share his thoughts and feelings with others, that he was much more interested in himself than in them and that perhaps he always had "preferred the pleasure" of his own company to that of others.

## CLINICAL PICTURE

Let us next turn to the characteristic features of the narcissistic personality using our four-way breakdown.

### Behavior

Rather typically the passive-independent conveys a calm and self-assured quality in his social behavior. His seemingly untroubled and self-satisfied air is viewed, by some, as a sign of confident equanimity.

Others respond to it less favorably; to them, it reflects immodesty, presumptuousness, pretentiousness, a haughty, snobbish, cocksure and arrogant way of relating to people. The narcissist appears to lack humility and to be overly self-centered and ungenerous; he exploits others, takes them for granted and expects them to serve him, but is unwilling to give in return. Moreover, his self-conceit is viewed as unwarranted to most; it is "uppish" and superior without the requisite substance to justify it.

### Phenomenological Reports

The passive-independent feels justified in his claim for special status; he has little conception that his behaviors may be unwarranted and even irrational.

His self-image is that of a superior person, someone "extra-special," entitled to unusual rights and privileges; this view is fixed so firmly in his mind that he rarely questions whether his assumption is valid. Anyone who fails to respect him is viewed with contempt and scorn.

Narcissistic individuals are cognitively expansive; they place few limits upon their fantasies and rationalizations; their imagination runs free of the constraints of reality or the views of others. They exaggerate their powers, freely transform failures into successes, construct lengthy and intricate rationalizations to inflate their self-worth, justify what they feel is their due and depreciate those who refuse to accept or enhance their self-image.

Spurred on by the facile workings of his imagination, the narcissist experiences a pervasive sense of well-being, a buoyancy of mood and an optimism of outlook. His affective tone, though based often on distorted interpretations of reality, is generally elevated, blithe, cheerful and carefree.

### Intrapsychic Processes

Passive-independents suffer few conflicts; their past experiences have supplied them, perhaps too well, with affection and encouragement. As a consequence, they are disposed to trust others and to feel a high degree of confidence that matters will work out well for them.

As will be detailed later, this sanguine outlook upon life is founded on an unusual set of early experiences that rarely can be duplicated in later life. The narcissist was misled by his parents into believing that he was lovable and perfect, regardless of what he did and how he thought. Such an idyllic life cannot long endure; the world beyond the boundaries of home will not be so benign and accepting.

As noted in the previous section, the passive-independent employs his boundless imagination to maintain his image of superiority and perfection; daydreams of achievement and glory characterize much of his waking time.

But reality bears down heavily at times; even the demands of shared everyday responsibilities prove troublesome to him. Such responsibilities are demeaning; they shatter the cherished illusion of his godlike qualities. Alibis to avoid such pedestrian tasks as "taking out the garbage" or "diapering the baby" are easy to muster since he is convinced of the superiority of *his* logic; what he believes is true, and what he wishes is right.

Not only does he display considerable talent in rationalizing his social irresponsibility but he is equally facile in utilizing other intrapsychic mechanisms. However, since he cares little for the opinions of others, his defensive maneuvers are transparent, a poor camouflage to a discerning eye. This failure to bother dissembling more thoroughly accounts in part for his overt immodesty and obvious arrogance.

### Biophysical Factors

There appear to be few characteristics at this level of analysis that distinguish the narcissistic personality. This is not to say that individual passive-independent personalities may not exhibit distinctive biophysical features; rather, as a group, they appear not to possess such traits in common.

## ETIOLOGY AND DEVELOPMENT

Bringing together the clinical features noted above suggests the following primary characteristics of the passive-independent pattern: *elevated affectivity* (buoyant, optimistic and carefree), *cognitive expansiveness* (boundless in imagination; facile in rationalizations), *admirable self-image* (egotistic; self-assured) and *interpersonal exploitation* (presumptuous in expectation of special considerations and good will). In this section we will attempt to trace some of the influences which have shaped these traits.

### Biogenic Factors

The role of biogenic influences in the narcissistic personality seems especially unclear. Although evidence adduced in support of biogenic determinants for most of the other personality patterns was largely of a speculative nature, there was some, albeit tenuous, logic for these speculations. In the case of the passive-independent pattern, however, where the existence of distinctive biophysical traits seems lacking, conjectures would have unusually weak grounding; thus, none will be proposed.

### Psychogenic Factors

Since little evidence for the development of the narcissistic personality can be provided from biological sources, we must trace the roots of this pattern among psychogenic influences.

**Parental Overvaluation and Indulgence.** For many and sundry reasons, some parents will view their child as "God's gift to man." They pamper, indulge and fawn over the youngster in such ways as to teach him that his every wish is a command to others, that he can receive without giving and that he deserves prominence without effort. In short order, the child learns to view himself as a special being, learns to expect subservience from others, begins to recognize that his mere existence is sufficient to provide pleasure to others and that his every action evokes commendation and praise. On the other hand, however, he fails to learn how to cooperate and share or to think of the desires and interests of others; he acquires no sense of interpersonal responsibility, no skills for the give-and-take of social life. The world revolves about him; he is egotistic in focus, and narcissistic in the expression of love and affect.

Exposed repeatedly to acquiescent and in-dulgent parents, he expects comparable treatment from others, and learns to employ the presumptuous and demanding strategies which effected favored reactions in the past. Should desire be frustrated, he can act only in one way—to demand and exploit. He has learned no alternative and has no recourse but to assume that his wishes automatically will be met.

Not only does this youngster learn to take others for granted and to exploit them for his benefit, but he learns also to view others as weak and subservient. By their obsequious and self-demeaning behaviors, the parents of the narcissistic child have provided him with an image of others as manipulable, docile, yielding and spineless. Not only does this view enhance his image of his own specialness and superiority, relative to others, but it serves to strengthen his disposition to exploit and use them; since they are so weak and submissive, he can tread and ride roughshod over them with impunity.

This feeling of omnipotence of extraordinary self-worth begins to take hold during the sensorimotor-autonomy stage. Every utterance and minor achievement on the part of the child is responded to with such favor as to give him a deluded sense of his own competence. Extreme confidence in one's child need not be a disservice to the child, if it is well earned. In the case of the passive-independent, however, a marked disparity will exist between the child's actual competence and the impression he has of it.

The failure of parental direction and control plays an important role during the intracortical initiative stage. The child is free to imagine, explore and act without discipline and regulation. Deluded by his sense of self-worth and power, and unrestrained by the imposition of parental limits, his thoughts and behaviors stray far beyond the accepted boundaries of reality. In short, untutored by parental discipline and unexposed to the constraints of fear, guilt and shame, he fails to develop those internal regulating mechanisms which we speak of as "self-control."

**Only Child Status.** Brief mention should be made of the high frequency with which the parental conditions noted above arise in the case of only children. Quite naturally, such children often are viewed by their parents as objects of special value. Not only are they often fawned over but they typically experience few of the restrictions and learn few of the responsibilities of sharing acquired by youngsters with siblings.

The preceding comments suggest that the popular notion of "only children being spoiled" has some merit in fact; needless to say, only children need not be exposed to parental over-valuation and indulgence, nor is such exposure limited to those who are only children.

## COPING STRATEGIES

We can easily understand why the instru-mental behaviors of the narcissist are so gratifying to him. By treating himself kindly, by admiring and imagining his own prowess, beauty and in-telligence and by reveling in his superiority and talents, he gains, through self-reinforcement, the rewards that most people must struggle to achieve through genuine attainments. He need depend on no one else to provide gratification; the rest of the world can go its merry or miserable way; he has himself to "keep him warm."

However, the narcissist does live in a world of others, and must relate to them, with all the complications and frustrations that such relation-ships entail. In the following sections we will turn to the manner in which the passive-independent copes with these complications as it manifests itself in interpersonal behavior and through the workings of intrapsychic processes.

**Exploitive Interpersonal Behavior.** Satisfying though it may be to reinforce oneself, it is all the more satisfying if one can arrange one's en-vironment so that others will contribute to these reinforcements. The narcissist seeks to accomplish this with minimal effort and reciprocity on his part. Thus, in contrast to the passive-dependent, who must submit and acquiesce to evoke favora-ble rewards, or the active-dependent, who must perform and be attractive and seductive in order to win praise from others, the passive-independent contributes little or nothing to others in return for the gratifications he seeks. Thus, as therapy progressed, Steven F. became increasingly aware of his lifelong assumption that others had been "honored" by his relationship to them, and re-ceived as much pleasure in providing for him as he received in accepting their attentions and favors.

The sheer presumptuousness and confidence exuded by the narcissist often elicit the admira-tion and obedience of others. Furthermore, he sizes up those around him and quickly trains those who are so disposed to pay tribute to him, e.g., the narcissist often will select a passive-dependent mate, one who will be obeisant, solic-itous and subservient, without expecting anything in return except his strength and assurances of fidelity.

Central to the narcissist's approach to others, then, is his assumption that good fortune will come to him without any effort at reciprocity. Since he feels entitled to get what he desires, and has been successful in maneuvering others to provide him with comforts and rewards he has not deserved, he has little reason to discon-tinue his presumptuous exploitive behavior.

**Fantasy, Repression, Rationalization and Pro-jection.** As with all of the mild pathological patterns, the narcissist can function successfully in life if he arranges his relationships in ways that both gratify his needs and are consonant with his interpersonal style. What happens, how-ever, if he is not successful, if he faces frustra-tion, deprecation and humiliation? What if events threaten to topple him from his illusory world of eminence and superiority? What behaviors and intrapsychic mechanisms does he employ to salve his wounds and anxieties?

Faced with such threats, he has no recourse but to turn to his fantasy life for solace. In con-trast to the active-independent, whom we will describe in the next section, he has not learned to be ruthless, to be competitively assertive and aggressive when frustrated. Neither has he ac-quired the intricate seductive strategies of the active-dependent to solicit rewards and protec-tions. Failing to achieve his aims with others, and at a loss as to what he can do next, he re-verts to himself to provide comfort and consola-tion.

At these periods, his lifelong and facile talents of imagination take over; these processes enable him to create a fanciful world in which he redeems himself and reasserts his pride and status. Since he is unaccustomed to self-control and reality testing, his powers of imagination have free rein to weave intricate resolutions to his difficulties.

What cannot be handled through fantasy resolutions simply are repressed, put out of mind and kept from awareness; otherwise, he invents alibis, excuses and "proofs" which seem to him plausible and consistent, and which convince him of his continued stature and perfection. These flimsily substantiated rationalizations are pre-sented to others with confidence and authority, but the narcissist may never have learned the skills of successful deception; he always said and did as he liked without a care for what others thought. Now his rationalizations may fail to bring relief and may evoke serious questioning and deprecating reactions from others. It is at this point that he may be pushed to the use of the projection mechanism. Unable to disentangle himself from lies and inconsistencies, and driven to maintain his illusion of superiority, he begins to turn against others and to accuse them of his own deceptions, his own selfishness and irrationalities. Thus, shortly before seeking marital counseling, Steven F. began to attack his wife's loyalty and faithfulness, accusing her of shirking her responsibilities and wasting her time on "silly civic activities," asserting that she was more interested in her own "personal affairs" than those of the family. Drained of his power and confidence, he became suspicious and hostile, and asserted that others sought to deprive him of his rightful stature.

## SELF-PERPETUATION OF PATTERN

The narcissist exhibits his personality style with persistence and inflexibility; he is unable to alter his strategy since these patterns are deeply ingrained. Rather than modifying his behavior, when failure looms, he may revert more intractably to his characteristic strategies; this only intensifies and fosters new difficulties. Thus, in his attempt to cope with stress, he sets up vicious circles which perpetuate his problems; three of these will be discussed in this section.

**Illusion of Competence.** Narcissists act as if belief in their superiority will suffice as its proof. Conditioned to think of themselves as competent and admirable, they see no reason to expend effort to acquire these virtues. Why bother engaging in hard work, why stoop to such demeaning labors as systematic and disciplined study if one already possesses talent and aptitude? Is it not beneath one's dignity to struggle as others must do?

Feeling well endowed at the start, the narcissist does not exert his energies to achieve what he desires; he simply assumes that whatever he aspires to will come easily to him. Some narcissists may sense that they cannot "live up" to their self-made publicity, and fear trying themselves out in the real world. Rather than facing genuine challenges, they temporize or boast, but never venture to test their adequacy; in this way they can retain their illusion of superiority without fear of disproof.

As a consequence of his illusions, the passive-independent paralyzes himself. His unfounded sense of confidence and his fantastic belief in his God-given perfection, may inhibit him from developing whatever natural aptitudes he may possess. Unwilling to expend the effort, he may slip increasingly behind others in realistic attainment. In due course, his deficits become pronounced, making him, as well as others, aware of his shortcomings. Since his belief in his intrinsic superiority is the bedrock of his existence—the underpinning of his coping strategy—the disparity between his genuine and illusory competence becomes increasingly painful. The strain of maintaining his false self-image may blossom to serious proportions, and result in the emergence of more severe pathological disturbances.

**Lack of Self-Controls.** The narcissist's illusion of competence is only one facet of a more generalized disdain for reality. These personalities are neither disposed to stick to objective facts nor to shape their actions and thoughts in accord with social custom or the demands of cooperative living. Unrestrained by parental discipline in childhood, and confident of their worth and prowess, they take liberties with rules and reality, and prevaricate and fantasize at will.

Apart from others and free to wander in his private world of fiction, he may begin to lose touch with reality, lose his sense of proportion and think along peculiar and deviant lines. His facile imagination, and the behaviors these thoughts may prompt, ultimately evoke comments and reactions from others concerning his "queer" way of thinking and acting. Ill-disposed to accept the validity of their judgments, and needful of retaining his admirable self-image, he turns increasingly to his habit of self-glorification. Lacking internal or self-controls, however, his fantasies take flight, and recede further and further from social and objective reality.

**Social Alienation.** If the narcissist were able to respect others, allow himself to value their opinions or see the world through their eyes, he would stand a good chance of having his tendencies toward illusion and unreality checked or curtailed. But the narcissist has learned to devalue others, not to trust their judgments and capacities, and to think of them as fools and knaves. Rather than questioning the correctness of his own actions and beliefs, he assumes that it is theirs that are at fault. The more disagreement he has with others, the more convinced he is of his own superiority, and the more isolated and alienated he becomes.

These difficulties are magnified by his inability to participate gracefully in the give-and-take of shared social life. His characteristic selfishness and ungenerosity often "pull" condemnation and disparagement from others. These reactions, unfortunately, drive him further into his world of fantasy and self-reinforcement, only to strengthen his alienation and his illusion of superiority.

Isolation prevents him from understanding the intentions and actions of others. He is increasingly unable to assess situations objectively, and fails to grasp why he has been rebuffed and misunderstood. Distressed by these repeated and perplexing social failures, he begins to elaborate new and fantastic rationales to account for his fate. But the more he ruminates, the more he loses touch, the more he distorts and the more he perceives things which are not there. He begins to be suspicious of others, to question their intentions and to criticize and attack them for their deceptions and cruelty. In time, these actions drive away potential well-wishers, creating unnecessary frictions, which then only "justify and prove" his suspicions.

Lacking the habitual controls of self-discipline and reality testing, his tendency to fantasize and distort speeds up. His air of grandiosity becomes more flagrant; he finds hidden and deprecatory meanings in the incidental behaviors of others and becomes convinced of their malicious motives, their claims upon him and their attempt to undo him. As his behavior and thoughts cross the line of reality, his alienation mounts and he must protect his phantom image of superiority more vigorously and vigilantly.

Trapped by the consequences of his own defensive maneuvers, he becomes bewildered and frightened, and the downward spiral progresses in an inexorable course. Losing touch with reality, he begins to accuse others, to hold them responsible for his failures. He builds up a "logic" based on irrelevant and entirely circumstantial "evidence"; ultimately, he constructs a delusional system to protect him from unbearable realities. At this point his behavior signifies more than a mild pathological pattern; he has decompensated into a severe disorder.

## REMEDIAL APPROACHES

Despite the chronic and pervasive nature of the narcissist's pattern, he often can function successfully in society if he possesses a modicum of substance and talent to back his confidence and social airs; difficulties arise only when a marked disparity exists between his presumptuousness and his actual competence. Strange as it may seem, his inexhaustible confidence and pride serves him in good stead. Thus, in contrast to many detached and dependent personalities, he has a tremendous reservoir of self-faith which can withstand considerable draining before it runs dry.

Passive-independents are not inclined to seek therapy; their arrogant pride disposes them to reject the "weakness" implied in the role of a patient. They are convinced that they can get along well on their own. How demeaning it would be to admit their shortcomings; why consider changing if one already is perfect. And to add insult to injury, why should one be guided by some less talented being, namely the therapist.

The passive-independent consents to therapy unwillingly. He maintains a well-measured distance from the therapist, resists the searching probes of therapeutic exploration, becomes indignant over implications of deficiencies on his part and seeks to shift the responsibility for them to others. His denials and evasiveness and his unwillingness to examine his illusions and destructive behaviors, intrude and interfere with progress. The treatment situation may become a struggle in which he attempts to outwit the therapist and to assert dominance and superiority; only with great patience and equanimity can the therapist establish a spirit of confidence and respect.

Narcissists are precipitated into therapy usually after a particularly painful blow to their pride; a severe occupational failure, an embarrassing loss of public esteem or a sudden change of attitude on the part of a previously idolizing marital partner illustrate the kinds of events which may prompt the voluntary acceptance of therapy.

Once involved in carrying out treatment, the therapist may hold the narcissist's interest by allowing him to focus attention upon himself; furthermore, by encouraging discussions of his past achievements, he may enable him to rebuild his recently depleted self-esteem. Not infrequently, the patient's self-confidence is restored merely by talking about himself, by recalling and elaborating his attributes and competencies in front of a knowing and accepting person.

If support is all that the therapist seeks as his goal, this can often be achieved in a few sessions. But the goals of therapy usually are more substantial, especially since the rebuilding of the patient's superiority illusions may prove, in the long run, to be a disservice to him.

As more fundamental goals, the therapist should seek to assist the patient in acquiring greater self-control, becoming more sensitive and aware of reality and learning to accept the constraints and responsibilities of shared social living. But first, the therapist must strengthen the patient's capacity to confront his weaknesses and deficiencies. Until he can accept himself on a more realistic basis than heretofore, it is not likely that the narcissist will be able to develop socially cooperative attitudes and behaviors.

As far as specific techniques are concerned,

the methods of environmental management, bio-physical treatment and behavior modification appear of limited value.

The changing of attitudes toward self and others may best be begun through procedures of phenomenological reorientation. Once a baseline of rapport has been established with nondirective techniques, the patient may be able to withstand directive methods designed to probe and modify his self-attitudes and social habits.

Techniques of intrapsychic reconstruction may be employed, although the narcissist's illusions often are reinforced too strongly by the freedom of imagination that this method fosters. Group therapy may prove profitable in assisting the patient to view himself in a realistic social light, and to learn the skills of interpersonal sharing and cooperation.

## THE AGGRESSIVE PERSONALITY: ACTIVE-INDEPENDENT PATTERN
(DSM-II: *Antisocial Personality*)

Independent personalities exhibit in common an inclination to view themselves as the primary source for achieving reinforcement. However, a major distinction must be drawn between the passive and active subtypes. Passive-independents, termed narcissistic personalities, are characterized by their sublime self-confidence, their deeply rooted faith in themselves as superior beings. In contrast, active-independents, referred to as aggressive personalities, are driven by a need to assert and prove their superiority; independence for them stems not so much from a belief in self-worth, as from a fear and mistrust of others. They have faith only in themselves and are secure only when they are independent of those who may undo, harm and humiliate them.

The *antisocial personality* diagnosis in the DSM-II parallels to some extent the "aggressive personality" syndrome described here. The DSM designation, we believe, places too great an emphasis on the undesirable social consequences of the patient's behavior, overlooking in great measure his "basic" personality style. In a later chapter, we will discuss, under the label "sociopathic disorder: antisocial type," those aggressive personalities who are openly and flagrantly hostile in their social behavior. Other aggressive personalities, however, "fit in" to the mainstream of the larger society, and are much more subtle in the expression of their hostile impulses. For comparative and descriptive purposes, we quote the following excerpt from the DSM-II.

This term is reserved for individuals who are . . . incapable of significant loyalty to individuals, groups, or social values. They are grossly selfish, callous, irresponsible, impulsive, and unable to feel guilt or to learn from experience and punishment. Frustration tolerance is low. They tend to blame others or offer plausible rationalizations for their behavior.

As noted above, aggressive personalities do not inevitably come into conflict with the law and are not a disreputable lot, composed exclusively of delinquents and criminals from the ranks of the "socially inferior." Rather, aggressive individuals often are commended and endorsed in our competitive society, where tough, hard-headed "realism" is admired as an attribute necessary for survival; thus, most aggressive personalities find a socially valued niche for themselves in the rugged side of the business, military or political world. This pattern often is found in the arrogant patriotism of nationalists, militarists and demagogues whose truculence is "justified" by the hostility of "alien" national and racial groups; rather sadly, it is all too evident in the machinations of smooth-tongued politicians whose benign facade cloaks a corrosive lust for power that drives them to espouse repressive legislation and militant foreign policies. Less dramatically, aggressive individuals participate in the ordinary affairs of everyday life: the punitive, "right-minded" father, the cunning, sweet-voiced salesman, the puritanical, "hell-and-damnation" minister, the picayune rule-abiding dean and the haughty, guilt-producing mother.

The anguish and pain engendered by the actions of these individuals have prompted philosophers and psychologists over the ages to search for a cause, a rationale that stirs these persons to behave in their hostile fashion. Such inquiries have led to innumerable "explanations," none of which alone is sufficient to account for the divergent forms in which aggressive behavior is displayed.

Most common among the more sophisticated explanations is the lack of trust and confidence in others which typifies these personalities. According to this thesis, their actions spring from an anticipation of hostility from others; thus, their aggression is a counterattack, a fending off of the malice and humiliation they have learned to expect; in short, they seek to "beat the other fellow to the punch."

To accomplish this goal, aggressive personalities grab as much control and power as they can so as to prevent others from using it to exploit and harm them. Once having seized power, however, they become ruthless and vindictive themselves; they employ their acquired strength for retribution; they "get back" at those who mistreated and betrayed them in the past.

The following case illustrates the development of a number of these features of the aggressive pattern:

**CASE 7-2**
*John W., Age 42, Production Supervisor, Married, Two Children*

The company for whom Mr. W. worked recently contracted with a management consulting firm to have their middle and senior level executives "talk over their personal problems" on a regular basis with visiting psychologists. Mr. W. was advised to take advantage of the arrangement because of repetitive difficulties with his subordinates; he had been accused of being "rough" with his secretaries, and excessively demanding of engineers and technicians directly responsible to him. The validity of these accusations was attested to by a rapid turnover in his department, and the frequent requests for transfer on the part of his professional staff.

Mr. W. was seen as a tall, broad-shouldered, muscular, but slightly paunchy, man with a leathery, large-featured face, large hands and brusque manner. He was the third child in a family of four; the oldest child was a girl, the others were boys. He recalled that his mother spoke of him as a strong-willed and energetic baby, one who fought to have his way right from the start. Until he left for college at 18 he lived with his family on a small ranch in Montana. His father struggled to "make a go of things" through the depression, and died just as he was "starting to make ends meet." Mr. W. spoke of his father as a tough, God-fearing man; he dominated the household, was a "mean" disciplinarian and showed no warmth or gentility. Toward the end of his life, while Mr. W. was in his teens, his father "got drunk three or four times a week," and often would come home and try to "beat up the kids and mom." He hated his father, but recognized that he served as a model for his own toughness and hardheaded outlook.

Mother was a background figure; she cooked, cleaned and helped out on the ranch when father asked her to do so. She never interfered with her husband's wishes and demands, turning over all decisions and responsibilities to him. Mr. W.'s older sister was quiet like his mother; they both "sort of faded into the wall." The three brothers were quite different; they fought "tooth and nail" ever since they were young. Mr. W. proudly boasted, "I could beat up my older brother when I was ten and he was 12"; he remained the dominant sibling from then on.

Mr. W. was given a "paid scholarship" to play college football, but was drafted into the Army between his freshman and sophomore years. He served in the final European phase of the war and recalled his harrowing experiences with considerable pride; he currently is an active member of a veterans organization. Upon returning home, he continued his education on the G.I. Bill of Rights, played football for two seasons and majored in business economics. Upon graduation he joined, as a field production assistant, the oil firm in which he is currently employed, married a girl he "picked up" some months before and moved about from one field location to another as assigned by his company.

On the job, Mr. W. was known as a "hard boss"; he was respected by the field hands, but got on rather poorly with the higher level technicians because of his "insistence that not a penny be wasted, and that nobody shirk their job." He was an indefatigable worker himself, and demanded that everyone within his purview be likewise. At times he would be severely critical of other production chiefs who were, as he saw it, "lax with their men." Mr. W. "couldn't stand lazy, cheating people"; "softness and kindness were for social workers"; "there's a job that's to be done and easy-going people can't get it done the way it should be." Mr. W. feared "the socialists" who were "going to ruin the country." He had a similar distaste for "lazy and cheating" minority and racial groups.

Mr. W. was assigned to the central office of his company on the basis of his profitable production record; for the first time in his occupational life he had a "desk job." His immediate superior liked the way Mr. W. "tackled problems" but was concerned that he alienated others in the office by his gruffness and directness. It was only after considerable dissension within his department that Mr. W. was advised, as he put it, "to unload on someone other than my secretaries and my pussy-footing engineers."

## CLINICAL PICTURE

Let us organize the major features of the active-independent pattern in line with the four levels of data used in previous sections.

### Behavior

Many people shy away from aggressive personalities, feeling intimidated by their brusque and belligerent manner. They sense that the aggressive individual is cold and callous, insensitive to the feelings of others and that he gains pleasure by competing with and humiliating anyone he can get his hands on.

Aggressive personalities tend to be argumentative and contentious; on occasion, they are abusive, cruel and malicious. They insist in discussions on being viewed as "right," tend to be dogmatic in their views and rarely give in on points, despite evidence negating their position.

Aggressive personalities behave as if the "softer" emotions were tinged with poison; they avoid expressions of warmth and intimacy and are suspicious of gentility, compassion and kindness, seeming to doubt the genuineness of these feelings.

When matters go their way, they may act in a gracious, cheerful, saucy and clever manner. But more characteristically, their behavior is guarded, reserved and resentful. Moreover, they have a low tolerance for frustration, and fear being viewed as indecisive and inadequate. When crossed, pushed on personal matters or faced with embarrassment, they respond quickly and become furious, revengeful and vindictive; they are easily provoked to attack, to demean and to dominate.

### Phenomenological Reports

Most active-independents are perceptually alert, finely attuned to the subtle elements of human interaction. There is a minor segment within this group that may constitutionally be gross and insensitive, but the great majority, though appearing to be coarse and imperceptive, are in fact quite keenly aware of the moods and feelings of others. Their seeming insensitivity stems from their tendency to use what they see for purposes of upsetting the equilibrium of others, that is, they take advantage of their acute perception of the weaknesses of others to be intentionally callous or manipulative.

The active-independent views himself as assertive, energetic, self-reliant and perhaps hard-boiled, but honest, strong and realistic. If we accept his premise that ours is a tough, dog-eat-dog world, we can understand why he values himself for being hard-headed, forthright and un-sentimental. In a jungle philosophy of life, where "might makes right," the only valid course for a person is to be on guard, suspicious, critical, aggressive and even ruthless.

He is adept at pointing out the hypocrisy and ineffectuality of do-gooders; he notes the devastating consequences of appeasement and submission; he justifies his aggressiveness by pointing to the hostile and exploitive behavior of others; he is contemptuous of the weak, and does not care if he is looked on with disfavor, claiming that "good guys come in last," and so on. To him, the only safe way to survive in this world is to dominate and control others; if you don't, they will.

The aggressive independent dreads the thought of being weak, of being deceived and of being humiliated. He expects no greater kindness from others than they should expect from him. He projects his own hostility, sees others as arrogant and bellicose and claims that he must be aggressive to defend himself. His principal task in life is to outsmart others, to get power over them before they outfox and dominate him. Perhaps, as he views it, if others were different he

could let his guard down, relax his striving for power. But people are ruthless; it is this "fact" that provokes him to act; he must outdo them at their own game. Personal feelings are irrelevant, at best; at worst, they are signs of weakness and of maudlin and sloppy sentimentality. No one can make a go of it in this life if he lets his feelings get in the way.

### Intrapsychic Processes

The aggressive personality is distinguished by his tendency to act out his impulses, rather than rework them, as is more usual, through intrapsychic mechanisms. He blurts out his feelings and vents his urges directly; rather than contain, inhibit or reshape his thoughts, he expresses them forcibly and precipitously. This directness may appear to some as commendable, an indication of forthrightness and openness; but the aggressive person expresses himself thusly, not out of "honesty and integrity," but from a desire to assert himself and intimidate others.

Despite the relative openness with which the active-independent expresses his feelings, there are times when he must restrain and transmute them. One cannot live harmoniously in society if one constantly bursts forth with one's hostile impulses; some measure of constraint and transformation must be invoked. To accomplish this, the aggressive personality utilizes three major mechanisms: rationalization, sublimation and projection.

The simplest and most expedient means of justifying one's aggressive urges is to find a plausible and socially acceptable excuse for them. Thus, the bluntness and gruff directness which characterize the active-independent are rationalized as signifying his frankness and honesty, his lack of hypocrisy, his willingness to face issues head-on, his being realistic and his not being mealy-mouthed and soft-headed; recall how clearly these are illustrated in the case of John W.

More long-range and less obvious resolutions of their hostile urges are seen in the occupations and professions to which aggressive personalities gravitate. Thus, they may sublimate their impulses by working in highly competitive business enterprises, by selecting a military career, joining the police force or the legal profession, becoming surgeons and so on.

The mechanism of projection is not uncommon among these personalities. Already sensitive to signs of potential danger from without, and well disposed to ward off threat by aggressive counteraction, the active-independent accentuates the fear of hostility he anticipates from others by projecting on to them his own hostility; this, of course, enables him to justify his aggressive actions since he perceives himself to be the object of unjust persecution. However, by attributing to others the hostility he feels toward them, he not only purges himself of any blame for his "defensive" actions, but, in a self-perpetuating cycle, aggravates his initial fears. Thus, the danger he now sees around him is a product of his own projections. More will be said of this mechanism and its destructive consequences in later sections.

### Biophysical Factors

There are a number of constitutional features which appear to occur with disproportionately high frequency among active-independent personalities.

In the realm of activation, these persons tend to be energetic, react with high intensity to stimuli and have a low threshold for responding. Unbounded in energy, they appear assertive and pushy and intrude upon others like the proverbial "bull in a china shop." Other active-independents display an irritability to stimulation; they respond before thinking, are impulsive, cannot delay or inhibit the first flush of feeling and therefore behave less reflectively and in a less controlled manner than those who can postpone and reevaluate their initial reactions.

With regard to affect and temperament, there are indications that aggressive personalities may possess what have been termed the parmic and choleric dispositions. Many appear constitutionally fearless (parmic), unblanched by events which most people experience as dangerous and frightening; they evidence a foolhardy courageousness, a venturesomeness seemingly blind to potentially serious consequences. Others appear easily provoked to intense anger (choleric); their biophysical make-up seems constituted to lead them to respond with hostility "at the drop of a hat"; their threshold for feeling angry is so low that the mildest of provocations can elicit intense rage reactions.

## ETIOLOGY AND DEVELOPMENT

Following the format laid down in discussing the previous patterns, we might note the following characteristics as typical of the aggressive personality: *hostile affectivity* (irritable and easily provoked to anger), *cognitive projection* (tending to ascribe one's own malicious motives to others), *assertive self-image* (proud of his energy, "realism," and hard-headedness) and *interpersonal vindictiveness* (socially blunt, intimidating and punitive). Let us next turn to those aspects of

their developmental background which may give rise to these features.

### Biogenic Factors

In previous discussions concerning the role of biogenic influences, we noted both the marked paucity of established empirical findings and the highly speculative nature of etiological propositions; the hypotheses to be presented below must be viewed in this light. Although plausible, they should be seen with a skeptical eye until they are adequately researched and verified.

**Heredity.** The high frequency of correspondence in overt hostile behavior commonly observed among family members suggests that constitutional dispositions traceable to genetic origins may play a role in the development of the aggressive pattern. Of course, observed similarities in family behaviors can be accounted for in large measure by shared experiences and common training methods. Nevertheless, it seems reasonable to posit that if there are biophysical substrates for aggressive tendencies, they may in part be transmitted by heredity.

**Choleric or Parmic Infantile Reaction Patterns.** Parents who bring their acting out and aggressive children to clinics often report that their youngsters "always were that way." A common complaint is that their child displayed temper tantrums even as an infant, would get furious and turn "red" when frustrated, either when awaiting the bottle or feeling uncomfortable in his wet diaper. As the child matured he is described as having had a "hot temper," and a bullying and demanding attitude toward other children. Not uncommonly, parents remark that these children seemed undaunted by punishment, unimpressionable, unbending and unmanageable. Furthermore, they evidenced a daring and boldness, an audacious and foolhardy willingness to chance punishment and physical harm; they seemed thick skinned and unaffected by pain.

The possession of such temperamental attributes from early life are significant not only in themselves but for the experiences they produce, and the reactions they evoke from others. Being more venturesome, such children explore the challenges and competitions of their environment more assertively; moreover, they intrude themselves and upset the peaceful existence that others seek. Not only are they likely to encounter and precipitate more conflict and trouble than most children, but their seeming recalcitrance in the face of punishment results in their receiving more punishment than that required to control most children. Thus, given a "nasty" disposition and an "incorrigible" temperament from the start, these children provoke a superabundance of exasperation and counterhostility from others. Their constitutional tendencies may, therefore, initiate a vicious circle in which they not only prompt frequent aggression from others, but, as a consequence, learn to expect frequent hostility.

**Mesomorphic-Endomorphic Body Build.** Although aggressive personalities may be found to possess all varieties of body build, there appears to be an especially high proportion who are either mesomorphic, or a mesomorphic-endomorphic mixture. Whether these body builds are constitutionally linked to the choleric and parmic temperaments, hypothesized above, cannot be assessed given our present state of knowledge and technology. Even if a genetic linkage between them does exist, it is likely that the presence of a heavy, muscular morphology would increase the probability that the individual will find that assertive and aggressive behaviors "pay off" for him. In other words, the powerful and sturdy youngster will more readily learn to utilize these behaviors since he is more likely to experience success in achieving his goals with them than a frailer youngster will.

**Neurological Characteristics.** Quite conceivably, a disposition to aggressive behavior may be based in part on low thresholds for activation. Should the reticular pathways for arousal be unusually dense, or should they be laid out so as to short-circuit the inhibitory and delaying effects of cortical intervention, the individual may exhibit both intense and impulsive behaviors, both of which are conducive to the learning of aggressive habits.

An unusual anatomical distribution in the limbic system also may contribute to the distinctive pattern of affectivity found in the active-independent. Conceivably, both "pleasure" and "pain" centers may be functionally sparse, accounting, in part at least, for the typical seriousness, hard-headedness and "lack of joy" seen in the aggressive personality, and also, for the bold and seemingly fearless quality of their outlook. Furthermore, we may speculate that the biophysical substrate for "rage and anger" may be either copious or extensively branched, resulting in more intense and more frequently activated hostile reactions.

*Psychogenic Factors*

Although aggressive characteristics may be traced in part to biogenic dispositions, psychogenic factors will shape the content and direction of these dispositions; moreover, psychogenic influences often are sufficient in themselves to prompt these behaviors. The following hypotheses focus on the role of experience and learning, but let us keep in mind that as far as personality patterns are concerned biogenic and psychogenic factors interweave in a complex sequence of interactions.

**Parental Hostility.** Infants, who for constitutional reasons, are cold, sullen, testy or otherwise difficult to manage, are likely to provoke negative and rejecting reactions from their parents. It does not take long before a child with this disposition will be stereotyped as a "miserable, ill-tempered and disagreeable little beast." Once categorized in this fashion, momentum builds up and we may see a lifelong cycle of parent-child feuding.

Parental hostilities may stem from sources other than the child's initial disposition; for example, children often are convenient scapegoats for displacing angers that have been generated elsewhere. Thus, in many cases, a vicious circle of parent-child conflict may have its roots in a parent's occupational, marital or social frustrations. Whatever its inital source, a major cause for the development of an aggressive personality pattern is exposure to parental cruelty and domination.

Before elaborating some of the features associated with parental hostility which lead to the aggressive personality, we might note some points which distinguish the experiences of the active-detached, as contrasted to the active-independent patterns. They are in many respects alike; both are exposed to parental rejection and both learn to be suspicious and to view the world as hostile and dangerous.

Two factors may account for why the active-detached learns to withdraw from others whereas the active-independent learns to rise up with counterhostility.

*First,* a close examination of the childhood of the *active-detached* personality indicates that parental rejection took the form primarily of belittlement, teasing and humiliation. Although these children may have borne the brunt of occasional physical cruelty, the essential nature of the message conveyed by the persecutor was that the child was weak, worthless and beneath contempt. As a result of this demeaning and deprecating attitude, the child learned to devalue himself, and developed little or no sense of self-esteem. Being worthless, derided and forlorn, he felt powerless to counterattack, to overcome the humiliation and ridicule to which he was exposed. The *active-independent* child was an object of similar aggression from his parents, but he received or experienced a different message than did the active-detached child. Rather than being devalued in the attack, he learned to feel that he was a "power" that had to be contended with, that he could cause others to be upset, that he had the wherewithal to influence the moods, attitudes and behaviors of others. Thus, instead of feeling humiliated and belittled, each reaction, each hostile onslaught to which he was exposed, served to reinforce an image of his influence and potency. Once viewing himself as possessing the power of "causing trouble," he was spurred on to more vigorous action and counterhostility.

The *second* distinction between the active-detached and active-independent may be traced to differences in temperamental attributes. It is not implausible that parmic (constitutionally fearless) and threctic (constitutionally fearful) youngsters would respond differently to parental hostility. This parental attitude would be likely to produce an avoidant pattern in a threctic youngster, thus an active-detached personality, and an aggressive pattern in a parmic youngster, thus an active-independent personality.

Let us now return to the rationale for believing that parental hostility can lead to the acquisition of an aggressive personality style.

Hostility breeds hostility, not only in generating intense feelings of anger and resentment on the part of the recipient, but, perhaps more importantly, in establishing a model for vicarious learning and imitation. It appears to make little difference as to whether or not a child desires consciously to copy parental hostility; mere exposure to these behaviors, especially in childhood when alternatives have as yet not been observed, serves as an implicit guide as to how people feel and relate to one another. Thus, impulsive or physically brutal parents arouse and release strong counter feelings of hostility in their children; moreover, they demonstrate in their roughshod and inconsiderate behavior both a model for imitation and an implicit sanction for similar behaviors to be exhibited whenever the child feels anger or frustration.

It may be useful next to trace the effects of parental hostility in line with the three major stages of neuropsychological development since this breakdown will provide us with additional insights into the complex pattern of habits and attitudes displayed by the aggressive personality.

1. The distinguishing feature of the sensory attachment stage is likely to have been *not* the amount of stimulation to which the infant was exposed, but rather its quality. Rough, abrupt or harsh treatment provides adequate, if not abundant, stimulation; but it also conveys a tone, a "feeling" in the neonate that the world is an unkind, painful and dangerous place, that discomfort and frustration are to be expected and to be prepared for. Early parental hostility is "felt"; it cues the infant to mistrust his environment and to view it with suspicion.

2. Having learned to expect that the world will treat him harshly, the child enters the sensorimotor-autonomy stage with a feeling that he cannot depend on the good will of others, that he must turn to himself to provide rewards and avoid discomforts. By virtue of constitutional strengths, or of parental reactions to his behavior which encourage a faith in his powers, the youngster rapidly acquires the skills of autonomy and self-reliance. Thus, by the end of the second neuropsychological stage, these children are both deeply mistrustful and substantially independent of their parents.

3. Being both suspicious of others and confident in their powers of self-sufficiency, these youngsters begin the intracortical-initiative stage with a determination to reject the directives and controls of others. Why should this child accept the restrictions and demands which others seek to impose upon him when he has nothing to gain and, in addition, is convinced that he can manage better on his own?

Subjected to persistent parental hostility throughout these growing years, he learns not only to reject them but to oppose actively the values and standards of much of the entire adult world. Thus, he sets out to shape his own identity, one that is contrary to those espoused by his "persecutors," and in so doing, embarks on a course of independence and mistrust, and one that is characterized by self-sufficiency.

Another consequence of rejecting "authorities" is to lose the guidance and controls society provides for handling and directing impulses. By failing to accept traditional values and customs, the youngster is left on his own. He must devise, anew, ways and means to handle his emotions. Going it alone is no simple task, and in this sphere, where these children are strongly driven by hostile impulses, we find that few of them acquire self-developed controls adequate to their emotions. For this, among other reasons, the active-independent youngster has difficulty in deferring gratifications, in resisting temptations and in inhibiting angry reactions to even the slightest frustrations; in short, he pursues his desires with little concern for the dangers or complications they invite.

**Deficient Parental Models and Social Ostracism.** Children who are exposed to parental hostility acquire enduring resentments toward others, and incorporate the parental model of aggression as a guide for venting these feelings. This background is among the most common found in the aggressive personality, but by no means is it the only psychogenic source for the development of this pattern.

Another set of experiences conducive to the aggressive personality is one in which there is a lack of parental models. In these cases, parents provide little or no guidance for the child, and he is left to fend for himself, to observe and to emulate whatever models he can find to guide him.

Broken families, especially those in which the father has abandoned his wife and children, characterize this state of affairs. With the model and authority of the breadwinner out of sight, and the mother harassed by overwork and financial insecurity, the youngster often is left to roam the streets, unguided and unrestrained by the affection and controls of an attending parent. The disappearance of the father and the preoccupations of a distracted mother are felt implicitly as signs of rejection. To find a model, a credo by which his fate can be mobilized and given meaning, he must often turn to his peers, to those other barren and lost souls who are bereft also of parental attention, and wander aimlessly in a hostile world.

Together with their fellow outcasts, these youngsters quickly learn that they are viewed as misfits in society, that their misfortunes will be compounded by the deprecatory and closed-minded attitudes of the larger community. They learn also that it is only by toughness and cunning that they will find a means of survival. But this adaptive strategy sets into play a vicious circle; as the youngster asserts himself, as he ventures into the deviant remains left for him and his fellow scavengers by the larger society, that very same society castigates and condemns him. His resentment mounts, and the circle of hostility and counterhostility gains momentum. With no hope of changing his fate, no promise of advancement, and struggling throughout to keep a foothold in the dog-eat-dog world into which he has been cast, he is driven further into an aggressive and vindictive style of life.

## COPING STRATEGIES

If we look at the world through the eyes of the aggressive personality—a place fraught with frustration and danger, a place where he must be on guard against the malevolence and cruelty of others—we can better understand why he behaves as he does.

His strategy is clear. You cannot trust others; they will abuse and exploit their power, they will dispossess you, strip you of all gratifications and dominate and brutalize you, if they can. To avoid this fate, one must arrogate all the power one can to oneself, one must block others from possessing the means to be belittling, exploitive and harmful. Only by alert vigilance to threat, only by vigorous counteraction can one withstand and obstruct their malice and hostility. Getting close to others, displaying weakness and being willing to appease and compromise, are fatal concessions to be avoided at all costs. Only by acquiring power for oneself can one be assured of gaining the rewards of life; only by usurping the powers which others command can one thwart them from misusing it. Given these fears and attitudes, we can readily see why they have taken the course of the active and independent strategy. Only through self-sufficiency and decisive action can they forestall the dangers of their environment and maximize achieving the bounties of life.

How are these aims manifested in social behavior, how does the aggressive personality justify these behaviors, and by what intrapsychic mechanisms does he maintain a modicum of peace with himself?

**Vindictive Interpersonal Behavior.** The aggressive act serves more than the function of counteracting hostility for the active-independent; he is driven to aggress by a desire to dominate and humiliate others, to wreak vengeance upon those who have mistreated him. Not only does he covet possessions and powers but he gains special pleasure in usurping and taking from others; what he can plagiarize, swindle and extort are fruits far sweeter than those he can earn through honest labor. And once having drained what he can from one source, he turns to others to exploit, bleed and then cast aside; his pleasure in the misfortunes of others is unquenchable.

Having learned to trust only himself, he has no feelings of loyalty, and may be treacherous and scheming beneath a veneer of politeness and civility. People are to be used as a means to an end; they are to be subordinated and demeaned so that he can vindicate himself for the grievances, misery and humiliations of the past. By provoking fear and intimidating others and by being ascendant and powerful, he will undo the lowly caste of his childhood. His search for power, then, is not benign; it springs from hate and the desire for retribution and vindication.

Not only does the strategy of assertion and domination gain release from past injustices, but, as with most coping maneuvers, it proves successful in achieving rewards in the present. Most people find themselves intimidated by hostile and sarcastic criticism and by the threat of emotional outbursts and physical violence. In using these behaviors, the aggressive personality possesses a powerful instrumentality at his disposal for coercing others, for frightening them into fearful respect and passive submission.

Most active-independents find a niche for themselves in society where their hostile and belligerent behaviors are sanctioned and admired. The cleverly conniving businessman, the physically brutal army sergeant, the stern and punitive school principal and the sadistic and self-righteous father, all illustrate roles which cloak outlets for vengeful hostilities under the guise of assuming a socially responsible function.

**Weak Intrapsychic Controls and the Mechanisms of Rationalization and Projection.** Threats, brute hostility and sarcasm are not endearing traits. How does one justify them to others, and by what means does the person rid himself of the fact that these behaviors may be unjust and irrational?

As noted in an earlier section, the aggressive personality has usually rebelled against controls his parents and society suggest to manage and guide his impulses. Rarely do these youngsters substitute adequate controls in their stead; as a consequence, they fail to restrain or channel the emotions that well up within them. As feelings surge forth, they are vented more or less directly; thus, we see the low tolerance, the impulsive rashness, the susceptibility to temptation and the acting out of impulses so characteristic of this pattern.

Obvious and persistent hostility cannot be overlooked. To make it acceptable, the aggressive individual fabricates rather transparent rationalizations. He espouses such philosophical balderdash as: "Might is right," "This is a dog-eat-dog world," "I'm being honest, not hypocritical like the rest of you," "It's better to get these kids used to tough handling now before it's too late" and "You've got to be a realist in this world, and most people are either foolish idealists, appeasers, commies or atheists." Thus, the most common intrapsychic device employed by aggressive personalities seeks not to negate their hostile feelings but to recast them in a favorable light. Seen in this way, they are fully justified, and need not be restrained; if anything, they are more valid than ever.

The active-independent's intense feelings occasionally surge forth irrationally, and he must supplement his intrapsychic apparatus with additional mechanisms.

Accustomed throughout life to hostility from others, and exquisitely attuned to the subtlest of signs of contempt and derision, he begins to interpret the incidental behaviors and innocent remarks of others as signifying fresh attacks upon him. Increasingly, he finds evidence that now, as before, others are ready to persecute, to slander and to vilify him.

Given this perception of his environment, he need not rationalize his outbursts; they are "justified" reactions to the malevolence of others. It is "they" who are contemptible, slanderous and belligerent and who hate and wish to destroy him. He is the victim, an innocent and indignant bystander subject to unjust persecution and hostility. Thus, John W. not only saw "socialists and commies everywhere" trying to undermine his way of life, but, more specifically, believed that most of his subordinates were purposely complaining and shirking their responsibilities . . . "in order to make me look bad." Through this projection maneuver, then, he not only disowns and purges his sadistic and malicious impulses but attributes this evil to others. He has absolved himself of the irrationality of his hostile outbursts; moreover, as a persecuted victim, he is free to counterattack and to gain restitution and vindication.

## SELF-PERPETUATION OF PATTERN

Despite the fact that the coping strategies of the aggressive personality have been learned as an optimum pattern for minimizing negative reinforcements and maximizing positive reinforcements, they produce, as do all pathological strategies, certain self-defeating actions. Not only are they adaptively inflexible and thereby ineffective in dealing with novel challenges, but they rest upon a rather tenuous and easily upset psychic balance. But perhaps their most destructive consequence is their tendency to foster rather than resolve problems.

**Perceptual and Cognitive Distortions.** Much of what is communicated and experienced in everyday life is fragmentary in nature—a few words, an intonation in voice or a gesture. On the basis of these incomplete odds and ends we usually extract a "message" or come to some conclusion or inference as to what others are conveying or intending; thus, we are constantly "filling in between the lines" on the basis of past experience, thereby enabling us to give these incidental cues a coherence and meaning.

Among the determinants of this "filling in" process are our own moods and anticipations. If we expect a particular person to be cruel and demeaning we are more likely to piece together the hazy elements of his communication in line with this expectancy. If we feel blue and down-hearted some days, it appears that the whole world is downcast and gloomy with us. Since the outlook and moods of most people are episodic and temporary, these intrusions tend to counterbalance each other; thus, we may be suspicious of certain persons but overly naive with others; we may feel dejected some days but cheerful and optimistic on others.

This variability and balancing of affects is not typical of pathological personality patterns. In the active-independent, for example, there is an everpresent undertone of anger and resentment; there is a persistent suspicion that others are devious and hostile. Because of the enduring nature of these moods and expectancies, the aggressive personality repeatedly distorts the incidental remarks and actions of others so that they appear to be deprecating and vilifying him. He consistently misinterprets what he sees and hears, and magnifies minor slights into major insults and slanders.

Despite the fact that the aggressive personality's vigilant sensitivity to the dangers of external threat is understandable, given his history and the function it serves of safeguarding him against present dangers, it tends, in the long run, to promote several self-defeating consequences.

By perceiving hostility where none exists he prevents himself from recognizing the objective good will of others. Phenomenologically speaking, *his* reality is what *he* perceives, not what factually exists. Thus, his extreme vulnerability to threat blocks him from recognizing the presence of non-threatening experiences, that is, experiences which might prove gratifying and thereby change the course of his outlook and attitudes. Moreover, these distortions aggravate his misfortunes by creating, through mood and anticipation, fictitious dangers which duplicate the past. Rather than avoiding anguish, his hypersensitivity uncovers them where, in fact, they do not exist. In effect, then, his moods and defensive strategies fabricate dangers engendered by his own actions, dangers from which he cannot escape since they derive from within himself.

**Demeaning of Affection and Cooperative Behavior.** The aggressive personality is suspicious of, and tends to depreciate, sentimentality, intimate feelings, tenderness and social cooperativeness. He lacks all sympathy for the weak and oppressed, and displays contempt toward those who express compassion and concern for the underdog.

Why should he be sentimental? What pleasures did he enjoy in childhood to look back upon so fondly? He learned all too well to trust no one. Why should he be sympathetic and kindly? Should he again chance the rebuffs he suffered at the hands of his parents and society? Won't others only undo him and infringe upon the freedom and autonomy which are so vital to his defense and his style of life?

By denying all tender feelings, the active-independent protects himself against the memory of painful parental rejections. Furthermore, feelings of sympathy and warmth would be entirely antithetical to the militant credo he has carved out for himself as a philosophy of life. To express "softer" emotions would only shake the foundations of his coping strategies and reactivate feelings that he has rigidly denied for years. Why upset the applecart? Why be rebuffed and exploited again? Moreover, sympathetic and tender feelings only "get in the way," only distract and divert him from being the well-oiled machine, the hard-headed realist he must be.

But this very attitude creates a vicious circle. By restraining positive feelings toward others and by repudiating the sharing and intimacy of co-operative social behaviors, he provokes others to withdraw from him. His cold and arrogant manner intimidates them and blocks them from expressing warmth and affection. Thus, once again, through his own actions, he creates experiences which perpetuate the frosty, condemning and rejecting environment of his childhood.

**Creation of Realistic Antagonisms.** The aggressive personality evokes hostility, not only as an incidental consequence of his behavior and attitude but because he often intentionally provokes others into conflict. He carries a "chip on his shoulder," seems to be spoiling for a fight and appears to enjoy tangling with others to prove his strength and to test his competencies and powers.

Having periodically been successful in past aggressive ventures, he now feels confident of his prowess; as a consequence, he displays a "repetition compulsion," a habit that is persistently exercised and nurtured. He seeks out dangers and challenges. Not only is he unconcerned and reckless but he appears poised and bristling, ready to vent resentments, to demonstrate his invulnerability, to restore his pride and vindicate himself.

But to what end? What does he accomplish besides reworking the tensions and resentments of the past? As with his perceptions and attitudes, his aggressive, conflict seeking behaviors only perpetuate his fears and his misery. More than merely fostering distance and rejection, he now has provoked others into justified counterhostility. By looking for a fight and by precipitous and irrational arrogance, he has created not only a distant reserve on their part but intense and well-reasoned animosity. Now he must face real aggression, and now he has a real basis for fearing retaliation. Objective threats and resentments do exist in his environment, and the vicious circle has been perpetuated anew. His vigilant state of mobilization cannot be relaxed; he must ready himself, no longer for suspected threat and imagined hostility, but for the real thing.

## REMEDIAL APPROACHES

The prognostic picture for the active-independent cannot be viewed as promising, unless he has found a socially sanctioned sphere of activities in which to channel his energies and hostilities. His chronic pattern will not readily be altered since his mistrust is deep, he resists exploring his own motives and his defensive armor is firm and resolute. However, unless he suffers repeated setbacks to his goals and strategies, he may not succumb to progressive decompensation.

The aggressive personality is not a willing participant in therapy; the submissive, help-seeking role of patient is anathema to these power oriented and mistrustful people. When they come for therapy it is usually under the pressure of marital discord or vocational friction; they may be in a jam as a consequence of undue harshness with subordinates, as in the case of John W., or as a result of incessant quarrels with and occasional brutality toward their spouse or children. Rarely do they experience guilt or accept blame for the turmoil they cause; to them, the problem can be traced to the other fellow's stupidity, laziness and hostility. Even when they voice some measure of responsibility for their difficulties, one senses an underlying defiance, a resentment and scorn toward their "do-gooder" therapist.

Aggressive personalities challenge the therapist and seek to outwit and defeat him. They set up situations to test the therapist's skills, to catch him in an inconsistency, to arouse his ire, to belittle and humiliate him. It is no mean task for the therapist to restrain his impulse to "do battle," or to express a condemning or disapproving attitude; great effort may at times be expended

to check these counterhostile and rejecting feelings. The therapist may have to remind himself periodically that his client's plight was not of his own doing, that he was the unfortunate recipient of a harsh and unkind upbringing and that only by a respectful and sympathetic approach can he ever be helped to get back on the right track.

To accomplish this goal the therapist must be ready to see things from the patient's point of view, he must convey a sense of trust, a feeling of sharing and alliance; it is imperative, however, that this building of rapport not be interpreted by the patient as a sign of the therapist's capitulation, of his having been intimidated by bluff and arrogance. He must maintain a balance of professional firmness and authority, mixed with understanding and a tolerance of the patient's less attractive traits. By building an image of a kind yet strong authority figure for himself, the therapist may guide the patient to change his expectancies. In his quiet manner and his thoughtful comments, the therapist may serve as a model of power, restraint and kindness, a model he desires to have his client learn to emulate. Hopefully, by this process, the patient may begin to develop more wholesome attitudes toward others, and be led to direct his energies into more constructive channels than he had in the past.

Among specific therapeutic techniques we may single out the biophysical pharmacological agents, the phenomenological and intrapsychic psychotherapies and group treatment methods. Various drugs are available to modulate the threshold and intensity of reactivity; these biological changes may minimize the frequency and depth of hostile feelings, and thereby decrease some of the self-perpetuating consequences of aggressive behavior. Some of the less directive phenomenological approaches may provide the patient with an opportunity to "vent his spleen"; once drained of venom, the patient may be disposed to explore his feelings and attitudes, and be guided into less destructive outlets than before. Intrapsychic procedures may be called for if a more thorough reworking of the patient's defensive strategies are sought. As far as group methods are concerned, aggressive patients often disrupt the functioning of therapeutic units. In time, however, many of these patients become useful catalysts for group interaction, and appear to gain insight and more constructive social attitudes.

# BASIC AMBIVALENT PATTERNS

Conflicts are an inevitable part of living. Each of us faces them periodically in the course of our daily life, and some unfortunate individuals are plagued with them for extended periods. Most conflicting desires and pressures are conscious to us, but some, the more painful ones, are kept from awareness, that is, are unconscious. What is true about the presence of conflicts in normal individuals certainly is true of those we label as pathological; perhaps their conflicts have been more intense or have endured longer than those experienced by normals.

For the most part, both normal and pathological personalities resolve their conflicts; allowing a conflict to remain uppermost in our thoughts is severely discomforting and debilitating. However, some of these resolutions are self-defeating, as in the case of a number of the pathological types thus far discussed.

Certain conflicts may be viewed as "basic" in the sense that they are either particularly disruptive, or last long or lead to resolutions that have wide ranging and enduring effects. One of these conflicts appears especially relevant to our discussion; it relates to the question of whether the person turns primarily to himself or to others to provide the reinforcements he seeks. Once an answer to this question has evolved, it will markedly influence the course of an individual's life.

Normal individuals, by virtue of their experiences, have learned to feel comfortable both with themselves and others; they are not in "basic conflict," and therefore can seek reinforcements from both sources. The pathological personalities previously discussed in this chapter and in chapter 6 have been forced by circumstance to face this conflict, and have opted, albeit unconsciously, for a consistent and single resolution. The *detached* individual, perhaps the most unfortunate of the lot, has found that he achieves positive reinforcements neither from others nor from himself; furthermore, as in the case of the active-detached, he may experience only negative reinforcements from both sources. For him, then, there is no conflict on this score; he looks neither to himself nor to others for satisfaction. The *dependent* individual is more fortunate in that he has learned that he can obtain reward and protection from others; however, he finds little pleasure or solace within himself. The conflict is resolved, then, by turning to the outer world. The situation is reversed in the case of *independent* personalities; their experience has taught them that it is best to look to themselves for protection and for the bounties of life.

Despite the fact that each of the aforementioned personalities will experience events through the course of their lives that will cause them to reconsider their decision, the probabilities are high that they will perceive these events in terms of their past and, therefore, will continue along the path they previously have followed. For them, the decision as to where one must turn for reinforcement has essentially been settled. They have learned to feel an optimum degree of comfort with their choice and have little or no doubt about the fact that it is best for them.

But this resoluteness is not true of all pathological patterns; in fact, it is the failure to come to terms with this conflict that characterizes the central difficulty of certain persons. We shall call those who experience this problem the "ambivalent pattern." Two types may be noted: those whose ambivalence is manifest in overt vacillation and inconsistency (active-ambivalent), and those who appear on the surface to have turned entirely to others, but are struggling to restrain an intense, unconscious desire to follow their own impulses (passive-ambivalent). Coexistent in both are strong, opposite desires and feelings toward others and themselves.

The *active-ambivalent,* or *negativistic personality* experiences the turmoil of his indecision daily. He gets into endless wrangles and disappointments as he vacillates emotionally between submissive dependency and conformity, at one time, and stubborn negativism and resolute autonomy, the next. The *passive-ambivalent* or *conforming personality* appears entirely different. He manifests an extraordinary consistency, a rigid and unvarying uniformity. This he accomplishes by overcontrolling and repressing all signs of autonomy and independence; he complies in every way to the strictures and rules set down by others. But this propriety and restraint are like a cloak with which he deceives himself and others, a straitjacket he places on himself to control intense impulses toward autonomy and self-assertion. Let us turn our attention to a fuller discussion of this passive-ambivalent pattern.

## THE CONFORMING PERSONALITY: PASSIVE-AMBIVALENT PATTERN
(DSM-II: *Obsessive-Compulsive Personality*)

Ambivalence connotes conflict, an opposition between contrary tendencies. We may better grasp the nature of the conflict within the passive-ambivalent by referring to the diametrically opposite trends displayed in two other pathological patterns, the passive-dependent (submissive personality) and active-independent (aggressive personality); in many respects, the passive-ambivalent reflects a mixture of these polar extremes. For example, he is like the active-independent in that he possesses a strong, albeit unconscious, desire to assert himself, to take the initiative and act autonomously of regulations imposed by others. Yet, at the same time, his conscious motivation is akin to the passive-dependent; he seeks to submit to others and submerge his individuality. To secure the support and comforts which others provide, he rigidly controls his impulses toward independence, and overcomplies to the standards and expectations they set down. He is like the aggressive personality, at the unconscious level; but consciously and behaviorally, he is like the submissive personality.

To assure that his aggressive impulses do not break through, the passive-ambivalent becomes overconforming and oversubmissive; he overorganizes and over-regulates his life in an effort to bind his unconscious, rebellious and oppositional urges. Moreover, he not only accepts societal rules and customs but vigorously espouses and defends them; he becomes moralistic, legalistic and righteous.

Certainly, morals and ethics are requisites to the civilized life, but the passive-ambivalent is so inflexible in his pursuit of them that one begins to wonder if he "protests too much." His obstinate insistence that life be systematized and regulated, whether appropriate or not, becomes a caricature of the virtues of order and propriety. He proceeds meticulously through his daily routines; he gets lost in the minutiae, in the form and not the substance of everyday life.

All these behaviors and attitudes are necessary to the passive-ambivalent's aim of controlling the seething antagonisms which lie beneath the surface. He must cling grimly to the prescriptions and rules of society; they are his protection against himself. He does not deviate from an absolute adherence to these injunctions lest his impulses burst out of control, and he expose to others and himself what he "really" feels.

The DSM-II employs the questionable label of *obsessive-compulsive personality* to characterize this syndrome. We consider this label questionable since many, if not most, of these patients exhibit neither obsessions nor compulsions; moreover, there is an "obsessive-compulsive neurosis" syndrome in the official nosology from which the obsessive-compulsive personality diagnosis must be distinguished (to facilitate this distinction, the

authors of the DSM-II suggest the alternate label of *anankastic personality,* a rather esoteric term for this syndrome). The DSM-II describes the syndrome as follows:

The behavior pattern is characterized by excessive concern with conformity and adherence to standards of conscience. Consequently, individuals in this group may be rigid, overinhibited, overconscientious, over-dutiful and unable to relax easily.

In the following case we may trace the clinical development and features of this personality.

*CASE 7-3*
*Wayne B., Age 40, College Dean, Married, No Children*

Wayne was advised to seek assistance from a therapist following several months of relatively sleepless nights and a growing immobility and indecisiveness at his job. When first seen, he reported feelings of extreme self-doubt and guilt and prolonged periods of tension and diffuse anxiety. It was established early in therapy that he always had experienced these symptoms; they were now merely more pronounced than before.

The precipitant for this sudden increase in discomfort was a forthcoming change in his academic post. New administrative officers had assumed authority at the college, and he was asked to resign his deanship to return to regular departmental instruction.

In the early sessions, Wayne spoke largely of his fear of facing classroom students again, wondered if he could organize his material well, and doubted that he could keep classes disciplined and interested in his lectures. It was his preoccupation with these matters that he believed was preventing him from concentrating and completing his present responsibilities.

At no time did Wayne express anger toward the new college officials for the "demotion" he was asked to accept; he repeatedly voiced his "complete confidence" in the "rationality of their decision." Yet, when face-to-face with them, he observed that he stuttered and was extremely tremulous.

Wayne was the second of two sons, younger than his brother by three years. His father was a successful engineer, and his mother a high school teacher. Both were "efficient, orderly and strict" parents. Life at home was "extremely well planned," with "daily and weekly schedules of responsibility posted" and "vacations arranged a year or two in advance." Nothing apparently was left to chance. Both boys were provided with the basic comforts of life, enjoyed the rewards of a well-run household, but knew exactly what was expected of them, and knew that their parents would be punitive and unyielding if they failed to adhere to these expectations.

Wayne perceived his brother as the more preferred and dominant child in the family. He felt that his brother "got away with things," was a "show-off" and knew how to "get around his mother." Begrudgingly, Wayne admitted that his brother may have been a brighter and more attractive child. Nevertheless, he asserted that there was "not much of a difference" between them, and that he had been "cheated and overlooked by the fraud." This latter comment spilled forth from Wayne's lips much to his surprise. Obviously, he harbored intense resentments toward his brother which he desperately tried to deny throughout his life. He feared expressing hostility in childhood since "mother and father would have nothing to do with emotions and feelings at home, especially angry feelings toward one another." The only way in which Wayne could express his resentment toward his brother was by "tattling"; he would experience great pleasure when able to inform his parents about things his brother had done with which they would disapprove. Not until therapy, however, did Wayne come to recognize that these self-righteous acts were less a matter of "sticking to the rules" than of trying to "get back at him."

Wayne adopted the "good boy" image. Unable to challenge his brother either physically, intellectually or socially, he became a "paragon of virtue." By being punctilious, scrupulous, methodical and orderly, he could avoid antagonizing his perfectionistic parents, and would, at times, obtain preferred treatment from them. He obeyed their advice, took their guidance as gospel and hesitated making any decision before gaining their approval. Although he recalled "fighting" with his brother before he was six or seven, he "restrained his anger from that time on and never upset his parents again."

Peer experiences were satisfactory throughout schooling, although he was known as a rather serious and overconscientious student. With the exception of being thought of as "a sort of greasy grind," his relationships during adolescence were adequate, if not especially rewarding.

At 27, Wayne completed his doctorate in political economics, married a rather plain but "serious-minded" girl and obtained his first regular academic appointment at a small college. Two years later he moved to his present institution. His "fine work" in advising freshmen students led to his appointment as Dean of Freshmen, and eventually to that of Dean of Students, a position he has held for seven years.

Although Wayne demonstrated a talent for "keeping the rules" and for assuming his responsibilities with utmost conscientiousness, he had been accused by both students and faculty as being a "stuffed shirt," a "moralist" with no real sympathy or understanding for the young. His lack of warmth, and frequent, harshly punitive decisions with students, was out of keeping with the new administration's policies and led to the request that he step down.

## CLINICAL PICTURE

Let us next organize the major features of the passive-ambivalent or conforming personality in terms of our four-fold clinical analysis.

### Behavior

One is often struck by the grim and cheerless demeanor of the passive-ambivalent; this is not to imply that they are invariably glum or downcast, but rather to suggest their typical air of formal austerity and serious-mindedness. Posture and movement reflect an underlying tightness, a tense control of emotions kept well in check.

Socially, they are viewed by others as industrious and efficient, though lacking in flexibility and spontaneity. They appear stubborn, stingy, possessive, uncreative and unimaginative; they tend to procrastinate, seem indecisive and are easily upset by the unfamiliar or by deviations from routines to which they have become accustomed.

They seem most content with their "nose to the grindstone," working diligently and patiently with activities that require their being tidy and meticulous. Some people perceive this as a sign of being orderly and methodical; others judge them as small-minded and picayune. They are especially concerned with matters of organization and efficiency, and tend to be rigid and unbending about rules and procedures; this often leads to the view that they are perfectionistic, compulsive and legalistic.

Their interpersonal behavior may be characterized as polite and formal. However, they appear to view and relate to others in terms of rank and status, that is, the conforming personality tends to be authoritarian rather than equalitarian in his outlook; this attitude is reflected in their contrasting behaviors with "superiors" as opposed to "inferiors." They are deferential, ingratiating and even obsequious with their superiors; they go out of their way to impress them with their efficiency and serious-mindedness, constantly seek their reassurance and approval and experience considerable anxiety and tension when they are unsure of their position. This contrasts markedly with their behavior when relating to subordinates; here the conforming personality is quite aggressive, autocratic and condemnatory. He acts often in a self-assured, pompous and self-righteous manner. This deprecatory attitude usually is hidden behind rules, regulations and legalities; he attempts to justify his aggressive intent by recourse to some authority higher than himself.

### Phenomenological Reports

The passive-ambivalent takes great pains not to recognize contradictions between his unconscious impulses and his overt behaviors. He protects himself from recognizing this disparity by avoiding and devaluing self-exploration; as a consequence, he exhibits little or no insight with regard to his motives and feelings. To accomplish this, he often adopts a philosophy that demeans the "personal equation." He may claim that insight and self-exploration are antithetical to efficient behavior, that introspective analysis of one's desires and emotions would intrude upon rational thinking and responsible self-control. As a protective device, then, he eschews looking into himself, and builds a rationale by which he can assert that such efforts are signs of immaturity and self-indulgence, traits which he views as anathema to the civilized life. Thus, despite his high intelligence, Wayne B. had no conscious awareness of the obvious precipitants of his recent malaise; moreover, he resisted and deprecated attempts to probe his emotions, both past and present, accused "modern day" students of being undisciplined and emotionally immature, and believed that they could "fulfill their promise" only if "they put aside their personal desires for the betterment of society."

The conforming individual is a good "organization man" and typifies what has been termed the "bureaucratic personality." His self-image is that of a conscientious, selfless, loyal, dependable, prudent and responsible person. Not only does he "willingly" accept the prerogatives and beliefs of institutional authorities but he believes that their coercive demands and expectations are right, are best for the "greatest good." Furthermore, he identifies with these attitudes and strictures, adopting them not only for himself, as a means of controlling his repressed impulses, but as a standard to regulate the behavior of others. His vigorous defense of institutional authority often brings him commendation and support, rewards which serve to reinforce his inclination toward obedience, autocratic behavior and self-righteousness.

The passive-ambivalent feels that he should be harsh in his self-judgments and that he should assess his accomplishments objectively and demand high standards for himself in achieving them. Additionally, he voices a strong sense of duty to others; he feels that he must not let them down, and more significantly, not engage in behaviors which might provoke their displeasure, so well illustrated in Wayne's relationship with his parents.

Although he may report feelings of self-doubt and guilt for having failed to live up to this ideal image, the conforming person has no conception that it may be his own ambivalence about achieving, his own unconscious resistance to the desires of authority, which block him from attaining his conscious goals. Thus, Wayne rationalized his indecision and procrastinations by the "wisdom" of being "careful before one leaps," of delaying action until one is sure that he is correct and of "shooting for high standards" which demand careful and reflective appraisal for their attainment; more likely, these cliché philosophies merely cloaked his unconscious desire to undo the rigid mold into which he had allowed his life to be cast.

The conforming personality expresses contempt for those who behave "frivolously and impulsively"; he considers emotional behavior as immature and irresponsible. Moreover, people must be judged by "objective" standards, by the time-proven rules and regulations of an organized society. He bases his reactions to others, then, according to the conventional values and customs of his group, claiming to make no "personal" judgments in his appraisal of others. What he fails to recognize, however, is that he judges others in accordance with rules that he himself unconsciously detests. It is as if he must impose harsh criteria upon others to convince *himself* that these rules can be adhered to. If he restrains the rebellious impulses of others, perhaps he can have confidence in being able to restrain his own.

### Intrapsychic Processes

Although appearing on the surface to be deliberate and well-poised, the passive-ambivalent sits atop an internal powder keg. He is beset by intense conflicts, an inner turmoil that threatens to upset the delicate balance he has so carefully wrought throughout his life. He must preserve that balance and protect himself against the intrusion into awareness and behavior of explosive contrary impulses and feelings. He must avoid events which might unleash these forces and cause him to lose favor with those in authority. Having opted for a strategy in which reinforcement is to be gained from those in power, he must, at all costs, prevent losing this primary source of reward and protection.

To accomplish this, he must take no risks, and operate with absolute certainty that no unanticipated event upsets his equilibrium. This aversion of external disruptions is difficult enough. But his greatest task is to control his own emotions, that is, to submerge the impulses that surge from within and from which he cannot escape. His only recourse for dealing with these incursions is either to transmute them or to seal them off; he executes this task by the extensive use of intrapsychic mechanisms. Because of the severity of his conflict and the imperative nature of its control, the passive-ambivalent employs more and varied unconscious mechanisms than any of the other pathological patterns.

The two most rewarding techniques for transforming negative impulses, yet finding outlets for them at the same time, are identification and sublimation. If the conforming personality can find a "punitive" model of authority to emulate, he can "justify" venting his hostile impulses toward others, and perhaps receive commendation as well. For example, in the case of Wayne we observed that as a child he identified with his parents' strict attitudes by "tattling" and reproaching his brother; this enabled him to find a sanctioned outlet for his otherwise unacceptable hostility. Sublimation serves a similar function. Unconscious feelings of hostility, which cannot be tolerated consciously, may be expressed in a socially acceptable way through occupations such as a judge, dean, soldier or surgeon. Likewise, becoming a fiercely moralistic father, or a "loving" but overcontrolling mother, are "approved" ways of restraint, but may camouflage hidden hostility toward one's children.

Three intrapsychic mechanisms—reaction-formation, isolation and undoing—do not provide an outlet for submerged hostile impulses but do serve the function of keeping them in check. For example, the ingratiating and obsequious manner of many passive-ambivalents, especially in circumstances which normally should evoke anger and hostility, may often be traced to a reversal, that is, a reaction formation, of their hidden, rebellious feelings. Not daring to expose their true impulses, they must bind them so tightly that their opposite comes forth. Conforming individuals often compartmentalize or isolate the emotional components of a situation. Thus, they neutralize or block off all feelings which would normally be aroused by events; in this way, they secure themselves against the possibility of reacting in ways that might cause them discomfort. Should the passive-ambivalent trespass the injunctions of authorities, or fail to live up to their expectations, they may engage in a variety of compulsively ritualistic acts which undo the evil or wrong they have done. In this manner, they seek expiation for their sins, and thereby regain the good will they fear they had lost.

### Biophysical Factors

There appear to be no distinguishing constitutional characteristics in the conforming personality. However, many exhibit a marked diminution of activity and energy expenditure, attributable in all probability to a lifelong habit of constraint and inhibition. Thus, few evidence a lively, energetic or ebullient manner; rather, most are rigid, controlled or plodding in their actions. This failure to release pent-up energies is likely to contribute to the development of psychophysiological disorders, commonly found among conforming personalities. Quite typically, they are besieged repeatedly with one psychosomatic ailment after another.

The speculation that passive ambivalence might reflect an intrinsic antagonism between threctic and choleric temperamental dispositions seems presumptuous. Yet we do observe an opposition between fear and anger among these individuals, that is, they appear to restrain intense anger because of intense fears. Conceivably, the biophysical disposition for both these reaction tendencies may be great, resulting in the frequent immobilization seen in their personalities. Given the grim and joyless quality observed in these persons, we might conjecture also that they possess a constitutionally anhedonic temperament, as well.

## ETIOLOGY AND DEVELOPMENT

The four features we would abstract from the foregoing as characterizing the conforming personality are: *restrained affectivity* (emotionally controlled; grim and cheerless), *cognitive constriction* (narrow-minded; overly methodical and pedantic in thinking), *conscientious self-image* (practical, prudent and moralistic) and *interpersonal respectfulness* (ingratiating with superiors; formal and legalistic with subordinates). Let us trace some of the roots of these and other traits of the passive-ambivalent pattern.

### Biogenic Factors

There is little evidence to suggest that biogenic influences contribute in any distinctive manner to the development of the conforming personality. Stated differently, a wide variety of overt physical traits, infantile reaction patterns and so on may be found among passive-ambivalents; no biogenic features are especially discriminable or highly correlated with this style of life.

Following the suppositions presented in the preceding section, we might hypothesize that the neurological regions of the limbic system associated with the expression of "fear" and "anger" may be unusually dense or well branched among these patients; these conflicting dispositions might underlie the hesitancy, doubting and indecisive behaviors seen in these patients. Speculations such as these, however, are highly conjectural, given the inchoate state of our knowledge.

*Psychogenic Factors*

The foundations of the passive-ambivalent pattern are rooted primarily in interpersonal experience and the coping behaviors with which the child learns to deal with these experiences. We will elaborate these coping strategies and the processes of self-perpetuation in a later section; for the present we will concern ourselves with influences that initiate the development of the conforming style.

**Parental Overcontrol by Contingent Punishment.** The notion of overcontrol as a concept of child rearing may best be understood by comparing it to other rearing practices; let us contrast it to practices associated with several of the pathological patterns that were previously described.

First, it differs from "overprotection" in that it stems from an attitude of parental firmness and repressiveness. Overprotection, most common in the history of the passive-dependent pattern, usually reflects a gentle and loving parental concern, a desire to cuddle and care for the child without harshness or hostility; overcontrolling parents may be "caring," but display this concern with the attitude of "keeping the child in line," of preventing him from causing trouble not only for himself but for them. Thus, overcontrolling parents, as illustrated in the case of Wayne B., frequently are punitive in response to transgressions whereas overprotective parents restrain the child more gently, with love, and not with anger and threat.

Overcontrol is similar in certain respects to the techniques of parental hostility, a training process more typical of the history of the active-independent pattern. But there is an important distinction here, as well. The hostile parent is punitive *regardless* of the child's behavior, whereas the over-controlling parent is punitive *only if* the child misbehaves. Thus, Wayne's parents expected him to live up to their expectations, and condemned him only if he failed to achieve the standards they imposed. We may speak of overcontrol as a method of contingent punishment, that is, punishment is selective, occurring only under clearly defined conditions.

The contingency aspect of parental overcontrol makes it similar to the methods of child rearing which characterize the history of the active-dependent personality. But, again, there are important differences. The active-dependent child experiences irregular *positive* reinforcements contingent on the performance of "good" behaviors, tending not to receive negative reinforcements for "bad behavior." In contrast, the passive-ambivalent child receives his reinforcements, *not* irregularly, but consistently, and he experiences mostly *negative* reinforcements rather than positive reinforcements. He learns what he must *not* do, so as to avoid negative reinforcements, whereas the active-dependent learns what he can do, so as to achieve positive reinforcements. The conforming child learns to heed parental restrictions and rules; for him, the boundaries of disapproved behaviors are rigidly set. However, as a function of experiencing mostly negative injunctions, he has little idea of what *is* approved; he seems to know well what he must *not* do, but does not know so well what he *can* do. Thus, Wayne's achievements were "taken for granted" and rarely acknowledged by his parents; comments and judgments were limited almost exclusively to pointing out his occasional infractions of the rules they set forth.

To summarize, then, parental overcontrol is a method of restrictive child rearing in which punitive procedures are used to set distinct limits upon the child's behavior. As long as the child operates within the parentally approved boundaries he is secure from parental criticism and condemnation. It is a highly efficient training procedure, but one that is fraught with pathological possibilities. Let us next examine some of these consequences in terms of the second and third neuropsychological stages of development (the first stage is likely to have been "highly scheduled," but this is neither pathogenic nor distinctive to the upbringing of the conforming personality).

1. In the second stage of development, the child begins his struggle to acquire autonomous skills and to achieve a sense of self-competence. During this period most children become assertive and resistant to parental direction and admonition. Overcontrolling parents will respond to these efforts with firm and harsh discipline; they will physically curtail the child, berate him, withdraw love and so on; in short, they will be relentless in their desire to squelch troublesome transgressions. Children who are unable to find an area of refuge from parental onslaught either will submit entirely, withdraw into a shell or be adamant and rebel. However, if the child uncovers a sphere of operation that leaves him free of parental condemnation, he is likely to reach a compromise; he will restrict his activities just to those areas which meet parental approval. This, then, becomes the action available to the conforming child; he sticks within circumscribed boundaries and does not venture beyond them.

But there are several consequences of taking this course. Autonomy has been sharply curtailed; he will not develop the full measure of self-competence that other, less restricted, children acquire. As a result, he will have marked doubts about his adequacy beyond the confines to which he has been bound, will fear deviating from the "straight and narrow path," will hesitate and withdraw from new situations and be limited in spontaneity, curiosity and venturesomeness. Thus, having little confidence in himself, and fearing parental wrath for the most trivial of misdeeds, he will submerge impulses toward autonomy and avoid exploring unknowns lest they transgress the approved boundaries. He is like the passive-dependent child in this regard but, in contrast, he has accepted his dependency not from the comfort of love and acceptance, but from the discomfort of punishment and the fear of rejection.

2. The third neuropsychological stage is characterized by the assumption of initiative on the part of the child, and the growing image of a distinctive personal identity. But a prerequisite to the emergence of these signs of individuality is a well-established sense of self-competence and autonomy, two features already lacking in the passive-ambivalent child.

To add insult to injury, overcontrolling parents continue to overtrain and overdirect their children. They provide constant advice and admonishments by which the child must guide his behavior. Not only is he enriched excessively by parental directives but these directives usually follow a narrow and well-defined course. As a consequence, he not only fails to learn to think for himself but is guided to think along conventional and adult lines. Rather than engaging in the usual imaginative explorations that are typical of childhood thinking, he is shaped to think and believe in an overly mature fashion. He proceeds at an accelerated pace toward adulthood, and is made to "toe the line" in acquiring proper and upright attitudes. For instance, Wayne recalled with some pride that he was referred to as a "little gentleman" ever since he was a young child; as a further indication of his premature adherence to adult conventions, he always wore a jacket and tie to class in high school and college, a sartorial style that helped fashion his prudish image among his peers.

Parental overcontrol at this stage has divested the child of the opportunity to learn initiative and to find his own identity; thus, he quickly becomes a caricature of adult propriety, a gentleman, but an automaton, as well. He is unable to face the novel and the unanticipated. He can act only if he is absolutely certain that his narrow band of established behaviors is applicable and correct. He does not venture on his own for

fear that he may be ill equipped to the task, or that he will overstep approved boundaries. His best course, then, is to simplify and organize his world, to be absolutely sure of what he can do and to eliminate complexities which require decisions and initiative. His environment must be one of familiarity, one guided by explicit rules and standards and one in which he knows beforehand what course of action is expected and approved.

Let us recapitulate the major learning experiences of the passive-ambivalent.

First, the child learns instrumentally to avoid punishment by acquiescing to parental demands and strictures; he has been "shaped" by fear and intimidation to be obedient and to conform to the expectations and standards set down by his elders.

Second, the child learns vicariously and by imitation; he models himself after the parental image; he incorporates "whole hog" the rules and inhibitions which characterize his parents' behaviors. Moreover, he learns to make a virtue of necessity; he becomes proud and self-satisfied in being a "good" and "proper" young man. This enables him not only to master his fear of parental rejection but to gain their approval and commendation. Adoption of the parental model has its seamy side, however. Along with their air of adult propriety, he incorporates his parents' strictness and punitive attitudes. He learns to place himself in a role parallel to theirs, and becomes a stern, intolerant and self-righteous tyrant who condemns the "immaturity and irresponsibility" of others.

The third characteristic of the passive-ambivalent's learning is its insufficiency, its narrow range of competencies and its inadequacies for dealing with novel and unforeseen events. Thus, the conforming personality not only is fearful of violating rules but lacks the wherewithal to chance the unknown. His behavioral rigidity is partly a matter of instrumental choice and partly a matter of having no alternatives.

**Guilt and Responsibility Training.** Another feature found commonly in the developmental history of the conforming personality is his exposure to conditions which teach him a deep sense of responsibility to others, and a feeling of guilt when these responsibilities have not been met. These youngsters often are "moralized" to inhibit their natural inclinations toward frivolous play and impulse gratification. They are impressed by the shameful and irresponsible nature of such activities, and are warned against the "terrifying" consequences of mischief and sin.

Others are told how pained and troubled their parents will be if they are inconsiderate, cause them embarrassment or deviate from the "path of righteousness." Long before the child can grasp the significance of these injunctions, he learns that he must adopt them as his own. In due course, he internalizes these strictures and develops a core of self-discipline and self-criticism, a "conscience" by which he prevents his behavior from transgressing the rights of others.

Guilt often is employed by overcontrolling parents as a means of diverting the early, rebellious behaviors of their offspring. The youngster is made to feel disloyal and disrespectful of his "well-meaning" parents when he balks at their impositions and restraints. How inconsiderate a child must be "after all the things they have done." By promoting a sense of guilt, the child's anger is diverted from its original object, and turned inward toward the self. Now it can be used in the service of further curtailing the child's rebellious feelings. Not only is the child made fearful of the consequences of his aggressive impulses but he learns in time to feel guilt for possessing them, an attitude that aids in their control. Moreover, by condemning himself, he demonstrates his "good" intentions, and thereby wards off or diminishes the intensity of reproach and criticism from others; thus, as his own persecutor, he may forestall a more devastating attack from his parents.

## COPING STRATEGIES

The driving force behind the behavior of the conforming personality is his intense fear of disapproval, his concern that his action will be frowned upon and punished. This fear can well be understood given his history of exposure to perfectionistic and condemnatory parents. One would think, however, that by "toeing the line" and by behaving properly and correctly at all times, he could put this concern aside and be relaxed and untroubled. But this does not prove to be the case since lurking behind his facade of submissiveness and propriety are deeply repressed and intense urges toward self-assertion and rebellion. It is the presence of these internal contrary impulses which causes him concern; it is the everpresent threat that these impulses will break into the open that serves as the basis for his fear of disapproval. He senses that he is pretentious and insincere in his overt behavior; he feels the marked disparity between the front he presents to others and the seething hostilities beneath. Thus, no matter how perfect his behavior, no matter how hard he attempts to prove himself, his inner ambi-

valence remains with him. He must always be on guard against detection; disapproval is a constant threat since his "true" feelings may be uncovered. To cope with these fears and impulses, the passive-ambivalent engages in certain characteristic, interpersonal behaviors and intrapsychic controls; it is to these that we next turn.

**Respectful Interpersonal Behavior.** We have addressed ourselves frequently in previous sections to this feature of the conforming pattern; here we will briefly summarize this characteristic and touch upon some aspects that were not earlier discussed.

The passive-ambivalent is extraordinarily careful to pay proper respect to authorities; he is not only polite and orderly but also ingratiating and obsequious. He takes great pains to display his loyalty to those in power; his conduct is beyond reproach, ever punctual and meticulous in fulfilling the duties and obligations expected of him.

These actions serve a variety of functions beyond those of gaining approval and avoiding displeasure. For example, the passive-ambivalent has marked doubts about his own adequacy and self-competence; through identification, that is, by allying himself with a "greater power," he gains considerable strength and authority for himself. Not only does he enjoy the protection and prestige of another, but by associating his actions with those of an external power, he is relieved of the burden of responsibility should these actions meet with disfavor. Thus, as justification for his harsh disciplinary action against students, Wayne invariably referred to the "long and fine traditions of the college," and the explicit rules dealing with "approved behaviors" set down by its Board of Trustees. Unfortunately, by submerging his individuality and by becoming a chattel of some greater authority, he alienates himself from genuine personal satisfactions and loses increasingly what remnants of personal identity he still possesses.

The conforming personality demands respect from subordinates. He insists on their recognizing his "rights," and despises them if they fail to pay proper heed to his due. This he does to bolster his deep feelings of inadequacy; signs of disrespect and disloyalty, especially on the part of subordinates, remind him all too painfully of his inner weaknesses and the shoddy foundation upon which his authority rests. Furthermore, his assertion of power over others provides him with a sanctioned outlet to vent his hostile impulses; should others fail to live up to his standards of perfection, he may justly reprimand and condemn them.

Another facet of interpersonal respect relates

to property and possession. The conforming personality displays the attitude "what is mine is mine and what is yours is yours; I will leave alone what you possess as long as you do likewise with mine." Just as he learned through the pain and anguish of parental restrictions to find a small sphere of behavior that is above reproach, so too does he gather and hold tight his bounty of meager possessions. He will hoard and protect against all intrusions those few prized belongings which he has struggled so hard to acquire. Having been deprived of so many desires and aspirations in childhood, he now nurtures, fondles and protects the little he has achieved. He fortifies himself to stave off the vultures who wish to deprive him of his skimpy resources, is miserly and ungiving and acts as if his "fortune" could never be replenished. "Respect my privacy," he states, "I have little enough; keep yours to yourself, and I will do the same."

But there is a more devious basis for the demand that his privacy be secure; he wishes no one to explore the emptiness of his inner self, and the truly barren quality of his attainments and competencies. Moreover, he dreads their uncovering his rebellious urges, the anger and hostility which lurk beneath his cloak of respectability and propriety. He must not let others expose the sham and pretense of his existence. Respect, then, is a means of maintaining distance, a way of hiding what he must keep from others and from himself.

**Intrapsychic Overcontrol.** The problems faced by the conforming personality cannot be resolved by external behavior alone; regardless of the success with which he complies with the demands and expectations of others, he continues to experience contrary inner impulses which remain a constant source of threat to the facade he presents. He must restrain these hostile urges for fear they will upset the security he has achieved; he cannot give up his dependence on others for he recognizes full well that he is totally inadequate without them; in short, he cannot give up his attachment to stronger authorities since he possesses no personal identity, and lacks the courage and means to act with initiative on his own.

How can he block out these conflicts and how can he submerge these contrary and disruptive urges?

In an earlier section, describing intrapsychic processes evident in the clinical picture, we discussed the central mechanisms which the passive-ambivalent employs to accomplish these aims.

Rather briefly, we may note again that the processes of identification and sublimation reflect a method by which troublesome impulses are transformed and redirected in such ways as both to vent them and gain commendation. The mechanisms referred to as reaction formation, isolation and undoing enable the individual either to bind or disown these contrary feelings, or to moderate their intensity should they become manifest.

## SELF-PERPETUATION OF PATTERN

It would not be unreasonable to ask the question of why, given the conflicts and anxieties engendered by his strategy, the passive-ambivalent fails to explore alternative coping methods. Of course, one answer is that he experiences less pain and anguish by continuing rather than changing his style of behavior; discomforting as his strategy may be, it is less discomforting than any other he can envisage.

But this is only part of the story. Much of what he does can be seen merely as the persistence of habit, the sheer continuation of what he learned in the past; thus, he perseveres, in part at least, not because his behavior is instrumentally rewarding in the present, but because it is deeply ingrained, so much so that it resists extinction and persists automatically.

None of what we have just said is unique to the passive-ambivalent pattern; it is equally true of all personality styles. Each style promotes a vicious circle such that the individual's adaptive strategy fosters similar conditions to those which gave rise initially to that strategy. In short, pathological strategies are traps, self-made prisons; they are self-defeating since they promote their own perpetuation. Let us next look at three self-perpetuating processes that characterize the plight of the conforming personality.

**Cognitive and Behavioral Rigidity.** The passive-ambivalent dreads making mistakes and he fears taking risks lest these provoke disapproval and punishment. As a defensive maneuver, he restricts himself to those situations with which he is familiar, and to those actions he feels confident will be approved. He operates within narrow boundaries and confines himself to the repetition of the familiar. He rarely allows himself to wander or to look at things with a different perception than he has in the past.

The conforming personality is single minded, has sharply defined interests and can stick to "the facts" without distraction or deviation. To obviate the ambiguity of the unknown, that is, the potentially dangerous, he maintains a tight, well-structured orientation toward life; he holds fast to the "tried and true" and keeps his nose to familiar grindstones.

The price the conformist pays for his rigid and narrow outlook is high. Certain areas of life, especially subtle tones of emotion and creative processes of imagination, simply are incompatible with the deliberate and mechanical quality of the conformist's style. More significantly, repetition, the continuous going over the same dull ground, prevents the passive-ambivalent from experiencing new perceptions and new ways of approaching his environment. By following the same narrow path, he blocks all chances of breaking the bonds of the past; his horizons are bound, confined to a duplication of the same old grind.

**Self-Criticism and Guilt.** By the time the passive-ambivalent has reached adolescence, he has learned to incorporate the strictures and regulations of his elders. Thus, even if he could "get away with it," even if he could be certain that no external power would judge him severely, he now has a merciless internal "conscience," a ruthless and inescapable inner gauge that serves to evaluate and intimidate him, one that intrudes at all times to make him doubt and hesitate before acting. The dictates of "proper" behavior have been well learned; he dares not deviate or act foolishly and irresponsibly; the onslaught of his own self-recriminations is adamant and forever present. He is trapped within the machinery of self-criticism; sources of external restraint have been supplanted with the inescapable controls of self-reproach and guilt. He now is his own persecutor, his own judge, ready to condemn himself not only for overt acts but, even more painfully, for thoughts of transgression. These inner controls hinder him from new and more venturesome actions, and thereby perpetuate the bonds and constraints of the past.

**Pursuit of Rules and Regulations.** Most people seek to minimize the constraints which society imposes; we all recognize the need for laws as the price for a civilized existence, but we prefer to keep as few as necessary.

The conformist is different; he lives by rules and regulations and goes out of his way to uncover legalities, moral prescriptions and ethical standards by which he can guide himself and judge others. This need is understandable; it derives from his intense struggle to control raging antisocial impulses which well up within him. The more restrictive the injunctions he finds in legalities and external authority, the less effort he must expend on his own to control his contrary impulses. But here again he traps himself in a self-defeating circle. By discovering new precepts and strictures to heed, he draws a tighter noose around himself, shrinks his world into an ever-narrowing

shell. Opportunities to learn new coping alternatives, to view the world afresh and more flexibly, are further curtailed; by his own hand he has narrowed the boundaries for change and growth.

## REMEDIAL APPROACHES

The prognostic future of the conforming personality is likely to remain unchanged; his strategies foster not as many new problems as repetitions of old ones. As long as the tasks he faces are those for which he is well prepared, it is likely that he will continue on an even keel most of his life. His ship is a "tight little island," unventuresome and well fortressed. His world has been surveyed and stabilized; his responsibilities and relationships usually are kept well within the bounds of his capacities; he hesitates exploring new directions and is reluctant, even obstinate, about change.

The extreme inflexibility of the conformist's approach may, however, become his Achilles' heel; his security and stability depend on the maintenance of a simple and well-ordered life. Should the unanticipated arise, or stress supersede his defenses, his equanimity and controls may falter. At these times, he may vacillate between periods of diffuse anxiety, explosive outbursts, expressions of marked self-doubt and contrition and a variety of bizarre compulsions. If pressures mount, or continue over a prolonged period, he may decompensate into a florid psychotic disorder, or a more advanced cycloid or paranoid personality pattern.

The passive-ambivalent often seeks therapy as a result of psychophysiological discomforts. These persons are frequently beset with psychosomatic difficulties since they have been unable to discharge their internal tensions; repressed impulses churn away within them, giving rise to numerous physical ailments.

Among the other reasons these personalities seek therapy are severe attacks of anxiety, and periodic spells of immobilization, sexual impotence or excessive fatigue. Symptoms such as these threaten the conformist's facade of efficiency and dedicated responsibility. They prefer, however, to view these symptoms as the product of an isolated physical "disease," failing to recognize, to the slightest degree, that they represent the outcroppings of internal ambivalence and repressed resentments.

The passive-ambivalent is likely to regard therapy as an encroachment upon his defensive armor; he seeks to relieve his symptoms but at the same time seeks desperately to prevent self-exploration and self-awareness. The patient's defensiveness in this matter must be honored by the therapist; probing and insight should proceed no faster than he can tolerate. Only gradually, and after building trust and self-confidence, may the therapist begin to bring to the open the patient's anger and hostile impulses. For every chink of defensive armor he removes, the therapist must be sure that he has bolstered the patient's autonomy two-fold; to remove more than the patient can tolerate is to invite disaster. Fortunately, the patient himself is often so well guarded that precipitous movement by the therapist may simply be ignored or intellectualized away. Nonetheless, caution is the therapist's byword with these personalities.

As is evident from the foregoing, supportive therapy is a major vehicle for treating these patients. In addition, several psychopharmacological tranquilizing agents may prove beneficial in alleviating periods of marked anxiety; these should be kept to a minimum, however, lest they cause the patient to feel a decrement in efficiency and coping alertness.

Quite useful also are behavioral modification techniques designed to desensitize the patient to previously discomforting or anxiety-provoking situations. As noted earlier, phenomenological methods, geared to developing insight, must be applied gradually and with discretion; these frequently fail to accomplish their purposes, however, since passive-ambivalents often display a grasp of their problems, but only at a verbal and intellectual level. To rework the foundations of their strategy may require the long-term procedures of intrapsychic therapy; however, personality reconstruction in these patterns is a slow, arduous and often fruitless process. Passive-ambivalents are not especially amenable to group therapy. Either they ally themselves too readily with the therapist, refusing to participate wholeheartedly as patients, or experience extreme threat and anxiety if forced to relinquish their defenses under the cross-examination of their fellow patients.

## THE NEGATIVISTIC PERSONALITY: ACTIVE-AMBIVALENT PATTERN
(DSM-II: *Explosive and Passive-Aggressive Personalities*)

The active-ambivalent pattern is perhaps the most frequent of the milder forms of pathological personality; it arises in large measure as a consequence of inconsistency in parental attitudes and training methods, a feature of experience that is not uncommon in our complex and everchanging society. What distinguishes life for the active-ambivalent child is the fact that he is subject to appreciably more than his share of contradictory parental attitudes and behaviors. His erraticism and vacillation, his tendency to shift capriciously from one mood to another, may be viewed as mirroring the varied and inconsistent reinforcements to which he was exposed.

The overt picture of the active-ambivalent is strikingly dissimilar from that of the passive-ambivalent. Both share intense and deeply rooted conflicts about themselves and others, but the passive-ambivalent vigorously suppresses his ambivalence, and appears, as a consequence, to be self assured, well controlled, and single minded in purpose; he is perfectionistic, inhibited, scrupulous, orderly and quite predictable. In contrast, the active-ambivalent fails either to submerge or to otherwise resolve his conflicts; as a consequence, his ambivalence and indecisiveness intrude constantly into the stream of everyday life, resulting in fluctuating attitudes, unstable and uncontrolled emotions and a general capriciousness and undependability. He cannot decide whether to seek reinforcements from others or from himself, whether to be dependent or independent, whether to take the initiative or sit idly by or whether to seek rewards or avoid punishment; he vacillates, then, like the proverbial donkey, first moving one way, and then the other, never quite reaching either bale of hay.

The pattern of erratic strategies employed by the active-ambivalent is similar to that observed in young children who explore, through trial and error, various instrumental behaviors in the hope of discovering which one succeeds for them; children display considerable spontaneity, shifting in an almost random fashion from assertion to submission, to avoidance, to exploitation, to obstinacy and so on. Most youngsters, however, meet up with fairly stable parental responses to their varied behaviors; as a consequence, they learn to discern which ones achieve their goals and which do not.

But the active-ambivalent child experiences little in the way of parental consistency; since he is unable to discern a clear pattern of consequences for his behaviors, he continues on his erratic "childish" course. For this and other reasons, these individuals frequently are referred to in adulthood as emotionally immature, a trait that can be traced in part to discordant conditions of learning that produced a deficiency in stable and predictable behaviors.

There are two diagnostic syndromes in the

DSM-II that relate to the principal clinical features of the active-ambivalent pattern: the *explosive personality* and the *passive-aggressive personality*. The characteristics described under these separate labels represent, we believe, the same basic coping pattern, and should be combined, therefore, into one syndrome. Excerpts from the DSM-II are quoted below; the first paragraph describes the "explosive" type, and the second that of the "passive-aggressive." Together, they provide a brief portrait of the typical behavior of the active-ambivalent pattern as we have conceived it.

This behavior pattern is characterized by gross outbursts of rage or of verbal and physical aggressiveness. These outbursts are strikingly different from the patient's usual behavior, and he may be regretful and repentant for them. These patients are generally considered excitable, aggressive and over-responsive to environmental pressures. It is the intensity of the outbursts and the individual's inability to control them which distinguishes this group.

The aggressiveness may be expressed passively, for example by obstructionism, pouting, procrastination, intentional inefficiency or stubbornness. This behavior commonly reflects hostility which the individual feels he dare not express openly. Often the behavior is one expression of the patient's resentment at failing to find gratification in a relationship with an individual or institution upon which he is overdependent.

As we perceive it, the active-ambivalent displays an everyday "passive-aggressive" style, punctuated periodically by "explosive" outbursts, for which he is subsequently regretful and repentant.

We shall refer to the active-ambivalent pattern as the negativistic personality since it is their general contrariness, their resistance to doing things which others wish or expect of them, their grumbling and sulky, unaccommodating and fault-finding pessimism that best characterize these people. Negativists dampen everyone's spirits; they tend to be sullen malcontents, "sourpusses" and perennial complainers, whose very presence demoralizes and obstructs the efforts and joys of others. Never do they appear satisfied, even in the best of circumstances; they see the "dark lining in the silver cloud." For example, if they are alone, they prefer to be with others; if with others, they prefer to be alone; if they receive a gift, they dislike being obligated; if they fail to receive a gift, they feel slighted and rejected; if they are given a position of leadership, they complain bitterly about the lack of support they get from others; if they are not in a position of leadership, they are critical and unsupporting of those who are.

The following case illustrates some of these features and their historical development.

### CASE 7-4
### Ann W., Age 27, Married, Three Children

For many years Ann had periodic "spells" of fatigue, backaches and a variety of discomforting gastrointestinal ailments. These recurred recently and, as in the past, no physical basis for her complaints could be established. In his interviews with her, Ann's physician concluded that there was sufficient evidence in her background to justify recommending psychiatric evaluation.

In his report, her physician commented that Ann had withdrawn from her husband sexually, implored him to seek a new job in another community despite the fact that he was content and successful in his present position, disliked the neighborhood in which they lived and had become increasingly alienated from their friends in past months. He noted the fact that a similar sequence of events had occurred twice previously, resulting in her husband's decision to find new employment as a means of placating his wife. This time Ann's husband was "getting fed up" with her complaints, her crying, her sexual rebuffs, her anger and her inability to remain on friendly terms with people. He simply did not want to "pick up and move again, just to have the whole damn thing start all over."

When Ann first was seen by her therapist she appeared contrite and self-condemning; she knew that the physical problems she had been experiencing were psychosomatic, that she caused difficulties for her husband and that she precipitated complications with their friends. This self-deprecation did not last long; almost immediately after placing the burden of responsibility on her own shoulders, she reversed her course, and began to complain about her husband, her children, her parents, her friends, her neighborhood and so on. Once she spilled out her hostility toward everyone and everything, she recanted, became conscience-smitten and self-accusing again.

The first item to which Ann referred when discussing her past was the fact that she was an unwanted child, that her parents had to marry to make her birth "legitimate." Her parents remained married, though it was a "living hell much of my life." A second girl was born two years after Ann, and a third child, this time a boy, five years thereafter. In the first two years of life, Ann was "clung to" by her mother, receiving a super-abundance of mother's love and attention. "It seems as if my mother and I must have stuck together to protect ourselves from my father." Apparently, parental bickering characterized home life from the first day of their marriage; Ann's father remained antagonistic to her from the very beginning, since Ann represented for him the "cause" of his misery.

The protection and affection that Ann received from her mother in her first two years was substantially reduced with the advent of her sister's birth; mother's attention turned to the new infant and Ann felt abandoned and vulnerable. She recalled the next several years as ones in which she tried desperately to please her mother, to distract her from her sister and recapture her affection and protection. This "worked at times." But as often as not, Ann's mother was annoyed with her for demanding more than she was able to provide.

By the time the third child appeared on the scene, parental conflicts were especially acute, and Ann was all the more demanding of support and attention as a means of assuaging her increased anxieties. It was not long thereafter that she began to hear the same comment from her mother that she had heard all too often from her father: "you're the cause of this miserable marriage." Mother would feel pangs of guilt following these outbursts, and would bend over backwards for brief periods to be kind and affectionate. But these moments of affection and love were infrequent; more common were long periods of rejection or indifference.

Ann never was sure what her mother's attitude would be toward her, nor what she could do to elicit her love and attention. Thus, at times when she attempted to be helpful, she gained her mother's appreciation and affection; at other times, when mother felt tired, distraught or preoccupied with her own problems, the same behavior would evoke hostile criticism.

Ann hated her sister "with a vengeance," but feared to express this hostility most of the time. Every now and then, as she put it, she would "let go," tease her unmercifully or physically attack her. Rather interestingly, following these assaults, Ann would "feel terrible" and be contrite, becoming nurturant and protective of her sister. She quickly recognized in therapy that her behavior with her sister paralleled that of her mother's. And, in time, Ann observed that this vacillating and ambivalent pattern served as the prototype for her relationships with most people.

Until college, Ann's peer relationships were not unusual, although she reported never having been a member of the "in group"; she had her share of friends nevertheless. Ann attended an all-girls college where she frequently experienced problems in social relationships. She had a sequence of ill-fated friendships; for example, during her first two years, she had four different room-mates. Typically, Ann would become "very close" to her room-mate; after a short period, usually less than a semester, she would become disillusioned with her friend, noting faults and finding her disloyal; eventually, Ann would become "blue," then "nasty" and hostile.

When Ann met her future husband, during the first semester of her junior year, she decided to move into a single room in her dormitory; though not a total isolate, she rarely mingled socially with the other girls. The courtship period with her boyfriend had its trying moments; Ann was inordinately jealous of his friends, and feared that he would leave her. Quite often, she would threaten to break off the romance so as not to be hurt should it progress further; this threat served to "bring him back" to her.

Ann's marriage has mirrored many of the elements she experienced and observed in her childhood. She is submissive and affectionate, then sickly, demanding and intimidating of her husband, a pattern not unlike the one she saw her mother use to control her father. Ann's husband spent much of his energies trying to placate her, but "Ann is never content." During the six years of their marriage, she seemed satisfied only when they first moved to a new location. But these "bright periods" dimmed quickly, and the same old difficulties emerged again. This time, however, her husband would have "none of this," and refused to budge. Ann again began to experience her physical symptoms, to withdraw affection, vent anger and vacillate in her moods.

## CLINICAL PICTURE

Let us next outline the central features of the negativistic pattern in accord with our four levels of clinical analysis.

### Behavior

The student, reading about the distinctive characteristics of a pathological personality type, often assumes incorrectly that these individuals always display the features that have been described. This is not the case, especially with regard to the milder personality patterns. Many of these persons behave "normally" much of the time, that is, their behaviors are appropriate to the reality conditions of their environment. What is stressed in presenting the clinical picture are those features, which by virtue of their frequency and intensity, *distinguish* these personalities. Thus, "sullenness" is a characteristic of the negativistic personality. But all persons are sullen sometimes, and the negativistic personality is *not* sullen much of the time. What does distinguish him is the ease with which he can be made to act in a sullen manner, and the regularity with which he evidences this behavior.

With this caveat in mind, let us turn to our description of the characteristic behaviors of the active-ambivalent.

The negativistic person displays a rapid succession of moods and seems restless, unstable and erratic in his feelings. These persons are easily nettled, offended by trifles and can readily be provoked into being sullen and contrary. There is a low tolerance for frustration; they seem impatient much of the time and are irritable and fidgety unless things go their way. They vacillate from being distraught and despondent, at one time, to being petty, spiteful, stubborn and contentious, another. At times they may appear enthusiastic and cheerful, but this mood is short lived. In no time, they again become disgruntled, critical and envious of others. They begrudge the good fortunes of others and are jealous, quarrelsome and easily piqued by indifference and minor slights. Their emotions are "worn on their sleeves"; they are excitable and impulsive and may suddenly burst into tears and guilt or anger and abuse.

The impulsive, unpredictable and often explosive reactions of the negativist make it difficult for others to feel comfortable in his presence, or to establish reciprocally rewarding and enduring relationships. Although there are periods of pleasant sociability, most acquaintances of these personalities feel "on edge," waiting for them to display a sullen and hurt look or become obstinate and nasty.

### Phenomenological Reports

The active-ambivalent can be quite articulate in describing his subjective discomfort, but rarely does he display insight into its roots. In speaking of his sensitivities and difficulties, he does not recognize that they reflect, in largest measure, his own inner conflicts and ambivalence.

Self-reports alternate between preoccupations with their own personal inadequacies, bodily ailments and guilt feelings, on the one hand, and resentments, frustrations and disillusionments with others, on the other. They voice their dismay about the sorry state of their life, their worries, their sadness, their disappointments, their "nervousness" and so on; they express a desire to be rid of distress and difficulty, but seem unable, or perhaps unwilling, to find any solution to them.

Cognitive ambivalence characterizes the thinking of negativistic persons; no sooner do they "see" the merits of solving their problems one way than they find themselves saying, "but . . . ." Fearful of committing themselves and unsure of their own competencies or the loyalties of others, they find their thoughts shifting erratically from one solution to another. Because of their intense ambivalences, they often end up acting precipitously, on the spur of the moment; for them, any other course would lead only to hesitation, vacillation and immobility.

The negative personality often asserts that he has been trapped by fate, that nothing ever "works out" for him and that whatever he desires runs aground. These persons express envy and resentment over the "easy life" of others; they are critical and cynical with regard to what others have attained, yet covet these achievements themselves. Life has been unkind to them, they

claim. They feel discontent, cheated and unappreciated; their efforts have been for naught; they have been misunderstood and are disillusioned.

The obstructiveness, pessimism and immaturity which others attribute to them are only a reflection, they feel, of their "sensitivity," the pain they have suffered from persistent physical illness or the inconsiderateness that others have shown toward them. But here again, the negativist's ambivalence intrudes; perhaps, they say, it is their own unworthiness, their own failures and their own "bad temper" which is the cause of their misery and the pain they bring to others. This struggle between feelings of guilt and resentment permeates every facet of the patient's thoughts and feelings.

### Intrapsychic Processes

A distinguishing clinical feature of the active-ambivalent is his paucity of intrapsychic controls and mechanisms. His moods, thoughts and desires rarely are worked out internally; few unconscious processes and maneuvers are employed to handle the upsurge of feelings; as a consequence, these emotions come directly to the surface, untransformed and unmoderated. Thus, negativistic personalities are like children in that they react spontaneously and impulsively to events on the passing scene; each new stimulus seems to elicit a separate and different emotion; there is no damping down, no consistency and no predictability to their reactions.

These behaviors are even more erratic and vacillatory than we might expect from the negativists' reinforcement history since they have long labored under a double handicap. Not only were they deprived of external sources of consistency and control in childhood, but as a consequence of these experiences they never acquired the techniques of internal control. Unsure of what to expect from their environment, and unable themselves to impose discipline and order, these persons seem adrift in their environment, and bob erratically up and down from one mood to another.

In a later section we will describe the alternating use by these patients of projection, and its converse, that of introjection. Here too, we see the operation of ambivalence and vacillation.

### Biophysical Factors

Negativistic personalities do not exhibit a distinctive or characteristic level of biological activation or energy. However, there is some reason to believe that they may possess an intrinsic irritability or hyper-reactivity to stimulation. These patients seem easily aroused, testy, high strung, thin skinned and quick tempered. All sorts of minor events provoke and chafe them; they get inflamed and aggrieved by the most incidental and insignificant behaviors on the part of others. Be mindful, however, that this hypersensitivity may result from adverse experiences as well as constitutional proclivities.

The speculative hypothesis may also be posited that these personalities possess some mixture of what we have termed the threctic, melancholic and choleric temperaments; thus, their behavioral ambivalences may reflect the workings of several conflicting dispositions, a situation which could easily give rise to the erratic and contradictory emotional reactions seen in these patients. Let us keep in mind, however, that we have no substantive evidence to warrant confidence in these conjectures.

Note should be made here of the high frequency of psychophysiological disorders found among these personalities. In addition to specific ailments, many negativistic individuals complain of ill-defined physical discomforts and generalized states of fatigue.

## ETIOLOGY AND DEVELOPMENT

As in the discussions of earlier patterns, we will list four major characteristics that distinguish the personality type under review. Several of these have been described in the "clinical picture"; others will be developed in later sections. These characteristics have been labeled as follows: *irritable affectivity* (is moody, high-strung and quick-tempered), *cognitive ambivalence* (holds incompatible ideas and shifts erratically among them), *discontented self-image* (feels misunderstood, disillusioned, a failure) and *interpersonal vacillation* (is impatient and unpredictable with others; switches from resentment to guilt). Let us next look at several etiological factors which may have contributed to their development.

### Biogenic Factors

As mentioned several times earlier, the role of biogenic influences in pathological personality development can only be speculated at this time. We know that these factors contribute a not insignificant share to the unfolding of behavioral traits, but we are far short of possessing the requisite data either for accepting this assertion with conviction, or specifying the character of the presumed biogenic effects. Nevertheless, as before, we will enumerate and describe briefly several plausible biogenic hypotheses.

**Heredity.** Many clinical features of the negativistic personality may be observed in common among family members. No doubt, this commonality can arise entirely from the effects of learning. But equally reasonable is the thesis that the biophysical substrate for affective irritability and for a sullen, peevish and testy temperament may be transmitted by genetic mechanisms.

**Irregular Infantile Reaction Pattern.** Infants whose behaviors and moods vary unpredictably may develop rather normal and stable patterns as they mature. The possibility arises, however, that a disproportionately high number of such "difficult to schedule" infants will continue to exhibit a "biologically erratic" pattern throughout their lives, thereby disposing them to develop the features of the active-ambivalent.

Fretful and "nervous" youngsters are good candidates for the negativistic pattern also because they are likely to provoke bewilderment, confusion and vacillation in parental training methods. Such "irregular" children may set into motion erratic and contradictory reactions from their parents which then serve, in circular fashion, to reinforce their initial tendency to be spasmodic and variable.

**Uneven Maturation.** Children who mature in an unbalanced progression, or at an uneven rate, are more likely to evoke inconsistent reactions from their parents than normally developing children. Thus, a "very bright" but "emotionally immature" youngster may precipitate anger in response to the "childish" dimensions of his behavior, but commendation in response to the "cleverness" he displayed while behaving childishly. Such a child will be confused whether to continue or to inhibit his behavior since the reactions it prompted were contradictory. Additionally, such children may possess "mature" desires and aspirations but lack the equipment to achieve these goals; this can lead only to feelings of discontent and disappointment, features associated with the active-ambivalent pattern.

**Neurological and Physiochemical Characteristics.** Conceivably, the affective excitability of the negativistic personality may arise in part from a high level of reticular activity or a dominance of the sympathetic division of the autonomic nervous system.

Equally speculative, but plausible, are hypotheses which implicate segments of the limbic system. Anatomically dense or well-branched centers subserving several different, and irreconcilable, emotions such as "anger," "sadness" and "fear" could account for the ambivalent behavioral proclivities seen in this pattern. Of interest in this regard is the recently uncovered "ambivalence" center in the limbic region; hypotheses concerning this area may also be considered as plausible.

Active-ambivalent personalities develop with appreciably greater frequency among women than men. Conceivably, many negativistic women may be subject to extreme hormonal changes during their menstrual cycles, thereby precipitating marked, short-lived and variable moods. Such rapid mood changes may set into motion sequences of erratic behavior and associated interpersonal reactions conducive to the acquisition and perpetuation of this pattern. Let us caution the student again that these hypotheses are merely unconfirmed speculations.

### Psychogenic Factors

Biogenic influences may dispose the individual to certain forms of behavior, but the ultimate form and pattern we observe clinically is largely a product of the environmental influences to which the person was exposed. These influences will be differentiated below for pedagogical purposes, but they often coexist in individual cases.

**Parental Inconsistency.** The central role of inconsistent parental attitudes and contradictory training methods in the development of the negativistic personality has been referred to repeatedly in our discussions. Although every child experiences some degree of parental inconstancy, the active-ambivalent youngster is likely to have been exposed to appreciably more than his share. His parents may have swayed from hostility and rejection, at one time, to affection and love another; and this erratic pattern has probably been capricious, frequent, pronounced and lifelong.

As a consequence, the child may develop a variety of pervasive and deeply ingrained conflicts such as trust versus mistrust, competence versus doubt and initiative versus guilt and fear. His self-concept will be composed of contradictory appraisals; every judgment he makes of himself will be matched by an opposing one. Is he good or is he bad, is he competent or is he incompetent? Every course of behavior will have its positive and its negative side. Thus, no matter what he does or thinks, he will experience a contrary inclination or value by which to judge it.

His internal ambivalence is paralleled by his inability to gauge what he can expect from his environment. How can he be sure that things are going well? Has he not experienced capricious hostility and criticism in the past when things appeared to be going well? His plight is terribly bewildering. Unlike the active-detached and active-

independent personalities, who can predict their fate, who "know" they will consistently experience humiliation or hostility, the active-ambivalent is unable to predict what the future will bring. At any moment, and for no apparent reason, he may receive the kindness and support he craves; equally possible, and for equally unfathomable reasons, he may be the recipient of hostility and rejection. He is in a bind; he has no way of knowing which course of action on his part will bring him relief; he has not learned how to predict whether hostility or compliance will prove instrumentally more effective. He vacillates, feeling hostility, guilt, compliance, assertion and so on, shifting erratically and impulsively from one futile action to another.

Unable to predict what kinds of reactions his behavior will elicit and having learned no way of reliably anticipating whether his parents will be critical or affectionate, he takes nothing for granted; he must be ready for hostility when most people would expect commendation; he must assume he will experience humiliation when most would anticipate reward. He remains eternally "on edge," in a steady state of tension and alertness. Keyed up in this manner, his emotions build up and he becomes raw to the touch, overready to react explosively and erratically to the slightest provocation.

We may summarize the effects of parental inconsistency as follows. *First,* the child learns vicariously to imitate the erratic and capricious behavior of his parents. *Second,* he fails to learn what "pays off" instrumentally; he never acquires a reliable strategy that achieves the reinforcements he seeks. *Third,* he internalizes a series of conflicting attitudes toward himself and others; for example, he does not know whether he is competent or incompetent; he is unsure whether he loves or hates those upon whom he depends. *Fourth,* unable to predict the consequences of his behaviors, he gets "tied up in emotional knots," and behaves irrationally and impulsively.

**Contradictory Family Communications.** Closely akin to parental inconsistency are patterns of intrafamilial communication which transmit simultaneous incompatible messages. Such families often present a facade of pseudomutuality which serves both to cloak and to control hidden resentments and antagonisms. This may be illustrated by parents who, although smiling and saying, "Yes, dear," convey through their facial expression and overly sweet tone of voice that they mean, "No, you miserable child." Overt expressions of concern and affection may be disqualified or negated in various subtle and devious ways. A parent may verbally assert his love for the child, and thereby invite the child to demonstrate reciprocal affection, but the parent always may find some feeble excuse to forestall or rebuff the affectionate response.

These children constantly are forced into what are termed approach-avoidance conflicts. Furthermore, they never are sure what their parents really desire, and no matter what course they take, they find that they cannot do right. This latter form of entrapment has been referred to as a double-bind; thus, the child is unable not only to find a clear direction for his behavior but to extricate himself from the irreconcilable demands that have been made of him. The double-bind difficulty is often compounded by the fact that the contradictions in the parental message are subtle or concealed. Thus, he cannot readily accuse his parents of failing to mean what they overtly say since the evidence for such accusations is rather tenuous; moreover, the consequences of making an accusation of parental dishonesty or deception may be rather severe. Unable to discriminate, and fearful of misinterpreting, the intent of these communications, the child becomes anxious, and may learn to become ambivalent in his thinking and erratic in his own behavior.

**Family Schisms.** Paradoxical and contradictory parental behaviors often are found in "schismatic" families, that is, in families where the parents are manifestly in conflict with each other. Here, there is constant bickering, and an undermining of one parent by the other through disqualifying and contradicting statements. A child raised in this setting not only suffers the constant threat of family dissolution, but, in addition, often is forced to serve as a mediator to moderate tensions generated by his parents. He constantly switches sides and divides his loyalties; he cannot be "himself" for he must shift his attitudes and emotions to satisfy changing and antagonistic parental desires and expectations. The different roles he must assume to placate his parents and to salvage a measure of family stability are markedly divergent; as long as his parents remain at odds, he must persist with behavior and thoughts that are intrinsically irreconcilable.

This state of affairs prevents the child from identifying consistently with one parent; as a consequence, he ends up modeling himself after two intrinsically antagonistic figures, with the result that he forms opposing sets of attitudes, emotions and behaviors. As is evident, schismatic families are perfect training grounds for the development of an ambivalent pattern.

**Guilt and Anxiety Training.** Schismatic families generate considerable anxiety and guilt on the part of children. They are in constant dread that the affections and supports of family life will dissolve; they are made to feel guilty for their contribution to family difficulties, and cannot help but feel dishonest and disloyal when they are forced to ally themselves first with one parent and then the other.

But guilt and anxiety, internal experiences which lead to hesitations in behavior and ambivalences in thought and feeling, can be produced in nonschismatic families. The child may learn these constraints through direct parental tuition. He may be taught to develop a "conscience" by which he must gauge the "correctness" of his behaviors and thoughts. The rationale and methods of inculcating such feelings were outlined in our discussion of the passive-ambivalent pattern; they are similar in most respects to that employed by the parents of the active-ambivalent child. But there is one significant difference. The passive-ambivalent child is likely to have been taught guilt in a consistent and unyielding manner whereas the active-ambivalent child experiences such training more irregularly. Thus, the guilt of the active-ambivalent is less firmly ingrained and it often fails to serve its control function; he "gives in" to his impulses more frequently than does the passive-ambivalent. As a consequence, he exhibits behavioral ambivalence, a vacillation between acting out, one moment, and feeling guilty, the next.

**Sibling Rivalry.** The case of Ann W., described previously, portrays a not uncommon feature in the developmental history of the negativistic personality. Many active-ambivalents felt that they had been "replaced" by a younger sibling and that their parents' affections were withdrawn and redirected to a newborn child.

Of course, such sibling relationships are experienced by many children, and what distinguishes the active-ambivalent in this regard is not clear. It would be plausible to hypothesize that these youngsters experienced a sharp and marked change between their initial feeling of parental security and its sudden termination upon the birth of the newborn child. It is not uncommon for mothers to become unusually preoccupied and attached to their "babies," at the expense of their older children. A child who previously experienced a deep bond with his mother may become severely upset upon the advent of a new child. This event may prove so distressing that it leads to a lifelong expectation that affection and security are not durable and that one must anticipate losing tomorrow what seemed safe and solid today.

How do these events and attitudes evolve into an active-ambivalent pattern?

The shock and pain of being "replaced" is likely to generate intense anxieties and strong feelings of jealousy and resentment. However, the child will hesitate venting these latter feelings for fear of provoking more of the parental rejection and withdrawal he has experienced; not infrequently, these children are made to feel guilty for their envious feelings and hostile outbursts. As a consequence, the "replaced" youngster may learn to restrain his emotions when his parents are present, but be "sneaky" and physically aggressive when his parents are absent. This erraticism in relating to his sibling may become a prototype for later relationships. We see this typical sequence of the active-ambivalent in the case of Ann W.: a friendly, even overly enthusiastic, early relationship with others that was followed by disappointment and hard feelings; in college, Ann became attached to a series of friends, only to find each of them "unlikable and disloyal" in short order; and as she moved with her husband from one community to the next, her early enthusiasms and friendships would quickly deteriorate into disillusionments and neighborhood animosities.

Adding further to their feelings of ambivalence is the fact that these children often are told how rewarding it is to "be a big sister"; however, they cannot help but observe that "baby" gets all of mother's attention and affection. Thus, the child faces another bind: should she desire to grow up and get the dubious rewards and powers of an older child or should she try to recapture the idyllic state of infancy? This, too, may set the stage for future ambivalent behaviors: assertive independence at one period and clinging dependency at the next.

## COPING STRATEGIES

Most persons acquire strategies which enable them to achieve an optimum level of reinforcement and maintain a reasonable degree of self-harmony. Normal personalities may be differentiated from pathological ones by the variety and character of the strategies they employ to achieve these goals; healthy individuals draw upon them flexibly as they face changing demands and pressures. Psychologically impaired individuals, in contrast, tend to be inflexible; they perceive different events as if they were the same, and utilize the same strategies they acquired in childhood, even though they are presently inappropriate. Once having learned a particular reinforcing strategy, it continues to serve as if it were a sacred rulebook for navigating the future.

The problem that faces the active-ambivalent pattern is quite different from that described previously as characteristic of most pathological personalities. Their difficulties stem *not* from the narrow and rigid character of their coping strategy but from its exaggerated fluidity. They have been unable to find a satisfactory direction or course for their behavior; they cannot decide, for example, whether to be dependent or independent or active or passive. Their dilemmas arise, then, not from an overcommitment to one strategy, but from a lack of commitment. As a consequence, they are indecisive, and vacillate in a tortuous and erratic manner from one course of action to another. They behave by fits and starts, shifting capriciously down a path leading nowhere, and precipitating them into endless wrangles with others and disappointments for themselves. Let us elaborate this troublesome pattern with reference to their interpersonal behavior and intrapsychic mechanisms.

**Vacillating Interpersonal Behavior.** It would appear from first impressions that the erratic course of the active-ambivalent pattern would fail to provide the individual with reinforcements; if this were the case, we would expect these persons to quickly decompensate into severe forms of pathology. Obviously, most do not, and we are forced to inquire, then, as to what gains, supports and rewards an individual can achieve in the course of behaving in the erratic and vacillating active-ambivalent pattern.

Being "difficult," quixotic, unpredictable and discontent can both produce a variety of positive reinforcements and avoid a number of negative reinforcements. It may be instructive to look at some examples, drawn from the sphere of marital life, of the ingenious, though unconscious, "games" these personalities "play."

1. An active-ambivalent woman who cannot decide whether to "grow up" or remain a "child," explodes emotionally whenever her husband expects "too much" of her. She then expresses guilt, becomes contrite and pleads forbearance of his part. By being self-condemning, she evokes his sympathy, restrains him from making undue demands and maneuvers him into placating rather than criticizing her.

2. Another wife, feeling both love and hate for her husband, complains and cries bitterly about his loss of interest in her as a woman. To prove his affection for her, he suggests that they go on a "second honeymoon," that is, take a vacation without the children. To this proposal,

she replies that this plan indicates that he is a foolish spendthrift, but, in the same breath, she insists that the children come along. That evening, when he makes affectionate advances to her, she abruptly turns him down, claiming that all he is interested in is sex. No matter what he does, it is wrong; she has him trapped and confused. Her ambivalence has maneuvered him, first one way, and then the other; it keeps him on his toes, always alert to avoid situations which may provoke her ire, yet never quite succeeding in doing so.

The strategy of negativism, of being discontent and unpredictable, of being both seductive and rejecting and of being demanding and then dissatisfied, is an effective weapon not only with an intimidated or pliant partner but with people in general. Switching back and forth among the roles of the martyr, the affronted, the aggrieved, the misunderstood, the contrite, the guilt-ridden, the sickly and the overworked, is a clever tactic of interpersonal behavior which gains the active-ambivalent the attention, reassurance and dependency he craves, while at the same time, it allows him to subtly vent his angers and resentments. Thus, for all the seeming ineffectuality of vacillation, it recruits affection and support, on the one hand, and provides a means of discharging the tensions of frustration and hostility, on the other. Interspersed with periods of self-deprecation and contrition, acts which relieve unconscious guilt and serve to solicit forgiveness and reassuring comments from others, this strategy proves *not* to be a total instrumental failure.

**Intrapsychic Undercontrol.** In an earlier section we noted the paucity of intrapsychic controls which characterize the active-ambivalent personality. These individuals failed to experience consistent parental discipline; if they learned anything, it was through an implicit modeling process by which they learned to copy the erratic and capricious style of their parents. Deprived of the requisite conditions for acquiring self-controls, and modeling themselves after their undisciplined parents, these personalities never learn to conceal their moods for long, and cannot bind or transform their emotions. Whatever inner feelings they sense, be it guilt, anger or inferiority, it spills quickly to the surface in pure and direct form.

This weakness of intrapsychic control would not prove troublesome if the active-ambivalent's feelings were calm and consistent, but they are not. Rooted in deep personal ambivalences, the negativist experiences an undercurrent of perpetual inner turmoil and anxiety. His equilibrium is extremely unstable; his lack of clarity as to

what the future will bring gives rise to a constant state of insecurity. Moreover, the frustrations and confusions he senses within himself turn readily to anger and resentment. And guilt often comes into play as a means of curtailing this anger. In short, the negativist suffers a wide range of intense and conflicting emotions which surge to the surface because of his weak controls and self-discipline.

The muddle and confusion of feelings that active-ambivalents experience prompt a variety of erratic and contradictory mechanisms. Thus, sometimes the negativist will turn his externally directed, hostile feelings back toward himself, a mechanism termed by some theorists as introjection, the converse of projection. For example, hatred felt toward others is directed toward the self, taking the form of guilt or self-condemnation. But, true to form, the active-ambivalent often alternates between introjection and projection. Thus, at one time, by projection, he ascribes his own destructive impulses to others, accusing them, unjustly, of being malicious and unkind to him. At other times, by introjection, he reverses the sequence, and accuses himself of faults which, justifiably, should be ascribed to others.

Thus, even in the use of unconscious mechanisms, the active-ambivalent behaves in an erratic and contradictory manner. Those at the receiving end of these bizarre intrapsychic processes cannot help but observe their irrationality, uncalled for outbursts and peculiar inconsistency.

## SELF-PERPETUATION OF PATTERN

Most of the pathological personalities described in this chapter and in chapter 6 feel some measure of stability and self-content with the style of life they have acquired; this is not so with negativistic personalities. Their attitudes and strategies provide them with little internal equilibrium or external gratification; they live in a constant state of phenomenological discontent and self-dissatisfaction. In addition, their irritability and misery provokes them to behave unpredictably, and to appear restless, sullen and obstructive much of the time. Thus, not only do they suffer an ever present sense of inner turmoil, but they act out their discontent for all to see and to share with them. In the following paragraphs we will describe three troublesome behaviors which perpetuate and intensify difficulties initially generated in childhood.

**Erratic and Negativistic Behaviors.** The mere process of behaving erratically, of vacillating from one course of action to another, is a sheer waste of energy. By attempting to secure his incompatible goals, the negativistic personality scatters his efforts and dilutes his effectiveness. Caught in his own cross currents, he fails to commit himself to one clear direction; he swings indecisively back and forth, performs ineffectually and experiences a paralyzing sense of inertia or exhaustion.

In addition to the wasteful nature of ambivalence, the negativistic person may actively impede his own progress toward conflict resolution and goal attainment. Thus, active-ambivalents often undo what good they previously have done. Driven by contrary feelings, they may retract their own "kind words" to others and replace them with harshness, or contaminate and undermine achievements they struggled so hard to attain. In short, their ambivalence may rob them of the few steps they secured toward progress.

The inconstant "blowing hot and cold" behavior of the active-ambivalent precipitates other persons into reacting in a parallel capricious and inconsistent manner; thus, by prompting these reactions he recreates the same conditions of his childhood that initially fostered the development of his unstable behavior.

People weary quickly of the moping, sulking, manipulative, stubborn and unpredictable explosive behaviors of the active-ambivalent. They are goaded into exasperation and into feelings of confusion and futility when their persistent efforts to placate the negativist invariably meet with failure. Eventually, these persons express hostility and disaffiliation, reactions which then serve to intensify the dismay and anxiety of the negativistic personality.

**Anticipation of Disappointment.** Not only does the active-ambivalent precipitate real difficulties through his negativistic behaviors, but he often perceives and anticipates difficulties where none in fact exists. He has learned from past experience that "good things don't last," that the pleasant and affectionate attitudes of those from whom he seeks love will abruptly and capriciously come to an end, and be followed by disappointment, anger and rejection.

Rather than be embittered again, rather than allowing himself to be led down the "primrose path" and to suffer the humiliation and pain of having one's high hopes dashed, it would be better to put a halt to illusory gratifications, to the futility, deception and heartache of short-lived pleasures. Protectively, then, he refuses to wait for others to make the turnabout; he "jumps the gun," pulls back when things are going well and thereby cuts off experiences which may have proved gratifying, had they been completed. His

anticipation of being frustrated and of being set back and left in the lurch, prompts him into creating a self-fulfilling prophecy. Thus, by his own hand, he defeats his own chances to experience events which may promote change and growth.

Cutting off the good will of others and upsetting their plans and pleasurable anticipations, gains for the negativist the perverse gratification of venting hostility and anger. But these acts prove to be Pyrrhic victories; not only does he sabotage his own chances for meaningful and rewarding experiences, but, inevitably, he provokes counterhostility from others, and increased guilt and anxiety for himself. His defensive maneuver has instigated reactions which perpetuate his original difficulty; he has set into motion a vicious circle in which he feels further self-discontent, and intensifies his anticipation of disappointment.

**Recreating Disillusioning Experiences.** Interpersonal vacillation, as noted earlier, gains partial reinforcements for the negativist, and partial reinforcements, as we know from experimental research, strengthen habits and cause them to persist and recur. In the active-ambivalent this pattern results in an unconscious repetition-compulsion to recreate disillusioning experiences that parallel those of the past.

The negativist operates on the premise that he can surmount the past and that he can recapture, in full measure, the love and attention he only partially gained in childhood. This search for full gratification cannot be achieved, however, since he now possesses needs and desires that are in fundamental opposition to one another, e.g., he both wants and does not want the affections of those upon whom he depends.

Nonetheless, the active-ambivalent enters new relationships as if a perfect and idyllic state of total symbiosis could be achieved. He goes through the motions of seeking a consistent and "forever true" source of love, one that will not betray him as his parents and others did in the past. He ventures into new relationships with a blind optimism; this time, he insists, all will go well.

Unsure of the trust he can place in others, and mindful of past betrayals and disappointments, the negativist begins to test his newfound "loves," to see if they are loyal and faithful. He cajoles them, frustrates them and withdraws from them, all in an effort to check whether they will prove as fickle and insubstantial as those of the past. Soon enough, these testing operations begin to exhaust the partner's patience; annoyance, exasperation and hostility follow as a consequence. The negativist quickly becomes disenchanted; he has found that his "idol" is marred and imperfect. He is again disillusioned and embittered. To protect himself, and to vent his resentment at having been a naive fool, the ambivalent turns against his betrayer, disavows, detests and recoils from him and, thereby, completes the vicious circle.

These crushing experiences recur repeatedly, and with each recurrence, the negativist further reinforces his pessimistic anticipations. In his effort to overcome past disillusionments, he has thrown himself blindly into new ventures that lead inevitably to further disillusion.

## REMEDIAL APPROACHES

Prognostically, these patients frequently decompensate into anxiety and agitated depression disorders. The therapist must always be on guard to anticipate and prevent suicide since the negativistic personality can act quite impulsively when he feels guilt, needs attention or seeks a dramatic form of retribution.

One of the major goals of therapy is to guide the patient into recognizing the sources and character of his ambivalence, and to reinforce a more consistent approach to life. Since these patients often come for treatment in an agitated state, a first task of treatment is to calm their anxieties and guilt. Once relieved of their tensions, however, many lose their incentive to continue treatment. Motivating the patient to pursue a more substantial course of therapy may demand formidable efforts on the part of the therapist since negativistic personalities are intrinsically ambivalent about dependency relationships. They may desire to be nurtured and loved by a powerful parental figure, but such submission poses a threat to their equally intense desire to assert their independence.

A seesaw struggle often ensues between patient and therapist; the negativist may exhibit an ingratiating submissiveness, at one time, and a taunting and demanding attitude, the next. Similarly, he may solicit the therapist's affections, but when these are expressed in the form of verbal assurances, the patient rejects them, voicing doubt about the genuineness of the therapist's feelings. In a different vein, when the therapist points out the patient's contradictory attitudes, the patient will evidence great verbal appreciation but not attempt to alter his attitudes at all.

Let us now turn to specific techniques.

First, undue environmental pressures which aggravate the patient's anxieties or increase his erratic behaviors should be removed. Intense anxieties often preoccupy the patient in the early phases of treatment; supportive therapy may usefully be employed in their relief, as may the pharmacological tranquilizing agents. If depressive features predominate, an antidepressant drug should be prescribed. In general, there is little indication for the use of formal behavior modification methods.

The more directive phenomenological techniques may be used to confront the patient with the obstructive and self-defeating character of his interpersonal relations; this approach must be handled with caution, however, lest the patient become unduly guilt ridden, depressed and suicidal. Perhaps the greatest benefit derived through these directive approaches is to stabilize the patient, to "set him straight" and put reins on his uncontrollable vacillations of mood and behavior. Nondirective phenomenological techniques usually are helpful only in the later stages of treatment when the patient already has "pulled himself together," and is ready to embark on a more constructive future course.

Because of the deep-rooted character of his problems and the high probability that unconscious resistances will impede the effectiveness of other therapeutic procedures, it often is necessary to recommend the more extensive and prolonged techniques of intrapsychic therapy. A thorough reconstruction of personality may prove to be the only means of altering this deeply rooted pattern. Group methods may fruitfully be employed to assist the patient not only in learning how to gain control over his interpersonal anxieties but also in acquiring more consistent social behaviors.

# CONCLUDING COMMENTS AND SUMMARY

The extensive coverage of clinical material in chapters 6 and 7 has provided us with a detailed description of the often overlooked patterns of mild personality pathology; moreover, it will serve us in good stead as a foundation for understanding the more severe patterns and disorders to be discussed in subsequent chapters.

It will be useful, prior to launching ahead,

## Table 7-1   Summary of Mild Pathological Personality Patterns

| | DETACHED | | DEPENDENT | |
|---|---|---|---|---|
| | *Asocial* | *Avoidant* | *Submissive* | *Gregarious* |
| **CLINICAL PICTURE** | Apathetic, flat, colorless, dull, aloof, distant, unconnected, vague, impersonal, impassive, complacent, irrelevant, unspontaneous, wandering, insensitive, uncommunicative. | Apprehensive, mistrustful, suspicious, lonely, shy, secretive, ill at ease, tense, hyper-alert, estranged, shrinking, self-preoccupied, alienated, oversensitive. | Docile, pliant, clinging, plaintive, polyanna-like, naive, dejected, mournful, self-effacing, inadequate, weak, unenergetic, timid, obsequious, generous, gentle, uncompetitive. | Sociable, charming, demonstrative, flirtatious, flighty, labile, dramatic, shallow, impressionistic, perceptive, manipulative, other-directed, uninsightful, superficial. |
| **ETIOLOGY AND DEVELOPMENT** <br> *Hypothesized Biogenic Factors:* | Passive infantile pattern, ectomorphic build, limbic and reticular deficits, parasympathetic dominance, synaptic dyscontrol. | Threctic infantile pattern, maturational irregularities, limbic imbalances, sympathetic dominance, synaptic acceleration. | Melancholic or threctic infantile pattern, ectomorphic or endomorphic build, imbalance between limbic and reticular systems, adrenal dysfunctions. | Hyperresponsive infantile pattern, low neurological and physiochemical arousal thresholds. |
| *Hypothesized Psychogenic Factors:* | Impoverished sensory attachment stage, parental indifference, fragmented family communications. | Parental rejection or deprecation, peer group alienation. | Parental attachment and overprotection, competitive deficits among peers and sibs, adoption of social roles. | Enriched and diverse sensory attachment stage, parental control by contingency and irregular reward, histrionic parental models, sibling rivalry, ease of interpersonal attraction, shifting values. and standards |
| **COPING STRATEGIES** <br> *Interpersonal Behavior:* | Distant: insensitive, imperceptive, and indifferent. | Aversive: hyperalert to avoid censure, derision and humiliation. | Compliant: abdicates responsibility and attaches self to others. | Seductive: manipulates others to provide approval and affection. |
| *Intrapsychic Processes:* | Impoverished intrapsychic world, minimal need and minimal use of mechanisms. | Cognitive interference, repression and disqualification of memories, thoughts and feelings. | Identification, denial of autonomous impulses. | Repression of contrary impulses, feelings of emptiness and social deceptions. |
| **SELF-PERPETUATION OF PATTERN** | Impassivity, insensitivity, and infrequent social activities decrease opportunities for growth stimulation. | Perceptual hyperalertness magnifies social rejection, cognitive interference alienates feelings of self, restricted social life precludes growth, fearful and suspicious behaviors evoke further rejection. | Avoidance of competence activities and self-deprecation perpetuate and deepen image of incompetence, plaintive behavior provokes exasperation and rebuffs. | Exteroceptive orientation results in scattered and unintegrated learning, massive repression retards inner growth, fleeting attachments perpetuate search for new approvals. |

to bring together some of the major themes presented in the last two chapters.

1. For pedagogical purposes, it has been necessary to separate biogenic from psychogenic factors as influences in personality development; this bifurcation does not exist in reality. Biological and experiential determinants combine and interact in a reciprocal interplay throughout life; for example, initial constitutional dispositions not only shape the character of experience but are themselves modified in a constant interchange with the environment.

This sequence of biogenic-psychogenic interaction evolves through a never-ending spiral; each step in the interplay builds upon prior interactions and creates, in turn, new potentialities for future reactivity and experience. Thus, as noted in chapter 5, the early environment of the maturing organism (e.g., variations in the quantity of stimulation) may produce partially irreversible biological abnormalities which, as a defective substrate, will then alter the impact of subsequent experiences.

Similarly, the infant's distinctive reactivity pattern will elicit distinctive counter-reactions from his parents; thus, these constitutional proclivities shape the nature of the experiences to which the youngster will be exposed.

The circular feedback and serially unfolding character of the developmental process defy simplification, and must constantly be kept in mind when analyzing the etiological background of personality. There are few unidirectional effects in development; it is a multideterminant transaction in which a unique pattern of biogenic potentials and a distinctive constellation of psychogenic influences mold each other in a reciprocal and successively more intricate fashion.

| INDEPENDENT | | AMBIVALENT | |
| --- | --- | --- | --- |
| Narcissistic | Aggressive | Conforming | Negativistic |
| Self-assured, haughty, spoiled, ungenerous, expansive, buoyant, optimistic, snobbish, boastful, immodest, pretentious, benignly arrogant, self-centered, disdainful, egocentric. | Hostile, vengeful, tough-minded, mistrustful, envious, sadistic, intimidating, controlling, fearless, unsentimental, competitive, power-oriented, vigorous, energetic, domineering. | Narrow-minded, overcontrolled, conscientious, methodical, rigid, disciplined, grim, cheerless, austere, compulsive, respectful, ingratiating, prudent, proper, orderly, legalistic. | Unpredictable, erratic, indecisive, restless, impatient, resentful, testy, stubborn, impulsive, irritable, contrary, disgruntled, high-strung, oppositional, bitter, sullen, obstructive, pessimistic, complaining. |
| No factors hypothesized. | Choleric or parmic infantile pattern, mesomorphic-endomorphic build, low reticular arousal threshold, limbic imbalances. | No factors hypothesized. | Irregular infantile pattern, uneven maturation, low neurological or physiochemical arousal thresholds, extreme and short-lived hormonal changes among women. |
| Parental overvaluation and indulgence, only child status. | Parental hostility, disorganized family and social systems. | Parental overcontrol by contingent punishment, guilt and responsibility training. | Parental inconsistency, contradictory family communications, family schisms, guilt and anxiety training, sibling rivalry. |
| Exploitive: presumptuous expectation of admiration and subservience from others. | Vindictive: dominates, controls and intimidates others. | Respectful: avoids anxiety and conflict by propriety and rigid adherence to conventions. | Vacillating: manipulates others by unpredictability and demanding attitudes. |
| Gratification by fantasy, repression, rationalization and projection of deficiencies. | Weak intrapsychic controls, rationalizes and projects sadistic impulses. | Intrapsychic overcontrol, transforms contrary impulses by identification, sublimation, reaction formation, isolation and undoing. | Lack of intrapsychic controls, impulses "acted out", alternates between projection and introjection. |
| Illusion of competence inhibits growth efforts, lack of self-controls lead to reality distortion, ungenerous behavior provokes social alienation. | Perceives hostility where none exists; rejects affection and cooperative experiences, provokes conflict and hostility. | Rigidity, internalized guilt and pursuit of restraining regulations preclude opportunities for change and growth. | Erratic and negativistic behaviors provoke inconsistent and rejecting reactions, anticipates and precipitates disappointments, creates unresolvable conflicts. |

Hopefully, scientific knowledge will advance beyond our present state of uncertainty and speculation; as research progresses, we may be able to specify with some measure of certainty the character of those interactions which result in the personality patterns described in chapters 6 and 7. What has been provided on this score are speculative hypotheses consistent with the limited findings of recent research and clinical observation.

2. All personality patterns, be they normal or pathological, are deeply etched and pervasive styles of functioning; they are anchored, in a general fashion, to the individual's biological constitution, and are refined, as a consequence of restricted and repetitive environmental experiences, into well-crystallized and distinctive modes of perceiving, feeling, thinking and behaving.

Although no sharp line may be drawn between normal and pathological patterns, we have highlighted certain features of personality functioning which both reflect and promote psychopathology. Three such characteristics were noted: *adaptive inflexibility,* that is, the rigid use of a limited repertoire of strategies for coping with different and varied experiences; *vicious circles,* that is, possessing attitudes and behaviors which intensify old difficulties, and which set into motion new self-defeating consequences; and *tenuous stability,* that is, a susceptibility and lack of resilience to conditions of stress. Together, these three features perpetuate problems and make life increasingly difficult for these unfortunate individuals.

3. All classification systems are presented in the form of "prototypes," that is, models which highlight the major or distinctive features of the cases described. Although each of the eight pathological syndromes discussed in chapters 6 and 7

tends to display personality characteristics and developmental histories in common, we must recognize that there are few, if any, perfect "textbook" cases; many variations inevitably are found among patients categorized in the same syndrome.

The eight-fold breakdown of patterns should be viewed merely as a provisional tool, a set of prototypes derived through an interpretive synthesis of data drawn from diverse sources such as hospital psychiatry, multivariate cluster studies, learning research and psychoanalytic theory. No doubt, this format will be revised as science progresses; it is hoped, however, that in the interim it may serve to clarify and systematize our understanding of clinical cases, and, perhaps, expedite such necessary objectives as prognosis, treatment and research.

4. Two features were stressed as central to an understanding of the eight patterns described in these chapters: (a) the patient's interpersonal style; and (b) the nature and source of the reinforcements he seeks, and the instrumental acts he utilizes to achieve them.

a. Interpersonal behaviors are considered important for several reasons. Most notably, they alert the clinician to significant relationships in the patient's developmental history, and provide suggestive leads for treatment. Moreover, interpersonal factors are especially relevant in the case of the mild personality patterns since these patients maintain active contact with others, meeting and interacting with people in normal everyday life. The character of the interpersonal behaviors they exhibit in these relationships will shape the kinds of reactions they evoke from others, and these reactions, in turn, will influence whether the patient's present degree of pathology will remain stable, improve or become worse.

b. The other major feature guiding our analysis relates to: the kinds of reinforcements the patient seeks (positive or negative); where he looks to find them (self or others); and how he behaves instrumentally to acquire them (active or passive).

Those patients who fail to seek positive reinforcements have been referred to as *detached;* within this category are those who seek neither to gain positive reinforcements nor to avoid negative reinforcements (passive-detached or asocial personality), and those who do not seek positive reinforcements but do seek to avoid negative ones (active-detached or avoidant personality). All the other personality syndromes seek

both to gain positive reinforcements and to avoid negative reinforcements.

Those who experience reinforcements primarily from sources other than themselves have been referred to as *dependent;* within this group are those who wait for others to provide these reinforcements (passive-dependent or submissive personality), and those who manipulate and seduce others to provide reinforcements for them (active-dependent or gregarious personality).

Patients who experience reinforcements primarily from themselves have been referred to as *independent;* within this category are those who are self-satisfied and content to leave matters be (passive-independent or narcissistic personality), and those who seek to arrogate more power to themselves (active-independent or aggressive personality).

The fourth major category, referred to as *ambivalent,* is composed of patients who have conflicting attitudes about dependence or independence; some submerge their desire for independence and behave in an overly acquiescent manner (passive-ambivalent or conforming personality) whereas others vacillate erratically from one position to another (active-ambivalent or negativistic personality).

5. A survey of the clinical features, etiology and development, coping strategies, self-perpetuation processes and remedial therapy for these eight patterns was presented in detail. A summary of these characteristics is provided in Table 7-1.

6. The classification system that has been formulated in these chapters is less novel than first meets the eye. Considerable similarities exist between the present syndromes of personality pathology and those systematized by other theorists and researchers. However, the variables we have postulated as central to the development and functioning of these patterns differ substantially from those proposed by other systematists, and it will be instructive for the serious student to explore the similarities and differences; such study should enable the student to become conversant with alternate diagnostic labels for essentially similar forms of psychopathology. Table 7-2 provides an outline of several of the better known classification systems of personality pathology that parallel those formulated in chapters 6 and 7.

7. Minimal reference was made to the professional research literature as a basis for drawing distinctions among the eight pathological patterns, and describing their developmental histories and clinical features. To have purloined data not di-

**Table 7-2  Some Diagnostic Typologies Resembling the Eight Mild Pathological Personality Patterns**

| TYPOLOGIES | DETACHED | | DEPENDENT | | INDEPENDENT | | AMBIVALENT | |
|---|---|---|---|---|---|---|---|---|
| | Passive | Active | Passive | Active | Passive | Active | Passive | Active |
| | Asocial Personality | Avoidant Personality | Submissive Personality | Gregarious Personality | Narcissistic Personality | Aggressive Personality | Conforming Personality | Negativistic Personality |
| Traditional Psychiatric Syndromes (DSM-II)[1] | Asthenic personality | Schizoid personality | Inadequate personality | Hysterical personality | | Antisocial personality | Obsessive-compulsive personality | Explosive and passive-aggressive personalities |
| Freudian Character Types[2] | | | Oral-dependent character | | | Anal-expulsive and phallic characters | Anal-retentive character | Oral-sadistic character |
| Horney's Neurotic Types[3] | | Detached type | Compliant type | | | Aggressive type | | |
| Fromm's Personality Orientations[4] | | | Receptive orientation | Marketing orientation | | Exploitative orientation | Hoarding orientation | |
| Leary's Interpersonal Personalities[5] | | Distrustful personality | Dependent personality | Over-conventional personality | Narcissistic personality | Sadistic personality | Hypernormal and autocratic personalities | Masochistic personality |
| Wolman's Character Neuroses[6] | | Hypervectorial character | | | | Hyperinstrumental character | Paramutual character | |
| McNair and Lorr Interpersonal Types[7] | Type E: flat, withdrawn | Type D: detached, mistrustful | Types F and G: passive, friendly | Type C: affiliative, sociable | | Type B: hostile, mistrustful | | |

1. American Psychiatric Association (1968).
2. Freud (1959); Abraham (1927); Brown (1940).
3. Horney (1945).
4. Fromm (1947).
5. Leary (1957).
6. Wolman (1965).
7. McNair and Lorr (1965).

rectly obtained for the system presented here would have been both presumptuous and dishonest. Any theorist, if he looks hard enough, can dredge up "facts" from diverse and entirely incidental research to "substantiate" his preconceived notions.

Avoidance of reference to the literature does not mean that the patterns formulated in these chapters are inconsistent with available data; they are not. Rather, we wish to stress that it would be more proper to present the schema simply as a provisional and heuristic model for organizing clinical data and stimulating future research. Future studies, designed and executed with the explicit intention of testing the hypothesis presented, will supply an objective and empirical foundation for evaluating the validity of the system, and for appraising its utility as a clinical tool.

8. A major theme stressed throughout the book is the intrinsic continuity of personality development. Granting the validity of this assertion, we propose that the more severe forms of psychopathology are elaborations and extensions of a patient's basic personality style, and that a successful analysis of his decompensated state rests on a thorough understanding of his basic personality. Severe states will be viewed, then, as logical outgrowths of a patient's lifelong style of coping seen under the pressure of intense or unrelieved adversity. No matter how dramatic or maladaptive a patient's behavior may be, it is best understood as an accentuation or distortion that derives from, and is fully consonant with, his premorbid personality pattern. In the following chapters we will explore these more severe, and obviously pathological, syndromes.

# Chapter 8

# PATHOLOGICAL PERSONALITIES OF MODERATE SEVERITY:

## Borderline Patterns

Willem de Kooning—*Woman 1* (1952). (Collection, The Museum of Modern Art, New York.)

## INTRODUCTION

In previous chapters, we referred to patterns of pathological personality as deeply etched and pervasive characteristics of functioning which unfold as a product of the interplay of constitutional and experiential influences. The attitudes, behaviors and strategies which derive from this transaction are embedded so firmly within the individual that they become the very fabric of his make-up, operating automatically and insidiously as his style or way of life. So much are they a part of him that the person often is blind to their fixed and self-destructive character. Present realities merely are catalysts that stir up longstanding habits and memories; he acts repetitively as he learned to act in the past, persisting inflexibly in his attitudes and strategies, irrespective of how maladaptive or irrational these behaviors now may be. Sooner or later his actions prove his undoing; his behaviors are self-defeating and promote vicious circles which involve him in difficulties that reactivate and aggravate the less favorable conditions of earlier life.

## SOME DISTINCTIONS BETWEEN THE MILD AND THE MORE SEVERE PATHOLOGICAL PATTERNS

Is there some line we can draw, some criteria we can use by which certain pathological patterns may be categorized as more severe or pernicious than others? Can we clearly distinguish between degrees of pathology in personality, when all of them display adaptive inflexibility, promote vicious circles and hang on a tenuous balance?

We asserted in chapter 3 that personality structure is best conceived of as a complex series of traits which lie on a continuum of adaptiveness. Adaptiveness, then, is a gradient, a matter of degree, and not a dichotomy; health versus disease, abnormal versus normal or psychotic versus nonpsychotic are polar extremes of a continuum that evidences many intervening shades and gradations between them.

Although an infinite number of discriminations may be made among degrees of severity, subtle refinements are difficult to justify, may not be feasible and usually are not necessary. As long as we keep in mind that psychopathology lies on a continuum, it will suffice to categorize patients into four broad classes: mild, moderate, marked and profound. This will not only be useful for pedagogical purposes, but it also corresponds roughly to a number of pragmatically therapeutic, legal and administrative functions. For example, mild (basic) pathological personalities, discussed in chapters 6 and 7, may benefit from therapy, but therapy may not be necessary for them to maintain an acceptable social adjustment. Treatment usually is mandatory, however, for the moderately ill (borderline patterns), but these persons can usually be treated without recourse to institutionalization. Markedly severe patterns (decompensated) can be treated satisfactorily only in the protective setting of an institution; thus, typically they must be subjected to the procedures of a legal commitment. Profoundly severe patterns signify the terminal stage of decompensation, and usually require arrangements for permanent institutionalization.

There are other more substantive grounds for differentiating patients in terms of severity. However, before we elaborate on these, let us be mindful again that the course of a patient's impairment may vary from time to time, progressing toward greater health in one period, and regressing toward greater illness the next.

### General Clinical Picture

As far as clinical behavior is concerned, moderately and markedly ill patients differ from mild patients in the frequency with which certain unusual and bizarre symptoms arise, such as explosive emotional outbursts, delusions and hallucinations.

Inner control over impulse has weakened in the more severe patient, and he employs rather extreme measures to maintain his homeostatic balance and psychological cohesion. These individuals cannot effectively mobilize their instrumental strategies, are less able to appraise the threats they face and are less flexible in drawing upon their coping resources. They become overly rigid and constrictive in their behaviors or, conversely, so confused and scattered as to nullify their chances for achieving their goals. Should their difficulties mount, and their restitutive efforts fail, they may abandon all attempts to mobilize their competencies or maintain their psychological cohesion.

Moderately and markedly ill patients frequently lose whatever insight they had into their difficulties, and may fail to discriminate between their inner subjective world and that of external reality. They are less and less able to fulfill their

social responsibilities, or respond appropriately in terms of conventional group standards and expectations. As reality recedes further into the background, rational thought and action is lost; previously repressed emotions erupt and are acted out, and an overwhelming sense of disintegration and demoralization may take hold. In the end, the profoundly deteriorated patient seems "burned out," totally devoid of life, in a state of petrification, without hope and without desire to recover.

### General Etiological Background

Why do some patients develop more disabling personality patterns than others? Are there differences in the quality, character or progression of pathogenic influences which result in a mild pattern of pathology for some, and a more severe level for others?

Three factors may be noted in this regard: more marked impairments in constitutional make-up; more destructive experiences in early life; and more repetitive and cumulative later difficulties. Let us briefly discuss each of these.

1. Whether the mechanisms are owing to heredity or other biogenic sources, some children are constitutionally constructed to perceive and react to events in ways conducive to severe pathology. Moreover, the extreme character of their temperamental reaction patterns provokes responses from others which parallel, but are more pernicious than, those generated by children with similar, but milder, constitutional tendencies. It is more probable that these youngsters will not only develop psychopathology in the first place, but that they will be inclined to decompensate to more severe impairments.

2. Biological distortions may be acquired during sensitive maturational stages of neural growth. The effects of extremes in stimulus *quantity* during these stages are not all-or-none, but matters of degree; marked deficits or intense overstimulation produce greater alterations of the biological substrate than do lesser degrees of impoverishment and enrichment.

If the *quality* of early experience is similar to those pathogenic conditions described in chapters 6 and 7, but is more powerfully concentrated or destructive, the youngster will learn more extreme attitudes and strategies, and, as a consequence, be impaired more seriously. Not only will his pathological development progress more rapidly under these injurious conditions, but the impairment is likely to attain more severe proportions.

3. Severe patterns stem from the interaction

of constitutional factors and adverse early experiences, but later events may aggravate the
damage caused by these initial conditions. These
later pathogenic events are in large measure repetitions of the same destructive experiences to which
the individual was exposed in early life; they
quietly and pervasively encroach upon every facet
of the individual's make-up, and their cumulative
weight wears down every healthy coping effort
the individual attempts to make.

Fostering this repetitive and cumulative adversity are the individual's own self-defeating
behaviors that perpetuate earlier difficulties, and
prompt new ones. By perceptual distortion, and
by acting in ways which recreate the conditions
of the past, he compounds his earlier troubles.
Moreover, these events revive and ignite the anguish of past anxieties, conflicts and inadequacies.
These pathologically disposed individuals are now
subject to a double strain since they are extremely
vulnerable to reminders of their painful past;
present events not only embody their own difficulties, but reactivate the residuals of faulty childhood learnings.

This upsurge of repressed feelings and memories, together with the cumulative repetition of
adverse experiences, combines to destroy the effectiveness of the individual's remaining coping
strategies. Unable to gain the reinforcements he
so desperately needs, fearful of losing his tenuous
hold on reality and threatened by the resurgence
of past feelings and thoughts, the individual gradually succumbs and decompensates. He may deteriorate to more primitive levels of control,
retreat to a less adequate relationship with reality
and fall into a more pathological pattern of life.

Throughout this pernicious sequence of decompensation, the individual continues to retain
the same basic perceptions, attitudes and behaviors he evidenced earlier in life; his advanced
state of psychopathology, no matter how bizarre
and maladaptive it may be, remains consonant
with his lifelong history and style of functioning.

## CLASSIFICATION OF THE MORE SEVERE PATHOLOGICAL PATTERNS

How can we organize the patterns into which
this deterioration unfolds? More specifically, what
system of classification will enable us to differ-
tiate the more severe states of psychopathology,
and maintain the theme of developmental continuity?

Several distinctive characteristics come to the
fore as a patient's lifelong coping strategies begin
to give way. He becomes concerned less with the

standards and guidelines of social reality than
with the fulfillment of his inner needs. Moreover,
he can no longer sit back and depend on his
strategies to do his work for him. Unsure of their
effectiveness, he must remain alert and vigilant
to assure receipt of some of the reinforcements
which he previously took for granted.

At the first stage of personality deterioration,
to be referred to as the "borderline pattern,"
most patients, both passive and active, mobilize
their resources, shore up their strategies and take
a more active role than before to secure the reinforcements to which they are accustomed. Under
these conditions, passive and active-dependents,
for example, become more alike than previously.
Both feel threatened by separation anxieties and
fear that they will be abandoned and left to their
own devices without the support, attention and
affection upon which they depend; as their former
strategies waver and stumble, they develop a common preoccupation, that of searching frantically
to recover the security they found in attaching
themselves to others.

Each of the other pairs of passive and active
personalities becomes more alike in a similar
fashion. Thus, narcissistic and aggressive personalities (independent patterns) become increasingly preoccupied with the fear of losing their
self-determination; asocial and avoidant personalities (detached patterns) suffer intense depersonalization anxieties, and attempt to maintain increased
distance from others; and both the conforming
and negativistic personalities (ambivalent patterns)
are forced to choose between independence and
dependence, becoming more clearly oriented toward one course than toward the other.

In each of these cases the individual is driven
to reinstate more actively the tenuous equilibrium
and rewards he achieved in the past. Individuals
who stabilize at this exceedingly uncomfortable
state of personality functioning will be referred
to as displaying a *borderline personality pattern*.
We will elaborate further on the features of this
moderately severe and pervasive pattern later in
this chapter.

At the second stage of personality decompensation the borderline patient's restitutive efforts have begun to fail; he achieves little or no
positive reinforcement from reality experiences,
and he begins to turn increasingly to the world
of inner fantasy. But as the inner world becomes
his world of experience, his already tenuous hold
on reality slips increasingly. He sinks into the
muddy and boundless world of illusion, submerged in a sea of bewildering impulses and fluid
fantasies. As in dreams, he finds himself in a

whirling abyss of confusion and irrationality, a frightening phantasmagoria of ethereal images and primitive feelings in which illusions dissolve, impulses surge forth, events seem suspended and objects have no meaning.

It is an odd, detached and unreal world to which the patient now has decompensated. At this more advanced state, all patients, regardless of initial distinguishing features, become more and more alike. Although their premorbid personality patterns continue to color their behaviors and perceptions, they have drawn increasingly into themselves, adrift from social reality. We shall refer to these markedly severe forms of deterioration as the *decompensated personality patterns;* they will be described in detail in chapter 9.

The third, or profound, stage of disintegration signifies more than an estrangement from outer reality. At this extreme point, there is a total estrangement from self, an inner void and a sense of nothingness and petrification. These patients contrast with decompensated personalities who, through fantasy and illusion, provide a measure of relief and reward for themselves. But should the patient's fantasies run dry, or should they prove only negatively reinforcing, that is, elicit nothing but painful reflections and memories, then, protectively, he will begin to avoid himself, "turn himself off," deaden his emotions and cut off all thought. In time, a flat, colorless, "burned-out" quality will emerge; he is now isolated and alienated not only from others, but from himself. These unfortunate persons have been labeled the *terminal personality patterns,* and will be further described in chapter 9.

## CONCEPT OF BORDERLINE PERSONALITY PATTERNS

In this chapter we will focus only on the first of the three stages of personality deterioration, termed the borderline pattern.

In the past, the label "borderline" has often been assigned when the clinician was uncertain about the status of his patient. Many a diagnostician faces the dilemma as to whether certain ominous symptoms he has observed signify the presence of a more severe form of pathology than first meets the eye. These patients display *both* "normal" and "psychotic" features, and the clinician handles this seeming incongruency by hedging, that is, "sitting on the fence." He waits until he can obtain a clearer picture of the patient, or until some change occurs in the patient's status, before making his decision as to whether the patient is suffering from a "neurosis" *or* a "psychosis."

This use of the borderline label rests on the false premise that patients *must* fall in either one of two categories of a dichotomy, that of "slightly sick" (neurosis) or "very sick" (psychosis). We contend, however, that personality pathology lies on a continuum, that is, that personality functions are not all-or-none phenomena, but may be found at any point along a continuous gradient. What we are suggesting, then, is that the "borderline" concept should not be used as a wastebasket for clinical indecision; rather, it is a meaningful clinical designation because it reflects a real and not a spurious or incongruous state of affairs: the patient's moderately maladaptive level of personality functioning. Moreover, the concept should not represent a transitory state between normality and frank pathology, that is, simply a way station leading inevitably to more severe illness; rather, it should signify a habitual level and style of behavior, a durable pattern of disturbed functioning that can stabilize and retain its principal characteristics for substantial periods of time. Useful discussions of the concept of the borderline pattern have been published by Wolberg (1952), Schmideberg (1959), Kernberg (1967) and especially Grinker et al. (1968).

Of course, patients who exhibit the borderline pattern may develop a healthier mode of adjustment, or decompensate into a more severe pattern or disorder. But barring the presence of change-inducing events, these patients are likely to preserve their characteristic level and style of functioning. Through all their ups and downs, and despite the admixture they display of both mild and marked pathological features, these patients are sufficiently different from both the less and more severe patient syndromes to justify our recognizing them as part of a distinctive clinical group. In the following sections we shall attempt to elaborate some of the clinical and etiological criteria which may enable us to better diagnose the borderline syndrome.

### General Clinical Picture

What central features, other than their moderate severity, distinguish the borderline band of the spectrum of personality pathology from the mild and markedly severe categories?

Two points deserve mention since they appear common to all of these patients, regardless of their other, more distinctive personality features: deficit social competence; and periodic, but reversible, psychotic episodes. Let us elaborate.

**Deficit Social Competence.** In reviewing the background of these patients, one frequently finds that they have had rather checkered histories in their personal relationships, in school and work performance; in other words, they have exhibited extreme unevenness in fulfilling normal social functions and responsibilities (Phillips, 1968). They rarely persevere and attain mature goals; their history shows repeated setbacks, a lack of judgment and foresight, a tendency to digress from earlier aspirations and a failure to utilize their natural aptitudes and talents. Here, we clearly can see the consequences of their basic adaptive inflexibility, and their involvement in self-defeating vicious circles. Many of these patients may have shown flashes of promise, stability and achievement, but these periods usually are short-lived. They appear incapable of learning from their experiences and involve themselves in the same imbroglios, quandaries and disappointments as they have before. Life seems to be a merry-go-round of getting into predicaments and discord, and then spending time trying to extricate oneself from them. Little is accomplished and so much is undone; the patient goes round in circles, covering the same ground as before, getting nowhere and then starting all over again.

In contrast to personalities at the mild level of pathological functioning, whose strategy, though self-perpetuating, is instrumentally successful much of the time, the borderline patient's strategy falters frequently, and leads him to endless impasses and serious setbacks. Thus, rather than finding and holding a secure niche for himself in society, as so many of the milder patterns do, he upsets his progress repeatedly, achieves a low level of social attainment and finds that he must start again from scratch.

Despite these ups and downs, the borderline patient manages to recoup, to get the wherewithal to pull himself together, to find an "out" and to gain enough of a foothold in normal life to prevent himself from slipping into a more pernicious and serious pattern. Thus, in contrast to the markedly severe or decompensated pattern, where realistic efforts to mobilize and defend oneself have been abandoned, the borderline patient gains enough reinforcement to motivate him to make a "go of it" again.

**Periodic but Reversible Psychotic Episodes.** Not infrequently, the borderline patient will experience transient periods in which bizarre behaviors, irrational impulses and delusional thoughts are exhibited; these confusing periods signify the tenuous character of the patient's stability and controls. During these disturbed states, he may "drift out" of contact with his environment as if he were caught up in a momentary dream in which reality is blurred, and fears and urges that derive from an obscure inner source take over and engulf him in an ocean of primitive anxieties and behaviors. Unable to grasp the illusory character of these inner stimuli, he may be driven to engage in erratic and hostile actions or embark on a wild and chaotic spree that he may only vaguely recall.

These brief episodes of emotional discharge serve a useful homeostatic function for the patient since they afford temporary relief from the mounting of internal pressures. When these pressures cumulate beyond tolerable limits, they erupt through the patient's tenuous controls, and are manifested in the form of bizarre acts and thoughts. Upon release, the patient may sense a feeling of easement and quiescence; he now can regain control and a measure of psychic equilibrium, until such time as tensions again cumulate beyond manageable proportions.

These transitory breaks from reality, which shall be termed "psychotic disorders" (discussed at length in chapter 11), occur *infrequently* in the mild pathological patterns. These less severely disturbed personalities occasionally lose control and engage in impulsive acting out, but they usually retain their awareness of reality; tenuous though their stability may be, they do not lose contact with their surroundings, or become engulfed in a world in which inner unconscious impulses dominate. This contrasts with the borderline patient who exhibits marked breaks with reality at moderately frequent intervals; every so often his intrapsychic world erupts into consciousness, blurring his awareness and releasing bizarre impulses, thoughts and actions.

How do the moderately and markedly severe patterns differ from each other, given the fact that both experience these bizarre episodes?

In essence, these episodes are transient and reversible in the borderline patient; he frequently is aware of their early signs, struggles to avoid them and often has the wherewithal to "get hold of himself." This contrasts with the markedly severe patterns. For this latter group, the confusion between reality and inner imagery has become a relatively permanent state, that is, they exhibit what we have termed the "decompensated personality pattern." Not only are more severely impaired patients undisturbed by their bizarre sensations and impulses, but they have come to accept their illusory world as objective reality. In contrast, the borderline patient not only recognizes the odd and discomforting nature of his psychotic episodes, but seeks to forestall the experience, and to overcome or "turn them off" when they occur, as illustrated in the following.

CASE 8-1
*Tony S., Age 39, Married, Two Children*

The normally affable exterior of this borderline active-dependent salesman would be disrupted by thoughts that his wife had learned of his infidelities (which she actually knew about for years), and would abandon him and his children. Unable to rid himself of these fears, he would succumb to brief psychotic episodes, lasting two to three weeks each, during which he would refuse to leave his home, pace back and forth in an agitated manner, tell everyone about the "devils" that were inside him and make plans for a dramatic form of suicide. Toward the end of these brief episodes, he would attempt to dismiss his recent disturbed behaviors as "just some silly notions," and begin to speak of "pulling myself together."

For him, the loss of control and the invasions of unconscious feelings and thoughts were most undesirable events. As soon as he was able to regain his composure, he rejected as alien to him what he had done and believed during his episode.

## General Etiological Background

In the introduction to this chapter we noted three etiological factors which may operate singly or jointly to produce pathological patterns: constitutional dispositions; early developmental experiences; and cumulative recent experiences, including those fostered by the patient's own behaviors and perceptions. Whatever the combination of pathogenic elements may be, the borderline patient has suffered more of them than have the mild patterns, and less of them than have the marked patterns. Differences in etiology, then, are not matters of the specific character of the pathogenic events, but rather of their intensity, frequency, timing or persistence.

As a consequence, in contrast to milder personality types, the borderline possesses an instrumentally less effective coping strategy; his stability and psychic integration are more tenuous; he seems less capable of mobilizing his resources to deal with the strains of interpersonal experiences, and is more vulnerable to the eruption of bizarre inner impulses and thoughts. Caught in this plight, he expends a great deal of energy and time seeking reinforcements and restraining disruptive urges. Preoccupied and distracted with these matters, he can attend only peripherally to the everyday events and relationships of life; as a consequence, he fails to take advantage of ordinary rewards and gratifications, and fails to learn more effective strategies for relating to the world. Should stress persist, he may turn increasingly to fantasy and illusion as a means of achieving the reinforcements he needs. With more frequent and prolonged episodes of unreality and dyscontrol, he may sink into a more severe, decompensated personality pattern.

## Comments

We have attempted in the preceding paragraphs to provide both a description and a rationale for the borderline, or moderately severe, pattern of personality pathology. These introductory remarks have served, however, only as a general background for the more specific forms of the borderline personality. Although borderline patients possess certain attributes in common, they are appreciably different in many fundamental respects.

We shall divide the borderline syndrome into three major subcategories: the *schizoid, cycloid* and *paranoid* personalities. Not only shall we describe the distinctive characteristics associated with each of these patterns, but we will attempt to show the intrinsic similarity and developmental continuity between them and their milder counterparts discussed in chapters 6 and 7.

Let us note, before we proceed, that the overt clinical picture of patients who previously employed active and passive strategies becomes sufficiently similar when they deteriorate to the borderline level to justify grouping them under single labels. In other words, the feature of instrumental activity or passivity is not as relevant and distinctive an aspect of borderline functioning as it is at the milder, and adaptively more successful, personality level. Bringing the active and passive-subtypes of detachment or dependency into single syndromes does not mean that we can overlook certain important distinctions which still exist between them. Thus, as we proceed in our discussions, we will continue to point out pertinent features which differentiate the clinical picture and etiological background of these patients.

# SCHIZOID PERSONALITY: DETACHED BORDERLINE PATTERNS
(DSM-II: *Schizoid Personality; Schizophrenia, simple and latent types*)

Detachment from others and alienation from self are the principal features of the schizoid personality. This patient parallels, but displays in more severe form, the two detached patterns (asocial and avoidant) described in chapter 6. They are akin, in the official DSM-II psychiatric nomenclature, to the term *schizoid personality,* and to the categories of *schizophrenia: simple* and *latent types,* from which the following excerpts are appropriately descriptive:

[The schizoid personality] manifests shyness, over-sensitivity, seclusiveness, avoidance of close or competitive relationships, and often eccentricity. Autistic thinking without loss of capacity to recognize reality is common, as is daydreaming and the inability to express hostility and ordinary aggressive feelings. These patients react to disturbing experiences and conflicts with apparent detachment.

[Schizophrenia, simple type] is characterized chiefly by a slow and insidious reduction of external attachments and interests and by apathy and indifference leading to impoverishment of interpersonal relations, mental deterioration, and adjustment on a lower level of functioning.

[Schizophrenia, latent type] is for patients having clear symptoms of schizophrenia but no history of a psychotic schizophrenic episode. Disorders sometimes designated as incipient, pre-psychotic . . . or borderline schizophrenia are categorized here.

It is our belief that all three official designations represent essentially the same clinical condition, and that distinctions made within the DSM-II reflect subsidiary discriminations that inevitably arise in all diagnostic syndromes, e.g., whether or not there had been a single psychotic episode, the issue that ostensibly separates the "simple" from the "latent" form of schizophrenia, or the presence of minor differences in the progression of personality deterioration, the distinction that differentiates the "schizoid personality" from "simple schizophrenia."

In general, all these patients are characterized by an impoverished interest in social affairs, an avoidance of close interpersonal relationships and an autistic but nondelusional pattern of thinking. They follow a meaningless, idle and ineffectual life, drift from one aimless activity to another, remain on the periphery of societal living and never develop intimate attachments or accept enduring responsibilities.

Using concepts provided in chapters 5 and 6, we might say that these patients neither anticipate receiving nor are capable of experiencing positive reinforcements either from themselves or others. The *passive-schizoid* is generally insensitive to

feelings; as a consequence, he often experiences a separation between his thoughts and his physical body, a strange sense of nonbeing or nonexistence, as if he carried along with his floating conscious awareness some depersonalized or identity-less human form. For the *active-schizoid,* who depreciates his self-worth, there is an abandonment of self and a disowning and remoteness from feeling and desire; his "real" self has been devalued and demeaned, something split off, cast asunder and rejected as humiliating or valueless. Not only are they alienated from others, then, but they find no refuge and comfort in turning to themselves. Thus, their isolation is two-fold; they gain little from others and experience a despairing sense of emptiness and isolation with themselves. Without these positive reinforcements to spur them, they drift into apathy and social withdrawal.

Denied the power or desire to experience the joy, love and vibrancy of a "personal" life, schizoids become devitalized and numb, wander in a dim and hazy fog and engage in activities and thoughts which have minimal purpose or meaning. Why should they participate in social activity, why should they desire, aspire or seek to achieve when nothing in life can spark their flat and spiritless existence or provide them with the feeling of personal pleasure and joy? Thus, they move through life like automatons, possessing impenetrable barriers to shared meanings and affections and estranged from the purposes and aspirations of society, or the spontaneity, delight and triumph of selfhood.

## CLINICAL PICTURE

Several features are found in common among patients classed in the schizoid category; these will be noted before specifying some of the characteristics that differentiate the active and passive subvarieties.

Three aspects of the borderline picture will be described in this and following sections: the source of anxiety that tends to prompt psychotic episodes; characteristic cognitive processes and preoccupations; and general mood and behavior.

### Depersonalization Anxiety

The deficient or disharmonious affect of these patients deprives them of the capacity to relate to things or to experience events as something different than flat and lifeless phenomena. Schizoids suffer a sense of vapidity in a world of cold and washed out objects.

Moreover, they feel themselves to be more dead than alive, insubstantial, foreign and disembodied. As existential phenomenologists might put it, schizoids are threatened by "nonbeing." Detached observers of the passing scene, these patients remain uninvolved, looking from the outside not only with regard to others but with regard to themselves, as well.

Many people may have experienced moments of inner void and social detachment at one time or another, but the feeling of estrangement and depersonalization is an ever-present and insistent feature of the schizoid's everyday existence. This persistent detachment or disavowal of self distinguishes the unreal and meaningless quality of his life, and may give rise to a frightening sense of emptiness and nothingness. Every so often, the schizoid may be overwhelmed by the dread of total disintegration, implosion, and nonexistence. These severe attacks of depersonalization may precipitate wild psychotic outbursts in which the patient frantically searches to reaffirm reality.

### Cognitive Autism and Disjunctiveness

The slippage and interference in thought processes which characterize the milder detached patterns are even more pronounced in the schizoid. When motivated or prompted to relate to others, they are frequently unable to orient their thoughts logically and they become lost in personal irrelevancies and in tangential asides which have no pertinence to the topic at hand. They lack "touch" with others and are unable to order their ideas in terms relevant to reciprocal, social communication. This pervasive disjunctiveness, this scattered and autistic feature of thinking, only further alienates them from others.

### Deficient Social Behaviors and Impoverished Affect

Examination of the developmental achievements of the typical schizoid will indicate an erratic course in which the person has continually failed to progress toward normal social attainments. School and employment history of these patients shows marked deficits and irregularities, given their intellectual capacities as a base. Not only are they frequent "drop outs," but they drift from one source of employment to another, and, if married, often are separated or divorced. This deficit in social competence and attainment derives from, and in part contributes to, their lack of drive and their feelings of unworthiness.

The colorfulness of personality is lost in the schizoid; there is a blandness of affect, a listlessness and a lack of spontaneity, ambition and interest in life. These patients are able to talk about only a few relatively tangible matters, usually things that demand immediate attention; rarely do they initiate conversation, or pursue it beyond what is necessary to be civil. Not only do they lack the spark to act and participate, but they seem enclosed and trapped by some force that blocks them from responding and empathizing with others. This inability to take hold of life, to become a member of society and to invest one's energies and interests in the world of others is well illustrated in the following case.

### CASE 8-2
### Jane W., Age 27, Unmarried, Hospitalized

Jane was the youngest of three sisters. Since early life, she was known to be quiet and shy, the "weakest" member of the family. Jane's father was a chronic alcoholic who, during frequent drinking sprees, humiliated and regularly beat various members of his family. Her mother seemed detached from Jane, but she often would be critical of her for being "stupid and slow."

Jane completed the tenth grade with better than average grades; however, she had to leave school shortly thereafter because of her mother's death. Jane was given a job as a seamstress as a means of contributing to the family income since her father had abandoned his family two years prior to his wife's death, never to be heard from again.

Unfortunately, Jane was unable to hold her position since the factory in which she worked had closed down; she failed to keep the next three jobs her sisters got for her over a two year period; as Jane put it, "I was not interested and slow."

Following dismissal from her last position, Jane simply withdrew from work, becoming entirely dependent on her older sister. Jane claimed that work was too difficult for her and, more significantly, that she thought that everyone felt, "I was stupid and would mess up the job." In a similar vein, several young men sought to court her, but she persistently refused their overtures since she knew "they wouldn't like me after they took me out."

For the next seven years, Jane took care of the house for her unmarried sister; however, Jane felt that she had never done a "good job" since, "I spent most of my time sleeping or watching TV." She reported further, "I don't like to read or to watch TV, but it's better than thinking about people or myself."

Upon her older sister's marriage, it was decided that Jane, who was both afraid and incapable of being on her own, should be institutionalized. The decision, made by both her sisters, was not responded to by Jane as a painful rejection; she accepted it, at least overtly, without protest.

Upon entrance to the hospital, Jane seemed hazy and disconnected, although she evidenced no hallucinations or delusions. She spoke minimally, answered questions with a yes or no, seemed rational, took care of herself reasonably well and fitted quietly into the admissions ward. She voiced relief to an attendant at being away from the expectations and demands of the outer world; however, she established no personal relationships with other patients or with the hospital personnel.

Were it not for the fact that no one wanted to assist her in making the transition back to society, Jane would have been recommended for discharge. Lacking such environmental support and recognizing her inability to relate easily with others or to assume independence, there was no option but to keep her hospitalized.

Let us next note some of the clinical features differentiating passive from active schizoids.

1. *Passive-schizoids* are drab, sluggish and inexpressive. They display a marked deficit in affectivity, are bland and appear untroubled, indifferent, unmotivated and insensitive to the external world. Their cognitive processes seem obscure, vague and tangential; they are either impervious to, or miss the shades of, interpersonal and emotional experiences. Social communications are responded to minimally or in a confused manner. Their speech is monotonous, listless or inaudible. Most people consider these schizoids to be unobtrusive and strange persons who fade into the background and are self-absorbed, aloof or lethargic.

Every so often the passive-schizoid will experience the awesome terror that he is "dead," nonexistent or petrified. Detached from the world and insensitive to his own feelings, he becomes aware of a frightening sense of "nothingness," a barren, cold, lifeless existence. The sense of impending disaster, of losing "self" or of being a walking automaton, a petrified object without meaning and experience, may overwhelm the patient and drive him into a bizarre psychotic episode in which he frantically searches to reaffirm his reality. Sinking into a lifeless void, he catches himself suddenly, struck by the sense of becoming a thing, not a being. This dread, this catastrophic sense of nothingness, causes him to flail out and to grasp objects, people and ideas by which he can convince himself that he does, in fact, exist. Thus, on the brink of total annihilation, he struggles wildly to confirm his being, clinging tenaciously to whatever meaning and feeling he can find or impute to his surroundings. These transient psychotic periods are attempts, then, to forestall the onrush of petrification and nothingness.

The passive-schizoid may also succumb to a brief psychotic disorder when he is faced with too much, rather than too little, stimulation. He is painfully uncomfortable with social obligations or personal closeness and will feel encroached upon if others press him into responsibilities beyond his tolerance. During these periods, he may either explode, bursting into frenetic activity to block the intrusions forced upon him, or simply "fade out," become blank, lose conscious awareness and "turn off" the pressures of the outer world. Several of these features are illustrated in the following brief sketch.

*CASE 8-3*
*Bernard K., Age 57, Unmarried*

This passive-detached schizoid man worked as a night watchman for many years, having maintained himself on the periphery of normal social life with but only two periods of brief institutionalization. Both episodes followed suggestions from his employer that a second watchman be hired to assist him in his nightly rounds. During these periods he became distraught and uncontrollably furious, "blanking out" shortly thereafter, and sank into a semi-stuporous state. When he regained his self-composure some weeks thereafter, he reported that "I feel better when I am by myself," "I don't want no one to talk to me about their problems" and "I like to work when it is quiet, with no other man around."

2. *Active-schizoids* are restrained, isolated, apprehensive, guarded and shrinking. Protectively, they have sought to "kill" their feelings and desires. They bind their impulses, withdraw from social encounters and prevent themselves from feeling the pain and anguish of interpersonal relationships. Thus, the apathy, indifference and impoverished thought we observe are not, as it is in the passive-schizoid, owing to an intrinsic lack of sensitivity but to an attempt to control, damp down or deaden excessive sensitivity.

Having given up the hope of gaining affection and security, the active-schizoid defensively denies feelings and aspirations. His cognitive processes are intentionally confused in an effort to disqualify and discredit rational thought and the distressful elements they contain. Thus, we see disharmonious affects, irrelevant and tangential thoughts and an increasing social bankruptcy and isolation produced as a function of building a tight armor of indifference around himself.

The active-schizoid will be precipitated into psychotic episodes for two reasons.

First, he is subject, like the passive-schizoids, to the devastating terror of "nothingness," the feeling of imminent nonexistence. In his effort to insulate himself and to shrink his world and deaden his sensitivities, he lays the groundwork for feelings of emptiness and unreality. To counter these frightening anxieties of depersonalization, he may strike out, engage in excited and bizarre

behaviors, cling to peculiar objects and utter unintelligible, beseeching words, all in an effort to
reaffirm his existence as a living being; he struggles to evoke responses from others, create a stir
and prove that life is real and not a mirage of
empty, floating automatons such as he senses
it to be.

Second, the active-schizoid may be precipitated into a psychotic disorder to avoid painful
negative reinforcements such as humiliation and
derogation from others. Although he has sought,
by active withdrawal and isolation, to minimize
his social contacts, this coping defense is not impenetrable. Should his armor be pierced and his
protective detachment assaulted and encroached
upon, he will not only experience the anguish of
the present, but will have ignited within him the
painful memories of past assaults. Under these
circumstances, the active-schizoid may burst into
a flood of erratic, hostile and bizarre reactions.
Fearful lest he be humiliated, injured and engulfed again and unable to govern the onrush of
previously repressed anxieties and angers, he may
lose control and be drowned in a chaotic wave
of primitive impulses. Simultaneously, then, his
external world has inundated him, and his inner
world has erupted; what we see during these episodes is his frantic struggle to escape being
swamped, smothered and submerged.

## ETIOLOGY AND DEVELOPMENT

We have stated repeatedly that personality
patterns arise from the complex interaction of
several biogenic and psychogenic factors. In describing the personality patterns presented in
chapters 6 and 7 we sought to identify the most
probable sources and combination of etiological
influences which contributed to the development
of each of these psychopathologies. Among the
major factors considered as significant were hereditary forces which shape the basic constitutional capacities and dispositions of the individual;
impoverished or enriched stimulation at each of
the three successive, sensitive periods of neurological maturation; the quality of parental feelings, communications and methods of behavior
control to which the growing child was exposed;
and the individual's tendency to perpetuate his
own self-defeating attitudes, behaviors and coping
strategies. In the following sections we will group
these influences into biogenic and psychogenic
factors, as was done in chapters 6 and 7, making
particular note of the similarities and differences
that we believe exist between the active and
passive variants of the schizoid personality.

### Biogenic Factors

Hypotheses ascribing personality functioning
to impairments in the biophysical substrate are
highly speculative. Conjectures may be offered,
but one must be mindful that present research
has not provided us with knowledge requisite to
definitive statements.

In the following discussion, we shall reiterate
several speculations proposed on pages 227 and
234 in chapter 6; we believe that the schizoid
patient will have similar but more serious biophysical impairments than the less severe asocial
and avoidant patterns. Since the biogenic influences ascribed to these two detached patterns
are substantially dissimilar, we shall divide the
presentation accordingly.

1. *Passive-schizoids* may be unfortunate
carriers of a defective family inheritance; genetic
factors conducive to affective and cognitive deficits may underlie many of these personalities.
There is ample evidence that families "breed"
the characteristics of the passive-schizoid personality, but it is difficult at present not only to
conceptualize the nature of the specific genetic
mechanisms which may be involved, but to state
unequivocally that these mechanisms do in fact
operate; stated differently, families may "breed"
the schizoid pattern through interpersonal contact and experience, and not through biological
inheritance.

Other biogenic factors indicative of, or conducive to, the development of this personality
are the following: a passive infantile reaction
pattern, which may set off a chain of impoverished stimulation and parental indifference; a
fragile ectomorphic build, requiring energy conservation, conducive to deficient physical competencies, and leading to vulnerabilities in situations of competitive stress; deficits or dysfunctions
in either reticular, limbic, sympathetic or synaptic
control systems, resulting in diminished activation, minimal reinforcement potentials and cognitive dysfunctions.

2. *Active-schizoids* often have a family history of apprehensive or cognitively "muddled"
relatives, suggesting the possibility that genetic
dispositions may be operative. A threctic infantile
reaction pattern is not uncommon in this personality, and often precipitates parental exasperation and rejection. Many have evidenced an
irregular sequence of maturation, resulting in
the development of an imbalance among competencies, an inability to handle superfluous
emotions and the emergence of social "peculiarities." The possibility that there may exist an

underlying excess in limbic and sympathetic system reactivity, or a neurochemical acceleration of synaptic transmission, likewise may be posited; such dysfunctions can give rise to the hypersensitivity and cognitive "flooding" which characterize these patients. It is suggested that the reader refer to chapter 6 for a more extensive discussion of these and subsequent speculative hypotheses.

### Psychogenic Factors

More extensive discussions of the hypotheses presented in these paragraphs may be found in parallel sections on pages 228 and 236 of chapter 6. What we will note regarding the psychogenic background of the passive and active-schizoids is in large measure a duplicate of what was said, respectively, about the passive-detached (asocial) and active-detached (avoidant) personalities. The essential difference between the psychogenic history of the mild and moderate detached patterns is the greater severity of injurious influences to which the moderately ill personality was exposed, or which he created for himself through his self-defeating strategies.

1. *Passive-schizoids,* especially those hindered in early life with constitutional insensitivities, often experience marked stimulus impoverishment in the sensory-attachment stage; this may result in an underdeveloped biophysical substrate for affectivity, and a deficit learning of interpersonal attachment behaviors. A family atmosphere of indifference, impassivity, or formality may have provided a model for imitative learning, thereby establishing the roots for a lifelong pattern of social reticence, interpersonal insensitivity and discomfort with personal affection and closeness. Parental styles of fragmented and amorphous communication may also be found; exposure to disjointed, vague and pointless interactions can result in the development not only of cognitive obscurity, but in the unfocused, irrelevant and tangential quality of the passive-schizoid's interpersonal relations.

Not only is it difficult to extinguish detached behaviors learned in early life, but they are further aggravated as the individual progresses through adolescence and early adulthood. Thus, experiences paralleling those of childhood often are repeated and tend to cumulate; stereotypes of the child's early "character" take firm root, shape subsequent social attitudes and preclude changes in interpersonal experience; these relationships often are caught in a web of destructive reciprocal reinforcements, which then serve to aggravate earlier maladaptive behavior tendencies. For example, the quiet, shy and ineffectual childhood behaviors of Jane W. led her family to stereotype her, that is, to expect that "she would always be that way"; had her family's attitudes and expectations been different, Jane might have "outgrown" this childhood image and attained a more normal social life.

Most pronounced among the processes which perpetuate the individual's initial experiences are his own behaviors and coping strategies. In the passive-schizoid, the following prove to be especially self-defeating: affective deficits that result in a "flattening" of emotional experiences; and perceptual insensitivities and cognitive murkiness that obscure the distinctions and highlights of events which otherwise might enhance and enrich his life. Thus, opportunities for a more stimulating and varied existence, so necessary to alter the schizoid's apathetic state, are diluted.

The impassive and cognitively insensitive behaviors of the passive-schizoid make him an unattractive and unrewarding member of social groups; unable to communicate with affect and clarity, he is shunned and overlooked and invited to share few of the more exciting and vibrant experiences to which others are drawn. Failing to interchange ideas and attitudes with others, he remains stationary and continues in his disjointed, amorphous and affectless state. Restricted to few social experiences, he acquires few social skills, finds it increasingly difficult to relate to others and perpetuates a vicious circle which not only fosters his isolated, dull life, but accentuates his social inadequacies and cognitive deficiencies.

Progressively alienated from others and a marginal member of society, he turns increasingly to solitary thoughts; in time, shared behaviors become fully subordinate to private fantasy. In solitude his thoughts are left to wander unchecked by the logic and controls of social communication and responsibility. Moreover, what he finds within himself hardly is rewarding; his past is a blank—a barren, colorless sequence of events and a void which offer no fabric for joyful fantasy; his inner personal world proves as "dead" and ungratifying as objective reality.

2. *Active-schizoids* have usually been exposed to a history of deprecation, rejection and humiliation; these result in feelings of low self-esteem and a marked distrust of interpersonal relations. Many have been subjected to belittlement, censure and ridicule, not only from parents but also from sibs and peers.

During the sensory-attachment stage they may have experienced the world as harsh and unwelcoming, thereby learning protectively to keep some distance from their environment and to insulate their feelings. Scorn and ridicule from others in response to their efforts at autonomy in the second developmental stage may have led to the acquisition of feelings of personal incompetence and low self-worth; as a further consequence, the child learns not only to avoid the appraisals of others, but to demean himself as a worthy source of positive reinforcement. Continuation of these experiences into the third developmental stage intensifies feelings of low self-esteem, and increases self-critical attitudes; the youngster now devalues, censures and belittles himself as others had in the past. Many are subjected to deprecation and humiliation at the hands of adolescent peers; experiences of social alienation, heterosexual failure and minimal vocational and competitive success during this period add further insult to the earlier injuries.

Unfortunately, the strategies that the active-schizoid acquires to fend off the painful experiences of life tend to foster rather than resolve his difficulties, as illustrated in the following case.

*CASE 8-4*
*Paul J., Age 26, Unmarried*

This young man had always been the butt of family teasing, an experience duplicated repeatedly at the hands of neighborhood peers. At the age of 14, both Paul's parents were killed in an automobile accident and he was sent to live with a kindly aunt in another city. Because of his past experiences and feelings of self-contempt and worthlessness, Paul insulated himself from potential friendships, circumscribing his life into a narrow sphere, and thereby precluded beneficial experiences that might have countered those of the past; similarly, he denied himself the chance to acquire social skills which might have facilitated more rewarding future relationships. Furthermore, in the effort to protect himself from future painful experiences, Paul remained hypervigilant to the threats he learned to anticipate from his environment. By focusing his attention only upon potential threats, and by accentuating minor social slights into major personal assaults, Paul reinforced his already distorted impression of the environment; thus, although he avoided certain objective dangers, his perceptual hypersensitivity attuned him to experience more threat than objectively existed.

In an effort to minimize his awareness of external discomfort, the active-schizoid turns inward to fantasy and rumination, but this also proves to be self-defeating. Not only are his inner conflicts intense, but he spends much of his reflective time reliving and duplicating the painful events of the past; thus, once more, his protective efforts reinforce his distress. Furthermore, since he has low self-esteem, his inner reflections often

take the form of self-reproval; he not only gains little solace from himself, then, but finds that he cannot escape from thoughts of self-derogation, from feelings of personal worthlessness or the futility of being himself.

In an effort to counter these oppressive, inner thoughts, he may seek to block and destroy his cognitive clarity, that is, to intrude and interfere with the anguish of his discordant, inner emotions and ideas. Not only does this protective maneuver prove self-defeating, in that it diminishes his ability to deal with events rationally, but it further estranges him from communicating effectively with others and experiencing the potentially gratifying rewards these might provide. Even more destructive, however, is the fact that the combination of self-reproval and intentional cognitive interference alienates the individual from himself; by his own protective strategy, then, he estranges himself from his own existence.

## COPING AIMS

In the preceding discussion of psychogenic factors we have referred to several of the coping strategies employed by the schizoid personality. This reflects the assertion made in chapter 5 that the adaptive efforts utilized by pathological personalities are themselves pathogenic, that is, that many of their instrumental strategies are self-defeating and foster new difficulties; all pathological patterns are alike in this regard. The central distinction between the more and less severe patterns is the fact that the strategies of the former group are instrumentally less successful and more self-defeating than those of the latter, either because they were never learned adequately, or because they have faltered under persistent and cumulative stress. Because of the inadequacy of their instrumental skills, we shall speak in this section of these patients' coping "aims," rather than their coping "strategies." Since their adaptive facilities are instrumentally so deficient, it seems best to focus on the restitutive and defensive efforts these patients employ; thus, these patients are distinguished from their milder counterparts, not in their strategies but in what they do to shore up these strategies when they begin to crumble.

As formerly effective strategies begin to falter, the schizoid may be driven to engage in a variety of extreme and frequently dramatic restitutive maneuvers; these are displayed in the form of brief psychotic episodes in which previously dormant or controlled thoughts and impulses break into consciousness, producing symptoms of bizarre ideation and behavior. If sufficient tension is discharged during these upsurges, and if environmental pressures are adequately relieved, the individual may regain his composure and equilibrium; his temporary "disordered state" has ended, and he returns to his previous level of pathological personality functioning. We will discuss in detail the characteristics of several of these more dramatic symptom disorders in chapters 10 and 11; for the present, however, we will focus our attention on the coping aims the schizoid seeks to achieve, that is, what he attempts to do to cope with stress now that his former strategies have failed him.

Earlier, we noted two sets of conditions which precipitate the schizoid into temporary psychotic disorders. One occurs when he feels a frightening sense of petrification, "deadness," depersonalization and emptiness, that is, a degree of outer and inner stimulation that is much *less* than that to which he is accustomed. The second occurs when he feels an oppressive sense of being encroached upon, pressured and obligated to others, that is, a degree of external stimulation that is much *more* than that to which he is accustomed. Let us next discuss the restitutive measures he employs to deal with these conditions. As we will see, these efforts exhibit themselves as "disordered" behavior.

### Countering Depersonalization

To cope with depersonalization, the schizoid frequently bursts into frenetic activity, becomes hyperactive, excited and overtalkative, spews forth a flight of chaotic ideas and is unrestrained, grabbing objects and running hurriedly from one thing to another, all in an effort to reaffirm his existence, to validate life, to avoid the catastrophic fear of emptiness and nothingness.

*Passive-schizoids* generally behave in a bland and apathetic manner since they experience few positive reinforcements and seek to avoid few negative reinforcements. As a result, they have little reason to acquire instrumental behaviors. Why then do they become active, frenetic and feverish and engage in vigorous coping efforts?

Passive-schizoids have enough awareness of the fruits of life to realize that other people do experience joy, sorrow and excitement whereas they, by contrast, are empty and barren. They seek to maintain the modest level of sensation and feeling to which they have become accustomed; although they avoid more than they can handle comfortably, they also feel considerable discomfort with less than they need, especially since less brings them close to nothing. Their

frantic, erratic and bizarre outbursts may be viewed, then, as a coping effort to counter the feeling that they are "going under," bereft of all life and meaning.

*Active-schizoids* control expressions of affect since they fear humiliation and rejection; they are bland and socially withdrawn, then, for protective reasons. Their overt appearance is similar to the passive-schizoid, not because of an intrinsic affectivity deficit, but because they have bound their emotions against possible rebuff. However, the consequences of their coping strategy are the same as those experienced by the passive-schizoid. Alienated from others and themselves, they may sense the terror of impending nothingness and of a barren, depersonalized and nonexistent self. Such feelings prompt them to engage in a frenetic round of behaviors to reaffirm reality.

### Deflecting Overstimulation

At the other extreme, both passive and active-schizoids may be faced with excess stimulation.

Unable to avoid external impositions, the *passive-schizoid* may react either by "blanking out," drifting off into another world, or by wild and aggressive outbursts. Undue encroachments upon his complacent world may lead him to disappear for prolonged periods of time, during which he seems confused and aimless, and which he only vaguely recalls. At other times, where pressure may be especially acute, he may instrumentally turn away these pressures by reacting with a massive outpouring of primitive impulses, delusional thoughts, hallucinations and bizarre behaviors.

As with passive-schizoids, external pressures may be too great for *active-schizoids,* going beyond their tolerance limits and leading them also either to "drift out" or to become wild and uncontrollable. During these outbursts, the probability of delusions, hallucinations and bizarre and aggressive behaviors is even greater than that found in the passive-schizoid. The active-schizoid has stored up intense repressed anxieties and hostilities throughout his life. Once released, they burst as in a rampaging flood; his backlog of fears and animosities has been ignited and now explodes in a frenzied, cathartic discharge. We may note several of these features in the following case.

### CASE 8-5
### George L., Age 37, Divorced

George was picked up as a vagrant in a town 70 miles from his home. He had been drinking, caused considerable commotion outside a bar, made lewd comments to passersby and seemed unclear as to his whereabouts. In police headquarters he seemed stuporous and apathetic, and was minimally communicative; he remained so for the following week, during which time he was remanded to a state hospital for observation.

Family history showed George to be the third of seven children; his mother, a hardworking woman, died when he was 11, and his father, a drifter and periodic drunkard, died when George was 16. George was the "queer" member of the family, always by himself, teased by his siblings and shunned by his peers. He left school at 16, wandered for a year, took odd jobs to sustain himself, joined the Navy for a four year tour of duty, did not care for it and has lived by himself since then in a rundown part of the city, working irregularly as a dish washer, cook and park attendant. He married a "pick-up" while in the Navy, and lived with her "miserably" for a few months. Upon his discharge, his wife disappeared; he has not seen her since, although he heard that she was remarried; she never legally divorced George.

When not in "trouble," George does not bother people; he simply prefers to be alone. Every couple of months he goes on a binge, a wild spree in which he spends all of his money, gets into a drunken brawl and usually lands in jail. Between these episodes, he does not drink and is quiet and unobtrusive.

Psychological tests and interviews with George showed that he was of better than average intelligence, had great mistrust of others and felt humiliated by his low status in life and the shame he brought to his more successful brothers in town. He admitted being suspicious of everyone's motives, having been made a fool of so much of the time. As he put it, "nobody gives a damn about you, especially if you're not worth a damn."

With regard to his wild sprees, he claimed that he "had to do something" every so often, so as "not to go crazy doing things that don't mean nothing." When his isolation and monotony became unbearable he would "hit the bottle, and start feeling some life again."

## REMEDIAL APPROACHES

In the following discussion we will differentiate, as we have before, the passive and active-schizoid varieties.

*Passive-schizoids* have poor prognoses for several reasons. Many are limited in their constitutional capacity for affectivity and activation: cognitive dysfunctions and interpersonal insensitivities may have their roots in irremediable biophysical deficiencies; few are motivated to seek or sustain a therapeutic relationship. Left to their own devices, they isolate themselves increasingly from social activities, thereby diminishing environmental controls and precluding beneficial interpersonal experiences.

The primary focus of therapy is the prevention of the self-defeating and deleterious consequences of social isolation. Through environmental management, the therapist may seek to increase the patient's awareness and involvement in interpersonal activities. Toward this end also, several psychopharmacological agents may be prescribed to stimulate activation and affectivity. However, efforts to enhance social interest must be undertaken in a slow, step by step manner, so as not to press the patient beyond tolerable limits. Among cognitively obscure patients, a clearer and more orderly style of thinking may be fostered by employing careful and well-reasoned therapeutic communications. Since passive-schizoids are not totally devoid of feeling, the therapist would do well to alert himself to those spheres of life in which the patient possesses constructive emotional inclinations, seeking to encourage activities that are consonant with these tendencies. Involvement in therapeutic groups may facilitate the development of social skills; it is wise, however, to precede or combine group therapy with individual sessions, so as to forestall undue social discomforts.

*Active-schizoids* have poor prognostic prospects. Their pattern is deeply ingrained; rarely do they live in an encouraging or supporting environment; probing into personal matters often is painful and terrifying; they have a marked distrust of close personal relationships, such as is inevitable in most forms of psychotherapy. Furthermore, therapy sets up false hopes, and often necessitates painful self-exposure; they would rather leave matters be, keeping to themselves, insulated from "unnecessary" humiliation and anguish. Should they engage in treatment, active-schizoids will tend to be guarded, and constantly test the therapist's sincerity; a "false" move will be interpreted as verification of the disinterest and deprecation they have learned to anticipate from others.

Trust is the essential prerequisite to therapeutic progress; without a feeling of confidence in the genuineness of the therapist's interests and motives, the patient will block his efforts and, ultimately, terminate treatment. Equally important is that the patient be settled in a supportive social environment; treatment will involve a long and uphill battle unless external conditions are favorable.

The primary focus of therapy with active-schizoids should be to enhance the patient's self-worth and to encourage him to recognize and utilize his positive attributes. The development of pride in self, that is, of valuing one's constructive capacities and feelings, is a necessary first step in rebuilding the patient's motivation to face the world; no longer alienated from himself, he will have a basis for overcoming his alienation from others. With a sense of valued self begun, the therapist may guide the patient into positively reinforcing social activities. The experience of positive reinforcements is what was lacking in the active-schizoid's life; initiating such experiences may prove to be the crucial turning point in what otherwise may have been an inexorable downward progression.

Both passive and active-schizoids should be aided to strengthen their controls and to curb the expression of irrational impulses; any precipitant of bizarre and socially destructive episodes, such as prolonged isolation, too rapid and intense personal relationships or the use of alcohol should be avoided when possible.

As far as specific techniques are concerned, supportive methods are primary in the early stages of therapy; phenomenological and group techniques are best employed in the midphases of treatment, that is, after adequate rapport and trust have been established. Intrapsychic therapy should not be considered until schizoid detachment is well under control; analytic procedures such as free association, the detached attitude of the therapist or the focus on dreams may only foster the schizoid's tendency to autistic reveries and social withdrawal. Institutionalization, when necessary, should be brief; hospital settings too often breed isolation and reward "quiet" behaviors, thus resulting in increased detachment and fantasy preoccupations.

How, then, does the schizoid learn new, more adaptive styles of behavior? In a nutshell, by acquiring a trust of the therapist, learning to relate to, and identify with, a receptive and encouraging person and hopefully, generalizing these experiences to others. With these learnings as a model, and with an increased sense of self-esteem, the patient may begin to test his newly acquired attitudes and skills beyond the therapeutic office.

## CYCLOID PERSONALITY: DEPENDENT AND AMBIVALENT BORDERLINE PATTERNS
### (DSM-II: *Cyclothymic Personality*)

The most obvious feature of the cycloid personality is the depth and variability of his moods. All these patients experience periods of dejection and disillusionment, frequently interspersed with temporary periods of elation or hostility.

Similarities exist between the present conception of the cycloid personality, that formulated under the same label by Kretschmer (1936), and the DSM-II syndrome termed the *cyclothymic personality,* characterized as follows in the official manual:

This behavior pattern is manifested by recurring and alternating periods of depression and elation. Periods of elation may be marked by ambition, warmth, enthusiasm, optimism and high energy. Periods of depression may be marked by worry, pessimism, low energy and a sense of futility. These mood variations are not readily attributable to external circumstances.

Common to each of these formulations is the alternation of moods. These moods are prompted less by external events than by internal factors; they are not so severe, however, as to be viewed as grossly pathological. Despite similarities in the clinical picture, fundamental differences exist between the present formulation of this personality and previous ones, especially with regard to their ostensive etiologies and basic coping strategies.

The present formulation will stress four divergent etiological backgrounds for the development of the cycloid personality, specifically those which parallel the two "dependent" and the two "ambivalent" patterns described in chapters 6 and 7. If these four patterns prove instrumentally deficient, or if they falter under the strain of persistent and intense environmental stress, the patient will deteriorate to the cycloid personality pattern. In each of these four strategies, he becomes less adept than previously in achieving the dependency reinforcements he seeks from others; as a consequence, he must try harder, must employ his characteristic strategy with greater fervor or abandon it and seek to institute new but equally ineffectual and self-defeating techniques.

Under these circumstances, for example, the *passive-dependent* person will experience a sense of helplessness and hopelessness, interspersed periodically with frantic efforts to stand on his own, or to recapture, by a cheerful outgoingness, the attachments and affections he seeks. Similarly, the characteristic gregarious strategy of the *active-dependent* may reach a feverish pitch of euphoric excitement, only to fall into the depths of futility, despondency and self-deprecation, should his restitutive efforts fail. Unsure of external approval and troubled by surging inner impulses, the *passive-ambivalent* may vacillate among marked self-condemnation, protestations of piety and good intentions, impulsive outbursts of hostility and feelings of intense guilt for his short-comings. The precycloid pattern of behavior vacillation in the *active-ambivalent* continues under increased stress, but at a more intense and erratic pace; he swings into profound gloom, at one time, and irrational negativism and chaotic excitement, at another. It is their extreme vacillation of behavior and mood and their common desperate seeking for esteem and approval from others that justifies bringing these patients together into a single "cycloid" syndrome, despite their divergent histories and coping strategies.

## CLINICAL PICTURE

Patients categorized as cycloid personalities display a wide variety of clinical features. However, certain elements stand out and are common to most; these will be noted hereafter. As with the schizoid personality, we will separate these features into three categories: primary source of anxiety; cognitive processes and preoccupations; and general mood and behavior. Characteristics which differentiate the four subvarieties will be described afterward.

### Separation Anxiety

Cycloid personalities are exceedingly dependent; not only do they require a great deal of protection, reassurance and encouragement from others to maintain their equanimity, but they are inordinately vulnerable to separation from these external sources of support.

Separation and isolation can be terrifying not only because cycloids do not value themselves or use themselves as a source of positive reinforcement, but because they lack the wherewithal, the know-how and equipment for independence and self-determination. Unable to fend for themselves, they not only dread signs of potential loss, but they anticipate it, and distort their perceptions so that they "see it" happening when, in fact, it is not. Moreover, since the cycloid devalues his own self-worth, it is difficult for him to believe that others can value him; as a consequence, he is

exceedingly fearful that others will depreciate him and cast him off.

With so shaky a foundation of self-esteem, and lacking the means for an autonomous existence, these patients remain constantly on edge, prone to the anxiety of separation and ripe for feelings of inevitable desertion. Any event which stirs up these feelings may precipitate a psychotic episode, most notably those of depression or excitement, as illustrated in the following brief case history.

### CASE 8-6
### Ruth S., Age 27, Married, One Child

This passive-dependent cycloid woman was admitted into a general hospital following a brief period of severe depression. For several years, Ruth would "go into a blue funk" whenever her husband was required to take short business trips away from home. In recent episodes, she could not perform even the simplest household chores and would sit in her bedroom with her two year old son and cry all day. Since this last episode, her husband requested a demotion to a job that required no traveling. However, in recent months, Ruth has again begun to exhibit her depressive moods whenever her husband would come home late from work or spend a few hours on a Sunday afternoon golfing with his friends.

### Cognitive Conflict and Guilt

Matters are bad enough for the cycloid, given his separation anxiety, but these patients are also in conflict regarding their dependency needs, and often feel guilt for having tried to be self-assertive. In contrast to their mildly pathological counterparts who have found a measure of success utilizing their strategies, cycloid patients have been less fortunate, and have struggled hard to achieve the few rewards they have sought. Moreover, in their quest for security and approval, most of them have been subjected to periods of isolation and separation; as a result, many have acquired feelings of distrust and hostility toward others.

The cycloid cannot help but be anxious. To assert himself would endanger the rewards he so desperately seeks from others and perhaps even provoke them to totally reject and abandon him; yet, given his past experiences, he knows he can never fully trust others nor hope to gain all the affection and support he needs. Should he be excessively anxious about separation and therefore submit to protect himself against desertion, he will still feel insecure; moreover, he will experience anger toward those upon whom he depends because of their power over him, for "forcing" him to yield and acquiesce. To complicate matters, this very resentment becomes a threat to him; if he is going to appease others as a means of preventing abandonment, he must take great pains to assure that his anger does not get out of hand. Should these resentments be discharged, even in so innocuous a form as displays of self-assertion, his security may be undermined and severely threatened. Thus, he finds himself in a terrible bind; should he "go it" alone, no longer depending on others who have been so unkind, or should he submit for fear of losing what little security he can eke out?

To secure his anger and constrain his resentment, the cycloid often turns against himself and is self-critical and self-condemnatory. He begins to despise himself and to feel guilty for his offenses, his unworthiness and his contemptibility. He imposes upon himself the same harsh and deprecatory judgments he anticipates from others. Thus, we see in these patients not only anxiety and conflict but overt expressions of guilt, remorse and self-belittlement.

### Mood and Behavior Vacillation

The most striking feature of the cycloid is the intensity of his moods and the frequent changeability of his behaviors, as illustrated in the following case history.

#### CASE 8-7
#### Leo P., Age 42, Married, Two Children

Leo has shown a lifelong development typical of an active-ambivalent cycloid. He claimed that he was never fully appreciated by anyone, especially his wife and his employers.

Desirous of seeking affection and approval from others, yet unsure of their feelings toward him, smothered by deep resentments, yet fearful of the consequences of assertion and anger, Leo would be in a state of turmoil, in an unresolvable conflict that precluded finding a single and stable course of action. Thus, for short periods, he would be acquiescent and ingratiating, but as soon as he felt unsuccessful, unloved and deserted he would burst into rage. When he momentarily felt confident and successful again, he became euphoric and was up in the clouds, making grandiose plans for the future; with his high hopes dashed shortly thereafter, he again became overtly hostile; then, protectively, he would turn his resentments inward and feel abject, worthless and guilty; but, to counter the oppressiveness of these feelings, he would divert his thoughts from himself, seek to buoy his spirits, run frenetically here and there and speak hurriedly and without pause, changing excitedly from one topic to another.

These *rapid* swings from one mood and behavior to another are *not* typical of the cycloid; they characterize periods in which there is a break in control or what we have referred to as a psychotic episode. More commonly, these patients exhibit a single dominant mood, usually a self-ingratiating and depressive tone that, on occasion, gives way to brief displays of anxious agitation, euphoric activity or outbursts of hostility.

The cycloid's typical, everyday mood and behavior reflect his basic personality pattern. In the following paragraphs we will note some of the clinical features that differentiate the four subvariants of the cycloid syndrome.

1. *Passive-dependent cycloids* typically are self-effacing, sweet, Pollyanna-like, pliant and submissive individuals who shun competition, are lacking in initiative and are easily discouraged. They attach themselves usually to one or two other persons upon whom they depend, with whom they can display affection and thoughtfulness and to whom they can be loyal and humble.

However, the cycloid's strategy of cooperation and compliance, in contrast to the less pathological *submissive* personality, has not been notably successful. He has put all his eggs in one basket, a specific loved one to whom he is excessively attached. But this attachment has not proved secure; his lifeline is connected to an unreliable anchor and his psychic equilibrium hangs on a thin thread and is in constant jeopardy. As a consequence, these patients exhibit a perennial preoccupation and concern with security; their pathetic lack of inner resources and their marked self-doubts lead them to cling tenaciously to whomever they can find, and to submerge every remnant of autonomy and individuality they possess.

This insecurity precipitates conflict and distress. These cycloids easily become dejected and depressed and feel hopeless, helpless and powerless to overcome their fate. Everything becomes a burden; simple responsibilities demand more energy than they can muster; life seems empty but heavy; they cannot go on alone; and they begin to turn upon themselves, feeling unworthy, useless and despised. Should their sense of futility grow, they may regress to a state of marked apathy and infantile dependency, requiring others to tend to them as if they were babies.

Sometimes, passive-dependent cycloids reverse their habitual strategy and seek actively to solicit attention and security. For short periods they may become exceedingly cheerful and buoyant, trying to cover up and counter their sense of underlying despondency. Other passives may disown their submissive and acquiescent past and display explosive though brief outbursts of angry resentment, a wild attack upon others for having exploited and abused them and for failing to see how needful they have been of encouragement and nurturance. At these times, a frightening sense of isolation and aloneness may overwhelm and panic these patients, driving them to cry out for someone to comfort and hold them, lest they sink into the oblivion and nothingness of self.

2. *Active-dependent cycloids* are similar to their mildly pathological counterparts, the gregarious personalities. Both are charming, histrionic, extravert, flighty, capricious, labile, evasive, superficial and seductive. However, the cycloid's strategies are instrumentally less successful than those of the gregarious personality; as a consequence, we observe more dramatic and extreme efforts to cope with events, many of which serve only to perpetuate and deepen their plight. For example, they may *not* have mastered the techniques of soliciting approval and ensuring a stream of constant support and encouragement; because of an excessively flighty and capricious style of personal relationships, they may experience long periods in which they lack a secure and consistent source of affection.

Deprived much of the time of the attentions and reinforcements they crave, these cycloids may intensify their basic strategy of gregariousness and seductiveness, and become dramatically histrionic and exhibitionistic. At these times, extreme hyperactivity, flightiness and distractibility are often evident; they exhibit a frenetic gaiety, an exaggerated boastfulness and an insistent and insatiable need for social contact and excitement. Frightened lest they lose attention and approval, they display a frantic conviviality, an irrational and superficial euphoria in which they lose all sense of propriety and judgment, and race excitedly from one activity to another.

At other times, they experience repeated rebuffs, or their efforts to solicit attention simply prove futile. Fearing a permanent loss of attention and esteem, they succumb to hopelessness and self-depreciation. Having lost confidence in their seductive powers, dreading a decline in vigor, charm and youth, they begin to fret and worry, to have doubts about their worth and attractiveness. Anticipating desertion and disillusioned with self, they begin to ponder their fate. Since worry begets further worry and doubts raise more doubts, their agitation turns to gloom, to increased self-derogation and to feelings of emptiness and abandonment; ultimately, they begin to distort reality so that everything, no matter how encouraging or exciting it formerly was, now seems bleak and barren.

3. *Passive-ambivalent cycloids* are extreme variants of the mildly pathological conforming personality. Both are methodical, rigid, industrious, conscientious and orderly persons; they overcomply to the strictures of society, display an air of moral rectitude, are overly respectful and deferential to authority and tend to be smallminded, perfectionistic, grim and humorless. They have learned to look to others for support and affection, but such rewards are contingent on compliance and submission to authority; they know that one *must* be good "or else." However, the passive-ambivalent cycloid is less certain than the conforming personality that he will receive rewards for compliance; try as he may, he is not confident that diligence and acquiescence will forestall desertion and that he will not be left adrift, alone and abandoned even when he submits and conforms.

Such insecurity may stem from several sources; for example, he may have been reproached unfairly by perfectionistic parents, or may not have been told with sufficient clarity "exactly" what was expected of him. Whatever the source, his compliant and conscientious strategies have not always "paid-off," and he is justly distressed and resentful; the pact he has made with his parents and other authorities has been abrogated too often, and they have failed to fulfill their share of the bargain.

The resentment and anger these cycloids feel for having been coerced into submission and then betrayed, churns within them and presses hard against their usually strong controls. Periodically, these feelings break through to the surface, erupting in an angry upsurge of fury and unbridled vituperation. This anger draws its strength not only from immediate precipitants but from their deep reservoir of animosity, filled through years of oppression and constraint. These outbursts of venom usually are directed toward weaker persons, innocent subordinates or children who, by virtue of their powerlessness, cannot retaliate.

Whether resentments are discharged overtly or kept seething near the surface, these cycloids experience them as a threat to their equanimity; feelings such as these signify weakness and emotionality, traits which are anathema to their self-image of propriety and control. Moreover, contrary impulses create anxiety because they jeopardize their security, that is, their basic dependency on others. Hostility is doubly dangerous; not only may it lead to an attack on the very persons upon whom they depend, thereby undermining the strength of those to whom they look for support, but it may provoke their wrath, which may result in outright rejection and desertion by these important persons.

To counter these hostile impulses, the passive-ambivalent cycloid may become excessively constrained and rigid, and engage in ritualistic and compulsive precautions to control all traces of resentment. Guilt and self-condemnation frequently become dominant features. Struggling feverishly to control their aggressive impulses, these patients often turn their feelings inward, and impose upon themselves severe punitive judgments and actions. Accusations of their own unworthiness are but mild rebukes for the guilt they feel. Self-mutilation and suicide, symbolic acts of self-desertion, may be a means of controlling their own expressions of resentment or punishing themselves for their anger.

4. *Active-ambivalent cycloids* are difficult to distinguish from their less severe counterpart, the negativistic personality. At best, we can say that the cycloids' overt symptoms are more intense and that their occasional psychotic episodes occur with somewhat greater frequency than in the negativist. Both groups may be characterized by their high unpredictability and by their restless, irritable, impatient and complaining behaviors. Typically, they are disgruntled and discontent, stubborn and sullen and pessimistic and resentful. Enthusiasms are short lived; they are easily disillusioned and slighted, tend to be envious of others and feel unappreciated and cheated in life.

Despite their anger and resentment, cycloids fear separation, and are desirous of achieving affection and love; in short, they are ambivalent, trapped by conflicting inclinations to "move toward, away or against others," as Horney (1950) might put it. They oscillate perpetually, first finding one course of action unappealing, then another, then a third, and back again. To give in to others is to be drained of all hope of independence, but to withdraw is to be isolated.

As with passive-ambivalent cycloids, the active-ambivalent has always resented his dependence on others, and hates those to whom he has turned to plead for love and esteem. Both types of ambivalent cycloids, in contrast with dependent cycloids, who have had a history of more consistent support from others, have never had their needs satisfied and have never felt secure in their relationships. The active-ambivalent has openly registered his disappointments, been stubborn and recalcitrant and vented his angers only to recant and feel guilty and contrite. He remains indecisive and continues to vacillate between apologetic submission, on the one hand,

and stubborn resistance and contrariness, on the other.

Unable to get hold of themselves and unable to find a comfortable niche with others, these cycloids may become increasingly testy, bitter and discontent. Resigned to their fate and despairing of hope, they oscillate between two pathological extremes of behavior. For long periods, they may express feelings of worthlessness and futility, become highly agitated or deeply depressed, develop delusions of guilt and be severely self-condemnatory and perhaps self-destructive. At other times, their habitual negativism may cross the line of reason, break out of control and drive them into maniacal rages in which they distort reality, make excessive demands of others and viciously attack those who have trapped them and forced them into intolerable conflicts. However, following these wild outbursts, these cycloids usually turn their hostility inward, are remorseful, plead forgiveness and promise "to behave" and "make up" for their unpleasant and miserable past. One need not be too astute to recognize that these "resolutions" will be short lived.

## ETIOLOGY AND DEVELOPMENT

The reader should refer to pertinent sections in chapters 6 and 7 for a more complete presentation of the points about to be summarized.

As frequently noted, a continuum exists between what we have termed the mild and moderately severe pathological personality patterns. This gradient refers not only to severity of symptoms but also to similarities in etiology and coping strategy. Thus, the major distinction between the asocial and avoidant patterns, discussed in chapter 6, and the schizoid pattern, discussed in this chapter, is one of degree; essentially identical pathogenic factors were experienced more intensely by the schizoid than the asocial and avoidant personalities and, as a consequence, their habits and attitudes unfolded as more maladaptive.

### Biogenic Factors

Constitutional dispositions to the cycloid pattern differ among the four subvariants.

1. *Passive-dependent cycloids* occur with considerable frequency in families with disproportionately numerous bland, sweet and unenergetic relatives. As infants many display both melancholic and threctic reaction patterns; the reticence and gentle sadness of these temperamental dispositions frequently evoke parental warmth and overprotection. Many of the patients

possess either ectomorphic or endomorphic builds, resulting in deficits in competitive abilities, and few positive reinforcements for assertiveness. Dysfunctions and imbalances in the reticular, limbic and adrenal systems may be hypothesized; specifically, the combination of low activation and high fear reactions may elicit dependency and bring forth protective and nurturant responses from others.

2. *Active-dependent cycloids* may frequently be found in families in which many members display high autonomic reactivity. A hyper-responsive infantile pattern is not uncommon among these patients; their alertness and activity in childhood not only exposes them to considerable stimulation, but evokes it from others. To account for their high sensory reactivity, one may posit the presence of neurally dense and responsive limbic, reticular and adrenal systems.

3. *Passive-ambivalent cycloids* evidence no distinctive pattern of biophysical functioning ascribable to biogenic sources.

4. *Active-ambivalent cycloids* frequently have shown an irregular infantile reaction pattern and an uneven course in the development of various capacities, both of which would increase the probability of inconsistent reactions from others. Low thresholds in neurological and physiochemical systems may be hypothesized to account, in part, for their hyperactivity and irritable affectivity.

### Psychogenic Factors

The following brief summary of the developmental experiences and self-perpetuation processes of the four subvariants of the cycloid personality may be supplemented by reference to pages 245, 253, 282 and 292, in chapters 6 and 7.

1. *Passive-dependent cycloids* have often been subjected to parental overprotection; during the first stage of neuropsychological maturation, many became unduly attached to a single caretaking figure with whom they developed a "symbiotic" dependence. This early attachment typically persisted through the second, or sensorimotor autonomy, stage, during which time the child's parents discouraged autonomy and venturesomeness. By the third stage, these youngsters had failed to develop a sense of self-identity, other than to view themselves as weak, inadequate and inept.

The psychogenic history of the passive-dependent cycloid differs from the mildly pathological submissive personality in matters of degree, rather than kind, e.g., the cycloid may have

been more attached or been given less opportunity for initiative. Cycloid children are also likely to have experienced less competence in the competitive give-and-take with siblings and peers; furthermore, their efforts to attach themselves in later life to new "caretakers" may have been less rewarding, resulting in greater insecurities and, in turn, to increasingly pathological coping behaviors.

These cycloid patients perpetuated their plight by abdicating self-responsibility and clinging tenaciously to others. This placed them in a most vulnerable position since they were increasingly devoid of capacities for autonomy, and they found themselves viewed with exasperation by those upon whom they depended. Failure to achieve support from others may have led either to marked self-disparagement or to frenetic efforts to solicit attention and approval. These erratic behaviors and mood swings fostered increased inner disharmony and maladaption, resulting in the loss of intrapsychic control and consequent brief psychotic episodes. Aspects of this sequence can be seen in the following case history.

### CASE 8-8
### Laura T., Age 29, Married, One Child

Laura was a housewife with a lifelong passive-dependent pattern that gradually deteriorated into a cycloid level of functioning following progressively severe conflicts with her physician husband who made greater demands of independence and sociability on her part than she could comfortably handle. In the early years of her marriage, Laura sought to fulfill his expectations by becoming involved in country club activities and entertaining his professional associates. The success of these efforts was short lived and, as a consequence, she became increasingly depressed and self-deprecating. Rather than support her during these periods, her husband became all the more critical and exasperated. In time, Laura's attempts to "brighten up" were less frequent and more abbreviated; she became more clinging and depressed, with periodic breaks that were severe enough to justify institutionalization. Upon her return home from these brief hospital stays, Laura would be jovial and enthusiastic about "asserting" herself again. Unfortunately, in what was usually less than a month or two, she would regress once more to her dependent and disconsolate state, beginning the cycle anew.

2. *Active-dependent cycloids* frequently had enriching and diverse experiences during their first years of life, leading to a penchant for stimulus variety and excitement and an inability to tolerate boredom and routine. Parental control by contingent and irregular reward was typical, that is, the child received periodic positive reinforcements for fulfilling parentally approved

expectations. This resulted in feelings of competence and security *only* when others acknowledged and encouraged one's performance. Furthermore, many of these youngsters were exposed to histrionic and exhibitionistic parental models; others were unusually attractive, and thereby learned to depend on favorable external comments as a basis for their feelings of adequacy. Another contributing factor may have been exposure to rapid changes in parental standards and societal values; this often results in the development of an exteroceptive orientation, a learning to be adept in "reading" what, where and when certain behaviors are approved. The acquisition of this radar system, geared to changing external stimuli, leads to an excessive flexibility and "other-directedness."

The skillful seductiveness of the active-dependent not only may foster new difficulties, but may falter as an instrumental strategy. This frequently is the case in cycloids, in contrast with their counterparts, the gregarious personalities. These personality patterns are not only shallow and capricious, but give little in return for their subtle though excessive demands upon others; as a result, they are unable to establish enduring close relationships. Furthermore, because of their exteroceptive orientation and their intrapsychic repressions, they fail to acquire inner resources from which they can draw sustenance. As a consequence, they are always on unsure footing, constantly on edge and never quite sure that they will secure the attention and esteem they require from others. Anxious lest they be cut adrift and left on their own, they proceed through cyclical swings of simulated euphoria in which they seek to solicit the attention they need, and periods of brooding dejection, hopelessness and self-depreciation. When their dread of desertion reaches monumental proportions, they lose all control, and are swept either into a chaotic and manic cry for help or into a deep and intransigent gloom.

3. *Passive-ambivalent cycloids* were likely to have been subject to parental overcontrol by contingent punishment; as a consequence, the child learned to conceive his worth in proportion to the degree of his success in meeting parental demands, feeling that he would be punished and abandoned if he failed to heed their strictures.

In childhood, cycloids may not have been guided with the same precision as their less severe counterparts, the conforming personalities; as a result, they feel especially vulnerable to error, knowing that they must keep within approved boundaries, yet unsure of exactly what these

boundaries are. Fearing transgression, they model themselves closely after authority figures, repressing all inclinations toward autonomy and independence lest these behaviors provoke wrath and desertion. They learned to follow rules, failed to develop initiative and lacked spontaneity and imagination; moreover, they were overtrained to be conventional and to feel guilt and self-reproach for failing to subscribe to the rigid prescriptions of their elders. In effect, they sacrificed their own identities to gain favor and esteem from others.

The strategy of the passive-ambivalent cycloid perpetuates his difficulties. His rigidity and conformity preclude growth and change, keep him from genuinely warm human relationships and alienate him from his own inner feelings. In a constant state of tension, for fear that he will overstep approved lines, he finds himself unable to make decisions and to act assertively. This indecisiveness readily turns to guilt, to feelings of having let others down and to thinking of himself as a fraud and a failure. As his feelings of self-derogation increase, his controls may weaken and his repressed angers and resentments may erupt, only to reinforce his fear and guilt, setting the cycle in motion again.

4. *Active-ambivalent cycloids* become negativistic, discontented and erratic persons as a function of parental inconsistency; they failed to be treated in even a moderately predictable fashion, being doted upon one moment and castigated the next, ignored, abused, nurtured, exploited, promised, denied and so on, with little rhyme or reason as they saw it. As a consequence, they learned to anticipate irrationality, to expect contradictions and to know, however painfully, that their actions will bring them rewards one time, but condemnation the next. Their parents may also have served as models for vacillation, capriciousness and unpredictability; moreover, schisms often existed between their parents, tearing their loyalties first one way and then the other. They learned that nothing is free of conflict, and that they are trapped in a bind. Yet, despite the feeling that they were mishandled and cheated, they received enough attention and affection to keep them hoping for ultimate harmony and secure dependency.

These hopes rarely are fulfilled in the lives of cycloids; external circumstances continue to be inconsistent. Furthermore, the cycloid himself creates inconsistency by his own vacillations, unpredictability, unreasonableness, sullenness and revengeful nature. Since he has learned to anticipate disappointment, he often "jumps the gun," alienating others before they alienate him. Moreover, his tensions keep churning close to the surface, leading him to act impulsively and precipitously. His lack of controls results in endless wrangles with others and precludes his achieving the affections he so desperately seeks. Dejected, angry and pessimistic he may become violent, exploding with bitter complaints and recriminations against the world or, conversely, turn against himself, become self-sacrificing, plead forgiveness and contrition and reproach and derogate his self-worth.

## COPING AIMS

The instrumental behaviors of moderately severe patients are similar but socially less adaptive than those utilized by the mild pathological patterns. Nevertheless, these strategies achieve enough positive reinforcement for the patient to lead him to persevere in their use.

It is difficult at first glance to grasp the functional utility of any of the cycloid's characteristic behaviors, let alone to see what gains he may derive by vacillating among them; clinging helplessness, resentful stubbornness, hostile withdrawal, pitiable depression and self-destructive guilt seem notably wasteful and self-defeating. No one should doubt that these represent genuinely felt emotions, but this does not preclude the possibility that they are also instrumentally useful in eliciting attention and approval, releasing tensions, wreaking revenge and avoiding permanent rejection by redeeming oneself through contrition and self-derogation.

It will be instructive to organize several of the cycloid's major strategies in terms of the goals they seek to achieve.

### Countering Separation

In contrast to his milder counterparts, the cycloid has been less successful in fulfilling his dependency needs, suffering, thereby, considerably greater separation anxieties. As a consequence, his concerns are not simply those of gaining approval and affection, but of preventing further loss; since he already is on shaky grounds, his actions are directed less toward accumulating a reserve of support and esteem, than of preserving the little security he still possesses.

At first, the cycloid will employ his characteristic strategies with even greater vigor than usual. Whichever of the four basic coping styles typifies his established personality pattern, will be applied with increased fervor in the hope of regaining his footing with others. Thus, *passive-dependent* and *passive-ambivalent cycloids* may

begin to view themselves as martyrs, dedicated and self-effacing persons who are "so good" that they are willing to sacrifice their lives for a higher or better cause. This they do, but not for the reasons they rationalize. Their goal is to insinuate themselves into the lives of others, to attach themselves to someone who will not only "use" them, but need them, and therefore not desert them. Self-sacrificing though they may appear to be, these cycloids have effectively manipulated the situation so as to assure against the separation they dread. Furthermore, by demeaning themselves, they not only assure contact with others, but often stimulate them to be gentle and considerate in return. Virtuous martyrdom, rather than being a sacrifice, is a means of exploiting the generosity and responsibility of others, a ploy of submissive devotion that strengthens attachments.

But what if the cycloid's efforts fail to counter the anxiety of separation? What occurs when exaggerations of his characteristic strategy fail to produce or strengthen the attachments he needs?

Under these conditions, we often observe a brief period in which the patient renunciates his lifelong coping style. For example, the *passive-dependent cycloid,* rather than being weak and submissive, reverses his more typical behaviors, and asserts himself, becoming either gay and frivolous or demanding and aggressive. He employs a new and rather unusual mode of coping as a substitute method for mastering the anxiety of separation. Unable to quiet his fears, faced with situations that refuse to be solved by his habitual, instrumental behaviors and discouraged and annoyed at the futility of using them, he disowns them, divests himself of these deficient coping devices and supplants them with dramatically new instrumentalities. His goal remains the same, that of denying or controlling his anxiety, but he has "found" a new strategy by which to achieve it, one that is diametrically opposed to that used before. It is this shifting from one strategy to another which accounts in part for the variable or cycloid pattern observed in these patients.

These novel efforts are not only often bizarre, but typically even less effective in the long run than the patient's more established strategies. He has sought to adopt attributes and behaviors which are foreign to his more "natural" self; unaccustomed to the feelings he tries to simulate and the behaviors he strives to portray, he acts in an "unreal," awkward and strained manner with others. The upshot of his reversal in strategy is a failure to achieve his goals, leading to increased anxiety, frustrations, dismay or hostility. Not only have his simulations alienated him from his real feelings, but the pretensions he displays before others have left him vulnerable to exposure and humiliation.

### Releasing Tensions

The ever-present fear of separation and the periodic failure of the cycloid to achieve secure and rewarding dependency relationships, cumulate an inner reservoir of anxiety, conflict and hostility. Like a safety valve, these tensions are released either slowly and subtly or through periodic and dramatic outbursts.

Since the cycloid seeks to retain the good will of those upon whom he depends, he tries, at first, to express indirectly the inner tensions he experiences. Dejection and depression are among the most common forms of such covert expression. The pleading, the anguish and the expressed despair and resignation of the cycloid serves to release his inner anxieties and to externalize and vent the fright and torment he senses within him.

But of even greater importance, depressive lethargy and sulking behaviors are means of expressing anger. In the *passive-dependent,* for example, depression may serve as an instrument to frustrate and retaliate against those who now seek to buoy his spirits. Angered by their previous failure to be thoughtful and nurturant, these cycloids employ their somber depression as a vehicle to "get back" at others or to "teach them a lesson." By exaggerating their plight and by moping about helpless and exhausted, the cycloid effectively avoids responsibilities, places added burdens upon others and thereby causes their families not only to care for them, but to suffer and feel guilt while doing so.

The *active-dependent cycloid* vents his anger in similar ways. Since others are accustomed to his gregarious and affable manner, his glum moroseness and sluggish and gloomy manner become doubly frustrating. By withdrawing into his dismal and sullen attitude, he constructs a barrier between himself and others in which they can no longer experience the pleasures of his dramatic and cheerful behaviors. Thus, in the form of recalcitrant depression, he gains revenge, punishes, sabotages and defeats those who have failed to appreciate him.

*Passive and active-ambivalents* are equally adroit in venting their tensions and expressing their angers. Their frequent fatigue and minor somatic ailments force others not only to be attentive and kind, but, by making them carry excess

burdens, to suffer, as well. Moreover, the dour moods and excessive complaints of these cycloids infect the atmosphere with tension and irritability, thereby upsetting the equanimity of those who have disappointed them. In the same way, the cycloid's cold and stubborn silence may function as an instrument of punitive blackmail, a way of threatening others that further trouble is in the offing or a way of forcing them to "make up" for the inconsiderations they previously had shown.

Despite the temporary gains achieved by these indirect forms of tension and hostility discharge, they tend to be self-defeating in the long run. The gloomy, irritable and stubborn behavior of the cycloid wears people down and provokes them to exasperation and anger which, in turn, will only intensify the anxieties, conflicts and hostilities which the patient feels.

As these more subtle means of discharging negative feelings prove self-defeating, the patient's tensions and depressions mount beyond tolerable limits and he may begin to lose control. Bizarre thoughts and psychotic behaviors may burst forth and discharge a torrential stream of irrational emotion. The *passive-dependent cycloid,* for example, may shriek that others despise him, are seeking to depreciate his worth and are plotting to abandon him. Inordinate demands for attention and reassurance may be made; he may threaten to commit suicide and thereby save others the energy of destroying him slowly. Under similar circumstances, the *passive-ambivalent cycloid* may burst into vitriolic attacks upon his "loved ones," as his deep and previously hidden bitterness and resentment surge into the open. Not unjustifiably, he accuses others of having aggressed against him, protesting that others are contemptuous of him and that they unjustly view him as a deception, a fraud and a failure. Utilizing the distorting process of intrapsychic projection, he ascribes to others the weakness and ineptness he feels within himself; it is "they" who have fallen short and who should be punished and humiliated. With righteous indignation he flails outward, castigating, condemning and denouncing others for their frailty and imperfections.

### Redemption Through Self-Derogation

The cycloid's hostility poses a serious threat to his security. To experience resentment toward others, let alone to vent it, endangers the patient since it may provoke the counterhostility, rejection and abandonment he dreads. Angry feelings and outbursts must not only be curtailed but condemned. To appease his conscience and to assure expiation, he must reproach himself for his faults, purify himself and prove his virtue. To accomplish this goal, hostile impulses are inverted; thus, aggressive urges toward others are turned upon oneself. Rather than express his anger he castigates and derogates himself, and suffers exaggerated feelings of guilt and worthlessness.

*Dependent cycloids,* for example, are notably self-recriminating; they belittle themselves, demean their competence and derogate their virtues, not only in an effort to dilute their aggressive urges, but also to assure others that they are neither worthy nor able adversaries. The self-effacement of these cycloids is an attempt, then, to control their hostile outbursts, and to stave off aggression from others. Among *ambivalent cycloids,* where hostile impulses are more profound and enduring than in dependents, the patient must counteract them more forcefully. Furthermore, since he has displayed his anger more frequently and destructively, he must work all the harder to redeem himself. Instead of being merely self-effacing and contrite, he turns upon himself viciously, viewing himself as despicable and hateful. Condemnatory self-accusations may reach delusional proportions in these patients; moreover, they often reject rational efforts to dissuade them of their culpability and dishonor. In some cases, the struggle to redeem oneself may lead to self-mutilation and destruction.

## REMEDIAL APPROACHES

Despite the many commonalities among cycloids, it is well to remind ourselves that each case is unique. At best, grouping individuals into syndromes will alert us to important features that certain patients share. But each individual possesses a distinctive history. Moreover, they are seen therapeutically at different stages in their disturbance; some are well-compensated, others are not. Some are bolstered by the support of their families whereas others face destructive environmental conditions. These and many other factors must be assessed before gauging the prognostic picture and recommending a remedial course of therapy.

The cycloid classification refers to a deeply ingrained personality pattern; nothing but the most prolonged and intensive therapy can produce substantial changes in basic patterns. Despite this tone of pessimism, the clinical prognosis of the cycloid is not too serious. In contrast to the schizoid personality, most cycloids seek and maintain a modicum of reasonably good social relationships. Their need for attention and approval,

their history of at least partial affection and encouragement in childhood, their skill in soliciting some measure of support and nurturance and their desire to restrain contrary and troublesome impulses, all presage an adequate future. Even following psychotic breaks, these patients tend to recover quickly, returning in short order to their former adaptive level. Moreover, if the cycloid can find an emotionally nurturant environment and is reinforced in his need for acceptance and attachment, he will manage to live in reasonable comfort and tranquility, and maintain a fairly secure hold on reality.

Should the attention and indulgence the cycloid requires be withdrawn, should his strategies prove wearisome and exasperating to others, precipitating anger and unforgiveness, his tenuous hold on reality will disintegrate, as his capacity to function will wither. At these times, he may succumb either to a somber depression or to an erratic and explosive surge of assertion and hostility; care must be taken to head off the danger of suicide during these episodes.

Among the first signs of a growing and imminent breakdown is marked discouragement and dejection. At this early phase, it is especially useful to employ supportive therapy and the phenomenological methods of reorientation. Efforts should be made to boost the patient's sagging morale, to encourage him to continue functioning in his normal sphere of activities, to build up his confidence in his self-worth and to deter him from ruminating and being preoccupied with his melancholy feelings. Care must be taken, however, not to press him beyond his capabilities, or to tell him to "snap out of it," since his failures to achieve such goals will only strengthen his growing conviction of his own incompetence and unworthiness.

Should a deeper depression take hold, it is advisable to prescribe one of the many psychopharmacological agents which may help in buoying his flagging spirits; these may be supplemented, where indicated, by a course of electroconvulsive treatments, a procedure notably useful in abbreviating depressive periods. Should suicide become a threat, or should the patient lose control and engage in hostile outbursts, it may be necessary to arrange institutionalization; however, the therapist must weigh the probabilities and consequences of these behaviors against the frequent disadvantages of prolonged hospitalization.

It is only during more quiescent periods that serious efforts to alter the cycloid's basic psychopathology can be instituted. A primary aim in this regard is the construction of capacities for autonomy, the building of confidence and initiative, and the overcoming of fears of self-determination and independence. No doubt, this will be resisted. Cycloids often feel that the therapist's attempt to aid them in assuming self-responsibility is a sign of rejection, an effort to "be rid" of them. The anxiety this engenders may evoke feelings of disappointment, dejection and even rage. These reactions must be anticipated and dealt with if fundamental personality changes are to be achieved.

Once a sound and secure therapeutic relationship has been established, the patient may learn to tolerate his contrary feelings and anxieties. Learning to face and handle these emotions must be coordinated, however, with the strengthening of healthier self-attitudes and instrumental strategies. This will be fostered if the therapist serves as a model to demonstrate how conflicts and uncertainties can be approached and resolved with equanimity and foresight. Group therapeutic methods may be utilized for purposes of testing these newly learned attitudes and strategies, and in refining them in a more natural social setting than is found in individual treatment.

# PARANOID PERSONALITY: INDEPENDENT AND AMBIVALENT BORDERLINE PATTERNS
## (DSM-II: *Paranoid Personality*)

The most prominent feature of these personalities is their mistrust of others, and their desire to remain free of close personal relationships in which they may lose the power of self-determination. Characteristically, they are suspicious, resentful and hostile, tend to misread the actions of others and respond often with anger to what they interpret as deception, deprecation and betrayal. Their readiness to perceive deceit and aggression precipitates innumerable social difficulties, which then confirm and reinforce their expectations. Their isolation from others, combined with their tendency to magnify minor slights, results ultimately in distortions that cross the boundary of reality; at this point, their thinking takes the form of delusions, a pathognomonic sign traditionally associated with these patients.

The present formulation of the paranoid personality is similar to that provided in the official DSM-II nomenclature under the diagnostic label of the same name, from which the following descriptive features have been excerpted:

> This behavioral pattern is characterized by hypersensitivity, rigidity, unwarranted suspicion, jealousy, envy, self-importance and a tendency to blame others and ascribe evil motives to them. These characteristics often interfere with the patient's ability to maintain satisfactory interpersonal relations.

In the days of Hippocrates, the term paranoia was used to designate most forms of mental illness. A more delimited usage, ascribed to Kahlbaum in 1863, reserved the label for conditions exhibiting conspicuous grandiose and persecutory delusions. Since then the appellation has been applied rather freely to several different categories of psychopathology in which delusions are evident, e.g., schizophrenia, paranoid type; paranoid states; paranoid personalities; and paranoia. In this text, the term will be applied exclusively to that *personality pattern* in which chronic delusions are a central feature; we will not use the label "paranoid" in other forms of psychopathology where delusions are secondary elements or relatively transitory phenomena.

Employing our basic reinforcement model, we may recall that "independent" personality patterns are characterized by their tendency to utilize themselves, rather than others, as the primary source of protection and gratification. The paranoid personality may be viewed as a moderately severe form of psychopathology founded on this strategy; they are akin to the two less pathological independent patterns, the narcissistic and aggressive personalities, and those with ambivalent patterns, the conforming and negativistic personalities, who have given up their dependency aspirations and opted for that of independence.

Entirely insignificant and irrelevant events are transformed so as to have reference to self in the paranoid patient; that is, tangential affairs and events take on personal relevance. As Cameron (1963) has described it so ably, the patient begins to impose his inner world of fantasy upon the outer world of reality; he creates a "pseudo-community" composed of distorted people and processes; an increasing number of situations and events lose their objective attributes and are seen in terms of subjective feelings and attitudes. Unable and unwilling to follow the dictates of others and accustomed to seeking gratification and power within himself, the paranoid reconstructs reality to make it suit his dictates. Threatened by a world in which others shape events, he creates a world in which *he* determines events and assumes the power and significance he desires.

This severe state of affairs arises if the paranoid patient's independent coping strategy has been inadequately learned or undermined. In contrast to his less severe counterparts, the paranoid's independence has been threatened, and he counters the anxiety he experiences by denying objective reality and substituting in its stead a new delusional reality in which he can affirm his stature and independence.

## CLINICAL PICTURE

Certain features are shared in common among paranoids. As in the two previous borderline patterns, we shall divide these characteristics into three areas: primary sources of anxiety; cognitive processes and preoccupations; and typical moods and behaviors. The four basic coping patterns which may unfold into the paranoid personality were discussed in detail in chapters 6 and 7. Characteristics distinguishing these four patterns at the paranoid level will be described later in this section.

### Attachment Anxiety

The paranoid detests being dependent not only because it signifies weakness and inferiority, but because he is unable to trust anyone. To lean upon another is to expose oneself to ultimate betrayal and to rest on ground which will only give way when support is needed most. Rather than chance deceit, the paranoid aspires to be the maker of his own fate, free of entanglements and obligations. Bad enough to place one's trust in others; even worse is to be subject to their control and to have one's power curtailed and infringed upon.

To be coerced by external authority and attached to a power stronger than himself provoke extreme anxiety. The paranoid is acutely sensitive to threats to his autonomy, resists all obligations and is cautious lest any form of cooperation be a subtle ploy to seduce him and force his submission to the will of others.

It is this attachment anxiety, with its consequent dread of losing personal control and independence, which underlies the paranoid's characteristic resistance to influence. Ever fearful of domination, he watches carefully to ensure that no one robs him of his will.

Any circumstance which prompts feelings of helplessness and incompetence, decreases his independence and freedom of movement or places him in a vulnerable position subject to the powers of others, may precipitate a psychotic episode. Trapped by the danger of dependency, struggling to regain his integrity and status and dreading deceit and betrayal, he may strike out aggressively, accuse others of seeking to persecute him, and ennoble himself with grandiose virtues and superiority. Should he find himself thinking, feeling and behaving in ways that are alien to his preferred self-image, he will claim that powerful sources have manipulated him and coerced him to submit to their malicious intent. That these accusations are pathological is evident by their vagueness and irrationality; for example, he safely locates these powers in unidentifiable sources such as "they," "a voice," "communists" or "the devil."

The paranoid's dread of attachment and fear of insignificance are similar to the anxieties of the schizoid. Both shy from close personal relationships and are vulnerable to the threat of "nothingness." These commonalities account, in part, for the difficulties that clinicians have faced in differentiating between these syndromes. There is, however, a crucial difference between these patients. Schizoids find little reinforcement in themselves; their fantasies generate feelings of low self-worth. Moreover, they turn away from others *and* from themselves; thus, they are neither attached nor possess a sense of self. Though paranoids turn away from others, as do schizoids, they find reinforcements within themselves. Accustomed to self-determination, they use their active fantasy world to create a self-enhanced image and rewarding existence apart from others. Faced with the loss of external recognition and power, they revert to internal sources of supply. Thus, in contrast to the schizoid, their inner world compensates fully for the rebuffs and anguish of experience; through delusional ideation they reconstruct an image of self that is more attractive than reality.

### Cognitive Suspicions and Delusions

The paranoid's lack of trust colors his perceptions, thoughts and memories. No doubt, all people selectively perceive events and draw inferences based on their needs and past experiences. But the feelings and attitudes generated in the life history of paranoids have produced an intense mistrust of others, creating within them a chronic and pervasive suspiciousness; they are oversensitive, ready to detect signs of hostility and deception, tend to be preoccupied with them and actively pick up, magnify and distort the actions and words of others so as to confirm their expectations. Moreover, they assume that events that fail to confirm their suspicions "only prove how deceitful and clever others can be." In their desire to uncover this pretense, they explore every nook and cranny to find justification for their beliefs, constantly testing the "honesty" of their "friends." Finally, after cajoling and intimidating others, the paranoid provokes them to exasperation and anger.

A number of these features are exemplified in the following graphic account.

### CASE 8-9
### Raymond R., Age 46, Married, One Child

This paranoid male was brought to a state hospital by the police following his merciless beating of his wife and 14 year old daughter. For some weeks prior to this event, he had been harboring the suspicion that his wife was in love with his best friend and had been poisoning his (Raymond's) food to be rid of him. On the evening of this episode, Raymond noticed that his wife served him a different meal than she took for herself and their daughter. Upon questioning, his wife informed him that she was merely, and quite obviously, eating the leftovers of the night before; knowing Raymond's dislike for leftovers, she had prepared him a fresh dinner. Raymond claimed that this was a ruse; no matter how his wife protested, Raymond twisted and distorted her words so as to make them reinforce his belief that she was, in fact, poisoning his food. When she refused to "prove her honesty" by eating the remains of his serving, and, then, exasperated, turned to leave the room, Raymond leaped up from the table, threw her to the floor and brutally attacked her; after rendering her bloody and unconscious, he assaulted his frightened daughter.

In short, the preconceptions of the paranoid rarely are upset by facts; they disregard contradictions, confirm their expectations by seizing upon real, although minute and irrelevant facts, or create an atmosphere which provokes others to act as they anticipated.

The unwillingness of the paranoid to attach himself to others or to share their ideas and points of view, leaves him isolated and bereft of the reality checks which might restrain his suspicions and fantasies. Driven to maintain his independence, he is unable to see things as others see them. Apart from others and with no one to counter the proliferations of his imagination, he concocts events to support his fears or his wishes, ponders incessantly along a single deviant track, puts together the flimsiest of evidence, reshapes the past to conform to his beliefs and builds an intricate logic to justify his anxieties and desires. Thus, left to his own devices, he cannot validate his speculations and ruminations; no difference exists in his mind between what he has seen and what he has thought; fleeting impressions and hazy memories become fact; a chain of unconnected facts is fitted together; conclusions are drawn. The inexorable course from suspicion to supposition to imagination has given birth to a delusion; a system of invalid and unshakable beliefs has been created.

Delusions are a natural outgrowth of the paranoid personality pattern. Two conditions, dependence on self for both stimulation *and* reinforcement, are conducive to the emergence of delusions. Insistent on retaining his independence, the paranoid isolates himself and is unwilling to share the perspective and attitudes of others. He has ample time to cogitate and form idiosyncratic suppositions and hypotheses; these then are "confirmed" as valid since it is he *alone* who is qualified to judge them.

The delusions of the paranoid differ from those seen in other pathological patterns. Accustomed to self-reinforcement and independent thought and "convinced" of his competence and superiority, the paranoid is both skillful in formulating beliefs and confident in their correctness; his delusions tend, therefore, to be systematic, rational and convincing. In contrast, the occasional delusions of the schizoid and cycloid appear illogical and unconvincing, tending to arise under conditions of unusual emotional duress; moreover, in further distinction, they are usually bizarre, grossly irrational, scattered and unsystematic.

### Defensive Vigilance and Veiled Hostility

Paranoids are constantly on guard, mobilized and ready for any emergency or threat. Whether faced with real dangers or not, they maintain a fixed level of preparedness, an alert vigilance against the possibility of attack and derogation. There is an edgy tension, an abrasive irritability and an ever-present defensive stance from which they can spring to action at the slightest hint of threat. This state of rigid control never seems to abate; rarely do they relax, ease up or let down their guard.

Beneath the surface mistrust and defensive vigilance in the paranoid lies a current of deep resentment toward others who "have made it." To the paranoid, most people have attained their status unjustly; thus, he is bitter for having been overlooked, treated unfairly and slighted by the "high and mighty," "the cheats and the crooks" who duped the world. Only a thin veil hides these bristling animosities.

Unable to accept their own faults and weaknesses, paranoids maintain their self-esteem by attributing their shortcomings to others. They repudiate their own failures and project or ascribe them to someone else. They possess a remarkable talent for spotting even the most trifling of deficiencies in others; both subtly and directly they point out and exaggerate, with great pleasure, the minor defects they uncover among those they despise. Rarely does their undercurrent of envy and hostility subside; they remain touchy and irascible, ready to humiliate and deprecate anyone whose merits they question, and whose attitudes and demeanor evoke their ire and contempt.

There are no universal attributes which may be spoken of as the "essence" of the paranoid personality. The great majority of these patients evidence the constellation of anxieties, cognitions and behaviors described above, but we must be careful not to let our focus upon these common symptoms obscure the variety of forms into which this impairment unfolds or the different coping patterns which underlie them. In what follows we shall describe some of the features which differentiate the four basic patterns of the paranoid personality. Despite the distinctions we shall draw, we must be mindful that distinctions are not well defined in reality; there are overlappings, with traces of the more distinctive features of each subvariety found often in the others. Few "pure" textbook cases ever are met.

1. *Passive-independent paranoids* are similar to their less severe counterparts, the narcissistic personalities. They seek to retain their admirable self-image, act in a haughty and pretentious manner, are naively self-confident, ungenerous, exploitive, expansive and presumptuous and display a supercilious contempt and benign arrogance toward others.

In contrast to the narcissist, who has achieved a modicum of success with his optimistic veneer and exploitive behaviors, the paranoid has run hard against reality. His illusion of omnipotence has periodically been shattered, toppling him from his vaulted image of eminence. Accustomed to being viewed as the center of things and to being a valued and admired figure among others, he cannot tolerate the lessened significance now assigned to him. His narcissism has been wounded.

Not only must the paranoid counter the indifference, the humiliation and the fright of insignificance generated by reality, but he must re-establish his lost pride through extravagant claims and fantasies. Upset by assaults upon self-esteem, he reconstructs his image of himself and ascends once more to the status from which he fell. To do this, he endows himself by self-reinforcement with superior powers and exalted competencies. He dismisses events which conflict with his newly acquired and self-designated importance; flimsy talents and accomplishments are embellished, creating a new self-image that supplants objective reality.

Since these patients lack internal discipline and self-control, they allow their reparative fantasies free rein to embroider a fabric of high sheen and appeal, caring little for the fact that their claims are unwarranted. These grandiose assertions become fixed and adamant; they are too important to the patient's need to regain importance and to become an identity of significance and esteem. The paranoid goes to great lengths to convince himself and others of the validity of his claims, insisting against obvious contradictions and the ridicule of others that he deserves to be catered to and that he is entitled to special acknowledgment and privileges.

But the evidence in support of the paranoid's assertions is as flimsy as a house of cards, easily collapsed by the slightest incursion. Unable to sustain this image before others and rebuffed and unable to gain the recognition he craves, he turns more and more toward himself for salvation. Taking liberties with objective facts and wandering further from social reality and shared meanings, he concocts an ever more elaborate fantasy world of grandiose delusions. Not uncommonly, he may begin to assume the role and attributes of some idolized person, someone whose repute cannot be questioned by others. As this identification takes root, the paranoid asserts his new identity, a noble and inspired leader, a saint or a god, a powerful and rich political figure or an awesome and talented genius. Grandiose missions are proposed for "saving the world"; plans are made for solving insurmountable geographic, social and scientific problems, for creating new societies, interplanetary arrangements and so on. These schemes may be worked out in minute detail, often correspond to objective needs and are formulated with sufficient logic to draw at least momentary attention and recognition from others. The following brief case illustrates this sequence of events in a passive-independent paranoid.

### CASE 8-10
### Charles W., Age 36, Married, No Children

Charles, an only child of poorly educated parents, had been recognized as a "child genius" in early school years. He received a Ph.D. degree at

24, and subsequently held several responsible positions as a research physicist in an industrial firm.

His haughty arrogance and narcissism often resulted in conflicts with his superiors; it was felt that he spent too much time working on his own "harebrained" schemes and not enough on company projects. Charles increasingly was assigned to jobs of lesser importance than that to which he was accustomed. He began to feel, not unjustly, that both his superiors and his subordinates were "making fun of him" and not taking him seriously. To remedy this attack upon his status, Charles began to work on a scheme that would "revolutionize the industry," a new thermodynamic principle which, when applied to his company's major product, would prove extremely efficient and economical. After several months of what was conceded by others as "brilliant thinking," he presented his plans to the company president. Brilliant though it was, the plan overlooked certain obvious simple facts of logic and economy.

Upon learning of its rejection, Charles withdrew to his home where he became obsessed with "new ideas," proposing them in intricate schematics and formulas to a number of government officials and industrialists. These resulted in new rebuffs which led to further efforts at self-inflation. It was not long thereafter that he lost all semblance of reality and control; for a brief period, he convinced himself of the grandiose delusion that he was Albert Einstein.

2. *Active-independent paranoids* may be seen as more severe variants of the aggressive personality described in chapter 7. They are characterized best by their power orientation, their mistrust, resentment and envy of others, and by their autocratic, belligerent and intimidating manner. Underlying these features is a ruthless desire to triumph over others, to vindicate themselves for past wrongs by cunning revenge or callous force, if necessary.

In contrast to his less severe counterpart, the paranoid has found that in his efforts to outwit and frustrate others, he has only prompted them to inflict more of the harsh punishment and rejection to which he was subjected in childhood. His strategy of arrogance and brutalization has backfired too often, and he now seeks retribution, not as much through action as through fantasy.

Repeated setbacks have confirmed the paranoid's expectancy of aggression from others; by his own hand, he stirs up further hostility and disfavor. Because of his argumentative and "chip-on-the-shoulder" attitudes, he provokes ample antagonism from others. Isolated and resentful, he increasingly turns to himself, to cogitate and mull over his fate. Left to his own ruminations, he begins to imagine a plot in which every facet of his environment plays a threatening and treacherous role. Moreover, through the intrapsychic mechanism of projection, he attributes his own venom to others, ascribing to them the malice and ill will he feels within himself. As the line draws thin between objective antagonism and imagined hostility, the belief takes hold that others intentionally are persecuting him; alone, threatened and with decreasing self-esteem, the suspicions of the active-independent paranoid now have been transformed into delusions. Not infrequently, persecutory delusions combine with delusions of grandeur; however, these latter beliefs play a secondary role among these patients, in contrast to their primacy among passive-independent paranoids.

Preeminent among these paranoids is their need to retain their independence; despite all adversity they cling tenaciously to the belief in their self-image. This need to protect their autonomy and strength may be seen in the content of their persecution delusions. Malevolence on the part of others is viewed neither as casual nor random; rather, it is designed to intimidate, offend and undermine the patient's self-esteem. "They" are seeking to weaken his "will," destroy his power, spread lies, thwart his talents, conspire to control his thoughts and to immobilize and subjugate him. These paranoids dread losing their independence; their persecutory themes are filled with fears of being forced to submit to authority, of being made soft and pliant and of being tricked to surrender their self-determination.

3. *Passive-ambivalent paranoids* are similar both to the mildly severe conforming personality and to the moderately severe passive-ambivalent cycloid personality. However, in contrast to these patients, who retain the hope of achieving gratification and protection through the good offices of others, the passive-ambivalent paranoid renounces his dependency aspirations and assumes a stance of independence. Despite his growing hostility and his repudiation of conformity and respect as a way of life, he retains his basic rigidity and perfectionism; he remains grim and humorless, tense, controlled and inflexible, small-minded, legalistic and self-righteous. Certain features of his make-up are deeply embedded, internalized as a fixed system of habits. Though he now may find it necessary to discard others as his primary source of reinforcement, the remnants of his lifelong habits of overcontrol and faultlessness are not so readily abandoned; the basic personality style remains immutable.

The passive-ambivalent paranoid continues to seek the clarity of rules and regulations, he cannot tolerate suspense and must create order and system in his life. Deprived of the guidelines he spurns from others, he learns to lean increasingly upon himself and to be his own ruthless slave driver in search of order, power and independence. This leads to an obsessive concern with trivial details and an excessive intellectualization of minor events, all to the end of obtaining internal perfection and faultlessness.

In his new found independence, this paranoid frees himself from the constraints of submission and propriety. He begins to discharge the reservoir of hostility he previously had repressed and imposes his self-created standards upon others, attacking them with the same demands and punitive attitudes to which he himself was earlier subjected. Impossible regulations set for others allow him to vent hostilities and condemnation for their failures to meet them; now he can give to others what he himself has received. He can despise and hate them for their weaknesses, their deceits and their hypocrisy—precisely those feelings which he previously had experienced within himself, had once sought to repress and which he still tries to conceal by condemning them in others.

Despite his overt repudiation of conformity and submission, the passive-ambivalent paranoid cannot free himself entirely of conflict and guilt; despite efforts to justify his aggressive manner, he is unable to square these actions with past beliefs. Furthermore, his present arrogance reactivates past anxieties; he cannot escape the memories of retaliation which his own hostile actions provoked in the past.

Deep within these paranoids, then, are the remnants of guilt and the fear of retribution; these two elements give rise to persecutory delusions. First, the passive-ambivalent paranoid has learned from past experience to anticipate disfavor and criticism in response to contrary and nonconforming behaviors; thus, as he looks about him he "sees," in the movements and remarks of others, the hostility he anticipates. Second, in order to deny or justify his behaviors, he projects his anger upon others; this mechanism, however, causes him to "find" hostile intent where none, in fact, exists. Lastly, his inner feelings of guilt reactivate his self-condemnatory attitudes; thus, part of him feels that he deserves to be punished for his resentments and behaviors. Thus, as a result of anticipation, projection and guilt, he begins to believe that others are "after him," seeking to condemn, punish, belittle and undo him.

There are certain encapsulated and well-defined delusions which often exist apart from the main body of a patient's "normal" beliefs.

These rare delusional systems are referred to as cases of classical *paranoia* (DSM-II). When they are seen, they tend to be found among passive-ambivalent paranoids. The overly rigid and tightly controlled thought processes of these paranoids often enable them to segment their beliefs and to keep them as separate and compartmentalized units. Thus, the patient may appear to function much of the time in a normal manner; however, once a topic associated with the delusion is broached, his irrational but normally hidden and encapsulated belief becomes manifest. The following brief example portrays a number of these characteristics.

CASE 8-11
Martin D., Age 50, Married, No Children

This passive-ambivalent paranoid, although known as a harsh, perfectionistic and overly legalistic probation officer, managed to maintain a moderately acceptable veneer of control and propriety in his relationships with his neighbors. In recent years, however, he became convinced that youngsters who "smoked pot" were part of a "communist plot to undo this great country." Whenever a "hippie" was brought to court on any charge, he would "make it his business to talk to the judge" about the plot, and attempt to ensure that he would impose a "proper jail sentence." After repeated failures to persuade the judge to see things his way, he began a personal campaign in the community to impeach the judge and to place "all hippies in a federal jail."

4. *Active-ambivalent paranoids* may be differentiated from their less severe counterparts, the negativistic personality, and the equally ill active-ambivalent cycloid, by the presence of both overt hostility and frank delusions. All three categories are noted by their discontent, pessimism, stubbornness and vacillation. However, the paranoid is more aggressively negativistic and faultfinding, appears sullen, resentful, obstructive and peevish at all times and openly registers his feelings of jealousy, of being misunderstood and of being cheated. As a consequence, he rarely can sustain good relationships, creating endless wrangles wherever he goes. Demoralized by these events, he foregoes all hopes of gaining affection and approval from others, and decides to renounce these aspirations in preference for self-determination.

Despite the strength with which he asserts his new found independence, the active-ambivalent paranoid remains irritable, dissatisfied and troubled by discontent and ambivalence. He rarely forgets his resentments, his feelings of having been mistreated and exploited. Not uncommonly, he begins to perceive the achievements of others as unfair advantages, preferential treatments which are undeserved, and which have been denied to him. His disgruntlement and complaints mount; his fantasies expand and weave into irrational envy; his grumbling turns to anger and spite; each of these feed into the central theme of his unjust misfortune, and are whipped, bit by bit, into delusions of resentful jealousy.

Erotic delusions are not uncommon among these patients. Although consciously repudiating their need for others, the ambivalent paranoid still seeks to gain affection from them. Rather than admit to these desires, however, he defensively projects them, interpreting the casual remarks and actions of others as subtle signs of their amorous intent. However, the paranoid is unable to tolerate these "attentions" since he dreads further betrayal and exploitation. Thus, in conjunction with these erotic delusions, the paranoid protests that he must be "protected"; he may accuse innocent victims of commiting indignities, making lewd suggestions or molesting him, as illustrated in the following case.

### CASE 8-12
### Belle G., Age 40, Divorced, No Children

This active-ambivalent paranoid woman, currently unmarried, but divorced twice following rather embittered and stormy marriages, began to accuse several men in her neighborhood of "peeking in" her bedroom windows while she slept at night. Despite their suspicion that her accusations were nothing more than fantasy, the local police, without her knowledge, assigned two officers to check her home several times each night. One evening, the two officers heard strange sounds within Belle's home (these turned out to be scuffling between her two cats); they quickly shined their flashlights into her open bedroom window, the one through which she claimed the accused men would peek, and found Belle sleeping nude and uncovered on her bed, a most unusual behavior for someone who anticipated and condemned the presence of voyeurs, but not surprising in pathologically ambivalent paranoid personalities.

## ETIOLOGY AND DEVELOPMENT

There is neither a unique set of determinants nor a uniform sequence of development in the etiological background of the paranoid personality; different combinations and orders of events can give rise to this condition. We have recognized some of these divergent lines by differentiating the paranoid personality into four basic variants; the following discussion will be arranged in terms of this four-way breakdown.

Let us be reminded, again, that the propositions to be presented below are provisional hypotheses, not facts; we have little in the way of dependable evidence from systematic and well-designed research to justify making definitive statements.

In the following paragraphs we will only summarize the highlights of paranoid biogenesis and psychogenesis, referring the reader for a more complete discussion of these points to pertinent sections on the independent and ambivalent personality patterns described in chapter 7.

### Biogenic Factors

These influences will be outlined below in accord with the four subvarieties of the paranoid personality.

1. *Passive-independent paranoids* evidence no clearly defined biogenic dispositions.

2. *Active-independent paranoids* appear to come from families with a disproportionately high number of members who display vigorous energy, an irascible choleric temperament or a fearless parmic temperament. As children, these patients tend to be active and intrusive, have frequent temper outbursts, are difficult to manage and precipitate difficulties with others by their thick-skinned, aggressive manner. Many possess a constitutional mesomorphic-endomorphic build, a physique which tends to reinforce the learning of assertive behaviors. It may be speculated that aspects of their temperament can be traced to low thresholds of reactivity in portions of the limbic and reticular systems.

3. *Passive-ambivalent paranoids* do not display in common distinctive biogenic histories.

4. *Active-ambivalent paranoids* often evidence irregular infantile reaction patterns and an uneven course of maturation, traits which tend to promote inconsistent and contradictory styles of parental behavior management. Their characteristic hyperactivity and irritable affectivity may be attributed to low neurophysiological thresholds for responsivity.

### Psychogenic Factors

The following summarizes and extends briefly several more extensive discussions provided in pages 263, 271, 282 and 292 of chapter 7.

1. *Passive-independent paranoids* typically were overvalued and indulged by their parents, given the impression that they were special creatures whose mere existence was worthy of note; many were "only" children. Few developed a sense of interpersonal responsibility, failing to

learn to cooperate, share or think of the desires and interests of others. Unrestrained by their parents and confident in their self-worth, their fantasies had few boundaries, allowing them to create fanciful images of their power and achievements.

The lack of social responsibility and exploitiveness of these paranoids led inevitably to interpersonal difficulties. Once beyond the protective and nurturant home setting, these individuals ran hard against objective reality; their illusion of omnipotence was challenged; their self-centeredness and ungiving attitudes were questioned and attacked; their image of eminence and perfection was shattered. Rather than face and adapt to reality, or build up their competencies to match self-esteem, they turned increasingly to the refuge of fantasy. Rationalizing their defects and lost in their dream gratifications, they retreated and became further alienated from others.

With new rejections and humiliations, the paranoid moved more into himself, and soon began to confuse his fantasy compensations for objective reality. In his world of imagination he redeemed himself and reasserted his pride and status. His lifelong habit of self-reinforcement and fantasizing stood him in good stead; with supreme facility he was able to weave alibis and proofs of his own perfection and grandiosity. Protected by his own fantasies, he learned to care little for the indifference of others, their jealous criticism and their malevolent lies and "distortions."

2. *Active-independent paranoids* typically were subjected to parental antagonism and harassment; they frequently served as scapegoats for displaced parental aggression. However, instead of anxiety, many, as a consequence of mistreatment, developed a sense of power; they acquired the feeling that they had "to be contended with" and that they could cause trouble and "get a rise" out of others through their obdurate and provocative behaviors. Additionally, many of these youngsters learned vicariously to model themselves after aggressive parents; moreover, what their parents did gave them implicit sanction to act with hostility toward others.

Let us next trace the sequence through which these attitudes and behaviors developed during each of the three neuropsychological stages. The aggressive paranoid learned, in the first stage, to perceive the world as harsh and unkind, a place demanding protective vigilance and mistrust. During the second stage, he acquired the self-confidence to fend for himself; he learned that through his own assertive actions he could disturb others and manipulate events to his suiting. The third stage was, in large part, a continuation of the first two; mistrustful of others, and confident in his autonomy and power, he began to reject parental controls and values, and to supplant them with his own. Unguided, and rebellious of parental authority, he developed few inner controls; as a consequence, he never learned to restrain his impulses, or to avoid temptations.

A similar sequence of learnings can be acquired by children who were reared in broken families and disorganized subcultures. Few impulse controls are taught; children gain their outlook on life wandering "on the street," in concert with equally destitute and disillusioned peers; few congenial and socially successful models exist for them to emulate; the traditional values and standards of society are viewed as alien, if not downright hypocritical and hostile. For these children, aggressive toughness is mandatory for survival; they learned quickly to adopt a "dog-eat-dog" attitude and to counter hostility and exploitation with the same.

Anticipating hostility and betrayal from others, the active-independent moved through life with a chip-on-his-shoulder, was bristling with anger and perceived hostility before it occurred. Resentments and antagonisms were projected upon others; moreover, dreading the thought of being attacked and humiliated or weak and powerless, he learned to attack first.

In contrast to his less severe prototype, the aggressive personality, the active-independent paranoid failed to acquire either confidence, skill or success in his assertive and vindictive strategy. Faced with repeated setbacks, he increasingly isolated himself from interpersonal relationships and withdrew into fantasy as a means of nurturing his wounds. It is this apartness from social life, this gnawing mistrust of others and the feeling of losing self-determination, that led these paranoids to their irrational suspicions, and to their delusions of persecution.

3. *Passive-ambivalent paranoids* frequently have a background of parental overcontrol through contingent punishment; they have striven to meet parental demands and to avoid errors and transgressions, and thereby minimize punitive treatment and the threat of abandonment. In their early years they sought to model themselves after authority figures, foregoing their independence, learning to "toe the line" and to follow rules with utmost precision. This paranoid pays a price for his rigid conformity; he lacks spontaneity and

initiative, is unable to form deep and genuine relationships and is indecisive and fearful of the unknown.

For various reasons, which differ from case to case, the security the paranoid sought to achieve through submission and propriety no longer works. Lacking adequate guidance and support from others, intolerant of suspense and dreading punishment and retribution lest his repressed anger erupts, he draws into himself, turns away from dependent conformity and seeks to find solace, if he can, within his own thoughts.

Although he renounced his dependency, the passive-ambivalent cannot relinquish his lifelong habits of perfectionism and faultlessness; moreover, feelings of guilt and fear become acute as he begins to assert himself. Anticipating punishment for his aggressive and nonconforming behaviors, and feeling deep within him that such actions deserve condemnation, he projects these self-judgments upon others, and now views them to be hostile and persecutory when they are not.

4. *Active-ambivalent paranoids* tend to acquire their negativistic irritability and discontent in response to inconsistent parental treatment; throughout early life, most were subjected to capricious vacillations in parental emotion and interest. Their parents were affectionate one moment and irrationally hostile the next; they were indifferent, then indulgent, exploitive, then generous and so on. These erratic behaviors often served as a model for vicarious learning and imitation.

Similar learnings may have been acquired in schismatic families where parents vie for their children's loyalties, creating not only confusion and contradictory behaviors in their children but feelings of guilt and anxiety.

These early learnings are perpetuated by the patient's own actions. His intransigence and disgruntlement and his own behavioral contradictions and inconsistency, result in difficult personal relationships and the persistence of chaotic and erratic experiences.

Should these events have led to painful setbacks or to severe disappointments and rejections, the active-ambivalent may have learned to forego his dependency needs, gradually relinquishing all hope of affection and approval from others. As he withdraws into himself, however, he sees others as having been given preferential and undeserved treatment. Soon his complaints and discontent take on an irrational quality; jealousy delusions come to the fore, and accusations of infidelity, deceit and betrayal are made against innocent relatives and friends.

## COPING AIMS

The instrumental behaviors of the moderately severe patterns are less adaptive and more self-defeating than those of the mildly ill. Moreover, they are more vulnerable to the strains of life, and are easily precipitated into psychotic disorders. Situations which promote the anxieties of attachment, expectations of sadistic treatment or the loss of self-determination result in defensive vigilance, withdrawal and ultimately in the delusions that are so characteristic of the paranoid personality. Not infrequently, the isolation and fantasy ruminations of the patient become deeply entrenched, leading to more permanent psychotic habits and attitudes. We will postpone to the next chapter a discussion of these decompensated paranoid patterns, termed "paraphrenia." For the present, we will discuss the coping aims of the paranoid, that is, the goals he seeks to achieve as a means of preventing further decompensation.

### Countering Attachment

The paranoid has reason to be mistrustful and to fear betrayal and sadistic treatment. To counter these sources of anxiety, he has learned to keep his distance from others and to remain strong and vigilant, not only as a protective stance but as a means of vindication and triumph over potential attackers. To assure his security, he engages in a variety of measures both to prevent the weakening of his resolve and to generate new powers for controlling others.

One of the major steps in this quest is a desensitization of tender and affectionate feelings. He becomes hard and obdurate and immune and insensitive to the suffering and pleading of others. By so doing he secures himself against entrapment and against being drawn into the web of deceit and subjugation. Assuming a callous and unsympathetic posture is not difficult for the paranoid; not only does it serve as a defensive maneuver against attachment, but it also allows for the discharge of his resentments and angers.

As a further means of affirming his self-determination, the paranoid assumes an air of invincibility and pride. He convinces himself that he has extraordinary capacities, that he can master his fate alone and overcome every obstacle, resistance and conflict. He dismisses all traces of self-doubt and repudiates the nurturant overtures of others; in this way he need never dread having to lean on anyone.

But the paranoid's autonomy is spurious. He maintains an illusion of superiority by rigid self-conviction and exaggerated bluff. Time and again, his competencies are proved defective and he is made to look foolish; thus, his precarious equilibrium, his self-appointed certainty and pride are upset too easily and too often. To redeem his belief in his invincibility, he begins to employ extreme and grossly pathological measures. Rather than accepting his obvious weaknesses and faults, he asserts that some alien influence is undermining him and causing him to fail and be humbled before others. Frailty, ineffectuality, shame or whatever predicament he finds himself in, must be attributed to an irresistible destructive power. As his suspicion of a "foreign force" grows and as his vigilance against belittlement and humiliation crumbles, he begins increasingly to distort reality. Not only can he not accept the fact that his failures are self-caused, but he is unwilling to ascribe these failures to "pedestrian" powers and events; rather, his loss reflects the malicious workings of devils, x-rays, magnetism, poisons and so on. His delusions of influence and persecution signify, then, both his dread of submission and his need to bolster pride by attributing his shortcomings to the action of insidious deceits or supernatural forces.

### Discharging Hostility

As we have just noted, the confidence and pride of the paranoid are but hollow shells; his pose of independence stands on insecure footings. He is extremely vulnerable to challenge, and his defensive facade is constantly weakened by real and delusional threats. To reassert his power and invincibility, he must resort to some course of action which will shore up his defenses and thwart his attackers. Hostility in the paranoid is such a defensive and restitutive measure, a means of countering threats to his equilibrium and a means of reestablishing his image of self-determination and autonomy.

Once released, the paranoid's hostility draws upon a deep reserve of earlier resentments. The fires of present angers are fed by animosities reactivated from the past; intense impulses for reprisal and vindication are brought to the surface and discharged into the stream of current hostility. Every trivial rebuff by others is a painful reminder of the past, part of a plot whose history he traces back to early humiliations and mistreatments. Trapped in this timeless web of deceit and malice, his fears and angers may mount to monumental proportions. With defenses down, controls dissolved and fantasies of doom running rampant, his dread and fury increase. A flood of frantic and hostile energies may erupt, letting loose a violent discharge, an uncontrollable torrent of vituperation and aggression.

These psychotic outbursts are usually of brief duration. As the swell of fear and hostility is discharged, the patient regains his composure and seeks to rationalize his actions, reconstruct his defenses and bind his aggression. But this subsiding of bizarre emotions does not lead to "normality"; rather, the patient merely returns to his former borderline personality pattern.

### Reconstructing Reality

The paranoid transforms events to suit his self-image and aspirations; delusions may be seen as an extreme form of this more general process of reality reconstruction. Even the passive-ambivalent, noted for his excessive rigidity, exhibits this lowering of controls, this loosening of boundaries between what is real and what is fantasied. These reconstructions take many forms, but it will suffice for us to describe the two that are most commonly found among paranoids: denial of weakness and malevolence, and their projection upon others; and aggrandizement of self through grandiose fantasies.

1.   Troubled by the mounting and inescapable evidence of his inadequacy and hostility, the paranoid must go further than mere denial; he not only disowns these objectionable traits, but throws them back at his accusers, real or imagined. It is "they" who are stupid, malicious and vindictive; "he," in contrast, is an innocent and unfortunate victim of the ineffectuality and malevolence of others. With this simple reversal, the paranoid not only absolves himself of fault, but finds an outlet and a justification for his resentment and anger. If he is in error, others should be blamed for their ineptness; if he has been aggressive, it is only because the evil in others has provoked him. He has been an innocent, and justifiably indignant, scapegoat for the blundering and the slanderous.

But the gains of the projection maneuver are short lived; moreover, it ultimately intensifies the paranoid's plight. By ascribing slanderous and malevolent urges to others, he now faces threat where none in fact existed; thus, by subjective distortion, he has created an everpresent hostile environment that surrounds him and from which there is no physical escape. Furthermore, his unjust accusations are bound to provoke in others feelings of exasperation and anger; thus, his strategy of projection has transformed what may have been overtures of good will from others into the hostility he feared.

2. Faced with genuine derogation and threat, the paranoid must redeem himself and reestablish his sense of autonomy and power. Once more, he may have no recourse but to turn to fantasy. Unable to confront his feelings of inadequacy and insignificance, he fabricates an image of superior self-worth and importance. Left alone to ruminate, he unfolds proofs of his eminence through intricate self-deceptions. He renounces or distorts objective reality and supplants it with a glorified image of self. Having endowed himself with limitless virtues, powers and talents, he need not now be ashamed of himself or fear anyone; he can "rise above" petty jealousies and can "understand all too clearly" why others seek to undermine and persecute him. The meaning of their malicious attacks is obvious; it is his eminence—his infinite superiority—which they envy and seek to destroy.

Step by step, his self-glorifications and persecutory delusions form into a systematic pattern; the "whole picture" comes into sharp relief. One delusion feeds on another, unchecked by the controls of social reality. Fabrications, employed initially to cope with the despair of reality, become more "real" than reality itself; it is at this point that we see the clear emergence of a psychotic phase.

## REMEDIAL APPROACHES

In estimating prognosis and recommending a course of therapy we must always take cognizance of the unique elements of each case. Although certain generalities about etiology and treatment apply to patients categorized under the same diagnostic label, we cannot embark on a treatment program without a thorough clinical study of the patient himself. With this caveat in mind, let us next discuss the prognosis and treatment of the paranoid personality.

As with all personality patterns, the prospects for a "thorough cure" of the paranoid are poor. His habits and attitudes are deeply ingrained and pervade the entire fabric of personality functioning. Modest inroads are possible, of course, but these only diminish the frequency of psychotic episodes rather than revamp the personality style.

Many paranoids do not succumb to serious reality distortions; nevertheless, these patients are usually regarded as suspicious, testy or supercilious people. A small number attain considerable vocational success, especially if they are genuinely talented or happen by good fortune to attract a coterie of disciples which seeks a supremely confident if somewhat deranged leader (witness some of the more notorious political leaders of the recent past).

Despite their poor social relationships and periodic delusional spells, the long-range prognosis for the paranoid is more promising than that of the schizoid. The reason is simple: paranoids draw sustenance from themselves whereas schizoids do not. Faced with external humiliation and derogation, the paranoid nurtures himself until his wounds are sufficiently healed; schizoids, lacking faith both in themselves and others, remain empty.

Compared to the cycloid, the paranoid has both an advantage and a disadvantage insofar as prognosis is concerned. Cycloids characteristically maintain reasonably good interpersonal relations; they gain, thereby, some portion of the support and encouragement they need. Furthermore, cycloids turn willingly to others during difficult periods, often soliciting enough affection and security to forestall a further decline. In contrast, paranoids tend to be socially obnoxious and keep to themselves when relationships turn sour; such behaviors increase their isolation, not only resulting in an intensification of their suspicions and hostility, but giving rise to further social estrangement. To the cycloid's disadvantage is his lack of internal reserves; this may result in his slipping into a helpless state of depression should he fail to evoke external support. This does not occur in the paranoid; he not only refuses to submit to weakness and indolence, but will struggle to "pull himself up by his own bootstraps," thereby forestalling a rapid decompensation.

The flagrant delusions and psychotic episodes of the paranoid tend to occur most often in mid and late life; this may be attributed to the loss of self-confidence associated with aging. Disappointments in life no longer are remediable, and the vigor and attractiveness of youth have begun to wane. Given the importance of strength and independence to the paranoid, he is especially vulnerable to signs of diminishing capacity, his growing inability to make up for lost time and a future of increased dependency on others.

Therapy with the paranoid is a touchy proposition at best. Few come willingly for treatment in the first place, for it signifies weakness and dependency, both of which are anathema to the paranoid. Furthermore, the therapist may fall into the trap of disliking and rejecting his patient since the suspicions and veiled hostility of the paranoid easily provoke displeasure and resentment. Also, the therapist must resist being intimidated by the patient's arrogance and demeaning comments; weakness is the last trait the paranoid could accept in one with whom he finally has placed his trust. There are other problems which can complicate the therapist's efforts. He must not display excessive friendliness and overt consideration; these behaviors often connote deceit to the patient, a seductive prelude to humiliation and deprecation; as the paranoid sees it, he has suffered undue pain at the hands of deceptively "kind" people. Nor can the therapist question the patient about his delusional beliefs; at best, this will drive the paranoid to concoct new rationalizations and distortions; at worst, it may intensify his distrust, destroy whatever rapport had been built, unleash a barrage of defensive hostility or precipitate an open psychotic break. His beliefs, his self-confidence and his image of autonomy and strength cannot be challenged; they are a too vital part of his coping system; to pierce them is to destroy his fragile equilibrium.

What approach and tactic then can the therapist take?

Essentially, he must aim to build trust through a series of slow and progressive steps. He must evidence a quiet, formal and genuine respect for the patient as a person; he must accept, but not confirm, his patient's beliefs, and allow him to explore his thoughts and feelings at whatever pace he can tolerate. Thus, the major goal of therapy is to free the patient of mistrust by showing him that he can share his anxieties with another person without the dread of humiliation and maltreatment to which he is accustomed. If this can be accomplished, the paranoid may learn to share with others, to look at the world not only from his own perspective but through the eyes of others; trusting the therapist, he can begin to relax, relinquish his defensive posture and open himself to new attitudes and points of view. Once he has accepted the therapist as a trusted friend, he will be able to lean on him and accept his thoughts and suggestions. This can become the basis for a more generalized lessening of suspicions and for a wider scope of trusting and sharing behaviors.

As regards specific modes of therapy, it is simplest to say that techniques are wholly secondary to the building of trust. Nevertheless, psychopharmacological drugs may be of value as calmatives during anxious or acting out periods. Institutionalization may be required if reality controls break down; it is best, however, not to place the patient in too confining a setting for too long, since this will only reinforce his anticipation of injustice and maltreatment.

During outpatient treatment, it is mandatory that environmental irritants be reduced; otherwise, therapy becomes an uphill battle. Behavioral and intrapsychic therapies cannot be employed without the prior development of trust; their effectiveness is dubious in any event. Nondirective phenomenological approaches are indicated as a first approach, to be followed, where appropriate, by other measures. The choice of specific second-stage therapeutic methods depends on practical considerations and ultimate goals. As noted earlier, therapy is likely only to moderate rather than reverse the basic paranoid personality pattern.

The conclusions and summary for this chapter will be found at the end of chapter 9.

# Chapter 9

# *PATHOLOGICAL PERSONALITIES OF MARKED SEVERITY:*

## Decompensated Patterns

Rico Lebrun–*Figure in Rain* (1949). (The Museum of Modern Art, New York.)

## *INTRODUCTION*

Little difficulty should be encountered in diagnosing the decompensated personality. In contrast to borderline patterns, in which patients exhibit "mixed" signs and fluctuate between relatively "normal" and distinctly pathological behaviors, decompensated patterns display a consistent and pervasive impairment which rarely is broken by lucid thoughts and conventional behaviors. Almost invariably, decompensated patients require institutionalization since they are unable to fend alone in everyday life, make few efforts to "get hold" of themselves and fail to fulfill any acceptable societal role.

The two central features of all severely deteriorated states are a *diminished reality awareness* and a *cognitive and emotional dyscontrol*. Both the psychotic disorders, to be described in chapter 11, and decompensated patterns fail to discriminate between subjective fantasy and objective reality; events take on a dreamlike quality, a hazy and phantasmagoric world of fleeting and distorted impressions colored by internal moods

and images. These patients cannot appraise correctly the threats they face or the rewards they may gain; the difference between positive and negative reinforcements is blurred, causing them to behave in a purposeless, irrational and bizarre manner. Control functions are markedly deficient; patients are unable to direct or coordinate an effective coping strategy. There is a sense of disunity and disorganization to their communications; ideas are inchoate and jumbled, or take the form of peculiar beliefs and delusions. Absurd and stereotyped behaviors are exhibited. Subjective images become reality and are projected upon the world as hallucinatory perceptions.

Before we proceed to systematize these general clinical features, let us note that the line we have drawn between the borderline and decompensated patterns is an arbitrary one, established for the purpose of alerting the reader to clinical features which characterize particular points along the continuum of pathological severity. Let us not forget that imperceptible gradations differentiate the points on this continuum, and that patients can fall anywhere along the way. In this section, we will be focusing on states which lie close to the extreme pole of severity, that is, those whose "decompensated" state is clear cut.

## GENERAL CLINICAL PICTURE

Psychotic disorders and decompensated personality patterns share a common level of pathological severity; both lack reality awareness and emotional and cognitive control. The principal distinction between them is the pervasiveness and relative permanence of these impairments among the decompensated personalities.

We will describe three major clinical features which further characterize the decompensated pattern in this section. These features present themselves regardless of other differences in personality make-up. They consist of: developmental immaturity and social invalidism; cognitive disorganization; and feelings of estrangement.

### Developmental Immaturity and
### Social Invalidism

In chapter 8 we noted that borderline patients display a deficit in social competence; they evidence an uneven attainment of conventional goals, experience repeated setbacks in their vocational and marital plans, get involved in foolish predicaments and spend much of their life extricating themselves from unnecessary difficulties, seeking to recoup the gains they once had achieved and then lost. Although borderline patients do not make appreciable progress, they have managed, at least, to attain some social success, and they do exert some effort to continue moving forward.

Such is not the case among decompensated patterns. A number of investigators (Zigler and Phillips, 1960; Phillips, 1966, 1968; Wishner, 1955; Cameron and Magaret, 1951) have indicated that these severely impaired individuals can best be described in terms of their social incompetence, inefficiency and immaturity. In both their history and current functioning, these patients evidence a profound deficit in social skills. These deficiencies develop usually in one of two ways: by a general *developmental immaturity,* or by a progressive decompensation to *social invalidism.* Let us briefly discuss these two processes.

1. The concept of *fixation* was formulated originally as an intrapsychic mechanism employed by children that resulted in an arrested development and in a persistence into adulthood of child-like behaviors. We need not agree with the specific rationale of this psychoanalytic formulation to recognize that early behaviors are perpetuated

throughout life; several alternative explanations for this persistence of early learning were provided in chapter 5.

Whatever the reason, or combination of reasons, the upshot of fixation or behavior perseveration is a consequent failure of the individual to acquire a fully mature repertoire of social skills. As new and greater tasks come to challenge his immature skills and as he fails more and more to fulfill expected roles, his incompetence and ineffectuality become increasingly apparent. Over time, the disparity between his competence and responsibility grows; he gets further and further behind others, becomes less able to "catch up" or to compensate for his already established lag. In individuals who have never achieved social maturity, the process of decompensation to a markedly severe level of functioning may progress both rapidly and early in life.

2. Many decompensated personalities have achieved a measure of social competence and maturity during their lives. Unfortunate circumstances, however, bore down heavily, and they deteriorated gradually into a more severe pathological state.

The concept of *regression* has been used in the psychoanalytic literature to signify a process of decompensation in which the individual returns under pressure to behaviors which characterized an early developmental stage; more specifically, the individual ostensibly reverts back to fixated childhood characteristics.

There is no need for us to accept the psychoanalytic formulation that decompensation is a backward retracing and revival of childhood fixations. Although elements of the past will emerge under extreme duress, there is no reason to assume that decompensation is a return to the past. Rather, it seems more reasonable to say that the individual's established repertoire of mature strategies disintegrates under pressure and gives rise to a wide range of deviant and generally *immature* behaviors. Among these behaviors is a "child-like" dependency and invalidism, colored no doubt by the particulars of the individual's own history.

*Invalidism,* a term coined by Cameron and Magaret (1951), underlies the regressive or child-like character of the decompensated patient. In the face of hopelessly adverse conditions, the patient withdraws into a totally dependent state, entirely devoid of social concerns and responsibilities. Unable to cope with the pressures of normal social life and unable to overlook his deficits, failures and humiliations, the patient retreats, accepting both the discomforts of total disability and the few gains it provides. No longer will he be burdened with life's struggles or face unfavorable comparisons, shame and vilification. Ultimately, he allows himself to slide into the security and the obscurity of a hospital environment. Cared for by others and excused from social expectancies and self-responsibilities, he begins to learn the "art" of the invalid. Within this controlled setting and its undemanding routines, he relinquishes progressively whatever competence and social maturity he previously achieved.

### Cognitive Disorganization

In most persons, ideas are associated in a logical and orderly progression so as to convey meaningful communications. This coherence and intent often are lost among the severely ill. Of course, disturbances in thought frequently are evident among certain patients long before they succumb to the decompensated level; this is especially the case among the less severely detached and schizoid patterns. However, no matter what the basic pattern may originally have been cognitive controls "loosen" as the patient decompensates. He displays an increasing number of irrelevant and bizarre notions; connections among thoughts become vague or involved; communications directed to others lose their focus and wander into generalities and abstractions, the significance of which is difficult to grasp. Sequences of ideas are disjointed and fragmented. Metaphorical and stereotyped phrases may be endlessly repeated; unrelated thoughts may be fused, creating neologisms which in turn may be thrown together in a "word salad" of disconnected nouns and verbs. The following illustrates the mumbo jumbo character of these disorganized flights of verbigeration:

Improper wave length-wave length changes, later visible death. That is a moving trollysis similar to circulation of life action. Born high focussating action may die through wave length charge and still live until visible death takes place.

Education comes from radiation of action. Anyone can study all science in a compositive way. It takes a compositive mind to be able to understand. Can tell compositive minds by stromonized conception. The mind at birth takes on a birthification, becomes environmental by the radiation to it. Metabolism to dimension differ in every person is of actions of metabolism and dimension balancing.

Quite commonly, delusions and hallucinations accompany cognitive disorganization. These tend to be loosely structured and transitory, in contrast to the more logical, ingrained and systematized delusional beliefs of the borderline paranoid. Decompensated patients piece together entirely unrelated observations and ideas from which they draw peculiar and bizarre inferences about the nature of the world. Typically, these unsystematized delusions and perceptions are dissolved and forgotten almost as readily as they were formed; some, however, seem to "stick," although they never attain the logic and coherence shown in the beliefs of the borderline paranoid patient.

The bizarre and chaotic thought processes of these patients are not wholly meaningless; their irrational quality stems from the fact that internal images are mixed in a rather chance-like manner with unrelated environmental events. Because of their lack of cognitive control, these patients allow stimuli from divergent origins to flow together into a common stream, resulting in odd perceptions, disjointed behaviors and incoherent verbalizations. In essence, by abandoning their cognitive controls, these patients have lost choice and selectivity. The hierarchy of potency which differentiated among stimuli and responses has been leveled; all stimuli have equal impact, and all responses have an equal probability of expression. Unable to scan their environment selectively and unable to distinguish the relevant from the irrelevant, their thoughts and actions become scattered and disorganized, a potpourri of fragmented delusions, transitory hallucinations and obscure tangential talk.

It will be instructive next to explore why cognitive disorganization occurs. Certainly, the patient has little reason to face reality or to perceive with clarity a life full of anguish and humiliation. Failing repeatedly to cope with adversity, he has no option but to withdraw, "tune out" reality and reduce contact with events that evoke nothing but shame and agony. The potency of inner thought and memory increases as he withdraws from external events, that is, the balance of his stimulus world shifts inward.

At first, he invites this respite from painful reality; memories and thoughts dominate his thinking, thereby shutting out the conflict and humiliation of external intrusions. Unchecked by logic or social consensus, his fantasies have free rein to salve his wounds unencumbered by realities. In time, these reveries blur into a dream-like state, lose their organization and become fragmented, discontinuous and ephemeral.

Despite the usefulness of fantasy in healing wounds and blocking reality, the patient finds, ultimately, that his dream world is not a haven but a nightmare. Whatever order and meaning he extracts from these disorganized reveries, remind him, in one way or another, of his misery, of past misfortunes and of being nothing but a failure, a humiliated invalid bereft of status and hope. His private world, then, proves no less painful than that of reality. Faced with the pain of self, he turns away, not only from others but also from himself. But this is no simple task; thoughts remain within one, fixed and adamant, cropping up no matter how hard one tries to deny them.

How can they be dismembered? Among the person's few alternatives is the capacity to destroy his own cognitive processes, befuddle his memories, block logic and meaning and create internal confusion where clarity, consensus and order existed; everything, then, is intentionally mixed up, disconnected, reversed and jumbled.

But this effort, like so many which preceded it, proves a further undoing of self. The patient becomes trapped in the web of his self-made confusion; try as he may, he cannot gain clear focus and cannot organize himself to find some meaning and purpose to existence. In the end he sinks further into an abyss of nothingness, an estrangement from both objective reality and subjective self.

### Feelings of Estrangement

The invalidism of the patient may be traced initially to a combination of causes including social disaffection, protective isolation and a final collapse of habitual coping strategies. Once invalidism is established, however, hopeless dependency and social incompetence become a basis for further alienation, and thus perpetuate the breach between the patient and the larger community.

As he succumbs to his new social role, the patient jettisons most traces of pride and self-control, abandoning whatever social amenities and facades he may have acquired; more importantly, he begins to lose touch with the meaning and structure of social behavior and with the form and syntax of language and communication. His actions and verbalizations take on a peculiar and idiosyncratic quality. The patterns and rules of interpersonal relations increasingly mystify him; he seems incapable of comprehending the sequence and purpose of social discourse, the reciprocal flow of person to person interaction. Unable to participate in or make sense out of his environment, he begins to experience life as something unreal, a game whose moves are made by unseen hands in accord with strange and unfathomable regulations. He senses a "nonbeing in the world," as the existentialists might phrase it. He is perplexed and bewildered, is unable to grasp the logic and significance of what surrounds him and feels doomed to wander in a vague, alien and frightening environment; he is homeless, an estranged nonparticipant at the mercy of enigmatic, capricious and hazardous powers; moreover, he stands alone, confused and devoid of any means of mitigating his despair and dread of the unknown or of the strange and ominous forces that surround him; at any moment, these unpredictable forces may destroy him or leave him totally isolated and helpless.

The decompensated patient's social estrangement is paralleled by an equally terrifying estrangement from self. As noted earlier, cognitive disorganization often reflects a process in which the patient seeks to destroy, disarrange or clutter painful thoughts and memories. He purposely makes his behavior incongruous, jumbles his ideas and swings fitfully from one mood to another without rhyme or reason. Cognitive disorganization as a strategy serves its function well; the patient successfully interferes with "real" thinking and feeling, and thereby protects himself from the anguish they produce.

But several disturbing consequences arise as a result of purposeful self-disjunction. As the patient observes his own behavior, he sees something foreign, a strange, unknown and peculiar being, a frightening and unpredictable creature he cannot recognize. Being both participant and spectator, he observes himself with terror and cannot match what now emanates from himself with what he knows to have been himself. He looks on aghast, unable to control his impulses, bizarre grimaces and strange outbursts. Perhaps, he concludes, some alien force resides within him, some power that causes him to act as he does; clearly, this body and these behaviors cannot be his.

Try as he may, the patient cannot escape the pain and fright of self-awareness. His divorce from self must be total; he must disembody himself and not only dismember his feelings and thoughts, but disown his behavior and body. It is at this point of self-abandonment, of rejecting self as a viable being, that the unfortunate patient disintegrates into the final and profoundly severe state we have termed the "terminal personality pattern." We shall elaborate differences between the terminal and decompensated patterns later in this chapter.

Before we proceed, we must note several marked similarities between the decompensated and the borderline schizoid patterns. As all personality patterns decompensate they begin to exhibit qualities of social detachment and self-estrangement, that is, traits found more commonly and permanently among schizoids. The schizoid, however, maintains reality contacts and often manages, albeit poorly, to function as a member of society.

The clinical similarity between schizoid and decompensated patients accounts in part for the common practice of labeling severely deteriorated patients as "schizophrenic"; this latter diagnostic label should be limited, however, to decompensated schizoid patterns, and should *not* be used for other, similar appearing patients who have followed a different developmental course before exhibiting schizoid-like symptoms. As we will point out later, sufficient differences exist among decompensated patterns to justify our making useful diagnostic distinctions.

## GENERAL ETIOLOGICAL BACKGROUND

It will be useful, as a précis, to outline briefly the principal determinants which contribute to the development of decompensated personalities; distinctions will later be made among the three subvarieties of this pattern. Several etiological factors have been discussed in detail in chapters 4 through 8.

### Constitutional Dispositions

A small but not insignificant portion of these patients are hampered by constitutional impairments or tendencies that strongly dispose them to psychopathology. Marked sensitivities, congenital injuries or any of a wide range of constitutional anomalies will increase both the probability and the likely severity of abnormal development.

Constitutional dispositions associated with decompensated personality patterns differ from those serious impairments described as "biophysical defects" in chapter 13. First, dispositions associated with pathological personality patterns are not identifiable by current diagnostic techniques, that is, their presence is inferred and is not known in fact. Second, where they are observable, they are not so severe as to preclude the possibility of a normal course of development.

### Pathogenic Early Experiences

Not all decompensated patients are constitutionally disposed to pathology. Some, born with entirely "normal" biophysical equipment, have been subjected to unusually destructive experiences during the years of early maturation and learning. Excessively impoverished or enriched stimulation and any number of pathogenic family attitudes and methods of behavior control may prepare the soil for the progressive unfolding of markedly pathological perceptions and strategies. The more intense, pervasive and enduring these experiences are, the more likely that they will result in a decompensated personality pattern.

### Cumulative and Self-Perpetuating Difficulties

Tendencies toward decompensation may be aggravated by the cumulation of repetitive pathogenic experiences. Not only are early behaviors and attitudes difficult to extinguish, but, in addition, the individual may be exposed to a continuous stream of destructive events which accelerate the pathological decline. Not the least of these accelerating factors are the patient's coping behaviors which foster new problems and perpetuate vicious circles.

### Prolongation of Psychotic Episodes

Borderline patients experience serious incursions upon their psychic equilibrium, giving rise usually to short-lived and reversible psychotic episodes. These bizarre periods normally subside following the ventilation of feelings and the reduction of stress.

In some cases, however, the psychotic episode persists until it becomes an ingrained and enduring pattern. Perhaps the conditions of stress did not diminish, or the patient may have become "caught" in the web of his own coping maneuvers. Perhaps the reinforcements he acquired during his episode were greater than those he obtained preceding it; for example, even though the conditions which precipitated the episode disappeared, the patient may have achieved unusually gratifying exemptions and privileges as a function of his illness which then reinforced its continuance.

Whatever the cause or combination of causes, some patients fail to "pull themselves together" or to over-ride what is usually a transient psychotic period. In these cases we may see a progressive deterioration into a more permanent decompensated personality pattern.

### Progressive Decompensation

It is evident from the preceding statements that the emergence of the decompensated personality pattern is a progressive and insidious process. Typically, the kernel of the pattern was set in place at childhood and developed into its manifest state through imperceptible steps. We need not elaborate each step in the developmental sequence preceding the formation of the final pattern; that can best be done by reviewing the clinical features and strategies of the mild and moderate personality patterns discussed in previous chapters. It will be useful, however, to describe the final step in the decompensation sequence.

The patient begins to slip into his deteriorated state when he feels that his "normal" relations with others have become bogged down and hopeless; he experiences at the same time an intolerable decline in his self-worth. As he protectively isolates himself from social contact, his feelings of hopelessness and self-derogation increase; yet he also senses a measure of relief as he assumes the pattern of invalidism. Minor gains have been eked out through collapse and withdrawal; others will care for him, and he need meet no responsibilities or struggle to achieve goals in a world with which he cannot cope. He has given up not only his aspirations but his struggle for a meaningful social existence; he allows himself to sink increasingly into a pervasive listlessness, a disorganization of control and thought, an emotional flatness and an invalidism in which he cares little and does little to care for himself.

At this stage, external events are seen as a distant screen upon which phantoms move in a strange and purposeless automaticity; voices emanate from alien sources, creating a muted cacophony of obscure and bewildering sounds; a fog descends, enshrouding his eyes and ears, dampening his senses and giving events a shadowy, pantomimic quality. Inner thoughts prove no more articulate or meaningful; within himself he finds a boundless region of fantasy, delusion, inchoate images and sensations; like an unanchored and rudderless ship in a whirling sea, he drifts without compass, hither and yon, buffeted by waves of past memories and future illusions; dreams, reality and the past and present, a potpourri of random pieces, merge and are then dismembered; his own physical presence seems foreign to him, a detached corpse; he senses himself floating, a disembodied mind with its rummage of fleeting, disconnected, jumbled and af-

fectless impressions. This frightening collapse of meaning and existence is shared by most decompensated patterns as their zest for life is drained.

Considerable space has been allotted thus far to a discussion of characteristics shared in common among each of the different decompensated patterns. This has been done in recognition of the notable similarity they exhibit in their clinical picture and in the final steps of their deterioration; despite appreciably different constitutional tendencies and developmental experiences, most patients become increasingly alike as they face repeated coping failures and social humiliation. These similarities have already been described, enabling us, therefore, to present a less extensive description of each of the separate decompensated patterns than was previously given to other personality patterns. As we have stated before, sufficient differences exist among these patterns to justify our making useful diagnostic distinctions. Thus, despite their overt commonalities, patients differ markedly in the content of their thinking, the strategies they previously employed, the type of reinforcements to which they may respond in a therapeutic regime and so on. In the following sections we will differentiate the three major decompensated patterns, noting their distinguishing clinical features and developmental histories.

We shall use the suffix "phrenic" for each of these decompensated patterns as a way of signifying their common level of marked severity; this decision parallels the uniform application of the suffix "oid" for the moderate level of severity. The choice of the "phrenia" suffix has no significance other than that of maintaining consistency with the well-recognized and established syndrome of schizophrenia. To point up the continuum that we believe exists between the borderline and decompensated personalities, we shall label the three markedly severe patterns with terms that parallel the moderately severe patterns, referring to them as *schizophrenia, cyclophrenia* and *paraphrenia*.

# SCHIZOPHRENIC PERSONALITY: DECOMPENSATED DETACHED PATTERNS
### (DSM-II: *Schizophrenia, Several Subtypes*)

It will be instructive to review the history and clinical conditions associated with the syndrome label "schizophrenia."

This term has been applied to almost 50 per cent of all hospitalized mental patients; such a striking statistic may signify either the impressive

prevalence of this particular impairment or the indiscriminate lumping into one gross category of equally disturbed but basically different patients.

It is our contention that the traditional category of "schizophrenia" should be subdivided into several classifications, only one of which (containing patients who have displayed a *lifelong and deeply ingrained pattern of detachment*) should be labeled as schizophrenic. Many severely decompensated patients, who previously were diagnosed as "schizophrenic," should be assigned to a psychotic "disorder" category since their impairments are only of brief duration. Other "schizophrenics" possess deeply ingrained personality patterns, but the pattern they exhibit is *not* characterized by a lifelong strategy of detachment. Rather, they may have possessed either dependent, ambivalent or independent styles of life; if so, they should be labeled, at the decompensated stage, either as cyclophrenic or paraphrenic.

### History

The English neurologist Willis, in 1674, made note of a pathological sequence in which "young persons who, lively and spirited, and at times even brilliant in their childhood, passed into obtuseness and hebetude during adolescence." The Belgian psychiatrist Morel, in 1856, described the case of a 14 year old boy who had been a cheerful and outstanding student, but who progressively lost his intellectual capacities and increasingly became melancholy and withdrawn. Morel considered cases such as these to be irremediable, ascribing them to an arrest in brain development stemming from hereditary causes. He gave the illness the name *dementia praecox* (démence précoce) to signify his observation that deterioration occurred at an early age.

Between 1863 and 1874, the German psychiatrists Kahlbaum and Hecker described two other forms of mental deterioration. They applied the term *hebephrenia* to conditions, arising in puberty and adolescence, that started with a quick succession of erratic moods, were followed by a rapid enfeeblement of all functions, and finally progressed to an unalterable psychic decline. The label *catatonia,* representing "tension insanity," was introduced for cases in which the patient displayed no reactivity to sensory impressions, lacked "self-will" and sat mute and physically immobile; ostensibly, these symptoms reflected structural brain deterioration.

Prior to 1896, the great German synthesist Emil Kraepelin considered hebephrenia and dementia praecox to be synonymous. However, in the fifth edition of his classic psychiatric text he concluded that the diverse symptom complexes of catatonia and hebephrenia, as well as certain paranoid disturbances, displayed a common theme of early deterioration and ultimate incurability; as he saw it, these illnesses were variations of Morel's original concept of dementia praecox. By subordinating the disparate symptoms of these syndromes to the common factor of an early and inexorable mental decline, Kraepelin brought order and simplicity to what previously had been diagnostic confusion and psychiatric dissension.

Following the tradition of German psychiatry, Kraepelin assumed that a biophysical defect lay at the heart of this syndrome; in contrast to his forebears, however, he hypothesized sexual and metabolic dysfunctions as probable causal agents rather than anatomical lesions.

Kraepelin's observations and syntheses were soon challenged and modified; Eugen Bleuler in Switzerland and Adolf Meyer in the United States were notable in this regard.

After observing hundreds of dementia praecox patients in the early 1900's, Bleuler concluded that it was entirely misleading to compare the type of deterioration they evidenced with that found among patients who were known to be suffering from brain deficiencies or degeneration. He observed that the reactions and thoughts of his patients were highly complex and differentiated, in marked contrast to the simple and gross behaviors of the feebleminded and organically diseased. Furthermore, many patients first displayed their illness in adulthood rather than adolescence, and others evidenced none of the signs of progressive deterioration which Kraepelin considered central to the syndrome. To Bleuler, then, the label "dementia praecox" seemed misleading as a designation since it characterized an age of onset and a course of development that were not supported by the evidence he had gathered. The significant features, as Bleuler saw it, were a "loosening of associations" and a "disharmony among affects." The patient's characteristic fragmentation of thought, feeling and action led Bleuler, in 1911, to propose the label "schizophrenia" to signify what he saw as a split (schism) within the patient's mind (phrenos).

Bleuler retained the Kraepelinian notion that the impairment was a unitary disease attributable to organic pathology. All schizophrenics shared a common neurological ailment which resulted in a common set of "primary" symptoms, notably that of loosened thoughts and disharmonious emotions. Beyond these, patients possessed a group of "secondary" symptoms, such as the content of their hallucinations and delusions, which Bleuler ascribed to the patients' distinctive life experiences and to their efforts to adapt to their neurological disease. Although Bleuler conceded that psychogenic influences shaped the particular character and color of the schizophrenic impairment, he asserted that these experiences could not in themselves "cause" the disturbance.

In 1906, Adolf Meyer suggested that dementia praecox was not an organic disease at all but a maladaptive way of "reacting" to stress, fully understandable in terms of the patient's life experiences; these maladaptive reactions led to a progressive "habit deterioration." Thus, these impairments reflected "inefficient and faulty attempts to avoid difficulties," and symptoms were seen as end products of abortive and self-defeating efforts to reestablish psychic equilibrium. Meyer did recognize, however, that constitutional weaknesses may prove to be serious handicaps to psychological adaptation, and thereby dispose the individual to future mental illness. His eclectic but well-reasoned "psychobiological" approach to schizophrenia (which he preferred to call "paregasia" to signify its distorted or twisted character) represented the first systematic recognition of the interactive and progressive nature of pathogenesis.

### Evaluation of the Syndrome Label "Schizophrenia"

The system of classification currently used in psychiatry retains the basic typology of dementia praecox as formulated by Kraepelin in the fifth edition (1896) of his text. However, for the greater part of this century, the label dementia praecox was replaced by the term "schizophrenic reaction types," representing modifications in accord with the thinking of Bleuler and Meyer. In the recently revised DSM-II, the nomenclature was simplified to that of "schizophrenia."

Despite the fact that Kraepelin's categories rested on dubious assumptions regarding etiology and prognostic course, they have been retained with minimal change, though clothed in more fashionable language. For many and divergent reasons, few diagnosticians are satisfied with the Kraepelinian typology; it remains in popular usage today largely as a result of habit and inertia. Like patients who are unable to extricate themselves from their past, perpetuating and fostering new difficulties as a consequence, so too does the profession of psychiatry find itself unable to break its old though admittedly poor classificatory habits. The Kraepelinian typology remains with us since no new formulation possessing sufficient distinction to overcome the inertia of the past has been proposed.

Since this text proposes a modification of the traditional nosology, a few words are in order to distinguish the Kraepelinian categories of schizophrenia from those to be provided here.

The term schizophrenia is applied in current practice to almost all patients who evidence chronic decompensation, without regard to the character of their premorbid personality pattern; in addition, it is used as a designation for almost all acute impairments that are noted by the primacy of disorganized thinking. The following descriptive statements are excerpted from the DSM-II classification of schizophrenia:

This large category includes a group of disorders manifested by characteristic disturbances of thinking, mood and behavior. Disturbances in thinking are marked by alterations of concept formation which may lead to misinterpretation of reality and sometimes to delusions and hallucinations, which frequently appear psychologically self-protective. Corollary mood changes include ambivalent, constricted and inappropriate emotional responsiveness and loss of empathy with others. Behavior may be withdrawn, regressive and bizarre.

We consider the application of the schizophrenic term to so wide a spectrum of ailments to be a serious limitation of the Kraepelinian system.

In the formulation presented in this text, all severely deteriorated personalities will be classified as *decompensated patterns* to signify nothing more than the pervasiveness, durability and severity of their pathology. Further distinctions, reflecting premorbid personality differences among these patients (e.g., detached, dependent and so on) will be made by reference to the labels schizophrenic, cyclophrenic and paraphrenic. Markedly severe though brief episodes, usually with acute onsets, will be noted as *psychotic disorders* and labeled in accord with the particular symptom that characterizes the disorder (e.g., delusion, depression and so on).

The term schizophrenia shall apply exclusively to decompensated personality patterns characterized by a lifelong and pervasive strategy of *detachment*. It is most akin in its developmental history and clinical features to the official schizophrenic subclassification of hebephrenia, with its early onset, social withdrawal, emotional blunting or disharmony, bizarre thinking and general disintegration of personality functions. The correspondence proposed between the present usage of the schizophrenic label and the official descriptive features noted as hebephrenia may be viewed as a return to Kraepelin's conceptions prior to the fifth edition of his classic work. We believe that Kraepelin was "carried away" by his attempt to subsume nearly all severe forms of decompensation under one label; this effort rested on the erroneous assumption that these divergent pathologies stem from a single constitutional defect, an oversimplication of the problem if there ever was one.

Because of differences between our formulations and those currently provided by the official DSM-II psychiatric nomenclature, it will be useful to note briefly our reinterpretation and reassignment of each of the traditional schizophrenic subclassifications. Ten varieties are listed.

As noted above, the *hebephrenic* category parallels in many respects what we shall term the "schizophrenic personality pattern"; as described in the DSM-II the hebephrenic subtype of schizophrenia

". . . is characterized by disorganized thinking, shallow and inappropriate affect, unpredictable giggling, silly and regressive behavior and mechanisms, and frequent hypochondriacal complaints. Delusions and hallucinations, if present, are transient and not well organized."

These clinical features typify the schizophrenic personality; however, they will apply only to chronic cases displaying early and pervasive decompensation. Brief episodes in which "hebephrenic" features are displayed will be described in chapter 11 under the psychotic disorder label "Fragmentation."

The two DSM-II schizophrenic subcategories referred to as the *simple* and *latent* types, noted by a "slow and insidious reduction of external attachments [with] clear symptoms of schizophrenia but no [necessary] history of a psychotic schizophrenic episode" may be juxtaposed with the "schizoid personality pattern" described earlier in chapter 8.

The DSM-II *catatonic* subcategory, divided into "excited" and "withdrawn" types, is characterized by a rapid onset and such varied symptoms as stupor, mutism, violent physical activity and overcompliance. This syndrome does not represent a personality pattern since it takes the form of rather short-lived psychotic episodes. Catatonic episodes will be noted in chapter 11 under psychotic disorder labels such as "Hostile Excitement," "Motor Rigidity" and "Impassivity."

The fifth of the classical or Kraepelinian varieties is the *paranoid* type of schizophrenia, distinguished by unsystematized and bizarre delusions, hallucinations, defensive suspiciousness and periodic hostile outbursts. Severely decompensated patients evidencing these as chronic traits compare with the "paraphrenic personality pattern," to be described later; those who display these same features following stress, and *without* a pervasive and severe deterioration of personality, will be listed in chapter 11 among such psychotic disorders as "Delusion" and "Hostile Excitement."

A sixth DSM-II schizophrenic subclassification, known as the *schizo-affective,* and divided into "excited" and "depressed" types, shows a mixture of cognitive disorganization, feelings of estrangement and a variety of intense and vacillating moods; patients who gradually decompensate to this state, after demonstrating a lifelong pattern of dependency or ambivalence, approximate what we shall term the "cyclophrenic personality pattern," to be described later. Those evidencing similar clinical features, but without pervasive and severe personality deterioration, will be referred to under such psychotic disorder labels as "Agitated Depression" and "Euphoric Excitement."

The seventh DSM-II syndrome, a new label in the official nomenclature, is termed *acute schizophrenic episode,* and is described as follows:

This condition is distinguished by the acute onset of schizophrenic symptoms, often associated with confusion, perplexity, ideas of reference, emotional turmoil, dreamlike dissociation, and excitement, depression, or fear. . . . In many cases the patient recovers within weeks, but sometimes his disorganization becomes progressive. More frequently, remission is followed by recurrence.

The acute category clearly recognizes that schizophrenic-like symptoms occur in patients who do not evidence a pervasive form of personality deterioration. In line with this important distinction between brief reversible episodes and chronic decompensated personality impairments, we have separated acute cases from the schizophrenic classification, and have placed them in a distinct major category termed "psychotic symptom disorders," to be discussed in chapter 11. The symptoms described under the DSM-II label of acute schizophrenic episode correspond most often to the psychotic disorder subcategories to be noted as "Impassivity," "Fragmentation," and "Hostile Excitement."

The last three varieties of schizophrenia in the current official classification include the *chronic undifferentiated* type, which "show mixed schizophrenic symptoms and which present definite schizophrenic thought, affect and behavior not classifiable under other types of schizophrenia"; the *childhood* type, for those cases occurring before puberty but not otherwise distinguished; and the *residual* type, for cases that have improved following a psychotic episode. These three categories have been included in the official nosology for reasons which we believe to be entirely secondary to the essential character of the pathological process itself. Thus, difficulties which clinicians experience in diagnosis, or the age or state of remission of a patient, deserve peripheral diagnostic notation; they are not substantive elements of the psychopathological process, and should not be included as an intrinsic part of syndrome classification.

With this historical review and comparison of diagnostic categories behind us, we next can turn to a description of the *schizophrenic personality pattern,* as conceived in this text.

## CLINICAL PICTURE

The schizophrenic is a markedly decompensated variant of the mild and moderately severe detached patterns; reference should be made to fuller descriptions on pages 224, 232 and 308.

Though the schizophrenic's clinical appearance is clearly more deteriorated than his schizoid counterparts, he still retains many of their attributes in addition to those he shares with the other decompensated patterns. His lack of social relatedness and competence is most striking. Cognitive processes are markedly disorganized, evidencing both autistic and fragmented qualities. Speech, when proffered, frequently is tangential if not incoherent, and tends to be scattered with neologisms mixed into rambling word salads. Behavior is extremely bizarre and spotted with peculiar mannerisms and automatisms. Emotional affect either is totally lacking, creating a drab and flat appearance, or is characterized by its inappropriateness and incongruity. Hallucinations and delusions are quite common, tending to be fleeting, unconnected and totally illogical.

The severity of the three cardinal signs noted in common among decompensated patterns is particularly pronounced in the schizophrenic personality since these traits have always existed as part of his make-up, although in less prominent form.

In the *passive-detached* pattern, for example, there is a premorbid affectivity deficit, cognitive slippage and interpersonal insensitivity; these patients always appeared perplexed, vacant and drab and were drawn within themselves, unable to communicate clearly and with feeling toward others. As conditions led them to retreat to what we have termed the schizoid pattern, they began to experience feelings of depersonalization and became even more unresponsive, socially inadequate, detached and inarticulate. Thus, prior to their advanced schizophrenic decompensation, they evidenced clear signs of cognitive disjunctiveness, depersonalization anxieties and deficient social behaviors, each of which parallels the cardinal traits of the markedly severe personality level. It is for these reasons, as we shall later discuss more fully, that disintegration into the decompensated pattern occurs with greater frequency and at an earlier age among detached personalities than among other premorbid personality types. Thus, we would expect to find that a major proportion of institutionalized psychotic patterns would be classified as schizophrenic personalities; similarly, the age at which the psychosis first becomes evident in these patients should be appreciably earlier than in that of other decompensated personality patterns.

Although the premorbid clinical picture of the *active-detached* pattern differs in certain fundamental respects from that of the passive-detached, these patterns progressively become more alike as they decompensate. As in the passive patterns, the active-detached is disposed to a rapid and early development of schizoid and schizophrenic features. His affective disharmony, alienated self-image, cognitive interference and interpersonal aversiveness are early forerunners of the estrangement feelings, cognitive disorganization and social incompetence of the decompensated level. The road toward schizophrenic disintegration has been well laid since childhood, and requires little external prompting to be traveled fully and rapidly in early life.

Although many more mildly detached personalities remain well compensated, a substantial proportion falter along the way, either deteriorating to the schizoid level, with its periodic psychotic eruptions, or decompensating further to the more chronically maladaptive schizophrenic pattern. At this stage of abject surrender and coping collapse, we see behavioral regressions, a frightening depersonalization and estrangement, bizarre and fragmented thinking and a marked social invalidism. The following case history depicts the development and the clinical characteristics of such an unfortunate being.

*CASE 9-1*
*Harold T., Age 27, Unmarried*

Harold was the fourth of seven children. His father, a hard-drinking coal miner, had been on relief throughout most of Harold's early life; his mother died giving birth to her seventh child when Harold was eight. The family was raised by two older sisters, ages 15 and 11 at the time of their motl.er's death; partial household assistance was provided by a widowed maternal aunt with eight children of her own.

"Duckie," as Harold was known, had always been a withdrawn, frightened and "stupid" youngster. The nickname "Duckie" represented a peculiar waddle in his walk; it was used by others as a term of derogation and ridicule. Harold rarely played with his sibs or neighborhood children; he was teased unmercifully because of his "walk" and his fear of pranksters. Harold was a favorite neighborhood scapegoat; he was intimidated even by the most innocuous glance in his direction.

His father's brutality toward the other children of the family terrified Harold. Although Harold received less than his share of this brutality, since his father thought him to be a "good and not troublesome boy," this escape from paternal hostility was more than made up for by resentment and teasing on the part of his older siblings. By the time Harold was ten or 11, his younger brothers joined in taunting and humiliating him.

Harold's family was surprised when he performed well in the first few years of schooling. He began to falter, however, upon entrance to junior high school. At about the age of 14, his schoolwork became extremely poor, he refused to go to classes and he complained of a variety of vague, physical pains. By age 15 he had totally withdrawn from school, remaining home in the basement room that he shared with two younger brothers. Everyone in his family began to speak of him as "being tetched." He thought about "funny religious things that didn't make sense"; he also began to draw "strange things" and talk to himself. When he was 16, he once ran out of the house screaming "I'm gone, I'm gone, I'm gone . . .", saying that his "body went to heaven" and that he had to run outside to recover it; rather interestingly, this event occurred shortly after his father had been committed by the courts to a state mental hospital. By age 17, Harold was ruminating all day, often talking aloud in a meaningless jargon; he refused to come to the family table for meals.

The scheduled marriage of his second oldest sister, who had been running the household for five years, brought matters to a head. Harold, then 18, was taken to the same mental hospital to which his father had been committed two years previously.

When last seen, Harold had been institutionalized for nine years; no appreciable change was evident in his behavior or prognosis since admission. Most notable clinically is his drab appearance, apathy and lack of verbal communication; on rare occasions he laughs to himself in an incongruous and peculiar manner. He stopped soiling, which he had begun to do when first admitted, and will now eat by himself. When left alone with pencil and paper, he draws strange religious-like pictures but is unable to verbalize their meaning in a coherent fashion. Drug therapy has had no effect upon his condition; neither has he responded to group therapeutic efforts.

### Childhood Variants

The great majority of schizophrenic personalities follow a gradual and slow course of decompensation, but there is a small number that exhibit *markedly* detached personality patterns in early childhood. Two types may be distinguished; they parallel, in their basic style, the passive- and active-detached patterns.

1. The first of these impairments, known in the literature as *infantile autism* (Kanner, 1954; Rimland, 1964), is an early and extreme variant of passive-detachment. These youngsters are identifiable within the first 18 months of life, and are usually referred to by their parents as "different" or perhaps "feebleminded."

Although appearing normal in all other respects, these infants seem totally unresponsive to human stimulation; however, they demand a consistency and sameness in their physical environment and display an intense preoccupation with inanimate objects. Their impenetrable aloneness and their apparent inner emotional vacuum is summarized well in Bettelheim's phrase "the empty fortress" (1967). Social isolation and a lack of personal identity are two notable features. If they speak at all, they rarely make reference to themselves; the term "I" frequently is lacking in their vocabulary. Presumably, this signifies their marked alienation, not only from others but from themselves.

Another characteristic of these children is their gross insensitivity to pain, further evidence of their affectivity deficit. Also notable is their tendency to engage in self-mutilating behaviors such as head-knocking and hand-biting; this may reflect a desperate need for external stimulation to overcome what may be an extreme deficit in sensory receptivity.

Many children display traits that are similar but less severe than those seen in the autistic infant. These youngsters should be labeled as "child autism: moderate severity," so as to distinguish them from the more serious infantile type. In a recent report these more moderate cases were referred to as "Isolated Personalities" (Group for the Advancement of Psychiatry, 1966). The recent DSM-II classifies these traits as a *withdrawing reaction of childhood,* with the following descriptive features:

This disorder is characterized by seclusiveness, detachment, sensitivity, shyness, timidity, and general inability to form close interpersonal relationships. The diagnosis should be reserved for those who cannot be classified as having *schizophrenia* and whose tendencies toward withdrawal have not yet stabilized enough to justify the diagnosis of *schizoid personality*.

2. The second of the childhood schizophrenias corresponds to the active-detached pattern. We shall refer to these impairments as *infantile threctism,* to represent their extraordinary fearfulness and vulnerability to threat.

In the very first months of life, these youngsters display an excruciating sensitivity to stimulation, whimpering or crying at the slightest noise and movement; parents invariably report them to be markedly colic and difficult to schedule.

Their tenseness and hyperirritability proves extremely discouraging and exasperating to their caretakers, often setting off a chain of parental reactions which intensifies the child's established pathological disposition.

Moderately severe variants of this picture are often seen. Here we would apply the label "child threctism: moderate severity." They parallel the diagnostic child categories "Anxious Personality" and "Overly Inhibited Personality" noted in a recent report (Group for the Advancement of Psychiatry, 1966), and the DSM-II classification labeled *overanxious reaction of childhood,* described as follows:

This disorder is characterized by chronic anxiety, excessive and unrealistic fears, sleeplessness, nightmares, and exaggerated autonomic responses. The patient tends to be immature, self-conscious, grossly lacking in confidence . . . and apprehensive in new situations and unfamiliar surroundings.

The following case illustrates several features of the more severe infantile threctic picture.

*CASE 9-2*
*Mary F., Age 5*

Mary was brought for diagnostic evaluation following withdrawal from nursery school. She was terrified at the prospect of leaving her bedroom each morning and whimpered, but did not otherwise resist being taken to school; she sat in the classroom shivering and in tears.

Her developmental history was presented by an extremely anxious mother whose speech and logic reflected her own apprehensiveness and cognitive disorganization. The father, an easily irritated and hostile man, came to the diagnostic conference only at the mother's insistence.

Though her parents were with her, Mary sat alone in the waiting room with her head turned downward, fidgeting and whimpering. She evidenced no parental attachment or clinging behaviors. Despite the fact that her mother was not indifferent to her, she made no effort to assuage Mary's apprehension and discomfort, leaving her completely alone in her anguish.

Mary could not be tested by conventional procedures. She failed to respond verbally to questions. According to her mother, Mary had not said a word for several months; she simply whimpered, cried or grunted. After much gentle prodding, it was possible to elicit several nonverbal responses to certain test items; it was evident, even from this limited performance, that Mary was not intellectually deficient.

Mary was the older of two girls by 18 months; rather interestingly, the younger sister displays a similar but less severe clinical picture. According to her mother, Mary was an extremely tense and colicky infant; she stiffened when she was held, cried "constantly" and even whimpered when asleep. The mother was always tired, and the father stayed away from home as much as he could in order to "turn off that screaming brat"; exhaustion and irritability permeated the household.

Mary never smiled; when she learned to recognize people, her face seemed to register "terror" no matter with whom she came into contact. Her days were spent fondling the few toys she had at her disposal; her eyes were always turned from others and focused downward, even when she walked.

Mealtime is a "disaster" period. The mother attempts to feed Mary as well as her younger sister; both children "pick at their food," frequently "spit out" what is given them and often vomit shortly after eating.

Mary began to speak a few words at about the age of two; her earliest verbal communications included such phrases as "I scared" and "no touch me." Fully developed sentences never were achieved, although her single word vocabulary was rather extensive; when she entered nursery school at age four, speech stopped completely.

A sense of inner terror and social aloneness are the most distinctive features of this youngster. She appears neither to seek nor to gain emotional support from her parents. From her viewpoint, the world seems to be a setting of strange and threatening sounds and movements. And this pattern of self-protective withdrawal was in clear evidence in the first months of her life.

## ETIOLOGY AND DEVELOPMENT

We shall not review in detail the background of schizophrenic personalities since their histories essentially duplicate conditions already discussed in our presentations of the mild detached and schizoid patterns (see pages 226, 234 and 311 to 313).

As has been stressed repeatedly throughout the text, markedly severe decompensated patterns lie at one polar extreme of a continuum of pathology, with the other extreme occupied by the mild personality types. The same complex of etiological factors that is found in mild pathologies is seen in the background of more severe variants; the principal differences are the greater intensity and frequency of pathogenic elements in the latter. Thus, where constitutional factors are operative, the presence of a severe biophysical impairment is more likely to result in a marked rather than a mild pathological pattern. Similarly, in the severely disabled patterns we are likely to discover a history of persistent and unrelieved environmental adversity. Let us briefly summarize some of the pathogenic elements associated with the passive- and active-patterns of schizophrenic development.

1. There is a reasonable likelihood that genetic anomalies conducive to affective and cognitive deficits are present in the biogenic back-

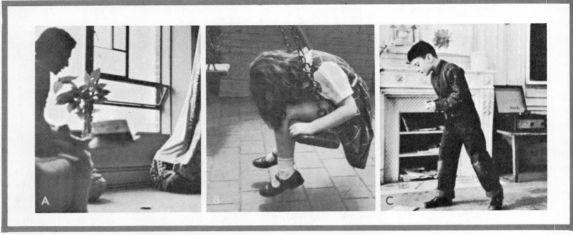

Figure 9-1    Severely withdrawn and psychologically mute children. (Parts A and C, courtesy of the St. Louis Post Dispatch; part B, courtesy of Ken Heyman from Magnum.)

ground of *passive schizophrenic personalities*. Many have shown a passive reaction pattern in infancy, which in turn may have initiated a sequence of impoverished stimulation and parental indifference. Fragile ectomorphic builds may have resulted in physical incompetencies and vulnerabilities to stress; speculations may be offered to the effect that deficits in reticular, limbic, sympathetic or synaptic control centers underlie their low activation, minimal capacity for reinforcement experiences and cognitive disorders.

In their psychogenic background, there is a reasonable probability of marked stimulus impoverishment during the sensory-attachment stage, reflecting either parental neglect or indifference; these experiences may lay the groundwork for a biophysical underdevelopment of affectivity substrates and a deficit learning of interpersonal attachment behaviors. A family atmosphere of cold formality may have served as a model for imitative learning, resulting in a lifelong style of social reticence and insensitivity and a discomfort with personal closeness. Fragmented and amorphous styles of parental communication may have prompted the development of disjointed and unfocused patterns of thinking.

Repeated exposure to these conditions and to peer experiences which aggravate them may cumulate to produce an inextricable web of pathogenicity. Once established, early styles of behavior and coping may perpetuate and intensify past difficulties. Social detachment, emotional impassivity and cognitively obscure thinking will progressively alienate the youngster from others and lead him to subordinate overt activity to autistic fantasy; unchecked by social consensus,

these inner thoughts begin to lose their logic and coherence, causing a new spiral of self-defeating processes that further the decompensation trend.

Ruminations of inner emptiness in these persons will prompt depersonalization anxieties. At the same time, they experience anxieties in response to social encroachments and responsibilities. Both depersonalization and encroachment result in periodic psychotic breaks. Ultimately, the slow and insidious process of personality deterioration will produce the social invalidism, cognitive disorganization and feelings of estrangement that characterize the decompensated level.

2.   The biogenic background of *active schizophrenic personalities* will often give evidence of apprehensive or cognitively obscure relatives, indicating the possible contribution of genetic factors to pathology. Threctic infantile patterns are common, often precipitating parental tension and derogation, which then aggravate the established temperament. Irregularities in maturation may frequently be noted, producing uneven competencies, difficult to handle emotions and notable social "pecularities." Low thresholds for sympathetic, reticular and synaptic functioning may be hypothesized to account for the hypersensitivity and cognitive "flooding" found among these patients.

Their psychogenic histories typically show a background of parental deprecation and peer group humiliation, resulting in lowered self-esteem and social distrust. These experiences often begin as early as the first or sensory-attachment stage of development, leading the youngster to protectively insulate his feelings. Ridicule in response to second-stage autonomy efforts contributes markedly to a sense of personal inadequacy and incompetence; the persistence of belittling and derogating attitudes through later childhood and adolescence leads eventually to self-criticism and self-deprecation. For example, Harold T. was subjected to relentless harassment and humiliation both at home and at school; by the time he was 13 or 14, Harold had "accepted" the inevitability of his fate, referred to himself as "stupid and ugly" and ultimately withdrew protectively from all social contacts.

The coping strategies these persons employ to protect against further social ridicule only perpetuate and intensify their plight. Thus, Harold denied himself opportunities for remedial experiences, perceived censure and threat where none existed and preoccupied himself with autistic fantasies that focused on past misfortunes. To counter these oppressive thoughts, he began to block or destroy his cognitive clarity, thereby fostering further self-estrangement and social incompetence. As feelings of depersonalization and unreality grew, periodic psychotic episodes blended into one another, and he deteriorated gradually into a more permanent decompensated state.

As noted in earlier sections, the prognostic picture for the mild detached patterns is extremely unfavorable; this contrasts with the dependent, ambivalent and independent personalities. Each of these latter patterns has gained a modicum of positive reinforcement through their coping strategies, and has sought and maintained some measure of social relatedness. Detached personalities, however, lack sources of positive reinforcement, and have disengaged themselves from reality and the controls of social interaction. Without positive reinforcements to motivate them and without the support and controls of social life, the prospects are high that they will undergo rapid personality decompensation. For these reasons, we find the schizophrenic personality pattern emerging typically early in life, usually, but not invariably, between the ages of 15 and 25. It is this same paucity of developed social skills and sense of deep unworthiness and incompetence that account for the fact that these patients often remain in a permanent decompensated state; schizophrenic personalities comprise the greater bulk of the chronic or "hard-core" patients in most mental institutions.

### Childhood Variants

Some thoughts concerning the etiology of infantile and childhood schizophrenic personalities may be instructive.

1. Both biogenic and psychogenic factors have been proposed as sources for the development of *infantile autism.*

Rimland (1964), on the basis of a well-reasoned speculation, contends that the impairment derives from a constitutional defect, probably that of a dysfunction in the reticular formation. Bettelheim (1967), based on a series of exhaustively studied case histories, suggests that the aberration stems from a failure on the part of parents to provide stimulation and encouragement in the first two years of life, followed by the child's "disappointment" and subsequent protective withdrawal. Kanner (1954) and Eisenberg and Kanner (1956) waver between the belief that autism has its origin in an inborn affective deficit and the thesis that the child has been exposed to a mother characterized by her "emotional refrigeration." Bender (1959) and Goldstein (1959) view the illness as a psychological defensive maneuver to counter the effects of a basic neurological impairment. In short, a whole range of etiological hypotheses has been posited, despite essential agreement as to the major clinical features.

We shall propose another etiological thesis in the hope that it will clarify rather than confuse matters. Specifically, we shall hypothesize that autistic pathology may arise *either* from biological or psychological conditions which may operate independently of each other, and which may be sufficient in themselves to produce the clinical picture. Dividing cases along this line of thinking, we shall propose the concepts of *primary autism* (biogenic) and *secondary autism* (psychogenic). Let us note, however, that regardless of which etiological source is primary in a particular case, the essential element in infantile autism is the failure of the child to acquire adequate human attachment behaviors.

In *primary autism,* we suggest that the infant lacks the biological equipment necessary either for experiencing or integrating stimulation during the sensory-attachment stage of neuropsychological development; such inferences would be appropriate in cases where there is evidence of ample parental warmth and affection. Since these youngsters ostensibly possessed infantile deficits in affect reception or integration, they were unable to learn the complex attachments required for establishing human relationships. The child's fate seems to have been sealed since he was constitutionally incapable of sensing or coordinating the requisite stimulation for the development of attachment behaviors at its crucial period in infancy; in effect, he now remains locked within himself. The following case depicts this autistic development.

### CASE 9-3
### Jimmy L., Age 6

This primary autistic youngster had been raised by highly intelligent parents and older siblings who showed great concern, attention and gentility in their care. Jimmy never evidenced any response to human overtures; he seemed totally oblivious of his parents and sibs, and would content himself in his first three or four years simply by rocking back and forth on his buttocks. At the age of four, he appeared to become fascinated by a number of drawings that an older sister had prepared for him in the hope of "breaking through his blankness." Since then, Jimmy has spent the better part of each day drawing highly complicated and colorful arrangements of squares, circles and triangles, done with extraordinary skill and artistry for his age. Despite this clear-cut sign of abstract intelligence, he still does not talk, smile, cry or otherwise respond to living or mobile objects.

Where marked affect deficits are evident in primary autistics, we would expect few or no attachment behaviors to develop. Attachments may be made in less severe cases, but only to simple inanimate objects; here we assume that sensory functions are intact, but the biological capacity for complex stimulus and emotional integrations is impaired.

The diagnosis of *secondary autism* assumes that the newborn's biophysical capacities have followed a normal sequence of maturation and are essentially intact. Defects arise as a consequence of unusual stimulation deficits; support for this diagnosis requires clear evidence of parental "coldness," neglect or incompetence. In these cases there is a marked developmental retardation of neural structures requisite to the learning of attachment behaviors. These youngsters appear similar to those whose difficulties are rooted in biogenic defects; however, since they began life with some normally matured affectivity capacities, their autism should become evident at a later period than those who suffer inborn impairments. These infants are likely to become attached to inanimate objects that provide them with the sensory stimulation they need.

Infantile autism is an unusual syndrome that arises from an extremely adverse set of conditions; most schizophrenic personalities have their origins neither in such severe biophysical defects nor such severe stimulation deficits. However, to a lesser degree, these same conditions can set the stage for the insidious development of a passive-detached pattern, which ultimately may unfold into schizophrenia.

2. The etiological basis for what we have termed *infantile threctism* also may be viewed as a quantitatively more extreme but qualitatively comparable set of conditions than those which give rise to adult schizophrenia; in the case of threctism, the parallel lies with the active-detached schizophrenic pattern. As with autism, we shall propose that *either* biogenic *or* psychogenic factors may take precedence; thus, terms such as primary threctism and secondary threctism may be in order.

In *primary threctism*, we observe infants who evidence extraordinary tension and fearfulness in the first months of life. In these cases, we infer the presence of either unusual sensory sensitivities, overendowed neural pain centers or aberrant structures of neural integration; such inferences, however, rest on the assumption of a benevolent caretaking environment during infancy. For these youngsters, attachment learning may be disrupted by the intensity, flooding or disjunctiveness of sensory impressions; thus, these infants must set up a protective barrier against what they sense to be an overwhelming influx of external stimuli. Though complicated by parental mismanagement, the case of Mary F. illustrates the clinical features and development of primary threctic children.

With less severe biological dispositions, the threctic child need not necessarily develop serious pathology. If he possesses parents who are exquisitely alert to his sensitivities, and thereby handle him with great care, the child's impairment may be surmounted, enabling him to acquire appropriate human attachments; thus, despite an inborn threctic disposition, the child's development may take a healthy turn under proper environmental conditions. We might note in this regard that the primary threctic child is more fortunate than the primary autistic youngster since the latter's insensitivity blocks the positive effects of a benevolent environment.

The etiology of *secondary threctism* is essentially psychogenic. These infants appear to possess normal sensibilities at birth, but are exposed in the very first months to extremely intense and painful sensory stimulation. To handle this stimulation, the infant protectively diminishes his contact with the world by reducing his sensory awareness; diagnosis of these cases should be based on evidence of particularly harsh or chaotic early environments. Many of these children acquire some form of attachment behavior; they discover a small sphere within their environment, usually neutral inanimate objects, which they draw upon repetitively as a "safe" source of sensory stimulation.

In general, these youngsters display their pathology at a somewhat later age than primary threctics. However, in cases of extremely harsh early handling, the pathological pattern may already be manifest at the age of one or two. Other less severely treated youngsters may not develop the full-blown disturbance until seven and ten years of age; these latter cases are referred to in the official DSM-II classification schema as *childhood schizophrenia*. This label, though pinpointing the age of occurrence, fails to draw distinctions which we contend should be made between primary and secondary types, and between autistic (passive) and threctic (active) types.

Let us again be mindful that most forms of schizophrenia evolve gradually, and reflect the interaction of both biogenic and psychogenic determinants; few cases have their origin in such markedly adverse biological or psychological handicaps as is found in infantile "autism" and "threctism." Adolescent or adult forms of schizophrenia may have their roots in conditions that are qualitatively comparable to those which produce the childhood impairment, but these adverse conditions were likely to have been quantitatively less severe. However, these less severe early difficulties may have been compounded and intensified throughout development, leading to a slow and inexorable decompensation that eventuates in an adult schizophrenic personality pattern that is no less severe than that found in childhood types.

# CYCLOPHRENIC PERSONALITY: DECOMPENSATED DEPENDENT AND AMBIVALENT PATTERNS
(DSM-II: *Schizophrenia, Schizo-Affective Type; Manic-Depressive Illness, Several Subtypes*)

The label "cyclophrenia" is a new term, coined in this text to represent a syndrome whose decompensation is deeply ingrained and pervasive; its distinguishing feature as a personality pattern is that it overlies a lifelong style either of dependency or of ambivalence. The estrangement, invalidism and cognitive disorganization of these patients emerge following the disintegration of a cycloid pattern of coping; thus, the syndrome reflects one further step in pathological severity that began with a mild dependent, or ambivalent, personality pattern.

There is no term in the psychiatric nomenclature for severely deteriorated patients whose earlier life style is noted by dependence strivings. It has been customary in psychiatric circles to label as "schizophrenic" all markedly decompensated patients, regardless of their premorbid personalities; for reasons noted earlier in the chapter, the failure to draw distinctions at the markedly severe level has been most unfortunate.

We have taken several steps to establish clarity along these lines. First, we have applied the general label "decompensated personality pattern" for all chronic and pervasively deteriorated states. And second, even though we recognize that clinical syndromes do not fall into sharply defined types, we have differentiated three severely deteriorated subpatterns in accordance with their dominant predecompensated style of coping.

The choice of the designation "cyclophrenia" has been made to match the established syndrome label of "schizophrenia"; both are decompensated personality patterns, as is "paraphrenia," to be discussed in a later section. Furthermore, the cyclophrenic term parallels that of "cycloid," the moderately severe variant of the dependent and ambivalent personality styles. In addition to maintaining consistency with both its decompensated and borderline counterparts, the cyclophrenic label means "cyclical minds," reflecting thereby an essential feature found among these patients —their vacillation in mood, thought and behavior.

### History

From the earliest literary and medical history, writers have recognized the coexistence within single persons of intense and divergent moods such as euphoria and depression. Homer, Hippocrates and Aretaeus described with great clarity and vividness the related character of mania and melancholia, noting both the periodic vacillation between these "spells" and the personality types likely to be subject to them. However, as with most medical and scientific knowledge, these early formulations were lost or suppressed in medieval times. With the advent of the Renaissance, the observations of Greek and Roman physicians were brought to light, and new systematic studies of the mentally ill were begun anew.

The first to revive the notion of the covariation between mood extremes in a single syndrome was Bonet, who applied the term *folie maniaco-mélancolique* in 1684. Schacht and Herschel noted similar patterns in the eighteenth century. In 1854, Falret published the results of thirty years' work with depressed and suicidal persons; he found that a large proportion of these patients showed a course of extended depression, broken intermittently by periods of marked elation and normality; he termed this syndrome *la folie circulaire* to signify its contrasting and variable character. It was Kahlbaum, however, whose genius for perceptive clinical classification has too often been overlooked, who clearly described in 1882 the typical covariation of mania and melancholia; to him, they were facets of a single disease which manifested itself in different ways at different times. He termed the milder form of this illness, notable for its frequent periods of normality, *cyclothymia* (essentially what we have labeled as the "cycloid personality"); a more severe and chronic variant of this same pattern was designated *vesania typica circularis* (essentially what we shall call the "cyclophrenic personality").

Although Kraepelin borrowed heavily from Kahlbaum's formulations, he rejected Kahlbaum's important distinction between mild and severe circular types; this reflected his attempt to find a set of simple common denominators for large groups of mental disorders. Thus, in 1896, he proposed the name manic-depressive insanity for "the whole domain of periodic and circular insanity," including such diverse disturbances and "the morbid states termed melancholia . . . [and] certain slight colorings of mood, some of them periodic, some of them continuously morbid." Asserting his conviction of the unitary character of this disease, Kraepelin wrote:

> I have become convinced all these states only represent manifestations of a single morbid process. It is certainly possible that later a series of subordinate groups may be . . . entirely separated off. But if this happens, then according to my view those symptoms will certainly not be authoritative which hitherto have usually been placed in the foreground.

Kraepelin left no doubt that he viewed the "circular insanity" to be a unitary illness; every disorder which gave evidence of mood disturbances was conceived to be a variant or "rudiment" of the same basic impairment. The common denominator for this group of disturbances was an endogenous metabolic dysfunction that was "to an astonishing degree independent of external influences."

To contrast these mood disorders with dementia praecox, which he characterized as progressing to an inevitable state of total personality disintegration, Kraepelin asserted that the manic-depressive had a favorable outcome. To reinforce this distinction more sharply, Kraepelin drew upon a valid but by no means consistent observation and made it into an irrefutable rule. It is well known that patients with mood disorders generally but not always have good prognoses. Kraepelin took this observation as a basis for claiming that *all* mood disorders have good prognoses; by a curious twist of logic, he then asserted that if a patient did deteriorate, he could not have had a mood, that is, a manic-depressive disorder, but rather dementia praecox. To fit the facts into his system, Kraepelin and his followers often changed their diagnoses. Thus, if a patient decompensated severely during the course of his illness, the character of his original personality make-up or the symptomatology he may initially have presented was cast aside; severe personality decompensation necessitated the diagnostic label of dementia praecox.

This cavalier juggling of diagnoses to fit the Kraepelinian formulation, not at all uncommon in present psychiatric practice, is most lamentable for another reason. Kraepelin completely overlooked a central feature in Kahlbaum's original formulation of the "circular insanities," a formulation which served as the basis of his category of the manic-depressive psychosis. In attempting to impose simplicity and symmetry on his classification system, and in an effort to convince others of the different nature of the biological causes which he believed distinguished dementia praecox and manic-depression, Kraepelin rejected Kahlbaum's thesis that the cyclical pattern can decompensate into a chronic and deteriorated form.

Simplicity is a commendable virtue in a classification system, especially if it clarifies the essential nature of seemingly divergent psychopathologies; but when it blurs distinctions or is founded on artificial or unsubstantiated differences in etiology or prognosis, there is reason to question a rigid adherence to the system. Kraepelin's etiological speculations have not proved valid; although most patients who display mood and cyclical disorders do not fully decompensate, there is no basis for asserting that they all do not.

There is every reason to assume that all forms of psychopathology can be expressed across the full continuum of severity; this position was held by Kraepelin's predecessor Kahlbaum in his original separation of the "circular insanities" into more and less severe variants. The categories of "cycloid" and "cyclophrenia" proposed in this text may be viewed, then, as a return to Kahlbaum's basic observation of differences in the chronicity and severity of the "circular insanities"; the separation of these syndromes picks up the thread of classificatory thinking where we believe Kraepelin went astray.

### Comparison of the Cyclophrenic and Similar Syndromes in the Official Classification

As noted above, we reject the common practice of classifying as schizophrenic most patients evidencing a progressive and marked decompensation. It is our contention that distinctions should be made in accord with premorbid personality styles.

There is one diagnostic label in the official DSM-II nosology that corresponds to the clinical picture of cyclophrenia; this designation, listed as *schizophrenia, schizo-affective type,* will be referred to later in this section. For the present, let us distinguish the cyclophrenic classification from other similar syndromes noted in the official APA Manual (1952, 1968).

The general classification *major affective disorders* is relevant in this regard. (As an aside, we might note that this label is a poor designation since the use of the term "affect" exclusively for this impairment implies that patients in other categories do not experience intense emotional feelings.) Impairments listed under the "affective" label were described in the 1952 manual as "psychotic reactions characterized by a primary, severe disorder of mood, with resultant disturbance of thought and behavior, in consonance with the affect." The major relevant subgroup of this syndrome is termed in the DSM-II as *manic depressive illness,* and is described as being "marked by severe mood swings, and a tendency to remission and recurrence."

The two phrases to note in the above quotes are those of "consonance with affect" and "a tendency to remission and recurrence." The first of these implies that the patient retains both cognitive control and reality awareness, that is, he does not evidence in notable form the two central elements of cognitive dyscontrol and loss of reality awareness which we consider the *sine qua non* for the designation of decompensated functioning. The second phrase indicates that the patient experiences only transitory and reversible psychotic episodes, that is, does not succumb to an enduring or chronic pathological state. These descriptive phrases correctly portray many patients, but these patients appear to be what we have termed "cycloid personalities," that is, per-

sonalities who are disposed to periodic and reversible psychotic episodes characterized by intense moods and erratic behaviors.

We believe that a separation should be made between the basic personality pattern of the patient and the episodic disorder he exhibits. These episodes will manifest themselves in any of a number of forms; among cycloids, for example, we might expect episodic psychotic disorders such as "agitated depression" or "euphoric excitement."

Let us illustrate the difference between the official nosology and the system we are proposing. A patient who manifests a transitory period of incongruous gaiety and irrational flights of ideas would be classified in the official nosology as *manic-depressive illness, manic type;* in the present system, he might be classified, given a basic active-dependent strategy, as "cycloid personality: active-dependent type; euphoric excitement disorder." Similarly, an apprehensive and depressed patient showing restless motor activity would be listed in the official nosology as *manic-depressive illness, depressed type;* depending on his lifelong coping style, we might designate him as "cycloid personality: passive-ambivalent type; agitated depression disorder." In short, the transitory psychotic disorder of the patient should be separated but correlated with his basic personality pattern; most "manic-depressions" are episodic psychotic disorders, not decompensated personalities.

Let us return to the main theme of the deteriorated cycloid personality, or what we have termed the cyclophrenic personality. The official DSM-II classification does include a clinical syndrome that is roughly comparable to cyclophrenia; not surprisingly, it is categorized under the schizophrenic rather than the affective label; it is listed as *schizophrenia, schizo-affective type.* The descriptive text for this impairment in the detailed 1952 manual states:

> For those cases showing significant admixtures of schizophrenic and affective reactions. The mental content may be predominantly schizophrenic, with pronounced elation or depression. Cases may show predominantly affective changes with schizophrenic-like thinking or bizarre behavior.

This brief description represents in crude form some of the overt clinical features of what we have termed the cyclophrenic; in essence, these patients exhibit cognitive disorganization, estrangement and invalidism (which are features of all decompensated patterns); in addition, they display both a strong affective tone and a social relatedness which are *not* found in schizophrenic personalities. The affectivity and sociability of cyclophrenics reflect their lifelong basic strategy of seeking interpersonal support, approval and nurture. Thus, cyclophrenics possess both the features of decompensated personalities and those of dependent or dependent-ambivalent strategies. This combination distinguishes them from the official classifications of manic-depression (episodic psychosis) and schizophrenia (detached strategy). Let us now elaborate the pattern.

## CLINICAL PICTURE

As indicated above, the cyclophrenic is a markedly decompensated variant of the mild, moderately dependent and ambivalent patterns; reference should be made to pages 242, 251, 279, 289 and 317 for a fuller description of the characteristics of these pre-decompensated clinical pictures. Despite his greater deterioration, the cyclophrenic retains many traces of the behaviors and moods which typified his earlier adjustment.

Most notable at this stage of his impairment is the emergence of a persistent social invalidism, as is evident in his inability to assume responsibility for his own care, welfare and health; thinking is difficult and speech may be limited, hesitant and indecisive; cognitive processes tend to be disjunctive and autistic, manifesting themselves either in sudden and erratic changes in focus or as inaudible and incoherent ramblings; behavior and emotion tend either toward the bizarre, with capricious bursts of energy and irrational exuberance, or toward the sluggish and lugubrious; there may be little or no motor activity, and a physical inertia, weighty and stooped posture and downcast and forlorn expression may come to dominate the clinical picture; fragmented as contrasted to systematized delusions and hallucinations are not uncommon, usually reflecting obsessive fears of impending disaster or strange and undiagnosable bodily ailments; self-deprecation, remorse and guilt are prominent as the content of their disorganized and fleeting delusions.

The following brief history depicts a number of these features.

*CASE 9-4*
*Louis M., Age 53, Married, Two Children*

Louis, an institutionalized cyclophrenic, would sit in his more typical daily behavior in a stooped manner, quietly bemoaning the fate of God, to whom he claimed he spoke the night before, and who had told him that because of his and God's sins, life for everyone would soon be even more "hellish" than living in a state hospital. Every several weeks, and rather unpredictably, Louis would suddenly be buoyed up, begin clapping his hands, and loudly sing to a cheerfully melodic refrain, a song with pleasant neologistic words (e.g., goody dum dum, happimush), but one that was otherwise totally incomprehensible. Following these brief euphoric episodes, Louis would succumb to his more usual depressive agitation, moaning incoherently about the wretched state of man's sinfulness, the coming of doomsday, the "tastelessness" of the weather, his "dramink" of hundreds of little girls and so on.

Acceptance of social invalidism as a way of life has not been difficult for these patients, given their lifelong orientation toward dependency. As the effort to maintain contact with the mainstream of social life is finally abandoned, they readily succumb to a state of helpless dependence.

Any withdrawal into self increases the probability of cognitive disorganization; in dependent patterns this process is accentuated. These personalities have habitually lacked the capacity to "think for themselves"; thus, they have great difficulty on their own in achieving self-reinforcements and in finding a consistent direction and order for thinking. Furthermore, whatever thoughts they do possess are colored by an oppressive and melancholy tone. To avoid these preoccupations, cyclophrenics may attempt to focus on deviant, cheerful thoughts; this accounts, in part, for their capricious and erratic ramblings. But these cognitive digressions cannot be sustained; sensing the futility of these efforts to change their mood, these patients may block or retard all thought processes, thereby producing the slow and laborious responses which often characterize them. Should these latter efforts fail, they may simply disassemble or disorganize their thoughts as a protective maneuver against the anguish which they evoke.

Estrangement in cyclophrenics has its roots largely in their growing sense of aloneness and apartness from the attachments they had previously established. Rebuffed and institutionalized, they experience not only the frightening anxieties of separation from "loved" ones but a new and strange environment. Geared throughout their lives to look to the outer world for guidance and support, cyclophrenics become keenly aware of their aloneness and the unfamiliarity of their surroundings. They feel lost, bewildered in a strange and unreal world, perplexed and removed.

Although cycloids and cyclophrenics lie on a continuum of severity, with only imperceptible shades of difference separating them, it will be useful to note certain features that distinguish at least the prototypes of these two impairments.

Cyclophrenics remain in a decompensated state, unable to survive without a total caretaking environment. Reality contact is minimal in these patients, preventing them from maintaining meaningful communications with others or gaining the benefits of their reassurance and support. Lifelong controls and coping strategies have collapsed, resulting in the total disintegration of personality functioning. In contrast, cycloids experience only transient and reversible psychotic episodes; at other times, reality contact is maintained, their controls and coping strategies are adequately preserved and they are able to evoke a modicum of positive reinforcement from interpersonal relationships.

Distinctions may also be noted between the schizophrenic and cyclophrenic personalities. Here the essential differences lie in their developmental histories, that is, the pattern of attitudes and strategies they have learned. Briefly, cyclophrenics have shown a capacity to relate to others, although in a dependent fashion; their thoughts focus on inadequacy, conflict, guilt and self-deprecation; frequent periods of extreme moods and mood swings are notable. In contrast, schizophrenics have characteristically been detached, self-contained and socially deficient; their cognitive processes have always been disjointed and autistic; affect has been either lacking or markedly apprehensive; periods of panic and bizarre impulses and feelings of alienation and depersonalization are notable.

Because of their social motivation and skills, the long-range prognosis for dependent personalities is considerably better than that for detached patterns; thus, the proportion of dependent (and ambivalent) patterns that decompensate to moderate and markedly severe levels of functioning is rather small, considerably less than that found among detached personalities. Dependent personalities have a built-in protection against decompensation stemming from their strong proclivity and skill in maintaining social relationships; for this reason, the incidence of cyclophrenia is substantially less than that of schizophrenia, but by no means zero.

Next, we will note some of the symptomatological features which distinguish the four basic personality types that decompensate to cyclophrenia.

1. *Passive-dependent cyclophrenics* tend to be consistent in their helpless invalidism and depression; earlier efforts to forego and reverse their pattern of submissive dependency, as evidenced in bursts of self-assertion or gregarious cheerfulness, have failed miserably. Convinced of their unworthiness and the inevitability of abandonment and desertion, they crumble and sink into a state of utter hopelessness. Though frightened by their separation from past sources of dependency, they quickly learn that they can gain a more consistent security in the "womb" of a totally nurtural hospital. Here they can comfortably regress to a child-like dependency, to a limpet-like attachment to whoever supplies their needs for protection and nurture. However, their infantile simpering and clinging behaviors often prove a drain upon their caretakers and fellow patients.

2. The picture of the *active-dependent cyclophrenic* tends at times to be distinctly different from that of the passive-dependent. Despite their social invalidism and the bizarre character of their thinking and behavior, these patients frequently make an effort to be charming, gay and attractive. Their lifelong pattern of soliciting attention and approval reemerges periodically in displays of irrational conviviality, often accompanied by garish clothes and ludicrous make-up. During these brief but wild flights into euphoria, there is a gushing forth of frenetic conversation and a latching on to any and all passers-by in a frantic effort to rekindle the human warmth they so desperately need. But these bizarre and hyperactive episodes usually are short lived, and the patient succumbs once more to a less agitated and more dolorous and downcast state. Even during these more prolonged and somber periods, we may observe that the active-dependent retains some of his former seductive and exhibitionistic features; thus, although his thoughts may be disorganized and irrational, one can see the histrionic quality of his complaints and self-deprecations, and one can sense that they are expressed in such ways as to solicit the listener's attention and compassion. Despite the genuineness of his misery and the obviously delusional nature of his thinking, habit systems acquired in earlier life still come through in discernible form. In the following case we may note several of these features.

### CASE 9-5
*Olive W., Age 49, Separated, Three Children*

Olive has been institutionalized three times, the first of which, at the age of 24, was for eight months; the second, at 31, lasted about three years; this third period has continued since she was 37.

Olive was the fifth child, the only girl, of a family of six children. Her early history is unclear, although she "always was known to be a tease" with the boys. Both parents worked at semiskilled jobs throughout Olive's childhood; her older brothers took care of the house. By the time she entered puberty, Olive had had sexual relations with several of her brothers and many of their friends. As she reported it in one of her more lucid periods, she "got lots of gifts," that would not otherwise have been received for "simply having a lot of fun." Apparently, her parents had no knowledge of her exploits, attributing the gifts she received to her vivaciousness and attractiveness.

A crucial turning point occurred when Olive was 15; she became pregnant. Although the pregnancy was aborted, parental attitudes changed, and severe restrictions were placed upon her. Nevertheless, Olive persisted in her seductive activities, and by the time she was 17 she again had become pregnant. At her insistence, she was married to the father of her unborn child. This proved to be a brief and stormy relationship, ending two months after the child's birth. Abandoned by her husband and rejected by her parents, Olive turned immediately to active prostitution as a means of support. In the ensuing six years, she acquired another child and another husband. Olive claims to have "genuinely loved" this man; they had "great times" together, but also many "murderous fights." It was his decision to leave her that resulted in her first, clear, psychotic break.

Following her eight month stay in the hospital, Olive picked up where she left off—prostitute, dance-hall girl and so on. Periods of drunkenness and despondency came more and more frequently, interspersed with shorter periods of gay frivolity and euphoria. For a brief time, one that produced another child, Olive served as a "plaything" for a wealthy ne'er-do-well, traveling about the country having "the time of her life." She fell into a frantic and depressive state, however, when he simply "dumped her" upon hearing that she was pregnant.

Hospitalized again, this time for three years, Olive's personality was beginning to take on more permanent psychotic features. Nevertheless, she was remitted to the home of her father and older brother; here she served as a housemaid and cook. Her children had been placed in foster homes; her mother had died several years earlier.

The death of her father, followed quickly by the marriage of her brother, left Olive alone again. Once more, she returned to her old ways, becoming a bar-girl and prostitute. Repeated beatings by her "admirers," her mental deterioration and her growing physical unattractiveness, all contributed to a pervasive despondency which resulted in her last hospitalization.

For the past several years she has been doing the work of a seamstress in the institution's sewing room; here, in addition to her mending chores, she makes rather garish clothes for herself and others. Every now and then, she spruces herself up, goes to the beauty parlor, puts on an excess of make-up and becomes transformed into a "lovely lady." More characteristically, however, her mood is somber; though responsive and friendly to those who show interest in her, her ideas almost invariably are bizarre and irrational.

3. Turning next to the *passive-ambivalent cyclophrenic,* we observe a much tighter and restrained picture than that found in either of the types discussed previously. The woebegone look has an air of tension; behaviors are more rigid and stereotyped and all sorts of mannerisms and grimaces may be displayed. On rare occasions they may exhibit explosive outbursts of rage directed at unseen persecutors; at other times they may assault themselves viciously. Many remain mute and unresponsive for long periods. Cognitive processes generally are labored, emitted in a slow and deliberate manner and tending, where coherent, to be self-deprecatory and tinged with delusions of persecution and guilt; their cognitive distortions usually are more organized or systematic than those of other cyclophrenics.

4. The clinical picture of the *active-ambivalent cyclophrenic* is not too dissimilar to that of the passive-ambivalent. However, tension and inner agitation are more manifest; conflicts and impulses are frequently acted out, and a stream of complaints is often voiced in irritable and disorganized commentaries. Behavior varies from listless pacing to hostile immobility. Delusions of guilt and self-condemnation may precipitate periodic flareups of violence and bickering. Most times, however, the patient is subdued and downcast, complaining in a quiet, almost unfeeling and automatic manner, as if by sheer habit alone. His sour pessimism, although now dissipated, still colors his attitudes and behaviors, making relationships with fellow patients and hospital workers difficult to sustain.

### Childhood Variants

The great majority of cyclophrenics decompensate more slowly than schizophrenics, typically reaching serious proportions in postadolescence or later. Nevertheless, a small number evidence the signs of marked personality disturbance in the early years of life. Two childhood cyclophrenic types will be noted in this regard.

1. The first impairment, known in the literature as *childhood symbiosis,* a term coined by Mahler (1952), parallels the passive-dependent personality pattern. The severe form of this disturbance occurs somewhat less frequently than autism, perhaps because the symbiotic child gains the rewards of a close personal relationship, something lacking in the autistic child. In these cases, there is an unusual attachment to the caretaking figure; the child brooks no separation and may be overwhelmed by panic should its mother leave. This contrasts markedly to autistic and threctic children, who seem indifferent to the presence of others or relieved when left alone. Parents describe these youngsters as extremely immature and fearful, as "cry-babies" who cling like appendages, unwilling or unable to stand and do things on

their own (these clinical symptoms do not draw notice usually until the second stage of neuropsychological development when the child fails to assume autonomous behaviors; they come to attention, then, between the ages of two and four).

Moderately impaired youngsters with similar features may properly be regarded as "child symbiosis: moderate severity"; mild cases of over-attachment at this age do not signify pathology since most of these youngsters "grow out of" the habit. A pattern similar to the moderate form of symbiosis has been described in the 1966 report of the Group for the Advancement of Psychiatry (GAP) under the label "overly dependent personalities." These cases may be difficult to differentiate from the moderately severe form of "childhood threctism" in that both groups of youngsters exhibit extreme apprehension; the threctic child, however, is pervasively anxious and tense whereas the symbiotic child is so only when parted from the person(s) to whom he is attached.

2.   The second childhood type is an early and extreme variant of the active-ambivalent pattern; we shall call this disturbance *childhood ambiosis* to reflect the centrality of ambivalence as a clinical feature. Similar descriptions have been proposed under the labels "oppositional personality" and "tension discharge disorder; neurotic personality" by the Committee on Child Psychiatry of the Group for the Advancement of Psychiatry (1966), and under the title "immature-labile" by Fish and Shapiro (1964). The recent DSM-II introduces a new and somewhat parallel diagnosis that is labeled *hyperkinetic reaction of childhood*, and is described as follows:

This disorder is characterized by overactivity, restlessness, distractibility and short attention span, especially in young children.

Most notable in these children are their behavioral unpredictability and erratic moods. There are prolonged periods of crankiness and testiness; at these times they display a hyper-mobility and restlessness, a sense of inner trouble and conflict and a tendency to severe temper tantrums for no apparent reason. At other times, these same youngsters become extremely attached and cling to their parents in a manner not dissimilar to that typical of the symbiotic child; this attachment seems to be born of fear, however, rather than of affection. Not uncommon are phobias and hypochondriacal traits. The impairment may be displayed as early as the end of the first year, but it is more frequently exhibited between the third and fifth years of life.

Many children display similar immature and negativistic behaviors in mild form; these less severe forms may evolve into a pattern of adolescent or adult active-ambivalence, that is, they may develop into negativistic personalities. The label of ambiotic should be reserved, however, for children whose impairment occurs in prepuberty and is so severe as to seriously upset the run of normal home life. Moderately severe cases may be categorized as "child ambiosis: moderate severity" to signify a nonpsychotic yet extremely troublesome pattern. The following case portrays the clinical picture and development of a properly diagnosed ambiotic child.

*CASE 9-6*
*Timothy R., Age 5*

Timothy was the older by three years of two boys in a family marked by a deep parental schism. Both parents were strikingly immature, having married at age eighteen when they were freshmen in college. Home life was noted by bitter fights. The father had little to do with his children, and even less, if possible, with his wife. The mother's relationship to her son was distinguished by its high pitch of emotionality and its extreme variability. She would fondle and cling to him one moment and scream and beat him in the next. The character of the relationship can be grasped by the following report of a typical round of feeding. The mother would attempt to coax Timmy to eat, promising candy bribes as a reward; Timmy would balk, and his mother would become exasperated; Timmy then cried; his mother began to "scream and beat him"; contrite almost immediately, his mother would then give Timmy a taste of the candy; Timmy would start to eat his regular food but "choke up" after taking a spoonful or two; his mother would become furious and storm out of the room, leaving Timmy alone. This sequence occurred almost every day; similar sequences characterized many of the other interactions between Timmy and his mother.

Timmy acted in a similar fashion when sent to nursery school; he refused to participate with other children, balked at every request, cried or had temper tantrums when frustrated, sat in a corner fidgeting or restlessly paced back and forth. His speech was grossly immature, monosyl-labic and practically incoherent; drawings were very primitive, more like a two year old's; he seemed awkward in his movements and clumsy in balance and coordination. He alternately clung to his teacher, or behaved in an obstinate and demanding manner; if he got his way, he would behave well for a brief period. At no time, however, would he tolerate sharing the attentions of the teacher with other children, constantly trying to draw her interest to him when she was involved elsewhere. After several weeks of this behavior, Timmy had maneuvered the teacher to act in an almost identical manner as his mother. Feeling exasperated, guilty and exhausted, the teacher requested that Timmy be withdrawn from nursery school.

At home, Timmy was "impossible to live with." He became an appendage to his mother and rarely would let her out of his sight, especially if he thought she was attentive to his younger brother. Even when mother gave her full attention to him, he seemed discontent and unsatisfied. Father's presence would send Timmy running to his mother, obviously fearing his father's ire and his demands that Timmy be disciplined firmly and "not be allowed to get away with all the things that mother allows."

Quite obviously, Timmy's inner ambivalence and impulsive and vacillating behaviors reflected the marked schism in the family, and the unfortunate model his mother provided through her own emotional inconsistencies and erratic discipline.

In concluding this discussion of the two childhood variants of cyclophrenia, we should alert the reader to the fact that we have not included disturbances that parallel the active-dependent (gregarious) and passive-ambivalent (conforming) patterns. The upbringing conducive to these adult personality patterns does not appear to produce psychopathology in childhood. Behavior control methods such as contingent and irregular reward (gregarious) and contingent punishment (conforming), though setting the seeds for the possible development of later impairments, rarely give rise to severe difficulties as long as the child remains within the family. It is in adolescence, when the child's environment markedly changes, that difficulties often arise.

With this brief reference to differences in developmental backgrounds, we next turn to a full discussion of that topic.

## ETIOLOGY AND DEVELOPMENT

We find the same complex of determinants in the cyclophrenic syndrome as we do in its less severe counterparts; the primary differences between them are the intensity, frequency, timing and persistence of pathogenic factors. Cyclophrenics may begin with less adequate constitutional equipment, or be subjected to a series of more adverse early experiences; as a consequence, they may fail to develop an adequate coping style in the first place or decompensate slowly under the weight of repeated and unrelieved difficulties. Most cyclophrenic cases progress sequentially through the basic and borderline patterns before deteriorating to the decompensated level. However, some patients, notably the childhood variants, never appear to "get off the ground," and give evidence of the cyclophrenic pattern from their earliest years.

We shall review next the developmental his-

tory of the four basic personalities that serve as foundations for cyclophrenia; with the exception of minor elaborations relevant to the final stages of decompensation, this review summarizes material already presented on pages 244 to 248, 252 to 256, 281 to 284, 291 to 294 and 320 to 323.

1. The biogenic background of *passive-dependent cyclophrenics* includes a disproportionately high number of bland and unenergetic relatives. A melancholic and threctic infantile reaction pattern is not infrequent, and often gives rise to parental overprotection. Ectomorphic or endomorphic body builds are more common than mesomorphic builds, predisposing deficits both in autonomy and competitive skills. Hypotheses may be proposed regarding various limbic, reticular or adrenal imbalances to account for their apparent lowered activation levels and their vulnerability to fear—both of which may elicit protective and nurtural responses in beneficent environments.

The central psychogenic influence appears to have been parental overprotection, leading to an unusually strong attachment to, and dependency on, a single caretaking figure. The perpetuation of overprotection throughout childhood fostered a lack in the development of autonomous behaviors and a self-image of incompetence and inadequacy. The growing child's own coping style accentuated these weaknesses; by abdicating self-responsibility and by clinging to others, they restricted their opportunities to learn skills for social independence.

In contrast to personalities who stabilize at the milder levels of pathology, future cyclophrenics found themselves frequently rebuffed by those upon whom they depended. The intense separation anxieties that these experiences engendered precipitated behaviors referred to as the cycloid pattern, characterized by mood vacillations, marked self-disparagements and guilt, and frequent psychotic episodes, as illustrated in the following case study.

*CASE 9-7*
*Helen A., Age 32, Married, No Children*

This cycloid woman decompensated over several years into a cyclophrenic pattern following persistent quarrels with her exasperated husband, a man she married in her teens who began to spend weeks away from home in recent years, presumably with another woman. For brief periods, Helen sought to regain her husband's affections, but these efforts were for naught, and she became bitterly resentful, guilt-ridden and self-deprecating. Her erratic mood swings not only increased feelings of psychic disharmony, but further upset efforts to gain her husband's attention and support. As she persisted in vacillating between gloomy despondency, accusatory attacks and clinging behaviors, more of her sources of support were withdrawn, thereby intensifying both separation anxieties and the maladaptive character of her behaviors. The next step, that of a regression to invalidism, was especially easy for her since it was consistent with her lifelong pattern of passive-dependence. Along with it, however, came discomforting feelings of estrangement and the collapse of all self-controls, as evidenced in her ultimate infantile-like behaviors and the total disorganization of her cognitive processes.

2. *Active-dependent cyclophrenics* often have numerous close relatives who exhibit high autonomic reactivity. Other evidence suggesting a biogenic predisposition is hyperresponsivity in early childhood; this temperamental factor not only exposed them to a high degree of sensory stimulation, but tended to elicit more frequent and intense reactions from others. It may be speculated further that neurally dense or low threshold limbic, reticular or adrenal systems underlie their sensory reactivity.

Among the more important psychogenic influences in this syndrome is an unusually varied and enriched sequence of sensory experiences in the first neuropsychological stage that built in a "need" for stimulus diversity and excitement. Parental control by contingent and irregular reward may also have occurred, establishing in these children the habit of feeling personally competent and accepted only if their behaviors were explicitly approved by others. Many of these youngsters were exposed to exhibitionistic and histrionic parental models. Another background contributor may have been exposure to variable and rapidly changing parental and societal values, resulting in an extreme of exteroceptivity, that is, an excessive dependence on external cues for guiding behavior. The emergent pattern of capriciousness and seductiveness in interpersonal relations fostered rather than resolved difficulties. Their emotional shallowness and excessive demands for attention and approval often resulted in a paucity of enduring relationships.

Unable to sustain a consistent external source of nurture and fearful that their capacity to elicit attention and support was waning, these patients began to evidence the cyclical mood swings that are characteristic of the cycloid level of functioning. Persistent shifts between brooding dejection, simulated euphoria and impulsive outbursts of resentment and hostility only resulted in further interpersonal complications and a mounting of separation anxieties. As these self-defeating behaviors and coping efforts failed repeatedly, there was a pervasive decompensation of all personality functions, and a gradual slipping into the more permanent cyclophrenic pattern.

3. The major developmental influence in the *passive-ambivalent cyclophrenic* is likely to have been parental control by contingent punishment and the resulting dread of abandonment lest authority expectations fail to be heeded. This dread may have been compounded by ambiguity in parental strictures; thus, the young, future cyclophrenic, unsure of what is and what is not approved, stood in constant fear of making errors. Many learned to model themselves as closely as they could to approved authority figures; they sacrificed all inclinations toward autonomy and independent action as a means of avoiding parental condemnation. In time, they came to judge themselves as harshly as their parents had done. To protect themselves against reproach, they vigorously repressed their assertive and hostile impulses, kept carefully within conventional guidelines, and even criticized themselves for minor digressions; a strong sense of guilt served as a further protection against error. Their coping strategy proved self-defeating; they became alienated from their own feelings and were unable to act decisively and confidently.

The sequence of decompensation in these patients is well illustrated in the following case study.

### CASE 9-8
### Thomas P., Age 43, Married, Two Children

Thomas, a passive-ambivalent cycloid, had a previous history of several brief depressive episodes, two of which required hospitalization. Shortly before his last institutionalization, he had been fired from his job and abandoned by his wife and children. According to the reports of other relatives, Thomas turned against himself at first. Quite obviously, with the mounting of his objective failures and shortcomings, his insecurity and guilt increased; Thomas felt like a fraud, a worthless creature who could not perform up to the expectations of others. The gloom and hopelessness of his mood was broken, however, by periodic eruptions of previously repressed anger and resentment. With his grip on reality wearing thin, he began to attack his "accusers" viciously, projecting onto them the weaknesses and defects which he felt within himself. In a constant state of tension, his prideful sense of order shattered, his dread of condemnation and rejection turning to reality and his rigid coping systems crumbling bit by bit, he slipped progressively into a state of confusion and invalidism; now his cognitive processes were in total disarray, and he was estranged both from self and reality. In time, left to drift alone in the back wards, he succumbed to the cyclophrenic pattern.

4. *Active-ambivalent cyclophrenics* often display both an irregular infantile reaction pattern and an uneven course of development, thereby increasing the likelihood of inconsistent treatment at the hands of others. Their hyperactivity and irritable affectivity may be hypothesized to be a consequence of various neurological and physiochemical imbalances or dysfunctions.

Primary among psychogenic influences was the role of parental inconsistency in upbringing; as youngsters, these patients are likely to have been exposed to extreme oscillations between smothering or guilt-laden affection on the one hand, and indifference, abuse or castigation on the other. Many were products of schismatic families. In addition to the emotional consequences of these experiences, parents served as models for learning erratic and contradictory behaviors. Such youngsters often were trapped in a "double-bind." Despite their discontent at having been mishandled and deceived, they obtained sufficient affection so as not to forego the hope that matters ultimately would improve.

Patients who decompensated beyond the mild (negativistic) pattern continued to be subjected to marked conflicts and disappointments. These difficulties were fostered by their own sullen and vacillating behaviors. Rarely could they sustain a prolonged harmonious relationship. As a consequence of their negativism and moodiness, they turned away the very affections and support they so desperately needed; this only intensified their erratic and troublesome behaviors. At this point, the cycloid pattern emerged in the form of violent and irrational outbursts of recrimination and revenge; interspersed with these bizarre episodes were periods characterized by severe self-reproaches and redemptive pleas for forgiveness.

Unable to "get hold" of themselves, control their churning resentments and conflicts or elicit even the slightest degree of approval and support from others, guilt-ridden and self-condemnatory, these patients slide from the cyclical episodes of the cycloid pattern into the more permanent abyss of cyclophrenia. Here they linger as invalids, away from the turmoil of reality; disorganized cognitively and estranged from themselves, they sink into the sheltered obscurity of institutional life.

### Childhood Variants

The etiology of both the symbiotic and ambiotic childhood patterns parallel in many respects their adult counterparts, the passive-dependent (submissive) cyclophrenic and the active-ambivalent (negativistic) cyclophrenic. However, the impact of pathogenic constitutional factors and adverse early experiences in these youngsters has been appreciably greater, thereby prompting the emergence of pathology in the first years of life.

1. The *symbiotic* child experienced a morbid parental attachment, producing marked separation anxieties, and a failure to acquire autonomous competencies; the child not only struggled to retain the symbiotic unity of the first developmental stage, but was incapable of functioning alone. Excessive dependency may have had its basis in a constitutional threctic temperament, that is, a biophysically based vulnerability to threat and anxiety. Parents who responded to their youngsters' pathetic fearfulness by coddling and overprotecting them set the stage for learning intense attachments. Furthermore, the constitutional fearfulness of these children disposed them to avoid venturing into the unknown, thereby further reinforcing their dependencies. At some critical period, such as when the child was enrolled in nursery school or when a new sibling was born, the severe nature of this dependency attachment was brought into sharp relief.

No constitutional disposition need have existed, however, for the development of excessive attachment and dependency; parental anxieties and an overprotective style of behavior management may have fostered the same condition. Here, too, the problem often first becomes manifest when the youngster panics at periods of separation or forced independence.

2. In the *ambiotic* child we see a picture of high distractibility, marked negativism, low tolerance for frustration, erratic mood swings and a mixture of demanding and clinging behaviors. Constitutional irregularities in infancy and an uneven sequence of maturation are not uncommon. Central to the impairment, however, was a history of markedly contradictory parental feelings and attitudes. These may have resulted from conflicting behavior styles between parents, as is often the case in schismatic families, or from the ambivalences and cyclical moods of a single parent. Rapid shifting between pampering and hostility, parental signals conducive to the "double-bind," and simultaneous exposure to easily manipulated and hostile caretakers, may have inflicted serious emotional damage and served as pathogenic models for these ambiotic children.

Let us conclude our discussion of this syndrome by noting that few of the mild dependent and ambivalent personalities decompensate into cyclophrenia; only a small number experience such adverse conditions as would lead to childhood symbiosis and ambiosis. The need for approval and the social skills acquired by adult dependent personalities serve as important buffers against their decline; they desire relating to others, display a measure of friendliness if approached by supporting persons and have a history of "good" human relationships which they can recall as a reminder that "life can be worth living." All these factors operate against serious decompensation, and account for their appreciably better prognosis than that of detached patterns.

# PARAPHRENIC PERSONALITY: DECOMPENSATED INDEPENDENT AND AMBIVALENT PATTERNS
(DSM-II: *Schizophrenia, Paranoid Type; Paranoid States*)

The label "paraphrenia" was first used by Kraepelin in 1893 to describe an insidiously developing pathology which he viewed as lying halfway between the paranoid conditions and dementia praecox (schizophrenia); we will discuss the history and logic for this syndrome, as Kraepelin viewed it, in a later section. The term shall be revived in this text since it seems especially appropriate for those cases of markedly severe personality decompensation which have been preceded by a premorbid history of strivings for independence, power and recognition. Paraphrenia parallels both schizophrenia and cyclophrenia in its insidious course of decompensation, and in the pervasiveness and severity of deterioration; it differs from these syndromes in that it applies to cases of paranoid deterioration rather than to cases of schizoid or cycloid deterioration.

As noted earlier, it is customary in current psychiatric practice to apply the label of "schizophrenia" to *all* cases of personality decompensation, regardless of differences in premorbid styles of functioning. This practice, we believe, has been most unfortunate since it unwisely groups widely divergent personalities into a single syndrome, causing endless diagnostic complications. To help resolve these difficulties, we have designated all severely and chronically deteriorated cases "decompensated personality patterns," reserving more specific labels to represent particular types of premorbid coping styles.

### History

In the present formulation, the paranoid and paraphrenic patterns are conceived of as syndromes which are similar in their developmental histories and basic personality orientation, but which differ in their degree of decompensation. A brief history of how previous theoreticians have applied these terms will be useful for purposes of clarifying their similarities and differences and for justifying our revival of the paraphrenic label.

The term "paranoia" can be traced back over 2000 years in medical literature, antedating the writings of Hippocrates. Translated from the Greek it means "to think beside oneself," and was used in ancient times as a general designation for any and all forms of serious mental disturbance. The word disappeared from the medical vocabulary in the second century and was not revived again until the eighteenth century. Heinroth, following the logic of Kantian psychology, utilized the term in 1818 to represent disorders of the intellect. Greisinger drew upon it in 1845 to signify pathological thought processes, and applied it to cases which exhibited persecutory and grandiose delusions. In 1863, Kahlbaum suggested that this label be reserved exclusively for delusional states. Kraepelin further refined its usage in 1893, restricting it to highly systematized and well-contained delusions in patients lacking other signs of a general personality deterioration.

Recognizing that paranoia, as he described it, applied to an extremely small number of cases, Kraepelin adopted a term first used by Guslain in the early nineteenth century, that of "paraphrenia," to signify impairments displaying a mixture of the delusional elements of paranoia and the deterioration features of dementia praecox (schizophrenia). Kraepelin believed that as many as 40 per cent of all patients who exhibited an early pattern of paranoid delusions ultimately deteriorated to dementia praecox, that the bulk of the remainder decompensated to the paraphrenic form and that a very small proportion retained the characteristic nondeterioration of pure paranoia.

From these observations, it would appear that Kraepelin conceived the systematized delusions of paranoia to be a first stage of what might turn out to be a general deterioration process. In the second stage, if it occurs, the patient decompensates to paraphrenia, identified by its bizarre thoughts (irrational delusions) and perceptual distortions (hallucinations); in this stage, Kraepelin specified that many functions of personality, not directly associated with thought and intellect, remain moderately well preserved, e.g., the patient's mood is not chaotic or fragmented, but is consistent with his disordered ideas. However, for many patients, paraphrenia was a transitional second stage that eventuated in a final stage of dementia praecox; in this last stage, all personality functions disintegrated, e.g., the patient's moods now are incongruous or random and are no longer consonant with the delusional content.

In his early writings, Kraepelin referred to totally deteriorated cases of paranoia by the name "dementia paranoides"; however, he subsequently claimed that "when the delusions and . . . emotions . . . may be observed with complete indifference to the natural relations of life . . . [these disorders] are more correctly to be brought under the head of dementia praecox."

In an earlier discussion we took the master synthesist to task for rejecting Kahlbaum's observation that moderately well-preserved cycloid patterns do, on occasion, decompensate; Kraepelin did not make this error, as we see it, with the paranoid patterns. Unfortunately, however, Kraepelin was consistent in one respect; he conceived the end point in this continuum to be that of dementia praecox (schizophrenia). Thus, once again, he categorized together, in one final group, deteriorated personalities with widely divergent developmental histories. As we have said before, a classification that includes all deteriorated personalities would be valid and useful; this grouping is what we have termed the "decompensated personality patterns." But we have contended further that this larger category be subdivided in accord with the premorbid histories and coping strategies which differentiate these patients. Thus, within the decompensated group, we have proposed schizophrenics, cyclophrenics and also paraphrenics.

It is important that we stress the fact that in contrast with his view of the "circular insanities," Kraepelin asserted that delusional states not only vary along a continuum of severity—from paranoia to paraphrenia to dementia praecox—but also often progress from one stage to another.

Kraepelin's use of the term "paraphrenia" is especially significant to our thesis since it represented his recognition that premorbid paranoid tendencies do decompensate to more severe levels; however, in his aspiration to simplify matters, Kraepelin once again assumed that if a final stage of deterioration was reached, the impairment *must* be that of dementia praecox. We are inclined to return to Kraepelin's earlier thinking on this score, suggested by his use of the term "dementia paranoides"; here Kraepelin recognized that the paranoid trend has its own developmental end point, independent of dementia praecox. We shall adopt Kraepelin's "paraphrenic" label rather than "dementia paranoides" for the severely decompensated paranoid states; the selection of this label parallels the terminology used in the severely decompensated states of schizophrenia and cyclophrenia.

### Comparison of the Paraphrenic and Similar Syndromes in the Official Classification

There are several listings in the DSM-II which resemble the paraphrenic syndrome as described in this section. Most relevant are *paranoia, paranoid states* and *schizophrenia, paranoid type*. All three syndromes are distinguished by the presence of persecutory and grandiose delusions. More specifically, the DSM-II description of the *paranoia* category states that "this extremely rare condition is characterized by gradual development of an intricate, complex and elaborate (delusional) system . . . [that] does not seem to interfere with the rest of the patient's thinking and personality." The *paranoid state* is differentiated in the detailed 1952 manual from paranoia by the fact that "it lacks the logical nature of (delusional) systematization . . . yet it does not manifest the bizarre fragmentation and deterioration of the schizophrenic reactions." And finally, the syndrome noted as *schizophrenia, paranoid type* is described in the 1952 manual by its "strong tendency to deterioration, . . . autistic, unrealistic thinking, with mental content composed chiefly of delusions."

In surveying these descriptions, one cannot help but be struck by the observation that the progression from "paranoia" to "paranoid state" to "schizophrenia: paranoid type" reflects, primarily, differences in degree of personality deterioration; all they have in common is the presence of delusions. Thus, in "paranoia" the delusions are highly systematized and the personality is intact; in the "paranoid state" the delusions lack the systematization seen in paranoia but fall short of the fragmentation and deterioration of the schizophrenic paranoid; in the latter, thinking is autistic and unrealistic, and the personality tends to be deteriorated. In effect, the distinctions in the APA Manual relate almost exclusively to degree of personality deterioration.

What appears especially peculiar in this regard, and is viewed as such by many clinicians, is the separation of these three subcategories into two different major syndromes: paranoid conditions and schizophrenia. This bifurcation into two syndromes of what is essentially a matter of degree of a single impairment reflects the persistence of Kraepelin's original notions reviewed earlier. It was inconsistencies such as these which prompted the revisions formulated for this text.

A few words are in order comparing the official syndromes with those proposed here.

The descriptive text associated with "paranoia" indicates that this is an extremely rare condition, and one likely to be found almost exclusively in what we have termed the passive-ambivalent variant of the paranoid personality; intricate delusions, isolated from the mainstream of consciousness, are entirely consistent with the coping style and intrapsychic mechanisms employed by this personality type.

The official description of the "paranoid state" is particularly ambiguous, and it is difficult to find comparisons in our classification schema. The 1952 manual states that the delusional system found in this disturbance is neither systematic nor fragmented, and may be of relatively short duration or persistent and chronic. This lack of descriptive clarity only points up the confusion that is bound to occur when the basis of a syndrome rests on the presence of a single symptom, that of delusions, and has no foundation in more general personality traits. At best, paranoid states may correlate with the disorder we have termed "delusions," to be described in chapter 12; it should be noted, however, that this disorder is associated with specific personality patterns.

The closest approximation to what we have termed paraphrenia may be found in the DSM-II descriptive text of "schizophrenia, paranoid type." However, as noted above, we do not consider the paraphrenic syndrome to be a variant of schizophrenia; rather, it is a parallel and equally decompensated personality pattern. It has its roots in a developmental history of independence strivings and follows the moderately severe paranoid pattern as the last of a series of personality decompensations of the independent coping strategy.

## CLINICAL PICTURE

The contrast in the clinical picture between the paranoid and paraphrenic patterns is more striking than that found between other borderline patterns and their decompensated counterparts. Although the transition is a gradual one, spotted along the way with several "disordered" episodes, the final decompensated state appears to reflect a major transformation. Actually, this is not the case; certain fundamental changes have taken place, of course, but superficial appearances tend to accentuate them. It is this overt and dramatic clinical difference which may, in part, have accounted for Kraepelin's decision to subsume

these cases, which he originally termed "dementia paranoides," under the dementia praecox label.

The air of independence and self-assertion which characterizes so many paranoid personalities is sharply deflated when they succumb to the paraphrenic pattern. In contrast to schizoids and cycloids, who have always appeared more or less ineffectual, weak or vacillating, the paranoid has fostered the image of being cocky, self-assured, willful and dominant; he falls a far distance when he finally topples, and the contrast is quite marked.

Despite these dramatic overt changes, the paraphrenic retains many elements of the basic personality style which characterized his earlier functioning; reference should be made to previous sections, notably pages 262, 268, 279, 289 and 327, for an extensive discussion of these premorbid features.

Though cognitively disorganized, estranged and invalided, the paraphrenic remains defensively on guard against influence, coercion or attachments of any kind. He still is mistrustful and suspicious, ever fearful that those upon whom he now must depend for his survival will be deceitful or injurious. Through the haze of his disorganized thought processes, he still distorts objective reality to fit his delusional "pseudo-community." Not only is he estranged from others, and therefore unable to share a common social perspective, but he continues his habit of actively resisting the other person's viewpoint. And despite the general collapse of his coping strategy, he persists, however feebly, in the struggle to retain his independence and to keep intact the remnants of his shattered self-image.

These traces of the paraphrenic's past assertiveness and self-assurance are submerged, however, in the ineffectualities and confusions of severe decompensation. Where self-determination and independence had characterized earlier behavior, we now observe a pervasive invalidism and dependence on others, an inability to assume responsibility for even the most mundane tasks of self-care and survival. Although cognitive processes were always distorted, delusional and narrow in focus, they possessed intrinsic order and logic to them; now they are fragmented, disjunctive and irrational. Previously, ideas were conveyed in a self-confident and often articulate manner; they now tend to be stated with hesitation and doubt; remarks frequently are tangential, expressed in incoherent phrases or scattered in disjointed flights of fancy. Emotions still retain their quality of veiled hostility but the "fight" is lacking, words of anger seem devoid of feeling and the spark of intense resentment has burned out. Behavior, once dominant, intimidating or contemptuous, has become aversive, secretive and bizarre. The whole complex of paranoid self-assurance and social belligerence has disintegrated, leaving an inner vacancy, a fearful hesitation and a fragmented shadow of the former being.

The role of invalidism in these patients has been hard for them to accept. Their mistrust of others and their lifelong orientation of hard-boiled self-determination make it difficult to accept the weakness and dependence which the role of "hospital patient" imposes upon them. But they have had no choice; their behavior has been grossly disturbing, impossible to tolerate in normal social life. For a few, institutional life is a sanctuary; "illness" may be a convenient rationalization to account for their repeated failures. Others assert that their "forced" hospitalization only proves the correctness of their persecutory delusions; it verifies the inevitable deceit of others, the inescapable resentment the world has always felt toward them. Distorted in this manner, many accept their fate of hospital invalidism and become less contentious and resistive; though still suspicious and easily affronted, they may no longer be as difficult to manage as when they were first committed.

The collapse of their formerly organized cognitive world has several roots. First, as their difficulties mounted, they became increasingly detached from social contact; lost in their own reveries, they had little need to maintain the logic of consensual thinking. They slipped, then, into the inchoate world of dream-like fantasy, with all its disjointed and phantasmagoric elements. In addition, as their formerly prideful self-image collapsed as a consequence of repeated social failures and the painful realities of their increasing dependence, they begin to engage in the destruction of their own cognitive processes; these patients would rather not think about their humiliations and the "shameful" state in which they find themselves. When these painful thoughts intrude into consciousness, they disassemble and twist them into digressive and irrelevant paths, ultimately creating disorganization where cognitive order and clarity previously existed.

Paraphrenics become estranged from self for similar reasons. Always apart from others by choice, they now disengage their thoughts and feelings from themselves. Unable to tolerate their present state of helpless dependency, they reject their own being and often adopt in its stead the identity of others.

There are many similarities in the clinical pictures of paraphrenics and active-detached schizophrenics, a fact which may result in diagnostic difficulties, especially if reference is not made to their different developmental histories. Paraphrenics exhibit many characteristics at this stage of decompensation which have existed throughout the life history of avoidant personalities. They now experience a deep sense of personal humiliation and low self-esteem where pride and high self-esteem existed before; cognitive interference and disjunctiveness have come to the foreground to replace their former clarity and logic; behaviors now are noted by aversiveness in contrast to dominance and directness; there is a growing impoverishment of affect, where once there was intense anger and resentment; and a sense of alienation and depersonalization has taken over from that of social involvement and self-assurance.

Both active-independent paraphrenics and active-detached schizophrenics learned in early life to be mistrustful and suspicious of others. The major difference between them is that the active-independent acquired a sense of self-confidence and learned to "fight back" whereas the active-detached youngster did not. But now that confidence and spirit have been shattered in paraphrenics, they experience in adulthood the same derogation and humiliation of self which was the lot of young, future schizophrenics. Thus, both types have not only been mistrustful of others, but both now lack a feeling of self-worth and self-confidence. Their clinical pictures begin to blend, making discriminations extremely difficult at the symptomatological level.

Because of these difficulties, it is important to differentiate paraphrenic and schizophrenic patients in terms of their developmental histories. Furthermore, from a prognostic point of view, the prospects for paraphrenics, though far from good, are more favorable than those for schizophrenics; they have had moderate success in their past social life and retain some residue of their former feelings of self-worth.

Let us next distinguish the clinical features of each of the four basic personality patterns that often decompensate to paraphrenia.

1. Before their final stage of decompensation, *passive-independent paraphrenics* usually construct delusional self-pictures of illustriousness and omnipotence as a means of countering the painful reality of their failures and embarrassments. But these efforts at narcissistic restitution have not been supported or encouraged; the patient has repeatedly been rebuffed and humiliated. As he progressively disengages himself from

reality, sinking further into a state characterized by autistic fantasy and feelings of futility, his overt behavior begins to lose its former color and his grandiose statements seem vapid, lacking the flavor of self-confidence; his delusional beliefs no longer seem inspired, suggesting that the patient himself may sense their emptiness and invalidity.

Quite typically, these paraphrenics spend endless hours ruminating over memories of a better yesteryear, such as when they experienced realistic adulation and encouragement in childhood. Many revert to child-like behaviors and attitudes, as if hoping that these reversions will revive the good will and commendation of the past. Most no longer act haughty and arrogant; on the contrary, they seem to accept their helpless invalidism and to bask in the care which others provide them; this transformation to a passive receptive role often is baffling to those who previously knew them. "Strange" as these behaviors may seem, they are not inconsistent with the narcissist's former exploitive strategy; moreover, the return to a role in which they benignly accept the good will of others may be an unconscious attempt to resurrect the rewards they experienced in childhood.

2.   Despite their common invalidism, disorganization and estrangement, *active-independent paraphrenics* exhibit a more strained and hostile demeanor than passive-independents. Though repeatedly humiliated and deflated, an undercurrent of suspicion and resentment remains in these patients and pervades their every mood and behavior. Each setback to their aspirations for power and revenge has only reinforced their persecutory delusions, and there is no diminishment in their tendency to project their anger upon others. However, because of their hospital confinement and their growing doubts of omnipotence, these paraphrenics become relatively subdued, usually working out their hostility and desire for retribution through fantasy and hallucination. Unconscious impulses may periodically erupt into bizarre and violent behavior; more often, however, these feelings are directed toward hallucinated images.

The following case portrays this deteriorated pattern.

CASE 9-9
*Joseph M., Age 52, Separated, Four Children*

Joseph lived in foster homes since the age of three months; at 8 years of age he settled with one family, remaining there until he was 15, when he left to go on his own. Eventually enlisting in the Navy, he was given a medical discharge on psychiatric grounds, after three years of service.

As a child, Joseph was known to be a "bully"; he was heavy, muscular, burly in build, had an inexhaustible supply of energy and prided himself on his physical strength and endurance. Though quite intelligent, Joseph was constantly in trouble at school, teasing other children, resisting the directives of teachers and walking out of class whenever he pleased.

Joseph was the foster son of a manager of a coal mine, and spoke with great pride of his capacity, at the age of 12, to outproduce most of the experienced miners. When he was 14, his foster mother died, leaving Joseph alone to take care of himself; his foster father, who lived periodically with a mistress, rarely came home. Joseph worked at the mine and quarreled bitterly with his father for a "fair" wage; when he was 15, he got into one of his "regular fights" with his father and beat him so severely that the man was hospitalized for a month. After this event, Joseph left his home town, wandered aimlessly for two years and enlisted in the Navy. In the service, Joseph drank to excess, "flew off the handle at the drop of a hat" and spent an inordinate amount of time in the brig. The persistence of this behavior and the apparent bizarre features which characterized some of these episodes resulted in his discharge.

For several years thereafter, Joseph appeared to make a reasonable life adjustment. He married, had four sons and started a small trash collecting business. Drinking was entirely eliminated, though Joseph remained a "hot-headed" fellow who happily "took on all comers" to prove his strength.

Greater success —and difficulty— followed when Joseph "took up" with a teen-age girl; this younger woman was quite attractive and built up Joseph's self-image. More importantly, she bore him, illegitimately, what his own wife failed to —a little girl. With mistress and child in hand, he left his legal family, moving some 600 miles to a new city where he "started life again." Within three years, Joseph founded a successful contracting company and became moderately wealthy; at 36, he ran for a local political office, which he won.

Trouble began brewing immediately thereafter. Joseph was unable to compromise in the give-and-take of politics; he insisted at public meetings, to the point of near violence, that his obviously impractical and grandiose plans be adopted. After many outbursts, one of which culminated in the assault of a fellow official, Joseph was asked to resign from office, which he refused to do. To assure his resignation, as he put it, "They dredged up all the dirt they could get to get rid of me"; this included his Navy psychiatric discharge, his abandonment of his legal family, his illicit "marriage," illegitimate child and so on. The final collapse of his world came when his present "wife," in whose name alone his business was registered, rejected him, sold the company and kept all of the proceeds.

Joseph became physically violent following these events, and was taken to a state institution. Here, his well-justified feelings of persecution were elaborated until they lost all semblance of reality. Joseph remained hospitalized for two years during which time he managed gradually to reorient himself, although still retaining his basic, aggressive paranoid pattern. Upon remission, he returned to his legal family, working periodically as a driver of heavy contracting equipment. He began drinking again and got involved in repeated fist fights in local bars. When Joseph came home after a night's drinking, he frequently attempted to assault his wife. To his dismay, his teen-age sons would come to their mother's defense; Joseph invariably was the loser in these battles.

After living with his family for four years, Joseph disappeared, unheard from for about 18 months. Apparently, he had lived alone in a metropolitan city some 90 miles from his home; the family learned of his whereabouts when he was picked up for vagrancy. After he was bailed out, it was clear that Joseph was a beaten and destitute man. He returned to the state hospital where he has since remained. Although subdued and generally cooperative, Joseph is still suspicious, tends to be easily affronted and occasionally flares up in a hostile outburst. He ruminates to himself all day, occasionally speaking in an angry voice to hallucinated images. The decompensation to the paraphrenic level now seems deeply entrenched.

3. The clinical picture of the *passive-ambivalent paraphrenic* is difficult to distinguish from the passive-ambivalent cyclophrenic, discussed earlier in the chapter. Although the basic passive-ambivalent style often splits in separate directions at the borderline level, taking either a cycloid or paranoid form, this divergence terminates as patients decompensate to the markedly severe or decompensated personality level. Basically alike in their personalities from early life, these ambivalent patients took different directions when faced with the threat of separation and abandonment; some asserted their independence, thereby turning in the paranoid direction; others clung to the hope of reestablishing their security through dependence on others, thus turning toward the cycloid pattern. Now, sharing a common fate of failure and personal devastation, they revert to similar decompensated characteristics. The clinical features they exhibit are essentially those of the passive-ambivalent cyclophrenic, noted on page 358. We maintain a distinction at the psychotic level primarily to indicate differences in the developmental course during the borderline, or moderate, stage of personality disintegration.

4. What has just been said about the clinical similarity between passive-ambivalent paraphrenics and their cyclophrenic counterparts is also true of *active-ambivalent paraphrenics* and their cyclophrenic counterparts; reference should be made to page 358 for a description of this clinical picture.

**Comment.** It should be noted that despite differences in their basic personalities, distinctions are difficult to make between the clinical pictures of the various decompensated patterns because their behaviors and moods, under the impact of external and internal pressures, have become appreciably similar. Moreover, the task of sorting patients on the basis of clinical symptomatology alone is complicated by the inevitable intrapatient variability in overt symptomatology. For example, delusions may be dominant in a patient at one time, but hardly noticed at other times. Thus, the only sound basis for differential classification, given overt clinical similarities among groups and intrapatient symptomatological variabilities, rests on the patient's developmental history. These background data should provide the diagnostician with a clear picture of a patient's basic personality pattern; with knowledge of the sources of reinforcement and the instrumental strategies the patient has experienced and habitually employed in the past, the clinician should have a sound foundation for recommending a plan of remedial treatment.

### Childhood Variants

Most paraphrenics deteriorate gradually, typically reaching the psychotic personality level after the age of 30 or 40. There are a small number of children, however, whose background and behaviors are similar in many respects to the active-independent variant of the paranoid and paraphrenic patterns; for the sake of maintaining a parallelism in terminology, we shall label this syndrome as *childhood pariosis*.

The clinical picture of these youngsters is dominated by impulsive and aggressive behaviors. These children, ranging in age from two through adolescence, are usually negativistic, belligerent and defiant; they exhibit little concern regarding the consequences of their behaviors. Most of them seem unable to restrain their hostility or postpone receiving gratification; they reject dependency attachments, seem devoid of fear, are suspicious of others and cleverly manipulative and tend to rationalize and project their socially deviant motives onto others.

The dominant clinical features of these youngsters have often been noted in the literature, usually under the labels of "character" or "behavior disorders." More recently, the Child Psychiatry Committee of the Group for the Advancement of Psychiatry (1966) has listed comparable syndromes under two titles, the "tension-discharge disorder: impulse ridden personality," and the "mistrustful personality"; Fish and Schapiro (1964) provide a somewhat similar picture in their "sociopathic-paranoid" type. The DSM-II provides a new classification that corresponds closely to the principal clinical features of what we have termed "child pariosis." Labeled *unsocialized aggressive reaction of childhood,* the description reads:

This disorder is characterized by overt or covert hostile disobedience, quarrelsomeness, physical and verbal aggressiveness, vengefulness, and destructiveness. Temper tantrums, solitary stealing, lying, and hostile teasing of other children are common.

**Comment.**   As with other childhood variants, there is no direct correlation between the pariotic child and comparable adult types. First of all, it is difficult to place this or any of the previously described childhood patterns at a specified level of severity. For example, different pariotic children will manifest different degrees of impulse control and reality adaptability; similarly, different symbiotic children may exhibit different degrees of overattachment and initiative. It may be useful in this regard to append the level of psychopathological severity to each of these youngsters; for example, "child pariosis: moderate severity." We would suggest limiting these notations to "moderate" and "marked" severity, since mild forms of these impairments may be only temporary affairs, given the relative fluidity of childhood personality.

For the most part, the personality of the child is less firmly fixed than that of adults; thus, not only will children fluctuate more than their older counterparts, but as time progresses, they may "grow out of" their earlier coping pattern. It seems wise, nevertheless, to view as moderately and markedly severe those children whose difficulties are so deviant as to warrant clinical treatment or hospitalization. This view is based on the belief that severe early patterns of pathology tend to be perpetuated and intensified over time; this consequence reflects the likely repetition of injurious parental influences and the child's own self-defeating and "provocative" behaviors. Unless remedial procedures are instituted early, "the twig" will grow in the direction it was "bent."

We might note, as was done earlier, that not all basic pathological personality patterns have counterparts in childhood disturbances. Thus, the child who is exposed to parental overvaluation and indulgence, that is, the passive-independent (narcissistic) child, rarely exhibits severe pathological traits in early life. Although this type of parental management builds a false sense of self-worth in the child, the consequences of having been "spoiled" do not usually reach severe proportions until adolescence or later.

## ETIOLOGY AND DEVELOPMENT

As should be evident from the general thesis presented in the text, the pathogenic determinants that shape the development of the paraphrenic pattern are similar to those found in its less severe counterparts, differing essentially only in their intensity, frequency, timing and persistence. The roots of these difficulties may be traced to a variety of sources: constitutional defects, adverse early experiences, periodically severe or unrelieved stress and so on. Thus, the patient's capacity to cope with his environment may never have been adequately developed, or it may have crumbled under the weight of persistent misfortune.

We shall next summarize the developmental background of the four variants of the paraphrenic personality; this review abbreviates more extensive discussions provided on pages 263, 270, 281, 291 and 332.

1.   An early pattern of parental overvaluation and indulgence is common among *passive-independent paraphrenics.* Many fail to learn interpersonal responsibility, rarely think of the desires and welfare of others and seem markedly deficient in group sharing and social cooperation. Undisciplined by parental controls and given an illusory sense of high self-worth, these youngsters place no reins on their imagination; they tend through excessive self-reinforcement to weave glorious fantasies of their own power and achievements; most of them, however, lack true substance to support their illusions and aspirations. Once beyond the confines of home, their haughty, exploitive, presumptuous and selfish orientation provokes repeated ridicule, humiliation and ostracism by peers. Unwilling to adjust to reality and accept a lowered self-esteem, they begin to withdraw from direct social competition and find consistent gratification in the refuge of fantasy. A vicious circle of rebuff, increased isolation and fantasy develops.

As these patients revert to the coping style characterizing the paranoid level, they harshly reject all forms of dependence, refuse to ally themselves with those whom they view as "inferior," and begin to suspect that others will undo them the first moment they can. Their resentment toward others for failing to appreciate them or to be willing subjects for their narcissistic exploitation comes to the surface in the form of overt anger and vituperation. Unable to gain recognition and humiliated time and again, they reconstruct reality to suit their desires and illusions. As fantasy supplants reality and as their delusions lead them further astray from others, the decompensation process speeds up. The more involved they become within their boundless and undisciplined inner world, the more their thoughts become fluid and disorganized. Repeated experiences of belittlement and censure take their toll; now their reveries are interrupted more and more with thoughts of persecution, dismay and anguish.

The final shameful collapse to the role of hospital invalid is a further blow to their once vaunted self-image. As they become conceptually more disorganized and as they try to deny and destroy the intrusions of their own painful thoughts and memories, they become increasingly estranged from themselves. All that remains is a thin thread connecting the present to memories of a happier yesteryear; these few mementos they hold fast to, turning them over and over again in their thoughts, embellishing and nurturing them, lost in the distant past which now becomes their only reality.

2. The background of the *active-independent paraphrenic* may include a number of biogenic factors. This is suggested by the frequent presence among family members of high levels of activation and energy, irascible choleric temperaments and fearless parmic temperaments. Along these lines, many of these patients as young children exhibited a vigorous aggressive and thick-skinned obtrusiveness; witness the early history of Joseph M. Mesomorphic-endomorphic physical builds are disproportionately frequent, serving to increase the likelihood that assertive and competitive behaviors will be positively reinforcing. Speculations may be made as to the neurological substrate of these tendencies in the limbic and reticular systems.

Many have been exposed to harsh parental treatment. These children apparently learned to counterattack in response to this experience rather than to withdraw into docility; this coping response may reflect the operation of a constitutional parmic temperament or a rapid learning that they possess the power to disrupt others by provocative behaviors or a simple process of imitating parental models. As a consequence of their experiences, these children acquire a deep mistrust of others, a desire for self-determination and a confident sense of competence and autonomy. With this as a base, they frequently reject parental controls and social values, developing in their stead an impulsive, aggressive and often hedonistic style of life.

Experiences such as these frequently arise in broken families and in disorganized subcultural groups. Here, children lack nurtural and consistent parental models, and acquire their outlook on life through contact with equally disillusioned and angry peers; as a consequence, they learn to emulate the "wrong" models; the customs and values of the larger society are viewed as alien, hypocritical and hostile; aggressive "toughness" becomes a necessary style of coping.

The expectations of attack and the chip on the shoulder attitudes of these youngsters provoke new tensions and conflicts, and thereby reactivate old fears and intensify new mistrusts. In decompensated cases, we see either deficiencies in the skill with which aggressive and vindictive strategies were learned or a gradual weakening of them as a result of repeated setbacks, as in the case of Joseph M. Under these conditions, inchoate suspicions of malignment and deceit gradually are transformed into irrational delusions of persecution. Unable to cope directly with the threats that surround them, their tensions either erupt into overt hostile attacks or are resolved in increasingly delusional fantasies. This paranoid stage with its periodic psychotic episodes may disintegrate further.

Unrelieved or severe stress may prompt a marked withdrawal from social contact; the shock and humiliation of hospitalization, the loss of self-determination and the terrifying dependence on others may shatter their fragile underpinnings and the last remnants of their delusional self-image. As they protectively withdraw further, they sink into a primitive and diffuse world of fantasy, unchecked by reality and social controls. The former logic of their delusional system loses its coherence and order; disorganized fantasies blur into objective reality. Hallucinations are projected and cognitive associations are dismembered; bizarre feelings and a sense of barrenness, disorientation and estrangement comes to the fore, as these patients now pass the line into paraphrenic decompensation.

3. With the exception of a divergency in coping aims during the borderline level of decompensation, the developmental history of the *passive-ambivalent paraphrenic* and the passive-ambivalent cyclophrenic is essentially alike; reference should be made in this regard to page 361 since there is no need to repeat this earlier discussion.

The major distinction between these decompensated personalities, as just noted, is that the ambivalent paraphrenic progressed through a paranoid period prior to his final decompensation whereas the ambivalent cyclophrenic followed a cycloid course. During this earlier phase of decompensation, the paraphrenic abandoned his basic ambivalence and shifted in the direction of independence; at this point in his deterioration, he exhibited overt hostility, and his psychotic episodes were marked by delusions of influence and persecution; all traces of dependency needs were denied, and inner conflicts and guilt feelings were projected onto others. As his coping efforts crumbled under repeated adversity, the patient disintegrated to the decompensated personality level; since his effort to assert his independence had failed, he reverted back again to his basic ambivalent personality pattern.

4. The parallel noted above also applies to the developmental course of the *active-ambivalent paraphrenic* and the active-ambivalent cyclophrenic. Again, the major distinction lies in directions taken during the borderline period; reference may be made to page 362 for a brief description of the characteristic background of these patients.

In general, the prognostic picture for paraphrenics is extremely grave; this is true of all four variants. The chronic and pervasive nature of their decompensation augurs a poor future adjustment. However, because of their earlier self-confidence and capacity to draw self-reinforcements, their prognosis is somewhat better than that of schizophrenics. But circumstance has devastated their self-image, leaving but a few remnants of self-esteem in its wake. Moreover, the undercurrent of mistrust and hostility in these patients makes it extremely difficult to establish therapeutic relationships which might alter the course of their illness.

### Childhood Variants

The role played by pathogenic constitutional dispositions or by adverse early experiences is likely to be more severe in the *pariotic* child than in his adult counterparts. As noted in the etiology of active-independent patterns, which pariosis most resembles, many of these children exhibit both choleric and parmic temperaments in early life, traits which readily give rise to parental exasperation and anger. Whatever the initial source, these youngsters are subject to intense parental antagonism in the first two or three years of life. For various reasons which were noted previously, these children do not yield to this harassment, but become contentious, arrogant and belligerent. Not only do they refuse defiantly to "knuckle under," but they even intentionally misbehave, engaging in a variety of conscious maneuvers to provoke and upset others. Their negativism, impulsiveness and deep mistrust of their parents generalize to all interpersonal relations, creating a vicious circle of social tension

and conflict. Many of these youngsters are labeled as "bad" early in life; this stereotype intensifies their resentment and anger, and often serves as an implicit "sanction" for continued arrogance and rebelliousness.

## REMEDIAL APPROACHES IN DECOMPENSATED PERSONALITIES

Most patients are institutionalized when they reach the markedly severe levels of personality decompensation; thus, treatment occurs within a hospital setting. In general, the initial focus of treatment is to relieve the patient of unbearable environmental tensions, rebuild his social skills and prepare him for approaches which may modify the distortions of his personality make-up; only after a modest degree of social rapport and cognitive clarity have occurred can the therapist begin to turn his attention to the attributes of the patient's specific personality pattern. Therapy for decompensated patients may be viewed, then, as a two-stage process. We shall concern ourselves in this section only with the first, that of preparing the groundwork for treatment methods geared to specific personality types.

As noted earlier, three central features characterize all decompensated personality patterns: social invalidism, cognitive disorganization and estrangement. It is these characteristics which are the focus of the first stage of this therapeutic sequence. Let us deal with them in order.

1. The hospital environment serves as an excellent protection against the incursions and stresses of reality; in this setting the patient is safe from further onslaught and anguish. But the supportive character of the hospital milieu may itself become a pathogenic influence. Specifically, the patient may be encouraged to slip into obscurity and relinquish whatever social skills he previously may have possessed; in other words, institutional life may foster a growth in *social invalidism*. Thus, although the important role that the hospital serves as a refuge must be granted, it should not blind us to the deleterious consequences of custodial overprotectiveness, social inactivity, personal idleness and physical vegetation.

Toward the end of countering these consequences, and for the purpose of rebuilding social competencies and motivations, it is advisable to encourage patients to participate in a variety of "normal life" activities, such as vocational therapy and social recreation. Involvement in even the simplest and most menial productive tasks will help forestall further regression to total invalidism and perhaps stimulate some growth toward feelings of adequacy and self-worth. Similarly, structured ward programs, group projects, attendance at social affairs, visits with congenial relatives and repeated contact with volunteers from outside the hospital will help to prevent the deterioration of social skills and possibly aid in learning new ones. Keeping in touch with the realities of normal productive and social life is a prerequisite to further therapy and an essential phase in the early handling of decompensated personalities.

2. The *cognitive disorganization* of these patients is extremely difficult to break through, and it may require months of laborious therapy to rebuild clearer and more orderly thinking. The therapist must pick up the patient's "symbolism" and trend of thought and grasp the elusive and jumbled threads of his communications. By listening carefully and responding in a "connected" yet logical manner, the therapist may help the patient to a more socially meaningful and disciplined way of thinking. Until some measure of cognitive control is established, and until a degree of consensual meaning replaces the patient's inchoate and confused communications, it will be almost impossible to utilize more focused therapeutic approaches.

3. The reestablishment of reality contact and the rebuilding of a sense of personal identity and self-worth are the two principal goals to counter the patient's *estrangement*. Attainment of these goals rests, first, on the development of trust between patient and therapist. Many hours of untiring perseverance, usually at a low key, are required before these patients will gain enough faith in their therapist to dare face the world of reality again. Having been humiliated, anguished and abandoned so often, the patient has learned to insulate himself; he has every reason to move cautiously before relating to others. The therapist must feel genuine respect for his patient; a sincere desire to be of assistance is needed to help carry the therapist through the long, slow and not too promising process of treatment. Should trust and a cognitively clear line of communication be developed, the therapist will have established the foundation for further progress.

Now feeling less estranged from others, the patient has taken the first step in learning to feel less estranged from himself. As the patient's cognitive processes take on greater clarity, and as his feelings of trust develop further, the therapist can begin to rebuild the patient's sense of self-worth. At this point, sufficient inroads have been made into the decompensation process itself so that the therapist may direct his attention to the specific features of the patient's personality and background. The therapist is no longer primarily concerned with the general state of the patient's decompensation; he can shift now to those features which distinguish his patient's lifelong attitudes and styles of coping, that is, his specific personality pattern.

We need not go into the problems and procedures of this second stage of therapy with decompensated personalities; the details and focus of this work have been discussed in previous "remedial approach" sections presented in conjunction with the mild and moderate personality patterns.

# TERMINAL PERSONALITY: PROFOUNDLY DECOMPENSATED PATTERN

It may be inappropriate to speak of this last and most decompensated state of psychopathology as a personality pattern since the syndrome represents the total disintegration of functions that normally comprise what we speak of as personality. These long-term and profoundly deteriorated patients are seen in every mental institution; some sit mutely on benches, vegetating and transfixed, attired in drab or peculiar garb; others wander aimlessly, seem unaware of the presence of other people and stare vacantly into space, absorbed in nothingness; occasionally they grimace or stop in a corner, rocking to and fro.

There is little in the recent literature or in the DSM-II to separate these more advanced states from those we have termed decompensated patterns. Kraepelin noted several end stages of dementia praecox, differentiating the last two of the series, "silly dementia" and "apathetic dementia," as terminal points. More recently, Menninger (1963) spoke of a "fifth order of dyscontrol" in the decompensation process; here the patient regresses to an irreversible impairment, exhibiting not even the feeblest and most ineffectual survival efforts.

## CLINICAL PICTURE

Distinctions cannot readily be made between the decompensated and terminal patterns since these lie on a gradient of severity; not only do they shade imperceptibly into one another, but there is enough intrapatient variability in the clinical picture to make clear-cut discriminations practically impossible. The essential distinction we seek to draw may be largely academic, yet there is reason to think that it may have its practical implications.

Basically, we would categorize as decompensated those who we believe exhibit signs which give promise, albeit small, that they can be rehabilitated. In contrast, in those we shall call the terminal pattern, the prognosis appears totally hopeless. These patients have been immersed in their disintegrated state for so long that their previous social habits and attitudes have largely been extinguished; they have deteriorated into a state of permanent invalidism. All efforts at self-care and self-determination have long since been relinquished, and the patient now seems devoid of any but the most rudimentary competencies necessary for survival. At this stage of decompensation, the fabric of former personality structures has completely decayed.

It is important to note that not all decompensated patterns deteriorate further over time, neither is there a simple one to one relationship between duration of illness and severity of deterioration. Many patients of longstanding chronicity not only adjust to the hospital routine, but assume a variety of simple tasks which help to deter further disintegration. Though they are social invalids according to any standard of normal behavior and responsibility, they perform these hospital chores with a reasonable measure of adequacy, e.g., changing their beds, eating without supervision or assistance, lining up to await medication and so on.

Among other features which may enable us to distinguish decompensated from terminal patterns is the persistence among the former of their distinctive premorbid attributes and coping styles. For example, decompensated patients tend to hallucinate actively and retain their "pet" delusional beliefs, characteristics which terminal patients rarely possess. Although the decompensated patient's distorted cognitive ideas and idiosyncratic behaviors indicate the severity of his illness, the continued presence of these "personal" processes signifies the preservation of some remnants of his former personality style. In contrast, carry overs from the past, in the form of "personal" delusions and behaviors, are "burned out" in the terminal patient; there is now a vegetable-like colorlessness, a loss of all those subtle features of thought and action which distinguished their former style of functioning. Some deteriorated cases continue to exhibit minor and peculiar habits and occasional bizarre acts, but these seem random and aimless, unrelated to their preterminal personality patterns. All terminal patients display, in common, a flat and insipid uniformity; those who were once identifiable as schizophrenics, cyclophrenics and paraphrenics now converge into a single, undifferentiated class.

## ETIOLOGY AND DEVELOPMENT

The downward spiral to deterioration occurs only after a prolonged period of hospitalization; prior to ultimate disintegration, each patient passes through one of the three decompensated patterns. There is no need, therefore, to review the long history of events which preceded this terminal stage; it simply picks up where the decompensated stage leaves off.

It will be instructive to separate the influences which contribute to the terminal stage of decay into those which arise from external as contrasted to internal sources, that is, those which derive from the conditions of hospitalization as opposed to those which stem from the patient's own thoughts and behaviors.

### Conditions of Hospitalization

Among the experiences of hospitalization which foster further deterioration are those of *social isolation* and *dependency training;* both of these are usually consequences of poor therapeutic planning or understaffed hospital management.

**Social Isolation.** Patients who are cut off from social contact, who are segregated or neglected and who are allowed to drift into the bleak back wards of institutions, without opportunities to communicate with fellow patients, staff and relatives, are bound to deteriorate with the passage of time. Long periods of social confinement not only perpetuate, but intensify deficits in cognitive organization and social skills; ultimately, under these stimulus deprivations, the patient loses whatever competencies he may have had as a participant of social life.

**Dependency Training.** At the other extreme, and perhaps no less damaging, is an excess in custodial care, a tendency to "overprotect" and coddle the patient. Though the decompensated patient is a "mental" invalid, he will not be helped to regain normal skills and responsibilities if he is exposed to a regime of inadvertent dependency training. Extreme devotion to the welfare of the patient may be of great value in many respects, but it may do him an ultimate disservice. Patients who are guided unwisely to relinquish their former interests and activities or to restrict themselves to the directives and suggestions provided by hospital personnel, may learn to lean too much on others and not enough on themselves. Under prolonged guidance and care of this kind, they may undergo a progressive impoverishment of competencies and self-motivations, resulting ultimately in a total lack of interest and an utter helplessness. In short, many decompensated patients are reinforced to learn dependency and apathy as a consequence of the "good care" to which they were exposed.

### Patient Behavior

Two factors which stem directly from the patient's own behavior foster further personality deterioration: *protective insulation* and *self-abandonment*.

**Protective Insulation.** It is not only through neglect and mismanagement that patients experience a decrease in social contact. To protect themselves from painful humiliation and rejection, decompensated patients learn to withdraw from reality and to disengage themselves from social give and take. Thus, even though they may be exposed to active and inviting hospital programs, many patients are reluctant to participate, preferring to keep to themselves. The consequences are no different for them than for those who are isolated by neglectful management. Without the controls and support of interpersonal relations, these patients recede further into a social stagnancy and become increasingly impoverished and deteriorated.

**Self-Abandonment.** The progressively decompensating patient cuts off his relationships not only with others but with himself as well.

Fantasy may have been an early refuge for many patients, but few of them gain consistent gratification from this source. As was noted in earlier discussions, the content of these fantasies turns too often into preoccupations with past misfortune and injustice. More importantly, the patient may find that he cannot escape the futility and anguish of being who he is. To protect himself from self-inflicted misery, he must destroy his thoughts, cluttering, blocking and disarranging his memories and feelings, and thus contributing to the cognitive disorganization that

characterizes the decompensated level. Confused and disoriented as he may be, however, the patient still senses the irrational and bizarre elements of his behavior. Try as he may to divert his awareness or to disorient himself, he cannot escape "being" what he is. Nothing less than a total divorce and abandonment of self will do. Humiliated and terror stricken, he jettisons himself and disavows his existence. In contrast to less severe personality patterns, the terminal patient accepts the calm and death-like emptiness that takes hold; depersonalization becomes a welcome relief, a permanent escape from being himself. He has "chosen" nothingness; he has disgorged his very being, with all of its turmoil and anguish.

In the following sequence we have recorded the responses of a terminal patient, 42 years of age, hospitalized for 17 years. Throughout the interview he stared blankly at a wall, his face turned away from the therapist. His voice was flat, hesitant and subdued; the therapist spoke quietly and in a gentle manner.

THER.: Could you tell me how you feel today?

PT.: Nothing . . . empty.

THER.: Do you remember your name? (repeated)

PT.: (No response)

THER.: What name did your parents call you when you were a child?

PT.: None . . . I'm not.

THER.: Who are you, then?

PT.: Nothing, no man, nobody.

THER.: What do you feel when you feel? (repeated)

PT.: Better dead . . . everything empty . . . nobody, nothing.

THER.: Is there someone here in the room with you? (repeated)

PT.: (long pause) You move.

THER.: Do you understand what I say when I speak to you? (repeated)

PT.: Everything is nothing . . . cold machines . . . dry . . . cardboard.

THER.: Do you feel that I want to help you? (repeated)

PT.: (long pause) Deadness . . . cold machines . . . cardboard . . . nothing better.

# CONCLUDING COMMENTS AND SUMMARY

In this chapter we complete our detailed coverage of the major types of *personality* psychopathology. These deeply etched and pervasive impairments have been given prominence since we believe that the study of personality and its development is basic to understanding all forms of psychopathology. This view contrasts with traditional texts which focus on the "symptom disorders," and then work backward, attempting to trace the patient's personality. Not only do we believe that the symptom disorders, to be discussed in the next two chapters, are merely caricatures and logical outgrowths of basic personality patterns, but we contend that personality pathology should be the foundation and primary focus of clinical study.

Let us summarize the central points provided in chapters 8 and 9 before progressing to our discussion of "disorders" in chapters 10 and 11.

1. A central theme both of text and chapter is the continuity and progressive character of pathological personality development. Moderately and markedly severe patterns of pathology are decompensated states that develop from several of the basic or mildly pathological personalities described in chapters 6 and 7; the traits which these patients exhibit are no less pervasive and integral a part of their make-up than those of the mild pathological patterns. Rooted in constitutional dispositions and progressively refined as a function of repetitive experiences, their personality becomes a distinctive and well-crystallized way of functioning in the environment; furthermore, each of these personality patterns perpetuates itself and evokes reactions which reinforce its continuance.

2. As far as etiology is concerned, the principal difference between the less and more severe patterns is the intensity, frequency, timing and persistence of essentially identical pathogenic influences. Thus, advanced states may arise as a consequence of initially more pernicious constitutional dispositions, notably more adverse early experiences or persistent and unrelieved later difficulties. These determinants interact in a complex and circular feedback system, producing an intricate sequence of "causes" that defy analytical simplification. Although the etiological hypotheses that have been proposed in these last two chapters must be viewed as speculative, they are consistent with current clinical research.

3. The diagnostic syndrome "borderline," discussed in chapter 8, has been a stepchild in the psychopathological literature; its use in the past has usually reflected a clinician's hesitation as to whether his patient is or is not severely ill. We have suggested that the concept of borderline be viewed neither as a wastebasket for diagnostic indecision nor merely as a way station between normality and total disintegration. Rather, we have conceived it as a crystallized, habitual and often enduring pathological personality pattern; although lying midway on a gradient of severity, it is sufficiently distinct from both the mildly (basic personality) and the markedly severe (decompensated personality) patterns to justify separate classification.

a. Two features distinguish the moderately pathological or borderline pattern from the basic or mildly pathological pattern. The first, noted as *deficit social competence,* refers to the erratic personal history of these patients and their failure to attain a level of social achievement commensurate with their natural aptitudes and talents. Faulty starts and repeated mishaps characterize their educational, vocational and marital life. In contrast to mildly pathological types, who progress and achieve a modicum of socially recognized success, borderline patients create endless complications for themselves and experience the same setbacks time and again. Despite these failures, however, they manage to "pull themselves together, and make a go of it again"; this contrasts to the fate of decompensated patterns where there has been a more uniform downhill progression, eventuating in total social invalidism.

The second distinguishing feature of borderline patients consists of *periodic but reversible psychotic episodes.* These patients experience severe transient disorders characterized by a loss of reality contact and by cognitive and emotional dyscontrol. These psychotic eruptions occur with notable frequency, in contrast to mild patterns where they arise only rarely. The reversibility of these episodes differentiates the disorders of the borderline from those of the decompensated pattern; in the borderline patient, the break from reality is brief and transitory whereas in the decompensated personality it is prolonged and often permanent.

b. Whether a function of constitutional or experiential factors, or both, borderline patients develop a less integrated and effective coping pattern than their milder personality counterparts. Since their strategies are less adequate and their stability more tenuous, they are especially vulnerable to the normal strains of interpersonal relationships. Caught in their own adap-

### Table 9-1   Summary of Borderline Pathological Patterns

| | SCHIZOID | CYCLOID | PARANOID |
|---|---|---|---|
| **CLINICAL PICTURE** | | | |
| Common Features: | 1. Deficit Social Competence | 2. Periodic but Reversible Psychotic Episodes | |
| Distinctive Features: | Depersonalization anxiety, cognitive autism and disjunctiveness, deficient social behaviors and impoverished affect. | Separation anxiety, cognitive conflict and guilt, mood and behavior vacillation. | Attachment anxiety, cognitive suspicions and delusions, defensive vigilance and veiled hostility. |
| **ETIOLOGY AND DEVELOPMENT** | Detached personality patterns. | Dependent and ambivalent personality patterns. | Independent and ambivalent personality patterns. |
| **COPING AIMS** | Countering depersonalization, deflecting overstimulation. | Countering separation, releasing tension, redemption through self-derogation. | Countering attachment, discharging hostility, reconstructing reality. |

tive inflexibilities and in their persistent tendency to foster new difficulties and self-defeating vicious circles, they experience constant upset of their equilibrium, and they are subject to frequent eruptions of uncontrollable thoughts and impulses. Once these emotions are discharged, these patients regain a modicum of homeostatic balance, until such time as tensions again mount beyond manageable proportions.

    c.   Three borderline patterns were distinguished; they parallel, in somewhat less discriminable form, the eight basic personality patterns described in chapters 6 and 7. The *schizoid* is a moderately severe variant of the detached pattern; the *cycloid* follows a moderately disintegrated, dependent or ambivalent orientation; and the *paranoid* is a moderately ill personality pattern characterized by an independent or ambivalent strategy. A detailed review of their clinical features, etiology and development, coping aims and remedial therapy was presented. These are briefly summarized in Table 9-1.

    4.   Decompensated personality patterns are deeply rooted, pervasive and relatively enduring states which require institutional care and treatment. They are distinguished from psychotic "disorders" by the breadth and persistence of their personality deterioration. Although psychotic disorders are of equal severity, they tend to be of relatively brief duration, are usually confined to a relatively limited sphere of functioning (e.g., mood, thought or behavior) and do not result in a general deterioration of the established pattern of personality; these disorders occur with notable frequency in borderline personalities, and with less frequency in the mild patterns.

    a.   Three clinical features may be noted in common among the decompensated patterns.

First, there is a marked *developmental immaturity or social invalidism*. Some patients appear to be "fixated," that is, their development has been arrested prior to full social maturity. For various reasons they do not acquire a repertoire of mature social skills; they fall increasingly behind their age-mates and tend to deteriorate relatively early in life. Other patients have achieved some measure of social competence during their lives, but under the weight of unrelieved stress, they begin to "regress," that is, revert to a more immature level of competence than they previously displayed; this process is termed invalidism.

The second feature distinguishing these patients is *cognitive disorganization;* this is noted by illogical, disjointed and fragmented thinking which gives rise to obscure communications, seemingly random or irrelevant flights of fancy and unsystematized delusions and hallucinations.

Feelings of *estrangement* comprise the third cardinal feature. Invalidism and cognitive disorganization combine to produce feelings of utter self-worthlessness and a sense of inner disorder and "nothingness." Under these conditions, the patients begin to view the world as alien, as a strange and mechanical nightmare of shapes and movements. Looking inward, they feel themselves to be disembodied shells, foreign and depersonalized objects that are unconnected to their thoughts and "being."

    b.   Deterioration in the decompensated pattern has the same biogenic and psychogenic roots as those found in less severe pathological personalities; these influences simply have been more injurious and persistent. Not infrequently, the more permanent decompensated pattern follows what might have been a transitory psychotic episode. For various reasons, not the least of which is poor hospital management and unreceptive family conditions, these patients remain institutionalized, only to disintegrate progressively into a more pervasive and enduring pathological state. Increasingly isolated from normal social affairs and gaining the habits and reinforcements of hospital invalidism, they begin to give up their struggle for a meaningful existence and allow themselves to deteriorate into the emptiness of permanent decompensation.

c. Three subvarieties of the decompensated pattern were discussed; they parallel the three borderline personalities. *Schizophrenia* is a markedly decompensated variant of the detached pattern, progressing downward from the schizoid personality; these patients often exhibit markedly severe clinical signs by the end of the second decade of life. *Cyclophrenia* represents the severely deteriorated dependent and ambivalent patterns and follows, in order, the less decompensated cycloid personality; there are appreciably fewer cyclophrenics than schizophrenics, and their decline generally occurs in the third and fourth decades. *Paraphrenia* refers to the markedly impaired independent and ambivalent personalities, and is a more severe variant of the moderately ill paranoid pattern; though more common in frequency than cyclophrenia, they occur less often than schizophrenia; this affliction arises most typically in the fourth and fifth decades.

Although these three decompensated patterns share as dominant features the cardinal signs noted earlier, they continue to exhibit, although somewhat less clearly and regularly, traces of their former, more distinctive, personality styles. Differential classification is difficult at this stage, however, and depends in large measure on the study of developmental histories.

d. A profoundly decompensated pattern, labeled the *terminal personality*, was briefly discussed. These patients have been immersed in their chronic state for so long that they seem devoid of any but the most rudimentary competencies for survival.

e. A comparison was made between the classification system provided in this chapter and that listed in the official DSM-II; points of similarity and difference were noted.

The historical roots of the official nosology were traced; a review of the writings of Kahlbaum and Kraepelin suggested that the system of syndromes presented in this chapter may be more consistent with their thinking than is the current official classification.

f. Childhood variants of personality pathology were briefly described; these were seen to parallel five of the eight basic personality patterns. *Infantile autism,* an established syndrome, correlates with passive-detachment (asocial); *infantile threctism,* proposed for the first time in this text, may be regarded as similar to the active-detached (avoidant) pattern; *childhood symbiosis,* also well known in the literature, corresponds to passive-dependence (submissive); *childhood ambiosis,* a new label for a previously described disturbance, has as its counterpart the active-ambivalent (negativistic) personality; and *childhood pariosis,* another new designation for a frequently reported syndrome, is related to the active-independent (aggressive) pattern.

5. Let us conclude by paraphrasing what was said in the summary of chapters 6 and 7.

All classification systems are composed of prototypes, that is, a set of models based on characteristics that are felt to be central to the understanding of certain types of cases; the system of personality syndromes formulated in this and previous chapters are "textbook" prototypes of this nature. Although all schemas tend to create a "false image" of logic, consistency and clarity, given the true variety and complexity of psychopathology, they may serve as useful tools to guide the analysis of real cases. But we must keep in mind that despite the fact that a system may "make sense" and be consonant with the theoretical, clinical and research literature, it *does* oversimplify the intricacies of personality development and the diversity of clinical symptomatology. It is hoped, nevertheless, that as a heuristic instrument, the classification system proposed in this text will better expedite the objectives of diagnosis, treatment and research than does the current official schema. Let us next proceed to the "disorder" syndromes.

# Chapter 10

# SYMPTOM DISORDERS

## I: Anxiety and Neurotic Disorders

Edvard Munch—*The Shriek* (1896). (Courtesy, The Museum of Modern Art, New York.)

## INTRODUCTION

It is a well-accepted assumption in science that the past can be related in a deterministic way to the present; unless he makes this assumption, no scientist can justify his pursuit for order and coherence in the empirical world. Psychopathologists follow this premise in their belief that a patient's present pathology can be traced logically and systematically to prior conditions, such as his initial constitutional disposition and the environmental experiences to which he was exposed. We have attempted to elucidate the particulars of this belief in previous chapters by hypothesizing relationships between specific types of influences and specific forms of clinical symptomatology. Though it is often difficult to trace the role of these influences in individual cases, it seems reasonable to expect in general that the presence of a lifelong biological temperament or of constant exposure to selectively reinforcing experiences would shape a distinctive and relatively stable personality pattern.

The learning of personality styles and behaviors is not a random process; unintentional and unplanned as most experiences may be, these events do not produce a hodgepodge of behaviors and attitudes. Rather, they forge a unified body of distinctive, generalized and stable traits. For example, the intrinsic biological make-up of an individual serves as a steady unifying force that gives a consistent coloration to the varied experiences of life. Furthermore, the events to which the child is exposed tend to be uniform and highly repetitive, giving rise to the acquisition of distinctive and deeply ingrained attitudes and behaviors. To these cohering influences may be added the self-perpetuating character of human behavior, that is, the tendency to revive or create experiences which duplicate those of the past. Thus, the features which begin to define the personality of childhood tend to become more sharply honed and distinctive as time progresses; by reciprocal interaction and circular influence, these early characteristics unfold progressively into a deeply ingrained, widely pervasive and notably characteristic pattern of personality. As described in the previous chapters, these patterns differ in their coping strategies and in the adequacy with which they succeed in dealing with the strains of life. Chapters 6 through 9 described pathological syndromes that represent the operation of these deeply ingrained personality patterns. As we have said, these patterns serve as the cornerstone for understanding a wide variety of forms of psychopathology.

Any classification system can go awry if its categories encompass too wide a range of clinical

378

conditions. There is need, therefore, to subdivide these broader categories in terms of notably discriminable features. This is done largely for practical clinical purposes since distinctions may be drawn among basically similar patients that will facilitate clinical functions; thus, to obliterate these distinctions is unwise because it results in the overlooking of useful clinical data.

For these and other reasons we shall next outline and describe what have been termed the "symptom disorders." As noted earlier, these are usually dramatic signs which stand out in sharp relief against the more prosaic background of everyday personality functioning.

To be consistent with our thesis that the patient's personality is the foundation for understanding his pathology, we shall relate these disorders to the major personality patterns described in previous chapters. Disorder syndromes are to be viewed, then, as extensions or disruptions in the patient's characteristic coping style; they are anchored to the patient's past history, and take on significance and meaning largely in that context. They are in contrast to the "behavior reactions," to be described in chapter 12, which are isolated and dramatic symptoms that crop up in otherwise normal personalities and which are largely unrelated to their general coping style. To clarify distinctions among the major types of pathological syndromes described in this text, it will next be useful to differentiate more sharply than before the "symptom disorders" from both the "personality patterns" and "behavior reactions."

## THE PROCESS-REACTIVE CONTINUUM

In an earlier chapter we referred to a growing body of literature dealing with what is known as "process and reactive schizophrenia"; a particularly fine summary and analysis of this work may be found in a paper by Garmezy (1968).

Starting with Bleuler, who rejected Kraepelin's thesis that the prognosis of schizophrenia was invariably poor, writers have increasingly referred to two prognostic pictures among these patients, dichotomizing them into "process" and "reactive" groups. *Process* schizophrenics are characterized by their poor prognosis; according to recent theorists, they exhibit an insidious course of development, and their illness stems from a biogenic source. The second or *reactive* group has a favorable prognosis; their illness has an acute onset, that is, their symptomatology comes on suddenly, and in response usually to conditions of psychogenic stress.

There is much to be said for the notion of process versus reactive schizophrenia; the goal of differentiating patients with similar overt symptomatologies is a worthy one, especially if these distinctions eliminate earlier confusions and facilitate a variety of clinical functions. Despite the useful purposes for which the process-reactive distinction was designed, it is based on certain faulty assumptions which may in the long run prove a disservice to clinical theory and practice. Let us note some of these objections, as well as some constructive alternatives.

### Dichotomy Versus Continuum

The process-reactive distinction was initially formulated as a dichotomy; patients were seen to fall into either "good" or "poor" prognostic categories. This dichotomy, however, is not only inconsistent with the more typical continuum found among psychological variables, but runs counter to clinical observation and research evidence. For example, clinicians find that patients fall on a gradient rather than into a dichotomy of prognostic promise; and recent research indicates substantial overlapping on many other significant variables between so-called process and reactive groups. In short, the facts justify abandoning the view that the process-reactive dimension is a dichotomy.

More consistent with clinical and research findings is that process and reactive groups represent prototypes at opposite extremes of a prognostic continuum; those at the "process" extreme evidence poor prognoses whereas those at the "reactive" extreme possess good prognoses. Between these polarities are impairments that vary in degrees of prognostic promise. As with the distinctions we drew previously between mild, moderate and marked severity, these intermediary prognostic degrees shade imperceptibly into one another; thus, no sharp line can be drawn to distinguish cases, as was implied in the original process-reactive dichotomy.

### Etiology Versus Embedment

It is held by many that the process-reactive dichotomy reflects different etiologies; the process group ostensibly is founded on biogenic factors whereas the reactive group is based primarily on psychogenic ones. Two points may be noted in this regard. First, there is no empirical evidence that cases with poor prognoses (process group) invariably have biogenic etiologies. Second, the assumption that reactive cases stem from psychogenic sources is largely a tautology, that is, patients are usually categorized as "reactive" in the first place because a clear psychogenic precipitant preceded their impairment, not because biogenic variables have been shown to be irrelevant or because their prognoses were found in fact to be good. Let us elaborate these comments.

It is well known that different etiologies may produce similar symptoms and prognoses. For example, the etiology of ingrained pathological personality patterns, which frequently have poor prognoses, may be either biogenic or psychogenic or more likely than not, both. There is no a priori reason for believing that cases with poor prognoses must be founded on a biogenic source; nothing in clinical theory precludes the possibility that psychogenic influences can produce impairments with unfavorable clinical prospects. Furthermore, there is no consistent body of research data to the effect that prognostically poor cases are exclusively the consequence of biogenic causes; to the contrary, ample evidence exists to indicate the central role of psychogenic factors in many of these cases. Although the presence of marked constitutional defects may dispose an individual to severe psychopathology, it seems evident that comparable consequences can stem from injurious environmental experiences. Until unequivocal data are gathered to the contrary, it would seem best to assume that "process," that is, slowly decompensating states may arise as a product of either biogenic or psychogenic determinants or both.

There is an important and valid idea that appears to be cloaked in the erroneous etiological distinction between process and reactive types. Rather than speak of biogenesis versus psychogenesis, it may be more fruitful to speak of pervasive and deeply ingrained characteristics that are resistant to extinction on the one hand versus more peripheral and circumscribed symptoms that may readily be extinguished on the other. In other words, the distinction that process-reactive theorists may be groping for is the degree of embedment of psychopathological traits. Conceived in this way, patients in the process group exhibit poor prognoses because their symptoms represent pervasive and deeply embedded personality traits; patients in the reactive group, in contrast, may have good prognoses because the symptoms they exhibit reflect more delimited or less deeply embedded characteristics.

The distinction we have suggested in the spread, permanence and strength of pathological traits need not be viewed as falling into a simple dichotomy, but rather as lying on a continuum, as noted above. Seen in this light, the process group corresponds essentially to our conception of "personality patterns"; here, a variety of different etiological histories give rise to pervasive and deeply rooted psychopathological traits. The reactive group, similar to what we shall term "behavior reaction" syndromes, to be discussed in chapter 12, represents behaviors that are narrowly delimited, minimally rooted and only slightly resistant to extinction. Along this gradient of embedment and between the two "pattern" and "reaction" extremes, are pathological syndromes which reflect events that have given rise to moderately embedded and moderately resistant symptoms. These clinical syndromes shall be termed "symptom disorders"; they are anchored in part to certain pervasive and deeply embedded personality traits, and in part to more transitory or circumscribed situational conditions.

### Generality of the Process-Reactive Continuum

The original formulation of the process-reactive distinction sought to account for differences in the prognosis of schizophrenic patients. It is clear, however, that the features and significance of the process-reactive concept, as redefined in the two previous sections, apply to *all* forms of psychopathology. Every type of impairment may usefully be characterized in terms of its prognosis, pervasiveness, embedment and degree of resistance to change.

According to our earlier discussions, all personality patterns, schizophrenic or not, would be seen as pervasive and embedded, and therefore have relatively poor prognoses. In contrast, behavior reactions should have good prognoses since these symptoms are either clearly circumscribed or minimally embedded in permanent personality traits.

With the preceding comments as a basis, we might conclude that all forms of psychopathology lie on a continuum of embedment, pervasiveness, resistance to extinction and prognosis. The deeply embedded and pervasive behaviors of the *personality patterns* are likely to persist, essentially unmodified, unless the entire fabric of the individual's style of functioning is reconstructed. Since *behavior reactions* are either narrowly delimited or weakly anchored in the individual's make-up, they can readily be uprooted by exposure to proper extinction procedures. *Symptom disorders* are characterized by well-delineated clinical features, such as are found in behavior reactions, but they also are anchored to embedded personality traits; their prognosis, therefore, falls somewhere between those of the patterns and the reactions. The manifest symptomatology of these disorders may be removed, given careful environmental management or exposure to proper extinction procedures; however, more complex therapeutic measures will be needed to rework the more basic personality traits to which they are rooted.

Let us next turn to other general features of the symptom disorders, contrasting them specifically with personality patterns and behavior reactions.

## DIFFERENCES BETWEEN SYMPTOM DISORDERS AND PERSONALITY PATTERNS

The behaviors and strategies which characterize personality patterns persist as permanent features of the individual's way of life and seem to have an inner momentum and autonomy of their own; they continue to exhibit themselves with or without external precipitants. In contrast, symptom disorders arise as a reaction to stressful external precipitants, tend to be transient, that is, of brief duration and subside or disappear shortly after these conditions are removed; we have chosen the label "disorder" to signify the fact that these symptoms occur when the patient's basic personality pattern has been upset.

The clinical features of the personality pattern are highly complex, varied and widely generalized, with many attitudes and habits exhibited only in subtle and indirect ways. In contrast, behaviors which characterize the symptom disorders tend to be isolated and dramatic, often simplifying, accentuating and caricaturing the more prosaic features of the patient's personality style; they stand out in sharp relief against the background of the patient's more enduring and typical mode of functioning.

The characteristic traits of the personality pattern "feel right" to the patient; they seem to be part and parcel of his make-up; the term *ego-syntonic* has been used to convey this sense of comfort, naturalness and suitability with which the patient experiences his traits. In contrast, symptom disorders often are experienced as *ego-dystonic*, that is, discrepant, irrational and uncomfortable to the patient; the behaviors, thoughts and feelings which denote his disorder seem strange and alien not only to others but to the patient himself; he often feels extreme anguish, as if he were caught or driven by forces beyond his control.

As far as therapy is concerned, personality patterns frequently require prolonged and extensive intrapsychic techniques because of their deep embedment and pervasive generality and the unconscious and automatic character in which these traits are expressed. In contrast, symptom disorders tend to be precipitated by external conditions which the patient is often aware of and wishes relief from. Moreover, the disordered patient's motivation to get rid of his "dystonic" and narrowly delimited symptom works hand in hand with highly focused therapeutic methods, resulting in the relative ease, speed and high frequency of symptom extinction.

## DIFFERENCES BETWEEN SYMPTOM DISORDERS AND BEHAVIOR REACTIONS

The symptoms of "behavior reactions" tend to be stimulus-specific, that is, linked primarily to external conditions; they are isolated behaviors, largely separated from the general pattern of personality functioning and elicited only in response to particular stimulus precipitants. Although "symptom disorders" are also prompted by external events, they are rooted in addition to the complex pattern of the individual's personality traits; these generalized traits intrude upon and complicate what otherwise might be a simple response to an external precipitant.

Behavior reactions tend to be durable and unvarying, displaying themselves in a uniform and consistent way each time the external precipitant occurs. This is not the case with symptom disorders. The clinical picture of disorders is contaminated not only by secondary symptoms, but entirely different symptoms may emerge and become dominant over time. At any one point, several subsidiary symptoms may covary simultaneously with the dominant symptom, e.g., in "phobic" cases one may find in addition to the phobia a mixture of depressive, obsessive and psychophysiological features. Moreover, the dominant symptom may subside and be replaced by previously unseen symptoms. This fluidity in the clinical picture of symptom disorders can be attributed to intrusions stemming from the patient's basic personality; as the varied and diverse elements of his habitual coping strategies become involved, waxing and waning over time, different symptoms may emerge and subside. Behavior reactions do not display these complications and fluidities since complicating personality processes do not intrude upon them.

Behavior reactions are not only simple and uncontaminated, but they tend to be understandable and appropriate, given the nature of the external precipitant. Symptom disorders, in contrast, are often irrational, overdriven and "symbolic"; they seem unnecessarily complicated and intricate and appear to bring surplus elements to bear on minimally troublesome situations. The reason, again, is the intrusion of deeply rooted attitudes and strategies.

Among these inner sources of aggravation are perceptual hypersensitivities and tendencies to over-react to events that only slightly duplicate disturbing conditions of the past. Because of the pervasive character of the disordered patient's personality pathology, a wide array of tangentially related feelings and memories are reactivated and unleashed in response to these "duplicates" of the past. More importantly, these inner forces over-ride present realities and become the primary stimulus to which the patient responds. His symptomatic behavior, then, is less a function of present precipitants than of the past associations they evoke. It is this primacy of the reactivated past which gives the disordered patient's symptomatic picture much of its irrational and symbolic quality; the bizarre or "hidden meaning" of his response can be understood if it is seen in terms of these "inner stimulus" intrusions.

In addition to eruptions of past memories and emotions, the patient's response is distorted in accord with habitual instrumental patterns. The behaviors which the patient exhibits are "rational and appropriate," *if* seen in terms of the emotions and memories that have been stirred up; however, they are quite bizarre and illogical if they are seen in terms of objective reality. In short, the patient's "symbolic" symptoms represent the direct consequences of intrusions of the past, and the complicated strategies the patient employed to deal with these past experiences. These behavioral and intrapsychic convolutions contrast markedly with the relatively direct and simple responses that characterize "behavior reactions."

In this chapter and the following one, we shall organize the symptom disorders into five general groups. These syndromes represent the varied ways in which pathological personalities respond to situations that threaten their tenuous equilibrium.

The first syndrome, the *anxiety disorders,* occurs in all personality patterns either as an initial response to unanticipated and moderately severe threat or as a disturbance following their inability to identify or cope with persistent threat.

The second group, the *neurotic disorders,* represents different ways of handling threat by the use of various intrapsychic mechanisms; these methods are employed most often by dependent, ambivalent and active-detached personalities; they attempt to resolve their tensions and hostilities internally, that is, without eliciting social reproval. Both anxiety and neurotic disorders will be described in this chapter.

*Psychophysiological disorders* comprise the third general syndrome to be discussed; these symptom disorders are found most commonly among ambivalent personalities; here, the patient's opposing inclinations and conflicts can find neither internal resolution nor external expression; tensions remain bound up within the individual and continue to churn away physiologically.

*Sociopathic disorders* comprise the fourth category; although these disorders arise in all personalities, they are most characteristic of independent personalities who have learned to handle threats and impulses by acting out; valuing reinforcement from themselves more highly than from others, they turn readily against the outside world to vent their feelings and are consequently drawn into social conflict and irresponsibility.

The last and markedly severe group of symptom syndromes is composed of the *psychotic disorders;* these disorders erupt in all personality patterns; they represent either extreme and bizarre attempts to cope with threat and anxiety or a collapse in the patient's coping efforts. Psychophysiological, sociopathic and psychotic disorders will be described in the next chapter.

# ANXIETY DISORDERS
(DSM-II: *Anxiety Neurosis*)

Among the most unpleasant yet common experiences is anxiety. Discomforting though it may be, anxiety plays a central role in the adaptive repertoire of all organisms; as a signal of danger, it mobilizes the individual's coping reaction to threat.

Anxiety is involved in all forms of psychopathology, either as a symptomatic expression of psychological tension or as a stimulant to adaptive coping. Because of its universality, however, we

must restrict the usage of the term to conditions in which extreme apprehension and diffuse emotional tension are dominant features of the clinical picture.

In the "anxiety disorders," as we shall describe them, the utility of anxiety as an alerting signal has been destroyed; the anxious patient is unable to locate the source of his apprehension; he experiences such unbearable distress as a consequence that his coping efforts become disorganized rather than organized. Thus, once anxieties are aroused, they continue to mount; unable to identify a reason for his fearful expectations, his anxiety generalizes and attaches itself to incidental events and objects in his environment. In this way, anxiety not only is disruptive in its own right, but it plants the seeds for its own perpetuation and growth.

The DSM-II, under the label *anxiety neurosis,* provides a succinct description of the syndrome as follows:

. . . anxious over-concern extending to panic and frequently associated with somatic symptoms . . . may occur under any circumstances and is not restricted to specific situations or objects. This disorder must be distinguished from normal apprehension or fear, which occurs in realistically dangerous situations.

We have begun our discussion of the "disorders" with anxiety since most of the other symptom syndromes are pathological maneuvers that patients utilize to control or diminish the experience of anxiety. In the other disorders, patients utilize devious and often complicated coping mechanisms to maintain their psychological cohesion against the disorganizing effects of anxiety. Should their defensive operations be deficient or without adequate compensatory measures, apprehension and tension will ensue.

We should note at the outset that marked anxiety occurs at two stages in the coping process: at the beginning and at the end.

In the early phase, we see anxiety as an initial reaction to impending threat; for most individuals, the precipitant subsides and they return to normal functioning. However, should the source of anxiety persist, the individual will learn to cope with it in whichever way he finds possible and expedient; these early ways of handling anxiety often turn out to be the precursors of later pathological personality patterns. Depending on the severity and persistence of the stress they face, and the coping methods which are available for them to learn, people may acquire either healthy adaptive strategies or pathologically maladaptive ones. Since chapters 6 and 7 have already dealt with the various pathological ways in which people learn to cope with threat, we need not discuss them further.

Our attention in this section will be directed to those cases of anxiety which arise *after* the individual has developed his adaptive coping pattern, that is, when his established and habitual style has been disrupted and disorganized. Here, sources of inner tension and anxiety that previously had been under control are released and rush to the surface. It is these cases of coping disorganization for which we reserve the term "anxiety disorder."

## CLINICAL PICTURE

The elements of which anxiety is composed are diverse and numerous, lending themselves to varied definitions and measures. Some clinicians focus on the subjective or *phenomenological* elements of the anxiety experience (reported feelings of diffuse fears and panic). Others concentrate on more objective *behavioral* signs (tremulousness, fidgeting and restless pacing). A third group attends to and defines the disorder with reference to its *biophysical* concomitants (excessive perspiration and rapid heart rate). The fourth group of clinicians prefers to represent anxiety in terms of repressed *intrapsychic* impulses that disrupt the individual's coping controls (upsurge of erotic and aggressive id instincts). Clearly, the concept of anxiety is not a singular dimension that can easily be pinpointed. Before we survey each of the four major levels of anxiety, it may be useful to differentiate three general forms in which anxiety is expressed; these distinctions reflect differences in the duration and intensity of the anxiety experience.

**Chronic Anxiety.** This is the most common of the anxiety disorders, characterized by prolonged periods of moderately intense and widely generalized apprehension and strain. The coping patterns of these patients are barely adequate to the challenges and impulses they must handle. Thus, they always seem on edge, unable to relax, easily startled, tense, worrisome, irritable, excessively preoccupied with fears and calamities and prone to nightmares and insomnia, have poor appetites and suffer undue fatigue and minor, but discomforting, physical ailments. Many patients learn to "adjust" to their chronic state, but their lives tend to be unnecessarily limited and impoverished, restricted by the need to curtail their activities and relationships to those few which they can manage with relative comfort.

**Acute Anxiety.** Brief eruptions of extreme and uncontrollable emotion often occur in patients who suffer a chronic state of anxiety. For varied reasons, traceable to some basic personality sensitivity or coping inadequacy, the patient feels a sense of impending disaster; he feels that he is disintegrating and powerless against forces which surge from within him. These feelings often climax a period of mounting distress in which a series of objectively trivial events were viewed as devastating and crushing; at some point, the patient's unconscious fears and impulses are reactivated, breaking through his crumbling controls and resulting in a dramatic upsurge and discharge of emotions. As the attack approaches its culmination, the patient's breathing quickens, his heart races, he perspires profusely and feels faint, numb, nauseous, chilly and weak. After a brief period, lasting from a few minutes to one or two hours, the vague sense of terror and its frightening sensations subside, and the patient returns to his more characteristic level of composure.

**Panic.** Here there is a sweeping disorganization and an overwhelming feeling of terror; the patient's controls completely disintegrate, and he is carried away by a rush of irrational impulse and bizarre thought, often culminating in wild sprees of chaotic behavior, violent outbursts of hostility, terrifying hallucinations, suicidal acts and so on. These extreme behaviors are similar but briefer forms of the psychotic state of "fragmentation"; panic, however, refers to transitory states of severe anxiety and decompensation which terminate after a few hours, or at most after one or two days, following which the patient regains his "normal" equilibrium. Should these shattering eruptions linger or recur frequently and their bizarre behaviors and terrifying anxieties persist, it would be proper to categorize the impairment as a psychotic disorder, notably that of "fragmentation," to be discussed in the next chapter.

Let us next turn to a more systematic analysis of the clinical signs of these disorders.

### Behavior

The overt actions of the anxious patient are easily observed. Most appear fidgety and restless, tend to pace excessively, engage in random movements, squirm in their seats and are jumpy, on edge, irritable and distractible. Others are overcontrolled, strained, muscularly tight; they bite their lips and exhibit minor hand tremors, facial tics or peculiar grimaces. The tone of their voice may be tremulous and denoted by rapid shifts in tempo and loudness; speech may be voluble and hurried one time, and quavering, blocked, distracted and paralyzed the next, as if extreme efforts at control have waxed and waned in their effectiveness.

### Biophysical Factors

Individual patterns of somatic discomfort differ widely, but in anxiety most of these symptoms reflect sympathetic system hyperactivity. Cardiovascular signs predominate in many patients; they experience chest pains, palpitations, increased blood pressure, throbbing sensations, undue perspiration and heat flashes. Among other visceral complaints are gastrointestinal symptoms such as nausea, vomiting, cramps, gas pains and diarrhea. In other patients, a constriction of the musculature prevails; here we see signs of body tightness with occasional spasms, a shortness of breath, tension headaches, wry necks and so on. A generalized picture of fatigue and exhaustion is a common residual of daily tension, and is often compounded by restless sleeping and insomnia.

### Phenomenological Reports

Apprehension is the most notable symptom reported by these patients; there is a vague and diffuse awareness that something dreadful is imminent, an experience compounded by the fact that they do not know what they dread and from where the danger may arise. This feeling of impending disaster periodically reaches intense proportions, as in the acute and panic forms of anxiety.

Apprehension and fear of the unknown distract the patient from matters of normal daily routine; he often complains of his inability to concentrate and is unable to maintain interest in previously pleasurable activities and pursuits. No matter what he does, he cannot avoid this pervasive and interminable apprehension. He finds himself unable to distinguish the safe from the unsafe, the relevant from the irrelevant; he is increasingly forgetful and irritable, and begins to view minor responsibilities as momentous and insurmountable tasks. His distress really begins to mount when he becomes self-conscious of his growing incompetence and tension. As this self-awareness increases, it becomes a preoccupation. Observing himself, he experiences tremors, palpitations, muscular tightness, "butterflies in the stomach," cold sweats, a feeling of foreboding and dreadful signs of imminent collapse. The fright of self-awareness not only perpetuates itself in a vicious circle, but feeds on itself and builds to monumental proportions. Unless he is able to distract and divert his attention, his controls give way or feel torn apart; there is an upsurge of unconscious fears and images which flood to the surface, further overwhelming the patient; at this point, we see an acute anxiety attack or panic.

### Intrapsychic Processes

Although anxiety is experienced by all individuals, why do pathological personality patterns experience it more frequently and severely than normal personalities?

To answer this question fully, we must turn to an analysis of the role of unconscious phenomena, that is, phenomena learned as a function of experience, but which now are either so automatic or repressed that they operate "beneath" the level of awareness.

Coping strategies are essentially automatic and beyond awareness; in pathological personalities they are characterized further either by being deficient or by their adaptive inflexibility. Furthermore, pathological types possess unconscious hypersensitivities to duplicates of their painful past. These coping inadequacies and reaction sensitivities contribute to the chronic, tenuous stability of these patients. If we extrapolate from these three characteristics—coping deficits, reaction sensitivities and tenuous stability—we may better understand why pathological personalities are disposed to anxiety disorders.

*First,* since the coping strategies of these personalities are deficient or inflexible, they cannot mobilize themselves effectively to handle a wide range of objective environmental threats. Unable to shield themselves adequately from many diverse sources of conflict and tension, the patient must keep up his guard, ever alert to dangers which may upset him; as a consequence, he may remain in a constant or chronic state of tension.

*Second,* the residues of past experiences, which comprise much of the unconscious, oversensitize him to situations that objectively are insignificant. Because he is generally unaware of the operation of these unconscious sensitivities, he finds himself unable to grasp the reason or source for his frequent apprehension. He knows only that his distress is grossly disproportionate to reality conditions; he does not know that the basis for his response is to be found in the derivatives of the past, now stirred up by objectively trivial events.

*Third,* once reactivated, these unconscious residuals upset the patient's tenuous controls; moreover, they in turn stimulate other emotions and impulses with which they were formerly associated. Thus, the individual not only feels a flood of seemingly unwarranted tension and fear, but he also experiences a variety of other strange and unreasonable emotions such as hostility and guilt. Several of these experiences are evident in the following brief sketch.

### CASE 10-1
### Simon B., Age 27, Unmarried

This chronically anxious young man began to experience, for no apparent reason, a mixture of intense anger and sexual impulses each morning as he entered the elevator that took him up to his office. The upsurge of these confusing emotions added a new dimension to his general state of anxiety. Not only was Simon unable to fathom

their sources, but being unable to identify them he could not counteract them; what was especially distressing about these unwarranted urges was the fear that they would provoke severe condemnation from others. Although he did not know from where these feelings arose, he did know that these surging impulses of rage and lust would destroy his tenuous personal and social stability. Simon's anxiety was compounded then by the very real consequences he could anticipate should these impulses find expression.

In the chronic anxious state, these bizarre thoughts and emotions churn close to the surface, but manage to be kept under control. If these feelings overpower the patient's tenuous controls, we will observe either an acute or a panic attack. These attacks often exhibit a mixture of terror and fury. In the less severe acute attack, there is more terror than fury; violent and lascivious urges are partially controlled or neutralized in these eruptions. In panic, however, these unconscious impulses rise to the foreground and account for the bizarre and turbulent picture seen during these episodes.

Although there is a marked loss of control during acute and panic episodes, these eruptions often serve as a useful safety valve. By discharging otherwise hidden and pent-up feelings, the patient's tensions may subside temporarily, and he may be able to relax for a while. For a fleeting moment, he has vented unconscious emotions and engaged in acts which he dares not express in the normal course of events; chaotic and destructive as they appear and as they basically are, these temporary "flings" serve a minor adaptive function.

Some patients adaptively utilize their chronic moderate tensions as a source of surplus energy. These individuals may be characterized by their seeming indefatigability, their capacity to "drive" themselves tirelessly toward achievement and success. There are others, however, who draw upon their tension surplus to intrude and disrupt the lives of their friends and families; they often become persistent and troublesome social irritants. Whether and how these tensions will be exploited depend on the basic personality pattern of the patient.

### PERSONALITY DISPOSITIONS

As was noted before, the label "anxiety disorder" is reserved for anxiety states found in pathological personality patterns; the term "fear reaction," to be described in chapter 12, refers to similar states arising in essentially normal individuals. The primary distinction between these two impairments is that the fear reaction is stimulus-specific, anchored to an observable and circumscribed object or event whereas the anxiety disorder is unanchored, free floating and precipitated by unobservable and essentially unconscious memories or impulses. Thus, in pathological personalities, minor and objectively insignificant precipitants not only reactivate past memories and emotions, but stir up and unleash a variety of associated secondary thoughts and impulses. These unconscious residuals of the past surge forward and become the primary stimulus that threatens the stability of the pathological personality, giving rise, then, to diffuse and acute states of anxiety.

Of course, no sharp line distinguishes normal from pathological personalities, but the differences in the pervasiveness and intensity of their respective painful past experiences make it less likely that normal personalities will subjectively perceive threat or have disruptive past feelings reactivated by the presence of real threat. Relatively free of these distortions and eruptions, normal persons rely on reality as the primary stimulus of the reaction; as a consequence, their responses are less diffuse and unanchored than those of pathological patterns. Since the concept of fear connotes a response made to external conditions of danger, we will reserve the term "fear reaction" for syndromes which correspond accordingly. In contrast, the term anxiety connotes a free-floating or objectless apprehension without apparent or tangible cause; in the "anxiety disorders," these causes are hidden, traceable to complicated and unconscious derivatives of the past.

What are the *specific* causes of anxiety in pathological personalities?

As we have said, objective precipitants play a secondary role to those which exist internally. It is the patient's anticipatory reaction sensitivities which dispose him to disorder; he transforms innocuous elements of reality so that they are duplicates of his past; and, as in a vicious circle, this distorted perception stirs up a wide range of associated past anxieties and reactions. To specify the source of anxiety, then, we must look not so much to the objective conditions of reality, though these may in fact exist, as to the deeply rooted personality sensitivities of the patient.

The task of identifying these sensitivities is a highly speculative one since no one can specify with assurance exactly what goes on in the unconscious. The best we can do is to make intelligent guesses as to which attitudes in each of the major personality types are likely to give rise to their anxiety proneness; this we shall attempt to provide in the following paragraphs.

It should be evident by now that there is no single "cause" for anxiety disorders, even in

patients with similar personality patterns; moreover, not only do anxiety precipitants differ from patient to patient, but different sensitivities may take precedence from time to time within a single patient. Let us proceed with this caution in mind.

1. *Passive-detached personalities* (asocial and schizoid) are characterized by their flat and colorless style; intense emotions are rarely exhibited, and states of chronic anxiety are almost never found. Two diametrically opposite sets of circumstances, however, may prompt a flareup of acute anxiety or panic: excess stimulation or marked understimulation. As was noted in chapter 8, schizoids may "explode" when they feel encroached upon or when they sense that they are being surrounded by oppressive social demands and responsibilities. Similar anxiety-provoking consequences follow from marked understimulation; here, the patient experiences feelings of depersonalization, a frightening sense of emptiness and nothingness, a state of self-nonexistence, stagnation, barrenness and unreality.

2. *Active-detached personalities* (avoidant and schizoid) may be precipitated into anxiety as a consequence of depersonalization and encroachment, in the same manner as their passive-detached counterparts. But, in addition, their histories have made them hypersensitive to social derogation and humiliation. They have acquired a marked distrust of others, but lack the self-esteem to retaliate against insult and derision. When repeated deprecations occur, reactivating past humiliations and resentments, these patients cannot respond or fear responding as they would like; their frustration and tension may mount, finally erupting into acute anxiety or panic. The following case, which might best be labeled "Schizoid Personality, active-detached type: Anxiety Disorder," points up a number of these elements.

*CASE 10-2*
*Gerald Y., Age 31, Unmarried*

This man, employed as a clerk in a large office, normally performed his work in a quiet and unobtrusive manner, keeping to himself and rarely speaking to anyone except to return a "hello" to a passing greeting. Every several weeks or so, Gerald would be found in the morning at his office to be sitting and "quaking" in a small back room, unable to calm himself or to describe why he felt as he did. Upon repeated probing, it was usually possible to trace his anxiety to some incidental slight he experienced at the hands of another employee the day before.

3. *Passive-dependent personalities* (submissive and cycloid) are extremely vulnerable to separation anxieties. Having placed their eggs in

someone else's basket, they have exposed themselves to conditions that are ripe for chronic anxieties; they may now experience the everpresent worry that they will be forsaken, abandoned by their sole benefactor and left to their own meager devices. Another potent factor, often giving rise to an acute anxiety attack, is the anticipation and dread of new responsibilities; their deep sense of personal inadequacy and the fear that new burdens may tax their limited competencies, thereby bringing forth disapproval and rejection from others, often precipitate a dramatic change from a calm and relaxed state to one of marked anxiety. Some of these features are illustrated in the following case, properly classified as "Submissive Personality: Anxiety Disorder."

### CASE 10-3
### Joanne L., Age 22, Unmarried

Joanne was to be married shortly; she had been overprotected throughout her life and felt generally ill-equipped to assume the various roles of a housewife. Her fiancé was a strong-willed man some 20 years her senior whose wife had died several months earlier. Joanne was advised to see a therapist for premarital counseling; it was clear, however, that her presenting problem was that of an anxiety disorder.

In recent weeks Joanne was unable to sleep and woke up frightened, tense and crying. She would sit at home in her favorite chair, anxious and fretful, preoccupied with a variety of "strange" thoughts, notably that her fiancé would die before the date of their planned marriage. She noticed that her hands trembled; she felt nauseated much of the time and had heart palpitations, feelings of dizziness and irregularities in her menstrual cycle. These symptoms began about ten days after her fiancé asked her to marry him, which she quickly agreed to do on the advice of her parents.

After several sessions, Joanne began to see that her anxiety was founded on her fear of leaving the protective security of her family and her dread that she might not be able to perform her new responsibilities in accord with her fiancé's expectations. As she gained some insight into the roots of her present state, and with adequate assurances of affection and support from her fiancé, Joanne's anxieties abated.

It should be noted that anxiety in these patients often serves as a means of evoking nurtural and supporting responses from others; in addition, it may become an instrumental ploy by which they can avoid the discomforting responsibilities of autonomy and independence.

4. *Active-dependent personalities* (gregarious and cycloid) are vulnerable to separation anxiety only to a slightly less extent than passive-dependents; however, the specific conditions which precipitate these feelings are quite different. Gregarious personalities promote their own separation anxieties by their tendency to seek diverse sources of support and changing sources of stimulation; they quickly get "bored" with old attachments and excitements. As a consequence, they frequently find themselves alone, stranded for extended periods with no one to lean on and nothing to be occupied with. During these "empty" times they are "at loose ends" and experience a marked restlessness and anxiety until some new excitement or attraction draws their interest. These patients experience genuine anxiety during these vacant periods, but they tend to overdramatize their distress as a means of soliciting attention and support; the use of anxiety histrionics as an instrumental tool of attention-getting is most notable in these patients.

5. *Passive-independent personalities* (narcissistic and paranoid) characteristically do not exhibit anxiety disorders; however, anxiety may be manifested for a brief period before these patients cloak or otherwise handle the expression of these feelings. The image of "weakness" conveyed in the display of this symptom is anathema to these persons; thus, it is rarely allowed to be expressed overtly, tending to be neutralized or contaminated by other symptoms.

The precipitants of anxiety in these patients usually relate to such matters as failures to manipulate and exploit others, or the growing disparity between their illusions of superiority and the facts of reality. Although they are not accustomed to inhibit emotions and impulses, their anxiety is manifested not in pure form but in an alloy of anxious hostility and resentment, as illustrated in the following brief history.

### CASE 10-4
### Alan P., Age 34, Unmarried

This narcissistic man was recently berated, and his work disparaged, by his employer. In previous years, discomforting events such as these were ameliorated by his adulating mother who assured him of the "stupidity" of others and, by contrast, his "brilliance and ability." Unfortunately, Alan's mother passed away several months prior to this work incident. Unable to replenish his self-esteem, Alan's feelings of anxiety began to mount. However, rather than admit his faults or "show" his inner tension, Alan began to criticize his boss to others in an agitated, bitter and deprecating tone.

6. *Active-independent personalities* (aggressive and paranoid) may experience appreciably greater and more frequent anxiety than their passive counterparts. The dread of attachment, of being controlled, punished and con-

demned by others is much more intense, and events which reactivate these memories evoke strong mixtures of anxiety and hostility. Severe attacks of panic will occur if the patient feels particularly powerless or at the mercy of the hostile forces he sees about him; we might note that the perception of these sources of influence and persecution, particularly in the paranoid, is often hallucinatory, that is, projections upon the environment of his own aggressive and vindictive impulses. Also notable is the fact that, in contrast to the "free-floating" anxiety found in most other personality patterns, these patients quickly find an external source to ascribe their inner discomfort to.

Chronic forms of anxiety are rarely seen in pure form in these patients; more commonly, the surplus tension and energy generated by anxiety are transformed and utilized to spur vigorous self-assertive action. Much of the drive and aggressiveness which characterize these patients reflect the exploitation of anxious energy in the service of their instrumental coping strategies.

We should be reminded that many, though not all, active-independents possess what we have termed the parmic temperament, that is, a constitutionally based fearlessness or insensitivity to threat. However, despite their relative imperviousness to anxiety, they are "human," and therefore do experience discomforting tensions. Nevertheless, their constitutional callousness decreases the probability of an anxiety disorder.

7. *Passive-ambivalent personalities* (conforming, cycloid and paranoid), along with their active-ambivalent counterparts, are, of all pathological patterns, the most frequent candidates for anxiety disorders. First, they experience a pervasive dread of social condemnation; every act or thought which may digress from the straight and narrow path is subject to the fear of punitive reactions from external authority. Second, this dread is compounded by their deeply repressed hostile impulses, which threaten to erupt and overwhelm their controls; without these controls, the tenuous social facade and psychic cohesion they have struggled to maintain may be torn apart at the seams. Thus, ever concerned that they will fail to fulfill the demands of authority, and constantly on edge lest their contrary inner impulses break out of control for others to see, these patients often live in a constant state of anxiety.

As will be recalled from chapter 7, the pervasive and chronic presence of this tension state was noted as a major feature of the personality of these patients; anxiety is so pervasive a part of their everyday functioning that one cannot say where personality ends and the anxiety symptom begins.

Many of these patients learn to utilize the excess energy they derive from their chronic hypertension to effective ends; the characteristic diligence and conscientiousness of the passive-ambivalent reflects, in large measure, the control and exploitation of anxious energy. However, should their tense and overcontrolled state be punctured, either by external precipitants or by an upsurge of disruptive internal impulses, there is a high probability that a manifest acute attack or panic will ensue.

8. *Active-ambivalent personalities* (negativist, cycloid and paranoid) experience frequent and prolonged states of anxiety. In contrast to their passive counterparts, however, their discomfort and tension are exhibited openly and are utilized rather commonly as a means either of upsetting others or of soliciting their attention and nurture; which of these two instrumental functions takes precedence depends on whether the dependent or the independent facet of their ambivalence comes to the foreground.

Typically, these patients color their apprehensions with depressive complaints, usually to the effect that others misunderstand them and that life has been full of disappointments. These complaints crystallize and vent their diffuse tensions and at the same time are subtle forms of expressing intense angers and resentments. Most commonly, these patients discharge their tensions in small and frequent doses, thereby decreasing the likelihood of a cumulative build up and massive outbursts; it is only when they are unable to discharge their hostile impulses or experience threatening separation, that these patients may be precipitated into a full-blown anxiety attack. Having learned to utilize anxiety as an instrument of subtle aggression or as a means of gaining attention and nurture, they often complain of anxiety for manipulative purposes, even when they do not genuinely feel it.

## REMEDIAL APPROACHES

Patients suffering from anxiety disorder typically seek therapy for the sole purpose of relieving their distressing symptom. Should this be the primary goal, sufficient in itself to reestablish the patient's disordered equilibrium, the therapist may focus his efforts appropriately, utilizing a variety of symptomatic treatment methods. Most prominent among these are the psychopharmacological tranquilizing agents. In conjunction with these, especially where objective precipitants are present, the therapist may engage in environmental manipulation, advising about, where feasible, the changing of jobs, taking of vacations, moving and so on. In addition, directive procedures of behavioral and phenomenological therapy may be especially effective as a means of modifying anxiety-producing attitudes; these techniques often achieve this goal in a relatively brief treatment course.

Should any of the aforementioned measures of symptom removal prove successful, the patient is likely to lose his incentive for further therapy; there is no reason to pursue treatment if the patient seems content, and experiences no secondary complications. However, should the patient desire to explore the "deeper" roots of his

disorder, or should symptom removal efforts have failed, it may be advisable to embark on the more extensive and probing techniques of intrapsychic therapy. Attention is directed here not to the relief of symptoms or to teaching the patient to accept and utilize his anxiety; rather, the task is to uncover the residuals of the past which have sensitized the patient to anxiety, and then to resolve or reconstruct these memories and feelings. This task often proves to be extremely difficult; not only may the patient be disinclined to relinquish his pathological defenses against anxiety, but the therapist must proceed with great caution, lest he release more of these feelings than the patient can tolerate; panic attacks and psychotic disorders are not an uncommon consequence of probing and releasing too much, too fast.

# NEUROTIC DISORDERS
## (DSM-II: *Neuroses*)

As an introduction and perspective for the various subtypes of neurotic disorder, it will be instructive to provide a brief history of theories concerning the concept of neurosis; some points which distinguish these disorders from other pathological states; the coping functions fulfilled by neurotic behaviors; and a rationale for the personality patterns that are disposed to develop these symptoms.

### HISTORY AND THEORIES

The term neurosis was first introduced in medical literature in 1781 by William Cullen; since then it has had a varied history, recently becoming a colloquial term for any and all forms of disagreeable, infantile or irrational behavior that falls short of a clear-cut psychosis. We will discuss the history of specific subvariants of this disorder in later sections, tracing for the moment the evolution only of the general concept itself.

1. As will be recalled from chapter 1, Charcot, the eminent French neurologist, began his seminal investigation of the age-old symptom termed "hysteria" in the last quarter of the nineteenth century; since the days of Hippocrates this impairment was viewed as a physical paralysis, somehow related to the emotions and found exclusively among women. Charcot knew, however, that hysterical symptoms occurred in men; more significantly, he discovered that these symptoms often shifted rather capriciously, could be

produced or removed through hypnosis and frequently made no sense when viewed in terms of known anatomical structures. It became clear to him that something other than a traumatic and direct nerve injury was involved. However, Charcot concluded, despite these facts, but true to his neurological orientation, that these patients had a degenerative nervous disease which disposed them both to hypnosis and to the shifting symptoms of hysteria.

Two of Charcot's students, Janet and Freud, picked up the threads of this puzzling disorder, evolving similar but significantly different theories for that group of symptoms we now refer to as neurotic disorders.

2. Janet focused on commonalities between cases of hysteria and memory dysfunction. What he observed led him to formulate the concept of "dissociation"; to him, the symptoms of both amnesia and hysteria were variants of the same dissociative process. This process signifies the separation and consequent insulation of functions and ideas which normally interact; thus, in dissociated states, streams of thought and emotion, which are interwoven in normal individuals, are split off from one another. Janet recognized that stress and exhaustion could precipitate such a split among functions; moreover, he proposed that certain insulated and "unconscious" ideas could persist for extended periods, and account for the symptoms of hysteria. Despite these insights into the psychogenesis of dissociated states,

Janet felt that the primary source of these difficulties lay in the patient's constitutional incapacity to organize and control divergent aspects of his experience.

3. Freud, in conjunction with Breuer, provided an alternative explanation, one that did not assume the presence of a constitutional weakness; moreover, they sought a psychogenic basis not only for the presence of these symptoms, but for the particular forms in which they would be expressed. In their early collaborative studies, they observed that the patient's symptoms often disappeared following the discharge of intense emotions during hypnosis. The consequence of this release of suppressed feelings, which they termed "abreaction," suggested that unconscious conflicts were at the root of neurotic symptoms; this view became the cornerstone of Freud's thesis. To him, the symptom represented an indirect and rather bizarre way of expressing unconscious tensions and impulses, without having to recognize the source and content of these tensions; the form in which the symptom was expressed was seen as a symbolic clue to the specific character of the patient's repressed problem. Freud investigated these overt clues as a means of deciphering the nature of the patient's unconscious strivings and conflicts.

Freud's disciples spoke of symptoms that represented the intrapsychic transformation of unconscious anxieties and impulses as *psychoneuroses*. They contrasted them with the *actual neuroses,* which represented the outcome of unconscious forces that were unexpressed and "dammed up," since they failed to be discharged through intrapsychic transformation and compromise solution; we shall make reference to the dammed-up symptoms of the actual neuroses along with the Freudian concept of "organ neuroses," in the next chapter, under the label of "psychophysiologic disorders."

The term "neurotic disorders," as used in this section, parallels the Freudian notion of the psychoneuroses. They are viewed as indirect symptomatic expressions of reactivated unconscious memories and emotions which have been recast into personally tolerable and socially acceptable forms through the operation of intrapsychic mechanisms. Freud connected the mechanisms involved in these symptoms to different stages of psychosexual development, viewing them as signs of a "fixation" or a "regression" to childhood sexual problems and their immature defensive solutions. This aspect of his formulation of the psychoneuroses may be seriously questioned, and need not be viewed as an integral

part of his general theory of neurotic symptom formation.

4. In 1915, Kraepelin organized the literature on the neuroses into three categories: neurasthenia; psychasthenia; and hysteria. This formulation remained in vogue until the 1950's and is still used in some quarters both in this country and on the continent. *Neurasthenia* represented states of fatigue, bodily symptoms and poor appetite, all of which ostensibly derive from a constitutional "nerve weakness." The *psychasthenia* group, signifying a "weakness of mind," included what we refer to as the phobic and obsessive-compulsive disorders. The third classification, *hysteria,* followed the thinking of Janet and Freud, and subsumed the conversion and dissociative disorders as we now distinguish them. Kraepelin's system served the purpose of unifying these symptom syndromes as milder variants of psychopathology; however, he offered no insights into other commonalities among them.

5. The next advance in the study of the neuroses stemmed from experimental research, specifically the attempt to relate Pavlov's conditioning studies to the clinical observations of Freud. In what is known as "experimental neurosis," investigators such as Masserman (1943), Liddell (1944), Maier (1949), Solomon and Wynne (1954) and Brady (1958) sought to create, through laboratory conditioning procedures, counterparts to the clinical neuroses. Other researchers studied experimentally produced analogues to the Freudian intrapsychic mechanisms (Miller, 1939; Sears, 1942).

As a consequence of these investigations, it became clear that behavior symptoms, comparable to those found in the psychoneuroses, could be induced as a *direct* function of environmental conditions, that is, without invoking the operation of unconscious forces. Moreover, these neurotic-like symptoms can also be acquired by vicarious learning and imitation (Bandura and Walters, 1963) and simple instrumental learning (Mowrer, 1950; Ullmann and Krasner, 1965). In short, there was no need to postulate unconscious forces, as Freud did, to account for "neurotic" behaviors.

Despite evidence for the direct learning of "neuroses," it is clear that the probability that these behaviors will emerge will be greater if the individual in question has had a long history of experiences which previously evoked comparable behaviors. That is, persons whose painful past experiences and "neurotic" habits of response have been repressed or "pushed out of mind" may be more readily provoked to respond in these neurotic ways than those who are not so vulnerable; thus, in cases with "repressed memories," minor precipitants may reactivate unconscious residuals, and thereby prompt the neurotic response.

What Freud spoke of as the psychoneuroses may be viewed, then, as cases in which painful elements of the patient's past have been stirred up and become primary stimuli for the neurotic behavior response. It is these impairments which we will discuss in the present chapter.

Neurotic dispositions occur primarily in pathological personality patterns since they possess unconscious reaction sensitivities to certain objectively innocuous environmental experiences. Moreover, they have a background of established and pathological coping strategies which they characteristically employ in response to these experiences. Faced with extreme stress—sufficient to upset or "disorder" their equilibrium —they are forced to apply their strategies in an appropriately extreme form; what we observe, then, are "neurotic" symptoms. Although these symptoms are similar to those seen in the "behavior reactions," those of the latter syndrome are less a product of reactivated unconscious feelings and habits than they are of objective reality or narrowly circumscribed learnings. The behavior reaction syndromes will be discussed in detail in chapter 12.

## SOME DISTINCTIONS BETWEEN NEUROTIC DISORDERS AND OTHER PSYCHOPATHOLOGICAL STATES

We have just reviewed some of the principal differences between neurotic disorders and behavior reactions. In essence, the distinction is traceable to the primacy of unconscious memories and coping strategies as behavior determinants in neurotic disorders. These residuals of the past intrude upon the individual's present perceptions and reactions, giving rise to seemingly bizarre and irrational symptoms.

Neurotic disorders are classed among the symptom disorders since they all reflect the intrusion into the present of pervasive unconscious emotions and strategies acquired as a function of past experience.

Neurotic, anxiety, psychophysiologic and sociopathic syndromes are alike in the moderate degree of their severity, which distinguishes them in this regard from the psychotic disorders. Despite the discomforts their symptoms may engender, these moderately disturbed patients maintain a sufficient measure of internal cohesion and balance to enable them to continue functioning in society; the psychotic's symptoms, however, are so disruptive or bizarre as to preclude such functioning.

Most neurotic, anxiety and psychophysiologic patients experience their symptoms as egodystonic, that is, they experience their feelings and behaviors as uncomfortable and view them as undesirable intrusions into their well-being. This ego-dystonic feature is usually not present in sociopathic patients, who tend to view their symptoms as neither unusual nor distressing.

There are important differences between neurotic, anxiety and psychophysiologic syndromes. In contrast to these other groups, neurotics manage to control their anxieties and to find some form, albeit indirect and symbolic, for discharging some of their inner tensions. Anxiety and psychophysiologic patients are unable to find internal or external measures either to control or to vent their tensions. In anxiety cases, tension is uncontrolled and consciously experienced, although its psychogenic source remains repressed or ambiguous. In psychophysiologic cases, tension is somaticized into bodily ailments; here, the patient banishes from consciousness both the disturbing emotion and its psychogenic source.

Neurotic and sociopathic disorders share in common the ability to discharge substantial portions of their unconscious anxieties and impulses. However, sociopathic patients discharge these feelings in pure and direct form, that is, without complicated intrapsychic transformations whereas neurotics neutralize or camouflage the true character of their emotions so as to make them personally more tolerable and socially more acceptable.

## COPING FUNCTIONS OF NEUROTIC BEHAVIORS

Let us briefly recapitulate and extend several of the points noted above.

As described in previous chapters, coping refers to processes of instrumental activity that are learned as a function of prior experience. These processes enable individuals to maintain an optimum level of psychological integration by increasing the number of positive reinforcements they achieve (e.g., attention, comfort, pleasure and status) and avoiding as many negative reinforcements as they can (e.g., punishment, frustration, rejection and anxiety).

Pathological personality patterns utilize "neurotic" coping behaviors to achieve four instrumental goals: counteracting external precipitants which threaten to upset their precarious equilibrium and tenuous controls; blocking reactivated unconscious anxieties and impulses from intruding into conscious awareness and provoking social condemnation; discharging tensions engendered by external stresses and unconscious residuals; and soliciting attention, sympathy and nurture from others.

It is the synthesis of these four instrumental goals which distinguishes neurotic from other symptom disorders. To discharge unconscious tensions while at the same time blocking awareness of their true sources, avoiding social rebuke and evoking social approval and support in their stead is a task of no mean proportions. It requires the masking and transformation of one's true thoughts and feelings by the intricate workings of several intrapsychic mechanisms, notably sublimation, rationalization, displacement, undoing, isolation and reaction formation; these mechanisms bolster the flagging controls of repression. The resulting neurotic symptom represents the interplay and final outcome of these unconscious maneuvers. Not only have the patient's anxieties and impulses been disguised sufficiently to be kept from conscious awareness, but they also managed to solicit attention and nurture and achieve a measure of tension discharge.

Alexander (1930) reports a classic case of "phobia" in which the patient's symptom achieved her instrumental neurotic goals through intrapsychic resolution.

A young woman dreaded going into the street alone, the thought of which made her feel faint and extremely anxious. Upon clinical investigation it became clear that a forbidden and unconscious sexual impulse was associated with her phobia; each time she would go out her impulse would be stimulated by the thought that a man might "pick her up" and seduce her. The thought both excited her and caused her intense anxiety. To avoid the true character of her forbidden desire and the tension it provoked she displaced her tension to an associated and more generalized activity, that of going into the street; thus, her phobia. However, she was able to venture out quite undisturbed if accompanied by a relative. In this way she could engage in fleeting sexual fantasies as she passed attractive men, without the fear that she might be carried away and shamed by her forbidden impulse. Her symptom was extremely efficient; not only did it enable her to maintain psychological cohesion by controlling her impulse, blocking her awareness of its true source and keeping her behavior within acceptable social boundaries, but, at the same time, it solicited the assistance of others who enabled her to find some albeit skimpy means of gaining both tension and impulse release.

The case just described brings us to another aspect of neurotic disorders, the tendency for symptoms to achieve what are known as *secondary gains*. According to traditional Freudian theory, the primary function of neurotic symptoms is the avoidance, control and partial discharge of anxiety, or as we would be inclined to call it, the elimination of a strong negative reinforcer stemming from unconscious sources. But, in addition, the neurotic coping maneuver may produce certain positive reinforcements; that is, as a consequence of his neurotic symptoms, the patient may obtain secondary advantages or rewards. In the case noted above, for example, the woman's phobic symptom achieved positive reinforcements above and beyond the reduction of the negatively reinforcing anxiety; in the role of a sick and disabled person, she solicited attention, sympathy and help from others, and was freed of the responsibility of carrying out many of the duties expected of a healthy adult. In this fashion her symptom not only controlled and partially vented her anxieties, but enabled her to gratify a more basic dependency need.

The distinction between primary gains (anxiety reduction) and secondary gains (positive rewards) may be sharply drawn at the conceptual level but is difficult to make when analyzing actual cases since the two processes intermesh closely in reality. However, to those who subscribe to Freudian theory, the conceptual distinction is extremely important. As they view it, secondary gains play no part in stimulating the formation of the neurotic symptom. To them, the patient is prompted to develop his symptom *not* as a means of gaining secondary or positive reinforcements, but as a means of avoiding, controlling or discharging the negative reinforcement of anxiety.

This sharp distinction between primary and secondary gains seems rather arbitrary and narrow. Although it is true that anxiety reduction is centrally involved in symptom formation, this, in itself, could not account for the variety of symptoms that patients display. We may ask: Why are certain intrapsychic mechanisms employed by some patients and different ones by others, and why do certain symptoms rather than others emerge? If the sole purpose of neurotic symptom formation were anxiety abatement, any set of intrapsychic mechanisms could fulfill that job, giving rise to any number and variety of different symptoms.

This, however, is not the case. Only certain types of symptoms are displayed in neurotic disorders, notably those which control or discharge anxiety *without provoking social condemnation,* and quite often *managing to solicit support and nurture* as well. It would seem, then, that neurotic coping maneuvers both reduce anxiety (primary gain) and at the same time achieve certain positive advantages (secondary gain).

We contend, therefore, in opposition to traditional Freudian theory, that neurotic symptom formation reflects the joint operation of both primary and secondary gain strategies (neither of which, we should note, is consciously planned). Furthermore, we have asserted that neurotic disorders have a common secondary gain characteristic that distinguishes them from most of the other disorder syndromes, that is, their symptoms not only serve to discharge tensions, but do so without provoking social condemnation, eliciting, in its stead, support, sympathy and nurture.

These features of neurotic symptomatology can best be understood if we examine which of the eight pathological personality patterns are disposed to develop these disorders.

## NEUROTIC PERSONALITY DISPOSITIONS

Neurotic disorders display themselves in such ways as both to avoid social derogation and to elicit support and sympathy from others. For example, the phobic patient, described previously, manipulated members of her family into accompanying her in street outings where she gained the illicit pleasures of sexual titillation; through her "unfortunate" disablement, she fulfilled her dependency needs, exerted substantial control over the lives of others and achieved partial impulse gratification *without social condemnation.* Let us look at two other examples. A neurotically depressed woman not only may be relieved of family responsibilities, but through her subtly aggressive symptom makes others feel guilty and limits their freedom while still gaining their concern, and yet not provoke anger. A hypochondriacal woman experiences diverse somatic ailments which preclude sexual activity; she not only gains her husband's compassion and understanding, but does so without his recognizing that her behavior is a subtle form of punishing him; she is so successful in her maneuver that her frustration of his sexual desires is viewed, not as an irritation or a sign of selfishness, but as an unfortunate consequence of her physical illness. Her "plight" evokes more sympathy for her than for her husband.

Why do the symptoms of neurotic disorders take this particular, devious route? Why are their hostile or otherwise socially unacceptable impulses masked and transformed so as to appear not only socially palatable but evocative of support and sympathy? To answer this question we must examine which of the various personality patterns tend to exhibit neurotic symptoms. When we do, we discover that they are found predominantly among five groups: both of the dependent personality patterns, both of the ambivalent personality patterns, especially those with strong dependency inclinations, and the active type of the detached patterns.

What rationale can be provided for the correspondence between these personalities and neurotic disorders?

We previously stated that a full understanding of symptom disorders requires the study of a patient's basic personality. Symptoms are but an outgrowth of deeply rooted sensitivities and coping strategies. What events a person perceives as threatening or rewarding and what behaviors and mechanisms he employs in response to them depend on the reinforcement history to which he was exposed. If we wish to uncover the reasons for the particular symptoms a patient "chooses," we must first understand the source and character of the reinforcements he seeks to achieve. As elaborated in chapter 5, the character of the reinforcements a patient chooses has not been a last minute decision, but reflects a long history of interwoven biogenic and psychogenic factors which have formed his basic personality pattern.

In analyzing the distinguishing reinforcement goals of neurotic behaviors, we are led to the following observations: neurotic patients appear especially desirous of avoiding the negative reinforcers of social disapproval and rejection; moreover, where possible, they wish to evoke the positive reinforcers of attention, sympathy and nurture. If we correlate this observation with personality dispositions, we find ourselves directed to the five patterns mentioned earlier.

Although each of these personality patterns has had different prior experiences, they share in common a hypersensitivity to social rebuff and condemnation, to which they hesitate reacting with counteraggression. In the *dependent patterns,* for example, there is a fear of losing the security and reinforcements which others provide; these patients must guard themselves against acting in such ways as to provoke disapproval and separation; rather, where feasible, they will maneuver themselves to act in ways which evoke favorable responses. The *ambivalent patterns,* particularly those in whom the dependency orientation is dominant, are similarly guided by the fear of provoking social condemnation. In the *active-detached pattern,* where dependency is not a factor, as it is in the previous four personalities, there has been a painful history of social ridicule and humiliation, to which they feel incapable of responding. This prompts patients to restrain or dilute their aggressive urges so as to avoid further derogation. In all five patterns, then, behaviors and impulses which might provoke social disapproval must be reworked internally. They can be vented publicly only if they have been recast by intrapsychic distortion and subterfuge.

Several observations may be drawn from the foregoing. *First,* neurotic symptoms do not arise in one personality pattern only. *Second,* we would expect, in many cases, the coexistence or simultaneous presence of several neurotic symptoms since they reflect the operation of the same basic coping process. *Third,* we would assume that neurotic symptoms would be transient since their underlying coping function would wax and wane as the need for them changes. And *fourth,* these symptoms should, in large measure, be interchangeable, with one symptom appearing dominant at one time and a different one at another.

Despite the fact that symptoms may covary and be interchangeable, we would expect some measure of symptom dominance and durability among different personality patterns. No one to one correspondence should be expected, of course, but on the basis of differences in lifelong coping habits, we would anticipate that certain personalities would be more inclined to exhibit certain symptoms than others. Thus, in the conforming personality, where ingrained intrapsychic mechanisms such as reaction formation and undoing have been present for years, we would expect the patient to display neurotic symptoms that reflect the operation of these mechanisms. Similarly, gregarious personalities should exhibit the more dramatic and attention-getting neurotic symptoms since exhibitionistic histrionics have always characterized their coping behaviors. It seems reasonable, then, that despite the common functions achieved through neurotic behaviors, differences will arise among these five patterns since patients will continue to draw upon the habitual mechanisms they employed in the past.

There are reasons, however, not to overstate the correspondence between personality and specific neurotic symptoms. *First,* neurotic-like symptoms, often indistinguishable from those exhibited by pathological personalities, arise in normal persons; these will be discussed in chapter 12 under the label of pathological "behavior reactions."

*Second,* there are endless variations in the specific experiences to which different members of the same personality syndrome have been exposed. Let us compare, for example, two individuals who have been "trained" to become conforming personalities. One may have been exposed to a mother who was chronically ill, a pattern of behavior which brought her considerable sympathy and freedom from many burdens. With this as a background factor, the person may be inclined to follow the model he observed in his mother when he is faced with undue anxiety and threat, thereby displaying hypochondriacal symptoms. A second conforming personality may have learned to imitate a mother who expressed endless fears about all types of events and situations. In his case, there is a greater likelihood that phobic symptoms would arise in response to stressful and anxiety-laden circumstances. In short, the specific "choice" of the neurotic symptom is not a function solely of the patient's personality pattern, but may reflect more particular and entirely incidental events of prior experience and learning.

**Comment.**   We are now ready to survey the various subforms of neurotic disorder: phobia, conversion, dissociation, obsession-compulsion, dejection and hypochondriasis. With minor exceptions, this grouping corresponds to the official DSM-II classification of the "neuroses." Points of difference, both substantive and semantic, will be noted in our discussion of each disorder.

Before we proceed, however, it should be noted that the classical symptoms of neuroses appear less common today than when first formulated some three quarters of a century ago. Moreover, a new set of neurotic disorders seems to be supplanting the old. For example, fewer cases of conversion and dissociation are reported today, but there are more reports of what are termed "existential nonbeing," "alienation" and "identity diffusion." There is no way of knowing whether these changes in symptomatology are real or apparent, e.g., changes due to new patterns of child rearing, a growing awareness of previously overlooked problems, social fashions in language, theoretical interests of modern-day clinicians and so on.

It seems to us that these changes are both real and spurious. No doubt, there are differences in child rearing practices and in the pressures and values of life, and between modern America and the turn of the century Europe to which Freud addressed his writings. We contend, however, that the basic processes and goals which underlie the formation of neurotic symptoms have not changed. It appears to us that the newer disorders are merely currently fashionable and acceptable ways of discharging anxieties and impulses, without provoking social condemnation. Symptoms such as conversion and dissociation are outmoded, and perhaps even suspect, in our sophisticated Freudian age. Sufferers of these disorders may gain only minimal compassion and approval as a consequence of their impairment. In contrast, everyone today knows "what a difficult world we live in," and "how hard it is to break out of the ruts of modern society"; thus, symptoms of "identity diffusion," "feelings of meaninglessness," "social alienation" and "existential anxiety" are likely to evoke approval and a sympathetic hearing, even though they may represent a subterfuge for dependency needs or overtly unacceptable aggressive impulses. In short, these new neurotic disorders appear to reflect the same intrapsychic maneuvers and reinforcement goals as were found in more classical neurotic forms. They are expressed, however, in ways that are suitable to present-day values and conditions.

We shall subsume several of these newer neurotic variants under the syndrome label "dejection" since we believe that their underlying character and manifest picture are best represented by this term. Also included within this category will be the traditional symptom disorder known as "neurotic depression." This latter term should be dropped, we believe, to avoid confusion with the psychotic disorder of the same name.

Let us terminate our review of the general features of neurotic syndromes, and turn our attention to the specific subvariants, both old and new.

## PHOBIC DISORDERS
(DSM-II: *Phobic Neurosis*)

Pathological fears were first reported in the writings of Hippocrates. Shakespeare referred to phobic reactions in *The Merchant of Venice* when he spoke of "Some, that are mad if they behold a cat." John Locke, in the early eighteenth century, speculated on their origin in his *Essays on Human Understanding*. In 1872, Westphal reported on three cases of peculiar fears of open public places. It was not until the writings of Freud, however, that the concept of phobia was presented, not as a simple although peculiar fear reaction, but as a displacement of an internal anxiety onto an external object. Phobias were

seen by Freud as the outcome of intrapsychic transformations and symbolic externalizations of inner tensions. The DSM-II describes this syndrome as follows:

. . . intense fear of an object or situation which the patient consciously recognizes as no real danger to him. . . . Phobias are generally attributed to fears displaced to the phobic object or situation from some other object of which the patient is unaware.

### CLINICAL PICTURE AND COPING FUNCTIONS

Phobias are unrealistic fears, that is, they appear to be unjustified by the object or event which prompts them. For example, most people would agree on the inherent danger and appropriateness of keeping distance from a large and wild animal or from a blaze that had gotten out of control. But it is not situations like these which evoke the phobic reaction. Rather, anxiety is prompted by such innocuous events as crossing a bridge, passing a funeral home, entering an elevator and so on.

Phobias signify perhaps the simplest of all intrapsychic transformations. Like other forms of neurotic behavior, they enable the disordered personality to achieve several of the four instrumental goals involved in symptom formation. In phobic disorders, the patient does not neutralize or dilute the experience of anxiety but simply displaces it to a well-circumscribed external source. In this way he blocks from conscious awareness the real "internal" reason for its presence, and by the simple act of avoiding the substitute or phobic object prevents himself from experiencing anxiety. In addition to mastering discomforting inner tensions, his symptom often achieves secondary gains such as avoiding responsibilities, gaining sympathy, controlling the lives of others, finding rationalizations for failures and so on.

As noted in an earlier section, entirely incidental experiences of the past may determine the particular focus of a neurotic symptom. But simple conditioned learning is not sufficient in itself to account for the presence of phobias. Phobias arise in pathological personalities, not in normal personalities, where conditioned fear reactions occur. In pathological patterns, the objects or events to which the phobic response is displaced have a "symbolical" significance, that is, the external source of fear crystallizes a range of more widely generalized and unconscious anxieties that have pervasive roots in past experiences. Thus, the phobic object is an external symbol that condenses and focuses diffusely anchored residuals of the past. By the processes of intra-psychic condensation and displacement, the patient projects his unconscious tensions onto a simple and tangible external source, enabling him thereby to cope with it by the direct act of physical avoidance.

Among the more common forms of phobia are the following:

Acrophobia: fear of heights
Agoraphobia: fear of open places
Claustrophobia: fear of closed places
Mysophobia: fear of dirt and germs
Xenophobia: fear of strangers
Zoophobia: fear of animals

The list of phobic precipitants is legion; as many as 180 have been identified in the literature. We refrain from elaborating the list, interesting though it may be, since we believe that the phobic object itself is of lesser significance than the coping functions it represents.

One study, seeking to find commonalities among diverse types of phobia, came to the conclusion that they may be grouped into two broad factors: separation phobias and harm phobias (Dixon et al., 1957). According to this study, one theme reflects a hypersensitivity to social rejection and isolation (being left alone, open spaces, train journey and dark places), and the other refers to the experience of pain in situations in which the individual is at the mercy of others (surgery, dental work or hospitals). Rather interestingly, these two factors are consistent with our contention that neurotic symptoms predominate in dependent and ambivalent personalities who need the support and nurture of others, and active-detached personalities who dread social mistreatment but lack the confidence or means to fight back. Let us turn next to these personality patterns, and explore the precipitants which give rise to their phobias and the coping strategies they employ to deal with them.

## PERSONALITY DISPOSITIONS

Not only may phobic symptoms develop in all pathological personalities, but the number of situations which can serve as the focus of fear is endless, as are the coping functions which the symptom may fulfill. But as previously noted, different probabilities exist as to who will exhibit these symptoms and why.

The following paragraphs survey the typical phobic precipitants and coping functions of those personality patterns which have a high probability of suffering a phobic disorder. In this and subsequent sections, an attempt will be made to present these personality patterns in descending order of probability of symptom formation, e.g., in phobic disorders, as listed subsequently, passive-dependents are the most vulnerable to this symptom, active-dependents are next and so on. (These rankings are based on limited observations and deductions from clinical theory, not on systematic empirical research.)

1. *Passive-dependent personalities* (submissive and cycloid) develop phobic symptoms when their dependency security is threatened or when demands are made which exceed their feelings of competence; they dread responsibility, especially those which require self-assertion and independence. For similar reasons of dependency security, they are motivated to displace or transform any internal impulse which may provoke social rebuke.

Not only does the phobic symptom externalize anxiety and avoid threats to security, but by anchoring tensions to tangible outside sources the patient may prompt others to come to his assistance. Thus, phobias, as external threats, may be used to solicit protection. In short, the phobic coping maneuver serves a variety of functions consonant with the patient's basic passive-dependent orientation.

2. *Active-dependent personalities* (gregarious and cycloid) exhibit phobic symptoms somewhat less frequently than their passive counterparts. Here, feelings of emptiness, unattractiveness and aloneness or the upsurge of socially unacceptable aggressive or erotic impulses, tend to serve as the primary sources of phobic symptom formation.

These symptoms often are displayed exhibitionistically, utilized as "dramatic" vehicles to gain attention and support from others. Active-dependents are quite open about their symptom, therefore, and try to get as much mileage out of it as they can, as is evident in the following case history.

*CASE 10-5*
*Charlotte B., Age 27, Divorced, Two Children*

This recently divorced active-dependent woman suddenly developed panic reactions while driving alone in a car. At home, Charlotte spent her days with her mother and two children; at work, she was busily engaged with fellow employees and customers. Charlotte was "isolated," however, without needed attention and support from others, when driving herself to and from work. To avoid these anxieties, she arranged to be picked up and driven home by a man whom she "found quite attractive." Her phobia symbolized her dread of aloneness; her resolution not only enabled her to travel without anxiety, but brought her into frequent contact with an "approving" and comforting companion.

3. *Passive-ambivalent personalities* (conforming and cycloid) develop phobias primarily as a function of three anxiety precipitants: stressful decision-making situations in which they anticipate being faulted and subjected to criticism; actual failures which they seek to rationalize or avoid facing again; and surging hostile impulses which they wish to counter, transform or externalize lest they overwhelm the patient's controls and provoke social condemnation.

In contrast to dependent personalities, these patients "hide" their phobias since their self-image would be weakened by such "foolish" and irrational symptoms. Similarly, they fear that these symptoms may provoke social ridicule and criticism. Thus, unbeknown to others, they displace their tensions onto a variety of external phobic sources. This enables them not only to deny the internal roots of their discomfort, but to make it tangible and identifiable, and thereby subject to easy control.

4. *Active-detached personalities* (avoidant and schizoid) are similar to passive-ambivalents in that their phobias tend to be private affairs. For them, the symptom does not serve as a means of evoking social attention, since they are convinced that attention will bring forth only ridicule and abuse. More commonly, it is a symbolic expression of feeling encroached upon or of being pressured by excessive stimuli and demands. Crystallized in this fashion, these patients possess an identifiable and circumscribed anxiety source which they can actively avoid. In a similar manner, phobias enable these patients to control the eruption of surging feelings of resentment and hostility which they dare not express openly. Dreading social rebuke, they must find some innocuous external source to keep their resentments in check. Through displacement and condensation, the phobic object comes to represent the true source of their anxieties and resentments. This feature of the phobic problem is illustrated in the following case.

### CASE 10-6
### Nelson C., Age 19, Unmarried

Nelson, an active-detached schizoid, experienced sudden surges of anxiety whenever reference was made to the name of a major shopping center in his home town. Crowded areas made him feel insignificant and worthless, and also often stimulated frightening erotic and hostile impulses. For some unknown reason, the shopping center came to symbolize these unwanted feelings. By avoiding the shopping center or refer-

ence to its name, Nelson felt as if his fears and impulses could be kept in check.

5. *Active-ambivalent personalities* (negativistic and cycloid) tend to be more open about discharging their feelings than other neurotically disposed personalities. This ready and diffuse discharge of anxiety and emotion has its self-defeating side. By venting tensions openly and connecting them freely to any and all aspects of their life, these individuals increase the likelihood that many formerly innocuous objects and events will become anxiety-laden. Moreover, these patients often utilize their phobic symptoms for secondary gain; they employ them to draw attention to themselves and as a tool to control and manipulate the lives of others, as portrayed in the following case.

### CASE 10-7
### Hermione K., Age 40, Married, One Child

This cycloid woman, with a history of two brief depressive episodes that required hospitalization, developed an "unreasonable" dread of entering the kitchen of her home. During a series of therapeutic sessions, it became clear that her phobia symbolized her growing feeling of incompetence as a wife, and enabled her to avoid facing her general fear of failure. Moreover, the phobia served to bring her sympathy and to punish her husband by forcing him to prepare most of the family's meals and to wash and dry the dishes, a chore he had always detested.

## CONVERSION DISORDERS
(DSM-II: *Hysterical Neurosis, Conversion Type*)

The discovery of the unconscious roots of conversion disorders was a turning point in the history of psychopathology. Let us begin our discussion with a review of this historical background.

### History

The concept of conversion disorder, in which physical symptoms serve as vehicles to discharge psychological tension, may be traced to the early Greeks. They identified a disease, termed by them *hysteria,* which represented a malady found in women, and which they attributed to abnormal movements of the uterus (hystera). A wandering uterus, they believed, could result either in the total loss of sensation in any of several body regions or in the experience of peculiar sensations and involuntary movements. Hysteria remained in the medical literature through the medieval period, although at that time it was attributed not to physical sources but to the operation of demonic spirits. In the sixteenth century, Lepois suggested that the disorder should not be attributed either to evil forces or to the wandering of the uterus but rather to lesions in the brain. Given this etiology, he claimed that the ailment should be found in both women and men. In the ensuing three centuries, however, no evidence of a pathological lesion was discovered, and the view persisted that the disease was limited to the female sex. As reported earlier in the chapter, a major breakthrough came in the late nineteenth century through the work of Charcot and the subsequent clinical studies of Janet, Breuer and Freud.

Freud proposed the first entirely psychological theory of hysterical symptom formation. On the basis of a few cases, he claimed that the symptom represented repressed emotions engendered by a traumatic incident, which failed to be discharged at the time of the trauma. These emotions and their associated thoughts were "dammed up" because they were morally repugnant to the patient's conscience. By disconnecting them from the mainstream of consciousness, the person was spared the pain of recognizing their contrary or immoral character. However, through the operation of several intrapsychic mechanisms, these emotions could be vented in disguised form. Phobias were one outcome; here, emotional energy was detached from its original source or idea, and displaced to some innocuous external object or event. In hysteria, the affective energy was displaced, converted and discharged through a body symptom; the hysterical symptom, though quite obscure in its psychic significance, did convey elements of the original unacceptable thought or impulse. To Freud, it symbolically represented the repressed and forbidden idea.

Although Freud later altered his views on the central role played by traumatic episodes, substituting in its stead the notion of repressed sexual attachments to the opposite-sex parent (Oedipus complex), his basic formulation of the genesis of the hysterical symptom remained essentially unchanged. His work on the "dynamics" of conversion disorders, presented at the turn of the century, became the cornerstone of his subsequent contributions. About the only significant extension of his original theory of symptom formation was the concept of secondary gain, developed to account for the fact that symptoms persisted even after their repressed emotions had been ventilated. This latter point is noted in the brief DSM-II description of this syndrome, which characterizes the *hysterical neurosis, conversion type* as follows:

. . . the special senses or voluntary nervous system are affected, causing such symptoms as blindness, deafness, . . . anesthesias . . . paralyses. . . . Often the patient shows an inappropriate lack of concern or *belle indifférence* about these symptoms, which may actually provide secondary gains by winning him sympathy or relieving him of unpleasant responsibilities.

## CLINICAL PICTURE AND COPING FUNCTIONS

Among the major overt symptoms of these disorders are the following (rarely is more than one evident in any patient): *loss of speech*—mutism, persistent or repetitive laryngitis or prolonged speech stammers; *muscular paralyses*—loss of voluntary control of major limbs or fingers; *tactile anesthesias*—total or partial loss of sensitivity in various external body parts; *visual or auditory defects*—total or partial loss of sight or hearing; and *motor tics* or *spasms*—eye blinks, repetitive involuntary grimaces and erratic movements or muscular or intestinal cramps. The list can be expanded endlessly since there is a tremendous number of body parts and functions which can be used as the focus of conversion displacement. The few we have noted are the most common and distinctive of these transformations. Other less frequent symptoms reflect the operation of the same coping processes. What is significant in these bodily ailments is the fact that there is no genuine physical basis for the symptom.

We have already covered several of the behavioral features and intrapsychic processes of conversion disorders. Recapitulating briefly, conversions are changes in body functions which crystallize and discharge tensions, and which represent symbolically the source of these tensions and the coping mechanisms which the patient utilizes to deal with them. They differ from anxiety disorders, in which tensions are discharged in essentially unmodified form and from phobic disorders in which tensions are condensed and displaced onto an external source, enabling the patient to avoid then the symbolic substitute for his anxiety.

The primary gain of the conversion maneuver is the blocking from awareness of the true source of anxiety. Despite the price he must pay in diminished bodily functioning, the patient remains relatively free of tension by accepting his disability. The "choice" of the symptom and the symbolic meaning it expresses reflect the particular character of the patient's underlying problem and the secondary gains he seeks to achieve. Both the problem and the gains he seeks stem from his basic personality and habitual coping style.

Let us illustrate these points with three brief examples: a "conforming" patient, whose pattern of life has been guided by the fear of social rebuke, may develop an arm paralysis to control the impulse to strike someone whom he hates; a "gregarious" personality may suddenly become mute for fear of voicing intense anger and resentment; and an "avoidant" schizoid may lose his hearing as a way of tuning out ridiculing voices, both real and imagined.

It is important to recognize that symptoms are rarely the end product of a single cause or coping function; they are *overdetermined,* that is, reflect a compromise solution for several different emotions and coping aims. For example, a paralyzed arm may not only serve to control a hostile impulse, but may attract social sympathy and express self-punitive guilt feelings.

It has often been reported in the literature that conversion patients evidence what is termed *la belle indifférence,* that is, a rather bland lack of concern about their bodily symptom. Although this indifference to illness is found in some cases of conversion, it is by no means typical of all. It would be expected to appear in patients who for some reason do not wish to draw attention to their ailment. Thus, it may be found in passive-ambivalent and active-detached personalities, both of whom have serious doubts as to how others might react to their infirmity. Other patients, however, voice open dismay about their impairment. Such public displays of discomfort would likely be exhibited among the dependent patterns where the desire for sympathy and nurture may play a part. It should be especially noted in the active-dependent, who characteristically seeks to draw attention to himself.

The view has often been expressed that the frequency of conversion symptoms has been on the wane in the past half century. Systematic research, limited though it is, seems to suggest, however, that the proportion of these cases in outpatient clinics has not changed during this period (Stephens and Kamp, 1962). If there is, in fact, a decline in the reporting of this variant of neurotic disorders, it may reflect changing habits of clinical diagnoses (e.g., terming these cases as psychophysiologic disorders) or changing theoretical interests of psychopathologists (e.g., focusing on "more basic" symptomatic features). Not to be overlooked, however, is the possibility that patients in modern-day America express their tensions in different ways than those exposed to cultures of a half century ago.

Another often held belief, recently reaffirmed (Guze and Perley, 1963), is that conversion is a woman's syndrome. This view persists, despite the fact that the disorder was exhibited by hundreds of soldiers during World War I, and is often found today among men. There is, however, a factual basis for the belief that women exhibit conversions to an appreciably greater extent than men. We are inclined to attribute this fact not to intrinsic physical characteristics that distinguish men from women but to the greater proportion of women who develop dependent personalities. Since conversions arise most frequently among dependent patterns, it would follow that more women would be subject to this syndrome. With this note on the role of personality factors, we are ready to turn our attention to correlations between personality and conversion disorders.

## PERSONALITY DISPOSITIONS

In the following paragraphs we shall by-pass extensive reference to the typical precipitants of conversion disorder. The events that trigger conversions are no different than those found in most other neurotic syndromes. These have been amply referred to in discussions of the anxiety and phobic disorders.

What does differentiate the conversion disorder from these other syndromes is the strategy the patient utilizes to cope with his distress. The discussion that follows will focus on instrumental behaviors which achieve significant reinforcers. Which reinforcers are sought and which strategies are used to attain them derive from a long history of experiences and learnings that have shaped the individual's personality pattern.

1. *Passive-dependent personalities* (submissive and cycloid) may develop conversions as a means of controlling an upsurge of forbidden impulses. However, more commonly, these symptoms serve to avoid onerous responsibilities and to recruit the secondary gains of sympathy and nurture. By demonstrating their physical helplessness, these patients often succeed in eliciting attention and care. Conversion symptoms may also represent self-punishment in response to feelings of guilt and worthlessness. However, these patients tend not to be too harsh with themselves. As a consequence, their conversion symptoms often take the form of relatively mild sensory anesthesias such as a generalized numbness in the hands and feet. Also notable is the observation that their symptoms are often located in their limbs. This may be a means of demonstrating to others that they are "disabled" and incapable of performing even the most routine of chores.

2. *Active-dependent personalities* (gregari-

ous and cycloid) tend to exhibit rather open and dramatic conversion symptoms. This is consistent with their basic style of attracting attention to themselves. Common symptoms among these patients are mutism and persistent laryngitis; this serves to prevent them from verbalizing hostile and erotic thoughts which might provoke social reproval. Moreover, these are extremely eye-catching symptoms, enabling the patient both to dramatize his plight and to draw total attention to his gesticulations and pantomime.

3. *Passive-ambivalent personalities* (conforming and cycloid) succumb to conversion symptoms primarily as a means of containing the upsurge of hostile or other forbidden impulses. The conversion disorder is not an easy "choice" for these patients, since to be ill runs counter to their image of self-sufficiency. However, in contrast to phobic symptoms, which prove especially embarrassing in this regard, conversions enable the patient to assume that his illness is of physical origin. Thus, it not only allows him to achieve the important secondary gain of dependence and nurture, but it enables him to continue to believe that he is basically self-sufficient, merely an unfortunate victim of a "passing" sickness.

These patients tend to underplay their ailment, acting rather indifferent and even comfortable with it. However, because of their need to cloak the pleasure they gain in their surreptitious dependency and to rigidly seal off the intense but forbidden impulses which well up within them, the symptoms they exhibit tend to be rather severe. Thus, in these personalities we often find the total immobilization of some body function, e.g., blindness, mutism or complete paralysis of both legs. The severity of these symptoms not only reflects the sweeping nature of their habitual controls and the need to "prove" the seriousness and unequivocal character of their illness, but it frequently represents in addition self-punishment for intense guilt feelings. By becoming blind or disabling their limbs, they sacrifice a part of themselves as penance for their "sinful" thoughts and urges.

4. *Active-detached personalities* (avoidant and schizoid) display a wide variety of conversion symptoms, ranging from minor tics, generalized sensory anesthesias and motor paralyses to the total loss of vision or hearing. These symptoms are not frequent since these patients avoid situations which promote tension. Nevertheless, when they are unable to avoid censure or excessive social demands and fear expressing their tensions overtly, they may bind their anxieties in the form of a conversion symptom. These symptoms are especially likely if circumstances stir up strong impulses of counterhostility which must be contained.

The loss of vision and hearing in these patients may be seen as an extension of their habitual avoidance strategy. By eliminating all forms of sensory awareness, they no longer see or hear others deriding them. Severance of body functions, by means of either sensory anesthesia or motor paralysis, may represent the condensation and displacement of depersonalization anxieties. Rather than experience a total sense of "nothingness," the patient may crystallize and contain this dreadful feeling by attaching it to one part of his body. Conversion symptoms may also reflect an act of self-repudiation. Since these patients tend to view themselves with derision and contempt, they may utilize conversion as an expression of self-rejection. By disconnecting some part of themselves, they symbolize their desire to disown their body.

The following case illustrates some of these elements.

*CASE 10-8*
*James L., Age 19, Unmarried*

This schizoid young man was seen for several years by his family physician in conjunction with periodic complaints of breathing difficulties associated with a numbness in the nasal region. Subsequent neurological examination proved negative, and he was referred on for psychiatric evaluation. The presence of an ingrained active-detached schizoid pattern was evident. The specific referring symptom of breathing difficulty remained a puzzle. Interviews revealed that James was extremely sensitive, and had frequently been taunted by his peers for his rather long and misshapen nose.

Once James began to trust his therapist, he voiced frequent derogatory remarks about his own unattractive physical appearance, particularly the humiliation he experienced when his fellow students called him "the anteater," a term of derision designed to poke fun at his long nose. The basis for his nasal anesthesia and its attendant breathing difficulties was soon apparent. The nose symbolized the source of both social and self-rejection. By conversion desensitization, he disowned it. Breathing difficulties naturally followed the failure to use his nasal musculature. But more significantly, it represented a hidden obsessive thought that he might "breathe in" ants.

After several therapeutic "conditioning" sessions, both conversion and obsessive symptoms receded. However, other features of his basic schizoid personality remained unmodified.

5. *Active-ambivalent personalities* (negativist and cycloid) express their feelings rather openly and directly. Thus, there is little build up

of tension. What tension does occur, is rarely camouflaged. When conversion symptoms form, they tend to be fleeting and exhibited in transitory intestinal spasms, facial tics or laryngitis. These represent sporadic efforts to control intense anger and resentment, which typically give way to more overt outbursts.

Many of these patients have been "trained" to use physical ailments as instruments for manipulating others. Complaints of vague sensations of bodily pain often draw attention and create guilt in others. These behaviors, however, are difficult to distinguish from the neurotic syndrome of hypochondriasis, to which we will address our attention in a later section.

## DISSOCIATION DISORDERS
(DSM-II: *Hysterical Neurosis, Dissociative Type; Depersonalization Neurosis*)

Dissociation is closely linked to both phobias and conversions; in fact, they are often subsumed under the more general label of "hysteria." Despite an overlapping in the personalities who exhibit them as well as in the underlying strategies which give rise to them, these disorders are sufficiently distinct in other regards to justify their separation. For example, in both phobias and conversions, inner tensions are displaced and discharged through a symbolic object or body part that both the patient and others are fully conscious of. In dissociation, however, the patient neither crystallizes his tensions into tangible forms nor gives evidence of being conscious of their expression. Rather, he vents his tension through transitory behavioral acts and does so in a dream-like state, that is, while completely unaware of what he is doing.

### History

Since the days of the early Greeks, observations have been made of individuals who seem to "drift off" and lose contact with their surroundings for varying periods of time. Some suffer total amnesia, forgetting who they are, what they have done and where they have been. Others experience trance-like dream states in which they engage in activities of which they have no recall.

The concept of dissociation and the first understanding of the processes involved began with the inquiries of Charcot and Janet. It was Charcot in the early 1870's who suggested that the stream of consciousness breaks up into divergent paths in cases of hysteria. As noted in an earlier section, he believed that this "splitting" process was traceable to a hereditary degeneration of the nervous system. Janet pursued this theme in the late 1880's in his clinical investigations of states of amnesia and somnambulism. He coined the term "dissociation" to represent what he viewed as the central process in these disorders. As Janet conceived it, the mental energy required to bind the diverse elements of personality had deteriorated or had been "exhausted." As a consequence, certain thoughts, feelings and memories, which normally cohere, drift apart and become lost to the principal core of the personality.

Janet's views were extended in 1905 by Morton Prince, an American psychologist who published a series of now famous inquiries into dramatic cases of "multiple personalities." Prince applied the term "co-consciousness" to represent aspects of thought which are not in the forefront of conscious attention. To him, hysteria, as found in cases of multiple personality, simply were extreme examples of independently acting co-conscious ideas.

Freud took exception to the views of both Janet and Prince, claiming that the mere process of "splitting" or "loosening" of associations, especially if attributed to neurological defects, was insufficient to account for both the timing and the content of the dissociative symptoms. He asserted that dissociation stemmed from an active process of repression in which forbidden impulses and thoughts are sealed into separate psychic compartments. These impulses are momentarily discharged during the dissociation state, providing the clinician thereby with clues into the character of the patient's repressed anxieties and conflicts. Upon a return to "normal" functioning, the memory of these ideas and emotions was again repressed and kept "out of mind."

### CLINICAL PICTURE

The DSM-II provides two separate syndromes for what we conceive to be the basic dissociative disorder. The first of these syndromes, *hysterical neurosis, dissociative type,* corresponds closely to the formulation to be presented, and is described as follows:

. . . alterations may occur in the patient's state of consciousness or in his identity, to produce such symptoms as amnesia, somnambulism, fugue, and multiple personality.

The second category, and one that is new to the official classification schema, is termed *depersonalization neurosis,* and is characterized:

. . . by a feeling of unreality and estrangement from the self, body, or surroundings.

The introduction of a separate depersonalization syndrome appears to us to be an unwise decision since we consider the symptom to be one of the minor variants of the more general dissociative category, as will be elaborated in later paragraphs.

For our purposes, the varieties of dissociation may be grouped into two categories: *minor dissociations,* including relatively prolonged dream-like states, in which events are experienced as hazy or unreal, and briefer states, in which the individual seems divorced from himself and his surroundings; *major dissociations,* including cases in which there is a sweeping amnesia of the past and cases known as multiple personality, in which entirely different features of the individual's psychic make-up separate and become autonomous units of functioning.

### Minor Dissociations

These include experiences of *estrangement* from self or environment. Here the patient senses familiar objects and events as strange or foreign or views himself to be unreal or unknown (depersonalization). *Trance-like states* are akin to estrangement, but here the patient's awareness is merely dimmed; he seems to be in a "twilight" dreamworld, totally immersed in inner events and entirely oblivious of his surroundings. *Somnambulism* refers to sleepwalking, a process of carrying out acts that are consistent with concurrent dream fantasies. In these states, the individual often searches for desired objects and relationships or works out tensions and conflicts that normally are unconscious. For example, a young man wanders nocturnally to the foot of the bed of his sleeping parents, seeking comfort and security; a woman runs every so often to the basement of her home to escape a nightmare fantasy of being taunted by her neighbors; a wealthy and respected man gets fully dressed, strolls into neighboring streets looking into trashcans and then returns home to sleep. Although somnambulists are able to get to wherever they are going, their thought processes tend to be hazy and incoherent during these episodes, and they rarely recall any of the events that happened. To be included also in the minor dissociations are *frenzied states* in which sudden, brief and totally forgotten bizarre behaviors erupt in the course of otherwise normal events. In these cases the person usually acts out forbidden thoughts and emotions which previously had been repressed.

### Major Dissociations

These include *total amnesia* in which the patient usually forgets both his past and his identity. These may occur in conjunction with a flight from one's normal environment, an event referred to as a *fugue.* Whether or not physical flight occurs, the amnesic patient has genuinely lost cognizance of his identity and the significant persons and places of his life. Most amnesic episodes terminate after several days, although a few prove to be permanent. *Multiple personalities* are extremely rare cases in which the patient's psychic make-up is reorganized into two or more separate and autonomously functioning units; the fictional characters of Doctor Jekyll and Mr. Hyde are a dramatic and simplified portrayal of the coexistence of diametrically contrasting features which often characterize the two personality units. In most cases, the patient's "normal self" is the dominant personality unit; it periodically gives way to, and is totally amnesic for, a contrasting but subsidiary unit of personality functioning. Appreciably less frequent are cases in which two equally prominent personality units alternate on a regular basis and with some frequency.

## COPING FUNCTIONS

What gives rise to dissociative phenomena?

To answer this question, it may be useful to go back first to Janet's original thesis: a lack of power for "psychic cohesion." Janet ascribed this deficiency to neural degeneration traceable either to hereditary weaknesses or to psychological "exhaustion." An alternative interpretation of Janet's thesis, one that is more consistent with current thinking, would assign the loss of "psychic cohesion" not to neural defects but to an acquired deficiency in cognitive controls. As a function of early training and experience, many individuals fail to acquire a coherent and well-integrated core of personality traits necessary for organizing their past and future experiences. We noted, for example, that active-dependent (gregarious) personalities lack an "inner identity," are empty or devoid of a past, tend to be over-reactive to external promptings and are deficient in self-controls. It would be consistent with their ingrained patterns for these patients to be subject to the splitting or disintegration of memories, impulses and thoughts, since they lack the equipment to bind or cohere divergent elements of their psychic make-up.

Another cause or function of dissociation may be found in the writings of Freud, who suggested that the disorder reflected the existence of strong and mutually incompatible elements of personality. Unable to contain these conflicting forces in a single cohesive unit, the personality is cleaved into separate systems, either with one system totally repressed (amnesia) or with two or more systems operating autonomously (multiple personality). This view, that dissociation reflects the preservation of the conscious self by banishing unacceptable traits from awareness, certainly seems reasonable as another determinant of the disorder.

Not to be overlooked as a third factor are secondary gains. Janet's thesis, as modified, suggests the operation of deficient cognitive controls. The Freudian thesis focuses on primary gains, that is, the isolation of thoughts and impulses which provoke anxiety, should they coexist consciously. The third hypothesis asserts that the dissociative act may provide positive reinforcements in the form of advantages such as a "new life," an escape from boredom, the attraction of attention, affection and nurture.

As in most pathologies, the dissociative symptom is likely to be overdetermined, an outcome representing a compromise of several determinants. These various combinations of influence will be seen when we turn next to the personality background of dissociated patients.

## PERSONALITY DISPOSITIONS

The personality patterns disposed to dissociative episodes are the same as those found in other neurotic disorders. The theme which unifies them in this regard is their common desire to avoid social disapproval. Other personalities, both pathological and normal, may exhibit dissociative symptoms, but the probability of such episodes in these cases is rather small. As noted earlier, our presentation will proceed in the order of the most to the least vulnerable of the five patterns in whom the disorder is most frequently exhibited.

1. *Active-detached personalities* (avoidant and schizoid) experience frequent and varied forms of dissociative phenomena. Feelings of estrangement may arise as protective maneuvers designed to diminish the impact of excessive stimulation or the pain of social humiliation. These symptoms may also reflect the consequences of the patient's devalued sense of self;

without an esteemed and integrated inner core to which experience can be anchored, events often seem disconnected, ephemeral and unreal.

Self-estrangement, termed depersonalization, may be traced to a characteristic coping maneuver of cognitive interference, which not only serves to disconnect normally associated events, but deprives the person of meaningful contact with his own feelings and thoughts.

Experiences of amnesia may occur as an expression of self-rejection. Forever to be oneself is not a cheerful prospect for these persons, and life may be started anew by disowning one's past identity.

Frenzied states are a common dissociative disorder in these patients, especially at the schizoid level of severity. Here, for a brief period, the patient may act out his frustrated and repressed impulses, as illustrated in the following case.

### CASE 10-9
#### Dolores J., Age 29, Unmarried

Dolores was seen after a series of "hysterical fits" at home. She lived alone with an elderly mother, had been unemployed for several years and spent most of her days sitting by the window, staring blankly. Her mother reported that Dolores had always been a quiet girl. However, since her older brother left home some two years earlier, Dolores rarely spoke to anyone, and often hid in her room when visitors came.

Her "fits" were repeated on an average of once a week while she was hospitalized. They would begin when Dolores shouted aloud, "I don't want to, I don't want to"; she then fell on her bed, vigorously fighting an unseen assailant who, she believed, sought to rape her. As she fended off her hallucinated attacker, Dolores would begin to tear at her clothes; finally, half denuded, she submitted to his desires, enacting a rather bizarre form of masturbation. After a brief period, mixed with tears and laughter, Dolores became quiet and subdued. Conscious awareness gradually returned, with no recall of the episode.

It is only in accord with tradition that we include these frenzied dissociative states among the neurotic disorders. There is no question but that the bizarre behavior and loss of reality evident during these episodes are severe enough to merit viewing them as psychotic. Custom and perhaps the brevity of the eruption and the rapid return to former functioning are the only justifications for placing them in the moderately severe categories.

2. *Passive-ambivalent personalities* (conforming and cycloid) succumb to dissociative episodes for a variety of reasons. Experiences of estrangement stem primarily from their charac-

teristic overcontrol and repression of feeling. By desensitizing their emotions or withdrawing them as a part of everyday life these patients may begin to experience the world as flat and colorless, a place in which events seem mechanical, automatic and unreal.

Episodes of total amnesia may occur if the patient is otherwise unable to isolate and control intense ambivalent feelings. The coexistence of conflicting habits and emotions may be too great a strain. Not only will the eruption of hostile and erotic impulses shatter the patient's self-image of propriety, but they may provoke the severe condemnation he dreads from others. Unable to restrain these urges, he must disown his identity and in the process obliterate all past associations and memories. The following brief sketch summarizes a typical case.

### CASE 10-10
#### George T., Age 38, Married, Four Children

This rather overcontrolled and highly tense police officer had recently become involved in an extramarital affair. After a few weeks, he began to suffer marked insomnia and unbearable guilt feelings. Unable to share his thoughts and emotions and refusing to go to confession at his church, he became increasingly disconsolate and depressed. One morning, he "forgot" who he was while driving to work, rode some 200 miles from his home town and was found three days later in a motel room, weeping and confused as to his whereabouts.

A frenzied state may be another form of discharge when tensions become unbearable. These allow the patient to vent his contrary impulses without conscious awareness.

Although rare, multiple personality disorders may be formed, enabling the patient to retain his "true" identity most of the time while gaining periodic release through his "other" self.

3. *Active-dependent personalities* (gregarious and cycloid) generally lack an adequate degree of personality integration, making it difficult for them even in normal times to unify the disparate elements of their lives. At times of strain and discord, this integrative deficiency may readily result in a dissociative state.

Somnambulism, a nighttime phenomenon, is not uncommon and usually takes the form of a search for attention and stimulation, when these patients feel otherwise deprived. Daytime trance-like episodes are rather unusual, however, since these patients desire to be alert to their environment. Also rare are amnesic fugues and multiple personality formations. When they do occur, they usually represent an attempt to break out of a confining and stultifying environment. Faced with internal poverty and external boredom or constraint, they may seek the secondary gains of a more exciting and dramatic life in which they can achieve the attention and approval they crave. These elements are nicely illustrated in the following brief history.

### CASE 10-11
#### Brenda S., Age 30, Married, No Children

This active-dependent woman had begun to feel "boxed in" by her suspicious husband; she suddenly disappeared from her home and was not located for several months. Brenda was found more than 1000 miles away working as a chorus girl in a run-down burlesque house, returning thereby to her vocation prior to marriage five years earlier. Although her claim that she had "blacked out" was doubted at first, further study revealed that she was totally amnesic for her life since her marriage, but recalled with great clarity her activities and relationships prior to that time.

4. *Passive-dependent personalities* (submissive and cycloid) may develop dream-like trance states when faced with responsibilities and obligations that surpass their feelings of competence; through this maneuver they effectively fade out of contact with threatening realities. Amnesic episodes, however, are extremely rare since these would prompt or intensify separation anxieties.

Repetitive somnambulistic states are not uncommon. Here the patient usually vents minor forbidden impulses or seeks to secure affect and nurture.

Brief frenzied states may arise at the moderately severe cycloid level if the patient experiences an upsurge of intense hostile impulses that may threaten his dependency security. In this way, contrary feelings may be discharged without the patient knowing it and therefore without having to assume blame. These irrational acts are so uncharacteristic of the patient that they tend to be seen by others as a sign of "sickness," often eliciting thereby nurtural and supporting responses.

5. *Active-ambivalent personalities* (negativistic and cycloid) are accustomed to expressing their contrary feelings rather directly, and will exhibit dissociative symptoms only if they are unduly constrained or fearful of severe retaliation. Even under these circumstances, the frequency of these disorders is rather low. Temper tantrums, which approach dissociative frenzied states in their overt appearance, are rather com-

mon. However, in these eruptions the patient does not lose conscious awareness and usually recalls the events that transpired.

## OBSESSION-COMPULSION DISORDERS
### (DSM-II: *Obsessive Compulsive Neurosis*)

Most people find themselves overly concerned and preoccupied when facing some real and troubling problem; they experience an inability to "get their mind off it" and turn to other matters. These events are similar to obsessive experiences, but in these cases the idea the person mulls over is rather picayune, absurd or irrational, yet it intrudes with such persistence as to interfere with his normal daily functioning. Compulsions are similar to obsessions; however, here the patient cannot resist engaging in certain acts, in performing some trivial behavioral ritual which he recognizes as ridiculous, humiliating or disgusting, but which he must execute to avoid the anxiety he experiences when he fails to do it.

Both obsessions and compulsions are similar to other neurotic symptoms in that they reflect the operation of intrapsychic mechanisms. Each neurotic disorder protects the individual from recognizing the true source of his anxieties, yet allows the anxiety a measure of release without damaging his self-image or provoking social rebuke. In phobias, the inner tension is symbolized and attached to an external object; in conversions, it is displaced and expressed through some body part; in dissociative symptoms, there is a blocking or splitting off of the anxiety source; in obsessions and compulsions, tension is controlled, symbolized and periodically discharged through a series of repetitive acts or thoughts.

### History

Commonalities among diverse neurotic symptoms were first proposed by Charcot. However, it was his student Janet who first made an effort to relate them systematically.

1. To Janet, all neurotic disorders were a consequence of a diminution of biological mental energies requisite to the integration of higher mental processes. Complex thoughts and emotions, which normally were connected and organized, drifted apart into a chaotic mental anarchy when these energies diminished or were drained. As a consequence of this weakness, primitive and subsidiary forces took over the personality and led to the scattering and disor-

ganization of formerly coordinated thoughts and emotions. Obsessions and compulsions were seen in this light. They were merely incidental expressions of a basic disintegration of organized higher mental processes.

2. As we noted earlier, Freud rejected Janet's thesis, claiming that both the timing and the choice of the symptom indicated the primacy of psychogenic rather than biogenic factors. All neuroses stemmed from intrapsychic mechanisms designed to control and alleviate anxieties traceable to early life experiences. The specific symptom reflected, symbolically, both the character of the anxiety source and the defensive maneuvers the patient employed to cope with it.

Obsessions and compulsions indicated to Freud that previously repressed thoughts and feelings of hostility and guilt had been reactivated. To counteract yet give partial ventilation to these ideas and emotions, the patient employs four defensive mechanisms—isolation, displacement, reaction formation and undoing.

Through "isolation" the patient disconnects the association that previously existed between a forbidden thought and its accompanying feeling. For example, he might have obsessional thoughts of murder without being aware of or experiencing an appropriate parallel emotion; conversely, he may feel a frightening and intense murderous urge without knowing its cause. By isolating an affect from its associated thought, the patient avoids confronting the real connection between them. Isolation may not be completely successful, however, and some residuals of the forbidden feelings and thoughts may still be experienced as distressful.

"Displacement" enables the patient to find a substitute activity or thought to attach his tensions to, something which camouflages his real discomfort and serves to focus his attention elsewhere. Thus, he becomes obsessed with some trivial thought, and thereby manages to divert himself from true reflection.

"Reaction formation" goes one step further toward self-deception; here, the individual thinks and behaves in ways that are diametrically opposite to his "true" but forbidden ideas and impulses. Through this mechanism, not only are feelings and thoughts disconnected and displaced, but their content is twisted into its exact opposite. Thus, instead of expressing an urge to soil and be messy, the patient becomes compulsively clean and neat.

"Undoing" parallels reaction formation. Having failed to reverse his attitudes and emotions beforehand, as in reaction formation, the patient finds that he must rescind and gain forgiveness for his transgressions. Thus, he attempts symbolically to redeem himself by various ritualistic acts. Through the undoing gesture, he not only pays penance for his forbidden thoughts, but seeks in a magical way to restore himself to a state of purity. For example, by compulsive or repetitive handwashing, the patient suffers the discomfort and embarrassment of his ritual and at the same time symbolically cleanses himself of his past misdeeds and evil intentions. However, since the real source of the patient's tension was not dealt with through the undoing maneuver, his relief is only temporary and he must repeat the ritualistic act time and again.

3. More recent views of obsessions and compulsions suggest that these symptoms reflect the simple overlearning of certain behaviors and thoughts. Thus, according to behavior theorists who eschew the role of unconscious processes in their formulations, these acts stem from either a conditioning sequence, in which the behavior in question reduced anxiety effectively, or from repeated exposure to certain models that were imitated. We will concern ourselves with these simple and straightforward learning habits in chapter 12 on the "behavior reactions."

Although learning is significantly involved in all forms of pathology, we shall focus our attention in this section on cases in which the symptom reflects the disruption or "disordering" of more generalized personality traits rather than the direct and simple product of overlearned behaviors. The distinction between these symptoms is a matter of the circumstances which give rise to them, and the persons in whom they appear rather than in the basic processes of how they may be learned. In both sets of conditions—disorder and reaction—learning and reinforcement principles are important theoretical tools for understanding symptom formation.

## CLINICAL PICTURE

Since several features of the obsessive-compulsive syndrome have already been elaborated, we need only detail in more systematic fashion what has been said.

*Obsessions* tend to be exhibited in two forms. The first, *obsessive doubting,* represents a state of perpetual indecision in which the patient interminably reevaluates a series of alternatives, rarely makes a clear-cut choice, and if he does, rescinds that choice, only to waver again. The uncertainty he feels leads him to brood about past

actions and reexamine them endlessly, to believe that they were ill conceived or poorly executed, and then to undo or recheck them repeatedly, e.g., a woman lies awake, uncertain whether she turned off the gas jets on the stove, proceeds to check them, finds them closed, returns to bed, thinks she may have inadvertently put them on, doubts that she could have done so, but must go and check again. *Obsessive thoughts* are intrusive, ideas which the person cannot block from consciousness. Some are meaningless (e.g., "where did I see a chair with one leg cut off?") and are experienced without emotion, but nonetheless are so persistent and distracting as to upset even the most routine of daily activities. Other recurrent thoughts are affect and tension-laden, pertain to forbidden aggressive impulses or to prohibited sexual desires and are experienced with shame, disgust or horror. The more desperately the patient tries to rid himself of these repugnant ideas, the more tormenting and persistent they become, e.g., a passing thought of poisoning a wayward husband becomes fixed in a wife's mind. No matter how much she seeks to distract her attention from it, the thought returns to hound her at every meal.

*Compulsions* are behavior sequences, usually in the form of some ritual that is recognized by the patient as absurd or irrational, but which, if not executed, will provoke anxiety. These rituals express themselves most frequently as bizarre stereotyped acts, e.g., touching one's nose with one's pinky before washing; repetition of normal acts, e.g., tying one's shoelace exactly eight times before feeling satisfied with the outcome; or insisting on cleanliness and order, e.g., being unduly concerned that ashtrays remain spotless or that one's books never be out of alphabetical sequence.

## COPING FUNCTIONS

The Freudian concepts of isolation, displacement, reaction formation and undoing are useful ways of referring to the principal intrapsychic methods by which the patient copes with his anxieties and forbidden impulses.

Obsessions relieve anxiety by isolating a thought from its associated feeling. In addition, by displacing the anxiety-provoking thought to a substitute and innocuous obsessional idea, the patient distracts himself, as in phobias, from the true source of his tensions. Reaction formation not only enables him to disconnect, but to counteract his forbidden feelings. In addition, by thinking and acting in ways that are diametrically opposite to his dangerous impulses, he may also be able to gratify these impulses with complete impunity, e.g., by actively engaging in the censoring of pornography, the patient provides himself, through his careful "examination" of this "disgusting literature," with an acceptable rationale to ventilate his otherwise repressed hostile and erotic impulses.

Compulsions achieve similar coping aims. The patient's irresistible preoccupation with a variety of absurd but "safe" activities distracts him from confronting his real source of discomfort. Moreover, through reaction formation, as illustrated in the case above, he may be able to pursue activities which serve as a subterfuge for his socially unacceptable impulses. Symbolic acts traceable to undoing mechanisms serve not only to void past sins, but to ward off anticipated future punishment and social rebuke. Thus, the self-punitive and redemptive aspects of the undoing ritual often discharge and diminish the oppressive build up of guilt feelings. In addition, the patient's insistence on order and cleanliness and the self-righteous air with which he performs these acts, evoke the secondary gains of attention and approval from others, e.g., the compulsively orderly and "proper" high school student will be viewed, both by parents and teachers alike, as a fine, well-disciplined and upright young man.

## PERSONALITY DISPOSITIONS

Obsessions and compulsions are exhibited by several pathological personalities; in the following we will list the five most common patterns, ranging from the most to the least vulnerable.

1. *Passive-ambivalent personalities* (conforming, cycloid and paranoid) exhibit these symptoms with appreciably greater frequency than any of the other pathological patterns; in fact, they are so typical of these patients that many clinicians, as well as the official DSM-II, refer to them as "obsessive compulsive personalities." Thus, in these individuals, the obsessive-compulsive symptomatology is not so much a matter of "disordered" coping as it is a deeply ingrained and learned strategy utilized throughout their lives to contain the upsurge of intense socially forbidden impulses. By a pattern of widely generalized reaction formations, they have learned not only to control their contrary inclinations, but to present a front of complete conformity and propriety.

Obsessive doubting may be so ingrained that these patients reevaluate and reexamine even the most trivial decisions and acts. This excessive preoccupation with minor irrelevancies enables them to distract their attention from the real source of their anxieties. Although doubting is a habitual aspect of their daily functioning, it may become quite distinctive as a symptom if there is a sudden eruption of feelings that may "give them away." Their pretense of equanimity and control is often disrupted by bizarre thoughts, usually of a hostile or erotic character. These stir up intense fears of social condemnation, which may be handled by a series of compulsive rituals, e.g., each morning, by washing his face three times and knotting his tie five times, a patient assured himself of his purity; moreover, by repeating some insignificant act in which he feels competent, he strengthened his confidence in his ability to control his impulses.

2. *Active-detached personalities* (avoidant and schizoid) develop these symptoms for various coping purposes. Obsessions may serve as substitute thoughts to distract these patients from reflecting on their "true" misery. Similarly, these thoughts may counter feelings of estrangement and depersonalization by providing schizoids, for example, with ideas and events that serve to assure them that life is real. Compulsive acts accomplish similar coping aims. They "fill up" time, diverting patients from self-preoccupations; moreover, these acts keep them in touch with real events and thereby help deter feelings of depersonalization and estrangement. Certain of these repetitive and superstitious acts may reflect attempts to cope with anticipated social derision. For example, a 30 year old schizoid patient made a complete 360 degree turn each time prior to his walking through a door. This, he felt, would change his personality, which in turn would disincline those he subsequently met from ridiculing him. These ritualistic behaviors often signify also a bizarre method of controlling socially condemned thoughts and impulses. Thus, the patient noted above put the index finger of his right hand to his lips, and then placed both hands in the back pockets of his trousers, whenever he felt the urge to shout obscenities or touch the breasts of women passers-by.

3. *Passive-dependent personalities* (submissive and cycloid) are often preoccupied with obsessive doubts. These usually derive from reactivated feelings of inadequacy and are precipitated by situations in which they must assume independence and responsibility. Here, they weigh interminably the pros and cons of the situation, thereby postponing endlessly any change in the status quo of

dependency. Obsessional thoughts and compulsive acts frequently are manifested when feelings of separation anxiety or repressed anger come to the fore. Here, the coping maneuver serves, through reaction formation or undoing, to counter tensions that would arise as a consequence of discharging their impulses. The symptoms displayed often take the form of "sweet" thoughts and approval-gaining acts, as illustrated in the following case.

### CASE 10-12
#### Myrna H., Age 32, Married, One Child

This woman could not rid herself of the obsessive image that her husband's face was "the most beautiful in the world"; she also took great pains each night to wash, iron and prepare every item of clothing he planned to wear the next day. Upon clinical study, she revealed an intense fear that her husband might discover that she once allowed a neighbor to kiss her while he was away on an extended business trip. Her obsessive symptom enabled her to block the visualization of her neighbor's face. Her compulsive acts of caring for her husband were an attempt to "prove" her faithfulness and devotion to him.

4. *Active-dependent personalities* (gregarious and cycloid) are disposed to have their thoughts and emotions rather scattered and disconnected as a function of their general deficit personality integration. They illustrate, in this regard, the modified dissociative thesis of Janet. They characteristically exhibit dramatic emotional feelings over matters of minimal import and significance. Conversely, they may discuss serious topics and problems with a rather cool detachment. This ease with which affect and idea can be isolated from each other is a primary factor in contributing to their obsessive symptoms. Thus, with little strain or tension, they readily disconnect an emotion from its associated content.

Quite often, these patients experience a "free-floating" erotic emotion, that is, a sexual impulse without precipitant or focus. Conversely, hostile obsessive thoughts may preoccupy them whereas the normally associated feeling of anger remains repressed. Which behavior or emotion is expressed and which is repressed is usually guided by their basic goal of gaining social approval and minimizing social rebuke, e.g., they rarely vent hostile feelings, but often manifest seductive emotions and behaviors.

5. *Active-ambivalent personalities* (negativistic and cycloid) tend to vent their contrary impulses rather openly. However, these feelings may be transformed intrapsychically into obses-

sions and compulsions if they are especially intense and likely to provoke either separation anxieties or severe social reproval. Obsessive thinking is a common resolution of this conflict, e.g., a normally outspoken patient was quietly obsessed with the thought that her husband's clothes were stained with lipstick and sperm; this symbolized her fear that he was having an affair and that others would discover this "fact," much to her shame; she did not dare confront him with her obsessive suspicion, dreading that he would admit it and leave her.

## DEJECTION DISORDER
### (DSM-II: *Depressive Neurosis*)

There is an obviously peculiar, even bizarre, quality to the neurotic disorders we have discussed so far. By discharging tensions through highly symbolic and indirect means, the patient's behavior appears clearly to fall beyond the province of "normality." For example, in phobic disorders, the patient's anxieties are displaced and transformed into a totally irrational fear; in the conversions, a strange and symbolic bodily ailment emerges; dissociation "splits off" tensions through trance-like states and memory loss; and obsessions and compulsions are insistent repetitions of peculiar acts and thoughts.

The next two disorders to be discussed, dejection and hypochondriasis, are more "normal," that is, seemingly understandable and rational. In these, the patient's tensions are vented through more or less conventional behaviors and by logical and coherent verbal communications which appear "sensible" to others. Despite the coherence and sensibility of these symptoms, however, they are just as pathological as other neurotic symptoms. They disguise the patient's true feelings and serve as a subterfuge to camouflage the real source of his tensions, both to himself and others. For example, hypochondriacal complaints focus on discomforts experienced in the person's body, but these "real" symptoms often cloak a hidden guilt and pervasive anger felt toward himself or others. In dejection, these same feelings of anger and guilt are voiced in the form of vague complaints of discontent and hopelessness.

Dejected patients alter their true feelings for fear that they might provoke social rejection and rebuke if openly expressed. Forbidden feelings are transformed in such ways as to recruit attention, support and nurture instead of reproval and condemnation. Although their "play for sympathy" may be seen through by some, these patients convey their sad plight with such genuineness or cleverness as to evoke compassion and concern from most. We shall deal first with the dejection disorder and turn in the next section to hypochondriasis.

## CLINICAL PICTURE

The precipitants and manifest form in which dejection is expressed depend largely on the premorbid personality of the patient. Some exhibit their depressive mood with displays of dramatic gesture and pleading commentary; others are demanding, irritable and cranky. Some verbalize their thoughts in passive, vague and abstract philosophical terms. Still others seem lonely, quiet, downhearted, solemnly morose and pessimistic. Common to all, however, is the presence of self-deprecatory comments, feelings of apathy, discouragement and hopelessness and a marked decline of personal initiative. Their actions and complaints usually evoke sympathy and support from others, but these reassurances provide only temporary relief from the prevailing mood of dejection.

All persons succumb, on occasion, to periods of gloom and self-recrimination, but these feelings and thoughts are usually prompted by conditions of objective stress, and tend to pass as matters take a turn for the better. In contrast, dejection, as a pathological disorder, appears either as an uncalled for and intense response of despondency to rather trivial difficulties or as an unduly prolonged period of discouragement following an objective, distressful precipitant.

A distinction must be made between the neurotic disorder of "dejection" to be described in this section and the psychotic disorder termed "depression" to be discussed in the next chapter. This distinction is largely a matter of degree. No sharp line can be drawn to separate what is essentially a continuum. Nevertheless, when the patient's moods and oppressive thoughts are so severe as to preclude meaningful social relationships or to foster total invalidism and dependency or to be accompanied by delusions and grossly bizarre behaviors, we may justly categorize the disorder as a psychotic depression.

In contrast to the DSM-II, which uses the label "depression" for both neurotic and psychotic states, we have chosen to employ the term "dejection" for the neurosis to signify more clearly its milder intensity.

## COPING FUNCTIONS

What aims are served by the patient's symptoms of morose hopelessness, ineffectuality and self-recrimination?

First and foremost, the moods and complaints of the dejected person summon nurtural responses from others. He recruits from both family and friends reassurances of his lovability and value to them, and gains assurances of their faithfulness and devotion.

As with other neurotic disorders, the dejection symptom may serve also as an instrument for avoiding unwelcome responsibilities. Dejection with its attendant moods and comments is especially effective in this regard since the patient openly admits his worthlessness and demonstrates his state of helplessness for all to see.

Along similar lines, some of these patients develop their impairment as a rationalization for indecisiveness and failure. Here, their complaints are colored with subtle accusations, claims that others have not supported or cared for them, thus fostering their sense of futility and their ineffectuality.

Overt expressions of hostility, however, are rarely exhibited by these patients, since they fear that these actions will prove offensive and lead others to rebuke or reject them. As a consequence, feelings of anger and resentment may be discharged only in subtle or oblique forms. This often is done by overplaying one's helplessness and futile state. His "sorrowful plight" may not only create guilt in others, but cause them no end of discomfort as they attempt to fulfill the patient's "justified" need for attention and care.

These devious coping maneuvers may prove fruitless or may evoke exasperation on the part of others. Under these circumstances, patients may discharge their tensions and also solicit the sympathy they otherwise failed to achieve by turning their anger upon themselves and condemning their own behaviors. It is at these times that protestations of guilt and self-reproval come to the fore. These patients voice a flood of self-deprecatory comments about their shortcomings, the inordinate demands they have made of others, their irresponsibility, unworthiness, evil thoughts and so on. Through self-derision and thinly veiled suicidal threats, they not only discharge their tensions, but manage to get others to forgive them and, once more, assure them of their lovability and worthiness.

The varieties of dejection exhibited in these patients reflect the particular sensitivities and coping strategies they acquired in the past. To better grasp these distinctions we must turn to the different personality backgrounds conducive to this syndrome.

## PERSONALITY DISPOSITIONS

As we noted previously, the common theme unifying the neurotic disorders is the fear of behaving or expressing thoughts and emotions which might provoke social condemnation. In addition, most of these patients seek to solicit attention, sympathy and nurture, as well. Neurotic patients attempt to avoid events which might precipitate a disordering of their precarious equilibrium. Toward this end also, they utilize intrapsychic mechanisms to keep disruptive and forbidden impulses from conscious awareness. Where feasible, these mechanisms are used in the service of venting these tensions and impulses in camouflage form. The strategies employed to achieve these aims are determined largely by a patient's central past experiences and learnings. In the following paragraphs we will survey the aims and coping styles of the five patterns most vulnerable to the dejection disorder.

1. *Passive-dependent personalities* (submissive and cycloid) are especially susceptible to separation anxiety. Feelings of helplessness and futility readily come to the fore when they are faced either with burdensome responsibilities or the anticipation of social abandonment. The actual loss of a significant person almost invariably prompts severe dejection, if not psychotic depression.

Anticipation of abandonment may prompt these patients to admit openly their weaknesses and shortcomings as a means of gaining reassurance and support. Expressions of guilt and self-condemnation typically follow since these verbalizations often successfully deflect criticism from others, transforming their threats into comments of reassurance and sympathy.

At the cycloid level especially, guilt may arise as a defense against the outbreak of resentment and hostility. Passive-dependent cycloids usually contain their anger since they dread provoking the retribution of abandonment and isolation. To prevent this occurrence they turn their aggressive impulses inward, discharging them through self-derisive comments and verbalizations of guilt and contrition. This maneuver not only tempers the exasperation of others, but often prompts them to respond in ways which make the patient feel redeemed, worthy and loved.

2. *Active-ambivalent personalities* (nega-

tivistic and cycloid) display an agitated form of dejection; they characteristically vacillate between anxious futility, despair and self-deprecation on the one hand, and a bitter discontent and demanding attitude toward friends and relatives on the other. Accustomed to the direct ventilation of impulses, these patients restrain their anger and turn it inward only when they fear that its expression will result in total rejection. One senses a great struggle between acting out and curtailing resentments. They exhibit a grumbling and sour disaffection with themselves and with others. Moody complaints and an attitude of generalized pessimism pervade the air. These serve as a vehicle of tension discharge, relieving them periodically of mounting inner and outer directed hostilities.

Instrumentally, the sour moods and complaints of these patients tend to intimidate others, and enable them to gain partial retribution for past disappointments by making life miserable for others. These manipulative characteristics and their consequences are illustrated in the following case.

### CASE 10-13
### Anna F., Age 50, Married, Two Children

Anna, a cycloid personality, employed a variety of complaints and intimidating maneuvers with her husband and children as a means of extracting attention and nurture from them, but she knew that these attentions were provided without genuine affection and compassion. Moreover, these expressions of support were received by her with a mixed welcome since Anna learned all too well from the past that people were inconsistent and fickle in their affectionate overtures. It was the unsureness of the durability and genuineness of support which, in large measure, gave her dejection its anxious and apprehensive coloring. This insecurity combined with Anna's restrained anger and mixed feelings of guilt to shape the restless and agitated character of her dejection.

3. *Passive-ambivalent personalities* (conforming and cycloid) exhibit a pattern of tense and anxious dejection that is similar to, but more tightly controlled than, that of their active-ambivalent counterparts. Faced with difficult decisions but unable to obtain either clear direction or approval from others, these patients experience a strong upsurge of anger and resentment toward themselves for their weakness and toward others for their unyielding demands and their unwillingness to provide support. They are fearful, however, of exposing their personal shortcomings and hostile feelings to others. On the other hand, they have been trained well to express self-reproval and feel guilt. Thus, rather

than vent their resentments toward others and suffer the consequences of severe social rebuke, these patients discharge their anger toward themselves. Severe self-reproval serves as a form of expiation for their forbidden contrary thoughts and feelings. Moreover, by being contrite they hope that no one will be so unkind as to attack and abandon them. Unfortunately, this hope rests on a poor foundation. Passive-ambivalents have experienced severe condemnation in the past for signs of weakness and incompetence. Thus, they cannot escape the "bind" they are in, cannot free themselves from the fear that their sorrowful state ultimately will provoke rejection. Their agitated and apprehensive dejection reflects, then, both their struggle to contain the expression of resentments and their fear that weakness and contrition will prompt derision and abandonment.

Passive-ambivalents, on occasion, display a benign and reflective moroseness. This may arise when they realize how empty their lives have been, how much they have denied themselves and how much they have given up as a consequence of external pressures. These "calm" periods of dejection are often interrupted by brief episodes of assertive self-determination. However, old feelings of anxiety are reactivated during these episodes, making them rather short lived. Almost invariably, these patients revert quickly to their established conforming ways.

4. *Active-dependent personalities* (gregarious and cycloid) overplay their feelings of dejection, expressing them through rather dramatic gestures and in fashionable jargon. This contrasts to the flat and somber picture of the passive-dependent, and the tense, guilt-ridden and agitated quality seen in the ambivalents. The histrionic coloring of their mood is a natural outgrowth of their basic coping style of actively soliciting attention and approval.

Episodes of dejection in these patients are prompted less by a deep fear of abandonment than by a sense of inner emptiness and inactivity. It arises most often when they feel stranded between one fleeting attachment and another, or between one transitory "exciting" preoccupation and the next. At these times of noninvolvement, they sense a lack of direction and purpose and experience a fearful void and aloneness.

Dejection in active-dependents tends to be expressed in popular jargon. The patient philosophizes about his "existential anxiety" or the alienation that one must inevitably feel in this "age of mass society." Their use of fashionable terms provides them with a bridge to others. It gives them a sense of belonging during those moments when they feel most isolated from the mainstream of active social life in which they so desperately crave to be. Moreover, their pseudosophistication about up to date matters and terminology not only enables them to rationalize their sense of emptiness and confusion, but also allows them to maintain their appeal in the eyes of "interesting" people. By attaching themselves to currently popular modes of group disenchantment, they reinstate themselves as participants of an "involved" cultural subgroup and manage, thereby, to draw interested attention to themselves. These expressions of social dissent also provide an outlet for venting some of their resentments and tensions. However, should these feelings of hostility be discharged without group support, as occasionally occurs at the cycloid level, they are quickly rescinded and replaced by dramatic expressions of guilt and contrition.

5. *Active-detached personalities* (avoidant and schizoid) are not viewed by most theorists as being among those who display the mood of dejection. This contention reflects, no doubt, the characteristic effort of these patients to flatten their affect. For purposes of self-protection, they suppress or otherwise interfere with the experience of any and all emotions. Despite the validity of this analysis, there are times when these patients sense genuine feelings of emptiness and loneliness. Periodically, they express a vague yet hopeless yearning for the affection and approval they have been denied. Adding to this mood are the contempt these patients feel for themselves and the self-deprecation they experience for their unlovability, weakness, ineffectuality and their failure to assert themselves and stand up for their rights. Though hesitant to express this self-contempt before others, lest it invite a chorus of further derision, close inquiry or tactful probing will frequently elicit both the self-deprecatory comments and moods of futility and dejection that we more commonly associate with other patterns.

## HYPOCHONDRIACAL DISORDERS
(DSM-II: *Hypochondriacal and Neurasthenic Neuroses*)

Interspersed between TV commercials for headache tablets, muscular relaxants, intestinal tonics and the like, we manage to see a few of the other forms of entertainment provided to meet the public demand. It has often been noted that more ingenuity is invested in attracting the

American populace to remedies for their non-existent ailments than in filling their impoverished imaginations. There are many reasons for the vast and continuous commercial success of these nostrums. Primary among them is the need of millions of Americans to find magical elixirs and balms by which they hope, rather futilely, to counter their lack of energy and a bevy of minor physical discomforts. These perennial states of fatigue and the persistence of medically undiagnosable aches and pains signify another of the neurotic disorders, one that runs to endless expenditures for drugs and physicians and disables, in one form or another, a significant portion of our populace.

Hypochondriacal disorders have been left as the last of the neurotic syndromes since they may be viewed as a bridge to the psychophysiological and sociopathic syndromes to be discussed next.

Hypochondriasis shares with psychophysiologic disorders a common focus on bodily distress and discomfort. However, the psychophysiological group has a demonstrable biological impairment that accounts for their physical discomfort; moreover, their symptomatology arises, in large part, from a failure to discharge hostile tensions whereas the symptoms of hypochondriacs reflect their way of discharging these same tensions.

It is this discharge of hostility which makes the hypochondriacal disorder similar to the sociopathic group. Both act out anger and tension in the form of overt complaints. However, sociopaths vent their hostility upon others in overt and direct forms since they concern themselves little with the consequence of social rebuke. In contrast, hypochondriacs divert part of their anger toward themselves, transforming their partially restrained emotions into bodily complaints. Instead of complaining to others about their psychic anger directly, they camouflage and complain about it in the form of a physical substitute. By turning their anger inward, they distract attention from their true hostile impulses; this prevents undue condemnation by others.

In this latter respect, hypochondriacs are similar to those with "dejection" disorders. The major difference between these syndromes is that in dejection, patients voice their discomforts in the form of emotion and mood whereas hypochondriacal patients represent their discomforts in terms of bodily aches and physical weariness.

Hypochondriacal disorders, as formulated in this text, subsume two separate syndromes listed in the DSM-II: *hypochondriacal neurosis* and *neurasthenic neurosis*. The following excerpts summarize their principal characteristics:

[Hypochondriacal neurosis] is dominated by preoccupation with the body and with fear of presumed diseases of various organs. Although the fears are not of delusional quality as in psychotic depressions, they persist despite reassurance.

[Neurasthenic neurosis] is characterized by complaints of chronic weakness, easy fatigability, and sometimes exhaustion.

It is our belief that hypochondriacal and neurasthenic symptoms represent two facets of the same syndrome; in one, the patient complains of *specific* bodily ailments and in the other, he complains of a *general* bodily weariness. Both symptoms often covary in a single patient since they serve essentially identical coping functions.

*History*

Although the clinical symptoms of neurotic fatigue and hypochondriasis were described in early Greek medical literature, it was not until the writings of George Miller Beard, in the mid-nineteenth century, that a specific theory was proposed to account for them. Beard coined the term "neurasthenia" to denote what he viewed to be the outcome of nervous exhaustion in these patients. His theory rested on the assumption that nerve cells operated like an electric battery, that is, they could run down or be depleted by overwork and inadequate psychic rest.

In his early writings, Freud agreed with Beard that the neurasthenic syndrome represented a physiological dysfunction. However, he hypothesized that the difficulty lay not in the depletion of neural energy but in the cumulation of excess sexual energies, which failed to be appropriately discharged. Freud subsumed neurasthenia in a single broader syndrome, termed the "actual neuroses," which included anxiety neuroses, neurasthenia and hypochondriasis. As he conceived it, these three disorders were, more or less, direct outcomes of undischarged or dammed-up physiological energies.

As noted earlier in the chapter, the actual neuroses were contrasted to the "psychoneuroses," whose origins lay in psychogenic trauma and whose tensions were transformed *and* discharged by the workings of the intrapsychic mechanisms. Freud altered some of these views in his later writings, proposing that psychogenic factors could play a role in the actual neuroses as well as the psychoneuroses. However, he continued to speak of the actual neuroses as bound and undischarged sexual energies, but began to see them as sources of focal irritation which could serve as the base for associated psychoneurotic symptoms. Specifically, he posited the view that neurasthenia (fatigue) might function as a somatic basis for a psychoneurotic withdrawal from social and sexual life. Similarly, hypochondriasis, which he conceived to be a mixture of anxiety and neurasthenia, reflected the withdrawal of sexual energies from their normal external objects, and their consequent attachment to narcissistically valued parts of the patient's own body.

More recent formulations of the hypochondriacal and neurasthenic syndromes have focused less on ostensive energy components and more on their interpersonal roots and coping functions. We shall base our presentation on these current viewpoints rather than on Freud's original thesis.

## CLINICAL PICTURE

The clinical features of the hypochondriacal and neurasthenic disorders are difficult to narrow down. Not only are the types of reported discomfort many and varied, but they almost inevitably combine with, complicate and blend into several other neurotic and psychophysiologic syndromes. They are given special note by the presence of prolonged periods of weariness and exhaustion, undiagnosable physical sensations, persistent insomnia, a state of diffuse irritability and reported pains in different, unconnected and changing regions of the body.

Phenomenologically, these patients experience a heaviness and a drab monotony to their lives. Despite this lethargy, they are exquisitely attuned to every facet of their normal physiology and markedly concerned with minor changes in bodily functioning.

Many patients, despite their preoccupation and concern with aches and pains, manage to function actively and with considerable vigor in the course of everyday life. Here, we may speak of hypochondriasis without neurasthenia. Other patients, however, are easily exhausted and cannot perform simple daily tasks without feeling that they have totally drained their meager reserves. This state of perpetual weariness, unaccompanied by specific body anxieties or discomforts, may be referred to as neurasthenia without hypochondriasis.

## COPING FUNCTIONS

As we have stressed before, neurotic symptoms reflect attempts to cope with tension and to achieve where possible a variety of secondary gains. Although our presentation of the coping maneuvers employed in these syndromes may sound as if patients plan them consciously, this is usually not the case. Strategies of coping are deeply ingrained and essentially unconscious habits and attitudes. They automatically "take over"

when the patient is confronted with current situations that he perceives as comparable to those of the past. They persist, in part, out of sheer inertia rather than because they are well-suited to meet the specifics of the current situation.

Among the principal goals of the hypochondriacal strategy are the patient's desires to solicit attention and nurture from others and to evoke reassurances that he will be loved and cared for, despite his weaknesses and inadequacies. By his "illness," the patient diverts attention from the true source of his dismay, usually the lack of interest and attention shown to him by others. Thus, without complaining directly about his disappointment and resentment, he still manages to rekindle their flagging interests and devotions. Moreover, these physical complaints are employed as a means of controlling others, making them feel guilty, and thereby retaliating for the disinterest and mistreatment the patient feels he has suffered.

In certain cases, these symptoms represent a form of self-punishment, an attack upon oneself disguised in the form of bodily ailments and exhaustion, as illustrated in the following case.

### CASE 10-14
### Ned R., Age 36, Married, Two Children

Ned, a passive-ambivalent personality, had recently begun to feel that his work at the office was "measurably" less than his colleagues' and that his exhaustion at the end of the day prevented him from being a "proper" father to his children. Although he voiced guilt for his failures, he was unable to face the real source of his recent distressing and depressing thoughts, the fact that he had begun to "fake" data to keep up with his associates; it was easier to tolerate weakness in his body than in his mind. Thus, he chose some symbolic physical substitute to punish himself for his guilt, "arthritic" aches in his fingers that made it increasingly difficult to write or to punch the keys of a calculator.

Not to be overlooked among the goals of coping are such secondary gains as avoiding responsibilities that threaten the patient's life style. Also prominent in this regard is the use of physical illness as a rationalization for inadequacies. Which of these varied coping aims are likely to be dominant in a particular patient depends on his basic personality, a topic to which we turn next.

## PERSONALITY DISPOSITIONS

As with the previously discussed neurotic disorders, we find the same five personality patterns to be most susceptible to hypochondriacal and neurasthenic symptoms. Let us be mindful again that these disorders are exhibited in other personalities, both normal and pathological, but that they occur with appreciably greater probability in the five following groups.

1. *Active-ambivalent personalities* (negativistic and cycloid) often display these symptoms in conjunction with a variety of psychophysiologic disorders. These basically discontent, irritable and fractious individuals use their physical complaints as a weak disguise for hostile impulses, a veil to cloak anger and resentment. Feelings of revenge for past frustrations often lie at the root of their excessive demands for special treatment. As household tyrants, they not only create guilt in others, but control the lives of family members and cause them considerable emotional anguish and financial cost.

Most of these patients were subjected in childhood to inconsistent parental treatment. Many learned, however, that they could evoke reliable parental attention and support when they were ill or complained of illness. As a consequence, whenever they feel the need for care and nurture, they revert back to this ploy of physical complaints as a means of evoking it.

Other patients, less successful in extracting the care and sympathy they desire, learn to nurture themselves and to attend to their own bodily needs. Disillusioned by parental disinterest or inconsistency, they provide, by a hypochondriacal ministering to themselves, a consistent form of self-sympathy and self-gratification.

2. *Passive-dependent personalities* (submissive and cycloid) have been well trained to view themselves as weak and inadequate. Overdependency and excessive parental solicitousness in childhood have taught them to protect themselves against overwork, not to exert their frail bodies and not to assume responsibilities that may strain their delicate physical equipment.

All sources of tension, be they externally precipitated or based on efforts to control forbidden inner impulses, lead to an anxious conservation of energy. Moreover, having learned that frailty and weakness elicit protective and nurtural reactions from others, they allow themselves to succumb to physical exhaustion and illness as a device to ensure these desired responses.

Genuine guilt feelings may crop up when these patients recognize how thoughtless and ineffectual they have been in carrying their burden of responsibilities. But here again, their physical state of weariness and bodily illness come to the rescue as a rationalization to exempt them from assuming their share of family chores.

3. *Passive-ambivalent personalities* (conforming and cycloid) also utilize these symptoms to rationalize failures and inadequacies. Fearful of being condemned for their shortcomings, they maintain their self-respect and the esteem of others by ascribing their deficiencies to a "legitimate" physical illness. This maneuver not only shields them from rebuke, but often evokes praise from others for the few meager accomplishments they have achieved. How commendable they must be for their conscientious efforts and attainments in the face of their illness and exhaustion.

Passive-ambivalents frequently suffer real fatigue and other psychophysiologic symptoms as a consequence of their struggle to control their anger and resentment. In addition, their bodily ailments often represent a turning inward of hostile impulses. Not infrequently, these ailments are a displaced and symbolic form of self-punishment, a physical substitute to vent feelings of guilt and self-reproval. Suffering not only discharges tension, then, but serves the function of expiation.

4. *Active-dependent personalities* (gregarious and cycloid) utilize hypochondriacal symptoms largely as an instrument for attracting attention. It also elicits approving comments for achievements which would not be offered were the patient well. To be fussed over and showered with favors is a rewarding experience for most individuals. In the active-dependents, however, this need for approval is "like a drug" that is required to sustain them. Because they feel a sense of emptiness and isolation without it, they seek a constant diet of attention and approval. If nothing else "works," illness can be depended on as a sure means to achieve these ends.

When life becomes humdrum and boring, physical ailments not only evoke interest and attention, but provide these patients with a needed source of stimulation. Bodily pains and aches are a preoccupation that can fill the empty moments.

Only rarely do these patients display weariness and fatigue, since these symptoms run counter to their active stimulus-seeking style of coping. Rather, through the use of dramatic hypochondriacal complaints they both draw attention to themselves and continue to participate in the mainstream of social life.

5. *Active-detached patients* (avoidant and schizoid) exhibit hypochondriacal symptoms to achieve a variety of different coping goals. For many it is a means of countering feelings of depersonalization. They may be overly alert to

## Table 10-1 Summary of Neurotic Disorders

### FEATURES COMMON TO ALL NEUROTIC DISORDERS

| Personality Background | General Coping Functions |
|---|---|
| Submissive, gregarious, conforming, negativistic, avoidant, cycloid, schizoid. | Maintain psychic and social equilibrium by counteracting external precipitants; block from awareness unconscious anxieties and impulses; vent tensions without provoking social condemnation; elicit attention, sympathy and nurture from others. |

### DISTINCTIVE FEATURES OF SPECIFIC NEUROTIC DISORDERS

| | Symptoms | Typical Coping Functions |
|---|---|---|
| PHOBIA | Strange and irrational fears that are recognized as absurd by the patient, but which must be avoided. | Distract self from inner sources of anxiety by displacing them to an external symbolic equivalent which can readily be avoided; deny and control forbidden impulses; solicit protection; avoid responsibilities. |
| CONVERSION | Bodily symptoms which simulate organic ailments, e.g., muscular paralysis; tactile anesthesia, mutism, visual and auditory defects, tics and spasms. | Crystallize and symbolize psychic tensions by displacement to body substitute; avoid responsibilities; control impulses; self-punishment by sacrificing body function. |
| DISSOCIATION | Estrangement, trance-like states, somnambulism, frenzied states, total amnesia, multiple personality. | Isolate and control ambivalent elements of a conflict; disown unacceptable feelings and memories; withdraw from environment; act out impulses. |
| OBSESSION-COMPULSION | Persistent and intrusive thoughts, repetitive and irresistible stereotyped acts, self-doubts, indecisiveness, need for orderliness. | Isolate and displace anxiety-producing thoughts to innocuous substitute; distract from and counteract forbidden feelings; discharge guilt by ritualistic undoing. |
| DEJECTION | Self-deprecation, feelings of futility, guilt and moroseness. | Solicit compassion; avoid responsibilities; create guilt in others; disguise expression of hostility. |
| HYPOCHONDRIASIS | Undiagnosable aches and pains, persistent complaints of physical discomfort, morbid concern over health, fatigue and weakness. | Attract attention; control others; rationalize failures and inadequacies; provide self-punishment and self-nurturance. |

bodily sounds and movements to assure themselves that they are "real" and alive. Not uncommonly, because of their habitual social isolation and self-preoccupation, they elaborate these bodily sensations into bizarre and delusional experiences.

Discomforting bodily sensations may be a symbolic expression of self-punishment. Thus, these symptoms often represent the disgust and hatred active-detached patients feel toward themselves.

Fatigue in these personalities may be viewed as an extension of their basic detachment strategy. Moreover, physical inertia can serve as a rationalization justifying withdrawal from social contact.

## REMEDIAL APPROACHES IN NEUROTIC DISORDERS

Despite overt differences in the symptomatology of the various neurotic disorders, we have viewed them as variations of a single large syndrome since they serve basically similar coping functions and since they arise most frequently in the same five personality patterns. These commonalities incline us to group them together for discussions of prognosis and therapy.

As far as prognosis is concerned, neurotic symptoms may persist long after their precipitating causes have abated. The primary reason for this persistence is the achievement of positive reinforcements, that is, secondary gains associated with the performance of neurotic behaviors. For example, a patient whose phobic response served initially to control and displace anxiety may retain his symptom after his anxiety has subsided if it gets him more attention and sympathy than he received without it. Since most neurotics seek the support and nurture of others, and since their "illness" often elicits these responses, the probabilities are high that the symptom will persist. Thus, neuroses are likely to remain unless environmental precipitants are removed and secondary gains are denied or achieved more effectively through other instrumental maneuvers.

Despite the short-term gains made by neurotic coping efforts, the symptoms they give rise to are frequently self-defeating in the end. By restricting his environment (e.g., phobias), limiting his physical competencies (e.g., conversions), preoccupying himself with distracting activities (e.g., obsessions-compulsions) or deprecating his self-worth (e.g., dejection), the patient avoids confronting and resolving his real difficulties and tends to become increasingly dependent on others. His neurotic maneuver, then, is a double-edged sword. It relieves for the moment passing discomforts and strains, but in the long run fosters the perpetuation of faulty attitudes and coping strategies.

Most neurotic patients exhibit a blend of several symptoms that rise and subside over time in their clarity and prominence. This complex and changing picture is further complicated by the fact that it is set within the context of the patient's broader personality pattern of pathological attitudes and strategies. In planning a remedial approach, the therapist is faced, then, with an inextricable mixture of focal and transitory symptoms that are embedded in a pattern of more diffuse and permanent traits.

Separating this complex of clinical features for therapeutic attention is no simple task. To decide which features comprise the "basic personality" and which represent the "neurotic symptomatology" cannot readily be accomplished since both are facets of the same system of vulnerabilities and coping strategies. Even when clear distinctions can be drawn, as when a symptom suddenly emerges in clear and sharp relief, a judgment must be made as to whether therapeutic attention should be directed to the focal symptom or to the "underlying" pattern from which it sprung. In certain cases, it is both expeditious and fruitful to concentrate solely on the manifest symptom disorder; in other cases, however, it may be advisable to rework the more pervasive and ingrained personality pattern.

Our interest in this chapter lies in the focal symptom, and we will now discuss some of the remedial approaches utilized in its relief. Recourse may be had to other techniques when more extensive personality changes appear appropriate.

Despite their coping efforts, many patients with neurotic disorders continue to experience considerable anxiety and tension. In these cases, any one of a number of biophysical tranquilizing agents may prove beneficial. In dejection, however, these drugs may have an adverse effect; it is advisable in these cases to utilize the pharmacological stimulants or antidepressants. At all times, the use of drugs should be considered with great care since they often upset the patient's own coping efforts and may result, thereby, in disturbances that are more serious than the one they were designed to alleviate. For example, dejection may serve to help the patient control his angry impulses, thereby preventing him from acting them out and experiencing serious repercussions such as separation and abandonment; by using a biophysical stimulant, hostile impulses may be released, precipitating fears of retribution and severe separation anxieties.

Behavior modification techniques are particularly promising as remedial measures for several of the neurotic disorders. These therapeutic procedures are especially suited for readily identifiable and clearly circumscribed symptoms which patients may be highly motivated to extinguish. Phobias and many of the obsessions and compulsions meet these basic criteria. Notable success has been reported in these syndromes with little or no deleterious consequences. Certain of the conversions (e.g., mutism, tics and some of the anesthesias and visual defects) have also been found amenable to behavior modification methods. These disorders, however, are more difficult to arrange within a program of extinction training than either phobic or obsessive-compulsive symptoms.

Dejection and hypochondriacal disorders may be treated suitably by a variety of phenomenological methods, both directive and nondirective. Intrapsychic techniques (e.g., psychoanalytic or hypnotic) may be the sole recourse available for handling most conversion symptoms and dissociation disorders.

The conclusions and summary for this chapter will be found at the end of chapter 11.

# Chapter 11

## *SYMPTOM DISORDERS*

### II:   Psychophysiologic, Sociopathic and Psychotic Disorders

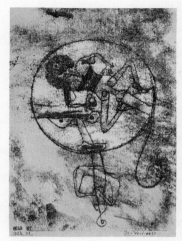

Paul Klee—*A Man in Love* (1923). (Philadelphia Museum of Art, photograph by A. J. Wyatt, staff photographer.)

Let us proceed directly from where we left off in chapter 10 and discuss the next three major syndromes of the symptom disorders.

## PSYCHOPHYSIOLOGIC DISORDERS

It is at times of illness or under conditions of excitement and stress that we become aware of many of the bodily functions we normally take for granted. If we stop to think for a moment we will recognize that each of the several systems which comprise our biophysical make-up —cardiovascular, gastrointestinal, respiratory, genitourinary and so on—is quietly carrying out a variety of functions requisite to organic survival.

Faced with threat, these systems are quickly activated to release and regulate energies which prepare the organism to cope efficiently with danger. Most frequently, the energy and tension that build up in response to these threats are discharged in the coping process. At other times, however, these physiological energies mount and persist since the individual is unable or unwilling to vent them. For example, fear and anger precipitate, among other things, a sharp rise in

blood pressure, which normally will subside if tension is expressed in the form of a rapid flight or a direct attack upon the threatening source. If fear or anger persists and tension is restrained and undischarged, a state of chronic high blood pressure may ensue, with eventual permanent tissue or organ damage.

Circumstances such as these are referred to as psychophysiologic disorders; the persistence of unrelieved physiological energies, precipitated initially by psychogenic agents, ultimately results in a fundamentally altered biological state. The central feature of these disorders, then, is the buildup of unexpressed protective physiological reactions; this upsets normal homeostatic balance and leads to irreversible organic diseases such as ulcer, hypertension and asthma. Thus, individuals who are subjected to persistent environmental stress or who are unable to resolve basic intrapsychic conflicts, may be afflicted with

**417**

bodily ailments that are no less severe than many that are caused by hereditary defects and infectious agents.

### Some Distinctions Between Psychophysiologic Disorders and Other Psychopathological States

Psychophysiologic and neurotic disorders display many similarities, and often coexist or covary in the same patient. As will be discussed in later paragraphs, both sets of disorders tend to crop up in the same five pathological personality patterns; however, psychophysiologic disorders are especially prominent in the two ambivalent personality types.

Psychophysiological symptoms differ from neurotic symptoms in that they do not represent symbolically the patient's intrapsychic problems. Moreover, these symptoms reflect the failure of the patient to circumvent the precipitants of his problems and to discharge tensions generated by them. In contrast, neurotic behaviors not only are symbolic expressions of unconscious problems, but are instruments, though indirect and circuitous ones, to avoid or to dissipate the buildup of associated physiological tensions. For example, the phobic person learns to avoid situations which may reactivate anxieties; the dissociative patient either drifts out of contact with provocative situations or discharges impulses during fugue and somnambulistic states; the compulsive restricts his activities to nonthreatening situations and releases tension through a variety of ritualistic acts. The psychophysiological patient, however, is unable to circumvent psychic distress or to vent the cumulation of psychic tensions. Thus, his visceral reactions are bottled up and churn away until they create irreversible bodily damage.

Psychophysiologic disorders are similar to anxiety disorders in that both signify failures to avoid precipitants of emotional tensions. However, in anxiety, the patient is quite conscious of his tension and discharges the buildup of physiological reactions through restless hyperactivity. By contrast, the psychophysiological patient neither experiences acute conscious apprehension nor vents his bodily tensions. He manages both to block awareness of his psychic discomfort and to suppress and somaticize his physiological reactions. In this way he remains unaware both of the psychic source of his tension and the anxieties they generate.

The contrast between psychotic and psychophysiologic disorders is fairly clear-cut. Although a small number of psychotic patients do evidence psychophysiologic disorders, the covariation of these syndromes is unusual since most psychotics tend to discharge their tensions rather openly. The overcontrol and internalization of emotions that characterize psychophysiological impairments contrast sharply with the typical free expression of feelings in psychotic disorders.

Psychophysiologic and sociopathic disorders differ for similar reasons. In the latter group, tensions and impulses are behaviorally acted out. As a consequence, these two disorders present appreciably different clinical pictures and tend not to coexist in the same patient.

## CLINICAL PICTURE

More than twenty somatic diseases have been ascribed, at least in part, to psychogenic causes. Which ones are influenced substantially by emotional factors remains a matter of dispute to be decided by future research. In the following paragraphs we shall list and briefly describe the symptoms of six psychophysiologic disorders which have been subjected to numerous theoretical and research studies.

1.   The *gastrointestinal system* is a frequent locale for psychophysiological impairment.

Particularly common are *peptic ulcers* in which the patient exhibits a crater-like lesion in the stomach or the upper part of the small intestine. Normally, a mucous lining protects the surface of these organs by blocking the corrosive effects of acid secretions that are requisite to digestion. However, should the lining be perforated or should excess secretions be produced, the patient will experience "burning" sensations, nausea and vomiting about one or two hours following meals. In these cases, the corrosive action of acids continues to dissolve the unprotected stomach and intestinal tissue. Where large open perforations are present there may be severe internal bleeding that may result in death. The following case history illustrates life history data for a typical peptic ulcer patient.*

### CASE 11-1
### Frederick B., Age 46, Married, Three Children

This man was admitted to a psychiatric hospital immediately after having been discharged from a senior executive position in a large company because of excessive drinking and unreliability in keeping appointments. Apart from a few years in military service Fred had been with this company for the preceding 25 years, had worked extremely

---

* From Gregory, I.: Fundamentals of Psychiatry. 2nd edition. Philadelphia, W. B. Saunders Co., 1968, p. 383.

hard, and felt personally responsible for much of the company's growth and expansion during the preceding 15 years. He had spent much time away from home traveling on company business and had worked evenings and weekends, and had not taken a vacation with his family for some years. However, Fred had come to feel that his talents and dedication were not appreciated or adequately rewarded. During the preceding five years he had perceived his future as bleak, with little or no opportunity for further advancement financially or in terms of prestige. Every morning he would feel sick over the dismal prospect of another day's exhausting demands. He would not express his feelings of frustration and resentment directly at work, but became increasingly irritable at home with his family. Fred started to drink excessively to relieve his tension and he developed peptic ulcers which were treated medically. He was given some sedative medication, but remained dependent on alcohol and became increasingly depressed, although he never reached the point of considering suicide.

Fred was born the fourth child in a family of five boys, and his father was an unsuccessful farmer whom he never respected and disliked from an early age. He felt much closer to his mother, who was nervous and physically frail, with numerous chronic bodily complaints that the family regarded as 90 percent emotional. This hypochondriacal mother, however, dominated her husband, criticized him, and nagged her sons into striving for the success that their father had never achieved.

Poverty and small physical stature contributed to making Fred feel inferior to other children in the neighborhood, but he overcompensated for this by striving for academic distinction. In spite of having to work in a store during noon hours, after school, and on Saturdays, he remained at the top of his class in school and graduated as valedictorian. He left home soon afterward, worked in an office during the daytime, and attended night school, where he claimed to have completed four years of college work, including two years of law school, although he never obtained a degree. At the age of 24 he married, and subsequently had three children, who he hoped would all go to college. It was a bitter blow to Fred when his eldest daughter got married shortly after leaving high school. Although his work always came ahead of his family, there was little conflict between him and his wife until the last few years during which he had been resentful, depressed, irritable, and drinking excessively.

At the time Fred was admitted to hospital after losing his job he was angry, tense, tremulous, and unhappy, but he showed no evidence of organic intellectual impairment, was in good contact with reality, and his depression appeared to be of neurotic intensity. The MMPI was valid and none of the clinical scales were elevated with the exception of scale 2 (depression). For several years he had been dissatisfied with his way of life, and the loss of his job freed him from its obligations and confronted him with the necessity of reevaluating his patterns of behavior and goals in life. Fred participated actively in individual and group psychotherapy, and rapidly acquired considerable

insight into developmental psychodynamics. His tension and depression diminished, his excessive smoking decreased, and he gained about seven pounds in weight. Fred was given a mild tranquilizing drug and after six weeks he left hospital much improved. There was no recurrence of his former symptoms during the next two years.

A similar disease, known as *colitis*, represents an inflammation of the colon (large intestine) and is typically accompanied by severe cramps and diarrhea.

2. *The cardiovascular system* exhibits two prominent psychophysiological disorders.

*Essential hypertension* consists of chronically elevated blood pressure, without organic cause, often resulting in serious circulatory and kidney ailments.

*Migraine* refers to repeated headaches, lasting several hours, attributable to arterial spasms; it is characterized by severe throbbing or pressure on one side of the head, and frequently is accompanied by nausea and other gastrointestinal upsets.

3. Certain *respiratory system* disorders are attributed in part to psychogenic influences.

*Bronchial asthma* is characterized by episodic attacks of wheezing, panting, gasping and a terrifying feeling of imminent suffocation. These symptoms reflect marked contractions or spasms in the bronchial muscles which cause the passages of the bronchi (lung tubes) to shrink, thereby creating a severe reduction in air intake. The background and experiences of an asthmatic woman with depressive inclinations are illustrated in the following history.*

### CASE 11-2
### Leah V., Age 34, Married, Four Children

This woman was admitted to a psychiatric hospital with a history of asthmatic attacks which had been increasing in frequency and severity during the preceding twelve years, together with feelings of fatigue, insomnia, and depression which had been increasing progressively over the preceding three months. She reported that her maternal grandmother and one maternal aunt had suffered from severe asthma, and she claimed that she was allergic to several fruits and vegetables. However, she had had extensive medical investigations and sensitivity tests but no program of desensitization had ever been recommended by the physicians caring for her, and her asthmatic attacks tended to be precipitated and aggravated by emotional stress.

Leah was the eldest of eight children and her mother was pregnant with her at the time of her

---

* From Gregory, I.: Fundamentals of Psychiatry. 2nd edition. Philadelphia, W. B. Saunders Co., 1968, p. 380.

marriage. This probably led to unconscious resentment and partial rejection of the patient by her mother who appeared to discriminate against the patient and favor some of the younger children. She perceived no such discrimination or favoritism on the part of her father who was a conscientious man, regularly employed, and well liked by everyone. In this home, however, he was rather passive and ineffectual, whereas the mother was dominant and aggressive. Leah described her mother as being moody and "a martyr type" who was critical and demanded high standards of behavior from all members of the family. During her childhood, Leah was given a great deal of responsibility in caring for her younger siblings and during adolescence she was frequently deprived of social activities with her friends in order to help at home. The patient was never able to express anger as a child and at the age of 34 she still felt that the opinion of her parents was as important as when she was a child.

Leah obtained little sexual information from her mother but started dating about the age of 15 and had a number of boy friends. During her junior year in high school she started going steady with a boy slightly older than herself and within six months she began a pregnancy which led to a forced marriage. Her parents disapproved of her husband, who was not a Catholic, but after marriage he changed his religion and their children were raised in this faith. During the first 12 years of her marriage the patient was pregnant 11 times. Six of these pregnancies terminated in spontaneous abortions and one child died a few days after birth, so that she was left with four living children. Pregnancy was always stressful for her and her first attack of asthma occurred shortly after the birth of her second child. The attacks became more frequent and severe during subsequent pregnancies, and after 12 years of marriage she submitted to a sterilization operation which freed her from this particular source of stress. However, a couple of years prior to this Leah became aware that her husband was going out with another woman. This made her feel nervous and angry inside, but she never confronted him with the fact or expressed her anger directly. Instead she punished him by denying him sexual relations, which she had in fact feared from the time of her first spontaneous abortion. Her husband's interest in the other woman was of very brief duration, but she continued to deny him sexual relations until about two years after her sterilization operation at which time he was involved in an automobile accident and sustained a whiplash injury to his neck. He felt unable to work and began drawing regular unemployment insurance which probably prolonged his disability. In addition, Leah became more solicitous of him and went out to work to supplement the family income. When the husband's insurance payments ran out, he looked for work sporadically but remained unemployed. He visited various employment offices and was offered several jobs, but turned them down for various reasons such as poor wages, no chance for getting ahead, or simply because he did not feel he would like the work.

In this situation Leah was unable to express resentment directly to the husband, but felt obliged to continue providing for the family and became increasingly worried about their financial situation. She became tired, had difficulty in sleeping, lost interest in her usual recreations, lost her appetite and some weight, and felt miserable. On admission to hospital her MMPI was technically invalid (21 F and only seven K responses), and it was considered that she was admitting to psychopathology that she did not in fact have. At interview she was in good contact with reality, and projective tests indicated neurotic constriction of personality with some hysterical denial and evidence of depression. Leah maintained that her husband and children were wonderful and initially she denied the marital conflict already outlined. During several weeks of psychotherapy, however, she was able to verbalize freely her sources of frustration and conflict and to gain considerable insight into previously unconscious psychodynamics. She also received antidepressive medication (Parnate) and gained about ten pounds in weight. Her husband was seen on several occasions, and eventually found employment. Leah left hospital much improved and was felt to be somewhat less vulnerable to developing overt psychopathology than formerly.

4. The *skin* is a major system of bodily functioning, centrally involved in mediating the organism's contact with the environment. As such, it is highly reactive not only to physical stimuli but to a whole range of psychologically significant events (e.g., blushing in embarrassment or blanching in fear).

Among the more prominent psychophysiological skin disorders is *neurodermatitis,* a chronic and nonallergenic inflammation accompanied by severe itching.

All psychophysiological symptoms mimic diseases that can be ascribed entirely to physical causes; thus, bronchial asthma or peptic ulcer may have its basis in hereditary defects or infectious agents. Many theorists contend that even where known psychogenic factors operate as causal agents, they merely aggravate and make manifest a latent biological vulnerability. Regardless of etiology, the final clinical picture is essentially the same, making the task of differential diagnosis an extremely difficult one at best. We label these diseases as psychophysiological when psychogenic factors are considered to play a significant etiological role. Table 11-1, presented on page 423, reviews several psychogenic hypotheses that have been proposed for the six disorders just described.

Let us next turn to some of the historical ideas which have shaped our understanding of the psychogenic roots of these disorders.

## HISTORY AND THEORIES

The label "psychosomatic" was first applied to cases of insomnia by Heinroth in 1818. This term remains a common synonym for the psychophysiologic disorders described in this section. Until the early twentieth century, however, little was known about the psychogenic mechanisms involved in these ailments, other than the fact that they appeared to be related to emotional stress.

### Early Psychoanalytic Concepts

Current thinking about psychophysiologic disorders may be traced to two notions first formulated by Freud.

In the concept of the "actual neuroses," Freud spoke of symptoms which were a direct consequence of the "damming up" of body energies. Here he included anxieties, neurasthenia and hypochondriasis, viewing them to be the simple result of a failure to discharge physiological sexual instincts. Although the three ailments he specified as resulting from this damming up process do not correspond to our present day list of psychophysiologic disorders, the notion that they reflect a blockage of physiological tensions may clearly be traced to Freud's "actual neurosis" hypothesis.

Several of Freud's disciples utilized the symbolism which he observed among the neurotic conversion disorders as a means of explaining psychosomatic symptoms, or what they called the "organ neuroses." To them, these symptoms symbolized, through a form of "body language," the character of the patient's repressed intrapsychic conflicts. For example, Ferenczi (1926) considered diarrhea to be an aggressive form of giving to others which substituted for real performance, and Garma (1950) conceived peptic ulcers to be symbolic attacks upon the mucous lining by the patient's introjected hostile mother. This symbolic conversion hypothesis for psychophysiologic disorders has been seriously questioned. It has been shown in recent years that the visceral organs, from which these symptoms arise, are not connected to higher cortical processes, and therefore do not lend themselves to the expression of symbolic ideas.

### Dunbar's Personality Profile Theory

The conversion model utilized by Freud's disciples attempted to account for the "specificity" of the symptom, that is, why patients with specific types of psychological problems developed certain psychophysiologic disorders rather than others. Since the conversion model of symbolic symptom expression was inapplicable to the visceral organs, alternate hypotheses had to be devised. This seemed necessary since it was believed that a correlation existed between particular pathogenic experiences and particular somatic disorders.

The first of these alternative models was provided by Flanders Dunbar (1935). As a consequence of her exhaustive studies of psychosomatic diseases, she was led to conclude that there was a direct correspondence between *personality types* and specific psychophysiological symptoms. For example, she proposed that ambitious and hard-driving executive personalities were especially vulnerable to coronary artery disease. Other personality profiles were found according to Dunbar to correlate specifically with migraines, peptic ulcers and so on.

Despite the plausibility and superficial validity of her thesis, subsequent evidence has indicated that there is no simple one to one correspondence between specific personality types and specific psychophysiologic disorders. Each psychosomatic symptom has been found in a variety of different personality profiles.

### Alexander's Conflict-Regression Theory

Franz Alexander (1950) agreed with Dunbar that psychophysiologic disorders should not be conceived as symbolic conversions, but disagreed with her view that direct correlations existed between particular personality types and specific somatic diseases. Instead, Alexander proposed that each psychosomatic disorder reflected a *specific* type of *unconscious conflict,* which could be found not in one but in a variety of different personality types.

Central to his thesis was the belief that a specific and different configuration of physiological reactions was activated in conjunction with each of several types of emotional states, e.g., rage was specifically associated with cardiovascular responses, dependency needs characteristically stimulated gastrointestinal activity and respiratory functions were notably involved in problems of communication. To Alexander, then, whatever correspondence existed between specific organs and specific psychological difficulties reflected neither a symbolic conversion process nor a personality style, but rather the presence of a specific emotional conflict; since certain physiological responses ostensibly correlated with these emotions, patients with particular conflicts will suffer corresponding physiological disorders.

In attempting to explain how the psychophysiological symptom arose in particular patients, Alexander invoked the Freudian concept of "regression," stating that psychosomatic patients had experienced traumatic conflicts in childhood which were "fixated," persist and are reactivated in the present. Current threats that stir up these fixated unconscious conflicts not only set into motion the person's "immature" psychological defenses, but in addition activate the *specific* physiological reactions that had been associated with these conflicts in childhood. Thus, to Alexander, adult psychophysiologic disorders reflect the consequence of chronic reactivations of the physiological reactions of childhood. For example, ulcer patients ostensibly suffered fixated dependency conflicts during the oral stage of psychosexual development. When present events reactivate this conflict, the patient's body responds with the same physiological reaction as when the conflict originally occurred in infancy. Specifically, these reactions took the form of excess gastrointestinal secretions since these occurred as a consequence of the infant's search for the security provided through maternal nutrition. Since "mother's milk" is not forthcoming in adulthood, the stomach and upper intestine are subjected, as a consequence of these physiological reactions, to a repeated flooding of gastric acids, causing the destruction of mucous lining and eventuating in a peptic ulcer.

The logic of Alexander's thesis has been modified by other theorists and extended to a variety of psychosomatic syndromes.

1. Margolin (1953) has been among those who have argued most eloquently for the view that psychophysiological illnesses can best be understood as regressions to infantile modes of physiological functioning. However, he does not accept fully the specific conflict facet of Alexander's theory. Rather, Margolin views the psychosomatic ailment as a consequence of the persistence of a generally immature physiological coping response which, though once appropriate in infancy, is now inappropriate for dealing with adult stress. He equates these inflexible and generalized infantile physiological reactions with immature and maladaptive childhood psychological coping maneuvers, both of which are equally inappropriate to present circumstance.

2. Ruesch (1946) has formulated another variant of Alexander's regression theory. In this proposal, he revives the conversion thesis that psychosomatic symptoms are a symbolic expression of unconscious conflicts transformed into the "language of the body." According to Ruesch, psychosomatic patients are either immature in their ways of communicating to others, having failed to learn to express ideas and feelings verbally, or have regressed as a consequence of stress to the use of primitive bodily forms of communication. As a consequence of his verbal inadequacies, the individual reverts to psycho-

somatic symbolism as a way of telling others about his psychological needs and conflicts. For example, chronic nausea would express an inability to "stomach" the unpleasant things which the person feels he must take from others; persistent back pains would be interpreted as a way of saying that he feels "overloaded" with pressure; neurodermatitis conveys the thought that others are "getting under his skin" and so on.

3. A third variation of Alexander's thesis has been proposed by Grace and Graham (1952). However, they by-pass the significance given to the regression notion and focus instead on the "specific attitudes" the patient has regarding difficult circumstances in his life. They claim that attitudes taken toward certain types of stressful situations activate specific constellations of physiological reactivity. For example, if an individual feels deprived and resentful and desires revenge as a consequence, then certain gastrointestinal secretions will be activated. Should these attitudes persist and their accompanying physiological reactions remain undischarged, correlated psychosomatic diseases, such as an ulcer, will eventuate.

Table 11-1 provides a summary of some of the psychogenic causes, personality characteristics and coping aims which theorists such as Alexander, Margolin, Graham and Ruesch, as well as others, have proposed as correlated with the six psychophysiologic disorders described earlier. We will comment on the validity of these hypotheses following our presentation of a number of alternate theories which reject the notion that psychosomatic symptoms are correlated with *specific* psychological needs or experiences.

### Nonspecificity Theories

A number of theorists (Mahl, 1953; Kaplan and Kaplan, 1959) state that there is insufficient evidence to warrant acceptance of any of the various "specificity" models that have been proposed. Despite impressive and intriguing theorizing, no clear-cut empirical relationship has been adduced to indicate that specific psychogenic factors are correlated with specific forms of psychophysiologic disorder.

The nonspecificity theorists offer an alternative. *First,* they contend that all sources of psychogenic stress, ranging from external realistic events (e.g., face to face warfare) to intrapsychic conflicts (e.g., repressed childhood hostilities), produce essentially similar *diffuse* physiological reactions. *Second,* should these generalized physiological states be prolonged or frequently repeated, one or several of a number of psychosomatic ailments may ensue. *Third,* the particular

**Table 11-1   Some Hypothesized Psychological Correlates of Psychophysiologic Disorders**

| DISORDER | PSYCHOGENIC CAUSES, PERSONALITY CHARACTERISTICS AND COPING AIMS |
|---|---|
| Peptic Ulcer | Feels deprived of dependency needs; is resentful; represses anger; cannot vent hostility or actively seek dependency security; characterizes self-sufficient and responsible "go-getter" types who are compensating for dependency desires; have strong regressive wish to be nurtured and fed; revengeful feelings are repressed and kept unconscious. |
| Colitis | Was intimidated in childhood into dependency and conformity; feels conflict over resentment and desire to please; anger restrained for fear of retaliation; is fretful, brooding and depressive or passive, sweet and bland; seeks to camouflage hostility by symbolic gesture of giving. |
| Essential Hypertension | Was forced in childhood to restrain resentments; inhibited rage; is threatened by and guilt-ridden over hostile impulses which may erupt; is a controlled, conforming and "mature" personality; is hard-driving and conscientious; is guarded and tense; needs to control and direct anger into acceptable channels; desires to gain approval from authority. |
| Migraine | Is unable to fulfill excessive self-demands; feels intense resentment and envy toward intellectually or financially more successful competitors; has meticulous, scrupulous, perfectionistic and ambitious personality; failure to attain perfectionist ambitions results in self-punishment. |
| Bronchial Asthma | Feels separation anxiety; was given inconsistent maternal affection; has fear and guilt that hostile impulses will be expressed toward loved persons; is demanding, sickly and "cranky" or clinging and dependent; symptom expresses suppressed cry for help and protection. |
| Neurodermatitis | Has overprotective but ungiving parents; has craving for affection; has conflict regarding hostility and dependence; demonstrates guilt and self-punishment for inadequacies; is a superficially friendly and oversensitive personality with depressive features and low self-image; symptoms are atonement for inadequacy and guilt by self-excoriation; displays oblique expression of hostility and exhibitionism in need for attention and soothing. |

ailment that the patient finally displays *cannot* be predicted by reference either to the content or to the source of the psychogenic precipitant.

The nonspecificity model has been criticized by many clinicians on the grounds that it fails to correlate psychosomatic disorders with psychological difficulties. This criticism is inaccurate. The model claims merely that the *specific* form of the psychophysiologic disorder cannot be predicted by the *specific* type of emotional difficulty experienced. The nonspecificity model asserts, quite clearly, that psychosomatic ailments *in general* are found to be associated with psychogenic problems. More specifically, its proponents claim that patients who are chronically unable to reduce anxiety are strongly disposed to exhibit *some form* of psychophysiologic disorder. This aspect of the nonspecificity view is nicely summarized in the following quote (Kaplan and Kaplan, 1959):

We believe that as long as a patient can deal with unpleasant emotions and with the anxiety engendered by his conflicts by means of various psychological defenses and mechanisms, there will be no abnormal psychogenic physical functioning nor resultant psychosomatic illness. If, however, a patient's psychological defenses are inadequate to reduce his excited or anxious state of emotional tension, then a variety of psychosomatic diseases may be produced in constitutionally

susceptible individuals as a result of the physiological concomitants of chronic tension. According to this view, many psychosomatic diseases are a consequence of the *breakdown* of psychological defenses. It should be added that we do not consider the aforementioned mechanism to account for all instances of psychosomatic illness; other mechanisms, such as conditioning, may play a role in certain diseases. Nor do we believe that there is sufficient evidence to indicate that the nature of the psychological stimulus setting off the emotional tension determines the type of disease that develops. The problem of "organ selection," i.e., what accounts for the type of disease suffered by a particular patient, is unsolved as yet.

### Constitutional Specificity Theories

The criticism that most psychological models fail to take account of constitutional differences as a factor in psychophysiologic disorders has led a number of researchers to propose the following alternate hypothesis: although specific psychogenic factors have not been shown to correlate with specific psychosomatic ailments, patients with distinctive and different physiological reaction patterns are disposed to develop specific types of ailments. This proposal may be spoken of as a "response specificity" thesis, resting on the well-accepted notion of intrinsic constitutional differences among individuals.

It was Adler, Freud's early disciple, who

first spoke of the role of "organ inferiorities" in psychological illness. However, Adler did not concern himself with psychosomatic ailments; rather, he drew upon the notion of bodily weaknesses to demonstrate mechanisms of compensatory striving.

It has only been in recent years, through the systematic experimental research of several investigators (Lacey and Lacey, 1958; Mirsky, 1958; Malmo, 1962), that evidence has accrued to show that individuals exhibit rather distinctive and stable types of physiological reactions to stress. For example, it has been shown that some individuals characteristically react with muscular rigidity to such varied conditions as embarrassment, pain and frustration whereas others react to the same variety of stressful events with intense gastrointestinal upsets. According to this thesis, the dominant sphere of physiological reactivity in an individual will dispose him to develop a specific type of correlated psychosomatic disorder; for example, "cardiovascular reactors" tend to experience heart palpitations and chest pains whereas "muscle reactors" are inclined to develop severe headaches.

The question may be posed as to whether these physiological reactivity patterns are acquired as a consequence of experience or whether they are inborn. As reported in chapter 4, studies by Murphy et al. (1962) and Thomas et al. (1964) indicate that distinctive autonomic behavioral patterns are exhibited shortly after birth and persist for many years thereafter. Since these styles of responding were evident prior to the effects of socialization, it would appear safe to assume that later patterns of reactivity are, at least in part, attributable to intrinsic constitutional tendencies.

Among the virtues of the constitutional specificity theory is that it rescues the notion of "symptom choice" from oblivion. Rather than depending on unverified clinical hypotheses, this theory is based on experimentally validated research, although much remains to be done in correlating physiological reaction patterns and vulnerabilities to particular psychosomatic ailments. It should be noted, further, that the constitutional thesis does not preclude the role of psychogenic influences. Combined with certain psychogenic hypotheses, it can account for which patients experience psychosomatic ailments in the first place, and which specific ailments they eventually will display. In short, psychophysiologic disorders are likely to reflect the interaction of both psychological experience and constitutional vulnerabilities; more on this point will be discussed in later sections.

## Evaluative Comment

What conclusions do we draw from our survey of the clinical picture, alternate theories and research data on psychophysiologic disorders?

1. Although the issue is not a closed one and is awaiting further and more detailed investigations for final judgment, the greater body of research evidence to date indicates that the *specific* type of psychophysiologic disorder exhibited by a patient *cannot* be predicted from the *specific* character of his psychological problem.

2. A fairly substantial body of data has accrued to the effect that psychosomatic disorders, *in general,* arise as a consequence of the failure to dissipate tensions, regardless of the content or source of these tensions. Individuals whose coping strategies lead them into repeated tension producing situations or prevent them from discharging the cumulative build up of tensions, are likely to succumb to one or several of a number of different psychophysiologic disorders.

3. Although failing to vent tension, the coping strategies which underlie psychophysiological symptom formation appear to achieve three functions: to keep from awareness the source and content of intrapsychic tension; to inhibit the expression of socially unacceptable impulses; and to obtain the secondary gains of attention, sympathy and nurture normally furnished to those who are sick.

4. Essentially identical psychogenic difficulties have been postulated as the cause of a wide variety of psychosomatic problems. A review of the literature, as summarized in Table 11-1, indicates that diverse psychosomatic disorders such as hypertension, ulcers, asthma and neurodermatitis, appear to derive from a single basic conflict, i.e., suppressing hostile impulses for fear that they may endanger dependency security. It is extremely difficult to uncover different etiologies among these disorders; the conflict between dependency security and hostile assertion seems to apply to all. This uniformity in psychogenesis leads us to conclude that most psychosomatic patients are trapped in an unresolvable dependency-independency ambivalence; they are unable to express feelings associated with one part of their conflict without increasing tensions in the other. As a consequence, their overall level of tension continues to mount and churn internally until it finally results in an irreversible psychophysiologic disorder.

5. Recent research indicates that the specific type of psychosomatic symptom the patient develops is likely to depend either on constitutional vulnerabilities or on his dominant physiological reaction pattern.

6.   We are led to conclude that the pathway which leads to a psychophysiologic disorder derives from a confluence of both psychogenic and physiogenic influences. In thinking about etiology, we must envision, then, a sequence of interactions in which the individual's learned coping strategies not only result in repeated disruptions of his homeostatic balance, but fail to dissipate chronic physiological tensions. A constitutionally predisposed individual will develop a specific type of psychosomatic disorder since his psychological problems, whatever their source or content, will have a selective physiological effect upon certain vulnerable organ systems.

7.   Definitive conclusions concerning the specific interplay of psychogenic and physiogenic factors must await further empirical research. Most of what has been published in the field of psychosomatic medicine can be faulted on a number of methodological grounds (Freeman et al., 1964). At the very best, these studies provide some rough guidelines for future systematic research.

## PERSONALITY DISPOSITIONS

It may be possible from what we have reviewed thus far to deduce which of the various pathological personality patterns are most susceptible to psychophysiologic disorders. Toward this end, it will be useful to examine first the various coping functions that underlie psychosomatic symptom formation.

One purpose of the psychosomatic patient's strategy is to block from awareness the content and source of his intrapsychic tensions; this aim, however, is neither distinctive to psychophysiologic disorders nor to any particular personality type. Since it is a basic coping function of most disorders, we must look to other factors to account for the psychosomatic symptom and its personality correlates.

Two other coping functions fulfilled by the psychosomatic symptom are the control or inhibition of hostile impulses and the eliciting of secondary gains such as attention, sympathy and nurture. However, these coping functions are also found in neurotic disorders, and are characteristic of the entire group of five personality patterns that are subject to these disorders, notably the two dependent patterns, the two ambivalent patterns and the active-detached pattern. Since various coping functions are found in common among these five personality patterns and two disorder syndromes, we are led to believe that psychosomatic symptoms would covary with neurotic symptoms in each of these personality patterns. Stated differently, we would hypothesize that psychophysio-

logic disorders will be found, not exclusively in one personality type, but in the five types that share these common coping goals; further, we would hypothesize that neurotic and psychosomatic symptoms will coexist or fluctuate interchangeably in the same patient. This latter finding has regularly been reported in the literature, but has not been systematically researched; it may reflect the fact that neurotic disorders often only partly discharge physiological tensions, therefore leaving a residue which may take the form of a psychosomatic ailment.

We believe not only that psychophysiologic disorders will arise most frequently in the five personality patterns mentioned previously, but that they are particularly characteristic of two types, the passive and active-ambivalents. Ample evidence exists for this view in the literature, but let us examine our reasons for believing it.

Among the central features of psychosomatic etiology are repetitive upsets of the body's physiological balance and a chronic failure to dissipate physiological tensions. These events will arise most often in patients who repeatedly find themselves in conflict situations, especially those in whom the discharge of tensions engendered by one side of the conflict will increase tensions engendered by the other. This state of affairs describes, in effect, the experiences of ambivalent personalities; they are trapped between acquiescent dependency on the one hand, and hostile or assertive independence on the other. When they allow themselves to submit to the wishes of others, they experience deep resentments and angers for having displayed weakness and given up their independence. Conversely, if they assert their independence and feelings of hostility, they experience intense anxieties for fear they will have further endangered their tenuous dependency security.

Let us next examine how this conflict develops into psychophysiologic disorders in each of the five vulnerable personality patterns.

1.   The *passive-ambivalent* personality (conforming and cycloid) keeps under close wraps most of the tensions generated by his dependence-independence conflict. Through repression and other mechanisms, his resentments and anxieties are tightly controlled and infrequently discharged. As a consequence, his physiological tensions are not dissipated, tend to cumulate and result in frequent and persistent psychophysiological ailments, as illustrated in the following brief sketch.

### CASE 11-3
### Peter S., Age 23, Married, No Children

This passive-ambivalent graduate student was admitted to the college infirmary following a recurrence of an old ulcer ailment. Peter's early history showed intense rivalries with an alcoholic but "brilliant" father who constantly demanded superior performances on the part of his son in both academic affairs and athletics. However, no matter how well Peter would perform, his father demonstrated "how much better he could do it now—or did it when he was young." Although Peter "quietly hated" his father, he dared not express it for fear of "being publicly humiliated by him."

In recent weeks, Peter's thesis proposal had been severely criticized by his departmental advisor. Peter believed that the professor was completely wrong in his judgments and suggestions, but dared not express these thoughts for "fear of further condemnation." Unable to vent his resentments, which were so much like those he felt toward his father, Peter's repressed emotions churned away inside and resulted in a flareup of his ulcer.

2. The precipitants and sequence of physiological tensions take a somewhat different turn in the *active-ambivalent* (negativistic and cycloid). Here, the patient periodically discharges his tensions, but because of his hypersensitivities and irritable behaviors, he creates an endless sequence of one troublesome problem after another. In other words, he accumulates tension faster than he dissipates it. Moreover, because of his fretful and contentious behaviors, his body is subject to constant vacillations in mood and emotion. As he swings erratically from one intense feeling to another, his homeostatic equilibrium, so necessary for proper physiological functioning, is kept constantly off balance. Not only is he likely to experience, then, an excess of chronic or repeated tension, but his system rarely settles down into a smooth and regularized pattern. As a consequence, the active-ambivalent is kept churning and sets himself up for a variety of psychosomatic disorders.

3. Although *passive and active-dependents* (submissive, gregarious and cycloid) are subject to psychophysiological ailments, they are not faced with the severe and unresolvable conflict that confronts ambivalents. In their case, dependency needs can be pursued without intensifying tensions associated with independence. Furthermore, although they are similar to ambivalents in their fear of expressing forbidden hostile impulses, the anger and resentment they feel are appreciably less. At the cycloid level, however, dependents have suffered frequent rebuffs and carry within them resentments no less intense than those found more characteristically in ambivalents.

4. *Active-detached personalities* (avoidant and schizoid) have strong but unexpressed resentments which may lead them to suffer psychosomatic ailments. However, the likelihood that they will

experience these disorders is less than that of ambivalents since their detached strategy enables them to avoid most anger arousing situations; in contrast, the ambivalent maintains active social contacts, and thereby subjects himself repeatedly to events that may reactivate his conflicts.

In conclusion, then, all five personalities are disposed to psychosomatic disorders, the specific form of which appears to depend on their particular constitutional vulnerabilities or physiological reaction patterns. As we have noted, the two ambivalent types seem especially susceptible to these disorders since their dependent-independent conflict disposes them to tensions which cannot either readily be resolved through intrapsychic mechanisms or easily be dissipated through behavioral discharge.

## REMEDIAL APPROACHES

Of all the pathologies described we can see most clearly the close interweaving of biological and psychological functions in the psychophysiologic disorders. Of course, every psychopathological ailment derives in part from the operation of both psychic and somatic factors; psychophysiologic disorders are notable in this regard only because they give evidence of this inseparable fusion in manifest physical form. What distinguishes them as disorders is not the fact that physiological processes are involved—a fact true of all disorders—but rather that they represent a failure to find a means of curtailing or dissipating the cumulation of these physiological processes. In other disorders, physiological tensions cumulate less rapidly and are discharged more efficiently.

Let us turn in this section to the general prognostic picture of the psychophysiologic disorders and to some of the therapeutic approaches that are taken to alleviate them.

The somatic symptoms of these disorders either persist for long periods or recur at frequent intervals. This state of affairs reflects in part the irreversible physical damage that often occurs in conjunction with the disorder, e.g., perforated stomach lining in peptic ulcers. In addition, unless the circumstances which led to the difficulty are resolved, tensions will continue to mount and disrupt normal biological functioning. Further complications arise since many of these patients fail to recognize the psychogenic roots of their disease, and some, notably the passive-ambivalents, often adamantly refuse to admit that they suffer any psychological discomfort or discontent. (We must be reminded, in this regard, that not all patients exhibiting ulcers or asthma, for example, suffer these ailments for psychogenic reasons; clinicians must not attempt to "convince" a patient that he may be emotionally troubled unless he has a sound reason for believing so.) Resistance to psychogenic interpretations is found among patients who fear to "open up," to become conscious of their forbidden and repressed impulses. In these cases, the prognosis is extremely poor since the patient will shy away from therapeutic involvements which threaten to "expose" his hidden feelings. Only if his physical symptoms become extremely discomforting, frightening or painful will he allow himself to be subjected to psychodiagnostic scrutiny.

Therapeutic attention must be directed first to remedying whatever physical impairments have occurred in conjunction with the disorder. Body pathology, as in ulcer perforations or severe hypertension, should be dealt with promptly by appropriate medical, nutritional or surgical means. When the physical disease process is under adequate control, attention may be turned to the management of environmental stresses and to the modification of detrimental attitudes and habits.

As we have said, psychosomatic symptoms arise as a consequence of the patient's inability to resolve his conflicts and discharge his tensions. Because of the patient's dread that these emotions will overwhelm him if released, the therapist must move slowly before exposing these conflicting attitudes or "opening the floodgates" to the onrush of these repressed feelings. Quite evidently, the patient has been willing to suffer considerable physical discomfort as the price for containing his unacceptable conflicts and impulses. The danger of precipitating a crisis is great if the patient gains

insight too quickly or if his previously hidden feelings are uncovered and unleashed too rapidly. Such exposure and release must be coordinated with a parallel strengthening of the patient's capacity to cope with these feelings.

The warning just noted points to the important role of supportive techniques in the early stages of treatment. At first, care should be taken to diminish tension and to help dissipate the cumulation of past tensions. Psychopharmacological tranquilizers may be useful in softening the response to tension precipitants. In addition, arrangements should be made where feasible to have the patient avoid those aspects of everyday living which prompt or aggravate unresolvable anxieties and conflicts.

Turning to the formal psychotherapeutic measures, the procedures of behavior modification and phenomenological reorientation may be used to extinguish attitudes and habits which have generated tensions, and to build in new ones which may facilitate discharging, avoiding or otherwise coping with them. Group therapy often serves as a valuable adjunct to help the patient explore his feelings, learn methods of resolving conflicts and liberate his tensions. As was noted earlier, the probing and uncovering methods of intrapsychic therapy should not be utilized in the early phases of treatment since they may prompt the surge of severely upsetting forbidden thoughts and impulses. However, should other procedures prove unsuccessful in alleviating tension or in diminishing the disturbing symptomatology, it may be necessary to employ intrapsychic processes, and to begin a slow and long-term process of reconstructing the patient's pervasive personality pattern.

# SOCIOPATHIC DISORDERS

The etiology and clinical features of this group of disorders have been formulated and reformulated innumerable times over the past century. Throughout its checkered history, to be described shortly, it has served to designate a rather varied collection of behaviors which have little in common other than the fact that they are viewed as contrary or repugnant to the social mores of the time. Despite the confusions that have characterized its past, few clinicians fail to "get the picture" when they hear the designation of "sociopath"; it was well summarized in the official 1952 nosology under the title *sociopathic personality disturbance, antisocial reaction,* which reads as follows:

This term refers to chronically antisocial individuals who are always in trouble, profiting neither

from experience nor punishment, and maintaining no real loyalties to any person, group, or code. They are frequently callous and hedonistic, showing marked emotional immaturity, with lack of a sense of responsibility, lack of judgment and an ability to rationalize their behavior so that it appears warranted, reasonable, and justified.

The term includes cases previously classified as "constitutional psychopathic state" and "psychopathic personality." As defined here the term is more limited, as well as more specific in its application.

## HISTORY AND THEORIES

A beginning recognition of the clinical features we now term as sociopathic may be traced to the eminent French psychiatrist, Philippe Pinel, who observed in the late eighteenth century that certain patients engage in impulsive and self-damaging acts, despite the fact that their reasoning abilities are unimpaired, and that they understand the irrationality of what they are doing. Benjamin Rush, the well-known American physician, wrote in the early 1800's of similar perplexing cases characterized by lucidity of thought combined with socially vicious or immoral behaviors. He spoke of these individuals as possessing an "innate, preternatural moral depravity" in which "the will becomes the involuntary vehicle . . . of the passions (1812)."

J. C. Prichard (1835) is generally credited with formulating the category of "moral insanity." These patients ostensibly lost the power of guiding themselves in accord with moral principles, yet retained their general intellectual grasp; as a consequence of this impairment, they conducted themselves cleverly, although irresponsibly and indecently, in the business of life. Henderson (1939) reports a statement, attributed to Mercier in the late nineteenth century, which summarizes well the perplexity shared by psychiatrists of the day: "There are persons who indulge in vice with such persistence, at a cost of punishment so heavy, so certain, and so prompt, who incur their punishment for the sake of pleasure so trifling and so transient, that they are by consent considered insane, although they exhibit no other indication of insanity."

Toward the end of the nineteenth century, Koch suggested the term "psychopathic inferiority" as a designation for these patients. Adolf Meyer separated psychopathic cases from psychoneurotic disorders. Although a strong exponent of the role of psychogenic factors in mental illness, he termed the former group as cases of "constitutional inferiority" to distinguish them from the neuroses, whose etiology he felt was colored less by an inborn defect. Kraepelin, at the same period, shared the popular view of the day that these patients were essentially constitutionally defective. As was characteristic of his penchant for systematization, he subdivided the "psychopathic personalities" into seven varieties such as "the liars and swindlers," "the unstable," "the born criminal" and so on.

Through the first quarter of this century, it was well accepted that psychopathic patients behaved as they did as a result of inborn constitutional defects. With the advent of Freud's psychoanalytic writings, which stressed the role of early experience as pathogenic factors, the view came to the fore that environmental events may be crucially involved in this disorder. This shift in etiological thinking was reflected in the changing labels assigned to these patients. The terminology of the disorder shifted from "constitutional psychopathic state," to "psychopathic personality," and most recently, to "sociopathic personality," the latter signifying the new focus on conditions of social unbringing.

Many intrapsychic theorists (Greenacre, 1945; Allen, 1950; Levy, 1951; Thorne, 1947) have traced the roots of sociopathic behavior to early parent-child relationships. Greenacre, for example, has stressed the role of the father. Allen speaks of maternal ambivalences. Levy divides these patients into two groups representing opposing types of early experiences: the "deprived psychopath" and the "indulged psychopath," the latter category described by Thorne as "the ego-inflated, defectively conditioned type."

Although there has been a recent shift to psychogenic hypotheses, the view that biological abnormalities underlie these disorders has not lost it adherents; rather than theorizing, as was the case in early writings, these men have sought to support their contentions through concrete research evidence. Despite the numerous investigators (e.g., Silverman, 1943; Hill, 1952) who have explored signs of possible brain damage in these patients, their work to date has proved of no avail, providing either negative, conflicting or unreliable findings.

About a quarter of a century ago, hypotheses were proposed to the effect that the larger sociopathic category includes several subtypes, each reflecting a different type of etiology and clinical picture (Karpman, 1941; Cleckley, 1950). Most frequently proposed is a group termed the "primary type" which presumably is of biogenic etiology and displays a minimal capacity for anxiety and an intractability to treatment. A "secondary type," or "neurotic psychopath" as some have termed it, ostensibly develops as a consequence of environmental factors.

The position that sociopathy may derive from different etiological origins is certainly an advance over the more simplistic and single-minded views espoused by earlier theorists. Despite their merits, the proposals of Karpman and Cleckley, for example, failed to stress the likely interaction of biogenic and psychogenic determinants. As we have often noted in this text, pathological syndromes usually arise from the complex interweaving of biological dispositions and environmental experiences. Along these lines, Eysenck (1957) provides the interesting thesis that all psychopaths possess an inherited tempermental disposition to extraversion which inclines them to learn sociopathic behaviors. According to the learning theory Eysenck espouses, extraverts condition slowly and therefore in contrast to normals, acquire only minimally the values and inhibitions of their social group. Eysenck's thesis leaves many details of psychopathic development unclear, and evidence for its central assumptions are scanty at best. Nevertheless, it may be viewed as a promising beginning toward the more sophisticated view that sociopathy, along with most psychopathological conditions, represents the interplay of both constitutional and experiential influences.

Although Eysenck's theory draws upon learning theory principles, it rests on the assumption of innate constitutional dispositions. Other learning theorists of sociopathy avoid this assumption, basing their interpretation solely in terms of concepts such as imitation and reinforcement (e.g., Bandura and Walters, 1959). Here, as with the early psychoanalysts, the role of parent-child interaction is central. For example, cold or hostile parents are viewed as models which the child imitates and uses to guide his "sociopathic" relationship with others. In other cases, parental styles of meting out reward and punishment may have shaped a pattern of superficial affability that cloaks a fundamentally devious and hostile attitude toward others.

As is evident from the foregoing, a wide range of theories has been proposed for this disorder. The thesis to which we shall subscribe will become evident as we proceed. But first, let us organize more systematically the major clinical features associated with this disorder. In addition, it will be useful to differentiate these cases from several of the other pathological impairments. Following these two sections, we will turn to a rationale and discussion of the various personality patterns which serve as the background for these socially troublesome disorders.

## GENERAL CLINICAL PICTURE

It was not difficult to pinpoint "symptoms" in presenting the neurotic disorders; in those syndromes, the symptom usually stood out in clear relief against the more generalized personality pattern of the patient. Unfortunately, the line between symptom and personality is more difficult to draw in the sociopathic disorder. There are no simple or clear-cut signs, such as phobias or obsessions, that emerge as distinctive features to contrast sharply with the more general and prosaic style of the patient's functioning. Rather, distinctions in the sociopathic disorder lie in the exaggeration or accentuation of his less striking and everyday personality pattern. The "symptom" therefore is neither unusual nor bizarre, but an extension or intensification of what the patient habitually does or thinks.

Because of the difficulty in separating personality from symptom, the American Psychiatric Association has dropped the "sociopathic" label in the recent DSM-II, incorporating this well-established disorder within the framework of the *antisocial personality* syndrome (or what we have termed the "aggressive personality"). This fusion of sociopathy and antisocial personality signifies a promising direction in the thinking of the APA nomenclature committee since it reflects an awareness of the interdependence of symptom and personality pattern, a theme we have stressed throughout the text. We believe, however, that there is merit in retaining the sociopathic syndrome as a separate diagnostic entity since, for example, the symptoms that characterize sociopathy arise not only in aggressive types, but also in other personalities, as will be illustrated in later paragraphs.

Despite the difficulties in separating "personality" and "disorder," we will attempt to note a few of the major features which clinicians view to be most characteristic of this syndrome. The items to be listed are not mutually exclusive. Neither do they provide a definitive picture of the disorder since the impairment will take different forms depending on the particular experiences and personality pattern of the patient.

It may be useful to begin with a brief paragraph summarizing the impressions of McCord and McCord (1964) who have undertaken a series of systematic studies of these patients:

His conduct often brings him into conflict with society. The psychopath is driven by primitive desires and an exaggerated craving for excitement. In his self-centered search for pleasure, he ignores restrictions of his culture. The psychopath is highly impulsive. He is a man for whom the moment is a segment of time detached from all others. His actions are unplanned and guided by his whims. The psychopath is aggressive. He has learned few socialized ways of coping with frustration. The psychopath feels little, if any, guilt. He can commit the most appalling acts, yet view them without remorse. The psychopath has a warped capacity for love. His emotional relationships, when they exist, are meager, fleeting, and designed to satisfy his own desires. These last two traits, guiltlessness and lovelessness, conspicuously mark the psychopath as different from other men.

If we combine the conclusions of the McCords with those of other researchers in the field, we are led to the following five characteristics as features of the sociopathic disorder.

**Disdain for Social Conventions.** Among the most notable characteristics of sociopaths is their tendency to flout conventional authority and rules. They act as if the established customs and guidelines for self-discipline and cooperative group behavior do not apply to them. In some, this disdain is evidenced in displays of petty disobedience or in the adoption of unconventional beliefs, values, dress and demeanor. Many, however, express their social arrogance and rebelliousness in minor illegal acts and deceits, coming into frequent difficulty with educational and law enforcement authorities. Still others are flagrantly aggressive and hostile, exhibiting a malicious physical brutality as they disrupt the peace, appearing to gain pleasure in intimidating and assaulting others.

**Deceptive Social Facade.**  Despite their disrespect for the rights of others, many sociopaths present a social mask, not only of civility but of sincerity and maturity. Untroubled by feelings of guilt and a sense of loyalty, they often develop a pathological talent for lying. Unconstrained by matters of honesty and truth, they learn with great facility to weave an impressive picture of their superior competencies and reliability. Many are disarmingly ingratiating and charming in their initial social encounters, becoming skillful swindlers and imposters. Their cleverness and alertness to the weaknesses of others may enable them to play their games of deception for long periods. Not uncommonly, however, the pleasure they gain from their ruse begins to flag. Before long their true insincerity and unreliability may be revealed by their failure to keep "working at" their deceptions or as a consequence of their need to let others know how cleverly deceptive they have been.

**Inability or Unwillingness to "Adjust" Following Punishment.**  Many sociopaths are of better than average intelligence, exhibiting both clarity and logic in their cognitive capacities. Yet they display a marked deficiency in self-insight, and rarely exhibit the foresight which one might expect, given their capacity to understand, at least intellectually, the implications of their behavior. In short, despite the fact that they voice a clear grasp of why they should alter their social misconduct, they fail repeatedly to make any modifications.

It is evident that many of these persons are unable to change because they possess deeply rooted habits and needs that are highly resistant to the effects of conscious reasoning and punitive consequences. In fact, punitive measures often reinforce those experiences and attitudes which initially gave rise to their misbehavior. To make their socially repugnant behavior more palatable to others, these persons concoct plausible explanations and excuses, usually those of "poor upbringing" and past "misfortunes." Thus, the unfortunate circumstances of their lives operated to lead them astray.

By utilizing their intelligence to feign innocent victimization, sociopaths absolve themselves of blame, remain calm and guiltless and have a "justification" for continuing their irresponsible attitudes and behaviors. Should these flippant rationalizations fail to convince others, as when they are caught in obvious and repeated lies and dishonesties, sociopaths may effect an air of total innocence, claiming without a trace of shame that they have been unfairly accused. Once more, their cognitive skills and pathological deceit are used to extricate themselves from difficulty and to absolve themselves from guilt.

**Impulsive Hedonism.**  Many sociopaths evidence a low tolerance for frustration, seem to act impetuously and cannot delay, let alone forego, prospects for immediate pleasure. They are easily bored and restless and are unable to endure the tedium of routine or to persist at the day after day responsibilities of marriage or a job. Quite characteristic is a proneness to taking chances and seeking thrills, acting as if they were immune from danger. Others jump from one exciting and momentarily gratifying escapade to another, with little or no care for potentially detrimental consequences.

**Insensitivity or Disregard for the Feelings of Others.**  Beyond their callous disdain for the social rights of others, the sociopath seems deficient in the capacity to share tender feelings, to experience genuine affection and love for another or to empathize with their needs and their distress. But even more, they appear to gain pleasure in the thought and process of hurting others, in seeing them downtrodden and suffering pain and misery. Thus, not only are they devoid of guilt and remorse as a consequence of their malicious acts, but they seem to obtain a degree of cruel satisfaction thereby. To achieve these malevolent ends, they often go out of their way to exploit others, enjoying not only the tangible fruits of their cunning and deceit, but the distress and pain they leave in its wake.

The following case illustrates a number of these clinical features.

*CASE 11-4*
*James F., Age 22*

James was arraigned at a county court for passing a series of forged checks. He was also thought to be the rapist of a 16 year old waitress. His previous record showed a list of minor burglaries, abandonment of a common-law wife and child and acquittal on two charges of passing bad checks.

Jim is a muscular, wiry and "sharply dressed" man who looked even younger than his 22 years. Although he presented an affable veneer when first seen, being both charming and verbally adroit, it was clear that he felt considerable inner tension and suspiciousness of those who sought to question him.

Disentangling Jim's real life from his fabrications was not done easily since he had no compunctions about lying when it suited his purposes. Factually, Jim was the only son of a family of three children. Both girls were younger. His father, a drunkard, abandoned the family when Jim was ten. There is evidence that he mercilessly assaulted both his wife and children. Jim's mother was killed in an auto accident shortly thereafter, and the family unit was separated and placed in different foster homes. When he was 15, Jim was accused of fathering the child of a twelve year old foster sister and was sent to a reformatory school.

In the three years at the reformatory, Jim was one of the "gang leaders," evidencing considerable skill in exploiting the weaknesses of his fellow delinquents. At 18, when he was freed to make his way alone, Jim was a skillful automobile mechanic. He never picked up this trade, however, having lasted but two weeks at a position arranged for him prior to leaving the reformatory.

Jim's whereabouts were not factually recorded for two years. At the age of 20 he was picked up for a minor theft. Despite a number of obscurities, it appeared that he lived with a 15 year old for several months, impregnating and then leaving her. From that point onward he drifted from job to job, lasting little more than a month at each. During that time, he maintained fleeting relationships with prostitutes and drunkards, managing each time to fleece them of their meager belongings, and then moving onward. When brought in for his most recent forgery offense, Jim admitted, confidentially, that he finally "had it good." He was living with and had complete control over three teen-age prostitutes whom he "protected" and solicited for.

### Some Distinctions Between Sociopathic and other Psychopathological Syndromes

Sociopathy is similar to other disorders in that it reflects a disruption of a deeply ingrained and pervasive pattern of personality functioning.

Distinctions between sociopathic and neurotic disorders can readily be made on the basis of their manifest clinical pictures. There is considerable dispute in the literature, however, as to whether they can be differentiated in terms of their etiology and development. A central issue in this debate is whether "anxiety" is present or absent in the sociopath. No disagreement exists as to the role of anxiety as a contributing factor in neurotic symptoms.

As we have conceived it, anxiety is a secondary factor in all symptom disorders. More central to the process of symptom formation are the patient's habitual coping strategies. Thus, symptoms primarily reflect how a patient has learned to control or discharge all forms of tension, e.g., anxiety, forbidden impulses, conflict, objective stress and so on, regardless of their particular source or specific content.

In neurotic symptom formation the patient attempts to discharge his tension through intrapsychic maneuvers and transformations. This strategy occurs in patients who wish to camouflage the source and content of their disturbing emotions so as to make them personally more tolerable, socially acceptable and capable of eliciting support and nurture from others. In contrast, the sociopathic symptom represents a relatively undisguised acting out of the patient's tensions. It tends to occur primarily in patients who not only care little for social approval, but appear to gain gratification in flouting convention and disturbing others. The difference between neurotic and sociopathic disorders, then, is not that patients classed in the former group experience anxiety and those in the latter do not; rather, it reflects the fact that most neurotics have learned to handle tensions by camouflaging them so as to gain social approval whereas most sociopaths have learned to act them out directly so as to scoff and deride social norms and values. Which symptom a patient "chooses," neurotic or sociopathic, depends then on his lifelong personality style. As we will elaborate later, sociopathic disorders occur most commonly in independent personality patterns whereas neurotic symptoms arise most frequently in dependent and ambivalent personalities.

A distinction must be drawn between sociopathic disorders and what shall be termed "dyssocial reactions," to be discussed in the next chapter. Let us be mindful, before we proceed, that there are no hard and sharp lines by which we can differentiate the various syndromes of psychopathology; points of distinction are matters of degree. This caveat is most appropriate with regard to distinctions between sociopathy and dyssocial reactions.

Both these syndromes are characterized by their disdain for social conventions. However, they can be differentiated in terms of the extent to which their behaviors reflect the operation of deeply ingrained and pervasive personality characteristics. As we conceive the distinction, "sociopathic disorders" arise in pathological personality types and reflect the reactivation of widely generalized sensitivities and coping distortions; "dyssocial reactions," in contrast, are stimulus-specific responses to circumscribed conditions, usually acquired by simple imitative learning. Although these reactions are learned as a consequence of faulty past experiences, these experiences did not permeate the entire fabric of the individual's personality make-up. As a consequence, these reactions arise only under special conditions and seem not to be compulsively driven, that is, they appear somewhat discriminating and understandable in terms of present needs and current realities.

Dyssocial reactions are seen most commonly in group delinquency behaviors and in planned criminal activities. In this pathology, the individual usually joins others in the expression of antisocial acts, or plans in a careful, logical but illegal manner the achievement of tangible profitable rewards. In contrast, the sociopath tends to be a "loner," with no genuine loyalty to anyone or anything, lacking the capacity to share and feel affection toward others. Furthermore, being driven primarily by the need to discharge tensions stirred up from the past, his goals appear indiscriminate and are pursued impulsively and irrationally. For example, a sociopath may pilfer worthless items from his place of employment or forge small checks, despite the fact that he has no financial need, may lose a good job if discovered and fall into public disgrace as a consequence. Compelled by the dictates of unconscious habits and attitudes, his behaviors are often foolish or purposelessly aggressive, enacted without apparent rhyme or reason. This is in contrast to patients with dyssocial reactions for whom goals are often substantial.

## PERSONALITY DISPOSITIONS AND CLINICAL SUBTYPES

The preceding paragraphs proposed that sociopathic disorders are rooted in pathological personality patterns. In the ensuing paragraphs we will turn our attention to those patterns described in chapters 6 and 7 which frequently give rise to this disorder. Since different patterns serve as a foundation for the sociopathic impairment, it will be instructive to differentiate the disorder into several personality correlated subtypes.

Subtype distinctions are especially needed since sociopaths have been described in the past by a parade of seemingly contradictory characteristics. Some clinicians have described sociopaths as impulsive, immature, naive, aimless and flighty; just as frequently, it has been said that they are sly, cunning and well-educated sorts who are capable of making clever long-range plans to deceive and exploit others. To complicate the picture further, sociopaths commonly have been noted for their cruel aggressiveness and for the keen pleasures they derive from disrupting and intimidating others; yet, at other times, these patients are pictured as lacking in hostile intentions and are believed to experience extreme discomfort when their actions prove harmful or upsetting to others. This confusion stems in part from a failure to recognize that sociopathic behaviors may spring from appreciably different personality styles, that is, that social deviation may arise as a consequence of fundamentally different coping strategies, each of which may lead, however, to similar repugnant actions.

To highlight these different pathways to sociopathy, we will describe in the following sections three variants of this disorder, each of which is found primarily in a single and different basic personality pattern. We believe that these three types comprise the greater majority of those currently classified as sociopathic. Although we will focus on those clinical features which distinguish each subtype, they do exhibit certain commonalities, notably a marked self-centeredness and a marked disdain for the needs of others. In addition to this central core, they often display in common several subsidiary features which make differential diagnoses extremely difficult. Nevertheless, it will be instructive for pedagogical purposes to highlight their more discriminable clinical characteristics and personality backgrounds.

### Antisocial Sociopath (active-independent personality)

We have frequently stated that if we wish to discern the logic of a patient's "choice" of his symptoms we must first grasp the source and character of the reinforcements he has learned to seek and the instrumental strategies he has acquired to achieve them. These fundamental determinants of his behavior do not arise fortuitously; rather, they reflect a long history of biogenic and psychogenic influences which interweave to form the central pattern of his personality.

An examination of the five clinical features of the sociopath reveals a common core of social disdain and self-centeredness. Stated in the conceptual terminology we have previously employed, these patients achieve their positive reinforcements from themselves, not from others. Translated into personality types, this means that sociopaths are likely to be "independent" personality patterns—the aggressive and the narcissistic types. Here, positive reinforcements are achieved primarily through the self, and the values and needs of others are likely to be viewed as negatively reinforcing. Thus, independents approach those with whom they come into contact as objects for exploitation, self-aggrandizement and self-gratification.

We will focus our attention in this section on the active-independent, or aggressive personalities, those whose past experiences have shaped vindictive attitudes and hostile behaviors. These personalities exhibit an "antisocial" form of sociopathic disorder since they possess impulses of retribution that are discharged in a hateful and destructive defiance of conventional social life.

Distrustful of others and anticipating betrayal and punishment, these personalities have acquired a cold-blooded ruthlessness, an intense desire to gain revenge for the mistreatment to which they were subjected in childhood. Here we see a total rejection of tender emotions and a deep suspicion of the good will offered by others. They assume a chip on the shoulder attitude, a readiness to attack and lash out at those whom they distrust, or those whom they can use as scapegoats for their seething hostile impulses. Dreading the possibility that others may think them weak or that others may manipulate them into a position of weakness, they must maintain an image of hard-boiled strength, carry themselves truculently and act tough, arrogant, brusque, callous and fearless. To "prove" their courage and manliness, they court danger and punishment. But punishment only verifies their expectation of unjust treatment. Rather than having a deterrent effect, then, it reinforces their rebelliousness and desires for retribution. In positions of power, they dare not exhibit weakness or feel remorse for their offenses. They must brutalize or intimidate others to vindicate themselves and to confirm their self-image of strength and independence.

Sociopathic features are close to the surface at all times in aggressive personalities. This latent tendency takes on manifest expression when the person finds himself unable to channel his aggressive and vindictive impulses into acceptable forms of social initiative and competition. Faced with persistent failures, beaten down in his attempts to dominate and control others and finding his aspirations outdistancing his talents and luck, his feelings of frustration, resentment and anger begin to mount until his controls give way to raw brutality and vengeful hostility. An episode of this nature is portrayed in the following case.

### CASE 11-5
### Guy L., Age 23, Married, No Children

This active-independent man had been employed for several months as a door to door sales representative for a rather disreputable magazine distribution company, known for its deceptive promotional methods. The sales commissions due him, according to his calculations, were quite substantial. However, Guy learned at the time of the quarterly settlement of his accounts that he had inaccurately completed a number of his invoice forms and would not be credited with these commissions, an amount totaling less than 20 dollars out of a total commission figure of close to 2500 dollars. His feeling of humiliation and anger was intensified that evening when his wife accused him of being a "fool" and "stupid." Furious about these events, Guy beat his wife that night; the following morning he went to the company's office, quietly gathered and systematically destroyed his and other salesmen's records, and "in a sudden fury" physically assaulted the office manager and his secretary.

Spurred on by repeated social rejection and punishment, driven by an increasing need for retribution and power, the aggressive impulses of these personalities surge unmodified into the open. At these times, they deliberately display their hostile feelings and openly flout the rights of others. They may become outrageously irresponsible and engage in flagrant excesses and antisocial acts. Not only are guilt and remorse lacking, but there is an arrogant contempt and abuse of others.

### Exploitive Sociopath (passive-independent personality)

The distinctive feature of hostile vindictiveness which characterizes the "antisocial" sociopath is usually lacking in the "exploitive" type. Here we see an indifferent conscience, a simple aloofness to truth and social responsibility which, if brought to the exploitive sociopath's attention, elicits an attitude of nonchalant innocence. Though totally self-oriented, many learn to become facile in the ways of social influence, are capable of feigning an air of dignity and confidence and are rather skilled in deceiving others with their clever glibness of tongue. Quite characteristically, they leave behind them a trail of outrageous acts such as swindling, sexual excesses, pathological lying and fraud.

This careless disregard for truth, this talent for exploitation and deception is often neither hostile nor malicious in intent. Rather, it derives from an attitude of omnipotence, superiority and self-assurance, a feeling that the rules of society do not apply to them and that they are above the discipline and responsibilities of shared living. As with their active-independent counterpart, the passive-independent gains his positive reinforcements from himself and is coolly indifferent to the welfare and rights of others, whom he uses as a means of enhancing and indulging his whims and desires.

Flagrant sociopathic behaviors emerge when the narcissistic individual realizes that in order to gain the respect of others, he must become a productive and contributing member of society. Having been accustomed to praise and commendation for his mere existence, as was typically the case in his childhood, he experiences considerable dismay at the fact that those outside the parental home will not be equally generous in their rewards.

Caring little to shoulder genuine responsibilities and unwilling to change his inflated self-concept, the narcissist refuses to "buckle down" like everyone else and expend real efforts to prove his worth. Since he has never learned to control his fantasies or to be concerned with integrity in social relationships, he maintains his feeling of superiority by deception and fraud, by lying and distorting his accomplishments and by charming others through craft and wit. Thus, rather than applying his talents and confidence toward the goal of tangible achievements, he devotes his energies to intricate lies and clever exploitations in which he slyly contrives to extract from others what he unjustly believes to be his due. Untroubled by conscience and self-discipline and needful of continued nourishment for his overinflated self-image, he fabricates stories which enhance his worth and seduces others into supporting his outrageous excesses. The following case depicts a number of these features.

### CASE 11-6
### Roger H., Age 44, Unmarried

This passive-independent male was reared in a well-to-do family, the only child of a doting mother. In the past ten years, Roger squandered a substantial inheritance and was beginning to "fall on hard times." Handsome, well-educated and suave in manner, he had always been skillful in charming and exploiting others, especially women. Faced with economic adversity, Roger allied himself with a group of stock promoters involved in selling essentially worthless shares of "sure-bet" Canadian mining stock. This led to other "shady deals"; and in time Roger became a full-fledged "love swindler" who intrigued, lived off and "borrowed" thousands of dollars from a succession of wealthy and lonely "mistresses."

Social criticism and punishment prove of no avail since this sociopath quickly dismisses them as the product of jealous inferiors. Driven to maintain his ever-expanding narcissistic needs and totally indifferent to the rights of others, he becomes a ne'er-do-well and develops a self-indulgent, grossly irresponsible and flamboyant sociopathic disorder.

### Impulsive Sociopath (active-dependent personality)

Impulsive and exploitive sociopaths are quite similar. Both tend to be clever, charming, flippant and capable of weaving fanciful images which intrigue and seduce the naive. They differ from the antisocial type in that their basic motivations are not those of hostility and revenge. They differ from each other in that the impulsive sociopath experiences intense anxiety if he fails to find an external source upon which he can depend for attention and approval. He "seduces" others merely to exploit their interest and involvement. Driven by a need for excitement and stimulation, he acts impulsively, is unable to delay gratification and evidences a penchant for momentary excitements and fleeting adventures, with minimal regard for later consequences.

The impulsive sociopath, then, is neither antisocial nor exploitive but simply thrill-seeking, easily infatuated and overly but transiently attached to one thing or person after another. What justifies the sociopathic label is his lack of loyalty and his social undependability, his disdain for the effects of his behaviors on those he abandons in his restless chase to satisfy one capricious whim after another. It is his desire for immediate gratification and his total disregard for the agreements and responsibilities he has hastily assumed, which lead to the view that his behavior is sociopathic. He leaves behind him a trail of broken promises and contracts, abandoned wives and children, squandered funds, distraught employers and so on.

It is when the gregarious person feels overly burdened with responsibility or suffocated by routine and boredom that he often begins the radical turn toward sociopathy. Lacking inner substance and self-discipline, tempted by new and exciting stimuli and skilled in attracting and seducing others, he foregoes his earlier attachments to travel an erratic course of irresponsibility, leaving in his wake the scattered debris of once promising but now abandoned hopes.

## REMEDIAL APPROACHES

It is commonly noted in the literature that sociopathic disorders are difficult cases, both in terms of prognosis and therapy. Let us briefly review current opinion on these two phases of the problem.

Sociopathy appears quite often in persons in their middle teens and recedes in frequency in later years. Most clinicians are pessimistic about the prospect of modifying sociopathic behaviors, especially during the peak early years. The apparent decline in incidence in middle age probably reflects two factors, entirely incidental to the intrinsic character of the disorder. First, those who have persisted in their sociopathic behaviors ultimately are imprisoned for prolonged periods as a consequence of repetitive immoral or illegal acts. Thus, they may be "out of commission" by the age of 35 or 40. Second, those who continue in the mainstream of society probably have learned to channel their antisocial, exploitive and impulsive tendencies more skillfully or into more socially acceptable endeavors. Despite these superficial changes, their basic personality remains unaltered, evidencing itself in a variety of less obvious and flagrant interpersonal difficulties.

Sociopaths are highly resistant to therapeutic efforts. Rarely are they convinced that they need treatment. Many are remanded by court action to their families with the stipulation that they engage in therapy. Once in treatment, however, they are either openly defiant and uncooperative or extremely congenial but cleverly evasive and deceptive. Also militating against therapeutic efforts are the many positive reinforcements the patient achieves while engaging in his impulsive, exploitive or hostile behaviors. This contrasts with the symptomatic behaviors of the neurotic who experiences discomfort with his ailment and is motivated, therefore, to pursue the relief that therapy promises.

Direct methods of treatment have proved of little value in controlling the sociopathic symptomatology. Nevertheless, efforts may be made to reduce the pernicious effects of environmental conditions that encourage and reinforce the continuation of destructive behaviors and attitudes. Psychopharmacological and other biophysical approaches make few, if any, inroads on these patients. Intrapsychic techniques seem equally ill-advised and fruitless. Supportive procedures may be of value in establishing rapport and phenomenological methods may be employed to help channel a more constructive form of tension discharge. The systematic methods of behavioral modification may prove useful in extinguishing particularly repugnant forms of acting out, although the effectiveness of these techniques in these cases has not been adequately documented. Of notable promise are group treatment procedures in which sociopathic patients freely discuss and share their attitudes, without feeling the implicit derogation they often experience when facing alone so conventional an authority figure as a therapist. Here, as they explore together their feelings and behaviors, they may learn a measure of loyalty and group responsibility which, hopefully, will generalize into constructive group oriented behaviors.

# PSYCHOTIC DISORDERS

Psychotic disorders are extremely severe forms of psychopathology and normally require inpatient or hospital treatment. The rather baffling symptoms we observe in these patients either represent extreme and bizarre efforts on their part to cope with threat and anxiety or signify the collapse of their habitual coping strategies. These disorders contrast with decompensated patterns, in which corrosive pathological processes have permeated the entire personality structure. In psychotic disorders the pathology tends to be episodic and reversible, and not as permanent and ingrained as the patterns.

The term "psychosis" has been in use for less than two centuries. Only since the classic texts of Kraepelin, in the first quarter of this century, has it been applied as a label to represent severe mental impairments. There is no need to discuss the history of these disorders. To all intents and purposes, it is one and the same with the history of psychopathology itself. Reference should be made to chapters 1 and 2 for a detailed exposition of both ancient and recent conceptions and theories.

## GENERAL CLINICAL PICTURE

The official DSM-II nomenclature refers to the *psychoses* as follows:

Patients are described as psychotic when their mental functioning is sufficiently impaired to interfere grossly with their capacity to meet the ordinary demands of life. The impairment may result from a serious distortion in their capacity to recognize reality.

Hallucinations and delusions, for example, may distort their perceptions. Alterations of mood may be so profound that the patient's capacity to respond appropriately is grossly impaired. Deficits in perception, language and memory may be so severe that the patient's capacity for mental grasp of his situation is effectively lost.

The range and variety of clinical features associated with psychotic psychopathology cannot be encompassed by a summary listing. Equally difficult and problematic are attempts to classify the complex and infinitely diverse clusters into which these symptoms may form. We will address ourselves to some of the issues connected with specific symptom clusters in conjunction with our later presentation of clinical types and their personality dispositions. For the present, we will note in general several features which justify the psychotic disorder label.

As was described in earlier chapters, the two distinguishing characteristics of the markedly severe states are a *diminished reality awareness* and a *cognitive* and *emotional dyscontrol*.

As the tide of uncontrollable anxieties and impulses surges forward, these patients begin to sink into a hazy and phantasmagoric world of fleeting, distorted and dream-like impressions in which subjective moods and images become fused with, and ultimately dominate, objective realities. Overt behaviors, stimulated primarily by these internal states, appear purposeless, disjointed, irrational, stereotyped and bizarre. There is a disunity and disorganization to their communications. Ideas and thoughts are conveyed in an inchoate and jumbled fashion, often taking the form of delusions or projected onto the world as hallucinatory perceptions. Controls are rendered useless or are abandoned as emotions break loose. There is no instrumental purpose or goal other than the ventilation of impulse and anxiety. Unable to grasp objective reality or coordinate feelings and thoughts, these patients regress into a totally helpless state of social invalidism.

To delineate more clearly the features of the psychotic disorders, it may be useful to differentiate them from those of the decompensated personality patterns; other symptom disorders; and the behavior reactions.

1. The distinction between psychotic disorders and decompensated personality patterns is difficult to make on the basis of overt clinical features alone. The principal distinction between them lies in the developmental history of the impairment. The emergence of psychotic disorders is usually of rapid onset and follows a period of reasonably adequate functioning. The disorder occurs most frequently in borderline pathological personalities. Although these individuals have evidenced many social difficulties and competency deficits, they have managed, at least for extended periods, to maintain some hold on social reality. By contrast, decompensated personalities have shown a consistent downward progression, with fewer and fewer intervening periods of reasonable social functioning.

Another distinction between markedly severe disorders and patterns is the role played by external precipitants. In the decompensated pattern, the patient's disturbance reflects the operation of internal and ingrained defects in his personality make-up whereas in the psychotic disorders there is evidence that current behaviors are, at least in part, a product of external or environmental stress. Futhermore, as the intensity of stress is reduced, the disordered patient begins, albeit slowly, to recoup his coping powers and to regain his former level of functioning. This is not in evidence among decompensated patterns. Thus, disorders are distinguished by their transitory character. They tend to be of relatively short duration whereas decompensated personality patterns are more permanent and fixed as a style of life.

This latter point brings us to another basis for distinguishing between these two markedly severe states. Among disordered patients, we frequently find a sense of disharmony and an effort "to fight off" their symptoms. The emotions and behaviors these patients experience are viewed by them to be

"ego-dystonic," that is, they are alien, strange and unwanted. In contrast, decompensated personalities appear indifferent to their state of pathology. Their traits have begun to be taken for granted and are "ego-syntonic," that is, they seem to be a natural part of their lives.

The naturalness with which bizarre traits are experienced in decompensated patterns reflects in large measure the insidious manner in which these traits developed. They evolved slowly, growing bit by bit into the very fabric of the personality make-up. In contrast, psychotic disorders come rather abruptly and are experienced as a marked disruption of the accustomed or "normal" mode of functioning. Either the symptoms stand out as isolated and dramatic deviations from a more typical style of behavior or they erupt as a bizarre accentuation or caricature of the more prosaic personality style.

Despite the distinctions noted, the line between psychotic disorders and decompensated personality patterns is often a blurred one. Man does not readily accommodate us in our desire for a simple system of classification. This diagnostic complication is compounded further in these cases by the fact that episodes of psychotic disorder may gradually blend into a more permanent decompensated pattern. Thus, for a variety of reasons—persistent stress, the "comforts" of hospitalization and so on —a patient may "get caught" in the web surrounding his psychosis and fail to "pull out" of what may otherwise have been a transitory episode.

2. Distinctions between psychotic disorders and other symptom disorders are not difficult to make. Psychotics evidence two central symptoms not found in less severe impairments, notably the loss of reality awareness and cognitive and emotional dyscontrol. Although psychotics often exhibit neurotic, psychophysiologic and sociopathic symptoms, such as obsessions, anxiety and a hostile acting out, they manifest in addition a variety of symptoms not found in these less severe disorders, such as social invalidism, perceptual hallucinations, irrational excitement, delusions, disorientation, total apathy and profound depression. With their coping strategies upset, distorted or shattered, their behaviors take on a chaotic and disorganized quality rarely seen in those who are able to maintain a moderate level of personality cohesion.

3. As has often been stated, psychopathological categories are not sharply defined classes, but represent positions along various continua which shade imperceptibly into one another. On one of these continuous gradients, psychotic disorders may be placed halfway between decompensated personality patterns and the more serious

behavior reactions. Thus, behavior reactions, in contrast to personality patterns, occur in direct response to specific stimulus precipitants. They operate independently of general personality traits, appearing largely as isolated and narrowly circumscribed behaviors. Psychotic disorders, although often prompted by external precipitants, are not as stimulus-specific as behavior reactions are. These disorders occur in response to a wide variety of stimulus conditions since they reflect the operation of pervasive personality sensitivities and vulnerabilities.

Behavior reactions tend to be consistent in their form of expression, manifesting themselves rather uniformly and predictably each time the distressing precipitant appears. In contrast, psychotic disorders tend to be inconsistent and contaminated with a mixture of different and interchangeable symptoms since they derive from a complex network of reactivated feelings, attitudes and strategies.

Behavior reactions are often understandable when viewed in terms of the precipitating stimulus. Furthermore, they tend to subside quickly when the disturbing event is removed. In contrast, the responses of psychotic disorders appear extremely complicated and irrational when viewed in terms of the precipitating event, and tend to "drag on" after the precipitant has been removed. Again, the overdriven character and surplus features that are seen in psychotic disorders can be traced to the intrusion of the patient's more generalized pattern of personality pathology. With each disturbing precipitant, no matter how specific and inconsequential it may be, a flood of tangentially related sensitivities and memories is stirred up. As a consequence, the patient's responses are determined less by the objective precipitating stimulus than by the subjective memories and emotions that were incidentally aroused. These disordered responses are complicated further by the intrusion of the patient's characteristic coping style. Moreover, given its current state of disarray, his coping effort produces behaviors that are grossly inappropriate and bizarre. In all, the baffling, obscure and symbolic nature of "disordered" responses contrasts markedly with the relatively simple and straightforward responses seen in the behavior reactions.

## CLINICAL TYPES AND PERSONALITY DISPOSITIONS

Disorders, according to the definitions furnished for this text, arise only in patients who possess pathological personality patterns. Repeated episodes of psychotic disorder, as described in chapter 8, occur primarily in borderline pathological patterns. Mild or basic pathological personalities are also subject to psychotic disorders, but with appreciably less frequency than is found in borderlines, and usually in response to extreme or persistent external stress.

Psychotic disorders are precipitated when pathological personalities are unable to control or discharge their tensions by means of a neurotic, psychophysiologic or sociopathic resolution. According to the definitions and rationale provided in preceding chapters, "normal" personalities do not experience psychotic disorders. Rather, they may be subject to severe behavior reactions. The overt features of these reactions may appear similar to those seen in the psychotic disorders; however, closer examination will reveal that they reflect responses to specific external stimuli rather than to widely generalized personality vulnerabilities, as is the case in the disorders.

Before we describe the various clinical types of psychotic disorder, we must point out that it is extremely difficult to predict the *particular* symptoms a patient will manifest when he succumbs to a psychosis. The first complication we face in this regard is the fact that the experiences of each individual are unique. Thus, the specific content and form of his symptoms will reflect the idiosyncratic character of his learnings. As a consequence of this individuality, no two persons will exhibit identical psychotic features. This presents a problem in organizing a classification system, since some reliable basis must be found to group together individuals who are, at least in part, dissimilar.

In a previous chapter we discussed this same issue with regard to the concept of personality patterns. In these syndromes, however, we were able to organize classification groups based on rather broad outlines of a patient's style of functioning; here we noted certain *general* and fundamental traits which gave rise to similar, but in their details, often overtly different behaviors and attitudes. Enough flexibility was built in to each category to allow for considerable variability. Thus, no single behavioral symptom was viewed to be the *sine qua non* of these basic personality patterns. Reference was made to specific symptoms only to illustrate the range and variety of certain fundamental characteristics.

Symptom disorders, in contrast to personality patterns, do *imply* the preeminence of a *particular* clinical feature, a singular symptom which emerges in clear fashion as the *sine qua non* of the impairment. However, the inevitable individual variability in the symptomatic picture of these cases produces a blurring of the "preeminent" symptom upon which the category label is based. For example, even in the neuroses, where rather distinctive and dramatic symptoms are often present (e.g., obsession or conversion), we pointed out that in most cases there is a coexistence of several symptoms which covary and are interchangeable over time; these symptoms wax and wane in their potency and clarity during the course of a disorder, thereby complicating efforts to assign a single symptom label to the disorder. Thus, despite the long-established tradition of referring to a disorder in terms of its most dramatic symptom, most patients exhibit "intra-individual variability," that is, display certain symptoms at one time and place and different symptoms at other times and places.

How then is the problem of symptom covariation and changeability to be resolved in the psychotic disorders?

Two directions seem reasonable toward the goal of finding a solution: systematic multivariate research designed to determine which symptoms covary or cluster together in the same patient; and systematic research to determine whether each of these multivariate symptom clusters are correlated with particular personality patterns whose basic traits (e.g., attitudes or coping strategies) could logically account for its correlated symptom cluster.

The eight clinical types to be described subsequently, and their corresponding personality dispositions, represent the results of such an effort. Here, we have attempted to bring together the findings of multivariate cluster studies (e.g., Overall, 1963; Lorr, 1963, 1966; Wittenborn and May, 1966) and the theoretical schema of pathological personality patterns described in chapters 6 through 9. Although extensive research has not been done to validate the specific typology to be presented, it may serve as a useful model for further systematic studies.

Let us note before we proceed that investigators utilizing multivariate analysis have not uncovered identical symptom clusters. This lack of correspondence arises for a number of reasons: the factorial methods they have employed have differed; the populations they have used for their respective samples often were not comparable; and the measures upon which they based their data tapped different clinical features. Thus, in the grouping presented below, we have taken a measure of liberty by selecting only those clusters which have recurred with fair regularity among different investigators and those which logically appear to correlate with the basic pathological patterns described in chapters 6 through 9.

It will be evident in the following discussion that we have *not* asserted that a one to one correspondence exists between a particular personality pattern and a particular psychotic disorder; rather, as the evidence of our own preliminary research suggests, certain personality patterns are *more likely* to exhibit certain disorders than they are others. This loosely fitting model of pattern-disorder correspondence was presented in our discussion of the neurotic disorders; for example, we noted that the obsessive-compulsive disorder occurred, not in one, but in several personality patterns, although with greater probability in some than in others.

Before turning to our discussion of the eight clinical forms of psychotic disorder, we must also note that the labels we have chosen as headings for these disorders differ from those listed in the official DSM-II. These new labels have been selected to stress the distinction which we contend must be made between decompensated personality *patterns* and psychotic *disorders,* a distinction not drawn in the categories of the official nosology. Disorders, according to our model, are distinguished from each other in terms of their dominant symptoms; thus, it would be logical to label them, as is done in the official listing of the neurotic disorders, with terms that describe these dominant symptoms. This approach to terminology and labeling has been utilized by most contemporary multivariate researchers. For example, we shall refer to these disorders with labels such as "impassivity," "euphoric excitement" and "agitated depression." To minimize confusion and to demonstrate the close correspondence that exists between the category groups formulated here and those in the official classification, frequent reference will be made regarding points of similarity between the two.

As we have done in previous sections, we shall list and describe the personality patterns that are most vulnerable to each of the disorders in descending order of frequency. For example, in the disorder labeled "impassivity," the passive-detached pattern is noted first since these personalities are more susceptible to this psychotic impairment than the other patterns that have been listed.

## IMPASSIVITY DISORDER
(DSM-II: *Schizophrenia, Catatonic Type, Withdrawn*)

These patients exhibit features similar to those classified in the official nosology as *schizophrenia, catatonic type, withdrawn* (stupor, mutism and waxy flexibility) and to a lesser extent, those of *manic-depressive illness, depressed type* (motor and mental retardation). Among multivariate researchers, Lorr et al. (1963, 1966), for example, have referred to a similar syndrome cluster as the "retarded" type.

## CLINICAL PICTURE

Most striking among these psychotics is their lethargy and seeming indifference to their surroundings. They move listlessly, are apathetic and even stuporous. Clothes are drab and their faces appear lifeless and mask-like. Speech is slow, labored and often blocked, whispered or inaudible. They seem passively withdrawn and unresponsive to their environment, cannot participate or feel involved and tend to perceive things about them as unreal and strange. There is an emotional poverty, a dreamy detachment, a tendency to stand immobile or fixed in one place for hours. They habitually sit in cramped, bent-over and peculiar positions, to which they return repeatedly if they are distracted or dislodged. Some not only show a total lack of initiative, but display an automatic obedience to the requests of others, even when these directives could result in severe physical discomfort or danger. Others are so profoundly detached that they fail to register reactions of distress to painful stimuli such as a slap or a pinprick.

All these behaviors signify a protective withdrawal, a retreat into indifference and a purposeful uninvolvement and insensitivity to life so as to avoid the anguish it has produced. By disengaging themselves totally, they need no longer feel the painful emotions they experienced before, no longer suffer the discouragement of struggling fruitlessly and no longer desire and aspire, only to be frustrated and humiliated again. Faced with a sense of hopelessness and futility, they have given up, become uncaring, neutral, flat, impassive and "dead" to everything.

## PERSONALITY DISPOSITIONS

Psychotic impassivity occurs in all personality patterns. The shutting off of emotions and the retreat into indifference are protective devices that can be employed easily by all individuals who have been overwhelmed by a sense of hopelessness and futility. Despite its ease as a coping maneuver, it appears with greater frequency among patients whose lifelong strategies dispose them to emotional detachment and withdrawal.

1. As a "logical" extension of their personality style, we find the impassive disorder arising often in the *passive* and *active-detached patterns* (asocial, avoidant and schizoid). Unable to handle even minor degrees of overstimulation, be it from unexpected responsibilities, objective threat or reactivated anxiety, they may overemploy their coping strategies and withdraw into an impassive, unresponsive and unfeeling state. These cases can usually be identified by their total muteness and their complete "tuning out" of the world, traits which result in an inner void and a picture of mask-like stupor, as portrayed in the following:

### CASE 11-7
#### Arthur O., Age 29, Unmarried

Arthur, an active-detached schizoid, was admitted to the psychiatric section of a general hospital after being found by a hotel chambermaid sitting on the edge of his bed, staring vacantly at a wall. When brought to the ward, he sat impassively in a chair, was unresponsive to questioning, indifferent to his surroundings and well-being, disinterested in food and unwilling to feed himself. He remained mute, withdrawn and immobile for several days, following which he slowly began to take care of himself without assistance, although he failed to speak to anyone for almost a month.

2. *Passive-dependent personalities* (submissive and cycloid) succumb on occasion to impassivity, but here we often see a coloring of sadness, a tone of inner softness, an inclination to "be nice" and to acquiesce in the wishes of others in the hope of maintaining some measure of affection and support from them. It is in these patients that we often observe a cataleptic waxy flexibility, that is, a tendency to maintain bodily positions into which others have placed them. This willingness to be molded according to the whims of others signifies their total abandonment of self-initiative and their complete dependence and submission to external directives. At the heart of their acquiescent impassivity is the deep need they have to counter their separation anxieties and to avoid actions which might engender disapproval and rejection.

Though impassivity occurs less frequently among *passive-ambivalents* (conforming and cycloid), they succumb for reasons similar to those of the passive-dependent.

3. In the *active-dependent* patterns (gregarious and cycloid), the impassivity psychosis usually reflects a collapse of their lifelong style of actively soliciting attention and approval. Rather than face failure and rejection, these patients may "retire" from their habitual strategy, disown their need for stimulation and excitement and temporarily reverse the course of their life style. Impassivity is usually of short duration in these patients, and can be re-

lieved by genuine assurances from others of their care, interest and affection.

## FRAGMENTATION DISORDER
(DSM-II: *Acute Schizophrenic Episode; Schizophrenia, Hebephrenic Type*)

Psychotic fragmentation, as we have formulated the syndrome, corresponds in its symptomatic picture to two of the official categories listed in the DSM-II: *acute schizophrenic episode* (confusion, emotional turmoil and perplexity) and *schizophrenia, hebephrenic type* (inappropriate affect, disorganized thinking and regressive behavior). Among multivariate studies, it closely approximates, for example, the "disorganized type" outlined by Lorr et al. (1963, 1966).

### CLINICAL PICTURE

These patients are identifiable by their incongruous and disorganized behavior. They seem disoriented and confused, unclear as to time, place and identity. Many exhibit posturing, grimacing, inappropriate giggling, mannerisms and peculiar movements. Their speech tends to ramble into word salads composed of incoherent neologisms and a chaotic mishmash of irrelevancies. The content of their ideas is colored with fantasy and hallucination and scattered with bizarre and fragmentary delusions that have no apparent logic or function. Regressive acts such as soiling and wetting are common, and these patients often consume food in an infantile or ravenous manner.

### PERSONALITY DISPOSITIONS

For most patients, fragmentation signifies a surrendering of all coping efforts. Thus, every pathological pattern may exhibit the disorder. In some personalities, however, fragmentation may be an active coping maneuver, thereby increasing the likelihood of its occurrence in these types. Furthermore, some patterns are more disposed than others to surrender their controls and thus collapse into a fragmented state. In short, although all personalities may succumb to the fragmentation disorder, some are more likely to do so than others. The following list includes these more vulnerable patterns.

1. *Active-detached personalities* (avoidant and schizoid) are especially inclined to this disorder not only because they can easily be overwhelmed by external and internal pressures, but because fragmentation is an extension of their

characteristic protective maneuver of interfering with their own cognitive clarity. By blocking the normal flow of thoughts and memories, they distract themselves and dilute the impact of painful feelings and recollections. Fragmentation may arise, then, as a direct product either of intolerable pressures, self-made confusion or both. What we see as a result is a picture of "forced" absurdity and incoherence and a concerted effort to disrupt cognitive clarity and emotional rationality. The following portrays such an episode.

#### CASE 11-8
#### Greta S., Age 22, Unmarried

Greta displayed an avoidant pattern ever since early adolescence. She was shy, somewhat fearful of all people, even those she had known all of her life, and preferred to spend her days at home helping her mother cook and clean for her father and younger brothers. One morning she became "silly and confused," began to talk "gibberishly," as her mother put it, became incontinent, grimaced and giggled for no apparent reason. When the family physician arrived, he noted that Greta placed herself into a series of contorted positions on the floor, sang incoherent songs and cried fitfully for brief periods. Greta continued this behavior, although more sporadically, for several weeks after institutionalization, following which she became quiet and withdrawn. About three months after hospitalization, she returned home and resumed her "normal" pattern of behavior.

2. Both *passive and active-dependents* (submissive, gregarious and cycloid) are disposed to fragmentation when faced with situations that seriously tax their limited capacity to function independently. Without external security and support and lacking a core of inner competence and self-determination, they may easily crumble and disintegrate, usually into regressive or infantile behaviors. Beneath their confusion and bizarre acts we often see remnants of their former coping strategies. For example, their regressive eating and soiling may reflect a continued seeking of care and nurture. Their stereotyped grimacing and giggling may signify a forced and pathetic effort to capture the good will and approval of those upon whom they now depend.

3. In the *passive and active-ambivalents* (conforming, negativistic and cycloid) fragmentation usually follows the shattering of controls previously employed to restrain deeply repressed conflicts. Unable to keep these divisive forces in check, these patients are torn apart, engulfed in a sea of surging memories and contrary feelings that now spew forth in a flood of incoherent verbalizations and bizarre emotions and acts. In their case, stereotyped grimacing, posturing and mannerisms

Figure 11-1    The process of fragmentation is vividly revealed in a series of paintings by an English artist, Louis Wain, an eccentric bachelor who had made a specialty of making portraits of his 17 cats before suffering a breakdown in middle life. The cat becomes more horrifying and the background more bizarre and abstract until finally the cat disappears entirely. (© Guttman Maclay Collection, Institute of Psychiatry, University of London.)

often signify feeble efforts to contain their impulses or to dampen the confusion and disharmony which they feel.

## RETARDED DEPRESSION DISORDER

(DSM-II: *Manic-depressive Illness, Depressed Type*)

The symptoms exhibited by these patients are similar to those labeled in the DSM-II as *manic-depressive illness, depressed type* (severely depressed mood; mental and motor retardation progressing occasionally to stupor). Corresponding syndromes based on multivariate research are noted as "intropunitive-retarded" types (Lorr et al., 1963, 1966) and "depressive retardation" (Wittenborn, 1962).

### CLINICAL PICTURE

There are several similarities between "impassivity" and "retarded depression." Both exhibit a generalized psychomotor inactivity, e.g., heavy and lugubrious movements, slow or dragged out speech and an everpresent air of fatigue and exhaustion. Careful observation, however, will uncover areas of considerable difference, even at the gross clinical level. For example, the retarded depressive patient experiences deep feelings, contrasting markedly with the emotional flatness of the impassive; his gloom and profound dejection are clearly conveyed as he slumps with brow furrowed, body stooped and head turned downward and away from the gaze of others, held in his hands like a burdensome weight. Various physical signs and symptoms further enable us to distinguish these disorders from impassive disorders. Retarded depressives lose weight and look haggard and drained. In their nighttime habits they follow a characteristic pattern of awakening after two or three hours of sleep, turn restlessly, have oppressive thoughts and experience a growing dread of the new day. Notable, also, is the content of their verbalizations, meager though they may be. They report a vague dread of impending disaster, feelings of utter helplessness, a pervasive sense of guilt for past failures and a willing resignation to their hopeless fate. As will be noted in the next section, retarded depressions occur most often among passive-dependent personalities whereas impassivity is more typical of the passive-detached type.

## PERSONALITY DISPOSITIONS

In discussing dispositions to "impassivity" and "fragmentation" disorders, we ranked the two detached patterns as the most vulnerable of the various personality types. In "retarded depression" and "euphoric excitement," the next psychotic syndrome to be described, we find a marked predominance of the dependent personality patterns.

1. *Passive-dependents* (submissive and cycloid) are especially susceptible to this disorder; *active-dependents* (gregarious and cycloid) are only slightly less vulnerable. Both patterns manifest these symptoms in response to essentially similar precipitants, notably a loss or the anticipated loss of an important source of their dependency security, e.g., the death of a parent or spouse or dismissal from a steady job. Their depression often represents a logical but overly extreme response to real or potentially threatening events. However, there is no question that the reaction is pathological; the depth of the response and the disposition to succumb to profound dejection, even before difficulties have arisen, clearly point to the presence of an unusual personality vulnerability.

Despite the genuineness of the depressive mood, dependent personalities do not forego their coping aims in their disordered state. Their displays of contrition and the deep gravity of their mood solicit attention, support and nurture from others. Moreover, their coping aims enable them to avoid unbearable responsibilities and provide them with the comforts and security of dependent invalidism. Aspects of this syndrome are depicted in the following brief example.

*CASE 11-9*
*Alma F., Age 34, Married, Two Children*

This cycloid woman was admitted to the psychiatric wing of a general hospital with her third depressive episode in eight years. When first seen she was markedly underweight, had been "unable" to eat for weeks and sat limply at the edge of her chair, weeping quietly and stating, over and over again, "What have I done to my family. . . ." Alma was observed to be quiet, although downcast when she was left alone. However, as soon as someone appeared, she began to moan aloud, deprecating herself for the harm and shame she had brought to her family. Needless to say, these lamentations evoked sympathetic and reassuring responses from others.

2. Both *passive and active-ambivalents* (conforming, negativistic and cycloid) succumb with some frequency to retarded depressions although, more characteristically, they lean toward the agitated form of depressive expression, to be discussed later. In the retarded form, ambivalents have managed to gain a measure of control over their inner conflicts and hostile impulses. This they have done by turning their feelings inward, that is, by taking out their hatred upon themselves. Thus, they persist in voicing guilt and self-disparagement for their failures, antisocial acts, contemptuous feelings and thoughts. In this self-punitive depressive disorder, they manage to cloak their "real" contrary impulses, seek redemption and ask absolution for their past behaviors and forbidden unconscious inclinations. Moreover, their illness solicits support and nurture from others. In a more subtle way it also serves as a devious means of venting their hidden resentment and anger. Their state of helplessness and their protestations of self-derogation make others feel guilty and burden others with extra responsibilities and woes.

# EUPHORIC EXCITEMENT DISORDER
(DSM-II: *Manic-depressive Illness, Manic Type*)

The cluster of symptoms we have termed "euphoric excitement" corresponds, in part, to the official classification listed as *manic-depressive illness, manic type* (excessive elation, talkativeness and flight of ideas). Among multivariate studies, it may be correlated, for example, with the "excited-grandiose" type described by Lorr et al. (1963, 1966).

## CLINICAL PICTURE

Certain commonalities may be noted between the "fragmentation" and "euphoric excitement" disorders. Most notable among these is that patients in both disorders tend to be rather disorganized, scattering their ideas and emotions in a jumble of disconnected thoughts and aimless behaviors. However, there is an exuberance, a zestful energy and jovial mood among euphorics that is lacking in fragmented patients. Furthermore, their ideas and hyperactivity, although tending to be connected only loosely to reality, have an intelligible logic to them and are colored by a consistent mood of affability and congeniality which evoke feelings of sympathy and good will on the part of others. In contrast, the behaviors and ideas of fragmented patients are extremely vague, disjointed and bizarre; moreover, their emotional moods are varied and changeable, inconsistent with their thoughts and

actions and difficult to grasp and relate to, let alone empathize with.

Euphorics tend, albeit briefly, to infect others with their conviviality and buoyant optimism. Many are extremely clever and witty, rattling off puns and rhymes and playing cute and devilish tricks. However, their humor and mischievousness begin to drain others who quickly tire of the incessant and increasingly irrational quality of their forced sociability. In addition to frenetic excitement and their impulsive and reckless race from one topic to another, these patients often display an annoying pomposity and self-

Figure 11-2.    Euphoric excitement. These pictures show the sequence of events during the first two days of a euphoric excitement episode in a 57 year old man. A. One day, while working on his farm, he suddenly jumped up shouting that the "spirit" had overtaken him. B. He said later that he had begun to get commands to jump up and roll over like a wheel, and then "to holler and praise the Lord and make a noise enough so He can hear you." C. He tried to get others to follow his lead, and eventually fell down exhausted. D. and E.   The next morning he started out to walk to a neighbor's house but was forcibly detained by his son, who carried him back. He told the doctors later, "I was joy at heart—That is why I couldn't stay still. I had to go talk with somebody and tell them how much joy." He was sent home from the hospital soon thereafter. (Reprinted from the American Journal of Psychiatry, 100(2): 781–787, 1944. Copyright, 1944, The American Psychiatric Association.

expansiveness as well. Their boundless conceit, pretense, boastfulness and self-aggrandizement become extremely trying and exasperating, and often destroy what patience and good will these patients previously evoked from others.

## PERSONALITY DISPOSITIONS

Euphoric excitement occurs with reasonable frequency in several pathological patterns; in most, it tends to last for periods of less than two to three months.

1. *Active-dependent patterns* (gregarious and cycloid) are particularly susceptible to this disorder since it is consistent with their characteristic gregarious coping style. Confronted with severe separation anxieties or anticipating a decline or loss of social approval, these personalities may simply intensify their habitual strategy until it reaches the rather forced and frantic congeniality we term euphoric excitement. Here we observe a frenetic search for attention, a release of tension through hyperactivity and a protective effort to stave off an undercurrent of depressive hopelessness, as illustrated in the following brief history.

*CASE 11-10*
*Jeri T., Age 37, Unmarried*

This active-dependent woman had been living alone for several months following the break up of an affair that had lasted five years. Jeri had been mildly depressed for some weeks thereafter, but claimed that she "was glad it was all over with." Her co-workers at the department store in which she was employed as a buyer began to notice a marked brightening of her spirits several weeks prior to her "breakdown." Jeri's "chipper mood" grew with each passing day until it became increasingly extreme and irrational. She would talk incessantly, skipping from one topic to the next and be uncontainable when telling lewd stories and jokes, not only to fellow employees but to customers as well. Her indiscretions and the frightening quality of her pseudo-exuberance prompted her supervisor to recommend that she be seen by the store nurse, who then suggested psychiatric treatment.

2. In the *passive-dependent pattern* (submissive and cycloid) we see a marked, although usually temporary, reversal of these patients' more subdued and acquiescent coping style. Their effusive hyperactivity, their happy go lucky air, their boundless energy and buoyant optimism comprise a front, an act in which they try to convince themselves as well as others that "all will be well"; in short, it is a desperate effort to counter the beginning signs of hopelessness and depression, a last-ditch attempt to deny what they really feel and to recapture the attention and security they fear they have lost.

3. *Passive-independent personalities* (narcissistic and paranoid) evidence a self-exalted and pompous variant of euphoric excitement. Faced with realities that shatter their illusion of significance and omnipotence, they become frightened, lose their perspective and frantically seek to regain their status. No longer secure in their image of superiority, they attempt through their euphoric behaviors to instill or revive the blissful state of their youth, when their mere existence was of value in itself. Thus, passive-independents are driven into their excited state in the hope of reestablishing an exalted status and not to recapture support and nurture from others, as is the case among the dependents.

4. *Active and passive-detached personalities* (avoidant, asocial and schizoid) exhibit brief and rather frenzied episodes of euphoric excitement in an attempt to counter the frightening anxieties of depersonalization. Here, for a fleeting period, they may burst out of their more usual retiring and unsociable pattern and into a bizarre conviviality. The wild, irrational and chaotic character of their exuberance tends to distinguish their euphoric episodes from those of others.

## *DELUSION DISORDER*
(DSM-II: *Schizophrenia, Paranoid Type; Paranoid States*)

The manifest symptomatology of this disorder parallels in several respects that which is listed in the official classification as *paranoid states* (transient delusions, not well systematized); to a somewhat lesser extent, these symptoms have been categorized under the label *schizophrenia, paranoid type* (unrealistic thinking, delusions of persecution or grandeur, ideas of reference and hallucinations). Among multivariate studies, the disorder is similar, for example, to the "paranoid-hallucinatory" type listed by McNair et al. (1964).

### CLINICAL PICTURE

Many psychotic disorders exhibit delusions. For the most part, however, delusions are subsidiary features in other impairments, an element that emerges as a secondary consequence following the effects of the primary disturbance, e.g., during "fragmentation" the patient confuses his fantasy world with reality, producing quite incidentally a variety of distorted impressions, which may then persist as delusional beliefs. In what we are terming the delusion disorder, however, the false belief usually takes shape first, leading in time to a cluster of secondary symptoms, e.g., for various reasons, the patient believes he possesses certain special powers and rights; these delusions may lead him to react to events in an excited, fragmented or otherwise irrational manner. Thus, in these episodes, the delusional system, no matter how disorganized it may be or become, is the primary component of the disorder, an intrinsic element producing subsidiary psychotic features, the most notable of which are the perceptual distortions of hallucination.

As implied above, delusions in these patients have a coherence and focus, in contrast to the more fragmented and incidental distortions which arise in other psychotic states. The focus of these delusions (persecutory or grandiose) and the tone and character of the secondary symptoms with which they are associated, depend largely on the patient's longstanding habits, needs and attitudes, that is, his prepsychotic personality pattern.

## PERSONALITY DISPOSITIONS

The foundation for delusional disorders is usually well established in the patient's characteristic mode of behaving and thinking. In the following survey of vulnerable personalities we will deal only with those patterns in which delusions are both dominant and an intrinsic part of the psychosis.

1. *Passive and active-independent personalities* (narcissistic, aggressive and paranoid) are well disposed to misinterpret events and to exhibit florid delusional beliefs. Unable to accept constraints on their independence and unwilling to accept the viewpoints of others, these patients isolate themselves from the corrective effects of shared thinking. Alone, they begin to ruminate and weave their suspicions into a network of fanciful and totally invalid beliefs. Among passive-independents, delusions often take form after a serious challenge or setback in which their image of superiority and omnipotence has been upset. These patients tend to exhibit compensatory grandiosity and jealousy delusions, in which they reconstruct reality to suit the image they cannot give up. The delusional system of the active-independent typically occurs following failures in their efforts to dominate others or as a

result of having felt betrayed and humiliated. In these cases we are likely to see a rapid unfolding of persecutory delusions, as portrayed in the following case.

### CASE 11-11
### Carl F., Age 40, Married, No Children

This paranoid personality, characterized throughout his life as arrogant and suspicious, was brought to a hospital following his refusal for several weeks to leave his bedroom at home. Carl had been in a competitive business, and over recent months had lost both money and important contracting jobs to another company that consistently underbid him. Forced to lay off many of his employees and feeling humiliated by the turn of events, Carl began to accuse others of having conspired to destroy him and his business. The more he accused others, the more his reputation and reliability were questioned. Unable to stem the tide against him by veiled threats and intimidation, Carl locked himself in his room at home "to think things over." His thoughts, however, turned increasingly irrational. After a few days, he "figured out" the plot that was "schemed up" by his competitors. He then sent a series of "blistering" letters to numerous city and state officials insisting that they "investigate the illegal methods" used against him. He refused to leave his room "until justice was done."

2. *Passive and active-ambivalent personalities* (conforming, negativistic, cycloid and paranoid) may be precipitated into a delusional psychosis as a consequence of anticipating or experiencing real mistreatment from those to whom they have turned for support and security. Shocked by betrayal and having foregone the hope of fulfilling their dependency needs, the repressed resentments and suspicions of the passive-ambivalent overwhelm their former rigid controls, break to the surface and quickly take delusional shape. During these episodes, usually brief and rather chaotic, the patient releases his anger and at the same time absolves himself of guilt by projecting his hostility upon others. Thus, his delusions tend to be persecutory. Active-ambivalents are accustomed to discharging their negative emotions more readily than passive-ambivalents. Thus, their tensions do not cumulate and burst out of control, as in the case of the passive type. Rather, they continue to be touchy and irritable. Their typical suspicions merely are aggravated until they form into a mixture of persecutory and jealousy delusions. The following detailed case illustrates the typical course of what appears to be an active-ambivalent cycloid personality with periodic delusional episodes (Rosen and Gregory, 1965).

*CASE 11-12*
*Magda Z., Age 42, Married, No Children*

This woman was admitted to the psychiatric ward of a general hospital six months after separation from her husband when she left home and moved into a single room. A few days prior to admission she told her sister that her food and cigarettes were being poisoned. In the hospital Magda said she could hear the voices of men and women engaged in sexual intercourse and she claimed her food was being doped so that she could be used sexually. She was extremely agitated by these hallucinations and delusions and felt anxious and miserable. After a few days she walked out of the hospital without permission. Magda went to a hotel, locked herself in her room and refused to let anyone in. The police were called and they broke down the door and took her to a state hospital.

Magda was born in Roumania. Her father died when she was nine years old. Her mother remarried two years later; the patient could not get along with her stepfather and claimed that he mistreated her. When she was 13 the whole family emigrated. She left school at 14 and worked in a factory until marriage at 18 to a much older man. She claimed that he was irresponsible and did not pay their bills so that she too had to work. Their sexual relationship was unsatisfying to her; in complete contrast to the erotic content of her delusions, she claimed that she had never wished to have intercourse with her husband or anyone else.

In the state hospital Magda was restless and agitated. She paced the floor and talked to herself or wept uncontrollably. In an evaluative interview her eyes were averted, her voice was quiet and monotonous, and at times she spoke inaudibly or answered questions with irrelevant comments. She was disoriented. Asked if she had inquired where she was, she replied, "I don't know whether they would tell me the truth or not. I locked the doors at my mother's and left the light on all night because I thought they were going to poison me and rob me when I was locked in that room. They asked me how I could talk, different ones, and I don't know how they could see me because the blinds were drawn. They were going to burn me to prove that I am what they say I am. You know what they are saying about me. I guess everybody does. They are saying that I am a prostitute and a bitch." She said she had been unhappy for a long time because she had been alone and added, "If you are not with the one you love, you are unhappy." Asked whom she loved, she replied, "Ray." (She was slightly acquainted with a man named Ray.) Asked how his name was spelled she said, "W-r-a-y, I think. There is x-ray, too. I don't know. They are forcing me to holler so they can say I am crazy."

Magda responded only temporarily to ECT and insulin coma therapy (her hospitalization occurred before tranquilizers were in general use). A year after admission, a lobotomy was performed; Magda's symptoms disappeared and she returned home to live with her husband. A few months later, however, her hallucinations and delusions reappeared. She was readmitted to the hospital and given chlorpromazine. She kept hearing voices, but they ceased to agitate her and she went home again, with instructions to continue the medication indefinitely. Soon Magda became seclusive and hostile again and then developed delusions of grandeur. She believes that she has been divorced from her husband and has married a king named Raymond; she herself was a princess, her father was Jesus, and she had given birth to quintuplets.

3. *Active-detached patterns* (avoidant and schizoid) exhibit less systematic and coherent delusions than those seen among other personality types. Distortions of reality are almost inevitable during periods of marked social isolation. An abrupt delusional formation may occur if these patients are faced with severe depersonalization feelings or are thrust into situations of excessive responsibility and stimulation. In general, however, other psychotic symptoms tend to predominate in the detached patterns. Their delusions, usually bizarre or nonsensical, are subsidiary features for the most part.

# HOSTILE EXCITEMENT DISORDER
(DSM-II: *Schizophrenia, Paranoid and Catatonic [Excited] Types*)

The features comprising this syndrome are found in the official DSM-II categories of *schizophrenia, paranoid type* (unpredictable behavior; frequently hostile and aggressive) and *schizophrenia, catatonic type, excited* (excessive and sometimes violent motor activity). Among multivariate studies, this disorder is similar to the "excited-hostile," "excited-grandiose" and "grandiose-belligerent-excited" types reported by McNair et al. (1964) and Lorr et al. (1963, 1966).

## CLINICAL PICTURE

In contrast to the rather cheerful and buoyant hyperactivity seen in "euphoric excitement," these patients move about in a surly and truculent manner and explode into uncontrollable rages during which they threaten and occasionally physically assault others with little or no provocation. They may unleash a torrent of abuse and storm about defiantly, cursing and voicing bitterness and contempt for all. Quite unpredictably, they may lunge at and assail passers-by and shout obscenities at unseen hallucinated attackers and persecutors. It is this quality of irrational belligerence and fury, the frenzied lashing out, which distinguishes this disorder from others. We might note, parenthetically, that since the advent of the major psychopharmacological tranquilizers, the incidence of such acting out in hospitalized patients has been markedly reduced.

## PERSONALITY DISPOSITIONS

Brief outbursts of hostile excitement may be observed in many of the pathological patterns. However, it arises with greater frequency and persistence in independent and ambivalent personalities.

1. *Active-independent patterns* (aggressive and paranoid) are particularly prone to this disorder since they are hypersensitive to betrayal and have learned to cope with threat by acting out aggressively. Faced with repeated failures, humiliations and frustrations, their limited controls may be overrun by deeply felt and undischarged angers and resentments. These forces, carrying with them the memories and emotions of the past, surge unrestrainedly to the surface and break out into wild and irrational displays and uncontrollable rage, as exemplified in the following case.

### CASE 11-13
### Barry J., Age 32, Divorced, No Children

This paranoid personality was remanded by the court to a psychiatric hospital after attempting to run down and shoot several innocent passers-by from his car. Barry was subdued after a violent struggle with several police officers who had side-swiped his auto off the road; fortunately, he had no ammunition left in his revolver at this point. For several hours after imprisonment, Barry continued to shout obscenities and to flail about in a strait jacket, finally succumbing to the effects of intravenously administered tranquilizers. No clear precipitant appeared to have set off his maniacal outburst, although it was learned that he had recently "been ditched" by a girlfriend. Despite the tempering effects of drugs, Barry was difficult to manage, would curse at hallucinated assailants and periodically attempt to assault the psychiatric aides that attended him.

2. *Passive-ambivalent personalities* (conforming, cycloid and paranoid) may exhibit brief but highly charged hostile outbursts should adverse circumstances lead them to relinquish their normal controls. The build up of repressed resentments, concealed for years under a veneer of conformity, occasionally erupts into the open when they have felt betrayed by those in whom they have placed their faith. During their rage, it is not unusual for these patients to brutalize themselves as well as others. For example, they may tear off their clothes, smash their fists and

lacerate their bodies, thereby suffering more themselves than do their assailants and betrayers. Their violent discharge of pent-up animosity is usually followed by a return to their former controlled state. In many cases, however, these patients may begin to exhibit one of the other psychotic disorders following their hostile episode. Most common among these are the disorders labeled "motor rigidity" and "agitated depression."

3. *Active-ambivalent personalities* (negativistic, cycloid and paranoid) also exhibit brief episodes of hostile excitement, often associated with self-mutilation. Their behaviors, however, do not come as a total surprise to former associates since the symptoms of the disorder are but extreme variants of their lifelong pattern of hostile irritability and behavioral unpredictability. Not uncommonly, these hostile discharges covary with "agitated depressions."

4. In *passive-independent patterns* (narcissistic and paranoid) we observe less of the physically vicious and cruel forms of excited hostility than is seen in the patterns noted previously. Rather, we observe an arrogant grandiosity characterized by verbal attacks and bombast. Anger and fury in these patients tend to take the form of oral vituperation and argumentativeness; there is a flow of irrational and caustic comments in which they upbraid and denounce others as inferior, stupid and beneath contempt. This withering onslaught has little objective justification, is chaotic and highly illogical, often colored by delusions and hallucinations, and is directed in a wild, scathing and hit or miss fashion in which they lash out at those who have failed to acknowledge the exalted status in which they view themselves.

5. *Active and passive-detached personalities* (avoidant, asocial and schizoid) often experience brief hostile episodes, usually as a consequence of excessive social demands and responsibilities or events that threaten to reactivate the anguish of the past. As in the case of the ambivalent patterns, these patients often brutalize themselves during their aggressive fury as much as they do others.

## MOTOR RIGIDITY DISORDER
(DSM-II: *Schizophrenia, Catatonic Type, Withdrawn*)

These cases are likely to be classified in the official nosology as *schizophrenia, catatonic type* (generalized inhibition, stupor, mutism and negativism). Multivariate studies by Overall (1963)

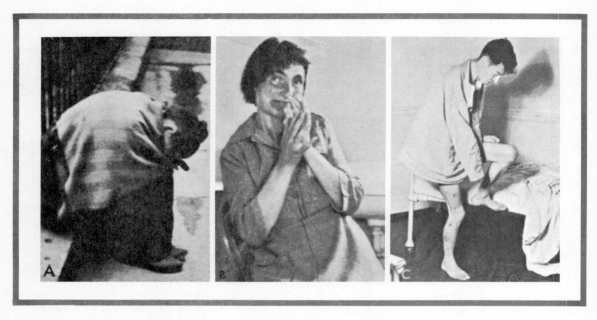

Figure 11-3 Some psychotic disorders. A. Retarded depression. (Roger-Viollet, Paris.) B. Fragmentation. C. Motor rigidity. (Parts B and C from Mayer-Gross, W., Slater, E., and Roth, M.: Clinical Psychiatry. London, Cassell, 1960.)

have discerned a distinctive diagnostic cluster, termed "catatonic schizophrenia," with the following four dominant features: mannerisms and posturing, emotional withdrawal, motor retardation and uncooperativeness; these correspond closely with the characteristics of the motor rigidity disorder.

## CLINICAL PICTURE

This syndrome is similar both to "impassivity" and "retarded depression" in that all three groups of patients exhibit minimal motor activity and often appear to be totally withdrawn and stuporous. (It may be of interest to note that these three disorders occur primarily in passive patterns.) The feature which distinguishes the "motor rigidity" disorder from the others lies in the patient's purposeful recalcitrance and manifest uncooperativeness; one senses that beneath the quiet and restrained exterior lies a seething but controlled hostility. The patient is not only mute and immobile, then, but "bullheaded" and adamant about remaining in certain fixed and preferred positions, opposing all efforts to alter them. This rigidity and restiveness are manifest in his body tension. For example, his fists may be clenched, his teeth gritted and his jaw locked tight and firm. Breaking periodically through his physical immobility, however, are stereotyped repetitive acts, bizarre gestures and grimaces and peculiar tics, grins and giggles. It appears that

every now and then his inner impulses and fantasies emerge briefly to be discharged or enacted through strange symbolic expressions. Quite evidently, there are active although confused thoughts and emotions churning beneath the passive exterior.

## PERSONALITY DISPOSITIONS

Periods of motor rigidity may be exhibited, in passing, by all personality patterns. In general, however, they occur rather infrequently and arise as a dominant symptom primarily in two pathological types.

1. *Passive-ambivalent personalities* (conforming, cycloid and paranoid) are especially subject to this form of psychotic disorder. Their physical uncooperativeness is a passive expression of their deeply felt resentments and angers. Their body tightness reflects an intense struggle to control against the outbreak of seething hostility, and their physical withdrawal and obduracy help them avoid contact with events that might provoke and unleash their aggressive impulses. Thus, motor rigidity both communicates and controls their anger, without provoking social condemnation. It may be viewed, then, as a bizarre extension of their habitual coping style, a means of controlling contrary impulses by protective restraint and rigid behaviors. The stereotype gestures and grimaces seen in these patients usually convey symbolically an abbreviated and imme-

diately retracted expression of their intolerable aggressive and erotic urges. Features of this disorder are illustrated in the following case history.

### CASE 11-14
### Arnold N., Age 28, Married, One Child

Arnold, a passive-ambivalent personality, was found one morning by his wife to be "staring in a funny way" outside his bathroom window. Not only did he refuse to reply to her concerned questions regarding his health, but he remained in a rigid position and refused to budge; no amount of pleading on her part was adequate to get him to relax or lie down. A physician was called to examine him shortly thereafter, but he was equally unable to penetrate Arnold's mutism or to alter his taut and unyielding physical posture.

Although Arnold did not resist being carried into an ambulance, he refused to change the body position in which his wife found him that morning.

Arnold's physical rigidity gave way under sedation and he spoke during these periods in a halting and confused manner. As soon as the effects of the drug wore off, however, he again was mute and resumed his immobile stance. Only after several weeks did he loosen up and begin to divulge his thoughts and feelings, both of which indicated a struggle to contain the rage he felt toward his father and his wife for the excessive demands he believed they imposed upon him.

2. *Active-detached personalities* (avoidant and schizoid) exhibit motor rigidity for reasons similar to those found in the passive-ambivalent. Here, however, the patient is motivated more by his desire to withdraw from external provocation than by the need to control his aggressive impulses, not that the latter is to be overlooked as a factor. Faced with unbearable derogation and humiliation, he draws into a shell, resistant to all forms of stimulation which may reactivate his past misery. The grimaces and giggling often observed in these patients clue us to their rather chaotic fantasy world.

# AGITATED DEPRESSION DISORDER

(DSM-II: *Manic-depressive Illness, Depressed Type; Schizophrenia, Schizo-affective Type, Depressed*)

The symptomatology of this disorder is likely to be categorized in the official classification as *manic-depressive illness, depressed type* (depressed mood, uneasiness, apprehension, perplexity and agitation). Depending on the presence of certain subsidiary features, it might be found to correspond to *schizophrenia, schizo-affective type* (affective changes with schizophrenic thinking or

bizarre behavior). Multivariate studies uncovering somewhat comparable syndromes have been reported as "intropunitive type" (Lorr et al., 1963, 1966) and "querulous, hypochondriacal type" (Friedman et al., 1963).

### CLINICAL PICTURE

The features of this disorder are rather mixed and erratic, varying in quality and focus in accord with the patient's basic personality pattern. In many respects, it is a composite of the previously described "retarded depression" and "hostile excitement" disorders, although not as extreme as either in their respective dominant characteristics. In all cases there is an incessant despair and suffering, an agitated pacing to and fro, a wringing of hands and an apprehensiveness and tension that are unrelieved by comforting reassurances. In some cases, the primary components are hostile depressive complaints and a demanding and querulous irritability in which the patient bemoans his sorry state and his desperate need for attention to his manifold physical illnesses, pains and incapacities. In other cases, the depressive picture is colored less by critical and demanding attitudes and more by self-blame and guilt; here we see anxious self-doubting, expressions of self-hate, a preoccupation with impending disasters, suicidal thoughts, feelings of unworthiness and delusions of shame and sin.

### PERSONALITY DISPOSITIONS

As was noted previously, the overall tone and subsidiary clinical details observed among the disorders depend on the particular history and personality pattern of the patient. Some of these differences may be noted in the following survey of the more vulnerable personality types.

1. *Active-ambivalent patterns* (negativistic and cycloid) are especially prone to agitated depressions. These disorders can be seen as an extension of their premorbid personality style—complaints, irritability and a sour grumbling discontent, usually interwoven with hypochondriacal preoccupations and periodic expressions of guilt and self-condemnation. Their habitual style of acting out their conflicts and ambivalent feelings becomes more pronounced, resulting in extreme vacillations between bitterness and resentment on the one hand, and intropunitive self-deprecation on the other. Self-pity and bodily anxieties are extremely common and may serve as a basis for distinguishing them from other agitated types. The following illustrates a typical case.

CASE 11-15
*Ethel S., Age 53, Married, Three Children*

Ethel, a cycloid personality with a prior history of several psychotic breaks, became increasingly irritable, despairing and self-deprecating over a period of one or two months; no clear precipitant was evident. She paced back and forth, wringing her hands and periodically shouting that God had forsaken her and that she was a "miserable creature, placed on earth to make my family suffer." At times, Ethel would sit on the edge of a chair, nervously chewing her nails, complaining about the disinterest shown her by her children. Then, she would jump up, move about restlessly, voicing irrational fears about her own and her husband's health, claiming that he was a "sick man," sure to die because of her "craziness."

Ethel's agitated and fretful behavior took on a more contentious and hypochondriacal quality in the hospital to which she was brought. During a course of electroconvulsive treatments and a regimen of antidepressant drugs, Ethel's composure gradually returned, and she came home seven weeks following hospitalization.

2. *Passive-ambivalent personalities* (conforming and cycloid) exhibit the more traditional form of agitated depression, noted by diffuse apprehension, marked guilt feelings and a tendency to delusions of sin and unworthiness. These patients do not exhibit the whining and querulous qualities seen in their active-ambivalent counterparts. Instead, they turn the aggressive component of their conflict toward themselves, claiming that they deserve the punishment and misery which they now suffer.

3. *Passive and active-dependent types* (submissive, gregarious and cycloid) evidence agitated depressions less frequently than the ambivalents. In their case, the primary precipitants tend to be anticipated losses in dependency security. They generally wail aloud and convey feelings of hopelessness and abandonment, all in the hope of soliciting support and nurture. Their agitation does not reflect an internal struggle of hostility versus guilt, as in the case of the ambivalents, but a more direct and simple expression of worrisome apprehension.

## REMEDIAL APPROACHES IN PSYCHOTIC DISORDERS

The various psychotic disorders differ in their prognoses and in their therapeutic management, but an extended discussion of these distinctions is beyond the province of this book. As a consequence, we shall mention only a few points applicable to the psychoses in general, and report some minor observations regarding specific disorders.

Before we proceed, let us again be reminded that the descriptive label given to each of the psychotic disorders is misleading in that it suggests that a single symptom stands alone, uncontaminated by others. This is not the case. Although a particular symptom may appear dominant at one time, it coexists and covaries with several others, any one of which may come to assume dominance. As a further complication, there is not only covariation and fluidity in symptomatology, but each of these psychotic disorders may arise in a number of different personality patterns.

Much of the confusion that has plagued diagnostic systems in the past can be attributed to this overlapping and changeability of symptom pictures. For reasons discussed in previous chapters, it has been argued that greater reliability and clarity can be achieved in diagnosis if we focus on the basic personality of the patient rather than on the particular dominant symptom he manifests. Moreover, by directing our attention to enduring and pervasive personality traits, we may be able to deduce the *cluster* of different symptoms he is likely to display and the sequence of symptoms he may exhibit over the course of his illness. For example, knowing the vulnerabilities and habitual coping strategies of the active-independent personality, we would predict that he will evidence either together or in sequence both delusions and hostile excitement, should he become psychotically disordered. Similarly, passive-ambivalents may be expected to manifest in their psychotic episodes cyclical swings between motor rigidity, agitated depression and hostile excitement. Focusing on ingrained personality patterns rather than transient symptoms enables us, then, to grasp both the cluster of symptoms a patient is likely to exhibit and the possible sequence in which they wax and wane.

Psychotics usually are hospitalized, remaining as inpatients for periods as wide-ranging as two to three weeks for some, and several years for others. Generally, psychotic disorders, as distinguished from decompensated personality patterns, run through the full course of their episode in less than a year, with a large proportion returning to their prepsychotic levels within a matter of a few months.

The determination of the length of hospitalization depends, in large measure, on a variety of factors that are not intrinsic to the disorder, for example, the administrative efficiency and policies of the institution, the willingness of the patient's family to accept his return home and so on. One finds all too often that patients who have recovered from their psychotic episode remain institutionalized because no one has made proper efforts to arrange their discharge. Many borderline and even mildly pathological personality patterns become immersed for years in the routine of the hospital as a consequence of institutional oversight or family disinterest.

An intrinsic deterrent to progress may be the disordered patient's basic personality. Certain of the patterns possess attitudes and coping styles which undermine chances for recovery; some resist therapeutic rapport whereas others are difficult to motivate. For example, detached personalities frequently deteriorate rapidly despite all treatment efforts. These personalities often succumb to "impassive" disorders with their flat and difficult to activate qualities or to "fragmentation" disorders which, given their characteristic cognitive disorganization, are highly resistant to meaningful therapeutic communication. Other patterns are conducive to better prognoses since they provide a handle, so to speak, that the therapist can use to relate to and motivate the patient. For example, dependent and ambivalent patterns are desirous of social approval and can be motivated by therapeutic attitudes of gentility and nurture during their typical disorders of "depression" and "euphoric excitement." For different reasons, notably the drive to assert themselves and to reestablish their autonomy, independent personality patterns, despite episodes such as "delusion" and "hostile excitement," have moderately promising prognostic pictures.

Practically every therapeutic modality and technique have been employed in the service of rehabilitating psychotic patients. In the following discussion we will note some of the measures that have been used and comment briefly on their respective merits.

Environmental management is a necessary step in the handling of psychotic disorders. This should consist of more than the mere removal of adverse conditions in life. Proper institutional placement should provide the patient not only with a refuge from environmental stress, but also with opportunities to resolve his tensions and programs to reorient him toward social recovery. In what is termed "milieu therapy," the patient's daily routine is scheduled to maximize both emotional support and the acquisition of attitudes and skills conducive to a better social adjustment than existed previously.

Biophysical treatment methods can be of notable value in several disorders. Psychopharmacological stimulants and antidepressants may fruitfully be utilized to reactivate patients suffering "impassive" and "retarded depressive" disorders. Similarly, tranquilizers are of extreme benefit in decreasing the tension and hyperactivity seen in "motor rigidity," and in both "euphoric and hostile excitement" disturbances. Worthy of note also are the beneficial results produced through electroconvulsive treatment among both "depressive" disorders. Each of these biophysical methods is of value not only in its immediate and direct effects, but in bringing the patient to a state in which other therapeutic measures may be employed, e.g., a lethargic and unresponsive depressed patient who has been stimulated by drugs may now be disposed to communicate in verbal psychotherapy.

Psychological therapeutic measures have not been especially successful in the early phases of psychotic disorder. Phenomenological and intrapsychic methods cannot be used effectively until the patient possesses a modicum of cognitive clarity and emotional quietude. Nevertheless, the sympathetic attitude, patience and gentle manner that these procedures employ may serve to establish rapport and build a basis for further therapy in the "depressions," "impassivity" and "motor rigidity."

Behavior modification techniques appear especially promising as instruments both for extinguishing or controlling specific symptoms and shaping more adaptive alternative responses. Although the durability of and the ability to generalize from these beneficial effects have not been adequately researched, these techniques are among the most encouraging of the newer treatment approaches to the psychotic disorders.

Group therapeutic methods are especially efficient and adaptable to hospital settings, given the shortage of professional institutional personnel and the feasibility with which sessions can be arranged. They are particularly valuable as vehicles for resocializing the patient and enabling him to express his confused attitudes and feelings in a highly controlled yet sympathetic environment.

# CONCLUDING COMMENTS AND SUMMARY

The syndromes presented in this and earlier chapters should be viewed as prototypes, that is, textbook models which highlight certain common and central features seen in otherwise dissimilar cases. By focusing primarily on these common attributes we have created the "false image" that patients classified under the same label exhibit a greater degree of uniformity in their etiology and symptomatology than actually exists. We must be mindful not to be misled into such simplifications. The schema we have furnished for the text, as with all classification systems, has not been designed as a rigid guide to "diseases," but as a pedagogical instrument to alert us to, and facilitate our understanding of, certain basic elements which are likely to be found in common among patients grouped in the same syndrome. In each of the "disorder" categories described in chapters 10 and 11 we will find patients who display divergent clinical characteristics. We believe, however, that by organizing them in terms of the features they share in common, we may expedite the process of clinical diagnosis and enhance the prospects for better treatment and research in the future. The format we have outlined, then, is a provisional tool whose utility will be decided through clinical use and empirical study. No doubt, it will be revised as psychopathological science progresses.

Let us next turn to some of the major themes discussed in chapters 10 and 11.

1. The "process-reactive" concept was discussed and evaluated with the conclusion that these two terms represent end points on a continuum of pathological embedment and pervasiveness. The *process* term reflects the presence of deeply ingrained and widely generalized pathological traits that are highly resistant to change and therefore indicate a poor prognosis; the process label corresponds roughly to the formulation of "personality patterns." The *reactive* term reflects the presence either of minimally rooted or well-circumscribed pathological features that usually can be extinguished or altered with ease, and therefore may be viewed as possessing a good prognosis; the reactive label may be correlated with our conception of the "behavior reactions" to be discussed in the following chapter. "Symptom disorders," comprising the body of the last two chapters, may be viewed as falling midway on the gradient of the process-reactive continuum, or as we would term it, the "pattern-reaction" continuum; they are anchored in part to pervasive and deeply ingrained personality traits and in part to more transitory or circumscribed situational conditions. Symptom disorders are more difficult to modify or extinguish than reactions, but less difficult than personality patterns. As such they may be said to have a fair prognosis.

2. The disorder syndromes were described as isolated, ego-dystonic and often dramatic symptoms which, although occasionally representing an abandonment of a patient's coping style, more often tend to accentuate or caricature the more prosaic features of his basic personality. They may best be viewed as either extensions or disruptions of the patient's habitual strategy, and are prompted by intense or unrelieved strain in spheres of vulnerability. No matter how adverse the conditions may be which precipitate a disorder, it can best be understood within the context of the patient's past history and personality pattern.

a. Despite the fact that we have affixed the label of a particular symptom to each of the disorder syndromes, the actual clinical picture we observe consists of a cluster of different symptoms which coexist and which may covary in their relative dominance during the course of an illness.

b. Since the same manifest disorder may crop up in different personality types, it was argued that greater reliability and clarity would be achieved in clinical analyses if attention were directed to uncovering the basic personality of the patient. By focusing on these more enduring and pervasive traits, the clinician may be able to anticipate both the cluster and the sequence of symptoms that a patient is likely to exhibit during his disordered episodes.

c. Most texts provide extensive discussions of the etiology and development of each symptom disorder. This was not done in chapters 10 and 11. We believe that disorders should *not* and *cannot* be traced directly to specific hereditary or early experience determinants. Rather, they are traceable to the patient's personality pattern, which reflects a complex sequence of interactions among both constitutional and environmental factors. To attempt to trace the thread of a disorder through this interwoven maze back to its "origins" in heredity and early experience is impossible and would be misleading. For both practical and theoretical reasons, the personality pattern must be viewed as an intermediary framework from which disordered states arise. Although specific current events may precipitate the emergence of a disordered state, the "real" etiology lies in the patient's lifelong personality vulnerabilities and maladaptive coping strategies. To stress this thesis, therefore, we have not discussed specific etiological variables (e.g., heredity or parental attitudes) when presenting the disorders, but rather have noted which personality dispositions are subject to them. We have sought in this way to demonstrate and reaffirm our conviction of the developmental continuity that exists in psychopathology. Details concerning etiological factors conducive to these personality vulnerabilities were presented in chapters 6 through 9.

d. For reasons similar to the above, we did not provide the usual four-fold breakdown of clinical signs (e.g., biophysical and intrapsychic) in presenting the clinical picture of the disorder syndromes. With the exception of their dominant symptom, the clinical picture of these syndromes is not uniform. It varies and changes in its symptomatology largely as a function of the basic personality of the patient. Primary attention should not be given, then, to the transitory symptom picture, but to the ingrained and pervasive personality traits from which it arises.

3. The symptom syndromes were divided into five major subgroups—anxiety, neurotic, psychophysiologic, sociopathic and psychotic disorders—each reflecting a different way in which various pathological personalities respond to situations that threaten their security and equilibrium.

a. *Anxiety disorders* occur in all personality types either as an initial response to unanticipated and moderately severe threat or as a disturbance following their inability to identify and cope with persistent threat. These patients exhibit a diffuse apprehensiveness and a disorganization of their habitual instrumental strategies. Three major forms were noted: chronic anxiety, acute anxiety and panic.

b. *Neurotic disorders* arise most often in dependent, ambivalent and active-detached personality patterns. These persons resolve and discharge their tensions largely through the use of intrapsychic mechanisms, employed to achieve the following four instrumental goals: counteract external precipitants which threaten to upset their precarious equilibrium and tenuous controls; block reactivated unconscious anxieties and impulses from intruding into conscious awareness and from provoking social condemnation; discharge tensions engendered by external stresses and unconscious residuals; and solicit attention, sympathy and nurture from others. Six neurotic syndromes and their subvarieties were described:

phobia, conversion, dissociation, obsession-compulsion, dejection and hypochondriasis.

c. *Psychophysiologic disorders* arise most frequently among ambivalent personalities, and to a lesser extent among dependent and active-detached personalities. These patients often experience conflicts which cannot be resolved and tensions which cannot be expressed. The bodily symptoms they exhibit occur as a result of repeated disruptions of their homeostatic balance and the failure to dissipate the buildup of chronic physiological reactions. Several psychophysiologic symptom disorders were briefly described, notably peptic ulcer, colitis, essential hypertension, migraine, bronchial asthma and neurodermatitis. A review of recent research led us to reject the thesis that a relationship exists between specific psychological problems and specific somatic symptoms. It was concluded that although certain personality patterns are more likely to suffer psychosomatic disorders than others, the particular physical disorder they exhibit arises as a function of constitutional vulnerabilities or physiological reaction patterns.

d. *Sociopathic disorders* occur in personality types who are inclined to act out their impulses with minimal regard for social consequences. Three subvarieties were described: the antisocial sociopath, usually an active-independent personality, who discharges through aggressive action his vindictive attitudes and hostile impulses; the exploitive sociopath, usually a passive-independent type, who expresses his disdain for others by outrageous acts such as swindling, pathological lying and sexual excesses; and the impulsive sociopath, frequently an active-dependent personality, who is driven to escape routine and boredom, feels little loyalty to those upon whom he previously depended and flits capriciously from one temptation and thrill to another.

e. *Psychotic disorders* may be experienced by all personality patterns. The symptoms observed reflect either extreme and bizarre attempts to cope with threat and anxiety or a collapse in the patient's coping efforts. Two features are found in common among all of these disorders: diminished reality awareness and cognitive and emotional dyscontrol. Eight clinical subtypes, based on a synthesis of the official classification system and various multivariate research studies, were described: impassivity, fragmentation, retarded depression, euphoric excitement, delusion, hostile excitement, motor rigidity and agitated depression. As with all symptom categories, several personality patterns were found to be susceptible to each of the psychotic syndromes.

4. Despite differences in rationale and terminology, considerable similarity exists between the disorder syndromes presented in this text and those found in the official psychiatric classification manual (DSM-II). Notations were made of points of correspondence between these two systems, thereby enabling the student to translate the terms of one schema to those of the other.

5. With this chapter we conclude our focus on syndromes that either reflect or derive from deep-seated and pervasive personality impair-

ments. In the following chapter we will turn to the "behavior reactions." As far as superficial appearances are concerned, these pathological reactions may be indistinguishable from the syndromes we have already discussed. However, a more careful study will uncover substantial differences in their etiology and development, differences which prove relevant to prognosis and treatment. Behavior reactions are not deep seated and pervasive impairments; rather, they are either transitory responses to brief, but stressful, conditions or they are more enduring responses that operate within a limited or circumscribed sphere of functioning.

# Chapter 12

# *PATHOLOGICAL BEHAVIOR REACTIONS*

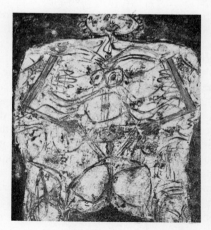

Jean Dubuffet—*Corps de dame* (1950).

## INTRODUCTION

The process-reactive dichotomy was discussed in the introduction to chapter 10. In our reformulation of this notion we proposed that it should be viewed not as a dichotomy but as a continuum; the personality patterns described in chapters 6 through 9 would correspond roughly to the "process" end of the gradient whereas the behavior reactions, to be described in this chapter, would correspond to the "reactive" pole. Clinical signs in personality patterns reflect the operation of deeply embedded and pervasive characteristics of functioning, that is, complicated, interwoven traits that color and manifest themselves automatically and unconsciously in all facets of the individual's everyday life. In contrast, we spoke of the behavior reactions as relatively direct responses to rather specific and distinctive stimulus experiences.

These reactions operate somewhat independently of the patient's personality style; their form and content are determined largely by the character of the external precipitant, that is, they are not contaminated by the intrusion of complex unconscious factors. Behavior reactions are best understood, then, *not* as a function of the intricate convolutions between intrapsychic mechanisms and repressed memories and impulses, but

as simple and straightforward responses to specific or circumscribed stimulus conditions. To paraphrase Eysenck (1959): there are no obscure "causes" which "underlie" pathological behavior reactions, merely the reaction itself; modify the reaction, or the conditions which precipitate it, and you have eliminated all there is to the pathology.

Two types of syndromes will be distinguished as comprising the behavior reactions: *transient situational reactions,* which consist of pathological responses to relatively brief and objectively stressful conditions, and *circumscribed learned reactions,* which consist of acquired and relatively permanent pathological responses to specific or narrowly delimited stimuli that ordinarily are innocuous. Before we elaborate the various subcategories of these two impairments, it may be useful to clarify further the distinctions we have made between the reaction syndromes and other forms of psychopathology.

### Some Distinctions Between Behavior Reactions and Symptom Disorders

Not only are the overt clinical features of the behavior reactions and symptom disorders often indistinguishable, but both tend to be prompted in part at least by external precipitants. How then are they different?

As noted in previous chapters, symptom disorders are rooted in pervasive personality vulnerabilities and strategies whereas behavior reactions are not. Symptom disorders arise when the established equilibrium of a pathological style of functioning has been upset or threatened.

Certain of the behavior reactions, those termed the *transient situational reactions,* are similar to disorders with regard to this "upsetting" feature. However, in these reactions, the disturbed behavior appears to be a "justified" response to realistically stressful precipitants, e.g., exhibiting anxiety or depression as a result of a financial catastrophe or severe physical trauma. Symptom disorders, in contrast, arise in response to what objectively is often an insignificant or innocuous event; despite the trivial character of the precipitant, the patient exhibits responses that are similar to those given by normal persons in response to severe stress. Thus, symptom disorders do not "make sense" in terms of actual present realities; they signify some unusual vulnerability on the part of the patient, that is, a tendency for certain objectively neutral stimuli to touch off and reactivate painful memories and pathological coping responses. Disorders occur, then, in pathological personality patterns, that is, in individuals who are encumbered with the residues of adverse past experiences. In contrast, transient situational reactions arise in "normal" individuals, who are relatively free of such past distortions.

As was just noted, unconscious memories and emotions intervene in the symptom disorders to complicate the connection between present stimuli and the patient's response to them. Similar intrusions occur in the behavior reaction subcategory that we have termed *circumscribed learned reactions.* Here, however, the patient's vulnerability is not widespread, but restricted to a specific and delimited class of stimulus conditions; for example, a 28 year old woman had a "deathly fear" of grasshoppers, but not of any other type of insect. Moreover, these pathological responses do not "pass through" a chain of complicated and circuitous intrapsychic transformations before they emerge in manifest form. Thus, in addition to the restricted number of precipitants which give rise to them, they are distinguished from symptom disorders in the direct stimulus to response route through which they are channeled.

In disorders, the precipitating stimulus stirs up a wide array of intervening thoughts and emotions which "take over" as the determinant of the response; reality stimuli serve, then, merely as catalysts that set into motion a complex chain of intermediary intrapsychic processes that transform what might otherwise have been a fairly simple and straightforward response. Because of the "contaminating" intrusion of these intrapsychic transformations the "disordered" response acquires an irrational and "symbolic" quality. For example, in phobias the object that is feared serves to represent something else; thus, a phobia of elevators might symbolize a more generalized and unconscious anxiety about being closed in and trapped by others.

Because of the pervasiveness of the disordered patient's vulnerabilities, intrapsychic elements become entangled in a wide variety of dissimilar stimulus situations, e.g., the feeling of being trapped may give rise not only to a phobia of elevators but also of rooms in which the doors are shut, of riding in cars in which the windows are closed, of tight clothes and so on. Moreover, these intrapsychic processes vary in their form and degree of intrusion; for example, a phobic patient may feel well on certain days and agree to the closing of room doors; on other days, however, all doors and windows must be wide open. Thus, the responses of symptom disorders not only are elicited by a wide variety of stimulus conditions, but these diverse responses wax and wane in their relative dominance.

All this fluidity and variability in clinical symptomatology contrast with the relative simplicity and uniformity of responses found in circumscribed learned reactions. Uninfluenced by the intricate and circuitous transformations of intrapsychic processes, these stimulus-specific responses tend to be consistent and predictable. They are manifested in essentially the same way each time the stimulus to which they have been attached occurs. Moreover, they are rarely exhibited at other times or in response to events which are dissimilar to the stimulus to which they originally were attached, e.g., the intense fear of grasshoppers noted above was experienced only if they appeared when the patient began to approach the door of a house; although there was some discomfort when live grasshoppers were seen elsewhere, the fear was considerably less. In short, circumscribed learned reactions are relatively ingrained but isolated responses to specific stimulus constellations. They tend not to vary or be influenced by the patient's general mood.

### Some Distinctions Between the Behavior Reactions and Pathological Personality Patterns

Behavior reactions are relatively compartmentalized stimulus-response habits that are isolated in large measure from the patient's characteristic style of functioning. Personality patterns refer to deeply ingrained and pervasive traits that color *all* aspects of an individual's functioning. In contrast, circumscribed reactions are narrowly focused behaviors, displaying themselves only in response to specific types of stimulus events. To use an analogy, we might speak of personality as both the body and the basic design of a fabric, and the behavior reaction as an embroidered decoration that has been sewn onto it. One may remove (extinguish) the embroidery with relative ease (as conditioning therapists have done in treating the behavior reactions) without involving or altering the body of the cloth (personality). Behavior reactions, then, do not permeate and intrude upon every facet of the individual's transactions with the world, as do his personality traits; rather they are stimulus-specific responses to a circumscribed class of stimuli.

Despite these differences in generality and pervasiveness, circumscribed behavior reactions and personality patterns are acquired essentially in the same ways. Both are learned as a function of the interaction of constitutional dispositions and environmental experiences, and the basic processes of conditioning, imitation and reinforcement apply with equal relevance to the development of both syndromes. The essential difference lies *not in how* they are acquired, but in the pervasiveness, scope or generality of experiences which give rise to them. In his personality pattern, the individual has acquired a wide range of highly generalized habits and attitudes. These were learned bit by bit as a consequence of repeated exposure to the many subtle events of early life. Immersed in the day to day environment of his parental home, the child quietly, undramatically and quite incidentally acquires innumerable impressions which cumulate insidiously to shape the character of his thoughts, feelings and ways of relating to others. These diffuse and piecemeal experiences derive from the repetition of incidental daily events and become the basis for deeply ingrained clusters of attitudes and behaviors which comprise his personality. Although circumscribed behavior reactions are acquired in exactly the same fashion, they tend to be learned in response to more specific and discriminable events. That is, they are behaviors learned *not* in response to everyday situations, since that would have led to the devel-

opment of a more generalized personality trait, but to clearly delimited and fairly unusual stimulus conditions. Thus, in the case mentioned previously, the fear of grasshoppers was traced to a particular incident when the patient was five years of age. Her older brother and his friends were dissecting grasshoppers on the front steps of her home; as she recalled the event under hypnosis, she was watching them curiously when they suddenly grabbed her and forced a live but decapitated grasshopper into her mouth. These learnings remain, for the most part, as permanent attitudes and response habits that are isolated from the main body of the individual's more general style of functioning, e.g., a specific fear of grasshoppers in an otherwise confident and courageous person.

It should be noted that the line between personality patterns and learned behavior reactions cannot be drawn with ease in describing characteristics of the first years of life. During this early period, learnings have not crystallized into an ingrained, pervasive, stable and consistent style of life. In many respects, then, childhood personality is a loose cluster of scattered behavior reactions learned in response to a wide variety of odds-and-ends experiences. Over time, however, as certain of the conditions which gave rise to these reactions are repeated and attached to an increasing variety of stimuli, and as the child's own self-perpetuating processes accentuate and spread the range of these events further, some of these behavior reactions become more dominant than others, until they take shape as pervasive and ingrained personality traits. Thus, early behavior reactions are the precursors of later personality patterns; it is a continuous developmental process.

In the next two sections we shall describe a variety of pathological behavior reactions. Although we include only those individuals who otherwise exhibit "normal" personalities in these categories, we must note that pathological personalities also display pathological behavior reactions—evidence again of the infinite variety and complexity of human behavior. Behavior reactions may occur in all personalities, normal or pathological. However, these reactions are only incidental aspects of the general pathology of personality patterns. With the exception of childhood, as noted above, they do not play an intrinsic role in the formation and expression of the basic coping strategy.

# TRANSIENT SITUATIONAL REACTIONS
### (DSM-II: *Transient Situational Disturbances*)

Earlier, we described the transient situational reactions as pathological responses to relatively brief and objectively stressful conditions. These syndromes correspond to the DSM-II description of the *transient situational disturbances* which reads as follows:

This major category is reserved for more or less transient disorders of any severity (including those of psychotic proportions) that occur in individuals without any apparent underlying mental disorders and that represent an acute reaction to overwhelming environmental stress. If the patient has good adaptive capacity his symptoms usually recede as the stress diminishes. If, however, the symptoms persist after the stress is removed, the diagnosis of another mental disorder is indicated.

For purposes of better understanding the source and character of these disturbing precipitations, it will be useful to differentiate two subvarieties of these reactions: *gross stress reactions,* which may take any form and which may occur at almost any point in life, and *age associated reactions,* which arise most commonly at particular periods in life and whose form of expression reflects the problems that are typically faced during these periods.

## GROSS STRESS REACTIONS

In previous chapters we concerned ourselves with impairments that were rooted in established and pervasive personality pathologies. In this section, we shall focus on equally severe, although brief, conditions which grow out of unusually stressful or sudden environmental stress, such as those prompted by war, civilian disaster or serious personal illness. These events are so terrifying and upsetting as to result in pathological behaviors among previously stable and well-adjusted individuals.

There is no single or characteristic clinical picture exhibited by patients reacting to these devastating events. Depending on the nature of the adversity and their premorbid personality features, these individuals will display symptoms that are not unlike those seen in more enduring pathological syndromes. However, in contrast to these other impairments, reactions quickly subside or disappear after the removal of the stress precipitant.

Stress reactions do *not* arise in response to the many minor and easily forgotten difficulties we all face in life; oversleeping before an important test, having to go out with a rather unappealing blind date, getting one's car stuck in a ditch or catching a severe cold before a big football weekend are all upsetting, but hardly reason to feel a sense of devastation and hopelessness. Rather, stress reactions occur in response to events that are genuinely deeply troubling and that shatter the person's self-image, security and hopes for the future; for example, a broken engagement after many years of courtship, the sudden death of a loved parent, dismissal from college as a result of poor grades in one's senior year, a dangerous but necessary surgical operation or a serious car accident. In short, these are experiences which cannot easily be dismissed or forgotten, and whose effects may change the course of one's life. The following brief case illustrates such a transient reaction.

### CASE 12-1
### James W., Age 19, College Junior

James was brought to the university health center in a state of visible anxiety and depression. He reported having been unable to sleep or eat and had spent the past several days fretting in his room, weeping whenever his room-mate entered or tried to talk to him. As he spoke to the physician, his head was bowed, his hands clenched and his face twisted and contorted in obvious anguish.

One month before, Jim had been a reasonably good student and a key member of the university football team (he had been admitted to the college on an athletic scholarship). He was a cheerful, energetic and well-liked young man on campus. One Saturday night, following a successful game, Jim went "partying," drank a bit too much, drove irresponsibly and had a serious car accident in which one of the passengers in his car was killed and two others were severely injured. Jim was only slightly bruised.

For the first few days following the accident, Jim seemed to handle his feelings rather well. Slowly, however, his mood turned morose. He stopped going to classes, refused to see anyone, sat still in his room or paced nervously back and forth. He had been dropped from the team, feared losing his scholarship, had nightmares about the accident, expressed deep guilt for what he had done and fretted about his future and what would become of him.

Jim was seen daily for three weeks, during which time he managed to "pull himself together" and began to face the world. Although he left the university that fall, he reentered another college shortly thereafter where, at last report, he has again made a good adjustment.

Of particular interest among the stress syndromes are traumatic conditions that are shared in common by many persons. For example, there are the well-publicized *civilian catastrophes,* such as those resulting from severe hurricanes, ship and plane disasters, floods, widespread and uncontrollable forest fires, earthquakes, rioting and so on. Depending on the severity of the disaster and the degree to which an individual is involved, one may see a variety of pathological reactions, ranging from total decompensation and amnesia to pathological grief, frenzied agitation and vicious, panicky acts of self-preservation; in short, a whole range of bizarre behaviors that are never observed in these same individuals at other times. Of course, those who are susceptible to feelings of anxiety, hostility or guilt are more prone to exhibit these behaviors than others, but by no means are these stress reactions limited to pathologically disposed personalities.

Another shared condition of unusual stress has been referred to under the euphemistic label of *combat exhaustion,* a term signifying severe decompensation among men involved in the strains of direct warfare. According to recent estimates, only 10 per cent of all servicemen are rendered unfit for further duty as a consequence of exposure to combat. The clinical picture exhibited by these men depends on the nature of their activities, the duration of their exposure to threat and their premorbid personality make-up. Although a few cases erupt rather suddenly, these pathological reactions tend to occur gradually, evidencing themselves in a slow erosion of confidence, energy and hope. What we observe is a marked weariness, sleeplessness, dejection and anxiety. Menninger describes the typical picture seen in infantry men as follows (1948):

In the majority of cases they followed a stereotyped pattern: "I just can't take it any more"; "I can't stand those shells"; "I just couldn't control myself." They varied little from patient to patient. Whether it was the soldier who had experienced his baptism of fire or the older veteran who had lost his comrades, the superficial result was very similar. Typically he appeared as a dejected, dirty and weary man. His facial expression was one of depression, sometimes of tearfulness. Frequently his hands were trembling or jerking. Occasionally he would display varying degrees of confusion, perhaps to the extent of being mute or staring into space.

As with civilian catastrophes and other forms of unusual stress, the prognosis for recovery in these cases is rather good, if efforts are made to remove the precipitant source and provide short-term therapeutic support.

## AGE ASSOCIATED REACTIONS

There are no fundamental differences between the impairments described in this section and those noted above as gross stress reactions. We differentiate them only to point up the fact that certain strains and crises will occur with greater probability at some points in life than others; it is the correlation of particular problems with particular age periods which justifies the distinction we shall make. It is likely not only that people will confront different problems and stresses as they progress through life, but that the way in which they react to these difficulties will differ as well. For example, adolescents, faced with the desire to assert their freedom from parental controls, are likely to exhibit aggressive and rebellious behaviors. In contrast, older people, faced with the prospect of increasing loneliness and infirmity, are more likely to display signs of depression and apathy. We shall divide these age associated reactions in the same manner as formulated in the DSM-II; they parallel the five major life periods—infancy, childhood, adolescence, adulthood and late life.

### REACTIONS OF INFANCY

The symptomatology of infantile reactions is rather limited and diffuse. The infant not only fails to register distinctions among the various difficulties to which he is exposed, but he lacks the means for conveying the nature of his discomfort with subtlety and precision. We infer the infant's experience of distress through a few gross forms of behavioral and emotional expression. These may be grouped in three categories: *a lack of responsiveness,* as in apathy, languor or somnolence; *a fearful tension,* as in body rigidity, sleeplessness and withdrawal from human contact; and *a cranky irritability,* as in colic, unrelenting and unrelievable crying, general negativism and a disagreeable petulance.

It is difficult to assert with confidence that these infantile reactions result primarily from external precipitants since constitutional dispositions can contribute a major share to their expression. We know that troublesome behaviors are shown in youngsters who have been exposed to genuinely "ideal" rather than adverse environments. This fact should caution us against looking for, and then "uncovering," entirely spurious psychogenic causes for their presence. In many cases, however, we may rightly ascribe the difficulty, at least in part, to adverse environmental conditions. These usually stem from the character and style of mother-child interactions or from a lack of caretaker-child contact. Let us briefly review some of the experiences conducive to the three infantile reactions noted above.

**Lack of Responsiveness.** Infants deprived of warm body contact, soothing voices, comfort and playful interaction often exhibit a flat, apathetic and languorous state. They frequently seem to be mentally retarded, lack awareness and interest in their environment, move about listlessly or are immobile and somnolent. They give evidence of what may be viewed as a mild form of "infantile autism." Barring an unusual degree of prior emotional deprivation, these infants can often be rehabilitated with ease. A period of compensatory petting and playful stimulation may ignite the child's social interest.

**Fearful Tension.** Hypertense, rigid and withdrawn infants may have experienced rather harsh parental treatment, "teaching" them to anticipate pain and discomfort in association with their environment. In early infancy, these youngsters are most likely to express their discomfort openly, through tears and crying. In time, however, they may acquire an instrumental protective reaction, a "freezing-up," a high-strung and hyperalert avoidance of all sources of potential threat. They may be viewed as exhibiting a mild variant of what we have termed "infantile threctism." Quiet, gentle and sincere affection over a brief period may often overcome the infant's anxious withdrawal.

**Cranky Irritability.** Most common among the infantile reactions is overt irritability and crankiness, especially at night and during feeding. These youngsters are extremely difficult to manage, schedule or placate. They are touchy, fretful, obstinate, moody and exasperating. Whatever the etiological source, once the child proves "difficult," a vicious circle may unfold; thus, parents may attempt time and again to assuage their infant's discontent, but fail repeatedly, and finally throw up their hands in disgust and exasperation. Many of these cranky reactions are fostered and perpetuated by parental vacillation between anxious pampering and angry resentment. These infants display in mild and preliminary form what has been called "childhood ambiosis." Calm and consistent management efforts often prevent these behaviors from growing into more permanent and crystallized pathological patterns.

Most infantile reactions are not extremely severe. Their importance lies in the fact that they may set the stage for the insidous development of more enduring and serious forms of pathology. The child's conception of his world,

shaped early in life, may often lead to the perpetuation and intensification of his initial problems.

## CHILDHOOD REACTIONS

As the child advances in maturity and experience, his capacity to perceive and react to the world becomes increasingly differentiated and refined. No longer are we limited to the rather gross behaviors and emotions seen in the infant; the growing child can now discriminate the source of his discomforts with increasing skill, and can express his feelings and thoughts with a more varied set of reactions than he did in infancy.

This growing variety in behavior expression, combined with the multitude of challenges and crises which characterize the years of childhood, makes the task of organizing and classifying behavior reactions extremely difficult. None of the many childhood classification systems which have been proposed has achieved any measure of acceptance. The schema prepared by the Committee on Child Psychiatry of the Group for the Advancement of Psychiatry (1966) is perhaps the most detailed and thoughtful of a long series of recent attempts to create order out of the chaos that exists in childhood nosology. A similar but less thorough classification has been formulated in the recent DSM-II. These new syndromes, labeled *behavior disorders of childhood and adolescence,* are distinguished from the listing that is labeled "reactions of childhood (and adolescence)" on the basis of degree of personality embedment; that is, the "behavior disorder" category is conceived as signifying an intermediary degree of pathological stability and internalization, falling between the "transient reactions" and what we have termed the "pathological personality patterns."

We have chosen not to follow the three-fold distinction between childhood reactions, disorders and personality as formulated in the DSM-II for several reasons. First, we consider the label "disorder" to signify an *upsetting* of an established personality pattern and not a degree or pervasiveness of personality embedment, as intended in the DSM nomenclature. Furthermore, we believe that moderately embedded and stable forms of disturbed behavior, both in children and adults, are best understood if viewed as moderately severe pathological personality patterns; when the personality style is reasonably entrenched, a greater depth and clarity concerning the etiology and basic coping strategies of the child will be gained if his behavior is seen as a variant of the extensively detailed personality pattern syndromes. Of course, clear-cut distinctions between transient childhood reactions and childhood personality patterns (e.g., childhood ambiosis, moderate severity) will often be difficult to draw in practice. The transient reaction category merely takes cognizance of the fact that most children exhibit a profusion of spontaneous and tentative efforts to deal with new challenges and tensions. These rudimentary and exploratory coping responses have not been crystallized or reinforced into stable and predictable patterns. Many are short lived, covarying and shifting rapidly with a variety of other equally sporadic reactions.

"Childhood reactions" may best be viewed, then, as exploratory coping responses, that is, preliminary and usually transitory instrumental efforts to avoid or otherwise overcome adverse experiences. Conceived in this way, they may be seen as *rudimentary forms* of several of the mild personality patterns described in chapters 6 and 7, that is, they derive from the interaction of the same constitutional and experiential factors, but have not crystallized into stable or fixed form.

For convenience and consistency, we may organize these reactive behaviors into five broad classes:

1. *Withdrawal reactions* (exploratory active-detached strategy), as seen in a fearful mistrustfulness of others, a generalized hesitancy and shyness, a marked introversion and a preference for social isolation.

2. *Overdependency reactions* (exploratory passive-dependent strategy), as shown by an immature clinging to parents and symptoms such as thumb-sucking and school phobias.

3. *Tension reactions* (usually a combination of exploratory active-detached and passive-ambivalent strategies) noted by a variety of symptoms such as nightmares, nailbiting, eating difficulties, unusual and excessive somatic complaints, compulsions and phobias.

4. *Oppositional reactions* (exploratory active-ambivalent strategy) characterized by behaviors such as quarrelsomeness, stubborness, petulance, disobedience and tantrums.

5. *Hostile reactions* (exploratory active-independent strategy) as exhibited in rebellious defiance, school truancy, malicious vandalism, physical cruelty and sadism.

As noted earlier, each of these exploratory strategies and reactions to specific sources of stress may generalize, initiate vicious circles of reciprocal reinforcement and stabilize eventually into a more habitual and pervasive personality pattern.

Let us next look at the typical precipitants

which give rise to childhood pathological reactions.

First and foremost are difficulties and tensions engendered within the *family setting*. A sudden awareness of or increment in parental discord may undermine what security the child previously experienced. Struggles over toilet training or other forms of imposed discipline may shatter the idyllic existence of infancy. Divorce or the death of one parent may also prompt a severe reaction. Dramatic changes in behavior may follow the birth of a sibling; here, youngsters may be confronted with marked decrements in parental interest and affection, leading to jealousy, resentment and insecurity.

Difficulties in *school adjustment* are notable sources of pathological reactions. Fear of leaving the security of the home, sharing attention and competing with others, submitting to forced discipline and experiencing the humiliation of academic failure or inadequacy may all serve as precipitants of behavior pathology.

New tensions are often prompted by difficulties in *peer relationships*. A lack of acceptance by neighborhood age-mates, becoming the butt of jokes and teasings, feeling alone and isolated at school, frequent residential changes and inadequacy in athletic competition may add to sources of stress already present, and result in pathological reactions.

It is difficult to predict the form of the behavioral reaction in children from the source and character of the stressful agent. There are children who withdraw when ostracized by their peers; some, however, will react with hostility, and others may become tense and agitated. Prior learning experiences and coping skills serve to shape the form into which the reaction will be cast. Although certain correlations exist between the nature of stress precipitant and the reaction that is evoked, e.g., depression and clinging behaviors following the death of a parent, the relationship tends to be far from simple and straightforward.

## ADOLESCENT REACTIONS

Many of the difficulties observed in adolescence are continuations of problems faced in childhood. Beyond these, however, are new strains and crises that are especially pronounced in this period of life; we shall concentrate in this section on these unique problems and reactions.

The primary and most troublesome tasks confronting the adolescent are his emancipation from parental control and his need to find a separate identity and an independent course in life. Adolescence is a period of transition and turbulence. The youngster must relinquish childhood standards and behaviors and replace them with something more suitable to his future role as an adult. Innumerable complications arise in this process, and few adolescents pass through this period without at least some degree of discomfort and awkwardness. Surging sexual impulses, heterosexual competition, concerns regarding choice and competence for a vocation and increased self-responsibility, all weigh heavily on the adolescent and make his outlook fraught with anxious anticipation and tension.

We shall focus on three types of behavior reaction which are common among the young today and which signify the presence of more than the usual amount of adolescent turbulence. In one way or another, each of these reactions is a response to the problem of parental liberation and growing independence. The first of these, what we shall term the *inadequacy reaction,* signifies that the youngster has accepted the established standards and goals of society, but feels that he cannot live up to them. The second, termed the *diffusion reaction,* represents an alienation from society and a passive refusal to accept any alternative set of values and guidelines. The third group, called the *rebellious reaction,* indicates that the youngster desires to forcefully upset the established customs of the larger society and does so through intentional antisocial acts. Let us elaborate these three reactions since they relate to experiences and feelings that are not foreign to the lives of many students reading this text.

**Inadequacy Reactions.** These are characterized by low self-esteem, an awkward self-consciousness, a timorous and hesitant manner in social situations and a tendency to view oneself as incompetent, unattractive, clumsy or stupid. These youngsters feel that they cannot "make the grade," become a part of the peer ingroup or be sought after and valued in the competitive give and take which characterizes adolescent relationships. They dread facing the social responsibilities and expectations that society has established for their age group and are fearful that they will falter in finding a mate, getting a job and so on. In short, they lack the confidence that they can function and be accepted on their own.

These youngsters do not question or reject the established values and goals of the larger society; they very much wish to achieve them and to be considered "regular guys" or attractive girls. However, they experience repeated failures in their quest and slip into increasingly more isolated behaviors, preoccupying themselves with watching TV, daydreams of glory and other forms of fantasy escape. In these, they see themselves as the "football hero" or as the girl with all the boys flocking about her. The more desirous they are of these conventional goals, the more envious they become of those who appear to possess them and the more often they view themselves as inadequate, unattractive and forlorn.

**Diffusion Reactions.** These are characterized by vague feelings of apathy and boredom, an inability to see any meaning or purpose to life other than momentary gratifications and an aimless and drifting existence without commitment or direction. In contrast to the inadequacy reaction, in which the adolescent desires but feels he cannot achieve the values and goals of this society, these youngsters feel estranged from society's traditions and believe them to be false or deceiving, but are unable or unwilling to find an alternative to replace them. They appear to be suffering from what Erikson (1950) speaks of as an "identity crisis," a sense of uncertainty as to who they are and where they are going.

As the adolescent liberates himself from the traditional roles and customs of his parents' society, he finds himself at loose ends and adrift, questioning whether any system of values can endure or be valid. In contrast to the "rebellious reaction" to be described below, the "diffused" adolescent's response is not one of hostility and anger, but of passive withdrawal, dejection, confusion and aimlessness. His dismay over the world of his parents is often mixed with feelings of compassion and concern for their plight. He views them as "fools," trapped in the rut of meaningless work and caught in a web of pretense and false and unrewarding material success.

As he ponders the grim realities of a society plagued with civil strife and engaged in hopeless and immoral wars, striving to maintain what he sees as adult hypocrisy and sham, as he senses the futility of long-range plans in a world that soon may be devastated in nuclear war, he convinces himself that nothing really matters, that nothing is worth laboring for or aspiring to. Unable to find a purpose in life, a goal for the future, his behavior becomes aimless, geared only to the pleasures of the moment, with little heed paid to their consequences. Lacking guidelines and goals, he has no reason to act and becomes paralyzed, unable to plan or to commit himself to anything.

Adolescent diffusion often remains latent until the age of 17 or 18, when the youngster goes off to college and is free of parental control and surveillance. Here he often learns "scientific" facts and the skills of critical thinking which enable him to question naive social dogma and archaic childhood beliefs. He becomes conditioned to think that the world of his parents is phony, stupid, self-defeating and meaningless. Moreover, among his peers, he finds many who share his dismay over the failures and deceptions of the society.

Unable to discipline himself and buckle down to the demands of academic life, lacking a coherent set of values by which he can channel his energies and resistant to the "absurdity" of conventional education, he fails to fulfill even the simplest assignments, and his grades sink precipitously. This event only "verifies" for him the stupidity and narrow conventions of the adult world. With his former self-image of "intelligence" shattered by poor academic performance, he seeks to reaffirm his status through promiscuous sexual activity, usually with minimal gratification or by the use of marijuana or LSD, which serves as an emblem of his "copping out" of society. Both of these "prove" his independence of his mortified parents. The following brief case history typifies this reaction.

### CASE 12-2
### Ted R., Age 18, College Sophomore

Ted entered one of the Ivy League colleges at the age of 16, the valedictorian of his high school class and a two-letter man in swimming and track. For the first time in his life, he found that he was not the center of attention among his peers; furthermore, his first semester final grades ranged between the B and D levels, greatly below those to which he was accustomed. More importantly, he was exposed to "really bright" upper classmen who had "turned against the system," were regularly cutting class, marching in peace and protest demonstrations and "smoking pot." Ted also began to question the values and traditions of his middle-class background. By the midpoint of his low sophomore year, he had become a "regular with grass," paid little attention to formal schoolwork, began to read avant-garde poets and philosophers, spent his days idly daydreaming and "sat around nights, just bulling about anything, especially the absurdity of life."

These youngsters often band together, providing each other with philosophical rationalizations for their shared attitudes and behaviors. Quite often, they assume the garb and style of the well-publicized "alienated generation," living together as "hippies" or "flower children." In this manner they gain not only a measure of notoriety and status among the "squares," but achieve a measure of support and begin to find a new system of values to replace their diffusion and sense of isolation.

**Rebellious Reactions.** These differ from the "diffusive" type in that the process of adolescent liberation is achieved by a vigorous attack upon established societal norms. This is done by intentional antisocial acts directed at representatives and symbols of the larger society. Thus, theirs is not a passive and semi-intellectual indifference to traditional customs, but a direct and brutal aggression against the powers that be. Their energies are channeled into opposition, toward the end of upsetting or destroying the customs and rules of a society they resent.

There are innumerable ways in which the strain of growing up can be reacted to rebelliously. A common and relatively mild form is running away from home, of simply picking up one day and leaving for a—hopefully—better world. These youngsters typically are responding to the pressures and expectations of their parents and use the running away mechanism not only as an escape, but as a means of causing their parents public embarrassment and forcing them to desist in their demands. Quite often this behavior arises as a consequence of intolerable parental conflicts that spill over into childhood scapegoating.

More severe rebellious reactions take the form of persistent truancy, vandalism and sexual misbehavior. These acts signify the youngsters' contempt for what they see as the oppressive rules and customs of a harsh or hypocritical society. Cases like these of so-called juvenile delinquency are found in all families and neighborhoods and are not limited by any means to the slums and the underprivileged. Every court is acquainted with privileged adolescents who have reacted to parental indifference, deception and hostility by stealing, drinking and a wide variety of other antisocial acts. Every school, both in "good" and "poor" communities, has its share of defiant, belligerent and truant youngsters. Deprived of affection and interest, many adolescent girls, for example, rebel against the narrow values of unkind and strict parents by acting out sexually. The increase of teen-age pregnancies in recent years attests to the number of unsatisfactory family relationships which precipitate this careless form of social defiance.

Although the three reactions we have just discussed arise under conditions of adolescent stress, it would be misleading if we left the impression that they were not connected, at least in part, to prior life experiences and more enduring personality traits. We categorize them as reactions rather than disorders, not because they occur independently of these background factors, but because they occur in youngsters who evidence no other deep-seated pathological impairments. Thus, although the initial impetus for these reactions may have its roots in the past, the residues of the past did

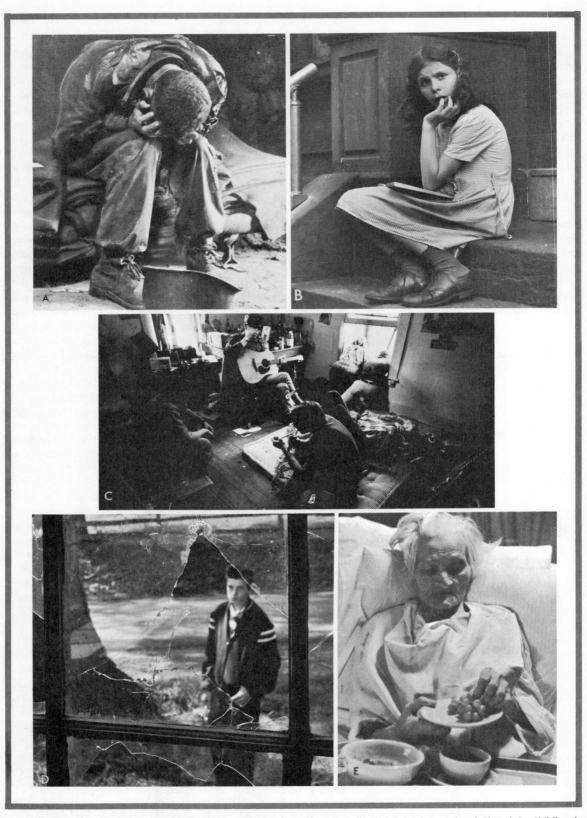

Figure 12-1 Transient situational reactions. *A*. Combat exhaustion. (United Press International Photo.) *B*. Childhood withdrawal reaction. (Courtesy of Esther Bubley.) *C*. Adolescent diffusion reaction. (Look Magazine, August 8, 1967— © Cowles Communications, Inc., 1967.) *D*. Adolescent rebellion. (Wyeth Laboratories.) *E*. Reactions of later life. (Abbott Laboratories.)

not result in the formation of a pervasive pathological pattern.

## ADULT REACTIONS

Many difficulties and strains are inevitable during the long span of adulthood. These crises are handled with relative equanimity by most individuals who manage to "ride through" the innumerable problems and responsibilities of marriage, family life and earning a living. On occasion, however, these pressures are unduly severe or erupt rather suddenly, leading to a "breakdown" in the individual's normal controls and mode of functioning. The symptoms into which these reactions form are determined by the character of the stressful agent and the individual's premorbid vulnerabilities and habitual coping style. Thus, objectively identical precipitants may prompt unbearable anxiety in one person, and depression, withdrawal or alcoholism in others. It would be fruitless and uninstructive to list the many and varied types of reactions possible; they encompass every conceivable form of expression. More useful in this regard would be a brief presentation of the three most frequent spheres of life in which adult stress occurs, notably family relations, earning a livelihood and physical illness.

*Strains of Family Life.* Complexities and tensions in family living are inevitable. They begin with the courtship process in which two persons attempt to coordinate their individual styles of life into a hopefully harmonious and balanced relationship; even at this stage conflicts and break ups occur, resulting not infrequently in marked feelings of anxiety, inadequacy and depression.

With the excitement and illusions of courtship behind them, many marital partners begin to face the hard realities of everyday life; the tasks of sharing and integrating personality differences in background, expectancies, interests and habits can often produce tension and discord in any sphere of interaction—practical daily routines, financial matters, food habits, sexual inclinations, preferences in friends and forms of recreation. The upshot of marked differences in these matters may be severe behavioral reactions such as violence, frigidity, depression, jealousy or indifference. The discovery that one's mate may be engaging in extramarital relations is a frequent precipitant of pathology. Divorce, although it may signify the presence of established difficulties, often serves to provoke a manifest breakdown.

Pregnancy is experienced by many women with fear and trepidation since it may represent a threat to marital security, awaken anxieties concerning the infant's health, be viewed as an in-

tolerable hindrance to freedom or revive thoughts of one's personal inadequacy. Concerns such as these often give rise to what are known as *postpartum reactions,* that is, pathological behaviors and feelings following childbirth.

The task of raising children is fraught with endless strains and concerns; persistent illnesses, difficulties in discipline, social misconduct and sibling conflicts, may not only lead to worry or anger, but reach a point of total collapse and breakdown, should they persist unresolved.

*Strains of Earning a Livelihood.* The struggle to make a living, find a secure form of employment and manage one's finances, is another sphere of adult strain and concern. The sudden loss of a job, repeated unemployment, mounting bills and the many associated tensions these problems create at home, illustrate events which can wear down an individual's resistance and precipitate a breakdown in his mental health. Not only are these problems difficult in themselves, but they often stir up painful secondary feelings such as inadequacy, resentment and futility, which only further aggravate the person's plight.

*Strains of Physical Illness.* The anguish of severe or prolonged illness or of undergoing major surgery is another of the many precipitants of adult pathological reactions. Fears of being permanently scarred, mutilated or debilitated and of losing one's vigor, attractiveness, femininity or youth, are serious matters to many adults who have learned to depend on these attributes for their psychological well-being. In these, as in the other forms of stress, we cannot predict in advance the reaction an individual will have to his disability. How he perceives these events depends on his lifelong needs and attitudes, and these in turn will determine if he will weather the crisis or react to it pathologically.

## REACTIONS OF LATE LIFE

There is no slackening of stress as people move into middle and old age. If anything, judging by incidence statistics, the frequency of severe behavioral reactions increases. Not only does the elderly person bring with him the residues of earlier problems, but added to these are a variety of new difficulties that are unique to late life.

Prominent among them is the marked decline of health and vigor; physical changes, diseases and dysfunctions inevitably occur with aging, and no longer can these individuals take their bodies for granted.

Innumerable physical ailments develop as the body's machinery begins to wear and falter. An increase in both the frequency and duration of illness and the likely prospects for at least one or two bouts of major surgery not only are distressing in themselves, but also activate endless anxieties about the possibility of permanent infirmity and impending death.

In their forties and fifties women experience menopause or "change of life" which is usually associated with a variety of disturbing symptoms such as hot flashes, dizziness and insomnia. Not only do these changes prove to be a distressing reminder to a woman that she can no longer bear children, but they are an inescapable sign that she has passed her peak of youthfulness and physical attractiveness. During this same period, men become increasingly aware of their inability to cope physically with the job they previously took in stride. They find that they tire easily at work and play and lack the sexual drive and capacity they exhibited in former years.

Between the late forties and sixties we often observe what are termed the *involutional reactions,* a period characterized by depressive melancholia and often mixed with hypochondriacal complaints, irritable petulance and persecutory delusions. The strain of declining health and vigor, of feeling empty and useless, of lost status and prestige, often bears down rapidly and heavily at this point in life.

The depressive and hypochondriacal involutional reaction is seen most often in women who have dedicated their lives to their families, have been meticulous and conscientious in their duties as housewives, have invested their affections and energies in bringing up their children and pleasing their husbands. With the advent of menopause and the progression of children into roles of independence, these women find themselves lost, at loose ends and unable to occupy their time in ways that previously gained them attention, security and approval. A similar quality of destitution, self-recrimination and melancholia arises in overconscientious and perfectionistic men who have committed their lives to their work and now begin to dread the prospects of decreased efficiency and retirement. The following history portrays this syndrome in a hypochondriacal involutional melancholic woman.

### CASE 12-3
#### Lilly N., Age 49, Married, Three Children

Lilly had recently traveled some distance to "deliver" her youngest child who was entering her freshman year at college. For months, she had "looked forward" to the "proud day when this last of my children was on her own." In the first few weeks following her daughter's departure, Lilly preoccupied herself with numerous household chores that had been postponed for the day "when I would be free." Upon completing these tasks (e.g., painting rooms and repairing upholstery), Lilly found that she "had nothing to do," that she would awaken "only to look at the four walls" and "feel lonely and blue." Quite in contrast to her "usual self," Lilly began to leave on her nightclothes all day, wander aimlessly around the house, "stare in" her children's empty rooms, reminisce about their childhood and weep.

At her husband's insistence, Lilly tried to busy herself with community activities, but to no avail. She stayed increasingly at home, dressed in her nightrobe and weeping all day, claiming that her body was "decaying," that she had hot flashes "ten times a day" and "aches in her head," none of which could be diagnosed by her physician. Her husband's growing exasperation with her "downcast mood and self-pitying behavior" only aggravated matters. She began to accuse him of viewing her as an "ugly shrew" and preferring to spend his time "playing around with the pretty, young secretaries" at his office. When she stated one morning that "you'll soon find me dead by my own hand," her husband had her put in a hospital, where she remained for several weeks and received antidepressant and electroconvulsive treatment.

The emergence of hypochondriacal symptoms in these patients signifies, in part, their increased self-centering of interests. Viewed instrumentally, these symptoms reflect on the one hand, a form of symbolic self-punishment for their growing inadequacies and on the other, a plea to forestall the loss of the attention and affection which they feel is inevitable.

Although critical, suspicious and persecutory symptoms often color the reactions of formerly conscientious and dedicated persons, they are found more commonly in individuals who previously exhibited domineering styles of behavior. Here, the involutional patient reacts to his waning powers and prestige by attributing the blame for his decline to others instead of accepting them as an inevitable part of the aging process. He cannot accept his lost status and is unwilling to move from the center of activity and control, to which he was accustomed, to that of a passive spectator on the sidelines.

Retirement and its associated feelings of aimlessness, worthlessness and financial insecurity, with its consequent increased dependence upon relatives, may add further anguish to the late years. To impose upon others for support and companionship may be worse than living alone and maintaining one's "pride." Since their mates and friends have died and their children have drifted away, these people may have been subjected to reluctant, indifferent or overtly hostile relatives who would prefer to abandon them and let them fend for themselves. These pressures and prospects add up to the awareness that life is approaching its end, that lost opportunities can no longer be retrieved, that there is little to look forward to and that everything from now on may be a slow and painful ride downhill.

Of course, aging need not be this distressing; many have planned well or are fortunate to have retained their physical well-being, good companionship, rewarding avocations, a supporting family and a financial nest egg, all of which they can now draw upon to maintain their self-esteem. However, for those who are ill prepared or who are beset by misfortune, the aging process becomes a period of anguish and discontent.

Pathological reactions occurring between the sixties and eighties are clinically similar to those found in the involutional period—hypochondriacal depressions and persecutory suspicions and delusions. However, these signs usually manifest themselves more gradually and insidiously than in the middle years. The process of erosion in self-worth and security may have progressed more slowly in these older patients, or perhaps events may have taken a turn for the worse later in life than those which prompted the involutional reaction. Complicating the problems of these patients are a variety of degenerative diseases which further weaken their capacities to cope with psychogenic strains. Thus, the source of the behavioral symptoms of these patients is especially difficult to determine since they almost invariably involve both emotional and physical factors. More will be said on these problems in chapter 13 under "defects associated with cerebral degeneration."

## REMEDIAL APPROACHES IN TRANSIENT SITUATIONAL REACTIONS

The prognostic course of these cases is relatively predictable and uncomplicated, assuming that the situational reaction diagnosis is correct. It can safely be expected that the patient will regain his normal composure and functioning shortly following the removal of the stressful precipitant.

Facilitating this process of rehabilitation are procedures of environmental management, biophysical treatment, supportive therapy and counseling.

Wherever appropriate and feasible, the therapist should seek to alter the environmental conditions which prompted and now aggravate the patient's pathological reactions; for example, in infancy this may lead to the removal of the child from an unhealthy setting to a benevolent foster home.

Not to be overlooked among available treatment measures are various biophysical techniques; for example, psychopharmacological tranquilizing agents may be of immediate benefit in calming anxieties generated in civilian catastrophes or in reducing turbulent emotions following other tension-producing situations. Of note, along these lines, is the unique benefits of electroconvulsive therapy in shortening the duration of involutional depressive reactions.

Supportive therapy is often needed to assuage the patient's anxieties and to shore up his flagging coping capacities. For example, a pathological reaction to a divorce may be abbreviated by the opportunity to share and discuss one's distress with a comforting and reassuring therapist. Counseling along practical lines often helps the patient reorient his attitudes and plan his future in ways more congenial to mental health. For example, in both adolescent and involutional reactions, where patients may be struggling to reorganize their self-image to meet the crisis of changing roles, the guidance of a wise counselor may suggest useful future directions which are consonant with their past and which may take the "sting" out of this period of painful transition.

## CIRCUMSCRIBED LEARNED REACTIONS

Let us reiterate several of the distinguishing characteristics of the circumscribed learned reaction noted earlier in the chapter.

These impairments consist of relatively permanent pathological behaviors learned in response to a narrowly delimited class of ordinarily neutral stimuli; they tend to be both stimulus-specific and uniform in their expression since they are relatively free of intruding and complicating intrapsychic processes.

Although circumscribed reactions are acquired in response to the same determinants and in accordance with the same learning principles as are personality patterns, they lack the pervasiveness or generality that characterizes personality traits, that is, they do not permeate and color every aspect of the individual's functioning. Rather, they are narrowly compartmentalized behavioral tendencies that are manifested in response to a restricted range of stimulus events.

Symptom disorders and circumscribed learned reactions are alike in that both are elicited in response to external events. However, in the learned reactions, the stimulus precipitant is not merely a catalyst to activate a chain of complex intrapsychic processes, as it is in the symptom disorders. Rather, the stimulus evokes, directly and simply, just those responses to which it was connected by learning. In other words, behavior reactions are not contaminated by intervening "unconscious" digressions and complications.

The two syndromes that comprise the behavior reactions should also be distinguished. Transient situational reactions are immediate and short-lived responses to brief but objectively stressful conditions. Circumscribed learned reactions differ on several counts. They are relatively ingrained or permanent response habits that persist long after the conditions which gave rise to them have passed. Moreover, they are acquired in response not only to stressful but to ordinarily neutral and trivial events. Thus, transient reactions are emotionally charged responses precipitated by adverse circumstances whereas circumscribed reactions may develop under rather calm and undramatic conditions, that is, without the presence of a stressful precipitant. For example, certain forms of misconduct (shoplifting, alcoholism and promiscuity) are often learned vicariously as a direct result of simple observation and imitation.

Let us next organize the clinical features of the circumscribed learned reaction syndrome into five major subcategories—fears, developmental habits, dyssocial behaviors, sexual deviations and addictions.

## FEAR REACTIONS

We need not elaborate the behavioral and phenomenological characteristics of intense fear since they are well known to all of us. These rather common reactions are not considered as pathological unless the response is entirely inappropriate or out of proportion to the objective seriousness of the stimulus that prompted it, as for example in reacting fearfully to the sight of a pine tree or becoming panicky when in the presence of an Oriental person.

There are many similarities between fear reactions and what we have labeled in previous chapters as anxiety and phobic disorders; elaboration of these distinctions will be instructive.

Anxiety and fear are alike in that both are characterized by phenomenological tension and by a rapid increase in sympathetic nervous system reactivity (perspiration, muscular contraction and rapid heartbeat). They differ in that anxiety disorders often tend to be unanchored or free-floating whereas fear reactions invariably are focused upon identifiable stimuli.

Phobic disorders and fear reactions are alike in that both are focused on or anchored to tangible external stimuli, leading many theorists to question whether any difference exists between them. As we conceive it, the difference is a matter of the degree and complexity with which intrapsychic factors contribute to shaping the pathological response. Phobias, as we have defined them, signify that intricate and highly convoluted intrapsychic processes have played a determinant role in "selecting" a provocative stimulus that subjectively symbolizes but is objectively different from that which is actually feared, e.g., a phobia for open places may symbolize a more generalized fear of assuming independence of others. In contrast, what we have termed fear reactions are direct, nonsymbolic responses to the actual stimulus the patient has learned to fear, e.g., a fear of Oriental persons that is traceable to distressing encounters in childhood with a Chinese teacher. Some measure of generalization occurs, of course, in learned fear reactions, but the individual tends to make the fear response only to objects or events which are essentially similar or closely associated with the original fear stimulus, e.g., learning to fear a cat in early life may be generalized into a fear of dogs since these are barely discriminable in the eyes of the very young. At most, then, fear reactions reflect simple and uncomplicated generalizations based on specific earlier stress situations. Although often appearing irrational to the unknowing outsider, they can be traced directly to these reality-based and well-circumscribed experiences.

Eysenck (1959) provides a classic illustration of how fear reactions are acquired in the following quotation (given the distinctions we have been making between fear reactions and phobic disorders, we should replace the terms "phobia" and "neurotic" in Eysenck's quote with "fear" and "behavior reaction"):

The paradigm of neurotic symptom formation would be Watson's famous experiment with little Albert, an eleven month's old boy who was fond of animals. By a simple process of classical Pavlovian conditioning, Watson created a phobia for white rats in this boy by standing behind him and making a very loud noise by banging an iron bar with a hammer whenever Albert reached for the animal. . . .

The fear of the rat thus conditioned is unadaptive (because white rats are in fact not dangerous) and hence is considered to be a neurotic symptom; a similarly conditioned fear of snakes would be regarded as adaptive, and hence not as neurotic. Yet the mechanism of acquisition is identical in both cases. This suggests that chance and environmental hazards are likely to play an important part in the acquisition of neurotic responses. If a rat happens to be present when the child hears the loud noise, a phobia results; when it is a snake that is present, a useful habit is built up.

Eysenck's example demonstrates beautifully what we conceive as circumscribed learned fear reactions, that is, a simple and direct learned response to an ordinarily innocuous stimulus object.

This simple and direct conditioned linkage between a stimulus and a response is *not* what is meant by the concept of "disorder," phobic or otherwise. As noted above, an intricate chain of intervening processes is involved in these disorders. They occur in personalities whose histories are replete with innumerable instances of adverse experience. Given their repeated exposure to mismanagement and faulty learning experiences, these individuals have built up an obscure intrapsychic labyrinth, a residue of complex, tangentially related, but highly interwoven memories, emotions, and coping responses that are easily reactivated under the pressure of new stress. Because these incidental intrapsychic processes are stirred up under stress conditions, no simple and direct line can be traced between the "disordered" response and its associated precipitant. The final outcome, as in a phobia, appears as a "symbolic" rather than as a simple "generalized" fear since the associative route is highly circuitous, involving both the residuals of the past and such intrapsychic distortion mechanisms as condensation and displacement. Phobias are formed, then, by the crystallization of diffusely anchored and unconsciously transformed past learnings acquired in response to a wide and diverse range of faulty experiences; this pervasively adverse background and the rather circuitous sequence of intrapsychic distortions that are activated are found in pathological rather than normal personality patterns. Since "normals" have not had such pervasively adverse experiences, they have little reason to employ a complex of intrapsychic maneuvers as a means of avoiding the reactivation of these distressing memories and emotions; as a result, what we observe in them are relatively "clean," simple and direct reactions.

Let us briefly note a number of conditions which give rise to the acquisition of circumscribed, learned fear reactions.

The simplest of these are situations in which a previously neutral stimulus has been paired, either intentionally or incidentally, with a noxious stimulus. In the example reported in Eysenck's quote, the fear response given "naturally" to the stimulus

of a sharp noise was "conditioned" to the stimulus of a white rat by the simple process of pairing the two stimuli through temporal contiguity.

Learned fear reactions need not have been based on direct prior experience with the fear-producing stimulus. Quite commonly, as in vicarious learning, children have merely seen or read about the "frightening" qualities of certain stimuli, e.g., a TV mystery in which a bloody murder occurs in a bathtub may build a persistent fear of taking a bath. In addition to visual pairings of noxious and neutral stimuli, children often acquire their fears through verbal association. For example, many youngsters who have never seen a snake have a dreadful fear merely of the thought of seeing one. They may have read about the "deadly poisonous" and "nauseatingly slimy" characteristics of these creatures or may have been told, in a tense and agitated voice by a fearful parent, "never to go near, let alone touch one." Along similar lines, children may acquire a variety of fearful attitudes simply by observing and imitating the behaviors, ideas and emotions of an apprehensive parental model. Thus, even though parents may never have directly told their children to be afraid of certain objects or events, children vicariously "soak in" attitudes merely by incidental observation. Through indirect associations such as these, a child may acquire within his behavioral repertoire a fearful expectancy of distress to stimuli that objectively are innocuous, despite the fact that he may never have had a direct or "real" experience with them.

If we think of the many incidental stimuli and chance-like conditions under which fears are learned, and add to it the effects of even simple stimulus generalization, we may begin to understand why so many of these fears appear irrational and peculiar. Despite their strange and nonsensical quality, however, they are a simple product of conditioned and vicarious learning, no more obscure in the manner of their acquisition than most of the attitudes and behaviors we take for granted as "normal."

## DEVELOPMENTAL HABIT REACTIONS
(DSM-II: *Special Symptoms*)

Any number and variety of peculiar and deviant habits can be acquired by the simple process of direct and indirect learning. As with the fear reactions, these behaviors and attitudes need not signify that complex intrapsychic mechanisms are working to resolve a "disordering" of personality equilibrium. Even compulsions and delusions, which most often signify the operation of "under-lying" intrapsychic processes, may on occasion represent the end product of simple vicarious learning through direct exposure and observation. It would be fruitless, then, to enumerate the many and diverse forms of habit pathology. Almost any kind of response can be learned and, if viewed as maladaptive by current societal standards, would be included in this psychopathological behavior inventory.

By what criteria should we narrow the list?

For practical purposes, if for no other, our choice should be based on frequency of occurrence, that is, pathological habits that are fairly common to large segments of the population. As we begin to uncover these common habits, we find that most of them were "normal" at one stage of development, that is, they were exhibited and considered appropriate by all persons early in their growth process, but were modified or extinguished by most individuals as they matured. Thus, these pathological developmental habits, as we shall label them, are acquired in the normal course of human growth and are not a consequence of experiences that are peculiar to just a few. What distinguishes them is *not* that they were learned in the first place, but that they failed to be modulated or unlearned during maturation.

Three spheres of development display these persistent or fixated habits: learning to eat, eliminate and speak. In the following paragraphs we will describe several pathological habits that were viewed initially as normal developmental behaviors.

Before we proceed, let us quote the section in the 1952 APA manual that refers to the impairments we shall be describing. These are listed in the DSM-II under the rather obscure label of *special symptoms*.

This category is useful in occasional situations where a specific symptom is the single outstanding expression of the psychopathology. This term will not be used as a diagnosis, however, when the symptoms are associated with, or are secondary to, organic illnesses and defects, or to other psychiatric disorders. Thus, for example, the diagnosis special symptom reaction, speech disturbance would be used for certain disturbances in speech in which there are insufficient other symptoms to justify any other definite diagnosis. This type of speech disturbance often develops in childhood. It would not be used for a speech impairment that was a temporary symptom of conversion hysteria or the result of any organic disease or defect. The diagnosis should specify the particular "habit."

As the preceding quotation implies, the "special symptom" classification applies when there are no other signs of psychopathology concurrent or "underlying" the habit reaction. Such impair-

ments correspond to the major syndrome we have labeled "circumscribed learned reactions." Since the specific impairments selected in the manual to illustrate "special symptoms" almost exclusively are those of childhood, it would seem quite appropriate to classify them under the subcategory label of "developmental habits."

## HABITS ASSOCIATED WITH EATING

Several troublesome behaviors may be acquired in conjunction with infantile and childhood feeding experiences. Thumbsucking, excessive eating, perverted appetites (pica), poor appetites (anorexia), gagging and vomiting are among the better known. These may stem from any number of biogenic or psychogenic causes, the latter including sucking indulgence or frustration in infancy, forced feeding, tension at meal times, maternal oversolicitude, nagging or excessive discipline. Many of these habits fade as the child matures, but occasionally they persist into adolescence and adulthood.

As was noted earlier, pathological behaviors need not indicate the presence of a general personality disturbance. Thus, many youngsters who continue to suck their thumbs into early adolescence exhibit no other signs of emotional disturbance. In these cases, the symptom is simply an isolated habit, learned as a function of a well-circumscribed set of experiences that did *not* pervade or disrupt the overall pattern of personality development. Whether the thumb was a primary source of sensory gratification and attachment learning during the first neuropsychological stage, or whether sucking was overlearned as a means of tension relief, the essential point that justifies the "developmental habit" label is the fact that the conditions which prompted its learning did not give rise to a more generalized pathological pattern. This is not to say that thumbsucking, appetite disturbances or other eating difficulties are not found in pathological personalities or that they may not occur with greater than chance probability in certain personality types; in fact, they do. However, in these latter cases, a diagnostic label other than "developmental habit" would be more appropriate since the habit is but one small facet of a larger constellation of pathological signs.

## HABITS ASSOCIATED WITH ELIMINATION

Infancy is a unique period of life in many respects. Not only does the child freely mouth, suck and eject objects with minimal concern for physical consequences or the opinions of others, but he is equally indiscriminate and careless in his practice of wetting and soiling at will. Only gradually are these universal eliminative habits of early life controlled and modulated. Through trial and error and parental persuasion and management, the child slowly learns to surrender his primitive ways and substitute more sanctioned modes of functioning.

This process of learning to relinquish the undisciplined freedom and pleasures of infancy may be fraught with tensions, misguidance and poor tuition. These adverse experiences may also result in the failure to regulate and inhibit infantile eliminative habits.

There are two forms of pathology reflecting the persistence of elimination habits, *enuresis* and *encopresis*. The latter refers to the rare habit of involuntary defecation or "soiling." This reaction often alternates with prolonged periods of retention and constipation. The former impairment occurs much more frequently and consists of habitual and involuntary urination, most notably at night. Because of its greater prevalence and because more is known about it, we shall limit our discussion to enuresis.

### Enuresis

Failure in bladder control is not considered to be an enuretic habit until the child is at least three years of age. Commonly, bed-wetting occurs from two to five nights a week. Over 80 per cent of reported cases have persisted since infancy. However, most parents do not seek professional assistance until the child is between eight and ten years of age. About 15 per cent of all children referred to mental health clinics have a history of enuresis. The problem occurs with appreciably greater frequency among males (about 2 or 3 to 1). Recent studies indicate the presence of enuretic problems in one fourth of all psychiatric discharges during military recruit training. The reported incidence of the problem declines rapidly with age. With the exception of cases with demonstrated organic pathology it appears to be extremely rare after the age of 30.

The assertion that constitutional factors may underlie or dispose a child to enuresis has not been proved, although there is evidence that monozygotic twins evidence greater concordance than dizygotics, and that a disproportionately high correspondence exists among children of the same family that have been reared in kibbutzim, where uniform toilet training methods are employed. Nevertheless, anatomical studies have not yielded conclusive supporting data. No doubt, any maturational dysfunction or delay will set into motion a variety of secondary psychogenic complications which can aggravate an existing physical weakness.

The problem of establishing the psychogenic etiology of developmental habits is not that of discovering the conditions which led the child to acquire his habit in the first place, as is the case in most forms of psychopathology; rather, the task is to determine the factors which *deterred the normal unlearning* of established and previously acceptable habits. Viewed in this way, enuresis reflects the operation of forces which resist or forestall change. With the exception of organically impaired cases, in which the sheer mechanics of sphincter control may be difficult, it appears that most enuretics retain their infantile habit in response to certain adverse experiences and in order to achieve some desired goal. Several such experiences and goals are notable.

Toilet training is often a struggle of power and wit in which coercion and threat are employed both by parents and child to achieve opposing ends. Forced to submit to his parent's wishes as a result of intimidation and harassment, the child may harbor deep resentments and desires for revenge. As a consequence, he may accede to daytime eliminative controls and inhibit any overt expression of his anger. However, at night, when he can deny responsibility for his acts, he may freely "get back" at his parents, wreak revenge, discharge his anger and quietly enjoy their futility and powerlessness to exert control over him.

Another instrumental goal associated with enuresis is the desire to prevent an anticipated or real loss of parental interest. The birth of a sibling during toilet training is a common precipitant for a regression to bed-wetting and soiling. Having learned through prior experience that wetting achieves prompt parental attention, and having their observations reinforced, these children often revert to their former careless ways of elimination. Whether prompted by a desire to recapture the "bliss" of infancy or merely to extract signs of continued parental solicitude, these youngsters find that enuresis is an effective coping instrument.

There is contradictory evidence in the literature dealing with personality traits and enuresis. Some writers assert that these youngsters are timid, shy and self-conscious. Others report them to be nervous, touchy and oversensitive. Still others view them as whining, disobedient, spiteful and stubborn. Finally, there are researchers who have found no differences in emotional adjustment and personality traits between enuretics and random groups of nonenuretic children. In short, enuretics appear to possess a variety of other psychological problems, but no more perhaps than is found in the population at large, and none that appears to be distinctive to or even highly correlated with their pathological habit. Where notable relationships do appear, they are often as much a consequence as a cause of the enuresis.

## HABITS ASSOCIATED WITH SPEECH

Learning to speak fluently and to give up the repetitive and stumbling word by word pattern of baby talk, is an achievement of no mean proportions, a difficult task of subtle motor, emotional and cognitive coordination that is subject to an endless variety of biological and psychological complications. Some of the innumerable difficulties which may arise during this learning venture are traceable to anatomical defects, but the majority are attributable to parental mismanagement and disruptive emotional experiences. These impairments include delayed speech, phonation and rhythmic difficulties and problems of articulation. The most interesting, from a psychological point of view, is stuttering. We shall confine our discussion of developmental speech reactions to this notoriously troublesome habit, not because the conditions which give rise to it are so unusual, but because it so often fosters secondary psychological problems that are more serious than the habit itself.

### Stuttering

This impairment, also referred to as stammering, is characterized by spasmodic interruptions in the normal flow of speech. The range of difficulty extends from mild and infrequent blocking of certain syllables at the one extreme to the prolonged failure to produce any words with brief intermittent bursts of unintelligible sounds at the other. Words beginning with the consonants b, d, t and s are typically the most troublesome. During periods of stuttering, the person may writhe, grimace and contort his mouth and face as if he were experiencing a deep internal conflict or struggle.

Stuttering symptoms do not appear in all situations calling for speech. For example, it often is not exhibited when the stutterer is relaxed or in the presence of people whom he feels to be his inferiors, or when he is singing, reading or whispering. It is most pronounced in situations that arouse fear or self-consciousness.

The impairment is found at all ages and in all social groups. Such famous figures as Aristotle, Demosthenes, Charles Lamb and Andrew Mellon were known to suffer from the disruptive effects of this habit. About 1 to 2 per cent of the population in the United States exhibit some form of stuttering. It is appreciably more frequent in males than in females, the ratio being roughly of the order of

5 to 1. The fact that the onset in over 90 per cent of the cases takes place before the age of six, with the majority of these between two and four, supports the view that the impairment is in most cases a prolongation of normal developmental speech disfluency, groping, blocking and repetition.

Several etiological theories have been proposed for the persistence of these disfluent speech habits. As was noted in earlier chapters, many diverse pathways may lead to the same form of psychopathology. In some cases, biogenic determinants may be primary and in others the disturbance may be generated largely by psychogenic causes. In most, however, there appears to be an interplay of both biogenic and psychogenic elements. Let us briefly elaborate this "interaction" thesis.

A review of research and theory on stuttering suggests that most, although by no means all, cases occur among youngsters who evidence a slight maturational lag in speech capacities. This delayed speech development often gives rise to parental anxieties, mismanagement or derogatory comments. Parental attitudes such as these in turn create tensions, self-consciousness and fears of speaking on the part of the child, which in circular fashion feed back to reinforce, intensify and perpetuate the original speech difficulty. This interactional hypothesis will be referred to again, after we review a number of alternate biogenic and psychogenic theories.

Several theorists contend that stuttering is a hereditary defect that will inevitably be triggered during the acquisition of speech. This position is supported by recent findings (Johnson, 1961) that children who stutter have nine times as many parents and siblings who have stuttered than does a matched group of nonstutterers. However convincing these data are, they do not "prove" the hereditary thesis. Johnson, who reported these findings, himself suggests that parents who are or have been stutterers are likely to be overly concerned and responsive to any sign of speech hesitation and awkwardness in their children. He proposes, therefore, that parental anxieties and over-reactions may create speech self-consciousness and tension on the part of these children, attitudes which lead to the prolongation and intensification of their "normal" disfluent speech.

Attempts to identify neurological or motor dysfunctions which might underlie the development of stuttering have proved fruitless. Various hypotheses, e.g., damage to brain regions associated with speech, disruptions in cerebral dominance and handedness, undeveloped speech musculature and so on have been shown to be either anatomically invalid (Penfield and Roberts, 1959) or empirically unsupported (Bloodstein, 1959). This failure to uncover uniform constitutional defects among stutterers does not mean, however, that defects may not exist as a factor in a number of stuttering cases. We may not be able to identify the presence of these defects because of the imprecision or limits of our diagnostic technology; moreover, a wide range of "normal" individual differences may exist in anatomy or maturational growth which may never be exhibited in the form of a tangible diagnostic sign. Thus, it is quite plausible, given the gradation or continuum along which differences exist in both physical and mental traits, that many youngsters who evidence stuttering behavior possess subtle deficiencies and minor developmental lags. Small though these minimal retardations or defects may be, they can set in motion a number of secondary complications, such as parental anxiety and condemnation, which then aggravate and perpetuate the original minor impairment.

The primacy of psychogenic factors in stuttering has been espoused by numerous theorists (e.g., Johnson et al., 1959; Sheehan, 1953; Barbara, 1962). They point to the fact that normal people often experience speech blocking when they are frightened or self-conscious, e.g., asking an instructor to excuse an absence for an examination or being suddenly faced with the need to introduce a group of people to each other. In these situations, the tension felt in conjunction with the task often decreases the adequacy of its performance. According to psychogenic theorists, these unusual tension situations parallel those which constantly confront the stutterer as he struggles to coordinate the many complex functions involved in the production of smooth and articulate speech. This highly generalized vulnerability was acquired, according to Johnson, when the child first began to speak at about the age of two. At this early stage, the entire complex of speaking was associated with extreme tension and self-consciousness. Complications such as parental indifference and derogation upset the delicate speech learning process, thereby fostering the continuation of the young child's normally hesitant speech. Parents who were unusually concerned or critical of the child's speech repetitiveness and stumbling and who interrupted and corrected his "mistakes," not only prevented the child from breaking out of the pattern of hesitant speech, but by communicating their anxieties or exasperation may have caused the child to become self-conscious and tense regarding his speech. As a consequence, he may have developed a generalized fear of speaking. Once established, these speech behaviors and attitudes may have set into motion a vicious circle. Fear and self-consciousness themselves increased the probability of stammering and speech hesita-

tion. Since fear induced stuttering, the child's expectation that he would stutter was reinforced, and with each reinforcement his dread of speaking was intensified, starting the vicious circle all over again.

Once the process of stuttering becomes an ingrained habit, it tends to spread and generate a variety of new psychological complications. We find, for example, that many stutterers are socially shy and hesitant and express the feeling that they are inferior to others. Beneath this overtly awkward and self-conscious style, stutterers frequently harbor deep feelings of resentment and anger toward others for the ridicule and embarrassment to which they have so often been subjected. Thus, stuttering is not only self-perpetuating, but leads frequently to secondary problems such as feelings of inadequacy, frustration and repressed anger. From what little evidence we have, it appears that the few personality traits that correlate with stuttering behavior are more a consequence than a cause of the impairment.

Let us return briefly to the previously mentioned thesis that stuttering arises in most cases from the interaction of biogenic and psychogenic factors. More specifically, we believe that it occurs most frequently in youngsters who display a maturational lag in speech development and who have experienced as a consequence undue parental concern or derogation. Evidence in support of this view is entirely circumstantial. First, it appears that children who show delayed speech are more likely to become stutterers than children who speak early. Second, boys are "slower" than girls in the development of speech; in line with our thesis, it is a well-established fact that boys outnumber girls in stuttering by about 5 to 1. The correlation between delayed speech, sex differences and stuttering suggests that children who experience some measure of difficulty in early speech development are more likely to arouse parental anxiety, to prompt critical and humiliating remarks from others and to develop a self-conscious sense of verbal inadequacy. Each of these produces tensions associated with speaking, and thereby reinforces and perpetuates the early and "normal" developmental habit of speech hesitation and repetition. Prolonged in this manner, these early habits eventually become "stuttering reactions."

## DYSSOCIAL REACTIONS
(DSM-II: *Dyssocial Behavior*)

Individuals falling into this category of the circumscribed learned reactions exhibit a marked disdain for social conventions. Their pathology, however, is *not* pervasively rooted in a generalized hostile or irresponsible personality pattern, as are the sociopathic disorders. With the exception of their habitual disregard, flouting and violation of social rules and customs, they tend to be well-balanced and psychologically integrated persons.

The category formulated here approximates that listed in the DSM-II nosological system under the descriptive label *dyssocial behavior* and is characterized in the 1952 APA manual as follows:

> This term applies to individuals who manifest disregard for the usual social codes, and often come in conflict with them, as the result of having lived all their lives in an abnormal moral environment. They may be capable of strong loyalties. These individuals typically do not show significant personality deviations other than those implied by adherence to the values or code of their own predatory, criminal, or other social group.

The term "dyssocial" reflects the fact that these behaviors are disapproved by those who determine the values and customs of the larger society. More significantly and in contrast to other forms of social misbehavior the basic personality of these individuals has *not* been distorted or undermined; rather, they have learned a relatively circumscribed habit, a way of conducting themselves that is considered socially contrary, repugnant and reprehensible.

Vicarious learning is the primary means by which dyssocial persons acquire their style of misconduct. The experiences to which these patients are exposed contrast with those experienced by aggressive personality patterns or their associated sociopathic disorders. Rather than being exposed to harsh and punitive parents, individuals displaying dyssocial reactions often have been brought up in a supporting and affectionate family environment. They learned through observation and modeling, however, to copy the socially unacceptable values and customs of their parents and the subcultural group of which they were a part. Their misconduct, then, is not a coping strategy worked out in a personal struggle to counter punitive parental treatment or social misfortune but rather a product primarily of simple exposure, observation and imitative learning.

Within the context of the patient's subcultural group, his behaviors and attitudes are considered not only acceptable, but preferable to those shared by members of the larger society. For example, the way of life pictured among members of the Mafia indicates the presence of strong family ties and affection, combined with the active promotion of antisocial and criminal behavior. Similar family and group styles, somewhat less publicized and socially destructive than those of the Mafia, provide security, mutual respect and loyalty among its members. Although they foster "healthy" personality growth, at the same time they lead to the acquisition of socially repugnant and reprehensible behaviors.

Many juvenile gang members, prostitutes and adult criminals may properly be classified within this syndrome (the particular form of the misconduct depends on the nature of the models to which they were exposed and reinforced). Whatever form their behavior takes, it represents a code of values and morals which runs contrary to the larger society. It is acquired, not because of adversity and mistreatment, but because it provided the individual with a sense of belonging and ingroup status. The following excerpts typify the background and attitudes of youngsters exhibiting the dyssocial syndrome (Shaw, 1930):

> When I started to play in the alleys around my home I first heard about a bunch of older boys called the "Pirates." My oldest brother was in this gang and so I went around with them. There were about ten boys in this gang and the youngest one was eleven and the oldest one was about fifteen. . . .
> Tony, Sollie, and my brother John were the big guys in the gang. Tony was fifteen and was short and heavy. He was a good fighter and the young guys were afraid of him because he hit them and beat them up. . . . My brother was fifteen and was bigger than Tony and was a good fighter. He could beat any guy in the gang by fighting, so he was a good leader and everybody looked up to him as a big guy. I looked up to him as a big guy and was proud to be his brother. . . .
> When I started to hang out with the Pirates I first learned about robbin (sic). The guys would talk about robbin and stealing and went out on "jobs" every night. When I was eight I started to go out robbin with my brother's gang. We first robbed junk from a junk yard and sometimes from the peddler. Sometimes we robbed stores. We would go to a store, and while one guy asked to buy something the other guys would rob anything like candy and cigarettes and then run. We did this every day. . . .
> The gang had a hangout in an alley and we would meet there every night and smoke and tell stories and plan for robbin. I was little and so I only listened. The big guys talked about going robbin and told stories about girls and sex things. The guys always thought about robbin and bummin from school and sometimes from home. . . .
> When I was ten the gang started to robbin stores and homes. We would jimmy the door or window and rob the place. I always stayed outside and gave jiggers. The big guys went in and raided the place. They showed me how to pick locks, jimmy doors, cut glass and use skeleton keys and everything to get into stores and houses. Every guy had to keep everything a secret and not tell anybody or he would be beat up and razzed. The police were enemies and not to be trusted. When we would get caught by the police we had to keep mum and not tell a word even in the third degree.
> I looked up to my brother and the other big guys because of their courage and nerve and the way they could rob. They would tell me never to say a word to

anybody about our robbin. My mother didn't even know it. Some kids couldn't be in the gang because they would tell everything and some didn't have the nerve to go robbin. The guys with a record were looked up to and admired by the young guys. A stool-pigeon was looked down on and razzed and could not stay in the gang. . . .

The guys stuck together and helped each other out of trouble. They were real good pals and would stick up for each other.

Dyssocial reactions contrast with sociopathic disorders. Sociopaths are "loners," isolated and resentful persons with no loyalty or group identification. Moreover, their actions are driven by unconscious tensions, leading them into indiscriminate and purposeless acts, often with no thought of tangible gain or social approval. In the dyssocial syndrome, however, patients behave thoughtfully and with planning, and do not engage in "senseless" or impulsive acts. Because of their relatively benign past, they are not driven by surging impulses of anger and resentment, neither are they compelled to gain vindication and triumph over those who have done them harm. Their antisocial acts are not "spur of the moment" irrational discharges, but well-developed learned habits of social misconduct which are approved and encouraged by those with whom they identify. Moreover, they are usually designed as a means of gaining financial or other tangible rewards. More notably, dyssocial patients exhibit, at least within the confines of their own social group, affection and concern for the welfare of others. In contrast to aggressive personalities and most sociopathic disorders, who display a generalized deficiency in group identification and loyalty, these individuals can be and are selectively nurtural, thoughtful and sharing.

Distinctions should be made also between the dyssocial reactions and adolescent rebellious reactions, described earlier in the chapter. *First,* in adolescent rebellion, the youngster adopts a form of behavior that is diametrically opposite to that espoused by his parents. It is a reaction against parental customs and values. In contrast, the dyssocial syndrome represents not rejection but, more commonly, adoption and imitation of parental attitudes and behaviors. *Second,* dyssocial styles are deeply ingrained and enduring habits, usually in evidence before the age of ten, and usually followed as a course of behavior well into adulthood. In contrast, adolescent rebellion is a transient age-specific reaction made in response to the task of assuming an independent identity. It is first displayed about the time of puberty and typically subsides, with or without treatment, by the early twenties. *Third,* rebellious adolescents engage typically in dramatic acting out behaviors, make it

a point to exhibit their flouting of authority, engage in boisterous bravado and are overtly hostile, intimidating and cruel to those who adhere to social conventions. In contrast, those categorized among the dyssocial reactions rarely are exhibitionistic, take their misbehavior in stride, tend not to be intimidating and brutal to others and execute their antisocial acts with greater control and aplomb.

In drawing these distinctions, we may have created the illusion that "real cases" can be neatly discriminated and placed into one or another of the behaviorally similar rebellious, dyssocial and sociopathic categories. These sharp lines are deceptive, sketched only for pedagogical purposes. When we review the clinical history and picture of a specific, socially troublesome individual, we find that his experiences and behaviors rarely lend themselves to unequivocal placement in one *or* another category. Rather, his background tends more often to display a mixture of features characteristic of several categories, a sad fact that defies our desire for diagnostic simplicity. Nevertheless, where the relative role of ingrained personality traits, transient stress conditions and circumscribed learned habits can be established, the clinician will be in a better position to distinguish his patients diagnostically and to determine the prognoses of his cases and the remedial approaches he should plan.

## SEXUAL DEVIATION REACTIONS
### (DSM-II: *Sexual Deviations*)

The 1952 APA Manual reserves this term "for deviant sexuality which is not symptomatic of more extensive syndromes." As implied in this diagnostic definition, sexual difficulties and perversions *do* occur in individuals who exhibit more pervasive pathologies. Thus, these same symptoms may be observed as one of a constellation of clinical signs of a more widely generalized pathological personality pattern. Inclusion in the *sexual deviation reaction* syndrome signifies, however, that the problem does *not* have its roots in personality pathology. Rather, it is a *circumscribed* learned reaction, a bizarre fragment that departs from an otherwise intrinsically "normal" personality style. In short, these deviations should be viewed as isolated habits acquired in response to an unusual combination of pathogenic circumstances that have distorted the learning of normal sexual behaviors, but have not intruded appreciably upon other spheres of personality development.

Before we discuss the various forms of sexual deviance included in this syndrome, let us briefly elaborate how personality factors often are or become involved in these habits. First, as was noted previously, sexual difficulties may reflect a wider pathological pattern. Second, and perhaps more importantly, sexual deviancy, although initally circumscribed, may lead to behaviors and problems that ultimately result in more pervasive problems. In other words, sexual deviance can be both a cause as well as a consequence of personality deviance. For example, a young and otherwise "healthy" homosexual must engage in furtive maneuvering, given the customs of our society, in order to gratify his needs. In addition to becoming exquisitely sensitive to receptive cues from potential partners, he is often fearful that others may have detected his behaviors. As a consequence of operating in this manner for some time, he may acquire generalized traits of hypersensitivity and suspiciousness concerning the hidden thoughts and feelings of others. These traits may become so ingrained that he begins to behave and think in ways that are similar to those seen in paranoid personalities.

In this section, we will focus our attention on persons whose deviance neither reflects nor has given rise to personality complications. Rather, we will limit ourselves to sexual deviancies that are circumscribed, that is, relatively free of associated personality impairments.

The popular view that sexual deviance is invariably associated with degeneracy, violence or other signs of marked antisocial pathology is grossly mistaken. Certain forms of perversion, such as rape-murders, usually indicate the presence of more general psychopathology, but the great majority of individuals who engage in deviant forms of sexuality are not different from anyone else in their general behaviors and attitudes. If anything, they tend to be socially reserved and timid rather than cruel and violent. Moreover, many deviates evidence only one form of sexual pathology. They repeat the same act time and time again and rarely explore or engage in other types of sexual deviance.

## ACQUISITION OF SEXUAL DEVIANCE

Before we specify factors conducive to the particular forms of sexual deviance, it will be instructive to present and evaluate some general hypotheses that have been proposed for the development of all forms of sexual impairment.

### Biogenic Factors

It is commonly believed that individuals disposed to sexual deviance must possess some biological abnormality. Hypotheses have been proposed to the effect that these impairments are of hereditary origin, that deviates are "oversexed," that is, suffer from some hormonal imbalance or possess other physical aberrations, such as a physique more appropriate to the opposite sex. To date, however, no evidence has been adduced in favor of any of these hypotheses.

Kallmann (1953), for example, provided data that show a greater concordance in homosexuality between monozygotic than dizygotic twins. However, these data did not prove the presence of hereditary factors in the great majority of homosexuals. First, although monozygotic twins showed greater concordance than dizygotics, there was greater discordance than concordance *among* monozygotic twins. Second, his studies failed to consider the greater commonality in environmental experience among monozygotic as contrasted to dizygotic twins. Third, one might postulate that the rather special conditions of upbringing among monozygotic twins could have fostered strong attachments on their part to members of the same sex.

Other genetic theorists have proposed that homosexuality may reflect a deviant chromosomal arrangement, more akin to that seen in the opposite sex. This proposition has been checked by the direct examination of chromosomal patterns in homosexuals (Pritchard, 1962) and has been found to be invalid.

Along other biological lines, the notion persists that homosexuals may have a hormonal imbalance, weighted toward an excess of opposite sex hormones. This has also been investigated and shown to be incorrect. Similarly, the popular view that homosexuals possess body physiques more characteristic of the opposite sex has likewise been refuted (Coppen, 1959). In short, no biogenic hypothesis concerning sexual deviancy, homosexual or otherwise, has been borne out by empirical research.

### Psychogenic Factors

It appears safe to assume that sexual deviance is a product of social learning, a result of some unusual and faulty set of environmental conditions which has blocked or distorted the acquisition of normal sexual attitudes and behaviors. Which one of an almost infinite number of sexual practices will come to the foreground during development depends on the cultural setting within which a child is born and the particular attitudes and experiences to which he is exposed. In some societies, such as early Greece, homosexuality was not only an accepted form of sexual behavior, but a preferred one among the intelligentsia and well-to-do. In contemporary Western societies, however, heterosexual intercourse is the preferred modality and goal of sexual behavior. Any form of sexual activity which does not result in coitus with an adult of the opposite sex as its ultimate objective is viewed as a sign either of immaturity or perversion.

What psychogenic determinants give rise to these deviations?

First, let us put aside discussing perversions that reflect pervasive personality impairments. In these cases, of which there are many and which have been interpreted rather ingeniously but debatably by psychoanalytic theorists (Fenichel, 1945), deviant sexuality "symbolizes" something else; it is the end product of a rather intricate, obscure and highly personalized set of memories, emotions and intrapsychic mechanisms. Whatever "causes" one ascribes to this form of sexual difficulty—and many are possible—it is an outgrowth of forces that can best be understood in terms of the larger pattern of needs, habits and strategies which comprises the individual's personality. It is *not* a circumscribed learned reaction, but an indirect symbolic expression of pervasive unconscious processes.

Sexual deviations, viewed as circumscribed learned habits, are acquired primarily in two ways: by conditioning and by imitative learning. Once acquired, these habits tend to be perpetuated and intensified as a consequence of a number of secondary reinforcing events. Let us elaborate this general thesis.

Neutral stimuli may acquire either sexually attractive or repulsive qualities simply by being paired through contiguity association with stimuli which previously were viewed as sexually attractive or repulsive. This process of learning is the standard paradigm of classical conditioning. For example, a child who was rather indifferent to his mother's undergarments may have his attitude changed when he hears "dirty jokes" about underclothes from his friends or becomes "infected" with sexual excitement as they titillate each other while viewing advertisements for brassieres and ladies' underpants.

Preadolescent and adolescent boys are especially prone to sexual arousal and erotic titillation. However, young adolescents rarely experience the act of coitus directly; more often, they associate their maturing sexual feelings with lurid stories, pornographic pictures, peephole observations and the like. Given the diverse and bizarre conceptions of sexuality experienced by adolescents, we should not be surprised that they learn to associate sexual responses with a peculiar array of stimuli. This early and largely incidental pairing of erotic excite-

ment with objectively neutral stimuli may create strong aversions to "real" sexuality and strange misconceptions of the nature of adult sexual activity. For example, if a young girl reads lurid stories in which sex is paired with brutal treatment, she may be conditioned to fear sexual activity, becoming in time not only hesitant in sexual matters, but totally unable to consummate the sexual act in marriage. Another young girl may have learned to believe, through the incidental comments and behaviors of her mother, that women must be "free with their bodies" if they ever wish to get and hold on to a man. This imitative learning may lead the child to pursue a promiscuous course when she begins heterosexual dating.

Sexual attitudes and behaviors need not be acquired in so direct a manner as those just illustrated. For example, a boy raised by an affectionate but controlling mother, and having minimal contact with a busy or rejecting father, may fail to acquire a sense of masculine identity; lacking in feelings of male competence and fearful of asserting himself in relation to women, he may gravitate into the role of a passive or feminine homosexual.

In summary, then, sexually deviant habits are often acquired as a result of faulty conditioning and imitative experiences. We will elaborate other types of learning conditions which foster the major variants of sexual deviance in a later section.

Before proceeding to specifics, let us ask the question: why do early deviant learnings persist? This question must be posed since most youngsters, somewhere along the way, usually acquire rather peculiar conceptions and habits of sexuality which they gradually relinquish in preference to more "mature" and conventional forms of sexual behavior. What factors contribute, then, to the persistence of deviant habits in certain individuals?

A rather general answer to this question was provided in chapter 5 when we outlined several factors which foster the continuity or perpetuation of early patterns of behavior. Let us briefly review several of those points, adapting them to the particular conditions surrounding sexual learning.

Foremost among these perpetuating factors are the consistency and sheer repetitiveness of certain environmental influences. For example, the child who is taught to "beware of sex" hears this admonishment not once but innumerable times, and not only in the form of stated precepts but in incidental ways such as the tone of voice and anxious questions of a worried parent.

Among the various forms of social reinforcement, we might mention the powerful impact of social stereotypes upon the development of homosexual behaviors. For example, an "effeminate" looking, nonathletic boy may be excluded from opportunities to acquire masculine traits and be shamed from attempting to date girls. As this stereotype shapes a feminine self-image within him and as his fears of heterosexual inadequacy grow, he may drift into homosexual relationships in which he neither is ridiculed nor feels inadequate.

It is not only external circumstances which serve to prevent the extinction of early deviant habits; many internal forces tend to perpetuate these behaviors. For example, feelings of fear and guilt often prevent youngsters from exploring new sexual outlets that could help alter their misconceptions and stimulate the acquisition of normal sexual behaviors. Similarly, many youngsters restrict their sexual life to masturbatory fantasies. Unfortunately, these fantasies may be limited to a few youthful misconceptions and distortions based on faulty or perverse experiences. As a consequence, masturbation only reinforces and strengthens their deviant conceptions. Thus, if new real life experiences are not available to extinguish these immature conceptions, these youngsters will continue, through self-reinforcement, to strengthen the same deviant notions each time they achieve pleasure in masturbation.

In the preceding paragraphs we have noted a few illustrations of how social reinforcement and self-perpetuation may strengthen early deviant habits and interfere with the acquisition of normal heterosexual behaviors. We will refer to these processes again when we next discuss the specific variants of sexual pathology.

## MAJOR VARIANTS OF SEXUAL DEVIANCE

Although the principles and processes of learning are essentially the same, it is common practice to differentiate the various forms of sexual deviance into several categories. Three groups of perversions may usefully be distinguished.

The *first* includes deviancies in the sexual object; among these are *homosexuality* (preferences for same sex mates), *pedophilia* (preferences for children) and *fetishism* (preferences for nongenital body parts or inanimate objects).

The *second* category refers to deviancies in the mode of sexual gratification; these include *exhibitionism* (exposing one's genitals before members of the opposite sex), *voyeurism* (observing the genitals or sexual behavior of others), *transvestitism* (wearing the clothes of the opposite sex) and *sadomasochism* (inflicting or suffering pain).

The *third* group pertains to deviancies in the intensity of desire and the frequency of sexual activity; among these are *nymphomania* in females

and *satyriasis* in males (excessive desire and activity) and *frigidity* in females and *impotence* in males (deficient desire and activity).

Let us keep in mind that these categories are not mutually exclusive; for example, many homosexuals (deviant object) suffer also from satyriasis (deviant intensity and frequency). We shall next discuss each of these three major categories, describing in some detail the typical conditions under which each of the variants is acquired.

### Deviations in the Sexual Object

Although the range of objects to which sexual feelings may become attached is endless (for example, toward animals or what is termed *bestiality*, or toward dead bodies referred to as *necrophilia*), we shall concern ourselves only with the three most commonly reported types—homosexuality, pedophilia and fetishism.

**Homosexuality.** Erotic relationships between members of the same sex were recorded in the earliest of ancient manuscripts. It is mentioned in the Bible, eulogized in the writings of the Greeks and Romans, commonly practiced and tacitly approved in a number of highly cultured civilizations and found among eminent historical and literary figures such as Alexander the Great, Michelangelo, Lord Byron, Oscar Wilde and Andre Gide.

Contrary to popular belief, homosexuality is neither a rare phenomenon nor a characteristic of "queer perverts." As Kinsey (1948, 1953) has shown, over 37 per cent of all males have had homosexual experiences to the point of orgasm after the onset of adolescence; 18 per cent of all males show as much homosexual as heterosexual behavior in their clinical histories; and 8 per cent have engaged exclusively in homosexual activities for at least three consecutive years after the age of 16. Although the frequency of homosexual behavior among women is about half that found among men, these figures are rather substantial and often come as a shock to those who view homosexuality as a rare phenomenon to be socially condemned and punished. Yet despite the high incidence of this habit and the fact that homosexuals manifest no greater degree of psychopathology than that found in the general population (Hooker, 1957), the view remains fixed in the public mind that these behaviors are a sign of degeneracy that calls for the arrest and incarceration of its practitioners.

Because they are subject to suspicion and potential derogation, many homosexuals live in constant fear that their habit will be exposed, resulting in their public disgrace. Not infrequently, these individuals acquire certain personality characteristics *as a consequence* of the subterfuge they invariably must practice to escape detection and the unusual pressures to which they are subject in their efforts to extract some measure of sexual gratification.

To minimize these tensions, young homosexuals tend to gravitate toward large urban settings where they may find a more congenial "homosexual community" in which to gain the emotional support and sexual outlets they need. Previously hounded and humiliated homosexuals can find in these communities a place to live and a "gay" bar or two where they may establish contacts for pursuing either a brief one night rendezvous or a more enduring "marital" relationship.

The great majority of practicing homosexuals are indistinguishable in speech, manner and dress from other people; most take great pains to avoid the appearance of effeminacy. Those who achieve the security of regular employment and the emotional gratifications available in a well-knit homosexual community, lead rather "ordinary" lives, preoccupied with the same run-of-the-mill concerns and problems that are found in the society at large. Many, however, have not been able to secure a comfortable niche for themselves in society. They experience prolonged periods of loneliness, remain apprehensive lest they be detected, grow increasingly insecure about their loss of "attractiveness" and so on. These homosexuals are in great conflict, troubled by the implacable nature of a habit they would like to be rid of but cannot.

What kinds of experiences have been shown to be related to the acquisition and the persistence of the homosexual habit? Although data relevant to this question are far from reliable or complete, several conditions, often in combination, appear with fair regularity in the histories of these patients.

*Imitation of Opposite Sex Parental Models.* Parental relationships which foster the imitation of the opposite sex is a common theme in the upbringing of many homosexuals. An early investigation of this thesis, carried out by Bender and Paster (1941), found that over 90 per cent of a group of 23 homosexuals were unable to identify with their same-sex parent because these parents were either physically absent from home, or grossly abusive or ineffectual and weak. By default, if nothing else, the opposite sex parent in these cases became the primary model for imitation. Bieber et al. (1962), in a more recent study comparing 106 homosexual males and 100

**Table 12-1 Parental Relationships of Homosexual and Heterosexual Male Patients***

| RELATIONSHIP | HOMO-SEXUALS | HETERO-SEXUALS |
|---|---|---|
| *Mother* | in per cent | |
| Demanded that she be prime center of patient's attention | 61 | 36 |
| Was seductive toward patient | 57 | 34 |
| Spent a great deal of time with patient | 65 | 27 |
| Tried to ally with patient against husband | 62 | 40 |
| Was more intimate with patient than with other male siblings | 56 | 29 |
| Encouraged masculine activities | 17 | 47 |
| Interfered with patient's heterosexual activity during and after adolescence | 58 | 35 |
| *Father* | | |
| Patient was father's favorite | 7 | 28 |
| Patient spent little time with father | 87 | 60 |
| Patient hated and feared father | 57 | 31 |
| Patient admired father | 16 | 47 |

* From Bieber (1962).

heterosexual males undergoing psychoanalysis, gave further support to this imitation thesis, and provided some details concerning how parents encourage the development of homosexual behaviors. Table 12-1 may be referred to for a comparative summary of these experiential influences. Basically, Bieber found that homosexual males spent appreciably less time with their fathers and feared and hated them to a greater extent than did equally troubled heterosexual males who suffered different forms of pathological impairments. As to their mothers, the homosexual group experienced less encouragement and more interference with masculine activities than the heterosexual group. In summary, then, male homosexuals appear not only to be deprived of adequate masculine identification, but concurrently are encouraged and even seduced to identify with the feminine role. (As a parenthetical note, we often find an early history among male homosexuals of having been dressed and groomed as little girls.)

*Aversion to the Opposite Sex.* Many homosexuals report feelings of disgust and revulsion in response to the thought or sight of the sexual anatomy of the opposite sex. These persons tend to be exclusively homosexual whereas those who experience no such distaste are often *bisexual* (homosexual *and* heterosexual).

Many factors may give rise to this aversive learning. The psychoanalysts refer to castration anxiety, a dreadful shock engendered within males upon first viewing what they believe to be the dismembered female genitalia. Whether, as the psychoanalysts assert, this provokes a fear that they also will suffer castration, leading them to avoid contact with the "mutilated" bodies of females, or whether this experience merely serves to condition an aversion to the strange and bizarre character of the female anatomy, is a point which may be debated endlessly. Rather than engage in this fruitless debate, it seems best to conclude simply that *any* event which connects opposite sex genitalia to aversive feelings will dispose the individual to avoid further contact.

White (1959) illustrates that homosexuality may be an incidental by-product of the typical attitudes conveyed by parents toward their children's early sexual interests. Thus, many a child is punished for his erotic curiosity and play with members of the opposite sex, but is never told in his early years that similar interests and activities with members of his own sex are forbidden; as a consequence, he may selectively learn to avoid heterosexual pursuits, without impairing comparable homosexual interests.

Aversions to heterosexuality may be acquired in more complex ways than simple aversive conditioning or selective punishment. As was previously noted, male homosexuals have often been dominated by affectionate but controlling mothers. The attitudes and feelings they acquire in this relationship are likely to be strong and to generalize to other women; some of these learnings may disincline them to heterosexual relationships. For example, they may have learned to fear women, to see them as demanding and "castrating" figures who control and manipulate men, as their mothers may have done both to them and to their fathers. Other homosexuals may have learned to view women as "saints," creatures who must never be defiled and besmirched by the coarse and lustful desires of men. A third group of homosexuals may have been overly attached to their "protectively loving" mothers, and now prove their endearing loyalty by avoiding the pursuit of a female replacement.

*Early Homosexual Experiences.* Bieber (1962) reports that more than half of his group of adult male homosexuals had their first homosexual experience prior to the age of 14; this contrasts with a figure of one fifth in a comparable group of adult heterosexuals. We must not conclude from this finding that early homosexual seduction must have been the "cause" of homosexuality since homosexual inclinations may already have been present before the age of 14. However, once such early involvements take place, especially if they occur prior to equivalent heterosexual gratifications, they may serve to reinforce and crystallize a rather weak and inchoate homosexual inclination. As we may recall from chapter 5, "first experiences" tend to weigh more heavily in shaping behavior than equivalent later experiences. Moreover, if these early homosexual relationships proved repeatedly pleasurable and served additionally as a source of emotional comfort and security, as Greco and Wright (1944) found in their study, then there is an increased likelihood that an early homosexual trend would be strengthened and perpetuated.

*Adolescent Peer Group Alienation.* Bieber (1962) found that over half of his group of homosexuals were isolated from normal peer relationships in adolescence. Less than one fifth engaged in competitive sports and social games, and most felt rebuffed and ridiculed by their male age-mates. Experiences such as these not only may have contributed to feelings of masculine inadequacy, but may have built a strong desire and longing for masculine acceptance and approval. Such youngsters may gravitate into homosexual relationships for a variety of reasons. First, among homosexuals they will be totally accepted despite their deficit masculinity. Second, in homosexual affairs they can receive the approval and affection from male peers that were denied them in earlier adolescent relations, as illustrated in the following segment of a more extensive case history.

*CASE 12-4*
*Isaac P., Age 46, Unmarried*

Isaac, a lifelong homosexual, was raised on an isolated farm until he was 12 years of age. His father was an alcoholic who ridiculed him for his "sissified" ways; most of Isaac's time was spent at home talking to and helping his mother and three older sisters. Isaac's sole contact with boys during this early period was limited to four hours of "strict academic work each weekday in a one-room schoolhouse" that contained first through sixth grades; there was only one other boy of his age at the school.

Isaac entered a regular junior high school at age 12 when his parents moved to a small city. In no time, he was dubbed a "sissy" since he spoke in an effeminate way and was extremely inept in sports. He recalled his desperate longing to be "like other boys" and to be "accepted by them." Unfortunately, his image was fixed in their eyes and his plight grew worse rather than better.

When he was 14, Isaac met a boy of his own age, similarly stereotyped and seeking male recognition and companionship. They became extremely close and dependent on each other, including the sharing of masturbatory fantasies. In time, they began to masturbate together and, ultimately, to masturbate each other. The "secret" they shared soon included another boy and as time progressed a number of older men. By the time Isaac was 17, his homosexual activities had become a deeply ingrained and highly rewarding pattern.

Before closing this discussion of homosexuality, we should note a few points concerning certain personality correlates of this form of sexual deviance.

A large segment of male homosexuals, but by no means all, exhibited a "soft" and non-assertive temperament in childhood. Of course, these traits in themselves do not produce homosexuality. However, youngsters who display these characteristics are more likely to fall prey to those experiences which Bieber has found to be typical of future homosexuals, e.g., rejection by their fathers, who may be disinclined to identify and associate with their "effeminate" sons, over-protection and identification with their mothers, who may be attracted to the soft and gentle temperament of their sons, and rebuff and ridicule by adolescent peers, who value competitive assertiveness and demean timidity and "weakness."

Other personality traits found among homosexuals may be acquired as a consequence of the deviant habit. Thus, the need to be alert to receptive cues on the part of potential partners and the everpresent fear of detection by a hostile society may result in the development of an exquisite hypersensitivity to the "underlying" intentions and motives of others, and to a generalized suspicion and anticipatory fear of rebuke and condemnation. Numerous homosexuals exhibit minor delusions of reference and persecution that stem, not from some deep and pervasive psychopathology, but from the kind of life they must lead in our society.

**Pedophilia.** This pathological habit focuses on children or young adolescents as sexual objects. The relationship, frequently forced upon the child, may be either of a heterosexual or homosexual nature, and usually involves the reciprocal manipulation of genitalia, or mouth-genital stimulation; heterosexual penetration and sodomy are not common except under the influence of alcoholic intoxication, or in cases of severe psychopathology where a marked loss of control is evident.

Statistics on the frequency of pedophiliac offenses are rather sparse, and etiological studies are limited essentially to case histories without systematic sampling or analysis. Pedophiliacs appear to comprise a highly diverse group in terms of age, education and socioeconomic background. Revitch and Weiss (1962) found a preference for young children among offenders over 50 and a preference for adolescents among those under 40. Kopp (1962) suggests that these men feel markedly deficient in masculine adequacy and turn toward children as a means of achieving gratification without incurring the rejection and ridicule they anticipate with adult partners. The apparent lack of interest in the act of intercourse among these men adds support to the view that they feel inadequate in adult sexuality.

Pedophilia, as a circumscribed habit, appears to represent a process of early conditioning that failed to be extinguished by more rewarding later experiences. The clinical history of most of these deviates indicates that they engaged in childhood and adolescent sexual play. These experiences, however, are not uncommon in the general population. What distinguishes pedophiliacs is the fact that they did not experience sufficient and satisfactory adult-like sexual activities which normally supplant these early behaviors. Whether a function of shyness, heterosexual inadequacy or a simple deficit of adult opportunities, the sexual practices of these individuals were restricted to masturbatory fantasies that fixated on the few satisfying sexual activities they engaged in with their childhood age-mates. The repetitive nature of these fantasies reinforced the immature level of sexual behavior previously enacted in conjunction with childhood partners.

Pedophilia frequently occurs in married adults who have children of their own; obviously, in these cases, sexual activity has not been restricted to the pedophiliac habit alone. What we find in most of these individuals is a persistent self-image of adult sexual inadequacy, a feeling that they are "performing" poorly, either by subjective evaluation, or as a consequence of repeated rejection and humiliation by their adult partners. The "regression" to pedophilia in these cases may be interpreted as an escape to earlier childhood sexual relationships in which they hope to recapture their feelings of competence and avoid the ridicule they anticipate from a more mature partner.

**Fetishism.** In this deviant habit the focus of sexual interest is either some nongenital body part, usually the foot, thighs, buttocks and hair or an inanimate object, usually an article of clothing such as undergarments, shoes and stockings. Not uncommonly, these objects acquire special powers of sexual stimulation if they were pilfered.

Minor degrees of fetishistic behavior are rather common, and within certain limits may even be viewed with respect and approval. For example, we often commend the attachment that lovers have for mementoes given to them by their mates (bracelets or locks of hair). Other fetishisms are conditioned by mass media and advertising. Thus, many men are aroused by fragrances and "seductive" garments which have been associated with sexual adventure and excitement. Somewhat closer to pathological fetishes are the habits of many adolescents who utilize photographs as a stimulus for masturbation.

The line between "acceptable" and deviant fetishism is drawn when the object involved becomes the primary source, and perhaps an indispensable one, for sexual gratification. For example, in some individuals the mere sight or feel of the fetish is sufficient to bring about an orgasm. In others, the presence of the object is a necessary adjunct to ensure ejaculation during coitus or masturbation.

The etiological origins of the fetishistic habit have been argued for over a century. One of the earliest hypotheses, proposed by Binet in 1888, viewed the perversion as a result of "accidental" circumstances in which incidental objects inadvertently were associated with periods of sexual excitement. Binet's thesis seems as valid today as when it was first formulated. Whether by direct tuition or incidental circumstance, the mere pairing of certain objects with sexual excitement may establish an association that can endure and become the preferred pattern of sexual release. This simple "conditioning" model may also account for the common practice of stealing the fetish as a means of enhancing its stimulating powers. Thus, it is not unusual for adolescents to pilfer undergarments from their mother's or their sister's wardrobes and use them as a tangible stimulus for their secretive masturbation. The whole sequence of stealing and using undergarments becomes conditioned to sexual excitement. Since adolescents usually do not find more mature sexual outlets, they may repeat the stealing prelude to masturbation over and over again, until it becomes a deeply ingrained habit.

Fetishistic habits may persist unextinguished if the individual is deprived of other forms of sexual opportunity or is hesitant by virtue of his personality about exploring different and more mature sexual outlets. In this regard, we often find that male fetishists tend to doubt their masculinity and often fear rejection and humiliation by women. However, these personality characteristics are found in common among many different types of sexual deviates. Although personality traits such as these may play some role in the initial acquisition of all these deviant habits, they appear of greater importance as factors in perpetuating the deviancy no matter what form it took, once it was acquired.

### Deviations in the Mode of Sexual Gratification

The "conditioning" model, noted previously, appears to apply as appropriately to the acquisition of deviant modes of sexual gratification as it does to deviant objects. In this section we will briefly describe four types of deviancy in line with this model: exhibitionism, voyeurism, transvestitism and sadomasochism.

**Exhibitionism.** In this perversion, perhaps second only to homosexuality as the most common of sexual deviations, gratification is obtained by exposing the genitals to members of the opposite sex in public or semipublic places such as parks, theaters, stores, and quite commonly, from a parked car along crowded streets. Children or young adolescent girls are the preferred objects for the great majority of male exhibitionists (female exhibitionists are extremely rare). Many exhibitionists engage in lewd gestures as a means of attracting viewers. Some expose themselves to induce tension and excitement for masturbatory activity. Exhibitionists tend to be consistent in the manner, setting, time of day and type and age of person to whom they expose themselves. A central element leading to the experience of gratification is a response of curiosity, embarrassment or shock on the part of the viewer. Failure to evoke such responses frequently results in feelings of deflation and disappointment; for example, Apfelberg et al. (1944) reported a case of a patient who achieved gratification only if the victim of his exhibitionistic act responded favorably to a question concerning the size of his penis. Exhibitionists often struggle to inhibit their impulse, but find that the more they restrain themselves, the more insistent their impulse becomes. Not uncommonly, they feel both shame and self-disgust following the act.

What experiences contribute to the acquisition and perpetuation of this deviation?

Certain facts strongly support the role of conditioning in acquisition. Once the behavior has been learned, it is reinforced by masturbatory fantasies and protected from extinction by personality traits which preclude the acquisition of substitute and more mature forms of sexual gratification. Let us briefly review these points.

The history of most male exhibitionists reveals a period of either preadolescent exposure to little girls in games such as "doctor and nurse," adolescent sexual play, in which reciprocal exposures take place, or some "accidental" event in which a state of inadvertent exposure gave rise to embarrassment or curiosity on the part of the female viewer. Henry (1955) reports the following recollections of an exhibitionist that illustrate such "accidents" well.

The exhibitionistic tendencies really started ten years ago. I remember one incident distinctly. I used to go bathing and undress in back of some rocks and shrubbery. While I was undressing, a woman about a block away was looking at me and was interested. I made note of this interest. I couldn't help but notice that she was of the opposite sex and that she had an interest in my body. It made me feel important and secure. Until this experience, I had been very modest and shy about showing any part of my body.

That first experience with the woman on the beach was very, very interesting. I got the impression that all women might feel the same way.

The exhibitionistic conditioning process includes not only the act of exposure itself, but an entire complex of incidental events and objects associated with the original learning experience. Quite often, we can infer the specific circumstances surrounding the initial acquisition of the habit by noting the setting and objects the exhibitionist utilizes repetitively for his act. It should not be surprising that children and adolescent girls are common victims since the original setting in which the habit was learned frequently involved exposure before one's playmates. Furthermore, the characteristic expectation among exhibitionists that their victim will register surprise or embarrassment may be seen as a replica of the curious or shocked response of the little girls to whom they exposed themselves in childhood.

Of course, many youngsters who never become exhibitionists engaged in childhood sex games or were involved in accidental exposures which proved exciting or stimulating. However, in these cases, subsequent experiences may have extinguished or overridden the exhibitionist response. To account for the failure of this habit to be extinguished among future exhibitionists, we must add to our formula a number of secondary factors. First, the experience may have been repeated innumerable times either in fact or in fantasy. Second, the individual may have possessed personality traits such as shyness or feelings of masculine inadequacy which precluded subsequent sexual experiences that could have diverted the exhibitionistic habit toward more adult forms of behavior.

**Voyeurism.** This perversion, also known as *scotophilia*, represents the habit of clandestine peeping as a primary mode of sexual stimulation. These individuals are popularly referred to as "peeping toms," a label drawn from the famous story of the tailor of Coventry who could not refrain from looking at Lady Godiva as she rode naked through the town market place (this tale portrays rather nicely the popular approval given to women who exhibit themselves and the harsh condemnation of men who seek to view her).

As practiced by voyeurs, the act usually centers on the surreptitious viewing either of women undressing or adults in the act of coitus. The acquisition and perpetuation of this habit can best be understood in terms of the learning model we previously formulated. Thus, we find in the histories of these patients that many of them gained their first exposure to the exciting and "illicit" phenomenon of sex either by peeking at their mothers and sisters as they undressed or by accidentally viewing their parents during intercourse. Repetitions of this type of event, either in reality or through masturbatory fantasies, reinforce the practice. If by virtue of their personality they failed to explore and engage in sexual activities which might have replaced this habit or if subsequent sexual experiences proved unsatisfactory or disheartening, there is a high probability that the voyeuristic habit will persist or recur.

**Transvestitism.** The term transvestitism literally means cross-dressing; it refers to the habit of achieving sexual gratification by wearing the clothing of the opposite sex or by genital contact with such clothing.

Fetishism and transvestitism are alike in that both employ objects as instruments of sexual excitement. However, the transvestite has no particular attachment for the object he utilizes; it is merely a means of facilitating a temporary self-image that he is a member of the opposite sex.

Because of these brief periods of self-identification with the opposite sex and the not infrequent covariation of homosexuality and transvestitism, many authors contend that these

Figure 12-2     Transvestitism. *A.* As a male. *B.* As a female. (From Olkon, D.: Essentials of Neuropsychiatry. Philadelphia, Lea and Febiger, 1945.)

perversions are merely two sides of the same coin. However, the great majority of transvestites do not display the cardinal sign of overt homosexuality, that of preferring members of their own sex as their sexual partners.

What are the etiological origins of this deviant habit?

Many of the case studies reported in the literature can be interpreted most parsimoniously in accord with the conditioning model provided earlier. Let us illustrate some of the typical features in the following case.

*CASE 12-5*
*John T., Age 20, College Student*

John reported numerous events in support of the view that he had been the object of maternal seduction, and recalled quite vividly that at the age of 13 or 14 his mother served as his primary source of sexual fantasies. These maternal experiences contrasted with those of a harshly rejecting father with whom he had no rapport. Thus, John was unsure of his masculine adequacy, having been subjected to repeated humiliation by his father; in relation to his mother, however, he felt both secure and wanted.

John recalled his constant state of confusion throughout childhood as to what sex he would rather be. At about the age of 14, he began to "borrow" his mother's undergarments for purposes of masturbation. Clothed in her brassiere

and panties, he was able both to be his accepting and kindly mother and, at the same time utilize her as a receptive object for his masculine sexual fantasies. The transvestitic act enabled him to be simultaneously both male and female. This "split" in sexual identification was illustrated nicely in the following description he provided:

"When I masturbate, I try to look at myself in the mirror as if I were two persons. The brassiere and panties make me feel as if I were a woman. At the same time I see my erect penis and know that I am also a man. I sort of switch back and forth so that I am a man masturbating with a woman at his side at the same time."

Whatever the original combination of psychogenic events, and it may be "pure chance" and nothing more, the process of viewing oneself as both a man and woman, as in a split screen, becomes the central focus of sexual fantasy and gratification. This initial habit is strengthened by repeated pleasurable reinforcements through these "mixed" masturbatory images. If the individual lacks the personality disposition or physical opportunities by which new habits can be acquired to supplant the practice, it may persist well into adulthood.

**Sadomasochism.** In this perversion the infliction of pain is a prerequisite for sexual excitement and gratification. Sadism, a term derived from the Marquis de Sade, who ostensibly practiced sexually motivated cruelty, refers to the act of inflicting pain upon a sexual partner. Masochism, a term derived from the novelist Leopold von Sacher-Masoch, whose fictional characters were obsessed with the sexual pleasures of pain, refers to the act of accepting and perhaps soliciting punishment as a necessary element of sexual gratification. It is common to combine these two deviant habits since they are frequently present in the same person. Where they do not coexist, sadism usually is found in men whereas masochism is more common in women. In some cases, sexual gratification is fully achieved as a consequence of the hostile act alone, e.g., achieving orgasm while being abused. In others, pain or the act of inflicting it serves as an exciting and energizing prelude to otherwise normal coitus.

Sadomasochism, as a circumscribed habit, can be understood well in terms of the conditioning model presented earlier. Of course, as we have noted before, these same behaviors may also reflect a direct or symbolic expression of pervasive personality pathology; these cases, however, may best be understood within the framework of one or another of the pathological personality syndromes.

What experiences, then, serve to condition

the sadomasochistic habit? Two types of events are frequently encountered in these cases.

First, many youngsters, either by direct observation or by exposure to books, TV and newspaper reports or by direct parental tutelage, come to associate sexuality with brutality and pain. The fear and tension generated by these learnings deeply impress children, and often result in the distorted image that sex is invariably connected either with the infliction or the suffering of physical and mental abuse. Armed with these bizarre conceptions, the youngster reinforces them through his own masturbatory fantasies, and pursues and expects them as an inevitable and necessary ingredient of the real sexual act.

The second source of this perverted habit may be traced to attitudes of shame, disgust and guilt toward sexual matters usually engendered by parental or religious teaching. Conditioned to view sex as "dirty" or as a sign of degradation and sin, the youngster reinforces this image through fantasy and carries it with him into the sexual act. Both sadistic and masochistic habits may arise as a consequence. The sadist handles his guilt by venting contempt for his partner's willingness to engage in the despised act; prior to intercourse, he degrades and even tortures her. The masochist, guilt-ridden for her "lascivious" intentions, must subject herself to physical flagellation and verbal abuse as an expiatory prerequisite to the forbidden and sinful act.

### Deviation in the Intensity and Frequency of Sexual Activity

Perversions included in this group represent extremes in sexual interest and desire, from marked aversions and deficits to incessant preoccupations and involvements. The discussion that follows does not apply to cases of brief duration. For example, temporary impotence or frigidity usually reflects not deeply ingrained habits but transient reactions to stressful circumstances of a temporary nature, e.g., a woman who becomes frigid after learning of her husband's extramarital affairs would not be classed in this syndrome. Similarly, we do not include among the categories of circumscribed habits those deficient or excessive sexual behaviors which derive from a more pervasive form of personality pathology; these disturbances are "symbolic" expressions of more generalized traits, not habits acquired in response to prior and specifically sexual experiences, e.g., the behavior of a negativistic female personality, who employs frigidity as a means of manipulating her husband, would not have her behavior properly understood or categorized as

a circumscribed learned habit since her frigidity is merely one among many instrumentalities of a more pervasive coping style.

**Impotence and Frigidity.** These disturbances refer to deficits either in the desire for sexual experiences or the capacity to fulfill them. Impotence is the term applied to men who suffer this impairment, and frigidity is its counterpart in women.

The difficulty may be relative or absolute, selective or pervasive. Some individuals not only lack all desire, but even have strong negative reactions merely to the thought of sex. Others desire relations and often make genuine attempts but succeed only on rare occasions. Many experience no sexual difficulties with certain partners, usually prostitutes or women they hold in contempt, but are completely blocked and impotent with their spouses. In short, there are innumerable variations in the pattern and particulars of these impairments.

What are the origins of these deficits of sexual desire or competence?

An extremely common source is faulty training in sex attitudes, especially prominent in the upbringing of girls. The view that sex is bad, dirty and sinful can establish deeply etched fears and guilt feelings which not only impair desire, but may create ineradicable aversions toward anything even remotely connected with sex. These distorted childhood habits and attitudes, reinforced throughout adolescence, persist into marriage where sexual relations are fully sanctioned. Even though the person may consciously be desirous, her ingrained fear of detection and punishment or the guilt she associates with sexual "lust and sin" remains unaltered, and results in a frustrating and disheartening frigidity.

Along similar lines, many women carry into marriage the tension and fear of pregnancy they acquired as a result of anxious premarital relationships. The dread and anguish associated with the act of coitus that was built up in these earlier experiences persist, and the grown woman finds herself unable to relax and "let go," despite the fact that it would now be perfectly proper for her to become pregnant.

Attitudes and feelings associated with the first sexual experience or set of experiences can play a crucial role in future sexual relations. As was noted above, a habitual fear of pregnancy may linger as a deterrent to sexual desire long after such concerns should have waned. In a different way, both men and women may have their "romantic" expectations shattered by the realities of a faulty early sexual experience. Intense pain, clumsy awkwardness, feelings of dissatisfaction and incompetence or other forms of unpleasantness and disillusionment, may set the stage for longstanding sexual anxieties and aversions. Once acquired in these initial ventures, these feelings perpetuate themselves in a vicious circle; thus, the mere anticipation of pain, tension or humiliation gives rise to these very feelings and becomes a self-fulfilling prophecy, thereby reinforcing the expectancy and starting the circle over again.

Whether a function of actual distressful experience or a result of a generalized anticipation of personal inadequacy or unattractiveness, many individuals come to the sexual act with fear and trepidation. As was noted above, the presence of worries and tensions precipitates unrewarding and humiliating sexual experiences which, in turn, reinforce the initial anxiety and self derogation and thereby perpetuate the problem.

**Satyriasis and Nymphomania.** Exaggerated or insatiable sexual desires is termed satyriasis in men and nymphomania in women. These sexual preoccupations and involvements may be confined to a single marital partner or may be pursued in a variety of promiscuous premarital and extramarital relations. Although most of these deviates center their attentions on members of the opposite sex, it is not uncommon for homosexuals to be overly engrossed with sexual activities.

These perversions, viewed as circumscribed habits, may be traced to a number of different learning experiences.

Prominent among them is exposure to models of imitation. In families in which mothers are excessively promiscuous with "strange" men or are sexually seductive with their husbands as a means of "cooling their tempers," the young girl may learn comparable habits and attitudes of sexual behavior. Similar patterns of imitation occur among "delinquent" and "hippie" groups in which promiscuous involvements become a "badge" of ingroup membership, a necessary pastime modeled in accord with group standards and values. Once initiated and reinforced by security and status, the habit may persist either of its own accord or on the basis of some rationalized belief such as "true love" is synonymous with "sexual freedom." Imitation of idealized models also follows from the popular belief among male adolescents that "masculine power and virility" correlate with frequent and varied conquests. The status and reputation of those who succeed in these exploits provide a model to be copied among those who need to "prove

their manliness." Insatiable habits may be acquired in this pursuit; and, since perfect success cannot be attained in one's pursuits, the person will feel that no matter how successful a "man" he has been, he can always do better.

Similar habits of sexual insatiability may have their origin in homes in which erotic feelings and affection were stimulated, but where strict parental attitudes forbade sex and the overt expression of warmth and tenderness. As a consequence of such deprivations, youngsters may have an acute need for outlets for their bottled-up erotic and affectionate emotions. Pained by parental aloofness and undemonstrativeness, they search not only for an outlet, but for the opposite of that to which they were accustomed. Out of desperation, if nothing else, they stumble upon a relationship in which "no holds are barred" in the expression of warmth, love and passion. The sharp contrast to the barren and cold home environment makes this experience doubly reinforcing; and to it, of course, are added the genuine pleasures of ardor and sexual intimacy. So reinforced, these youngsters continue to pursue more of the same, sliding bit by bit into a habitual pattern of nymphomania or satyriasis, as illustrated in the following case.

*CASE 12-6*
*Desi T., Age 16, High School Student*

Desi was admitted to the psychiatric ward of a general hospital following an attempted suicide; upon examination, it was found that she was pregnant. Interviews with the girl, her parents, two brothers and one of her boyfriends revealed the following.

Desi's parents were extremely "proper and strict" about sex and gave their children no leeway in dating and attending school dances; home in general was a cold and formal place. Although all the children felt deprived of affection, the two older brothers "accepted" their fate and submitted to their parents' strictures. Desi, however, had "always been sort of rebellious."

When Desi was 13 she met a 15 year old boy with whom she "fell in love." Petting activities began within a few weeks, and after three or four months, Desi experienced coitus for the first time. The event was referred to by her as "marvelous." To keep her parents from being unduly suspicious, she informed them that she was in a "special honors" club that met four times a week after school (Desi was in fact an excellent student). This story enabled her to visit her boyfriend's home almost every afternoon; both his parents worked, and he had no siblings at home. For three years, they engaged in intercourse nearly every school day. When Desi was 15, she met another boy whom she began to see one or two evenings a week for similar purposes. A third, older man had appeared on the scene in recent months and she pursued her pleasures with him as well. Upon learning that she was pregnant, Desi felt her "goose was cooked," thought of running away, became confused and distraught and then tried to "do away" with herself by taking an overdose of sleeping pills.

## ADDICTION REACTIONS
(DSM-II: *Alcoholism; Drug Dependence*)

The "addiction" label has been used rather freely to describe a number of diverse preoccupations with activities such as golf, TV and gambling. There are similarities between these normal social absorptions and those traditionally subsumed under the addiction label, e.g., the needs they fulfill, the way in which they are acquired and so on. However, the official definition within psychopathology restricts the addiction term to involvements with certain chemical substances, notably alcohol and drugs.

The general literature dealing with drugs has grown rapidly in recent years owing to their increased use among college and high school students. Despite the marked concern of parents and authorities and the fascination and intrigue that young people exhibit with regard to the newer drugs, these chemicals are of little intrinsic interest in themselves to psychopathologists, although their effects and manner of acquisition are worthy of attention. Concern and fascination notwithstanding, however, we shall deal with drugs only briefly. The incidence of alcoholism, a consequence largely of public sanction and active promotion, makes it a problem even more serious than that of drugs. Despite its wide prevalence, however, alcoholic addiction is acquired in a fairly simple and straightforward way; thus, it too requires but a brief discussion as a topic of psychopathology.

## ALCOHOLISM

Although early civilizations used and identified alcoholic intoxication with religious fervor and ecstasy, persistent inebriation was almost invariably condemned as a sign of moral degradation. Nevertheless, numerous figures of historical eminence were plagued with extended bouts of alcoholic indulgence, an ailment that apparently must have aided as well as impaired their attainments.

We shall focus on five aspects of this syndrome: incidence, effects, phases, coping functions and correlated personality traits and etiology.

**Incidence.** Upwards of 75 million Americans imbibe alcoholic beverages in varying degrees. Alcoholic addiction, however, defined essentially by an insatiable craving and by the fact that an individual's work efficiency and social functioning have been chronically impaired, occurs in about 5 million cases, ranking the habit as the fourth most prevalent of all medical problems. Two hundred thousand new cases are reported each year, and about 15 per cent of first admissions to mental hospitals are diagnosed as suffering from this impairment. The addiction is found in all races and nationalities, but its incidence is unevenly distributed; for example, the rate is especially high among the Irish and the French, but rather low among Jews, Chinese and Italians. In general, more men than women are alcoholics, the ratios varying from 2 to 1 in some countries to as high as 25 to 1 in others.

**Effects.** Among the major and immediate effects of alcoholic intake is a numbing or depressing of the higher centers of the brain (the precise physiology involved is irrelevant to the purposes of our discussion). This results, generally, in (a) a lessening of inhibitions, often evidenced in increased sociability and self-confidence, (b) a reduction in felt tensions and worries, typically sensed as feelings of warmth, relaxation and well-being and (c) an impairment of intellectual and perceptual functions, manifested in faulty judgments, blurred vision and physical incoordination. Severe or pathological intoxication may result from a brief or extended alcoholic debauch; during these acute episodes the patient is markedly confused and disoriented. In some cases there is active hallucination and an acting out of perverse or violent behaviors. Not uncommonly, there is total amnesia for the events of the episode. Numerous effects may be traced to the long-term addiction to alcohol. Among them are delirium tremens, Wernicke's syndrome and Korsakoff's psychosis; these symptoms, however, reflect the presence of permanent biophysical defects and will be described therefore in the following chapter.

**Phases.** Jellinek, in his authoritative studies of alcoholic addiction (1952, 1960), suggests that the sequence from moderate social drinking to chronic alcoholism follows a fairly predictable sequence, which he breaks down into four stages.

1. The first stage, labeled the *prealcoholic symptomatic phase,* begins with conventional social drinking. Here the individual may be faced with the normal stresses of life, but he learns to his pleasure that alcohol can diminish his tensions and bolster his confidence. Acquainted now

with this agreeable means of escape from pressure and tension, he no longer bothers to tolerate or "put up with" the everyday strains which most people take in stride. With but minimal provocation, he turns increasingly to his morale booster, his dissipator of minor as well as major woes. This transition, manifesting itself ultimately in daily indulgence, proceeds imperceptibly, step by step, over a period of several months to two years.

2. The second, or *prodromal phase,* begins with a rather sudden and unexplainable amnesic experience in which the individual does not lose consciousness, but has no recall afterward of his actions and surrounding events. These episodes, often repeated, do not necessarily follow a heavy bout with alcohol. As this phase continues, the person begins to engage in surreptitious drinking, becomes preoccupied with plans for his "next" drink, starts to "gulp down" rather than sip his glassful and evidences the first signs of an awareness and concern that his habit has progressed beyond simple social drinking.

3. In the third, or *crucial phase,* the individual has "lost control"; once he takes a drink he does not stop until he is too uncoordinated to hold the bottle, or too ill to imbibe more. Despite his inability to stop once he has started, he is still able to control whether or not to take that first drink. This measure of control enables him periodically to "give up" alcohol for periods of weeks or even months. Ultimately, however, he "gives in" just once, with the inevitable consequence of complete intoxication.

The inevitable downward spiral picks up momentum and the alcoholic begins the practice of drinking heavily during the day. Faced with impaired work efficiency, dismay and reproval from family and friends, he begins to concoct alibis to himself and others to justify his habit and its consequences. His deceptions and alibis lead to exasperation and recrimination from others. His inability to control himself leads not only to guilt but to job dismissals, abandonment by friends, resentments and conflicts at home.

Now he anticipates failure and humiliation, begins protectively to withdraw from social contact and thereby increases his isolation and his dependency on alcohol. This vicious, perpetuating circle of increased alcoholic dependency ultimately involves the deterioration of physical health. Alcohol serves now as the primary source of dietary sustenance, resulting in severe nutritional deficiencies and distressing physical ailments.

When he ventures into those prolonged bouts

of intoxication, known as "benders," his limited physical reserves are strained beyond their limits, resulting in his first hospital admission for alcoholism. His dependence on alcohol is no longer merely psychological. He has become a true addict, suffering "withdrawal symptoms" that can be alleviated only by further alcoholic indulgence. Beset by guilt, recrimination and a physical need for alcohol, he no longer is able to abstain, starts the habit of drinking upon awakening each morning and crosses the line into the final phase of addiction.

4. The fourth, or *chronic phase,* is characterized by continual drinking and repeated benders. Judgment, responsibility and ethical considerations are cast to the wind. Life is composed of drinking and more drinking, with no thought to its consequence upon family and future. A function of habit, expectancy and physiochemical body changes, he is now precipitated into a state of stupor with half the alcohol previously required. Despite prolonged periods of oblivion, he returns to the bottle, not so much to dilute the impact of his memories and his sorry state, as to avoid physical withdrawal symptoms such as "the shakes," violent nausea, hallucinated images and bizarre fears. The circle is now complete; he is totally addicted, both psychologically and physically.

**Coping Functions and Personality Correlates.** The question arises, given the devastating effects of alcoholic addiction, of why the habit persists, that is, what functions does it fulfill to compensate for its many inevitable and crushing losses. In contrast to other pathological habits and their disastrous consequences, the solution to the alcoholic habit is so simple and uncomplicated: stop drinking. What propels the addict to persist in his "foolishness" with so simple a solution at hand? Does this perverse habit reflect a deeper and more pervasive pathology, and if so, is there a particular personality pattern disposed to alcoholism? Let us address ourselves to these questions in the following paragraphs.

A literature review (Fenichel, 1945; Menninger, 1938; Levy, 1958; Zwerling and Rosenbaum, 1959; Coleman, 1964) will provide us with an endless number of coping functions associated with the use of alcohol. These varied and diverse aims of the alcoholic habit can be grouped into four categories: *self-image enhancement,* e.g., providing a feeling of well-being and omnipotence and bolstering self-esteem and confidence; *disinhibition of restraints,* e.g., allowing previously controlled impulses such as hostility or extramarital and homosexual inclinations to be released without feeling personal responsibility and guilt; *dissolution of psychic pain,* e.g., alleviating the anguish of frustration and disappointment, as in a "dead-end" job or a hopeless marriage, or blotting out awareness of one's loneliness, meaningless existence and feelings of futility; and *masochistic self-destruction,* e.g., relieving one's sense of guilt and worthlessness by destroying one's career or breaking up one's family. It is evident, then, that there is no single purpose or function to which the alcoholic habit is directed; in fact, some of them, e.g., dissolution of psychic pain and masochistic self-destruction appear at odds.

Given this diversity in alcoholic coping functions, it is not surprising that no one has been able to pinpoint an "alcoholic personality type." Some are impulsive, expansive and hostile; others are withdrawn and introverted; still others are plagued with guilt, tension and worry. Zwerling and Rosenbaum (1959), for example, include such varied characteristics among alcoholics as schizoid traits, dependent traits, depressive traits, hostile and self-destructive impulses and sexual immaturity. In short, research and clinical observation lead us to conclude that almost all forms of "troubled and maladjusted personalities" may be found among alcoholics, none of them distinctive or unique to alcoholism, and none of them necessarily a cause rather than a consequence of the habit. Moreover, no evidence has been adduced to tell us why alcohol rather than other means has become the primary instrument for adaptive coping in these patients. In the following section, however, we will offer some tentative hypotheses that are specific to the development of the alcoholic habit.

**Etiology.** Disentangling the web of interacting determinants in behavior habits that involve biochemical properties, such as alcoholism, is especially difficult. The interplay between predisposing constitutional factors and experiential determinants is so intricate and subtle that no one as yet has been able to trace its relations. Most studies seeking to implicate a role for biogenic influences either have been poorly designed or achieve results that lend themselves to psychogenic as well as biogenic interpretations. As matters now stand, experiential determinants are believed to be primary.

Conceived as a circumscribed learned habit, although one in which there is an inevitable involvement of biological factors, alcoholism may be traced through a sequence of three etiological influences. *First,* incidental observation and imitation usually serve as the *original* source that gives rise to the practice of drinking. *Second,* a variety of positive reinforcements occur in conjunction with drinking, strengthening the habit and ultimately leading to what may be termed a "psychological addiction." *Third,* prolonged psychological addiction leads to biochemical changes of cell metabolism which result in a physiological craving for alcohol, that is, a "physiological addiction." Let us elaborate this sequential etiological hypothesis.

1. Vicarious learning seems to be a universal source for the original acquisition both of drinking habits and its use as a coping instrument. Most notable in this regard is exposure to parental models and to the well-advertised image of drinking as a social lubricant and dilutor of tension. Youngsters may learn to believe that drinking is sanctioned for purposes of coping with frustration or dissolving guilt and responsibility, simply by observing similar uses on the part of their parents. In a relevant study showing the impact of parental modeling, Roe et al. (1945) found that children who were separated from their alcoholic parents and placed in foster homes were no more likely to become alcoholic than were children of nonalcoholic parents, and much less likely than those who remained with alcoholic parents (this study demonstrates also the invalidity of the argument that alcoholism is a hereditary disease).

Not to be overlooked among the forces of vicarious learning and imitation are common social stereotypes regarding the drinking habits of certain ethnic groups. Thus, the popular image that "the Irish are drunks" may not only serve as an implicit model to copy for youngsters of Irish descent, but also be a form of encouragement and sanction for drinking. When faced with the normal strains of life, an Irish youngster may turn to alcohol rather than to other forms of coping, because he feels that this course of behavior is not only expected, but inevitable among members of his ethnic background.

2. Once the practice of "normal" social drinking has become established, the powers of positive reinforcement become more significant than those of imitation. Given the presence of any of the various coping needs which alcohol can reward, drinking if practiced repetitively can become deeply ingrained as a habit. Alcohol not only serves as a useful source of reinforcement, but it is especially powerful in this regard since its effects are immediate, in contrast to the slow and delayed character of other, more complicated, forms of coping. Because of this distinctive feature of immediacy, the drinking response pre-

empts all other coping methods. Progressively, then, the individual's alternatives for dealing with tension and discomfort are narrowed to this one preeminent response.

Of course, there are negative consequences of drinking (hangovers, wives' complaints and loss of job), but these negative effects are not as immediately experienced as its positive rewards. Moreover, if the person pauses to reflect on these troublesome consequences, he can quickly turn off these thoughts simply by taking another drink.

Given the rapid and tremendously reinforcing properties of alcohol, why is it that most people who take an occasional drink do not become alcoholics?

For the main part, the answer is that they either have found other, more suitable, ways of coping with their discomforts or are not so troubled in the first place that alcohol proves strongly reinforcing. There is a third explanation, however, one that stems from individual differences in the biological tolerance for alcohol. Although the evidence favoring a constitutional *disposition* to alcoholism is equivocal at best, there is no question that many individuals have a constitutional *aversion* to alcohol, experiencing numerous biological discomforts such as nausea, dizziness and sleepiness. These discomforts are *immediate negative reinforcers* that come more quickly and outweigh the positive rewards, serving therefore to preclude any possible development of the alcoholic habit. In contrast, those who do *not* experience these aversive effects, consume substantial quantities of alcohol, achieve their associated positive reinforcements and find themselves on the road to alcoholism.

3. The final stage of addiction follows a long-term psychological addiction. Ultimately, there are changes in the individual's cell metabolism which result in severe withdrawal symptoms (tremors, nausea, fevers and hallucinations) when drinking is terminated. At this stage, alcohol has become more than a psychological habit; it is a substance which the alcoholic craves to ward off a physiologically induced suffering. Now, as the vicious circle expands, he drinks not only for psychological reasons, but to avoid the negative reinforcements of physiological withdrawal. He is both a psychological and physiological addict.

## DRUG DEPENDENCE

Alcohol has not been the only instrument for **facilitating man's** need to relieve pain and mo-

notony. Drugs also have served since ancient times to moderate the discomforts of life and to expand its illusory possibilities.

Alcohol is a drug, although Western customs have guided our thinking otherwise. There are as many differences in chemical composition and effects between drugs as there are between alcohol and most drugs. In short, were it not for our customary practices, alcohol would be viewed as just one of a number of chemical substances to which people become habituated and addicted. Viewed in this way, the preceding discussion on "alcoholic addiction" applies in large measure to "drug addiction."

Because of condemnatory and legal attitudes toward drugs in this country, the incidence of drug abuse is much less than that found with alcohol. However, in recent years there has been a marked rise in the usage of certain hallucinogens and stimulants, especially among "privileged" adolescents. This increased incidence has given rise to a flood of public concern and consternation. For these reasons, it may be instructive to differentiate the major types of drugs and their effects. In addition, we will touch upon certain features of acquisition, coping and personality correlates that distinguish drug dependence from alcoholism.

The World Health Organization has suggested a useful distinction between drug *addiction* and drug *habituation*. The addictive drugs, notably those listed as "narcotics" and "sedatives" in table 12-2, sooner or later, *always* produce an overpowering craving. Ultimately, there is a need for increased dosages, followed by severe physical symptoms upon drug withdrawal. In contrast, habit-forming nonaddictive drugs, such as those included under the labels "hallucinogens" and "stimulants" in table 12-2, do not generate compulsive cravings, although the individual ordinarily acquires a strong inclination to continue the habit. Furthermore, there usually is no increased tolerance for the drug which would produce a need for higher dosages. Crucial to the distinction between addiction and habituation is the fact that the termination of the habituation drugs does not result in physical withdrawal symptoms.

Table 12-2 provides a brief summary of the major types of drugs; these are grouped into four major categories: narcotics, sedatives, hallucinogens and stimulants. The first two meet the criteria of addictive drugs whereas the latter two are viewed as habituation drugs.

*Narcotics,* and in particular heroin, are notably harmful in that tolerance builds up rapidly

## Table 12-2   Drugs: Their Sources and Effects

| DRUG | SLANG NAME | SOURCE | EFFECTS |
|------|-----------|--------|---------|
| **Narcotics** | | | |
| Opium | | Dried, coagulated milk of unripe opium poppy pod | Pain relief; drowsy indifference; aimless and drifting feeling; loss of appetite; temporary impotence; severe withdrawal symptoms such as cramps and tremors lasting four to five days. |
| Morphine | M; Miss Emma | 10–1 Reduction of crude opium | |
| Heroin | H; Horse; Junk | Converted morphine | |
| **Sedatives** | | | |
| Nembutal | Yellow jackets | | Calm, subdued, relaxed state; dull, depressive mood; incoherency and confusion; withdrawal symptoms such as convulsions and vomiting lasting seven to ten days or more. |
| Seconal | Red devils | Barbituric acid derivatives | |
| Luminal | Purple hearts | | |
| Amytal | Blue heavens | | |
| **Hallucinogens** | | | |
| Marijuana | Pot; Grass | Resinous female hemp plant | Euphoric relaxation; altered perceptions; impaired judgment. |
| Peyote | Cactus | Dried cactus buttons with mescaline | Visual hallucinations; feelings of omnipotence; marked anxieties lasting six to twelve hours. |
| LSD | Acid; Hawk | Synthetic chemical | |
| STP | | Atropine-like synthetic | Same as above, but more intense and lasting three to four days. |
| **Stimulants** | | | |
| Cocaine | Coke; Snow | Alkaloid of cocoa leaf | Temporary blissful state preceded by headaches and followed by insomnia |
| Benzedrine | A; Bennies | Synthetic chemical | Energy and exuberance, followed by hypertension, confusion and anxiety. |
| Dexedrine | Pep pills; Dexies | | |
| Methedrine | Speed; Crystals | Synthetic chemical | Rapidly mounting exhilaration, followed by marked anxiety and delirium. |

and results in an increasing need for this highly expensive addictive. It is not uncommon to find, within an extremely short period, that every aspect of the addict's life is centered on ways to acquire the drug. Because of the expense involved, the heroin addict, often a member of an underprivileged minority, gives up his few valued belongings, becomes careless about his diet and health and is drawn by a desperate search for funds into illegal activities. *Sedative* addictions produced by barbiturate drugs are more common than generally recognized, especially among middle and upper class adults. In contrast to heroin, this addiction can be controlled and stabilized with minimum dosages. However, should the addiction be prolonged, severe brain dysfunctions may result, and marked withdrawal symptoms are inevitable.

*Hallucinogens* and *stimulants* are associated neither with increased body tolerance, physiological cravings nor severe withdrawal symptoms upon termination, that is, they are not addiction drugs. However, the individual may become psychologically dependent on these agents in the sense that he finds himself unwilling or unable to "chuck the habit" he has built up. Marijuana and cocaine are among the oldest and best known drugs used to induce temporary euphoria and relaxation (cocaine has been listed in some quarters as an addictive drug, but it does not fulfill the criteria of physiological dependence and withdrawal symptoms). In recent years, marijuana, better known as "pot" or "grass," has attained great popularity among "liberated" college students. Here, it is used as a means of "cooling it," that is, gaining a pleasant interlude of mild euphoria to block out what are felt to be the absurd values and oppressive regulations of a dehumanized adult society. This drug has no known harmful physical effects, but it often serves as a prelude to the use of other less benign agents. LSD (lysergic acid diethylamide), although not a narcotic, has proved a mixed blessing to many youths who have dabbled with it. Unquestionably,

LSD is an instrument capable of evoking a dramatic experience, a means of expanding and sensitizing conscious awareness, but it may also precipitate extremely frightening hallucinations and emotions that can last well after the chemical residues of the drug have worn off. Among the various amphetamines—benzedrine, dexedrine and methedrine—the last-named, known as "speed," has recently come into prominence as a source of rapidly induced exhilaration. However, it may also induce severe anxieties and delirium, not uncommonly resulting in homicide, rape and suicide.

What coping functions are fulfilled by these drugs?

As was stated earlier, drugs and alcohol appear to fulfill essentially similar purposes, although perhaps in somewhat different population groups. Thus, we would include "self-image enhancement," "disinhibition of restraints," "dissolution of psychic pain" and "masochistic self-destruction" among the various coping aims of drug use.

Next, we may ask if there are differences between those who become addicted to alcohol rather than to drugs.

There is a considerable overlap, of course, but it appears that drug reactions, with the exception of sedative addictions, is primarily a problem of the young. Relatively few people over 40 are frequent users of narcotics, hallucinogens and stimulants. This disproportionate difference between age groups reflects in part the relative recency of the discovery and popularity of certain drugs. Thus, older people who were "addictively disposed" years ago could not have been exposed to these agents until well after they had been "hooked" on something else, in all likelihood alcohol. Moreover, until fairly recently, the image of the drug addict was that of a "lower class degenerate," hardly an inviting model for the young of the past to identify with. This contrasts with the "alienated intellectual hippie" image associated with current-day users, an attractive model to be emulated by "ingroup" college students. (We might note parenthetically that this model is associated only with the use of marijuana, LSD and other mild or "mind-expanding" drugs; it does not extend to heroin, which still is associated with "lower class degeneracy" or to methedrine, which prompts "mindless" hyperactivity and delirium.)

Are there differences in personality among those who use different drugs?

No clinical research or data have accumulated to provide an answer to this question. From the few unsystematic studies available, it would appear that drug choice may be influenced in part by the characteristic coping style of the individual. In other words, addicts may "select" a drug that is consonant with and facilitates their preferred mode of dealing with stress. If there is merit to this speculative hypothesis, we would expect to find a disproportionate number of detached personalities among narcotic users, since these drugs would facilitate their tendencies to social withdrawal and indifference. Similarly, sedatives might be preferred among the passive-dependent and ambivalent patterns to aid in controlling impulses that can upset their equanimity and dependency status. Hallucinogens, to extend this series of conjectures, might be found more commonly among passive-independent types who characteristically turn inward to enlarge their world of experience. And lastly, stimulants may be preferred by active-dependents who seek excitement, change and adventure, or by active-independents who dread feelings of weakness and lassitude, and desire energy to act out their assertive impulses.

We have touched previously on some of the etiological factors conducive to the development of drug habits. They appear, essentially, to be the same as those found in alcoholism: imitation as the source of habit origination; positive reinforcement of coping aims as a means of strengthening the habit; and finally, body chemical changes resulting in physiological addiction. Narcotic and sedative addictions often have their origin in medical treatment; thus, morphine may have been prescribed to relieve pain, and seconal recommended to counter insomnia. The hallucinogenic habit is most commonly acquired as an incidental by-product of peer group involvement; thus, "smoking pot" or "tripping with LSD" has come to be expected of everyone associated with the "alienated" adolescent subculture.

## REMEDIAL APPROACHES IN CIRCUMSCRIBED LEARNED REACTIONS

Despite differences in their form of expression, circumscribed learned reactions are alike in their stimulus specificity, e.g., an individual suffering a circumscribed fear reaction behaves "normally," that is, fearlessly, except when confronted with a particular stimulus. Furthermore, each reaction tends to be manifested in a uniform and consistent fashion, e.g., a sexual deviate manifests the same perversion time and again, and usually in the same environmental settings. Each of these response habits is repeated innumerable times until it becomes a deeply ingrained form of behavior. Moreover, these reactions are strongly reinforced upon repetition, e.g., fear and sexual responses are associated with intense activation levels; addiction reactions provide rapid if not immediate gratification; developmental habits are acquired early in life, tending to preempt other alternative responses. In short, unless it is superseded by stronger incompatible responses or extinguished by deconditioning experiences, it is highly likely that these learned reactions will persist unmodified, as many of them do.

What therapeutic methods can be employed to eliminate or moderate these pathological reactions? Several approaches, either alone or in concert, may be recommended.

First, the stimulus conditions to which the pathological habit is a response may be altered by "environmental management." For example, parents may be counseled in the case of a stuttering child to terminate their destructive practice of interrupting and criticizing the youngster's speech efforts. Similarly, a severe addict may be removed to a hospital, not only to facilitate withdrawal, but to prevent his being "tempted" by available drugs. In a different fashion, youngsters who have acquired dyssocial reactions may be exposed to more wholesome models than before, such as "big brothers," athletic clubs and so on.

Biophysical methods may usefully be employed in several of these learned disturbances. For example, pharmacological tranquilizing agents may serve to alleviate tensions associated with a patient's fear reaction. Other pharmaceuticals may overcome the uncomfortable side effects and withdrawal symptoms of alcoholic and drug addiction.

Most promising among the therapies for these learned reactions are techniques based on extinction principles associated with various "behavioral modification" and directive "phenomenological reorientation" methods. These procedures are highly efficient in that they "zero in" on the target habit without becoming involved in circuitous intrapsychic explorations or tangential personality traits. Various techniques, e.g., systematic desensitization, seek through cognitive suggestion to pair neutral feelings and attitudes, such as relaxation, with formerly provocative stimuli. Similarly, aversive conditioning methods have been used to associate negative reinforcements with responses that previously were positively reinforcing, e.g., drugs such as "antabuse" and a variety of emetics are given to alcoholics to produce intense physical discomfort in conjunction with drinking; repetition of this experience will condition pain rather than pleasure with the habit, thereby fostering its extinction.

Intrapsychic therapies are of dubious value in dealing with circumscribed pathological reactions. Although they may be useful in cases in which pervasive personality trends are involved, they are unnecessarily circuitous and inefficient for extinguishing stimulus-specific reactions.

Group methods may be employed with moderate success in reactions that originated as a function of social imitation or that have been reinforced by group activities. Thus, alcoholics and drug addicts often benefit by extinction techniques generated in group settings, e.g., Alcoholics Anonymous or the Synanon for narcotic addicts. The special value of these group procedures is that the individual's habit is negatively reinforced in a setting that previously encouraged and provided reinforcements for it.

## CONCLUDING COMMENTS AND SUMMARY

Chapters 6 through 11 focused on personality patterns and symptom disorders; in these syndromes, biogenic and psychogenic factors interweave in a complex sequence of interactions to produce the final clinical picture. This interaction also occurs in the behavior reactions, discussed in this chapter, but in these impairments the role of experiential determinants is especially prominent. Pathological reactions are anchored to specific environmental stimuli, that is, they are evoked in response to a circumscribed set of external conditions. Only through the most indirect evidence and the most circuitous rationales, can they be ascribed even in part to biogenic influences. The rather straightforward stimulus-response specificity of these reactions makes them particularly amenable to the concepts and research of psychological "learning theories." We have found it notably clarifying and expedient, therefore, to formulate and analyze these impairments with such terms and principles as "imitation" and "conditioning."

It will be useful to note again that the syndromes presented in this chapter, as with those provided before, are best viewed as textbook prototypes that simplify the true variety and complexity of "real" cases. Classification systems are pedagogical instruments which expedite our understanding and treatment of patients; they are heuristic tools to facilitate a variety of clinical and research goals, and should not be viewed as fixed and immutable guides to "disease entities."

The content and major themes of the chapter may be summarized as follows:

1. As far as superficial appearances are concerned, behavior reactions may be indistinguishable from syndromes discussed in previous chapters. Careful study will uncover substantial differences, however, between reactions and other syndromes, especially with regard to etiology and development. Moreover, the form and content of the reactions are determined largely by the character of their external precipitants rather than by the patient's more general personality style or the reactivation of complex and intruding intrapsychic factors.

Two types of behavior reactions were distinguished: *transient situational reactions* which consist of pathological responses to brief and objectively stressful conditions, and *circumscribed learned reactions* which consist of acquired and relatively permanent pathological responses to narrowly delimited and ordinarily innocuous stimuli.

2. *Transient situational reactions* arise in "normal" personalities when their established equilibrium and habitual style of functioning have been upset or threatened by realistically stressful precipitants. Two subvarieties were discussed— gross stress reactions and age associated reactions.

*Gross stress reactions* may take almost any form of psychopathology and may occur at almost any point in life. They grow out of unusually severe or sudden conditions of environmental stress such as war, civilian disasters or physical illness.

*Age associated reactions* are similar to gross stress reactions except for the fact that they occur with greater probability at certain points of life and are likely to take forms consistent with the age of the patient and the character of the problem faced. Five major age periods were distinguished— infancy, childhood, adolescence, adulthood and late life.

Three *infancy* reactions were noted: lack of responsiveness, fearful tension and cranky irritability.

Five *childhood* reactions were outlined: withdrawal reactions, overdependency reactions, tension reactions, oppositional reactions and hostile reactions.

Three *adolescent* reactions were described: inadequacy reactions, diffusion reactions and rebellious reactions.

*Adult* reactions encompass almost every conceivable form of expression and tend to reflect both the character of the stressful agent and the individual's premorbid vulnerabilities and habitual coping style. Among the sources most likely to produce pathological behaviors are: strains of family life, strains of earning a livelihood and strains of physical illness.

Reactions of *late life* reflect primarily the loss of physical health and feelings of unworthiness and loneliness. Notable during the transitional menopause period is "involutional melancholia."

3. *Circumscribed learned reactions* are ingrained but narrowly compartmentalized behavioral tendencies; they are stimulus-specific and uniform in their expression since they are relatively free of intruding and complicating personality traits and intrapsychic processes. Five major subcategories were distinguished—fears, developmental habits, dyssocial behaviors, sexual deviations and addictions.

*Fear* reactions are aversions to ordinarily neutral stimuli acquired as a consequence of direct conditioning or learned vicariously through observation and imitation. Distinctions between fears and the symptom disorders of anxiety and phobia were discussed.

*Developmental* habit reactions are behaviors that are "normal" at one stage of maturation, but are usually modified or extinguished during development; what makes these habits pathological is not that they were learned in the first place, as is the case with other reactions, but that they failed to be modulated or unlearned.

Three spheres of development were noted and their associated habits discussed: eating, including persistent behaviors such as thumbsucking; elimination, including the problem of enuresis; and speech, including stuttering.

*Dyssocial* reactions are characterized by a marked disdain and violation of social regulations and customs. In contrast to the sociopathic disorders, to which they are overtly similar, these reactions are not rooted in a pervasively hostile or irresponsible personality pattern. They are exhibited in psychologically "normal" individuals and are acquired primarily as a consequence of social imitation.

*Sexual deviation* reactions are isolated habits acquired in response to an unusual combination of pathogenic circumstances. These events have distorted the learning of normal sexual behaviors, but have not necessarily intruded upon other spheres of personality development. Several variants of deviancy were described, as were their probable etiologies. Three broad categories were distinguished: deviancies in sexual object, including homosexuality, pedophilia and fetishism; deviancies in mode of sexual gratification, including exhibitionism, voyeurism, transvestitism and sadomasochism; and deviancies in the intensity of desire and frequency of sexual activity, including nymphomania and satyriasis and frigidity and impotence.

*Addiction* reactions were divided into two types, alcoholism and drug dependence. The incidence, types, effects, phases, coping functions and etiology of these impairments were described. The role of vicarious learning and imitation in the initial acquisition of these habits was noted; positive reinforcement of coping aims was stressed as a factor in strengthening the habit; body chemical changes are central in the third step of the sequence, that of physiological addiction.

4.  Despite differences in terminology, organization and rationale, considerable similarity exists between the reaction syndromes presented in this chapter and those found in the official classification manual. Notations were made of points of correspondence between these two systems.

5.  With this chapter we conclude our focus on syndromes in which psychogenic factors contribute a major share to the development of psychopathology. In the following chapter we will turn to "biophysical defects," in which biogenic factors are preeminent. Although psychological habits and attitudes may color the form and content of these impairments, their basic pathological character is determined by the presence of some fundamental alteration in the individual's anatomy, physiology or chemistry. In contrast to the syndromes described in this chapter, biophysical defects can best be formulated and understood with reference to neurological and physiochemical concepts rather than those of psychological learning theories.

# Chapter 13

# BIOPHYSICAL DEFECTS

Pablo Picasso—*Seated Woman* (1959).

## INTRODUCTION

The syndromes discussed in preceding chapters may be traced, in large measure, to psychogenic factors. Where biogenic influences were involved, they neither assumed a paramount role in precipitating the impairment nor were necessary elements in shaping the character of the disturbance; rather, they were either entirely subsidiary, as in the behavior reactions, or complexly interwoven with a variety of environmental learning experiences, as in the personality patterns and symptom disorders.

To contrast with these impairments, our attention shall turn in this chapter to syndromes in which biogenic factors are preeminent. Psychogenic influences may color the particular form and content of these aberrations, but the basic pathology itself has been precipitated and shaped by neurological defects or physiochemical dysfunctions.

As noted in the introduction to chapter 4, psychopathologists trained exclusively in the behavioral sciences often neglect the role that biological factors may play in the etiology of mental disorders. This deemphasis is lamentable for it signifies a cognitive narrow-mindedness that does not befit the role of a scientist. Moreover, the tendency to "impose" psychogenic hypotheses has not only proved irrelevant or misleading in many forms of psychopathology, but is often injurious.

Overlooking the role of biophysical factors in pathological personality patterns is bad enough, but it is worse still in syndromes in which there are clear-cut organic involvements; the tendency to obfuscate matters in these cases by placing primary stress on ostensive psychogenic factors is nothing less than gross medical negligence and scientific irresponsibility. Every psychopathologist must be open-minded enough to explore the potential contribution of biophysical elements in each case he encounters, even where psychological factors are centrally involved.

Most texts in psychiatry devote as much as one half of their total volume to the identification and elaboration of biophysical defects. Such attention is appropriate in the training of psychiatrists since these men must be prepared to recognize and discriminate among even the most obscure diseases. Since the primary focus of this text is not to prepare professionals for refined neurological diagnosis, we are free to by-pass detailed presentations. However, this does not allow us to take the liberty of overlooking *all* biophysical impairments; rather, we must survey the most frequent varieties of organic impairments in order to broaden our understanding of the psychopathological process. Moreover, it is important that we see more clearly differences between the major classes of syndromes, labeled patterns, disorders, reactions and defects.

Syndrome distinctions are not only of pedagogical or academic interest, but are relevant to a number of significant clinical goals. Since the overt clinical signs of basically divergent syndromes often overlap, the diagnostician must learn to separate impairments rooted in biophysical defects from those that stem principally from learning experiences. With these distinctions in hand, the clinician can better gauge a patient's prognosis and more effectively plan a course of treatment.

In the preceding paragraphs we have sought to justify the importance of studying pathologies rooted in part to biophysical defects. Let us swing back the pendulum for a moment and note that the *particular* form and content of these syndromes are shaped by innumerable psychogenic influences. Eugen Bleuler was the first to formally note this relationship when he referred to the immediate and direct consequences of the biophysical defect as *primary* symptoms, and the more elaborate psychological form and content through which it was manifested as *secondary* symptoms. In this regard, let us quote what was said in the introduction to chapter 5:

> Although behavior pathology may be triggered by biogenic abnormalities, the mere specification of a biogenic cause is not sufficient for an adequate etiologic analysis. Even in cases where clear-cut biogenic factors can be identified, it is necessary to trace the developmental sequence of experiences which transform these defects into a manifest form of psychopathology; the need for this more extensive developmental analysis is evident by the fact that some individuals with biological defects function effectively whereas other, similarly afflicted individuals, succumb to maladaptation and psychopathology. Clearly, the biological defect, in itself, cannot account for such divergences in development. Pathological behaviors that are precipitated initially by biological abnormalities are not simple and direct products of these defects; rather, they emerge through a complex sequence of interactions which include environmental experience and learning.
> . . . biological influences are not uniform from one situation to the next, but vary as a function of the environmental conditions within which they arise. The position we take then is that both factors contribute to all (psychopathologies), and that their respective contributions are determined by reciprocal and changing combinations of interdependence.

Let us state clearly, here at the outset of the chapter, that the consequences of biogenic disturbances often depend less on the type, location or extent of the physical defect than on the premorbid personality of the patient and the situational environment within which he continues to function. We never see an individual whose impaired functioning is directly a product of his biophysical defect. Rather, the presenting clinical picture is a composite of the disorganizing consequences of his disability, set in the context of his premorbid experiences and behavior styles and his postmorbid coping reactions and environmental circumstances. For example, the same type of brain tumor may lead to a morose and withdrawn depression in one person, to hypochondriacal irritability in a second, severe delusions in a third and a quiet but cognitively confused set of responses in a fourth. In short, the severity and specific content of the disturbance are, in large measure, a function of the patient's personality and coping style.

## VARIETY OF CLINICAL SIGNS

Some biophysically impaired patients exhibit no perceptible signs of illness, despite the presence of a clear-cut organic disease. There are limits, however, to the degree to which restitutive and compensatory functions can contain or camouflage the defect. At some point in neural dysfunction, differing from person to person, the individual begins to display psychopathological features. These clinical signs may be manifested in any of a variety of functions, and may range from mild disturbances to the most markedly severe. Some of these features follow directly from the nature of the underlying defect, although their particular character and content are always colored by premorbid personality trends. In this section, we will focus on some of the more common signs that reflect the organic process itself, apart from its more personal "psychological" components.

Before we outline these common signs, let us note that the identification and diagnosis of biophysical syndromes often present numerous difficulties. In many cases, especially where no clear-cut precipitant is evident, the presence of a defect must be "pieced together" into a coherent cluster from diverse, obscure and seemingly unrelated signs. The imprecision of these inferred diagnoses is compounded by the fact that nonorganic syndromes exhibit features that are indistinguishable from those seen in organic cases, e.g., cognitive disorientation arising from cerebral degeneration may not readily be discernible from schizophrenic cognitive interference. To complicate matters, it is often impossible to separate the extent to which a particular patient's symptoms reflect his organic defect from his psychological response to his defect. And further, mild neurological diseases frequently exacerbate an existent but previously latent pathological personality trait into clinical form.

The diagnostic process must also take cognizance of the intricate interdependence of organic functions with the body. Any localized biophysical defect will disrupt not only the specific system that has directly been injured, but other functionally connected systems whose processes are partially subserved by the impaired region. Thus, any impairment, whatever its locale, may produce both *specific* dysfunctions, as well as nonspecific or *general* dysfunctions. In addition, the clinical picture will reflect not only these specific and general disturbances, but the wider coping efforts of the patient to adjust and compensate for his "disordered" state. To overcome these and other difficulties, the diagnostician must make his judgments on the basis of a total clinical history, a battery of both psychological tests and neurological procedures as well as overt behavioral signs.

Before presenting the principal biophysical syndromes, let us summarize the various types of symptoms found in these defects. These clinical signs may be grouped conveniently into three categories: those associated with the loss of *general integrative functions,* those reflecting a loss of *specific functions* and those representing the patient's *compensatory coping efforts.* In no single case should we expect to find more than a few of the signs mentioned.

### General Integrative Impairments

Certain processes are prerequisites to wakeful brain activity; others represent the brain's capacity to coordinate and synthesize its diverse functions. Defects that disrupt these fundamental operations of the nervous system shall be termed losses of general integrative functions. In contrast with other more specific spheres of neural function, these overarching processes are essential to those higher capacities we associate distinctively with man. We shall divide them into three subcategories: those concerned with levels of activation, manifesting themselves in *impairments of consciousness;* those associated with the brain's monitoring and regulating functions, exhibiting themselves in *impairments of control;* and those relating to the processes of memory retrieval and cognitive learning, displaying themselves in *impairments of abstraction.*

**Impairments of Consciousness.** A prerequisite to all higher forms of brain functioning is a minimal level of central nervous system arousal. Various injuries, toxins and infections may result in the rapid or progressive faltering of neural activation, leading to decrements in attentiveness and awareness. These vary in intensity from the relatively mild forms of "clouding of consciousness" to the severe, stuporous states of coma. Clouded consciousness is signified by a hazy, almost somnolent, level of awareness in which the patient is awake but extremely difficult to reach; he seems unable to attend to external stimuli, to think clearly or to maintain a consistent focus on one set of ideas or events without "drifting off" into a dream-like state. At the extreme end of these impairments are states of coma in which even dream processes, as well as those of conscious awareness, are suspended.

**Impairments of Control.** Activation and consciousness, although prerequisites to higher brain functioning, are no assurance that the brain will monitor and order the events to which it attends. Any number of biophysical disturbances may impair the overall mastery and control of thoughts, emotions and behaviors. The basic processes of inhibiting, separating and directing the concurrent streams of impression, memory and impulse which bombard the brain may be either mildly or markedly disrupted. This general breakdown in the sequential regulation of perceptions and behaviors ranges from mild distractibility to the markedly severe state of delirium.

Less severe degrees of brain dyscontrol are seen in such clinical signs as labile emotions, perceptual distractibility and physical hyperactivity. These patients attend in rapid succession to one or another element of the multiple stimuli that surround them and are unable to focus on anything for too long a period. In addition, they are typically restless, shift capriciously from one activity to another and exhibit sudden outbursts of impulsive and changeable emotions. In short, they seem incapable of stemming or otherwise governing the flow of both external and internal stimulation, responding to these stimuli as if they were short-circuited through the brain without benefit of assimilation or control.

More severe forms of brain dyscontrol are noted by verbal incoherence, confusion and bewilderment, agitated hyperactivity and fearful illusions and hallucinations. Cameron (1963) described these processes of disorganization with reference to concepts such as *interpenetration, fragmentation* and *overinclusion.* Thus, as the overall regulatory mechanisms of the brain falter in their monitoring capacities, stimuli penetrate one another, that is, feelings and impressions arising from one source invade or intrude upon other sources, causing a confluence of normally segregated ideas, behaviors and emotions. Similarly, sequentially successive actions or thoughts may be fragmented, that is, aborted or broken off from their normal progression. Overinclusion represents a third variation in the breakdown of brain modulation and control; here the patient cannot discriminate and exclude irrelevant from relevant thoughts and perceptions, leading his ideas and behaviors to lose their salience and to diffuse aimlessly without focus or direction.

In the milder states of disorientation, this disorganized and drifting process may be sustained for extended periods; although flustered and distractible, the patient has some measure of control and some cognizance of reality. In the more severe states of delirium, however, brain dyscontrol is marked, and the patient seems utterly confused and perplexed such that fleeting perceptions and weird inner sensations fuse in a distorted, bewildering and often frightening manner.

**Impairments of Abstraction.** Consciousness and control are but preliminaries to the distinctively human capacity of abstraction. The vast network of intracortical systems in the brain allows for the coordination, retrieval and synthesis of diverse memories and cognitive processes. Damage to higher cerebral centers may cause a marked decrement in this overarching integration of symbolic material.

In less severe form, the loss of abstraction is seen in an inability both to grasp and to retain new information; old memories are functionally operative in these patients, but new learnings fail to be registered with clarity and precision and tend not to be recalled, even in their simplest form. This impairment is most evident in tasks that require the sequential integration of both past and present knowledge; here, patients appear to forget the problem solving goal to which their efforts are directed, as well as the facts and steps necessary for its attainment. It is as if their brains lack the capacity both to consolidate immediate symbolic memory and to sustain extended sequences of cognitive coordination.

Goldstein (1939) refers to this disintegration of the brain's higher synthesizing and symbolic functions as a "loss of the abstract attitude." With severe injury, the patient succumbs to the "concrete attitude," noted by the tendency to be oriented only by the immediate and tangible, without recourse to memory retrieval and cognitive reflection. The normal brain, with its capacity to draw upon and coordinate widely diverse neural systems, enables the individual to transcend the immediately given aspects of sense impressions and internal impulse and to evaluate present tangible realities from a reflective and conceptual point of view—in short, to adopt an abstract attitude. Among the behaviors which are likely to suffer first and most severely under conditions of cerebral disturbance, Goldstein lists the following. The patient is unable to: give an account of his acts and thoughts, shift reflectively from one aspect of a situation to another,

keep in mind various aspects of a task simultaneously, analyze and then synthesize the essentials of a given whole, evoke or retrieve memories and conceive and anticipate the "merely possible."

### Specific Functional Impairments

All parts of the nervous system work together as a unit. The scientist's separation of "general" versus a variety of different "specific" functions is largely artificial, a conceptual distinction representing, in the main, his need to organize his subject matter into convenient categories. The subdivision of psychological functions into separate categories is misleading in that it suggests a parallel subdivision in the brain in which identifiable loci correspond to each function. Although there is some substantive basis in the differentiated structures of the brain for making these distinctions, any defect in one part of the brain alters in some manner every psychological function. There is a "gradient of neural specialization," however, such that focal brain defects impair certain functions to a greater extent than others. Only in this sense of a specialization gradient can we speak of impairments as *specific* rather than general.

Let us briefly review a few of the many and varied specific psychological processes which may be disturbed by biophysical defects. We shall group them into three categories: *single function impairments, perceptual-motor impairments* and *cognitive-language impairments*.

**Single Function Impairments.** In addition to paralyses of *motor* capacities, patients often exhibit a variety of spontaneous involuntary movements, e.g., rhythmic tremors in the extremities known as parkinsonism; slow writhing and twisting movements of the hands and feet, referred to as athetosis; rapid, irregular, and asymmetrical jerking motions in extremities, termed chorea.

Innumerable *sensory* and *perceptual* dysfunctions may be diagnosed through neurological, visual and auditory examinations; the labels and details of these clinical symptoms are beyond the province of this textbook. It will suffice to note that specific sensory defects usually stem from damage to the peripheral regions of the nervous system, those concerned with the initial receipt of stimuli. Perception is a more complex function than sensation; in these processes, the central nervous system is involved in the organization of sensory stimuli into "meaningful" patterns or units. Disturbances in those regions of the brain subserving the perception of organized stimulus patterns and relationships may be evident in numerous pathological distortions.

Disturbances of *gross motor coordination* may

reflect nervous system defects in regions requisite to kinesthesis and body equilibrium; among their consequences are prolonged states of vertigo, periodic and sudden losses of balance and tendencies to drift to one side in walking. Among other coordination dysfunctions are a variety of gait disturbances such as spastic, staggering or scissors steps.

Impairments in regions such as the limbic system or reticular formation usually have pervasive consequences; however, in rare cases, such defects exhibit markedly excessive or deficient *emotional* behaviors.

**Perceptual-Motor Impairments.** The attempt to coordinate one's motor responses in line with one's perception of stimuli is a higher order activity of the brain that is basic to a wide variety of psychological functions. In certain respects, impairments of this type may properly be viewed as "general integrative" disturbances. However, in many cases, the injury is relatively circumscribed, affecting only activities which require the sequential act of perceiving an event and reacting to it in a manner consonant with one's desires; thus, the individual may be able to abstract symbolically what he perceives and may possess the capacity to conceptualize what he wishes to accomplish, but be incapable of producing the desired response. It is as if some segment of internal wiring is missing, resulting in repetitive deflections or digressions in the progression from sensory input to motor output. Not uncommonly, these persons are extremely awkward or deficient in physical coordination, speech articulation, reading and writing. Many also exhibit disturbances of body image, weakly established handedness and right-left confusions.

**Cognitive-Language Impairments.** Few disturbances have remained in so chaotic a state of scientific knowledge as those relating to man's symbolic linguistic functions. This confusion stems in part from the difficulty of differentiating the effects of neural dysfunctions in the central cognitive mechanisms from those owing to the peripheral instrumental mechanisms of sensory reception and motor response. Unfortunately, psychopathologists cannot depend on animal experimentation to supply them with the precise details of neural functioning in these distinctively human capacities. Having to rely on the "muddled" clinical pictures of diseased and injured patients for their data, theorists have come up with only crude guesses as to the precise structures which subserve cognitive-language functions.

The major category of cognitive language defects is labeled *aphasia;* ostensibly, this stems from impairments in the parietotemporal area of the dominant, usually the left, cerebral hemisphere.

The diagnosis of aphasia assumes that peripheral sensory and motor mechanisms are intact. Several subvarieties of aphasia have been differentiated, each of which represents a different facet of disturbance in the complex process of symbolic verbalization.

*Motor or expressive aphasia* refers to an inability to verbalize spontaneously letters, words or sentences; the ability to comprehend language remains intact in pure cases. Quite commonly, expressive aphasia, which refers to vocalized speech, is often accompanied by an inability to write, known as *agraphia*.

*Sensory or receptive aphasia* denotes an inability to understand words and sentences. In some cases, the spoken word can be understood, but written symbols are experienced as obscure and meaningless; this latter impairment is referred to as *alexia*.

*Amnestic aphasia* is signified by an inability to recall the names of familiar objects and events. Other types of aphasia have been differentiated, but the list we have supplied covers the major varieties.

The cognitive deficits seen in aphasic patients represent a loss in the most complex of man's specialized spheres of cortical functioning, symbolic thinking. Because of the scope and complexity of this function, it is often assumed to be a form of higher order integration. This is not the case. Most of these patients are fully cognizant of their impairment, and retain, in large measure, the capacity to assume the "abstract attitude." Thus, despite deficits in this highest of evolutionary capacities, aphasic defects are *specific* to linguistic symbolism and are not general integrative dysfunctions. Of course, this specific language deficit may be accompanied by concomitant sensory and perceptual-motor impairments. At some point, the combination of these more specific impairments is so far-reaching as to be properly conceived as a general integrative impairment.

Before concluding, let us reiterate the fact that "real" cases of biophysical defect do not lend themselves to such neat pedagogical discriminations as we have previously outlined. Moreover, the intrinsic organic unity of the brain means that focal injuries invariably disrupt more than one psychological function. In addition to the fact that several specific processes are usually impaired simultaneously, we find that some "reorganization" of general integrative processes is almost always involved, even in minor focal injuries. These biophysical reorganizations are paralleled by a variety of psychological coping adjustments, a topic to which we turn next.

## Compensatory Coping Efforts

Until now, we have focused our attention on symptoms that represent the direct effects of the biophysical disturbance. The clinical picture we observe, however, is complicated by numerous secondary signs that reflect the damaged individual's attempt to compensate or otherwise cope with his defects. These restitutive measures are employed to enable him to continue to function in his accustomed way, despite his structural limitations.

There are interesting differences between biophysically disturbed adults and children in the manner in which they respond to their impairments. In the adult, in whom established and preferred styles of behavior have developed over many years, the person struggles, so to speak, to reorganize his remaining capacities so as to regain those competencies he was once capable of performing; he does not yield to his defect, therefore, but rather seeks to build in or strengthen counteracting mechanisms by which he can compensate for his loss. This contrasts, in large measure, with what is seen in biophysically impaired children. Having developed neither an established or fully matured pattern of functioning to which they are accustomed nor a well-defined style of coping upon which to base restitutive efforts, they tend more readily to "give in" to the direct effects of their injuries. As a consequence, we see in relatively pure and unmodified form many of the symptoms that were described in the previous two sections, those of dyscontrol and distractibility, restlessness and emotional lability, perceptual-motor disturbances and so on.

The compensatory coping efforts of some adults are sufficient to counteract or camouflage the direct effects of their physical impairment. We shall *not* be concerned in this section with those persons whose competencies are such as to enable them to make the adjustment process a successful one. Our interest lies with those who fail to cope in a "healthy" fashion. In general, they exhibit one or more of three types of responses: *catastrophic reactions* as they become aware of their illness and their marked incompetencies; a marked *accentuation of established personality dispositions;* and a *withdrawal* from tasks that tax their limited capacities, and a consequent *rigidity* and *perseveration* in behavior.

**Catastrophic Reactions.** The inability to think, feel and act as one could prior to illness poses a serious threat to the biophysically impaired individual. Every task which he fails to execute as well as he did in the past is a reminder, so to speak, of his altered state, tangible evidence of his permanent decreased competence. Each experience of failure carries more meaning to a defective individual than to a normal one since it makes the patient aware of the fundamental change that has taken place. Goldstein illustrates the seriousness of these experiences in the following quote (1942):

Here is a man with a lesion of the frontal lobe, to whom we present a problem in simple arithmetic. He is unable to solve it. But simply noting and recording the fact that he is unable to perform a simple multiplication would be an exceedingly inadequate account of the patient's reaction. Just looking at him, we can see a great deal more than this arithmetical failure. He looks dazed, changes color, becomes agitated, anxious, starts to fumble, his pulse becomes irregular; a moment before amiable, he is now sullen, evasive, exhibits temper, or even becomes aggressive. It takes some time before it is possible to continue the examination. Because the patient is so disturbed in his whole behavior, we call situations of this kind catastrophic situations.

**Accentuation of Personality Dispositions.** There are many ways in which individuals may attempt to cope with "catastrophic" anxiety. As was amply illustrated in chapters 10 to 12, unusual stress seriously upsets the equilibrium of both normal and pathologically disposed individuals, giving rise to a variety of different clinical symptoms.

The symptoms that a patient exhibits will tend to reflect his characteristic way of coping with difficulties. Thus, as a consequence of his physical impairment and the anxieties it evokes, we would expect that a basically dependent person would become notably security oriented and develop a variety of secondary symptoms, such as phobias and conversions, as a means of assuring increased support and nurture from others. An independent personality, in contrast, may resist "submitting" to his diminished competence; he may react by becoming more aggressively assertive and domineering than before.

Biophysically impaired individuals are more likely to exhibit a more marked accentuation of their personality trends in response to stress than normal persons. This stems from the fact that their cerebral impairments place a physical limit on their capacity to behave flexibly and weaken their capacity to control their ingrained and "automatic" habits and attitudes. Deprived of normal regulating mechanisms, personality dispositions come to the fore in relatively pure and unmodulated form. Thus, as a consequence of their inability to monitor and inhibit their habitual responses, the established response traits of these patients assume an increasingly dominant role.

**Withdrawal, Rigidity and Perseveration.** The repetition of catastrophic anxiety in chronically impaired individuals and their progressive inability to cope with the affairs of life often "force" them to react by what Goldstein has referred to as a "shrinking of the milieu." In order to preserve the few remnants of their psychological cohesion and to avoid the painful distress of repeated failures, these patients restrict their activities to those which do not tax their limited resources.

Many defective patients begin to take on characteristics that typify the active-detached and passive-ambivalent personality patterns, and for somewhat similar reasons. All these individuals dread making mistakes and fear the consequences of the unknown. In the passive-ambivalent personality, these concerns stem primarily from learning experiences, usually reflecting the training discipline of overcontrolling parents; in the active-detached, we see the consequences of repeated social humiliation and decreased self-esteem. In the biophysically injured individual, however, these concerns arise from a growing awareness of his marked incompetencies, embarrassing failures and a sensed social ridicule. As a consequence, the organically damaged person narrows his world to activities in which he feels safe, maintains a rigidity in his behavior, perseverates in the few things in which he feels competent and rarely ventures beyond secure boundaries. Goldstein describes the process in the brain-injured as follows (1959):

> Observation shows that the patient is withdrawn from the world around him so that a number of stimuli, including dangerous ones, do not arise. He avoids company. He is as much as possible doing something which he is able to do well. What he is doing may not have any particular significance for him, but concentration on activities which are possible for him makes him relatively impervious to dreaded stimulation. Particularly interesting is his excessive orderliness in all respects. Everything in the surrounding world has a definite place. Similarly, he is very meticulous in his behavior as to time, whereby the determination as to when he should do something is related to events and to activities of his which always occur at the same time, or to a definite position of the hands of a clock. This orderliness enables him to prevent too frequent catastrophes.

## DIMENSIONS OF ETIOLOGICAL ANALYSIS

The causes of biophysical impairments are many and varied. In certain cases, several factors and influences may be involved; in others, there is a single major precipitant. Unfortunately, there is no simple way to group the pathogenic sources of biophysical defects; any arrangement will result either in overlaps or serious omissions.

In this section we shall summarize several vantage points or dimensions from which we may approach biophysical etiology. Each of these dimensions represents only one way of analyzing the determinants or influences of these impairments; in other words, the pathogenesis of most syndromes may be approached and conceptualized from several points of view. For example, *mongolism,* a form of mental retardation, can be spoken of as an endogenous disease from genogenic sources; each term in this statement—endogenous, disease and genogenic—signifies a different but not mutually exclusive dimension of etiological analysis.

### Pathogenic Agents

Cobb (1943) proposed a four-fold classification of biophysical defects which we may usefully borrow for purposes of differentiating etiologies. Although Cobb recognizes that most cases exhibit the influence of several sources, the distinctions he draws do help in separating the principal components of pathogenesis.

*Genogenic* agents refer to sources of hereditary or genetic origin. Among the various forms of mental retardation, for example, the "garden variety" type can be ascribed to deficiencies transmitted directly from parent to offspring whereas others, such as mongolism, are due to nonhereditary aberrations in chromosomal genetic make-up. Both, however, are due to genogenic factors.

*Histogenic* agents are those which produce lesions in the nervous system, excluding hereditary or genetic factors. Tissue changes resulting from cerebral infections or injuries would fall in this category.

*Chemogenic* agents refer to pathogenic factors in the biochemistry of neurophysiological functioning. These include alterations in the magnitude, balance or sequence of metabolic, nutritional, or endocrinological processes. Similar pathological effects may result from the intrusion of various toxins or drugs upon bodily tissues.

*Psychogenic* agents are those which arise from interpersonal or learning experiences. For example, sparseness in the density and branching of neural tissues, known as aplasia, may result from inadequate environmental stimulation during sensitive periods of neuropsychological development.

### Deviance Versus Disease

Some defects are traceable to what Williams (1956) has termed "biochemical individuality"; in chapter 4, we extended this concept to include the notion of "neuroanatomical individuality." These labels signify the fact that people differ in the composition of their intrinsic biophysical make-up.

Some individuals *deviate naturally* from so-called average chemical and anatomical patterns in ways that dispose them to psychopathology. These deviations may be spoken of as "abnormalities," that is, statistical extremes in the normal distribution of bodily traits which are so severe as to be functionally impaired or limiting.

Natural deviances may be contrasted to what we term *diseases*. For example, some persons are short because of their natural constitutional disposition to be of short stature, not because they suffered some infection or malnutrition. Similarly, many of the mentally retarded fall at the low end of the normal distribution of intelligence simply because their naturally endowed internal apparatus is inadequate for performing complex tasks, and not because of some injury, infection or chemical toxin.

The "disease" label signifies the operation of some unusual process or agent in an otherwise average or normal body structure or function; it reflects a marked intrusion or disruption in an individual's make-up that sets him apart from those who vary in accord with the bell-shaped curve of natural individual differences. Thus, deviations represent extreme positions along this bell-shaped curve whereas diseases represent a break in a new direction that is not part of the usual range of natural individual differences.

The distinction between deviance and disease may be viewed as similar to the distinction between qualitative and quantitative differences. Disease connotes a difference in quality. For example, there is no "natural" continuum of states, nor intermediate conditions, between cancer and no-cancer; the patient either has cancer or he has not. Deviance, however, refers to characteristics which differ on a naturally occurring continuum that possesses many intervening shades; it reflects, then, not a qualitative difference in kind, but a quantitative difference in degree.

Some forms of mental retardation are diseases whereas others are deviances. For example, *phenylketonuria* is a disease, a metabolic disturbance traceable to an all-or-none aberration in a single genetic structure. Other types of mental retardation are deviances, representing statistical extremes in a naturally occurring continuum of biophysical structures that subserve intellectual functions.

### Endogenous Versus Exogenous Sources

The etiological concepts of endogenous (originating from within the organism) and exogenous (originating outside the organism) are useful in denoting whether the pathogenic factor is of constitutional origin or whether it stems from an external or environmental source. Infections or toxins that produce psychopathology would be referred to as exogenous agents whereas genetic aberrations or severe metabolic dysfunctions would be labeled as endogenous.

Because these dimensions are often confused, we might note that there is no necessary correspondence between the terms disease and exogenous or between deviance and endogenous. Although many diseases have an exogenous origin (e.g., infection or toxin), others have an endogenous base (e.g., a genetic aberration that results in a metabolic dysfunction). Similarly, deviances often have endogenous roots (e.g., inherited constitutional inadequacies conducive to mental retardation); however, they may also stem from exogenous sources (e.g., intellectual deficiences arising from early nutritional or stimulus impoverishment).

### Intracranial Versus Systemic Locus

A further distinction may be made in accord with whether the pathogenic agent focuses its destructive action specifically and primarily upon brain tissues or whether it arises from and has a general destructive impact on the body as a whole. The former may be spoken of as intracranial pathogenesis, the latter as systemic pathogenesis. Among the former are the following: head injuries which lacerate cerebral matter; infectious syphilitic parasites which invade and destroy, more or less specifically, the protective lining and neural tissue of the central nervous system; toxins that have minor general body effects, but which pass through the blood-brain barrier and result in severe cerebral damage. In contrast, systemic impairments produce changes in central nervous system functioning only as an incidental part of their more pervasive damage, e.g., infections such as typhoid and pneumonia may give rise to transient periods of feverish deliria; chronic nutritional deficiencies due to an inborn metabolic disease may result in a variety of bodily impairments, including the maldevelopment of cerebral cells.

### Focal Versus Diffused Cerebral Locus

This dimension of etiological analysis narrows the distinction noted above to discriminations within the brain itself. The issue here is whether the pathogenic source is localized in a circumscribed region of the brain, or is more pervasive.

As was discussed in an earlier section, there is an intricate interdependence among the structural regions of the brain such that any focal defect will disrupt not only the more or less specialized function it subserves, but other functions that it only indirectly subserves. Because of this interdependence, the psychological consequences of focal versus diffused impairments cannot be sharply differentiated; focal lesions are more far-reaching than would seem the case given their immediate anatomical limits. The major clinical distinction between diffused and focal defects is that the former are more likely to produce disturbances in the brain's overall control and abstraction functions.

Illustrative of agents resulting in diffused impairments are the following: toxic substances which filter through the blood-brain barrier and pervade all tissues through the circulatory system; metabolic dysfunctions which curtail either nutrition or oxygen in both cerebral spheres; general bodily degeneration that afflicts unselectively and equally several functional regions. Focal impairments such as the following may be noted: lesions in specifiable zones resulting from head injuries; a selective maturational retardation following disease during a specific sensitive developmental period; and aplasia in a delimited anatomical region traceable to inherited family characteristics.

## CLASSIFICATION OF BIOPHYSICAL SYNDROMES

All biophysical defects reflect a relatively nonspecific alteration of neural tissue: it is simply the amount and locale of tissue destruction, no matter what the pathogenic source, that determine the basic impairment. However, the raveled and awesome complexity of the brain, its involved and intricate relationship to behavior, and the numerous pathogenic factors which can disrupt the varied functions it subserves, preclude the possibility of formulating a simple unidimensional classification system. Moreover, the final clinical picture is shaped by the patient's current environment and his premorbid style of coping.

On what basis, then, can these defects be differentiated?

An attempt was made toward this end in the 1952 APA classification manual. Here, biophysical syndromes were organized primarily in terms of the reversibility of the underlying tissue pathology. Certain impairments were labeled as *acute* to signify that the biophysical disturbance was likely to be transitory, that is, reversible. Others were termed *chronic* to represent the belief that the damage to the nervous system was relatively permanent, that is, irreversible. Certain characteristic features were noted as distinguishing acute from chronic impairments.

Unfortunately, the division between acute and chronic did not prove especially fruitful and led to numerous diagnostic complications. Symptoms, viewed as characteristic of acute syndromes, such as disorientation and delirium, are often exhibited in chronic impairments. In addition to the overlap of acute and chronic symptomatology, both types of impairments are traceable to the same pathogenic factors. Moreover, prognostic statements of reversibility or irreversibility, the essential distinction that defines the acute and chronic categories, often cannot be made; many so-called chronic syndromes develop following what appears initially to be an acute impairment. In a substantial proportion of cases there is no independent means of telling whether a syndrome is acute or chronic other than by waiting to see if the clinical signs do or do not abate in time. Valuable though the concept of reversibility and irreversibility may be, the diagnostic difficulties involved in its application and the limited discriminations it would provide, were it reliable, indicated that the acute-chronic distinction would not suffice as a basis for a nosological arrangement. As a consequence, the distinction was dropped in the recent DSM-II.

In recognition of its potential utility, the writers of the DSM-II have divided the organic syndromes in accord with their primary causes. Etiology, however, is a secondary and often misleading factor. As was noted earlier, it makes little difference as to what the source of the impairment might be. The primary determinants of most biophysical syndromes are how much and which tissues were damaged and the environment and coping style of the patient. Whether damage is of toxic, infectious or traumatic origins is largely irrelevant; the end product, in terms of pathological behavior, thought and emotion, is essentially the same, no matter what the etiology may have been.

If every major dimension by which distinctions can be drawn among biophysical defects is either unreliable or misleading, how then shall we organize these syndromes?

Unfortunately, there is no answer other than to follow in general the format provided in the DSM-II. Despite our basic adherence to this nosological system, we must keep in mind that it is the extent and locale of neuronal damage and the setting and coping style of the patient that are the paramount determinants of his clinical picture.

The major syndromes in the DSM-II have been organized implicitly in accord with two different principles: one set of syndromes is defined in terms of common *etiological origins;* the other is grouped on the basis of common *clinical signs.* We shall divide our presentation in line with this etiological-clinical sign distinction, not because we believe it to be fundamental to an understanding of these impairments, but because it will alert the reader to the primary data used to define these syndromes—in the one case that of cause, and in the other that of clinical picture.

# SYNDROMES ORGANIZED IN TERMS OF ETIOLOGICAL ORIGINS

The following syndromes are classified according to the primary cause of the impairment. The symptomatology may be mild, moderate or marked in severity; this is determined largely by the extent of tissue damage. Each category includes both acute and chronic forms of the defect.

## *DEFECTS ASSOCIATED WITH INTRACRANIAL INFECTION*

Numerous aberrations in behavior may be traced to the invasion of exogenous bacteria and viruses within the body. In certain acute systemic infections, such as typhoid and pneumonia, we observe marked disturbances during periods of high fever; most notable in this regard is delirium. It is the more chronic intracranial infections, however, which are of primary interest and concern to the psychopathologist; among these are *neurosyphilis* and *encephalitis.*

### NEUROSYPHILIS
(DSM-II: *General Paralysis*)

We may recall from chapter 1 that the discovery of the role of syphilis as a psychopathogenic agent was the first tangible source of support for the medical-disease model in psychiatry. Prior to the mid-nineteenth century, no relationship was seen to exist between syphilis, viewed then as a skin disease, and psychological impairments. The sequence of insights and laboratory findings which led to the discovery of its psychiatric significance must be recognized as a major step toward the diagnostic differentiation of psychopathological syndromes.

The clinical importance of neurosyphilis has decreased in recent years owing to advances in antibiotic therapies; until the advent of this treatment, over one fourth of all admissions to mental hospitals were ascribed to neurosyphilis. High fever therapy, induced by malarial infection, was employed in the second quarter of this century; this method activated the body's defensive system, which then destroyed the infectious syphilitic spirochete, preventing further neural damage and arresting the deterioration process before it led to complete paralysis and death. Since antibiotic therapy was devised in the 1940's and is prescribed today with the first symptoms of bacterial infection, the progressive effects of the syphilitic infection usually are abruptly terminated; as a result of this early preventive treatment, neurosyphilis accounts now for less than 2 per cent of new hospital admissions.

#### *Etiology and Course*

The syphilitic spirochete enters the body through minute abrasions of the skin or through mucous membranes such as are found in the surface tissue of the mouth and genitals. A directly contagious disease, most commonly transmitted during sexual intercourse, the syphilitic spirochete may also be transferred through kissing, contact with open infected sores and infiltration from mother to fetus during pregnancy.

Once the spirochete enters the body, it spreads with great rapidity, giving evidence of its presence through a sequence of five-stages: in the *first* stage a hard chancre or lesion appears at the point of infection ten to 40 days after the contraction of the disease; the *second* stage, appearing one or two months following the chancre, is characterized by a diffuse copper-colored rash over the entire body, and is often accompanied by fever, indigestion and headache; overt symptoms disappear in the *third* stage, although internally the spirochetes continue to destroy bodily tissue and organs, especially blood vessels and nerve cells; the *fourth* stage becomes evident five to 20 years after the initial infection, manifesting itself in a wide variety of symptoms, to be discussed shortly, stemming from the pervasive destruction of vascular and neural tissue; and the *fifth* stage is noted by increasing motor paralysis, confusion and delirium, followed by death.

## Syndrome Subcategories

Two types of neurosyphilitic syndromes are differentiated in modern psychiatric practice: the *meningoencephalitic* and *meningovascular* types.

The meningoencephalitic classification, formerly labeled *general paresis,* signifies the fact that the primary damage has been to the neural tissue of the brain. In contrast, the primary involvement in the meningovascular type has been with the surrounding membranes and blood vessels of the brain rather than with the nerve tissue itself. The overt symptomatology observed in chronic cases of both encephalitic and vascular types is essentially indistinguishable. Meningovascular impairments, however, are often of an acute, that is, reversible nature; in these cases, the symptomatology is characterized by a relatively short period of marked confusion and delirium, usually occurring shortly after the onset of the infection.

A subcategory of *juvenile paresis* is often distinguished from its adult counterpart. These cases stem from congenital neurosyphilis, that is, they are transmitted from the mother to the fetus. As a consequence of modern medical treatment, only about 1 per cent of these infected children develop the general neurosyphilitic syndrome. The symptomatology of these children is not dissimilar to that seen in the adult form. However, it is likely that many infected embryos do not survive to full-term births. Also, because of the detrimental effects of the infection during neurological maturation, many of these children suffer marked visual defects, mental retardation and a host of other, often grotesque, physical impairments that are not seen in adult cases.

## Clinical Picture

Among the obvious neurological signs of damage are marked degenerative changes and atrophy of cerebral tissue. The overall size of the brain is often decreased, shrunken and filled in with a turgid cerebrospinal fluid. A common symptom is the *Argyll-Robertson* sign in which the pupil of the eye fails to respond to light, but does accommodate to distance.

Notable impairments to *specific functions* are tremors of fingers, tongue, eyelids and facial muscles. Motor control of speech begins to weaken and falter, resulting in slurring, disarticulation and stuttering. The fine coordination required in writing often gives way. At first, there is an unsteadiness in handwriting; later, writing becomes crude and heavy and finally, there is no more than a few coarse and tremulous lines. Gross motor coordination is gradually eroded, exhibiting itself in the loss of balance and a shuffling unsteady gait, referred to as *locomotor ataxia.* Perceptual-motor dysfunctions are evident in such signs as an inability to button clothes, thread a needle or catch a ball.

Among *general-integrative* impairments are periodic convulsions and loss of consciousness. Less dramatic, but increasingly present, is a decrement in control, at first seen in a general carelessness and slovenliness about personal matters, and later in a gross social tactlessness, hyperdistractibility and emotional impulsivity. Also common are impairments in abstraction, poor retrieval of memories and confusion in thought.

The following case depicts a number of the typical neurosyphilitic features (Kolb, 1968).

### CASE 13-1
#### Marjorie W., Age 26, Married

Marjorie was brought to the hospital because she had become lost when she attempted to return home from a neighboring grocery store. About seven months before the patient's admission, her husband noticed that she was becoming careless of her personal appearance and neglectful of her household duties. She often forgot to prepare the family meals, or, in an apparent preoccupation, would burn the food. She seemed to have little appreciation of time and would not realize when to get up or go to bed. The patient would sit idly about the house, staring uncomprehendingly into space.

At the hospital Marjorie entered the admission office with an unsteady gait. There, by way of greeting, the physician inquired, "How are you today?" to which she replied in a monotonous, tremulous tone, "N-yes-s, I was-s op-er-a-ted on for 'pen-pendici-ci-tis." She never made any spontaneous remarks and when, a few days after her admission, she was asked if she were sad or happy, she stared vacantly at the physician and, with a fatuous smile, answered, "Yeah." Marjorie sat about the ward for hours, taking no interest in its activities. Sometimes she would hold a book in her lap, aimlessly turning the pages, never reading but often pointing out pictures like a small child and showing satisfaction when she found a new one to demonstrate. Neurological examination showed dilated pupils that reacted but slightly to light and on convergence. There was a tremor of lips and facial muscles on attempting to speak. The protruded tongue showed a coarse tremor. All deep tendon reflexes were hyperactive. The Wasserman reaction was strongly positive in both blood serum and cerebrospinal fluid.

Neurosyphilitics often do not give evidence of "catastrophic reactions" since their pathology develops in a rather slow and insidious fashion. Because of the gradual and pervasive character of their defect, they often fail to sense the changes that have taken place within them or to grasp its full significance. As their ailment progresses, there is a growing accentuation of their premorbid personality coping styles. This accentuation occurs not only because of the increased stress they experience as they confront the ordinary tasks of life, but because they have lost the integrative controls with which to adapt to events flexibly, and to inhibit their more automatic and ingrained habits of response.

It was once thought that as neurosyphilitics decompensated, their personalities were molded into one of three classic types: an *expansive* type, noted either by extreme euphoria or grandiose delusions; a *depressed* type, characterized by symptoms of melancholia, agitated dejection or hypochondriacal delusions; and a *demented* type, exhibiting a general personality deterioration, social withdrawal and emotional apathy. The organization of neurosyphilitic personality types into these three categories is misleading. The range of premorbid personality dispositions "released" by the physical impairment is much more varied than is characterized by these three classic types. In fact, many of these patients exhibit no psychopathological traits other than the "standard" symptoms of neurological disease.

## ENCEPHALITIS

This syndrome, representing the inflammation and frequent destruction of brain tissue, may be traced to a variety of infectious sources, the most probable of which are filterable viruses; on occasion, similar effects are produced by immunization serums and systemic infections such as measles and hepatitis.

Different forms of the disease have been described, the most prominent of which is known as *epidemic encephalitis*. This contagious variety spread throughout Europe and to the United States between 1915 and 1919. Although rarely seen in true epidemic form, another outbreak was reported in India in 1958. Because a marked lethargy and somnolence are common during the early phase of the disease, it originally was termed encephalitis lethargica; however, these symptoms are not always present.

Although the neurological and psychological consequences of encephalitis are similar to those observed in neurosyphilis, there are certain distinguishing features worthy of note.

### Clinical Picture in Acute Cases

Most patients react with high fever and drowsiness immediately following the infection. A few succumb to prolonged sleep for periods of weeks; this sleep is *not* stuporous since they can be roused to take nourishment or converse briefly. Neurological signs are displayed during this stage, particularly in the motor and ocular mechanisms. An irritable hyperactivity often follows the termination of the somnolent period. Patients are restless and agitated, cannot sleep, suffer periodic convulsions, become disoriented and delirious and may experience frightening hallucinations.

### Clinical Picture in Childhood Chronic Cases

The effects of encephalitis in children are often severe and permanent; this depends largely on the age of the child. The normal maturation of intellectual capacities may be seriously impaired in children under the age of five or six; the younger the child and the more prolonged the acute phase, the more severe the deficiency. Perhaps as many as five per cent of all institutionalized cases of mental retardation can be ascribed to the effects of early encephalitis.

Children, both young and older, often display a postencephalitic impulsiveness and distractibility; they become difficult to discipline, neglectful of personal responsibilities and emotionally erratic, agitated and hyperactive—in short, they exhibit a loss of integrative controls. Some retain the "abstract attitude," but find considerable difficulty in monitoring external stimuli and regulating internal impulses. As a result of the disruptive and chaotic effects of the impairment, their chances for developing a coherent personality are seriously hampered; thus, many continue into adulthood as undisciplined, erratic and moody persons.

### Clinical Picture in Adult Chronic Cases

The consequences of encephalitis in adulthood are considerably less severe than they are in childhood. For the great majority, they are limited to motor symptoms such as motor rigidity, spontaneous tremors of the musculature, a staring, mask-like facial expression and a propulsive and quivering gait.

*Oculogyric crises,* a symptom in which the eyes are involuntarily turned upward for several minutes, are part of a minor cluster of neuro-ocular impairments. The loss of psychological control and abstraction capacities is minimal in adults. However, the illness may precipitate pathological coping reactions; when they do occur, it is the patient's premorbid personality which determines their severity and character.

## DEFECTS ASSOCIATED WITH TOXIC AGENTS

In this section we shall review three chemogenic cripplers of brain tissue: alcohol, drugs and poisons. Before we begin, let us note that alcoholic and drug addiction syndromes, discussed in chapter 12, differ from alcoholic and drug defects, listed in this chapter. An addiction does not, in itself, signify that a patient has suffered neural tissue damage. Individuals may be both addicted and defected, but these need not covary, and therefore must be distinguished.

There is no relationship between the chemical make-up of a toxin and the content of the clinical symptoms that a patient exhibits. The specific pathological behaviors displayed are determined by the patient's premorbid personality and present environment, *not* by the particular toxin to which he has been subjected. Different toxic agents vary, however, in the potency and duration of their effects; thus, they may produce different symptoms on these accounts.

All toxins, if ingested in sufficient quantities, cause severe *acute* impairments. These are characterized chiefly by a clouding of consciousness and a loss of integrative controls. Concentration is difficult; there may be disorientation as to time and place; recent memory often is impaired; emotions are labile and erratic; a restless hyperactivity may covary with marked fatigue; periods of delirium are not uncommon and are often accompanied by visual hallucinations and delusions.

*Chronic* syndromes are characterized by diminished abstraction capacities, motor and language deficits, accentuated premorbid personality traits and, if sufficiently prolonged, social withdrawal, incompetence and behavioral rigidity.

Let us next examine the three major toxic syndromes.

## ALCOHOLIC SYNDROMES
(DSM-II: *Alcoholic Psychosis*)

Seven subcategories have been distinguished in the DSM-II to represent the disruptive effects of alcohol. Only four will be discussed here: pathological intoxication, delirium tremens, alcoholic hallucinosis and alcoholic deterioration. Of these, the first two are acute impairments, the fourth is chronic, and the third may be either. Another defect, known as Korsakoff's syndrome, is often included among alcoholic impairments; however, alcohol is only one of several different factors which can give rise to this "dysmnesic-confabulatory" disturbance; the syndrome will be presented under the category of "nutritional defects."

### Pathological Intoxication

This is an acute disruption of normal brain functioning following immediately after the ingestion of relatively moderate amounts of alcohol. It occurs in individuals whose tolerance is especially low either as a function of neurological disease (e.g., epilepsy), general emotional instability (e.g., paranoid personality) or physical susceptibilities (e.g., states of exhaustion). Disorientation, confusion and delirium are prominent symptoms. During these periods, patients may act out violently, experience intense anxiety, perceive hallucinations or be plunged into a state of depression. The content of these ancillary psychological symptoms usually reflects a release and accentuation of the patient's predelirious personality. Delirium typically lasts a few hours, although, on occasion, it may extend to a day or two, following which the patient succumbs to a prolonged and deep sleep; upon awakening, the patient recalls little or nothing of what happened.

The following case demonstrates the type of behavior that might be observed during these intoxicated states (Kolb, 1968).

### CASE 13-2
#### Nathan W., Age 28, Divorced

Nathan was seen in jail while awaiting trial on a charge of drunkenness and disorderly conduct. The patient's father had committed suicide as he was about to be sent to a hospital for mental diseases. Nathan himself was described as being a friendly but quick-tempered and restless individual whose marriage had terminated in early divorce. He was said never to have been particularly alcoholic, but one July 4 he celebrated the holiday by drinking two bottles of beer and a glass of wine. Soon afterward he attempted to fling himself down an 80-foot embankment and was so greatly excited that he was taken to the police station for the night. The next morning he had no recollection of the affair. Ten months later Nathan called late one afternoon to see friends who invited him to sample what they considered choice varieties of whiskey and gin. He accepted their invitation and drank somewhat more heavily than usual. Soon after leaving the home of his friends he was observed by a police officer to be acting strangely. As the officer spoke to him he attacked him. While the officer was calling for help, Nathan disappeared. About 15 minutes later two women were startled to see a strange man thrust his head through a closed window of their living room and shout, "Help! Murder!" It was Nathan, who then ran on to another house where he rang the doorbell insistently. As the occupant answered the summons he again screamed, "Murder!" and ran to the street once more, where he broke the windshields and headlights of several parked automobiles and tore out the seats and pulled parts from other cars. At this point he was seized and taken to the police station where, on awakening the following morning, he had no recollection of his experiences of the previous night.

### Delirium Tremens

This well-publicized and dramatic syndrome is likely to be superimposed upon a pattern of chronic alcoholic addiction. It usually takes the form of a withdrawal symptom following a prolonged binge of heavy drinking; on occasion, it may appear in an addicted individual in conjunction with a minor head injury or systemic infection.

As the phase of delirium approaches, the patient senses a diffuse apprehensiveness, uncomfortable restlessness and insomnia, and may become distraught over slight noises or sudden movements. Several covarying symptoms appear as the impairment proceeds to its more serious phase.

1. *Physical symptoms:* body temperature rises, perspiration becomes profuse, there is a rapid heart rate, nausea, unsteady gait, physical weakness and coarse tremors of hands, tongue and lips.

2. *Concentration symptoms:* consciousness becomes clouded, there is disorientation for time and place, and memory for well-known events and people become blurred.

3. *Perceptual symptoms:* visual and tactile hallucinations come to the fore, the patient sees strange small objects twisting and running; he feels lice, roaches and spiders crawling all over him.

4. *Anxiety symptoms:* experiences of extreme fear and terror are common, mostly in response to the menacing objects and movements which appear to surround him, but also as a general foreboding that he is doomed to remain forever in his frightening state.

This delirious episode usually lasts for three to six days, and is followed by a deep sleep. Physical symptoms disappear upon awakening, but there is a slight residual of anxiety and a hazy recall of terrifying hallucinations. These tend to deter further drinking for a short period.

The following description illustrates the typical experiences and behaviors of such a patient.

#### CASE 13-3
#### James Z., Age 47, Married, No Children

Jim is a moderately successful lawyer, despite his chronic alcoholism. He "goes off on a bender" about once a month, disappearing for several days to a week. In the past ten years, Jim has been briefly hospitalized more than 20 times in conjunction either with delirium tremens or some other alcohol-related difficulty.

In a recent episode, his "girl-friend" called the emergency ward at the local hospital because Jim was jabbing himself with a fork "to get those miserable gnats off" his body. He was screaming and delirious upon admission to the hospital, terrified not only of the hallucinated gnats, but of the "crazy shapes" and "smelly queeries" that were "coming after" him. Nothing could be done to comfort Jim for several hours; he continued to have tremors, sweated profusely, cowered in a corner, drew his blankets over his head, twisted and turned anxiously, vomited several times and kept screaming about hallucinated images which "attacked" him and "ate up his skin."

After three days of delirium, with intermittent periods of fitful sleep, Jim began to regain his normal senses. He was remorseful, apologized to all for his misbehavior and assured them of his "absolute resolution never to hit the bottle again." Unfortunately, as was expected, he again was hospitalized three months later as a consequence of a similar debauche that was followed by delirium tremens.

### Alcoholic Hallucinosis

The major symptom in this disturbance is auditory hallucination; in a few cases, this is accompanied by delusions. In contrast to delirium tremens, these patients are not disoriented or confused and are able to carry out their everyday responsibilities, except those involving their particular hallucination.

It is highly probable that the syndrome occurs only in individuals already disposed to psychopathological tendencies; alcohol serves merely as a "releaser," a weakener of fragile controls that otherwise barely manage to contain the pathological process.

There is no clear understanding as to why auditory hallucinations in particular come to the fore in these cases. Quite possibly, alcohol may have selective chemical effects upon constitutionally disposed individuals, giving rise to disturbances specifically in the auditory apparatus. Patients will interpret these strange sensations in line with their latent pathological tendencies. Thus, some "hear" threatening voices or pistol shots whereas others recognize comforting sounds or voices, as in the famous play *Harvey*, about a genial drunk and his friendly invisible rabbit.

### Alcoholic Deterioration

This chronic condition is difficult to separate from prolonged alcoholic addiction since they almost invariably coexist. We attach this label to cases which give evidence both of a progressive destruction of cortical cells and an insidious decline of premorbid personality traits. In chronic alcoholic addiction, the habit need not have progressed to the stage of pervasive cellular atrophy.

The clinical picture seen in these patients is a composite of their various neural and psychological complications; abstraction capacities are impaired and exhibited in memory defects, poverty of ideas, illogical reasoning and poor judgment; controls progressively give way and the patient displays emotional impulsiveness, crudeness and irresponsibility and a growing slovenliness in personal appearance; depending on premorbid personality traits, he may become irritable and hostile or servile and dependent; a variety of specific functional impairments become evident, notably a loss of fine motor control, speech disarticulation, sluggish reflexes and aphasic symptoms.

## DRUG SYNDROMES

Many of these impairments are difficult to differentiate from drug addictions. Distinctions, although largely academic and impossible to make in acute cases, are justified in chronic drug syndromes in which permanent alterations have occurred in the biophysical apparatus.

It should be noted that drugs taken for euphoric and hallucinogenic purposes, e.g., heroin, marijuana and LSD, are not viewed as toxic agents, although they do alter, perhaps even permanently, the biophysical substrate of psychological functioning.

Three drugs typically are included as toxic agents—morphine, barbiturates and bromides. Moderate levels of these drugs over several months may produce confusion, drowsiness, moodiness, fitful sleep, faulty memory and sluggish reactivity; these are often accompanied by a variety of discomforting physical ailments. Prolonged use of these drugs, even with doses below the level capable of producing acute disturbances, may develop into serious addictions; withdrawal symptoms as well as possible irreversible changes in neural tissue are inevitable. With the exception of decreased controls, most of the specific and integrative functions of the brain are not severely impaired. There are likely to be a number of personality disturbances, however, usually accentuations of premorbid traits.

## POISON SYNDROMES

A variety of both acute and chronic symptoms may occur in response to the ingestion or inhalation of several metals, liquids and gases. Notable among these are lead, mercury, manganese, carbon monoxide and carbon disulfide. Most acute forms of poison intoxication are accidental; chronic varieties usually arise as a consequence of prolonged occupational exposure. As is typical of most acute syndromes, these patients exhibit confusion, irritability, fatigue, hallucinations, delirium and, where high dosages are involved, severe coma. In chronic cases, the principal symptoms are a progressive deterioration of controls and abstraction capacities. Personality complications, when present, reflect an accentuation of preclinical traits.

## DEFECTS ASSOCIATED WITH BRAIN TRAUMA

Injuries to the head provided ancient man with his first source of data concerning the role of the brain in consciousness and intelligence. Hippocrates identified the connection between these accidents and a variety of perceptual and motor disabilities. Galen was the first to propose that head injuries were a primary cause of mental disorders. Today we know that there are perhaps as many as one million accidents each year in the United States involving the head region; many result in severe although usually temporary mental abberations. An unknown number of seemingly minor falls and head wounds may cause unrecognized and permanent harm to the developing nervous systems of young children.

### TYPES OF INJURY AND THEIR IMMEDIATE EFFECTS

Trauma to the brain produces several immediate consequences, the nature of which depends on the overall extent and severity of the accident, and on whether it includes the destruction of brain tissue and its supporting blood vessels. Head injuries have been grouped into four types: concussions, contusions, lacerations and vascular accidents.

**Concussions.** These rather common and temporary impairments stem from blows to the head which neither penetrate the skull nor damage brain tissue. There is a brief loss of consciousness followed by a period, ranging from several minutes to a few days, in which the patient seems confused, may be nauseated and dizzy and experiences both focal and diffuse headaches. The knockout blow in boxing typifies this acute syndrome.

It is unclear as to what mechanisms underlie

the brief and seemingly reflexive episode of unconsciousness that characterizes concussions. Among the more plausible speculations are that blood circulation is sharply curtailed to minimize pressure and reduce potential bleeding; another is that the reticular activating system is abruptly inhibited to prevent further strain on the nervous and circulatory apparatus.

**Contusions.** These are abrasions of brain tissue resulting from violent or jolting head motions, severe cerebral compressions or skull fractures. Contusions are more serious than concussions since they represent an actual bruising of neural matter. A period of coma is not uncommon, lasting from a few hours to several weeks. Upon regaining consciousness, the patient remains somewhat disoriented, may become delirious and almost invariably experiences both headaches and dizziness. Convulsions are not infrequent, and there may be a temporary loss of speech, as well as other relatively specific impaired functions.

**Lacerations.** The most serious exogenous brain traumas are accidents which penetrate the skull and rupture or tear through brain tissue. If the patient survives his injury, he is likely to remain in a coma for an extended period. The immediate postcoma symptoms are essentially the same as were noted for contusions. The nature of specific functional impairments, ranging from total paralysis to aphasia to minor motor deficits, depends essentially on the locus of injury. Premorbid personality traits and the general extent of neural damage, determine whether the patient will remain quiescent or be hyperactive and anxious.

**Vascular Accidents.** In this acute, endogenous impairment, the defect arises either from a blocking or a bursting of a cerebral blood vessel.

The sudden blocking of circulation, termed *cerebral thrombosis,* prevents the receipt of nourishment or the removal of waste products within associated brain regions. A similar defect, but one that develops much more gradually, is termed "cerebral arteriosclerosis"; this degenerative defect, to be discussed later, occurs as a consequence of the progressive narrowing of the blood vessels. In both impairments, there may be a paralysis of the musculature, a variety of sensory anesthesias and cognitive-language deficits.

The rupture of a circulatory vessel, termed *intracranial hemorrhaging,* results in a flooding of blood throughout the surrounding brain field. If the vessel involved is a major one or essential to the neural activation of vital organs, the result is usually death. In less severe cases, there is a strong likelihood that the recovery phase will be characterized by paralysis, confusion and other marked functional limitations.

## POST-TRAUMATIC SYMPTOMS

Most cases of brain concussion and contusion in adults are followed by a rapid recovery, with no long-term or chronic consequences. Although the evidence is unclear, severe concussions or contusions in childhood, especially during periods of early neurological maturation, may produce developmental retardations; these defects are likely to be limited to spheres of brain capacity that are undergoing rapid neural proliferation at the time of trauma.

Disturbing aftereffects in cases of laceration and vascular accident are rather common but by no means inevitable. The most frequent of the enduring symptoms are headaches and dizziness. Specific functional defects are determined by the locus of tissue damage. Convulsive seizures persist in about five per cent of these cases. Deterioration of integrative abstraction and control functions are not common in adults unless there has been extensive neural destruction or bilateral (both hemispheres) damage to the frontal lobes. Here, we observe memory deficits, inabilities to grasp and discriminate concepts, defective judgment and a lack of insight and planning. As was noted earlier, severe injuries to the maturing child produce more serious consequences than in the adult. Not only are control functions critically impaired, resulting in symptoms such as hyperdistractibility and emotional lability, but the entire developmental sequence of higher abstraction capacities may be retarded.

Personality changes observed in posttraumatic cases are colored by premorbid traits and attitudes. Some patients exhibit a chronic irritability; others appear to be in a state of permanent fatigue and invalidism. There is no way to determine the extent to which these changes can be ascribed specifically to neural damage. However, if the lesion is located in the reticular system, we would expect to see distortions in activation, either a general apathy and dullness or an increased intensity of prior behavioral tendencies. Similarly, injuries to limbic regions may give rise to any number and variety of alterations in emotional reactivity. In general, nonfocal lesions decrease inhibitory controls, releasing and accentuating premorbid personality trends.

The following history is more or less typical

of the behavioral consequences of brain trauma (Gregory, 1968).

This farmer was admitted to the psychiatric unit of a general hospital with a history of marked personality changes following a serious automobile accident ten months previously. Prior to the accident he had been healthy, hard working, sociable, and easy to get along with. In the automobile accident, he sustained fractures of the arm and skull with severe concussion and brain damage, so that he was unconscious for ten days afterward.

On awakening from the coma, Carl had no recollection of events that had occurred immediately preceding the accident, and he continued to have difficulty in remembering certain events that happened after he recovered consciousness. What his family noticed most, however, were the marked changes in his behavior that occurred after he left the hospital and returned home to his farm. They found him extremely irritable, easily angered, and unpredictable in his behavior. Carl drove the chickens as though they were cows, and made them so nervous that egg production dropped drastically. He fed the cows just enough for them to stay alive. He carefully locked up empty fuel drums which he had never done previously. He wrecked some of the farm machinery so badly that his son could not repair it. He would not talk to members of his family at all except to berate and swear at them, and he threatened his wife with physical violence many times. He blamed his family for poor crops which were really due to drought, and he frequently got up at night and slammed doors.

Carl's unusual behavior had already improved considerably by the time he was admitted to the psychiatric unit, and throughout the three weeks he remained there, he was pleasant, cooperative, and sociable, with no evidence of depression or paranoid ideation. However, he did show mild disorientation for time and impairment of memory for recent events, which remained fairly constant throughout his hospital stay and did not show the marked changes that sometimes occur in certain types of organic brain syndrome.

Because of the abrupt nature of their impairment, many patients recognize their decreased competence and experience repeated "catastrophic anxieties." As a consequence, they begin to "shrink their milieu," drawing more and more into a narrow world of activities and relationships in which they feel both able and secure. It is not uncommon, therefore, that the long-term post-traumatic personality picture in adult patients, once having passed through an initial period in which their preclinical traits were accentuated, begins to be characterized by a pervasive social detachment and behavioral rigidity.

## DEFECTS ASSOCIATED WITH NUTRITIONAL DEFICIENCIES

The role of malnutrition as a factor producing psychopathology has decreased sharply throughout the western world, although it continues to be of significance in certain underdeveloped and primitive societies. Several sources of dietary inadequacy and their associated clinical syndromes will be discussed briefly.

*Thiamine deficiencies* produce the disease known as *beriberi,* which usually affects only the peripheral nervous system. In addition to a number of minor physical impairments, it is characterized by increased irritability, fatigue and insomnia. Should the pathology extend to the destruction of central nervous system tissue, we observe a cluster of clinical symptoms known as *Wernicke's syndrome.* Neurological signs of oculomotor disturbance, pupillary sluggishness and tremors in the extremities are common in this impairment. Consciousness may be clouded for prolonged periods, and delirium and convulsion are often seen in advanced cases. Wernicke's syndrome is a frequent consequence of nutritional inadequacies stemming from a long-term alcoholic habit.

*Niacin deficiencies* give rise to the syndrome known as *pellagra.* Before preventive dietary measures were introduced, this nutritional inadequacy accounted for as much as 10 per cent of all first admissions to state hospitals in the southern United States. In addition to a variety of physical effects such as dermatitis, diarrhea, headaches and fatigue, patients frequently experience depressions and anxiety as well as occasional delirium and hallucinosis.

*Vitamin B complex deficiencies* often give rise to the clinical syndrome referred to as *Korsakoff's psychosis.* Although the cluster of symptoms grouped under this label has traditionally been associated with advanced forms of alcoholism, the syndrome is not limited to cases of chronic alcoholic toxicity; in fact, even in these cases, the symptomatology is a consequence not of alcohol but of vitamin deficiencies associated with the eating habits of chronic alcoholics. The psychosis, first described in 1887 by Sergei Korsakoff, is merely a descriptive cluster of symptoms whose origins may be found in a number of different etiological sources. Known also as the "dysmnesic-confabulatory syndrome," it is characterized by marked decrements in the retention of new learning, an inability to sustain attention and alertness and a tendency to falsify reminiscences so as to fill in memory gaps. Quite frequently, the symptoms noted earlier under the label of Wernicke's syndrome are superimposed upon the Korsakoff cluster. The overall clinical picture typically is compounded by a generalized blunting of higher integrative capacities and progressive personality accentuations and distortions.

# DEFECTS ASSOCIATED WITH METABOLIC AND ENDOCRINOLOGICAL DYSFUNCTIONS

Many differences among people in rate and pattern of metabolic and endocrinological functioning remain within "normal" limits. These biochemical differences give shape to distinctive individual temperaments and reactivity patterns. Our concern in this section, however, is not with "normal" variations; these constitutional differences are relevant primarily to general personality development. Rather, our focus here is on pathologically deviant or diseased biochemical functions.

The defects presented in the previous four sections—infections, toxic agents, trauma and nutritional deficiencies—are, with few exceptions, due to exogenous causes. Beginning with this section, the primary etiological sources are endogenous; thus, metabolic and endocrinological dysfunctions, intracranial neoplasms and cerebral degeneration, although occasionally prompted or fostered by external precipitants, more commonly derive from constitutional or internal origins.

Although the number of anomalies associated with metabolic and endocrinological functioning is legion, we will limit ourselves to brief discussions of three groups of syndromes: *porphyria, thyroid dysfunction* and *adrenal dysfunction.* The first is a metabolic disease, the latter two are basically endocrinological disorders.

**Porphyria Syndromes.** This condition is a result of an inborn error of metabolism resulting in the production of abnormal types of porphyrins which appear in the urine. Two types may be distinguished: acute intermittent porphyria, more common in females, and transmitted by a Mendelian dominant trait; and congenital porphyria, a rare condition, more common in males, and transmitted as a recessive trait.

Porphyrin compounds are found throughout the body. Production of excessive and chemically malformed compounds leads primarily to a patchy demyelinization of the spinal nerves and the motor cells of the central nervous system; changes in bone marrow, liver and blood composition are also common physical sequelae. The typical clinical picture in the more frequent *intermittent type* begins with an acute attack of severe abdominal pain that fails to subside within 24 hours; it is often accompanied by marked behavioral irritability and argumentativeness. The early physical symptoms wax and wane, but most patients continue to exhibit agitation, depression, disturbances of memory and, on occasion, delirium and hallucinosis. The long-term prognosis of this impairment depends on the extent of nervous system involvement, the patient's personality vulnerabilities and the environmental reinforcements to which he is exposed.

**Thyroid Syndromes.** The thyroid is an endocrine gland centrally involved in regulating body metabolism. Over or underproduction of its major hormone, known as *thyroxin,* results in a variety of pathological consequences.

In *hyper*thyroidism there is an oversecretion of thryroxin, causing an acceleration of metabolic activity and giving rise to emotional irritability and excitability, as well as a host of physical signs such as insomnia, tremors and weight loss. In about 10 per cent of these cases, symptoms of a severe psychopathological nature are evidenced. These include severe apprehension and agitation, fleeting hallucinations and, in rare cases, periods of delirium. The probability and character of these psychological symptoms appear to be less a function of the endocrinological disturbance than of the personality vulnerabilities and dispositions of the patient.

*Hypo*thyroidism, frequently termed "myxedema," usually stems from an endogenous deficiency in iodine production. Among the more common symptoms are increased weight, physical sluggishness, an inability to concentrate and a poor memory for recent events. Individuals with established personality defects respond to this impairment in accord with their premorbid tendencies. For example, passively inclined persons are more likely to yield to their physical state and become lethargic, retiring or depressed whereas formerly active individuals may react by becoming anxious, restless or irritable.

**Adrenal Syndromes.** Diseases of the adrenal glands are likely to result in marked behavioral changes since this endocrine organ is centrally involved in the activation of emergency biological responses and the rapid metabolism of energy needs.

Chronic insufficiencies in the adrenal cortex, known as *Addison's disease,* are associated with both physical and psychological changes. Characteristic physical symptoms include weight loss, darkened skin pigmentation, lowered blood pressure, fatigability and lassitude; among the more notable psychological signs are moderate depression and a decreased sociability and ambition. Coping responses to these changes will reflect the patient's premorbid personality tendencies; we observe quiet "sensible" adjustments in some, and anxiety, irritability, severe depression and invalidism in others.

*Hyper*functions of the adrenal cortex give rise to unusual physical aberrations, especially during puberty; precocious sexual development may be exhibited should this rare disease occur at this point in maturation. In another impairment, known as *Cushing's syndrome,* there are abnormal growths in the adrenal cortices resulting in excessive secretions of the organ's hormones; among the psychological sequelae of this defect are severe mood swings, ranging from marked apathy and depression to irritability and overt hostility.

## DEFECTS ASSOCIATED WITH INTRACRANIAL NEOPLASM

In this classification we include endogenous impairments resulting from abnormal growths within the brain or its surrounding tissues. These are found in about 2 per cent of all autopsied cases and are encountered at all ages, but predominantly in the forties and fifties. *Malignant* growths tend to interfere directly with cellular functioning, result in the paralysis of associated biological and psychological processes and almost inevitably result in death. *Benign* tumors, in contrast, usually exert their effects by intracranial pressure; because the cranium is a rigidly enclosed region, expansion of any part will cause compression of both near and far brain tissue.

The clinical picture associated with neoplasms is extremely varied, reflecting the location, size and rapidity of tumor growth and, as with all biophysical defects, the preclinical personality of the patient. The well-known triad of symptoms —headache, vomiting, and "choked disc" (a narrowing of the fovea of the retina due to intracranial pressure and the swelling of the optic nerve)—may occur too late to be of preventive value.

Among the more prominent signs of a loss of integrative functions are clouding of consciousness, inability to concentrate, convulsive seizures and memory impairments; acute symptoms such as delirium may follow a sudden increase in intracranial pressure.

Signs of general impairment are usually intertwined with a number of more specific disturbances; the nature of these circumscribed symptoms depends on the primary locus of tissue damage or pressure. Although tumors in the frontal lobes may result in behaviors that are at variance with a patient's premorbid personality, it is more likely that preclinical traits will simply be accentuated. Temporal and parietal lobe neoplasms are often associated with perceptual motor and cognitive language dysfunctions whereas occipital lobe tumors frequently give rise to visual hallucinations.

Because the brain can accommodate to slowly expanding neoplasms for long periods, no signs of pathology may be evident until the disease process has progressed beyond controllable proportions. In some of these insidiously developing cases, the emergence of pathognomonic symptoms is so closely interwoven with subtle psychological changes as to be overlooked even to a discerning clinical eye. Moreover, it is not difficult to misinterpret the universal and persistent neoplasm symptoms of headache and nausea as "just another" sign of a minor and insignificant psychophysiological or hypochondriacal disorder.

## DEFECTS ASSOCIATED WITH CEREBRAL DEGENERATION

Increased longevity is one of the many beneficial consequences of recent advances in medical science. However, this has not been an unmixed blessing since the prolongation of life means that man will be confronted with more of the disabling impairments of old age. Three times as many people survive beyond the age of 65 than they did a century ago, only to suffer now the ravaging effects of physical and mental deterioration. We have seen a sharp upturn in recent years in the total number and percentage of cases admitted to hospitals in conjunction with the degenerative effects of aging. In the past twenty years alone, the proportion of patients over 65 admitted to mental hospitals has increased five times as rapidly as those below that age; at present, almost one fourth of all first admissions are in this age bracket. These figures only touch the surface of the devastating and desolating psychological consequences of growing old. Perhaps as many as a third of a million persons in nursing homes for the aged are there as a result of mental as well as physical deterioration. In addition, there are untold numbers of older persons who are sheltered within their families and communities, despite severe degenerative psychopathology. In short, aging is a major psychological health problem of growing proportions.

Before detailing the subsyndromes of cerebral degeneration, let us consider some of the determinants which contribute to the aging process.

## GENERAL ETIOLOGY

Medical science is still unclear as to why men age, and why people differ in both the rapidity and character of the aging process. It was once believed that the progression of bodily deterioration was as intrinsic a biological process in old age as was growth in youth. Recent thought suggests that degeneration, although ultimately inevitable, is fostered by avoidable environmental conditions, such as toxins, faulty nutrition, psychic stress, climate and irradiation, each of which impairs the organism's regenerative powers. Thus, it is not inconceivable, given proper preventive habits and the expected advances of medical science, that an average age of more than 120 years may be common in the near future.

Although life may be prolonged, the question will still remain as to why some people continue to be productive and alive in spirit during old age, many others simply manage to "hold on" and others deteriorate rapidly. Until the recent growth of interest in gerontology—the study of old age—differences among men in the rapidity and character of aging were viewed to be a product primarily of the pattern in which the various components of their bodies degenerated. We now know that the deterioration process is more complicated than that of the distribution of regional body degeneration alone; clinical symptomatology in aged patients is influenced greatly by psychological and social factors. As evidence of this biogenic-psychogenic interplay, gerontologists point out that severe psychopathology is often present in old age with but minimal evidence of neuropathological disease; and conversely, they find cases of pervasive brain degeneration with but few minor psychological disabilities. Clearly then, psychopathology in old age is not simply biogenic or psychogenic; it is a complex interaction of both factors. If we keep this interactive point of view as a framework, we may proceed to the pedagogical task of separating these two classes of determinants.

### Biogenic Factors

There are numerous neurological and circulatory changes associated with aging. The total weight of the brain is reduced, with a definite decrease in the number of neuronal cells, especially in the cortex. Both large and small blood vessels lose their elasticity and appear convoluted. Fatty deposits and calcifications proliferate, lining and surrounding both cells and vessels, occluding normal blood flow, retarding the delivery of oxygen and nutrient materials and resulting in the reduction of cellular metabolism and the elimination of waste products. Not only do these changes lead to tissue degeneration and decreased cellular efficiency, but they upset homeostatic balances and set into motion secondary strains which exhaust the body's tenuous energy reserves.

Associated with these internal changes is a general decline in physical energy, a diminished muscular strength, speed and coordination, a weakened sensory acuity and an increased vulnerability to illness compounded by slow and arduous periods of recuperation. Prominent among changes in general integrative functions is a failing memory, with all of its disconcerting effects. Similarly, older persons display an increased intellectual rigidity, a decline in the capacity for new learning or for solving problems that require reflection and imagination. Fortunately, many are still able to draw upon their storehouse of accumulated experience to master the everyday tasks of life.

### Psychogenic Factors

The importance of psychosocial factors is usually secondary in advanced cases of cerebral degeneration. However, the role played by psychological attitudes and social resources is extremely important during the earlier phases of degeneration and may determine the entire course of the aging process. Many an older person remains vigorous, productive and intellectually alert, despite substantial biophysical deterioration; witness the spirited writings of George Bernard Shaw and Bertrand Russell when they were well into their nineties or the physical stamina and clarity of mind of Amos Alonzo Stagg who continued his football coaching career to the age of 100.

For most individuals, later life is a period of transition that demands adjustments even more challenging than those faced during the turbulent years of adolescence. In contrast to the adolescent, the aging person is not physically robust and pliant, and, more importantly, does not look forward with bright anticipation to his future prospects; most envision only increasing infirmity and inescapable death. Such cheerfully euphemistic labels as "senior citizen," designed to "soften the blow," only tell him that he is past his peak and is expected to sit on the sidelines while others carry on the game of life. Added on to the realities of failing health and retirement from meaningful work, the realization of a loss of personal status and significance may come as a profound shock. As aging persons look about them, they see the values they cherished throughout their lives simply cast aside by "new fangled" ideas and customs. Having little else to hold to than their memories and increasingly distraught by the "arrogance and irreverence" of the young, they begin to exhibit an intolerance and conservatism that irritates others and becomes a source of interpersonal tension that further endangers the affection and respect they so desperately crave. Feelings of alienation and isolation are further compounded by the death of peer group companions, and the older person suffers increased demoralization and draws ever more into himself. The prospect of loneliness and poverty and of being an unwelcome burden to unreceptive children adds to their fears and to the indignity of having to depend for survival on the patronizing good will of others. Psychologically isolated, their sense of self-worth destroyed and anticipating a future beset by increased incompetence, infirmity and inescapable death, many older persons "give up" and allow themselves to sink into the "inevitable."

Whether or not the individual's life assumes the bleak sequence of events just outlined depends on his lifelong personality style and outlook and the degree of support and encouragement he finds in his environment. Possessing an aliveness of spirit, a capacity for self-renewal, an active interest in contemporary affairs and a wholesome family and community environment, the probability is small that the person will succumb readily to the degenerative changes of aging. However, given few inner resources or a discouraging family life, the likelihood of rapid psychological and physical deterioration markedly increases. As we progress in our description of the various clinical subdivisions of degeneration, let us keep in mind this complex background of psychosocial factors which determine the manner and extent to which the individual copes with the inevitable bodily degenerations of aging.

## PRESENILE DEVIANCES AND DISEASES
(DSM-II: *Presenile Dementia*)

For the most part, biophysical degeneration is a normal process, a sequence of events to which all individuals succumb sooner or later. However, some persons exhibit presenile syndromes, that is, give evidence of biological deterioration earlier in life than usual. These individuals may suffer from *deviances* rather than diseases; they lie at the low end of the bell-shaped curve, that part of the statistical continuum which indicates extremes in natural individual differences in the degenerative process. Their decline, then, is *not* due to some special and qualitatively unusual disease process, but is simply a quantitative deviation from the average.

"Individuality" in degeneration is an important but as yet unexplored region of research. The notion, however, is neither strange nor new. We clearly recognize individual differences in the degeneration of bodily organs other than the nervous system; thus, some individuals exhibit failing eyesight rather early in life; others suffer degenerative heart ailments, liver dysfunctions, auditory impairments and so on, at a younger age than is "average." Although many defects like these may be traced to disease processes, that is, qualitatively unusual agents such as genetic errors, toxins, infections and the like, a similar number may simply represent extremes in the normal distribution of biophysical traits. Similarly, many of the psychopathologies of midlife may be due in part to the early degeneration of selected regions of the nervous system. For example, the gradual "flattening of affect" seen in some forty year olds may stem from an inherited tendency for segments of the limbic system to atrophy somewhat prematurely; in a like manner, the "fuzziness" in thinking and the "impaired memory" of some fifty year olds may simply reflect a natural early decline in associated neural substrates.

Although speculation concerning constitutional differences in degeneration can become too facile as an explanation for behaviors of unknown etiology, the role of these "normal" individual differences cannot be overlooked. Despite the obscure nature of these individual variations and the subtle and complex effects they produce, a full understanding of the degenerative process will never be achieved until their role is clearly established; their study promises to be a significant new endeavor in the field of research.

Most presenile degenerative syndromes described in the past century are *diseases* rather than deviances, since they are associated with rare neurological or metabolic defects. In the following sections, we will describe briefly four of these well-delineated disease syndromes. As medical science progresses, the character and details of other presenile groups, both disease and deviance, will no doubt be identified.

### Huntington's Chorea

This is a relatively rare chronic disease characterized by progressively severe and uncontrollable jerking movements. First described by the American neurologist George Huntington in 1872, it is transmitted genetically in the form of a Mendelian dominant gene, is found in all races and parts of the world and occurs in persons between the ages of 30 and 50. Behavioral symptoms frequently precede demonstrable neurological signs; many patients exhibit increased irritability, defective attention and memory and depression several years prior to the emergence of the choreiform twitching. The first definitive signs are seen in facial grimacing, head nodding and an involuntary smacking of the tongue and lips. As the disease progresses, there is a gradual spreading to the trunk and limbs of irregular and stretching movements; in addition, there is a disjointed and bizarre gait and explosive speech. The progressive nature of this disease is illustrated in the following case (Kolb, 1968).

### CASE 13-5
### Rachel A., Age 56, Married, One Child

Rachel was admitted to a mental hospital at the age of 56. The familial incidence of Huntington's chorea was striking. A maternal grandmother, a maternal uncle and his daughter, the patient's mother and four of the patient's siblings exhibited definite symptoms of Huntington's chorea. Two members of the family committed suicide after they had developed the disease. Prior to her illness Rachel was apparently an attractive, well-adjusted person. She was a Girl Scout leader and took part in community affairs. Shortly before she was 35 years of age she began to show an insidious change of personality. She discontinued her church, Girl Scout, card club and other activities; she lost interest in her family and at times wandered away from home, returning at night but giving no information as to where she had been. In this same period she began to drop articles and to show twitching of her hands. Rachel became neglectful of her personal appearance, refused to comb her hair, bathe, or change her clothes. She refused to launder soiled garments and would hide them in closets or corners. The choreiform movements increased in extent, and she occasionally fell. At times she

showed temporary alertness and interest in anticipation of a visit from her daughter, but after one or two days she drifted back into her former seclusiveness and deteriorated habits.

On many occasions Rachel threatened and even attacked her husband, sometimes with a knife, and on one occasion inflicted a four-inch scalp wound. She became profane and her favorite term in addressing her husband was, "You G-d-fool." She was subject to tantrums in which she would threaten to jump from a window. She came to be known to the children in the neighborhood as "the old witch on the third floor." Finally, the choreiform movements became so extreme that it was difficult for her to go up and down stairs and she often fell.

On arrival at the hospital, Rachel's facial expression was vacant and she showed such uncoördinated and choreiform movements of her legs that she had difficulty in walking without assistance. There were gross choreiform movements of the head and all extremities. Her constant grimacing, blinking of her eyes, and twitching of her fingers were quite striking. The coördination of her hands was so poor and the movements of her head were so extreme that she had difficulty in eating. Her speech was explosive and difficult to understand. Although somewhat irritable, demanding, and distrustful, she adjusted to the hospital environment without serious difficulty.

The disease is characterized neurologically by diffuse cerebral atrophy, notably in the small ganglion cells. Psychological disturbances are almost inevitable during the mid and later stages of the defect. In some measure, these are a direct product of cerebral changes, especially those associated with the loss of bodily controls. For the greater part, however, they reflect the patient's premorbid personality and the attitude he develops toward his ailment. Some become grossly apathetic, others become severely depressed and still others appear either anxious, delusional, aggressive or hallucinatory. The course of the impairment is irreversible; hospitalization is inevitable and death usually follows within 15 to 20 years of the onset of symptoms.

### Alzheimer's Disease

This form of diffused cerebral atrophy was first described by the German neurologist Alois Alzheimer in 1906. Although the defect is not clearly a familial disease, research suggests that in some cases a hereditary disposition may be operative. At present, however, the exact etiology, assuming there is one, is not known.

Some investigators believe the defect to be a premature variant of senile dementia which will be described later, but there are several features which tend to differentiate the course and symptomatology of these two syndromes. First, Alzheimer's disease occurs abruptly and at an appreciably earlier age than senility, usually in the 40's or 50's; second, it is distinguished by the presence of certain pathognomonic symptoms such as marked speech impairments, involuntary movements in the extremities and occasional convulsions, none of which are notably present in senile dementia; third, degeneration is rapid, with death likely within four or five years after the initial onset of symptoms.

In the early stages, preceding the deterioration in speech and motor functions, patients exhibit impaired reasoning and memory. Both receptive and expressive aphasia are not uncommon as the disease progresses. Accompanying this may be a decrement in control functions, giving rise to disorganized thought, general restlessness, distractibility and emotional lability. In the advanced stage there is an overall deterioration with bodily emaciation, intellectual decline and psychological resignation. The physical exhaustion and distressing awareness of hopelessness and impending death foster a rapid psychic collapse in these patients.

### Pick's Disease

The initial description of this extremely rare disease was made by the Czechoslovakian neurologist Arnold Pick in 1892. Neurologically, the degenerative process is limited at first to the frontal and temporal lobes; as the disease advances, atrophy becomes more pervasive, spreading throughout the central nervous system. The age of onset is approximately the same as in Alzheimer's disease; however, in the latter impairment, the degenerative process is pervasive from the beginning. Other distinctions between the two syndromes may be noted. In contrast to Alzheimer's symptom cluster, patients suffering Pick's disease give less evidence of early memory and speech difficulties and tend to be apathetic and indifferent rather than agitated and restless; also, they are more likely to have ancestors with similar pathological histories. As with Alzheimer's disease, these patients deteriorate rapidly, becoming confused and disorganized in their thinking as degeneration progresses; death occurs about four years after onset.

### Parkinson's Disease

First described by the English physician James Parkinson in 1817, this defect occurs most often between the age of 50 and 70, and arises from a relatively well-circumscribed disease process that affects primarily either the basal ganglia, thalamus or reticular activating system. In contrast to other presenile impairments, it is not associated with a general deterioration of personality and intellect, nor does it inevitably eventuate in death.

The parkinsonian symptoms of muscular rigidity and tremors, propulsive gait, mask-like facies and indistinct speech have been observed in patients following encephalitis, viral infections and exposure to toxins; in most cases, the symptomatology either disappears in time or fails to be progressive. The presenile form of Parkinson's disease, however, is progressively debilitating and appears to result from an endogenous dysfunction of brain metabolism, the etiology of which is unknown. Despite its basic biophysical character, the symptoms of the disease are aggravated by emotional stress. This latter phenomenon may be explained, psychogenically, as a consequence of a general weakening of behavioral controls during periods of emotional upset; it is consistent also with the biogenic view that defective metabolic processes may be aggravated and intensified at times of sympathetic nervous system arousal. Personality changes, such as social withdrawal and apathy, are frequently associated with this syndrome, but do not appear to be an intrinsic part of the disease process; rather, they seem to reflect the patient's attitude toward his physical disability.

## SYNDROMES OF ADVANCED AGE

These impairments stem largely from "normal" processes of cerebral degeneration and are not viewed as products of disease. Neuropathological changes are highly individual, however, each patient exhibiting a pattern of degeneration that is consonant with his distinctive genetic, nutritional and psychological history. To complicate matters, the final clinical picture is often less a result of this "unique" pattern of neurological deficit than the patient's present coping behaviors and environmental conditions.

Two major syndromes are differentiated in conventional practice: *senile dementia and cerebral arteriosclerosis*. As the DSM-II points out, the clinical differentiation of these syndromes may be impossible, especially since both pathological processes often are present simultaneously. We shall draw distinctions between them for pedagogical if not for practical purposes.

### Senile Dementia

These cases comprise about 10 per cent of first admissions to mental hospitals. Although the average age of admission is about 75, the onset of dementia is probably earlier since most patients are cared for by their families prior to hospitalization. No sharp line can be drawn as to when the senile process occurs since degeneration is gradual; imperceptible changes cumulate slowly until an inescapable picture exists to justify the syndrome label. Despite the fact that no two patients exhibit the same clinical picture, certain common features are found.

The brains of senile patients are reduced markedly in size as a function of pervasive cerebral tissue atrophy. Gross neurological examination shows a narrowing of cortical convolutions, a widening of fissures and the presence of numerous scar cells and hydrocephalic accumulations.

Diminished control and abstraction powers are evident on the psychological level. In less severe cases, there is an ineptness in regulating impulses, an increased carelessness and untidiness in personal habits and a tendency to erratic emotional outbursts. A notable early feature is pronounced forgetfulness, especially for recent events.

As the degenerative process advances, thinking becomes illogical, ideas interpenetrate or are fragmented, speech is often rambling and incoherent, and there is a growing disorientation, confusion and loss of identity; periods of terror, bewilderment and delirium may not be uncommon. Although deficits in general control and abstraction processes characterize the deteriorations of senile dementia, specific disabilities in circumscribed functions may be notable if certain regions of the brain are more severely impaired than others; these may take any number of forms, from a loss of speech to minor paralyses to a total amnesia for a particular life period.

Emotional behavior usually is consistent with premorbid traits. However, since these patients are lacking in normal inhibitory controls, their feelings are expressed in accentuated and peculiar form. What often appears as strange and unanticipated behaviors on the part of the elderly usually reflects the expression of previously repressed needs and conflicts, which are now manifest since integrative regulating capacities have deteriorated.

It was once common to classify the "psychotic personality" of senile patients into five groups: the *simple deteriorated type,* noted by an uncomplicated decline in personality functions; the *depressed and agitated type,* who exhibits hypochondriacal delusions, is self-accusatory, guilt-ridden and vacillates between dejection and anxious restlessness; the *presbyophrenic type,* typified by a gregarious sociability and verbosity, especially as he attempts to "cover up" marked memory impairments; the *delirious and confused type,* who is totally disoriented, restless and incoherent; and the *paranoid type,* characterized by grandiosity and delusional suspicions.

This "personality" classification usefully points out some of the major behavioral features of senile dementia, but it tends to be misleading in several regards. *First,* it suggests that patients can be neatly separated into one or another of these subcategories; this does not prove to be at all possible since most advanced cases of senility display, at different times, the features of each of these categories. *Second,* the system implies that the five categories of psychotic behavior are more or less characteristic of senility, when in fact they merely represent a few of the many states seen in "disordered" patients of all ages. Older patients display no less a variety of disordered states than those found among younger persons; thus, the five-fold schema is deficient in that it fails to include other clinical syndromes exhibited during senility. *Third,* the classification breakdown overlooks the developmental continuity between the patient's premorbid personality and the behavior he shows during senility; as we have noted before, the weakening of integrative controls in defects such as senile dementia usually releases and accentuates previously restrained or more prosaic personality tendencies.

As the degenerative process continues its downward trend, the patient slips progressively into a severely deteriorated physical and mental state. He is now totally disoriented, bedridden and reduced to a minimal or vegetable-like existence. With few reserves left to resist disease and with recuperative powers severely weakened, he succumbs readily to some minor infection and dies shortly thereafter.

### Cerebral Arteriosclerosis

Although this disease is by no means inevitable, most elderly people show signs of a hardening and thickening of the blood vessels, causing a cumulative deprivation of oxygen and nutrients to the brain. Approximately 15 per cent of first admissions to mental hospitals are designated as suffering from this form of arteriosclerotic defect.

The symptom picture and clinical course of these patients are difficult to distinguish from those of senile dementia, especially in cases of slow and progressive development. For the most part, the features noted in the section on senility apply to the arteriosclerotic condition. Several

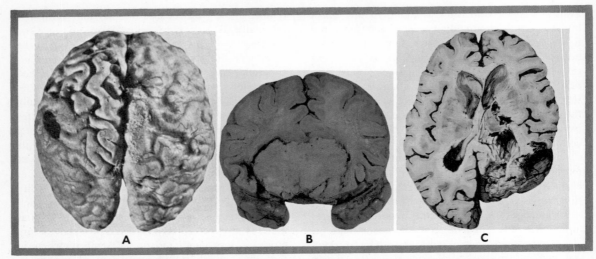

Figure 13-1    Some brain diseases. *A.* Neurosyphilis. (From Wechsler, I. S.: Clinical Neurology. 9th edition. Philadelphia, W. B. Saunders Co., 1963.) *B.* Tumor. *C.* Cerebral arteriosclerosis. (Parts *B* and *C* from Bruetsch, W. L.: Mental disorders arising from organic disease. *In* The Biology of Mental Health and Disease. New York, Hoeber-Harper, 1952.)

points of distinction may be noted, however. *First,* senile dementia progresses almost invariably in a gradual and insidious fashion; changes in cerebral arteriosclerosis, however, often occur in a rapid and dramatic way, usually as a consequence of a sudden occlusion of a major artery. *Second,* the impairments of senile dementia are pervasive in nature and usually affect most prominently the individual's general integrative capacities such as memory retrieval and control and abstraction functions; arteriosclerotics more often give evidence of selective and specific functional impairments, with general integrative capacities remaining relatively intact. *Third,* the symptomatology of senile patients is, more or less, even

and predictable, evidencing slow, almost imperceptible, changes; the clinical picture of arteriosclerotics tends to fluctuate erratically, flaring up into acute confusional episodes at some times, and then quieting down into equanimity and coherence at others. *Fourth,* few seniles experience pain and discomfort in conjunction with their neurological impairment; in contrast, the arteriosclerotic suffers repeated headaches, dizziness and occasional convulsions.

In the later stages of degeneration, seniles and arteriosclerotics are difficult to distinguish; both deteriorate to a bed-ridden state and are confused, emaciated and subject to physical diseases, one of which inevitably proves fatal.

## SYNDROMES ORGANIZED IN TERMS OF CLINICAL SIGNS

The preceding sets of biophysical syndromes were arranged in accord with their etiological origins. Each syndrome exhibited a wide variety of symptoms and progressed through different clinical courses. Nevertheless, despite the fact that their precipitating biogenic agents contributed but a small share to the complex symptom picture that emerged, they were classified in terms of these pathogenic sources.

In the syndromes to be discussed in this section, classification is based on certain features of the symptomatological picture rather than the etiological precipitants of the disturbance. There is no logic to the practice of separating these and the etiological classification groups insofar as the

intrinsic character of their pathologies. The distinction is essentially a matter of convention.

The syndromes discussed in this section arise from a variety of different etiologies, yet exhibit similarities in symptomatology. This should not be taken to mean, however, that the entire clinical picture of a particular syndrome is identical in all respects. Nevertheless, for practical clinical purposes and in keeping with the conventional nosology, we shall view these cases as if they were more homogenous than they in fact are.

The three syndromes to be discussed are: *epilepsy,* characterized by periodic cerebral convulsions; *mental retardation,* noted by pervasive deficiencies in intellectual capacity; and *circumscribed brain dysfunctions in childhood,* distinguished by integrative dyscontrol and deficits specific to cognitive-language and perceptual-motor capacities.

## EPILEPSY

This rather common syndrome incorporates a variety of recurrent clinical states that stem neurologically from an excessive discharge of brain cells; it is characterized chiefly by periods of unconsciousness, involuntary movements or bizarre sensory hallucinations. The terms "seizures" and "convulsions" are often used as synonyms for epilepsy. The term *idiopathic* epilepsy has been applied in the past to cases in which the etiology of the seizure is unknown and presumed to be inherent in the constitutional make-up of the individual. Convulsions are common, however, to many of the syndromes discussed in previous sections. The epileptic classification, to be described here, represents the idiopathic variety, that is, the etiology of these cases has not been identified. Those which are symptomatic of known causes are classified under the heading of the appropriate etiological syndrome.

Epilepsy was well known to the early Greeks. Although popular opinion viewed the impairment to be a "sacred disease" divined by the gods, Hippocrates in the fourth century B.C. considered it to be an ailment of organic origins. This more rational view did not survive, and in the medieval period epilepsy was thought to be a sign of evil spirits within the body. Other naive notions have characterized the history of this impairment; among its ostensive causes were the movements of the stars and perversions of sexual life. Proposals of a similar level of sophistication were made concerning its treatment; these included trephining (boring holes in the skull), drinking pigeon's soup, bleeding and so on. Many eminent historical figures who suffered the ailment, such as Caesar, Napoleon, de Maupassant and Lord Byron, managed to survive the remedial efforts of their physicians.

It was not until the second half of the nineteenth century that the English neurologist Hughlings Jackson speculated that the symptoms of the disease might derive from irritations within the brain that led to excessive discharges of nerve cells. This thesis was essentially confirmed through the use of the electroencephalogram in the late 1920's.

Epilepsy affects about two million Americans, has its onset at any age (many newborn infants give evidence of the disease) and is found in about the same proportions among various so-called racial groups and among men and women. With minor exceptions, epileptics exhibit the same distribution of intellectual capacities as found in the general population, and do not give evidence of progressive neural or personality deterioration. The proportion of epileptics in mental hospitals is only a shade higher than that of nonepileptics.

### SYMPTOMATOLOGY AND CLINICAL VARIETIES

Neurologically, the epileptic process consists of spontaneous and massive discharges of groups of brain cells. Whatever its stimulus, locale or route of spread, the patient experiences in rather intense form the same behaviors, thoughts and feelings that normally are activated by the cerebral tissues involved. Thus, if motor regions are activated, as is so often the case, the patient will spontaneously engage in some kind of physical activity; should the discharge involve visual areas, he may experience visual hallucinations; if regions of the brain that subserve memory are stimulated, then he may suddenly recall some long-forgotten past event.

Before losing consciousness, as is the case in most types of epilepsy, many patients experience what is known as the *aura,* a brief warning of an impending convulsion. This prodromal sign may take different forms depending on the initial site of cellular discharge and the learned attitudes the patient has acquired toward his convulsive experiences. Some simply feel a diffuse apprehensiveness; others become dizzy or get an abdominal cramp; still others sense some unpleasant odor, strange sounds in their ears or an uncontrollable twitching in their legs. These initial signs often provide a useful clue to the primary site of the underlying neural defect. Depending on the locus of the impairment and the extent to which the discharge spreads, the patient may or may not lose consciousness. Periods of unconsciousness are inevitable when brain centers subserving conscious control are flooded. Since neuronal discharges temporarily inactivate the involved cells, the patient remains unconscious for a short period and often experiences minor discomforting residuals upon awakening.

The problem of differentiating the various "types" of epilepsy has plagued clinicians ever since its true character was discovered. In contrast to the syndromes discussed in previous sections, attempts to classify the impairment in terms of etiology have proven extremely cumbersome and impractical; not only is there a great divergence of causes, but for the most part etiological origins cannot be identified. Efforts to distinguish epileptic types in accord with the anatomical locus of the initial discharge present similar complications since, in most cases, the area from which the discharge originates cannot be pinpointed.

Despite recent efforts to develop a classification that coordinates etiology and the primary site of anatomical involvement (Penfield and Jasper, 1954; Symonds, 1955; Goldensohn, 1965), the traditional practice persists of differentiating these patients in terms of clinical symptomatology. We shall follow the traditional schema in the following descriptions. Let us be mindful, however, that the categories to be presented do not exhaust the varieties of epilepsy nor are they mutually exclusive; several "types" may be found in the same patient.

### Grand Mal

This is the commonest and most dramatic form of epilepsy and involves a generalized seizure throughout the brain. Its most prominent psychological correlates are the loss of consciousness and convulsive motor activity. In some cases the patient may undergo vague changes in mood and sensation several hours prior to the seizure; about two thirds experience the aura phenomenon. Just prior to the loss of consciousness, the patient may emit a cry or scream when air is forced from the lungs as a consequence of the involuntary contraction of respiratory muscles. Concurrent with unconsciousness, the patient falls to the ground, displays *tonic* muscular contractions such that the body is rigid with the legs outstretched, arms flexed and fists clenched. This first phase lasts about a minute and is accompanied by respiratory stoppage and marked facial pallor. Immediately thereafter, air is inhaled and the *clonic* phase commences with spasms and rapid jerking movements, during which time the patient thrusts his limbs back and forth and vigorously opens and closes his jaws; many patients inadvertently harm themselves in this phase, either by biting their tongues or bruising themselves while thrashing about. Following the clonic phase, which also lasts about a minute, convulsive movements gradually ebb and the patient regains consciousness although he usually remains a bit confused, has a headache and feels sleepy. The frequency of these episodes varies from several times a day to as few as once every several years.

### Jacksonian Type

This syndrome, named after Hughlings Jackson, is often a prelude to a grand mal seizure. It is characterized by a preliminary motor spasm or sensory disturbance in a circumscribed region of the body, probably due to a focal impairment, which then spreads to encompass a wider sphere of functions; as noted above, it may eventuate in a full-blown or generalized grand mal convulsion. Patients are conscious as the muscular twitching or sensory tingling begins and then "marches" across the body. Although the subsequent loss of consciousness may reflect a spreading of the initial focal discharge, it is often a product of a psychogenic "blanking out," an anticipatory fainting when the step by step advance of these distressing symptoms is viewed. Of course, in these cases the typical grand mal tonic and clonic symptoms are lacking. These latter features of Jacksonian epilepsy are notable in the following brief sketch.

### CASE 13-6
### Dora S., Age 27, Two Children

Dora suffered periodic Jacksonian seizures in her left arm since childhood that were not controllable with medication. By the time she was 13 or 14, she "learned" to faint whenever she felt the beginning signs of tremor. At no time did she ever display the traditional grand mal reaction; rather, she would clutch her left hand and quickly sink to the ground in an unconscious state, during which time the arm continued to twitch. Dora would regain consciousness a few minutes following the termination of the tremor, quite aware of what had occurred prior to her faint, and would usually be in good spirits since she had "got away from that crazy feeling that crawled all over me."

### Petit Mal

The term "petit mal" was coined originally to denote a minor or small seizure, but it has come to represent states in which there is a momentary diminution rather than a total loss of consciousness. During these ten to 15 second episodes, occurring as often as 20 or 30 times a day, the patient is completely out of touch with his surroundings, stares vacantly ahead, drops whatever he may be doing or holding and then resumes his activity with no awareness of what has happened.

Traditionally included in the petit mal syndrome are *akinetic* attacks which refer to an abrupt loss of muscle tonus, resulting in such consequences as a sudden falling to the ground, dropping of objects and head nodding. Also included are *myoclonic* spells characterized by brief motor jerking or muscular contractions. Petit mal symptoms rarely appear for the first time after adolescence and usually disappear before the age of 30.

### Psychomotor Types

The principal feature of this condition is a clouding of consciousness during which the patient engages in a rather inappropriate but well organized sequence of activities, following which he returns to full awareness with total amnesia for his intervening behaviors. For example, in the middle of a conversation, the person may suddenly turn from his companion, stroll into a garden and begin weeding the grass; in a few minutes he may return, continue the conversation as if nothing unusual has occurred and have no awareness of his unusual acts. Kolb (1968) reports the following typical case history.

#### CASE 13-7
#### Marie T., Age 20, Unmarried

When 10 years old, Marie was brought to the clinic by her mother after she had suffered a number of episodes of loss of consciousness. These were described by the mother in the following way.

She awakened with a headache, seemed listless, and then was noticed by her mother to develop a twitching movement of the left side of her mouth and eyes. Her arms assumed an "odd," stiff position and became unresponsive. This condition persisted 5 minutes, to be followed by another similar episode 10 minutes later in which she urinated and defecated. These attacks were followed by five others preceded by an aura of "fear"—as the child stated, being "scared." The patient had total amnesia for the attacks.

For years Marie reported only daily brief episodes of "scary feelings." It was necessary to increase the dosage of the anticonvulsant medication, and Mebaral was prescribed as well. At age 14 she was admitted to the hospital with an acute delirious state due to barbiturate overdosage. Following this hospital admission, her mother noticed a character change in that she became resentful and hostile, expressed the attitude that she was disliked, and seemed depressed. Then "slow spike waves" were observed over the left temporal region during periods of sleep.

At this time Marie commenced to have episodes of loss of consciousness, occurring without warning and with subsequent amnesia, in which she suddenly rushed away from her place of work, walking rapidly and aimlessly through the streets, impulsively removing her stockings and placing them in her purse or suddenly staring blankly, smacking her lips, giggling foolishly, and then mumbling incoherently.

It has been reported that psychomotor patients, on occasion, engage in violent or other antisocial acts during their seizures. Such events are extremely rare, and it is not at all unlikely that these seemingly senseless aggressive episodes are more a function of a concurrent psychogenic disorder than of the basic epileptic defect.

### ETIOLOGY

Epilepsy is a symptom, not a disease, and there are almost as many determinants of this symptom as there are diseases and deviances which can disturb brain functioning. Among the exogenous factors which may give rise to convulsions are birth traumas, infectious diseases, toxins, vascular accidents, neoplasms and tissue degeneration. Hereditary susceptibilities, congenital defects and errors of metabolism and endocrine function are among the more probable endogenous origins of the seizure symptom. It is general practice to diagnose convulsions which are symptomatic of known etiological agents in the syndrome category associated with that agent, e.g., "defects associated with brain trauma." The so-called idiopathic type, usually of an unknown endogenous source, represents the kind of epileptic cases normally included in the syndrome discussed in this section.

It is not uncommon for seemingly innocuous stimuli to provoke a convulsive episode. Thus, external precipitants may serve to trigger some unusual biophysical sensitivity; for example, certain musical notes or the flickering of lights often activates vulnerable regions and sets off a focal discharge which may then spread into a full-fledged seizure.

Along similar lines, it appears that unusual psychic stress increases the frequency of convulsions among chronic epileptics. It is plausible to speculate in these cases that any situation that taxes the individual's monitoring and control functions will lower the threshold for a seizure. During these periods also, excessive and undischarged tension may cumulate. With lowered controls and a mounting tension, the epileptic's vulnerable region may "give way," resulting in an explosive and convulsive discharge.

### PERSONALITY AND BEHAVIOR CORRELATES

There appears to be a more than chance frequency of *mild* personality disturbances among epileptics, especially in the psychomotor type. However, there is no distinctive "epileptic personality" (Tizard, 1962). Although these patients exhibit somewhat more than their share of emotional difficulties and social maladjustments, these traits are likely to be a psychogenic correlate of their defect rather than something intrinsic to it. Many epileptics are overprotected by concerned parents and experience social stigmatism and humiliation and frustrating discriminations and restrictions in both their educational and vocational pursuits. It should not be surprising, then, that many develop feelings of inadequacy, self-contempt and interpersonal suspiciousness and hostility.

The correspondence between personality difficulties and psychomotor epilepsy may very well reflect inaccurate diagnoses. What often passes as psychomotor behavior may not stem from biophysical causes at all; rather, it may be a dissociative disorder that mimics this form of epilepsy. Since dissociative disorders derive from one of several pathological personality patterns, the frequently reported covariation between these "epileptic" types and personality disturbances should not be surprising.

Many investigators have noted that personality disturbances are especially prominent among patients with temporal lobe epilepsy. Ostensibly, these persons seem deficient in regulatory control and evidence notable hyperactive, egocentric and aggressive behaviors (Gibbs, 1958; Bingley, 1958). In a recent study (Small et al., 1962), however, no differences in personality impairment were found between epileptics with temporal lobe lesions and those with lesions localized in other regions.

## MENTAL RETARDATION

Children who lack the intellectual capacity to profit from the teachings of their elders, and adults who seem incapable of grasping many of the basic elements of self and social responsibility have been known to man since earliest history; they are found today in every culture and stratum of society. These unfortunate people are grouped together under the single syndrome label of "mental retardation," despite an immense variety in their clinical characteristics, degrees of deficit and etiological backgrounds. Other labels have been used over the years to describe this syndrome: *feeble-mindedness, mental deficiency, amentia, hypophrenia* and most recently, *mental subnormality.* Each of these descriptive terms has something to commend it, but the label of "mental retardation" appears to be the most common and preferred term in current use.

Although the average incidence of mental retardation is estimated at 3 per cent, there is considerable variation in reported figures depending on the type of population sampled (e.g., urban versus rural, white versus Negro or northern versus southern), the criteria used for diagnosis (e.g., intelligence-test scores, academic achievement, family history or social competence) and the arbitrary "cut-off" point selected to demarcate "normal" intelligence from retardation. Of the four million children born annually in the United States, approximately 120,000 ultimately will be classed among the mentally retarded, although only 15,000 of these will require complete custodial care. About 200,000 retardates (roughly 4 per cent of the total retarded population) are currently institutionalized; the others manage to maintain themselves within the community or are cared for by their families.

### History

Until the past half century, the mentally retarded were treated as fools or simpletons; they were made fun of, exploited and scorned; for brief periods, notably in medieval times, they were feared and punished. In general, however, the lot of the retarded was better than that of the emotionally disturbed since the former were occasionally objects of pity and charity rather than apprehension and distrust.

The first systematic study of a mentally retarded person was undertaken by the educationist Jean Itard (1801) at the suggestion of Philippe Pinel, the eminent psychiatrist of the French Revolution. Itard's work on the "wild boy of Aveyron," a feral child found in the forest in 1798, is now a classic treatise on the education of children deprived of early human stimulation. Over a five year period, Itard was able to teach the youngster to communicate with words rather than with grunts and gestures, but could not aid him to control his "crude and uncivilized" emotions and habits.

Although Itard felt pessimistic about the prospects of training these youngsters to become full-fledged citizens of society, other clinicians and educators undertook to explore new methods for uplifting their lives. Most prominent among these was Edouard Sequin, a former student of Itard, who developed in the 1830's and 1840's a variety of systematic procedures for retraining the basic perceptual and motor functions of the retarded. His work coincided with the opening of institutions devoted to the custodial care and treatment of the "feeble-minded." By 1876, there were twelve such residential "schools" in the United States.

Advances were minimal in the ensuing 60 or 70 years; work with the retarded remained essentially custodial, with few efforts to accomplish more than the training of habits of cleanliness and the curtailment of destructive behaviors. Little was done either in prevention or rehabilitation. In the past one or two decades, however, more optimistic attitudes have come to the fore. The adaptation of higher level retardates to the Armed Services and industrial employment, medical progress in the early diagnosis and remediation of certain defects, mounting parental concern and legislative pressure and a consequent marked increase in research funds and facilities have given the field a new impetus that was sorely lacking in previous years. The fruits of this revived interest remain a matter of future progress, however.

Much confusion still reigns as to the best means for differentiating and grouping the many varieties of retardation. Classification, although not an end in itself, is an important step in clinical analysis, and is often a useful guide in research, prevention and treatment. Several nosological schemas have been proposed with regard to mental retardation; we shall outline the four most prominent: gross physical characteristics, etiology, measured intellectual ability and social competence.

## CLASSIFICATION ACCORDING TO GROSS PHYSICAL CHARACTERISTICS

Man's earliest attempts to group the varieties of mental retardation reflected his crude observation of gross or manifest physical characteristics. It was well known that many who exhibited severe deficits in intellectual and social competence also displayed physiognomic and morphological aberrations. These overt anomalies varied from minor irregularities in skeletal structure to extremely repulsive distortions of both trunk and head. The following classification schema rests on these identifiable physiognomic features. As will be evident, similarities in gross physical appearance do not necessarily signify similarities either in etiology or degree of retardation.

### Garden Variety "Familial" Types

In contrast to the popular image, more than 75 per cent of all mentally retarded individuals display neither overt nor covert physical signs that correlate with their mental defect. In all physical regards they appear "like everyone else," some are attractive, most are "average looking" and some are unattractive. Not only do they fail to exhibit gross structural aberrations, but their brains give evidence neither of tissue pathology nor abnormal electroencephalographic rhythms.

Yet, these "seemingly normal" people, when faced with simple intellectual tasks, become confused and inept and perform in a manner more appropriate to a chronological age much less than theirs.

These "garden variety" retardates do not suffer the more severe types of intellectual deficiency; many are capable of a basic elementary school education, and often find employment later in life in some routine or unskilled job. For the most part, these milder retardates come from families in which retardation is rather common.

The correspondence among family members of this type of defect suggests two etiological hypotheses. *First,* it is quite probable that many of these cases have inherited "normal" genes which endow them with abilities that fall at the lower end of the bell-shaped continuum of intelligence; they do not appear to be suffering the consequences of a disease, but seem merely to *deviate* statistically in accord with natural individual differences from the average. The *second* hypothesis is that children who are reared in families in which parents are intellectually dull and educationally disadvantaged are likely to be deprived of the experiential stimulation necessary for the full development of their higher mental abilities. These youngsters and their siblings are likely to continue the family pattern *not* for genetic but for environmental reasons.

Since development is a product of a complex and interwoven set of biogenic and psychogenic influences, the probabilities are that both the "genetic deviance" and "experiential impoverishment" theses are correct. Parents of limited intellectual endowment pass on their deficit genetic equipment to their children; also, by virtue of their deficient educational and cultural achievements, they fail to stimulate the limited potentials their children possess. Together, these disadvantages set off a vicious circle that perpetuates the impairment from generation to generation.

### Microcephaly

In this and the following "physical types," the degree of mental subnormality is usually much greater than that found among garden variety retardates. The impairment is likely to stem from a "disease process" and tends to be characterized by gross morphological deformities.

Microcephaly is a physical descriptive term subsuming diseases with different etiologies and of varying severity. It represents one of the more common types of institutionalized mentally retarded, comprising about 20 per cent of this

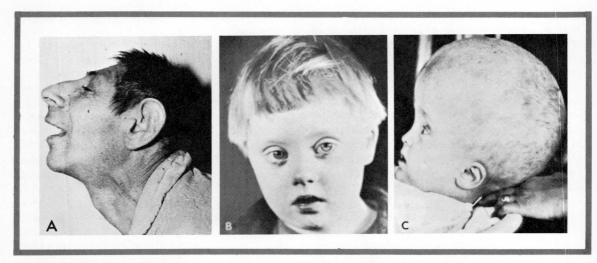

Figure 13-2    Some physical types of mental retardation. A. Microcephaly. (Columbus State School, Columbus, Ohio.) B. Mongolism. (Courtesy of Dr. Clemens Benda.) C. Hydrocephaly. (From Wechsler, I. S.: Clinical Neurology. 9th edition. Philadelphia, W. B. Saunders Co., 1963.)

population. The major distinguishing feature is a cone-shaped cranium with a circumference of less than 17 inches in adulthood, as contrasted to a normal figure of 22 inches. Although physiognomic variations are present, most possess a sharply receding forehead that is set in contrast to otherwise normally developed facial features. Microcephalics vary intellectually from moderate to profound retardation; all levels are notably deficient in abstract and language functions. In some cases, the impairment may be traced to a genetic disease; most, however, appear to arise as a consequence of intrauterine or perinatal complications.

The genetic group, also known as "true" or "primary" microcephalic, is extremely rare, shows less marked physical distortion and, in general, is of less severity in retardation than the nongenetic or "secondary" type of microcephalic. Among the probable etiological factors in the latter group are x-ray radiation and infections transmitted in utero during early fetal development. These microcephalics display numerous symptoms accompanying their retardation, notably convulsions, blindness, deafness and cardiac malformations. Postmortem examinations suggest that cerebral development has failed to progress after the fourth or fifth month of fetal life. In cases of perinatal injury or anoxia, the major postmortem signs are maldevelopments in the cortex, specifically a failure of cerebral convolution formation.

Microcephalics have been characterized as hyperactive but good-natured. However, since the impairment stems from different etiologies and

structural pathologies, and patients have been exposed to different environmental conditions, it is unlikely that this description of temperament could be uniformly applicable. For example, Brandon et al. (1959) found microcephalics to be as varied in their personalities as other retarded types.

### Mongolism (Down's Syndrome)

This physical classification represents a distinct disease entity since its characteristic features are found in conjunction with only one etiological agent. It was given its popular name in 1866 by a British physician, Langdon Down, who was struck by the similarity in facial characteristics between these children and members of the "mongolian race"; the resemblance, however, is limited strictly to the eyes which are almond-shaped and slope upward toward their outer corners.

Estimates suggest that there are over 100,000 cases in the United States alone; proportionately equal numbers are found throughout the world. The disease appears about once in every 500 births, and comprises between 10 to 15 per cent of institutionalized retardates. The great majority of cases are cared for at home since these patients are usually not severely impaired, are relatively easy to manage and preoccupy and often are of an unobtrusive or pleasant temperament.

In addition to the almond-shaped eyes, the physiognomy of these retardates is conspicuous by a flattening of the back of the head, a heavily fissured tongue that tends to protrude through thin, similarly fissured lips and a broad nose that is depressed at the bridge. Hair is sparse and thin, and the skin is delicate and milk-white or rosy. Hands and feet are stubby and clumsy; overall stature is small. They stand stoop-shouldered, are physically uncoordinated and their gait is heavy and shuffling. Other distinctive signs are frequent cardiac malformations, fingerprint L-shaped loops rather than whorls and a deeply resonant and somewhat croaky voice. Mongoloid brains on autopsy give evidence of diffuse undevelopment and suggest the consequences of a basic metabolic deficiency.

Mongoloids tend to be only moderately impaired intellectually. Most can be toilet-trained and are capable of learning simple chores and routine skills. Speech, however, is rather limited, consisting at best of a few meaningful words. Their daily activities often consist of idle TV watching or hours of repetitive play such as putting a set of blocks in a preferred arrangement, destroying the design and commencing again.

The etiology of this syndrome is well on the way to being established. About 95 per cent of mongoloids have been found to possess 47 chromosomes instead of the normal complement of 46. Most are trisomic (three rather than two units) for chromosome 21; the remaining 5 per cent exhibit other defects, all of which are related to chromosomal disjunctions. There is minimal evidence of familial correspondence in mongolism; the disease appears to be a mutational aberration occurring during fertilization or shortly thereafter. The well-known fact that mothers beyond the age of 35 are appreciably more likely to give birth to mongoloid children indicates that some anomaly associated with maternal age is centrally involved in many of these cases. Degeneration of hormonal processes requisite to proper gametogenesis or metabolic dysfunctions causing an error in mitosis in an early embryonic cell, are among the more prominent hypotheses proposed to bridge the unknown facts. Further research is needed to clarify the precise mechanisms by which this anomaly develops. Despite advances in the understanding of its etiology, no effective treatment or preventive measure has been uncovered.

### Cretinism

As with mongolism, cretinism may properly be classed as a disease entity traceable to a distinct etiological background. In contrast with mongolism, however, preventive and remedial measures are known, with strikingly effective results even in severe cases.

These patients appear normal at birth. Toward the end of the first year, there are signs of a general sluggishness and apathy. Normal growth is stunted with the exception of a disproportionately large head. Hands and feet are noticeably stumpy and malformed; the abdomen is swollen and bulgy, legs are bowed and the spine is curved. The face of adult cretins is characterized by a flat nose, widely spaced eyes, large and flabby ears, thick lips and a broad, frequently protruding, tongue. Skin texture is dry and rough and often cold to the touch. Hearing frequently is defective and sexual development is delayed, if not totally arrested. The intellectual level of these patients correlates with the degree of their biological defect.

Cretinism is a result of a lack of iodine. This may stem either from an inadequacy in diet or from a congenital defect in the thyroid gland. Cretinism was once common in regions of the world where natural iodine was lacking in the soil, and therefore lacking in the food it supplied. Since this dietary deficiency usually affected several members in a family, it was thought at first to be a hereditary disease. At the turn of the century, however, it was discovered that thyroid extracts countered the deleterious effects seen in cretinism. Shortly thereafter, the crucial role of iodine deficiency was noted; families that had been subject to the disease as a result of dietary or thyroid deficits were soon rid of its consequences.

Cretinism still arises in cases of congenital hypothyroidism. Here the patient is lacking the biophysical equipment to metabolize normally ingested iodine, and may suffer consequences similar to those deprived of the nutrient through dietary deficiencies. Early signs of this disease can now readily be identified; with proper administration of thyroxin in the first year of life, the afflicted child may develop free of both physical and psychological effects. Deleterious consequences will occur, however, if remedial measures are delayed until later life; although the impairment can be arrested and partly counteracted, most of the damage wreaked in adult cases is not reversible.

### Hydrocephalus

Like microcephaly and in distinction to mongolism and cretinism, this physical type is a descriptive category subsuming similar clinical pictures that stem from different etiological origins. Hydrocephalic cases are noted by a globular enlargement of the cranium resulting from the accumulation of abnormal amounts of cerebrospinal fluid; both face and body remain normal

528

BIOPHYSICAL DEFECTS

in size, giving the upper part of the head a grotesque appearance. The expansion of the cranial region reduces the pressure exerted upon the brain by the excess fluid; however, any degree of pressure capable of enlarging the cranium must be sufficient also to produce cerebral maldevelopment and tissue atrophy. The extent to which the brain is impaired correlates with age of onset and severity and duration of pressure. Operative procedures in early life, designed to remove accumulated fluid and reestablish normal circulation, may be effective in curtailing the progression of the disease.

The etiology of hydrocephalus is varied. Some cases may be traced to genetic factors, probably a single recessive gene. Most stem from prenatal or early postnatal inflammatory infections or neoplasms which block the cerebrospinal aqueducts; this results in a progressive accumulation of fluids that normally are discharged or absorbed. Physical abnormalities are seldom noted before the second or third month of life. However, owing to the plasticity of the infant's cranium, the excess fluid quickly forces enlargements in all directions. Unless relief is rapidly forthcoming, neuronal damage during the early maturational stages is likely to result in severe retardation.

### Other Physical Types

Among the many variants in physiognomy and stature observed among the mentally retarded, brief mention should be made of two relatively distinct but rare syndromes.

*Macrocephaly* is characterized by an increase in the size and weight of the brain itself rather than by an accumulation of cerebrospinal fluid, as in hydrocephaly. The enlarged brain, often noted at birth, does not reflect an abundance of neural tissue, but is due to a proliferation of glial cells that serve as the supporting structures for neural tissue. In further contrast to the hydrocephalic, the head tends to be square rather than globular, and facial features often are well developed and prominent. The etiology or etiologies of this physical type are unknown. Most victims are severely retarded.

*Gargoylism* (*Hurler's Disease*) is noted by a protruding forehead, bushy eyebrows, saddle-shaped nose, coarse and thick lips, perpetually flexed limbs, stubby hands and feet and a stunted body. The level of retardation ranges between mild and profound. Etiologically, this disease can usually be traced to a single recessive gene that causes dysfunctions in lipid metabolism. Few cases survive beyond adolescence.

## CLASSIFICATION ACCORDING TO ETIOLOGY

It is a cliché that "you can't judge a book by its cover." Similarly, gross physical features may be a poor guide to the basic character of different types of mental retardation. Just as the same book jacket may cover texts of significantly different contents, so too may commonalities in overt appearance cloak substantively divergent pathologies.

Most medical scientists believe that the best system of classification is one founded on etiology; with this knowledge as a basis, they can design preventive and therapeutic measures in a rational and focused rather than a purely empirical and random manner. Physical features, as we have seen in our previous discussion, *sometimes* do correspond to distinct etiological origins (e.g., mongolism or cretinism); however, in most cases, there is little or no correlation. The guidelines offered by physique and physiognomy have brought us just so far and no further. From this point forward, they will provide us with little assistance in uncovering the causes of mental retardation.

Fortunately, with advances in medical knowledge, we may be ready to classify most patients on the basis of etiology; in fact, the DSM-II nosological schema is organized on these grounds. However, as with all classification systems, there are deficiencies and complications here, as well. The etiology of many defects is unknown, and in others several etiological factors often covary. Nevertheless, this schema furnishes a basic framework within which further advances in etiological knowledge may be subsumed.

The outline to be presented deviates from the DSM-II; it represents what we believe to be a more logical synthesis of the two etiological systems upon which the manual was based. George Jervis (1959) provided a classification framed in terms of the well-established distinction between endogenous and exogenous factors. The American Association of Mental Deficiency in the same year (Heber, 1959) published a manual incorporating over 100 causal agents grouped into eight major categories. In what follows, we have attempted to coordinate and summarize these two systems; it corresponds on essential points to the DSM-II, but differentiates syndromes in terms of endogenous versus exogenous etiologies.

### Endogenous Categories

Patients in this category show *no* evidence that their defects are due to external causes such as toxins, infections or injuries. From various aspects of their case histories, it appears safe to conclude that their retardation stems from genetic origins. This group has been referred to as "primary" or "hereditary" deficiency. We shall divide them into two subtypes depending on whether defects derive from deviances within the range of "normal" individual differences, or reflect the transmission of a genetic disease or chromosomal aberration.

**Genogenic Deviance.** These retardates usually show mild severity and comprise the larger part of the "garden variety" type. Although complex psychosocial variables interact in shaping the final picture, the role of an inherited intellectual "weakness" cannot be overlooked. These individuals fill out the major bulk of the lower part of the normal distribution of individual differences in intelligence on the basis of the same genetic units which endow others with higher capacities. The only difference is that the particular units they receive construct a morphological and neurophysiological substratum that is less well designed for "intellectual" tasks than those obtained by more able individuals. These inherited units comprise a complex mosaic of polygenic elements, each of which contributes a small part to the overall development of that composite of functions we call intelligence.

No study can fully separate the interwoven mixture of biogenic and psychogenic elements involved in producing mental ability, but there is ample evidence (Roberts, 1952; Penrose, 1964) that the *milder* forms of retardation, those that comprise the lower bulk of the bell-shaped continuum, cluster in families whereas the more severe levels, those which are "off the curve," do not. These facts suggest that the garden variety retardates, that is, those who are slightly impaired and lack notable physical pathology, are part of man's "natural" variability; they merely *deviate* from the average. They contrast with retardates who evidence both gross physical aberrations and severe intellectual deficits; these cases appear to be the product of some genetic or exogenous *disease*.

**Genogenic Disease.** In this category we include inborn errors of functioning traceable to genetic or chromosomal defects. We speak of them as genetic diseases rather than deviances, because they indicate the presence of some unusual factor that lies outside the range of normal individual variability. Two subclasses may be noted.

*First,* there are diseases which arise from genetic characteristics that are transmitted from parent to child. These genogenic "family diseases" usually take the form of a single recessive gene. When two such genes are paired, the normal metabolic mechanisms requisite for growth are disturbed, giving rise to a variety of developmental defects, of which mental retardation is frequently one. Gargoylism and certain types of microcephaly and cretinism, each of which was briefly discussed previously, are among these defects. Perhaps the best known syndrome of this type is *phenylketonuria* (PKU), a disease of amino acid metabolism; fortunately, this defect can be identified shortly after birth and treated successfully by a proper dietary regime. Other forms of retardation attributable to normally transmitted single recessive genes are *Tay-Sachs* disease and *Niemann-Pick* disease, both of which exhibit dysfunctions in fat metabolism.

The *second* class of genogenic diseases are chromosomal aberrations. In these cases the parents' normal chromosomal complement fails to be transmitted intact to the child. For a variety of reasons, largely unknown, mutations or structural dislocations occur giving rise to an impaired genetic composition. The best known of these diseases is *mongolism,* discussed previously. In this defect, some disturbance in the mother's reproductive functions causes a trisomic or disjunctive formation usually in chromosome 21. Similar effects may occur as a consequence of prior ionizing radiation in the mother or in the embryo shortly after fertilization.

### Exogenous Categories

In this group, occasionally referred to as "secondary" or "acquired" mental deficiency, there is usually no notable history of retardation within the family. Subcategories are differentiated in accord with the primary etiological agent.

**Toxic Factors.** A wide variety of toxic agents may result in cerebral dysfunctions and malformations, either pre or postnatally. Maternal toxemias of pregnancy or maternal intoxications due to carbon monoxide or various immunological vaccines are among the rarer causes of retardation. Incompatibility between maternal and fetal blood types can result in a number of developmental defects; the retardation syndrome known as *kernicterus,* characterized by jaundice and hearing deficits, is an illustration of the consequence of this incompatibility. Although extremely rare, postnatal brain damage may follow exposure to highly toxic substances during early stages of neurological maturation.

**Infectious Agents.** The probability of retardation from infectious sources is greatest during early life. Few maternal infections cross the placental barrier; those that do, notably syphilis and German measles, especially within the first three months of pregnancy, may result in an irreversible retardation. Postnatal diseases associated with encephalitis may give rise to intellectual deficits of sufficient severity to be categorized as retardation.

**Trauma.** Prenatal trauma is extremely rare. More significant as a source of retardation are birth injuries associated with prolonged labor and difficult deliveries; these consequences are especially frequent in premature infants since they lack the developmental apparatus to withstand even "normal" complications. Cerebral hemorrhaging and anoxia are the two most prominent sources of defects. Extremely severe postnatal head trauma may produce generalized mental retardation; more commonly, where these events do have sequelae, they are of a circumscribed nature, that is, affect only those functions subserved by the injured region.

**Endocrine Dysfunctions.** Many of these impairments are genetic in origin. *Hypothyroidism,* the most common of these defects, may stem from either endogenous or exogenous sources. Cretinism, described earlier, may arise as a consequence of inborn defects of the thyroid gland or of dietary deficiencies in iodine.

**Psychosocial Deprivation.** As discussed in chapter 5, appropriate stimulation in the young child is necessary for normal maturation. It appears clear that a variety of environmental experiences are crucial to the development not only of interpersonal sensitivity and emotional responsiveness, but of language and abstract thinking. Children reared in intellectually and economically disadvantaged homes are frequently exposed to a drab and monotonous life. Most relevant in this regard is the paucity of complex verbal stimulation and reasoning during the early phases of intracortical development; as a consequence, the growth of structural pathways which subserve symbolic communication and abstract thinking may be retarded. Unless the degree of deprivation is unusually marked, however, as may be the case in institutionalized children or children who have been cruelly isolated from human contact, the extent of retardation is likely to be relatively delimited or circumscribed and of only mild severity.

The currently well-publicized view that children from economically underprivileged families are intellectually impoverished is only partly true. No doubt, they are less likely to be guided and stimulated in line with the verbal styles and abstract modes of thought that characterize the dominant middle class. And, as a consequence, they do perform poorly in middle-class schools and on most standard intelligence tests, which likewise mirror the values and modes of the majority population. However, many of these youngsters do acquire nonconventional forms of intelligent expression and thought; thus, they are not necessarily subject to an impoverishment of stimulation, but a "difference" in stimulation. Because the character and content of their thought does not fit the mold of the middle-class majority and the test and school criteria this group establishes, these underprivileged children *appear* "retarded" when they are not.

These comments should not be construed as favoring a lessened concern for the formal education and enrichment of the underprivileged; they are offered to alert us to the fact that their poor test and school performances may signify a difference in "styles" of intelligence and not a deficiency in it. With this caveat in mind we can turn next to classifications based on test-measured ability.

## CLASSIFICATION ACCORDING TO MEASURED INTELLECTUAL ABILITY

Retardation is commonly classified by reference to intelligence test scores. As was noted above, there are differences in "styles of intelligence"; therefore, questions are justifiably raised as to what behaviors and test items should be included as criteria for its assessment. Without elaborating the issue at this point, let us note that most instruments used for intelligence appraisal are weighted heavily in verbal-symbolic materials and tend to tap experiences that are common to the dominant middle-class culture. As such, they may be biased devices for assessing the mental abilities of persons who are not part of the mainstream of American life.

Nevertheless, the value of establishing *degrees* of intellectual ability cannot be overlooked as part of the clinical study of retardation. The same etiology may produce a severely retarded child or a mildly retarded child; the same gross physical appearance may be exhibited by persons of widely divergent abilities. Thus, the two classification systems discussed previously are insufficient for the categorization of retardation. Whatever the etiology, whatever physical form in which the patient appears, it is the degree of intellectual impairment which is the relevant factor in determining the diagnosis of retardation. The most frequent basis for making this appraisal is an I.Q. score on an intelligence test. Unfortunately, this single criterion continues to be

**Table 13-1    Correspondence of Various Mental Retardation Terminologies to Measured Intelligence**

| APPROXIMATE IQ SCORE RANGE | DSM-II, AND AAMD MANUAL TERMINOLOGY, 1961 REVISION* | COMMON FORMER LABELS | EDUCATIONAL TERMINOLOGY |
|---|---|---|---|
| 68–85 | Borderline | Borderline | Slow learner (sometimes included in educable range) |
| 52–67 | Mild | Moron | Educable retarded |
| 36–51 | Moderate | Imbecile | Trainable retarded |
| 20–35 | Severe | Imbecile | Trainable retarded |
| Below 20 | Profound | Idiot | Total-care group |

* Heber (1961)

used despite repeated warnings of its limited and biased utility.

The notion of measurement of individual differences, as may be recalled from chapter 1, dates back to the nineteenth century English statistician and psychologist Sir Francis Galton. However, it was the French psychologists, Binet and Simon, who devised in 1905 the first scale for predicting academic potential. This scale not only became the model for subsequent instruments of intelligence appraisal, but in modified form, has remained the primary tool of assessment. In 1910, the Binet scale was translated into English and published as the Vineland Revision. William Stern, a German psychologist, suggested in 1912 that a *ratio* be calculated between a child's age-equivalent performance level on the scale and his actual chronological age; thus, the "intelligence quotient" was born. In 1916, Lewis Terman updated the Binet scales, selecting his items so that they were applicable to an American population; the basic format, however, remained essentially Binet's. The Stanford-Binet, as Terman's revision was termed, was again revised in 1937 and 1960. Along with the several Wechsler scales of intelligence, they are the primary instruments in use today for calculating I.Q. scores. It is on the basis of these test results that youngsters in most quarters of this country are judged to be retarded. Table 13-1 presents a summary of the retardation classification terms that have been applied to I.Q. score categories.

The simplicity of determining retardation by a test procedure and the quantitative precision of degree of retardation implied by a numerical score are quite illusory and have given intelligence tests their totally undeserved status as *the* diagnostic criterion. Despite their unquestioned utility as one element in the evaluation of retardation, these instruments are notoriously biased; they overlook cultural differences, are lim-

ited in the range of the relevant functions they tap and rest on questionable assumptions regarding the structure and development of intellectual capacities. Moreover, identical I.Q. test scores fail to differentiate individuals in ways relevant to the diagnosis of retardation. Used as the sole criterion, as is so often the case, they neglect etiological considerations, intellectual potential and, most important, may mislead us with regard to the individual's capacity for coping with "real life" problems. In short, test scores, when used alone, create a false sense of relevancy and accuracy and often compound the problems of the marginally retarded rather than facilitate their solution.

## CLASSIFICATION ACCORDING TO SOCIAL COMPETENCE

Discontent with the narrow focus and limited applicability of I.Q. scores has led to a renewed interest in classifying retardates by reference to social competence criteria rather than quantitative test scores. Competence criteria are not new. The eminent English authority A. F. Tredgold wrote in the sixth edition of his text on mental deficiency (1937) that these impairments should be classified in accord with the degree to which the individual can adapt himself to a normal environment, independent of supervision and support. Similarly, a prominent American specialist in the field, Edgar Doll, wrote (1941) that retardation is best viewed in terms of social maturity. More recently, the U. S. Department of Health, Education and Welfare has outlined a chart that coordinates quantitative I.Q. scores with degrees of functional efficiency and social competence (Table 13-2).

To date, however, no completely satisfactory system has been devised to classify retardates in terms of social competence, although the British

## Table 13-2 Functional Competence of the Mentally Retarded*

This table integrates chronological age, degree of retardation, and level of intellectual, vocational, and social functioning.

| DEGREE OF MENTAL RETARDATION | PRESCHOOL AGE 0–5 MATURATION AND DEVELOPMENT | SCHOOL AGE 6–20 TRAINING AND EDUCATION | ADULT 21 AND OVER SOCIAL AND VOCATIONAL ADEQUACY |
|---|---|---|---|
| Profound (IQ Below 20) | Gross retardation; minimal capacity for functioning in sensorimotor areas; needs nursing care | Some motor development present; may respond to minimal or limited training in self-help | Some motor and speech development; may achieve very limited self-care; needs nursing care |
| Severe (IQ 20–35) | Poor motor development; speech minimal; generally unable to profit from training in self-help; little or no communication skills | Can talk or learn to communicate; can be trained in elemental health habits; profits from systematic habit training | May contribute partially to self-maintenance under complete supervision; can develop self-protection skills to a minimal useful level in controlled environment |
| Moderate (IQ 36–51) | Can talk or learn to communicate; poor social awareness; fair motor development; profits from training in self-help; can be managed with moderate supervision | Can profit from training in social and occupational skills; unlikely to progress beyond 2nd grade level in academic subjects; may learn to travel alone in familiar places | May achieve self-maintenance in unskilled or semiskilled work under sheltered conditions; needs supervision and guidance when under mild social or economic stress |
| Mild (IQ 52–67) | Can develop social and communication skills, minimal retardation in sensorimotor areas; often not distinguished from normal until later age | Can learn academic skills up to approximately 6th grade level by late teens; can be guided toward social conformity | Can usually achieve social and vocational skills adequate to minimum self-support but may need guidance and assistance when under unusual social or economic stress |

* Adapted from *Mental Retardation Activities of the U. S. Department of Health, Education, and Welfare*, p. 2. United States Government Printing Office, Washington, 1963

nosology makes an attempt in this direction (Lyons and Heaton-Ward, 1953). Nevertheless, it is mandatory that criteria be included to represent the individual's capacity to learn the fundamentals of self-sufficiency and to acquire attitudes requisite to shared social living.

Our discussion of the varied criteria by which retardation may be classified points up again the futility of approaching psychopathology from a single frame of reference. As with other pathologies, retardation is a complex phenomenon that may be viewed and understood from several vantage points. Only when taken together can these seemingly divergent approaches facilitate our complete understanding of the problem, and a better means for its remediation.

## CIRCUMSCRIBED BRAIN DYSFUNCTIONS IN CHILDHOOD

(DSM-II: *Nonpsychotic Organic Brain Syndromes in Childhood*)

We began this chapter on biophysical syndromes with a discussion of neurosyphilis, known formerly as general paresis. Neurosyphilis, as pointed out in chapter 1, was the first successfully diagnosed disease entity in the history of psychiatry; the sequence of steps which led to its differentiation and etiological specification represents one of the finest pages in the research literature of psychopathology. Since we began with the first of the historically significant biophysical defects, it is appropriate that we conclude this chapter with the most recently studied biophysical syndrome.

An entirely new cluster of clinical characteristics has been recognized in the last ten years, tentatively labeled "circumscribed brain dysfunctions in childhood." While there is much to be learned about this impairment, and much research that still lies before us, there is reason to believe that scientific studies associated with this syndrome will prove to be an even greater step toward the understanding of psychopathology than that achieved by the discovery of neurosyphilis. Elucidation of the obscure and subtle elements which comprise this syndrome should provide us with a deeper insight into the complex dimensions of neuropsychological development and the role of inborn constitutional differences associated with their maturation. The importance of this biophysical classification lies, then, not only in its value as a discriminable clinical syndrome, but in its promise as a heuristic concept leading to significant scientific advances.

Briefly, these children are characterized by one or more of the following features. They exhibit deficits in integrative and regulatory controls; thus, for many clinicians, they are best depicted as hyperactive, impulsive, hyperdistractible and behaviorally disorganized. Another significant symptom cluster focuses on specific developmental and learning deficits; thus, in some quarters, these youngsters are noted by their sensory handicaps, perceptual-motor dysfunctions and speech and reading disabilities.

Youngsters classified in this syndrome display these signs in more subtle forms than are seen in children with gross nervous system defects. Thus, they do not present the severe motor impairments seen in children with cerebral palsy. Also notable is the fact that their learning deficits are often unrelated to general decrements in intelligence. Brain dysfunctions will inevitably disrupt some facet of intellectual performance, but these need not result in the loss of higher abstraction capacities. Thus, most cases of brain dysfunction evidence specific or circumscribed deficits rather than generalized deficits, as in the case of mentally retarded children.

### History

The concept of "brain dysfunction" grew out of efforts some 25 years ago to differentiate children with severe developmental impairments who previously were lumped together and categorized as "defective." As more attention and more refined diagnostic procedures were applied to these cases, they gradually were separated and subdivided into several subcategories such as childhood schizophrenia, infantile autism and culturally deprived, retarded or brain-injured children.

The label given to the last named of these categories, "brain-injured," was coined by Heinz Werner and Alfred A. Strauss, the former an eminent developmental psychologist, the latter a neuropsychiatrist; these men collaborated for more than ten years in the 1930's and 1940's at the Wayne County (Michigan) Training School. Their aim was to separate "defective" children into two categories, an *exogenous* group, in which perinatal or early childhood cerebral damage could be identified, and an *endogenous* group, in which no evidence of such injury to the nervous system could be discerned from their histories.

Despite the inevitable overlap, they concluded that the exogenous group exhibited greater behavioral hyperactivity, emotional lability and perceptual handicaps than the endogenous group. They distinguished this group from the main body of "defective" children, and labeled them "brain-injured." Two volumes were published on the basis of these early and subsequent studies (Strauss and Lehtinen, 1947; Strauss and Kephart, 1955).

The research of Strauss and his colleagues was based on a population consisting of mentally retarded youngsters. Other investigators believed that the features observed among brain-injured retardates might be found to characterize other similarly injured children who were not retarded. Works by Cruickshank (1965), Kephart (1960), Birch (1964) and Rappaport (1966) typify this newer direction.

In the past few years there has been a tremendous rise in the number of children assigned to the brain dysfunction category; in fact, despite the recency of the concept and the difficulty of detection, studies place the incidence of "brain-injured" children at more than 25 per cent of outpatient clinic populations (Paine, 1962; Lezak and Dixon, 1964). This striking figure reflects in part a growing awareness of the diagnostic features of this clinical entity and the increased precision of assessment techniques and skills. Moreover, the increased incidence of these cases may be a rather perverse and unintentional product of medical advances; thus, physicians are able to save infants today who would have succumbed to infections and trauma just a few years ago, but many of these youngsters now suffer the residuals of their early ailments. Not to be overlooked as a factor in the increased "identification" of these cases is its appeal to parents who would prefer to think that their children have succumbed to a personally nonimplicating "brain-injury" disease rather than a personally implicating and emotionally threatening "mental illness." Similarly, physicians, inclined by training to look for physical causes or confused and disenchanted by complicated and obscure psychological explanations, may readily affix the brain dysfunction label to these difficult to diagnose cases.

Whatever the reasons for its sudden prevalence, there is a renewed optimism concerning these children, as evidenced by increased research funds, a brighter and less guilt-ridden outlook on the part of parents and promising new rehabilitative approaches. This is not to say that the lines of future research have been well defined or that what has been uncovered will withstand the test of time. In fact, as of the time of this writing, a vigorous debate continues among professionals as to which of several labels best describes these cases.

Reflecting this state of confusion, the DSM-II subsumes these cases under the category *non-psychotic organic brain syndromes,* describing the childhood variant as follows.

In children, mild brain damage often manifests itself by hyperactivity, short attention span, easy distractibility and impulsiveness. Sometimes the child is withdrawn, listless, perseverative and unresponsive. In exceptional cases there may be great difficulty in initiating action. These characteristics often contribute to a negative interaction between parent and child. If the organic handicap is the major etiological factor and the child is not psychotic, the case should be classified here. If the interactional factors are of major secondary importance, supply a second diagnosis under *behavior disorders of childhood and adolescence;* if these interactional factors predominate give only a diagnosis from this latter category.

Historically, the term "brain-injured" was the first to be applied to children who exhibit the characteristic developmental and learning disabilities of this syndrome. As youngsters who suffer these impairments were further studied, new terms came into being. "Brain-damaged" children, perhaps the most frequent label in the current literature, has been used synonymously with brain-injury. Other terms have become increasingly popular. These appear to be divided in two groups: the first stresses the biophysical aspect of the impairment whereas the second focuses on its consequences. Notable among the former are "cerebral dysfunction" and "minimal brain damage"; in the latter, we have "hyperkinetic behavior syndrome" and "learning disabilities."

This proliferation of descriptive and diagnostic labels is most lamentable and confusing. Given our present state of knowledge, the failure to settle on one term can only inhibit constructive research designed to disentangle the complex of symptoms associated with this syndrome and achieve a better understanding of its manifold etiologies.

There is reason to question the advisability of retaining the term "brain injured" first proposed by Strauss and Werner, as well as its synonym of "brain-damaged." First, in many cases that typify the syndrome, evidence of anatomical damage or a history of an injuring episode is often absent and entirely presumptive. Second, many children with demonstrable brain damage do not exhibit the symptoms that characterize the syndrome.

Diagnosis in most cases is based on func-tional disruptions rather than structural defects. The suggested label "brain-dysfunction" would seem especially appropriate, therefore, since it avoids the presumptive etiological hypothesis contained in terms such as "damage" and "injury," and focuses on the primary source of data used to diagnose the syndrome.

The adjective "minimal," often attached to the term "brain dysfunction," aids us in differentiating this syndrome from other more severe forms of dysfunction. As on a continuum, "minimal" suggests that these youngsters possess a limited degree of impairment. Unfortunately, this adjective may not only prove confusing in certain regards, but fail to be as differentially descriptive a term as "circumscribed." Minimal brain dysfunction" may be interpreted as meaning *mild mental retardation;* however, this retardate subsyndrome is characterized by a *general* intellectual impairment. Thus, minimal may mean an across the board lowering of functional capacities. More consistent with the deficits that presumably characterize the youngsters discussed in this section is the presence of selective or *circumscribed* impairments, that is, learning or behavior deficiencies that are present *without* a general lowering of intellectual capacity. Were the deficits of a wider or more pervasive character, these children would properly be diagnosed as mentally retarded. Thus, the label "circumscribed brain dysfunctions" seems most accurate in distinguishing these children from other similar clinical groups. Let us note, however, that people do not fall into neat pigeonholes. There will be many cases in which circumscribed defects combine to form a picture of a more general retardation; the line between these two syndromes is bound to be murky and tenuous in numerous patients. Nevertheless, it is necessary to highlight theoretical distinctions between them, if for no other reason than pedagogical clarity.

## GENERAL CLINICAL PICTURE

As a diagnostic entity, "circumscribed brain dysfunctions" includes children of near average, average or above average general intelligence who exhibit specific or narrowly delimited developmental, learning or behavioral deficiencies; these deficits may be of mild or moderate but not of marked severity, and be traceable primarily to functional limitations of the central nervous system. Several dysfunctions may coexist in the same child; however, they should not be so pervasive as to decrease markedly the overall level of intellectual functioning.

Despite the value of referring to this syndrome under one label, no uniform pattern is to be observed among these cases. The sheer complexity of the brain itself argues against such simplifications as a *single* clinical prototype of circumscribed brain dysfunction. In short, the classification comprises a multiplicity of syndromes subsumed under one diagnostic label. The features of each subgroup reflect the particular locus, extent, duration and developmental period in which the nervous system was affected. Complicating the possibilities further, the final clinical picture takes shape not only as a function of neural deficits, but the child's compensatory coping responses and the psychosocial environment within which he lives.

The complex network of influences which often interact are illustrated in the following case.

*CASE 13-8*
*Mark Y., Age 9*

Mark was the second of three children in a socioeconomically upper middle-class family with strong intellectual and social aspirations. His father is a successful lawyer and his mother is a former school teacher.

His birth was uneventful and Mark appeared to be a "normal" youngster until, at the age of 18 months, his mother became increasingly concerned that he had walked "late and awkwardly" and that his speech was "rather delayed." She began to "teach him" to speak more articulately, but with little success. At the age of three and a half, when he was first sent to nursery school, Mark spoke in a "babyish manner," slurred words, was still physically awkward and seemed "hypertense and slow" according to his teacher. A "psychological test" was given to Mark when he was four and a half and his parents were told that he might be "slightly retarded." This news "frightened" Mark's mother and she immediately set out to "raise his I.Q."

Over the following two year period, Mark's mother "drilled him" on a variety of verbal and numerical "training programs." The tension that pervaded this teaching process hardly helped Mark's sense of competence and comfort with academic materials. Nevertheless, he progressed quite well in certain spheres, notably in arithmetic where he was able to multiply and divide simple numbers by the time he entered kindergarten.

In first grade, his teacher noted Mark's physical clumsiness and inarticulate speech. More importantly, Mark seemed to have great difficulty in discriminating among many of the letters in the alphabet, and had no facility at all for reading words. He was at a total loss when asked to identify visually the numbers he could readily multiply in his head.

The diagnosis of "minimal brain damage" was given following a detailed neurological and psychological evaluation. Currently, Mark remains tense and self-conscious about his academic impairments, dislikes school, has begun to read haltingly, still confuses letters, has difficulty writing

with a pencil and is inept in all sports, but can converse quite intelligently and continues to demonstrate excellent "oral" mathematical ability.

Despite the many varieties of cerebral dysfunction, certain typical features are seen with sufficient regularity to justify using them as diagnostic criteria. Two broad classes of symptoms may be distinguished: general deficits in integrative and regulatory controls, and specific developmental and learning deficits.

### Deficits in Integrative and Regulatory Controls

There is a complex of behavior symptoms in these children that reflects a general inability to modulate and control both internal and external stimuli. These youngsters seem to be "at the mercy" of environmental distractions, fleeting thoughts and impulses. These control deficits may be subdivided into three areas.

**Behavioral Disinhibition and Disorganization.** Many clinicians have referred to these children as hyperactive or hyperkinetic since they appear to be always in motion, restless, constantly on the go and rushing headlong into one activity after another. Closer examination, however, reveals that the actual amount of motor behavior in these children is no greater than that found in normal youngsters of the same age. What appears to distinguish brain dysfunction children is the lack of focus and direction to their behavior and their inability to inhibit impulses or restrain themselves from reacting to distractions which other youngsters can do with ease. Thus, it is *not* the amount of physical energy and hyperactivity which differentiates these children, but their disorganized behavior, their meddlesomeness and their capricious changeability.

**Perceptual and Cognitive Distractibility.** As in their behavior, these children may exhibit an inability to sustain attention for prolonged periods and are diverted by fleeting and extraneous stimuli, shuttling back and forth in rapid succession from one trivial distraction to another. This, too, reflects their deficient regulative and integrative controls and their powerlessness to put aside the inconsequential and maintain focus on the pertinent and relevant.

Not only do they evidence scattered responses to external stimuli, but they are overly influenced by transient inner thoughts. Communication and thinking display what have been termed interpenetration, fragmentation and overinclusiveness; ideas run upon one another with no logic, the sequence of thought is broken in midstream and they include unselectively every random notion or passing fancy that crosses their mind. Such digressions may prevent these children from utilizing their higher order "abstraction" capacities; they cannot sustain and organize their thoughts sufficiently to reflect and "plan ahead," to put things together and "see" larger concepts, to draw upon past learnings or solve sequentially complex problems. Thus, although they may possess the potential for integrative abstractions, they fail to utilize and develop them fully as a consequence of their chaotic perceptual and cognitive activities.

**Emotional Lability.** The consequences of regulatory deficits may extend to the sphere of feelings and impulses, as well. The tendency to be impulsive, to be unable to delay gratification and to act out emotions with little or no modulation is evident in capricious moods, temper tantrums and episodes of unprovoked aggressive outbursts. The character of these emotional expressions depends, of course, on the total life experiences to which these children are exposed. Given support and encouragement in ways that maximize feelings of competence and adequacy, these outbursts are likely to be transient, few and far between. However, should their relationships prove humiliating and frustrating, feelings of self-deprecation and anger will cumulate and be "touched off" by seemingly trivial events. In general, then, the emotions these youngsters feel will be released with relative ease due to their regulatory and control deficits; the content and frequency of these expressions, however, depend on the particular character of their environmental relationships.

We should note that some of these youngsters exhibit a behavioral torpidity and a cognitive and emotional rigidity. In contrast to most children with brain dysfunctions, this particular subgroup tends to be overcontrolled and overinhibited rather than undercontrolled and disinhibited. This flat and contained demeanor may reflect the particulars of their biophysical defect, but more often it is a compensatory coping reaction, a shrinking of their milieu, a withdrawal into a narrow sphere in which they feel a measure of competence and security. Usually this adaptive response is seen in adolescents and may be observed to unfold gradually as the child gets older. Although by no means universal, many of these children learn bit by bit to cope with their defect; they no longer "yield" to the transient stimuli and impulses that previously disrupted their lives and complicated their relationships with others.

*Specific Developmental and Learning Deficits*

The second cluster of pathognomonic symptoms refers to relatively specific functional impairments, notably evident in maturational lags and deficiencies in the acquisition of certain skills and competencies. Many of these youngsters are characterized as "being slow" at school but only in well-delimited subjects rather than in all areas. They frequently are thought to be lazy and obstreperous because they achieve so much more poorly than they "score" on intelligence tests. Others are spoken of as "immature" since they function both physically and socially at a level appreciably below their age and measured intelligence; they seem inordinately clumsy and inept, and often behave in an "infantile" and petulant manner with their peers.

A careful evaluation of their behaviors and performances indicates a marked unevenness in their functioning, that is, they do not display a uniform or generalized retardation. It is this circumscribed or delimited nature of their deficit that distinguishes them from the mentally retarded. The specific impairments they exhibit will depend on the locus, size, duration and developmental age in which the brain was affected. The character of the circumscribed deficit varies from child to child; no two children exhibit the same pattern of maturational lags or learning disabilities since the impaired biophysical substrate will vary from case to case, as will the environmental conditions to which they must adapt. In the following discussion, we will note some of the more common spheres in which these deficits are exhibited.

**Single Function Impairments.** It is not likely that disturbances will be restricted to single functions in the growing child; brain regions are highly dependent upon one another for their proper maturation and development. Dysfunctions, initially centered in one zone, are likely to lead to maldevelopments in associated spheres; this "spread of developmental dysfunction" will vary appreciably depending on the age of the child.

Despite this spread, a "gradient" of dysfunction may be observed in many patients, with certain functions more markedly impaired than others. Since we have excluded from this syndrome cases of severe disability, such as cerebral palsy and blindness, we are left with children who exhibit subtle or minor disturbances. These youngsters may evidence any number of visual, auditory, tactile or other sensory deficiencies. Others exhibit minor paralyses, tremors and awkwardness in fine and gross motor coordination.

**Perceptual-Motor Impairments.** Many children with brain dysfunctions have difficulty in discriminating visual patterns such as letters or words; Mark Y. obviously suffered from this impairment. Others cannot fuse or bring basic perceptual units together in larger configurations, tending to separate and focus on only the discrete parts. Problems of figure-ground and right-left confusion, spatial disorientation and visual reversals are not uncommon in these youngsters. Difficulties in coordinating perception and response are notable in many cases. Many seem incapable of reproducing what they see and understand; others react inconsistently to the same visual configuration. Physical balance is frequently impaired; this seemingly simple and basic act requires the smooth and facile integration of visual and kinesthetic stimuli, and often is accomplished by these youngsters with a proficiency characteristic of children of a much younger age. Problems in speech and articulation and difficulties in visual-motor coordination requisite for legible writing are frequently evident.

**Cognitive-Language Impairments.** Irregularities or developmental lags in communication skills are another sphere in which defects might center. Here we see a variety of minor aphasias, spoken and written language confusions, discrepancies between oral reading and comprehension of what has been read and defective memory for symbolic concepts, both mathematical and verbal. In short, many of these children exhibit an inability to grasp and utilize language anywhere near the facility expected, given their overall intellectual level.

## GENERAL ETIOLOGY

The level of neurological organization in humans is in a relatively primitive state at birth; most biophysical substrates for complex functions have not yet matured. Because these functions are not normally displayed until later in life, severe constitutional limitations and injuries may be present within the neonate *without* any observable indication for months or years. Defects become obvious only when the child is "expected" normally to perform certain activities such as walking, talking, reading and so on. The delayed recognition of these defects makes it extremely difficult to identify etiological origins. For example, if the dysfunction does not become evident until the child enters school and displays an inability to learn letters and words, the diagnostician will be at a loss to know whether the "cause" is constitutional, a birth injury or an aftermath of a childhood infection. Because of the subtle and delayed nature of these symptoms,

and because of the difficulty in differentiating disease-caused dysfunctions from natural individual differences in capacity and aptitude, the task of identifying the etiological source is a complex one indeed.

Despite these difficulties and the paucity of reported empirical research in the literature, it will be useful to summarize briefly the more probable origins of this syndrome. They range from subtle genetic deviances to known and explicitly demonstrable brain injuries. The format provided in our discussion of the mental retardation syndrome will be useful in discussing the etiology of these more circumscribed deficits. As will be recalled, the principal distinction drawn was between endogenous and exogenous factors.

### Endogenous Factors

Because of the brief period that has elapsed since this syndrome was described, few, if any, systematic studies have been executed with regard to the role of genetic or constitutional factors. It is plausible to speculate, despite the paucity of data, that differences among individuals in circumscribed functions may reflect *genetic deviances* transmitted in the normal course of fertilization from parent to child. Consistent with this thesis would be findings to the effect that youngsters who evidence such deficits as developmental motor lags, speech disarticulation or reading problems are the progeny of parents who exhibited similar childhood deficits. Whether the biophysical substrate for these deviances are tissue aplasias in selected regions of the brain, delayed maturational rates, peculiar interneuronal "wirings" or biochemical anomalies can only be conjectured.

Speculations are in order also with regard to the role of *genetic diseases,* either in the form of parentally transmitted units or chromosomal aberrations. It would appear reasonable to think that recessive genes may be centrally involved in many circumscribed dysfunctions since their effects are likely to be of a limited and nonsevere nature. By contrast, mutations and structural chromosomal disjunctions are likely to produce impairments that are more severe and pervasive than those found in circumscribed cases.

### Exogenous Factors

Sources foreign to the organisms's natural or endowed neurological make-up may cause either mild and focal or severe and pervasive damage. The exogenous determinants of brain dysfunctions, therefore, are essentially the same as those described in the section on mental retardation. Relatively little research has accumulated, however, to verify the specific role of any of these factors.

Toxic, infectious, traumatic and endocrinological disturbances may affect certain selected regions of the brain more severely than others, thus eventuating in a circumscribed dysfunction rather than a general mental retardation. As noted in our discussion of the "psychophysiologic disorders," there are individual differences in which bodily systems are vulnerable to stress. Thus, children may possess differential vulnerabilities, causing certain regions of the nervous system to succumb more seriously than others to the impact of an infectious or toxic assault.

The maturational stage during which the damage occurred may also be a factor; thus, the character of the circumscribed dysfunction may be a matter of *when* the toxic or infectious event assaulted the body. In most cases, however, damage at a particular sensitive stage of neuropsychological development results not only in a loss to the rapidly maturing region but to the entire matrix of interconnections associated with that region. Moreover, several neural systems simultaneously proliferate at any one developmental period; it is likely, therefore, that the impact of a pathogenic event will affect several regional zones, although some more than others. Because of the relative undifferentiation of some structures, and their still to be developed potentials, the child, despite the presence of an early injury, may be able to reconstruct certain spheres of his damaged nervous system to a greater extent than others.

Psychosocial deprivation may also turn out to be selective in its effects. Deficits in "stimulus nutriment" may slow down developmental progressions, not across the entire brain but only in fairly delimited functional regions, e.g., parental restrictions and overprotectiveness may lead to developmental lags only in sensorimotor competencies; similarly, severely limited verbal symbolic experiences, stemming from a pervasive "cultural deprivation," may result in deficits in cognitive and language functions but not in others.

## REMEDIAL APPROACHES IN BIOPHYSICAL DEFECTS

Biophysical defects, for the most part, are matters requiring medical and surgical treatment, and are more appropriately discussed in textbooks in these fields. Nevertheless, it will be instructive to provide a summary of the various factors involved in the prognosis of these cases and to review some of the more general principles and goals of therapy.

**Prognosis.** The prognosis for these defects depends on several factors: the type of disease, the location and diffuseness of tissue disturbance, the age at the time of occurrence, whether the impairment is acute or chronic and, in a wider context, the patient's premorbid personality and the environmental conditions within which he lives.

Briefly, certain *progressive diseases* for which no effective treatment is known ultimately prove fatal, e.g., Huntington's disease and malignant cerebral neoplasms. Most other types of diseases are either nonprogressive or can be arrested if not reversed.

In general, the *location and diffuseness* of tissue damage have little bearing on prognosis. However, losses in regions subserving certain critical functions, e.g., speech or integrative controls, may demand coping adjustments that are greater than the impaired individual can muster, resulting thereby in a prognosis that is grim indeed.

Prognosis, as far as *age of occurrence* is concerned, exhibits a curvilinear pattern; defects in both the very young and those past middle age have a poorer prognosis than those occurring in adolescence and early maturity. In prenatal life, infancy and early childhood, where considerable interdependencies exist among simultaneously developing neural systems, minor disruptions in one region "spread" and retard the maturation of other brain regions. In late life, coping resources have begun to falter and the person is less able than before to compensate for his defect and to reorganize his remaining capacities.

Acute impairments are reversible and likely to have a better prognosis than irreversible chronic conditions. Similarly, nonprogressive cases in which the disease process has run its full course present a more promising outlook than progressive states in which the prospects are for further deterioration and increasingly serious impairments.

One might expect, upon first thought, that personality factors and environmental conditions are less relevant in determining the prognosis of biophysical defects than they are in psychopathologies without physical damage. In fact, the converse is true; biophysically impaired individuals are especially vulnerable to the influence of their premorbid tendencies and present environmental conditions. Unable to master or regulate the flow of stimuli around and within them, they are subjected to the full impact of forces that non-damaged persons are physically able to modulate and control.

**Therapy.** As was noted earlier, therapy in most biophysical defects are principally matters of medical and surgical responsibility. This is especially true in diseases attributable to infections, toxins, trauma, nutritional and metabolic dysfunctions, neoplasms and convulsions. We shall review approaches to these syndromes as a unit; in a later section, we will discuss degenerative defects, mental retardation and circumscribed brain dysfunctions, in which psychological remedial measures are primary.

1. Disturbances treated principally by medical and surgical procedures are approached in different ways depending on the stage of the impairment. "Active" states, comprising acute disturbances or chronic impairments undergoing a temporary flareup, are handled differently than quiescent "static" states, which consist primarily of stabilized chronic conditions.

In *active states,* the two central goals of treatment are the removal of the precipitating or aggravating agent (e.g., the infectious or toxic invader), and the elimination or diminution of the manifest symptomatology (e.g., delirium, coma or convulsions). As an illustration of the first goal, physicians prescribe a regimen of penicillin for neurosyphilis since this drug effectively destroys the invading spirochete; similarly, in brain trauma or neoplasm, surgical procedures are employed to remove blood clots, siphon excess fluids and reconstruct circulatory pathways necessary to supply blood to brain tissue. The symptomatic facet of treatment is illustrated by the use of medications to curb the hyperactivity of delirium or to reduce the frequency of convulsions in epilepsy; similarly, a quiet and subdued atmosphere may be arranged during periods of confusion and agitation in cases of cerebral degeneration.

In *static* states, in which the disease process has been halted or reversed, the primary focus of treatment is symptomatic relief such as the reduction of pain or the calming of anxiety.

In both active and static states, there may be need to remove the patient to an institutional setting. This should be avoided, when possible, since physically impaired patients tend to recover more rapidly in their home surroundings. However, if the family cannot control a severely disturbed patient, or if they aggravate the problem, the patient is best committed to the care of hospital personnel. In these settings, active cases are treated through direct medical techniques and are usually remitted after a short stay. Static cases often remain hospitalized, in order to undergo programs of long-term milieu therapy.

2. *Degenerative defects* of advanced age with few exceptions represent admixtures of both biophysical impairments and psychosocial deterioration. Until recently, it was believed that the process of decompensation in the elderly was irreversible and that little could or should be done other than to make them comfortable, keep them out of trouble and help them bide their remaining time.

Today, it is recognized that the rapid decline and troublesome behaviors of many elderly patients have little relation to their organic condition. Rather, these problems more often reflect feelings of isolation and hopelessness, a loss of self-worth and usefulness and their realization that no one "really cares" and at best is reluctantly "putting up with them."

The growing awareness that psychosocial factors are more crucial to the continued health and longevity of these patients has led to new therapeutic attitudes, centered largely on social rehabilitation. "Senior citizen" clubs, adult education programs, special homes and hospital wards designed to provide the aging person with helpful counseling, social companionship, worthwhile activities and a sense of purpose and self-worth have begun to "take the edge off" the psychic pain of old age. Feeling accepted and useful and engaging in stimulating and worthwhile activities day after day enable the elderly person to regain his self-respect and to feel that he is of value to others.

3. Most *mental retardates* are not benefited by medical or surgical treatment; among the exceptions are special diets or medications for cases of phenylketonuria and cretinism and operative procedures for hydrocephalus. There are no known techniques which can "raise" the capacities of retardates. Most treatment methods, then, are designed to help these persons establish a meaningful and gratifying social and vocational life by training and encouraging the maximum development of their given capacities. To achieve this goal, there must be a total commitment involving medical, educational, psychological, community, family and socioeconomic programs. More than the average person, who stands a fair chance of "making a go" of life, the retardate with his intellectual handicaps and social deficits needs the support, guidance and respect of those who raise, educate and socialize with him.

Discouraged, guilt-ridden or overprotective parents will only aggravate the retardate's natural limitations. Thus, parental counseling is often required to assure a maximum of warmth, acceptance and encouragement.

Educators often need prodding. Many are "bothered" by these "stupid and troublesome" youngsters and frequently shunt them into ill-equipped and poorly taught ungraded classes. School administrators and teachers must be helped to recognize the many achievements that are possible among these children *if* they are provided with programs geared to their pace and style of development. Given proper training, milder retardates can acquire vocational skills which enable them to become productive, self-respecting and well-adjusted members of the community. More severely retarded youngsters can be educated to perform simple household chores, thereby preparing them to be useful participants within their families.

Community "sheltered workshops" have been developed in many cities, enabling mildly retarded youngsters to find social companionship and to make the transition to an independent adult life. These centers can provide moderately retarded adults with a useful and self-fulfilling vocation, while they still reside at home. Other community, state and federal programs have been established to assess the aptitudes of retardates, train them and then locate employment opportunities in which they may achieve a sense of accomplishment, while they fulfill a useful occupational role.

4. Remedial approaches for children with *circumscribed brain dysfunctions* are designed primarily to establish greater regulatory controls and to overcome deficits in development and learning.

Various psychopharmacological agents may be employed to dampen the hyperdistractibility and emotional lability of these children, but this medical regimen tends to treat only the surface symptom rather than the basic control deficit.

Several educational and psychological procedures have been employed to achieve this goal of more effective self-regulation. They seek to minimize disruptive environmental stimulation and to structure the child's activities and daily routine. The normal stimuli of home and classroom usually prove to be excessively distracting to these youngsters; they cannot "get their bearing" in these environments and are flooded with more distractions than they can possibly cope with. As a consequence, efforts to learn the rudiments of regulatory and discriminative controls are constantly disrupted. To enable such children to acquire these functions, they are provided with settings of minimal stimulation. Step by step, as they learn to modulate their responses to simple stimulus situations, the complexity and variety of the environment are increased. To strengthen this progression toward regulatory controls, the child is exposed to an unvarying daily routine in which the time for awakening, eating and so on is highly systematized. Likewise, the teaching programs and materials to which they are exposed are highly organized so as to maximize the development of logical routines, focused perception and structured thinking. Important, also, is parental consistency, firm direction and the establishment of clear limitation in behavior. Not only do these measures aid the youngster directly in controlling his erratic ways, but they serve as models which he may incorporate through imitation.

The developmental and learning deficits of these children are attacked best through systematic remediation programs focused on perceptual-motor and speech training. In recent years, numerous procedures have been devised to upgrade these and other circumscribed deficiencies (e.g., Cruickshank, 1965; Kephart, 1960; Frostig, 1964).

# CONCLUDING COMMENTS AND SUMMARY

In this, our last chapter on clinical syndromes, attention has been turned to impairments in which biogenic factors are primary. In contrast to most psychiatric texts, in which as much as half the volume is devoted to biophysical defects, we have presented in detail only those more prevalent impairments which may further our understanding of psychopathology. Let us summarize the major themes and facts of the chapter.

1. With the exception of a few relatively clear-cut syndromes, the diagnosis of biophysical defects is not nearly as simple a matter as one might initially think. Pathological processes may have been triggered originally by biogenic influences, but the "final" clinical picture is never a simple and direct consequence of the physical disturbance itself; rather, we see the composite end product of the defect as it develops through a complex sequence of interactions with premorbid personality trends and postmorbid coping adjustments.

2. Clinical signs reflecting the presence of

a biophysical defect vary depending on its location, size, diffuseness, activity, maturational stage of occurrence, the patient's age, premorbid personality and the environmental setting within which he lives. Despite innumerable differences among individuals and syndromes, the principal signs of these defects can be distinguished and categorized in three groups.

a. *General Integrative Impairments:* These include alterations in the level of *consciousness,* from decreased activation to stuporous coma. The loss of regulatory *controls* is a frequent clinical sign, ranging in severity from distractibility and emotional lability to markedly confused and delirious states. Decrements in *abstraction* capacities are the third indication of higher integrative impairment; these losses are observed in concept-formation and problem-solving deficits and in an inability to "transcend the immediate" through memory recall, cognitive reflection and anticipatory planning.

b. *Specific Functional Impairments:* Among these losses are deficits in highly circumscribed functions such as motor paralyses and sensory anesthesias. More often, especially in central nervous system involvement, impairments are shown in perceptual-motor difficulties and cognitive-language aphasias.

c. *Compensatory Coping Efforts:* The defective individual must reorganize his life in response to the impairment he has suffered. In the early phases of difficulty, many of these individuals experience "catastrophic reactions" as they recognize the severity of their limitations. Quite commonly, these reactions are accompanied by a release and accentuation of premorbid and previously controlled personality tendencies. As a final adaptation, some "shrink their milieu," withdrawing to a narrow and secure environment where they engage rigidly and perseveratively in the same safe and unvarying activities.

3. The etiologies of biophysical defects are many and varied; in some cases, several factors are simultaneously involved. There is no single system of classification which encompasses all of the etiological dimensions by which these syndromes can be analyzed. Among the several ways of distinguishing their pathogenic sources, the following were presented: distinctions that reflect the source of the causal agent were differentiated into *genogenic, histogenic, chemogenic* and *psychogenic;* defects that represent quantitative extremes of normal individual variability were termed *deviances;* these were contrasted to defects which stem from qualitative changes in bodily functions, referred to as *diseases;* another

distinction referred to whether the etiological source originated within the individual, termed *endogenous* or outside the individual, termed *exogenous; intracranial locus,* signifying that the primary effect of the pathogenic agent was centered within the brain, was differentiated from *systemic locus,* in which the primary attack focused on other parts of the body; and the distinction between *focal* and *diffused* cerebral locus attempted to differentiate defects within circumscribed regions of the brain from those which are within the brain, but are more pervasive and widespread.

4. The extraordinary complexity of the brain, its intricate relationship to behavior and the numerous pathogenic factors which can disrupt the varied functions it subserves preclude the possibility of formulating a simple, unidimensional classification system of biophysical defects. The traditional nosological schema does not surmount these complexities. A review of the DSM-II indicates that most syndromes are organized with reference to their primary etiological origins; others are categorized on the basis of commonalities in their clinical picture.

a. Among syndromes organized in terms of "etiological origins" are those arising from *intracranial infections* (notably neurosyphilis and encephalitis), *toxins* (primarily alcohol, drugs and poisons), *head trauma* (concussions, contusions, lacerations and vascular accidents), *nutritional deficiencies* (mostly in the vitamin B complex), *metabolic and endocrinological dysfunctions, intracranial neoplasm* and *cerebral degeneration* (including presenile syndromes such as Pick's and Alzheimer's diseases, and advanced age syndromes such as senile dementia and cerebral arteriosclerosis). The typical clinical picture and course, as well as details concerning the various subtypes and conditions, were provided.

b. Among syndromes organized in accord with their common "clinical signs" were *epilepsy, mental retardation* and *circumscribed brain dysfunctions in childhood.* Each category was further subdivided into its major clinical varieties. Etiological hypotheses and data were presented, as were signs that aid in their diagnostic differentiation. Difficulties were noted regarding the identification of pathogenic agents and the criteria to be utilized for syndrome classification.

5. The prognosis of biophysical defects was considered to be a function of several factors, notably the type of disease, location and diffuseness of tissue disturbance, developmental age of

occurrence, premorbid personality trends and current environmental conditions. Treatment methods differ for "active" as opposed to "static" defects. Although therapy in most of these syndromes is largely the concern of physicians and surgeons, patients often require supportive and reeducative psychological procedures as well. The role of social and educational therapeutic measures is especially important in syndromes of cerebral degeneration, mental retardation and circumscribed brain dysfunction.

With this chapter we conclude our presentation of the clinical syndromes. Four major groups were elaborated. Chapters 6 through 9 focused on *personality patterns,* characterized by deeply ingrained and pervasive attitudes and coping strategies that are founded on a complex developmental interaction of both biogenic and psychogenic determinants. In chapters 10 and 11, the *symptom disorders* were presented; these impairments are seen as relatively distinctive clinical signs that occur during periods of stress in pathological personalities and stand out in sharp relief against the patient's more prosaic pattern. *Behavior reactions,* discussed in chapter 12, were seen as pathological responses arising in essentially normal personality types, either in response to situations of unusual but transient stress or as ingrained learned responses to circumscribed stimulus situations. The fourth major category, *biophysical defects,* was described in this chapter and incorporates disturbances attributable to impairments in the organism's biological make-up.

In each of the preceding chapters we have attempted, albeit briefly, to outline some of the therapeutic measures appropriate to the conditions discussed. The following two chapters will enable us to distinguish these treatment methods more clearly and to understand more fully their rationale and utility.

# Part 4

## THERAPY

*Introduction*

## Introduction

No book on "mental illness" would be complete without surveying in some depth the therapeutic techniques which practitioners employ to alter psychopathology; this is the objective of the next two chapters.

As we noted in the first paragraphs of the book, man has always been intrigued by the bizarre actions and emotions displayed by his fellow man. Along with this curiosity, man sought to devise remedies that might alleviate the anguish of these unfortunate beings. For the greater part of history, techniques were based on superstition and magic. In preliterate times and in the early Egyptian civilizations the shaman or priest served as the therapist; his tools were those of ritualistic incantation, "medicinal" herbs and spiritually healing objects such as amulets and charms. The early Greeks, led by Hippocrates and Aristotle, turned from these fruitless rituals and instituted what proved to be a sound although short-lived approach of "rational" therapy. Although retaining the view that mental illness stemmed from spiritual forces, the Greeks and Romans em-

ployed such therapeutic practices as rest, dietetics and the sympathetic counsel of physician-priests. This humanistic approach came to an end during the latter phases of the Roman period. Throughout the centuries of the Middle Ages, "scientific" and compassionate methods gave way to cruel measures based on fear, witchcraft and a punitive Christian theology. Not until the late eighteenth century, commencing with Pinel's "open door" and "fresh air" policies, was a more benign era again ushered in. For roughly the next century advances were limited, however, to programs of custodial care.

Treatment as we know it today did not begin until the discovery of hypnosis and its relation to hysteria. The early work of Charcot and Bernheim was instrumental in leading Freud to the thesis that mental illness was essentially a psychological process traceable to the persistence of unconscious memories and conflicts. Psychoanalysis, the first of the systematic and rationally grounded treatment techniques, was designed by Freud to release these intrapsychic forces and reconstruct the self-defeating defenses that patients employed to deal with them. For many years, well into the midpart of this century, psychotherapy was viewed as synonymous with Freud's psychoanalytic procedure. Although new techniques were conceived, they were for the most part modifications of the Freudian approach.

It was not until the 1930's, with the resurgence of "medical" therapy, that alternatives to "intrapsychic" treatment came to the fore. This new movement began with the development of convulsive and surgical procedures; these early biophysical techniques were followed in the 1950's by the discovery of psychopharmacological methods.

Newer psychological methods were also devised in the 1940's and 1950's; they differed substantially in both rationale and technique from psychoanalysis. Among them are the several procedures that we shall group under the labels of phenomenological reorientation and behavior modification.

Thus, as man begins the latter third of the twentieth century, he has at his disposal for the first time a variety of alternative treatment techniques. Although their efficacy has not been fully validated, these methods provide the clinician with a real choice as to which tools he can use to achieve the goals of therapy.

## GOALS OF THERAPY

It was Hippocrates, the first of the great "scientific" physicians, who outlined the basic goals of medical treatment: to do no harm or wrong to the patient, relieve his suffering and assist "nature's" healing processes. Phrased in more contemporary terms, the therapist *first* must be sure that his techniques will not make matters worse than they already are; *second,* he must alleviate the patient's present discomfort; and *third,* he must facilitate the development of a healthier and more resilient state. In these three guidelines, Hippocrates set down treatment goals that are applicable to all health professions and to all varieties of illness. How can we translate them in terms more relevant to psychopathology?

To achieve this translation we must recognize first that psychopathology encompasses a wide range of problems. What is best for one type of difficulty may be damaging to another. Treatment goals and techniques must be geared, then, to the specific nature of the problem. To illustrate from general medicine, one case may require

antibiotics, another call for surgery and a third require simple rest in a changed climate. In a similar manner, therapy in psychopathology must be selected in terms of the patient's specific problem. Psychopathology is no less varied than physiopathology; each subvariety of illness may call for different treatment goals and techniques.

Let us turn now to Hippocrates' first goal, that of doing no harm or wrong to the patient. Therapists may do their patients a disservice if they employ treatment techniques that are inapplicable and inefficient, thereby worsening the situation or postponing the employment of more effective procedures. This occurs all too frequently since many therapists apply the same treatment methods regardless of the specific nature of the patient's presenting problem. Psychotherapeutic inflexibility is no different than the often condemned chiropractic practice of utilizing bone manipulation for such diverse cases as asthma, urinary infections and myopia.

The achievement of Hippocrates' second goal, relief from suffering, is shared both by therapist and patient. Although the particular methods selected to achieve this objective differ among therapeutic "schools," all desire to reduce discomforting symptoms. Some accomplish this by dislodging the "unconscious roots" of the symptom, others by modifying its biophysical substrate, others by changing attitudes which give rise to it and still others through direct behavior extinction procedures.

Hippocrates' third goal, to facilitate the development of a healthier and more resilient state than before, presents a number of ethical as well as practical problems. Many patients, having achieved the immediate goal of symptom relief, do not foresee the possibility that further therapy may assist them in attaining a degree of "positive" mental health substantially greater than that which they achieved previously. Therapists who seek to fulfill this goal are faced with the ethical question of whether or not to guide their patients, either through open discussion or implicit therapeutic procedures, into pursuing the aim of "deeper" insight and "self-actualization." Therapists differ as to the emphasis they give to these more sweeping goals. Some consider "personality growth" to be the primary objective of psychotherapy; others, although they value positive mental health no less, orient their methods to more circumscribed objectives. As matters now stand, there is no evidence that techniques explicitly designed to effect growth and self-actualization are appreciably more successful in achieving these objectives than methods with more modest aims (Frank, 1961).

## LEVELS OF THERAPEUTIC FOCUS

One would think from the disparate techniques employed by the various schools of therapy that they would have substantially different goals. This is not the case. Psychoanalysts, existentialists, pharmacologists and behaviorists, despite conceptual and procedural differences, seek to "do no harm," "to relieve suffering" and "to promote growth and durable health." How then do they differ?

Numerous scholars have sought to classify alternative therapies in the hope of discerning basic commonalities and divergencies (McNair and Lorr, 1964; Sundland and Barker, 1962; Wallach and Strupp, 1964; London, 1964; Patterson, 1967). No simple and agreed upon classification has emerged as a consequence of these efforts since each of the so-called schools are far from "pure" or consistent within themselves. For example, within the same "school," therapists may be distinguished in terms of their underlying philosophy of man, e.g., some view him to be no more than a composite of habit systems; others conceive man as a responsible choice-making agent. Another distinction relates to the therapist's conceptions of psychopathology and its development, e.g., some place importance on early childhood experiences, others do not. A major division among therapists lies in the sphere of treatment process, e.g., some believe that therapeutic techniques should be based on experimentally derived principles whereas others give primacy to clinical theory; some believe that the therapist should take the lead in directing the course and goals of treatment, others allow the patient to assume this role; in some approaches the therapist is impersonal, acting in accord with certain strict and unvarying procedures, in others he acts in a warm, personal or spontaneous manner.

It is our contention that the techniques employed by therapists are determined first and foremost by the kind of data they focus upon in therapy. As noted in chapter 2, alternative approaches to psychopathology and its treatment are shaped primarily by the "level" of data that the scientist has chosen to emphasize. Once a particular class of data has been selected, the types of concepts and theories he will formulate and the therapeutic techniques and procedures he utilizes follow logically and inevitably. If he chooses to stress overt behavior, his theoretical schema and treatment approach will perforce be different than if he focuses on the biophysical substrate, phenomenological experience or intrapsychic mechanisms.

We shall organize the next two chapters in accord with these four levels. Let us briefly note here their principal characteristics.

*Biophysical* therapists consider the biological substrate to be the most fruitful level for therapeutic modification. These men, trained usually in the tradition of psychiatric medicine, often contend that the primary source of pathology lies in the anatomical or neurophysiological make-up of the individual. It follows logically, then, that the biological defect should be treated directly. Thus, these therapists employ pharmacological agents as a means of altering biochemistry and physiological thresholds, surgical management as a way of destroying pathological tissue or electrical stimulation to modify patterns of neural organization.

*Intrapsychic* therapists focus on the data of unconscious processes. These men, trained in the tradition of psychodynamic psychiatry, often assert that the primary source of difficulty stems from the persistence of repressed childhood anxieties and defensive maneuvers. The task of therapy, then, is to bring these residues of the past into consciousness where they can be reevaluated and reworked in a constructive fashion. To accomplish these goals, these therapists assume a passive role and attempt to revive early memories and conflicts through methods such as free association and dream interpretation.

*Phenomenological* therapists turn their attention to the data of conscious experience, that is, to the patient's subjective perception of events. These men, most of whom follow in the tradition of clinical personology, believe that the root of psychic disturbances lies in the individual's cognitive distortions of himself and others. The primary role of therapy, then, is not to explore the unconscious or to remove overt symptoms, but to "free" the patient so that he may develop an enhanced image of his self-worth and a constructive outlook on life. To accomplish this task, phenomenological therapists engage in "free-wheeling" discussions in which the patient is guided or encouraged to find more wholesome attitudes.

*Behavioral* therapists concern themselves with the data of overt action and performance. Their focus in treatment is the patient's socially maladaptive or deficient behaviors, not internal states such as phenomenological experience, unconscious conflicts or constitutional dispositions. These men, trained in the tradition of academic-experimental psychology, conceive their techniques in terms like stimulation and reinforcement. They assert that differences between adaptive and maladaptive behaviors reflect differences in the reinforcement experiences to which individuals were exposed. Therapy consists of the direct application of experimentally derived principles of learning and unlearning. The therapist seeks neither to remove "underlying causes" nor to give the patient free rein to explore his attitudes and feelings; rather, he arranges a program in which the behaviors he wishes to eliminate are unlearned, and those he wishes to enhance are strengthened through reinforcement or imitation. (Parenthetically, we must note that although behavior therapists utilize techniques devised initially in experimental learning research and concepts derived from learning theories, there is no justification for the common practice of exclusively restricting the term "learning therapies" to their methods. Phenomenological and intrapsychic approaches are also "learning therapies" since they, too, proceed in accord with principles that deal with how patients "learn" psychopathology and how these pathologies may be "unlearned" in therapy. Learning concepts and principles, then, are not the exclusive province of behavior therapy; therapists who focus on phenomenological and intrapsychic data levels utilize their own "brand" of learning theory, and do so with equal justification, if not with equal consistency or explicitness.)

## EVALUATION OF THERAPY

The ultimate test of a treatment program is not its rationale, theory or philosophy, but whether or not it works. Facile, even ingenious, explanations as to why and how beneficial changes *should* occur cannot replace the simple empirical fact that a treatment is or is not successful.

Every advocate of a therapeutic method claims a significant measure of success for his cherished technique, including those who espouse faith healing, warm baths, a diet of soy beans or the manipulation of bones. The question of successful treatment is not whether one achieves success, but whether the degree of success is significantly greater than that attained by patently "unscientific" methods, or through the mere passage of time alone. Moreover, the results of

therapy should be gauged, at least in part, by objective as well as subjective criteria, and should be judged repeatedly through long-term follow-up evaluations to assure that changes are more than transitory.

Until the last decade or two, most therapists paid little attention to questions of effectiveness; either they took success for granted or they themselves served as judges of therapeutic effectiveness. Heavily involved in direct clinical service, few therapists had time for evaluative studies, and fewer still were trained to undertake objective, controlled and systematic research.

This sorry state of affairs has begun to be remedied. In the last ten years, increasing numbers of investigators have brought their methodological talents to bear on the problem of therapeutic evaluation. This rapidly proliferating body of research has focused on two interrelated problems: the *efficacy* of therapy, that is, whether or not beneficial changes do take place in conjunction with treatment (often referred to as "outcome" studies); and the therapeutic *mode of action,* that is, the features or ingredients of the treatment procedure that are centrally involved in effecting beneficial changes (often referred to as "process" studies).

Much of the research done in the past has suffered from weak experimental design, inadequate sampling, ill-defined criteria, poor measuring instruments and unjustified generalizations. Thus, before we discuss the two principal issues of evaluative research, outcome and process, we will briefly discuss two subsidiary problems, the selection of relevant *evaluative criteria* for assessing therapeutic change, and the nature of the *patient sample* selected for research.

### EVALUATIVE CRITERIA

How does one determine if beneficial changes have taken place? Who makes the judgment, what measures are used, and at what point in the treatment program are they applied?

Establishing criteria for evaluating change is not a simple matter, nor is there consensus as to what criteria should be employed. Few would take issue with amorphous generalities such as "relief from suffering" and a "healthier, more resilient state than before." But how are these generalities to be spelled out and given the form of explicit and judicable criteria, gauged in accord with precise and objective measures? It is at the point of detailed criteria specification that consensus among researchers breaks down, and the need for reasonable agreement is so much needed.

Numerous and varied criteria of therapeutic change have been employed. These range from self-reports, therapist ratings, symptom check lists, intratherapy verbalizations, psychological test data and physiological indices, but many problems exist with regard to the reliability and validity of these criteria.

In addition to utilizing valid criteria and establishing a measure of consensus and uniformity in their application, it is important that several different criteria be used in evaluating the efficacy of therapy. Most forms of psychopathology are highly complex and manifest their features in varied ways. Different aspects of pathology may exhibit different degrees of change, even producing contrasting results. For example, the patient's subjective appraisal of change may fail to correspond with judgments made by others; thus, he may claim to be feeling better, having begun to express his formerly restrained hostile attitudes, but, as a consequence, may be judged by his family to be increasingly destructive socially. In short, single criterion measures may provide a misleading picture of improvement.

Multiple criteria are particularly important in studies designed to compare different therapeutic approaches. For example, after 15 or 20 sessions, behavior therapy may be judged quite successful if gauged by a symptom check list whereas intrapsychic therapy, oriented to the goal of "basic personality reconstruction," will in all likelihood be evaluated as unsuccessful at this point in treatment and according to this criterion. In short, since different forms of therapy focus on different levels of personality functioning and seek to achieve their aims after different lengths of treatment, it is important to utilize a comprehensive and repeated set of criteria so as to specify the precise nature of their impact and to delineate the timing and sequence of these beneficial effects.

Despite the value of combining criteria such as therapist ratings, test scores and intratherapy communications, the most significant criterion, *manifest changes in real-life situations,* is often neglected or bypassed because of difficulties involved in obtaining relevant data. Signs of improvement exhibited in institutional settings or changes noted within the therapeutic office, may or may not be "transferred" to everyday family, vocational and community relationships. The crucial test of therapeutic effectiveness, then, is *not* what can be reported, measured or seen in the therapeutic setting, but what is generalized to and carried out in extratherapeutic life.

## PATIENT SAMPLE

The effect of therapy, whether it be biological or psychological, varies as a function of who is treated; what works with one patient may not work with another. Despite the obvious character of this observation, many investigators have pursued their research on the unwarranted assumption that their clinical sample was homogeneous, with each patient equally disposed to respond favorably or unfavorably to the treatment to which he was subjected. In short, patients were not differentiated either in terms of their prognoses or other significant variables such as types of problems, target symptoms or chronicity. Those who have attempted to differentiate their patients have done so in accord with the traditional system of diagnostic categories. As was noted in earlier chapters, the official nosological schema is notoriously unreliable, and groups together patients who differ in significant if not crucial variables. As a result, most studies have produced data that confuse rather than clarify judgments of efficacy, and provide no information concerning which forms of pathology are most receptive to the therapy being investigated. Keisler comments on this point as follows (1966):

Because of these initial patient differences, no matter what the effect of psychotherapy in a particular study (be it phenomenally successful or a dismal failure), one can conclude very little if anything. At best, one can say something such as: for a sample of patients coming to this particular clinic over this particular period, psychotherapy performed by the clinic staff during that period on the average was either successful or unsuccessful. No meaningful conclusions regarding the types of patients for whom therapy was effective or ineffective are possible. This is inevitably the case since no patient variables crucially relevant for subsequent reactivity to psychotherapy have been isolated and controlled.

Meaningful evaluations of therapy require, then, that research patients be distinguished so that those who respond favorably can readily be identified. With this information in hand, it may be possible to learn which patients and problems are benefited most by which treatment techniques.

Once a comprehensive set of objective and reliable criteria has been selected and relevant distinctions drawn within the patient sample, the investigator has met two of the central requirements needed to determine whether or not certain treatment approaches are associated with beneficial changes, and which ingredients of the therapeutic procedure are instrumental in achieving them. These two sides of the same evaluative coin were referred to previously as "efficacy" and "mode of action." Let us turn to some of the issues and problems involved in each.

## EFFICACY (OUTCOME STUDIES)

Investigations that seek an answer to the question of whether or not therapy is effective have been termed "outcome studies." What must be achieved in the design of these studies is some assurance that observed changes in patients can be attributed to therapy rather than to nontherapeutic factors. Confounding factors can affect the results of these studies in two opposite ways; they may obscure what otherwise might have been valid positive findings or give a false impression of positive results when, in fact, there were none. Proper design requires that all extraneous and obscuring effects that might distort the results should be placed under careful control; with confounding variables removed or accounted for, the precise consequences of the therapeutic intervention itself can be properly gauged.

Biased results will be obtained if the patient sample possesses either a notably good or poor prognosis at the start of therapy, e.g., were the patients relatively healthy college students faced with pressing although minor and transitory problems of a social or vocational nature, or were they hard-core, back ward hospital patients with ingrained personality patterns of long duration? The first group is likely to resolve current problems with or without therapy in a relatively short period; the problems of the second group, however, are pervasive, longstanding, deeply entrenched and therefore highly resistant to solution, even with the "best" and most concerted of therapeutic programs.

Another set of factors confounding research data are incidental environmental events that take place concurrently with therapy, e.g., the death of a close relative, finding a boyfriend, flunking out of college, receiving a long sought for job promotion and so on. There is need to control or account for extratherapeutic events which are *not* a direct consequence of therapy, but which often influence the course of therapeutic progress.

How can these inevitable and invariably confounding variables be prevented from distorting the assessment of therapeutic efficacy?

This crucial aspect of research design is accomplished by employing a "control-group," that is, a group of *comparably ill* patients who do not receive therapy, but are likely to be subject to the same random collection of incidental experiences as those who are involved in therapy. The progress or lack of progress of the control group serves as a base line of improvement against which the therapeutic group can be compared.

Other potential difficulties which should be resolved in the planning of efficacy studies relate to the frequency and time intervals between evaluations. Long-term assessments should be scheduled to appraise the durability of therapeutically induced change. Short-term evaluations cannot be overlooked, however, since immediate albeit temporary relief has its values as well, e.g., preventing suicide. It is wise, then, to obtain repeated measurements of efficacy rather than a single "end point" evaluation, especially since end point evaluations often reflect entirely random fluctuations in pathology and lead the investigator to mistake a transient episode for a "final" state. Moreover, repeated measurements may be useful since different patients may respond to treatment at varying and uneven rates.

In summary, evaluations of therapeutic efficacy require "matched" control groups that serve as base lines for comparison. Furthermore, both therapeutic and control groups should be subjected to repeated evaluations; this will provide a picture of the course as well as the "outcome" of treatment and will eliminate the misleading effects of transitory or unreliable findings.

## MODE OF ACTION (PROCESS STUDIES)

If therapy is *un*related to outcome, that is, if it fails to be associated with beneficial change, then there is little reason to explore in detail the ingredients of the therapeutic regimen. On the other hand, if treatment is beneficial, there is good reason to distinguish those elements of the therapeutic "process" which contributed to the beneficial outcome from those which are entirely specious; certainly, not all the events that occur in the treatment setting can be assumed to be of therapeutic value. To achieve this goal, the total matrix of intratherapeutic variables must first be disentangled. Once this is accomplished, the investigator can set out to observe or manipulate each of these variables until he can determine which ones are crucial to therapeutic change.

Before we proceed, let us note that the distinction between process and outcome research is often misleading in that it creates the illusion that the process of therapy is independent of its outcome. Many investigators have become engrossed in "process" for its own sake, in methodological refinements and technology, and lose sight of the primary goal of evaluative research. The purpose of process studies, insofar as it refers to therapeutic evaluation, is not to record how frequently a patient makes remarks that indicate anxiety and hostility or to measure the relationship between these remarks and a host of physiological indices such as heart rate and respiration, but to isolate the ingredients of a therapeutic technique and correlate them with outcome criteria. Although events that take place in therapy provide an excellent research laboratory for investigating the interplay and correlates of human interaction, the primary goal of process studies is to delineate therapeutic variables that are crucial to favorable change in psychopathology.

The job of unraveling the complex and interwoven elements which comprise even the simplest of therapeutic procedures is enormously difficult. Determining what exactly is going on in therapy, and isolating, weighing and evaluating the components involved, e.g., separating the therapist's attitude and "personality" from the content of what he says, is a much more challenging task than that of verifying the "overall" outcome itself. However, if meaningful discriminations are to be made between alternative therapeutic approaches, and if maximally efficient techniques are ever to be devised, it is mandatory that this challenge be faced and surmounted. We know that many contemporary treatment methods, despite differences in theory and despite acrid controversies about their respective merits, are substantially alike with regard to certain basic ingredients, e.g., the therapist's sympathetic and seemingly "all-knowing" attitude; the process of implicit if not explicit reinforcement of "healthy" behaviors; and the therapist as a model of "reason" and emotional and cognitive control. On the other hand, alternative therapies do entail distinctive procedural features; these must be isolated and studied if we are to construct techniques in the future that are more efficacious than those of the present.

Numerous methodologies have been utilized to disentangle the flow of process variables. "Real" therapy as it unfolds in its natural setting is extremely complex, comprising several simultaneously operating variables that are often inextricably interwoven. The task of analyzing and separating these components calls for highly refined methods of observation and assessment.

In recent years, experimental procedures have been designed to decrease the complexity of "real" therapy and to isolate, in relatively uncomplicated form, what are believed to be its essential ingredients. In what is termed "analogue research," a simulated therapeutic interaction is arranged so that researchers can systematically explore specified variables of the natural treatment complex without the interference of extraneous factors. This is done most often in a laboratory mock-up with experimental subjects rather than with real patients, although the latter practice is becoming commoner. Questions have been raised concerning the generalizability to real therapy of findings obtained in these simulated analogue studies. Whatever its limitations, it does provide a useful technique for delineating with precision several of the crucial variables that operate in natural therapy. Moreover, it allows investigators to experiment with entirely new therapeutic procedures based on a growing body of research dealing with the processes of behavior change.

## A PROPOSED ECLECTIC ORIENTATION

Before we proceed to the details of the principal forms of therapy, it will be useful, as a précis, to propose that they be viewed from a multitherapeutic perspective.

The "science" of therapy is in its infancy, despite popular illusions and professional pretensions to the contrary. For the most part, the efficacy of the principal techniques employed today is yet to be proved. Much more research is needed. Newer techniques must continue to be explored and older ones subjected to systematic evaluation. Such research and the rewards it promises will occur only if practitioners are willing to reexamine their traditional methods and bring the same refreshing objectivity to them as they hope their patients will bring to the solution of their habitual behaviors. The disinclination of clinical practitioners to submit their cherished techniques to detailed study or to revise them in accord with critical empirical findings is most lamentable. Therapeutic advances, so vital to the welfare of hundreds of thousands of patients, cannot take place unless practicing therapists give up their inertia and resistance to outside scrutiny.

Despite the fact that the theories underlying most therapeutic approaches are burdened with irrelevant conceptualizations and that most research leaves much to be desired in the way of proper controls, sampling and evaluative criteria, there is one overriding fact about therapy that comes through clearly: therapeutic techniques must be suited to the patient's problem. Simple and obvious although this statement is, it is repeatedly neglected by therapists who persist in utilizing and argue heatedly in favor of *a* single approach to *all* forms of psychopathology. No "school" of therapy is exempt from this notorious attitude.

It should be elementary, given the history of medicine, that no single treatment method works for all problems. Would it not be ludicrous and shocking if a physician prescribed his favorite remedy for all patients, regardless of the disease or difficulty they suffered? Should it not be equally distressing if a psychotherapist did likewise? Obviously, the diversity of psychopathological problems calls for a variety of different therapies, singly or in combination, geared to deal with the specific problem at hand.

The primary reason most approaches to therapy appear to be equally "good or bad" is that they succeed with only a small proportion of the many varieties of psychopathology they set out to treat. The probability of success in a mixed or varied patient population will be increased, it seems to us, if several approaches, rather than one approach, are employed.

As we review the specific techniques described in the next two chapters, let us keep in mind that no single approach is sufficient to deal with all the types and multidimensional complexities that comprise the body of psychopathology. Each therapeutic approach carves out a small slice of this vast complex for its special province. Let us remember that conceptual systems, as pointed out in chapter 2, are "inventions" created by man to aid him in understanding nature, and are not realities themselves. Theories and the therapies they generate must fit reality, not the other way around.

Given the paucity of current knowledge, there can be no justification for employing one therapeutic technique to the exclusion of others; multiplicity and flexibility in approaches are mandatory. Until unequivocal data exist to enable us to exclude as ineffective certain therapeutic methods and to specify the optimal matching of treatment to problem, we must assume an eclectic approach, employing the best for each case and continuing to experiment with alternative methods.

The following two chapters will be divided in the same manner as was done in part 2 on "etiology and development." Chapter 14 will focus on *biological* treatment methods, that is, therapeutic approaches designed to alter the biophysical substrate of psychopathology. Chapter 15, *psychological* treatment methods, includes procedures designed primarily to alter behavioral, phenomenological and intrapsychic functions.

# Chapter 14

## BIOLOGICAL APPROACHES TO TREATMENT

Conrad Marca-Relli—*Seated Figure* (1954).

## INTRODUCTION

No relationship need exist between the belief in a biogenic cause of psychopathology and the use of biological methods of treatment. Nevertheless, most biologically oriented therapists favor the "disease model" discussed in chapter 2. They contend that psychopathology is an overt manifestation of underlying anatomical lesions or biochemical aberrations; from this premise it follows quite logically that methods that remedy the defect directly (e.g., repairing lesions, altering chemical thresholds or rearranging neural circuitries) would be the most successful treatment technique.

We need not be committed to the view that psychopathology is of biogenic origin in order to believe that biological therapies may be usefully employed; biological methods may prove efficacious in conditions in which the etiology is unequivocally psychogenic. For example, pharmacological "tranquilizers" may be fruitfully employed to ease "psychological" tension caused by the loss of a job or the death of a relative.

Let us be clear at the start, then, that the therapeutic approach to be described in this chapter does *not* assume a biogenic etiology to pathology. These techniques are distinguished from other methods only by the fact that their primary mode of action is at the biological substrate level.

Biologically oriented procedures are only one of several sets of tools that comprise the multitherapeutic armamentarium of an experienced and well-rounded therapist. They should not be employed to the exclusion of other therapeutic modalities and methods, as is too often the case. The practice of applying a single cherished treatment procedure, whether it be biological or psychological, to every form and variety of pathological condition is a sad commentary on the maturity of the profession, a sign of cognitive and behaviorial rigidity most unbefitting to those who seek to aid others in achieving adaptive flexibility.

### HISTORICAL REVIEW

Before we proceed to a discussion of the major biological treatment methods, it will be useful to refresh our memory of the historical development of "somatotherapies" first presented in chapter 1.

The most striking historical fact to be noted is the role played by serendipity (the art of accidental discovery). In the main, those who discovered the principal somatic methods in use today chanced upon them while exploring therapies for other diseases. Insulin coma therapy, employed initially to treat morphine addiction and to aid emaciated patients to gain weight, was observed, quite fortuitously, to benefit psychotics as well. Similarly, the major psychopharmacological drugs were designed originally to control blood pressure, muscular tension and allergic disorders; only incidentally were they recognized to have psychological consequences as well. For the most part, then, it has been a combination of chance and good fortune that made alert clinicians stumble on the beneficial effects of their methods. Only in the past decade or so has rational scientific planning and experimental investigation, based on a moderately sophisticated grasp of the intricate neurological and physiochemical processes of the body, been employed in the development of biological therapies.

The early history of biological techniques was based mostly on religious and mystical beliefs. Trephining, involving insertions through the skull, was designed to release evil spirits which ostensibly resided in the patient's brain. Egyptian "medications" used in 1500 B.C., such as lizard's blood, crocodile dung and fly specks were not disease cures but magic potions.

Natural plants, known for centuries and still used today, served as folk remedies and as forerunners of our present biotherapies. Alcohol, in the form of wine, was used "to confirm hopes . . . and to ease the anxious mind of its burdens" centuries before Christ. The Ebers papyrus makes mention of opium, and Homer spoke of it as the "sorrow-easing drug." Cocaine, chewed in the form of coca leaves, was taken by Peruvian indians more than two thousand years ago. The dried leaves of the hemp plant *Cannabis sativa,* better known as marijuana, was known in the Orient as a "healer of life's discontents" long before Marco Polo brought it to the European continent.

The rationale for treating diseases by counteracting the defect directly rather than by relieving its symptoms, was established during the Renaissance. Medical reasoning, however, was extremely naive at that time, e.g., the fat of a bear, a hairy animal, was prescribed as a cure for baldness. Paracelsus, in the sixteenth century, classified diseases in accord with the treatments that ostensibly cured them, a rather sophisticated notion and one that still has its merits. Unfortunately, the remedies employed during the Renaissance included such worthless concoctions as Egyptian mummy, unicorn's horn and bezoar stones. Not all physicians were so blind as to accept the value of these crude measures. Never-

theless, despite frequent warnings to the effect that many of these "medications" were harmful, patients continued to be subjected to strange herbs and potions and to blistering, cupping, bleeding, ducking and twirling well into the nineteenth century.

Although preceded by bromide "nerve tonics" in the mid-nineteenth century and by barbiturates (notably phenobarbital) for convulsions in the early decades of this century, the first "scientific" form of biological therapy was Wagner-Jauregg's use of a malarial infection in 1917 to curtail the destructive advance of neurosyphilis. Another early form of biotherapy was devised in 1921 by Jacob Klaesi who used barbiturates to induce prolonged sleep as a form of rest for "irritated" nerve cells.

The modern era of somatotherapy began in the 1930's with the almost simultaneous development of insulin coma therapy, convulsion treatment and cerebral surgery. In none of these techniques did their discoverers understand the biophysical processes that accounted for the efficacy of their methods; they either stumbled on them by accident or formulated them on the basis of erroneous conceptions concerning their mode of action.

Sakel's insulin procedure, first described in 1933, rested on the now disproved thesis that psychoses resulted from excessive adrenaline; ostensibly, this overabundance of adrenaline was neutralized by the administration of insulin.

Meduna's contention that epilepsy and schizophrenia were mutually exclusive diseases has been shown to be in error; yet it led him to induce convulsions in schizophrenics by metrazol with the thought that this would reestablish "normal" chemical balances. In 1937, Cerletti induced convulsions by electrical means, a technique popularly known as "electric shock" treatment, but more appropriately termed today as electroconvulsive therapy (ECT). Meduna and Cerletti believed that their techniques were maximally beneficial in cases diagnosed as schizophrenia; empirically, however, their value seems limited to depressive disorders.

Surgical incursions into the brain were first attempted in 1890 by Burkhardt who sought to dismember those parts of the cortex which ostensibly harbored the hallucinations and delusions of paranoid patients. This operative approach was discontinued due to medical and public objections, and was not attempted again until Moniz performed the first of his "prefrontal lobotomies" in 1935. Surgical procedures, together with insulin coma and electroconvulsive therapies, continued to be the principal forms of biotherapy until the mid-1950's.

The aimless advance of somatotherapies progressed in its course of serendipidity with the discovery of two psychopharmacological agents: chlorpromazine and reserpine. In 1952, Delay and Deniker reported the general "tranquilizing" effects of chlorpromazine, a drug synthesized for use with surgical and hypertensive patients. During the same year, reserpine, an extract of the Rauwolfia Snakeroot plant, which had been used for general medical purposes since the 1920's by Indian physicians, was noted to be effective in calming hyperactive and assaultive patients. Because of the ease of administration, the economy and the highly impressive early reports of their efficacy, these two pharmacological substances ushered in a new wave of optimism in psychiatric medicine. Although this early period of enthusiasm has since subsided, these as well as other drugs have taken a solid place in the physician's kit. A secondary consequence of this boom in psychopharmacological interest has been the growth of sophisticated studies of brain biochemistry and a correlated development of new compounds designed to alter neurophysiological functioning. In recent years, scientific rationales and experimental research rather than aimless chance discoveries have begun to play an increasing role in the design of pharmacological agents.

# PSYCHOPHARMACOLOGICAL AGENTS (CHEMOTHERAPY)

In preceding paragraphs we briefly outlined the recent emergence of drug methods as the most promising of the biotherapies. In this section we will note some of the theoretical rationales that have been proposed regarding their mode of action, list and briefly describe some of the principal agents employed in contemporary psychiatric practice, provide an evaluation of their efficacy and suggest their probable line of future development. But first, it will be instructive to make a few comments about current attitudes and practices in this expanding field.

An early period of irrational optimism, characterized by the belief that psychiatric "wonder drugs" would cure all mental illnesses and deplete the rolls of every state hospital, has passed. Nevertheless, the field continues to be subjected to a flood of new products, each of which is preceded by massive and tantalizing advertisements that promise "a new life" for the psychiatric patient. Despite this bewildering array of highly touted medications, we note that psychiatrist's offices, guidance clinics and mental hospitals are no less busy than before. Formerly agitated and assaultive patients are easier to handle, but there has been no sweeping change in the frequency or variety of psychopathological conditions. In short, these "wonder drugs" have assumed their place as one of many tools in the therapist's treatment kit.

## THEORETICAL RATIONALES

When a psychopharmacological agent has been shown to exert an effect upon an organism, questions arise as to the precise nature of its psychological consequences, e.g., whether it influences, singly or in combination, motor behavior, sensory processes, perception, discrimination, learning, memory, conceptual thinking and so on; the specific biophysical mechanisms altered by the drug, e.g.; whether it activates or inhibits certain neurohormonal transmitter substances or has different kinds of effects on cortical regions, reticular pathways, limbic divisions and so on; and the relationship between these psychological and biophysical changes and the "final" clinical effect.

Answers to the first question are largely obtained through animal laboratory studies, although certain functions, e.g., higher cognitive processes, can be appraised only in human clinical trials. Answers to the second question involve the use of exceedingly complex technical procedures which specify the anatomical site of action and trace the precise character and sequence of the induced chemical changes; the task of unraveling the neurophysiological concomitants of drugs must disentangle effects throughout the awesomely intricate histological structure of the brain and the complicated network of interactions which operates among its diverse components. Attempts to answer the third question are even more difficult since the observed "final" clinical outcome reflects not only the action of interacting chemical and neurological pathways, but the individual's learning and adaptive history and the conditions prevailing in his current environment.

Because of the varied questions that can be posed regarding the nature of pharmacological action, and because of the complexity of the factors involved, theorists have had a relatively open field to speculate on "why" and "how" these drugs produce their effects. These formulations may be grouped into three categories: *neurohormonal defect theories,* which hypothesize that drugs overcome endogenous chemical dysfunctions in synaptic transmission; *neurophysiological imbalance theories,* which assume that these agents reestablish equilibrium among ill-matched functional systems; and *psychological reaction theories,* which posit that these substances result in energy and temperament changes that alter the patient's coping competencies and lead him to modify his self-image.

### Neurohormonal Defect Theories

Speculations of drug action formulated in accord with this viewpoint assume that pharmacological agents counteract endogenous defects in synaptic transmission. Implicit, if not explicit, in this thesis is a belief that the major forms of psychopathology stem from disturbances in one or another of the neurohormonal transmitter substances. Among the more prominent speculations of this type are those referred to as the serotonin, adrenolutin and taraxein hypotheses discussed in chapter 4. According to these theories, drugs reestablish normal synaptic transmission by facilitating the release of formerly bound transmitter substances, by blocking competing but faulty metabolites or by inhibiting enzymes that have depleted crucial neurotransmitters.

It is likely that endogenous disturbances of neurohormones would result in intensely maladaptive behaviors and place the person at a marked disadvantage in regulating events, even in benign social environments. Any drug that would compensate for these chemical aberrations would be expected to improve the patient's coping competencies and enhance his prospects for normal functioning. However, the thesis that psychopathology has its roots in neurohormonal defects is far from proved, and the imaginative speculations concerning serotonin, adrenolutin and taraxein have been seriously questioned or sharply revised in light of new empirical evidence. In short, there are no data to support the notion that specific endogenous chemical defects play a determinant role in the major psychopathologies. Thus, the thesis that pharmacological substances achieve their beneficial effects by repairing existent biochemical disturbances is of dubious validity, given our present state of knowledge.

### Neurophysiological Imbalance Theories

One of the major complications of neurohormonal defect theories is the fact that synaptic transmitter substances may be unevenly distributed in the brain and produce opposite effects in several of the principal regions of the nervous system. The architectural complexity of the limbic, midbrain, cortical and reticular systems and the vast number of pathways which chemicals traverse make it evident that drug effects are varied and complicated. Moreover, the fact that pharmacological agents can release endogenous chemical substances in one neurological system and suppress those of other systems argues for a thesis formulated in terms of neurophysiological *relationships* rather than singular or localized effects. Accordingly, some theorists have proposed that these drugs reestablish disturbed homeostatic balances among neurophysiological systems. Equilibrium, according to these speculations, is achieved by the drugs' *selective* facilitation and inhibition of neural regions that have been either out of phase with one another or weighted unequally in their regulative powers.

These formulations contend that the principal forms of psychopathology stem from endogenous imbalances among functional neural groups. For example, the normal interplay between sympathetic and parasympathetic components of the autonomic nervous system may have been impaired; Rubin's thesis (1962) of adrenergic-cholinergic imbalances, discussed in chapter 4, represents a formulation of this type. Along similar lines, Lehmann (1959) proposes that pharmacological agents restore balances among *visceropsychic systems* (structures subserving consciousness of affect), *sensoripsychic systems* (consciousness of objects and reality) and *corticopsychic systems* (consciousness of concepts and symbols). According to Lehmann's conjecture, psychopharmacological agents can best be described in terms of their ability to counteract different patterns of disequilibria among these three psychophysiological systems through selective excitatory and inhibitory effects.

The intricate relationships among intracerebral regions are gradually being unraveled through refined technical procedures, but the precise role and sequence through which pharmacological substances traverse these topologically complex systems is still far from thoroughly understood. As such, neurophysiological imbalance models, consistent though they are with the fact that chemical substances have varying effects throughout the nervous system, must be viewed as only a plausible schema, and not a verified theory.

### Psychological Reaction Theories

Although the direct action of pharmacological drugs is chemical and their effects formulable in terms of altered neurophysiological relationships, there are those who believe that the crucial variable is not chemical or neurophysiological, but psychological. To them, the factors that determine the patient's response are not molecular events or processes, but the patient's prior psychological state and the environment within which he currently functions. According to this view, biophysical changes induced by drugs take on a "meaning" to the patient, and it is this meaning which determines his "final" clinical response.

Theorists of this persuasion pay less attention to specifying the mechanisms and pathways of biophysical change than to the impact of these changes on the patient's self-image, coping competencies, social relationships and the like. To support their thesis, they note that barbiturates, which typically produce sedative reactions, often produce excitement and hyperactivity. Similarly, many persons exhibit a cheerful state of intoxication when given sodium amytal in a congenial social setting, but succumb to a hypnotic state when the drug is administered to them in a therapeutic environment. Of even greater significance than social factors according to this view, is the patient's *awareness* of the energy and temperamental changes that have taken place within him as a consequence of drug action. Freyhan (1959), discussing the effect of "tranquilizers" in reducing mobility and drive, states that patients with compulsive traits, who need intensified activity to control their anxiety, may react unfavorably to their loss of initiative, resulting thereby in an upsurge rather than a decrement in anxiety. Other patients, who are comforted by feelings of reduced activity and energy, may view the drug's tranquilizing effect as a welcome relief. Thus, even if a drug produced a uniform biophysical effect on all patients, its psychological impact would differ from patient to patient, depending on the meaning these changes have in the larger context of the patient's needs, attitudes and coping strategies. As Sarwer-Foner remarks (1959):

If the pharmacologic effect threatens the patient by interfering with vital defenses, new waves of energy are produced, alerting and disturbing him. Here these arise *precisely because of the medication* he is receiving. . . . When the changes produced affect the patient,

physician, hospital, and their interrelations in a way that makes the patient feel *less* inferior, worthless, and dangerous, a new opportunity for a more adult level of functioning is produced. When this situation continues for a sufficiently long time, further ego reintegration can take place. The symptomatic action of the drugs leads therefore to a variable therapeutic effect.

In short, the "psychological reaction" model contends that the effectiveness of pharmacological agents is determined primarily by the patient's premedication self-image and coping strategy. If the drug facilitates the control of disturbing impulses or if it activates a new sense of competence and adequacy, then it may be spoken of as beneficial. Conversely, if the effect is to weaken the patient's defenses and upset his self-image, it may prove detrimental. The key to the effectiveness of a drug, then, is not its chemical impact, but the psychological significance of these changes.

The three theories of psychopharmacological action we have just presented focus on different facets of a broad constellation of factors that contribute to drug efficacy. Although resting on different etiological premises, they are not nearly as divergent as they appear to be in the writings of their exponents. As we see it, they merely stress different levels and variables of the same process, each of which is an important dimension of psychopharmacological study: neurohormonal changes, alterations in neurophysiological balance and their psychological significance.

## DRUG CLASSIFICATION

The proliferation of new pharmacological agents, each exhibiting minor changes from prior variants in their chemical composition, and producing difficult to detect differences in their physiochemical action and clinical effects, has made the grouping of drugs into an orderly and logical classification a nightmare. Criteria which once served to distinguish categories of agents no longer suffice, and new arrangements and boundary lines are constantly drawn. Even if there were no new drugs to contend with, classification would still be a difficult task since criteria for categorizing agents fail to line up in a simple logical system.

The three major criteria that have been employed in classifying psychopharmacological drugs are the following: *chemical composition; neurological site* and *mode of physiochemical action;* and *effects upon clinical behavior* and *mood.* This tripartite division parallels to some extent the three-fold breakdown in theories discussed previously.

## Table 14-1   Major Psychopharmacological Agents

### TRANQUILIZERS

**Phenothiazine Derivatives**

*Dimethylamine Series*

Chlorpromazine (Thorazine)*
Methoxypromazine (Tentone)
Promazine (Sparine)
Promethazine (Phenergan)
Propiomazine (Largon)
Triflupromazine (Vesprin)
Trimeprazine (Temaril)

*Piperazine Series*

Acetophenazine (Tindal)
Carphenazine (Proketazine)
Fluphenazine (Permitil)
Perphenazine (Trilafon)
Prochlorperazine (Compazine)
Thiopropazate (Dartal)
Thiothixene (Narvane)
Trifluoperazine (Stelazine)

*Piperidine Series*

Mepazine (Pacatal)
Thioridazine (Mellaril)

**Rauwolfia Alkaloids**

Alseroxylon (many trade names)
Deserpidine (Harmonyl)
Rescinnamine (Moderil)
Reserpine (many trade names)

**Substituted Diols**

Emylcamate (Stratran)
Mephenesin (Tolserol)
Meprobamate (Miltown, Equanil)
Phenaglycodol (Ultran)

**Miscellaneous Compounds**

Azacyclonol (Frenquel)
Benactyzine (Suavitil)
Buclizine (Softran)
Captodiamine (Suvren)
Chlordiazepoxide (Librium)
Chlormezanone (Trancopal)
Diazepam (Valium)
Ectylurea (Nostyn, Levanil)
Ethchlorvynol (Placidyl)
Haloperidol (Haldol)
Hydroxyzine (Atarax, Vistaril)
Mephenoxalone (Trepidone)
Oxanamide (Quiactin)
Oxazepam (Serax)
Promoxolane (Dimethylane)
Tybamate (Solacen)

### ANTIDEPRESSANTS

**MAO Inhibitors—Hydrazines**

Iproniazid (Marsilid)
Isocarboxid (Marplan)
Nialamide (Niamid)
Phenelzine (Nardil)
Pheniprazine (Catron)

**MAO Inhibitors—Nonhydrazines**

Etryptamine (Monase)
Pargyline (Eutonyl)
Tranylcypromine (Parnate)

**Iminodibenzyl Derivatives**

Amitryptyline (Elavil)
Desipramine (Norpramin)
Imipramine (Tofranil)
Nortryptaline (Aventyl)
Opripramol (Ensidon)

**Miscellaneous Compounds**

Deanol (Deaner)
Methylphenidate (Ritalin)
Pipradol (Meratran)

* Names listed in parentheses are trade names.

**Chemical Composition.** A detailed discussion of the similarities and differences in the chemical structure of pharmacological agents would not be appropriate in a text such as this. All we need to know is that these drugs are derived from an impressively wide range of chemical groups, e.g., amine, ergot and piperidyl derivatives, phenothiazine variants and numerous amine oxidase inhibitors. Despite the ease with which groupings can be based on the chemical lineage of agents, minor modifications in structure can produce strikingly different clinical consequences, e.g., the substitution of a single sulphur atom in certain phenothiazines, which normally produce a tran-quilized response, will transform the drug into a stimulant. In short, similarities in chemical composition may be misleading since they suggest commonalities in clinical effects that may not exist.

**Neurological Sites and Physiochemical Action.** Despite recent progress, the task of grouping drugs in accord with commonalities in anatomical locus and physiological effect is a most forbidding one indeed. Only a few rough parallels can be drawn at this stage of our knowledge. Future research along these lines may advance this approach to classification, but questions will still remain as to whether such schemas will have any relationship to the clinical efficacy of pharmacological substances.

**Clinical Behavior and Mood.** The most common basis for distinguishing and grouping pharmacological agents is in terms of the symptoms they modify. Efforts to classify drugs in terms of "target" symptoms or broad clinical syndromes, however, tend to be misleading. Rarely is just one target symptom affected; rather, these drugs have a pervasive impact, influencing several clinical features simultaneously. In a different way, classifying drugs in terms of which clinical syndromes they influence implies incorrectly that the drug deals with all facets of that diagnostic group. Moreover, it implies that the drug does not produce meaningful effects with patients in other diagnostic categories; for various reasons, notably the heterogeneity and unreliability of diagnostic categories, such drug classifications are bound to be ill conceived and invalid.

More in line with clinical evidence is the view that some drugs tend to decrease activity and subdue mood whereas others appear to increase activity and brighten mood. The former group has been referred to as "tranquilizers" and "sedatives," and the latter as "antidepressants"

and "stimulants." But even this gross differentiation fails to account for individual variations in reaction that are due to personality factors such as coping styles and a host of relevant socioenvironmental conditions.

Despite difficulties in establishing uniform criteria for classification, some schema must be employed for pedagogical purposes. We refer the reader to Tables 14-1 and 14-2 where these agents are grouped in terms of each of the criteria discussed above. These tables provide a multidimensional perspective which will allow the reader to review each of the major drugs from several vantage points. In Table 14-1, agents are organized in accord with the first and third criteria presented, those of chemical composition (e.g., phenothiazine derivatives, dimethylamine series and so on) and clinical effects (e.g., tranquilizers versus antidepressants). Table 14-2 attempts to specify the various neurological sites affected by several of these drugs, and notes whether they excite or inhibit associated physiological functions.

Let us next turn to the two principal drug types, tranquilizers and antidepressants, and review their distinguishing features and clinical in-

## Table 14-2 Physiochemical Effects of Various Psychopharmaceutical Drugs*

| BRAIN AREA | FUNCTIONS | PHYSIO-CHEMICAL EFFECT | ILLUSTRATIVE DRUGS |
|---|---|---|---|
| Neocortex | Thinking and reasoning | Excitatory<br>Inhibitory | Amphetamines and methylphenidate<br>Barbiturates |
| Thalamus | Integration of sensation, transmission and modulation of alerting impulses | Excitatory<br>Inhibitory | Barbiturates and phenothiazines<br>Meprobamate |
| Reticular Formation | Arousal, integration of emotional responses to stimuli | Excitatory<br>Inhibitory | Rauwolfia alkaloids (Small doses)<br>Phenothiazines, barbiturates and iminodibenzyl derivatives |
| Limbic System | Regulation of emotions | Excitatory<br>Inhibitory | Phenothiazines and rauwolfia alkaloids<br>Meprobamate, calordiazepoxide, diazepam, oxazepam, tybamate and hydroxyzine |
| Hypothalamus | Control of autonomic and endocrine functions | Excitatory<br>Inhibitory | MAO inhibitors and amphetamines<br>Phenothiazines and rauwolfia alkaloids |
| Synapses | Nerve impulse transmission | Excitatory<br>Inhibitory | Rauwolfia alkaloids<br>Amphetamines, iminodibenzyl derivatives, LSD and mescaline |
| Interneuronal Circuits | Coordination of neuronal masses | Inhibitory | Meprobamate |
| Neurohormonal Depots (Serotonin and Norepinephrine) | Regulation of brain metabolism | Excitatory<br>Inhibitory | MAO inhibitors and iminodibenzyl derivatives<br>Phenothiazines and rauwolfia alkaloids |

* Modified from Wolberg (1967)

dications. We will mention only a few examples of each for illustrative purposes.

## TRANQUILIZERS

As was noted earlier, the discovery of the clinical utility of *chlorpromazine* and *reserpine,* reported in 1952, ushered in a new wave of optimism in psychiatric medicine. Many investigators, spurred by the impressive results of these two agents, began to manipulate their basic molecular structure in the hope of discovering variants that would be even more efficacious than the parent models. Modifications of these, as well as other, chemical substances have resulted in over 100 new psychopharmacological products in the past 15 years. Despite differences in structure, most of these agents affect essentially the same clinical behaviors as do chlorpromazine and reserpine, that is, they are "tranquilizers."

Tranquilizers may be distinguished from a variety of compounds termed sedatives that have been used for over a century to moderate tension and agitation. Tranquilizers, in contrast to sedatives, relieve anxiety and reduce hyperactivity without markedly dulling cognitive alertness and clarity; thus, they appear more selective in their dampening effects than sedatives, focusing on emotional and motor functions and operating minimally on cognitive functions. Let us briefly discuss the major subtypes of the tranquilizer group.

### Phenothiazine Derivatives

Chlorpromazine, chemically part of the dimethylamine series, was the first and is still thought to be the most effective phenothiazine for handling markedly disturbed patients characterized by emotional tension, cognitive confusion and motor hyperactivity. Numerous structural modifications of the basic chlorpromazine molecule have been made, producing drugs that differ from the parent model in both potency and side effects. In general, the greater the potency, the more severe and dangerous are the toxic consequences. For example, the addition of a piperazine ring to the basic molecule, as in prochlorperazine, results in a compound that is five to ten times more potent than chlorpromazine, but increases the incidence of severe secondary complications. At the other end of the scale, in the piperidine series, significant alterations are made in the basic side chain and nucleus of chlorpromazine, decreasing both the potency of the compound and its associated side effects.

In the main, the various phenothiazine derivatives are alike in their clinical utility. Their primary indication is with the more severe reactions, disorders and patterns in which a reduction in activity level and a dampening of heightened moods, such as anxiety and hostility, is desired.

### Rauwolfia Alkaloids

The rauwolfia tranquilizers are extracted from the *rauwolfia serpentina* plant, named after the sixteenth century German botanist, Leonhard Rauwolf. Although used for centuries as a medicinal, it was not until 1951, when a crystalline alkaloid termed *reserpine* was extracted from the plant, that its utility in psychopathology received recognition. Early reports on the drug were extremely enthusiastic, especially in psychotic syndromes characterized by anxiety and agitation. However, with increased clinical experience, it became evident that the drug often produced dangerous psychological as well as physiological side effects; severe depressive disorders were precipitated all too frequently. As a consequence, the drug's use has diminished, giving way to the less troublesome phenothiazines. Efforts to modify the structural composition of the basic reserpine molecule, e.g., *deserpidine* and *rescinnamine,* have not proved successful in eliminating the depression complication. Recently, rauwolfia alkaloids have reverted to their original use in treating hypertensive diseases, especially in cases where anxiety is a component.

### Minor Tranquilizers

For the most part, agents listed in table 14-1 under the headings "substituted diols" and "compounds of miscellaneous structure" are both less potent and produce fewer troublesome side effects than the phenothiazine derivatives. These drugs are of lesser utility than phenothiazines in treating markedly disturbed patients, but they do fulfill a function with moderately anxious and agitated patients. They influence the same spectrum of symptoms as do the phenothiazines, but to a lesser degree.

*Chlordiazepoxide* and *meprobamate* are perhaps the most frequently prescribed of these minor agents. In addition to its use in subduing moderate degrees of agitation, chlordiazepoxide appears to achieve a lifting of mood in dejection disorders and in cases of mild agitated depression; similar effects have been reported with *diazepam, oxazepam* and *tybamate.* Meprobamate is not indicated in depressive moods and may exacerbate these symptoms; it is notably effective, however, in milder anxieties, especially when relaxation of muscular tension and the facilitation of restful sleep are among the clinical goals.

## ANTIDEPRESSANTS

An early report indicating that the antitubercular drug, isoniazid, produced a beneficial stimulant effect in a psychiatric patient was drowned in the vast sea of medical literature (Flaherty, 1952). It was not until the late 1950's that the role of a similar drug, *iproniazid,* was recognized as an agent that could produce "euphoric" behaviors. Evidence was gathered shortly thereafter that these drugs inhibit monoamine oxidase, an enzyme centrally involved in the metabolism of neurohormonal transmitter substances. This discovery in part gave impetus to the neurohormonal defect theories discussed previously.

Also in the late 1950's several Swiss chemists synthesizing new variants of phenothiazine noted that one of their compounds, *imipramine,* produced an effect opposite to what they anticipated; it did not decrease tension or control hyperactivity as was expected, but did brighten the mood of depressed patients. New "antidepressant" compounds were quickly formulated on the basis of modifications of the iproniazid and imipramine molecules.

Antidepressants should be distinguished from compounds known as stimulants that have been employed for over a century to increase motor activity and mental alertness. In contrast to stimulants, the effects of antidepressants begin slowly and last appreciably beyond the termination of treatment. Also, and more important, antidepressants not only activate cognitive alertness and motor behavior, but favorably influence the mood of the patient; stimulants, in contrast, often aggravate negative moods. Let us briefly outline the major categories of antidepressant drugs.

### MAO Inhibitors

Iproniazid, the first widely used monoamine oxidase inhibitor, produced dangerous side effects, notably liver toxicity; this led to its early removal from the prescription market. In the interim, several chemically similar substances were synthesized, of which several were hydrazine compounds such as iproniazid (e.g., isocarboxazid and phenelzine) and others nonhydrazines (e.g., etryptamine and pargyrine).

The therapeutic effect of these agents upon retarded depressive symptomatology is well estab-

lished. In general, *tranylcypromine* seems superior to other agents of this type; its clinical efficacy, however, is somewhat dampened by discomfiting physical side effects. It should be noted also that MAO inhibitors frequently convert a retarded depression into an agitated one, and on occasion, patients may be precipitated into fragmented or excitement disorders.

### Iminodibenzyl Derivatives

These agents often produce striking behavioral and mood changes in retarded depressions, usually within a week after the onset of treatment; those who fail to show improvement following a two to three week course of therapy tend not to respond at all. *Imipramine* and *amitriptyline,* the two major iminodibenzyl derivatives, appear somewhat superior to other compounds of the antidepressant group. Retarded depressions do not respond as frequently with secondary agitation and excitement disorders as they do with the MAO inhibitors. There is little evidence, however, that any of the antidepressants is effective in agitated depressions or in the dejection disorders.

## MISCELLANEOUS AGENTS

This section includes several drugs grouped according to the symptoms they influence. Some, the *sedatives* and *stimulants,* are less effective and selective than tranquilizers and antidepressants, although they act on the same symptomatological features. Others, the *anticonvulsants,* have a very narrow band of clinical utility. A few, *convulsion-inducing* and *coma-inducing* agents, are included for their historical interest. The last group, *psychotomimetics* and *hallucinogens,* are discussed because of their potential value as experimental tools.

### Sedatives

These compounds, previously employed to calm anxiety and agitation, have been replaced in the past 15 years by tranquilizers. Two of the oldest "hypnotics" in medicine, *chloral hydrate* and *paraldehyde,* are rarely used today. Sodium and potassium *bromides,* popular years ago, have been made obsolete both by tranquilizers and other sedatives with less troublesome side effects.

*Barbiturates* are the most frequently prescribed and useful of the sedatives. However, they dampen sensory, cognitive and motor functions, and therefore are not as selective in their effects as are the minor tranquilizers; moreover, problems of addiction may ensue as a result of prolonged use. For the most part, the shorter-acting barbiturates (thiopental and secobartital) are employed to induce sleep whereas the long-acting barbiturates (phenobarbital and barbital) are used primarily as calmatives and anticonvulsants. Some of the short-acting barbiturates (sodium amytal and sodium pentothal) are administered intravenously for purposes of "narco-therapy"; in this procedure, a hypnotic state is induced by the drug, allowing the therapist to explore otherwise unconscious memories and emotions.

### Stimulants

The major group of stimulants is the *sympathomimetic amines* (amphetamine, dextroamphetamine and methamphetamine). These act directly on the nervous system; their effects are rapid and brief and wear off in a matter of a few hours. Although since the 1930's they were believed to counter depressive disorders, recent studies show that they are no more effective, and often worse, than placebos. During their brief period of chemical action, they tend to accelerate motor behavior and increase energy; this momentary surge is short lived and deceptive, and patients often slump into a more acute depressive mood when the drug is withdrawn. Despite its many limitations, not the least of which is the problem of addiction, these drugs are of occasional clinical utility as "energizers."

A number of slower-acting stimulants (deanol, methylphenidate and pipradrol) have shown some benefit among mildly depressed or dejected patients; they appear to be of minimal value in more severe depressions. In contrast to the sympathomimetic amines, these stimulants have a more enduring effect in brightening the patient's outlook, are not followed by a sharp letdown of mood following withdrawal and do not appear to be addictive.

### Anticonvulsants

Numerous drugs have been used to control epilepsy. Bromides, noted previously among the sedatives, were introduced in 1857 to moderate the symptoms of this syndrome. Unfortunately, this agent has a wide inhibitory effect on the nervous system, producing a clouding of consciousness and a pervasive dampening of behavior and mood. It was not until 1912 that a more effective anticonvulsant was synthesized, phenobarbital, one of the barbiturates mentioned earlier; phenobarbital is still employed in selected cases of grand mal seizures. With the synthesis of *sodium diphenyl hydantoinate* (Dilantin) in 1937,

a major advance took place in treatment of grand mal; along with several newer compounds (methyl hydantoin and primidione) it remains the most potent agent for this defect.

Drugs to control the petit mal form of epilepsy have also been formulated. The first of these, *trimethadione,* was developed in 1938; however, it was not known to be an effective agent in these disturbances until 1945. Since then, several new drugs (paramethadione and phensuximide) have been synthesized and have proved to be of notable value in petit mal disturbances.

### Convulsion-Inducing Agents

It may seem strange to follow a discussion of anticonvulsants by presenting drugs whose purpose is to produce convulsions. The impression that these two sets of drugs may be working at cross purposes is deceptive since they are not employed in the same patients; an analogy may be made with stimulants and sedatives which can counteract one another, but are rarely used concurrently. Although the short-term impact of a convulsion-inducing drug may appear to be detrimental to patients, the ultimate goal is to produce beneficial effects.

Camphor was used by Paracelsus in the sixteenth century to produce "magnetic" changes in the brain; others, guided by equally primitive conceptions, employed this drug for a variety of physical ailments. It was not until 1935, however, that Meduna induced convulsions in mental patients with camphor injected intramuscularly. Since camphor proved to be slow and unreliable, creating unpredictable and uncontrollable consequences as well, he turned to a synthetic camphor preparation, pentylenetetrazol, more commonly known as *metrazol;* this drug was both quick-acting and more reliable than camphor. However, it was also proved to cause complications. Convulsions were severe, even violent, and patients often suffered bone fractures and dislocations; also, because patients remained partly conscious during the first phases of early clonic movement, they developed great fears of treatment, reporting a frightening sense of impending doom as they awaited the loss of consciousness. Because ECT avoids these complications, it has replaced the metrazol convulsion technique.

Undaunted by the efficacy and simplicity of ECT, some chemists continued their search for a new pharmacological convulsant and chanced upon hexafluorodiethyl ether, known under the trade name of *Indoklon.* This agent is applied as an inhalant by means of a mask and a vaporizer. Its primary advantage over other chemical convulsants is that the patient loses consciousness rapidly, well before the onset of tremors and clonic movements. In this respect, it parallels the almost immediate action of ECT. There have been few controlled studies of Indoklon, and its efficacy as compared with ECT has not been established.

### Coma-Inducing Agents

The therapeutic value of sleep for medical ailments has been known for centuries. It was commonly used also for emotional disturbances by both the early Egyptians and Greeks. The imaginative eighteenth century therapist, Herman Boerhaave, in addition to numerous other treatment suggestions, was among the first to propose "deep" sleep as a means of treating depressions.

Chemical induction of deep sleep, employing the then newly discovered bromides, was first reported in the late nineteenth century. This technique was adapted by Klaesi in 1921, using a cocktail of various sedatives. He extended the period of sleep to eight to ten days, interrupted only for food intake and elimination. The method, termed *prolonged narcosis,* was considered effective with schizophrenic patients. It was Klaesi's belief that the sleep period allowed fatigued or overly irritated neural cells to regain their balance, thereby strengthening the patient's capacity to deal with his psychological difficulties.

Klaesi's sedative sleep treatment did not bring the patient to a comatose state. It was not until Sakel stumbled upon the possibilities of inducing reversible hypoglycemia (lowered blood sugar) through large doses of insulin that a true physiological coma was employed as a therapeutic method. The sequence of Sakel's discoveries proceeded as follows. He observed that insulin was effective in reducing the hyperactive withdrawal symptoms of newly abstinent morphine addicts; this led him to the notion in the late 1920's that similar benefits might be achieved with excited schizophrenics. In attempting to establish an optimal dosage for these patients, many quite by accident fell into a comatose state. Sakel noted to his surprise that when several of his patients emerged from their coma, not only had their excitement diminished, but other pathological symptoms abated as well. Recalling the work of Klaesi on prolonged narcosis, Sakel reasoned that *insulin coma therapy* (ICT) achieved similar but more beneficial results since it *directly* altered chemical dysfunctions which he then speculated to be the basis of the schizophrenic syndrome. As noted in earlier chapters, Sakel's early conjectures as to the mode of action of ICT were either biochemically illogical or disproven by experimental findings. Subsequent hypotheses, in-

volving both physiochemical and psychological explanations, have been shown to be either empirically invalid or impossible to confirm. Nevertheless, Sakel's technique received wide acclaim and was heralded in its first years of use as the most effective treatment method for all forms of severe psychopathology.

Sakel's original procedure was modified only slightly in ensuing years. The technique is time consuming, often complicated and requires the presence of well-trained medical personnel. After the initial injection of insulin, the patient succumbs to coma in about three hours; the patient is awakened after two hours in the comatose state by tubefeeding him with a sugar solution. The typical treatment course calls for 30 to 50 such sessions.

Despite the flush of early optimism and the continued confidence of several deeply committed adherents (Rinkel and Himwich, 1959), evidence gathered in several large scale studies indicates that ICT is only slightly superior to routine hospital care (Brannon and Graham, 1955; West et al., 1955). Staudt and Zubin (1957) report that the improvement rate immediately following treatment is about 60 per cent. This early level does not hold, however, and trails off within two to three years to about the same proportion (30 to 40 per cent) as found in comparable control patients who received no therapy at all; moreover, the relapse rate in insulin-treated groups is higher than that of controls. Definitive conclusions concerning the efficacy of ICT are difficult to draw since most of the optimistic studies failed to employ proper design procedures and based their data on dubious evaluative standards. In recent years, owing to questions concerning its efficacy, its time-consuming and complicated procedures and the growing employment of more economical and effective pharmacological agents, the use of ICT has sharply declined.

Brief mention might be made of *carbon dioxide* as a coma-inducing agent. Although employed with psychotics since the late 1920's, it was abandoned with the advent of ICT and ECT. Not until Meduna (1950) suggested its use in cases of anxiety disorder did it again achieve a small measure of popularity. The technique requires the inhalation of a mixture of 30 per cent carbon dioxide and 70 per cent oxygen, resulting in a loss of consciousness following about 25 respirations. The rationale for this treatment rests on the assumption that anxiety disorders are due to an unusually low threshold for sensory stimulation; ostensibly, the treatment raises the threshold by building a physiological "resistance" to carbon dioxide, which then generalizes to other noxious stimuli, both physical and psychological. No evidence has been adduced in support of this speculative thesis. More importantly, there is no evidence that patients subjected to carbon dioxide improve to a greater degree than the base line control rate (Hargrove, Bennett and Steele, 1953).

### Psychotomimetics and Hallucinogens

Although commonly viewed as "mind-expanding" drugs by the public, clinicians consider hallucinogens such as LSD, mescaline and psilocybin to be experimental tools that simulate psychotic behaviors; thus, professionals have dubbed these drugs "psychotomimetics."

Numerous investigators have created experimental "model psychoses" with these agents in the hope of gaining insight into the etiology and treatment of "real" psychopathologies. As was mentioned in previous chapters, the impact of LSD and mescaline upon neurohormonal substances led several theorists to speculate that dysfunctions of serotonin and adrenolutin were central to natural psychoses. Not only have these conjectures been sharply revised in light of subsequent chemical research, but early enthusiasms concerning the value of "model psychoses" have also waned in recent years since these states do not faithfully duplicate either the physical processes or the subjective experiences of a true psychosis.

Some therapists have claimed that hallucinogens facilitate other treatment techniques (Cholden, 1956; Shlien et al., 1968). Schmneige (1963) summarized the rationale for their therapeutic use as follows: it helps the patient recall and vent repressed early experiences; it intensifies the patient's affectivity; and it allows him to observe and better understand his attitudinal distortions and so on.

Despite these commendable features and frequent subjective reports by patients of new "transcendental" feelings following repeated hallucinogen intake, there have been few well-controlled studies proving their efficacy either as a form of therapy or as an adjunct to other therapeutic methods.

## EVALUATION

There are several advantages of psychopharmacological therapy that are not shared by other treatment techniques:

1. The ease of administration, minimal time demands upon professional personnel and the small financial cost of these agents allow more patients to be treated more efficiently and economically than with other forms of therapy.

2. Therapeutic regimens can be programmed with considerable precision since dose levels and rates can be administered exactly as desired and regulated to produce optimum effects.

3. Pharmaceuticals can be used not only as an adjunct to other therapeutic techniques, but to enhance or counteract effects produced by other techniques.

4. The efficacy of drugs can be evaluated more rapidly than other therapies since their effects are usually evident within a few days.

5. In contrast to other treatment methods (surgery or intrapsychic therapy), detrimental effects can readily be reversed by the simple expedient of withdrawing the drug.

6. Since the chemical composition of pharmacological drugs can be deciphered quickly, modifications in molecular structure can be devised and tested rapidly to see if they are superior to established agents.

## EFFICACY (OUTCOME STUDIES)

Despite differences among drugs, the presence of discomfiting side effects and the need to tailor the therapeutic regimen to suit individual response patterns, there can be no question but that these agents successfully alter a broad spectrum of troublesome symptoms, ranging from rage and agitation through hallucinations and delusions to apathy and social withdrawal. The phenothiazines and iminodibenzyl derivatives, in particular, produce more impressive beneficial effects with markedly disturbed patients than that achieved by psychological therapies, even at the best staffed institutions. Not only do they facilitate patient management, and thereby make patients more accessible to other forms of treatment, but they moderate the intensity of disruptive emotions, help calm bizarre behaviors and often stabilize disordered thought processes.

Since "basic" pathological attitudes and habits are not directly altered by drugs, we cannot say that they have been "cured." Nevertheless, the downward progression of psychic decompensation fostered by the presence of chaotic emotions and behaviors is often stopped, enabling the patient to regain a measure of psychic control and thereby increase his chances of developing adaptive coping responses. Pharmaceuticals often prevent prolonged episodes if administered in the early stages of disorder. Improvement may be sustained for years, without impairing the patient's capacity to think effectively or to experience the full range of normal emotions.

Although evaluative criteria have differed widely, these impressive results have been demonstrated consistently in well-controlled research. For example, Davis (1965), reviewing the findings of over 400 investigations on both tranquilizers and antidepressants, concluded that the evidence *in psychotic populations* overwhelmingly supports the superiority of these agents when compared to stimulants, sedatives and placebos. Even when inadequately designed studies were deleted and the effects of beneficial nondrug influences were cancelled out, the picture of unquestioned efficacy in psychotic states remained substantially unchanged. Among these findings are those gathered in the extremely well-controlled studies of the Psychopharmacology Service Center of the National Institute of Mental Health (Cole et al., 1964; Cole and Davis, 1967).

The efficacy of pharmacological agents in nonpsychotic states has *not* been convincingly demonstrated. Minor tranquilizers appear of value in ameliorating the discomforts of anxiety, but for the most part, milder personality patterns and neurotic and psychophysiologic disorders benefit only slightly with these agents. The paucity of properly designed studies with these patient populations prevents us from drawing definitive conclusions concerning drug efficacy.

Certain features of gross symptomatology respond best to certain types of drugs. Tranquilizers are medications of choice in cases of manifest anxiety, hyperactivity and hostility; antidepressants are indicated in cases noted by dejection, guilt and suicidal threats.

Other than the broad target symptoms of anxiety, hostility and depression, there is little research enabling us to specify which patients benefit most from which drugs. Individual differences in drug response have repeatedly been observed, but formal research has been limited, for the most part, to group statistics, with little or no indication of which medications suit the overall pattern of a patient's personality. Moreover, few investigators have sought to identify predictor variables which would indicate whether or not a given patient will benefit from drug therapy; among exceptions in this regard is the work of Katz and Cole (1961); Wittenborn and May (1966) and Glueck (1968).

The importance of personality factors in drug choice is pointed up by the fact that the amelioration of surface symptoms may result in a worsening of the patient's pathological state. Alterations in target symptoms may give rise to secondary reactions that are more troublesome and problematic than those they replaced. For example, as Sarwer-Foner (1959) has shown, agitated patients with deeply rooted fears of passivity and dependency will react adversely to the inactivating and restraining effects of tranquilizing drugs.

On the other side of the ledger, "fundamental" changes may occur in patients as a function of "surface" symptom changes. For example, the remission of delusions following a drug will, in all likelihood, not reflect the direct impact of the chemical upon thought processes; the delusional network may simply have been subdued or masked by drug-induced apathy. More fundamentally, the diminution of delusions may be a secondary consequence of the reduction of behavioral hyperactivity and assaultiveness; as a result of reduced assaultiveness, the patient's social relationships may improve and this, in turn, may decrease his anticipation of hostility from others, thereby calming his suspicions and diluting the basis of his delusions.

In summary, since the complex and sequential effects of these drugs have not been thoroughly explored, there is little empirical basis for knowing which patients will *ultimately* be benefited, and which will be fundamentally unaltered or worsened.

Deserving of final note in this review of efficacy are some of the physiological side effects and psychological complications which often impede the potentially beneficial consequences of drugs.

Many agents produce deleterious reactions such as severe allergic responses, pigment alterations and cardiac changes; other drugs can lead to habituation. These troublesome side effects may not require the discontinuance of the drug since most of them can be controlled by varying the dosage level or administering counteracting medicaments.

Some therapists hesitate employing drugs since patients frequently become dependent on them and learn to accept symptom palliation instead of seeking more fundamental resolutions to their difficulties. A judicious handling of prescriptions and a sharing with the patient of the reasons for decreasing drug dependence may avoid this complication without depriving him of its benefits.

## MODE OF ACTION (PROCESS STUDIES)

In the preceding section, some thoughts were noted concerning the circuitous manner in which pharmacological agents can produce their beneficial outcomes. Thus, many changes stem not so much from direct drug effects, but from secondary social and psychological consequences. Important though secondary effects may be in accounting for the overall efficacy of a drug, they are not intrinsic ingredients of pharmacological treatment. The "process" of drug action is its more direct influence upon organismic biochemical processes. Research attention must focus, then, on the specific biophysical alterations these agents produce and on their direct correlates in activation level, temperament and energy.

The first step in this appraisal is to identify the specific anatomical sites within which these compounds act; for example, is the action of a drug localized in one neural region such as specific tracts of the reticular formation, or is it distributed somewhat evenly throughout several systems? Once the pattern of drug concentration has been mapped, the next step is to specify the character and sequence of pathways of its primary effects; for example, does the drug inhibit reticular activating fibers and does it simultaneously or subsequently excite those of the limbic region?

The task of elucidating the pattern of drug action appears simple and straightforward in theory, but is a formidable technical job. The anatomical and physiochemical complexity of the central nervous system and the intricate and subtle interdependencies among its various regions make for an awesomely tangled web. Except for a few gross studies limited largely to specifying the primary sites of drug concentration, efforts to unravel the sequence and interactions of drug pathways have not proven notably successful to date. As a consequence, formulations concerning intracranial sites of action and their associated enzymatic machinery are either crude simplifications or imaginative conjectures (see Table 14-2).

Even if the neurological sites and physiochemical effects of these drugs were well mapped, the task of translating these findings into their correlated behavioral consequences would remain an arduous one. We know in only a rather primitive way that several of these drugs raise the threshold of psychic pain and confusion, and seem to disconnect thoughts and memories from their normally associated emotional correlates. It will be some time, however, before the wide-ranging complex of neurochemical changes will be matched with clarity to their corresponding behavioral consequences. This will require considerably greater theoretical sophistication and a more ingenious technical know-how than currently exist. Moreover, the job of formulating an overarching process schema for psychopharmacology faces the problem of coordinating different data levels and conceptual languages. Few practicing clinicians are conversant with the events of molecular neurochemistry, and even fewer biochemists grasp the subtleties of intrapsychic strategies and pathological behaviors. As increasing numbers of psychopathologists learn to bridge these formerly separated disciplines, the goal of making more explicit the intricate relationships between altered pathophysiology and psychopathology will no longer be a vague possibility, but an attainable reality.

## ELECTRICAL STIMULATION METHODS

Electricity was used as a therapeutic instrument long before its physical properties were understood. Its first application may be traced to early Rome where physician-priests placed live electric eels across the forehead of patients to relieve persistent headaches. Although employed by medical experimenters throughout the ensuing centuries, electricity did not attain official status as a treatment method until 1744, when the Royal Academy of Science in France initiated an annual report dealing with medical "electrotherapy." Among the early procedures recommended by this august body were spark treatments, mild shocks transmitted by vibrators, globes and percussive instruments, electric baths and so on. Needless to say, whatever benefits were gained by these "treatments" were likely to have been the consequence of "placebo" suggestibility.

Electrical magnetism, developed by Anton Mesmer, swept the French nation in the mid and latter part of the eighteenth century and gave rise to a brief period of pseudoscience, charlatanism and rampant medical quackery. Although the invention of an electrical condenser in the 1740's allowed physicians to transmit "real" currents to patients, it was Mesmer's intangible hypnotic magnetism that caught the eye of most psychopathologists of the day. Nevertheless, a number of imaginative physicians explored the use of mild electric shocks in the mid-1700's for cases of epilepsy and hysteria. And by the mid and late nineteenth century, numerous psychiatrists had experimented with electrical procedures, reporting allegedly good results with mental retardation, apathy and depression. For a short period, the renowned neurologist, Charcot, employed low voltage electrical currents in hysteria. In the early 1900's, electrical techniques were utilized for the first time to promote prolonged sleep and to induce epileptic-like convulsions; this work, undertaken by Leduc and Robinovitch, was limited largely to experimentation with sheep and dogs. Cerletti, the founder of electroconvulsive treatment, had investigated electrically produced seizures with animals for several years prior to testing its potential therapeutic effects on humans in the mid 1930's.

## ELECTROCONVULSIVE THERAPY

Electroconvulsive therapy (ECT), one of the few genuine techniques to emerge from the long medical history of "electrotherapy," developed not as a form of electrical treatment, but as an incidental method to induce therapeutic convulsions. In other words, the convulsion and not the electricity is the therapeutic agent.

### HISTORY AND RATIONALE

As described previously, Cerletti and his associate Bini experimented with electrically induced convulsions in animals for several years. Learning in 1935 of Meduna's success in treating schizophrenics with camphor and metrazol, they decided to investigate whether similar beneficial effects could be produced by electrical means. Thus, at no time did Cerletti and Bini believe that the electrical current per se was the essential therapeutic element. Rather, electricity was seen merely as a more efficient and less complicating method than metrazol for inducing the alleged therapeutic benefits of convulsions (Cerletti and Bini, 1938).

Cerletti accepted the importance given to the convulsive experience by Meduna, but did not share Meduna's theory that schizophrenia and epilepsy were intrinsically antagonistic disease entities. It was Meduna's belief, as we may recall, that the seizures of the epileptic signified the presence of biophysical abnormalities which precluded the development of a schizophrenic psychosis. In his alternative, Cerletti proposed that the convulsion brought the patient close to a state of death; this aroused extraordinary biological defenses in the form of a still unidentified substance that Cerletti termed *agonine,* which led to a generalized strengthening of adaptive capacities and, ultimately, to therapeutic recovery. Attractive though Cerletti's theory may be, it is yet to be verified.

Numerous clinicians and researchers have proposed plausible rationales concerning the mechanisms underlying the ECT technique. Within ten years of its discovery, Gordon (1948) reported 50 different theoretical formulations, and many others have since been published. They range from obscure hypotheses of psychoanalytical symbolism, e.g., convulsions revive and overcome the "birth trauma," to unverifiable neuroanatomical conjectures, e.g., convulsions create capillary spasms that selectively destroy pathogenic neural cells. These formulations may be divided into two broad categories, biological and psychological, and within these classes, certain recurrent themes occur with fair regularity.

### Biological Theories

Most of these formulations are modeled after Cerletti's original proposals. The convulsion presumably "shocks" the organism and produces an alarm reaction, similar to that suggested by Selyé in his "general adaptation" schema. Aroused in this manner, the organism is galvanized to counteract and cope more effectively with the strains of everyday life; as a consequence, he overcomes his current pathological state and begins to exhibit a more vigorous adaptive style. Implicit in this thesis is the assumption that those who benefit by ECT must have exhibited deficits either in stress reactivity or sympathetic arousability prior to treatment.

Another group of biological theories postulates that ECT destroys neural traces of recent memories to a greater extent than those of distant memories. This thesis, based on the dubious data of post-ECT "retrograde amnesia," asserts that the residuals of recent experiences, attitudes and emotions are more markedly disrupted by convulsive treatment than older and ostensibly healthier patterns; as a consequence, the patient "forgets" the current precipitants and reactions of his disorder, and thereby returns to his premorbid level of adjustment.

### Psychological Theories

These formulations fall into two categories.

The first, espoused primarily by intrapsychic theorists, considers the ECT experience to be a form of expiation. According to this view, the patient is relieved of intense guilt feelings by being "punished" repeatedly with the "electric shock." Since depressive patients often exhibit intense guilt feelings and are among those who profit most by ECT, the thesis possesses at least some measure of logical plausibility. Unfortunately, subconvulsive electrical procedures, which render the patient unconscious and are experienced phenomenologically as identical to ECT by the patient, do not produce equivalent therapeutic effects. In other words, although the guilt-ridden patient believes he is undergoing the punitive "shock" in the subconvulsive method, he fails to show the improvement evidenced in the convulsive form. The intrapsychic thesis is difficult to sustain in light of this evidence.

A second group of psychological theories follows a conditioning model. One of these theories conceives ECT to be a punitive stimulus, a view not dissimilar to that proposed by intrapsychic theorists. However, this model suggests that the negative effect of the shock is conditioned to the patient's current symptomatology, e.g., his depressive complaints, behavioral languor and so on. To avoid the punitive discomforts of treatment, the patient "learns" to inhibit behaviors to which the ECT has been conditioned, namely his clinical symptomatology. Thus, he camouflages or represses his depressive attitudes and feelings, brightens up and thereby avoids the negatively reinforcing ECT experience.

Other conditioning theorists take a diametrically opposite view of the effects of ECT. To them, ECT conditions formerly stressful environments to the "relaxed" state of the induced coma. Thus, what is conditioned is not "punitive fear," as proposed in the previously described conditioning thesis, but lowered emotional arousal and tension. Since this reduced arousal and tension have been conditioned by ECT to his present environment, the patient begins to face his current life with equanimity.

Both conditioning theories run into the same empirical difficulty as the intrapsychic "guilt-expiation" thesis; that is, why is subconvulsive electrical therapy less effective than ECT when both produce equivalent degrees of "psychological fear" and "physical relaxation?"

It should be obvious from the variety of rationales presented here that no agreed upon theory of ECT action has been formulated; it remains essentially an empirical rather than a theoretically rational procedure.

## PROCEDURE

Despite minor variations in method, the basic ECT technique has remained essentially unchanged since Cerletti and Bini originally devised it. The patient rests comfortably on a well-padded mattress. To avoid unpleasant associations with treatment, patients are administered a quick-acting anesthetic such as intravenous sodium pentothal. A reversible muscular relaxant such as anectine may also be injected to minimize the intensity of seizure activity, decreasing thereby the danger

of dislocations or fractures. Electrodes are attached to the head and a current from 70 to 130 volts is administered for a period of 0.1 to 0.5 seconds, permitting between 200 to 1600 milliamperes to flow through the brain. When the convulsion begins, a resilient mouth piece is inserted to avoid serious tongue bite. Trunk and upper extremities are gently restrained during the seizure to prevent undue or dangerous movements. The convulsion is of the *grand mal* variety; there is a sudden flexion of the body, followed by a tonic or rigid phase lasting about ten to 15 seconds; next, the clonic phase ensues, characterized by rapid jerking movements lasting about 30 seconds. Following the convulsion, most patients remain unconscious from five to 30 minutes and awake in a somewhat hazy and confused state with minor and generalized aches, but with no recall for the episode. This experience is repeated from eight to 20 times in a typical course of therapy, with sessions spaced usually at three per week.

## EVALUATION

ECT has several advantages as a method of inducing convulsions when compared to pharmacological convulsants. As Kalinowsky and Hoch have put it (1961):

(1) the method is technically simpler and cleaner than the repeated intravenous injections of a drug which easily lead to thrombosis of the veins; (2) there is an immediate loss of consciousness which spares the patient any discomfort; (3) failure to respond with the desired convulsive manifestations can be avoided.

In addition to these points, electrical stimulation can be focused on specific brain regions whereas convulsant drugs are diffuse in their action. Furthermore, no potentially troublesome toxins are introduced into the body with ECT, thereby minimizing chemical aftereffects such as nausea and allergic responses.

Since the advent of oral pharmacological agents (tranquilizers and antidepressants), however, the use of ECT as a treatment technique has sharply declined. Even with muscular relaxants and anesthetics, ECT patients still experience postconvulsion discomforts, memory loss and possible brain damage.

### Efficacy (Outcome Studies)

In the main, studies investigating ECT have been poorly designed and controlled. Some of these inadequacies may be traced to the fact that research on this technique preceded the more sophisticated methodology of the past two decades. Thus, in contrast to recent studies of psychopharmacological agents, most evaluations of ECT are characterized by shoddy research procedures. Undifferentiated patient populations typically were grouped together; evaluative criteria were ill defined or their reliability suspect; control groups were generally lacking or inappropriate; and follow-up studies, for the most part, were of brief duration or not reported.

Despite the paucity of well-executed studies, enough data have been gathered over the years to enable us to draw fairly reliable conclusions of ECT efficacy (Huston and Locher, 1948; Alexander, 1953; Staudt and Zubin, 1957; Kalinowsky, 1967).

*First,* the *short-term* benefits of ECT in *depressive disorders* are highly impressive, making it the treatment of choice, especially in cases of "involutional melancholia" and in episodes of "agitated depression." Rapid improvement figures are in the vicinity of 60 to 90 per cent, as compared to spontaneous remission rates of 40 to 50 per cent. Long-term improvement levels, however, do not support the superiority of ECT treatment over matched controls. It appears, then, that ECT only hastens recovery time in those cases that it benefits. On the negative side, patients who improve with ECT relapse more frequently than do those who remit spontaneously, although the recovery rate still remains at about 40 per cent after a five year follow-up. Despite the high relapse rate, there are definite advantages to early recovery, e.g., alleviating patient anguish and reducing the possibility of suicide.

*Second,* except for cases of markedly severe depression, the evidence of ECT efficacy is minimal or negative. Where it does facilitate remission in nondepressed cases, these patients are likely to have profited equally well under less drastic therapeutic regimens.

*Third,* efforts to identify variables predictive of ECT efficacy have not been successful (Thorpe, 1962). Despite the unquestioned success of ECT in abbreviating short-term depressive episodes, not all these cases respond favorably to this treatment. Numerous physiological indices, e.g., the sedation-threshold and the mecholyl tests, as well as several psychological measures, e.g., the MMPI, have been employed with this prognostic goal in mind. Evidence gathered to date has been either equivocal or of lesser predictive accuracy than that achieved by gross clinical analysis.

The use of ECT has waned sharply since the advent of psychopharmacological agents. Not only have the iminodibenzyl derivatives and MAO inhibitors shown almost equal efficacy in producing rapid improvement and with fewer dangers and side effects, but long-term remissions can be achieved more feasibly with the simple expedient of maintenance drug dosages.

## Mode of Action (Process Studies)

In an earlier discussion of the rationale of ECT, we noted several alternative hypotheses concerning the manner in which convulsions produce their therapeutic effect. As was described earlier, most biotherapies were "stumbled upon" with little planning or rational forethought; theories were concocted afterward in an effort to "make sense" out of what was found by accident.

In the following paragraphs, we shall summarize research findings dealing with the mode of ECT action and reevaluate some of the theories that have been proposed to account for its clinical effects.

Efforts to elucidate the mode of action of a biophysical therapy require that we first specify the relevant neurological and physiochemical changes that have been produced. Once these data are established, reasonable speculations can be proposed as to "how therapy works."

Among the early ECT findings was a marked reduction of oxygen consumption during treatment (Wortis et al., 1941). This led to the thesis that ECT accomplished its effects by producing cerebral anoxia. Unfortunately for its proponents, this speculation had to be abandoned when induced anoxia, created through nonconvulsive means, failed to produce reactions comparable to ECT; moreover, when medications were introduced to prevent ECT anoxia, there was no appreciable change in treatment efficacy.

Kalinowsky (1946) proposed the thesis that the primary site of ECT action centered on the diencephalon; stimulation of this region, without inducing generalized convulsions, has resulted in no therapeutic benefits.

Formulations have been based on the belief that ECT "reactivates" deficient adrenal systems (Gellhorn, 1957). There is no convincing empirical evidence to support this thesis; moreover, this theory runs up against the fact that depressive patients, who respond best to ECT, do not exhibit adrenal insufficiency.

The view that ECT is a gross form of frontal lobe psychosurgery has been proposed by Fulton (1943). Although cellular damage is often found among those treated by ECT, these effects are not limited to the frontal lobes. Moreover, the therapeutic benefits are found primarily among depressive disorders; if treatment was centered in the frontal lobes, we would expect its greatest benefits to be with patients who evidence marked thought disturbances, e.g., delusional and fragmentation disorders.

Meduna's original theory of an intrinsic biological antagonism between schizophrenia and epilepsy possesses no merit for several reasons; these two pathological syndromes do overlap, despite Meduna's contentions to the contrary, and ECT has proven effective in depressive rather than schizophrenic conditions.

Cerletti's thesis that convulsions are biological stressors that activate a defensive chemical substance capable of strengthening the patient's adaptive capacity remains unproved since no such substance has been uncovered. Similar models based on Selyé's general adaptation syndrome have the appeal of postulating no special substance other than the body's own natural defensive properties; however, this thesis fails to account for why beneficial effects are found in only one pathological state, that of depressive disorders.

Questions have been raised as to whether it is the convulsion rather than the electric current which is responsible for the therapeutic effect. Several lines of evidence suggest that seizure activity is at least a necessary if not a sufficient ingredient, and that the electrical current is neither sufficient nor necessary. First, metrazol-induced convulsions produce only slightly less beneficial effects than ECT, and in predominantly the same type of patient. Second, subconvulsive electrical stimulation achieves minimal or no therapeutic effect. Third, if seizure activity is controlled by drugs as the standard ECT current is administered, clinical improvement is sharply reduced (Ottoson, 1960). These data suggest that the convulsion is a significant process ingredient whereas the current is not.

Several theorists have speculated that the effective agent of ECT is the deep coma into which the patient slips. This thesis cannot be sustained in light of the failure of other coma or deep sleep treatments to produce equivalent therapeutic effects.

The view that ECT produces a *selective* memory loss has had considerable support in the literature (Janis, 1950; Hunt and Brady, 1951; Williams, 1961; Lewis and Maher, 1965). Numerous animal experiments, as well as careful interviews with patients both pre- and post-ECT, have suggested that induced convulsions disrupt recent memory traces and experiences that are emotionally arousing. A variety of physiological and conditioning models have been proposed to explain these two forms of selective "amnesia." Fascinating though many of these hypotheses may

be, they do not "explain" why ECT is beneficial almost exclusively in depressive states, but exhibits little or no impact on other "recently disordered" or "emotionally aroused" conditions.

In summary, there are no confirmed or generally accepted explanations of the process of ECT efficacy. Most theorists have singled out one aspect of the total ECT experience such as partial memory loss or occasional patient fears, and have formulated their ideas on this factor alone. None has drawn the diverse biophysical and psychological threads of ECT treatment together into an all-embracing theory—not that such a theory would ensure an answer either. As matters now stand, ECT continues as a valued treatment technique, not by force of theoretical logic, but by its proved empirical efficacy in selected cases of depressive disorder.

## MISCELLANEOUS TECHNIQUES

Brief mention may be made of other procedures that employ electrical currents for purposes of therapeutic gain. These techniques have proved to be either of limited efficacy (electronarcosis and subconvulsive methods) or of experimental rather than clinical utility (focal stimulation implants).

### ELECTRONARCOSIS

In an attempt to control the violent muscular discharge of ECT, several investigators designed procedures that "soften" the convulsive reaction and allow the therapist to control the character and timing of the electrically induced discharge.

Leduc, whose work was referred to earlier in the chapter, attempted a controlled input of electrical current both in animals and himself long before the advent of ECT. By means of a rheostat, he was able to build up the current slowly, preventing a convulsion but producing an induced state of sleep.

It was Frostig et al. (1944) who first explored the possibility of supplanting ECT with a modification of Leduc's "electric sleep" method. In Frostig's procedure, the patient is subjected to a current sufficient to produce a mild tonic spasm for about 30 seconds; unconsciousness, muscular rigidity and an arrest of pulse and respiration result. Following this initial phase, the current is reduced, but maintained at a level capable of maintaining the patient in a "narcosis state" for seven or more minutes.

Frostig's procedure differs from the standard

ECT on several minor points. Both procedures generate an initial tonic convulsive state, although the response in electronarcosis is usually milder. The essential distinction lies in the prolongation of the period of unconsciousness, controlled by the continued presence of a reduced current. Upon the termination of the narcotic state, patients often exhibit the usual clonic phase characteristic of ECT.

Several theorists have argued that electronarcosis "should be" superior to ECT (Azima, 1953). In essence, they believe that the gains achieved by ECT should be enhanced by the extended and more "restful" state of electronarcosis, e.g., "exhausted" neural cells have more time to be replenished, biological defensive reactions can build up more firmly and the symbolic act of guilt expiation is prolonged. Despite the plausible nature of these rationales, the facts are that in the few clinical (uncontrolled) studies reported in the literature (Bowman and Simon, 1948; Kalinowsky and Hoch, 1961), electronarcosis is of lesser efficacy than ECT. Since the method is technically more cumbersome than ECT, and since patients have experienced more discomforts with it, electronarcosis has never attained the status of an established therapeutic procedure.

## SUBCONVULSIVE METHODS

Both ECT and electronarcosis induce seizures. Other methods have been devised which render the patient unconscious, but do not generate convulsive activity. Three varieties of subconvulsive stimulation have been studied.

The first, designed by Hirschfeld (1950) and termed *electrostimulatory treatment,* focuses on selected regions within the brain and activates these structures without inducing a generalized convulsion. Since patients are not rendered unconscious during treatment, many experience painful sensations and require an anesthetic prior to the administration of the current. Encouraging results have been reported by its proponents, but there are no well-controlled studies to support these contentions.

The notion of stimulating peripheral body regions can be traced back to the early Romans,

and to the French of the eighteenth century. More recently, the technique has been investigated by Jones et al. (1955) on the assumption that electrical stimulation of the legs and lumbosacral region may serve to activate the reticular system, thereby "arousing" withdrawn and lethargic patients. Efficacy studies have been few and for the most part equivocal.

The use of the *electrosone,* developed and employed extensively by the Russians, attempts to induce a nonconvulsive "deep sleep," somewhat akin to Leduc's procedure devised at the turn of the century. In this technique, a low voltage rhythmic current is passed between the eyes and the occipital region of the brain. Reports that "nervous" and "depressed" patients awaken refreshed and invigorated are yet to be demonstrated in properly controlled studies.

## FOCAL STIMULATION IMPLANTS

Long and narrow electrodes have been inserted by investigators into localized and well-defined brain regions, thereby enabling them to stimulate with considerable precision just those neural systems which they believe subserve pathological behaviors. Of particular interest in this regard are Heath's studies on septal stimulation (1954) and intracranial self-stimulation (1962). In his earlier studies, Heath reported that stimulation in the septal region proved of therapeutic value in one third of a selected group of "anhedonic" patients. In subsequent work, Heath equipped several patients with small portable self-stimulators, permitting them to transmit electrical stimuli to any of several regions of the brain; rather consistently, preferences were shown for the septal implants.

That self-stimulating methods such as these may prove effective in overcoming not only moods but behaviors and attitudes as well is a fascinating prospect, but one fraught with weighty, ethical implications. For the present, however, the neurological skills and technology required for successful implanting prevent its development as an everyday therapeutic technique. It remains largely an experimental tool, enabling researchers to elucidate the substrate and mechanisms of mood and memory.

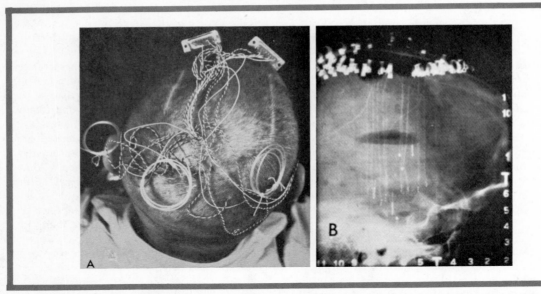

Figure 14-1  Focal stimulation implants. *A.* Patient with wires. *B.* X-ray of patient showing electrodes. (Parts *A* and *B* from Nodine, J. H. and Moyer, J. H. [eds.] : Psychosomatic Medicine. Philadelphia, Lea and Febiger, 1962.)

# SURGICAL PROCEDURES

Appearances to the contrary, the ancient technique of *trephining* cannot be viewed as a forerunner of modern day psychosurgery. For the most part, this primitive procedure, consisting of chipping out a small segment of the skull, was conceived not as a medical technique, but as a method by which "evil spirits" were expunged. There is some evidence, albeit tenuous, that a procedure somewhat akin to trephining was employed both by Greek and Roman physician-priests; by opening the skull, toxic humors that ostensibly caused irrational behaviors were discharged. Trephining was used again in medieval times to purge the insane of demons; other more humane physicians of the time considered the procedure useful in relieving noxious poisons. These physicians made no effort to alter the brain itself, but merely perforated the cranium to "drain off" infectious matter. In a sense, this procedure is a variant of venesection or blood-letting, an equally ill-conceived purgative method that achieved great popularity between the sixteenth and nineteenth centuries.

## HISTORY AND RATIONALE

The first true antecedent of contemporary psychosurgery was the work of the Swiss neurologist G. Burkhardt who reported the results of two brain operations on psychotic patients in 1890. Burkhardt believed that the root of mental aberrations were abnormally high intensities of neural activity in specific regions of the brain. He set out to relieve these neural abnormalities and their psychological correlates (e.g., impulsiveness and hallucinations) by severing the connection between pathological and normal regions, or by excising tissue segments from the afflicted part. Although he reported success in reducing violent and hallucinatory behaviors in five cases, his work was abandoned because of adverse criticism from his medical colleagues.

Burkhardt's early studies were unknown to a group of neurosurgeons who reported the results of comparable work at the 1935 meeting of the Second International Neurological Congress in London. At these sessions, Fulton and Jacobsen (1935) described the elimination of experimentally induced "neuroses" in two chimpanzees following the surgical removal of large segments of the frontal lobes. Brickner (1936), at these same meetings, noted marked behavioral changes in one of his patients following the removal of a frontal region tumor. Although Fulton and Jacobsen stressed the serious loss of cognitive functions in their chimpanzees, and although Brickner conveyed but a few fragmentary clinical impressions, the idea was revived that surgical procedures could moderate pathological behaviors.

Egas Moniz, a Portuguese psychiatrist, later

to obtain the Nobel Prize for his work, attended the 1935 Congress. He reported in later years (1954) that the ideas and research of Fulton, Jacobsen and Brickner crystallized thoughts of utilizing a surgical procedure for psychotics that he had been mulling over for some time. Starting with the thesis that psychotics suffer from "abnormally fixed arrangements" in the brain, first formulated in this fashion by the eighteenth century psychiatrist Hermann Boerhaave, Moniz concluded that the destruction or isolation of these arrangements would free the patient of his fixation and enable him to reorganize his attitudes and behaviors in a normal fashion.

Fortunately, since the days of Burkhardt's technically crude methods, great advances had taken place in neurosurgical procedures. Together with Almeida Lima, a neurosurgeon, Moniz was able to devise several sophisticated surgical methods, finally selecting what they termed the *prefrontal leucotomy* technique (1936), a procedure that severed connections between the frontal lobes (alleged thought center) and the thalamus (alleged emotion center). As with Burkhardt a half century earlier, there was resistance in many quarters of the medical profession to Moniz's "barbaric" treatment. Nevertheless, this time psychiatry was ripe for a new therapeutic panacea, a simple cure-all that would reduce the growing population of "hopeless" psychotics.

Psychosurgery was given a marked impetus in this country by Walter Freeman and James Watts (1942) who reported rather striking results with procedures similar to those of Moniz and Lima. Patients who had for years been confined to institutions as uncooperative or utterly hopeless were reported to have become manageable, capable of working efficiently by themselves and even improved enough in some cases to take on jobs and assume a normal social life. The surgical procedure employed by Freeman and Watts, which they termed the *prefrontal lobotomy,* differed slightly from that of Moniz. They refined Moniz's general statement that mental difficulties were pathologically "fixed" neural pathways, claiming that psychopathology was a product of the patient's tendency to overelaborate, by means of the reflective processes of the frontal lobes, emotions generated in the thalamic region. In accord with this theoretical rationale, they assumed that severing the pathways between these centers would prevent the patient from "worrying" about his emotional discomforts; as a consequence, he could no longer expand minor distresses into pathological proportions.

Other rationales have been proposed for the ostensive efficacy of surgical procedures. Most are variants of the theses formulated by Moniz and by Freeman and Watts; they are no less speculative and equally difficult to confirm or refute. Essentially, they fall into two types. One group of rationales stresses the thesis that surgical management reduces the patient's power to elaborate emotional experiences; the other contends that the destruction of established and pathological neural patterns enables the patient to acquire new "healthier" behaviors and thoughts. Neither of these hypotheses can be tested, given our present technology and our limited grasp of neural relationships within the brain. We will discuss the modus operandi of psychosurgical techniques in a later section. First, however, let us review the major operative procedures devised in the past 30 years.

## PROCEDURES

Since Moniz's original procedure, numerous techniques have been fashioned in the hope of both maximizing the efficacy of psychosurgery and minimizing its troublesome complications. These methods may be conveniently grouped into four categories: thalamofrontal sectioning, cortical undercutting, cortical excisions and subcortical ablations.

**Thalamofrontal Sectioning.** These procedures were the first and most widely employed psychosurgical techniques, and include the *prefrontal leucotomy* of Moniz, the *prefrontal lobotomy* of Freeman and Watts and the *transorbital lobotomy* devised by Fiamberti in 1937. The primary intent of these operations is to sever nerve tracts between the frontal cortex and the thalamus. In both prefrontal leucotomy and lobotomy methods, small drill holes are made on the side or top of the skull (see Figure 14-2) and a sharp instrument is inserted and rotated in about a 35 degree arc anterior to the frontal lobes. The transorbital technique differs from the others in that the cutting instrument is inserted through the thin, bony structure separating the eye and the brain; it has the advantage, relative to other thalamofrontal methods, that it is simpler to execute surgically and tends to produce fewer postoperative complications. Variations of these three procedures have been tried; they differ from the standards in the location of sectioning and in whether one or both lobes are severed.

**Cortical Undercutting.** This method, devised by Scoville in 1948, involves cleaving the frontal cortex at the junction between the gray and white matter, thereby severing the underlying long as-

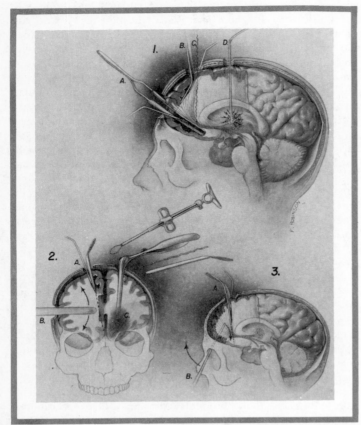

Figure 14-2 Psychosurgical techniques. 1.A. Orbital undercutting. B. Undercutting of superior convexity. C. Electrocoagulation of inferior median quadrant. D. Electrocoagulation of thalamic nucleus. 2.A. Cingulate gyrus undercutting. B. "Closed" standard lobotomy. C. Electrocautery method and suction and spatula method. 3.A. "Open" standard lobotomy. B. Transorbital lobotomy. (Entire set, courtesy of Dr. William B. Scoville.)

sociation fibers and precluding the "reverberation" of complex thought sequences. As indicated in Figure 14-2, undercutting may be performed in different sections of the cortex.

**Cortical Excisions.** These procedures, variously termed *lobectomies, gyrectomies, topectomies* and *cingulectomies,* represent operations involving the surgical removal of selected exterior segments of the cortex. Symmetrical bilateral excisions are usually made of clearly defined anatomical areas in the hope of eliminating functions subserved by the extirpated region.

**Subcortical Ablations.** The methods described previously focus on structures that can be approached surgically with relative ease. Deeper anatomical regions cannot be "seen" nor can they be altered surgically without severely impairing intervening and presumably healthy brain tissue. A variety of ancillary tools have been employed to minimize these complications and still allow the destruction of selected recessed structures. Many of these "hidden" regions can be localized with considerable precision by stereotaxic techniques. Properly pinpointed, these target areas may be ablated by inserting long and narrow instruments that carry electrical current. The operative procedures of *thalamotomy, hypothalamotomy* and *amygdalotomy* represent the application of this method to the thalamus, hypothalamus and amygdaloid areas. Various chemical solutions, such as formalin and procaine, have been inserted with the same goal in mind. More recently high frequency sound waves have been used to destroy recessed structures with minimal disruption of intervening tissue. Similarly, through modern radiosurgery, proton rays have been beamed into narrowly delimited regions without producing impairments to enveloping structures.

## EVALUATION

As was done in previous sections, two questions must be raised in evaluating psychosurgery. What is the efficacy of surgical treatment, that is, does it succeed in remediating psychopathology as gauged by properly designed and controlled "outcome" studies? What ingredients comprising the surgical intervention account for its beneficial effects, that is, can we elucidate the "process" or mode of therapeutic action?

## Efficacy (Outcome Studies)

The variety of operative procedures, the diversity of patient types studied and the discouraging yet everpresent methodological inadequacies of most research make it almost impossible to draw generalizations about the results of psychosurgery.

Efficacy studies that are worthy of scientific confidence require that patient populations be distinguished in accord with relevant diagnostic and prognostic variables, that explicit, reliable and meaningful criteria of change be established and that precise and objective instruments by which these criteria can be measured be employed. Of utmost importance is the presence of properly matched control groups exposed to comparable "extratherapeutic" experiences and evaluated at equivalent time intervals. Much of the controversy over psychosurgical efficacy can be traced to design inadequacies on each of the aforementioned points.

Adding to the evaluative problem in psychosurgery are the multiplicity and technical imprecision of operative techniques. Without precise and detailed information concerning the exact site and extent of tissue destroyed by each method, it is impossible to make comparative judgments of their efficacy or evaluate the types of pathology they are most likely to benefit.

With these discouraging comments as a précis, let us briefly review the results of a few of the better known efficacy studies.

The first exhaustive and detailed studies of lobotomy procedures were undertaken by Freeman and Watts (1942, 1950). In summary, they found that their patients fell roughly into three equal categories of improvement: one third benefited greatly, one third only slightly and one third not at all. These percentages, we may note, are what we have learned to expect in most patient groups *without therapeutic intervention.* Freeman and Watts, however, failing to employ a proper control group for comparative evaluation, and utilizing rather gross criteria for improvement, considered their results to be quite encouraging.

Let us next note the findings of three studies that at least begin to approximate the canons of sound evaluative design.

One group of researchers associated primarily with Columbia University (Mettler, 1949; Mettler, 1952; Lewis et al., 1956) initiated a series of studies on the efficacy of topectomy procedures, although several other techniques were investigated as well. Their first reports were highly favorable. Subsequent work, including a careful reappraisal of the control methods they employed in their earlier studies, led them to question the efficacy of psychosurgical procedures. In their final report, they concluded that psychosurgery: *if effective at all,* is of minimal use with deteriorated patients, the group with whom it is most frequently employed; has as its most significant consequence the reduction of excess affect; and should *not* be attempted until all other therapies have been exhausted.

In contrast to the rather pessimistic conclusions of the Columbia group, investigators at the Boston Psychopathic Hospital (Greenblatt et al., 1950; Greenblatt and Solomon, 1953; Paul, Fitzgerald and Greenblatt, 1957), comparing three lobotomy procedures over a five year follow-up period, concluded that "significant improvement" was found in 46 per cent of a chronic schizophrenic population. More specifically, 67 per cent of those subjected to the "bimedial" lobotomy operation maintained their significant improvement after five years. Based on these data, the Boston associates claimed that the bimedial technique should be viewed as the procedure of choice in chronic schizophrenic patients, an assertion that runs diametrically counter to that of the Columbia group (unfortunately, the surgical procedures employed in these studies are not comparable). The sanguine conclusions of the Boston group must be qualified in light of the questionable "control" methods they employed. There was no "nontreatment" control group; instead, they compared three different lobotomy procedures, judging efficacy on a comparative scale that had no base line from which to appraise the contribution of extratherapeutic influences such as physician expectations, hospital milieu, postoperative care and so on.

To confuse the picture of surgical efficacy further, Robbin (1958, 1959) compared changes observed in 198 lobotomy patients and an equal number of controls matched for chronicity, age on admission and so on. In general, he found that lobotomy patients had a slightly improved chance of hospital discharge, but that more of them were subsequently readmitted than in the matched controls. Among those who remained hospitalized, lobotomy cases evidenced no differences in ward behavior when compared to control patients.

Summarizing this rather confusing mass of research, we may conclude that psychosurgery has as its primary consequence the reduction of intense affect. Thus, it should be of greatest value with patients characterized by severe anxiety and agitation or by emotional impulsiveness and hos-

tility. However, since the advent of psychopharmacological agents, the need to employ so radical
a technique as surgery for these cases has been
markedly reduced. It would appear, then, that
psychosurgery can be justified only when all other
therapeutic procedures have failed. Even then, it
should be employed with great reluctance since
its effects are irreversible, and the possibility always exists that less drastic and more effective
methods may soon be discovered.

### Mode of Action (Process Studies)

Since the efficacy of psychosurgery may be
seriously questioned, there is little reason to attempt to elucidate its presumed mode of action.
Even if this were a worthy goal, we would be
led to conclude that these procedures are comparable, given the intricately raveled character
of the brain, to the use of a well-placed axe or
carefully directed blowtorch in the repair of computer circuitry.

Not only are surgical methods gross and
inexact, but we lack sufficient knowledge of the
neurological substrates of behavior to employ
them with greater precision. If we combine the
fact that the exact neurological consequences of

these procedures are blurred with the fact that
we lack adequate knowledge concerning functions
subserved by even well-defined substrates, we can
only conclude that current explanations of the
"process" of psychosurgery must be either highly
speculative or crude simplifications.

Nevertheless, several researchers have set out
to study the "precise" consequences of various
surgical procedures, both in animals and man
(Willett, 1961). Hypotheses concerning cognitive
changes, alterations in affect and disruptions of
inhibitory controls have been proposed on the
basis of numerous laboratory studies. Illuminating
though these investigations may be regarding certain of the varied sequelae of psychosurgery, they
tend to be narrowly conceived, that is, to focus
on but one facet of a complicated mosaic of
effects. None has provided a comprehensive rationale of how surgical intervention can be of
genuine therapeutic merit. It seems best to view
these theoretical schemas as interesting by-prod-
ucts of research that have little bearing on the
question of surgical efficacy.

In conclusion, psychosurgery should not be
employed as a therapeutic tool since its effects
may prove more disastrous than the impairment
it was intended to relieve.

## CONCLUDING COMMENTS AND SUMMARY

Before we launch into the vast sea of psychological treatment methods in the next chapter,
let us summarize the principal topics and facts
of this chapter.

1. Although the chief exponents of biological treatment contend that biogenic factors
are primary in psychopathology, there is no need
to accept this view in order to recognize that
biological approaches can be of therapeutic value.
Thus, these procedures may prove efficacious in
conditions in which the etiology is unequivocally
psychogenic.

2. The history of "somatotherapies" is characterized by serendipity, the unwitting discovery
of beneficial treatment methods by fortuitous
events. Only in the past decade have rational
foreplanning and experimental research characterized the development of biological therapies.

3. Psychopharmacological agents have
come to the fore as the primary instruments of
biological treatment in the last two decades.

a. Three rationales for the efficacy of
these drugs were described: *neurohormonal defect theories,* which assume that these agents over-

come endogenous chemical dysfunctions in synaptic transmission; *neurophysiological imbalance
theories,* which posit that they reestablish equilibrium among ill-matched functional systems; and
*psychological reaction theories,* which hypothesize
that chemical substances create energy and temperament changes that alter the individual's coping competencies and lead him to modify his
self-image.

b. Two major categories of drugs were
reviewed in some detail: *tranquilizers* and *antidepressants.* Among the principal agents in the
former category are phenothiazine derivatives,
rauwolfia alkaloids and numerous so-called minor
tranquilizers. In the latter category, the principal
compounds are MAO inhibitors and iminodibenzyl derivatives. Miscellaneous substances were
also described, notably sedatives, stimulants, anticonvulsants, psychotomimetics and a variety of
convulsion- and coma-inducing drugs.

c. Efficacy studies of tranquilizer action strongly support their utility in cases of
marked agitation and hostility, especially among
psychotic patients. Antidepressants, although not

as efficacious as electroconvulsive therapy, have been shown to be of distinct value in moderating depressive mood disorders.

Studies seeking to elucidate the mode of action of these drugs have provided only the barest outlines, not only of their direct physiological consequences, but of the complicated chain of effects they produce.

4. Electroconvulsive therapy is the major treatment technique employing electric stimulation. However, the essential feature of this procedure is not the electric current per se, but the convulsion it induces. Most efficacy studies of ECT can be faulted on methodological grounds, but sufficient data have accumulated over the years to justify the conclusion that ECT is the treatment of choice in depressive disorders. Although it produces a rapid remission of these symptoms, ECT does not decrease the probability of relapse.

Other electrical stimulation techniques were briefly described, namely electronarcosis, subconvulsive methods and focal stimulation implants.

5. Several procedures of surgical intervention were described. Serious questions were raised concerning the efficacy of these techniques. Since the advent of psychopharmacology, psychosurgery has lost whatever status it possessed as a treatment method, becoming an instrument of last resort.

# Chapter 15

# PSYCHOLOGICAL APPROACHES TO TREATMENT

Francis Bacon—*Study of Velasquez' Portrait* (1953).

## INTRODUCTION

Until that day in the distant future when practitioners can specify exactly which "pill" will dissolve the discomforts of psychopathology, patients will continue to be treated with drugs whose mode of action is only partially understood and whose effectiveness is highly limited. Unfortunately, this state of confusion and minimal efficacy is paralleled among the equally perplexing and inefficacious psychological therapies.

Beset with troublesome "mental" difficulties, patients are given a bewildering "choice" of psychotherapeutic alternatives that might prove emotionally upsetting in itself, even to the well-balanced individual. Thus, patients may not only be advised to purchase this tranquilizer rather than that one or told to take vacations or leave their jobs or go to church more often, but if they explore the possibilities of formal psychological therapy, they must choose among myriad "schools" of treatment, each of which is claimed by its adherents to be the most efficacious and by its detractors to be both ineffective and unscientific.

Should a patient or his family evidence a rare degree of "scientific sophistication," they will inquire into the efficacy of alternative therapeutic approaches. What they will learn, assuming they chance upon an objective informant, is that the "outcome" of different treatment approaches is strikingly similar, and that there is little data available to indicate which method is "best" for the particular difficulty they face. Moreover, they will learn the startling fact that most patients improve *without benefit of psychotherapy* almost as frequently as those who are subjected to prolonged psychological treatment.

This state of affairs is most discouraging. However, the "science" as opposed to the "art" of psychotherapy is relatively new, perhaps no older than one or two decades. Discontent concerning the shoddy empirical foundations of therapeutic practices was registered in the literature as early as 1910 (Patrick and Bassoe), but systematic research did not begin in earnest until the early 1950's, and has become a primary interest of able investigators only in the last five or ten years (Rubinstein and Parloff, 1959; Strupp and Luborsky, 1962; Hoch and Zubin, 1964; Goldstein and Dean, 1966; Gottschalk and Auerbach, 1966; Stollak, Guerney and Rothberg, 1966; Shlien et al., 1968).

Given the confusing picture that prevails among psychological treatment methods, it may appear that a logical ordering of techniques at

576

this time would be both unwise and premature. Nevertheless, it is necessary that we set forth as clearly as possible the basic rationales that differentiate the alternative therapies in practice today. To accomplish this in a reasonably useful pedagogical fashion requires first, that we review briefly the historical development of psychological procedures and second, that we outline the major dimensions by which they can be analyzed. With this as a foundation, we will have a perspective from which the principal types of psychological treatment can be described and evaluated.

## HISTORY

Psychotherapy has a long history, although the concept of treatment by psychological methods was first formally proposed in 1803 by Johannes Reil. In this section we will briefly review some of the relevant points presented in chapter 1, arranging the history of psychotherapy into six phases or periods, several of which overlap and extend into the present.

1. "Psychological" treatment was first recorded in the temple practices of early Greeks and Egyptians in the eighth century B.C. In Egyptian "hospices," physician-priests interpreted dreams and suggested solutions both to earthly and heavenly problems. In the Grecian Asclepiad temples, located in regions remote from sources of stress, the sick were provided with rest, given various nourishing herbs, massaged and surrounded with soothing music. During the fifth century B.C., Hippocrates suggested that exercise and physical tranquility should be employed to supplant the more prevalent practices of exorcism and punishment. Asclepiades, a Roman in the first century B.C. devised a variety of measures to relax patients, and openly condemned harsh "therapeutic" methods such as bloodletting and mechanical restraints. The influential practitioner Soranus (120 A.D.) suggested methods to "exercise" the mind by having the patient participate in discussions with philosophers who could aid him in banishing his fears and sorrows. Although doubting the value of "love" and "sympathy" as a therapeutic vehicle, Soranus denounced the common practices of keeping patients in fetters and darkness and depleting their strength by bleeding and fasting. The value of philosophical discussions espoused by Soranus may be viewed as a forerunner of many contemporary psychological therapies.

Humane approaches to the treatment of the mentally ill were totally abandoned during medieval times when witchcraft and other cruel and regressive acts were employed as "therapy." In the early years of the Renaissance, medical scientists were preoccupied with the study of the body and its workings and paid little attention to matters of the mind or the care of the mentally ill. Institutions for the insane were prevalent throughout the continent, but they continued to serve as places to incarcerate and isolate the deranged rather than as settings for medical or humane care.

2. The second phase of psychological treatment, what may be termed the period of "hospital reformation" and "moral treatment," began with the pioneering efforts of Philippe Pinel following the French Revolution. Guided by the belief that institutionalized patients could be brought from their state of degradation and depravity by exposure to a physically attractive environment and by contact with socially kind and moralistically proper hospital personnel, Pinel initiated an approach to mental hospital care that took hold, albeit gradually and fitfully. Moral treatment as practiced by responsible and considerate hospital personnel failed to take root for many years. This occurred for several reasons: there was a decline in the nineteenth century of psychiatric "idealism"; innumerable practical difficulties prevented the staffing of institutions with adequately motivated workers; and there was a resurgence from the mid-nineteenth to the early twentieth century of the medical disease model, turning the attention of psychiatrists to methods of physical rather than psychological treatment.

3. The practice of office psychiatry, characterized by treatment techniques that focus on one patient at a time and attempt to uncover the unconscious basis of his problems, may be said to have begun with Mesmer's investigations of "animal magnetism," i.e., hypnotism. Although the concept of magnetic forces was soon dispelled, Mesmer's occult procedures set the stage for a more scientific study of unconscious processes and strengthened the view that "suggestion" can be a potent factor in influencing mental symptoms. Moreover, Mesmer's enormous success with well-to-do "neurotics" in his private salon may be viewed as a precursor of modern day office practice.

As was recounted in earlier chapters, Charcot explored the use of hypnotism in his studies of hysteria. Exposed to the ideas of Charcot and Bernheim and to the discovery by Breuer of emotional "abreaction," Freud elaborated an intricate theory of psychic development and a highly original system of therapeutic practice, both of which he termed "psychoanalysis." Subjected soon thereafter to dissenting views, even among its early adherents, the practice of psychoanalysis splintered into numerous subvarieties. Despite these deviations, the focus on unconscious processes and the office practice model with individual patients remained well entrenched as a treatment prototype still in vogue today.

4. The fourth stage of psychological treatment may be said to have begun with the opening of mental health clinics for the young. This movement led to a new therapeutic goal, "freeing" the patient to develop his full potentials without the constraints of misguided and inhibiting social forces.

"Clinics" were common in medicine for many centuries. But it was not until Lightner Witmer opened the first psychoeducational clinic in 1896 at the University of Pennsylvania that the problems of the young became a major focus of psychological treatment. Therapy until then had been practiced almost exclusively with institutionalized psychotics. Together with psychoanalysis, which concentrated on the "strange" physical maladies of adults, the emergence of school guidance and college counseling centers extended psychological treatment to the full range of psychopathological difficulties.

The character and problems of children and adolescents led inevitably to a therapeutic philosophy that differed from those formulated in the service of hospital psychotics and adult neurotics. The clientele of school and college clinics was composed of moderately well-compensated young people who appeared to be suffering from parental, social and educational forces that interfered with and blocked their efforts to develop natural "growth" potentials. To remedy these difficulties, clinical therapists began to devise techniques which would "free" the patient to be himself, to "actualize" his capacities and to develop a sense of "personal self-regard." Thus, by the early 1940's, the ideas of Rank on "will therapy," and those of Rogers on "client-centered" therapy, gradually came to the fore as the primary psychological methods employed in outpatient clinics and school counseling services. In time, their views took root as a worthy philosophy not only in clinic centers, but in office practice and hospital settings as well.

5. Concurrent with the development of "office psychoanalysis" and "clinic self-actualizing therapy," laboratory scientists were gathering a body of empirical data on the basic processes of learning and behavior change. It was many years, however, before the early work of Pavlov,

Thorndike and Watson and the later concepts of Hull and Skinner began to be translated into principles applicable to therapy. By the mid-1950's, a variety of "behavior modification" techniques, employing procedures such as reinforcement and extinction and eschewing notions such as "unconscious forces" or "actualizing needs," were devised and promulgated by men such as Mowrer, Wolpe, Eysenck and Ferster. The emergence of these treatment methods, in contrast to other psychological techniques, grew not out of clinical need and observation, but out of systematic laboratory research. Although less than two decades old, behavior techniques quickly rose to the status of one of the major alternatives of psychological therapy.

6. The most recent stage in this historical progression has not been the development of new therapeutic procedures, but the application of research methodology in the evaluation of the "efficacy" and "process" of established procedures.

Until the 1950's, the efficacy of alternative therapies was, for the most part, an article of faith rather than proof. At best, the merits of these techniques were "demonstrated" in crudely designed and easily faulted clinical studies. "Success" was gauged subjectively by the therapist himself according to ambiguous criteria rather than through objective measures undertaken by independent judges. Rarely were controls employed, and improvement rates were presented without reference to such relevant variables as chronicity, symptomatology and so on. In short, what little had been done was done poorly.

Despite questions concerning effectiveness, proponents of each technique were not only convinced of the utility of their cherished procedures, but prospered and confidently inculcated each new generation of fledgling clinicians. Disputes among "schools" of therapy were evident, of course, but they were handled by verbal polemics rather than empirical research.

As long ago as 1910, Hoche noted that therapists were not scientists but cultists, willing promulgators of dubious measures that rested on the most unreasonable of assumptions (Patrick and Bassoe, 1910). Despite these early warnings, it was not until the late 1940's that clinicians such as Carl Rogers and J. McV. Hunt, trained both in scientific method and therapeutic practice, pioneered the first controlled studies of psychological therapy (Rogers and Dymond, 1954; Hunt, 1952). Spurred further by the critical reviews of Eysenck (1952), Zubin (1953) and Levitt (1957), increasing numbers of investigators began to reexamine the empirical under-pinnings of psychotherapy and set out to design efficacy and process studies that employed proper controls, criteria and measurement techniques. The fruits of this newest phase in history of psychotherapy have not yet materialized, but the seeds of the "scientific" era of psychotherapy have finally been well-planted.

## MAJOR DIMENSIONS OF PSYCHOLOGICAL TREATMENT

As was pointed out earlier in the text, we can approach any complex subject from a variety of vantage points, focusing first on one feature or characteristic and then on another. Thus, no single organizational format can do justice to the diverse attributes that comprise each variant of psychotherapy. In the following paragraphs, we will outline four of the many dimensions by which alternative therapies can be differentiated—setting, goals, process and data focus. Each of the principal techniques can be analyzed in accord with these factors. For example, "client-centered" therapy is practiced in an individual treatment *setting;* its *goals* are determined by the patient and are oriented toward the objective of "growth"; the therapeutic *process* consists of techniques which foster self-insight and the ventilation of emotions; and the therapist *focuses* his attention on phenomenological *data*.

### Setting

Although by no means mutually exclusive, therapy is usually practiced in one of three settings: *individual patient-therapist relationships, small group interactions* and *institutional milieus.*

The first of these settings, the treatment by a therapist of one patient at a time, is the most common arrangement in which psychotherapy is carried out. All systems and schools of therapy have employed this arrangement (e.g., behavior modification and psychoanalysis), and every type of psychopathology has been treated within it.

Small group interactions, generally referred to as group treatment methods, usually have one therapist working simultaneously with several patients. Central to this setting is the interplay among patients and the unfolding of social attitudes and interpersonal styles of behavior. Several variants of group treatment have been devised (e.g., analytical group therapy and psychodrama) and employed with numerous types of pathological conditions. Group procedures are often carried out in conjunction with individual therapy.

In contrast to the two arrangements just noted, in which patients are seen several hours a week at most, the institutional milieu setting encompasses the management and therapeutic planning of every aspect of the patient's life. Each day, from waking to sleeping, activities are coordinated to provide a "total push" toward rehabilitation; this includes ward schedules, occupational therapy, educational programs and physical and recreational games, as well as more formal individual and group therapy sessions.

### Goals

Two elements comprise the character of therapeutic goals. The first deals with *who* selects the goals, the second refers to *what* these goals are.

1. The problem of who determines the goals of treatment distinguishes what have been termed "directive" and "nondirective" therapies.

In directive approaches, the therapist, by virtue of his professional knowledge and the patient's emotional state, assumes responsibility for choosing the objectives and procedures of treatment; the "doctor" diagnoses what is wrong and guides the patient through what he decides is the best course of action.

In nondirective approaches, the patient decides more or less the steps and aims of the therapeutic process; in fact, it is the patient's increasing capacity to choose his life goals that is considered central to the therapeutic experience. Nondirective therapists intrude minimally into the patient's commentaries and reminiscences; at most, he helps the patient clarify his discursive thoughts and inchoate feelings.

2. Therapists may be distinguished by the goals they emphasize.

Some therapists focus on extinguishing maladaptive behaviors or relieving pathological emotions; the aim of treatment is to bring the patient back to a nonpathological state rather than to spur him to a "better" way of life. If growth should occur, it is expected to follow of its own accord, once the troublesome symptomatology has been eliminated.

Other therapists exert their primary efforts in the direction of developing new, more effective behaviors, considering the reduction of symptomatology to be of less significance than the acquisition of "better" ways of life. As they view it, current symptoms should fade of their own accord once the patient has gained alternative and more adaptive ways of resolving difficulties and achieving fulfillments.

Few therapists are committed firmly to one *or* another of these divergent goals; however, predilections toward "symptom extinction" versus "constructive response alternatives" may be noted among different therapies.

### Process

Of the several dimensions in which therapies are differentiated, none is more crucial to our understanding than the process by which they seek to produce beneficial changes. The major distinction here is between *insight-expressive* and *action-suppressive* processes.

Those inclined to the *insight-expressive* end of the continuum maintain that improvement is facilitated by new self-understandings and by the ventilation of highly charged but previously unexpressed emotions. To them, overt behaviors are merely surface phenomena that represent deeply rooted attitudes and feelings which must be understood and discharged. The process of therapy, then, consists of methods to uncover and release these attitudes and feelings. With insight and emotional ventilation achieved, it is expected that the patient will be able to confront life's tasks with equanimity, new powers of rational thinking and rapid personality growth.

Therapists inclined to the *action-suppressive* end of this dimension devalue the significance of self-understanding and emotional ventilation. They do not believe that insight is the sine qua non of therapy or that emotional ventilation leads to adaptive changes. Self-understanding and emotional catharsis are viewed at best as adjuncts to the ultimate goal of treatment, that is, producing demonstrable alterations in *real life behaviors*. The principal task of therapy, then, is to effect adaptive *actions* or responses. If necessary, the therapist will intervene in the patient's social environment, advising as many significant persons as needed to facilitate the patient's opportunity to alter his pathological behaviors.

### Data Focus

The four-fold breakdown in data that has been followed throughout the text may be employed to increase our understanding of the various forms and techniques of psychotherapy. In chapter 14, procedures which focused on the *biophysical* level were outlined. In this chapter, therapies may be differentiated in accord with *behavioral, phenomenological* and *intrapsychic* data levels. Which of these classes a therapist considers to be his province of interest will, in large measure, determine his treatment goals and the processes he will employ to attain them. Let us briefly examine these three data levels of therapy and their consequences; a more detailed discussion will be provided in later sections.

Therapists who subscribe to the *behavioral* orientation emphasize variables that can be directly observed. As a consequence, their interest centers on environmental stimuli and overt behavioral responses. They avoid where possible reference to unobservable or subjective processes such as intrapsychic conflicts or phenomenological attitudes. Since inner states are anathema to them, they are inclined to an action-suppressive rather than an insight-expressive process. Since the most clearly formulated schema of "behavior" change has been developed in the laboratories of learning theorists, they borrow their methods and procedures from that body of research. Most pathologies are considered to be deficient or maladaptive learned behaviors. It follows logically, they contend, that these behaviors can best be altered by the same learning principles and procedures that were involved in their acquisition. Thus, behavior therapists design their treatment programs in terms of conditioning and imitative modeling techniques which provide selective rewards and punishments. In this way, pathological behaviors that had been connected to provocative stimuli are systematically eliminated, and more adaptive alternatives are carefully formed.

*Phenomenological* therapists believe that treatment should be conceived in terms of the patient's conscious experience of events. Since the individual reacts to his present world in accord with his current perception of it, phenomenologists contend that the goal of treatment should not be to unravel the early causes of his difficulties, but to assist him in developing insight into his distorted attitudes and beliefs. As his perception of events and people is clarified, he will be able to approach his life with fewer difficulties and will act in ways that fulfill his "true" potentials.

*Intrapsychic* therapists focus their efforts on the elusive and obscure data of the unconscious. To them, the crucial elements "underlying" pathology are repressed childhood anxieties and the unconscious adaptive processes that have evolved to protect against their resurgence. The task of therapy, then, is to unravel these hidden residues of the past and to bring them into consciousness where they can be reevaluated and reworked in a constructive fashion. Shorn of insidious unconscious forces through the unfolding of self-insight and the uprooting of forbidden feelings, the patient may now explore a more wholesome and productive way of life.

The varied settings, goals, processes and data levels which differentiate psychological treatment methods may lead one to conclude that the field of psychotherapy comprises a motley assemblage of techniques. However, despite substantive differences in verbalized rationales and technical procedures, psychotherapies "sound" more dissimilar than they are in practice. Close inspection reveals that their aims are fundamentally alike and that their methods, although focusing on different facets or levels of psychological functioning, deal essentially with the same pathological processes.

It may be appropriate at this point to comment on the student's inevitable desire to find a single "definition" of psychological treatment. It should be evident from the foregoing, as was the case in defining psychopathology, that no single descriptive phrase will do. Wolberg (1967), for example, lists 26 different definitions in the recent literature. Obviously, psychotherapy means different things to different people. Definitions of psychotherapy cannot be formulated by reference to an abstract set of principles; rather, therapy is more or less whatever data, goals, setting and process a therapist employs in his practice. Thus, a behaviorally oriented therapist, who adheres to an action-suppressive process, will define psychotherapy differently than an intrapsychically oriented therapist, who is inclined to follow an insight-expressive procedure. Definitions *follow*, then, rather than precede the orientation adopted by the therapist. No single definition can fully convey the variety of philosophies and techniques with which psychotherapy is executed.

Since there is no simple way to define therapeutic techniques, it may be argued that it would be best simply to catalogue the myriad approaches currently in use, leaving their classification to some later date when a clear-cut organizational logic may have evolved. However, as was noted in earlier discussions concerning the classification of pathological syndromes, no format will ever be fully satisfactory since it is impossible to encompass all of the many dimensions and features by which a complex set of phenomena can be grouped.

Despite the inevitable limitations of classification, there are certain logical relationships among therapies which enable us to coordinate techniques in a reasonably systematic fashion. Unless we employ some rational format, advances in therapeutic science will become lost in a sea of incidental and scattered observations. Some frame of reference must be employed, then, to ensure that alternative techniques will be differentiated; in this way, we may accumulate a body of evaluative data that will enable therapists to determine the methods that are "best" for different types of psychopathology.

For the remainder of the chapter we will classify psychological therapies into six groups. The first, termed *environmental management*, refers to procedures that are designed to change the patient indirectly by manipulating and exploiting the surrounding conditions of his life for therapeutic purposes. The second, labeled *supportive therapy*, focuses directly on the patient; however, these procedures seek only to reestablish the patient's equilibrium without altering his premorbid make-up. The next four parts comprise techniques that are designed to promote fundamental changes in the patient. The first three deal with therapies that are practiced most often in the setting of an individual patient-therapist relationship. These methods—*behavior modification, phenomenological reorientation* and *intrapsychic reconstruction*—correspond to descriptions provided earlier in the "data focus" section. In addition to discussing the rationale and typical techniques of these "schools" of therapy, we will provide an evaluative review of relevant outcome and process studies. A similar format will be employed in the sixth and concluding part, comprising the various *group methods* of psychological treatment.

# ENVIRONMENTAL MANAGEMENT

Little progress can be expected in therapy if the patient's everyday environment provides few gratifications and is filled with tension and conflict. Like the proverbial high priced automobile that uses up gasoline faster than it can be pumped in, an unwholesome life situation may set the patient back faster than therapy can move him forward. For these reasons, it may be necessary to control or modify disruptive home or work influences, or perhaps remove the patient entirely from these disorganizing effects.

Beyond "relief and protection," environmental manipulation may be employed to achieve positive therapeutic ends such as "releasing" potentials or developing social skills. These two elements, the alleviation of situational stress and the exploitation of situational opportunities for constructive change constitute the chief goals of environmental management.

We will divide the methods by which these goals are achieved into two types. The *first*, termed "outpatient casework therapy," refers to procedures for patients who live in a normal community setting. The *second,* termed "inpatient milieu therapy," is employed for patients in hospital or other institutional settings.

## OUTPATIENT CASEWORK THERAPY

The profession of "social work" has traditionally played a central role in planning and controlling extratherapeutic elements of patient life which influence the progress of formal treatment; appropriately enough, social workers are viewed as integral members of the total "therapeutic team."

There are two goals of outpatient casework. First, to assist either the patient or his family in removing deleterious economic and interpersonal conditions and second, to facilitate the patient's opportunities to cope with the affairs of his life.

Achieving these ends may entail direct counseling on practical matters such as daily habits and routines and the budgeting of family finances. More importantly, caseworkers can be of considerable assistance in pointing out to relatives how they may be contributing to interpersonal tensions and resentments within the family. The one or two hours of face to face therapy with the patient may be completely negated by the attitudes of relatives whose verbalized good intentions are no guarantee that they will be carried out. Where necessary, then, direct intervention in the form of weekly counseling sessions may be recommended for relatives who precipitate difficulties. The efforts of a skillful psychiatric social worker can be of inestimable value in this regard.

Where occupational or social problems exist, caseworkers may be instrumental in arranging patient participation in community agencies such as sheltered workshops and recreational centers. In sheltered occupational programs, the patient may learn to cope with tensions he may have previously experienced in relating to fellow employees and employers; the understanding and tolerant attitudes of the professional supervisory staff at these centers ensure against harsh reprimands for poor performance which reinforce feelings of self-inadequacy (Olshansky, 1960). For essentially similar goals, caseworkers may recommend participation in recreational clubs so as to remotivate social interests and develop interpersonal skills; these settings are relatively free of the personal and competitive tensions of normal group relationships (Bierer, 1948; Lerner, 1960).

Caseworkers can be of invaluable service in smoothing the transition of patients from hospital to home and community. Practical arrangements may be made for the patient's employment, follow-up therapy and guidance to the family as to their expectations and ways of reacting to the patient. To ease the strain of resuming normal responsibilities that may be too taxing for the patient, arrangements may be made for *halfway house* or *night or day* hospital programs. In a halfway house, the patient lives with other former patients in a home within the community that is supervised by professional personnel; in this setting, he may begin to relearn the skills of normal social life without facing undue family expectations and occupational pressures (Wechsler, 1960). Similarly, in night hospital programs, patients begin their re-entry to community life by working at a "regular job" during the day, but still have the refuge and support of hospital services and personnel in the evening (Harris, 1957). In a parallel day program, the pattern of transition to community life is reversed; here, patients live at home, but spend their days in the sheltered environs of the hospital where deviant behaviors are tolerated and where they can continue to be helped in coping with everyday problems (Odenheimer, 1965).

Facilitative although outpatient casework may be, it is usually not sufficient in itself to rehabilitate the patient. Except in cases of transient situational stress, environmental vexations and complications are often only precipitants, tending merely to aggravate deeply established pathological patterns. In other words, the source of the patient's difficulties are "internal," ingrained attitudes and habits that persist and perpetuate themselves with little external prompting. Thus, caseworkers find all too often that following the removal of one environmental irritant, the patient involves himself in another that is as destructive as the first. Without modifications of the patient's pathological expectancies and behaviors, the benefits of casework alone, in all likelihood, will prove shortlived.

## INPATIENT MILIEU THERAPY

Until the last two or three decades, institutionalized patients were provided with kind and thoughtful custodial care at best and at worst, were incarcerated in filthy wards, shackled, crammed together and isolated from the interests and activities of the larger community. Even among the better hospitals, little effort was expended to see that the setting, routines and per-

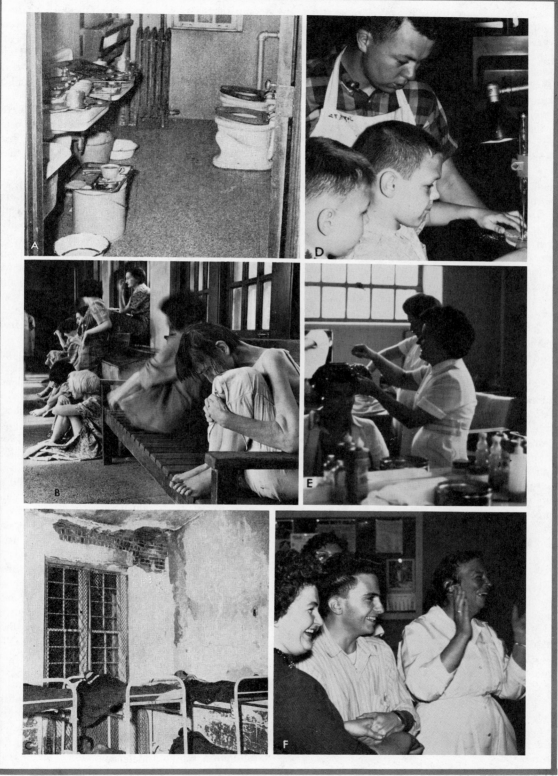

Figure 15-1  Contrasting hospital milieus. (Parts *A* and *C* from Deutsch, A.: The Shame of the States. New York, Harcourt, Brace and Company, 1948. Part *B* courtesy of Jerry Cooke. Parts *D*, *E* and *F* courtesy of Allentown State Hospital, Allentown, Pa.)

sonnel of the institution provided more than a comfortable asylum, a refuge from strains of everyday existence, a place where patients could withdraw quietly into themselves. Despite the pioneering efforts of Pinel in the eighteenth century and Dorothea Dix in the nineteenth century, Deutsch (1948) could report in his book, *The Shame of the States,* that most hospital patients in the mid-twentieth century sat out their lives in dreary environments, abandoned by unsympathetic families and exposed to uninterested personnel.

The change from inhumane to custodial to genuine therapeutic environments came about, not through public outcries, but through the fortuitous advent of psychopharmacological treatment. These drugs "contained" difficult patients, encouraging and enabling hospital workers to turn their attention from problems of restraint to those of therapy. At the same time, state legislative bodies became convinced that a massive infusion of funds for psychopharmaceuticals might ultimately unburden the taxpayer of costly long-term patient incarceration. The increased ease of patient management, together with the influx of additional funds, combined to spur a new attitude on the part of both public and hospital personnel.

The transformation from "custodialism" to "humanism" was not an easy one since hospital staffs were accustomed to viewing their charges as hopelessly chronic (Greenblatt, Levinson and Williams, 1957; von Mering and King, 1957). Only gradually was the "legend of chronicity" replaced by the "legend of recovery," that is, the attitude that patients can be rehabilitated. Today, the well-run mental hospital is no longer a place of incarceration or a refuge for social invalids, but a total "therapeutic community," a miniature environment that simulates the life and activities of the outside social world; it differs from a "true society" only in that it is designed intentionally to assist its members to learn to replace maladaptive and deficient behaviors with more appropriate ones.

Two aspects of institutional life promote these ends.

The first is the simple act of removing the patient from normal environmental stresses and placing him in a quiet and tolerant setting. "Safe" from external sources of humiliation and hostility, and able to "act out" his disturbed feelings without condemnation, the patient's anxieties subside and he may begin to regain a measure of composure.

The achievement of this first goal prepares the patient for the second and more important one of milieu therapy, developing increased social competence. Every facet of hospital life, e.g., cafeteria routine, housekeeping schedules, recreational programs and so on, becomes a therapeutic experience. Two aspects of institutional therapy have been stressed to achieve the goal of increased competence, occupational rehabilitation and the group planning of shared activities.

In years past, occupational therapy served the function of keeping patients busy by using them as cheap labor to reduce the costs of institutional management. At the very best, these activities countered the tendency of patients to disintegrate into idleness and invalidism. Such limited aims have been repudiated; occupational programs are designed today with the patient's special rehabilitative needs in mind. Industrial training is meaningful and goal-oriented, suited to the talents and interests of the patient and arranged to provide him with new skills that will enhance his self-esteem and prepare him to find a rewarding vocation in the larger social community.

The former practice of isolating patients from each other and from the larger community is a thing of the past. Modern day hospitals not only practice "open ward" policies, but encourage social contact among patients and the outside world. Moreover, patients who live together in ward units establish their own "governments" through which they plan daily routines and recreational activities (Jones, 1953; Denker, 1960; Rapaport, 1963). Through these self-organized and administered groups, patients begin to gain a sense of citizenship and social responsibility, achieve a renewed sense of self-respect, acquire a modicum of interpersonal skills and learn to assume a participant role in an environment that parallels the give-and-take interactions of normal community life. Although group ventures such as these can prove a strain upon the fragile controls of certain patients, for the greater number it furnishes an opportunity to strengthen their self-controls and regain the perspective of shared living that was lost during earlier phases of their illness.

Inpatient milieu therapy is a relatively recent innovation (there are few studies concerning its efficacy), but there can be little question that it has opened the door to methods of rehabilitating large numbers of patients who cannot be handled by more conventional and formal techniques of therapy. At the very least, programs of active stimulation and patient participation should ensure that fewer patients than heretofore will "regress" into the vicious circle of self-perpetuating invalidism and social incompetence.

# SUPPORTIVE THERAPY

Whereas the procedures of environmental management focus on the situational context of the patient, seeking to exploit the persons and activities surrounding his daily life for therapeutic purposes, the procedures of supportive therapy focus directly on the patient himself. In contrast to other individual treatment approaches, however, supportive therapy does not seek to make fundamental changes in the patient's premorbid attitudes and strategies, but to strengthen these patterns so that he can again function as he did prior to his current disorder.

Supportive procedures are employed either as the principal mode of therapy or as adjuncts to other treatment methods. In his monumental text on psychotherapy, Wolberg (1967) outlines the chief indications of the supportive approach, distinguishing between principal and adjunctive uses; we will summarize several of his recommendations in the following paragraphs.

As the *principal* form of treatment, supportive therapy is especially well-suited for the following categories:

1. Basically "normal" persons who have succumbed temporarily to a transient situational reaction. A brief period of therapeutic intervention, designed to alleviate disturbing symptoms and to shore up formerly adequate behaviors and attitudes, may suffice to bring the patient to his habitual level of equilibrium and stability.

2. Patients whose current outlook and actions constitute a serious threat to themselves and others. As a necessary expedient, supportive measures may serve to prevent suicidal impulses, calm intense anxieties and panic reactions or deter the acting out of homicidal and other destructive tendencies.

3. Borderline personalities whose stability is perpetually in doubt, and who may be kept from more severe disorders through a long-term therapeutic relationship. In these ongoing treatments, patients are so guided as to avoid and "ride through" recurring conflicts and tensions that might otherwise precipitate psychotic episodes.

As *adjuncts* to other forms of therapy, supportive measures may be fruitfully employed to strengthen the patient's coping resources during periods of marked or unanticipated anxiety or depression. During these exigencies, supportive approaches may revive the patient's flagging hopes, bolster his coping strategies and ameliorate tensions that can seriously disrupt the normal progress of treatment.

Central to the varied techniques which comprise supportive therapy is the patient's acceptance of the therapist's "benevolent authority," as Wolberg puts it. The therapist must maintain a sympathetic but firm attitude, exhibiting a tolerance of the patient's deviance, yet inspiring strength through the force of his authority and his forthright honesty. As a consequence, the patient will be inclined to trust the therapist's judgments and view him as an ally worthy of identification and respect. With this as a foundation, the therapist may achieve the ends he seeks.

Supportive therapy may be separated into three basic procedures: *ventilation, reassurance* and *persuasion*. These may be employed separately, concurrently or sequentially. Let us examine each.

## VENTILATION

People often gain a measure of emotional relief by simply unburdening their woes to a sympathetic listener; the therapeutic value of much of what a friendly physician or minister achieves is obtained by the expedient of listening without reproval as the troubled person "gets things off his chest."

Emotional ventilation comprises an important element of supportive therapy. Distressing ideas and impulses often cannot be banished from one's thoughts, and keep cropping up to disrupt one's daily life. To relieve the pressure of these "bottled up" emotions, the patient is encouraged to share his thoughts with the therapist and to feel free to express the pent-up tensions they generate. He is assured that everyone experiences discomfiting impulses and ideas, and that he can feel confident that they will be accepted and understood by the therapist without reproach. It is hoped that exposure of these suppressed conflicts and urges will not only serve to decrease tension, but also assist the patient in learning to accept them and develop a more constructive approach to their solution. Wolberg describes the benefits of ventilation in this succinct statement (1967):

> The ability to share his troubles with a sympathetic and understanding person robs them of their frightening quality. In addition, the patient may find that his judgment as to the viciousness of his experiences is distorted. The very act of translating inner feelings into words helps restore mastery. The fact that he has not been rejected by the therapist, even though he has revealed shortcomings, encourages him to re-examine himself.

Discussion of the patient's problem is continued until he no longer reacts emotionally to it. Repeated verbalization of unpleasant and disagreeable attitudes and experiences permits him to face his past fears and conflicts with diminished turmoil.

Where therapeutic goals are limited to the restitution of equilibrium without changes in premorbid behavior and personality, the patient is *not* urged to reveal more than he himself is inclined to do. Although the patient is encouraged to express whatever he desires, the therapist refrains from probing and uncovering repressed emotions and thoughts that can aggravate the very discomforts he is seeking to relieve.

## REASSURANCE

The mere act of participating in therapy is a form of implicit reassurance that all is not hopeless, that there is someone knowledgeable and understanding who can be turned to for solace and strength in moments of anxiety and despondency.

Supportive therapists provide reassurance in more direct ways by pointing out how baseless are the patient's beliefs and feelings, such as his unwarranted apprehensions of "going insane," and how unjust he has been in condemning himself for minor social digressions or excesses. He diverts the patient's preoccupations with past regrets, has him recall his more commendable achievements and directs his attentions to potentially constructive and self-enhancing activities in the present.

Although reassurance is part and parcel of every therapeutic encounter, its indiscriminate use can only backfire. A consistent Pollyanna-like approach to therapy will ultimately raise questions in the patient's mind as to his therapist's grasp and appreciation of the problems he faces; even worse, it may lead the patient to doubt his therapist's sincerity or judgment. On the other hand, should the patient learn to accept these superficial pacifications, he may become unduly dependent on them and be unwilling to face reality or to examine genuine solutions to his problems. Inevitably, he will be in for rude shocks when objective diffi-

culties and personal inadequacies simply cannot be "reassured" away.

## PERSUASION

In this supportive technique the therapist seeks to convince the patient that he, the patient, possesses within him the will and the wherewithal to reorient his pathological attitudes and behaviors. By dint of his authority and by the use of subtle ploys, the therapist enjoins the patient to "get hold of himself" and reject the irrational assumptions and habits which consistently disrupt his life. By appealing to the patient's reason and "common sense," he is led to see the logic for abandoning his deviant ways, developing a fresh outlook on life and rebuilding a sense of self-esteem. Concrete suggestions are made to aid the patient in redirecting his goals, dissipating his "worry habits," mastering his muddled thoughts, assuming responsibilities with confidence and authority and facing adversity with an objective attitude. By the sheer force of the therapist's convictions and the picture of self-assurance and firm resolve which he paints, the patient is inspired to see the virtues and rewards of a poised and outgoing style of life and to exhibit a high self-regard; hopefully others will view him in the same way.

Persuasive measures often reap immediate benefits in that they strengthen the patient's self-confidence and brace his weakened coping defenses. But not all patients possess the means for reorienting themselves successfully or the competence to master their distraught emotions effectively; moreover, for a variety of both conscious and unconscious reasons, many will resist the therapist's facile prescriptions. Although persuasion can serve as a fruitful if temporary expedient for well-integrated personalities, the probability is small that its benefits can long be sustained even in these cases, or that mere exhortation can make any inroads with patients who suffer severe forms of pathology. As with reassurance, persuasion often backfires; thus, patients may lose their "faith" in all types of psychotherapy should the exhortations of their therapist come to naught.

# BEHAVIOR MODIFICATION APPROACHES

With the exception of a few scattered pioneers, "behavior modification" therapy has risen to the status of a major treatment alternative only in the last ten years. There are differences in theory and technique among adherents of this

approach, but they share certain important beliefs in common, a few of which will be noted here by way of an introduction.

*First,* the data emphasized by behaviorists differentiate them from other therapeutic "schools."

Behaviorists consider objectively observable actions and events to be the primary subject matter of psychological science; they eschew, where possible, all reference to subjective or unconscious processes which play a central role in phenomenologically and intrapsychically oriented therapies.

*Second,* behaviorists argue that the procedures of therapy should consist of the systematic application of experimentally derived and corroborated principles. They avoid "loosely formulated" techniques derived from unverifiable clinical observations which they contend typify the methodology of other treatment approaches.

*Third,* despite certain theoretical differences, behavior therapists subscribe in common to the concepts and methods of learning research. This orientation reflects both their desire to adhere to "scientific" principles and their belief that psychopathology is learned behavior that is viewed to be socially maladaptive or deficient. According to this view, whatever has been learned, adaptive or maladaptive, can be "unlearned" by the therapeutic application of the same principles and conditions that led to its initial acquisition.

*Fourth,* to achieve the goals of treatment, the therapist must first specify both the maladaptive behaviors (overt symptoms) and the environmental conditions (stimuli and reinforcements) that sustain them. Once these have been identified, the therapist can arrange a program of "learning" procedures tailored specifically to the elimination of the maladaptive responses and to the institution of more adaptive ones.

## HISTORICAL REVIEW

Pavlov and Thorndike discovered the principles of classical conditioning and trial and error reward learning in the early years of this century, but the value of these principles as tools for understanding and modifying psychopathology was only slowly recognized. Not until the early 1920's were efforts made to demonstrate conditioning procedures in the acquisition of pathological behaviors (Watson and Rayner, 1920; Bagby, 1922; Smith and Guthrie, 1922). Soon thereafter, in 1924, behavior principles were first applied to treatment. Two publications of that year signaled the beginning of the behavior modification approach: the research of Mary Cover Jones and the theoretical notions of William Burnham.

Jones (1924) tried two ways of extinguishing a child's fear of white furry animals. The child, a two and a half year old dubbed Little Peter, was seen to exhibit less fear when he observed other children calmly handling a white

rat. By introducing several such "fearless" children as models for Peter to observe, Jones was the first to demonstrate empirically the contemporary behavior modification technique of "model imitation." In another study with Peter, Jones progressively exposed the child to a formerly feared white rabbit by a series of graduated steps that brought him into closer and closer contact with the animal; in due course, Peter was able to fondle the rabbit calmly. By following a course of progressive "toleration" of what previously was anxiety-producing, Jones' technique was the forerunner of the now well-established behavioral procedure termed "desensitization."

Burnham (1924) preceded much of the work of Miller and Dollard (1950) by "translating" psychoanalysis into learning concepts such as stimulus and reinforcement; similarly, he proposed a number of "counterconditioning" procedures which anticipated the techniques of Wolpe (1958).

By the late 1930's, behavior theories and research had taken firm root. Tolman, Guthrie, Hull and Skinner provided a rich fund of knowledge concerning the principles and processes of learning. Pavlov's early studies of experimentally induced conflict "neuroses" (1927) had stimulated numerous investigators such as Liddell, Gantt and Maier to explore how pathological behaviors can be conditioned. In 1943, Masserman reported the first of a long series of animal studies employing behavioral procedures to overcome experimentally produced pathologies. Several years earlier, Max (1935) paired an electric shock with evocative stimuli as a method to extinguish homosexual thoughts, and Mowrer and Mowrer (1938) utilized a similar procedure to control night time enuresis. It was during the same decade that Dunlap (1932) proposed a habit extinction procedure termed "negative practice," a precursor of modern counterconditioning techniques.

Many academic "learning" psychologists were called upon to perform "clinical" psychological services during World War II. Upon their return to academia, several sought to bridge these two fields and provided thereby a fresh momentum to the behavioral movement. It was hoped that learning principles might furnish a firm scientific basis for the nebulous concepts of therapy and at the same time that clinical processes might provide a new source of data to enrich the rather narrow sphere within which learning research had long been confined.

The first of these "integrative" efforts (Shaw, 1946; Shoben, 1948; Dollard and Miller, 1950) limited themselves to translating therapeutic processes into the language of learning theory. Although these writings suggested a new way of conceptualizing and explaining traditional forms of therapy, they suggested no new techniques as to how therapy might be executed.

During the late 1950's, stimulated largely by the provocative writings of Skinner (1953), Wolpe (1958) and Eysenck (1959), the coalescence of learning and psychotherapy took a new turn. Instead of merely restating accepted forms of treatment in the vernacular of learning concepts, investigators began to utilize principles that were derived first in behavioral learning research to create entirely new forms of therapy. It is these new approaches, based on the direct application of experimental learning principles, that comprise the treatment methods to be discussed in this section.

Before describing the major variants of behavior modification therapy, let us briefly summarize the general rationale of these approaches, outline their typical sequence of treatment planning and review the logic for the format of classifying techniques that we will follow.

## RATIONALE

As was noted earlier in this section, behavior therapists share a number of beliefs. They consider overt actions and observable events to be the most fruitful data for their concepts and treatment variables. Therapy, to them, consists of the systematic application of experimentally corroborated learning principles. Psychopathology is viewed to be deficiently learned or maladaptively learned behaviors which can be unlearned or relearned in accord with the same principles by which they were first acquired.

Behaviorists assert that nonbehavioral therapists unwittingly apply learning principles in their treatment procedure. Nonbehavioral therapists formulate their methods in elaborate conceptual systems and engage in circuitous maneuvers, such as providing interpretations and promoting the release of repressed emotions, but the crucial element in their technique, according to behaviorists, is the selective if inadvertent manner in which they reinforce the patient's adaptive behaviors and extinguish those which are maladaptive. Behaviorists contend that the benefits of psychological treatment will be maximized if therapists knowingly apply these learning principles in a planned and systematic fashion.

Accordingly, behavior therapists take great care to unburden themselves of all of the more traditional therapeutic activities considered to be peripheral to effective treatment. They make no effort to trace and unravel the developmental roots of the patient's problem, considering this historical analysis to be an unnecessary diversion from the task at hand. Similarly, they do not "waste their time" exploring unconscious conflicts or facilitating patient insights since these are considered nonproductive of therapeutic gain. In short, they divest themselves of all the superfluous and time-consuming paraphernalia associated with other treatment procedures, and concentrate exclusively on those basic learning principles which are proved to be scientific and efficacious.

Behaviorists contend further that other therapeutic approaches are method-oriented rather than problem-oriented. Nonbehaviorists are seen to proceed in a uniform fashion regardless of the particular character of the patient's difficulty, utilizing the same "psychoanalytic" or "client-centered" procedure with all forms and varieties of pathology. In contrast, they claim that behavioral approaches are flexible and problem-oriented. There is no "fixed" technique in behavior therapy; rather, the therapist identifies the distinguishing elements of each problem and then fashions a procedure designed specifically to effect changes in just that problem.

## TREATMENT PLANNING AND PROCEDURE

As was just noted, behavior therapists arrange their methods in accord with the presenting problem, limiting and focusing their attention to those features only. For example, if the patient complains of a phobia, procedures are designed to eliminate just that symptom, and therapy is completed when it has been removed.

The planning and procedures of behavior modification typically take the following course:

*Explicit Specification of Pathological Behaviors.* Although clinical assessments usually are limited to patient self-reports with their characteristically vague and global descriptions, efforts are made to translate these verbal generalities into their precise behavioral correlates. Thus, a general phrase such as "I'm just tense much of the time" is carefully probed until it yields more specific and tangible features such as "chest tightness," "cold, clammy hands," "fear of fainting" and so on.

*Explicit Specification of Stimulus Conditions Which Provoke and Reinforce Pathological Behaviors.* In a similar manner efforts are made to identify precisely the antecedent circumstances that precipitate the disturbed behaviors and the consequent reinforcements that sustain them or cause them to persist.

*Explicit Formulation of Treatment Goals and Procedures.* Following these assessments the therapist specifies which behaviors and stimulus conditions should and can be altered, and then designs a program of systematic procedures to achieve these well-defined objectives.

## CLASSIFICATION

Behavior therapy is a spirited and vital new direction in psychological treatment that has caught the interest of thousands of younger psychologists and psychiatrists; this recent and rapid growth continues unabated right into the present. Unfortunately, the proliferation of new methods makes it difficult to formulate a simple and durable classification taxonomy. Although numerous schemas have been devised in the past ten years (Eysenck, 1960; Bandura, 1961; Rachman, 1963; Grossberg, 1964; Franks, 1964; Ullmann and Krasner, 1965; Mowrer, 1966; Kanfer and Phillips, 1966; Wolberg, 1967; Shlien, 1968; Thomas, 1968), none has taken hold as *the* way to organize this growing body of treatment techniques.

Part of the difficulty of classification stems from the variety of learning theories to which behavior therapists subscribe; thus, distinctions may be drawn between methods that stress the role of contiguity learning or reinforcement learning or learning by imitation.

Perhaps the most common basis for separating procedures depends on whether they follow the paradigm of classical (respondent) conditioning or instrumental (operant) conditioning. Other systematists, however, differentiate techniques that deal with disrupting stimulus events from those that focus on the maladaptive response. Each schema possesses certain merits, as well as its share of difficulties.

In the following sections we will follow a classificatory format that emphasizes the primary *objectives* of therapeutic intervention. The *first* set of approaches, termed "behavior elimination methods," consists of procedures that are limited to but especially well-suited for the task of weakening existent pathological responses. The *second* group, labeled "behavior formation techniques," includes procedures that can fulfill several goals; they can be employed not only to eliminate pathological behaviors, but also to strengthen existent adaptive responses and acquire entirely new adaptive ones. Although this two-fold division is not without overlap, it possesses the merit of stressing the utility of methods as instruments for achieving the two primary objectives of behavior modification—the elimination of maladaptive behaviors and the formation or strengthening of adaptive ones.

# METHODS OF BEHAVIOR ELIMINATION

The most expedient and direct procedures for eliminating or overcoming maladaptive responses have been termed "counterconditioning" and "extinction." Let us review some of the techniques classed under these labels.

## COUNTERCONDITIONING METHODS

The rationale of counterconditioning is based on the fact that incompatible responses cannot coexist; for example, you can walk forward or backward, but you cannot do both at the same time. Translating this into therapeutic terms, if a patient exhibits a maladaptive feeling or behavior in response to certain stimuli, that response can be neutralized or blocked by evoking responses that are antithetical to it; for example, if a particular stimulus habitually elicited an anxiety response in a patient, the therapist may train the patient to associate an incompatible response to that stimulus, such as intense pleasure or deep relaxation, in the hope of precluding or counteracting anxiety.

Counterconditioning methods have been employed to achieve two goals, eliminating feelings and thoughts, such as anxiety or fear, which inhibit desirable and adaptive behaviors; and eliminating personally objectionable or socially unacceptable behaviors, such as compulsive rituals or alcoholism. To countercondition an emotion that inhibits an adaptive response, the technique of "desensitization" may fruitfully be applied; to countercondition a maladaptive response itself, methods of "aversive learning" can be used. Let us examine both procedures.

### Desensitization

This technique, most fully developed by Joseph Wolpe (1958), seeks to counteract the discomforting and inhibitory effects of fear-producing stimuli by interposing and associating a relaxation response to these stimuli; hopefully, by repeated counterconditioning, the fear response will be replaced by its antagonist, relaxation. Not only are the discomforts of fear eliminated thereby, but the patient may now be free to

### Table 15-1   Typical Desensitization Hierarchies*

| FEAR OF DEATH | FEAR OF PHYSICAL SYMPTOMS |
|---|---|
| a. Seeing first husband in his coffin | a. Irregular heartbeat |
| b. Attending a burial | b. Shooting chest pains |
| c. Seeing a burial assemblage from afar | c. Pains in left shoulder and back |
| d. Reading an obituary notice of a young person dying of heart attack | d. Pain in top of head |
| e. Driving past a cemetery | e. Buzzing in ears |
| f. Seeing a funeral | f. Tremor in hands |
| g. Passing a funeral home | g. Numbness or pain in fingertips |
| h. Reading an obituary notice of an old person | h. Difficulty in breathing after exertion |
| i. Being inside a hospital | i. Pain in left hand (old injury) |
| j. Seeing a hospital | |
| k. Seeing an ambulance | |

\* From Wolpe (1958)

acquire adaptive responses that had previously been blocked.

Wolpe's procedure follows a precise and well-planned sequence.

*First,* on the basis of interviews and psychological tests, stimulus events that evoke marked emotional discomforts are identified. These events are grouped and ranked into one or more "hierarchies" (a graded list with a common theme ranging from the least to the most disturbing event). It is Wolpe's contention, shared by other behavior therapists, that the typical, vague and inarticulate complaints of patients must and can be differentiated into a set of discriminable responses (e.g., types of fears, fears of varying intensity and so on) to specific stimulus antecedents (e.g., particular scenes, thoughts and memories). On the basis of such discriminations, lists comprising separate classes of fears, differentiated further in terms of intensity, are constructed. Table 15-1 illustrates two fear "hierarchies" devised for a housewife concerned with death and physical illness. The items in each list progress upward from the least to the most distressing.

In the *second* phase of desensitization training, the patient is taught deep muscle relaxation in accord with Jacobson's (1938) progressive body relaxation technique; occasionally, hypnosis or drugs are employed to facilitate a calm state. This period of training proceeds for several sessions until the patient is able to achieve a state of total relaxation rapidly and on his own.

The *third* and central treatment phase consists of pairing the relaxed state with each of the anxiety-producing stimuli on the hierarchy list. This is accomplished by starting with the lowest ranking, that is, the least discomforting item.

While the patient feels calm and relaxed, he is asked to imagine a vivid and life-like representation of the stimulus event. Should the patient experience even the slightest degree of anxiety at this time, he signals the therapist who then instructs him to discontinue the image until the relaxed state is regained. When the patient can visualize the stimulus image without experiencing discomfort, the entire sequence of relaxation and imagination is repeated with the next and slightly more disturbing stimulus item from the hierarchy. The procedure continues for as many sessions as necessary until the most distressing stimulus from the list can be visualized calmly.

The logic of Wolpe's counterconditioning procedure is simple and straightforward: relaxation is incompatible with fear; by arranging a properly graded sequence, the previously conditioned association between each stimulus item and the response of fear is eliminated. Wolpe claims with some justification (see "evaluation" section) that the relaxed attitude acquired in the consulting room generalizes to real-life situations, that is, the patient is able to face the actual, previously feared environmental event without reacting as he had in the past.

Although Wolpe considers his method to be a behavioral approach, it should be noted that his desensitization technique deals essentially with phenomenological processes. His procedure employs the data of symbolic imagination, not overt behavior. It would be more correct, therefore, to classify his therapeutic technique among the "cognitive learning" procedures, a subdivision of the "phenomenological approaches." The status of Wolpe's formulations as a behavioral approach may be seriously questioned also on the grounds of his partial allegiance to a neurological etiology, a view that contrasts sharply with the "pure behaviorism" of Skinner and his disciples. Nevertheless, tradition, brief though it has been in this field, assigns Wolpe's methods to the behavior classification.

### Aversive Learning

Whereas desensitization attempts to eliminate responses (e.g., fear) that inhibit desirable behaviors (e.g., facing and solving previously feared situations), aversive learning seeks only to eliminate undesirable responses (e.g., aggressive sexual acts). This distinction may be seen more clearly by the fact that desensitization achieves its aims by counterconditioning an *unpleasant* response (fear) with a pleasant one (relaxation); in contrast, aversive learning counterconditions a formerly *pleasant* response (drinking or sexual excitement) with an unpleasant one (nausea or pain).

The classic example of aversion therapy is the use of nauseant drugs in the treatment of alcoholism (Lemere and Voegtlin, 1950). In this procedure, the patient first ingests the drug. Then,

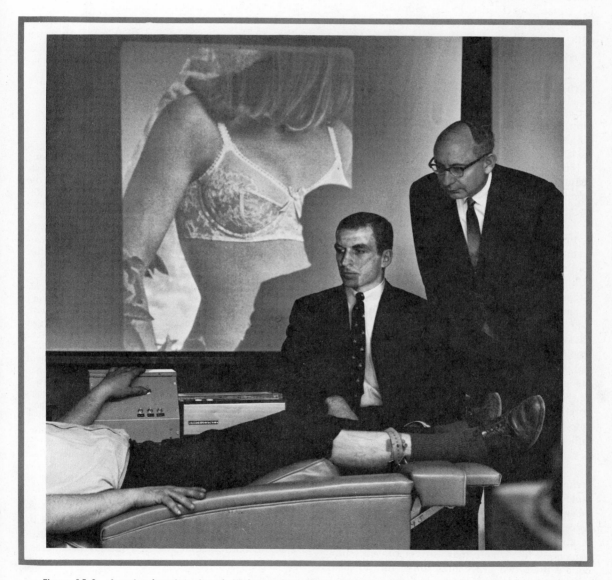

Figure 15-2 Aversive learning. Joseph Wolpe, right, and an associate, administer electric shocks to a homosexual man through an electrode strapped to his calf. When a nude male figure is on the screen, the shocks begin; when a female figure is projected, they cease. The idea is that the homosexual stimulus will be associated with, and eventually inhibited by, the pain. (New York Times Magazine Section, June 4, 1967, © Bernie Cleff.)

moments prior to the onset of nausea, he is given a drink of liquor. Since the drink immediately precedes the sickening nausea and vomiting, the patient learns over a number of such sessions to associate drinking with an unpleasant rather than a pleasant experience.

Aversive procedures have been utilized to combat numerous maladaptive habits. For example, male homosexuals have been given a moderately painful shock in conjunction with photographs of nude men; the shock is terminated when a picture of a nude woman replaces that of a man (see Figure 15-2). Hopefully, the patient learns not only to associate feelings of pain with homosexuality, but to view heterosexuality as a comforting alternative.

## EXTINCTION METHODS

Counterconditioning procedures eliminate inhibitory emotions and maladaptive behaviors indirectly, that is, they do not attack the response itself, but interpose an incompatible response to a formerly provocative stimulus. Extinction procedures, in contrast, work directly on the disruptive behavior itself, that is, without employing an antithetical response.

There is a parallel between the two major forms of extinction and the two methods of counterconditioning. "Implosive therapy" is akin to desensitization in that it has as its primary utility the elimination of responses that inhibit adaptive behaviors. "Reinforcement withdrawal" is similar to aversive learning in that it is most useful in eliminating socially undesirable behaviors. A forerunner of both methods was known as "negative practice" (Dunlap, 1932), a procedure in which the patient voluntarily produced the unacceptable response, time and again, until he "got tired of it" or began to think it was "pretty silly" or "stupid"; negative practice was employed most frequently in extinguishing speech difficulties and other motor disturbances, such as tics.

Both implosive and reinforcement withdrawal techniques rest on the well-known learning principle that the strength of a response decreases when it fails to be followed by its expected reinforcement. The manner in which this principle is applied, however, and the divergent types of behaviors for which they are employed, differentiate these two procedures sufficiently to justify separating them.

### Implosive Therapy

This technique is similar to desensitization in that it has as its goal the elimination of inhibitory responses such as fear and anxiety. The procedural steps of these two methods are quite alike also in that the patient's most disturbing thoughts and feelings are identified, and he is asked to imagine them during treatment sessions. In contrast to desensitization, however, the innovator of the implosive technique, Stampfl (London, 1964; Stampfl and Levis, 1967), introduces the *most* anxiety-arousing event immediately, seeking thereby to frighten the patient overwhelmingly rather than to calm and relax him. Stampfl argues that by flooding the patient's imagination with the very worst of his fears, *in a setting in which no actual harm does occur,* the patient will gradually learn that his fears are unfounded (unreinforced) since nothing really detrimental happens to him. The following outlines a typical sequence in the extinction of a phobia through implosive methods.

### THERAPY EXCERPT 1
#### Implosive Therapy

A female college student of 19 with a lifelong fear of spiders was introduced to two therapists and given a general idea in her first session of the purpose and procedure of implosive therapy. Returning a few days later for her second session, she was asked to close her eyes and imagine herself in her room alone, suddenly confronted with a spider on her window curtain. Following that, one of the therapists suggested that she visualize seeing several spiders surging rapidly out of a hole in the wall next to the window . . . .

Hundreds of them begin to creep over her furniture, around the walls and up the ceiling. She can't escape them—the door is bolted and covered with menacing spiders. One by one, the spiders crawl toward her. The first spider, a particularly large creature, creeps onto her leg—another suddenly lands on her head. Then five, 20, 50, a 100 of them creep all over her—into her eyes, nostrils, up her dress, into her mouth—fat, hairy, monstrous spiders swarming on her body, into her clothes, down her throat, into her vagina, anus, intestines, stomach . . . .

Needless to say, the patient is extremely tense, at her wit's end. Then, suddenly, the patient is "awakened" from her nightmarish vision. The spiders are gone—she's "all right"—nothing, in fact, has happened to her.

Two approaches as contrasting as implosive and desensitization therapy for the same types of problems would be hard to conceive, yet adherents of both methods report substantial success in achieving their common goals.

### Reinforcement Withdrawal

Rather than forcing the patient to be flooded and overwhelmed by his disturbing thoughts and feelings as in implosive therapy, the reinforcement withdrawal tactic allows the undesirable behavior to dissipate naturally, simply by failing to provide the reinforcements it previously evoked. In further contrast to implosive therapy, in which the therapist seeks to overcome *inhibiting* responses such as fear, reinforcement withdrawal is most suitable for combating behaviors that *should be inhibited,* such as aggression and compulsive acts. To illustrate, Walton (1960) was able to extinguish a woman's severe habit of scratching her skin by advising her family to refrain from providing sympathy and attention in conjunction with her ailment; withdrawal of these positive reinforcements led to a rapid cessation of the habit. In another study, Williams (1959) achieved the control of bedtime tantrum behavior in a child by advising his parents to pay no attention to him as he cried and raged; by the eighth night, the youngster not only failed to whimper, but even smiled as he quietly went to bed.

## METHODS OF BEHAVIOR FORMATION

Until recently, most types of therapy had as their principal goal the elimination of faulty attitudes, feelings and behaviors. It was argued or assumed implicitly that when these symptoms were removed the patient would be "free" to utilize or develop more adaptive habits. Such constructive consequences do follow for many patients, but not all. Many lack the means for acquiring new adaptive habits, e.g., autistic children or other patients whose past experiences may not have supplied them with a repertoire of healthy behaviors that will flourish, so to speak, when their inhibiting fears and maladaptive responses are removed.

The notion of "forming" new constructive behaviors by direct procedures is an important departure from more traditional therapeutic methods. Although many therapies have "positive growth" as a desired aim, few are designed to achieve this goal explicitly and in a systematically planned fashion.

Our attention will turn in this section to two behavioral methods employed to achieve the goal of response "formation": *selective positive reinforcement* and *model imitation.* Although acquisition and strengthening of adaptive behaviors are the distinguishing objectives of these procedures, both may be used to eliminate maladaptive responses as well.

## SELECTIVE POSITIVE REINFORCEMENT

As was discussed earlier, "pure" behaviorists eschew reference to subjective or internal mediating processes; to them, the patient's actions are best conceived as a product *not* of intrapsychic conflicts or phenomenological attitudes but of observable environmental conditions. Accordingly, changes in behavior must be achieved by manipulating external events. Central to these manipulations are reinforcements, that is, environmental rewards and punishments. By a judicious arrangement of reinforcing consequences, behaviors can be either strengthened or weakened.

The most fully developed schema based on the selective reinforcement model is operant conditioning, a technique devised by B. F. Skinner (1938) and his many associates and disciples (e.g., Ferster, 1958, 1964; Ayllon and Michael, 1959; Bachrach et al., 1965). Briefly, operant methods provide rewards when the patient exhibits the desired behavior and withhold them when undesired responses occur. Through this selective application of positive reinforcement, present adaptive behaviors are fortified, and through sequences of "successive approximation" and "shaping," new adaptive responses are built into the patient's behavioral repertoire.

The utility of this procedure as a means of restoring social competence and self-reliance among decompensated patients has been demonstrated in a number of hospital studies. King et al. (1960), for example, reinforced at first simple motor acts in a group of withdrawn "schizophrenics"; gradually, they built these simple responses into more complicated cooperative and communicative behaviors by making the receipt of reinforcement contingent on adequate performance. In another study, Ferster (1961) set out to overcome one of the major problems of autistic children—the lack of variety of their behavioral repertoire (many of these youngsters spend their days engaged in the same repetitive act such as rocking or fondling a particular toy). To enlarge and diversify the range of their behaviors, Ferster arranged a selective reinforcement sequence in which the children received rewards only upon the performance of increasingly complex and varied activities which they ultimately did. Along similar lines, Ayllon and Azrin (1965) were able to condition self-care and productive work among hospitalized psychotics by making the receipt of desired comforts and privileges contingent on the execution of these behaviors. The investigators noted, as part of their research design, that these same patients quickly abandoned their responsi-

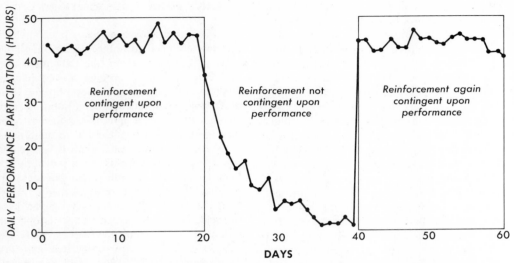

Figure 15-3    Control of rehabilitative activities as a function of selective reinforcement. (After Ayllon, T., and Azrin, N. H.: The measurement and reinforcement of behavior of psychotics. J. Exper. Anal. Behav., 8:357–383, 1965.)

bilities and lapsed into their habitual lethargy and invalidism when these same rewards were made available to them regardless of their performance. Adaptive and productive behaviors were reacquired quickly when special privileges once more were made dependent on self-care and productive performance (see Figure 15-3).

## MODEL IMITATION

According to Bandura (1962, 1965), the primary exponent of behavior modification through imitative modeling, selective positive reinforcement is an exceedingly inefficient method for promoting the acquisition of *new* adaptive learnings. Effective though operant procedures may be for strengthening and building upon responses that *already exist* in the patient's behavioral repertoire, they demand extremely ingenious and time-consuming manipulations to generate new response patterns. Contributing to this difficulty is the fact that the patient must perform the desired response or some close approximation of it *before* the therapist can apply the appropriate reinforcement. Where the sought for response is highly complex (e.g., speaking meaningful sentences), the probability is likely to be zero that it will be spontaneously emitted. Approximations of complicated responses may be achieved by an intricate chain of reinforced steps, but this sequence is bound to be both laborious and prolonged. Rather than struggle through this tiresome and at best unreliable procedure, the task of forming *new* responses can be abbreviated and accelerated by arranging conditions in which the

patient simply observes and imitates a model performing the desired act. The sheer simplicity of the modeling procedure, Bandura argues, justifies its use in preference to operant methods.

Modeling sequences are designed most often in combination with reinforcement; thus, in a typical procedure, the patient will obtain a reward when he imitates an act performed by a model. To illustrate, Lovaas et al. (1966, 1968) taught "mute" schizophrenic children to talk by rewarding only those vocalizations which duplicated *sounds* articulated first by the therapist. Gradually, rewards were provided only in response to *words* and then to *phrases* modeled by the therapist; ultimately, it was possible to teach the *meaning* of words, as well as a variety of complex communicative skills and social behaviors. Similar effects, generating a wide range of newly acquired responses, have been produced not only with live models, but with models presented through the medium of films. Imitative modeling has also proved efficacious and economical in the elimination of inhibitory (fear) and socially undesirable (aggression) responses (Bandura, Grusec and Menlove, 1967; Chittenden, 1942).

## *EVALUATION*

Behavior modification techniques can be analyzed in accord with several of the principal dimensions that distinguish alternative therapies; let us briefly examine these.

The *data focus* of behavior methods, needless to say, is behavioral, although it should be noted again that several of these procedures are really phenomenological in focus (e.g., Wolpe's "desensitization" method).

Individual patient-therapist relationships are the *settings* within which behavior treatment is carried out most often. Not uncommonly, however, these procedures are part of institutional milieu programs. Demonstrations of behavior techniques in small group interactions have also been reported.

There is some question as to whether the patient or the therapist selects the *goals* in behavior treatment. The patient's complaints are primary, but the therapist plays an indirect role in that he accepts these complaints, limiting the goals of treatment to their resolution and nothing more. Behaviorists are flexible, however, as to what goals should be pursued; they focus on the elimination of clinical symptoms and the formation of adaptive alternatives.

The feature that most clearly distinguishes behavior therapies from other approaches is their commitment to an action-suppressive *process*. Behaviorists consider emotional ventilation and insight, the bedrocks of other schools of therapy, to be of dubious value; not only are these two procedures viewed as time-consuming digressions, but they are often thought to be counterproductive, that is, to strengthen rather than weaken maladaptive behaviors (Kahn, 1960; Bandura, 1965). As behaviorists see it, the task of therapy is to achieve as directly as possible changes in real-life *action*, not greater self-understanding.

Behaviorists point to a number of *advantages* inherent in their approach.

*First,* they argue that the principles which guide their methods are anchored to "scientific" laboratory data and can be tested and revised, therefore, in an objective and systematic fashion. Moreover, the correspondence between behavior procedures and basic research will enable therapists of this persuasion to translate new laboratory data into novel treatment approaches, facilitating, thereby, the development of alternative empirically grounded techniques.

*Second,* since behaviorists focus their efforts on clearly delimited and carefully defined symptom problems, they will soon accumulate a body of quantitative data concerning the efficacy of their approach, not "in general," but with specific and identifiable syndromes. These data can then be used as base lines against which alternative treatment techniques can be compared.

*Third,* if behavioral methods can be shown to be of equal or superior efficacy to other treatment approaches, their benefits will be two-fold since they achieve their results in far fewer sessions. This advantage is especially significant for patients in lower socioeconomic groups who can ill afford the greater expense and time involved in traditional therapies.

*Fourth,* behavior therapy can be carried out by persons who are appreciably less sophisticated psychologically than those who can perform other types of therapy. The need for more therapists in our society is great, and the expediency and economy of employing hospital nurses and attendants, as well as parents, teachers and other auxiliary persons, cannot be readily overlooked.

Nonbehavioral therapists do not accept the contentions of behaviorists. They note numerous *disadvantages* and objections.

*First,* critics assert that behaviorists ennoble themselves by falsely appropriating the prestige of "scientific" learning theories. Not only is their distinctive affinity to principles of learning questioned (other therapists adhere to learning theories as well), but the very existence of established "laws" of learning is doubted. These critics ask whether such dubious laws can be systematically applied to complex therapeutic processes when their applicability to simple situations is still a matter of dispute. To "prove" their point, they note that behavior therapists devise different forms of therapy from the same learning theory, and that therapists adhering to different theories often utilize similar techniques (Colby, 1964; Breger and McGaugh, 1965; Keisler, 1966; Wolberg, 1967).

*Second,* questions are raised as to whether the sparse language of learning theories—stimuli, conditioning, response and reinforcement—is a sufficiently sensitive conceptual instrument for dealing with the subtle and complex processes of psychological treatment. Although learning and environmental events are central to an understanding of therapeutic interactions, "forcing" these processes into the meager verbal formulations of behavior theories will blunt rather than sharpen the clinician's powers of observation and analysis (White, 1964).

*Third,* it is noted that the actual processes of behavior therapy are far from "pure" applications of learning principles. Most behavior modification procedures include elements that are incidental to the theoretically formulated plan of therapy (Breger and McGaugh, 1965). For example, in desensitization, is therapeutic gain entirely a function of counterconditioning learning or is it at least in part attributable to the therapist's personality and enthusiasm and his powers of suggestion?

The *fourth,* and perhaps the most vigorously

argued criticism of behavior therapy, contends that these procedures deal only with superficial and narrowly defined symptoms; they ignore not only the "underlying causes" of overt symptoms, but many important although difficult to define syndromes such as "existential anxiety," "identity crises" and "personality patterns." Since deeper and more pervasive difficulties are left untouched, behavior therapy is considered a technique of markedly limited utility. Moreover, it is felt that new symptoms, perhaps different in form and content than those removed by behavior therapy, will inevitably appear since their underlying functions have not been resolved. In short, the ostensive benefits of behavior methods are considered to be either limited, temporary or illusory.

A feverish debate over the advantages and disadvantages of behavior approaches continues to rage in professional journals (Breger and McGaugh, 1965; Rachman and Eysenck, 1966), shedding as the old saying goes more heat than light. Let us next turn, not to theoretical arguments, but to empirical research, reviewing briefly efficacy studies and studies of the essential mode of therapeutic action.

## EFFICACY (OUTCOME STUDIES)

A review of the efficacy of behavior therapy must be brief in a general text such as this. Attention will be limited to three questions: How effective are these procedures? Are therapeutic changes generalized to real life situations? Do beneficial effects endure without generating new difficulties?

**Effectiveness.** Published reports indicate that the clinical effectiveness of behavior procedures is in the region of 75 to 90 per cent, a range strikingly higher than that reported for other treatment approaches; what is impressive additionally is the short period of time required to achieve these results.

Wolpe (1964) cites data on 200 cases, reporting a figure of 89 per cent recovered; Hussain (1964) achieves an even higher success rate in 105 cases; a slightly lower magnitude of improvement was found in a study by Marks and Gelder (1966). General reviews by Grossberg (1964), Eysenck and Rachman (1965), and Bergin (1966) summarize numerous reports, most of them exhibiting approximately the same level of success. Most of these findings were obtained in uncontrolled studies, using ambiguous criteria and rated by therapists who judged their own cases (Gelfand and Hartmann, 1968). Several well-designed studies, however, substantiate these

clinical reports. Lazarus (1961), Lang and Lazovik (1963) and Paul (1966) demonstrated the superiority of *desensitization* methods when compared both to controls and to other forms of therapy. Hogan and Kirchner (1967) and Levis and Carrera (1967) found *implosive therapy* far more effective than no treatment control groups. The impact of *selective positive reinforcement* methods has been unequivocally established in numerous studies (Ullmann and Krasner, 1965). Similarly, there is a growing body of properly controlled studies illustrating the impressive merits of *imitative modeling* procedures (Bandura, 1965; Mischel, 1968).

Behavior approaches have been employed most frequently for the removal of clearly circumscribed symptom disorders (anxiety and phobias) and behavior reactions (enuresis and stuttering); for the most part, they have not been applied to the solution of more diffuse and complex forms of pathology (identity diffusions and basic coping strategies).

Wolpe (1964, 1968) has contended, however, that behavior methods can be and have been employed successfully in complex pathologies. He notes that the cases that behaviorists treat may "look" simple because behavioral concepts and procedures transform the data of psychopathology into more precise and salient terms than do therapies that employ the "obscure" concepts of other theoretical schools. Thus, he asserts that behaviorists extract from the manifold components of psychopathology just those elements that are "essential" to therapy; this clarification process creates the appearance that they have unjustly simplified matters, when in fact they have merely done away with obscurities and unessentials.

To justify this contention, Wolpe set out to show that desensitization works as well with complex as with simple "neuroses." He employed the same procedure in 65 complex cases and 21 simple cases; the rate of improvement was identical, 89 per cent, although the so-called complex cases required a greater number of sessions to achieve their goals. Wolpe's study is not without its faults; his criteria for distinguishing between simple and complex disorders may be questioned, and his data are subject to the usual criticisms of uncontrolled research, especially when conducted and evaluated by a therapist so partisan as Wolpe himself. Even if his particular findings were confirmed by other workers using more adequate research procedures, they could not be assumed to be valid for other forms of behavior therapy; neither would these results be necessarily applicable to other types of pathologies. Suggestive though Wolpe's study may be, much work remains to be done before we can specify the particular types of problems for which each of the various behavior methods is most efficacious.

As matters now stand, counterconditioning and extinction procedures appear to be the treatment of choice in symptom disorders and behavior reactions characterized by inhibitory anxiety, phobia and fear. Selective reinforcement techniques seem especially well suited for strengthening and shaping adaptive behaviors in decompensated or otherwise behaviorally deficient patients. Although research on imitative modeling is still sparse, these techniques may prove to be the most powerful and widely applicable method for both eliminating and forming behavioral responses.

**Generalization.**   Two questions may be raised concerning "generalization." First, do behaviors learned in the consulting room transfer to "real life," and second, does the patient achieve benefits beyond those specifically dealt with in therapy.

Since one of the major theses guiding the behavioral movement is action rather than insight, behaviorists are keenly interested in translating treatment changes into the sphere of "reality." Rachman (1966) has demonstrated this transfer in a *desensitization* procedure dealing with the fear of spiders. Bandura, Grusec and Menlove (1967), employing an *imitative modeling* technique, executed their study in a natural rather than a treatment setting. Among the numerous studies of selective reinforcement that have taken place in "reality," reference may be made to the study by Ayllon and Azrin (1965) mentioned earlier.

No systematic data exist with regard to secondary or additional benefits following direct behavior therapy; what evidence can be found is largely composed of clinical reports. The logic for this form of generalization may be illustrated as follows. The elimination of a behavior reaction such as stuttering may enable the patient to feel at ease in social situations that previously were discomfiting. Since the tension and awkwardness that accompanied his former disability no longer intrude in his personal relationships, he can better enjoy social activities, and ultimately develop greater confidence and skills in this sphere of life.

**Permanence.**   According to critics of the behavioral approach, symptoms are merely surface expressions of underlying conflicts; thus, if one removes the symptom, the effects either will be temporary, that is, eventuate in a return of the original symptom, or lead to the substitution of a new symptom. What evidence is there that such ill effects do occur? The answer is little or none.

For the most part, research data on the permanence of change favor the behavioral view. However, most of the studies reported (Wolpe, 1961; Lazarus, 1963; Rachman, 1967) have been limited to techniques of behavior elimination, primarily desensitization. In addition, with few exceptions (Lang and Lazovik, 1963; Paul, 1967, 1968), follow-up studies have not been carried out in a carefully designed manner, employing proper controls, explicit criteria and objective appraisal methods. Despite these defects, and although negative findings are scattered in the literature (Agras, 1965; Cooper, 1963), the overall record of lasting effects with behavior elimination reflects an impressive figure, and one that is appreciably greater than that achieved with other therapeutic approaches.

According to reviews provided by behaviorists (Eysenck and Rachman, 1965; Rachman, 1967), symptom substitution following behavior therapy is "of minimum importance and occurs very rarely." These reports, needless to say, cannot be regarded as objective; quite different judgments might have been obtained if the criteria and identification of symptom substitution had been made by therapists from other theoretical schools.

In accord with distinctions drawn in early chapters between "symptom disorders" and "behavior reactions," we would expect that behavior therapy would achieve permanent results without symptom substitution among the reactions. In disorders, however, in which the symptom is but a single salient expression of a pervasive personality style, we would expect that its removal would *at least sometimes* be associated with the development of new symptom expressions (Cahoon, 1968). It should be noted, however, that as new symptoms emerge, they, too, may be amenable to behavior elimination methods.

## MODE OF ACTION (PROCESS STUDIES)

Which of the complex of variables comprising behavior therapy are essential to its success and which are irrelevant? Elements such as the therapist's attitudes and personality are considered to be incidental ingredients in behavior treatment. Are these factors, considered to be crucial in many nonbehavioral procedures, irrelevant to the success of behavior therapy? Behavior theorists say yes, supporting their contention with data from three sources.

The first source of support comes from

laboratory learning research. The ease of producing behavior changes with animal and human subjects in experimental settings, in which therapeutic "empathy" and "suggestion" do not play a part, lends credence to the view that they are not essential ingredients of the behavioral therapeutic technique. Of course, laboratory learning studies do not simulate real-life therapy; natural therapeutic interactions contain innumerable "confounding" factors that are never found in experimental research. Laboratory derived principles may be employed in the behavioral treatment situation, but there is no assurance that they operate there in a form as pure as they do in rigorously controlled learning research.

The second source of support comes from laboratory analogues of therapy; these especially arranged conditions are devised to simulate "real" therapy. Only those ingredients which represent the principles of behavior treatment (frequency and sequence of reinforcements and stimulus properties) are included, thereby eliminating all nonbehavioral sources of influence. In this manner, researchers are able to trace the impact of "pure" behavioral principles in a therapeutic-like setting. Studies such as these (Goldstein and Dean, 1966; Stollak, Guerney and Rothberg, 1966) provide considerable support for the role of conditioning and extinction processes in shaping behavioral change. However, as critics of this type of research note, experimental analogue settings with normal subjects are not the same as real patients in real therapy; behaviors modified in these studies do not represent "true" therapeutic events.

It is the third source, controlled research in real treatment settings, that enables behaviorists to speak of their therapeutic "process" with confidence. In these studies, limited, however, largely to desensitization procedures (Lang and Lazovik, 1963; Lang, Lazovik and Reynolds, 1965; Davison, 1965, 1968; Rachman, 1965; Paul, 1966, 1967), several of the ingredients of alternative treatment techniques were carefully isolated and compared. In summary, these investigations have shown that: counterconditioning is the essential vehicle of desensitization treatment; the "therapeutic relationship" is neither a sufficient nor a necessary element in effecting behavior change; suggestibility is not a factor in producing the benefits of desensitization; and short-term procedures designed to explore "causes" or develop insight prove inferior to desensitization as a method for reducing anxiety (see Figure 15-4).

Little research has been done to elucidate the process of behavior therapy, except in the technique of desensitization. Potentially confounding influences in operant conditioning procedures have not been parceled out and systematically examined in real therapeutic settings. For example, the impressive findings reported by Ayllon and Azrin (1965) referred to earlier, may reflect the influence of several factors (e.g., suggestion, empathy and modeling) other than selective reinforcement. Similarly, few investigations of imitative learning have separated and evaluated the relevant ingredients of the modeling process; several such studies are currently under way by Bandura and his associates at Stanford (Mischel, 1968).

Let us summarize our review of the behavior modification approach with the following observations:

1. The techniques of behavior modification have been subjected to more systematic research despite their brief history than all other psychological treatment approaches combined. This reflects, in part, the strong academic-experimental orientation of those who practice behavior therapy; most behaviorists have sought to provide a firm link between the scientific discipline of psychology proper and the applied problems of clinical treatment. Since behavior therapies will continue to be rigorously examined at each stage of their development, it is likely that most of them, once established, will withstand the test of time.

2. Despite the fact that most published studies of behavior therapy represent reports of clinical rather than controlled experimental research, the overall picture of efficacy that emerges is extremely impressive. More specifically, the effectiveness of counterconditioning methods for eliminating circumscribed learned reactions and symptom disorders is well documented. Similarly, selective reinforcement and imitative modeling techniques have proved suitable for strengthening and forming adaptive social behaviors among several patient groups (e.g., severely decompensated and antisocial syndromes) that have failed to yield to other therapeutic approaches. That these attainments have been achieved rapidly, economically and in the hands of only moderately sophisticated agents (e.g., nurses or attendants) adds further to the value of these methods.

3. On the debit side of the ledger, behavioral approaches have not demonstrated efficacy with diffuse and pervasive pathological impairments such as personality patterns, maladaptive coping strategies or "existential crises." Many of these difficult to pinpoint problems

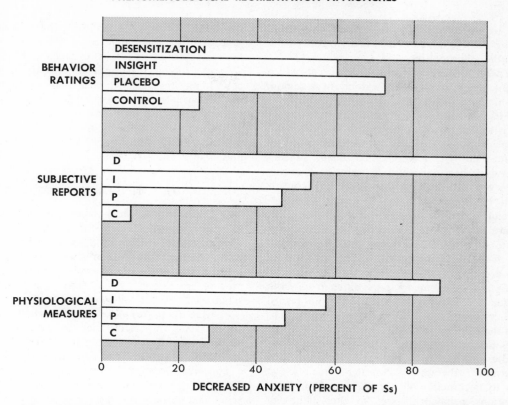

Figure 15-4   Relative efficacy of four procedures of anxiety reduction. College students who dreaded public speaking were assigned to one of four conditions: desensitization; insight-oriented psychotherapy; placebo "tranquilizers"; and a control group that received no treatment. Each group was given pre- and posttreatment assessment batteries consisting of behavior ratings, subjective reports and a variety of physiological measures. As is noted above, desensitization was consistently superior to the other procedures. Follow-up evaluations, both six weeks and two years later, revealed that these improvements were sustained (Paul, G. L., 1966, 1967).

simply do not lend themselves to the sharply focused procedures of behavior therapy. Although advances in treatment methodology may ultimately bring these forms of disturbed functioning within the purview of behavior therapy, for the present they seem more suitably handled by phenomenological and intrapsychic approaches.

4.   With the flush of early treatment successes, many behavior therapists heralded the rapid demise of other schools of therapy. Little attention was given in their zeal to the possibility

that other treatment approaches were not necessarily incompatible with behavior techniques. It is more in keeping with the "scientific" attitude, so central to the ethos of behaviorism, to await the gathering of a more substantial body of empirical evidence before drawing definite conclusions of the relative efficacy of different therapies. Such data, especially as they apply to the comparative utility of alternative approaches in each of the various impairments which comprise psychopathology, are far from complete.

## PHENOMENOLOGICAL REORIENTATION APPROACHES

Behavior therapists employ different procedures and ally themselves with different theories of learning, but they share a number of deeply held beliefs. Not only do they possess in common their focus on behavioral data and their heritage in the "scientific" traditions of academic-experimental psychology, but they firmly adhere to the view that laboratory derived learning

principles are central to both an understanding of the causes of psychopathology and to its remediation.

There are no bonds of strength among phenomenological therapists equal to those that hold behaviorists together. Phenomenologically oriented therapists inherit their views from widely divergent sources; many are offshoots of psychoanalysis;

some are strongly influenced by one or another learning theory; others derive their impetus from existential philosophies.

There are three factors, however, which phenomenological therapists exhibit in common, and which set them apart from other schools.

*First,* in contrast to behaviorists and in common with intrapsychic therapists, phenomenologists place heavy emphasis on internal processes that mediate overt actions. To them, psychopathology is best conceived in terms of enduring and pervasive traits that shape and give consistency to behavior. No matter how widely generalized and consistent certain behaviors may be, they are but "surface" derivatives of these inner mediators. It follows, therefore, that phenomenologists focus their therapeutic efforts on *internal* dispositions.

*Second,* phenomenologists differ from both behavior and intrapsychic therapists with regard to which events and processes they consider central to the etiology and treatment of psychopathology. Behaviorists emphasize the role of environmental events such as stimuli and reinforcements; intrapsychic therapists consider unconscious forces to be crucial. As a consequence of these orientations, behaviorists seek to alter pathology by manipulating stimulus events and reinforcement contingencies, and intrapsychic therapists direct their efforts toward uprooting and reconstructing the elements of the unconscious. In contrast to both, phenomenologists concern themselves with the data of *conscious perceptions and attitudes,* believing that these cognitive processes are crucial to both the development and perpetuation of psychopathology. Therapy, then, is directed to the reorientation of consciously discordant feelings and erroneous beliefs, and not to the modification of isolated behaviors or to the disgorging of the past and its associated unconscious derivatives.

*Third,* given their emphasis on conscious attitudes and perceptions, it follows that phenomenological therapists are inclined to follow an insight-expressive rather than an action-suppressive treatment process. Both phenomenological and intrapsychic therapists employ the insight-expressive approach, but the focus of their explorations differs, at least in theory. Phenomenologists attend to dissonant social attitudes and self-perceptions which can be consciously acknowledged by an examination of the patient's everyday relationships and activities. In contrast, intrapsychic therapists view consciously acknowledged attitudes to be "superficial verbalizations" that cloak hidden beliefs and emotions; to them,

the task of therapy is to bring into awareness repressed materials that resist conscious examination. Phenomenologists consider intrapsychic "depth" probing to be both unnecessary and time consuming; they believe that a reorientation of the patient's conscious assumptions and feelings, without exploring their historical origins or dissolving their unconscious roots, will more than suffice to enable him to rectify his difficulties and find a more constructive way of life.

## COMMONALITIES IN THERAPEUTIC PROCESS

Phenomenological therapists employ the face to face discussion interview as their principal treatment format. Despite important differences in patient-therapist interaction styles and treatment goals, the sequence and content of the therapeutic process are essentially the same; these may be subdivided into the following five steps.

**Establishing Rapport.** An important part of all therapies, especially face to face interview procedures, is the patient's feeling of comfort and trust in his therapist. This is achieved by providing a congenial treatment atmosphere and by the therapist's genuine concern for the patient's well-being and respect for his potential as a valued person. Once rapport has been established, the patient will more readily discuss his troubles with a measure of ease and confidence.

**Exploration of Thoughts and Feelings.** By word and gesture, the therapist conveys to the patient that he can express his concerns, knowing that they will be fully accepted and sympathetically understood. At this stage of treatment, the therapist serves as an interested listener whose efforts are limited to encouraging the patient to explore any thoughts and feelings related to his difficulty. At most, the therapist will act to prompt the flow of ideas or interrupt the patient's discourse to have a point clarified or elaborated. For example, in the following brief excerpt, a male patient is led to explore more fully his thoughts and feelings about both himself and his second wife (Rosen and Gregory, 1965).

*THERAPY EXCERPT 2*
*Phenomenological Exploration*

*Patient.* Joan [the second wife] is different from what Alice [the first wife] was like. I never got along with Alice. We fought all the time. (*Pause*) Sometimes I wonder why she married me—I don't think she really liked me. (*Pause*) I guess with Joan—I have arguments with her and I wonder if the whole thing is starting over, like with Alice.

*Therapist.* You feel Joan is different but you're worried this marriage will go bad too.

*Pt.* (*Spoken with heat.*) That's right. We argue and argue and I think maybe it's my fault. I just can't get along with anybody—I hate Joan's father, I - I - I can't stand my stepfather—I get jealous when anybody so much as looks at Joan, and I get mad at myself when I get jealous. I guess I just wreck things—spoil them. (*Tears appear in his eyes.*)

*Th.* You hate other people and you hate yourself—*nothing* is any good.

*Pt.* I don't like having to come here either—I ought to be able to manage things better. I'm the boy who always louses things up. (*Said in a sarcastic and bitter tone.*)

*Th.* You feel you always were a failure and still are.

*Pt.* Yes—well—maybe some things I manage better. (*Pause*) For instance. . . .

**Selective Focusing.** Once the "clinical picture" takes shape in the therapist's mind, he will attempt to orient the patient to certain core themes whose further exploration is considered essential to treatment progress. Selective focusing may be achieved in several ways: by pointed questioning, by reflecting or rephrasing certain of the patient's "passing comments," as illustrated partially in the previous excerpt and by planning discussion topics prior to sessions.

**Developing Insight.** Therapists have at their disposal a number of maneuvers by which they assist the patient to translate his discursive reflections into crystallized formulations called "insight"; which of these maneuvers are emphasized depends on the therapist's "school" of treatment. Some guide the patient gently and indirectly by bringing his attention to certain themes time and again until their significance and meaning gradually unfold. Others facilitate insight by providing tentative interpretations that "suggest" connections between events that seem unrelated in the patient's eyes. Still others are direct, bringing the "reasons" for his difficulties clearly and forcefully to the patient's attention.

**Promoting Constructive Alternatives.** As insight develops, the patient begins to recognize the possibility that he can assume attitudes and employ strategies that are different than those of his past. However, awareness of these possibilities is not often sufficient in itself to motivate change. To promote change, some therapists assure the patient that these new alternative behaviors are both reasonable and feasible, leaving it entirely to him, however, to decide if and when he will carry them out. Other therapists take a more vigorous role, exhorting the patient to stop dallying, to "get on the ball" and initiate some positive action.

## CLASSIFICATION

Differences arise among phenomenologists as to the style or manner of the therapist-patient interaction, and whether the therapist or the patient determines the goals of treatment. On the basis of these two elements of the therapeutic relationship, we find sufficient divergences to categorize three variants of the phenomenological approach.

The *first group*, labeled "self-actualization" methods, assumes that each person possesses an inherent wisdom for choosing a life course that is most suitable for him. Psychopathology arises because this capacity for self-fulfillment has been blocked or distorted by adverse circumstances. The task of therapy is to provide the patient with a permissive and encouraging atmosphere that will facilitate the emergence of his potentials. By behaving in a nondirective and equalitarian manner, and by respecting the patient's capacity to choose his own goals, the patient will ultimately discover ways to actualize the promise that inheres within him.

The *second* phenomenological approach, termed "confrontation-directive," is diametrically opposite in style to that of the self-actualizing procedure. Here, the therapist assumes an authoritarian role; the patient is considered to be inept, irresponsible or sick, unable or unwilling to choose for himself what his goals should be. Not only does the therapist take an active part in deciding the objectives of treatment, but he employs persuasive or commanding tactics to influence the patient to adopt a system of values that is deemed, more or less, universally appropriate.

Between the two polarities just mentioned is the *third* or "cognitive-learning" approach. These procedures tend to be neither directive nor nondirective; rather, therapist and patient come to agree on which of the patient's habitual attitudes perpetuate and aggravate his difficulties. The therapist employs certain broad principles of learning theory to eliminate these self-defeating attitudes and to develop more wholesome alternatives. In contrast to confrontation-directive therapists, those who follow the cognitive-learning approach are not committed to the achievement of a particular value system.

Let us next review these three approaches and their subvariants.

## SELF-ACTUALIZATION METHODS

The chief goal of treatment, according to this approach, is not to understand the causes or to remove the symptoms of psychopathology, but to "free" the patient to develop a confident image of his self-worth. This will enable him to explore and test his own values in the world, unconstrained by the conventions of mass society. Liberated in this manner, the patient will learn to act in ways that are "right" for him, and thereby "actualize" his inherent potentials. To promote these objectives, the therapist views events from the patient's frame of reference and conveys both a "caring" attitude and a genuine respect for the patient's worth as a human being.

Two "schools" of phenomenological therapy stress the goal of self-actualization—the *client-centered* and the *existential* approaches. The client-centered approach, associated most closely with Rogers' "self theory" discussed in chapter 2, is based on the optimistic premise that man possesses an innate drive for socially constructive behaviors; the task of therapy is to "unleash" these wholesome growth forces. The existential school, also discussed in chapter 2, possesses a less sanguine view of man's inherent fate, believing that he must struggle to find a valued meaning to life; therapy, then, attempts to strengthen the patient's capacity to choose an "authentic" existence. Let us examine both schools in greater detail.

## CLIENT-CENTERED THERAPY

The thesis that man is driven to "actualize his potentials" may be traced to the seminal writings of Carl Jung and Otto Rank. Jung (1916, 1923) contended that man possessed a singular "life urge" that craved self-realization. Rank (1929, 1936) translated the notion of a drive for self-fulfillment into a philosophy of therapy. To Rank and his disciples—the social worker Jessie Taft (1933) and the child psychiatrist Frederick Allen (1942)—the paramount aim of therapy was to free the patient's "will," a somewhat mystical but powerful energy that leads to self-reliance and uniqueness in personality. This end could best be achieved, according to Rank, by making the patient the central figure in the therapeutic relationship. In effect, the patient became his own therapist and his professional helper became, not an all-knowing authority, but a catalyst to strengthen the patient's will toward growth.

Carl Rogers (1942, 1951, 1961, 1967), working independently of Rank and his associates, developed the notion of "client-centered" therapy most clearly and effectively. According to Rogers, patient "growth" is a product neither of special treatment procedures nor professional know-how; rather, it emerges from the quality and character of the therapeutic relationship. More specifically, it occurs as a consequence of certain attitudes of the therapist, notably his: *genuineness,* that is, his ability to "be himself" in therapy and to express his feelings and thoughts without pretensions or the cloak of professional authority; *unconditional positive regard,* that is, his capacity to feel respect for the patient as a worthy being, no matter how unappealing and destructive his behaviors may be; and *accurate empathic understanding,* that is, his sensitivity to the patient's subjective world, and his ability to communicate this awareness to the patient.

In line with these three attitudes, the patient assumes full responsibility for the subject and goals of therapeutic discussion; the therapist reflects rather than interprets the patient's thoughts and feelings and encourages, but does not recommend, efforts toward growth and individual expression. The nondirective therapist's willingness to allow the patient to determine his own goals is nicely illustrated in the following (Rogers, 1951).

### THERAPY EXCERPT 3
#### Client-centered Therapy

*S [Subject or Client]:* I've never said this before to anyone—but I've thought for such a long time —This is a terrible thing to say, but if I could just—well (*short, bitter laugh; pause*), if I could just find some glorious cause that I could give my life for I would be happy. I cannot be the kind of a person I want to be. I guess maybe I haven't the guts—or the strength—to kill myself —and if someone else would relieve me of the responsibility—or I would be in an accident—I —I—just don't want to live.

*C [Counselor]:* At the present time things look so black to you that you can't see much point in living—

*S:* Yes—I wish I'd never started this therapy. I was happy when I was living in my dream world. There I could be the kind of person I wanted to be—But now—There is such a wide, wide gap—between my ideal—and what I am. I wish people hated me. I try to make them hate me. Because then I could turn away from them and could blame them—but no—It is all in my hands—Here is my life—and I either accept the fact that I am absolutely worthless—or I fight whatever it is that holds me in this terrible conflict. And I suppose if I accepted the fact that I am worthless, then I could go away someplace —and get a little room someplace—get a mechanical job someplace—and retreat clear back to the security of my dream world where I could do things, have clever friends, be a pretty wonderful sort of person—

*C:* It's really a tough struggle—digging into this like you are—and at times the shelter of your dream world looks more attractive and comfortable.

*S:* My dream world or suicide.

*C:* Your dream world or something more permanent than dreams—

*S:* Yes. (*A long pause. Complete change of voice.*) So I don't see why I should waste your time—coming in twice a week—I'm not worth it —What do you think?

*C:* It's up to you, Gil—It isn't wasting my time —I'd be glad to see you—whenever you come— but it's how you feel about it—if you don't want to come twice a week—or if you do want to come twice a week?—once a week?—It's up to you. (*Long pause.*)

*S:* You're not going to suggest that I come in oftener? You're not alarmed and think I ought to come in—every day—until I get out of this?

*C:* I believe you are able to make your own decision. I'll see you whenever you want to come.

*S:* (*Note of awe in her voice.*) I don't believe you are alarmed about—I see—I may be afraid of myself—but you aren't afraid of me— (*She stands up—a strange look on her face.*)

*C:* You say you may be afraid of yourself— and are wondering why I don't seem to be afraid for you?

*S:* (*Another short laugh.*) You have more confidence in me than I have. . . . I'll see you next week—(*that short laugh*) maybe. (*Her attitude seemed tense, depressed, bitter, completely beaten. She walked slowly away.*)

Self-actualization unfolds gradually. We may condense the several stages of this progression into two broad phases. First, the patient, sensing the therapist's complete and unshakable belief in his worth, begins to value himself, as well. Second, as he adopts this new self-image, he is increasingly willing to test in reality behaviors that are in keeping with his "true" feelings, without fear of censure and humiliation; hence, he begins to "actualize himself."

## EXISTENTIAL THERAPY

Therapists of this persuasion are committed to the view that man must confront and accept the inevitable dilemmas of life if he is to achieve a measure of "authentic" self-realization. Themes such as these were first formulated in the philosophical writings of Kierkegaard, Nietzsche, Husserl, Heidegger and, more recently, in those of Jaspers, Buber, Sartre and Tillich. From these sources also, may be traced the foundations of existential therapy, notably those advanced by Ludwig Binswanger (1942, 1947, 1956), Medard Boss (1957, 1963), Viktor Frankl (1955, 1965) and Rollo May (1958, 1963). Despite differences in terminology and philosophical emphasis, these existential variants are very similar insofar as their approach to therapy.

Important to all existential therapists is the "being-together encounter" between patient and therapist. This encounter, characterized by mutual acceptance and self-revelation, enables the patient to find an authentic meaning to his existence, despite the profound and inescapable contradictions that life presents. The focus both in *logotherapy* (Frankl) and *daseinsanalyse* (Binswanger and Boss), the two major variants of existential treatment, is to utilize the insoluble predicaments and suffering of life as a way of discovering self-meaning and purpose. By facing the "inevitable" with equanimity, the patient rises above petty frustrations and discovers the fundamentals upon which his genuine self can unfold.

## CONFRONTATION-DIRECTIVE PROCEDURES

The philosophy underlying confrontation-directive procedures contrasts sharply with that of self-actualization methods. Patients are viewed to be inept, irresponsible or sick, and therefore unwilling or unable to choose the course they must take for their own well-being. The therapist not only assumes full authority for deciding the objectives of treatment, but confronts the patient with the irrationalities of his thinking; moreover, he employs commanding tactics to indoctrinate the patient with a value system that is considered universally beneficial.

The first systematic formulation of what may be called a confrontation-directive procedure was published by DuBois (1909) and Dejerine (1913), both of whom sought to impart "reason" to patients whose emotions had confused or distorted their capacity to think sensibly. It was DuBois' belief that mental disorders were irrational preoccupations with minor symptoms, causing these symptoms to become "mountains, instead of molehills." To counter these foolish absorptions, DuBois enjoined the patient to disregard his troubles and reorient his thoughts in the direction of his virtues and accomplishments. The therapist inspired his patients to believe that happiness was best achieved through self-denial and a dedication to others. DuBois' philosophy of "positive thinking" and "selfless altruism" was promptly borrowed as a guiding principle among pastoral counselors, but it had little impact on clinical practitioners.

In the mid-1940's, Thorne (1944, 1948), viewing the growth of what he considered to be the narrow-minded and sentimentalistic practices of nondirective client-centered therapy, proposed an approach that revived modern confrontation-directive procedures. In contrast to DuBois, who sought to smooth over the strains and vexations of life, Thorne induced conflicts deliberately by confronting the patient with his contradictory and self-defeating attitudes. Provoked in this manner, the patient was forced to examine his destructive habits and to explore more adaptive alternatives.

Two features distinguish confrontation-directive approaches from other phenomenological procedures: the practice of "forcefully" exposing the patient's erroneous or irrational attitudes and "imposing" a particular philosophy of life in its stead. Of interest in this regard are the diametrically opposite philosophies espoused by the two approaches to be next discussed.

## RATIONAL-EMOTIVE THERAPY

This approach has been most clearly formulated by Ellis (1958, 1962, 1967), although its origins may be traced to the writings of Alfred Adler. Ellis considers the primary objective of therapy to be countering the patient's tendency to perpetuate his difficulties through illogical and negative thinking. The patient, by reiterating these unrealistic and self-defeating beliefs in a self-dialogue, constantly reaffirms his irrationality and perpetuates his distress. To overcome these implicit but pervasive attitudes, the therapist confronts the patient with them and induces him to think about them consciously and concertedly and to "attack them" forcefully and unequivocally until they no longer influence his behavior. By revealing and assailing these beliefs and by "commanding" the patient to engage in activities which run counter to them, their hold on his life is broken and new directions become possible.

The following transcript, in which a patient recounts an experience in which his golf partners expressed their dislike of him, illustrates the technique nicely (Ellis, 1962).

### THERAPY EXCERPT 4
#### Rational-emotive Therapy

*Therapist:* You think you were unhappy because these men didn't like you?

*Patient:* I certainly was!

*Th.* But you weren't unhappy for the reason you think you were.

*Pt.* I wasn't? But I was!

*Th.* No, I insist: you only think you were unhappy for that reason.

*Pt.* Well, why was I unhappy then?

*Th.* It's very simple—as simple as A, B, C, I might say. A, in this case, is the fact that these men didn't like you. Let's assume that you observed their attitude correctly and were not merely imagining they didn't like you.

*Pt.* I assure you that they didn't. I could see that very clearly.

*Th.* Very well, let's assume they didn't like you and call that A. Now, C is your unhappiness—which we'll definitely have to assume is a fact, since you felt it.

*Pt.* Damn right I did!

*Th.* All right, then: A is the fact that the men didn't like you, C is your unhappiness. You see A and C and you assume that A, their not liking you, caused your unhappiness, C. But it didn't.

*Pt.* It didn't? What did, then?

*Th.* B did.

*Pt.* What's B?

*Th.* B is *what you said to yourself* while you were playing golf with those men.

*Pt.* What I said to myself? But I didn't say anything.

*Th.* You did. You couldn't possibly be unhappy if you didn't. The only thing that could possibly make you unhappy that occurs from without is a brick falling on your head, or some such equivalent. But no brick fell. Obviously, therefore, you must have *told yourself* something to make you unhappy.

*Pt.* But I tell you . . . Honestly, I didn't say anything.

*Th.* You did. You must have. Now think back to your being with these men; think what you said to yourself; and tell me what it was.

*Pt.* Well . . . I . . .

*Th.* Yes?

*Pt.* Well, I guess I did say something.

*Th.* I'm sure you did. Now what did you tell yourself when you were with those men?

*Pt.* I . . . Well, I told myself that it was awful that they didn't like me, and why didn't they like me, and how could they not like me, and . . . you know, things like that.

*Th.* Exactly! And that, what you told yourself, was B. And it's *always* B that makes you unhappy in situations like this. Except as I said before, when A is a brick falling on your head. *That,* or any physical object, might cause you real pain. But any mental or emotional onslaught against you—any word, gesture, attitude, or feeling directed against you—can hurt you only if *you* let it. And your letting such a word, gesture, attitude, or feeling hurt you, your *telling yourself* that it's awful, horrible, terrible—that's B. And that's what *you* do to *you*.

*Pt.* What shall I do then?

*Th.* I'll tell you exactly what to do. I want you to play golf, if you can, with those same men again. But this time, instead of trying to get them to love you or think you're a grand guy or anything like that, I want you to do one simple thing.

*Pt.* What is that?

*Th.* I want you merely to *observe,* when you're with them and they don't love you, to observe what you say to you. That's all: merely watch your own silent sentences. Do you think you can do that?

*Pt.* I don't see why not. Just watch my own sentences, what I say to me?

*Th.* Yes, just that.

When the patient came in for his next session, I asked him if he had done his homework and he said that he had. "And what did you find?" I asked. "It was utterly appalling," he replied, "utterly appalling. All I heard myself tell myself was self-pity; nothing but self-pity."

"Exactly," I said. "That's what you keep telling yourself—nothing but self-pity. No wonder you're unhappy!"

Ellis contends that patients exhibit certain almost universal self-defeating assumptions. Among them are the following: that it is necessary to be loved and approved; to be worthwhile as a person, one must be thoroughly good and competent; many people are wicked and sinful and should be blamed and censured for their villainy.

Underlying these destructive attitudes, according to Ellis, is the tendency of patients to blame themselves for their limitations and wrongdoings; that is, to subscribe to the false and self-defeating assumption that they are "no good and therefore deserve to suffer." The principal goal of therapy is to challenge and destroy this belief, to liberate the patient, to free him from such irrational notions as shame and sin and to live life to the fullest despite social shortcomings or the disapproval of others.

## REALITY-INTEGRITY THERAPY

The underlying theme of "rational-emotive therapy" is that man is too harsh with himself, tending to blame and judge his actions more severely than is necessary. No more opposite a philosophy could be found than that espoused in Glasser's "reality therapy" (1961, 1965) or Mowrer's "integrity therapy" (1961, 1965, 1966). In effect, these men claim that patients are sick because they are irresponsible; they are *not* "oversocialized" victims of too rigid standards, but "undersocialized" victims of a failure to adhere to rigid moralistic standards. Anguish stems not from too much guilt, but from an unwillingness to admit guilt, sin and irresponsibility.

The task of therapy, according to this view, is to confront the patient with his past misbehaviors and irresponsibilities and make him "confess" his wrongdoings. The therapist does not accept the patient's facile rationalizations or other efforts to find scapegoats for his misfortunes. Only by facing and admitting the "reality" of his deceit and guilt can the patient regain self-integrity and learn to deal with the future truthfully and objectively. No longer needing to hide his sins, he can rectify past mistakes and find a more moralistic and responsible style of life without shame or the fear of being discovered.

## COGNITIVE-LEARNING TECHNIQUES

Therapists grouped in this category are neither directive nor nondirective insofar as treatment goals or style of therapeutic interaction is concerned. Rather, therapist and patient conjointly agree that the latter possesses attitudes which promote and perpetuate his difficulties in life.

Cognitive-learning therapists are more active in the treatment process than those who follow the self-actualization philosophy; they encourage the patient to alter his self-defeating perceptions and cognitions instead of allowing him to work things out for himself. In contrast to confrontation-directive therapists, however, they do not prejudge the patient's problem in accord with a fixed philosophy such as "integrity" or "rationality"; they have no particular "axe to grind," so to speak, no set of beliefs they seek to inculcate. Rather, they plan merely to reorient the patient's misguided attitudes, whatever these may be and toward whatever direction may prove constructive, given his personal life circumstances.

Although subscribing to learning principles, cognitive-learning therapists differ from behavior-learning therapists in that treatment is focused not on overt symptom behaviors, but on those internal mediating processes (perceptions and attitudes) which give rise to and perpetuate these behaviors.

Cognitive-learning approaches have recently begun to gain favor among many professionals since they bridge the gap between laboratory learning principles and the primary vehicle of most therapies, verbal discussion. Several formal systems have been proposed along these lines (Kelly, 1955; Miller, Galanter and Pribam, 1960; Breger and McGaugh, 1965; Kanfer and Saslow, 1965); we shall limit our discussion, however, only to two, those known as expectancy-reinforcement (Rotter, 1954) and assertion-structured (Phillips, 1956) therapies.

## EXPECTANCY-REINFORCEMENT THERAPY

Formulated by Rotter (1954, 1962), this approach seeks to alter the patient's expectancies (cognitive anticipations) that particular forms of behavior are followed by positive or negative reinforcements of varying strengths. Maladaptive behaviors stem from the presence of erroneous expectancies, learned largely as a consequence of faulty past reinforcements which generalize into current situations and relationships.

Therapy is viewed as a specially arranged process of unlearning and relearning that is no different in its fundamental character and principles than that of other learning settings. In fact, as Rotter notes, formal therapy, despite its concentrated and focused nature, is often a less efficient vehicle for change than repetitive everyday experiences, since it is limited to a few hours a week at most and takes place in a setting that is appreciably different than that to which its effects must be generalized.

Therapeutic processes are designed to change maladjustive reinforcement-expectancies, or as Rotter has put it (1954):

lowering the expectancy that a particular behavior or behaviors will lead to gratifications or increasing the expectancy that alternate or new behaviors would lead to greater gratification in the same situation or situations. In general learning terms we might say we have the choice of either weakening the inadequate response, strengthening the correct or adequate response, or doing both.

Of utmost importance as a therapeutic goal is strengthening the expectancy that problems can be resolved, which Rotter formulates as follows:

It is the purpose of therapy not to solve all of the patient's problems, but rather to increase the patient's ability to solve his own problems. . . . From a social learning point of view, one of the most important aspects of treatment, particularly face to face treatment, is to reinforce in the patient the expectancy that problems are solvable by looking for alternative solutions.

Although the role of the therapist is to selectively reinforce adjustive expectancies and problem-solving skills, he is not:

. . . merely a mechanical verbal conditioner, but rather a person whose special reinforcement value for the particular patient can be used to help the patient try out new behaviors and ways of thinking. The patient ultimately determines for himself the value of new conceptualizations and alternate ways of behaving in his experiences outside of therapy.

## ASSERTION-STRUCTURED THERAPY

According to Phillips' model (1956), behavior is best understood in terms of the person's "assertions" concerning himself and others. These assertions, which are essentially cognitive hypotheses or assumptions about the world in which the person lives, have varying probabilities of "confirmation" (correctness) or "disconfirmation" (incorrectness). Should these assertions be disconfirmed frequently, as occurs in persons inclined to psychopathology, the individual will

experience "tension," with its accompanying symptoms. Rather than resolving these tensions, Phillips believes that the disturbed person reiterates his faulty assertions more strongly than before. This results in a self-defeating vicious circle termed "redundancy" and leads to a progressive inflexibility and narrowing of behavior alternatives.

Phillips illustrates the pathological sequence in the following example (1956):

1. Assertion. Child's expectations are for constant attention, accord, interest; he expects to get his way; expects to have others give in to him in the interest of his comfort and his immediate demands.
2. Disconfirmation. The school and other out-of-the-home environments cannot treat the child in this way; therefore they act to disconfirm the child's expectations. These social facts conflict with the expectations themselves.
3. Tension. At school or in other atypical situations (i.e., not typically like the home setting) tensions develop from this conflict.
4. Redundancy. Child redoubles efforts to get attention, refuses to make academic effort, becomes a behavior problem owing to tension and partly to his fighting back at disconfirming experiences. The child now falls behind in school work in real and formidable ways; this failure, in turn, becomes more disconfirming to him and his original assertions. Thus the vicious circle proceeds; and until it is entered into in effective ways, it continues.

The chief task of therapy is to discover the nature of these faulty assertions, and then to "interfere" with their perpetuation by teaching the patient alternative beliefs and hypotheses that have a greater probability of confirmation. Thus, therapeutic interference reduces the vicious and evernarrowing circle of redundancy, thereby enabling the person to explore on his own increasingly effective problem-solving attitudes and behaviors. This process of actively "teaching" the patient to examine his assertions and to explore alternatives is well illustrated in the following transcript from the eighth therapy hour with a college student (Phillips, 1956).

***THERAPY EXCERPT 5***
*Assertion-structured Therapy*

*Patient.* I had a hard time getting to school this morning.
*Therapist.* Oh, you did?
*Pt.* Couldn't get out of bed.
*Th.* This is pretty early for you, eh?
*Pt.* It is bad on Saturdays but on school days it is just misery. Ah . . . Saturdays and Sundays. The main thing I want to talk about today is responsibility.

*Th.* Yeah.

*Pt.* You've been saying it is a matter of my thinking something else is more important—

*Th.* Momentarily—

*Pt.* Well, even momentarily . . . well, the only thing I can say is . . . well, the . . . I just can't see this.

*Th.* OK, what's your notion about it?

*Pt.* The only thing I can see is . . . ah . . . and it seems very obvious to me . . . Well, this one course, B—, is giving me trouble and I'm afraid of it. I'm afraid because I know there are a lot of other smart people who are going to get *A's* and I don't think I can get *A's*.

*Th.* Shying away from competition?

*Pt.* Yeah . . . because I don't want the superiority notions I have disconfirmed.

*Th.* Yeah.

*Pt.* But . . . ah . . . it certainly is a compulsion . . . it certainly is . . . I mean . . if I were doing something like watching TV, that would be fine . . but I'm sitting there thinking *I gotta get to the work, I gotta get to the work,* but I can't, I can't . . . then . . . I mean, doing nothing certainly isn't more important than doing something like studying—

*Th.* But you are doing something, you aren't ever doing nothing, are you?

*Pt.* Well, I mean——

*Th.* You're delaying, or you're saying "I can postpone it," or momentarily you're saying it isn't quite *that* important although the long-range is important—the grades at the end of the semester or your preparation as a prelaw student. But isn't your momentary behavior one that says, "This can be delayed," "This can be pushed back," "This can be handled some way other than studying it right now"?

*Pt.* Well, the behavior, I guess, would indicate that . . . but, as far as what I've done, what I see myself it's a definite compulsion. Here I have so much homework, I'm so far behind, how am I going to do it?

*Th.* Uh huh.

*Pt.* How am I going to start? I have so much to do I don't know where to start.

*Th.* You have so much to do?

*Pt.* Yeah, then maybe I could get up and walk around . . . and think about it and get my wits together.

*Th.* Well, now do you say something like that when you have a long distance to go? Travelling? You don't say, "Oh, it's so far I can't get started —I'll never get there.". . because before you could get there you'd have to take three steps, I'll have to take two, and you can pose the problem of Zeno's arrow here and never get going. That's the problem that says that before you can shoot an arrow a given distance, it has to travel half that distance; before it can travel the remaining distance, it has to travel half *that* distance, and so on and on, and the arrow can never reach its destination because it always has half the remaining distance to go.

*Pt.* Uh huh.

*Th.* Maybe you kinda look at your B—— course that way?

*Pt.* Uh huh. But I should look at it different . . . I should get going.

*Th.* But you don't look at travelling . . . going some place that is important to you that has no conflict connected with it, no alternatives . . . you don't look at those tasks that way . . . figure out how far you have to go before you get there and let that discourage you——

*Pt.* You mean thinking beforehand how much there is to do?

*Th.* Um huh. "It's so overwhelming I can't do it—I'll do something else," you are saying—"It's just so much, I can't compete with these people, I'm behind already, so why knock myself out, it's all settled, it's a lost battle."

*Pt.* Of course, if I were going to Florida . . . ah . . . and my parents wouldn't let me have the car, I'd see it was too far for me and therefore I wouldn't go.

*Th.* That's right, the alternative in the conflict of not going would be so overwhelming you wouldn't pursue the goal. The alternative to going would be so important . . . and that's what we're saying here with respect to your study of B——: the alternatives are more important, however momentary they are, however weak they seem to be as you think of your ultimate goals like grades at the end of the semester. (Pause.) You see my point?

*Pt.* Uh huh. Course I don't see how to get rid of these.

*Th.* Well, let's talk about it from that vantage point now. What you're saying is it's not important for you to knock yourself out in a situation where you're behind. If in a race you fall behind, your tendency is to give up if you cannot gain enough ground to win. Or to let it slack so much that there's no more conflict any more, no contest— you're out of it. There are too many people competing with you in B—— that are doing better than you, so you're saying: "OK, I'm so far behind I can't compete with you people, so I'll just call it no contest." But that's a choice, isn't it? That's an assertion . . . that's the choice that says that's more important than staying in there and battling it out and doing whatever I can, or retrieving my losses, or whatever. (Pause.) Does that get over to you at all?

*Pt.* Why yes, sure. Actually, though . . . ah . . . ah . . . though I may think that calling it no contest, it actually isn't any contest——

*Th.* But there is.

*Pt.* Yes there is——

*Th.* There is in reality as far as your matriculation in the course is concerned, and it is in terms of your own reality as the course and the semester move on. But *at the time* you're supposed to get down to study, you find something else to do because these other "something elses" are more attractive, more compatible, stronger at the moment, they have less conflict connected with them, and so on. (Pause.) That's part of the business of your responsibility and self-discipline, isn't it?

*Pt.* It's all the same thing.

*Th.* Yeah. All part and parcel. (Pause.) You're saying, "I'll get in the contest when I can win, or when I can achieve the high-level perfor-

mance I deem my prerogative . . . but . . . I won't
. . . if there's anything against me . . . I mean really
formidably against me.

## EVALUATION

The variety of philosophies, goals and therapeutic procedures which differentiate the several
phenomenological approaches make it difficult to
group and evaluate these therapies as a unit.
Despite these substantive differences, however,
there are certain merits and criticisms which may
be assigned in common to all of these methods.
Let us note them briefly.

Among the *merits* ascribed by proponents
are the following.

*First,* the language of phenomenological discourse represents events in terms that are "meaningful" to patients rather than in the obscure
vernacular of intrapsychic therapies or the overly
objectivized terminology of behavioral schools.
Consequently, patients understand what is "going
on" in the consulting room, and can readily
translate into reality what they have learned.
Discussions at the phenomenological level, then,
facilitate both the acquisition of insight and its
application to current realities.

*Second,* phenomenological therapies are carried out in a face to face interpersonal interaction
that resembles "normal" extratherapeutic relationships to a greater degree than those of other
therapeutic schools. Consequently, what is learned
in the setting of phenomenological treatment
should more readily generalize to the natural interpersonal settings for which they are ultimately
intended.

*Third,* phenomenological approaches focus
on internal mediating processes that "underlie"
behavior. Consequently, they are more efficient
instruments for solving pervasive or complex difficulties than are behavior therapies which deal
primarily with isolated or well-circumscribed
symptoms. Similarly, phenomenological therapies
can grapple with such nebulous symptom clusters
as "existential dilemmas" and "identity crises"
that are further obscured by the conceptual
schema of intrapsychic schools and resist formulation in the overly precise language of behavior
therapies.

Among the many *criticisms* leveled at
phenomenological therapies, we might note the
following.

*First,* phenomenologists formulate their procedures in a vague and unsystematized manner,
presenting a discursive mélange of sporadic recom-

mendations as to how therapy should be conducted. Upon careful analysis, these recommendations prove to possess no more substance than
those of supportive reassurance, ventilation and
persuasion, although they are cloaked in pretentious semantics and specious social philosophies.
Critics note that all psychotherapies employ the
processes that phenomenological therapists consider essential; thus, phenomenologists make a
virtue out of the commonplace.

*Second,* phenomenological therapies fail to
deal with the historical course and the unconscious
roots of psychopathology. According to intrapsychic therapists, consciously acknowledged attitudes and feelings, which characterize the data of
phenomenological therapy, are but "superficial"
verbalizations that cloak deeper motives and emotions. As they see it, unless the patient comes to
grips with these "hidden" events, "true" insight
will constantly be subverted and therapeutic
progress will be blunted or prove illusory.

*Third,* phenomenological approaches are of
minimal value in cases of marked anxiety or with
patients who otherwise are unable to face or
analyze their attitudes and emotions. In short,
these procedures are limited to relatively stable
and moderately intelligent adults whose functional
capacities are sufficiently intact to enable them to
engage in calm self-exploration or symbolic verbal
discourse.

Let us turn from these pro and con theoretical arguments to matters of empirical research,
discussing first, findings concerning the "efficacy"
of phenomenological therapies and second, those
relating to their "mode of action."

### EFFICACY (OUTCOME STUDIES)

There is a shocking paucity of phenomenological outcome and process research, much less
than in behavior procedures; this sad fact is all
the more dismaying since phenomenological
techniques have an appreciably longer history than
behavior techniques. Moreover, what research has
been done can be faulted on numerous methodological grounds. Among the better studies, few
though they may be, are those by Carl Rogers
and his associates on client-centered techniques.

Most research employing control groups fails
to support the view that phenomenological procedures produce beneficial effects (Eysenck, 1952,
1960, 1965; Levitt, 1957; Cross, 1964; Dittman,
1966). Not all the data are negative, but they are
for the most part highly discouraging.

The fact that phenomenological therapists
observe improvement among the patients they

treat has been explained by reference to "spontaneous remission," that is, the tendency of many people to get better "naturally," with or without therapeutic intervention. To prove that therapy contributes a share to patient improvement, it must be shown to accomplish *more* than that observed in comparable control groups. This minimal criterion for research design has been met in less than ten studies dealing with phenomenological methods; the results, unfortunately, have not been heartening.

One such investigation, carried out by Paul (1966), was described earlier in the behavior modification section; he showed that a counterconditioning procedure was superior to phenomenological "insight" as a means of eradicating a fear symptom. Phillips (1956) reports results favoring his assertion-structured therapy in the short-term treatment of children when compared to a psychoanalytic approach; the validity of his findings may be questioned, however, on numerous grounds. Similarly, Ellis (1957) concluded that rational therapy resulted in greater improvement than two matched groups receiving "orthodox psychoanalytic" and "psychoanalytically oriented" therapies; these data are highly suspect inasmuch as Ellis himself was the therapist for all three groups and performed all of the ratings upon which his findings were based.

A study reported in Rogers and Dymond (1954), once considered the finest example of proper evaluative research, found that client-centered therapy produced significant favorable changes in self-perception among treated "neurotics." Unfortunately, they employed nontreated "normals" rather than nontreated "neurotics" as their control group; the necessary base rate of spontaneous remission against which to compare the results of their treated group required a neurotic and not a normal control population. Quite apart from this serious methodological flaw, they found little evidence concerning changes in specific symptomatology, behaviors in everyday situations or attitudes toward others. In short, Rogers and Dymond showed that client-centered therapy altered patient's attitudes toward themselves, but had little if any effect on other features of their pathology.

The findings of an unusually well-designed, five-year project employing client-centered therapy with schizophrenics have recently been reported (Rogers et al., 1967). As with earlier studies, the overall outcome data proved discouraging, that is, approximately the same number of treated patients improved as did the untreated controls. A careful analysis of this overall result, however, showed a *greater variability in outcome* among treated as compared to control patients. More specifically, when the treated group was divided in terms of who did the therapy, it was found that patients who were seen by therapists characterized by "high empathy and positive regard" had improved significantly whereas those treated by therapists low in these attributes had actually deteriorated, that is, *they became significantly worse*. This important result indicates that changes associated with phenomenological therapy are more than matters of spontaneous remission alone. Therapy or, perhaps more accurately, therapists produce both positive and negative consequences which, unless properly separated, cancel themselves out when outcome data are pooled into an overall average. We will return to the implications of this interesting finding in a later section.

## MODE OF ACTION (PROCESS STUDIES)

If beneficial effects are produced by phenomenological treatment, what ingredients of technique or therapeutic interaction give rise to them?

For an answer to this question, we must turn again to the work of Rogers and his associates; no other phenomenological therapist has sought to provide the requisite empirical data.

It appears clear from numerous studies, summarized in excellent reviews by Gardner (1964) and Bergin (1966, 1967), that the "process" ingredients essential to treatment success, at least in the client-centered approach, are the therapist's *genuineness* (self-honesty and unpretentiousness) *warmth* (acceptance of the patient) and *empathy* (accurate awareness of the patient's feelings). Of particular note, as was pointed out above, is the fact that therapists who lack these attributes tend to make their patients worse.

There is evidence also that "experienced" therapists in general are more successful than highly inexperienced therapists (Cartwright and Vogel, 1960). Although this finding may suggest that experienced therapists are better because they have learned the "treatment technique," research shows that experience is correlated with beneficial results independently of technique (Fiedler, 1950, 1951); in other words, experience per se is the crucial factor, not the theory that therapists espouse or its associated treatment procedure. Several factors may account for the superior performance of experienced therapists. *First,* inexperienced therapists are often self-conscious and anxious, two factors which impede the ostensibly important process ingredients of empathic accuracy and warmth. *Second,* experienced therapists are a relatively select population, comprising the "best" of a more heterogeneous and formerly inexperienced group, following years of "weeding out." *Third,* experienced therapists, regardless of their original orientations, may have learned certain common elements of "good" therapeutic behavior; they now employ these behaviors, wittingly or unwittingly, with greater frequency than do less experienced therapists who have yet to "learn the ropes."

Let us note several points in summarizing this review of phenomenological approaches.

1. With the exception of client-centered procedures, few outcome and process studies have been carried out on phenomenological therapies. The little that has been done fails frequently to meet even the rudiments of proper research design and control.

2. For the most part, theorists have formulated their treatment procedures in a discursive, vague and sporadic manner; it is extremely difficult to determine the exact techniques and sequence of steps involved in the therapeutic process. Social commentaries and philosophies are provided rather than specific and tangible recommendations as to the execution of treatment. Cutting through this verbal persiflage, one often finds these techniques merely to be "dressed-up" variants of the supportive procedures of reassurance, ventilation and persuasion.

3. In general, outcome data are negative or equivocal, although there is some evidence that these therapies promote *either* beneficial *or* detrimental changes in patients. Recent research suggests that certain characteristics displayed by the therapist in the treatment relationship are the essential process ingredients. Much work remains to be done, however, before we can isolate the contribution of the individual ostensive ingredients, specify their interrelationships and demonstrate their efficacy in each of the many varieties of psychopathology.

## INTRAPSYCHIC RECONSTRUCTION APPROACHES

Intrapsychic therapy had its formal beginning in the pioneering studies of Freud during the last decade of the nineteenth century. We have discussed both frequently and at length the history, rationale and variants of intrapsychic theory; there is no need to review these matters again.

Despite inevitable controversies and divergencies in emphasis, often appearing more divisive upon first than later examination, intrapsychic therapists share certain beliefs and goals in common that distinguish them from other orientations; two will be noted below.

*First,* intrapsychic therapists focus on internal mediating processes that ostensibly "underlie" and give rise to overt behavior. In contrast to phenomenologists, however, their attention is directed to those mediating events that operate at the "unconscious" rather than the conscious level. To them, overt behaviors and phenomenological reports are merely "surface" expressions of repressed emotions and their associated defensive strategies. Since unconscious processes are impervious to "surface" maneuvers, techniques of behavior modification are seen as mere palliatives, and methods of phenomenological reorientation are thought to resolve only those difficulties which are so painless as to be tolerated consciously. "True" insight occurs only when the deeply in-grained forces of the unconscious are unearthed and analyzed. The task of intrapsychic therapy, then, is to circumvent or pierce resistances that shield these insidious elements, bring them into consciousness and rework them into more constructive forms.

*Second,* intrapsychic therapists see as their goal the reconstruction of the patient's personality, not the removal of a symptom or the reorientation of an attitude. Disentangling the underlying structure of psychopathology, forged of many interlocking elements that build into a network of pervasive strategies and mechanisms, is the object of their therapy. To extinguish an isolated symptom or to redirect this or that perception, is too limited an aim, one that touches but a mere fraction of a formidable pathological system whose very foundations must be reworked. Wolberg illustrates this philosophy in the following analogy (1967):

A leaky roof can expeditiously be repaired with tar paper and asphalt shingles. This will help not only to keep the rain out, but also ultimately to dry out and to eliminate some of the water damage to the entire house. We have a different set of conditions if we undertake to tear down the structure and to rebuild the dwelling. We will not only have a water-tight roof, but we will have a better house. . . . If our object is merely to keep the rain out of the house, we will do better with the short-term repair focused on the roof, and not bother with the more hazardous, albeit ultimately more substantial reconstruction.

Reconstruction, then, rather than repair is the option chosen by intrapsychic therapists. They set for themselves the laborious task of rebuilding those functions and structures which comprise the substance of personality, not merely its "facade."

## CLASSIFICATION

Despite commonalities in data focus and reconstructive goals, intrapsychic therapists part company on several matters, notably the extent to which they emphasize the developmental roots of pathology and the particular techniques they employ in conducting treatment. Let us briefly examine these differences.

1. A significant number of intrapsychic therapists believe that successful treatment is contingent on the exploration and resolution of the infantile origins of adult psychopathology. This necessitates probing and uncovering the "conflicts" of early instinctual "psychosexual" development and the myriad "neurotic" defenses that the patient has devised to keep them from consciousness.

This emphasis on uprooting the past is not shared by all who follow the intrapsychic persuasion. Rather than attending to childhood experiences, some therapists focus on current-day events and relationships. Efforts are directed toward the end of refashioning the patient's unconscious style of interpersonal behavior, rather than to tracing its origins in infantile development.

2. Therapists who seek to revive the infantile roots of pathology depend exclusively on treatment techniques that are employed only occasionally by those who concentrate on contemporary events.

Those who focus on infantile conflicts maintain total passivity in the treatment relationship; the therapist becomes a "blank screen" upon which the patient "transfers" the feelings and attitudes he acquired toward significant persons of his childhood. To further facilitate the reliving of the past, the patient reclines on a couch, faces away from the therapist, becomes immersed in his own reveries and is allowed to wander in his thoughts, undistracted by external promptings. Significant childhood memories and emotions are revived during these "free associations," guided only by the therapist's occasional questions and carefully phrased interpretations; these comments

are employed selectively to circumvent or pierce the patient's defensive resistances to the recall of repressed material.

Therapists who deemphasize the revival of infantile memories make only occasional use of the recumbent couch position or the technique of free association. It is more convenient to explore realistic current problems by employing the "natural" face to face discussion interview. Moreover, the therapist does not assume the role of a totally neutral figure; rather, he becomes an active participant in a semireal relationship, serving as a catalyst who brings the patient's unconscious attitudes and strategies into awareness.

The distinctions noted previously between past and present focus, and passive and active techniques, lie on continua, with some intrapsychic approaches at the extremes, and others falling between. Five variants will be presented in the following sections, beginning with *classical psychoanalysis,* characterized by a "passive" reworking of infantile psychosexual conflicts, and progressing through *ego analysis, character analysis, interpersonal analysis* and *transactional analysis,* the last of which is characterized by the "active" reworking of the patient's current social roles.

## *CLASSICAL PSYCHOANALYSIS*

In their joint studies of hysteria, published in 1895, Breuer and Freud concluded that the neurotic symptom represented a repressed painful emotion that had been converted into a symbolic bodily form. They observed that by discharging (abreaction) these repressed emotions during hypnotic sessions, the patient's hysterical symptom frequently and suddenly disappeared. This confirmed, for Freud at least, the notion that hysteria was "bound energy" stemming from a repressed emotion. The technique of its release was referred to as the "cathartic" method.

Freud explored alternative methods by which to achieve the cathartic effect since many of his patients were unreceptive to hypnosis. He soon discovered that comparable results could be obtained simply by having patients recall and ventilate emotions associated with their painful experiences. However, he ran against new complications since many patients seemed unable to bring their memories and feelings into consciousness. To overcome this obstacle, he devised the method of "free association," having the patient relax on a couch and articulate any thoughts which crossed his mind, no matter how trivial or embarrassing. This procedure circumvented many of the memory blocks that had precluded the recall of significant past events and the discharge of their associated emotions. The following transcript indicates the typical flow of verbalizations in free association; comments noted in parentheses represent unverbalized observations and interpretations by the therapist (Wolberg, 1954).

### THERAPY EXCERPT 6
#### Free Association

*Patient* So I started walking, and walking, and decided to go behind the museum and walk through Central Park. So I walked and went through a back field and felt very excited and wonderful. I saw a park bench next to a clump of bushes and sat down. There was a rustle behind me and I got frightened. I thought of men concealing themselves in the bushes. I thought of the sex perverts I read about in Central Park. I wondered if there was someone behind me exposing himself. The idea is repulsive, but exciting too. I think of father now and feel excited. I think of an erect penis. This is connected with my father. There is something about this pushing in my mind. I don't know what it is, like on the border of my memory. (*pause*)

*Therapist* Mm hmm. (*pause*) On the border of your memory?

*Pt.* (*The patient breathes rapidly and seems to be under great tension.*) As a little girl, I slept with my father. I get a funny feeling. I get a funny feeling over my skin, tingly-like. It's a strange feeling, like a blindness, like not seeing something. My mind blurs and spreads over anything I look at. I've had this feeling off and on since I walked in the park. My mind seems to blank off like I can't think or absorb anything. [*This sounds like a manifestation of repression, with inhibition of intellectual functioning, perhaps as a way of coping with the anxiety produced by a return of the repressed.*]

*Th.* The blurring of your mind may be a way of pushing something out you don't want there. [*interpreting her symptoms as resistance*]

*Pt.* I just thought of something. When father died, he was nude. I looked at him, but I couldn't see anything, I couldn't think clearly. I was brought up not to be aware of the difference between a man and a woman. I feared my father, and yet I loved him. I slept with him when I was very little, on Saturdays and Sundays. A wonderful sense of warmth and security. There was nothing warmer or more secure. A lot of pleasure. I tingle all over now. It was a wonderful holiday when I was allowed to sleep with father. I can't seem to remember anything now. There's a blur in my mind. I feel tense and afraid.

*Th.* That blur contaminates your life. You are afraid of something or afraid of remembering something. [*focusing on her resistance*]

*Pt.* Yes, yes, but I can't. How can I? How can I?

*Th.* What comes to your mind?

Freud's search for residuals of the past led him next to the discovery of dreams as the "royal road to the unconscious." As he viewed it, repressed fears and desires filtered through the patient's defenses at night, although they took form in various symbolic disguises. By an introspective analysis of his own dreams, Freud in 1900 was able to present a technique for deciphering the unconscious significance of typical dream symbols. Wolberg (1954) provides the following transcript to demonstrate the character of dream recall, and the insight it often furnishes the patient regarding previously repressed emotions.

### THERAPY EXCERPT 7
#### Dream Recall and Analysis

*Patient* I dreamt my father was quite ill and I was taking care of him. I don't know what was the matter with him, but he was ill. I guess my sisters were around there somewhere, but I seemed to be feeding him and giving him his medicine. And there's one thing that sticks in my mind—a view of a spoon, an ordinary tablespoon, leaning up against something—in jelly or something along that line, something gelatinous. And I thought I was sort of half awake and I thought: "Well, Jesus Christ what am I doing—what can I say to that dream? It means that I am being my mother; I'm carrying out the functions of my mother, taking care of my father." And this is what I know it means: I have a desire or fear of being homosexual. I'm taking my mother's place. It hit me hard between the eyes and I almost fainted. And the next night I dreamt about a hasp, kind of a lock—you know, the kind where the hasp drops over a part when you drop a padlock into it. And I thought there was something about the hasp, and I thought I'm on this side of it; somebody is on the other side and can't get in, and I can't get over there. I could be turned around the other way. I could be over there, couldn't get in and, *he* could be here and not get out. It was not in any way a menace or anything like that, but it was that I'm here, and the presence of this hasp keeps *him* out and keeps *me* in. I can't get to him and he can't get to me. It's possible that you can turn it around, and the same thing would be true. In other words, it's an equation. (*pause*)

*Therapist* What are your associations to this dream?

*Pt.* That is, if I were on the other side, the hasp would prevent me from getting inside. He would be inside, and he would be prevented from getting outside. I just remembered that I had another dream. I dreamed about a man I worked for about the time I got married the second time. I had worked for him once before. He was very fond of me, and I of him. Now I suspect there was a funny component in that relationship. He was, himself, in analysis. We had a lot in common for artistic reasons, philosophic and political reasons. However, in the end he turned out to be a heel. In spite of this guy's glowing promises, and so on and so on, I hadn't been married a month before I was fired. It wasn't his fault; he was just going broke.

But the slob didn't even buy me a drink when I got married. This was a pal, wept on my shoulder when his wife left him, and I used to go up there to spend all the evenings with him. When he was very bad I'd stay over, you know, that kind of thing. He was going through what I went through with Anna, only I didn't know it then. You know I'd get flashes—now I know what they mean—that maybe he and I would be better off without women.

The last major feature of what Freud termed his therapy of "psychoanalysis" followed from his observation that patients often expressed totally unwarranted attitudes toward the therapist. Freud noted that these seemingly irrational emotions and thoughts reflected hidden attitudes toward significant persons of the past. This "transference" phenomenon, which illuminated important aspects of the repressed unconscious, could be facilitated if the therapist remained a totally neutral object; by assuming this passive role, the therapist "forced" the patient to attribute traits to him drawn from earlier relationships with parents or other significant childhood figures. The transference process is well illustrated in this excerpt; here, a female patient gains insight into the childhood roots of her inability to express aggressive feelings (Wolberg, 1954).

### THERAPY EXCERPT 8
*Transference Analysis*

*Patient* I want to talk about my feeling about you.

*Therapist* Mm hmm.

*Pt.* You sit here, a permissive person who lets me go on. I want to do something now, but I'm afraid you will be disappointed in me if I upset the apple cart, if I explode. I think we are too nice to each other. I'm ready not to be nice. My greatest fear of you is that you are potentially going to be severe with me if I let loose. Also, I fear I will let you down by not performing well, by not being nice. I feel I will gain your disapproval. And yet I see you don't condemn and don't criticize. It is still important to me to gain a nod from you or a smile. (*pause*)

*Th.* It sounds as if you would like to let loose with me, but you are afraid of what my response would be. [*summarizing and restating*]

*Pt.* I get so excited by what is happening here. I feel I'm being held back by needing to be nice. I'd like to blast loose sometimes, but I don't dare.

*Th.* Because you fear my reaction?

*Pt.* The worst thing would be that you wouldn't like me. You wouldn't speak to me friendly; you wouldn't smile; you'd feel you can't treat me and discharge me from treatment. But I know this isn't so, I know it.

*Th.* Where do you think these attitudes come from?

*Pt.* When I was nine years old, I read a lot about great men in history. I'd quote them and be dramatic. I'd want a sword at my side; I'd dress like an Indian. Mother would scold me. Don't frown, don't talk so much. Sit on your hands, over and over again. I did all kinds of things. I was a naughty child. She told me I'd be hurt. Then at fourteen I fell off a horse and broke my back. I had to be in bed. Mother then told me on the day I went riding not to, that I'd get hurt because the ground was frozen. I was a stubborn, self-willed child. Then I went against her will and suffered an accident that changed my life, a fractured back. Her attitude was, "I told you so." I was put in a cast and kept in bed for months.

*Th.* You were punished, so to speak, by this accident.

*Pt.* But I gained attention and love from mother for the first time. I felt so good. I'm ashamed to tell you this. Before I healed I opened the cast and tried to walk to make myself sick again so I could stay in bed longer.

*Th.* How does that connect up with your impulse to be sick now and stay in bed so much? [*The patient has these tendencies, of which she is ashamed.*]

*Pt.* Oh ... (*pause*)

*Th.* What do you think?

*Pt.* Oh my god, how infantile, how ungrown up. (*pause*) It must be so. I want people to love me and be sorry for me. Oh, my god. How completely childish. It is, *is* that. My mother must have ignored me when I was little, and I wanted so to be loved. [*This sounds like insight.*]

*Th.* So that it may have been threatening to go back to being self-willed and unloved after you got out of the cast. [*interpretation*]

*Pt.* It did. My life changed. I became meek and controlled. I couldn't get angry or stubborn afterward.

*Th.* Perhaps if you go back to being stubborn with *me,* you would be returning to how you were before, that is, active, stubborn but unloved.

*Pt.* (*excitedly*) And, therefore, losing your love. I need you, but after all you aren't going to reject me. The pattern is so established now that the threat of the loss of love is too overwhelming with everybody, and I've got to keep myself from acting selfish or angry.

To Freud, psychopathology represented the persistence of repressed instinctual drives that had generated severe conflicts during psychosexual development. Not only did the individual expend energies to control the resurgence of these memories, but since the conflicts they engendered remained unresolved, they persisted into adulthood and caused the individual to act as if he were living in the past. The task of therapy was to uproot the unconscious and to free potentially constructive energies that had been tied up in the task of keeping it repressed. To do this, Freud employed the procedures of free association, dream interpretation and most importantly, the analysis of the "transference neurosis," to be discussed shortly. Adherence to these goals and procedures is variously termed orthodox, Freudian or "classical psychoanalysis."

The feature which distinguishes the classical procedure from "neo-analytic" methods is the central role given to the elucidation and resolution of the *transference neurosis*. All intrapsychic therapists recognize that patients project onto the therapist attitudes and emotions that derive from past relationships. Classical analysts go one step further; they consider these transference phenomena to represent the nucleus of the patient's infantile conflicts and pathological defenses. Accordingly, classical therapists seek to foster the expression of transference materials, revealing not only their current manifestations, but exposing, analyzing and reworking their infantile roots. Unless these origins are thoroughly resolved, treatment is considered incomplete.

To "force" a transference neurosis, which ostensibly duplicates with the therapist the "infantile neurosis" generated in early psychosexual conflicts, the therapist assumes the passive role, requests that the patient recline on the couch and verbalize by free association, analyzes dream materials and schedules no less than five sessions per week to assure intense contact. Should transference phenomena be actively resisted, the therapist attempts to break through resistances by interpreting their character. As transference materials become manifest, their irrational and infantile basis is thoroughly analyzed, and their persistent effects since childhood demonstrated. Insight into these transference distortions is expected to free the patient from their pernicious effects by breaking the hold of infantile misconceptions and fears, liberating energies that had been tied up in repression and providing a renewed sense of self-mastery.

## EGO ANALYSIS

As was described in chapters 1 and 2, "ego" theorists believe that the infant possesses innate adaptive capacities which, if properly stimulated, enable him to develop in a healthy fashion. Although ego theorists accept Freud's "id" theory, which states that the seeds of pathology are the conflicts between libidinous instincts and the demands of society, they assert that an equal if not greater cause of pathology is the failure of adaptive potentials to develop adequately. Accordingly, ego therapy focuses not only on the resolution of the infantile neurosis, but also on the reconstruction of the patient's deficit adaptive capacities.

Although ego analysts pay less attention to infantile id conflicts than to infantile ego deficien-cies, they retain the classical psychoanalyst's emphasis on the revivification and resolution of the past. To elicit early memories and provide the patient with insights into the roots of his difficulties, ego analysts adhere closely to the classical techniques of free association, recumbent position, dream interpretation and transference analysis. However, in addition to these procedures, they actively promote the strengthening and expansion of the patient's repertoire of adaptive behaviors. By various interpretive suggestions, they seek not only to eliminate the destructive and energy-consuming consequences of id conflicts, but also to build up the patient's deficient ego capacities. The manner in which this is done and how these active steps intermesh with the passive procedures required to foster transference, have not been spelled out in the writings of the ego analysts.

## CHARACTER ANALYSIS

"Character analysts," together with the "interpersonal" and "transactional" analysts to be discussed in the next two sections, pay less heed to matters of the past than they do to the resolution of present difficulties. Moreover, according to these "social" theorists, psychopathology does not arise from conflicts or deficiencies associated with instinctual sources, but from the interpersonal character of early experience. In another deviation from the doctrines of Freud, they assert that adult pathology is not simply a repetition of "nuclear" infantile neuroses. Early experiences are recognized as the basis for later difficulties, but intervening events are thought to modify their impact; coping behaviors learned early in life promote new difficulties which, in turn, provoke new adaptive strategies. By adulthood, then, an extensive series of events have occurred, making present behaviors and attitudes far removed from their initial childhood origins. Consequently, and in contrast to both classical and ego analysts, "social" analysts consider it digressive and wasteful to reconstruct either the infantile neuroses of the id or the adaptive deficiencies of the infantile ego. In their stead, efforts can more fruitfully be expended in uncovering and resolving *current* unconscious attitudes and strategies.

Karen Horney (1937, 1950), although preceded by Alfred Adler and Wilhelm Stekel in this philosophy, was the most successful theorist in pointing out the importance of current life conflicts. As conceived by Horney, neuroses were rooted in infantile anxieties. Stress in childhood led initially to the development of a wide variety of spontaneous coping mechanisms. Ultimately, these early mechanisms were narrowed down to a single ingrained "character trait" that became the core of the patient's coping style. However, a "basic conflict" remained as to which coping mechanisms should be employed. To resolve this conflict, the patient repressed the distracting alternatives, and formed an "idealized self-image." This fictional self-concept forced the patient to misrepresent the true variety of his inner feelings and thoughts. In his struggle to retain this false image, the patient's available energies for constructive growth were drained, and he was caught in vicious circles that intensified his difficulties and estranged him further from his "real" self.

Character analysis consists of breaking through the patient's idealized self-image by exposing him to the true variety and contradictory nature of the impulses and attitudes that rage within him. To achieve this, the therapist puts the patient through a self-disillusioning process in which the "neurotic pride" with which he holds his idealized self is shown to be both irrational and self-destructive.

Although face to face discussion is the more typical treatment procedure, free association is often used to uncover the character of the patient's repressed conflicts. Similarly, relevant childhood experiences are probed and unraveled, but not for the purpose of resolving them, as in classical analysis. Rather they are exposed to demonstrate both the foundations of current difficulties and the repetitive sequence of destructive consequences they have caused. The therapist actively interprets the patient's transference distortions, not only in the treatment interaction, but as they are expressed in the patient's everyday relationships with others. The focus on the current ramifications of character trends and the direct mode of attack upon the vicious circles they engender, further distinguish Horney's treatment approach from both classical and ego analysis.

## INTERPERSONAL ANALYSIS

Foremost among the "social" therapists is Harry Stack Sullivan (1953, 1954), whose interpersonal-anxiety theory was described in chapter 2. Sullivan's interpersonal approach to analysis was formulated more systematically than that of Horney's character therapy. He directed his efforts not only to "parataxic distortion," a process akin to the classical transference phenomenon, but to

a host of other habitual and anxiety-reducing unconscious maneuvers such as selective inattentions, memory dissociations and inaccurate self-evaluations. The task of therapy was to unravel this unconscious pattern of self-protective but ultimately self-defeating measures.

Like Horney, Sullivan's approach to therapy is considerably more flexible than that of classical analysis. Free association in the recumbent position may be employed, but more often the patient sits upright in face to face discussion interviews. At times, the therapist will attempt to elicit childhood memories and dream materials; however, his focus is directed primarily to present reality problems. Sullivan believed that the classical passive or blank-screen attitude should be replaced by a more natural expression of the therapist's real feelings and thoughts. Beyond this, he proposed that certain attitudes be simulated by the therapist so as to throw the patient "off guard," thereby provoking therapeutically illuminating responses. In short, Sullivan enjoins the therapist to participate actively in an interpersonal treatment relationship, exploiting his own reactions and feigning others, as a means of uncovering the patient's current distortions and unconscious styles of behavior.

The primary instrument of Sullivan's therapy is skillful interviewing. By this Sullivan means subtly drawing out the patient's unconscious distortions by careful listening and questioning, suggesting that the patient may harbor unwarranted preconceptions of himself and others, and offering tentative speculations as to how these self and interpersonal attitudes may have caused problem relationships in the past and how they may be altered in the future. The interpersonal interview interaction, then, rather than the passive free association technique, was considered by Sullivan to be the most fruitful means of disentangling the web of unconscious distortions, along with suggestions to prevent its perpetuation.

## TRANSACTIONAL ANALYSIS

A progressive shift from a biological to a sociocultural orientation may be seen in the several intrapsychic therapies discussed so far. The classical approach concentrates on the libidinous instincts of the id; ego analysts turn their attention to the instinctual reservoir of the ego's socially adaptive behaviors; in character analysis, it is the person as a complete entity rather than that segment associated with his instinctual drives and potentials that is the focus of attention; the

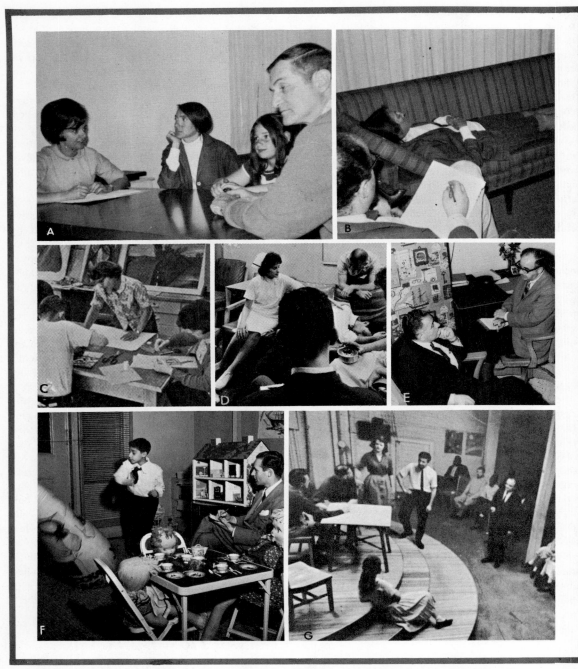

Figure 15-5   Therapeutic techniques and settings. *A*. Family therapy. *B*. Classical psychoanalysis. (Parts *A* and *B* from Lincoln Consultation Center, Bethlehem, Pa.) *C*. Activity therapy. *D*. Discussion group therapy. (Parts *C* and *D* from National Institute of Mental Health, Bethesda, Md.) *E*. Phenomenological interview therapy. (Courtesy of Allentown State Hospital, Allentown, Pa.) *F*. Play therapy. (From Monkmeyer Press Photo Service, New York.) *G*. Psychodrama. (Courtesy of J. R. Black.)

interpersonal approach advances from the person's total "character" pattern to those features which represent his relationships to others; and in transactional analysis, to be discussed be-

low, the progression continues toward the sociocultural end of the continuum by directing attention to the "roles" assumed by the patient in societal groups.

Employing patient-therapist communications as their data and drawing their models from either mathematical game theorists such as von Neumann and Morgenstern (1944) or social role theorists such as Mead (1934), a number of recent therapists have formulated an approach to treatment that is best depicted by the label "transactional analysis." Among them are Grinker (1961), Berne (1961; 1964) and Haley (1963); the best known of these men, due largely to the witty and phrase-making character of his popular works, is Eric Berne, whose views we shall summarize to illustrate the transactional approach.

According to Berne, patient-therapist interactions provide insight into the patient's characteristic interpersonal maneuvers and mirror the several varieties of his everyday social behaviors. These maneuvers are translated into caricature forms known as "pastimes" or "games," each of which highlights an unconscious strategy of the patient to defend against "childish" anxieties or to secure other equally immature rewards. This analytical process is akin to that contained in the analysis of transference phenomena, although Berne dramatizes these operations by tagging them with rather clever and humorous labels (e.g., "schlemeil," "ain't it wonderful" or "do me something").

Berne contends, as did Horney, that contradictory character trends coexist within the patient; however, in contrast to Horney, no single trend or "ego state" as Berne puts it, achieves dominance. Rather, these ego states are fluid, with one or another coming to the fore depending on the nature of the social maneuvers of others. Three ego states may be elicited as a consequence of these reciprocal maneuvers or "transactions": archaic or infantile behaviors, known as the *child* state within the patient; attitudes reflecting his parent's orientation, termed the *parent* ego state; and mature qualities the patient has acquired throughout life, termed the *adult* state.

The unconscious attitudes and strategies of these conflicting ego states are exposed and interpreted in transactional analyses. In order to promote insight into the patient's more immature maneuvers, the therapist allows his own parent, child and adult states to transact with those of the patient. This procedure strengthens the patient's adult state since it serves to teach him to withstand manipulations by others that formerly evoked his child and parent trends. As a consequence of these therapeutic transactions, the patient gains insight into the foolish "games" he "plays" in current relationships, and reinforces those skills and attitudes that comprise his mature adult state.

## ADJUNCTIVE INTRAPSYCHIC PROCEDURES

Several techniques have been devised to facilitate the exposure and manipulation of unconscious processes in cases that are resistant to traditional analytical procedures. Three will be briefly noted: hypnotherapy, art therapy and play therapy.

**Hypnotherapy.** Hypnotic induction, either through verbal means or by use of drugs (narcotherapy), may be employed to circumvent barriers to both insight and action (Wolberg, 1967). During the trance state, achieved at the hands of a trusted therapist, the patient may be able to ease his repressive controls and thereby revive memories and emotions that resist interview and free association techniques. Similarly, posthypnotic suggestions may provide a needed impetus to behaviors for which the patient is psychologically prepared, but unable to muster the "courage" to carry out. As a rule, hypnosis should be utilized as an adjunct to rather than the primary instrument of a treatment program.

**Art Therapy.** Drawings and paintings as instruments for deciphering unconscious processes have been valued diagnostic tools for over a half century. More recently, these "artistic" activities have shown themselves to be useful vehicles for achieving emotional catharsis and insight, especially among patients who have difficulties in discharging their tensions or in translating their inchoate thoughts into words (Bender, 1937; Naumberg, 1966); once stated in pictorial terms, the patient may more readily grasp the character of his unconscious inclinations.

Spontaneous art productions are most commonly executed in the treatment setting, where the patient can be observed as he engages in the process, and where therapeutic discussions can follow immediately after completion of the work. Some therapists suggest, additionally, that the patient draw and paint at home where he can discharge and symbolically represent diffusive feelings when these emotions are "naturally" provoked.

**Play Therapy.** These procedures achieve ends similar to those of art therapy; their utility, however, is limited to children primarily between the ages of two and 12. Given opportunities to handle a variety of "suggestive" toy materials, the youngster often vents a wide range of emotions and attitudes that he normally dare not or cannot express (A. Freud, 1928; Axline, 1947; Woltman, 1959).

For some therapists, the primary value of play activity is diagnostic, providing insights into the child's repressed or otherwise unverbalized feelings. Others see it as a cathartic device to release pent-up emotions. A third group employs the data of the child's actions and associated fantasies as a basis for interpretation, translating the unconscious meaning of these behaviors directly to the child in the hope thereby of disintegrating his "infantile neurosis." Still others consider play as a vehicle through which the child can establish a wholesome relationship with a benevolent and accepting adult, thus counteracting unfortunate parental experiences. Many therapists view the play situation as an opportunity to achieve several of the previously mentioned gains, exploiting one or another as fits the case.

## EVALUATION

Intrapsychic therapists contend that treatment approaches designed "merely" to reduce behavioral symptoms and phenomenological complaints fail to deal with the root source of pathology and are bound therefore to be of short-lived efficacy; as they view it, therapy must reconstruct the "inner" processes that underlie overt behaviors and complaints. Intrapsychic treatment undertakes this difficult task. It does not sacrifice the goal of personality reconstruction for short-term symptom relief; reworking the source of the problem rather than controlling its effects is what distinguishes intrapsychic therapy as a treatment procedure. Once the unconscious roots of the impairment are disclosed and dislodged, the patient will no longer precipitate new difficulties for himself and will be free to develop strategies that are consonant with his healthy potentials.

No one can question the goals of intrapsychic therapy; they are highly commendable, if difficult to achieve. It is not the goals of the intrapsychic approach which are viewed critically; rather, dissent arises with regard to the theoretical rationale, technique and feasibility of these methods. Let us note several of the objections.

*First,* and perhaps the most persistent criticism, is the assertion that intrapsychic data are both vague and inaccessible. Therapists are expected to manipulate "metaphysical" entities whose very existence is unverifiable and whose

modification can never be empirically confirmed. Exerting efforts to alter these unobservable processes is considered nothing less than foolishness, and claiming success in such ventures is nothing but an article of faith. In short, dealing with matters of the unconscious is a throwback to the days when mysticism flourished, a continuation of a prescientific way of thinking from which psychopathology must be liberated.

*Second,* the process of intrapsychic treatment is considered unnecessarily involved and digressive, dredging up facts and events which are entirely subsidiary if not irrelevant to the nature of the patient's problem. Rather than focusing directly on the difficulty, as do therapists of other schools, the intrapsychic therapist pursues a host of activities that turn the patient's attention to his past, his unconscious mechanisms and his "deeper" motivations. Such circuitous pathways to the resolution of pathology are seen not only as wasteful and time consuming, but as a sign of presumption and arrogance on the part of the therapist since he asserts that the patient is troubled by something other than he claims to be. By his therapeutic maneuvers, the therapist "forces" the patient to accept ostensible ailments that fit the therapist's theoretical presuppositions. The fact that the "discovery" of these "underlying problems" proves to be a laborious and prolonged task and one of doubtful therapeutic value is further reason to question the intrapsychic approach.

*Third,* even if intrapsychic therapies were shown to be efficacious, few patients are able to devote the time or expend the funds required to pursue a full course of treatment. Most analytical techniques demand at least three or four sessions per week over a two to five year span. Assuming treatment was feasible on these accounts, problems would arise since there are too few trained therapists to make this approach available to the masses. In short, intrapsychic therapies must be relegated to a secondary position among treatment techniques on wholly practical grounds, if on no other.

Let us turn next to questions of effectiveness since the justification for this form of therapy must rest on its superior efficacy rather than its practical feasibility.

### EFFICACY (OUTCOME STUDIES)

The number of efficacy studies on intrapsychic therapy is shockingly small; moreover, of the few investigations scattered in the literature, none fulfills even the minimum desiderata of proper research design and control. Available are miscellaneous clinical reports based on heterogeneous patient populations subjected to poorly described clinical procedures; none is compared to control groups or evaluated in accord with objective criteria of improvement.

That there are formidable difficulties involved in the planning and execution of therapeutic studies cannot be denied. However, there can be no justification for the failure to carry out thorough studies of analytical techniques, especially in light of their 70 year history and the more than one hundred thousand patients who have been exposed to treatment. It behooves practitioners of the intrapsychic approach to undertake these studies since existing research, inadequate though it is, suggests that patients subjected to analytical therapies improve to no greater extent than patients who receive no treatment at all.

Eysenck has convincingly demonstrated in his systematic literature reviews (1952, 1960, 1964, 1965) that intrapsychic therapies are associated with no better than between 39 to 67 per cent significant improvement in cases for which they are ostensibly best suited, that of the neurotic disorders. If we compare these figures with the published base rate level of improvement shown among similarly disturbed individuals who did not receive formal therapy, that is, the so-called "spontaneous remission" percentage of two thirds improved (Denker, 1946; Schorer et al., 1966), we are led to the rather disconcerting conclusion that analytical treatment is no better and perhaps even *less* efficacious than no treatment.

Those who rise to the defense if not the support of analytical therapies (Rosenzweig, 1954; DeCharms et al., 1954; Strupp, 1964; Keisler, 1966; Wolberg, 1967) are unable to adduce empirical evidence favoring the efficacy of intrapsychic procedures. What they do point out quite correctly is that evidence used in criticism of these therapies is itself based on shoddy research.

In short, the data and arguments for and against analytical techniques are entirely equivocal since no adequately designed studies have been done. Definitive conclusions regarding efficacy simply cannot be drawn at the present time.

## MODE OF ACTION (PROCESS STUDIES)

Data concerning the intrapsychic mode of action, that is, the ingredients that contribute to treatment change, are no more available than those concerning efficacy. Not only is there a total lack of research on this score, but intrapsychic therapists have failed to specify which aspects of the treatment technique are crucial in achieving their objectives. Moreover, no theorist has translated the various elements of these procedures in terms conducive to research investigation. In his penetrating essay on the "myths" of therapy research, Keisler poses the following incisive questions concerning the classical analytical approach (1966):

What is the attitude, technique, or personality characteristic essential before a therapist can be said to be doing analytical therapy? The answer seems quite unclear and at best multifaceted and inexplicit. It seems to be an attitude: the therapist must present himself as a neutral and ambiguous stimulus to the patient, in order not to distort the patient's task of free-association and dream production or hamper the appearance of transference phenomena. Yet, at subsequent stages of the interaction the analyst apparently becomes quite non-ambiguous, offering interpretations of childhood experiences and the transference relationship. Where does the one attitude (or complex of attitudes) end, and the other begin? What are the behavioral cues which determine the shift of set? What is the interrelationship of the various attitudes (inaction, ambiguity and/or neutrality) prevailing in the earlier stages of therapy? How do these attitudes relate to the interviewing techniques of questioning and clarification which seem to prevail concurrently?

Since there are no theoretical answers to these questions each researcher attacks the variables most interesting to himself (e.g, interpretation, therapist ambiguity, therapist general activity, counter-transference, insight, resistance, anxiety, and the like). Although Freudian theory seems to generate many constructs, the explicit integration or description of the essential ingredients nowhere occurs.

In summary, then, published outcome research offers little support for the view that intrapsychic therapies achieve significantly beneficial results. Moreover, there are few process data available to indicate the essential ingredients of analytical techniques. Research on these methods is both skimpy and of poor methodological quality. Given the equivocal character of the evidence, no conclusions can be drawn until additional and appreciably more sophisticated research is undertaken.

# GROUP TREATMENT METHODS

The impact of group factors in molding and sustaining behaviors and attitudes has been thoroughly researched in recent decades. During this same period, there has been a growing awareness of the paucity of trained personnel to meet the increasing need for therapeutic services, especially in cutting the backlog of chronic, institutionalized cases; spurred by practical considerations, psychopathologists sought to devise new and more expeditious ways of treating patients for whom individual therapy was neither feasible nor available. The combination of "group dynamics" research and the need for more expedient forms of therapy led to the rapid growth of group treatment methods.

A small band of therapists had begun to employ group procedures more than a half century ago. J. H. Pratt, a Boston physician, held special classes as early as 1905 for tubercular patients, advising them not only on proper habits of physical care, but on methods to deal with the emotional complications that accompanied their illness. In 1909, L. C. Marsh, a minister, delivered inspirational lectures to groups of state hospital patients; he noted that therapeutic benefits were greatly enhanced if patients were enjoined to participate in discussions following his talks. Similar group discussion therapies were instituted by J. L. Moreno, a Viennese psychiatrist, in 1910. In the late 1920's, S. R. Slavson initiated programs of "activity group therapy" for children between eight and 15 years of age. In the early 1930's, L. Wender and P. Schilder employed a psychoanalytically oriented approach in the treatment of hospital groups. A rapid spurt of interest in these methods quickly followed; thus, although there were less than 125 publications on group techniques between 1906 and 1940, the number increased between 1946 and 1950 to more than 500; almost 900 articles were published between 1951 and 1955, and from 1961 to 1965, the figure approaches two thousand.

## Rationale

Group therapists contend that in the semirealistic group setting patients display most clearly those attitudes and habits that intrude and complicate their real, everyday relationships with others. The interplay among group members provides numerous opportunities to observe distortions in perception and behavior which aggravate and perpetuate interpersonal difficulties. Since the atmosphere and intent of the group are characterized by mutual support, these distortions can be rectified and more socially adaptive alternatives acquired in their stead. Moreover, since each patient expresses his deeper feelings and attitudes with the knowledge that similar experiences are shared by fellow group members, he gradually learns to tolerate himself and to be sympathetic to the needs of others. As a consequence, he develops greater self-acceptance, a capacity to view things from the perspective of others, a freedom from self-defeating interpersonal strategies and the ability to participate more effectively in social relationships.

Let us enumerate the advantages of group therapy as seen by its exponents. *First,* and perhaps most significant, is the fact that the patient acquires his new learnings in a setting that is similar to his "natural" interpersonal world; relating to peer group members is a more realistic experience than that of the authoritarian therapist-patient relationship. It is easier to "generalize" to the extratherapeutic world what one learns in peer-group settings since it is closer to "reality" than is the individual treatment setting. *Second,* since the patient must cope with a host of different personalities in his group, he acquires a range of flexible interpersonal skills; in this way, he learns to relate not only to the neutral or uniform style of a single therapist, but to a variety of disparate personality types. *Third,* the semirealistic atmosphere of the group provides the patient with ample opportunities to try out his new attitudes and behaviors; group therapy serves, then, as a proving ground, an experimental laboratory within which the formative stages of new learnings can be rehearsed and refined. *Fourth,* by observing that his feelings are shared by others, the patient is not only reassured that he is not alone in his suffering, but regains thereby some of his former self-confidence and self-respect. *Fifth,* no longer ashamed of his thoughts and emotions, he can give up the barriers he has defensively placed between himself and others, enabling him to relate to them without fear and embarrassment. *Sixth,* able to accept criticism and to forego his pathological interpersonal defenses, he begins to see himself as others do and develops a more realistic appraisal than heretofore of his social strengths and weaknesses. *Seventh,* concurrent with increased accuracy of self-perception, he learns to observe others more objectively and gradually relinquishes his previous tendencies to distort his interpersonal judgments. *Eighth,* now able to respect the feelings of others, he can share their perspectives and begin to provide them with assistance in resolving *their* difficulties.

Despite these advantages, critics of group therapies note that "deeper" personal problems are often by-passed and unresolved, lost in the shuffle of the many voices that compete in the struggle to gain ascendancy within the group. The fluid and rapid process of group interchange may not allow for the prolonged probing needed to expose and rework the roots of problems, especially among more hesitant or retiring patients. Other critics note that the free-wheeling expression of attitudes among group members can seriously undermine the security of certain patients, many of whom may withdraw from treatment before these injuries can be repaired.

### Classification

The advantages and disadvantages just noted do not apply with equal force to the several varieties of group therapy. In the following sections we will not deal with "inspirational" and lecture type group procedures (e.g., Alcoholics Anonymous) that are designed to alleviate special circumscribed problems such as alcoholism, drug addiction, obesity and the like. Rather, we will limit ourselves to methods that seek to rework more pervasive problems and which employ professional leaders as therapists.

There is no single dimension along which group therapies can be aligned; almost as many variants and combinations thereof exist as there are practitioners of the art. Some therapists are directive; others are nondirective. Among these therapists, some are inclined to offer interpretations whereas others await their formulation by the patient. Many therapists become "equals" in group discussions, unburdening their own feelings and attitudes; others remain aloof and detached. Some therapists employ group methods as adjuncts to concurrent individual treatment; others dispense entirely with individual sessions. Many recommend that group members meet in sessions without the therapist; others oppose such meetings. There are "closed" and "open" groups, the former maintaining the same group members through fixed periods of treatment, the latter continuing indefinitely with new members added as old members "graduate." Some groups are formed on the basis of a common problem such as delinquency or marital difficulties; others are planned to be as heterogeneous as possible. Obviously, no simple classification is possible.

Nevertheless, we will describe in the following sections what we believe are the five basic variants of group therapy. They differ, essentially, in the "process" of treatment; some engage in "activities" thought to be of therapeutic value; others "discuss" interpersonal feelings and attitudes; some "play roles" that simulate real life situations.

## ACTIVITY GROUPS

In this therapeutic arrangement, patients join in a club-life situation to pursue a common set of activities and interests such as games, handicrafts, travel, painting or dancing. Developed first by Slavson (1943) as a technique for the remediation of social difficulties in children and adolescents, activity therapy has taken root as a model for group programs of occupational and social rehabilitation in hospitals and outpatient clinics. The method is most applicable to patients with social deficits (e.g., shy, isolated or chronically withdrawn cases) or those whose behaviors have been socially troublesome (e.g., ungiving, impulsive or acting out cases). The outward appearance of these groups is not unlike a normal social club; it is designed, however, to expand and strengthen each patient's repertoire of adaptive and wholesome interpersonal skills.

In contrast to other treatment groups, activity therapy makes little or no attempt to expose and discuss the patient's pathological attitudes and emotions; it simply provides a social behavior-learning environment. Although feelings may be freely vented within broad limits, there is no effort to develop insight into the roots or character of these feelings. Rather, adaptive learning accrues by the simple process of participating and sharing in group projects. Guided subtly but firmly by an observant and sympathetic therapist, patients are gradually led to acquire a sense of increased self-initiative and group responsibility. By quietly and indirectly discouraging untoward behaviors and by facilitating and openly rewarding constructive alternatives, the therapist molds the pattern of group interaction in directions suitable to the varied "growth" needs of each member.

## DISCUSSION GROUPS

This category includes the most common varieties of group therapy. In it, usually six to ten patients participate in leader-directed or nondirected discussions; some groups focus on specific topics whereas others have open discourse in which "anything goes."

Among the earlier variants of this technique were "directive-didactic" sessions, usually employed in hospital settings; here, the therapist, often a minister, presented an uplifting lecture, followed by a group discussion during which each patient was exhorted to see the "errors of his way," to regain his "will" and to bring himself back to the mainstream of normal life. More recent and sophisticated forms of this inspirational therapy have provided patients with educational insights into the causes of their pathology, in the hope of making their anxieties less ominous and to suggest more "reasonable" and positive outlooks on life.

Nondirective methods, based on a self-actualization philosophy, have been another recent variant of the group discussion approach. Here, the therapist plays a passive role, assuming a congenial and nonjudgmental attitude that encourages patients to expose and explore their feelings until they discover better ways than before to resolve them.

Central to most discussion therapies is the reciprocal exposure and expression of each member's attitudes and feelings. As topics and events unfold, each person brings into the open, as candidly as he can, the various emotions and thoughts he experiences toward other members. The patient becomes cognizant of his idiosyncratic sensitivities by contrasting his reactions with those of others to the same set of circumstances. Not only does he become aware of his selective distortions, but he begins to see how these reactions perpetuate his difficulties and create new ones.

Another feature that characterizes discussion groups is the way in which patients interpret each other's difficulties; this interpretive interplay is well illustrated in the following transcript (Hinckley and Hermann, 1951).

### THERAPY EXCERPT 9
### Discussion Group Therapy

*Therapist.* Will you review for us what happened last time, Alice?

*Alice.* I was scared. I didn't like getting together with people I hardly knew. Telling things about myself was awful.

*June.* Well, I felt just the opposite. I loved it. I suppose the lesson of the session was that by listening to others and helping them, we learn about ourselves.

*Ellen.* I'm having a bad day. Someone bumped my car, and I've been fuming. I'm not sure I can contribute much today at all.

*June.* Now that I think about it, I don't know where to start in regard to my problems. I'm too fat. I know it's from eating too much, but there must be some reason behind it, I know. Why do I pick at food all the time?

*Therapist.* Tell us something more about your background, if you will.

*June.* Well, everybody in our family have beautiful figures. They all disapprove of my over-eating.

*Sara.* You mean you have to fight it? You don't look overweight to me.

*June* (in great surprise).  Won't you all come home with me?

*Alice.* Are you hungry all the time? Are you hungry when you're happy and satisfied?

*June.* No, I guess not. I was with a fellow over the weekend and had a wonderful time, and I wasn't hungry at all.

*Therapist.* Sounds psychological. Perhaps you know something of the psychology of overeating.

*Alice.* My little niece has the same sort of trouble.

*June.* Well, I suppose when you keep on eating all the time and never really get satisfied, it can't be food you want at all. (Silence) Maybe—maybe—the eating is a substitute for something else that is lacking.

*Therapist.* You feel something else is lacking?

*Alice.* She is right. Something else probably is lacking. She wants something, but it's not food. She feels OK—at least not hungry—when she is with her boyfriend. (Laughing) Maybe it's love she is looking for.

*June* (surprised). Why, yes, that could be, couldn't it? How reasonable that seems! But why should I need to look for love?

*Alice.* Guess I can't help there. I don't know.

*June.* There must be something wrong in the family—something lacking. Can it be love there, too? Oh, I'm getting confused.

*Sara.* No, I think you are on the right track. I've got trouble along that line, too, but I don't try to solve mine by eating. I do it in other ways.

*Karen.* Well, what is this trouble at home? I've got troubles with my boy friend, and I never can get along at home. My mother nags if I don't jump when she wants me to. My boy friend used to take my part, but since my father died, he sides with my mother when he knows about our arguments. My mother ends up crying all the time. Something is wrong.

*Therapist.* Conflict with parents sometimes does cause painful behavior symptoms.

In contrast to analytical groups, to be described next, no effort is made in discussion therapies to uncover and trace the childhood roots of these interpersonal distortions. Rather, the focus is on the here and now and, quite often on just those events that take place in the ongoing interactions within the group itself.

### ANALYTICAL GROUPS

Analytical groups take their inspiration from one or another of the many varieties of intrapsychic theory. In common with individual analytical approaches, the focus of group analysis is the exposure of unconscious attitudes and strategies, the discharge of repressed emotions and the reconstruction of childhood-rooted pathological trends. This is accomplished, as in classical techniques, by the use of free association, the interpretation of dreams and the analysis of the complex network of multiple transference relationships that emerge between patients.

Several therapists in the mid-1920's formulated the processes of group interaction in terms of intrapsychic concepts, but it was Schilder (1939) who first applied classical analytical techniques to group treatment. Slavson, the founder of activity therapy, in both early and later writings (1943, 1964) contributed a systematic rationale for resolving the multiple transferences that arise in group settings. More recently, Wolf (1949, 1950, 1962) has advanced a step by step technique for uprooting early memories, penetrating unconscious conflicts and defenses and working through the intricate pattern of group transference relationships. He contends that the exposure and resolution of unconscious materials and transference phenomena occur more rapidly and thoroughly in groups than is possible in individual analytical treatment.

## ROLE-PLAYING GROUPS

The model for this group approach is Moreno's technique of *psychodrama* (1934, 1946), a method designed to stimulate the open portrayal of unconscious attitudes and emotions through spontaneous playacting. In a typical procedure, several patients and therapists enact an unrehearsed series of scenes in which they assume roles simulating people that are significant in their real lives. Patients are encouraged to relive and express with dramatic intensity feelings and thoughts that ostensibly could not be tapped or vented through normal conversational methods.

Many role-playing techniques have been devised through the years (Corsini, 1966). Some seek to reenact earlier problem relationships; the intent, here, is to aid the patient to discharge repressed feelings and to test out new, more liberated reactions. For example, a shy patient, who previously allowed his father to degrade his efforts toward independence, will assume the role of his former self and assert dramatically what he could not express in real life. Another method, termed "role reversal," is intended among other goals to aid patients in gaining insight into how others view them; thus, two patients take the role of one another and portray in caricature form the attitudes and behaviors they believe depict the person whose role they assume. Other techniques focus on preparing the patient for future difficulties, hoping thereby to desensitize

inner fears and bolster skills necessary for their successful resolution.

The primary value of the role-playing group is that it simulates more closely than conversational expression ever can real problem situations; in other words, generalization from the therapeutic situation to the extratherapeutic world can readily be achieved. Additionally, patients can be "carried away" in their role portrayals, enabling their deepest emotions and attitudes to be brought to the surface. As a consequence, unconscious forces surge forth, come into sharp focus and can be dealt with immediately and effectively through "on the spot" manipulations by therapeutic co-actors. Thus, its exponents contend, psychodramatic methods are more powerful and efficient than are the "pallid" insight-discussion techniques for exposing and resolving deeply repressed unconscious materials.

## FAMILY GROUPS

The patient who seeks therapy is often but one member of a pathological family unit. Not uncommonly, interactions between family members form a complex of shared psychopathology, the patient being merely its most dramatic "symptom."

The "primary" patient is enmeshed in his daily encounters in a system of interlocking attitudes and behaviors that not only intensify his illness, but sustain the pathological family unit. Each member, through reciprocal perceptual and behavioral distortions, reinforces pathogenic reactions in others, thus contributing to a vicious circle of self-perpetuating responses. It follows logically from this premise, that therapy must intervene not only with the patient himself, but with the total family; in short, what is needed is family therapy, not individual therapy.

Several variants in technique have been proposed to achieve the goal of disentangling these reciprocally reinforcing pathological family relations (Ackerman, 1958; Jackson and Weakland, 1961; Satir, 1964; Boszormenyi-Nagy and Framo, 1965). Essentially, the therapist brings several members of the family together, explores major areas of conflict and exposes the destructive behaviors that have perpetuated their difficulties. The therapist clarifies misunderstandings, dissolves barriers to communication and neutralizes areas of prejudice, hostility, guilt and fear. In this manner, he gradually disengages the pathogenic machinery of the family system and enables its members to explore healthier patterns of relating. By recommending new, more wholesome attitudes and behaviors and by supporting family members as they test out these patterns, the therapist may succeed in resolving not only the difficulties of the primary patient, but pathological trends that have taken root in all members.

The following transcript illustrates a typical interchange in family therapy. It is drawn from the fourth session of a group that was formed because of the mother's concern that her son (Dick), a 13 year old boy, was becoming increasingly rebellious and potentially delinquent. The treatment unit consists of the therapist, the mother and father (Mr. and Mrs. Clay), Dick and his ten year old sister, Janet (Sundberg and Tyler, 1962).

### THERAPY EXCERPT 10
*Family Therapy*

*Therapist.* I think last time one thing that was mentioned was that we need a lot more understanding, and that's our task here—to try to understand each other. The purpose of this kind of meeting is to help the family to talk together and to see how each other feels about things.

*Mrs. Clay.* I felt that something was brought out last time that was really helpful to me and that is that I spend too much time moralizing and talking. I think I have overdone that.

*Therapist (to Dick and Janet).* How did the rest of you feel about that? Do you agree with Mom on that? (Janet laughs.) On the moralizing and talking? Both of you?

*Janet.* Well, I think that she talks a little bit too much, but not too much. I mean she talks a little too much at times, but it isn't too bad.

*Mrs. Clay.* Janet felt this week that I dug into her about eating too much and gaining weight. (Laughs.)

*Therapist.* Oh, is that right? Would you tell us about that?

*Janet.* Oh, it was yesterday at the party. I had some cookies and I started to eat them. She'd say, "Now Janet, don't you eat any of those."

*Mrs. Clay.* I said, "Now don't eat all of them." (Laughs.) She had a whole pile of them. (Laughs again.)

*Therapist.* And this is something that you would just as soon not be reminded of.

*Janet.* Oh, I might be reminded but not every single second.

*(Pause.)*

*Therapist.* How about you Dick. How have you been?

*Dick.* Oh, I wasn't home hardly any of the time. When she (the mother) was home, I wasn't and when I was home, she wasn't, so I didn't have hardly any trouble.

*Mr. Clay.* I think that it has been a little easier week this time. I don't know how Dick is coming out on his school problems, but I think that it has been a little better, partly because he has had his own way.

*Dick.* The teachers sent me five times to the office this week. That's an improvement.

*Mr. Clay.* Improvement? Do you mean that you've gone to the office more times? How many times? Once a day?

*Dick.* No, I went three times in one day. Twice. One time in two different days.

*Mr. Clay.* The average has been worse than that?

*Dick.* It's usually been about two times every day.

*Mr. Clay.* Do they come from the same or different teachers?

*Dick.* Oh, it's usually the same one. I have my ideas and I'm not going to back down. If you do back down you are a lost soul. You've got to have your own head.

*Mr. Clay.* You have a point there. But sooner or later you back up against something you can't control and then what are you going to do?

*Dick.* I'm going to just push right forward.

*Mr. Clay.* You can't sometimes.

*Dick.* Hmmm.

*Mr. Clay.* I wonder what the answer is. It seems to me that everyone is going to have to knuckle down some place sometime. It's just a matter of when and how quick.

*Mrs. Clay.* It has been awful easy for me to have a high standard in life. I have it for myself as well as others, but I think that I am coming to realize that I can't influence others—that if I keep my standard for myself that then I'll have to let others choose their standards. I think I have been getting a little more peace in my mind and realizing that I am responsible to God for myself and to train others, but the results are not my——

*Dick (interrupts).* Mother, this isn't church. Good night!

*Mrs. Clay.* Well, those things have to be said.

*Dick.* She can do it in church—not here. A bunch of preaching!

*Mr. Clay.* Most people have to learn the hard way, but they'd like you to learn some other way than the hard way, but I kind of think that you are going to have to learn the hard way, however hard it is. If you're going to fall, you'll just have to fall.

*Mrs. Clay.* Well, I've just wanted to prevent that, but I don't think that can be done.

*Therapist.* Is it that you feel irritated with Dick or that you feel that the children need to learn on their own?

*Mr. Clay.* I kind of feel, maybe I'm sounding off here against Dick, but that's not necessarily the case, that not the last couple of years but previous to that he didn't get all that was coming to him, not only him but the rest of us in this room. Their discipline wasn't as tough as it might have been. And now that it is starting to tighten up again, they are kind of behind the eightball and they don't know what to do about it. They don't want to give in—they have had their own way for a while—and now the fun begins.

*Therapist.* How do you feel about this, Dick?

*Dick.* I'm not backing down.

*Therapist.* That seems to be your theme, doesn't it?

*Dick.* Boy, there's going to be something that's really going to come up. Someone is going to have to work hard. I'm not going to back down.

*Therapist.* It's important for you to keep your own head all the way.

*Dick.* Yeah.

*Mr. Clay.* I think Dick has said exactly what his major trouble is, if you call that a trouble—Dick doesn't think so—he thinks it's a good point. Well, nobody can be boss all the time— there isn't any question. That is the reason I say that everybody is going to have to lower their head and get it bloody sometime in order to learn that they can't run the whole show. The sooner we realize it, the better off we are. I don't mean that they should cow-tow to everybody, but at the same time sooner or later they are going to run up against somebody that's not going to fool with that kind of stuff. If it's on the job, they may get canned, and if it's other places there are other results.

*Therapist.* I wonder what Dick could tell us to help us to feel how it feels to have to fight to keep from being pushed around.

*Dick.* When I was in school did I tell you how I got to the office?

*Therapist.* How?

*Dick.* Well, we were—yeah, I'll tell about yesterday. There was a party at school. A friend and I, we were passing out the punch and I was doing okay. One of the other guys started talking to me and he was talking and we got to laughing about something. The teacher got mad and after the party was all over he said, "Would you mind going to the office?" So we went to the office and he said, "I don't want you guys to make a fool of us anymore." I said, "Well, if I knew I was making a fool of you I'd of made a big one." And then at the time I said that he came over to me and said, "If you are going to say any more I'll bend you over." So I went back and sat down. As soon as we got out I said, "The next time I go to the office I'll bend *him* over," and I think he heard me—I'm pretty sure he did.

### EVALUATION

The advantages and disadvantages of individual and group therapies have been debated for years. Obviously, these two approaches are different and can be justified on rational grounds by their exponents. Group methods save personnel time and if effective can expedite the treatment of a greater number of patients than can individual methods. Decisions as to their special spheres of utility cannot truly be made since there have been few empirical studies demonstrating their comparative efficacies. Therapists make their choices on the basis of theoretical or personal preferences; on these dubious grounds, some utilize one or the other treatment approach exclusively for all patients.

Among the few outcome studies, note may be made of two that satisfy certain minimal criteria of sound research design. Powdermaker and Frank (1953) compared two groups, one receiving individual therapy only, the other receiving both individual and group therapy. The results were not notably different. Using physician judgments as a criterion, 52 per cent of the former group were improved as contrasted to 62 per cent of latter. In a population of hospital patients, Fairweather et al., (1960) studied the effectiveness of four therapeutic regimens: a nontherapy control, individual therapy, group therapy and group living with periodic group therapy. Notable in the design was the systematic differentiation and matching of patient "types," the use of a battery of several objectives criterion measures and periodic follow-up evaluations. The results were complicated; the efficacy of alternative treatment techniques varied as a function of type of disorder and length of hospitalization. Essentially, all therapeutic modalities proved superior to the control group. Differences among treatment procedures were minimal, although they appeared to favor the group-living and individual therapy approaches.

Few studies have been undertaken to tease out the "process" ingredients of each of the various forms of group therapy. What little has been done provides no insight into their role as factors contributing to treatment efficacy.

In summary and as is true with most types of individual therapy, virtually no studies of a systematic and properly designed nature have been published on group treatment approaches. Stated differently, there are no empirical data from which we can judge with confidence the efficacy or mode of action of these therapies. Although good reasons can be cited for the paucity of sound research (e.g., the complexity and number of the variables involved or the difficulty in matching patients), it is the responsibility of group treatment proponents to show that the value of their preferred method is more than an article of faith.

## CONCLUDING COMMENTS AND SUMMARY

It is inevitable that controversies exist among exponents of different treatment methods. However, so prominent a figure as Carl Rogers (1961) has stated rather woefully that "the field of psychotherapy is in a mess," and Ungersma (1961) has concluded that "the present situation in psychotherapy is not unlike that of a man who mounted his horse and rode off in all directions. . . . Individual practitioners of any art are expected to vary, but some well-organized schools of therapy also seem to be working at cross purposes." Messy though matters may be, divergent approaches need not work at cross purposes. As will be noted in our final conclusions, alternate therapies are not intrinsically contradictory; rather, they may be seen as complementary approaches, each focusing on one facet of the multidimensional complex we call psychopathology. Before elaborating this thesis, let us summarize the principal distinctions and features of the many techniques described in this chapter.

1. The historical development of psychotherapy was traced, beginning *first* with the ancient practices of the Greeks and Romans. With pioneering hospital programs that stressed "moral treatment," exemplified by Pinel and his followers in the late eighteenth century, psychological methods moved into their *second* stage, taking on many qualities that persist into modern times. The *third* historical phase began with the advent of Mesmer's hypnotic technique in the mid-eighteenth century, and took firm root with Freud's psychoanalytic procedures in the early twentieth century; in this period, the practice of "office psychiatry" became the model setting for psychological treatment. The opening of "clinic services" for the young in the second quarter of this century, concentrating on the liberation of "growth potentials" in patients, may be viewed as the *fourth* stage of psychological therapy. The *fifth* period, developing rapidly in the mid-1950's, was characterized by the application of laboratory-derived learning principles to psychotherapeutic practice. The most recent, or *sixth,* period, no more than ten years old, has shifted the attention of therapists to the systematic evaluation of the "outcome" and "process" of alternative treatment methods.

2. Alternative therapies may be differentiated in terms of four major dimensions. First is the therapeutic *setting.* Three were noted: individual patient-therapist relationships, small group interactions and institutional milieus. Second, the *goals* of therapy were described; distinctions were drawn in terms of who sets the goals and what goals therapy seeks to achieve. Third, differences in the *process* of therapy were noted; the principal division here being the insight-expressive versus the action-suppressive approach. Fourth, therapies were differentiated in accord with their *data focus;* distinctions were drawn between behavioral, phenomenological and intrapsychic levels.

3. *Environmental management,* the first of the psychological treatment methods discussed,

refers to procedures that change the patient *indirectly* by manipulating and exploiting for therapeutic purposes the surrounding conditions of his life. Two approaches were described: *outpatient casework therapy,* for patients who are not institutionalized and function in their normal everyday setting; and *inpatient milieu therapy,* for patients who reside in an institutional setting.

4. *Supportive therapy,* in contrast to environmental management, focuses directly on the patient. However, in contrast to other direct treatment techniques, which seek to promote fundamental changes in the patient's premorbid personality, supportive procedures have as their primary aim the reestablishment of the patient's premorbid equilibrium. Three principal methods of support were described: *ventilation, reassurance* and *persuasion.*

5. *Behavior modification* therapists consider overt or objectively observable actions and events to be the primary subject matter for treatment. They contend that psychopathology is simply maladaptive or deficient learning; consequently, the task of therapy is to arrange systematic programs of "unlearning" and "relearning" so as to eliminate maladaptive behaviors and to institute adaptive ones in their stead.

The many subvarieties of behavior modification were divided into two major groups: "behavior elimination" methods, which are suitable only for the removal of maladaptive behaviors, and "behavior formation" methods, which are suitable also for the acquisition of new behaviors. The "elimination" category includes several varieties of *counterconditioning* and *extinction* procedures. Among the "formation" methods, emphasis was given to *selective positive reinforcement* (operant conditioning) and *model imitation* procedures.

Studies of the efficacy and mode of action of behavior techniques were reviewed. These reported in general rather impressive statistics, indicating highly favorable results in symptom disorders, behavior reactions and cases evidencing chronic social deficits.

6. *Phenomenological reorientation* procedures have as their primary focus those conscious perceptions and attitudes of patients which tend to perpetuate their pathology. In contrast to behavior therapists, who are inclined to pursue an action-suppressive process, phenomenologists usually employ insight-expressive techniques.

Three major variants of the phenomenological approach were described. The first, entitled "self-actualization," provides a congenial and essentially nondirective atmosphere designed to facilitate the growth of the patient's intrinsically constructive potentials; two subvarieties were described: *client-centered* and *existential* therapy. In the second major phenomenological approach, termed "confrontation-directive," the therapist assumes an authoritative role in which he decides the treatment goals and exhorts the patient to achieve them; two subtypes were presented: *rational-emotive* and *reality-integrity* therapy. The third variant, labeled "cognitive-learning," attempts to discern which of the patient's attitudes perpetuate his difficulties, employing a variety of learning principles to eliminate these outlooks and to inculcate more adaptive ones; two subvarieties were described: *expectancy-reinforcement* and *assertion-structured* therapy.

Research studies evaluating these techniques show them to be of variable efficacy. Notable in this regard are findings that some therapists promote beneficial changes in patients whereas others cause patient deterioration; differences in several therapist characteristics have been related to these divergent effects.

7. *Intrapsychic reconstruction* therapists assume that treatment can be effective only when the deeply ingrained and pervasive forces of the unconscious have been unearthed, analyzed and rebuilt.

Five therapeutic variants of this persuasion were described. *Classical analysis,* in which the therapist becomes a neutral screen for patient projections, seeks to revive childhood memories and resolves infantile conflicts by the induction of a "transference neurosis." *Ego analysis* is similar in procedure to the classical technique, but emphasizes the liberation of adaptive capacities that had been thwarted in the patient's childhood. In *character analysis* there is a shift toward contemporary problems and a more active role on the part of the therapist; the goal here is to break through the patient's self-defeating "idealized image." *Interpersonal analysis,* akin in rationale and technique to character analysis, emphasizes the therapist's skill in interviewing as the primary instrument for disengaging the patient's distortions of self and others. *Transactional analysis* focuses on the habitual roles the patient "plays" in his current social relationships and attempts to counter those which stem from childhood origins. In addition to the preceding, brief mention was made of three adjunctive intrapsychic methods: *hypnotherapy, art therapy* and *play therapy.*

Research evaluations of intrapsychic therapies are few and far between. What little outcome data can be found are equivocal, at best; adequately designed process studies are non-existent.

8. The rationale and procedures of several *group treatment* methods were described. A primary contention of group therapists is that their techniques more closely approximate "real-life" situations than do individual procedures, thereby facilitating generalizations to the extratherapeutic world.

Five variants were presented: *activity, discussion, analytical, role-playing* and *family groups.* The few outcome and process studies that have been published do not provide indications of their efficacy or clarity as to the essential features of their action.

9. Although each of the treatment approaches described in this chapter centers its attention on one facet of the psychopathological process, the effect upon the patient is broader than that intended by his therapist. In "reality," every patient, no matter which theory or procedure his therapist subscribes to, will as a consequence of treatment unlearn certain behavioral habits, alter aspects of his phenomenological self-image and have elements of his intrapsychic world realigned. In other words, the patient is a unified natural entity, not a compartmentalized mechanism that can be subdivided in accord with certain theoretical practices; beneficial interventions at one point or level of this unitary complex will feedback and have secondary salutary effects at other levels and points as well.

Unfortunately, therapists of divergent schools share the narrow-minded conviction that *their* particular focus and technique is "the best." This view simply is not borne out by empirical research. Not only do alternative approaches produce treatment effects in common, making it difficult to draw distinctions among them, but no single approach has a monopoly of success with all types of pathology. Rather, each method is likely to have limited spheres of utility, proving more efficacious with some cases than with others. The task facing the profession is to discern common areas of utility and to demonstrate empirically where special areas of efficacy lie.

10. The internecine warfare that rages between practitioners of "opposing" therapeutic schools can be resolved only by more and better research, not by elegantly phrased rationales or by arrogant assertions of scientific purity. Rather sadly, considering the magnitude and importance of the problem, there have been shockingly few empirical studies that fulfill even the basic rudiments of adequate research design. This state of affairs is rapidly changing. In recent years an

increasing number of rigorously trained students have been attracted to the task of evaluating alternative therapies. Not only have earlier methodological obstacles to "outcome" research been identified and controlled, but the many components that comprise the "process" of therapy are gradually being disentangled. As this new research orientation takes firm root, we may expect in the near future not only to specify which patients respond best to which therapeutic techniques, but to devise novel procedures that are more efficacious than those in current use.

# GLOSSARY

The glossary has been included with two purposes in mind: (1) to define terms that may not be found in standard and more complete psychological and psychiatric dictionaries, and (2) to provide a quick reference for terms that occur repeatedly in sections of the text other than those in which they are fully discussed.

**Ablation:** Surgical removal of body tissue.

**Abnormal:** Deviating from the norm or average; extraordinary or unusual; often but not necessarily maladaptive.

**Abreaction:** Discharge of emotions when consciously recalling previously repressed unpleasant experiences.

**Abstract thinking:** Capacity to generalize, to transcend immediate experiences and to reflect and plan logically.

**Acetylcholine:** Chemical neurohormone associated with synaptic transmission.

**Acting-out:** Direct and overt expression of unconscious emotions and conflicts that normally are controlled or moderated by intrapsychic mechanisms.

**Activation:** Energy arousal and mobilization associated with increased alertness and physical vigor.

**Active:** Engaging in overt instrumental behaviors.

**Active-ambivalence:** A basic coping strategy characterized by erratic and negativistic behaviors, and by the vacillation of attitudes and moods.

**Active-dependence:** A basic coping strategy characterized by gregarious and seductive behaviors, and by the pursuit of interpersonal attention and approval.

**Active-detachment:** A basic coping strategy characterized by the avoidance of social relationships, and by feelings of self-alienation.

**Active-independence:** A basic coping strategy characterized by domineering, aggressive and vindictive social behaviors.

**Addiction:** Psychological or physiological dependence on drugs or alcohol.

**Adient:** Pertaining to a drive that orients the person positively or toward some object or activity.

**Adrenal glands:** Endocrine glands located adjacent to the kidneys; the inner portion is termed the adrenal medulla and the outer portion is termed the adrenal cortex.

**Adrenaline:** See *Epinephrine*. The principal hormone secreted by the adrenal medulla; it stimulates energy mobilization and body alertness. Also known as epinephrine.

**Adrenergic:** Tending to activate the sympathetic nervous system.

**Affect:** Feeling tone or mood.

**Aggressive personality:** Mildly severe or basic pathological pattern associated with active-independent coping strategy.

**Agitated depression disorder:** Psychotic disorder characterized by apprehensiveness, restlessness, verbalized guilt, controlled hostility and depressed mood.

**Agnosia:** Impaired ability to recognize familiar objects or persons.

**Agraphia:** Impaired ability to express language in writing.

**Alexia:** Impaired ability to understand written language.

**Allergy:** Hypersensitivity of body tissue to physical or chemical stimuli.

**Ambivalence:** Coexistence of conflicting feelings or attitudes toward the same object or person.

**Amnesia:** Partial or total loss of memory.

**Anesthesia:** Impaired sensitivity to stimuli.

**Anhedonia:** Dimension of temperament signifying a marked and chronic inability to experience pleasure; also, a general although less severe inability to experience most emotions.

**Anoxia:** Insufficiency of oxygen.

**Anterograde amnesia:** Memory loss following psychic trauma or physical shock.

**Antidepressant drugs:** Pharmaceuticals designed to relieve dejection and depressive moods.

**Anxiety:** Psychogenic apprehension and tension, the source of which is usually unknown or unrecognized.

**Anxiety disorder:** A clinical syndrome characterized either by a state of chronic and moderately severe apprehension or by acute and intense anxiety and panic attacks.

**Aphasia:** Impaired ability to speak and communicate language (expressive or motor aphasia), or to comprehend language (receptive or sensory aphasia), attributable usually to brain defects.

**Aplasia:** Deficient development of body tissue.

**Apraxia:** Impaired ability to carry out purposeful movements, usually without demonstrable organic defects.

**Arteriosclerosis:** Loss of elasticity and hardening of the arteries, usually associated with aging.

**Asocial personality:** Mildly severe or basic pathological pattern associated with passive-detached coping strategy.

**Atrophy:** Shrinking and weakening of a body organ.

**Attachment:** The state of being bound to and dependent on another.

**Attitude:** A learned readiness to perceive and react in a particular way to a person, object or situation.

**Aura:** Sensations signifying an impending convulsion.

**Autistic thinking:** Grossly unrealistic fantasies consonant with pathological needs.

**Automatism:** Mechanical and repetitious actions, usually of a symbolic nature, carried out without conscious intent or control.

**Autonomic nervous system:** The portion of the nervous system not subject to voluntary control, serving to regulate major internal organs such as the viscera, glands and smooth muscles. It consists of sympathetic and parasympathetic divisions.

**Autonomy:** Capacity for self-reliance and independent functioning.

**Avoidant personality:** Mildly severe or basic pathological pattern associated with active-detached coping strategy.

**Basic personality patterns:** The mild level of pathological severity in personality functioning. There are eight subtypes, each characterized by the presence of pervasive, ingrained and self-perpetuating maladaptive attitudes and coping strategies. Patterns develop gradually as a function of the interaction of both constitutional and experiential influences.

**Behavioral level:** Data and concepts reflecting the observable responses or actions of patients.

**Behavior control:** Actions taken by others designed to shape the content of what people learn and the style in which these learnings will be expressed.

**Behavior modification:** Therapies based largely on the application of "learning" principles, and focusing on the alteration of overt actions rather than on subjective feelings or unconscious processes.

**Behavior reactions:** A group of syndromes noted by the stimulus-specificity of the pathological response; they include *transient situational reactions* and *circumscribed learned reactions.*

**Belle indifférence:** A lack of concern for the implications of one's own disabilities, occasionally seen in patients with conversion disorders.

**Biogenic:** Traceable to physical and biological sources.

**Biophysical defects:** A group of syndromes in which there is a clear-cut impairment of the biological substrate.

**Biophysical level:** Data and concepts representing the biological substrate of psychological functioning.

**Biophysical treatment:** Pharmaceutical, electrical and surgical therapeutic methods employed to alter the biological substrates of behavior, emotion and thought.

**Blocking:** Emotionally based and involuntary interruption of a train of thought or speech.

**Borderline personality patterns:** The moderate level of pathological severity in personality functioning; there are three major subtypes—schizoid, cycloid and paranoid—each characterized in part by deficits in social competence and by periodic but reversible psychotic episodes.

**Bronchi:** Lung vessels that permit the passage of air.

**Cardiovascular:** Pertaining to the circulatory system (heart and blood vessels).

**Case history:** All available biographical data that facilitate the understanding of a patient's current state.

**Catastrophic anxiety:** A term coined by Goldstein to signify the frightening awareness of one's incompetence. It is experienced by patients following severe brain injury.

**Catatonia:** Traditional nomenclature for a subdivision of schizophrenia. It is characterized chiefly by motor rigidity and withdrawal, but punctuated periodically with brief periods of excitement.

**Catalepsy:** Lack of motor responsiveness; patients are characterized by their resistance to change from an assumed semirigid and trance-like position.

**Catharsis:** Recalling and describing painful experiences and attitudes, and venting their associated emotions.

**Cathexis:** A psychoanalytic term signifying the attachment of intense emotions to a particular object or person.

**Cerebral cortex:** The surface layer of gray matter of the brain associated with higher mental processes.

**Childhood ambiosis:** Moderately and markedly severe active-ambivalent personality patterns evidenced in childhood, and characterized by crankiness, pouting, behavioral unpredictability and erratic moods.

**Childhood pariosis:** Moderate and markedly severe active-independent personality patterns evidenced in childhood, and characterized by irrational suspiciousness, belligerence, impulsiveness and aggressive defiance.

**Childhood symbiosis:** Moderate and markedly severe passive-dependent personality patterns evidenced in childhood, and characterized by a gross immaturity and a pathological attachment to caretakers.

**Chemotherapy:** Pharmaceutical treatment.

**Choleria:** Dimension of temperament signifying a disposition to irritability and hostility.

**Cholinergic:** Tending to activate the parasympathetic nervous system.

**Chorea:** Involuntary spasmodic movements of head and extremities.

**Chronic disorder:** Longstanding impairments that are likely to be permanent.

**Chromosome:** Separable rod-like bodies in the nucleus of cells that contain the genes.

**Circumscribed learned reactions:** A group of syndromes, found in basically nonpathological personalities, characterized by the presence of an ingrained pathological reaction that is limited to a specific and narrow band of stimulus precipitants.

**Circumstantiality:** Intruding and elaborating irrelevant or trivial details in conversation.

**Claustrophobia:** Anxiety displaced symbolically in a fear of closed places.

**Clinical picture:** Current status of patient based on a cross-sectional analysis of behavioral, phenomenological, intrapsychic and biophysical data.

**Cognitive processes:** Modes of thought, knowing and symbolic representation, including comprehension, judgment, memory, imagining and reasoning.

**Coma:** Stupor and unconsciousness.

**Commitment:** Legal procedure for mandatory hospitalization of persons suffering severe mental impairments.

**Compensation:** Intrapsychic mechanism by which undesirable traits are cloaked and overcome by accentuating or strengthening a more desirable one.

**Competence:** Capacity to function in one's environment independent of assistance and supervision.

**Compulsion:** Irresistible and repetitive urge to engage in an act that is recognized as irrational.

**Concepts:** Symbols or labels employed to represent phenomena relevant to a theory.

**Concordance:** Presence of a trait in both members of a twin pair.

**Concrete thinking:** Impaired ability to reflect and generalize; thinking limited to the world of immediate stimuli.

**Conditioning:** A process of learning in which a response comes to be elicited by a stimulus that formerly did not elicit that response.

**Conflict:** Presence of opposing or incompatible desires or demands.

**Conforming personality:** Mild pathological pattern associated with passive-ambivalent coping strategy.

**Confusion:** Disturbed orientation, clouded consciousness and muddled thinking.

**Congenital:** Present from birth.

**Consciousness:** State of awareness.

**Consonance:** Attitudes, emotions or events that are compatible.

**Constitution:** Intrinsic and relatively enduring biological characteristics.

**Contingent:** Signifying dependence on special associated circumstances.

**Continuum:** A continuous dimension or scale such that additional points may always be found between any two points.

**Control group:** Subjects used for comparison purposes in research to insure that incidental variables do not account for the study's results.

**Control level:** Capacity to cope effectively under conditions of stress.

**Conversion disorder:** Neurotic syndrome in which anxiety is converted, unconsciously and symbolically, into a loss or alteration of a sensory or motor function.

**Coping strategy:** A person's basic and characteristic pattern of approaching his environment so as to maximize achieving positive reinforcements and minimize experiencing negative reinforcements.

**Correlate:** Characteristics or scores that are related or vary such that changes in one are accompanied by predictable changes in the others.

**Correspondence rules:** A formal set of procedures for coordinating concepts to the empirical world and linking them to each other.

**Criterion:** A measure or event that serves as a standard for judging other measures or events.

**Critical period:** A stage in neuropsychological maturation when certain forms of experience have notably pronounced effects; also known as "sensitive periods."

**Cycloid personality:** Moderately severe or borderline pathological patterns associated with various dependent and ambivalent coping strategies.

**Cyclophrenic personality:** Markedly severe or decompensated pathological pattern associated with various dependent and ambivalent coping strategies.

**Decompensated personality patterns:** A marked level of pathological severity in personality functioning; there are three major subtypes— schizophrenia, cyclophrenia and paraphrenia —each characterized in part by social invalidism, cognitive disorganization and feelings of estrangement.

**Decompensation:** Progressive personality disintegration evidenced in the loss of cognitive and emotional controls and in decreased reality awareness.

**Dejection disorder:** A neurotic syndrome characterized by worrisomeness, guilt feelings and mild depression.

**Delirium:** A markedly confused state characterized by excitement, incoherence and disorientation; illusions and hallucinations are often present.

**Delusion:** A false belief maintained despite objective evidence to the contrary.

**Delusion disorder:** A psychotic syndrome characterized chiefly by the presence of delusions.

**Dementia praecox:** Obsolescent term for schizophrenia.

**Denial mechanisms:** A group of intrapsychic processes that enable the individual to keep from consciousness intolerable thoughts, perceptions or feelings, e.g., repression, isolation or projection.

**Dependence:** Reliance on others for support and the satisfaction of needs.

**Depersonalization:** Feeling of self-estrangement and unreality.

**Detachment:** Social disaffiliation or self-alienation.

**Deviancy:** Traits at the quantitative extremes of the normal curve.

**Diagnosis:** Description, identification and labeling of a pathological condition.

**Discordance:** Presence of a trait in only one member of a twin pair.

**Discrimination:** In perception, the ability to detect or react differently to objectively dissimilar stimuli.

**Diseases:** Pathological conditions traceable primarily to impairments in the biological substrate.

**Displacement:** Intrapsychic mechanism by which emotions are transferred from their original object to a more acceptable substitute.

**Dissociation disorder:** A neurotic syndrome in which normally associated segments of memory and thought are split off from each other, e.g., amnesia or somnambulism.

**Dissonance:** Attitudes, emotions or events that are incompatible.

**Distortion mechanisms:** A group of intrapsychic processes that enable the person to transform and disguise intolerable thoughts, feelings and memories so as to make them personally and socially more acceptable, e.g., fantasy, rationalization and sublimation.

**Dizygotic twins:** Twins from separate ova; fraternal twins.

**Double bind:** Communications containing intrinsically contradictory requests that "trap" the recipient since he cannot provide a satisfactory response.

**Drives:** Innate or learned forces that prompt certain forms of behavior and sensitize the organism to respond to relevant associated stimuli.

**DSM-II:** The official classification of psychopathological conditions published in 1968 under the title "Diagnostic and Statistical Manual of Mental Disorders" by the American Psychiatric Association.

**Dysfunction:** Impaired or disturbed functioning.

**Echolalia:** Automatic and meaningless repetition by a patient of what is said to him.

**Echopraxia:** Repetitive and automatic imitation by a patient of another person's movements.

**Ectomorphy:** Term employed by Sheldon to represent the body dimension of thinness, linearity and fragility.

**Ego:** Term employed by intrapsychic theorists to represent that division of the personality structure associated with mediating and resolving conflicts between the instinctual drives of the "id," the prohibitions and ideals of the "super-ego" and the reality conditions of the environment.

**Egocentric:** Preoccupied with self needs, and lacking interest and concern for those of others; in contrast to narcissism, egocentricity does not necessarily signify a high opinion of self.

**Ego-dystonia:** Feelings and behaviors exhibited by the patient which are experienced as alien or repugnant to his conception of himself.

**Ego strength:** The capacity of the patient to cope with the stresses of life.

**Ego-syntonia:** Feelings and behaviors exhibited by the patient which are experienced as consonant with his conception of himself.

**Electroconvulsive therapy (ECT):** A form of biological treatment in which an electric current is passed through the brain to produce a convulsion.

**Electroencephalograph (EEG):** Graphic recording of brain potentials.

**Empathy:** Insightful awareness of and ability to share the emotions, thoughts and behaviors of another person.

**Empirical:** Pertaining to observable and tangible events.

**Endocrine glands:** Ductless glands that secrete hormones into the lymph or blood stream.

**Endogenous:** Pertaining to causal influences that originate from sources within the patient.

**Endomorphy:** Term employed by Sheldon to represent the body dimension of fat, softness and rotundity.

**Environment:** External conditions capable of influencing an organism.

**Environmental management:** A general category of therapy referring to methods that exploit the patient's family, social and work surroundings for purposes of treatment and rehabilitation, e.g., casework or milieu therapy.

**Enzyme:** Organic catalysts that modify other organic substances.

**Epidemiology:** Study of the statistical location and distribution of pathological conditions.

**Epinephrine:** The principal hormone secreted by the adrenal medulla; it stimulates energy mobilization and body alertness.

**Erotic:** Pertaining to sexual impulses.

**Estrangement:** A variant of the dissociative disorder signifying a feeling that ordinarily well-known objects, persons and events seem different, unreal or distant.

**Etiology:** Study of the causation of pathological conditions.

**Euphoric excitement disorder:** A psychotic syndrome characterized by exaggerated feelings of well-being and a lack of inhibition.

**Exogenous:** Pertaining to causal influences that originate from sources other than from within the patient himself.

**Exorcism:** An ancient practice of incantation designed to purge demonic spirits from the minds of men.

**Extinction:** In learning, the elimination of an acquired response.

**Extravert:** A personality type formulated by Jung to represent highly sociable, impulsive and emotionally expressive persons.

**Factor:** (a) A generic term for a distinctive psychological function, trait or influence; (b) In statistics, an independent psychological attribute derived from commonalities exhibited in behavior or test performance.

**Familial:** Pertaining to the family or to characteristics that tend to occur frequently in particular families.

**Fantasy:** Daydreaming; an intrapsychic mechanism in which unconscious conflicts are resolved and unconscious desires are gratified through fanciful imagination.

**Fixation:** An intrapsychic mechanism in which the normal developmental progression is arrested and the patient persists in behaving at an immature level in order to avoid the conflicts and challenges typical of his chronological age.

**Flexibility:** Capacity or inclination to change habitual behaviors in accord with changing circumstances.

**Flight of ideas:** Fragmentary skipping from one verbalized but unfinished idea to another with no logical progression.

**Focal lesion:** A defect that is localized in a circumscribed brain area.

**Fragmentation disorder:** A psychotic syndrome characterized by marked cognitive, emotional and behavioral disorganization.

**Free association:** An intrapsychic technique of therapy in which the patient is asked to relax his usual controls and to verbalize every passing thought and emotion.

**Frontal lobe:** The most anterior region of the cerebral cortex, serving as the primary substrate for higher thought processes.

**Frustration:** Experiencing the thwarting of a desire or need.

**Ganglia:** Nerve net or center, most often located outside the spinal cord.

**Gene:** A submicroscopic unit of inheritance arranged within the chromosomes.

**General paresis:** Synonym for chronic neurosyphilis.

**Generalization:** Transfer of learnings acquired in one situation to another situation that is somewhat similar to the first.

**Genetic factors:** Inherited influences or dispositions.

**Genital:** Pertaining to the sexual organs.

**Gerontology:** Study of old age.

**Gregarious personality:** Mildly severe or basic pathological pattern associated with active-dependent coping strategy.

**Guilt:** Feelings of self-depreciation and apprehension stemming from engaging in thoughts or behaviors that are forbidden or run contrary to one's conscience.

**Habit:** A repetitive mode of response.

**Hallucination:** A perception that has no basis in external reality.

**Hallucinogen:** Chemical agent that produces hallucinations; also known as psychotomimetic drug.

**Heredity:** Genetic transmission of traits from parent to child.

**Heterogeneous:** Composed of dissimilar characteristics throughout.

**Heterozygous:** Carrying both a dominant and recessive gene for a particular trait.

**Homeostasis:** Maintaining optimal constancy and balance among physiological processes.

**Homogeneous:** Composed of similar characteristics throughout.

**Hormone:** Chemical substance secreted by endocrine glands to stimulate and regulate physiological processes.

**Hostile excitement disorder:** A psychotic syndrome characterized by irrational anger and uninhibited aggressiveness.

**Hyperkinesia:** Excessive motor activity.

**Hypermnesia:** Unusually retentive memory.

**Hypnosis:** Trance-like state of high suggestibility induced artificially by another person.

**Hypochondriacal disorder:** A neurotic syndrome in which there is a persistent and exaggerated concern about diminished health and energy in the absence of demonstrable organic pathology.

**Hypothalamus:** Complex of neural cells at the base of the brain involved in the regulation and expression of emotion and motivation.

**Hypothesis:** A provisional explanation set forth for purposes of empirical confirmation or disconfirmation.

**Hypothetical construct:** A term for concepts of heuristic theoretical value, but linked tenuously to observable phenomena.

**Hysteria:** Traditional diagnostic label for conversion and dissociative neurotic disorders.

**Id:** Term employed by intrapsychic theorists to represent that division of the personality structure associated with primitive instinctual impulses.

**Identification:** An intrapsychic mechanism in which the individual associates himself with another person, group or movement, usually as a means of enhancing his feelings of self-worth.

**Idiographic:** A scientific orientation that focuses on the unique features of a situation or personality.

**Idiopathic:** Of unknown causation, and presumed to be inherent in the individual's constitutional make-up.

**Illusion:** Misinterpretation or false perception of a real sensory experience.

**Impassive disorder:** A psychotic syndrome characterized by mutism, emotional apathy and social withdrawal.

**Implicit learning:** Acquiring new ideas and behaviors through reflective thought and imaginative self-reinforcement.

**Imprinting:** Learning to associate a biologically disposed response to a specific stimulus pattern in early maturation.

**Impulse:** With reference to behavior, the urge to act.

**Impulsive:** Pertaining to the tendency to act out desires without reflecting on their consequences.

**Incidence:** Frequency or rate of occurrence of new cases in a specified time period.

**Incoherence:** Disconnected and difficult to understand communications.

**Incontinence:** Loss of bladder or bowel control.

**Independence:** Capacity or disposition for self-reliance.

**Infantile autism:** A markedly severe passive-detached personality pattern evidenced in early childhood, and characterized by mutism, interpersonal indifference and repetitive meaningless acts.

**Infantile threctism:** A markedly severe active-detached pattern evidenced in early childhood, and characterized by extraordinary fearfulness, tenseness and vulnerability to threat.

**Inferred concepts:** Terms representing deductions or generalizations based on observable clinical signs.

**Inhibition:** The restraint of urges, usually those considered to be socially disapproved.

**Innate:** Inborn.

**Inpatient:** Institutionalized patient.

**Insanity:** A legal term for severe mental impairments in which the person is judged incapable of assuming responsibility for his actions.

**Insight:** Seeing meaningful relationships and understanding their psychological significance.

**Instinct:** Inherited disposition to behavior that is characteristic of all members of a species.

**Instrumental behavior:** Activities that are executed to effect changes in the environment.

**Instrumental learning:** Acquiring new responses on the basis of their capacity to produce reinforcements.

**Intervening variable:** A term for concepts representing unobservable or mediating processes which are anchored or defined in terms of observables.

**Intracortical-initiative stage:** Third stage of neuropsychological development beginning at about four years of age and extending through adolescence; characterized by the rapid proliferation of higher cortical connections, and enabling the growing child to reflect, plan and act in novel ways independent of parental supervision.

**Intrapsychic level:** Data and concepts representing processes that take place beneath the level of awareness, i.e., in the unconscious.

**Intrapsychic reconstruction:** Therapies designed to make the patient aware of his unconscious drives and conflicts, and to rework them for purposes of reorganizing the patient's personality.

**Introjection:** An intrapsychic mechanism in which the attributes of other persons are internalized and assumed to be true of one-self.

**Introvert:** A personality type formulated by Jung to represent socially awkward, emotionally reserved and self-absorbed persons.

**Isolation:** An intrapsychic mechanism in which the association between a thought and its accompanying emotion is separated.

**Labile:** Pertaining to instability or changeability, especially with regard to emotions.

**Latent:** Pertaining to a disposition that is dormant or inactive.

**Lesion:** Neural tissue damage due to injury or disease.

**Life style:** Roughly, personality pattern.

**Limbic system:** Neural structures located at the base of the cerebral hemispheres (notably the amygdala, septal nuclei and hypothalamus) involved in the activation and expression of emotions.

**Linkage:** Connection between two or more genes that increases the probability that they will be inherited together.

**Logorrhea:** Excessive and often incoherent speech.

**Maladaptive:** Pertaining to deficient or inappropriate responses to environmental circumstances.

**Mania:** A suffix denoting extreme preoccupation with a specific idea or activity, e.g., kleptomania (inclinations to steal) or nymphomania (excessive desire of females for intercourse).

**Manic-depressive illness:** Official DSM-II syndrome for markedly severe psychopathological conditions characterized by intense and often alternating moods.

**Mannerism:** A repeated, peculiar and stereotyped gesture or posture.

**Masochism:** Obtaining gratification, usually sexual, through the experience of pain.

**Masturbation:** Genital self-stimulation for sexual pleasure.

**Maturation:** Sequence of ontogenetic development in which initially diffuse and inchoate structures of the body progressively unfold into specific functional units.

**Mechanism:** Intrapsychic (unconscious) processes employed to deny or distort discomforting thoughts or emotions, e.g., repression, rationalization and sublimation.

**Mecholyl:** A chemical agent that leads to a brief drop in blood pressure.

**Melancholia:** Dimension of temperament signifying a tendency to experience sadness and pain; also used as a synonym for depression.

**Menopause:** Period in middle life when menstruation stops.

**Mesomorphy:** Term employed by Sheldon to represent the body dimension of skeletal breadth and muscularity.

**Milieu therapy:** Environmental management within a hospital setting to promote the patient's social rehabilitation.

**MMPI (Minnesota Multiphasic Personality Inventory):** An empirically designed self-report personality questionnaire designed to facilitate psychopathological diagnosis.

**Model:** (a) A person whose behavior and attitudes are imitated. (b) A schema or system that provides a suggestive framework for a theory.

**Monozygotic twins:** Twins developed from a single ovum; identical twins.

**Mood:** Prevailing or characteristic emotional state.

**Morbid:** Pathological.

**Morphology:** The study of body structures; also employed to represent the manifestations of body forms.

**Motivation:** A state characterized by increased activation and drive-fulfillment. See *Drives*.

**Motor rigidity disorder:** A psychotic syndrome characterized by mutism, the assumption of inflexible postures and resistance to social suggestions.

**Multidimensional approach:** An orientation that takes into consideration several variables and theoretical schemas in the analysis of a problem.

**Mutism:** Inability or refusal to speak.

**Narcissistic personality:** Mildly severe or basic pathological pattern associated with passive-independent coping strategy.

**Negative reinforcement:** Any condition that weakens the strength of a response with which it is associated, leading usually to the acquisition of alternative responses.

**Negativistic personality:** Mildly severe or basic pathological pattern associated with active-ambivalent coping strategy.

**Neologism:** A new word, usually condensed from several conventional words, and having special meaning to the patient who coined it.

**Neurohormone:** Chemical substance involved in neural impulse transmission; also known as neurohumor.

**Neuron:** Individual nerve cell.

**Neuropsychological stages:** Broad periods of development during which stimulus experiences have particularly pronounced effects on the maturation of neural structures and their associated psychological functions.

**Neurotic disorders:** A group of syndromes often seen in patients with only mild degrees of personality decompensation; characterized by dramatic symptoms (e.g., phobias or conversions) that reflect attempts to solicit social support while discharging unconscious anxieties and hostilities in disguised form. Also referred to as neurosis and psychoneurosis.

**Nomothetic:** A scientific orientation that focuses on those features of psychological functioning presumed to be common to all persons.

**Nosology:** Systematic classification of pathological conditions.

**Obsession:** Repetitive idea that is recognized as irrational, but cannot be dismissed from thought.

**Obsession-compulsion disorder:** A neurotic syndrome characterized by the persistence of unwanted thoughts or impulses which cannot be terminated by reason or without a consequent feeling of anxiety.

**Operational definition:** A term for concepts derived from the procedures by which empirical objects or events are measured.

**Organic impairments:** Psychopathology due primarily to tissue damage or physiological dysfunction.

**Outcome research:** Studies concerned with the overall efficacy or success of treatment techniques.

**Outpatient:** A noninstitutionalized patient receiving treatment.

**Overdetermination:** A term signifying the confluence of several influences in shaping a single symptom.

**Overt signs:** Observable clinical indices.

**Paranoid personality:** Moderately severe or borderline pathological pattern associated with various independent and ambivalent coping strategies.

**Paraphrenic personality:** Markedly severe or decompensated pathological pattern associated with various independent and ambivalent coping strategies.

**Parasympathetic nervous system:** Division of the autonomic nervous system that is generally inhibitory in function.

**Parmia:** Dimension of temperament signifying a disposition to fearlessness and venturesomeness.

**Passive:** Pertaining to minimal engagement in overt instrumental behaviors.

**Passive-ambivalence:** A basic coping strategy characterized by rigid behavior, social conformity and the repression of all contrary thoughts and feelings.

**Passive-dependence:** A basic coping strategy characterized by socially submissive and clinging behaviors, and by a self-image of inadequacy and incompetence.

**Passive-detachment:** A basic coping strategy characterized by emotional apathy and social indifference.

**Passive-independence:** A basic coping strategy characterized by narcissistic attitudes, self-confidence and interpersonal exploitation.

**Pathogenic:** Conducive to pathology.

**Pathognomonic:** Characteristic of symptoms that are typical and somewhat distinctive to a particular diagnostic syndrome.

**Pathological personality pattern:** A broad class of syndromes characterized by deeply ingrained and pervasively maladaptive styles of life.

**Pathology:** The study of impaired mental or physical functions. Also employed as a general synonym for the manifestations of these conditions.

**Perseveration:** Involuntary continuation and repetition of a behavioral response once it has been initiated.

**Phases of epigenesis:** Erikson's formulation of the stages of psychosocial and ego development; these parallel but extend the range of Freud's psychosexual stages.

**Phenomenological level:** Data and concepts representing subjective states or reports of conscious experience.

**Phenomenological reorientation:** Therapies that focus on redirecting the patient's self-defeating attitudes toward life.

**Phenylketonuria** (PKU): A congenital defect of protein metabolism resulting in profound mental retardation.

**Phobic disorder:** A neurotic syndrome in which unconscious anxiety is kept from awareness by displacing it onto a symbolic substitute in the environment that can be actively avoided.

**Placebo:** A procedure or inactive substance that simulates a form of treatment; although possessing no intrinsic therapeutic merit, it is often associated with beneficial results.

**Polygenic:** Signifying the influence of several simultaneously operating genes in the expression of a manifest trait.

**Positive reinforcement:** Any condition that strengthens the learning of a response with which it is associated.

**Posturing:** Unusual positions maintained for long periods.

**Precipitating cause:** A stressful event occurring shortly before the overt manifestation of psychopathology.

**Predisposing cause:** A source of influence in the patient's past, or a latent disposition within his personality make-up, that inclines him to succumb to psychopathology under conditions of stress.

**Premorbid:** Existing prior to manifest pathology.

**Prenatal:** Pertaining to development before birth.

**Prepotent:** Dominant or ascendant.

**Prevalence:** Total number of cases currently existing in a given population at any particular time.

**Process research:** Studies concerned with unraveling those ingredients of a therapeutic technique associated with its efficacy or success.

**Prodromal:** Pertaining to an early sign of pathology.

**Prognosis:** Prediction of the course and outcome of a pathological condition.

**Projection:** An intrapsychic mechanism in which the person denies his own unacceptable traits and impulses and ascribes them to others.

**Projective technique:** A personality test consisting of partially unstructured stimuli designed to reveal the subject's unexpressed attitudes, conflicts and coping strategies.

**Psychiatric social work:** Field of social work concerned with the environmental management and counseling of psychiatric patients.

**Psychiatry:** Field of medicine concerned with the diagnosis and treatment of psychopathological conditions.

**Psychoanalysis:** A school of psychopathology founded by Sigmund Freud oriented to the understanding of intrapsychic processes and their development, and to the treatment of psychiatric conditions by methods that expose the unconscious elements of personality functioning.

**Psychogenic:** Traceable to psychological experiences and learning.

**Psychopathology:** Field of medicine and psychology concerned with the study of maladaptive behavior, its etiology, development, diagnosis and therapy. Also employed as a general synonym for the manifestations of these conditions.

**Psychophysiologic disorders:** A group of syndromes signifying the presence of structural organic impairments attributable to psychogenic influences and their accompanying persistent physiological tensions. Also known as psychosomatic disorders.

**Psychotherapy:** A general term for treatment by psychological procedures.

**Psychotic disorders:** A group of syndromes signifying a transient episode of markedly severe psychopathology, and characterized by bizarre coping efforts or the disintegration of such efforts (e.g., agitated depression, motor rigidity or fragmentation).

**Puberty:** Period during early adolescence when secondary sex characteristics appear.

**Randomization:** Method of selecting research samples and assigning subjects to them that assures that each member of the population has an equal chance of being chosen and assigned to the various groups, thereby minimizing the possibility of bias in the results.

**Rapport:** Reciprocal feelings of comfort, acceptance and confidence between therapist and patient.

**Rationalization:** An intrapsychic mechanism in which consciously logical explanations and justifications are provided to account for unconsciously unacceptable feelings, thoughts and actions.

**Reaction formation:** An intrapsychic mechanism in which intolerable feelings or thoughts are repressed and their converse are expressed.

**Regression:** An intrapsychic mechanism in which the patient retreats to an earlier and less mature style of functioning in response to current stress.

**Reinforcement:** Any condition that alters the strength of a response with which it is associated. See *Positive reinforcement* and *Negative reinforcement*.

**Reliability:** The degree to which a measuring device produces the same results with the same subjects from one time to another.

**Remedial approach:** A general term for methods of management and treatment of pathological conditions.

**Remission:** A period of significant improvement following a pathological condition.

**Repetition compulsion:** An unconscious tendency to recreate earlier experiences and to engage again in the maladaptive responses with which they were formerly approached.

**Repression:** An intrapsychic mechanism in which painful memories and impulses are expunged and kept from consciousness.

**Resistance:** Opposition to therapeutic efforts, especially a defensive reluctance to explore repressed material.

**Retarded depression disorder:** A psychotic syndrome characterized by a sad and woeful look, a stooped posture and gloomy disconsolate verbalizations.

**Reticular formation:** Neural fibers that sweep between the brain and spinal cord and are known to be involved in maintaining and controlling alertness and arousal; they are believed by some theorists to serve as a relay station for coordinating impulses among lower and upper brain centers.

**Retrograde amnesia:** Loss of memory for experiences that occurred shortly prior to a trauma or shock.

**Rigidity:** Inability or resistance to change habitual behaviors in accord with changing circumstances.

**Rorschach test:** A projective technique consisting of ten standard inkblots.

**Sadism:** Obtaining gratification, usually sexual, by inflicting pain upon others.

**Sample:** A group of subjects selected for research purposes; preferably, they should be representative of the population to which the results will be generalized.

**Schizoid personality:** Moderately severe or borderline pathological pattern associated with detached coping strategies.

**Schizophrenic personality:** Markedly severe or decompensated pathological pattern associated with detached coping strategies.

**Secondary gain:** Advantages gained through a neurotic symptom other than the reduction of anxiety.

**Self-actualization:** The drive to realize one's inherent potentials.

**Self-image:** The person's conception of his own traits and their worth.

**Self-perpetuation:** Tendency to create conditions that accentuate and intensify traits already present within oneself.

**Sensitive developmental period:** See critical period.

**Sensorimotor-autonomy stage:** Second stage of neuropsychological development, extending in its peak development roughly between 12 months and six years of age; noted by the rapid differentiation of motor capacities and their integration with established sensory functions, enabling the young child to assume a measure of independence through increasingly skillful locomotion, manipulation and verbalization.

**Sensory-attachment stage:** First stage of neuropsychological development, generally from birth to 18 months, evidencing rapid maturation of sensory capacities and characterized by dependency of the infant upon others.

**Sequelae:** Residual symptoms following an acute pathological condition.

**Serendipity:** The art of accidental discovery.

**Sibling:** Offspring of the same parents.

**Social competence:** Range of skills for living effectively in normal community life.

**Sociopathic disorders:** A group of syndromes characterized by a disdain for social responsibilities and conventions, and a lack of interpersonal loyalty.

**Somatotype:** Physique or body build.

**Stereotype:** A prejudiced and difficult to alter conception of the traits of others.

**Stimuli:** Events that impinge upon the organism.

**Stimulus nutriment:** Concept formulated by Rapaport to signify the periodic stimulation needed to facilitate the development of ego capacities.

**Stress:** Any condition—biological or psychological—that taxes the coping capacities of a person.

**Stupor:** State of lethargy or unresponsiveness.

**Sublimation:** An intrapsychic mechanism in which unacceptable or thwarted impulses are channeled into socially approved substitute activities.

**Submissive personality:** Mildly severe or basic pathological pattern associated with a passive-dependent coping strategy.

**Superego:** Term employed by intrapsychic theorists to represent that division of personality structure associated with social prohibitions and morality.

**Supportive therapy:** Methods designed to reestablish the patient's normal equilibrium or mode of functioning, usually during periods of stress.

**Symbolization:** An unconscious process by which one idea or object comes to represent another.

**Sympathetic nervous system:** That division of the autonomic nervous system active in preparing the individual for emergency situations.

**Symptom:** A clinically significant sign.

**Symptom disorders:** A broad group of syndromes characterized by the emergence of distinctive and often dramatic clinical signs; these disorders occur in pathological personality patterns under conditions of special stress; the symptoms exhibited stand out in sharp relief against the patients' more prosaic symptomatology.

**Synapse:** Junction where impulses from one neuron pass to another.

**Syndrome:** A constellation of symptoms that covary and are more or less distinctive of a particular pathological condition.

**Systemic:** Pertaining to or affecting the body as a whole.

**Temperament:** Constitutional disposition to react emotionally.

**Terminal personality:** Profoundly decompensated pathological pattern observed in chronically ill institutionalized patients.

**Theory:** A framework of concepts and hypothesized propositions from which empirical events can be explained and predicted.

**Therapy:** Generic term for treatment of pathological conditions.

**Threctia:** Dimension of temperament signifying a disposition to fearfulness.

**Toxic:** Poisonous.

**Trait:** A more or less enduring characteristic of a person.

**Transference:** In therapy, an unconscious tendency to generalize to the therapist attitudes and feelings learned in relation to one's parents.

**Transient situational reactions:** A group of syndromes, found in basically nonpathological personalities, characterized by pathological responses, usually of relatively brief duration, to objectively stressful stimulus conditions.

**Trauma:**  Severe physical or psychological injury.

**Tremor:**  Continuous and involuntary spasms involving a small group of muscles.

**Typology:**  A system for grouping persons into relatively distinctive classes on the basis of a single dominant characteristic.

**Unconscious:**  Out of awareness; in intrapsychic theory, the portion of the psyche containing repressed memories and emotions that cannot be brought to awareness except through special techniques such as hypnosis and free-association.

**Undoing:**  An intrapsychic mechanism in which guilt for past misdeeds is atoned for through symbolic acts of expiation.

**Vacillation:**  Fluctuating between two or more choices.

**Validity:**  In general, the extent to which a hypothesis is empirically verified, or a test measures what it purports to measure.

**Variable:**  A trait or characteristic in which events or people differ.

**Verbigeration:**  Meaningless repetition of words or sentences.

**Vicarious learning:**  Acquisition of behaviors or attitudes without direct experience, usually through incidental observation or imitation.

**Vicious circle:**  Sequences in which certain attempts to solve problems tend to perpetuate these problems and create new ones.

**Waxy flexibility:**  A willingness to assume any physical position molded by others.

**Withdrawal symptoms:**  Clinical signs which appear upon the termination of drug use among those who have been physiologically addicted to it.

**Word salad:**  Incoherent jumble of meaningful words and neologisms.

# BIBLIOGRAPHY

## PART 1

## Chapter 1

Cameron, N. *Personality Development and Psychopathology.* New York: Houghton Mifflin, 1963.

Grimm, J. F. C. *The Works of Hippocrates.* Vol. 2. Glogau, 1838.

Jones, E. *Life and Works of Sigmund Freud.* Vol. 1. New York: Basic Books, 1953.

Latham, R. G. *The Works of Thomas Sydenham, M.D.* London: Sydenham Society, 1848.

Meehl, P. E. Some ruminations on the validation of clinical procedures. *Canad. J. Psychol., 13,* 102-128, 1959.

Menninger, K. Psychiatric diagnosis. *Bull. Menninger Clin., 23,* 226-240, 1959.

Noyes, A. P. *Modern Clinical Psychiatry.* Philadelphia: Saunders, 1953.

Pavlov, I. D. *Lectures on Conditioned Reflexes.* Vol. 1. New York: International Publishers, 1928.

Roe, A. Integration of personality theory and clinical practice. *J. Abnorm. Soc. Psychol., 44,* 36-41, 1949.

Stern, J. A., and McDonald, D. G. Physiological correlates of mental disease. *Ann. Rev. Psychol., 16,* 225-264, 1965.

Szasz, T. S. The problem of psychiatric nosology. *Amer. J. Psychiat., 114,* 405-413, 1957.

Thorndike, E. L. *The Elements of Psychology.* New York: A. G. Seiler, 1905.

## Chapter 2

Adams, H. B. Mental illness—or interpersonal behavior. *Amer. Psychol., 19,* 191-196, 1964.

Altschule, M. *Bodily Physiology in Mental and Emotional Disorders.* New York: Grune and Stratton, 1953.

Bandura, A. Psychotherapy as a learning process. *Psychol. Bull., 58,* 143-159, 1961.

Bandura, A. A social learning interpretation of psychological dysfunctions. In London, P., and Rosenhan, D. (eds.), *Foundations of Abnormal Psychology.* New York: Holt, Rinehart and Winston, 1968.

Bandura, A., and Walters, R. H. *Social Learning and Personality Development.* New York: Holt, Rinehart and Winston, 1963.

Beck, S. J. The science of personality: Nomothetic or idiographic? *Psychol. Rev., 60,* 353-359, 1953.

Bindra, D. Experimental psychology and the problem of behavior disorders. *Canad. J. Psychol., 13,* 135-150, 1959.

Binswanger, L. Existential analysis and psychotherapy. *Psychoanal. and Psychoanal. Rev., 45,* 79-83, 1958.

Bleuler, E. The physiogenic and psychogenic in schizophrenia. *Amer. J. Psychiat., 87,* 203-211, 1930.

Boss, M. *The Psychology of Dreams.* New York: Philosophical Library, 1958.

Campbell, J. D. *Manic-Depressive Disease.* Philadelphia: Lippincott, 1953.

Cattell, R. B. *The Scientific Analysis of Personality.* Baltimore: Penguin Books, 1965.

Cronbach, L. J. The two disciplines of scientific psychology. *Amer. Psychol., 12,* 671-684, 1957.

Dallenbach, K. The place of theory in science. *Psychol. Rev., 60,* 33-44, 1953.

Delgado, J. M. R. Emotions. In Vernon, J. (ed.), *Introduction to Psychology: A Self-Selection Textbook.* Dubuque, Iowa: W. C. Brown, 1966.

Delgado, J. M. R., Roberts, W. W., and Miller, N. Learning motivated by electrical stimulation of subcortical structures in the monkey brain. *J. Comp. Physiol. Psychol., 49,* 373-380, 1954.

Dollard, J., and Miller, N. *Personality and Psychotherapy.* New York: McGraw-Hill, 1950.

Erikson, E. *Childhood and Society.* New York: Norton, 1950.

Erikson, E. Identity and the life cycle. In Klein, G. S. (ed.), *Psychological Issues.* New York: Int'l Univ. Press, 1959.

Estes, W. K. From chipmunks to bulldozers to what? *Contemp. Psychol., 10,* 196-199, 1965.

Eysenck, H. J. The science of personality: Nomothetic! *Psychol. Rev., 61,* 339-342, 1954.

Eysenck, H. J. (ed.) *Behavior Therapy and the Neuroses.* London: Pergamon Press, 1960.

Eysenck, H. J., and Rachman, S. *Causes and Cures of Neurosis.* London: Routledge and Kegan Paul, 1965.

Fairbairn, W. R. D. *Psychoanalytic Studies of the Personality*. London: Tavistock, 1952.

Festinger, L. *A Theory of Cognitive Dissonance*. Evanston, Ill.: Row, Peterson, 1957.

Fish, F. A neurophysiological theory of schizophrenia. *J. Ment. Sci., 109,* 828-838, 1961.

Ford, D., and Urban, H. *Systems of Psychotherapy*. New York: Wiley, 1963.

Fromm, E. *Man for Himself*. New York: Rinehart, 1947.

Gellhorn, E. *Physiological Foundations of Neurology and Psychiatry*. Minneapolis: U. of Minnesota Press, 1953.

Hartmann, H. *Ego Psychology and the Problem of Adaptation*. New York: Int'l. Univ. Press, 1958.

Heath, R. G., et al. *Studies in Schizophrenia*. Cambridge: Harvard U. Press, 1954.

Heath, R. G. Schizophrenia: Biochemical and physiologic aberrations. *Int'l. J. Neuropsychiat., 2,* 597-610, 1966.

Hebb, D. O. Alice in Wonderland, or psychology among the biological sciences. In Harlow, H., and Woolsey, C. (eds.), *Biological and Biochemical Bases of Behavior*. Madison: U. of Wisconsin Press, 1958a.

Hebb, D. O. The motivating effects of exteroceptive stimulation. *Amer. Psychol., 13,* 109-113, 1958b.

Heilbrunn, G. Psychoanalysis, yesterday, today and tomorrow. *A.M.A. Arch. Gen. Psychiat., 4,* 321-330, 1961.

Hoagland, H. Metabolic and physiologic disturbances in the psychoses. In *Biology of Mental Health and Disease*. New York: Hoeber, 1952.

Hoffer, A., and Osmond, H. The adrenochrome model and schizophrenia. *J. Nerv. Ment. Dis., 128,* 18-35, 1959.

Hoskins, R. G. *The Biology of Schizophrenia*. New York: Norton, 1946.

Katkovsky, W. Social-learning theory and maladjustment. In Gorlow, L., and Katkovsky, W. (eds.), *Readings in the Psychology of Adjustment*. Second edition. New York: McGraw-Hill, 1968.

L'Abate, L. *Principles of Clinical Psychology*. New York: Grune and Stratton, 1964.

Maslow, A. *Toward a Psychology of Being*. Princeton: Van Nostrand, 1962.

May, R., Angel, E., and Ellenberger, H. F. (eds.) *Existence: A New Dimension in Psychiatry and Psychology*. New York: Basic Books, 1958.

Mowrer, O. H. Learning theory and behavior therapy. In Wolman, B. (ed.), *Handbook of Clinical Psychology*. New York: McGraw-Hill, 1965.

Olds, J. Pleasure centers of the brain. *Sci. Amer., 195,* 104-116, 1956.

Olds, J. Hypothalamic substrates of reward. *Physiol. Rev., 42,* 554-604, 1962.

Osmond, H., and Smythies, J. Schizophrenia: A new approach. *J. Ment. Sci., 98,* 309-315, 1952.

Rapaport, D. The theory of ego autonomy: A generalization. *Bull. Menninger Clin., 22,* 13-35, 1958.

Rapaport, D. The structure of psychoanalytic theory: A systematizing attempt. In Koch, S. (ed.), *Psychology: A Study of a Science*. Vol. 3. New York: McGraw-Hill, 1959.

Rashkis, H. A. The organization factor as an explanatory principle in functional psychosis. *A.M.A. Arch. Neurol. Psychiat., 80,* 513-519, 1958.

Riesman, D. *The Lonely Crowd*. New Haven: Yale, 1950.

Rogers, C. A theory of therapy, personality, and interpersonal relationships, as developed in the client-centered framework. In Koch, S. (ed.), *Psychology: A Study of a Science*. Vol. 3. New York: McGraw-Hill, 1959.

Rosenzweig, N. A mechanism in schizophrenia. *A.M.A. Arch. Neurol. Psychiat., 74,* 554-555, 1955.

Rotter, J. B. *Social Learning and Clinical Psychology*. Englewood Cliffs: Prentice-Hall, 1954.

Rotter, J. B. Generalized expectancies for internal versus external control of reinforcements. *Psychol. Monogr., 80,* 1-28, 1966.

Rubin, L. S. Patterns of adrenergic-cholinergic imbalance in the functional psychoses. *Psychol. Rev., 69,* 501-519, 1962.

Shlien, J., et al. (eds.) *Research in Psychotherapy*. Vol. 3. Washington, D.C.: American Psychological Association, 1968.

Singer, R. D. Organization as a unifying concept in schizophrenia. *A.M.A. Arch. Gen. Psychiat., 2,* 61-74, 1960.

Skinner, B. F. What is psychotic behavior? In *Theory and Treatment of the Psychoses*. St. Louis: Washington University Press, 1956.

Skinner, B. F. *Cumulative Record*. New York: Appleton-Century-Crofts, 1959.

Spitz, R. A. *The First Year of Life*. New York: Int'l. Univ. Press, 1965.

Szasz, T. The myth of mental illness. *Amer. Psychol., 15,* 113-118, 1960.

Ullmann, L., and Krasner, L. (eds.) *Case Studies in Behavior Modification*. New York: Holt, Rinehart and Winston, 1965.

Williams, R. J. The biological approach to the study of personality. *Berkeley Conference on Personality Development*, 1960.

Woolley, D. W. *The Biochemical Bases of Psychoses*. New York: Wiley, 1962.

Woolley, D. W., and Shaw, E. A biochemical and pharmacological suggestion about certain mental disorders. *Sci., 119,* 587-588, 1954.

Wolpe, J. *Psychotherapy by Reciprocal Inhibition*. Stanford: Stanford Univ. Press, 1958.

## Chapter 3

American Psychiatric Association, *Diagnostic and Statistical Manual of Mental Disorders*. Washington, D.C.: Mental Hospitals Service, 1952, 1968.

Ash, P. The reliability of psychiatric diagnosis. *J. Abnorm. Soc. Psychol., 44,* 272-277, 1949.

Cameron, N. *Personality Development and Psychopathology*. New York: Houghton Mifflin, 1963.

Cattell, R. B., and Scheier, I. H. *The Meaning and Measurement of Neuroticism and Anxiety*. New York: Ronald, 1961.

Delgado, J. M. R. In Vernon, J. (ed.), *Introduction to Psychology; A Self-selection Textbook*. Dubuque, Iowa: W. C. Brown, 1966.

Duffy, E. *Activation and Behavior*. New York: Wiley, 1962.

Fulkerson, S. C., and Barry, J. R. Methodology and research on the prognostic use of psychological tests. *Psychol. Bull., 58,* 177-204, 1961.

Gill, M., and Brenman, M. Research in psychotherapy. *Amer. J. Orthopsychiat., 18,* 100-110, 1948.

Glueck, B. C., et al. The quantitative assessment of personality. *Comp. Psychiat., 5,* 15-23, 1964.

Gottschalk, L. A., and Auerbach, A. H. (eds.) *Methods of Research in Psychotherapy*. New York: Appleton-Century-Crofts, 1966.

Grunbaum, A. Causality and the science of human behavior. *Amer. Scientist*, 665-676, 1952.

Katz, M. M., and Cole, J. O. A phenomenological approach to the classification of schizophrenic disorders. *Dis. Nerv. Syst., 24,* 1-8, 1963.

Katz, M. M., Cole, J. O., and Barton, W. E. (eds.) *Role and Methodology of Classification in Psychiatry and Psychopathology*. Washington, D.C.: Public Health Service, 1968.

Leary, T., *Interpersonal Diagnosis of Personality*. New York: Ronald, 1957.

Lorr, M. (ed.) *Explorations in Typing Psychotics*. New York: Pergamon, 1966.

Lorr, M., Bishop, P. F., and McNair, D. M. Interpersonal types among psychiatric patients. *J. Abnorm. Psychol., 70,* 468-472, 1965.

Lorr, M., Klett, C. J., and McNair, D. M. *Syndromes of Psychosis*. New York: Macmillan, 1963.

McNair, D. M., Lorr, M., and Hemingway, P. Further evidence for syndrome-based psychotic types. *A.M.A. Arch. Gen. Psychiat., 11,* 368-376, 1963.

Meehl, P. E. *Clinical Versus Statistical Prediction*. Minneapolis: U. of Minnesota Press, 1954.

Meehl, P. E. When shall we use our heads instead of the formula? *J. Counsel. Psychol., 4,* 268-273, 1957.

Meehl, P. E. Seer over sign: The first good example. *J. Exp. Res. Personality, 1,* 27-32, 1965.

Menninger, K., Pruyser, P., and Mayman, M. *The Vital Balance*. New York: Viking Press, 1963.

Moruzzi, R. S., and Magoun, H. W. Brain stem reticular formation and activation of the EEG. *EEG Clin. Neurophysiol., 1,* 455-473, 1949.

Murphy, L. B. Discussion of papers in the light of research in human development. In Katz, M., et al. (eds.), *The Role and Methodology of Classification in Psychiatry and Psychopathology*. Washington, D.C.: Public Health Service, 1968.

Olds, J. Pleasure centers in the brain. *Sci. Amer., 195,* 105-116, 1956.

Overall, J. E. A configural analysis of psychiatric diagnostic stereotypes. *Behav. Sci., 8,* 211-219, 1963.

Overall, J. E., Hollister, L. E., and Pichot, P. Major psychiatric disorders: A four-dimensional model. *A.M.A. Arch. Gen. Psychiat., 16,* 146-151, 1967.

Pasamanick, B., Dinitz, S., and Lefton, M. Psychiatric orientation and its relation to diagnosis and treatment in a mental hospital. *Amer. J. Psychiat., 116,* 127-132, 1959.

Phillips, L. *Human Adaptation and its Failures*. New York: Academic Press, 1968.

Phillips, L., and Rabinovitch, M. Social role and patterns of symptomatic behaviors. *J. Abnorm. Soc. Psychol., 57,* 181-186, 1958.

Rado, S. *Psychoanalysis of Behavior*. New York: Grune and Stratton, 1962.

Roe, A. Integration of personality theory and clinical practice. *J. Abnorm. Soc. Psychol., 44,* 36-41, 1949.

Rosenthal, R. Experimenter outcome-orientation and the results of the psychological experiment. *Psychol. Bull., 61,* 405-412, 1964.

Rotter, J. *Social Learning and Clinical Psychology*. New York: Prentice-Hall, 1954.

Sarbin, T. R. A contribution to the study of actuarial and statistical methods of prediction. *Amer. J. Sociol., 48,* 593-602, 1943.

Sarbin, T. R., Taft, R., and Bailey, D. E. *Clinical Inference and Cognitive Theory*. New York: Holt, Rinehart and Winston, 1960.

Shakow, D., and Huston, P. E. Studies of motor function in schizophrenia. *J. Gen. Psychol., 15,* 63-106, 1936.

Silverman, J. The problem of attention in research and theory in schizophrenia. *Psychol. Rev., 71,* 352-379, 1964.

Thompson, E. T., and Hayden, A. C. (eds.) *A.M.A. Handbook on Standard Nomenclature of Diseases and Operations*. 5th ed. New York: McGraw-Hill, 1961.

Windle, C. Psychological tests in psychopathological prognosis. *Psychol. Bull., 49,* 451-482, 1952.

Wittenborn, J. Holzberg, J., and Simon, B. Symptom correlates for descriptive diagnosis. *Genet. Psychol. Monogr., 47,* 237-301, 1953.

Wittenborn, J. R., and May, P. R. A. (eds.) *Prediction of Response to Pharmacotherapy*. Springfield, Ill.: Thomas, 1966.

Zigler, E., and Phillips, L. Psychiatric diagnosis. *J. Abnorm. Soc. Psychol., 63,* 607-618, 1961a.

Zigler, E., and Phillips, L. Psychiatric diagnosis and symptomatology. *J. Abnorm. Soc. Psychol., 63,* 69-75, 1961b.

# PART 2

Hartmann, H., and Kris, E. The genetic approach to psychoanalysis. In *The Psychoanalytic Study of the Child*. Vol. I. New York: Int'l. Univ. Press, 1945.

Krech, D., and Crutchfield, R. *Theory and Problems of Social Psychology*. New York: McGraw-Hill, 1948.

Lewin, K. Defining the field at a given time. *Psychol. Rev., 50,* 292-310, 1943.

## Chapter 4

Altschule, M. D. *Body Physiology in Mental and Emotional Disorders*. New York: Grune and Stratton, 1953.

Anastasi, A. Heredity, environment, and the question "how"? *Psychol. Rev., 65,* 197-208, 1958.

Becker, W. C. The process-reactive distinction: A key to the problem of schizophrenia. *J. Nerv. Ment. Dis., 129,* 442-449, 1959.

Belmont, I., et al. Perceptual evidence of CNS dysfunction in schizophrenia. *A.M.A. Arch. Gen. Psychiat., 10,* 395-408, 1964.

Bergman, P., and Escalona, S. Unusual sensitivities in very young children. In *Psychoanalytic Study of the Child*. Vols. 3-4. New York: Int'l. Univ. Press, 1949.

Böök, J. A. Genetical aspects of schizophrenic psychoses. In Jackson, D. (ed.), *The Etiology of Schizophrenia*. New York: Basic Books, 1960.

Böök, J. A. Schizophrenia as a gene mutation. *Acta Genetica, 4,* 133-139, 1953.

Chess, S., Thomas, A., Birch, H. G., and Hertzig, M. Implications of a longitudinal study of child development for child psychiatry. *Amer. J. Psychiat., 117,* 434-441, 1960.

David, P. R., and Snyder, L. H. Some interrelations between psychology and genetics. In Koch, S. (ed.), *Psychology: A Study of a Science.* Vol. 4. New York: McGraw-Hill, 1962.

Davidson, M. A., et al. The distribution of personality traits in seven-year-old children: A combined psychological, psychiatric, and somatotype study. *Brit. J. Educ. Psychol., 27,* 48-61, 1957.

Delafresnaye, J. F. (ed.) *Brain Mechanisms and Learning.* Springfield, Ill.: Thomas, 1961.

Delgado, J. M. R. Emotional behavior in animals and humans. *Psychiat. Res. Repts., 12,* 259-266, 1960.

Escalona, S. *Roots of Individuality.* Chicago: Aldine, 1968.

Escalona, S., and Leitch, M. *Early Phases of Personality Development: A Non-normative Study of Infancy Behavior.* Evanston, Ill.: Child Development Publications, 1953.

Escalona, S., and Heider, G. *Prediction and Outcome.* New York: Basic Books, 1959.

Essen-Moller, E. Psychiatrische Untersuchungen an einer Serie von Zwillingen. *Acta Psychiat. Neurol. Suppl., 23,* 1941.

Essen-Möller, E. *Psychiatrische Geisteskranken Elternpaare.* Stuttgart: Thieme, 1952.

Eysenck, H. J. *Dimensions of Personality.* London: Routledge and Kegan Paul, 1953.

Eysenck, H. J. *The Structure of Personality.* London: Methuen, 1957.

Fabing, H. Trends in biological research in schizophrenia. *J. Nerv. Ment. Dis., 124,* 1-7, 1956.

Feldstein, A., Hoagland, H., and Freeman, H. Blood and urinary serotonin and 5-hydroxyindoleacetic acid levels in schizophrenic patients and normal subjects. *J. Nerv. Ment. Dis., 129,* 62-68, 1959.

Franks, C. M. Conditioning and abnormal behavior. In Eysenck, H. J. (ed.), *Handbook of Abnormal Psychology.* New York: Basic Books, 1961.

Fuller, J. L., and Thompson, W. R. *Behavior Genetics.* New York: Wiley, 1960.

Garmezy, N. Process and reactive schizophrenia: Some conceptions and issues. In Katz, M., et al. (eds.), *The Role and Methodology of Classification in Psychiatry and Psychopathology.* Washington, D.C.: Public Health Service, 1968.

Gellhorn, E. *Autonomic Regulations: Their Significance for Physiology, Psychology and Neuropsychiatry.* New York: Interscience, 1943.

Gesell, A., et al. *The First Five Years of Life.* New York: Harper, 1940.

Glueck, S., and Glueck, E. *Family Environment and Delinquency.* Boston: Houghton Mifflin, 1962.

Gottesman, I. I., and Shields, J. Schizophrenia in twins: 16 years' consecutive admissions to a psychiatric clinic. *Brit. J. Psychiat., 112,* 809-818, 1966.

Gregory, I. Genetic factors in schizophrenia. *Amer. J. Psychiat. 116,* 961-972, 1960.

Gregory, I. *Fundamentals of Psychiatry.* Philadelphia: Saunders, 1968.

Halevy, A., Moss, R. H., and Solomon, G. F. A relationship between blood serotonin concentrations and behavior of psychiatric patients. *J. Psychiat. Res., 3,* 1-10, 1965.

Hartmann, H. *Ego Psychology and the Problem of Adaptation.* New York: Int'l. Univ. Press, 1958.

Heath, R. G., et al. Effect on behavior in humans with the administration of taraxein. *Amer. J. Psychiat., 114,* 14-24, 1957.

Heath, R. G. A biochemical hypothesis on the etiology of schizophrenia. In Jackson, D. D. (ed.), *The Etiology of Schizophrenia.* New York: Basic Books, 1960.

Heath, R. G. Schizophrenia: Biochemical and physiologic aberrations. *Int'l. J. Neuropsychiat., 2,* 597-610, 1966.

Higgins, J. The concept of process-reactive schizophrenia: Criteria and related research. *J. Nerv. Ment. Dis., 138,* 9-25, 1964.

Hoffer, A., and Osmond, H. The adrenochrome model and schizophrenia. *J. Nerv. Ment. Dis., 128,* 18-35, 1959.

Hoskins, R. G. *The Biology of Schizophrenia.* New York: Norton, 1946.

Kallmann, F. J. *The Genetics of Schizophrenia.* New York: J. J. Augustin, 1938.

Kallmann, F. J. *Heredity in Mental Health and Disorder.* New York: Norton, 1953.

Kantor, R., Wallner, J., and Winder, C. Process and reactive schizophrenia. *J. Consult. Psychol., 17,* 157-162, 1953.

Kety, S. Biochemical theories of schizophrenia. *Sci., 129,* 1528-1532; 1590-1596, 1959.

Kety, S. The relevance of biochemical studies to the etiology of schizophrenia. In Romano, J. (ed.), *Origins of Schizophrenia.* Amsterdam: Excerpta Medical Foundation, 1968.

Krech, D., and Crutchfield, R. S. *Theory and Problems of Social Psychology.* New York: McGraw-Hill, 1948.

Kretschmer, E. *Physique and Character.* New York: Harcourt Brace, 1925.

Kringlen, E. Discordance with respect to schizophrenia in monozygotic male twins: Some genetic aspects. *J. Nerv. Ment. Dis., 138,* 26-31, 1964.

Kringlen, E. Schizophrenia in twins: An epidemiological-clinical study. *Psychiatry, 29,* 172-184, 1966.

Lacey, J. I. The evaluation of autonomic responses: Toward a general solution. *Annals N.Y. Acad. Sci., 67,* 123-164, 1956.

Leonhard, K. Cycloid psychoses—endogenous psychoses which are neither schizophrenic nor manic-depressive. *J. Ment. Sci., 107,* 633-648, 1961.

Lindegard, B. Variations in human body-build. *Acta Psychiat. Neurolog., 86,* 1-163, 1953.

Lindegard, B., and Nyman, G. E. Interrelations between psychologic, somatologic, and endocrine dimensions. *Lunds Universitets Arsskrift, 52,* 1-54, 1956.

Lipton, E. L., Steinschneider, A., and Richmond, J. B. Autonomic function in the neonate. *Psychosom. Med., 23,* 472-9, 1961.

Lombroso, C. *L'Uomo Delinquente.* Bocca: Torina, 1889.

Lombroso, C. *Crime: Its Causes and Remedies.* Boston: Little, Brown, 1911.

Luxenburger, H. Die Schizophrenie und ihr Erbkreis. In Just, G. (ed.), *Hdbh. d. Erbbiologie.* Vol. 5. Berlin: Springer, 1939.

Lynn, R. Russian theory and research on schizophrenia. *Psychol. Bull., 60,* 486-498, 1963.

MacMahon, B., and Sowa, J. M. Physical damage to the fetus. In *Causes of Mental Disorder: A Review of Epidemiological Knowledge*. New York: Milbank Memorial Fund, 1961.

Malmo, R. B., and Shagass, C. Physiological studies of reaction to stress in anxiety states and early schizophrenia. *Psychosom. Med., 11*, 9-24, 1949.

Malmo, R. B., Shagass, C., and Davis, F. H. Electromyographic studies of muscular tension in psychiatric patients under stress. *J. Clin. Exper. Psychopath., 12*, 45-66, 1951.

Meehl, P. Schizotozia, schizotypy, schizophrenia. *Amer. Psychol., 17*, 827-838, 1962.

Meili, R. A longitudinal study of personality development. In Jessner, L., and Pavenstedt, E. (eds.), *Dynamic Psychopathology of Childhood*. New York: Grune and Stratton, 1959.

Montague, M. F. A. *Prenatal Influences*. Springfield, Ill.: Thomas, 1962.

Murphy, L. B., et al. *The Widening World of Childhood*. New York: Basic Books, 1962.

Newman, N. H., Freeman, F. N., and Holzinger, K. J. *Twins: A Study of Heredity and Environment*. Chicago: U. of Chicago Press, 1937.

Osborne, R. H., and DeGeorge, F. V. *Genetic Bases of Morphological Variation*. Cambridge: Harvard U. Press, 1959.

Osmond, H., and Smythies, J. Schizophrenia: A new approach. *J. Ment. Sci., 98*, 309-315, 1952.

Pasamanick, B., and Knoblach, H. Epidemiologic studies on the complications of pregnancy and the birth process. In Caplan, G. (ed.), *Prevention of Mental Disorders in Children*. New York: Basic Books, 1961.

Pavlov, I. P. *Lectures on Conditioned Reflexes*. New York: Int'l. Univ. Press, 1941.

Penrose, L. S. Research methods in human genetics. In *Congrès International de Psychiatrie: VI. Psychiatrie Sociale*. Paris: Hermann et Cie, 1950.

Penrose, L. S. The genetical background of common diseases. *Acta Genetica, 4*, 257-265, 1953.

Pincus, G., and Hoagland, H. Adrenal cortical responses to stress in normal men and in those with personality disorders. *Amer. J. Psychiat., 106*, 641-650, 1950.

Rapaport, D. The autonomy of the ego. *Bull. Menninger Clin., 15*, 113-123, 1951.

Rees, L., and Eysenck, H. J. A factorial study of some morphological and psychological aspects of human constitution. *J. Ment. Sci., 91*, 8, 1945.

Rees, L. Physical characteristics of the schizophrenic patient. In Richter, D. (ed.), *Somatic Aspects of Schizophrenia*. London: Pergamon, 1957.

Rees, L. Constitutional factors and abnormal behavior. In Eysenck, H. J. (ed.), *Handbook of Abnormal Psychology*. New York: Basic Books, 1961.

Rosanoff, A. J., et al. The etiology of so-called schizophrenic psychoses. *Amer. J. Psychiat., 91*, 247-286, 1934.

Rosenthal, D. Some factors associated with concordance and discordance with respect to schizophrenia in monozygotic twins. *J. Nerv. Ment. Dis., 129*, 1-10, 1959.

Rosenthal, D. An historical and methodological review of genetic studies in schizophrenia. In Romano, J. (ed.), *Origins of Schizophrenia*. Amsterdam: Excerpta Medical Foundation, 1968.

Rostan, L. *Cours élémentaire d'hygiène*. Paris, 1828.

Scheibel, A., and Scheibel, M. Substrates for integrative action in the brain stem reticular formation. In *International Symposium on Reticular Formation*, Ford Foundation. Boston: Little, Brown, 1958.

Schulz, B. Kinder manisch—depressiven und anderer Affektiv psychotischer Elternpaare. *Zeitschr. Neurol., 169*, 311-328, 1940.

Selyé, H. *The Stress of Life*. New York: McGraw-Hill, 1956.

Shaw, E., and Woolley, D. W. Some serotonin-like activities in lysergic acid diethylamide. *Sci., 124*, 121-122, 1956.

Sheer, D. (ed.) *Electrical Stimulation of the Brain*. Houston: U. of Texas Press, 1961.

Sheldon, W. H., et al. *The Varieties of Human Physique: An Introduction to Constitutional Psychology*. New York: Harper, 1940.

Sheldon, W. H., and Stevens, S. S. *The Varieties of Temperament: A Psychology of Constitutional Differences*. New York: Harper, 1942.

Sheldon, W. H., et al. *Varieties of Delinquent Youth: An Introduction to Constitutional Psychiatry*. New York: Harper, 1949.

Sheldon, W. H., et al. *Atlas of Men: A Guide for Somatotyping the Male at All Ages*. New York: Harper, 1954.

Shields, J., and Slater, E. Heredity and psychological abnormality. In Eysenck, H. J. (ed.), *Handbook of Abnormal Psychology*. New York: Basic Books, 1961.

Slater, E., and Shields, J. *Psychotic and Neurotic Illnesses in Twins*. London: H. M. Stationery Office, 1953.

Sontag, L. W. The possible relationship of prenatal environment to schizophrenia. In Jackson, D. (ed.), *The Etiology of Schizophrenia*. New York: Basic Books, 1960.

Thomas, A., et al. *Behavioral Individuality in Early Childhood*. New York: New York University Press, 1963.

Thomas, A., Chess, S., and Birch, H. G. *Temperament and Behavior Disorders in Children*. New York: New York Univ. Press, 1968.

Thompson, W. R. Influence of prenatal and maternal anxiety on emotionality in young rats. *Sci., 125*, 698-699, 1957.

Tienari, P. Psychiatric illnesses in identical twins. *Acta Psychiat. Scand., 39*, Suppl. 171, 1-195, 1963.

Toderick, A., Tait, A. C., and Marshall, E. F. Blood platelet 5-hydroxytryptamine levels in psychiatric patients. *J. Ment. Sci., 106*, 884-890, 1960.

Vandenberg, S. G. Contributions of twin research to psychology. *Psychol. Bull., 66*, 327-352, 1966.

Venables, P. Input dysfunction in schizophrenia. In Maher, B. A. (ed.), *Progress in Experimental Personality Research*. Vol. I. New York: Academic Press, 1964.

Viola, G. *La Constituzione Individuale*. Bologna: Capelli, 1932.

Walter, G. Electroencephalographic development of children. In Tanner, J. M., and Inhelder, B. (eds.), *Discussions on Child Development*. New York: Int'l. Univ. Press, 1953.

Weinberg, I., and Lobstein, J. Inheritance in schizophrenia. *Acta Psychiat. Neurolog., 18*, 93-140, 1943.

Wilder, J. The law of initial values. *Psychosom. Med., 12*, 392-401, 1950.

Wittman, P., Sheldon, W. H., and Katz, C. J. A study of the relationship between constitutional variations and fundamental psychotic behavior reaction. *J. Nerv. Ment. Dis., 108,* 470-476, 1948.

Woolley, D. W. *The Biochemical Bases of Psychoses.* New York: Wiley, 1962.


*Chapter 5*

Bandura, A., and Huston, A. C. Identification as a process of incidental learning. *J. Abnorm. Soc. Psychol., 63,* 311-318, 1961.

Bateson, G., Jackson, D. D., Haley, J., and Weakland, J. Toward a theory of schizophrenia. *Beh. Sci., 1,* 251-264, 1956.

Bateson, G., and Ruesch, J. *Communication, the Social Matrix of Psychiatry.* New York: Norton, 1951.

Beach, F., and Jaynes, J. Effects of early experience upon the behavior of animals. *Psychol. Bull., 51,* 239-262, 1954.

Beck, A. T. Thinking and depression: Idiosyncratic content and cognitive distortions. *A.M.A. Arch. Gen. Psychiat., 9,* 324-333, 1963.

Becker, W. C. Consequences of different kinds of parental discipline. In Hoffman, M., and Hoffman, L. (eds.), *Review of Child Development Research.* Vol. I. New York: Russell Sage, 1964.

Bibace, R., Kaplan, B., and Wapner, S. *Developmental Approaches to Psychopathology.* New York: McGraw-Hill, 1969 (in press).

Bowlby, J. *Maternal Care and Mental Health.* Geneva: World Health Organization, 1952.

Butler, J. M., and Rice, L. N. Adience, self-actualization and drive theory. In Wepman, J., and Heine, R. (eds.), *Concepts of Personality.* Chicago: Aldine, 1963.

Caldwell, B. M. The effect of infant care. In Hoffman, M., and Hoffman, L. (eds.), *Review of Child Development Research.* Vol. I. New York: Russell Sage, 1964.

Cameron, N. *The Psychology of Behavior Disorders.* New York: Houghton Mifflin, 1947.

Cairns, R. B. Attachment behavior in mammals. *Psychol. Rev., 73,* 409-426, 1966.

Cameron, N., and Magaret, A. *Behavior Pathology.* New York: Houghton Mifflin, 1951.

Carothers, J. C. The African mind in health and disease. *World Health Organization Monograph, 17,* Geneva: World Health Organization, 1953.

Child, C. M. *Patterns and Problems of Development.* Chicago: U. of Chicago Press, 1941.

Clark, R. E. Psychoses, income and occupational prestige. *Amer. J. Sociol., 54,* 433-440, 1949.

Clausen, J. A. Family structure, socialization, and personality. In Hoffman, L., and Hoffman, M. (eds.), *Review of Child Development Research.* Vol. II. New York: Russell Sage, 1966.

Clausen, J. A., and Kohn, M. L. Relation of schizophrenia to the social structure of a small city. In Pasamanick, B. (ed.), *Epidemiology of Mental Disorders.* Washington, D.C.: American Association for the Advancement of Science, 1959.

Conel, J. L. *The Postnatal Development of the Human Cerebral Cortex.* Five Volumes. Cambridge, Mass.: Harvard U. Press, 1939-1955.

Dohrenwald, B. S., and Dohrenwald, B. P. Stress situations, birth order, and psychological symptoms. *J. Abnorm. Psychol., 71,* 215-223, 1966.

Dunham, H. W. Epidemiology of psychiatric disorders as a contribution to medical ecology. *A.M.A. Arch. Gen. Psychiat., 14,* 1-19, 1966.

Eisenberg, L. Normal child development. In Freedman, A., and Kaplan, H. (eds.), *Comprehensive Textbook of Psychiatry.* Baltimore: Williams and Wilkins, 1967.

Erikson, E. H. Growth and crises of the healthy personality. In Klein, G. S. (ed.), *Psychological Issues.* New York: Int'l. Univ. Press, 1959.

Faris, R. E. L., and Dunham, H. W. *Mental Disorders in Urban Areas.* Chicago: U. of Chicago Press, 1939.

Frank, G. A. The role of the family in the development of psychopathology. *Psychol. Bull., 64,* 191-208, 1965.

Frank, L. K. Society as the patient. *Amer. J. Sociology, 42,* 335-344, 1936.

Fromm, E. *The Sane Society.* New York: Rinehart, 1955.

Frumkin, R. M. Occupation and mental disorder. In Rose, A. M. (ed.), *Mental Health and Mental Disorder.* New York: Norton, 1955.

Gewirtz, J. L. A learning analysis of the effects of normal stimulation upon social and exploratory behavior in the human infant. In Foss, B. M. (ed.), *Determinants of Infant Behavior II.* New York: Wiley, 1963.

Glidewell, J. C. (ed.) *Parental Attitudes and Child Behavior.* Springfield, Ill.: Thomas, 1961.

Goldberg, E. M., and Morrison, S. L. Schizophrenia and social class. *Brit. J. Psychiat., 109,* 785-802, 1963.

Goldfarb, W. Emotional and intellectual consequences of psychologic deprivation in infancy: A reevaluation. In Hoch, P., and Zubin, J. (eds.), *Psychopathology of Childhood.* New York: Grune and Stratton, 1955.

Goldhamer, H., and Marshall, A. W. *Psychosis and Civilization.* Glencoe, Ill.: Free Press, 1953.

Goldman, A. E. A comparative-developmental approach to schizophrenia. *Psychol. Bull., 59,* 57-69, 1962.

Goldstein, K. *The Organism.* New York: American Book Co., 1939.

Goodman, P. *Growing Up Absurd.* New York: Random House, 1960.

Gregory, I. An analysis of familial data on psychiatric patients: Parental age, family size, birth order and ordinal position. *Brit. J. Prev. Soc. Med., 12,* 42-59, 1958.

Hardt, R. H., and Feinhandler, S. J. Social class and mental hospital prognosis. *Amer. Sociol. Rev., 24,* 815-821, 1959.

Harlow, H. F. Primary affectional patterns in primates. *Am. J. Orthopsychiat., 30,* 67-84, 1960.

Harlow, H. F. The maternal affectional system. In Foss, B. M. (ed.), *Determinants of Infant Behavior II.* New York: Wiley, 1963.

Harlow, H. F., and Harlow, M. K. The affectional systems. In Schrier, A., et al. (eds.), *Behavior of Non-Human Primates.* Vol. 2. New York: Academic Press, 1965.

Hebb, D. O. *The Organization of Behavior.* New York: Wiley, 1949.

Helson, H. Adaptation-level as a basis for a quantitative theory of frames of reference. *Psychol. Rev.,* *55,* 297-313, 1948.

Hess, E. H. Imprinting. *Sci., 130,* 133-141, 1959.

Hollingshead, A. B., and Redlich, F. C. *Social Class and Mental Illness.* New York: Wiley, 1958.

Kanner, L. Problems of nosology and psychodynamics of early infantile autism. *Amer. J. Orthopsychiat., 19,* 416-426, 1949.

Kelly, G. A. *The Psychology of Personal Constructs.* New York: Norton, 1955.

Langner, T. S., and Michael, S. T. *Life Stress and Mental Health.* Glencoe, Ill.: Free Press, 1963.

Leary, T. *Interpersonal Diagnosis of Personality.* New York: Ronald, 1957.

Lefcourt, H. M. Internal versus external control of reinforcement: A review. *Psychol. Bull., 65,* 206-220, 1966.

Lidz, T., Cornelison, A., Terry, D., and Fleck, S. The intrafamilial environment of the schizophrenic patient: VI. The transmission of irrationality. *A.M.A. Arch. Neur. Psychiat., 79,* 305-316, 1958.

Linton, R. *Culture and Mental Disorders.* Springfield, Ill.: Thomas, 1956.

Lorenz, K. Der Kumpan in der Umwelt des Vogels. Der Artgenosse als auslösendes Moment Socialzer Verhaltungsweissen. *J. orn. Ipz., 83,* 137-213; 289-413, 1935.

Lu, Y. C. Contradictory parental expectations in schizophrenia. *Psychiat., 19,* 231-236, 1956.

Lystad, M. H. Social mobility among selected groups of schizophrenic patients. *Amer. Sociol. Rev., 22,* 282-292, 1957.

Mahler, M. S. On child psychosis and schizophrenia: Autistic and symbiotic infantile psychosis. In *Psychoanalytic Study of the Child.* Vol. 7. New York: Int'l. Univ. Press, 1952.

Malzberg, B. *Social and Biological Aspects of Disease.* Utica: State Hospitals Press, 1940.

Malzberg, B. Important statistical data about mental illness. In Arieti, S. (ed.), *American Handbook of Psychiatry.* New York: Basic Books, 1959.

McClelland, D. C. *Personality.* New York: Dryden, 1951.

McClelland, D. C., et al. *The Achievement Motive.* New York: Appleton-Century-Crofts, 1953.

McGraw, M. B. *The Neuromuscular Maturation of the Human Infant.* New York: Columbia U. Press, 1943.

Melzack, R. Effects of early experience on behavior: Experimental and conceptual considerations. In Hoch, P., and Zubin, J. (eds.), *Psychopathology of Perception.* New York: Grune and Stratton, 1965.

Milner, E. *Human Neural and Behavioral Development.* Springfield, Ill.: Thomas, 1967.

Moltz, H. An epigenetic interpretation of the imprinting phenomenon. In Newton, G., and Levine, S. (eds.) *Early Experience and Behavior.* Springfield, Ill.: Thomas, 1968.

Murphy, G. *Personality: A Biosocial Approach to Origins and Structures.* New York: Harper, 1947.

Murphy, L. B., et al. *The Widening World of Childhood.* New York: Basic Books, 1962.

Myers, J. K., and Roberts, B. H. *Family and Class Dynamics in Mental Illness.* New York: Wiley, 1959.

Newton, G., and Levine, S. (eds.) *Early Experience and Behavior.* Springfield, Ill.: Thomas, 1968.

O'Connor, N. Children in restricted environments. In

Newton, G., and Levine, S. (eds.), *Early Experience and Behavior.* Springfield, Ill.: Thomas, 1968.

Odegaard, O. New data on marriage and mental disease: The incidence of psychosis in the widowed and the divorced. *J. Ment. Sci., 99,* 778-785, 1953.

Orlansky, H. Infant care and personality. *Psychol. Bull., 46,* 1-48, 1949.

Parker, J. B., et al. Factors in manic-depressive reactions. *Dis. Nerv. Syst., 20,* 1-7, 1959.

Pasamanick, B., et al. Socioeconomic status: Some precursors of neuropsychiatric disorders. *Amer. J. Orthopsychiat., 26,* 594-601, 1956.

Phillips, L. *Human Adaptation and its Failures.* New York: Academic Press, 1968.

Piaget, J. *The origins of intelligence in children.* New York: Int'l. Univ. Press, 1952.

Rapaport, D. The theory of ego autonomy: A generalization. *Bull. Menninger Clin., 22,* 13-35, 1958.

Reisman, D. *The Lonely Crowd.* New Haven: Yale U. Press, 1950.

Renaud, H., and Estess, F. Life history interviews with one hundred normal American males: Pathogenicity in childhood. *Amer. J. Orthopsychiat., 31,* 786-802, 1961.

Rheingold, H. L. The effect of environmental stimulation upon social and exploratory behavior in the human infant. In Foss, B. M. (ed.), *Determinants of Infant Behavior II.* New York: Wiley, 1963.

Ribble, M. A. *The Rights of Infants.* New York: Columbia U. Press, 1943.

Riesen, A. H. Stimulation as a requirement for growth and function in behavioral development. In Fiske, D., and Maddi, S. (eds.), *Functions of Varied Experience.* Homewood, Ill.: Dorsey, 1961.

Rogers, C. R. A theory of therapy, personality, and interpersonal relationships, as developed in the client-centered framework. In Koch, S. (ed.), *Psychology, a Study of a Science.* Vol. 3. New York: McGraw-Hill, 1959.

Rose, A. M., and Stub, H. R. Summary of studies on the incidence of mental disorders. In Rose, A. M. (ed.), *Mental Health and Mental Disorder.* New York: Norton, 1955.

Rosen, E., and Rizzo, G. Preliminary standardization of the MMPI for use in Italy: A case study of inter-cultural and intracultural differences. *Educ. Psychol. Measmt., 21,* 629-636, 1961.

Rosenzweig, M. R., et al. Effect of environmental complexity and training on brain chemistry and anatomy: A replication and extension. *J. Comp. Physiol. Psychol., 55,* 429-437, 1962.

Scott, J. P. Comparative social psychology. In Waters, R. H. (ed.), *Principles of Comparative Psychology.* New York: McGraw-Hill, 1960.

Scott, J. P. *Early Experience and the Organization of Behavior.* Belmont, Calif.: Brooks-Cole, 1968.

Scott, W. A. Social psychological correlates of mental illness and mental health. *Psychol. Bull., 55,* 65-87, 1958.

Scheibel, M. E., and Scheibel, A. B. Some neural substrates of postnatal development. In Hoffman, M., and Hoffman, L. (eds.), *Review of Child Development Research.* Vol. I. New York: Russell Sage, 1964.

Sears, R. R., Maccoby, E. E., and Levin, H. *Patterns of Child Rearing.* Evanston, Ill.: Row, Peterson, 1957.

Sherif, M., and Sherif, C. (eds.) *Problems of Youth: Transition to Adulthood in a Changing World*. Chicago: Aldine, 1965.

Short, J. F. Juvenile delinquency: The sociocultural content. In Hoffman, L., and Hoffman, M. (eds.), *Review of Child Development Research*. Vol. II. New York: Russell Sage, 1966.

Singer, M. T., and Wynne, L. C. Thought disorder and family relations of schizophrenics, III: Methodology using projective techniques. *A.M.A. Arch. Gen. Psychiat., 12,* 187-212, 1965.

Spitz, R. A. *The First Year of Life*. New York: Int'l. Univ. Press, 1965.

Srole, L., et al. *Mental Health in the Metropolis; the Midtown Manhattan Study*. Vol. I. New York: McGraw-Hill, 1962.

Stainbrook, E. Some characteristics of the psychopathology of schizophrenic behavior in Bahian society. *Amer. J. Psychiat. 109,* 330-335, 1952.

Stevenson, I. Is the human personality more plastic in infancy and childhood? *Amer. J. Psychiat., 114,* 152-161, 1957.

Thompson, W. R., and Schaefer, T. Early environmental stimulation. In Fiske, D., and Maddi, S. (eds.), *Functions of Varied Experience*. Homewood, Ill.: Dorsey, 1961.

Weinberg, S. K. *Society and Personality Disorders*. New York: Prentice-Hall, 1952.

White, R. W. Competence and the psychosexual stages of development. In Jones, M. R. (ed.), *Nebraska Symposium on Motivation*. Lincoln: U. of Nebraska Press, 1960.

Whorf, B. *Language, Thought and Reality*. New York: Wiley, 1956.

Yarrow, L. J. Maternal deprivation: Toward an empirical and conceptual reevaluation. *Psychol. Bull., 58,* 459-490, 1961.

Yarrow, L. J., and Goodwin, M. S. Some conceptual issues in the study of mother-child interactions. *Amer. J. Orthopsychiat., 35,* 473-481, 1965.

# PART 3

American Psychiatric Association. *Diagnostic and Statistical Manual of Mental Disorders*. Washington, D.C.: Mental Hospitals Service, 1952, 1968.

## Chapters 6 and 7

Abraham, K. *Selected Papers*. London: Hogarth Press, 1927.

American Psychiatric Association. *Diagnostic and Statistical Manual of Mental Disorders*. Washington, D.C.: Mental Hospitals Service, 1952, 1968.

Brown, J. F. *Psychodynamics of Abnormal Behavior*. New York: McGraw-Hill, 1940.

Buss, A. H., and Lang, P. J. Psychological deficit in schizophrenia, I: Affect, reinforcement, and concept attainment. *J. Abnorm. Psychol., 70,* 2-24, 1965.

Freud, S. *Collected Papers*. Vol. IV. New York: Basic Books, 1959.

Fromm, E. *Man for Himself*. New York: Rinehart, 1947.

Garmezy, N. Process and reactive schizophrenia: Some concepts and issues. In Katz, M., et al. (eds.), *The Role and Methodology of Classification in Psychiatry and Psychopathology*. Washington, D.C.: Public Health Service, 1968.

Haley, J. An interactional description of schizophrenia. *Psychiatry, 22,* 321-332, 1959.

Horney, K. *Our Inner Conflicts*. New York: Norton, 1945.

Horney, K. *Neuroses and Human Growth*. New York: Norton, 1950.

Lang, P. J., and Buss, A. H. Psychological deficit in schizophrenia, II: Interference and activation. *J. Abnorm. Psychol., 70,* 77-106, 1965.

Leary, T. *Interpersonal Diagnosis of Personality*. New York: Ronald, 1957.

Leary, T., and Coffey, H. S. Interpersonal diagnosis: Some problems of methodology and validation. *J. Abnorm. Soc. Psychol., 50,* 110-124, 1955.

Lorr, M., Bishop, P. F., and McNair, D. M. Interpersonal types among psychiatric patients. *J. Abnorm. Psychol., 70,* 468-472, 1965.

McNair, D. M., and Lorr, M. Differential typing of psychiatric outpatients. *Psychol. Rec., 15,* 33-41, 1965.

Noyes, A., and Kolb, L. *Modern Clinical Psychiatry*. 7th ed. Philadelphia: Saunders, 1968.

Silverman, J. Scanning-control mechanism and "cognitive filtering" in paranoid and non-paranoid schizophrenia. *J. Consult. Psychol., 28,* 385-393, 1964a.

Silverman, J. The problem of attention in research and theory in schizophrenia. *Psychol. Rev., 71,* 352-379, 1964b.

Wolman, B. (ed.) *Handbook of Clinical Psychology*. New York: McGraw-Hill, 1965.

## Chapters 8 and 9

American Psychiatric Association. *Diagnostic and Statistical Manual of Mental Disorders*. Washington, D.C.: Mental Hospitals Service, 1952, 1968.

Bender, L. Autism in children with mental deficiency. *Amer. J. Ment. Defic. 63,* 81-86, 1959.

Bettelheim, B. *The Empty Fortress*. New York: Free Press, 1967.

Cameron, N. *Personality Development and Psychopathology*. New York: Houghton Mifflin, 1963.

Cameron, N., and Magaret, A. *Behavior Pathology*. New York: Houghton Mifflin, 1951.

Eisenberg, L., and Kanner, L. Early infantile autism, 1943-1955. *Amer. J. Orthopsychiat., 26,* 556-566, 1956.

Fish, B., and Schapiro, T., A descriptive typology of children's psychiatric disorders, II: A behavioral classification. In Jenkins, R. L., and Cole, J. O. (eds.), *Diagnostic Classification in Child Psychiatry*. Psychiat. Res. Report No. 18. Washington, D.C.: American Psychiatric Association, 1964.

Goldstein, K. Abnormal conditions in infancy. *J. Nerv. Ment. Dis. 128,* 538-557, 1959.

Grinker, R. R., Werble, B., and Drye, R. C. *The*

*Borderline Syndrome.* New York: Basic Books, 1968.

Group for the Advancement of Psychiatry. *Psychopathological Disorders in Childhood: Theoretical Considerations and a Proposed Classification.* New York: Group for the Advancement of Psychiatry, 1966.

Kanner, L. To what extent is early infantile autism determined by constitutional inadequacy? *Proc. Assoc. Res. Nerv. Mental Dis., 33,* 378-385, 1954.

Kernberg, O. Borderline personality organization. *J. Amer. Psychoanal. Assoc., 15,* 641-685, 1967.

Kraepelin, E. *Psychiatrie: ein Lehrbuch für Studierende und Ärtze.* (various editions) Leipzig: Barth, 1888-1927.

Kraepelin, E. *Lectures on Clinical Psychiatry.* New York: William Wood, 1904.

Kretschmer, E. *Physique and Character.* New York: Macmillan, 1936.

Mahler, M. S. On child psychosis and schizophrenia: Autistic and symbiotic infantile psychosis. In *Psychoanalytic Study of the Child.* Vol. 7. New York: Int'l Univ. Press, 1952.

Menninger, K., Mayman, M., and Pruyser, P. *The Vital Balance.* New York: Viking, 1963.

Phillips, L. Social competence, the process-reactive distinction, and the nature of mental disorder. In Hoch, P., and Zubin, J. (eds.), *Psychopathology of Schizophrenia.* New York: Grune and Stratton, 1966.

Phillips, L. *Human Adaptation and its Failures.* New York: Academic Press, 1968.

Rimland, B. *Infantile Autism.* New York: Appleton-Century-Crofts, 1964.

Schmideberg, M. The borderline patient. In Arieti, S. (ed.), *American Handbook of Psychiatry.* Vol. 1. New York: Basic Books, 1959.

Wishner, J. The concept of efficiency in psychological health and in psychopathology. *Psychol. Rev., 62,* 69-80, 1955.

Wolberg, A. The "borderline patient." *Amer. J. Psychother., 6,* 694-701, 1952.

Zigler, E., and Phillips, L. Social effectiveness and symptomatic behaviors. *J. Abnorm. Soc. Psychol., 61,* 231-238, 1960.


## Chapters 10 and 11

Alexander, F. *Psychoanalysis of the Total Personality.* New York: Nervous and Mental Disease Publications, 1930.

Alexander, F. *Psychosomatic Medicine.* New York: Norton, 1950.

Allen, F. The psychopathic delinquent child: Round table. *Amer. J. Orthopsychiat., 20,* 223-265, 1950.

American Psychiatric Association. *Diagnostic and Statistical Manual of Mental Disorders.* Washington, D.C.: Mental Hospitals Service, 1952, 1968.

Bandura, A., and Walters, R. H. *Adolescent Aggression.* New York: Ronald, 1959.

Bandura, A., and Walters, R. H. *Social Learning and Personality Development.* New York: Holt, Rinehart and Winston, 1963.

Brady, J. V. Ulcers in "executive" monkeys. *Sci. Amer., 199,* 95-100, 1958.

Cleckley, H. *The Mask of Sanity.* St. Louis: Mosby, 1950.

Dixon, J. J., et al. Patterns of anxiety: The phobias. *Brit. J. Med. Psychol., 30,* 34-40, 1957.

Dunbar, H. F. *Emotions and Bodily Changes.* New York: Columbia U. Press, 1935.

Eysenck, H. J. *The Dynamics of Anxiety and Hysteria.* New York: Praeger, 1957.

Ferenczi, S. *Further Contribution to the Theory and Technique of Psychoanalysis.* London: Hogarth, 1926.

Freeman, E. H., et al. Psychological variables in allergic disorders: A review. *Psychosom. Med., 26,* 543-576, 1964.

Friedman, A. S., Cowitz, B., Cohen, H. W., and Granick, S. Syndromes and themes of psychotic depression. *A.M.A. Arch. Gen. Psychiat., 9,* 504-512, 1963.

Garma, A. Gastric neurosis. *Int'l. J. Psychoanal., 31,* 53-61, 1950.

Garmezy, N. Process and reactive schizophrenia: Some conceptions and issues. In Katz, M., et al. (eds.), *The Role and Methodology of Classification in Psychiatry and Psychopathology.* Washington D.C.: Public Health Service, 1968.

Grace, W. J., and Graham, D. T. Relationship of specific attitudes and emotions to certain bodily diseases. *Psychosom. Med., 14,* 242-251, 1952.

Greenacre, P. Conscience in the psychopath. *Amer. J. Orthopsychiat., 15,* 495-509, 1945.

Gregory, I. *Fundamentals of Psychiatry.* Philadelphia: Saunders, 1968.

Guze, S. B., and Perley, M. J. Observations on the natural history of hysteria. *Am. J. Psychiat., 119,* 960-965, 1963.

Henderson, D. K. *Psychopathic States.* New York: Norton, 1939.

Hill, D. EEG in episodic psychotic and psychopathic behavior. *EEG Clin. Neurophysiol., 4,* 419-422, 1952.

Kaplan, H. I., and Kaplan, H. S. Current theoretical concepts in psychosomatic medicine. *Amer. J. Psychiat., 115,* 1091-1096, 1959.

Karpman, B. On the need for separating psychopathy into two distinct clinical types: Symptomatic and idiopathic. *J. Crim. Psychopath., 3,* 112-137, 1941.

Lacey, J. I., and Lacey, B. C. Verification and extension of the principle of autonomic response stereotype. *Amer. J. Psychol., 71,* 50-73, 1958.

Levy, D. M. Psychopathic behavior in infants and children: Round table. *Amer. J. Orthopsychiat., 21,* 223-272, 1951.

Liddell, H. S. Conditioned reflex method and experimental neurosis. In Hunt, J. McV. (ed.), *Personality and the Behavior Disorders.* New York: Ronald, 1944.

Lorr, M. (ed.) *Explorations in Typing Psychotics.* New York: Pergamon, 1966.

Lorr, M., Klett, C. J., and McNair, D. M. *Syndromes of Psychosis.* New York: Macmillan, 1963.

Mahl, G. F. Physiological changes during chronic fear. *Annals N.Y. Acad. Sci., 56,* 240-249, 1953.

Maier, N. R. F. *Frustration: A Study of Behavior Without a Goal.* New York: McGraw-Hill, 1949.

Malmo, R. B. Activation. In Bachrach, A. J. (ed.), *Experimental Foundations of Clinical Psychology.* New York: Basic Books, 1962.

Margolin, S. G. Genetic and dynamic psychophysiological determinants of pathophysiological process. In Deutsch, F. (ed.), *The Psychosomatic Con-*

cept in Psychoanalysis. New York: Int'l. Univ. Press, 1953.

Masserman, J. H. Behavior and Neurosis. Chicago: U. of Chicago Press, 1943.

McCord, W., and McCord, J. The Psychopath: An Essay on the Criminal Mind. Princeton: Van Nostrand, 1964.

McNair, D., Lorr, M., and Hemingway, P. Further evidence for syndrome-based psychotic types. A.M.A. Arch. Gen. Psychiat., 11, 368-378, 1964.

Miller, N. E. Experiments relating Freudian displacement to generalization of conditioning. Psychol. Bull., 36, 516-517, 1939.

Mirsky, I. A. Physiologic, psychologic, and social determinants in the etiology of duodenal ulcer. Amer. J. Digest. Dis., 3, 285-314, 1958.

Mowrer, O. H. Learning Theory and Personality Dynamics. New York: Ronald, 1950.

Murphy, L. B., et al. The Widening World of Childhood. New York: Basic Books, 1962.

Overall, J. E. A configural analysis of psychiatric diagnostic stereotypes. Beh. Sci., 8, 211-219, 1963.

Prichard, J. C. A Treatise on Insanity and other Disorders Affecting the Mind. London: Sherwood, Gilbert, Piper, 1835.

Ruesch, J., et al. Chronic disease and psychosomatic invalidism. Psychosom. Med. Monograph, Whole #9, 1946.

Rush, Benjamin. Medical Inquiries and Observations upon the Diseases of the Mind. Philadelphia: Grigg, 1812.

Sears, R. R. Survey of Objective Studies of Psychoanalytic Concepts. New York: Social Science Research Council, 1942.

Silverman, D. Clinical and electroencephalographic studies of criminal psychopaths. A.M.A. Arch. Neurol. Psychiat., 50, 18-33, 1943.

Solomon, R. L., and Wynne, L. C. Traumatic avoidance learning: The principles of anxiety conservation and partial irreversibility. Psychol. Rev., 61, 353-385, 1954.

Stephens, J. H., and Kamp, M. On some aspects of hysteria: A clinical study. J. Nerv. Ment. Dis., 134, 305-315, 1962.

Thomas, A., et al. Behavioral Individuality in Early Childhood. New York: New York Univ. Press, 1963.

Thomas, A., Chess, S., and Birch, H. G. Temperament and Behavior Disorders in Children. New York: New York Univ. Press, 1968.

Thorne, F. C. Etiological studies of the psychopathic personality: The ego-inflated, defectively conditioned type. J. Consult. Psychol., 11, 299-310, 1947.

Ullmann, L. P., and Krasner, L. (eds.) Case Studies on Behavior Modification. New York: Holt, Rinehart and Winston, 1965.

Wittenborn, J. R. The dimensions of psychosis. J. Nerv. Ment. Dis., 134, 117-128, 1967.

Wittenborn, J. R., and May, P. R. A. (eds.) Prediction of Response to Pharmacotherapy. Springfield, Ill.: Thomas, 1966.

## Chapter 12

American Psychiatric Association. Diagnostic and Statistical Manual of Mental Disorders. Washington, D.C.: Mental Hospitals Service, 1952, 1968.

Apfelberg, B., Sugar, C., and Pfeffer, A. Z. A psychiatric study of 250 sex offenders. Amer. J. Psychiat., 100, 762-800, 1944.

Barbara, D. (ed.) The Psychotherapy of Stuttering. Springfield, Ill.: Thomas, 1962.

Bender, L., and Paster, S. Homosexual trends in children. Amer. J. Orthopsychiat., 11, 730-744, 1941.

Bieber, I., et al. Homosexuality: A Psychoanalytic Study. New York: Basic Books, 1962.

Binet, A. Études de psychologie expérimentale: le fétichisme dans l'amour. Paris: Doin, 1888.

Bloodstein, O. A Handbook on Stuttering for Professional Workers. Chicago: National Society for Crippled Children and Adults, 1959.

Coleman, J. C. Abnormal Psychology and Modern Life. 3rd edition. Chicago: Scott, Foresman, 1964.

Coppen, A. J. Body-build of male homosexuals. Brit. Med. J., 2, 1443-1445, 1959.

Erikson, E. H. Childhood and Society. New York: Norton, 1950.

Eysenck, H. J. Learning theory and behavior therapy. J. Ment. Sci. 105, 61-75, 1959.

Fenichel, O. The Psychoanalytic Theory of Neuroses. New York: Norton, 1945.

Greco, M. C., and Wright, J. C. The correctional institution in the etiology of chronic homosexuality. Amer. J. Orthopsychiat., 14, 295-308, 1944.

Group for the Advancement of Psychiatry. Psychopathological Disorders in Childhood: Theoretical Considerations and a Proposed Classification. New York: Group for the Advancement of Psychiatry, 1966.

Henry, G. W. All the Sexes: A Study of Masculinity and Femininity. New York: Holt, Rinehart and Winston, 1955.

Hooker, E. The adjustment of the male overt homosexual. J. Proj. Tech. 21, 18-31, 1957.

Hooker, E. The homosexual community. In Proceedings of the XIV International Congress of Applied Psychology. Vol. II: Personality Research. Copenhagen: Munksgaard, 1962.

Jellinek, E. M. Phases of alcohol addiction. Quart. J. Stud. Alcohol, 13, 673-678, 1952.

Jellinek, E. M. The Disease Concept of Alcoholism. New Haven: Hillside Press, 1960.

Johnson, W. Stuttering and What You Can Do About It. Minneapolis: U. of Minn. Press, 1961.

Johnson, W., et al. The Onset of Stuttering. Minneapolis: U. of Minnesota Press, 1959.

Kallmann, F. J. Heredity in Health and Mental Disorders. New York: Norton, 1953.

Kinsey, A. C., Pomeroy, W. B., and Martin, C. E. Sexual Behavior in the Human Male. Philadelphia: Saunders, 1948.

Kinsey, A. C., Pomeroy, W. B., and Martin, C. E. Sexual Behavior in the Human Female. Philadelphia: Saunders, 1953.

Kopp, S. B. The character structure of sex offenders. Amer. J. Psychother., 16, 64-70, 1962.

Levy, R. I. The psychodynamic functions of alcohol. Quart. J. Stud. Alc., 19, 649-659, 1958.

Menninger, L. Man Against Himself. New York: Basic Books, 1938.

Menninger, W. C. Psychiatry in a Troubled World. New York: Macmillan, 1948.

Penfield, W., and Roberts, L. Speech and Brain-mechanisms. Princeton: Princeton U. Press, 1959.

Pritchard, M. Homosexuality and genetic sex. J. Ment. Sci., 108, 616-623, 1962.

Revitch, E., and Weiss, R. G. The pedophiliac offender. Dis. Nerv. Syst., 23, 73-78, 1962.

Roe, A., Burks, B., and Mittleman, B. Adult adjustment of foster children of alcoholic and psychotic parentage and the influence of the foster home. *Memoirs of the Section on Alcohol.* Yale Univ., 1945.

Shaw, C. R. *The Jack-Roller.* Chicago: U. of Chicago Press, 1930.

Sheehan, J. G. Theory and treatment of stuttering as an approach-avoidance conflict. *J. Psychol., 36,* 27-49, 1953.

White, R. W. *The Abnormal Personality.* 3rd ed. New York: Ronald, 1964.

Zwerling, I., and Rosenbaum, M. Alcoholic addiction and personality. In Arieti, S. (ed.), *American Handbook of Psychiatry.* New York: Basic Books, 1959.

## Chapter 13

American Psychiatric Association. *Diagnostic and Statistical Manual of Mental Disorders.* Washington, D.C.: Mental Hospitals Service, 1952, 1968.

Bingley, T. Mental symptoms in temporal lobe gliomas. *Acta Psychiat. Neurol. Scand. Suppl., 33,* 1-151, 1958.

Birch, H. G. (ed.) *Brain Damage in Children: The Biological and Social Aspects.* Baltimore: Williams and Wilkins, 1964.

Brandon, M. W. G., Kirman, B. H., and Williams, C. E. Microcephaly. *J. Ment. Sci., 105,* 721-747, 1959.

Cameron, N. *Personality Development and Psychopathology.* New York: Houghton Mifflin, 1963.

Cobb, S. *Borderlands of Psychiatry.* Cambridge: Harvard U. Press, 1943.

Cruickshank, W. M. (ed.) *The Teacher of Brain-Injured Children: A Discussion of the Bases for Competency.* Syracuse: Syracuse Univ. Press, 1966.

Doll, E. A. The essentials of an inclusive concept of mental deficiency. *Amer. J. Ment. Def., 46,* 214-221, 1941.

Frostig, M., and Horne, D. *The Frostig Program for the Development of Visual Perception: Teacher's Guide.* Chicago: Follett, 1964.

Gibbs, F. A. Abnormal electrical activity in the temporal regions and its relationship to abnormalities in behavior. *Res. Publ. Assn. Res. Nerv. Ment. Dis., 36,* 278-294, 1958.

Goldensohn, E. Seizures and convulsive disorders. In Wolman, B. (ed.), *Handbook of Clinical Psychology.* New York: McGraw-Hill, 1965.

Goldstein, K. *The Organism.* New York: American, 1939.

Goldstein, K. *Aftereffects of Brain Injuries in War.* New York: Grune and Stratton, 1942.

Goldstein, K. The organismic approach. In Arieti, S. (ed.), *American Handbook of Psychiatry.* New York: Basic Books, 1959.

Gregory, I. *Fundamentals of Psychiatry.* Philadelphia: Saunders, 1968.

Heber, R. A manual on terminology and classification in mental retardation. *Amer. J. Ment. Def., 64,* Monog. Suppl. 2, 1959.

Itard, J. M. G. *The Wild Boy of Aveyron.* Translation. New York: Appleton-Century, 1932.

Jervis, G. A. The mental deficiencies. In Arieti, S. (ed.), *American Handbook of Psychiatry.* New York: Basic Books, 1959.

Kephart, N. C., *The Slow Learner in the Classroom.* Columbus: Merrill, 1960.

Kolb, L. *Noyes' Modern Clinical Psychiatry.* 7th ed. Philadelphia: Saunders, 1968.

Lewis, N. D. C. *A Short History of Psychiatric Treatment.* New York: Norton, 1941.

Lezak, M. D., and Dixon, H. H. The brain-injured child in a clinic population: A statistical description. *Except. Children, 30,* 237-240, 1964.

Lyons, J. F., and Heaton-Ward, W. A. *Notes on Mental Deficiency.* Bristol: Wright, 1953.

Paine, R. S. Minimal chronic brain syndromes in children. *Devel. Med. Child Neurolog., 4,* 21-27, 1962.

Penfield, W., and Jasper, H. *Epilepsy and the Functional Anatomy of the Human Brain.* Boston: Little, Brown, 1954.

Penrose, L. S. *The Biology of Mental Defect.* 2nd ed. New York: Grune and Stratton, 1964.

President's Panel on Mental Retardation. *A Proposed Program for National Action to Combat Mental Retardation.* Washington, D.C.: U.S. Government Printing Office, 1963.

Rappaport, S. R. (ed.) *Childhood Aphasia and Brain Damage.* Narberth, Pa.: Livingston, 1965.

Roberts, J. A. F. The genetics of mental deficiency. *Eug. Rev. 44,* 71-83, 1952.

Shlien, J. (ed.) *Research in Psychotherapy.* Vol. III. Washington, D.C.: American Psychological Association, 1968.

Small, J. G., Milstein, V., and Stephens, J. R. Are psychomotor epileptics different? A controlled study. *A.M.A. Arch. Neurol., 7,* 187-194, 1962.

Strauss, A. A., and Kephart, N. *Psychopathology and Education of the Brain Injured Child.* Vol. II. New York: Grune and Stratton, 1955.

Strauss, A. A., and Lehtinen, L. *Psychopathology and Education of the Brain Injured Child.* Vol. I. New York: Grune and Stratton, 1947.

Symonds, C. Classification of epilepsies. *Brit. Med. J., 1,* 1235-1238, 1955.

Tizard, B. The personality of epileptics: A discussion of the evidence. *Psychol. Bull., 59,* 196-210, 1962.

Tredgold, A. F. *A Textbook of Mental Deficiency.* 6th ed. Baltimore: Williams and Wilkins, 1937.

Williams, R. J. *Biochemical Individuality.* New York: Wiley, 1956.

# PART 4

Frank, J. D. *Persuasion and Healing: A Comparative Study of Psychotherapy.* Baltimore: Johns Hopkins Press, 1961.

Keisler, D. J. Some myths of psychotherapy research and the search for a paradigm. *Psychol. Bull., 65,* 110-136, 1966.

London, P. *The Modes and Morals of Psychotherapy.* New York: Holt, Rinehart and Winston, 1964.

McNair, D. M., and Lorr, M. An analysis of professed psychotherapeutic techniques. *J. Consult. Psychol., 28,* 265-271, 1964.

Patterson, C. H. *Counseling and Psychotherapy: Theory and Practice.* New York: Harper and Row, 1959.

Sundland, D. M., and Barker, E. N. The orientations of psychotherapists. *J. Consult. Psychol., 26,* 201-212, 1962.

Wallach, M. S., and Strupp, H. H. Dimensions of psychotherapists' activities. *J. Consult. Psychol., 28,* 120-125, 1964.

## Chapter 14

Alexander, L. *Treatment of Mental Disorder.* Philadelphia: Saunders, 1953.

Azima, H. Prolonged sleep treatment in mental disorders. *J. Ment. Sci., 101,* 593-599, 1955.

Bowman, K. M., and Simon, A. Studies in electronarcosis therapy. *Amer. J. Psychiat., 105,* 15-21, 1948.

Brannon, E. P., and Graham, W. L. Intensive insulin shock therapy: A five year survey. *Amer. J. Psychiat., 11,* 659-663, 1955.

Brickner, R. M. *The Intellectual Functions of the Frontal Lobes.* New York: Macmillan, 1936.

Cerletti, U., and Bini, L. Electric shock treatment. *Boll. Accad. Med. Roma, 64,* 36, 1938.

Cholden, L. (ed.) *Lysergic Acid Diethylamide and Mescaline in Experimental Psychiatry.* New York: Grune and Stratton, 1956.

Cole, J. O., et al. Phenothiazine treatment in acute schizophrenia: Effectiveness. *A.M.A. Arch. Gen. Psychiat., 10,* 246-261, 1964.

Cole, J. O., and Davis, J. M. Antidepressant drugs. In Freedman, A. M., and Kaplan, H. I. (eds.), *Comprehensive Textbook of Psychiatry.* Baltimore: Williams and Wilkins, 1967.

Davis, J. M. Efficacy of tranquilizing and antidepressant drugs. *A.M.A. Arch. Gen. Psychiat., 13,* 552-572, 1965.

Flaherty, J. A. The psychiatric use of isonicotinic acid hydrazine: A case report. *Del. Med. J., 24,* 198-201, 1952.

Fleming, T. C. An inquiry into the mechanism of action of electric shock treatments. *J. Nerv. Ment. Dis., 124,* 440-450, 1956.

Freeman, W., and Watts, J. *Psychosurgery.* Springfield, Ill.: Thomas, 1942.

Freeman, W., and Watts, J. *Psychosurgery in the Treatment of Mental Disorders and Pain.* Springfield, Ill.: Thomas, 1950.

Freyhan, F. A. Clinical and investigative aspects. In Kline, N. S. (ed.), *Psychopharmacology Frontiers.* Boston: Little, Brown, 1959.

Frostig, J. P., et al. Electronarcosis in animals and in man. *A.M.A. Arch. Neurol. Psychiat., 51,* 232-237, 1944.

Fulton, J. F. *Physiology of the nervous system.* New York: Oxford, 1943.

Fulton, J. F., and Jacobsen, C. F. The functions of the frontal lobes: A comparative study in monkeys, chimpanzee and man. *Abstr. 2nd Int'l. Cong.,* London, 1935.

Gellhorn, E. *Autonomic Imbalance and the Hypothalamus: Implications for Physiology, Medicine, Psychology, and Neuropsychiatry.* Minneapolis: U. of Minnesota Press, 1957.

Glueck, B. Personal communication. 1968.

Gordon, H. L. Fifty shock therapy theories. *The Military Surgeon, 3,* 397-401, 1948.

Greenblatt, M., Arnot, A., and Solomon, H. C. *Studies in Lobotomy.* New York: Grune and Stratton, 1950.

Greenblatt, M., and Solomon, H. C. *Frontal Lobes and Schizophrenia.* New York: Springer, 1953.

Hargrove, E. A., Bennett, A. E., and Steele, M. An investigational study using carbon dioxide as an adjunct to psychotherapy in neuroses. American Psychiatric Association Meetings, May 7, 1953.

Heath, R. G. *Studies of Schizophrenia.* Cambridge: Harvard U. Press, 1954.

Heath, R. G. Brain centers and control of behavior—man. In Nodine, J., and Moyer, J. H. (eds.), *Psychosomatic Medicine.* Philadelphia: Lea and Febiger, 1962.

Hirschfeld, G. Observations with non-convulsive electric-stimulation. *Psychiat. Quart. Suppl.,* part 2, 1950.

Hunt, H. F., and Brady, J. W. Some effects of electro-convulsive shock on a conditioned response ("anxiety"). *J. Comp. Physiol. Psychol., 44,* 88-98, 1951.

Huston, P. E., and Locher, L. M. Manic-depressive psychosis: Course when treated and untreated with electric shock. *A.M.A. Arch. Neurol. Psychiat., 60,* 37-48, 1948.

Janis, I. L. Psychological effects of electric convulsive treatments. *J. Nerv. Ment. Dis., 3,* 359-397; 469-489, 1950.

Jones, C. H., et al. Peripheral electrical stimulation: A new form of psychiatric treatment. *Dis. Nerv. Syst., 16,* 323-332, 1955.

Kalinowsky, L. B. *Shock Treatments, Psychosurgery and other Somatic Treatments.* New York: Grune and Stratton, 1946.

Kalinowsky, L. B. The convulsive therapies. In Freedman, A. M., and Kaplan, H. I. (eds.), *Comprehensive Textbook of Psychiatry.* Baltimore: Williams and Wilkins, 1967.

Kalinowsky, L. B., and Hoch, P. *Somatic Treatments in Psychiatry.* New York: Grune and Stratton, 1961.

Katz, M. M., and Cole, J. O. Research conference in drugs and community care: A review and analysis. *Psychopharm. Serv. Cent. Bull.,* 1-13, December 1961.

Lehmann, H. E. Concepts, rationale, and research. In Kline, N. S. (ed.), *Psychopharmacology Frontiers.* Boston: Little, Brown, 1959.

Lewis, N. D. C., Landis, C., and King, H. E. *Studies in Topectomy.* New York: Grune and Stratton, 1956.

Maher, B. A. *Principles of Psychopathology.* New York: McGraw-Hill, 1966.

Moniz, E. Prefrontal leucotomy in the treatment of mental disorder. *Amer. J. Psychiat., 93,* 1379-1385, 1936.

Moniz, E. How I succeeded in performing the prefrontal leukotomy. *J. Clin. Exp. Psychopath., 15,* 373-379, 1954.

Ottoson, J. O. Experimental studies of the mode of action of electroconvulsive therapy. *Acta Psychiat. Neurolog. Scand., 35,* Supplement 145, 1960.

Paul, N. L., Fitzgerald E., and Greenblatt, M. The long-term comparative results of three different lobotomy procedures. *Amer. J. Psychiat., 113,* 808-814, 1957.

Rinkel, M., and Himwich, H. (eds.) *Insulin Treatment in Psychiatry.* New York: Philosophical Library, 1959.

Robbin, A. A. A controlled study of the effects of leucotomy. *J. Neurol. Neurosurg. Psychiat., 21,* 262-269, 1958.

Robbin, A. A. The value of leucotomy in relation to diagnosis. *J. Neurol. Neurosurg. Psychiat., 22,* 132-136, 1959.

Rubin, L. Patterns of adrenergic-cholinergic imbalance in the functional psychoses. *Psychol. Rev., 69,* 501-519, 1962.

Sarwer-Foner, G. J. Theoretical aspects of the modes of action. In Kline, N. S. (ed.), *Psychopharmacology Frontiers.* Boston: Little, Brown, 1959.

Schmneige, G. R. The current status of LSD as a therapeutic tool: A summary of the clinical literature. *J. Med. Soc. N.J., 60,* 203-207, 1963.

Staudt, V., and Zubin, J. A biometric evaluation of the somatotherapies in schizophrenia. *Psychol. Bull., 56,* 171-196, 1957.

Thorpe, J. G. The current status of prognostic test indicators for electroconvulsive therapy. *Psychosom. Med., 24,* 554-567, 1962.

Weigert, E. V. Psychoanalytic notes on sleep and convulsion treatment in functional psychoses. *Psychiat., 3,* 189-194, 1940.

West, F. H., et al. Insulin coma therapy in schizophrenia: A fourteen-year follow-up study. *Amer. J. Psychiat., 11,* 583-589, 1955.

Willett, R. The effects of psychosurgical procedures on behavior. In Eysenck, H. J. (ed.), *Handbook of Abnormal Psychology.* New York: Basic Books, 1961.

Williams, G. J. The effect of electroconvulsive shock on an instrumental conditioned emotional response ("conflict"). *J. Comp. Physiol. Psychol., 54,* 633-637, 1961.

Wittenborn, J. R., and May, P. R. A. (eds.) *Prediction of Response to Pharmacotherapy,* Springfield, Ill.: Thomas, 1966.

Wolberg, L. R.: *The Technique of Psychotherapy.* 2nd edition. New York: Grune and Stratton, 1967.

Wortis, S. B., et al. Brain metabolism: The effects of electric shock and some newer drugs. *Amer. J. Psychiat., 98,* 354-361, 1941.

## Chapter 15

Ackerman, N. W. *The Psychodynamics of Family Life.* New York: Basic Books, 1958.

Agras, W. S. An investigation of the decrement of anxiety responses during systematic desensitization therapy. *Beh. Res. Ther., 2,* 267-270, 1965.

Allen, F. *Psychotherapy with Children.* New York: Norton, 1942.

Axline, V. M. *Play Therapy.* Boston: Houghton Mifflin, 1947.

Ayllon, T., and Michael, J. L. The psychiatric nurse as a behavioral engineer. *J. Exp. Anal. Beh., 2,* 323-334, 1959.

Ayllon, T., and Azrin, N. H. The measurement and

reinforcement of behavior in psychotics. *J. Exp. Anal. Beh., 8,* 357-383, 1965.

Bachrach, A. J., Erwin, W. J., and Mohr, J. P. The control of eating behavior in an anorexic by operant conditioning techniques. In Ullmann, L., and Krasner, L. (eds.), *Case Studies of Behavior Modification.* New York: Holt, Rinehart and Winston, 1965.

Bagby, E. The etiology of phobias. *J. Abnorm. Soc. Psychol., 17,* 16-18, 1922.

Bandura, A. Psychotherapy as a learning process. *Psychol. Bull., 58,* 143-159, 1961.

Bandura, A. Social learning through imitation. In Jones, M. R. (ed.), *Nebraska Symposium on Motivation.* Lincoln: Univ. of Nebraska Press, 1962.

Bandura, A. Behavioral modification through modeling procedures. In Krasner, L., and Ullmann, L. (eds.), *Research in Behavior Modification.* New York: Holt, Rinehart and Winston, 1965.

Bandura, A., Grusec, J. E. and Menlove, F. L. Vicarious extinction of avoidance behavior. *J. Pers. Soc. Psychol., 5,* 16-23, 1967.

Bender, L. Art and therapy in the mental disturbances of children. *J. Nerv. Ment. Dis., 86,* 249-263, 1937.

Bergin, A. E. The effects of psychotherapy: Negative results revisited. *J. Counsel. Psychol., 10,* 244-250, 1963.

Bergin, A. E. Some implications of psychotherapy research for therapeutic practice. *J. Abnorm. Psychol., 71,* 235-246, 1966.

Bergin, A. E. An empirical analysis of therapeutic issues. In Arbuckle, D. S. (ed.), *Counseling and Psychotherapy.* New York: McGraw-Hill, 1967.

Berne, E. *Transactional Analysis in Psychotherapy.* New York: Grove, 1961.

Berne, E. *Games People Play.* New York: Grove, 1964.

Bierer, J. *Therapeutic Social Clubs.* London: Lewis, 1948.

Binswanger, L. *Grundformen und Erkenntnis menschlichen Daseins.* Zurich: Niehaus, 1942.

Binswanger, L. *Ausgewählte Vorträge und Aufsätze.* Berne: Francke, 1947.

Binswanger, L. Existential analysis and psychotherapy. In Fromm-Reichmann, F., and Moreno, J. L. (eds.), *Progress in Psychotherapy.* Vol. 1. New York: Grune and Stratton, 1956.

Boss, M. *Psychoanalyse und Daseinsanalytik.* Berne: Hans Huber, 1957.

Boss, M. *Psychoanalysis and Daseinsanalysis.* New York: Basic Books, 1963.

Boszormenyi-Nagy, I., and Framo, J. L. *Intensive Family Therapy.* New York: Harper and Row, 1965.

Breger, L., and McGaugh, J. L. Critique and reformulation of "learning-theory" approaches to psychotherapy and neurosis. *Psychol. Bull., 63,* 338-358, 1965.

Burnham, W. H. *The Normal Mind.* New York: Appleton. 1924.

Cahoon, D. D. Symptom substitution and the behavior therapies: A reappraisal. *Psychol. Bull., 69,* 149-156, 1968.

Cartwright, R. D., and Vogel, J. L. A comparison of changes in psychoneurotic patients during matched periods of therapy and nontherapy. *J. Consult. Psychol., 24,* 121-127, 1960.

Chittendon, G. E. An experimental study in measuring and modifying assertive behavior in young children. *Monogr. Soc. Res. Child Develop., 31*, 1942.

Colby, K. M. Psychotherapeutic processes. In Farnsworth, P., et al. (eds.), *Annual Review of Psychology*. Vol. 15. Palo Alto, Calif.: Annual Reviews, 1964.

Cooper, J. E. A study of behavior therapy in thirty psychiatric patients. *Lancet, 1,* 411-415, 1963.

Corsini, R. J. *Role-playing in Psychotherapy: A Manual.* Chicago: Aldine, 1966.

Cross, A. J. The outcome of psychotherapy: A selected analysis of research findings. *J. Consult. Psychol., 28,* 413-417, 1964.

Davison, G. C. The influence of systematic desensitization, relaxation, and graded exposure to imaginal stimuli in the modification of phobic behavior. Unpublished doctoral dissertation, Stanford University, 1965.

Davison, G. C. Systematic desensitization as a counterconditioning process. *J. Abnorm. Psychol., 73,* 91-99, 1968.

Dejerine, J., and Gaukler, E. *Psychoneurosis and Psychotherapy.* Philadelphia: Lippincott, 1913.

Denber, H. C. B. (ed.) *Research Conference on the Therapeutic Community.* Springfield, Ill.: Thomas, 1960.

Denker, P. G. Results of treatment of psychoneurosis by the general practitioner: A follow-up study of 500 cases. *N.Y.S.J. Med., 46,* 2164-2166, 1946.

Deutsch, A. *The Shame of the States.* New York: Harcourt, Brace and Co., 1948.

Dittman, A. T. Psychotherapeutic Processes. In Farnsworth, P. R., et al. (eds.), *Annual Review of Psychology*. Vol. 16. Palo Alto: Annual Reviews, 1966.

Dollard, J., and Miller, N. E. *Personality and Psychotherapy.* New York: McGraw-Hill, 1950.

DuBois, P. *The Psychic Treatment of Mental Disorders.* New York: Funk and Wagnall, 1909.

Dunlap, K. *Habits: Their Making and Unmaking.* New York: Liveright, 1932.

Ellis, A. Outcome of employing three techniques of psychotherapy. *J. Clin. Psychol., 13,* 344-350, 1957.

Ellis, A. Rational psychotherapy. *J. Gen. Psychol., 59,* 35-49, 1958.

Ellis, A. *Reason and Emotion in Psychotherapy.* New York: Lyle Stuart, 1962.

Ellis, A. Goals of psychotherapy. In Mahrer, A. R. (ed.), *The Goals of Psychotherapy.* New York: Appleton-Century-Crofts, 1967.

Eysenck, H. J. The effects of psychotherapy: An evaluation. *J. Consult. Psychol., 16,* 319-324, 1952.

Eysenck, H. J. Learning theory and behavior therapy. *J. Ment. Sci., 105,* 61-75, 1959.

Eysenck, H. J. *Behavior Therapy and the Neuroses.* New York: Pergamon, 1960.

Eysenck, H. J. The effects of psychotherapy. In Eysenck, H. J. (ed.), *Handbook of Abnormal Psychology.* New York: Basic Books, 1961.

Eysenck, H. J. The outcome problem in psychotherapy: A reply. *Psychotherapy, 1,* 97-100, 1964.

Eysenck, H. J. The effects of psychotherapy. *Int'l. J. Psychiat., 1,* 99-142, 1965.

Eysenck, H. J., and Rachman, S. *The Causes and Cures of Neurosis.* London: Routledge and Kegan Paul, 1965.

Fairweather, G. W., et al. Relative effectiveness of psychotherapeutic programs: A multicriteria comparison of four programs for three different patient groups. *Psychol. Monogr,* Whole #492, 1960.

Ferster, C. B. Reinforcement and punishment in the control of human behavior by social agencies. *Psychiat. Res. Repts., 10,* 101-118, 1958.

Ferster, C. B. Positive reinforcement and behavior deficits in autistic children. In Franks, C. M. (ed.), *Conditioning Techniques in Clinical Practice and Research.* New York: Springer, 1964.

Fiedler, F. E. A comparison of therapeutic relationships in psychoanalytic, nondirective, and Adlerian Therapy. *J. Consult. Psychol., 14,* 436-445, 1950.

Fiedler, F. E. Factor analyses of psychoanalytic, nondirective, and Adlerian Therapeutic relationships. *J. Consult. Psychol., 15,* 32-38, 1951.

Ford, D. H., and Urban, H. B. *Systems of Psychotherapy.* New York: Wiley, 1963.

Frankl, V. E. *The Doctor and the Soul: An Introduction to Logotherapy.* New York: Knopf. 1955.

Frankl, V. E. Logotherapy and existential analysis: A review. *Amer. J. Psychother., 20,* 252-260, 1966.

Franks, C. M. (ed.) *Conditioning Techniques in Clinical Practice and Research.* New York: Springer, 1964.

Freud, A. *Introduction to the Technique of Child Analysis.* Washington, D. C.: Nerv. Ment. Dis. Publ., 1928.

Gardner, G. G., The psychotherapeutic relationship. *Psychol. Bull., 61,* 426-437, 1964.

Gelfand, D. M., and Hartmann, D. P. Behavior therapy with children: A review and evaluation of research methodology. *Psychol. Bull., 69,* 204-215, 1968.

Glasser, W. *Mental Health or Mental Illness.* New York: Harper and Row, 1961.

Glasser, W. *Reality Therapy.* New York: Harper and Row, 1965.

Goldstein, A. P., and Dean, S. J. (eds.) *The Investigation of Psychotherapy.* New York: Wiley, 1966.

Gottschalk, L. A., and Auerbach, A. H. (eds.) *Methods of Research in Psychotherapy.* New York: Appleton-Century-Crofts, 1966.

Greenblatt, M., Levinson, D. J., and Williams, R. H. (eds.) *The Patient and the Mental Hospital.* Glencoe, Ill.: Free Press, 1957.

Grinker, R. R. A demonstration of the transactional model. In Stein, M. I. (ed.), *Contemporary Psychotherapies.* Glencoe, Ill.: Free Press, 1961.

Grossberg, J. M. Behavior Therapy: A review. *Psychol. Bull., 62,* 73-88, 1964.

Haley, J. *Strategies of Psychotherapy.* New York: Grune and Stratton, 1963.

Harris, A. Day hospitals and night hospitals in psychiatry. *Lancet, 729,* 1951.

Hinckley, R. G., and Hermann, L. *Group Treatment in Psychotherapy.* Minneapolis: Univ. of Minnesota Press, 1951.

Hoch, P. H., and Zubin, J. (eds.) *The Evaluation of Psychiatric Treatment.* New York: Grune and Stratton, 1964.

Hogan, R. A., and Kirchner, J. H. Preliminary report of the extinction of learned fears via short-term implosive therapy. *J. Abnorm. Psychol., 72,* 106-109, 1967.

Horney, K. *The Neurotic Personality of Our Time.* New York: Norton, 1937.

Horney, K. *Neurosis and Human Growth.* New York: Norton, 1950.

Hunt, J. McV. Toward an integrated program of research on psychotherapy. *J. Consult. Psychol., 16,* 237-246, 1952.

Hussain, A. Behavior therapy in 105 cases. In Wolpe, J., et al. (ed.), *Conditioning Therapies.* New York: Holt, Rinehart and Winston, 1964.

Jackson, D. D., and Weakland, J. H. Conjoint family therapy: Some considerations on theory, technique and results. *Psychiat., 24,* 30-45, 1961.

Jacobson, E. *Progressive Relaxation.* Chicago: U. of Chicago Press, 1938.

Jewish Board of Guardians. *Conditioned Environment in Case Work Treatment.* New York, 1944.

Jones, M. *The Therapeutic Community: A New Treatment Method in Psychiatry.* New York: Basic Books, 1953.

Jones, M. C. The elimination of children's fears. *J. Exper. Psychol., 7,* 383-390, 1924.

Jung, C. G. *Psychology of the Unconscious.* New York: Moffat, Yard, 1916.

Jung, C. G. *Psychological Types or the Psychology of Individuation,* New York: Harcourt, Brace, 1923.

Kahn, M. A polygraph study of the catharsis of aggression. Unpublished doctoral dissertation, Harvard Univ., 1960.

Kanfer, F. H., and Phillips, J. S. Behavior therapy. *A.M.A. Arch. Gen. Psychiat., 15,* 114-127, 1966.

Kanfer, F. H., and Saslow, G. Behavioral analysis: An alternative to diagnostic classification. *A.M.A. Arch. Gen. Psychiat., 12,* 529-538, 1965.

Kasius, C. (ed.) *A Comparison of Diagnostic and Functional Casework Concepts.* New York: Family Service Association of America, 1950.

Keisler, D. J. Some myths of psychotherapy research and the search for a paradigm. *Psychol. Bull., 65,* 110-136, 1966.

Kelly, G. A. *The Psychology of Personal Constructs.* New York: Norton, 1955.

King, G. F., Armitage, S. G., and Tilton, J. R. A therapeutic approach to schizophrenics of extreme pathology. *J. Abnorm. Soc. Psychol., 61,* 276-286, 1960.

Lang, P. J., and Lazovik, A. D. Experimental desensitization of a phobia. *J. Abnorm. Soc. Psychol., 67,* 519-525, 1963.

Lang, P. J., Lazovik, A. D., and Reynolds, D. J. Desensitization, suggestibility, and pseudotherapy. *J. Abnorm. Psychol., 70,* 395-402, 1965.

Lazarus, A. A. Group therapy of phobic disorders by systematic desensitization. *J. Abnorm. Soc. Psychol., 63,* 504-510, 1961.

Lazarus, A. A. The results of behavior therapy in 126 cases of severe neurosis. *Beh. Res. Ther., 1,* 69-79, 1963.

Lemere, F., and Voegtlin, W. L. An evaluation of the aversion treatment of alcoholism. *Quart. J. Stud. Alc., 11,* 199-204, 1950.

Lerner, R. C. The therapeutic social club: Social rehabilitation for mental patients. *Int'l. J. Soc. Psychiat., 6,* Nos. 1 and 2, 1960.

Levis, D. J., and Carrera, R. Effects of ten hours of implosive therapy in the treatment of outpatients. *J. Abnorm. Psychol., 72,* 504-508, 1967.

Levitt, E. E. The results of psychotherapy with children: An evaluation. *J. Consult. Psychol., 21,* 189-196, 1957.

London, P. *The Modes and Morals of Psychotherapy.* New York: Holt, Rinehart and Winston, 1964.

Lovaas, O. I. Some studies on the treatment of childhood schizophrenia. In Shlien, J. (ed.), *Research in Psychotherapy.* Vol. III. Washington, D. C.: American Psychological Association, 1968.

Lovaas, O. I., et al. Acquisition of imitative speech by schizophrenic children. *Sci., 151,* 705-707, 1966.

Marks, I. and Gelder, M. A controlled retrospective study of behavior therapy in phobic patients. *Brit. J. Psychiat., 111,* 561-573, 1966.

Masserman, J. H. *Behavior and Neurosis.* Chicago: Univ. of Chicago Press, 1943.

Max, L. W. Breaking up a homosexual fixation by the conditioned reaction technique: A case study. *Psychol. Bull., 32,* 734, 1935.

May, R., et al. (eds.) *Existence.* New York: Basic Books, 1958.

May, R., and Van Kaam, A. Existential theory and therapy. In Masserman, J. H. (ed.), *Current Psychiatric Therapies.* Vol. 3. New York: Grune and Stratton, 1963.

Mead, G. H. *Mind, Self, and Society.* Chicago: U. of Chicago Press, 1934.

Miller, G. A., Galanter, E., and Pribam, K. H. *Plans and the Structure of Behavior.* New York: Holt, Rinehart and Winston, 1960.

Mischel, W. *Personality and Assessment.* New York: Wiley, 1968.

Moreno, J. L. *Who Shall Survive?* Washington, D.C.: Nerv. Ment. Dis. Publ., 1934.

Moreno, J. L. *Psychodrama.* Vol. 1. Beacon, N.Y.: Beacon House, 1946.

Mowrer, O. H. *The Crisis in Psychiatry and Religion.* Princeton: Van Nostrand, 1961.

Mowrer, O. H. Integrity therapy: A self-help approach. *Psychother., 3,* 14-19, 1965.

Mowrer, O. H. Learning theory and behavior therapy. In Wolman, B. (ed.), *Handbook of Clinical Psychology.* New York: McGraw-Hill, 1965.

Mowrer, O. H. The behavior therapies, with special reference to modeling and imitation. *Amer. J. Psychother., 20,* 439-461, 1966.

Mowrer, O. H., and Mowrer, W. M. Enuresis: A method for its study and treatment. *Amer. J. Orthopsychiat., 8,* 436-459, 1938.

Naumberg, M. *Dynamically Oriented Art Therapy: Its Principles and Practice.* New York: Grune and Stratton, 1966.

Odenheimer, J. F. Day hospital as an alternative to the psychiatric ward. *A.M.A. Arch. Gen. Psychiat., 13,* 46-53, 1965.

Olshansky, S. The transitional sheltered workshop: A survey. *J. Soc. Issues, 16,* 33-39, 1960.

Patrick, H. T., and Bassoe, P. *Nervous and Mental Diseases.* Chicago: Year Book Publishers, 1910.

Patterson, C. H. *Theories of Counseling and Psychotherapy.* New York: Harper and Row, 1966.

Paul, G. L. *Effects of Insight, Desensitization, and Attention Placebo Treatment of Anxiety.* Stanford: Stanford Univ. Press, 1966.

Paul, G. L. Insight versus desensitization in psychotherapy two years after termination. *J. Consult. Psychol., 31,* 333-348, 1967.

Paul, G. L. Two-year follow-up of systematic desensitization in therapy groups. *J. Abn. Psychol., 73,* 119-130, 1968.

Pavlov, I. P. *Conditioned reflexes: An Investigation of the Physiological Activity of the Cerebral Cortex.* London: Oxford Univ. Press, 1927.

Phillips, E. L. *Psychotherapy: A Modern Theory and Practice.* Englewood Cliffs, N.J.: Prentice-Hall, 1956.

Powdermaker, F. B., and Frank, J. D. *Group Psychotherapy.* Cambridge, Mass.: Harvard Univ. Press, 1953.

Rachman, S. Introduction to behavior therapy. *Beh. Res. Ther., 1,* 3-15, 1963.

Rachman, S. Studies in desensitization: I. The separate effects of relaxation and desensitization. *Beh. Res. Ther., 3,* 245-252, 1965.

Rachman, S. Studies in desensitization: III. The speed of generalization. *Beh. Res. Ther., 4,* 205-208, 1966.

Rachman, S. Systematic desensitization. *Psychol. Bull., 67,* 93-103, 1967.

Rachman, S., and Eysenck, H. J. Reply to a "critique and reformulation" of behavior therapy. *Psychol. Bull., 65,* 165-169, 1966.

Rank, O. *The Trauma of Birth.* New York: Harcourt, Brace, 1929.

Rank, O. *Will Therapy: An Analysis of the Therapeutic Process in Terms of Relationship.* New York: Knopf, 1936.

Rapaport, R. N. Principles for developing a therapeutic community. In Masserman, J. (ed.), *Current Psychiatric Therapies.* Vol. 3. New York: Grune and Stratton, 1963.

Reil, Johannes C. *Rhapsodies in the application of psychic methods in the Treatment of Mental Disturbances.* 1803.

Rogers, C. R. *Counseling and Psychotherapy.* Boston: Houghton Mifflin, 1942.

Rogers, C. R. *Client-Centered Therapy.* Boston: Houghton Mifflin, 1951.

Rogers, C. R. *On Becoming a Person.* Boston: Houghton Mifflin, 1961.

Rogers, C. R. Psychotherapy today or where do we go from here? *Amer. J. Psychother., 17,* 5-16, 1963.

Rogers, C. R., et al. *The Therapeutic Relationship and Its Impact.* Madison: U. of Wisconsin Press, 1967.

Rogers, C. R., and Dymond, R. F. (eds.) *Psychotherapy and Personality Change.* Chicago: U. of Chicago Press, 1954.

Rosen, E., and Gregory, I. *Abnormal Psychology.* Philadelphia: Saunders, 1965.

Rosenzweig, S. A transvaluation of psychotherapy: A reply to Hans Eysenck. *J. Abnorm. Soc. Psychol., 49,* 298-304, 1954.

Rotter, J. B. *Social Learning and Clinical Psychology.* Englewood Cliffs, N.J.: Prentice-Hall, 1954.

Rotter, J. B. Some implications of a social learning theory for the practice of psychotherapy. Mimeographed paper, 1962.

Rubenstein, E. A., and Parloff, M. B. (eds.) *Research in Psychotherapy.* Washington, D.C.: American Psychological Association, 1959.

Satir, V. M. *Conjoint Family Therapy.* Palo Alto, Calif.: Science and Behavior Books, 1964.

Schilder, P. Results and problems of group psychotherapy in severe neuroses. *Ment. Hyg., 23,* 87-98, 1939.

Schorer, C. E., et al. Improvement without treatment.

Paper presented at *American Psychiatric Association Meetings.* May, 1966.

Shaw, F. J. A stimulus-response analysis of repression and insight in psychotherapy. *Psychol. Rev., 53,* 36-42, 1946.

Shlien, J. M., et al. (eds.) *Research in Psychotherapy.* Vol. III. Washington, D.C.: American Psychological Association, 1968.

Shoben, E. J. A learning-theory interpretation of psychotherapy. *Harvard Educ. Rev., 18,* 129-145, 1948.

Skinner, B. F. *Science and Human Behavior.* New York: Macmillan, 1953.

Slavson, S. R. *An Introduction to Group Therapy.* New York: The Commonwealth Fund, 1943.

Slavson, S. R. *A Textbook in Analytic Group Psychotherapy.* New York: Int'l. Univ. Press, 1964.

Smith, S., and Guthrie, E. R. Exhibitionism. *J. Abnorm. Soc. Psychol., 17,* 206-209, 1922.

Stampfl, T. G., and Levis, D. J. Essentials of implosive therapy: A learning-theory-based psychodynamic behavioral therapy. *J. Abnorm. Psychol., 72,* 496-503, 1967.

Stollak, G. E., Guerney, B. G., and Rothberg, M. (eds.) *Psychotherapy Research.* Chicago: Rand McNally, 1966.

Strupp, H. H. The outcome problem in psychotherapy revisited. *Psychother., 1,* 1-13, 1963.

Strupp, H. H., and Luborsky, L. (eds.) *Research in Psychotherapy.* Vol. II. Washington, D.C.: American Psychological Association, 1962.

Sullivan, H. S. *The Interpersonal Theory of Psychiatry.* New York: Norton, 1953.

Sullivan, H. S. *The Psychiatric Interview.* New York: Norton, 1954.

Sundberg, N. D., and Tyler, L. E. *Clinical Psychology.* New York: Appleton-Century-Crofts, 1962.

Taft, J. *The Dynamics of Therapy in a Controlled Relationship.* New York: Macmillan, 1933.

Thomas, E. J. Selected sociobehavioral techniques and principles: An approach to interpersonal helping. *Social Work, 13,* 12-26, 1968.

Thorne, F. C. A critique of nondirective methods of psychotherapy. *J. Abnorm. Soc. Psychol., 39,* 459-470, 1944.

Thorne, F. C. Principles of directive counseling and psychotherapy. *Amer. Psychol., 3,* 160-165, 1948.

Ullmann, L. P., and Krasner, L. (eds.), *Case Studies in Behavior Modification.* New York: Holt, Rinehart and Winston, 1965.

Ungersma, A. J. *The Search for Meaning.* Philadelphia: Westminster, 1961.

Von Mering, O., and King, S. H. *Remotivating the Mental Patient.* New York: Russell Sage Foundation, 1957.

Von Neumann, J., and Morgenstern, O. *The Theory of Games and Economic Behavior.* New York: Princeton, 1944.

Walton, D. The application of learning theory to the treatment of a case of neurodermatitis. In Eysenck, H. J. (ed.), *Behavior Therapy and the Neuroses.* New York: Pergamon, 1960.

Watson, J. B., and Rayner, R. Conditioned emotional reaction. *J. Exper. Psychol., 3,* 1-4, 1920.

Wechsler, H. Half-way houses for former mental patients: A survey. *J. Soc. Issues, 16,* 20-26, 1960.

White, R. *The Abnormal Personality.* 3rd ed. New York: Ronald, 1964.

Williams, C. D. The elimination of tantrum behavior by extinction procedures. *J. Abnorm. Soc. Psychol.*, *59*, 269, 1959.

Wolberg, L. R. *The Technique of Psychotherapy.* New York: Grune and Stratton, 1954.

Wolberg, L. R. *The Technique of Psychotherapy.* 2nd ed. New York: Grune and Stratton, 1967.

Wolf, A. The Psychoanalysis of groups. *Amer. J. Psychother.*, *3*, 525-558, 1949; *4*, 16-50, 1950.

Wolf, A., and Schwartz, E. K. *Psychoanalysis in Groups.* New York: Grune and Stratton, 1962.

Wolpe, J. *Psychotherapy by Reciprocal Inhibition.* Stanford, Cal.: Stanford U. Press, 1958.

Wolpe, J. The prognosis in unpsychoanalyzed recovery from neuroses. *Amer. J. Psychiat.*, *117*, 35-39, 1961.

Wolpe, J. Behavior therapy in complex neurotic states. *Brit. J. Psychiat.*, *110*, 28-34, 1964.

Wolpe, J. Behavior therapy in complex neurotic states. In Shlien, J. (ed.), *Research in Psychotherapy.* Vol. III. Washington, D.C.: American Psychological Association, 1968.

Woltman, A. G. Play therapy and related techniques. In Brower, D., and Abt, L. (eds.), *Progress in Clinical Psychology.* Vol. 3. New York: Grune and Stratton, 1959.

Zubin, J. Evaluation of therapeutic outcome in mental disorders. *J. Nerv. Ment. Dis.*, *117*, 95-111, 1953.

# INDEX OF NAMES

# INDEX OF SUBJECTS

Page numbers in *italic* type refer to illustrations.
Page numbers in **bold** type refer to tables.

Behavioral theories, 64–68
  evaluation of, 69
Behaviorism, 33, 64–68
Beliefs and goals, regulatory, disintegration of, 205–206
Beriberi, in biophysical defects, 512
Bestiality, 478
Biochemical research, mental disorders and, 15
Biogenic factors, 115–157
Biological functions, in infantile reaction patterns, 127
Biological substrate, plasticity of, 160–162
Biophysical defects, 218, 496–542
  as clinical syndrome, 103
  brain trauma and, 510–512
  cerebral degeneration and, 514–520
    etiology of, 515–516
  cerebral location of, local *vs.* diffused, 503–504
  chemogenic agents in, 502
  cranial concussion in, 510
  cranial contusions in, 511
  cranial lacerations in, 511
  endocrinological dysfunctions and, 513–514
  endogenous *vs.* exogenous, 503
  etiology of, 502–504
  genogenic agents in, 502
  histogenic agents in, 502
  intracranial infection and, 505–507
  intracranial neoplasm and, 514
  intracranial *vs.* systemic, 503
  metabolic dysfunctions and, 513–514
  nutritional deficiencies and, 512–513
  prognosis of, 538
  psychogenic agents in, 502
  therapeutic approaches to, 538–540
  thiamine deficiencies in, 512
  toxic agents and, 508–510
  vascular accidents in, 511
Biophysical theories, 44–49
  evaluation of, 70
Body build, ectomorphic, 227
  ectomorphic or endomorphic, in passive-dependent submissive personality, 245
  in personality disorders, 46
  mesomorphic-endomorphic, 271
Borderline personality, 304
  characteristics of, 305–307
  clinical features of, 305–307
Brain, impairment of, 498
Brain cell degeneration, 141
Brain dyscontrol, fragmentation in, 498
  interpenetration in, 498
  overinclusion in, 498
Brain dysfunctions, circumscribed, in childhood, 532–538, 541. See also *Childhood brain dysfunctions.*
Brain lesions, in limbic system, 47
  in psychopathology, 46–47
  in reticular formation, 47
Brain syndromes, nonpsychotic, organic, in childhood, 532–538, 541

Caelius Aurelianus, medical translations of, 6
Catalepsy, 80
Catastrophic reactions, in mental disorders, 501
Cerebral arteriosclerosis, 518–520, *520*
Cerebrotonia, 134

Character analysis, 614–615, 627
Character traits, psychosexual, 53
Chemogenic agents, in biophysical defects, 502
Chemotherapy, 553–564. See also *Psychopharmacological agents.*
Child rearing, guilt and anxiety training in, 293
Child's position in family, as source of pathogenic learning, 186
Childhood, ambiosis in, 377
  pariosis in, 368–369, 377
  schizophrenia in, 353
  symbiosis in, 377
Childhood brain dysfunctions, background of, 533–534
  behavioral disinhibition and disorganization in, 535
  clinical features of, 534–537
  cognitive-language impairments in, 537
  distractibility in, perceptual and cognitive, 535
  emotional lability in, 536
  etiology of, 537–538
  genetic deviances in, 537
  genetic diseases in, 537
  perceptual-motor impairments in, 536
  single function impairments in, 536
Childhood experiences, traumatic, Freud's view of, 22
Childhood reactions, 460–461, 494
  family setting in, 461
  peer relationships in, 461
  school adjustment in, 461
Choleria, 94
Chromosomes, 117
  abnormalities of, 118
Cingulectomy, 572, *572*
Classical psychoanalysis, 611–614, 627
Clinical analysis, 74–110
  elements of, 77–78
  objectives of, 75
  problems of, 75–77
Clinical syndromes, 97–99, *105*
  nosological classification of, 99–101
    evaluation of, 100–101
    suggestions for revision of, 101–107
Cognitive-language mechanisms, impairment of, in childhood brain dysfunctions, 537
  in mental disorders, 500
Cognitive-learning techniques, 605–608
Combat exhaustion, as gross stress reaction, 459, *464*
Communication, family styles of, 185
Compulsions, 79
  in obsession-compulsion disorders, 406
Conceptual terminology, as component of scientific theories, 38–39
Concordance among twins, 119
Concussion, cranial, post-traumatic symptoms of, 511–512
Conditioning, in learning, 64
Conflict, cognitive, of cycloid personality, 317
  psychosexual, Freud's theory of, 52–54
Conflict-regression theory, of Alexander, 421
Conforming personality, 196
  passive-ambivalent, 277–287
    clinical features of, 279–281
    coping strategies in, 284–285
    etiology and development of, 281–284
    guilt and responsibility training in, 283
  passive-ambivalent, parental overcontrol in, 282
    self-perpetuation of, 285–286
    therapeutic approaches to, 286–287